Lecture Notes in Computer Science 14081

The series Lecture Notes in Computer Science (LNCS), including its subseries Lecture Notes in Artificial Intelligence (LNAI) and Lecture Notes in Bioinformatics (LNBI), has established itself as a medium for the publication of new developments in computer science and information technology research, teaching, and education.

LNCS enjoys close cooperation with the computer science R & D community, the series counts many renowned academics among its volume editors and paper authors, and collaborates with prestigious societies. Its mission is to serve this international community by providing an invaluable service, mainly focused on the publication of conference and workshop proceedings and postproceedings. LNCS commenced publication in 1973.

Helena Handschuh · Anna Lysyanskaya
Editors

Advances in Cryptology – CRYPTO 2023

43rd Annual International Cryptology Conference, CRYPTO 2023
Santa Barbara, CA, USA, August 20–24, 2023
Proceedings, Part I

Editors
Helena Handschuh
Rambus Inc.
San Jose, CA, USA

Anna Lysyanskaya
Brown University
Providence, RI, USA

ISSN 0302-9743 ISSN 1611-3349 (electronic)
Lecture Notes in Computer Science
ISBN 978-3-031-38556-8 ISBN 978-3-031-38557-5 (eBook)
https://doi.org/10.1007/978-3-031-38557-5

This Springer imprint is published by the registered company Springer Nature Switzerland AG
The registered company address is: Gewerbestrasse 11, 6330 Cham, Switzerland

Preface

The 43rd International Cryptology Conference (CRYPTO 2023) was held at the University of California, Santa Barbara, California, USA, from August 20th to August 24th, 2023. It is an annual conference organized by the International Association for Cryptologic Research (IACR).

A record 479 papers were submitted for presentation at the conference, and 124 were selected, including two pairs of soft merges, for a total of 122 speaking slots. As a result of this record high, CRYPTO 2023 had three tracks for the first time in its history.

For the first time in its history as well, CRYPTO benefited from the great advice and tremendous help from six area chairs, covering the main areas of focus for the conference. These were Lejla Batina for Efficient and Secure Implementations, Dan Boneh for Public Key Primitives with Advanced Functionalities, Orr Dunkelman for Symmetric Cryptology, Leo Reyzin for Information-Theoretic and Complexity-Theoretic Cryptography, Douglas Stebila for Public-Key Cryptography and Muthuramakrishnan Venkitasubramaniam for Multi-Party Computation. Each of them helped lead discussions and decide which ones of the approximately 80 submissions in their area should be accepted. Their help was invaluable and we could not have succeeded without them.

To evaluate the submissions, we selected a program committee that consisted of 102 top cryptography researchers from all over the world. This was the largest program committee that CRYPTO has ever had, as well. Each paper was assigned to three program committee members who reviewed it either by themselves or with the help of a trusted sub-referee. As a result, we benefited from the expertise of almost 500 sub-referees. Together, they generated a staggering 1500 reviews. We thank our program committee members and the external sub-referees for the hard work of peer review which is the bedrock of scientific progress.

The review process was double-blind and confidential. In accordance with the IACR conflict-of-interest policy, the reviewing software we used (HotCRP) kept track of which reviewers had a conflict of interest with which authors (for example, by virtue of being a close collaborator or an advisor) and ensured that no paper was assigned a conflicted reviewer.

In order to be considered, submissions had to be anonymous and their length was limited to 30 pages excluding the bibliography and supplementary materials. After the first six or so weeks of evaluation, the committee chose to continue considering 330 papers; the remaining 149 papers were rejected, including five desk rejects. The majority of these received three reviews, none of which favored acceptance, although in limited cases the decision was made based on only two reviews that were in agreement. The papers that remained under consideration were invited to submit a response (rebuttal) to clarifications requested from their reviewers. Two papers were withdrawn during this second phase. Each of the 328 remaining papers received at least three reviews. After around five weeks of additional discussions, the committee made the final selection of the 124 papers that appear in these proceedings.

We would like to thank all the authors who submitted their papers to CRYPTO 2023. The vast majority of the submissions, including those that were ultimately not selected, were of very high quality, and we are very honored that CRYPTO was the venue that the authors chose for their work. We are additionally grateful to the authors of the accepted papers for the extra work of incorporating the reviewers' feedback and presenting their papers at the conference.

This year the Best Paper Award was awarded to Keegan Ryan and Nadia Heninger for their paper "Fast Practical Lattice Reduction Through Iterated Compression." The Best Early Career Paper Award went to Elizabeth Crites, Chelsea Komlo and Mary Maller for their paper "Fully Adaptive Schnorr Threshold Signatures." The runner up Best Early Career Paper was by Ward Beullens on "Graph-Theoretic Algorithms for the Alternating Trilinear Form Equivalence Problem." These three papers were subsequently invited to be submitted to the IACR Journal of Cryptology.

In addition to the presentations of contributed papers included in these proceedings, the conference also featured two plenary talks: Hugo Krawczyk delivered the IACR Distinguished Lecture, and Scott Aaronson gave an invited talk titled "Neurocryptography." The traditional rump session, chaired by Allison Bishop, took place on Tuesday, August 22nd, and featured numerous short talks.

Co-located cryptography workshops were held in the preceding weekend; they included the following seven events, "Crypto meets Artificial Intelligence—The Glowing Hot Topics in Cryptography," "MathCrypt—The Workshop on Mathematical Cryptology," "CFAIL—The Conference for Failed Approaches and Insightful Losses in Cryptography," "PPML—The Privacy-Preserving Machine Learning Workshop," "WAC6—The Workshop on Attacks in Cryptography 6," "ACAI—Applied Cryptology and Artificial Intelligence," and "RISE—Research Insights and Stories for Enlightenment." We gladly thank Alessandra Scafuro for serving as the Affiliated Events Chair and putting together such an enticing program.

All of this was possible thanks to Kevin McCurley and Kay McKelly without whom all of our review software would be crashing non-stop, and all of the Crypto presentations would be nothing but static. They are the true pillars of all of our IACR Crypto events and conferences. Last but not least we thank Britta Hale for serving as our General Chair and making sure the conference went smoothly and attendees had a great experience. Thank you to our industry sponsors, including early sponsors a16z, AWS, Casper, Google, JPMorgan, Meta, PQShield, and TII for their generous contributions, as well as to the NSF Award 2330160 for supporting Ph.D. student participants.

August 2023

Helena Handschuh
Anna Lysyanskaya

Organization

General Chair

Britta Hale	Naval Postgraduate School, USA

Program Co-chairs

Helena Handschuh	Rambus Inc., USA
Anna Lysyanskaya	Brown University, USA

Area Chairs

Lejla Batina *(for Efficient and Secure Implementations)*	Radboud University, the Netherlands
Dan Boneh *(for Public Key Primitives with Advanced Functionalities)*	Stanford University, USA
Orr Dunkelman *(for Symmetric Cryptology)*	University of Haifa, Israel
Leo Reyzin *(for Information-Theoretic and Complexity-Theoretic Cryptography)*	Boston University, USA
Douglas Stebila *(for Public-Key Cryptography)*	University of Waterloo, Canada
Muthu Venkitasubramaniam *(for Multi-Party Computation)*	Georgetown University, USA

Program Committee

Shweta Agrawal	IIT Madras, India
Ghada Almashaqbeh	University of Connecticut, USA
Benny Applebaum	Tel-Aviv University, Israel
Marshall Ball	New York University, USA
Fabrice Benhamouda	Algorand Foundation, USA

Nina Bindel	SandboxAQ, USA
Allison Bishop	Proof Trading and City University of New York, USA
Joppe W. Bos	NXP Semiconductors, Belgium
Raphael Bost	Direction Générale de l'Armement, France
Chris Brzuska	Aalto University, Finland
Benedikt Bünz	Stanford and Espresso Systems, USA
David Cash	University of Chicago, USA
Gaëtan Cassiers	TU Graz and Lamarr Security Research, Austria
Yilei Chen	Tsinghua University, China
Chitchanok Chuengsatiansup	The University of Melbourne, Australia
Kai-Min Chung	Academia Sinica, Taiwan
Carlos Cid	Simula UiB, Norway, and Okinawa Institute of Science and Technology, Japan
Sandro Coretti	IOHK, Switzerland
Geoffroy Couteau	CNRS, IRIF, Université Paris-Cité, France
Luca De Feo	IBM Research Europe, Switzerland
Gabrielle De Micheli	University of California, San Diego, USA
Jean Paul Degabriele	Technology Innovation Institute, UAE
Siemen Dhooghe	imec-COSIC, KU Leuven, Belgium
Itai Dinur	Ben-Gurion University, Israel
Christoph Dobraunig	Intel Labs, Intel Corporation, USA
Thomas Eisenbarth	University of Lübeck, Germany
Sebastian Faust	TU Darmstadt, Germany
Ben Fisch	Yale University, USA
Pierre-Alain Fouque	IRISA and University of Rennes, France
Georg Fuchsbauer	TU Wien, Austria
Chaya Ganesh	Indian Institute of Science, India
Rosario Gennaro	City University of New York, USA
Henri Gilbert	ANSSI, France
Niv Gilboa	Ben-Gurion University, Israel
Mike Hamburg	Rambus Inc., the Netherlands
David Heath	University of Illinois Urbana-Champaign, USA
Naofumi Homma	Tohoku University, Japan
Abhishek Jain	Johns Hopkins University, USA
Bhavana Kanukurthi	Indian Institute of Science, India
Shuichi Katsumata	PQShield, UK, and AIST, Japan
Jonathan Katz	University of Maryland and Dfns, USA
Nathan Keller	Bar-Ilan University, Israel
Lisa Kohl	CWI, the Netherlands
Ilan Komargodski	Hebrew University, Israel and NTT Research, USA

Alexander Russell	University of Connecticut, USA
Paul Rösler	FAU Erlangen-Nürnberg, Germany
Kazue Sako	Waseda University, Japan
Alessandra Scafuro	North Carolina State University, USA
Patrick Schaumont	Worcester Polytechnic Institute, USA
Thomas Schneider	TU Darmstadt, Germany
André Schrottenloher	Inria, Univ. Rennes, CNRS, IRISA, France
Dominique Schröder	FAU Erlangen-Nürnberg, Germany
Benjamin Smith	Inria and École Polytechnique, France
Ling Song	Jinan University, China
Mehdi Tibouchi	NTT Social Informatics Laboratories, Japan
Yosuke Todo	NTT Social Informatics Laboratories, Japan
Alin Tomescu	Aptos Labs, USA
Dominique Unruh	University of Tartu, Estonia
Gilles Van Assche	STMicroelectronics, Belgium
Damien Vergnaud	Sorbonne Université, France
Jiayu Xu	Oregon State University, USA
Arkady Yerukhimovich	George Washington University, USA
Yu Yu	Shanghai Jiao Tong University, China

Additional Reviewers

Kasra Abbaszadeh
Behzad Abdolmaleki
Masayuki Abe
Ittai Abraham
Hamza Abusalah
Amit Agarwal
Akshima
Gorjan Alagic
Martin Albrecht
Bar Alon
Miguel Ambrona
Prabhanjan Ananth
Megumi Ando
Yoshinori Aono
Paula Arnold
Gal Arnon
Arasu Arun
Gilad Asharov
Renas Bacho
Matilda Backendal
Christian Badertscher
Shi Bai
David Balbás
Paulo Barreto
James Bartusek
Andrea Basso
Jules Baudrin
Balthazar Bauer
Carsten Baum
Josh Beal
Hugo Beguinet
Amos Beimel
Sana Belguith
Thiago Bergamaschi
Olivier Bernard
Sebastian Berndt
Ward Beullens
Tim Beyne
Rishiraj Bhattacharyya
Ritam Bhaumik

Mengda Bi
Alexander Bienstock
Bruno Blanchet
Olivier Blazy
Maxime Bombar
Xavier Bonnetain
Jonathan Bootle
Samuel Bouaziz-Ermann
Katharina Boudgoust
Alexandre Bouez
Charles Bouillaguet
Christina Boura
Clémence Bouvier
Ross Bowden
Pedro Branco
Anne Broadbent
Olivier Bronchain
Andreas Brüggemann
Anirudh Chandramouli
Eleonora Cagli
Matteo Campanelli
Pedro Capitão
Eliana Carozza
Kévin Carrier
Wouter Castryck
Pyrros Chaidos
Andre Chailloux
Suvradip Chakraborty
Gowri Chandran
Rohit Chatterjee
Albert Cheu
Céline Chevalier
Nai-Hui Chia
Arka Rai Choudhuri
Hien Chu
Hao Chung
Michele Ciampi
Valerio Cini
James Clements
Christine Cloostermans
Benoît Cogliati
Andrea Coladangelo
Jean-Sébastien Coron
Henry Corrigan-Gibbs
Craig Costello
Elizabeth Crites
Eric Crockett
Jan-Pieter D'Anvers
Antoine Dallon
Poulami Das
Gareth Davies
Hannah Davis
Dennis Dayanikli
Leo de Castro
Paola De Perthuis
Rafael del Pino
Cyprien Delpech de Saint Guilhem
Jeroen Delvaux
Patrick Derbez
Zach DeStefano
Lalita Devadas
Julien Devevey
Henri Devillez
Jean-François Dhem
Adam Ding
Yevgeniy Dodis
Xiaoyang Dong
Nico Döttling
Benjamin Dowling
Leo Ducas
Clément Ducros
Céline Duguey
Jesko Dujmovic
Christoph Egger
Maria Eichlseder
Reo Eriguchi
Andreas Erwig
Daniel Escudero
Thomas Espitau
Andre Esser
Simona Etinski
Thibauld Feneuil
Pouria Fallahpour
Maya Farber Brodsky
Pooya Farshim
Joël Felderhoff
Rex Fernando
Matthias Fitzi
Antonio Flórez-Gutiérrez
Cody Freitag

Sapir Freizeit
Benjamin Fuller
Phillip Gajland
Tarek Galal
Nicolas Gama
John Gaspoz
Pierrick Gaudry
Romain Gay
Peter Gaži
Yuval Gelles
Marilyn George
François Gérard
Paul Gerhart
Alexandru Gheorghiu
Ashrujit Ghoshal
Shane Gibbons
Benedikt Gierlichs
Barbara Gigerl
Noemi Glaeser
Aarushi Goel
Eli Goldin
Junqing Gong
Dov Gordon
Lénaïck Gouriou
Marc Gourjon
Jerome Govinden
Juan Grados
Lorenzo Grassi
Sandra Guasch
Aurore Guillevic
Sam Gunn
Aldo Gunsing
Daniel Günther
Chun Guo
Siyao Guo
Yue Guo
Shreyas Gupta
Hosein Hadipour
Mohammad Hajiabadi
Shai Halevi
Lucjan Hanzlik
Aditya Hegde
Rachelle Heim
Lena Heimberger
Paul Hermouet
Julia Hesse
Minki Hhan
Taiga Hiroka
Justin Holmgren
Alex Hoover
Akinori Hosoyamada
Kristina Hostakova
Kai Hu
Yu-Hsuan Huang
Mi-Ying Miryam Huang
Pavel Hubáček
Andreas Hülsing
Akiko Inoue
Takanori Isobe
Akira Ito
Ryoma Ito
Tetsu Iwata
Jennifer Jackson
Joseph Jaeger
Zahra Jafargholi
Jonas Janneck
Stanislaw Jarecki
Zhengzhong Jin
David Joseph
Daniel Jost
Nathan Ju
Seny Kamara
Chetan Kamath
Simon Holmgaard Kamp
Gabriel Kaptchuk
Vukašin Karadžić
Ioanna Karantaidou
Harish Karthikeyan
Mustafa Khairallah
Mojtaba Khalili
Nora Khayata
Hamidreza Khoshakhlagh
Eda Kirimli
Elena Kirshanova
Ágnes Kiss
Fuyuki Kitagawa
Susumu Kiyoshima
Alexander Koch
Dmitry Kogan
Konrad Kohbrok

Sreehari Kollath
Yashvanth Kondi
Venkata Koppula
Marina Krcek
Maximilian Kroschewski
Daniël Kuijsters
Péter Kutas
Qiqi Lai
Yi-Fu Lai
Philip Lazos
Jason LeGrow
Gregor Leander
Ulysse Léchine
Yi Lee
Charlotte Lefevre
Jonas Lehmann
Antonin Leroux
Baiyu Li
Chaoyun Li
Hanjun Li
Wenjie Li
Xin Li
Xingjian Li
Zhe Li
Mingyu Liang
Xiao Liang
Damien Ligier
Wei-Kai Lin
Helger Lipmaa
Guozhen Liu
Jiahui Liu
Linsheng Liu
Meicheng Liu
Qipeng Liu
Zeyu Liu
Chen-Da Liu-Zhang
Alex Lombardi
Johanna Loyer
Ji Luo
Vadim Lyubashevsky
Yiping Ma
Varun Madathil
Bernardo Magri
Luciano Maino
Monosij Maitra
Christian Majenz
Jasleen Malvai
Marian Margraf
Mario Marhuenda Beltrán
Erik Mårtensson
Ange Martinelli
Daniel Masny
Loïc Masure
Takahiro Matsuda
Kotaro Matsuoka
Christian Matt
Krystian Matusiewicz
Noam Mazor
Matthias Meijers
Fredrik Meisingseth
Pierre Meyer
Daniele Micciancio
Elena Micheli
Marine Minier
Helen Möllering
Charles Momin
Atsuki Momose
Hart Montgomery
Tal Moran
Tomoyuki Morimae
Kirill Morozov
Fabrice Mouhartem
Koksal Mus
Saachi Mutreja
Michael Naehrig
Marcel Nageler
Rishub Nagpal
Yusuke Naito
Anand Kumar Narayanan
Shoei Nashimoto
Ky Nguyen
Georgio Nicolas
Raine Nieminen
Valeria Nikolaenko
Oded Nir
Ryo Nishimaki
Olga Nissenbaum
Anca Nitulescu
Julian Nowakowski
Adam O'Neill

Sai Lakshmi Bhavana Obbattu
Maciej Obremski
Arne Tobias Ødegaard
Morten Øygarden
Cavit Özbay
Erdinc Ozturk
Jiaxin Pan
Dimitrios Papachristoudis
Aditi Partap
Anat Paskin-Cherniavsky
Rafael Pass
Sikhar Patranabis
Stanislav Peceny
Chris Peikert
Angelos Pelecanos
Alice Pellet-Mary
Octavio Perez-Kempner
Guilherme Perin
Trevor Perrin
Giuseppe Persiano
Pessl Peter
Spencer Peters
Duong Hieu Phan
Benny Pinkas
Bertram Poettering
Guru Vamsi Policharla
Jason Pollack
Giacomo Pope
Alexander Poremba
Eamonn Postlethwaite
Thomas Prest
Robert Primas
Luowen Qian
Willy Quach
Håvard Raddum
Shahram Rasoolzadeh
Divya Ravi
Michael Reichle
Jean-René Reinhard
Omar Renawi
Joost Renes
Nicolas Resch
Mahshid Riahinia
Silas Richelson
Jan Richter-Brockmann
Doreen Riepel
Peter Rindal
Bhaskar Roberts
Wrenna Robson
Sondre Rønjom
Mike Rosulek
Yann Rotella
Lior Rotem
Ron Rothblum
Adeline Roux-Langlois
Joe Rowell
Lawrence Roy
Keegan Ryan
Mark Ryan
Sherman S. M. Chow
Eric Sageloli
Antonio Sanso
Practik Sarkar
Yu Sasaki
Robert Schaedlich
Jan Schlegel
Martin Schläffer
Markus Schofnegger
Peter Scholl
Jan Schoone
Phillipp Schoppmann
Jacob Schuldt
Mark Schultz
Marek Sefranek
Nicolas Sendrier
Jae Hong Seo
Karn Seth
Srinath Setty
Yannick Seurin
Dana Shamir
Devika Sharma
Yaobin Shen
Yixin Shen
Danping Shi
Sina Shiehian
Omri Shmueli
Ferdinand Sibleyras
Janno Siim
Mark Simkin
Jaspal Singh

Amit Singh Bhati
Sujoy Sinha Roy
Naomi Sirkin
Daniel Slamanig
Christopher Smith
Tomer Solomon
Fang Song
Yifan Song
Pratik Soni
Jesse Spielman
Srivatsan Sridhar
Damien Stehlé
Marc Stevens
Christoph Striecks
Patrick Struck
Adam Suhl
Chao Sun
Siwei Sun
Berk Sunar
Ajith Suresh
Moeto Suzuki
Erkan Tairi
Akira Takahashi
Katsuyuki Takashima
Abdul Rahman Taleb
Quan Quan Tan
Er-Cheng Tang
Qiang Tang
Stefano Tessaro
Justin Thaler
Yan Bo Ti
Tyge Tiessen
Junichi Tomida
Dilara Toprakhisar
Andreas Trügler
Daniel Tschudi
Yiannis Tselekounis
Ida Tucker
Balazs Udvarhelyi
Rei Ueno
Florian Unterstein
Annapurna Valiveti
Gijs Van Laer
Wessel van Woerden
Akhil Vanukuri
Karolin Varner
Javier Verbel
Tanner Verber
Frederik Vercauteren
Corentin Verhamme
Psi Vesely
Fernando Virdia
Quoc-Huy Vu
Benedikt Wagner
Roman Walch
Hendrik Waldner
Han Wang
Libo Wang
William Wang
Yunhao Wang
Zhedong Wang
Hoeteck Wee
Mor Weiss
Weiqiang Wen
Chenkai Weng
Luca Wilke
Mathias Wolf
David Wu
Lichao Wu
Zejun Xiang
Tiancheng Xie
Alex Xiong
Anshu Yadav
Sophia Yakoubov
Hossein Yalame
Shota Yamada
Avishay Yanai
Kang Yang
Qianqian Yang
Tianqi Yang
Yibin Yang
Kan Yasuda
Eylon Yogev
Yang Yu
Arantxa Zapico
Hadas Zeilberger
Bin Zhang
Jiang Zhang
Ruizhe Zhang
Zhenda Zhang
Chenzhi Zhu
Jens Zumbraegel

Contents – Part I

Consensus, Secret Sharing, and Multi-party Computation

Completeness Theorems for Adaptively Secure Broadcast 3
Ran Cohen, Juan Garay, and Vassilis Zikas

Bingo: Adaptivity and Asynchrony in Verifiable Secret Sharing and Distributed Key Generation 39
Ittai Abraham, Philipp Jovanovic, Mary Maller, Sarah Meiklejohn, and Gilad Stern

Network-Agnostic Security Comes (Almost) for Free in DKG and MPC 71
Renas Bacho, Daniel Collins, Chen-Da Liu-Zhang, and Julian Loss

Practical Settlement Bounds for Longest-Chain Consensus 107
Peter Gaži, Ling Ren, and Alexander Russell

New Bounds on the Local Leakage Resilience of Shamir's Secret Sharing Scheme 139
Ohad Klein and Ilan Komargodski

Arithmetic Sketching 171
Dan Boneh, Elette Boyle, Henry Corrigan-Gibbs, Niv Gilboa, and Yuval Ishai

Additive Randomized Encodings and Their Applications 203
Shai Halevi, Yuval Ishai, Eyal Kushilevitz, and Tal Rabin

How to Recover a Secret with $O(n)$ Additions 236
Benny Applebaum, Oded Nir, and Benny Pinkas

On Linear Communication Complexity for (Maximally) Fluid MPC 263
Alexander Bienstock, Daniel Escudero, and Antigoni Polychroniadou

Cryptography with Weights: MPC, Encryption and Signatures 295
Sanjam Garg, Abhishek Jain, Pratyay Mukherjee, Rohit Sinha, Mingyuan Wang, and Yinuo Zhang

Best of Both Worlds: Revisiting the Spymasters Double Agent Problem 328
Anasuya Acharya, Carmit Hazay, Oxana Poburinnaya, and Muthuramakrishnan Venkitasubramaniam

Perfect MPC over Layered Graphs ... 360
Bernardo David, Giovanni Deligios, Aarushi Goel, Yuval Ishai, Anders Konring, Eyal Kushilevitz, Chen-Da Liu-Zhang, and Varun Narayanan

Round-Optimal Black-Box MPC in the Plain Model ... 393
Yuval Ishai, Dakshita Khurana, Amit Sahai, and Akshayaram Srinivasan

Reusable Secure Computation in the Plain Model ... 427
Vipul Goyal, Akshayaram Srinivasan, and Mingyuan Wang

List Oblivious Transfer and Applications to Round-Optimal Black-Box Multiparty Coin Tossing ... 459
Michele Ciampi, Rafail Ostrovsky, Luisa Siniscalchi, and Hendrik Waldner

Security-Preserving Distributed Samplers: How to Generate Any CRS in One Round Without Random Oracles ... 489
Damiano Abram, Brent Waters, and Mark Zhandry

One-Message Secure Reductions: On the Cost of Converting Correlations ... 515
Yuval Ishai, Mahimna Kelkar, Varun Narayanan, and Liav Zafar

A Framework for Statistically Sender Private OT with Optimal Rate ... 548
Pedro Branco, Nico Döttling, and Akshayaram Srinivasan

Malicious Secure, Structure-Aware Private Set Intersection ... 577
Gayathri Garimella, Mike Rosulek, and Jaspal Singh

Threshold Cryptography

Secure Multiparty Computation from Threshold Encryption Based on Class Groups ... 613
Lennart Braun, Ivan Damgård, and Claudio Orlandi

Two-Round Stateless Deterministic Two-Party Schnorr Signatures from Pseudorandom Correlation Functions ... 646
Yashvanth Kondi, Claudio Orlandi, and Lawrence Roy

Fully Adaptive Schnorr Threshold Signatures ... 678
Elizabeth Crites, Chelsea Komlo, and Mary Maller

Snowblind: A Threshold Blind Signature in Pairing-Free Groups ... 710
Elizabeth Crites, Chelsea Komlo, Mary Maller, Stefano Tessaro, and Chenzhi Zhu

Practical Schnorr Threshold Signatures Without the Algebraic Group Model 743
Hien Chu, Paul Gerhart, Tim Ruffing, and Dominique Schröder

Author Index 775

Consensus, Secret Sharing, and Multi-party Computation

Completeness Theorems for Adaptively Secure Broadcast

Ran Cohen[1(✉)], Juan Garay[2], and Vassilis Zikas[3]

[1] Efi Arazi School of Computer Science, Reichman University, Herzliya, Israel
cohenran@runi.ac.il
[2] Texas A&M University, College Station, USA
garay@cse.tamu.edu
[3] Purdue University, West Lafayette, USA
vzikas@cs.purdue.edu

Abstract. The advent of blockchain protocols has reignited the interest in adaptively secure broadcast; it is by now well understood that broadcasting over a diffusion network allows an adaptive adversary to corrupt the sender depending on the message it attempts to send and change it. Hirt and Zikas [Eurocrypt '10] proved that this is an inherent limitation of broadcast in the simulation-based setting—i.e., this task is impossible against an adaptive adversary corrupting a majority of the parties (a task that is achievable against a static adversary).

The contributions of this paper are two-fold. First, we show that, contrary to previous perception, the above limitation of adaptively secure broadcast is **not** an artifact of simulation-based security, but rather an inherent issue of adaptive security. In particular, we show that: (1) it also applies to the property-based broadcast definition adapted for adaptive adversaries, and (2) unlike other impossibilities in adaptive security, this impossibility cannot be circumvented by adding a programmable random oracle, in neither setting, property-based or simulation-based.

Second, we turn to the resource-restricted cryptography (RRC) paradigm [Garay *et al.*, Eurocrypt '20], which has proven useful in circumventing impossibility results, and ask whether it also affects the above negative result. We answer this question in the affirmative, by showing that time-lock puzzles (TLPs)—which can be viewed as an instance of RRC—indeed allow for achieving the property-based definition and circumvent the impossibility of adaptively secure broadcast. The natural question is then, do TLPs also allow for simulation-based adaptively secure broadcast against corrupted majorities? We answer this question in the negative. However, we show that a positive result can be achieved via a *non-committing* analogue of TLPs in the programmable random-oracle model.

Importantly, and as a contribution of independent interest, we also present the first (limited) composition theorem in the resource-restricted setting, which is needed for the complexity-based, non-idealized treatment of TLPs in the context of other protocols.

H. Handschuh and A. Lysyanskaya (Eds.): CRYPTO 2023, LNCS 14081, pp. 3–38, 2023.
https://doi.org/10.1007/978-3-031-38557-5_1

1 Introduction

A physical broadcast channel enables a set of n parties to communicate as if talking via a megaphone: Once a party speaks, all other parties are guaranteed to hear its message. In a *broadcast protocol* (aka Byzantine Generals [66,76]) the parties are asked to realize this "megaphone" capability over point-to-point channels, even when a subset of them collude and actively disrupt the protocol's execution. The standard formulation of a broadcast protocol requires two core properties: *agreement* (all honest parties output the same value, even if the sender is cheating) and *validity* (if the sender is honest, then all honest parties output its message). A broadcast protocol is t-resilient if both properties hold facing any set of (up to) t misbehaving and colluding parties.

Broadcast is one of the most studied problems in the context of fault-tolerant distributed computing and cryptographic protocols, leading to numerous breakthrough results. For example, classical results show that while t-resilient broadcast protocols can be constructed in the plain model for $t < n/3$ [44,76], a larger corruption threshold cannot be tolerated [16,40,66]. Overcoming this lower bound requires working in weaker models. A common approach is to assume a setup assumption in the form of a *public-key infrastructure* (PKI) for digital signatures [35] (where every party generates a pair of signing/verification keys, and publishes its verification key during the setup phase), or more involved *correlated randomness* (where a trusted party generates correlated secrets to the parties before the protocol begins; e.g., an "information-theoretic PKI" [77]); this approach enables broadcast protocols tolerating $t \leq n$ corruptions.[1]

Simulation-Based vs. Property-Based Definitions. Broadcast can be thought of as a concrete instance of secure multi-party computation (MPC) [53,86]. MPC protocols enable a set of mutually distrusting parties to compute a function on their private inputs, while guaranteeing various properties such as correctness, privacy, independence of inputs, and more. While the original security definitions had the above property-based flavor, nowadays standard definitions formalize the above requirements (and others) in a simulation-based manner [20,21,52]. Informally, in the simulation paradigm for security, the protocol execution is compared to an ideal world where the parties have access to a trusted party (the "ideal functionality") that captures the security properties the protocol is required to achieve. The trusted party takes the parties' inputs and performs the computation on their behalf. A protocol is then regarded secure if for any adversary attacking it, there exists an ideal-world adversary (the "simulator") attacking the execution in the ideal world, such that no external distinguisher (environment) can tell the real and the ideal executions apart.

Simulation-based definitions provide several advantages compared to the property-based approach. First, in a property-based definition, it may be the case that an important property is missed (e.g., one may require privacy of the inputs but neglect to require input independence); this may be subtle to

[1] For the related *consensus* problem (aka Byzantine *agreement*), where all parties have an input, the best achievable bound is $t < n/2$ [41].

notice since the properties should capture both the guarantees towards the honest parties as well as the influence the adversary may have over the computation. Second, the holistic approach provides a simple and clear definition that can be applied in complex settings, such as adaptive corruptions and concurrent executions. Third, many simulation-based security definitions guarantee security under composition, which enables analyzing a complex task where sub-protocols are modeled as ideal functionalities, and later replaced by protocols securely realizing them.

For the specific case of broadcast, the commonly used ideal functionality (e.g., [25,54]) mimics an ideal megaphone in a rather simple way: First, the sender provides its message to the ideal functionality, which later hands it out to the adversary and to all other parties.

Adaptively Secure Broadcast. It is not hard to see that a broadcast protocol which is secure according to the property-based definition (requiring *agreement* and *validity*) also realizes the ideal megaphone functionality when the set of corrupted parties is defined at the onset of the protocol (i.e., when the adversary is *static*). However, as observed by Hirt and Zikas [58], this no longer holds in the adaptive-corruption setting. The issue is that a *rushing* adversary may be the first to learn the sender's input message, in which case it can corrupt the sender and replace its message (i.e., "bias" the content of the message), or simply crash it, in case of fail-stop adversaries. For example, the protocol of Dolev and Strong [35] (and the vast majority of the protocols in the literature) begins by having the sender send its message to all other parties, who then proceed to make sure they all agree on the output value. In case the first party receiving this message is corrupted, the adversary can decide whether to corrupt the sender (thus preventing all other parties from learning it) as a function of that message.

Hirt and Zikas [58] defined a weaker functionality that captures this capability of the adversary to influence the output. In this *corruption-unfair broadcast* functionality, once the functionality receives the input from the sender, it first hands it to the adversary, who can now corrupt the sender and replace its input *before* the functionality sends the output to the remaining honest parties. Such a broadcast protocol is *corruption-unfair* because the adversary gets a "double dipping" capability to both learn the sender's input before the other parties *and* to change it. This is in contrast to the megaphone functionality that allows the adversary to *either* be the first to learn the message *or* to corrupt the sender (without first learning the message) and choose the output, but not both. This difference is best illustrated when each party broadcasts a random bit: if corruption-unfair broadcast is used the adversary has the capability to bias the agreed-upon bits towards 0 by corrupting only senders that broadcast 1 and flipping their bit, whereas if the ideal megaphone is used the adversary does not get any advantage over simply randomly guessing which parties broadcast 1.[2]

[2] In the context of collective coin tossing, the capability of the adversary to first learn the sender's message and later to corrupt the sender and change its input has been referred to as *strongly adaptive* [55,56,60,64].

Hirt and Zikas [58] further showed that the megaphone functionality can be realized for $t \leq n/2$ (i.e., when the adversary cannot corrupt a majority of the parties); the idea is for the sender to "commit" its message into the system using verifiable secret sharing (VSS), and later use corruption-unfair broadcast to reconstruct the original message (as observed in [31,32], robust secret sharing can be used instead of VSS). But for the dishonest-majority setting, as mentioned above, Hirt and Zikas showed that realizing the megaphone functionality in the case of adaptive adversaries is impossible.

The fact that the problem statement (and proof) of the impossibility of adaptively secure broadcast in [58] were both given only with respect to a simulation-based definition, created the (as we prove, inaccurate) perception that this impossibility is an artifact of simulation-based security, and would not carry-over to property-based definitions—see, for example, [12,83,84]. In particular, the first central question of our work, which we answer in the affirmative, is:

Does the impossibility of adaptively secure broadcast in [58] *also apply to the property-based setting?*

In fact, the quest to answer the above question reveals a deeper issue one needs to account for when addressing adaptive security of a protocol using a property-based definition. In particular, as discussed below, in order to answer this question, we distill a natural property that secure computation protocols—not just broadcast protocols—tolerating adaptive adversaries should satisfy, which we term *corruption fairness.*[3]

Atomic vs. Non-atomic Multisend. The attack from [58] applies in the so-called *non-atomic multisend* model, where sending multiple messages to the network are considered as separate operations. This is the classical model considered in the distributed-computing literature since the '80s (e.g., [35,39,40]), where the adversary could corrupt a party and make it "crash" (or change its input [38]) right after the party sends its messages to some of the parties, but before it completed sending to all parties. This is also the standard model for capturing adaptive corruptions in the MPC literature (e.g., [20,21,24,27]). The ability of the adversary to corrupt a party in such a manner has also been referred to as *strongly rushing* [1,2,83].[4]

In passing, we note that one can also motivate the non-atomic multisend model by modern message diffusion protocols, such as the one used in distributed-ledger constructions: for example, consider the setting where a party's outgoing communication goes through a router (e.g., an ISP) that may

[3] Although in this work we focus on broadcast, corruption fairness can easily be defined—and is a natural requirement—for any adaptively secure MPC task.

[4] In this work we refrain from using the term "strongly rushing," because we believe it creates the misconception of an assumption on the adversary. We view the non-atomic multisend model as the *"plain"* model for a rushing adversary, a view which is consistent with the literature [20,21], and atomic multisend as an assumption on the network which limits the adversary's adaptivity.

queue (or even block) some (or all) outgoing messages. If we view such diffusion protocols as emulating send-to-many communication (i.e., multisend), then by corrupting the router the adversary can achieve the same message delivery patterns as in a non-atomic multisend scenario.[5]

In [47], Garay *et al.* noticed that this attack does not carry over to the *atomic multisend* model where the sender is guaranteed not to be corrupted in the time between sending its first message for a given round and the time it completes sending all messages for that round, and, further, a message that has been sent is guaranteed to arrive at its destination. Interestingly, Garay *et al.* showed another variation of this attack illustrating that the protocol of Dolev and Strong [35] (and all other protocols in the literature) does not realize the megaphone functionality even in the atomic-multisend model. Complementarily, they presented an adaptively secure broadcast protocol tolerating $t < n$ corruptions in this model.

Even though the atomic-multisend model has recently gained popularity with many consensus protocols that seek security against adaptive corruptions (e.g., [1,13,28,29,82,84]), the non-atomic-multisend model is the one that corresponds to the "plain" network model, as it makes less assumptions on the underlying communication network.[6] This model is more challenging as it admits more powerful adversaries; indeed, certain impossibility results in the non-atomic multisend model do not translate to the atomic-multisend regime [1,17,58]. Let us stress that it is neither the goal nor the intention of this work to dismiss the atomic multisend model, which is frequently used in the distributed-computing literature. Our point here is that atomic multisend is a network assumption limiting the rushing power of the adversary (and, therefore, its adaptivity), by effectively posing a restriction on the adversary's ability (speed) to corrupt.

The Resource-Restricted Paradigm. A more recent approach to overcome the impossibility results of broadcast [16,40,66] without using "private-state setup assumptions"[7] (such as a PKI) is the *resource-restricted cryptography* (RRC) paradigm [50], where instead of considering arbitrary adversaries that run in probabilistic polynomial time (PPT), additional restrictions are assumed on their capabilities. For example, when the computational power of the adversary is assumed to be smaller than the combined computational power of the honest parties, Nakamoto-style consensus [48,75] employs proofs of work (PoWs) [36] to overcome the aforementioned lower bounds without relying on PKI-like setup assumptions. This is a fruitful promising approach that has led to broadcast protocols [4] and secure multi-party computation protocols [50] that can tolerate any dishonest minority, given only a "public-state setup."

[5] We stress that the above is orthogonal to the synchrony assumption: Consider for example a synchronous setting, where a round takes 60 s (i.e., any message sent by an honest party is delivered within 60 s) and corrupting a party takes 30 s. Then delaying messages at the router gives the adversary time to corrupt the sender and crash it based on messages it sends, dropping all pending messages.

[6] We view non-atomic multisend as the *"plain"* model for a rushing adversary, a view which is consistent with the literature on security models for MPC [20,21].

[7] Terminology taken from [43].

Another example of resource-restricted cryptography is *time-based hardness.* Here there is no restriction on the overall computational power of the adversary (other than being PPT); instead, there is an assumed bound on the number of parallel steps that the adversary can take within a given time interval. This assumption enables the usage of *time-lock puzzles* (TLPs) [11,79] and has been used for example by Boneh and Naor [14] to overcome the lower bound by Cleve [30] and construct a fair coin-tossing protocol between two parties. This approach has led to several interesting results, such as "resource fairness" [45], non-interactive non-malleable commitments [67], and round-efficient randomized broadcast [83]. Another use case of time-based hardness which has been shown to be sufficiently strong to overcome Cleve's impossibility is *verifiable delay functions* [15,78,85].

Thus, the second main question we ask in this paper is:

> *Can the impossibility of adaptively secure broadcast* [58] *be circumvented in the resource-restricted cryptography paradigm?*

Intriguingly, the answer to the above seemingly innocent question is different depending on the definition of (adaptively secure) broadcast one adopts—property-based vs. simulation-based—and/or on how strong a setup we are willing to assume. In particular, we answer this question in the affirmative in the case of property-based definition via TLPs, which can be viewed as an instance of RRC. However, in the case of simulation-based security, it turns out that TLPs do not suffice. Nonetheless, we show that a positive result—i.e., simulation-based adaptively secure broadcast against corrupted majorities—can be achieved based on *non-committing* TLPs, which use access to a programmable random oracle.

1.1 Our Contributions

In this paper we carry out a thorough investigation of adaptively secure broadcast for a wide class of common setups, both in the property-based and in the simulation-based security settings. In the property-based setting, we devise a characterization of the feasibility landscape covering a broad class of protocols—effectively, all known broadcast protocols from the literature; for simulation-based security, our characterization is *complete*—i.e., it covers all possible protocols. Our results are summarized in Table 1.

We proceed to describe our contributions in more detail.

A Property-Based Definition of Adaptively Secure Broadcast. Our first contribution towards investigating the applicability of the impossibility results of Hirt and Zikas [58] to the property-based setting, is to come up with a property-based definition of secure broadcast that captures the essence of an adaptive attack (like the one from [58]). We stress that one might be able to come up with several variants of such a definition, that capture different aspects of corrupting a party in an adaptive fashion. Our goal, however, is not to answer the question "What is

Table 1. Feasibility of adaptively secure broadcast with non-atomic multisend, synchronous communication. All negative results (lower bounds) hold for any dishonest majority of fail-stop corruptions and any correlated-randomness setup; (∗) negative results for property-based broadcast are for protocols in the class $\Pi_{\mathsf{step\text{-}rel}}$ (that includes all known broadcast protocols), see Definition 9. All positive results (protocol constructions) tolerate an arbitrary number of malicious corruptions and require a PKI for signatures. TLP stands for a weak time-lock puzzle and RO for programmable random-oracle model.

	property-based	**simulation-based**
PKI	✗* **Theorem** 2	✗ HZ [58]
PKI+RO	✗* **Corollary** 3	✗ **Corollary** 2
PKI+TLP	✓ **Theorem** 3	✗ **Theorem** 5
PKI+TLP+RO	✓ **Theorem** 3	✓**Theorem** 6

the *right* property-based definition of adaptively secure broadcast?"[8]; rather, any such definition that extends the standard property-based definition to capture natural effects of adversarial adaptivity is well suited for understanding applicability of lower bounds to the property-based setting, because they highlight different attack surfaces that might be exploited by an adaptive adversary.

In a nutshell, the new definition aims to capture the following natural property of adaptively secure protocols (which has thus far not been made explicit in the analysis of adaptive security): The (adaptive) adversary should not be able to corrupt a party—in our case the sender—and influence this party's input value based on this value.[9] One can easily see the importance of such a property for randomized tasks beyond just broadcast, such as for example leader election. In fact, as it will become apparent from our property-based impossibility proof, the corruption fairness property is related to the existence of a *committal round* [72], i.e., a fixed round in which all inputs to the protocol are committed. As proven by Canetti et al. [26], a committal round is necessary for boosting static security to adaptive security, generically, in perfectly secure MPC.

We name the new property *corruption fairness with respect to inputs* (*corruption fairness* for short). In more detail, following [58] and with the illustrating example of broadcasting a random bit in mind (where the adversary's goal is to corrupt only parties who broadcast a given value, say 1, and flip their bit), our definition goes as follows (see Definition 5 for a formal version).

Definition (Broadcast, property-based definition, informal). An n-party protocol is an *adaptively secure t-resilient broadcast protocol* according to the property-based definition if, in addition to agreement and validity, it satisfies the following:

[8] In fact, we conjecture that it might be impossible to capture *all* natural properties of adaptive security in *one* property-based definition, i.e., without effectively resorting to the simulation-based paradigm.

[9] It might be useful to make a distinction here between *corruption fairness* and *input independence*: The latter requires that the adversary cannot bias corrupted parties' input based on the honest parties' input, and, unlike corruption fairness, applies both to static and adaptive adversaries.

- **Corruption fairness with respect to inputs:** The probability of any PPT adversary to win the following game is bounded by $1/2 + \mathsf{negl}(\kappa)$ (where κ denotes the security parameter). When attacking an execution of the protocol where the sender begins with a random bit $b \leftarrow \{0,1\}$ as its input, we say that the adversary wins the game if one of the following events occurs:
  - $b = 0$ and the sender remained honest at the end of the protocol;
  - $b = 1$ and the common output of the honest parties is 0.

We emphasize that the definition can easily be generalized to deal with arbitrary, polynomial-length messages, and to any message x_0 that the adversary wishes to bias towards. That is, where the goal of the adversary is to keep the sender honest whenever sending the message x_0, but corrupt the sender when sending a message $x \neq x_0$ and force the output to be x_0.

We illustrate the power of this definition compared to the weaker definition (that guarantees only *agreement* and *validity*) via the following use cases:

- The first is *collective coin flipping* where each party broadcasts a random bit. When corrupting an arbitrary set of t parties the adversary can set their inputs to 1, but on expectation $t/2$ of them already started with 1, so on expectation $(n+t)/2$ values will be 1 and $(n-t)/2$ values will be 0. Using a broadcast protocol satisfying the definition above, the adversary gains no more power. However, using the weaker definition, the adversary can dynamically choose to corrupt t parties who broadcast 0, thus on expectation $n/2+t$ values will be 1 and $n/2-t$ values will be 0.
- The second is *hiding a small number of senders in a large population.* In many settings a small set of initially unpredictable parties should reliably broadcast their messages. Using a broadcast protocol satisfying the weaker notion, the adversary can monitor the system and immediately corrupt any party who sends a message, thus executing a DoS attack. This can be overcome using a broadcast protocol satisfying the definition above, where each sender broadcasts its message while adding '1' as a prefix, whereas all other parties broadcast the zero string; messages starting with '0' are later discarded.[10] A similar approach was used in the broadcast protocol of Wan et al. [83] to achieve a single-round reliable communication by a small set of unpredictable senders; however, as we explain below, their construction still does not satisfy the *corruption-fairness* property.

Impossibility of Property-Based Adaptively Secure Broadcast. It is not hard to verify that any broadcast protocol that is secure according to the simulation-based definition (i.e., realizes the ideal megaphone functionality) is also secure according to the property-based definition of (adaptively secure) broadcast. The intuition is that a simulator that interacts with the megaphone functionality can win the corruption-fairness game only with probability 1/2 (by guessing

[10] Note that in our model the adversary can corrupt a party after sending a message and drop the message from the network, but this is done *independently* of the content of the message; therefore, we require all other parties to broadcast dummy messages.

the input), and therefore any adversary that can win the corruption-fairness game with a noticeable probability over 1/2 can be translated to a distinguisher between the real and ideal computations. We formally prove this result in Lemma 1.

However, one may ask whether the property-based definition is actually weaker than the simulation-based definition, or if it is equivalent. Stated differently, does the property-based definition above capture the attack from [58]? The attack from [58] rules out the simulation-based definition, but that may perhaps be due to another feature of the megaphone functionality.

Our second contribution is extending the impossibility result from [58] to rule out the property-based definition for a large class of protocols that includes all published approaches to construct broadcast protocols, in particular recent ones explicitly targeting adaptive security [28,82–84]. Intuitively, this covers all protocols that define an *a-priori*-known round R such that prior to round R it is guaranteed that no set of size $\lfloor n/2 \rfloor - 1$ "knows" the sender's input (in the sense that if this set emulates in its head a continuation of the protocol where all other parties crash, it has a noticeable error probability), and at round R there exists a set of size $\lfloor n/2 \rfloor - 1$ that "knows" the sender's input (i.e., by emulating the continuation, the set errs only with negligible probability).[11] In the sequel, we will denote this class of "step-release" protocols by $\Pi_{\mathsf{step\text{-}rel}}$. It is worth noting that existence (but not *a-priori* public knowledge) of such a round is guaranteed in any *execution* of any broadcast protocol, which follows from the fact that at the beginning of the protocol only the sender knows his input, whereas at the end everyone learns it.

This means that in term of *feasibility*, the simulation-based definition and the property-based definition are *equivalent* for all protocols from the class $\Pi_{\mathsf{step\text{-}rel}}$: i.e., for $t \leq n/2$ both definitions can be satisfied, and for $t > n/2$ both definitions cannot be satisfied. Note that this does not imply that any protocol that satisfies the property-based definition also satisfies the simulation-based definition.

Theorem 2 (Impossibility of property-based broadcast, informal). *Let $t > n/2$. Then, there is no adaptively secure broadcast protocol (from the class $\Pi_{\mathsf{step\text{-}rel}}$) tolerating a fail-stop, PPT t -adversary that satisfies the property-based definition of (adaptively secure) broadcast.*

We note that the impossibility result holds even assuming any correlated-randomness setup and/or secure data erasures.

Overcoming the Property-Based Impossibility via TLPs. Next, we study whether the RRC paradigm can overcome the impossibility of adaptively secure broadcast. We use TLPs [11,79] for this task. The idea is quite simple: the sender "hides" its message inside a TLP and uses a protocol for corruption-unfair broadcast (e.g., [35,83]) to send the puzzle to all parties; every recipient can open the puzzle after investing a polynomial amount of computation and obtain the output. We note that our usage of TLPs is similar to Wan et al. [83] with the difference that in [83]

[11] In most broadcast protocols from the literature (e.g., [28,35,46,83,84]), the sender starts by sending its input to all parties, meaning that $R = 1$.

the TLP was hidden for a duration of a round, whereas we hide it for the duration of the entire protocol; see Appendix 1.2 for a detailed comparison.

The guarantee provided by a TLP with gap $\varepsilon < 1$ (see Definition 2) is that when setting the puzzle with difficulty parameter $T^{1/\varepsilon}$, any adversary that can evaluate circuits of polynomial size, but of depth bounded by $T(\kappa)$, cannot solve the puzzle with better than negligible probability. We will say that an adversary is (R, T)*-bounded* if the number of parallel steps it can take within R rounds is bounded by $T(\kappa)$. Therefore, if the corruption-unfair broadcast protocol takes R rounds, we are guaranteed that any (R, T)-bounded adversary cannot win the corruption-fairness game with more than $1/2 + \mathsf{negl}(\kappa)$ probability.

In fact, our protocol does not require a "lightweight" generation of the puzzle, and can use a puzzle generation that is as computationally expensive as solving the puzzle. Therefore, we only require the *weak* variant of time-lock puzzles [11,69] that allows for parallelizable, yet computationally expensive puzzle generation, and can be based on one-way functions and the existence of non-parallelizing languages [11]. We show:

Theorem 3 (Feasibility of property-based broadcast via TLPs, informal)**.** *Let $t \leq n$, let T be a polynomial, assume that weak time-lock puzzles exist, and that corruption-unfair broadcast can be computed in R rounds. Then, there is an adaptively secure broadcast protocol tolerating an (R, T)-bounded t-adversary that satisfies the property-based definition of (adaptively secure) broadcast.*

TLP Barriers for Simulation-Based Broadcast. Next, we ask whether TLPs are also sufficient to satisfy the simulation-based definition of broadcast. Somewhat surprisingly, the answer to this question is negative, thus posing a separation between the two definitions. The main reason is illustrated when trying to simulate the protocol that satisfies the property-based definition. When the sender is honest and a simulator tries to simulate the TLP without knowing the message, it gets stuck, since the TLP is a committing object: Once the puzzle is generated it can only be opened to a unique value. Therefore, the simulator's success probability is again restricted to correctly guessing the sender's input, which results in a noticeable distinguishing probability between the real and ideal executions.

In Sect. 5.1 we extend this argument to rule out *any* adaptively secure broadcast protocol even facing an (R, T)-bounded adversary. In turn, this implies that TLPs are not sufficient for realizing simulation-based broadcast.

Theorem 5 (Impossibility for simulation-based broadcast from TLPs, informal)**.** *Let $t > n/2$, and let R and T be polynomials. Then there is no adaptively secure broadcast protocol tolerating an (R, T)-bounded, fail-stop, PPT t-adversary that satisfies the simulation-based definition of broadcast.*

The impossibility result can be extended to hold even assuming any correlated-randomness setup, secure data erasures, and/or a non-programmable random oracle, in addition to TLPs.

Overcoming the Simulation-Based Impossibility of Adaptively Secure Broadcast. We note that the above "barrier" resembles other barriers in achieving adaptive security of committing cryptographic primitives, such as commitments [23,26] and public-key encryption [73]. Next, we show that a programmable random oracle can be used to construct a non-committing variant of TLPs, which in turn allows us to overcome the above barrier. Namely, instead of hiding the message m inside the puzzle, the sender samples a random one-time pad key x, hides x inside the puzzle, and corruption-unfairly broadcasts the puzzle along with $c = m \oplus H(x)$. Now the simulator can simulate a puzzle when the sender is honest, and upon a corruption request of the sender (or after R rounds have elapsed, and it can safely ask the megaphone functionality for the output), the simulator can program the random oracle appropriately.

This approach is similar to the one in [5,9] who used a programmable RO to model composable TLPs. What **substantially differentiates** our treatment is that we rely on the *complexity-based* definition of TLPs [11], which is realizable from computational hardness assumptions, rather than requiring, as [5,9] do, access to an ideal functionality which is **not** (and arguably *cannot* be) implemented from such assumptions in the plain model. This forces us to explicitly treat the composability issues of (complexity-based) TLP constructions. This turns out to be non-trivial and may be of independent interest.

Theorem 6 (Feasibility of simulation-based broadcast via TLPs in the RO model, informal). *Let $t < n$, let T be a polynomial, assume that weak TLPs exist, and that corruption-unfair broadcast can be executed in R rounds. Then, there is an adaptively secure broadcast protocol, according to the simulation-based definition, tolerating an (R, T)-bounded t-adversary in the programmable random-oracle model.*

Random Oracle (RO) Barriers. Given the simulation-based impossibility even assuming TLPs and the above possibility when assuming TLP in tandem with a programable RO, one might wonder whether just assuming a programable RO would do the trick. We answer this question in the negative, by showing how to adapt the impossibility of Theorem 5 to hold when we replace TLPs with an (even programable) RO (see Corollary 2). To complete the picture, we also show how to derive the impossibility of property-based adaptively secure broadcast even assuming an RO, as a simple corollary of Theorem 2 (see Corollary 3).

Composition in Resource-Restricted Settings. The protocols in our positive results (Theorems 3 and 6) rely on delivering a TLP to all parties via an ideal corruption-unfair broadcast functionality $\mathcal{F}_{\mathsf{ubc}}$; indeed, one can later use the protocol of Dolev and Strong [35] as a concrete instantiation of corruption-unfair broadcast in the PKI model. It might be tempting to use an off-the-shelf composition theorem for claiming security of the derived protocol. However, it turns out that standard composition theorems no longer apply in the RRC setting since the adversary may take advantage of the honest parties' resources in the sub-protocol when attacking the higher-level execution. For example, given a corruption-unfair broadcast protocol π, consider a new protocol π' where some party P_i sends a TLP to another party P_j who solves the puzzle and returns the solution to P_i; otherwise, all parties proceed according to π. Clearly, π' has the same security guarantees as π; however, when used to instantiate $\mathcal{F}_{\mathsf{ubc}}$ in our broadcast constructions, the adversary can corrupt P_i and send the sender's TLP to P_j and this way learn the underlying message.[12]

As an additional contribution, we prove a limited composition theorem (Theorems 4 and 7) that is sufficient for instantiating $\mathcal{F}_{\mathsf{ubc}}$ in our setting by protocols that also consider a bound on the parallel computational resources of honest parties; for example, in the case of Dolev and Strong [35], honest parties only sign and verify signatures, but do not perform other computations, so the adversary cannot "outsource" solving the puzzle to honest parties. We leave the quest for a more general composition theorem as an interesting open problem.

Summary of Our Contributions. Taken together, our results distill the essence and extend the reach of the impossibility result from [58]. This establishes that the impossibility of adaptively secure broadcast is not just an artifact of the simulation-based definition, but it also applies to an extension of the property-based broadcast definition to the adaptive-corruptions case. Further, we show how the resource-restricted paradigm separates the property-based definition from the simulation-based definition, which serves as yet another motivation for using simulation-based security, especially when designing adaptively secure protocols. Finally, we prove the first composition theorem in the RRC setting, where UC composition no longer holds.

1.2 Related Work

Recently, Wan et al. [83] used TLPs to construct adaptively secure **corruption-unfair** broadcast protocols (i.e., not the adaptively secure primitive we are after) in the non-atomic multisend model, with the goal of reducing the round complexity of randomized broadcast from linear to poly-logarithmic, facing a constant fraction of corrupted parties. As pointed out by the authors, their goal was *not* to realize the megaphone functionality, but only to satisfy the property-based definition of (corruption-unfair) broadcast. The main idea in [83] is to use TLPs to "hide" the contents of the messages *for one round at a time* in a way that essentially provides atomic-multisend guarantees. Given this, they run the polylogarithmic-round protocol of Chan et al. [28], which in turn is based on Dolev and Strong [35].

We note that although the protocol in [83] relies on similar assumptions as the ones in this work, it **does not** answer our question as it is vulnerable to the attack from [47], showing that the Dolev-Strong protocol (DS) [35] is **not** adaptively secure even in the atomic-multisend model. Specifically, the adversary waits for the completion of the first round of DS, in which the sender sends its input to all parties. Before the second round begins, the adversary (who learns

[12] The UC composition theorem in [22] applies to *balanced* environments, i.e., environments that do not give honest parties much more resources than to the adversary. In [22] the focus is on running time, whereas in this work it is on *parallel* running time; hence, by abusing the terminology from [22], one can say that the environment in our protocol is not balanced with respect to parallel running time.

the content of the message at that point) can decide whether to corrupt the sender and "inject" a signature on a different message to some of the second-round messages (thus forcing the protocol to abort and output a default value), or keep the sender honest and let the protocol successfully complete with the original input message. In contrast, in our construction we hide the message using a TLP for the entire duration of DS protocol (not in a round-by-round way), and this enables overcoming the attack from [47].

Baum et al. [9] study a stronger version of TLPs that provides universal composability. They define an ideal TLP functionality, and prove that realizing it inherently requires a programmable random oracle. Next, they realize the TLP functionality based on generic-group-style formalization of the repeated-squaring technique from [79] as well as a restricted programmable and observable random oracle [19]. In contrast to the weaker, property-based definition of TLP [11,79] (used in this paper), the reliance on a random oracle in [9] enables the TLP functionality to define a fixed and *a priori* known step with the guarantee that the adversary learns nothing about the content of the TLP prior to that step and that once that step is reached, the content of the puzzle is fully revealed. The ideas from [9] that apply to the two-party setting were extended in [10] to capture the multi-party case, as well as verifiable delay functions.

In more detail, Baum et al. [9] give an elegant argument showing that coin-flipping protocols based on TLPs, such as the one of Boneh and Naor [14], cannot be simulated without resorting to a programmable RO, even facing so-called *computationally restricted environments.* Essentially, when simulating a TLP-based coin-flipping protocol, the environment may first get the information needed to learn the output (possibly after the conclusion of the protocol) and then abort with probability 1/2. Next, it can check whether the output learned from its view matches the honest party's output; if so it outputs 'ideal' and if not 'real'. The simulator who receives the honest party's output must simulate the view using this output bit without knowing whether the environment will abort or not; in case of abort, the simulator must equivocate the output obtained from the committed view by the environment to be a random bit—a task that cannot be achieved in the standard model.

Although our proof technique and overall reasoning are very different from those in [9], the source of the impossibility in both cases is the fact that TLPs are non-equivocable. Such equivocality turns out to be essential in both simulation arguments, despite the inherent difference of the primitives and the statements themselves. For example, as the impossibility of [9] relies on Cleve's impossibility [30], the attack applies even with static corruptions; further, when considering the multiparty setting it is oblivious to the underlying network (e.g., it applies even given a broadcast channel). In contrast, in our setting, the attack crucially relies on the adversary's adaptive and rushing capabilities, and is very sensitive to the underlying network assumptions (e.g., the attack no longer holds in the atomic-multisend model).

Matt et al. [71] formalized the notion of delayed adaptive corruptions in UC, where the adversary, who wishes to corrupt a certain party, gets hold of the newly corrupted party only after some time has elapsed. The goal of their paper is to prove security of various flooding protocols (that inherently require a strong form of atomic multisend capabilities) in this model. In contrast to [71] we do not restrict in the model the time it takes the adversary to corrupt a party, but instead rely on cryptographic assumptions.

Arapinis et al. [5] presented a UC modeling of TLPs in the UC framework. To overcome the non-equivocation barrier of TLPs, they follow Nielsen [73] and use a programmable random oracle to equivocate the content of the TLP; our construction for overcoming the impossibility of simulation-based adaptively secure broadcast from TLPs essentially uses the same technique as [5] for equivocating the TLP using a programmable RO. As opposed to [9], they do not rely on generic-group-style assumptions and rely solely on a programmable random oracle; however, to restrict the computational capabilities of the adversary, the authors use a functionality wrapper that limits the number of evaluation queries that can be done in a round in the spirit of [6,50].

We remark that [5,9,10] use an **ideal functionality** to model TLPs, but it is unclear how to **compose** a realization of the TLP functionality in a protocol that invokes it without resorting to generic-group-style assumptions or a functionality wrapper (as discussed above, standard UC composition does not apply in the resource-restricted setting). In contrast, our composition theorem provides a fine-grained analysis of a limited "plug-and-play" design for TLPs.

2 Preliminaries

In this section we first present the network model, followed by some basics on simulation-based security, and conclude with the definition of time-lock puzzles.

2.1 The Model

An n-party protocol $\pi = (P_1, \ldots, P_n)$ is an n-tuple of PPT interactive Turing machines (ITMs). The term *party* P_i refers to the ith ITM; we denote the set of parties by $\mathcal{P} = \{P_1, \ldots, P_n\}$. Each party P_i starts with input $x_i \in \{0,1\}^*$ and random coins $r_i \in \{0,1\}^*$. Without loss of generality, the input length of each party is assumed to be the security parameter κ. We consider protocols that additionally have a setup phase (used, e.g., to model a public-key infrastructure (PKI)) where a trusted dealer samples (possibly correlated) secret values $(\mathbf{r}_1, \ldots, \mathbf{r}_n) \leftarrow D_\pi$ from some efficiently sampleable distribution D_π, and hands party P_i the secret string $\mathbf{r}_i$ (referred to as the correlated randomness of P_i). While our lower bounds hold with respect to any distribution for correlated randomness, our upper bounds rely on a weaker setup assumption of a PKI for digital signatures, where each party generates a pair of signing/verification keys and publishes its verification key.

An *adversary* $\mathcal{A}$ is another PPT ITM describing the behavior of the corrupted parties. It starts the execution with input that contains the security parameter (in unary) and an additional auxiliary input. At any time during the execution of the protocol the adversary can corrupt one of the honest parties, in which case the adversary can read its internal state (containing its input, random coins, correlated randomness, and incoming messages) and gains control over it. A t-adversary is limited to corrupt up to t parties.

The parties execute the protocol over a fully connected synchronous network of point-to-point channels. That is, the execution proceeds in rounds: Each round consists of a *send phase* (where parties send their messages from this round) followed by a *receive phase* (where they receive messages from other parties). The adversary is assumed to be *rushing*, which means that it can see the messages the honest parties send in a round before determining the messages that the corrupted parties send in that round. The communication lines between the parties are assumed to be ideally authenticated (and thus the adversary cannot modify messages sent between two honest parties but can read them).

Throughout the execution of the protocol, all the honest parties follow the instructions of the prescribed protocol, whereas the corrupted parties receive their instructions from the adversary. In our positive results, the adversary is considered to be actively malicious, meaning that it can instruct the corrupted parties to deviate from the protocol in any arbitrary way. Our lower bounds, however, only rely on fail-stop adversaries that can crash parties, but not cheat in any other way. At the conclusion of the execution, the honest parties output their prescribed output from the protocol, the corrupted parties do not output anything and the adversary outputs an (arbitrary) function of its view of the computation (containing the views (internal states) of the corrupted parties).

Atomic Multisend. A subtle point that is central to this work is the capabilities of the adversary when corrupting a party that has just sent its messages for the round. Two central models are considered in the literature:

- In the *atomic multisend* model [47] a message that has been sent to the network is guaranteed to be delivered to its recipients even if the sender becomes corrupted shortly after sending; further, the messages are sent to the network as an atomic operation in the sense that once the sender begins sending its messages for the round it cannot become corrupted until it has finished sending all of its messages for the round. This model has gained popularity in many recent consensus protocols (e.g., [1,13,28,29,82,84]).
- In the standard (*non-atomic multisend*) model, the operation of sending messages to the channel is not atomic, and the adversary may corrupt a sender *after* it sent its message to some party P_i and *before* it has sent its message to another party P_j; further, the adversary can drop the message the newly corrupted sender sent to P_i and replace it with another. This is the model that has been used in classical models of distributed computation (e.g., [35,38–40]) and cryptographic protocols [20,21,24,27]. This models has also been referred to as *strongly adaptive* [55,56,60,64] and *strongly rushing* [1,2,83].

In this work we consider the non-atomic multisend model. Clearly, this is the preferred one as it requires less assumptions on the underlying communication. However, this model is more challenging as it considers more powerful adversaries; indeed, certain impossibility results in the non-atomic-multisend model do not translate to the atomic-multisend realm [1,17,58]. In fact, as proven by Katz et al. [61], atomic multisend is a strictly weaker model facing dishonest-majority as it cannot be realized from the basic ingredients needed for synchronous communication (bounded-delay channels and a synchronizing clock).

Secure Data Erasures. Two models are normally considered in the adaptive-corruption setting, depending on the ability of honest parties to securely erase certain parts of their memory (i.e., from their internal state) without leaving any trace; see [20,24] for a discussion. While some impossibility results of adaptively secure cryptographic protocols crucially rely on parties *not* being able to erase any information, and completely break otherwise (e.g., [49,51,57,73]), other impossibility results are stronger and do not rely on the absence of secure erasures (e.g., [17,33,58,62]).

In this work we do not assume secure erasures for our protocol constructions; however, our impossibility results hold even in the secure-erasures model. This makes for the strongest statements; to avoid confusion we will state the model explicitly in each section.

2.2 Simulation-Based Security

Some of the results in this work consider a simulation-based definition of broadcast, where security is defined via the real vs. ideal paradigm. Namely, a protocol is considered secure if every attack that can be executed by a PPT adversary in the real-world execution, can be simulated by a PPT simulator in an ideal world, where an incorruptible trusted third party (aka, the *ideal functionality*) receives inputs from the parties and carries out the computation on their behalf. For the specific task of broadcast, the trusted party receives the input from the broadcaster and delivers it to all other parties (see Sect. 3.2).

We consider a *synchronous* model with an online distinguisher (aka, the *environment*); this is the prevalent model in many frameworks for cryptographic protocols; see, e.g., [7–9,21,59,65,68,74]. Such a model requires the simulator to report its view to the distinguisher in every round. We do not rely on any other specific properties of the model, but for concreteness, we state our results in the synchronous model of the UC framework as defined in [8,61,65].

Loosely speaking, we consider protocols that run in a hybrid model where parties have access to a simple "clock" functionality $\mathcal{G}_{\mathsf{clock}}$. This functionality keeps a counter, which is incremented once *all honest parties* request the functionality to do so, i.e., once all honest parties have completed their operations for the current round. In addition, all communication is done over bounded-delay channels, where each party requests the channel to fetch messages that are sent to him, such that the adversary is allowed to delay the message delivery by a bounded and *a priori* known number of fetch requests. Stated differently, once the sender has sent some message, it is guaranteed that the message will be delivered within a known number of activations of the receiver. For simplicity, we assume that every message is delivered within a single fetch request.

We note that when considering online distinguishers, a resource-restricted adversary may bypass its limitations by delegating some of its computation to the environment. It is therefore standard to restrict the resources of the environment as well, see e.g., [45]. In this work, when considering a resource-restricted adversary in the simulation-based setting, we will consider the pair of an adversary and an environment as resource restricted, in the sense the their joint resource is bounded.

To simplify the presentation we describe the functionalities and protocols in a less technical way than standard UC formulations (e.g., we do not explicitly mention the session id and party id in every message, and somewhat abuse the activation policy by batching several operations together).

2.3 Time-Lock Puzzles

Time-lock puzzles [79] enable a sender to "lock" its message in a way that "unlocking" requires an inherently sequential computation. This is a powerful primitive that has led to many results, and has been extensively studied; see, e.g., [3,9,11,14,18,37,42,45,63,67,69,70,80,81,83]. While the standard definition requires the puzzle generation to be "lightweight" compared to solving the puzzle, our feasibility results can be based on the weaker notion in which puzzle generation is as computationally expensive as solving the puzzle (yet, as opposed to puzzle solving, the puzzle generation is parallelizable). Such weak time-lock puzzles are known from the minimal assumption of one-way functions and the existence of non-parallelizing languages [11,69]. In this paper we follow the formulation by Bitansky et al. [11].

Puzzles. A puzzle is associated with a pair of parameters: A security parameter κ determining the cryptographic security of the puzzle, as well as a difficulty parameter T that determines how difficult it is to solve the puzzle.

Definition 1 (Puzzle). *A* puzzle *is a pair of algorithms* $(\mathsf{PGen}, \mathsf{PSol})$ *satisfying the following requirements.*

- Syntax:
  - $Z \leftarrow \mathsf{PGen}(T, s)$ *is a probabilistic algorithm that takes as input a difficulty parameter* T *and a solution* $s \in \{0,1\}^\kappa$*, where* κ *is a security parameter, and outputs a puzzle* Z*.*
  - $s = \mathsf{PSol}(Z)$ *is a deterministic algorithm that takes as input a puzzle* Z *and outputs a solution* s*.*
- Completeness: *For every security parameter* κ*, difficulty parameter* T*, solution* $s \in \{0,1\}^\kappa$ *and puzzle* Z *in the support of* $\mathsf{PGen}(T, s)$, $\mathsf{PSol}(Z)$ *outputs* s*.*
- Efficiency:
  - $Z \leftarrow \mathsf{PGen}(T, s)$ *can be computed in time* $\mathsf{poly}(\log T, \kappa)$*.*
  - $\mathsf{PSol}(Z)$ *can be computed in time* $T \cdot \mathsf{poly}(\kappa)$*.*

Time-Lock Puzzles. In a time-lock puzzle, we require that the parallel time required to solve a puzzle is proportional to the time it takes to solve the puzzle honestly, up to some fixed polynomial loss.

Definition 2 (Time-lock puzzle). *A puzzle* $(\mathsf{PGen}, \mathsf{PSol})$ *is a* time-lock puzzle with gap $\varepsilon < 1$ *if there exists a polynomial* $T_1(\cdot)$*, such that for every polynomial* $T(\cdot) \geq T_1(\cdot)$ *and every polysize adversary* $\mathcal{A} = \{\mathcal{A}_\kappa\}_{\kappa \in \mathbb{N}}$ *of depth* $\mathsf{depth}(\mathcal{A}_\kappa) \leq$

$T^{\varepsilon}(\kappa)$, there exists a negligible function μ, such that for every $\kappa \in \mathbb{N}$, and every pair of solutions $s_0, s_1 \in \{0,1\}^{\kappa}$:

$$\Pr\left[b \leftarrow \mathcal{A}_{\kappa}(Z) \;\middle|\; b \leftarrow \{0,1\}, Z \leftarrow \mathsf{PGen}(T, s_b)\right] \leq 1/2 + \mu(\kappa).$$

Definition 3 (Weak puzzle). *A weak puzzle is a pair of algorithms* ($\mathsf{PGen}, \mathsf{PSol}$) *satisfying the* Syntax *and* Completeness *requirements as per Definition 1, and the following* weak efficiency *requirement.*

- Weak Efficiency:
  - $Z \leftarrow \mathsf{PGen}(T, s)$ *can be computed by a uniform circuit of size* $\mathsf{poly}(T, \kappa)$ *and depth* $\mathsf{poly}(\log T, \kappa)$.
  - $\mathsf{PSol}(Z)$ *can be computed in time* $T \cdot \mathsf{poly}(\kappa)$.

Mahmoody et al. [69] showed how to construct a weak time-lock puzzle in the random-oracle model while Bitansky et al. [11] showed how to construct it from any one-way function and non-parallelizing language.

Definition 4 (Non-parallelizing language). *A language $\mathcal{L} \in \mathsf{DTime}(T(\cdot))$ is* non-parallelizing with gap $\varepsilon < 1$ *if for every family of non-uniform polysize circuits $\mathcal{B} = \{\mathcal{B}_{\kappa}\}_{\kappa \in \mathbb{N}}$ where $\mathsf{depth}(\mathcal{B}_{\kappa}) \leq T^{\varepsilon}(\kappa)$ and every large enough κ, $\mathcal{B}_{\kappa}$ fails to decide $\mathcal{L}_{\kappa} = \mathcal{L} \cap \{0,1\}^{\kappa}$.*

Theorem 1 ([11]). *Let $\varepsilon < 1$. Assume that one-way functions exist, and that for every polynomially bounded function $T(\cdot)$ there exists a non-parallelizing language $\mathcal{L} \in \mathsf{DTime}(T(\cdot))$ with gap ε. Then, for any $\varepsilon_1 < \varepsilon$ there exists a weak time-lock puzzle with gap ε_1.*

3 Broadcast Protocols: Definitions

Intuitively, a broadcast protocol should emulate a "megaphone" functionality in the sense that when the sender speaks, all recipients receive its message. This is traditionally captured via the *agreement* and *validity* properties. However, as observed in Hirt and Zikas [58], such a property-based definition falls short of capturing the ideal megaphone functionality when facing adaptive corruptions. Namely, the ideal megaphone functionality does not allow the adversary to corrupt the sender after learning its input message, and change it retrospectively. Hirt and Zikas [58] further showed that the ideal megaphone functionality cannot be realized in the dishonest-majority setting in the standard (non-atomic-multisend) communication model.

3.1 Property-Based Broadcast

With the goal of distilling the essence of the impossibility result in [58], we provide a weaker, property-based definition that is complete in the presence of adaptive corruptions. In addition to *termination*, *agreement*, and *validity*, this definition requires another property: *corruption fairness with respect to inputs* (corruption-fairness for short). As discussed in the introduction, even though this definition is weaker than the simulation-based one, it is still stronger than the traditional definition of broadcast and enables realizing tasks for which traditional broadcast is not sufficient.

Recall that when broadcasting a random bit via a "corruption-unfair" broadcast (where only *termination*, *agreement*, and *validity* are guaranteed), the adversary gets to learn the input bit *before* deciding whether to corrupt the sender and change its input; for example, the adversary may corrupt the sender when the input is 1 and flip it to 0, but when the input is 0 the adversary may continue without corrupting the sender. Informally, a broadcast protocol should not concede this capability to the adversary.

Without loss of generality, we consider the message space to be $\{0,1\}^{\kappa}$. Looking ahead, our lower bounds hold even in the simpler, Boolean case where the message space is $\{0,1\}$, while our upper bounds hold for any polynomial-length messages. The goal of the adversary in the corruption-fairness experiment is to force the output to be some predetermined message $x_0 \in \{0,1\}^{\kappa}$ but without corrupting the sender in case it begins with input x_0. Again, without loss of generality, we let $x_0 = 0^{\kappa}$, and to simplify the definition consider two potential messages in the experiment: 0^{κ} and 1^{κ}.

Definition 5 (Broadcast, property-based definition). *An n-party protocol π, where a distinguished sender holds an initial input message $m \in \{0,1\}^{\kappa}$, is a* broadcast protocol *(according to the property-based definition) tolerating adaptive PPT t-adversaries, if the following conditions are satisfied for any adaptive PPT t-adversary $\mathcal{A}$:*

- ***Termination:*** *There exists an a-priori-known round R such that the protocol is guaranteed to complete (i.e., every so-far honest party produces an output value) within R rounds.*
- ***Agreement:*** *All honest parties (at the end of the protocol) output the same value, with all but negligible probability.*
- ***Validity:*** *If the sender is honest (at the end of the protocol) then all honest parties (at the end of the protocol) output m, with all but negligible probability.*
- ***Corruption fairness with respect to inputs:***

$$\Pr\left[\mathsf{Expt}^{\mathsf{fair\text{-}bcast}}_{\pi,\mathcal{A}}(\kappa) = 1\right] \le \frac{1}{2} + \mathsf{negl}(\kappa),$$

where the experiment $\mathsf{Expt}^{\mathsf{fair\text{-}bcast}}_{\pi,\mathcal{A}}(\kappa)$ is defined in Fig. 1.

Note that, as observed in [58], the protocol of Dolev and Strong [35] (as well as most broadcast protocols in the literature) allows an adversary to first learn the sender's input message m, and later change the common output as a function of m. Therefore, this protocol does not satisfy the *corruption-fairness* property (even in the atomic-multisend model [47]). The broadcast protocols from [31,32,58] satisfy this property for $t \le n/2$ in the standard model, and similarly, the protocol from [47] for $t < n$ in the atomic-multisend model.

Experiment $\mathsf{Expt}^{\mathsf{fair\text{-}bcast}}_{\pi,\mathcal{A}}(\kappa)$

1. The challenger samples a uniformly random bit $b \leftarrow \{0,1\}$ and invokes $\mathcal{A}$ on input 1^κ.
2. The challenger samples randomness[a] $(\mathbf{r}_1,\ldots,\mathbf{r}_n) \leftarrow D_\pi$ and simulates the protocol π on sender-input b^κ toward $\mathcal{A}$, who can adaptively corrupt parties throughout the execution. (The challenger simulates all honest parties, and upon a corruption request reveals the internal state of the corrupted party to the adversary, as well as the control over that party.)
3. The output of the experiment is set to 1 if:
   - $b = 0$ and the sender is honest at the end of the protocol;
   - $b = 1$ and the output value of an arbitrary honest party is 0^κ.

   Otherwise, the output of the experiment is set to 0. (If all parties are corrupted, the output is set to be 0.)

[a] Without loss of generality this includes both the protocol's random coins and any potentially correlated randomness (setup) parties might use.

Fig. 1. The corruption-fairness experiment for adaptively secure broadcast

We shall refer to the commonly used property-based definition of broadcast as *corruption-unfair broadcast.*

Definition 6 (Corruption-unfair broadcast, property-based definition). *An n-party protocol π tolerating an adaptive PPT t-adversary, is a corruption-unfair broadcast protocol if* agreement, validity *and* termination *hold, but* corruption-fairness *does not necessarily hold.*

3.2 Simulation-Based Broadcast

While the property-based definitions provide the core requirements of broadcast, they are weaker than simulation-based definitions and are therefore more suitable for lower bounds. We next present the stronger simulation-based definitions which are better suited for proving the security of protocol constructions.

Definition 7 (Broadcast, simulation-based definition). *An n-party protocol π, is a broadcast protocol (according to the simulation-based definition) tolerating an adaptive PPT t-adversary, if π securely realizes the broadcast functionality, defined in Fig. 2.*

We note that our functionality captures causality of corruption vs. information release—the two events that affect corruption-fairness—in an explicit manner, as opposed to [47,58]. Concretely, we specify the causality of the events that the adversary asks to learn the output and that the output value is locked. In particular, in [58], once the input is handed to the functionality, it is automatically locked (so the adversary is not allowed to corrupt the sender and change it). Although this does not make a difference in a standalone setting with an "offline distinguisher" (as the simulator can decide whether to corrupt the sender before the sender hands its input to the ideal functionality), in a UC-like setting the simulator might not be informed when the (honest) input is given. This might enable the design of protocols which artificially reduce the simulator's choice to corrupt and erase; e.g., if the sender chooses one of polynomially many rounds to start broadcasting its input.

The functionality $\mathcal{F}_{\mathsf{bc}}$

- **Initialization:** The functionality initializes the output message $m_{\mathsf{out}} := \bot$ and a Boolean flag $\mathsf{isOutputLocked} := \mathsf{false}$.
- **Input:** The sender sends an input message $m \in \{0,1\}^\kappa$. The functionality sets the output message $m_{\mathsf{out}} := m$.
- **Output request:** If the adversary asks to receive the output value and there exists at least one corrupted party, the functionality hands the adversary the message m_{out} and sets $\mathsf{isOutputLocked} := \mathsf{true}$. If all parties are honest, the functionality ignores this request.
- **Corruption request:** If the adversary corrupts the sender, the functionality hands the adversary the message m_{out}. The adversary can provide the functionality a message m' and if $\mathsf{isOutputLocked} = \mathsf{false}$, the functionality sets the output message to be $m_{\mathsf{out}} := m'$.
- **Output:** The functionality sends m_{out} as output to all parties and sets $\mathsf{isOutputLocked} := \mathsf{true}$.

Fig. 2. The broadcast functionality

Next, we provide the simulation-based definition of corruption-unfair broadcast, where the adversary can first learn the message and later corrupt the sender and replace its message.

Definition 8 (Corruption-unfair broadcast, simulation-based definition) *An n-party protocol π, is a corruption-unfair broadcast protocol (according to the simulation-based definition) tolerating an adaptive PPT t-adversary, if π securely realizes the corruption-unfair broadcast functionality, in Fig. 3.*

The functionality $\mathcal{F}_{\mathsf{ubc}}$

- **Input:** The sender sends an input message $m \in \{0,1\}^\kappa$. The functionality sets the output value $m_{\mathsf{out}} := m$ and sends m to the adversary.
- **Corruption request:** If the adversary corrupts the sender, the adversary can provide the functionality a message m' and if no honest party received the output yet, the functionality sets the output message to be $m_{\mathsf{out}} := m'$.
- **Output:** The functionality sends m_{out} as output to all parties.

Fig. 3. The corruption-unfair broadcast functionality

As a sanity check, we prove that a protocol that satisfies the simulation-based definition (Definition 7) also satisfies the property-based definition (Definition 5). The proof can be found in the full version of the paper [34].

Lemma 1. *If an n-party protocol π is a broadcast protocol according to the simulation-based definition tolerating an adaptive PPT t-adversary, then π is a broadcast protocol according to the property-based definition tolerating an adaptive PPT t-adversary.*

4 Property-Based Adaptively Secure Broadcast

In this section we analyze the property-based definition of adaptively secure broadcast. In Sect. 4.1 we extend the impossibility result of Hirt and Zikas [58] to this regime, and in Sect. 4.2 we show how to overcome this impossibility using resource-restricted cryptography; namely, via time-lock puzzles.

First we observe that although the impossibility statement in Hirt and Zikas [58, Lemma 8] is for all protocols, the proof presented there uses an implicit assumption that for an invocation of broadcast with sender P_s, the adversary is aware of the first subset of $\mathcal{P} \setminus \{P_s\}$ of size $t-1$, which receives information about the input that P_s is attempting to broadcast, and the actual round in which this occurs. An analogue of this property can also be defined for computationally secure protocols, where information might be available to a set but *computationally inaccessible.* In fact, all published dishonest-majority broadcast protocols have such a "release" round, which is not only defined, but also publicly known by the protocol structure; e.g., where the sender sends its input to everyone in the first round (e.g., [35,44]), the first round is actually this public round. We denote this class of protocols as $\Pi_{\mathsf{step\text{-}rel}}$ (see Definition 9 below).

In our treatment of simulation-based security in Sect. 5.1, we provide an argument, inspired by the MPC literature, which allows us to extend our simulation-based impossibility to arbitrary protocols, i.e., beyond the class $\Pi_{\mathsf{step\text{-}rel}}$ (see Step 2 in the proof of Theorem 5). We note in passing that this argument can easily be adapted to complete the argument of Hirt and Zikas [58, Lemma 8]. However, it turns out that the class $\Pi_{\mathsf{step\text{-}rel}}$ is even more relevant in the property-based setting. Therefore, we next formally specify this class and prove our impossibility results for all protocols that satisfy it.

For any given protocol π in the correlated-randomness model, any subset of parties $\hat{\mathcal{P}} \subseteq \mathcal{P}$, and any round ρ, let $\textsc{view}^{\rho}_{\pi,\hat{\mathcal{P}}}(x,\kappa)$ denote the joint view of the parties in $\hat{\mathcal{P}}$ at the beginning of round ρ in an honest execution (i.e., without the adversary corrupting anyone) on sender-input x, where κ is the security parameter. In particular, $\textsc{view}^{1}_{\pi,\hat{\mathcal{P}}}(\cdot)$ consists of the inputs and the setup (including randomness) of all parties in $\hat{\mathcal{P}}$ at the beginning of the protocol (before any message is exchanged). For simplicity—to capture also randomized protocols with non-simultaneous termination—we allow the view to be defined even after a party terminates: if for some $P \in \hat{\mathcal{P}}$, party P terminates in some round $\rho \le R$ (where R is the upper bound of the protocol's round complexity guaranteed by the *termination* property of Definition 5), then $\textsc{view}^{R}_{\pi,\hat{\mathcal{P}}}(\cdot)$ includes the view of this party up to termination (round R). We also assume for simplicity (again wlog) that for any such party, its view includes the party's output.

The definition of the class $\Pi_{\mathsf{step\text{-}rel}}$ ensures that a round $\hat{r}_\pi$ and a set $\hat{\mathcal{P}}_\pi \subseteq \mathcal{P} \setminus \{P_s\}$ of size $|\hat{\mathcal{P}}_\pi| < \lfloor n/2 \rfloor$ are defined by the protocol, such that the set $\hat{\mathcal{P}}_\pi$ is the first set of parties that are able to learn the actual input and this happens in round $\hat{r}_\pi$; i.e., no other set of parties (of the same size) is able to output the input of the sender based on its view from rounds $1, \ldots, \hat{r}_\pi - 1$. Formally:

Definition 9 (The protocol class $\Pi_{\mathsf{step\text{-}rel}}$). *For any protocol π in the class $\Pi_{\mathsf{step\text{-}rel}}$, there exists some round number $\hat{r}_\pi$, a set $\hat{\mathcal{P}}_\pi \subseteq \mathcal{P} \setminus \{P_s\}$ of size $|\hat{\mathcal{P}}_\pi| < \lfloor n/2 \rfloor$, and a PPT algorithm $\hat{B}_\pi$ such that the following properties hold:*

1. *There exists a negligible function ν such that for any input x it holds that*
$$\Pr\left[\hat{B}_\pi\left(\text{VIEW}^{\hat{r}_\pi}_{\pi,\hat{\mathcal{P}}_\pi}(x, \kappa)\right) = x\right] \geq 1 - \nu(\kappa).$$
2. *Let D be the input domain of the protocol (the set of possible inputs). If the input x is chosen uniformly at random from D, then the output of the honest parties in the following experiment is $y \neq x$ with noticeable probability:*
   (a) Initiate the protocol π with sender P_s receiving a uniform input $x \leftarrow D$, and sample and distribute the correlated randomness according to π.
   (b) Consider a fail-stop adversary that corrupts the parties in $\hat{\mathcal{P}}_\pi \cup \{P_s\}$ in round $\hat{r}_\pi$ and crashes them before sending their round-$\hat{r}_\pi$ messages.
   (c) Have the honest parties complete their protocol and set y to the output of any honest party (e.g., the one with the smallest index).

We stress that such a set $\hat{P}_\pi$ and round r_π is well defined in the execution of *any* broadcast protocol, not just protocols in $\Pi_{\mathsf{step\text{-}rel}}$. This follows directly from the validity property of broadcast—at the beginning only the sender knows the input and at the end everyone outputs it. What makes $\Pi_{\mathsf{step\text{-}rel}}$ a subclass of all protocols, is the assumption that $\hat{P}_\pi$ and r_π are defined by the protocol itself (and not at execution time). This seemingly strong restriction is sufficient to capture all published broadcast protocols and is therefore sufficient for the statement we are making in this section, that without assumptions limiting the adaptive corruption ability of the adversary—e.g., atomic multisend or slow corruption [71]—such broadcast protocols are *not* adaptively secure, not even according to the property-based definition.

4.1 Impossibility of Property-Based Adaptively Secure Broadcast

We start by adapting the impossibility result of Hirt and Zikas [58] to work with the property-based definition. In particular, we present a simpler argument than [58] that extends the impossibility to: (1) capture a smaller, Boolean input domain (as opposed to exponential-size domain in [58]), and (2) we show the impossibility with respect to a property-based definition (as opposed to the simulation-based definition in [58]). We also observe that this proof strategy works both for deterministic and randomized protocols assuming any correlated-randomness setup and/or secure data erasures. We note that by Lemma 1 an impossibility of a broadcast protocol according to the property-based definition also rules out such protocols secure according to the simulation-based definition.

Theorem 2. *Let $t > n/2$. Then, there exists no broadcast protocol in the class $\Pi_{\mathsf{step\text{-}rel}}$ (secure according to the property-based definition) tolerating an adaptive, fail-stop PPT t-adversary. The theorem holds both for deterministic and randomized protocols assuming any correlated-randomness setup and/or secure erasures.*

The proof can be found in the full version of the paper [34].

4.2 Property-Based Adaptively Secure Broadcast Protocol

Next, we proceed to show that the property-based definition of broadcast can be realized assuming a time-lock puzzle. The high-level idea is quite simple. The sender hides its message inside a (weak) time-lock puzzle, and uses a corruption-unfair broadcast protocol (e.g., Dolev and Strong [35]) to deliver the puzzle to all parties. The TLP parameters should guarantee that the adversary cannot solve the puzzle before the corruption-unfair broadcast completes.

We start by defining the protocol in a hybrid model where a trusted party is in charge of executing corruption-unfair broadcast, and later proceed to prove a composition theorem that enables securely replacing the trusted party with a corruption-unfair broadcast protocol, e.g., Dolev and Strong [35].

Adaptively Secure Broadcast Given Ideal Corruption-Unfair Broadcast. In the spirit of resource-restricted cryptography, we will not consider arbitrary PPT adversaries, since otherwise the impossibility results from Sect. 4.1 will kick in. Instead we will assume an upper bound on the number of parallel steps an adversary can perform during the protocol's execution.

Definition 10 ((R, T)-bounded adversary). *A PPT adversary $\mathcal{A}$ is (R, T)-bounded if for every $\kappa \in \mathbb{N}$, the maximal depth of a circuit that $\mathcal{A}$ can evaluate within R communication rounds is bounded by $T(\kappa)$.*

Protocol $\pi_{\mathsf{bc\text{-}prop}}(T, \kappa)$

- **Hybrid model:** The protocol is defined in the corruption-unfair broadcast $\mathcal{F}_{\mathsf{ubc}}$-hybrid model, where $\mathcal{F}_{\mathsf{ubc}}$ produces an output within R rounds.
- **Public parameters:** A puzzle $(\mathsf{PGen}, \mathsf{PSol})$ with gap $\varepsilon < 1$, a difficulty parameter T, and the security parameter κ.
- **Private input:** The sender has a private input $m \in \{0, 1\}^{\kappa}$.
- **The protocol:**
  - **Lock:** The sender computes $Z \leftarrow \mathsf{PGen}(T^{1/\varepsilon}, m)$.
  - **Corruption-unfair broadcast:** The sender broadcasts Z via $\mathcal{F}_{\mathsf{ubc}}$.
  - **Recover the output:** Upon receiving Z, each party computes $m = \mathsf{PSol}(Z)$ and outputs m.

Fig. 4. Adaptively secure, property-based broadcast protocol

Theorem 3. *Let $t \leq n$ and let $T(\cdot)$ be a polynomial. Assume that weak time-lock puzzles with gap $\varepsilon < 1$ exist and that corruption-unfair broadcast can be computed in R rounds against an adaptive PPT t-adversary. Then, Protocol $\pi_{\mathsf{bc\text{-}prop}}$ (Fig. 4) is a broadcast protocol (according to Definition 5) that is secure against an (R,T)-bounded adaptive PPT t-adversary.*

The proof of Theorem 3 can be found in the full version of the paper [34].

Realizing Ideal Corruption-Unfair Broadcast. Next, we would like to instantiate $\mathcal{F}_{\mathsf{ubc}}$ with the protocol of Dolev and Strong [35]. However, as discussed in the introduction, standard composition theorems no longer apply in the resource-restricted setting. We therefore prove the following limited composition theorem that is sufficient for instantiating $\mathcal{F}_{\mathsf{ubc}}$ with the protocol of Dolev and Strong [35] in $\pi_{\mathsf{bc\text{-}prop}}$; we leave the quest for a more general composition theorem as an interesting open problem.

Similarly to standard composition theorems (e.g., [21]), given a protocol π in the $\mathcal{F}$-hybrid model and another protocol ρ that realizes $\mathcal{F}$, we wish to argue security for the protocol $\pi^{\mathcal{F}\to\rho}$ where the call to $\mathcal{F}$ is replaced by an invocation of ρ. Given an adversary $\mathcal{A}$ to $\pi^{\mathcal{F}\to\rho}$ we derive an adversary to π by considering the induced adversary to ρ and "replace" the execution of ρ with the induced adversary by an ideal computation of $\mathcal{F}$ with the simulator that is guaranteed to exist by the security of ρ. However, as opposed existing composition theorems, we need to ensure that the simulator does not use too many resources. Many simulation strategies have the simulator run in its head the honest parties along with the adversary; in the following two definitions we capture the requirement that such simulators do not use additional resources.

Definition 11 **((R,T)-bounded protocol).** *Let $\rho = (P_1, \ldots, P_n)$ be an n-party protocol. We say that ρ is (R,T)-bounded if for every κ, the maximal depth of a circuit that can be evaluated by any P_i within R communication rounds is bounded by $T(\kappa)$.*

Definition 12 (Resource-respecting simulation). *An (R,T_1)-bounded protocol ρ securely realizes a functionality $\mathcal{F}$ against PPT t-adversaries with* resource-respecting simulation, *if every PPT adversary $\mathcal{A}$ can be simulated by a PPT simulator $\mathcal{S}$, and further, if $\mathcal{A}$ is (R,T_2)-bounded then $\mathcal{S}$ is (R,T_1+T_2)-bounded.*

We are now ready to state the limited composition theorem. The proof can be found in the full version of the paper [34].

Theorem 4. *Let π be a protocol in the $\mathcal{F}$-hybrid model, where $\mathcal{F}$ is invoked exactly once and all communication is conveyed via $\mathcal{F}$ (i.e., the parties do not send any other messages), and assume that π is a broadcast protocol (according to Definition 5) that is secure against (R,T)-bounded adaptive PPT t-adversaries. Let $0 < \alpha < 1$ be a constant and let ρ be an $(R,\alpha \cdot T)$-bounded protocol that realizes $\mathcal{F}$ against PPT t-adversaries with resource-respecting simulation.*

Then, the protocol $\pi^{\mathcal{F}\to\rho}$ *that is obtained by replacing the call to* $\mathcal{F}$ *with an execution of* ρ*, is a broadcast protocol (according to Definition 5) that is secure against* $(R,(1-\alpha)\cdot T)$*-bounded PPT* t*-adversaries.*

Note that in the corruption-unfair broadcast protocol π_{ubc} of Dolev and Strong [35], honest parties need only to sign, verify, and send signatures, and further, the simulator essentially runs the code of the honest parties towards the adversary. Consider an instantiation of π_{ubc} with some signature scheme such that the number of sequential steps made by each honest party in the protocol is bounded by $T = T(n,\kappa)$; stated differently, the protocol is (n,T)-bounded (i.e., $R = n$). Let $0 < \alpha < 1$ and denote $T' = \frac{1}{\alpha}T$. By Theorem 3, Protocol $\pi_{\mathsf{bc\text{-}prop}}(T',\kappa)$ is a broadcast protocol (according to Definition 5) that is secure against an (n,T')-bounded adaptive PPT t-adversary. By Theorem 4, the protocol π that is obtained by replacing the call to $\mathcal{F}_{\mathsf{ubc}}$ with an execution of π_{ubc}, is a broadcast protocol (according to Definition 5) that is secure against $(n,(1-\alpha)\cdot T)$-bounded PPT t-adversaries. We derive the following corollary.

Corollary 1. *Assume that weak time-lock puzzles with gap* $\varepsilon < 1$ *exist, let* $t \le n$*, let* $0 < \alpha < 1$ *be a constant, and let* T *be a polynomial such that* $\pi_{\mathsf{bc\text{-}prop}}(T,\kappa)$ *is a broadcast protocol (according to Definition 5) that is secure against an* (n,T)*-bounded adaptive PPT* t*-adversary, and that* π_{ubc} *is an* $(n,\alpha T)$*-bounded corruption-unfair broadcast protocol.*

Then, the protocol π *that is obtained by replacing the call to* $\mathcal{F}_{\mathsf{ubc}}$ *with an execution of* π_{ubc}*, is a broadcast protocol (according to Definition 5) given a PKI for digital signatures, that is secure against* $(n,(1-\alpha)\cdot T)$*-bounded PPT* t*-adversaries.*

5 Simulation-Based Adaptively Secure Broadcast

In this section we analyze the simulation-based definition of broadcast. In Sect. 5.1 we show that the assumptions used in Sect. 4.2 that satisfy the property-based definition are not sufficient to realize the simulation-based definition, and in Sect. 5.2 we show how to overcome the new impossibility via the new notion of non-committing time-lock puzzles.

5.1 Impossibility of Simulation-Based Adaptively Secure Broadcast

We next demonstrate that assuming time-lock puzzles does not help in realizing adaptively secure broadcast according to the simulation-based definition. We remark that our impossibility applies to all (polynomial-time) protocols and not just protocols in the class $\Pi_{\mathsf{step\text{-}rel}}$. This impossibility combined with Corollary 1 demonstrate a separation between the two definitions, property-based and simulation-based, but also the fact that time-lock puzzles are less effective in a simulation-based setting. Intuitively, the reason is that the puzzle is a non-interactive object which has a *binding* property (once handed over, its solution cannot be changed) and a *temporary hiding* property (while the solver works to solve the puzzle, they cannot distinguish it from a puzzle with another solution). In fact, once one observes these properties, the limits of the strength of TLPs for simulation-based adaptive security becomes less of a surprise, as it resembles analogous issues displayed by primitives with similar properties, such as commitments [23,26] and public-key encryption [73].

Before stating our results we first extend the notion of (R, T)-bounded adversaries to the simulation-based setting, where the adversary can use the computational resources of the environment. We consider the pair of environment $\mathcal{Z}$ and adversary $\mathcal{A}$ to be (R, T)-bounded, meaning that for every $\kappa \in \mathbb{N}$, the maximal depth of a circuit that $\mathcal{Z}$ and $\mathcal{A}$ can jointly evaluate within R communication rounds, is bounded by $T(\kappa)$.

We note that by restricting the joint resources of the environment and the adversary, we actually obtain a stronger impossibility result, since even a weaker distinguisher can distinguish between the real execution and the simulated one. Moreover, the result is in fact even stronger since we do not restrict the simulator to be (R, T)-bounded.

We are now ready to state the impossibility result, showing that even TLPs cannot help circumvent the impossibility of adaptively secure broadcast under simulation-based security. Recall that this impossibility holds for any polynomial-time protocol. Nonetheless, for ease in exposition, we prove the statement in two steps: First we prove it for protocols in the class $\Pi_{\mathsf{step\text{-}rel}}$, and then we extend it to protocols besides this class.

In a nutshell, the first (and most involved) step above is proven by using the fact that, by definition of $\Pi_{\mathsf{step\text{-}rel}}$, in round $\hat{r}_\pi$ the adversary attacking π and corrupting $\hat{\mathcal{P}}_\pi$ has all the information it needs to recover the output (even when the sender is honest). This means that, in order to simulate, the simulator needs to give its adversary this information. But the only way the simulator can ensure this is by asking the functionality $\mathcal{F}_{\mathsf{bc}}$ for the sender's input. This gives rise to the following distinguishing strategy for the environment: Once the environment gets its $\hat{r}_\pi$-round messages, it attempts to flip the output by corrupting the sender and all parties in the set $\hat{\mathcal{P}}_\pi$ defined by class $\Pi_{\mathsf{step\text{-}rel}}$. What complicates things is that, unlike the proof of Theorem 2, the environment cannot set a trap for the simulator by making its choice to corrupt the sender depend on the output of $\hat{B}_\pi$. The reason is that the input (to $\hat{B}_\pi$) view of round $\hat{r}_\pi$ might include TLPs, which the environment cannot quickly solve (within round $\hat{r}_\pi$) by the time it decides whether or not to corrupt the sender and try to flip the output.

Instead the environment does the following: It always, optimistically, corrupts the sender and tries to flip the output; it then uses *input-dependent* check-events to distinguish as follows. If the input is 0 the environment checks that the simulator gave it consistent $\hat{r}_\pi$-round messages by running algorithm $\hat{B}_\pi$;[13] otherwise, if the input is 1 then it checks if the simulator managed to flip the bit by looking at the output of $\mathcal{F}_{\mathsf{bc}}$. As discussed above, the only way the simulator can ensure that the first check succeeds is by asking the functionality $\mathcal{F}_{\mathsf{bc}}$ for the input; however, when this happens, the output of $\mathcal{F}_{\mathsf{bc}}$ gets locked

[13] The environment can take its time running $\hat{B}_\pi$ after the protocol terminates.

which will make it impossible for the simulator to flip the output. Hence, one of the two check events will occur noticeably more frequently in the real than in the ideal world, rendering the protocol insecure. We proceed with formal statement; the proof can be found in the full version of the paper [34].

Theorem 5. *Let $t > n/2$. Then, there exists no broadcast protocol which is secure according to the simulation-based definition and tolerates an adaptive, fail-stop, PPT, t-adversary. The theorem holds both for deterministic and randomized protocols assuming any (even inefficient[14]) correlated-randomness setup and/or secure data erasures, and holds even for (R,T)-bounded environments and adversaries and assuming time-lock puzzles.*

Replacing TLPs with a (Programable) Random Oracle. One can verify that replacing, in Theorem 5, the time-lock puzzle (and the (R,T)-bounded environment assumption) with a random oracle—even a programmable one—does not affect the impossibility. Indeed, the proof of this statement follows the same line of arguments as Theorem 5, where Step 1 is even simpler and uses the simpler attack from Theorem 2—i.e., at round $\hat{r}_\pi$, the environment who corrupts the parties in $\hat{\mathcal{P}}_\pi$ evaluates $\hat{B}_\pi$ (the environment can now do that as it is not (R,T)-bounded) on their view, and depending on the output of $\hat{B}_\pi$, either corrupts the sender and crashes all corrupted parties, or lets the protocol complete. It is easy to verify that the probabilities of the events in the proof will remain (asymptotically) the same, and are not affected by adding a random oracle.

Indeed, the real-world events are defined in a way which does not alter their distribution when a random oracle is assumed; and in the ideal world, programmability cannot help the simulator alter the events, as (1) the environment does not change its behavior depending on the RO, and (2) the ideal-world events depend only on the environment and the behavior of the ideal functionality (which is also independent of the RO). Thus we can derive the following corollary:

Corollary 2. *Let $t > n/2$. Then, there exists no broadcast protocol in the (programable) random-oracle model, which is secure according to the simulation-based definition and tolerates an adaptive, fail-stop, PPT, t-adversary. The theorem holds both for deterministic and randomized protocols assuming any (even inefficient) correlated-randomness setup and/or secure data erasures.*

In passing, we note that a similar corollary can also be derived for the property-based definition. In particular, we can extend the property-based model of execution by allowing all relevant machines (the parties, the adversary, and the challenger from Definition 5) oracle access to a random function. Then, for all such protocols, as long that they satisfy Definition 9, it is straightforward

[14] Classical correlated randomness setup assumes efficient sampling and distribution mechanisms. By removing such restrictions here we can even capture non-programmable random oracle, as an exponential-space correlated randomness functionality that samples the entire random table of the RO.

to verify that all the events involved in the proof of Theorem 2 remain intact. Indeed, the probability of these events is derived directly from Definition 5. This proves the following simple corollary of Theorem 2.

Corollary 3. *Let $t > n/2$. Then, there exists no broadcast protocol in the class $\Pi_{\mathsf{step\text{-}rel}}$ (secure according to the property-based definition) tolerating an adaptive, fail-stop PPT t-adversary in the random-oracle model. The theorem holds both for deterministic and randomized protocols, and assuming any correlated-randomness setup and/or secure erasures.*

5.2 Simulation-Based Adaptively Secure Broadcast Protocol

The main reason why the protocol from Sect. 4.2 does not realize the simulation-based definition is that once the simulator simulates an honest sender broadcasting the puzzle Z (without knowing the real input value), it cannot equivocate the content of the puzzle upon corruption of the sender, or when the protocol completes and the output is revealed. We now proceed to construct an adaptively secure broadcast protocol that satisfies the simulation-based definition in the programmable random-oracle model. First off, we introduce the notion of time-lock puzzles that are *non-committing.*

Non-committing Time-Lock Puzzles. Standard constructions of time-lock puzzles are committing in the sense that once a puzzle is generated, it can be opened into a unique message with all but negligible probability. In contrast, a *non-committing* time-lock puzzle enables a simulator to initially simulate a puzzle, and later, given an arbitrary message m, to "explain" the puzzle as containing m. We show how to achieve this notion given a standard time-lock puzzle and a programmable random oracle, by generating $Z = \mathsf{PGen}(T, x)$ for a random $x \leftarrow \{0,1\}^\kappa$ and attaching $c = H(x) \oplus m$ to the puzzle. Once the simulator is asked to equivocate the new puzzle (Z, c) to the message m, it can program the random oracle to return $H(x) = c \oplus m$. We note that a similar idea was used in [5,9] to model TLPs in the UC framework.

We proceed to state the theorem. The proof can be found in the full version of the paper [34].

Theorem 6. *Assume that weak TLPs with gap $\varepsilon < 1$ exist and that corruption-unfair broadcast can be computed in R rounds against an adaptive, PPT t-adversary, for $t \leq n$. Let $T(\cdot)$ be a polynomial. Then, Protocol $\pi_{\mathsf{bc\text{-}sim}}$ (Fig. 5) is a broadcast protocol according to the simulation-based definition (Definition 7) that is secure against an adaptive t-adversary in the programmable random-oracle model, where the adversary and the environment are PPT and (R, T)-bounded.*

Similarly to Theorem 4, we prove a limited composition theorem for the simulation-based setting. The proof can be found in the full version of the paper [34].

Theorem 7. *Let π be a protocol in the $\mathcal{F}$-hybrid model, where $\mathcal{F}$ is invoked exactly once and all communication is conveyed via $\mathcal{F}$ (i.e., the parties do not send any other messages) that realizes a functionality $\mathcal{G}$ against an adaptive t-adversary, where the adversary and the environment are PPT and (R,T)-bounded. Let $0 < \alpha < 1$ be a constant, and let ρ be an $(R, \alpha \cdot T)$-bounded protocol that realizes $\mathcal{F}$ against PPT t-adversaries with resource-respecting simulation.*

Then, the protocol $\pi^{\mathcal{F} \to \rho}$ that is obtained by replacing the call to $\mathcal{F}$ with an execution of ρ, realizes $\mathcal{G}$ against an adaptive t-adversary, where the adversary and the environment are PPT and $(R, (1-\alpha) \cdot T)$-bounded.

Protocol $\pi_{\mathsf{bc\text{-}sim}}(T, \kappa)$

- **Hybrid model:** The protocol is defined in the corruption-unfair broadcast $\mathcal{F}_{\mathsf{ubc}}$-hybrid model, requiring R rounds. The parties have access to a random oracle $H : \{0,1\}^\kappa \to \{0,1\}^\kappa$.
- **Public parameters:** A puzzle $(\mathsf{PGen}, \mathsf{PSol})$ with gap $\varepsilon < 1$, a difficulty parameter T, and the security parameter κ.
- **Private input:** The sender has a private input $m \in \{0,1\}^\kappa$.
- **The protocol:**
  - **Lock:** The sender samples a random $x \leftarrow \{0,1\}^\kappa$ and computes $Z \leftarrow \mathsf{PGen}(T^{1/\varepsilon}, x)$.
  - **Corruption-unfair broadcast:** The sender sets $c = m \oplus H(x)$ and broadcasts (Z, c) via $\mathcal{F}_{\mathsf{ubc}}$.
  - **Output:** Upon receiving (Z, c), compute $x = \mathsf{PSol}(Z)$ and outputs $c \oplus H(x)$.

Fig. 5. Adaptively secure, simulation-based broadcast protocol

Consider an instantiation of the corruption-unfair broadcast protocol π_{ubc} of Dolev and Strong [35] with some signature scheme such that the protocol is (n,T)-bounded. Let $0 < \alpha < 1$ and denote $T' = \frac{1}{\alpha} T$. By Theorem 6, Protocol $\pi_{\mathsf{bc\text{-}sim}}(T', \kappa)$ is a broadcast protocol (according to Definition 7) that is secure against an (n, T')-bounded adaptive PPT t-adversary. By Theorem 7, the protocol π that is obtained by replacing the call to $\mathcal{F}_{\mathsf{ubc}}$ with an execution of π_{ubc}, is a broadcast protocol (according to Definition 7) secure against $(n, (1-\alpha) \cdot T)$-bounded PPT t-adversaries. We therefore derive the following corollary.

Corollary 4. *Assume that weak TLP with gap $\varepsilon < 1$ exist, let $t \le n$, let $0 < \alpha < 1$ be a constant, and let T be a polynomial such that $\pi_{\mathsf{bc\text{-}sim}}(T, \kappa)$ is a broadcast protocol that is secure against an (n, T')-bounded adaptive PPT t-adversary, and that π_{ubc} is an $(n, \alpha T)$-bounded corruption-unfair broadcast protocol.*

Then, the protocol π that is obtained by replacing the call to $\mathcal{F}_{\mathsf{ubc}}$ with an execution of π_{ubc}, is a broadcast protocol (according to Definition 7) in the programmable random-oracle model and given a PKI for digital signatures, that is secure against $(n, (1-\alpha) \cdot T)$-bounded PPT t-adversaries.

Acknowledgments. Ran Cohen's research is supported in part by NSF grant no. 2055568. Juan Garay's research is supported in part by NSF grants no. 2001082 and

2055694. Vassilis Zikas's research is supported in part by NSF grant no. 2055599 and by Sunday Group. The authors are also supported by the Algorand Centres of Excellence programme managed by Algorand Foundation. Any opinions, findings, and conclusions or recommendations expressed in this material are those of the author(s) and do not necessarily reflect the views of Algorand Foundation.

References

1. Abraham, I., et al.: Communication complexity of Byzantine agreement, revisited. In: 38th ACM PODC, pp. 317–326 (2019)
2. Abraham, I., Devadas, S., Dolev, D., Nayak, K., Ren, L.: Synchronous byzantine agreement with expected $O(1)$ rounds, expected $O(n^2)$ communication, and optimal resilience. In: Goldberg, I., Moore, T. (eds.) FC 2019. LNCS, vol. 11598, pp. 320–334. Springer, Cham (2019). https://doi.org/10.1007/978-3-030-32101-7_20
3. Alexandru, A.B., Loss, J., Papamanthou, C., Tsimos, G.: Sublinear-round broadcast without trusted setup against dishonest majority. Cryptology ePrint Archive, Report 2022/1383 (2022). https://eprint.iacr.org/2022/1383
4. Andrychowicz, M., Dziembowski, S.: PoW-based distributed cryptography with no trusted setup. In: Gennaro, R., Robshaw, M. (eds.) CRYPTO 2015, Part II. LNCS, vol. 9216, pp. 379–399. Springer, Heidelberg (2015). https://doi.org/10.1007/978-3-662-48000-7_19
5. Arapinis, M., Lamprou, N., Zacharias, T.: Astrolabous: a universally composable time-lock encryption scheme. In: Tibouchi, M., Wang, H. (eds.) ASIACRYPT 2021, Part II. LNCS, vol. 13091, pp. 398–426. Springer, Cham (2021). https://doi.org/10.1007/978-3-030-92075-3_14
6. Badertscher, C., Maurer, U., Tschudi, D., Zikas, V.: Bitcoin as a transaction ledger: a composable treatment. In: Katz, J., Shacham, H. (eds.) CRYPTO 2017, Part I. LNCS, vol. 10401, pp. 324–356. Springer, Cham (2017). https://doi.org/10.1007/978-3-319-63688-7_11
7. Badertscher, C., Gazi, P., Kiayias, A., Russell, A., Zikas, V.: Ouroboros genesis: composable proof-of-stake blockchains with dynamic availability. In: ACM CCS 2018, pp. 913–930 (2018)
8. Badertscher, C., Canetti, R., Hesse, J., Tackmann, B., Zikas, V.: Universal composition with global subroutines: capturing global setup within plain UC. In: Pass, R., Pietrzak, K. (eds.) TCC 2020, Part III. LNCS, vol. 12552, pp. 1–30. Springer, Cham (2020). https://doi.org/10.1007/978-3-030-64381-2_1
9. Baum, C., David, B., Dowsley, R., Nielsen, J.B., Oechsner, S.: TARDIS: a foundation of time-lock puzzles in UC. In: Canteaut, A., Standaert, F.-X. (eds.) EUROCRYPT 2021, Part III. LNCS, vol. 12698, pp. 429–459. Springer, Cham (2021). https://doi.org/10.1007/978-3-030-77883-5_15
10. Baum, C., David, B., Dowsley, R., Kishore, R., Nielsen, J.B., Oechsner, S.: CRAFT: composable randomness beacons and output-independent abort MPC from time. In: Boldyreva, A., Kolesnikov, V. (eds.) PKC 2023, Part I. LNCS, vol. 13940, pp. 439–470. Springer, Cham (2023). https://doi.org/10.1007/978-3-031-31368-4_16
11. Bitansky, N., Goldwasser, S., Jain, A., Paneth, O., Vaikuntanathan, V., Waters, B.: Time-lock puzzles from randomized encodings. In: ITCS 2016, pp. 345–356 (2016)
12. Blum, E., Katz, J., Loss, J.: Synchronous consensus with optimal asynchronous fallback guarantees. In: Hofheinz, D., Rosen, A. (eds.) TCC 2019, Part I. LNCS,

vol. 11891, pp. 131–150. Springer, Cham (2019). https://doi.org/10.1007/978-3-030-36030-6_6
13. Blum, E., Katz, J., Liu-Zhang, C.-D., Loss, J.: Asynchronous byzantine agreement with subquadratic communication. In: Pass, R., Pietrzak, K. (eds.) TCC 2020, Part I. LNCS, vol. 12550, pp. 353–380. Springer, Cham (2020). https://doi.org/10.1007/978-3-030-64375-1_13
14. Boneh, D., Naor, M.: Timed commitments. In: Bellare, M. (ed.) CRYPTO 2000. LNCS, vol. 1880, pp. 236–254. Springer, Heidelberg (2000). https://doi.org/10.1007/3-540-44598-6_15
15. Boneh, D., Bonneau, J., Bünz, B., Fisch, B.: Verifiable delay functions. In: Shacham, H., Boldyreva, A. (eds.) CRYPTO 2018, Part I. LNCS, vol. 10991, pp. 757–788. Springer, Cham (2018). https://doi.org/10.1007/978-3-319-96884-1_25
16. Borderding, M.: Levels of authentication in distributed agreement. In: 10th International Workshop on Distributed Algorithms WDAG, pp. 40–55 (1996)
17. Boyle, E., Cohen, R., Data, D., Hubáček, P.: Must the communication graph of MPC protocols be an expander? In: Shacham, H., Boldyreva, A. (eds.) CRYPTO 2018, Part III. LNCS, vol. 10993, pp. 243–272. Springer, Cham (2018). https://doi.org/10.1007/978-3-319-96878-0_9
18. Brakerski, Z., Döttling, N., Garg, S., Malavolta, G.: Leveraging linear decryption: rate-1 fully-homomorphic encryption and time-lock puzzles. In: Hofheinz, D., Rosen, A. (eds.) TCC 2019, Part II. LNCS, vol. 11892, pp. 407–437. Springer, Cham (2019). https://doi.org/10.1007/978-3-030-36033-7_16
19. Camenisch, J., Drijvers, M., Gagliardoni, T., Lehmann, A., Neven, G.: The wonderful world of global random oracles. In: Nielsen, J.B., Rijmen, V. (eds.) EUROCRYPT 2018, Part I. LNCS, vol. 10820, pp. 280–312. Springer, Cham (2018). https://doi.org/10.1007/978-3-319-78381-9_11
20. Canetti, R.: Security and composition of multiparty cryptographic protocols. J. Cryptol. **13**(1), 143–202 (2000)
21. Canetti, R.: Universally composable security: a new paradigm for cryptographic protocols. In: 42nd FOCS, pp. 136–145 (2001)
22. Canetti, R.: Universally composable security. J. ACM **67**(5), 28:1–28:94 (2020)
23. Canetti, R., Fischlin, M.: Universally composable commitments. In: Kilian, J. (ed.) CRYPTO 2001. LNCS, vol. 2139, pp. 19–40. Springer, Heidelberg (2001). https://doi.org/10.1007/3-540-44647-8_2
24. Canetti, R., Feige, U., Goldreich, O., Naor, M.: Adaptively secure multi-party computation. In: 28th ACM STOC, pp. 639–648 (1996)
25. Canetti, R., Lindell, Y., Ostrovsky, R., Sahai, A.: Universally composable two-party and multi-party secure computation. In: 34th ACM STOC, pp. 494–503 (2002)
26. Canetti, R., Damgård, I., Dziembowski, S., Ishai, Y., Malkin, T.: Adaptive versus non-adaptive security of multi-party protocols. J. Cryptol. **17**(3), 153–207 (2004)
27. Canetti, R., Cohen, A., Lindell, Y.: A simpler variant of universally composable security for standard multiparty computation. In: Gennaro, R., Robshaw, M. (eds.) CRYPTO 2015, Part II. LNCS, vol. 9216, pp. 3–22. Springer, Heidelberg (2015). https://doi.org/10.1007/978-3-662-48000-7_1
28. Chan, T.-H.H., Pass, R., Shi, E.: Sublinear-round byzantine agreement under corrupt majority. In: Kiayias, A., Kohlweiss, M., Wallden, P., Zikas, V. (eds.) PKC 2020, Part II. LNCS, vol. 12111, pp. 246–265. Springer, Cham (2020). https://doi.org/10.1007/978-3-030-45388-6_9
29. Chen, J., Micali, S.: Algorand: a secure and efficient distributed ledger. Theoret. Comput. Sci. **777**, 155–183 (2019)

30. Cleve, R.: Limits on the security of coin flips when half the processors are faulty (extended abstract). In: 18th ACM STOC, pp. 364–369 (1986)
31. Cohen, R., Coretti, S., Garay, J., Zikas, V.: Probabilistic termination and composability of cryptographic protocols. In: Robshaw, M., Katz, J. (eds.) CRYPTO 2016, Part III. LNCS, vol. 9816, pp. 240–269. Springer, Heidelberg (2016). https://doi.org/10.1007/978-3-662-53015-3_9
32. Cohen, R., Coretti, S., Garay, J.A., Zikas, V.: Round-preserving parallel composition of probabilistic-termination cryptographic protocols. In: ICALP 2017. LIPIcs, vol. 80, pp. 37:1–37:15. Schloss Dagstuhl (2017)
33. Cohen, R., Shelat, A., Wichs, D.: Adaptively secure MPC with sublinear communication complexity. In: Boldyreva, A., Micciancio, D. (eds.) CRYPTO 2019, Part II. LNCS, vol. 11693, pp. 30–60. Springer, Cham (2019). https://doi.org/10.1007/978-3-030-26951-7_2
34. Cohen, R., Garay, J., Zikas, V.: Completeness theorems for adaptively secure broadcast. Cryptology ePrint Archive, Report 2021/775 (2021). https://eprint.iacr.org/2021/775
35. Dolev, D., Strong, H.R.: Authenticated algorithms for Byzantine agreement. SIAM J. Comput. **12**(4), 656–666 (1983)
36. Dwork, C., Naor, M.: Pricing via processing or combatting junk mail. In: Brickell, E.F. (ed.) CRYPTO 1992. LNCS, vol. 740, pp. 139–147. Springer, Heidelberg (1993). https://doi.org/10.1007/3-540-48071-4_10
37. Eckey, L., Faust, S., Loss, J.: Efficient algorithms for broadcast and consensus based on proofs of work. Cryptology ePrint Archive, Report 2017/915 (2017). http://eprint.iacr.org/2017/915
38. Feldman, P.: Optimal Algorithms for Byzantine Agreement. Ph.D. thesis, Stanford University (1988). https://dspace.mit.edu/handle/1721.1/14368
39. Fischer, M.J., Lynch, N.A.: A lower bound for the time to assure interactive consistency. Inf. Process. Lett. **14**(4), 183–186 (1982)
40. Fischer, M.J., Lynch, N.A., Merritt, M.: Easy impossibility proofs for distributed consensus problems. Distrib. Comput. **1**(1), 26–39 (1986)
41. Fitzi, M.: Generalized communication and security models in Byzantine agreement. Ph.D. thesis, ETH Zurich, Zürich, Switzerland (2003). http://d-nb.info/967397375
42. Freitag, C., Komargodski, I., Pass, R., Sirkin, N.: Non-malleable time-lock puzzles and applications. In: Nissim, K., Waters, B. (eds.) TCC 2021, Part III. LNCS, vol. 13044, pp. 447–479. Springer, Cham (2021). https://doi.org/10.1007/978-3-030-90456-2_15
43. Garay, J., Kiayias, A.: SoK: a consensus taxonomy in the blockchain era. In: Jarecki, S. (ed.) CT-RSA 2020. LNCS, vol. 12006, pp. 284–318. Springer, Cham (2020). https://doi.org/10.1007/978-3-030-40186-3_13
44. Garay, J.A., Moses, Y.: Fully polynomial Byzantine agreement in t+1 rounds. In: 25th ACM STOC, pp. 31–41 (1993)
45. Garay, J., MacKenzie, P., Prabhakaran, M., Yang, K.: Resource fairness and composability of cryptographic protocols. In: Halevi, S., Rabin, T. (eds.) TCC 2006. LNCS, vol. 3876, pp. 404–428. Springer, Heidelberg (2006). https://doi.org/10.1007/11681878_21
46. Garay, J.A., Katz, J., Koo, C.-Y., Ostrovsky, R.: Round complexity of authenticated broadcast with a dishonest majority. In: 48th FOCS, pp. 658–668. IEEE Computer Society Press (2007)
47. Garay, J.A., Katz, J., Kumaresan, R., Zhou, H.-S.: Adaptively secure broadcast, revisited. In: 30th ACM PODC, pp. 179–186 (2011)

48. Garay, J., Kiayias, A., Leonardos, N.: The bitcoin backbone protocol: analysis and applications. In: Oswald, E., Fischlin, M. (eds.) EUROCRYPT 2015, Part II. LNCS, vol. 9057, pp. 281–310. Springer, Heidelberg (2015). https://doi.org/10.1007/978-3-662-46803-6_10
49. Garay, J., Ishai, Y., Ostrovsky, R., Zikas, V.: The price of low communication in secure multi-party computation. In: Katz, J., Shacham, H. (eds.) CRYPTO 2017, Part I. LNCS, vol. 10401, pp. 420–446. Springer, Cham (2017). https://doi.org/10.1007/978-3-319-63688-7_14
50. Garay, J., Kiayias, A., Ostrovsky, R.M., Panagiotakos, G., Zikas, V.: Resource-restricted cryptography: revisiting MPC bounds in the proof-of-work era. In: Canteaut, A., Ishai, Y. (eds.) EUROCRYPT 2020. LNCS, vol. 12106, pp. 129–158. Springer, Cham (2020). https://doi.org/10.1007/978-3-030-45724-2_5
51. Garg, S., Sahai, A.: Adaptively secure multi-party computation with dishonest majority. In: Safavi-Naini, R., Canetti, R. (eds.) CRYPTO 2012. LNCS, vol. 7417, pp. 105–123. Springer, Heidelberg (2012). https://doi.org/10.1007/978-3-642-32009-5_8
52. Goldreich, O.: Foundations of Cryptography: Basic Applications, vol. 2. Cambridge University Press, Cambridge (2004)
53. Goldreich, O., Micali, S., Wigderson, A.: How to play any mental game or A completeness theorem for protocols with honest majority. In: 19th ACM STOC, pp. 218–229. ACM Press (1987)
54. Goldwasser, S., Lindell, Y.: Secure multi-party computation without agreement. J. Cryptol. **18**(3), 247–287 (2005)
55. Goldwasser, S., Kalai, Y.T., Park, S.: Adaptively secure coin-flipping, revisited. In: Halldórsson, M.M., Iwama, K., Kobayashi, N., Speckmann, B. (eds.) ICALP 2015, Part II. LNCS, vol. 9135, pp. 663–674. Springer, Heidelberg (2015). https://doi.org/10.1007/978-3-662-47666-6_53
56. Haitner, I., Karidi-Heller, Y.: A tight lower bound on adaptively secure full-information coin flip. In: 61st FOCS, pp. 1268–1276 (2020)
57. Hazay, C., Lindell, Y., Patra, A.: Adaptively secure computation with partial erasures. In: 34th ACM PODC, pp. 291–300 (2015)
58. Hirt, M., Zikas, V.: Adaptively secure broadcast. In: Gilbert, H. (ed.) EUROCRYPT 2010. LNCS, vol. 6110, pp. 466–485. Springer, Heidelberg (2010). https://doi.org/10.1007/978-3-642-13190-5_24
59. Hofheinz, D., Müller-Quade, J.: A synchronous model for multi-party computation and the incompleteness of oblivious transfer. Cryptology ePrint Archive, Report 2004/016 (2004). http://eprint.iacr.org/2004/016
60. Kalai, Y.T., Komargodski, I., Raz, R.: A lower bound for adaptively-secure collective coin-flipping protocols. In: DISC, pp. 34:1–34:16 (2018)
61. Katz, J., Maurer, U., Tackmann, B., Zikas, V.: Universally composable synchronous computation. In: Sahai, A. (ed.) TCC 2013. LNCS, vol. 7785, pp. 477–498. Springer, Heidelberg (2013). https://doi.org/10.1007/978-3-642-36594-2_27
62. Katz, J., Thiruvengadam, A., Zhou, H.-S.: Feasibility and infeasibility of adaptively secure fully homomorphic encryption. In: Kurosawa, K., Hanaoka, G. (eds.) PKC 2013. LNCS, vol. 7778, pp. 14–31. Springer, Heidelberg (2013). https://doi.org/10.1007/978-3-642-36362-7_2
63. Katz, J., Loss, J., Xu, J.: On the security of time-lock puzzles and timed commitments. In: Pass, R., Pietrzak, K. (eds.) TCC 2020, Part III. LNCS, vol. 12552, pp. 390–413. Springer, Cham (2020). https://doi.org/10.1007/978-3-030-64381-2_14

64. Khorasgani, H.A., Maji, H.K., Mukherjee, T.: Estimating gaps in martingales and applications to coin-tossing: constructions and hardness. In: Hofheinz, D., Rosen, A. (eds.) TCC 2019, Part II. LNCS, vol. 11892, pp. 333–355. Springer, Cham (2019). https://doi.org/10.1007/978-3-030-36033-7_13
65. Kiayias, A., Zhou, H.-S., Zikas, V.: Fair and robust multi-party computation using a global transaction ledger. In: Fischlin, M., Coron, J.-S. (eds.) EUROCRYPT 2016, Part II. LNCS, vol. 9666, pp. 705–734. Springer, Heidelberg (2016). https://doi.org/10.1007/978-3-662-49896-5_25
66. Lamport, L., Shostak, R.E., Pease, M.C.: The Byzantine generals problem. ACM Trans. Program. Lang. Syst. **4**(3), 382–401 (1982)
67. Lin, H., Pass, R., Soni, P.: Two-round and non-interactive concurrent non-malleable commitments from time-lock puzzles. In: 58th FOCS, pp. 576–587 (2017)
68. Liu-Zhang, C.-D., Maurer, U.: Synchronous constructive cryptography. In: Pass, R., Pietrzak, K. (eds.) TCC 2020, Part II. LNCS, vol. 12551, pp. 439–472. Springer, Cham (2020). https://doi.org/10.1007/978-3-030-64378-2_16
69. Mahmoody, M., Moran, T., Vadhan, S.: Time-lock puzzles in the random oracle model. In: Rogaway, P. (ed.) CRYPTO 2011. LNCS, vol. 6841, pp. 39–50. Springer, Heidelberg (2011). https://doi.org/10.1007/978-3-642-22792-9_3
70. Malavolta, G., Thyagarajan, S.A.K.: Homomorphic time-lock puzzles and applications. In: Boldyreva, A., Micciancio, D. (eds.) CRYPTO 2019, Part I. LNCS, vol. 11692, pp. 620–649. Springer, Cham (2019). https://doi.org/10.1007/978-3-030-26948-7_22
71. Matt, C., Nielsen, J.B., Thomsen, S.E.: Formalizing delayed adaptive corruptions and the security of flooding networks. In: Dodis, Y., Shrimpton, T. (eds.) CRYPTO 2022, Part II. LNCS, vol. 13508, pp. 400–430. Springer, Heidelberg (2022). https://doi.org/10.1007/978-3-031-15979-4_14
72. Micali, S., Rogaway, P.: Secure computation. In: Feigenbaum, J. (ed.) CRYPTO 1991. LNCS, vol. 576, pp. 392–404. Springer, Heidelberg (1992). https://doi.org/10.1007/3-540-46766-1_32
73. Nielsen, J.B.: Separating random oracle proofs from complexity theoretic proofs: the non-committing encryption case. In: Yung, M. (ed.) CRYPTO 2002. LNCS, vol. 2442, pp. 111–126. Springer, Heidelberg (2002). https://doi.org/10.1007/3-540-45708-9_8
74. Nielsen, J.B.: On protocol security in the cryptographic model. Ph.D. thesis, University of Aarhus (2003). https://www.brics.dk/DS/03/8/BRICS-DS-03-8.pdf
75. Pass, R., Seeman, L., Shelat, A.: Analysis of the blockchain protocol in asynchronous networks. In: Coron, J.-S., Nielsen, J.B. (eds.) EUROCRYPT 2017, Part II. LNCS, vol. 10211, pp. 643–673. Springer, Cham (2017). https://doi.org/10.1007/978-3-319-56614-6_22
76. Pease, M.C., Shostak, R.E., Lamport, L.: Reaching agreement in the presence of faults. J. ACM **27**(2), 228–234 (1980)
77. Pfitzmann, B., Waidner, M.: Unconditional Byzantine agreement for any number of faulty processors. In: Finkel, A., Jantzen, M. (eds.) STACS 1992. LNCS, vol. 577, pp. 337–350. Springer, Heidelberg (1992). https://doi.org/10.1007/3-540-55210-3_195
78. Pietrzak, K.: Simple verifiable delay functions. In: ITCS 2019, vol. 124, pp. 60:1–60:15 (2019)
79. Rivest, R.L., Shamir, A., Wagner, D.A.: Time-lock puzzles and timed-release crypto. Technical report, Massachusetts Institute of Technology, USA (1996)

80. Rotem, L., Segev, G.: Generically speeding-up repeated squaring is equivalent to factoring: sharp thresholds for all generic-ring delay functions. In: Micciancio, D., Ristenpart, T. (eds.) CRYPTO 2020, Part III. LNCS, vol. 12172, pp. 481–509. Springer, Cham (2020). https://doi.org/10.1007/978-3-030-56877-1_17
81. Srinivasan, S., Loss, J., Malavolta, G., Nayak, K., Papamanthou, C., Thyagarajan, S.A.K.: Transparent batchable time-lock puzzles and applications to byzantine consensus. In: Boldyreva, A., Kolesnikov, V. (eds.) PKC 2023, Part I. LNCS, vol. 13940, pp. 554–584. Springer, Cham (2023). https://doi.org/10.1007/978-3-031-31368-4_20
82. Tsimos, G., Loss, J., Papamanthou, C.: Gossiping for communication-efficient broadcast. In: Dodis, Y., Shrimpton, T. (eds.) CRYPTO 2022, Part III. LNCS, vol. 13509, pp. 439–469. Springer, Heidelberg (2022). https://doi.org/10.1007/978-3-031-15982-4_15
83. Wan, J., Xiao, H., Devadas, S., Shi, E.: Round-efficient byzantine broadcast under strongly adaptive and majority corruptions. In: Pass, R., Pietrzak, K. (eds.) TCC 2020, Part I. LNCS, vol. 12550, pp. 412–456. Springer, Cham (2020). https://doi.org/10.1007/978-3-030-64375-1_15
84. Wan, J., Xiao, H., Shi, E., Devadas, S.: Expected constant round byzantine broadcast under dishonest majority. In: Pass, R., Pietrzak, K. (eds.) TCC 2020, Part I. LNCS, vol. 12550, pp. 381–411. Springer, Cham (2020). https://doi.org/10.1007/978-3-030-64375-1_14
85. Wesolowski, B.: Efficient verifiable delay functions. In: Ishai, Y., Rijmen, V. (eds.) EUROCRYPT 2019, Part III. LNCS, vol. 11478, pp. 379–407. Springer, Cham (2019). https://doi.org/10.1007/978-3-030-17659-4_13
86. Yao, A.C.-C.: Protocols for secure computations (extended abstract). In: 23rd FOCS, pp. 160–164. IEEE Computer Society Press (1982)

Bingo: Adaptivity and Asynchrony in Verifiable Secret Sharing and Distributed Key Generation

Ittai Abraham[1], Philipp Jovanovic[2], Mary Maller[3], Sarah Meiklejohn[2,4], and Gilad Stern[5(✉)]

[1] Intel Labs, Petach Tikva, Israel
[2] University College London, London, UK
[3] Ethereum Foundation and PQShield, Bern, Switzerland
mary.maller@ethereum.org
[4] Google, Mountain View, USA
[5] The Hebrew University of Jerusalem, Jerusalem, Israel
gilad.stern@mail.huji.ac.il

Abstract. We present Bingo, an adaptively secure and optimally resilient packed asynchronous verifiable secret sharing (PAVSS) protocol that allows a dealer to share $f + 1$ secrets with a total communication complexity of $O(\lambda n^2)$ words, where λ is the security parameter and n is the number of parties. Using Bingo, we obtain an adaptively secure validated asynchronous Byzantine agreement (VABA) protocol that uses $O(\lambda n^3)$ expected words and constant expected time, which we in turn use to construct an adaptively secure high-threshold asynchronous distributed key generation (ADKG) protocol that uses $O(\lambda n^3)$ expected words and constant expected time. To the best of our knowledge, our ADKG is the first to allow for an adaptive adversary while matching the asymptotic complexity of the best known static ADKGs.

1 Introduction

The ability of a party to distribute a secret among a set of other parties (i.e., *secret sharing*) is a fundamental cryptographic primitive, with applications such as Byzantine agreement, threshold cryptography, and secure multiparty computation [1–5]. At its most basic level, secret sharing involves one honest dealer, sharing one secret among a set of n parties, so that if at least t parties coordinate they can reconstruct the secret (where notably an adversary is assumed to control strictly fewer than t parties).

There are many functional enhancements of secret sharing, including *verifiable* secret sharing (VSS) [6], where parties can verify the validity of their shares even in the face of a malicious dealer, and *packed* secret sharing [7], where a dealer can deal m secrets in a way that is more efficient than just running m iterations of the protocol. In terms of enhancements to the network model, *asynchronous* secret sharing [8,9] requires no assumptions about the delay on

H. Handschuh and A. Lysyanskaya (Eds.): CRYPTO 2023, LNCS 14081, pp. 39–70, 2023.
https://doi.org/10.1007/978-3-031-38557-5_2

messages between parties or the order in which they are received. Finally, and crucially for systems that are expected to run for long periods of time, *adaptively secure* secret sharing protocols [10] allow the adversary to corrupt parties over time rather than starting with a static set of parties that it controls.

Verifiable secret sharing has traditionally seen many applications in multiparty computation [4,11,12]. In recent years, people have also noticed the potential of VSS for preventing malicious MEV (*maximal extractable value*) in blockchains [13,14]. Indeed, frontrunning-as-a-service companies such as Flashbots are able to extract millions of dollars of value by reordering transactions on the Ethereum blockchain,[1] and in doing so increase overall costs for users. Using VSS, parties could share their transactions among a set of validators rather than sending them in the clear. It is crucial in this and many other real-world settings for the VSS to be not only efficient but also adaptively secure even when operated over an asynchronous network such as the internet.

Our main construction, Bingo, fills exactly this gap: it is an adaptively secure packed asynchronous verifiable secret sharing (PAVSS) protocol that allows a dealer to share $f + 1$ secrets with a total communication complexity of just $O(\lambda n^2)$ words, where n is the total number of parties and f is the number of malicious parties. Additionally, Bingo is *optimally resilient* in assuming that $n = 3f + 1$, and supports three different types of reconstruction:

- Reconstruction of a single secret, which does not reveal any information about any non-reconstructed secrets.
- Given an index k, reconstruction of the sum of the k-th secrets shared by several different dealers, which does not reveal any information about any non-reconstructed secrets.
- Reconstruction of all secrets at once, which can be viewed as reconstructing a degree-$2f$ sharing.

Each of these has a word complexity of $O(\lambda n^2)$ and requires a constant number of rounds. In terms of assumptions, Bingo requires a PKI and a univariate powers-of-tau setup [15] (of size $O(\lambda n)$ words) and is proved secure against algebraic adversaries [16].

Using Bingo, we construct two more advanced primitives: *validated asynchronous Byzantine agreement* (VABA) and *distributed key generation* (DKG). These are both essential protocols in constructing secure distributed systems, with DKG in particular emerging as an important tool for supporting a variety of distributed applications [3,5,17]. Again, for both of these protocols to be run in realistic distributed environments like the internet, it is essential that they be asynchronous and adaptively secure.

We first use Bingo to construct an adaptively secure VABA protocol that reaches agreement on messages of size $O(n)$ and requires just $O(\lambda n^3)$ words. Second, we use Bingo and our VABA protocol to construct an adaptively secure high-threshold *asynchronous* distributed key generation (ADKG) protocol. Our ADKG protocol requires just $O(1)$ expected rounds and $O(\lambda n^3)$ expected words,

[1] https://explore.flashbots.net/.

and has a secret key that is a field element (which in particular makes it compatible with standard threshold signature schemes like BLS [18]). We rely on the one-more discrete log assumption and prove security with respect to algebraic adversaries [16]; recent work by Bacho and Loss suggests that these relatively strong assumptions may be needed to support adaptively secure DKG for BLS [19]. To the best of our knowledge, ours is the first asynchronous protocol to be proven adaptively secure, and even previous synchronous adaptively secure protocols required $\Omega(n^4)$ sent words [19,20].

1.1 Technical Overview

The conceptual decomposition of distributed protocols to a distributed computing part against a weaker adversary and a cryptographic commitment and zero-knowledge part goes back to the foundational result of Goldreich, Micali, and Wigderson [21]. Here we present a high-level overview of Bingo by decomposing it into two parts: an efficient distributed protocol that is resilient to *omission failures* (i.e., failures that are non-malicious) and an efficient polynomial commitment scheme that essentially forces the malicious adversary to behave as an omission adversary. We start in Sect. 3 with our polynomial commitment scheme, then show in Sect. 4 how to use it to get an AVSS, Bingo, that tolerates adaptive malicious adversaries. Our construction builds on the KZG polynomial commitment scheme [22], which means relying on a powers-of-tau setup [15]. Our public parameters are backwards compatible with prior universal setups [23].

Step One: Bingo for Omission Failures. In this setting, the goal is to share a degree-$2f$ polynomial among $3f+1$ parties, f of which may suffer omission failures. Due to asynchrony, the dealer can interact with only $2f+1$ parties, and since f of them may have omission failures, the remaining $f+1$ honest parties need to enable all honest parties to eventually receive their share of the secret. Here we use the known technique [4,24–26] of having the dealer share a bivariate polynomial $\phi(X,Y)$ of degree at most $2f$ in X and degree f in Y. Visually, we think of a matrix of size $n \times n$ of the evaluations of $\phi(X,Y)$ at roots of unity $\{\omega_1,\dots,\omega_n\}$, as shown in Fig. 1. As such, we think of the polynomial $\phi(X,\omega_i)$ as the i-th *row* of the polynomial, which we denote by α_i, and the polynomial $\phi(\omega_i,Y)$ as the i-th *column* of the polynomial, which we denote by β_i. The dealer then sends each party i the i-th row. Each party can then wait for $2f+1$ parties to acknowledge receiving their rows before knowing that they will be able to complete the protocol. This works because once $f+1$ honest parties have their row we are guaranteed that all honest parties will eventually be able to recover their share in the following way: First, each honest party i that received a row from the dealer sends each party j the value $\phi(\omega_j,\omega_i)$. Hence each honest party j receives at least $f+1$ points on its j-th column and is able to reconstruct it. Second, once party j reconstructs its column, it sends each party i the value $\phi(\omega_j,\omega_i)$. In this way, all honest parties eventually reconstruct their columns, so each honest party i hears at least $2f+1$ values for row i and can reconstruct it.

As described, each party needs to send just $O(n)$ words and the protocol takes a constant number of rounds.

	β_1	β_2	β_3	β_4	β_5	β_6	β_7
α_1	v_{11}	v_{12}	v_{13}	v_{14}	v_{15}	v_{16}	v_{17}
α_2	v_{21}	v_{22}	v_{23}	v_{24}	v_{25}	v_{26}	v_{27}
α_3	v_{31}	v_{32}	v_{33}	v_{34}	v_{35}	v_{36}	v_{37}
α_4	v_{41}	v_{42}	v_{43}	v_{44}	v_{45}	v_{46}	v_{47}
α_5	v_{51}	v_{52}	v_{53}	v_{54}	v_{55}	v_{56}	v_{57}
α_6	v_{61}	v_{62}	v_{63}	v_{64}	v_{65}	v_{66}	v_{67}
α_7	v_{71}	v_{72}	v_{73}	v_{74}	v_{75}	v_{76}	v_{77}

	β_1	β_2	β_3	β_4	β_5	β_6	β_7
α_1	v_{11}	v_{12}	v_{13}	v_{14}	v_{15}	v_{16}	v_{17}
α_2	v_{21}	v_{22}	v_{23}	v_{24}	v_{25}	v_{26}	v_{27}
α_3	v_{31}	v_{32}	v_{33}	v_{34}	v_{35}	v_{36}	v_{37}
α_4	v_{41}	v_{42}	v_{43}	v_{44}	v_{45}	v_{46}	v_{47}
α_5	v_{51}	v_{52}	v_{53}	v_{54}	v_{55}	v_{56}	v_{57}
α_6	v_{61}	v_{62}	v_{63}	v_{64}	v_{65}	v_{66}	v_{67}
α_7	v_{71}	v_{72}	v_{73}	v_{74}	v_{75}	v_{76}	v_{77}

Fig. 1. A graphical representation of Bingo's sharing process showing the two ways in which party i can obtain their secret polynomial. The row polynomials are denoted by $\alpha_i = \phi(X, \omega_i)$ whereas the column polynomials are denoted by $\beta_i = \phi(\omega_i, Y)$. On the left-hand side, party 2 receives α_2 directly from the (honest) dealer. On the right-hand side, party 2 did not receive their polynomial from the dealer. Instead i receives evaluations of the column polynomials β_j from at least $2f + 1$ other parties. Because $\beta_j(\omega_2) = \alpha_2(\omega_j)$, this is equivalent to obtaining $2f+1$ evaluations of α_2, meaning party 2 can obtain α_2 by interpolation.

Step Two: Bingo for Malicious Failures. In order to move from omission failures to malicious failures with adaptive security, we use a perfectly hiding bivariate *polynomial commitment scheme* (PCS) that essentially forces the malicious parties to act as if they can only have omission failures.

Our bivariate PCS has five desirable properties: (1) it requires a standard $O(\lambda n)$ univariate powers-of-tau setup; (2) a commitment has size $O(\lambda n)$; (3) given a commitment to $\phi, \hat{\phi}$, one can generate commitments to all rows; (4) given $f + 1$ evaluations on column j, one can generate evaluation proofs for all points of column j; and (5) given $2f + 1$ evaluations on row i, one can generate evaluation proofs for all points in row i. Perhaps surprisingly, our PCS commits to a bivariate polynomial $\phi(X, Y)$ of degree f in each column and degree $2f$ in each row by simply committing to $f + 1$ specific rows, where a commitment to row i is just a KZG univariate polynomial commitment for $\phi(X, \omega_i)$ of degree $2f$. It is easy to see that this fulfills the first two properties. For the third property, we prove that interpolation in the exponent of any $f + 1$ row commitments generates commitments to all rows. In order to reduce computation costs, it is also possible to compute the interpolated coefficients and send them instead of sending the commitments. Every party can then evaluate commitments in the exponent instead of interpolating $f + 1$ commitments and evaluating the rest.

From Bingo to VABA and ADKG. We detail how to use Bingo to obtain a VABA protocol and an ADKG protocol in Sect. 5. Using Bingo's $O(n^2)$ word complexity for packing $O(n)$ secrets allows us to associate with each party a random value based on secrets from $f + 1$ parties at a total cost of just $O(n^3)$ words. This random value, when used as a party's rank, allows us to construct adaptively secure *leader election* and *proposal election* protocols, which in turn allow us to build a VABA protocol with $O(n^3)$ expected word complexity for

Table 1. A comparison of AVSS schemes, in terms of: (1) the best amortized word complexity and (2) the batch size needed to obtain that complexity; (3) the need to rely on a CRS setup (where ● means there is no trusted setup and ○ means there is); (4) the maximum degree of the shared polynomial (where the schemes with maximum degree $2f$ can be used for sharing any degree between f and $2f$); and (5) the cryptographic assumptions needed to prove security. None of the prior schemes have been proved secure against an adaptive adversary, and all schemes have a constant round complexity.

Scheme	Word complexity	Batch size	CRS setup	Max degree	Assumptions
Cachin et al. [1]	$O(\lambda n^3)$	$O(1)$	●	$2f$	DL
Backes et al. [27]	$O(\lambda n^2)$	$O(1)$	○	f	q-SDH, q-polyDH
Haven [28]	$O(\lambda n)$	$O(n \log n)$	●	$2f$	DL, ROM*
hbACSS [29]	$O(\lambda n)$	$O(n^2)$	○	f	q-SDH
Bingo (this work)	$O(\lambda n)$	$O(n)$	○	$2f$	q-SDH, AGM

* Haven requires the secret to be distributed uniformly at random.

$O(n)$ sized inputs. This construction uses the ability to individually reconstruct sums of secrets shared by different dealers.

To obtain an ADKG, each party uses Bingo's $O(n^2)$ word complexity for a *high threshold* secret; i.e., with a threshold of $2f + 1$ (or more generally any threshold between $f+1$ and $2f+1$). Using the VABA protocol above on inputs formed from $f + 1$ completed high-threshold sharings allows us to reach agreement on a common BLS secret key formed from the sum of $f+1$ high-threshold secret sharings. Once agreement is reached, we reveal the BLS public key by using the standard "recovering in the exponent" technique. We prove that the resulting BLS signature scheme is adaptively secure using the framework of Bacho and Loss [19], relying on the $2f + 1$-one-more discrete log assumption and the algebraic group model.

1.2 Related Work

Tables 1 and 2 provides a comparison with the most relevant prior AVSS and ADKG schemes. Cachin et al. [1] study asynchronous verifiable secret sharing (AVSS) in the computational setting. The earlier works of Feldman and Micali [35] and Canetti and Rabin [9] study AVSS in the private channel setting. Backes, Datta, and Kate [27] provide the first construction with asymptotically optimal $\mathcal{O}(\lambda n^2)$ word complexity for AVSS. They use the seminal pairing-based polynomial commitment scheme due to Kate, Zaverucha, and Goldberg (KZG) [22]. Compared to Backes et al., we provide the same asymptotically optimal $O(\lambda n^2)$ word complexity with an $O(n)$ improvement in the size of the secret and a scheme that is proven to be adaptively secure.

AlHaddad, Varia, and Zhang [28] obtain a high-threshold AVSS, Haven, for uniformly random secrets with $O(n^2)$ word complexity. Moreover, their scheme can be instantiated with a setup-free polynomial commitment scheme [36–39] at

Table 2. A comparison of ADKG schemes, in terms of: (1) the best word complexity; (2) the expected number of rounds; (3) the need to rely on a CRS setup (where ● means there is no trusted setup and ○ means there is); (4) the maximum reconstruction threshold; and (5) the cryptographic assumptions needed to prove security. None of the prior schemes have been proved secure against an adaptive adversary.

Scheme	Word complexity	Rounds	CRS setup	Max threshold	Assumptions
Kate et al. [30]	$O(\lambda n^4)$	$O(n)$	●	f	DL, ROM
Kokoris-Kogias et al. [17]	$O(\lambda n^4)$	$O(n)$	●	$2f$	DL
Abraham et al. [31]	$O(\lambda n^3)$	$O(1)$	●	f	SXDH, BDH, ROM†
Das et al. [32]	$O(\lambda n^3)$	$O(\log n)$	●	$2f$	DDH, ROM
Groth and Shoup [33]	$O(\lambda n^3)$	$O(1)$	●	f	DL, ROM
This work	$O(\lambda n^3)$	$O(1)$	○	$2f$	q-SDH◇

† Abraham et al. require the secret key to be a group element.
◇ We prove that our protocol satisfies oracle-aided simulatability [19], as opposed to the more general notions of secrecy [34] or key expressability [3]. To some extent, this can be thought of as introducing a reliance on the one-more discrete logarithm (OMDL) assumption.

a $O(n^2 \log n)$ word complexity. Because our construction enables packed secret sharing and allows for arbitrary secrets, we can share n arbitrary secrets with the same word complexity ($O(n^2)$) that it takes AlHaddad et al. to share one random secret.

Yurek et al. [29] provide three variant protocols called hbACSS, which are proved secure against a static adversary. These protocols achieve batching rather than packing (because they use an f-by-f polynomial), but for each shared secret they are (quasi)linear in both computation and communication overhead in an amortized sense. While AVSS protocols with efficient batching allow for sharing many secrets more efficiently than sharing them separately, packed secret sharing protocols [7] do so by sharing them on the same high-degree polynomial. These sharings can then be used where high-degree polynomials are needed (e.g. in high-degree DKGs), whereas simple batching does not suffice for these purposes. Because Bingo is packed (due to its use of a $2f$-by-f polynomial) it achieves linear overheads after sharing $O(n)$ secrets (which we rely on in our leader election protocol), whereas the hbACSS protocols achieve the same overheads after sharing $O(n^2)$ secrets. A construction using a $2f$-by-f bivariate polynomial has previously been suggested in [40].

There has been considerable recent interest in practical ADKG and the building blocks needed to support it. Kokoris-Kogias, Malkhi, and Spiegelman [17] obtain a high threshold ADKG with $O(n^4)$ communication complexity and $O(n)$ rounds. Gurkan et al. suggest an aggregatable publicly verifiable secret sharing (PVSS) scheme [3] that builds upon the SCRAPE PVSS of Cascudo and David [41]. When combined with the consensus protocol of Abraham et al. [31], the result of Gurkan et al. yields a high-threshold ADKG with $O(n^3 \log n)$ communication complexity and $O(1)$ expected time that is secure against static adversaries. Their secret key is a group element, however, which makes it incompatible with commonly used threshold cryptography schemes, such as BLS, that require field elements as secrets. Cascudo and David [42] introduce Albatross, which uses packed secret sharing to build a randomness beacon that shares $O(n^2)$ random values. Albatross also uses the SCRAPE PVSS as a backend and thus cannot be used to share a field element (and has a static security proof).

Das, Xiang, and Ren [43] provide a reliable broadcast protocol that, among other improvements, removes the logarithmic factor from the consensus protocol of Abraham et al. [31] to get $O(n^3)$ communication complexity and $O(1)$ expected time. Das et al. [32] provide a high-threshold DKG that has a field element as a secret key, $O(n^3)$ word complexity, and is secure against a static adversary. In the optimistic case it runs in $O(1)$ rounds, but in the face of a Byzantine attacker it requires an expected $O(\log(n))$ rounds.

Groth and Shoup [33] provide a DKG that has $O(n^3)$ word complexity and avoids a trusted setup. There is a rigorous security analysis only for static corruptions, however, and their scheme doesn't support high-threshold reconstruction. In terms of their underlying AVSS, it has an amortized linear cost with a batch size of $n \log n$. We get the same amortized cost for a batch size of n, which we need in our weak leader election protocol (in the full version of the paper [44]).

2 Definitions

In this section we start by defining basic notation, and then defining polynomial commitment schemes and reliable broadcast as basic building blocks to be used in our constructions. Following that, we discuss the way we model interactive protocols in order to finally define packed asynchronous verifiable secret sharing.

2.1 Preliminaries

For a finite set S, we denote by $|S|$ its size and by $x \xleftarrow{\$} S$ the process of sampling a member uniformly from S and assigning it to x. Further, $\lambda \in \mathbb{N}$ denotes the security parameter and 1^λ denotes its unary representation. For two integers $i \leq j$, we define $[i,j] = \{i,\ldots,j\}$, and for every $n \in \mathbb{N}$ we define $[n] = \{1,\ldots,n\}$. We define $\omega_1,\ldots,\omega_n$ to be n different roots of unity of order $n+f$. In a slight abuse of notation, we define ω_0 to be 0 and $\omega_{-f},\ldots,\omega_{-1}$ to be the remaining f roots of unity of order $n+f$. PPT stands for probabilistic polynomial time. By $y \leftarrow A(x_1,\ldots,x_n)$ we denote running algorithm A on inputs $x_1,\ldots,x_n$ and assigning its output to y, and by $y \xleftarrow{\$} A(x_1,\ldots,x_n)$ we denote running $A(x_1,\ldots,x_n;R)$ for a uniformly random tape R. Adversaries are modeled as randomized algorithms. We use code-based games in our security definitions [45]. A game $\mathsf{G}^{\mathsf{sec}}_{\mathcal{A}}(\lambda)$, played with respect to a security notion sec and adversary $\mathcal{A}$, has a MAIN procedure whose output is the output of the game. $\Pr[\mathsf{G}^{\mathsf{sec}}_{\mathcal{A}}(\lambda)]$ denotes the probability that this output is equal to 1.

Our constructions rely on the discrete logarithm assumption (dlog) which says that it is hard to output x given g^x, where g is a generator of a group $\mathbb{G}$ of prime order p and $x \xleftarrow{\$} \mathbb{F}_p$. We also rely on the *q-strong Diffie-Hellman* assumption (q-sdh) [46], which says that it is hard to output a pair $(c, g^{1/(x+c)})$ given $(g, g^x, g^{x^2}, \ldots, g^{x^q}, \hat{g}, \hat{g}^x) \in \mathbb{G}_1^{q+1} \times \mathbb{G}_2^2$, where $\mathbb{G}_1$ and $\mathbb{G}_2$ are groups of prime order p, generated by g and $\hat{g}$, and form a bilinear group, q is an integer, and $x \xleftarrow{\$} \mathbb{F}_p$. Finally, our DKG application relies on the k-one-more discrete logarithm (omdl) assumption [47], which says that it is hard to output $(x_1, \ldots, x_k) \in \mathbb{F}_p^k$ given $(g, g^{x_1}, \ldots, g^{x_k}) \in \mathbb{G}^{k+1}$, where g is a generator of a group $\mathbb{G}$ of prime order p and $x_1, \ldots, x_k \xleftarrow{\$} \mathbb{F}_p$, and at most $k-1$ queries to a discrete log oracle DL that on input X outputs $\log_g(X)$. We use bp to denote the parameters defining a bilinear group with extra generators; i.e., $\mathsf{bp} = (g, \hat{g} \in \mathbb{G}_1, h \in \mathbb{G}_2, \mathbb{G}_T, e)$.

Some properties of our constructions are proved secure in the algebraic group model (AGM) [16]. In the AGM, whenever an adversary outputs a group element it must output the algebraic representation of that element relative to all the group elements it has seen thus far; i.e., if it has seen $X_1, \ldots, X_m$ then upon outputting a new element Y it must output $a_1, \ldots, a_m$ such that $Y = \prod_i X_i^{a_i}$.

2.2 Polynomial Commitments

We define a *polynomial commitment scheme* (PCS) as consisting of the following algorithms:

- $\mathsf{srs} \xleftarrow{\$} \mathsf{Setup}(1^\lambda)$ takes as input a security parameter and outputs a commitment key srs.
- $\boldsymbol{C} \xleftarrow{\$} \mathsf{Commit}(\mathsf{srs}, \phi)$ takes as input the commitment key and a polynomial ϕ and outputs a commitment $\boldsymbol{C}$. We often specify the randomness $\hat{\phi}$ explicitly using the notation $\boldsymbol{C} \leftarrow \mathsf{Commit}(\mathsf{srs}, \phi, \hat{\phi})$.
- $m, \hat{m}, \pi \leftarrow \mathsf{Eval}(\mathsf{srs}, \phi, \hat{\phi}, \omega)$ takes as input a commitment key, a pair of polynomials, and a point on which to evaluate. It returns $m = \phi(\omega)$, $\hat{m} = \hat{\phi}(\omega)$ and a proof π that $m, \hat{m}$ are consistent with ω.
- $0/1 \leftarrow \mathsf{Verify}(\mathsf{srs}, \boldsymbol{C}, \omega, m, \hat{m}, \pi)$ takes as input a commitment key, a commitment, an opening point, a pair of openings, and a proof π. It returns 1 if it is convinced that $(m, \hat{m})$ is a valid opening of $\boldsymbol{C}$ at ω and 0 otherwise.

In what follows, we often omit the commitment key srs as an explicit input to the other algorithms. Following Kate et al. [22], we require that a PCS satisfies *correctness*, meaning that $\mathsf{Verify}(\mathsf{Commit}(\phi, \hat{\phi}), \omega, \mathsf{Eval}(\phi, \hat{\phi}, \omega)) = 1$ and both *polynomial binding* and *evaluation binding*. These say, respectively, that an adversary cannot open a single commitment to two different values and that an adversary cannot output two valid but incompatible evaluations of the same pair of polynomials, as represented by a single commitment.

Definition 1 (Polynomial binding). [22] *Consider a game* $\mathsf{G}_{\mathcal{A}}^{poly\text{-}binding}(\lambda)$ *in which an adversary* $\mathcal{A}$ *takes* 1^λ *as input and outputs the tuple* $(\phi_1, \hat{\phi}_1, \phi_2, \hat{\phi}_2)$, *and wins if (1)* $\mathsf{Commit}(\phi_1, \hat{\phi}_1) = \mathsf{Commit}(\phi_2, \hat{\phi}_2)$ *and (2)* $(\phi_1, \hat{\phi}_1) \neq (\phi_2, \hat{\phi}_2)$. *We say the PCS satisfies* polynomial binding *if for all PPT adversaries* $\mathcal{A}$ *there exists a negligible function* $\nu(\cdot)$ *such that* $\Pr[\mathsf{G}_{\mathcal{A}}^{poly\text{-}binding}(\lambda)] < \nu(\lambda)$.

Definition 2 (Evaluation binding). [22] *Consider a game* $\mathsf{G}_{\mathcal{A}}^{eval\text{-}binding}(\lambda)$ *in which an adversary* $\mathcal{A}$ *takes* 1^λ *as input and outputs* $(\boldsymbol{C}, \omega, m_1, \hat{m}_1, \pi_1, m_2, \hat{m}_2, \pi_2)$*, and wins if (1)* $\mathsf{Verify}(\boldsymbol{C}, \omega, m_i, \hat{m}_i, \pi_i) = 1$ *for* $i \in \{1, 2\}$ *and (2)* $(m_1, \hat{m}_1) \neq (m_2, \hat{m}_2)$*. We say the PCS satisfies* evaluation binding *if for all PPT adversaries* $\mathcal{A}$ *there exists a negligible function* $\nu(\cdot)$ *such that* $\Pr[\mathsf{G}_{\mathcal{A}}^{eval\text{-}binding}(\lambda)] < \nu(\lambda)$.

We define another important property for a PCS, *interpolation binding*, which says that given enough evaluations of a committed pair of polynomials, the interpolated polynomials obtained from these evaluations must be the ones contained inside the commitment. For this we use the notation $p \leftarrow \mathsf{Interpolate}(\{\omega_i, y_i\}_i)$ to denote using Lagrange interpolation to obtain a degree-d polynomial given $d+1$ evaluation points and their corresponding evaluations.

Definition 3 (Interpolation binding). *Consider the game* $\mathsf{G}_{\mathcal{A}}^{int\text{-}binding}(1^\lambda)$ *defined as follows*

$\underline{\text{MAIN}(1^\lambda, d)}$
$\mathsf{srs} \xleftarrow{\$} \mathsf{Setup}(1^\lambda, d)$
$(\boldsymbol{C}, \{(\omega_i, m_i, \hat{m}_i, \pi_i)\}_{i\in[d+1]}) \xleftarrow{\$} \mathcal{A}(\mathsf{srs})$
$p(X) \leftarrow \mathsf{Interpolate}(\{(\omega_i\, m_i)\}_{i\in[d+1]})$
$\hat{p}(X) \leftarrow \mathsf{Interpolate}(\{(\omega_i, \hat{m}_i)\}_{i\in[d+1]})$
check $\omega_i \neq \omega_j$ *for all* $i \neq j$
check $\mathsf{Verify}(\mathsf{srs}, \boldsymbol{C}, \omega_i, m_i, \hat{m}_i, \pi_i) = 1$ *for all* $i \in [d+1]$
check $\boldsymbol{C} \neq \mathsf{Commit}(\mathsf{srs}, p(X); \hat{p}(X))$
if all checks pass return 1*, else return* 0

We say the PCS satisfies interpolation binding *if for all PPT adversaries* $\mathcal{A}$ *there exists a negligible function* $\nu(\cdot)$ *such that* $\Pr[\mathsf{G}_{\mathcal{A}}^{int\text{-}binding}(1^\lambda)] < \nu(\lambda)$.

In our construction of Bingo, we do not use the hiding property defined by Kate et al. as it did not fit our use case. We instead provide a new hiding definition, capturing the ability of a simulator to both open commitments and provide evaluations without knowledge of the underlying polynomials. As this definition is somewhat specific to our usage of KZG within Bingo, and in particular to the way in which it is embedded in a bivariate polynomial commitment (as described below), it can be found in the full version of the paper [44].

In a *bivariate* PCS, ϕ is a polynomial in indeterminates X and Y. This means we consider an additional algorithm:

- $\boldsymbol{A} \leftarrow \mathsf{PartialEval}(\mathsf{srs}, \boldsymbol{C}, V_n)$ takes as input the commitment key, the bivariate commitment, and a set of partial evaluation points V_n of size n. It outputs n partial evaluations, consisting of commitments to univariate polynomials $\alpha(X) \leftarrow \phi(X, v)$ and $\hat{\alpha}(X) \leftarrow \hat{\phi}(X, v)$ for each $v \in V_n$.

To prove evaluations of ϕ and $\hat{\phi}$, we can use these univariate polynomials as input to Eval, and their commitments as input to Verify (which must now take in two evaluation points ω and ω_v rather than a single one). In terms of correctness, we define an algorithm $\boldsymbol{A} \leftarrow \mathsf{CPE}(\phi, \hat{\phi}, V_n)$ that first runs Commit on ϕ and $\hat{\phi}$ and then runs PartialEval on its output $\boldsymbol{C}$ and V_n. We then require that $\mathsf{Verify}(\mathsf{CPE}(\phi, \hat{\phi}, V_n), (\omega, v), \mathsf{Eval}(\phi(X, v), \hat{\phi}(X, v), \omega)) = 1$ for all $v \in V_n$.

2.3 Reliable Broadcast

A *reliable broadcast* is an asynchronous protocol with a designated *sender*. The sender has some input value m from a known domain $\mathcal{M}$ and each party may output a value in $\mathcal{M}$. A reliable broadcast has the following properties assuming all *nonfaulty* (i.e., uncorrupted) parties participate in the protocol:

- **Validity.** If the sender is nonfaulty, then every nonfaulty party that completes the protocol outputs the sender's input value m.
- **Agreement.** The values output by any two nonfaulty parties are the same.
- **Termination.** If the dealer is nonfaulty, then all nonfaulty parties complete the protocol and output a value. Furthermore, if some nonfaulty party completes the protocol, every nonfaulty party completes the protocol.

2.4 Packed Asynchronous Verifiable Secret Sharing (PAVSS)

We define a packed AVSS using two interactive protocols that take place between n parties: Share and Reconstruct. In Share, the designated dealer receives as input a set of secrets $s_0, \ldots, s_m$ from a finite field $\mathbb{F}$ and all other parties receive no input. None of the parties have any output at the end of Share, but they do update their local state. Because the AVSS is packed, there are $m+1$ possible invocations of Reconstruct, one for each index k. Each party thus provides k as input to the protocol, and has as output a field element $v_k \in \mathbb{F}$, which represents their local view of the k-th secret shared by the dealer.

We formally define the environment for a PAVSS in the full version of the paper, in terms of capturing the ways in which the adversary can control the network (i.e., when honest parties receive messages) and the other actions the adversary can take. We then formally define three security properties for a PAVSS, which we informally summarize here.

Our first definition, *termination*, sets the conditions under which nonfaulty parties can be guaranteed to complete Share and Reconstruct. Briefly, it says that (1) if the dealer is nonfaulty then all nonfaulty parties will complete Share; (2) if one nonfaulty party completes Share then all nonfaulty parties will; and (3) if all nonfaulty parties complete Share and invoke Reconstruct(k) then they all will complete Reconstruct(k). Our next definition, *correctness*, captures the requirement that all nonfaulty parties who complete Reconstruct(k) should agree on the same secret, which in turn should be the same as the one used by the dealer (if it was also nonfaulty). Our final definition, *secrecy*, captures the requirement that an adversary should not be able to learn anything about the k-th secret until the point at which some nonfaulty party invokes Reconstruct(k).

Our specific PAVSS scheme, Bingo, is also *complete* in the sense that every party has a share of each of the secrets (this can be seen in the proof of Theorem

$\underline{\mathsf{KZG.Setup}(\mathsf{bp}, d_1)}$	$\underline{\mathsf{KZG.Eval}(\mathsf{srs}, \alpha(X), \hat{\alpha}(X), \omega_i)}$
$\tau, x \xleftarrow{\$} \mathbb{F}$	$m \leftarrow \alpha(\omega_i)$
$\hat{g} \leftarrow g^x$	$\hat{m} \leftarrow \hat{\alpha}(\omega_i)$
$\mathsf{srs} \leftarrow (\mathsf{bp}, h, h^\tau, \{g^{\tau^i}, \hat{g}^{\tau^i}\}_{i=0}^{d_1})$	$q(X) \leftarrow (\alpha(X) - m)/(X - \omega_i)$
return srs	$\hat{q}(X) \leftarrow (\hat{\alpha}(X) - \hat{m})/(X - \omega_i)$
	$\pi \leftarrow g^{q(\tau)}\hat{g}^{\hat{q}(\tau)}$
	return $(m, \hat{m}, \pi)$
$\underline{\mathsf{KZG.Commit}(\mathsf{srs}, \alpha(X); \hat{\alpha}(X))}$	
$C \leftarrow g^{\alpha(\tau)}\hat{g}^{\alpha(\tau)}$	$\underline{\mathsf{KZG.Verify}(\mathsf{srs}, C, \omega_i, m, \hat{m}, \pi)}$
return C	if $e(Cg^{-m}\hat{g}^{-\hat{m}}, h) = e(\pi, h^{\tau - \omega_i})$ return 1
	else return 0

Fig. 2. The hiding univariate KZG polynomial commitment scheme.

3, in which every party guarantees it has a share before terminating). Beyond the above three properties, this thus makes Bingo a packed asynchronous complete secret sharing (ACSS) scheme [4].

3 A Bivariate Polynomial Commitment Scheme

3.1 Construction

Our construction for a bivariate polynomial commitment scheme, given in Fig. 3, builds heavily on top of the univariate PCS due to Kate et al. [22]. As such, we first present this construction in Fig. 2.

In both commitment schemes, the setup outputs universal powers-of-tau parameters [15], meaning they are backwards compatible with prior trusted setups [23]. Let $\phi(X,Y)$ be a bivariate polynomial with degree d_1 in X and degree d_2 in Y. A commitment to $\phi(X,Y)$ first decomposes $\phi(X,Y)$ into d_2+1 univariate polynomials $\phi_i(X)$ such that $\phi(X,Y) = \sum_{i=0}^{d_2} \phi_i(X)Y^i$. The randomness $\hat{\phi}(X,Y)$ is decomposed in the same manner. Then each of the $\phi_i(X)$ are committed to using KZG.Commit with randomness $\hat{\phi}_i(X)$. A commitment C such that $|C| = d_2$ has maximum degree d_2 in Y and d_1 in X.

The partial evaluation algorithm takes as input a commitment C and a set of distinct points V_n of size n. It then runs a discrete Fourier transform (DFT) that maps a polynomial to a set of evaluations. Because the DFT/iDFT algorithm is a linear transformation, it can be applied to (homomorphic) group exponents in the exact same way as it is run for field elements, without having to know the discrete logarithms. To avoid confusion, we nevertheless denote the algorithms acting on field elements as DFT and iDFT and the algorithms acting on group elements as DFTExp and iDFTExp. PartialEval thus runs and outputs

$\underline{\mathsf{Setup}(\mathsf{bp}, d_1)}$
return $\mathsf{KZG.Setup}(\mathsf{bp}, d_1)$

$\underline{\mathsf{PartialEval}(\mathsf{srs}, \boldsymbol{C}, V_n)}$
$\boldsymbol{A} \leftarrow \mathsf{DFTExp}(\boldsymbol{C}, V_n)$
return $\boldsymbol{A}$

$\underline{\mathsf{Eval}(\mathsf{srs}, \alpha(X), \hat{\alpha}(X), \omega_i)}$
return $\mathsf{KZG.Eval}(\mathsf{srs}, \alpha(X), \hat{\alpha}(X), \omega_i)$

$\underline{\mathsf{Commit}(\mathsf{srs}, \phi(X,Y); \hat{\phi}(X,Y))}$
$\sum_{i=0}^{d_2} \phi_i(X)Y^i \leftarrow \mathsf{parse}(\phi(X,Y))$
$\sum_{i=0}^{d_2} \hat{\phi}_i(X)Y^i \leftarrow \mathsf{parse}(\hat{\phi}(X,Y))$
$\boldsymbol{C} \leftarrow \{g^{\phi_i(\tau)}\hat{g}^{\hat{\phi}_i(\tau)}\}_{i=0}^{d_2}$
return $\boldsymbol{C}$

$\underline{\mathsf{Verify}(\mathsf{srs}, \boldsymbol{A}, (i,j), m, \hat{m}, \pi)}$
return $\mathsf{KZG.Verify}(\mathsf{srs}, \boldsymbol{A}_j, \omega_i, m, \hat{m}, \pi)$

$\underline{\mathsf{GetProofs}(\{(w_i, y_i, \hat{y}_i, \pi_i)\}_{i\in[f+1]}, V_n)}$
$\beta(X) \leftarrow \mathsf{Interpolate}\left(\{(w_i, y_i)\}_{i\in[d_1+1]}\right)$
$\hat{\beta}(X) \leftarrow \mathsf{Interpolate}\left(\{(w_i, \hat{y}_i)\}_{i\in[d_1+1]}\right)$
$\boldsymbol{P} \leftarrow \mathsf{InterpolateExp}\left(\{(w_i, \pi_i)\}_{i\in[d_1+1]}\right)$
$z_1, \ldots, z_n \leftarrow \mathsf{DFT}(\beta(X), V_n)$
$\hat{z}_1, \ldots, \hat{z}_n \leftarrow \mathsf{DFT}(\hat{\beta}(X), V_n)$
$\bar{\pi}_1, \ldots, \bar{\pi}_n \leftarrow \mathsf{DFTExp}(\boldsymbol{P}, V_n)$
return $\{(z_i, \hat{z}_i, \bar{\pi}_n)\}_{i\in[n]}$

Fig. 3. Our bivariate PCS, built on top of the KZG univariate PCS. The set V_n consists of n roots of unity, i.e., values ω_i such that $\omega_i^n = 1$.

$$\mathsf{DFTExp} : ((g^{a_0}, \ldots, g^{a_{d_1}}), \mathbb{F}^n) \mapsto \{g^{\sum_{j=0}^{d_1} a_j \omega_i^j}\}_{i=0}^{n-1}.$$

If V_n is a multiplicative subgroup of $\mathbb{F}$ containing roots of unity, then DFT and DFTExp run in time $n\log(n)$. Note that it is possible to replace the DFTs with simple Lagrange interpolation in any field without using roots of unity, but DFTs are used to improve efficiency. If $W \subset V_n$ is a subset of roots of unity, then interpolation over W runs in time $n\log^2(n)$ [48]. In addition to the interpolation algorithm $p \leftarrow \mathsf{Interpolate}(\{(\omega_i, y_i)\})$, we denote by $P \leftarrow \mathsf{InterpolateExp}(\{(\omega_i, Y_i)\})$ the algorithm that performs these operations in the exponent (i.e., by acting on group elements). We also denote by $Y \leftarrow \mathsf{EvalExp}(\omega, P)$ the algorithm that performs polynomial evaluation in the exponent.

To verify that a commitment opens at (ω_i, ω_j) to $(m, \hat{m})$, we take as input the partial evaluation $\boldsymbol{A}$ over the set V_n where $\omega_j \in V_n$. Then $\boldsymbol{A}_j = g^{\phi(\tau,\omega_j)}\hat{g}^{\hat{\phi}(\tau,\omega_j)}$ is a KZG commitment to $\phi(X, \omega_j)$ under randomness $\hat{\phi}(X, \omega_j)$. The prover can thus provide a KZG opening proof that $\boldsymbol{A}_j$ opens at ω_i to m under randomness $\hat{m}$ (i.e., the output of $\mathsf{KZG.Eval}$), which the verifier can check using $\mathsf{KZG.Verify}$.

The security of our bivariate PCS follows directly from the security of the KZG univariate PCS, in terms of polynomial binding, evaluation binding, and hiding, which follow in turn from the $\mathsf{q\text{-}sdh}$ assumption. We next prove, in the algebraic group model [16], that the underlying univariate PCS also satisfies interpolation binding. A proof of this lemma can be found in the full version of the paper [44].

Lemma 1. *If the* dlog *and* q-sdh *assumptions hold, then interpolation binding (Definition 3) holds for the KZG PCS.*

3.2 Commitment and Proof Interpolation

For any bivariate polynomial $\phi(X, Y)$ of degree d_1 in X we have that the points $\phi(\omega_{v_1}, \omega_j), \ldots, \phi(\omega_{v_{d_1+1}}, \omega_j)$ suffice to interpolate the partial evaluation $\phi(X, \omega_j)$. A special property about our bivariate PCS is that, given a commitment $\boldsymbol{C}$ and $d_1 + 1$ openings (with respect to the same ω_j), parties can also compute the opening proofs for $\boldsymbol{C}$ at (x, ω_j) for any $x \in \mathbb{F}$. This will be useful in Bingo when the dealer is dishonest.

In Fig. 3 we describe an additional algorithm $\{(z_i, \hat{z}_i, \bar{\pi}_i)\} \leftarrow \mathsf{GetProofs}(\{(v_i, y_i, \hat{y}_i, \pi_i)\}, V_n)$ that takes as input $d_1 + 1$ opening points, their evaluations and associated proofs, and a set V_n, and outputs n evaluations and their associated proofs over the bigger set V_n. In Lemma 2 we prove the correctness of this algorithm, namely that if every opening $(y_i, \hat{y}_i, \pi_i)$ verifies with respect to the commitment $\boldsymbol{C}$ and the indices (j, w_i), then every output $(z_k, \hat{z}_k, \bar{\pi}_k)$ also verifies with respect to $(\boldsymbol{C}, k, j)$. A proof of this lemma can be found in the full version of the paper [44].

Lemma 2. *Let $\boldsymbol{C}$ be a bivariate polynomial commitment, let $\boldsymbol{A}$ be such that $\boldsymbol{A} \leftarrow \mathsf{PartialEval}(\boldsymbol{C}, V_n)$, let v_i be indices such that $w_i = \omega_{v_i}$ for every $i \in [d_1 + 1]$, and let $\{(v_i, y_i, \hat{y}_i, \pi_i)\}_{i \in [d_1+1]}$ be values such that $\mathsf{VerifyEval}(\boldsymbol{A}, (j, v_i), y_i, \hat{y}_i, \pi_i) = 1$ for all $i \in [d_1 + 1]$. If*

$$\{(z_i, \hat{z}_i, \bar{\pi}_i)\}_{i \in [n]} \leftarrow \mathsf{GetProofs}(\{(w_i, y_i, \hat{y}_i, \pi_i)\}_{i \in [d_1+1]}, V_n)$$

then $\forall k \in [n]$, $\mathsf{VerifyEval}(\boldsymbol{A}, (j, k), \beta_j(\omega_k), \hat{\beta}_j(\omega_k), \bar{\pi}_k) = 1$.

Below we prove an additional useful property of our bivariate PCS, namely that by performing interpolation in the exponent on the partial (univariate) commitments we can recover the bivariate commitment.

Lemma 3. *Let $v_1, \ldots, v_{d_2+1} \in [n]$ be distinct values, and let $\alpha_{v_1}(X), \ldots, \alpha_{v_{f+1}}(X)$ and $\hat{\alpha}_{v_1}(X), \ldots, \hat{\alpha}_{v_{f+1}}(X)$ be polynomials of degree no greater than d_1. Define $\phi(X, Y), \hat{\phi}(X, Y)$ to be the unique bivariate polynomials of degree d_1 in X and d_2 in Y such that $\forall i \in [d_1 + 1]$ $\alpha_{v_i}(X) = \phi(X, \omega_{v_i}), \hat{\alpha}_{v_i}(X) = \hat{\phi}(X, \omega_{v_i})$. If $\forall i \in [d_2 + 1]$ $D_i = \mathsf{Commit}(\alpha_{v_i}(X);\ \hat{\alpha}_{v_i}(X))$ and $\boldsymbol{C} = \mathsf{InterpolateExp}(\{(\omega_{v_i}, D_i)\}_{i \in [f+1]})$, then $\boldsymbol{C} = \mathsf{Commit}(\mathsf{srs}, \phi(X, Y);\ \hat{\phi}(X, Y))$.*

Proof. First note that $\phi(\tau, Y) = \mathsf{Interpolate}(\{(\omega_{v_i}, \phi(\tau, \omega_{v_i})\}_{i \in [f+1]})$. By construction $D_i = \mathsf{Commit}(\mathsf{srs}, \alpha_{v_i}; \hat{\alpha}_{v_i}) = g^{\alpha_{v_i}(\tau)} \hat{g}^{\hat{\alpha}_{v_i}(\tau)} = g^{\phi(\tau, \omega_{v_i}) + x\hat{\phi}(\tau, \omega_{v_i})}$, where $\hat{g} = g^x$. Thus

$$(g^{\phi_0(\tau) + x\hat{\phi}_0(\tau)}, \ldots, g^{\phi_f(\tau) + x\hat{\phi}_f(\tau)}) = \mathsf{InterpolateExp}\left(\{(\omega_{v_i}, D_i)\}_{i \in [f+1]}\right).$$

This shows the lemma because

$$(g^{\phi_0(\tau) + x\hat{\phi}_0(\tau)}, \ldots, g^{\phi_f(\tau) + x\hat{\phi}_f(\tau)}) = \mathsf{Commit}(\mathsf{srs}, \phi(X, Y);\ \hat{\phi}(X, Y)).$$

4 Bingo: Packed Asynchronous Verifiable Secret Sharing

In this section we present Bingo, our packed AVSS scheme. We discuss its design in Sect. 4.1 and its security in Sect. 4.2.

4.1 Design

Bingo consists of a sharing protocol BingoShare (Algorithm 2), and a reconstruction protocol BingoReconstruct (Algorithm 3). Additional reconstruction protocols for reconstructing sums of secrets and batch reconstructing are presented in Algorithm 4 and Algorithm 5, respectively. Moreover, BingoShare uses a subprotocol BingoDeal (Algorithm 1), that describes the steps performed by the dealer. In more detail:

BingoDeal. The dealer receives secrets $s_k \in \mathbb{F}$ for $k \in [0, m]$ as inputs. It then uniformly samples two bivariate polynomials $\phi, \hat{\phi}$ over $\mathbb{F}$ of degrees $2f$ in X and f in Y such that $\phi(\omega_{-k}, \omega_0) = s_k$ for $k \in [0, m]$. This can be done by uniformly sampling values for $\phi(\omega_i, \omega_0)$ for $i \in [f]$ and interpolating the resulting $\phi(X, \omega_0)$. Following that, the dealer simply uniformly samples $\phi(X, \omega_i)$ for $i \in [f]$ by directly sampling their coefficients, and interpolating the resulting $f + 1$ polynomials into a bivariate polynomial ϕ. The dealer then computes the *row projections* $\alpha_i(X) = \phi(X, \omega_i)$ and $\hat{\alpha}_i(X) = \hat{\phi}(X, \omega_i)$, and the *column projections* $\beta_i(Y) = \phi(\omega_i, Y)$, and $\hat{\beta}_i(Y) = \hat{\phi}(\omega_i, Y)$ for all $i \in [n]$. Looking ahead, the asymmetric degrees of the polynomials (α of degree $2f$ and β of degree f) help parties know that if they complete the BingoShare protocol, every other party will eventually do so as well. By definition, $\alpha_i(\omega_j) = \beta_j(\omega_i)$ and $\hat{\alpha}_i(\omega_j) = \hat{\beta}_j(\omega_i)$ for any $i, j \in [n]$. The dealer then broadcasts a commitment to this polynomial (formed using our bivariate PCS), using reliable broadcast, and privately sends every party $i \in [n]$ its pair of row polynomials α_i and $\hat{\alpha}_i$.

Algorithm 1. BingoDeal$(s_0, \ldots, s_m)$

```
uniformly sample φ(X,Y) with degree 2f in X and f in Y s.t. φ(ω_{-k}, ω_0) = s_k ∀k ∈ [0, m]
uniformly sample φ̂(X,Y) with degree 2f in X and f in Y
CM ← Commit(φ; φ̂)
for all i ∈ [n] do
    α_i(X) ← φ(X, ω_i), α̂_i(X) ← φ̂(X, ω_i)
(reliably) broadcast ⟨"commits", CM⟩
send ⟨"polynomials", α_i, α̂_i⟩ to every i ∈ [n]
```

BingoShare. The goal of BingoShare (Algorithm 2) is for each party i to learn their row polynomials α_i and $\hat{\alpha}_i$. As depicted in Fig. 1, there are two ways this can happen. First, if the dealer is honest, they send the polynomials in BingoDeal and party i learns them directly (lines 7-10).

If the dealer is corrupt, however, party i may never receive a "polynomials" message. In this case other nonfaulty parties can help i as follows. First, they use their α polynomials to help other parties learn their β column polynomials (lines 15-23), taking advantage of the fact that $\alpha_j(\omega_\ell) = \beta_\ell(\omega_j)$ (we omit the $\hat{\alpha}$ and $\hat{\beta}$ polynomials in this description, but the process for them is identical). In other words, if party ℓ is given $\alpha_j(\omega_\ell)$ by enough other parties j then it can use $\mathsf{GetProofs}$ to compute evaluations and proofs for all other parties, as shown in line 21. Importantly, while party ℓ could interpolate β_ℓ and compute the evaluations directly, it would be unable to form the proofs using Eval as the proof for each party j needs to verify against cm_j (i.e., a commitment to α_j and not β_ℓ).

In the previous step, each party ℓ thus sends evaluations $\beta_\ell(\omega_i)$ to each party i. After receiving enough of these polynomials, party i can then interpolate α_i (in line 31). Before completing the protocol, parties make sure that enough parties have received their row and column polynomials and are helping everybody reach the end of the protocol. This is done by parties sending "done" messages after having received their row and column polynomial, and terminating only after $n - f$ such messages have been received, guaranteeing that at least $f + 1$ nonfaulty parties shared their information. Note that if one party receives its row and column polynomials, it does not know that all parties will eventually receive enough information to interpolate their polynomials as well. Therefore, parties have to wait to actually receive $n - f$ "done" messages before terminating, even if they received enough information to send their own "done" message.

$\mathsf{BingoReconstruct}$. Once parties have finished the sharing phase, they can start recovering the shared secrets for all $k \in [0, m]$. The execution of $\mathsf{BingoReconstruct}$ may not be required in all cases, however, as it depends on the concrete application in which Bingo is used. To start recovery of the secret at index k, each party i evaluates its polynomials α_i and $\hat{\alpha}_i$ at position ω_{-k} and creates a proof $\pi_{\alpha,i,-k}$ showing that the evaluations are correct with respect to the commitment cm_i. Afterwards, party i sends a "rec" message with the evaluations $\alpha_i(\omega_{-k})$, $\hat{\alpha}_i(\omega_{-k})$ and the proof $\pi_{\alpha,i,-k}$ to all other parties j. Once party i receives its first "rec" message from party j, it verifies that the included shares are correct and, if so, stores the tuple $(j, \alpha_j(\omega_{-k}))$ in a set $\mathsf{shares}_{i,k}$. Finally, once party i has received $f + 1$ different correct shares for the shared secret at index k, it interpolates $\mathsf{shares}_{i,k}$ to a polynomial β_{-k}, outputs $\beta_{-k}(\omega_0)$ as the secret, and terminates. Note that the points $\alpha_j(\omega_{-k})$ should equal $\phi(\omega_{-k}, \omega_j)$. Interpolating $f + 1$ such points (with different values for j) yields the polynomial $\beta_{-k}(Y) = \phi(\omega_{-k}, Y)$, so $\beta_{-k}(\omega_0) = \phi(\omega_{-k}, \omega_0) = s_k$ as required.

Algorithm 2. $\mathsf{BingoShare}_i()$

if i is the dealer with input $s_0, \ldots, s_m$ **then**
$\mathsf{BingoDeal}(s_0, \ldots, s_m)$
$\alpha_i \leftarrow \bot, \hat{\alpha}_i \leftarrow \bot, \mathsf{cm} \leftarrow \emptyset$
$\mathsf{points}_{\alpha,i} \leftarrow \emptyset, \mathsf{points}_{\hat{\alpha},i} \leftarrow \emptyset, \mathsf{proofs}_{\beta,i} \leftarrow \emptyset$
upon receiving a $\langle$"commits", $\mathsf{CM}\rangle$ broadcast from the dealer, **do**
$\mathsf{cm} \leftarrow \mathsf{PartialEval}(\mathsf{CM}, \{\omega_1, \ldots, \omega_n\})$ ▷ $\mathsf{cm} = (\mathsf{cm}_1, \ldots, \mathsf{cm}_n)$
upon receiving the first $\langle$"polynomials", $\alpha_i', \hat{\alpha}_i'\rangle$ message from the dealer, **do**
upon $\mathsf{cm} \neq \emptyset$, **do**
if $\alpha_i = \bot$ and $\mathsf{KZG.Commit}(\alpha_i', \hat{\alpha}_i') = \mathsf{cm}_i$ **then**
$\alpha_i \leftarrow \alpha_i', \hat{\alpha}_i \leftarrow \hat{\alpha}_i'$ ▷ save $\alpha_i, \hat{\alpha}_i$ if consistent with cm
upon $\alpha_i \neq \bot$ and $\mathsf{cm}_i \neq \bot$, **do** ▷ upon having row, help others with columns
for all $j \in [n]$ **do**
$\alpha_i(\omega_j), \hat{\alpha}_i(\omega_j), \pi_{\alpha,i,j} \leftarrow \mathsf{Eval}(\alpha_i, \hat{\alpha}_i, \omega_j)$
send $\langle$"row", $\alpha_i(\omega_j), \hat{\alpha}_i(\omega_j), \pi_{\alpha,i,j}\rangle$ to party j
upon receiving the first $\langle$"row", $\alpha_j(\omega_i), \hat{\alpha}_j(\omega_i), \pi_{\alpha,j,i}\rangle$ message from j, **do**
upon $\mathsf{cm}_j \neq \bot$, **do** ▷ collect points and interpolate column
if $|\mathsf{proofs}_{\beta,i}| < f+1$ **then** ▷ no need to collect points if interpolated
if $\mathsf{Verify}(\mathsf{cm}, (i,j), \alpha_j(\omega_i), \hat{\alpha}_j(\omega_i), \pi_{\alpha,j,i}) = 1$ **then**
$\mathsf{proofs}_{\beta,i} \leftarrow \mathsf{proofs}_{\beta,i} \cup \{(\omega_j, \alpha_j(\omega_i), \hat{\alpha}_j(\omega_i), \pi_{\alpha,j,i})\}$
if $|\mathsf{proofs}_{\beta,i}| = f+1$ **then** ▷ enough to interpolate column proofs
$(y_1, \hat{y}_1, \pi_1), \ldots, (y_n, \hat{y}_n, \pi_n) \leftarrow \mathsf{GetProofs}(\mathsf{proofs}_{\beta,i}, \{\omega_1, \ldots, \omega_n\})$
for all $j \in [n]$ **do**
send $\langle$"column", $y_j, \hat{y}_j, \pi_n\rangle$ to party j ▷ help others with rows
upon receiving the first $\langle$"column", $\beta_j(\omega_i), \hat{\beta}_j(\omega_i), \pi_{\beta,j,i}\rangle$ message from j, **do**
upon $\mathsf{cm} \neq \emptyset$, **do** ▷ collect points and interpolate row
if $\alpha_i = \bot$ **then** ▷ no need to collect points if already have α_i
if $\mathsf{Verify}(\mathsf{cm}, (j,i), \beta_j(\omega_i), \hat{\beta}_j(\omega_i), \pi_{\beta,j,i}) = 1$ **then**
$\mathsf{points}_{\alpha,i} \leftarrow \mathsf{points}_{\alpha,i} \cup \{(\omega_j, \beta_j(\omega_i))\}$
$\mathsf{points}_{\hat{\alpha},i} \leftarrow \mathsf{points}_{\hat{\alpha},i} \cup \{(\omega_j, \hat{\beta}_j(\omega_i))\}$
if $|\mathsf{points}_{\alpha,i}| = 2f+1$ **then** ▷ enough to interpolate row
$\alpha_i \leftarrow \mathsf{Interpolate}(\mathsf{points}_{\alpha,i}), \hat{\alpha}_i \leftarrow \mathsf{Interpolate}(\mathsf{points}_{\hat{\alpha},i})$
upon $\alpha_i \neq \bot, \hat{\alpha} \neq \bot$ and $|\mathsf{proofs}_{\beta,i}| = f+1$, **do**
send $\langle$"done"$\rangle$ to all parties
upon receiving $\langle$"done"$\rangle$ messages from $n-f$ parties, **do**
upon $\alpha_i \neq \bot, \hat{\alpha}_i \neq \bot$, and $|\mathsf{proofs}_{\beta,i}| = f+1$, **do**
terminate

Algorithm 3. $\mathsf{BingoReconstruct}_i(k)$ for $k \in [0, m]$

$\mathsf{shares}_{i,k} = \emptyset$
$\alpha_i(\omega_{-k}), \hat{\alpha}_i(\omega_{-k}), \pi_{\alpha,i,-k} \leftarrow \mathsf{Eval}(\alpha_i, \hat{\alpha}_i, \omega_{-k})$
send $\langle$"rec"$, k, \alpha_i(\omega_{-k}), \hat{\alpha}_i(\omega_{-k}), \pi_{\alpha,i,-k}\rangle$ to all parties
upon receiving the first $\langle$"rec"$, k, \alpha_j(\omega_{-k}), \hat{\alpha}_j(\omega_{-k}), \pi_{\alpha,j,-k}\rangle$ message from j, **do**
  if $\mathsf{Verify}(\mathsf{cm}, (-k, j), \alpha_j(\omega_{-k}), \hat{\alpha}_j(\omega_{-k}), \pi_{\alpha,j,-k}) = 1$ **then**
    $\mathsf{shares}_{i,k} \leftarrow \mathsf{shares}_{i,k} \cup \{(\omega_j, \alpha_j(\omega_{-k}))\}$ ▷ $\alpha_i(\omega_{-k}) = \phi(\omega_{-k}, \omega_i) = \beta_{-k}(\omega_i)$
    if $|\mathsf{shares}_{i,k}| = f + 1$ **then** ▷ enough to interpolate $-k$'th column
      $\beta_{-k} \leftarrow \mathsf{Interpolate}(\mathsf{shares}_{i,k})$
      output $\beta_{-k}(\omega_0)$ and **terminate**

4.2 Security

The security of Bingo scheme is captured in the following main theorem.

Theorem 1. *If the underlying commitment scheme is secure, then the pair* ($\mathsf{BingoShare}, \mathsf{BingoReconstruct}$), *as specified in Algorithms 2 and 3, is an f-resilient packed AVSS for $m+1$ secrets, for any $m \leq f < \frac{n}{3}$.*

To prove this, we argue for correctness, termination, and secrecy in turn. To prove correctness and termination, we first prove a series of lemmas that consider the relationship between the committed polynomials represented by CM and the polynomials $\alpha_i, \hat{\alpha}_i, \beta_i, \hat{\beta}_i$ held by a nonfaulty party i at the point at which they complete Share. In all of the following lemmas we consider many instances of the BingoShare and BingoReconstruct protocols running simultaneously with both faulty and nonfaulty dealers. Each of the lemmas focuses on one of those instances and argues that certain values are consistent within that one instance. We first show that the existence of an extractor that can, for both faulty and nonfaulty dealers, output polynomials ϕ and $\hat{\phi}$ such that $\mathsf{CM} = \mathsf{Commit}(\phi;\ \hat{\phi})$.

The following lemma demonstrates the existence of an extractor that outputs polynomials consistent with the dealers broadcast commitment CM whenever a single nonfaulty party completes BingoShare. Where the polynomial commitment scheme is binding, this ensures that the output of BingoReconstruct is fully determined once an honest party completes. A proof of this lemma can be found in the full version of the paper [44].

Lemma 4. *Assume some nonfaulty party completed the* BingoShare *protocol with respect to the commitment* CM *broadcast from the dealer. Suppose the (univariate) polynomial commitment scheme satisfies interpolation binding. There exists an efficient extractor* Ext *that receives the views of the nonfaulty parties and outputs a pair of bivariate polynomials $\phi(X,Y)$ and $\hat{\phi}(X,Y)$ of degree $2f$ in X and f in Y such that $\mathsf{CM} = \mathsf{Commit}(\phi(X,Y);\ \hat{\phi}(X,Y))$. Furthermore, if the dealer is nonfaulty, then $\forall k \in [0,m]$ $s_k = \phi(\omega_{-k}, \omega_0)$.*

Corollary 1. *Assume some nonfaulty party completed the* BingoShare *protocol, that the extractor from Lemma 4 returns* $\phi(X,Y), \hat{\phi}(X,Y)$*, and the PCS satisfies polynomial binding. If some nonfaulty party* i *updates* $\alpha_i(X), \hat{\alpha}_i(X)$ *to values other than* $\perp$*, then* $\alpha_i(X) = \phi(X,\omega_i)$ *and* $\hat{\alpha}_i(X) = \hat{\phi}(X,\omega_i)$.

Proof. Suppose a nonfaulty party updates $\alpha_i(X), \hat{\alpha}_i(X)$ and an extractor outputs $\phi(X,Y)$ and $\hat{\phi}(X,Y)$ such that $\mathsf{CM} = \mathsf{Commit}(\phi(X,Y);\ \hat{\phi}(X,Y))$. By the correctness of PartialEval we have that $\mathsf{cm}_i = \mathsf{Commit}(\phi(X,\omega_i);\ \hat{\phi}(X,\omega_i))$. If $(\alpha_i(X), \hat{\alpha}_i(X)) \neq (\phi(X,\omega_i), \hat{\phi}(X,\omega_i))$, then the adversary could simulate all nonfaulty parties, find two openings of cm_i and thus break polynomial binding.

Now assume that some nonfaulty party completes the protocol and define $\phi(X,Y)$, $\hat{\phi}(X,Y)$ to be extracted polynomials. The next lemma demonstrates that any point accepted by any nonfaulty party is consistent with $\phi(X,Y)$, $\hat{\phi}(X,Y)$. A proof of this lemma can be found in the full version of the paper [44].

Lemma 5. *If (1) the dealer broadcasts a* $\langle$*"commits"*, $\mathsf{CM}\rangle$ *message and it gets received by a nonfaulty party, and (2) the underlying PCS satisfies evaluation binding and interpolation binding, and (3) some nonfaulty party completes the* BingoShare *protocol at time* t*, then define* $\phi(X,Y), \hat{\phi}(X,Y) \leftarrow \mathsf{Ext}(\mathsf{view}_t)$ *for* Ext *as in Lemma 4. Then the following properties hold:*

- *if a nonfaulty party* i *adds* (j, y_j) *and* $(j, \hat{y}_j)$ *to* $\mathsf{points}_{\alpha,i}$ *and* $\mathsf{points}_{\hat{\alpha},i}$ *respectively in lines 28 and 29, then* $y_j = \phi(\omega_j, \omega_i)$ *and* $\hat{y}_j = \hat{\phi}(\omega_j, \omega_i)$*, and*
- *if a nonfaulty party* i *adds* $(j, y_j, \hat{y}_j, \pi_j)$ *to* $\mathsf{proofs}_{\beta,i}$ *in line 19, then* $y_j = \phi(\omega_i, \omega_j)$ *and* $\hat{y}_j = \hat{\phi}(\omega_i, \omega_j)$.

Proofs of the following theorems can all be found in the full version of the paper. For the correctness property, we start by extracting $\phi, \hat{\phi}$ at the time the first nonfaulty party completes BingoShare and define $r_k = \phi(\omega_{-k}, \omega_0)$ for every $k \in [0, m]$. Parties reconstruct by sending the values $\phi(\omega_{-k}, \omega_i)$, interpolating the polynomial $\phi(\omega_{-k}, Y)$ and evaluating it at ω_0. Therefore, as long as Lemma 5 holds, reconstruction is successful.

Theorem 2. *If* q-sdh *and interpolation binding (Definition 3) hold, then Bingo satisfies correctness.*

For the termination property, showing that if the dealer is nonfaulty then all nonfaulty parties complete the BingoShare protocol and that all nonfaulty parties complete the BingoReconstruct protocol is straightforward and is done by following the messages the dealer and nonfaulty parties are guaranteed to send. Proving that all nonfaulty parties complete the BingoShare protocol if one does, on the other hand, is more subtle and requires leveraging the asymmetric degrees of $\phi, \hat{\phi}$. We start by noting that if some nonfaulty party completed the protocol, at least $f+1$ nonfaulty parties updated their row polynomials $\alpha_i, \hat{\alpha}_i$. These parties send "row" messages to all parties, allowing all nonfaulty parties to receive at least $f+1$ evaluation on their columns $\beta_i, \hat{\beta}_i$. Since those polynomials are of degree f, this is enough to interpolate the polynomials and proofs and send "column" messages. After receiving such a message from all $n - f \geq 2f + 1$ nonfaulty parties, every party will be able to interpolate their rows, which are of degree no greater than $2f$, and complete the BingoShare protocol.

Theorem 3. *If* q-sdh *and interpolation binding (Definition 3) hold, then Bingo satisfies termination.*

To argue for secrecy, we need to rely on one additional property of the polynomial commitment scheme: that there exist algorithms SimCommit, SimPartialEval and SimOpen that allow for the simulation of bivariate commitments, partial evaluations, and openings of commitments respectively. We note that SimOpen works as follows: $\psi, \hat{\psi} \xleftarrow{\$} \mathsf{SimOpen}(\tau_s, \mathsf{cm}_\psi, \{y_i, \hat{y}_i\}_i)$ takes in a trapdoor τ_s, a commitment cm_ψ, and a set of evaluations of $y_i, \hat{y}_i$, and outputs a pair of polynomials ψ and $\hat{\psi}$ such that $\mathsf{cm}_\psi = \mathsf{Commit}(\psi, \hat{\psi})$, $\psi(v_i) = y_i, \hat{\psi}(v_i) = \hat{y}_i$ for all i, and the distribution over $(\psi, \hat{\psi})$ is uniform, given the above restriction. Importantly, this must hold even for adversarially chosen evaluation points v_i and evaluations y_i, (representing the adversary's ability to see points from this party before corrupting it). For completeness, we provide a formal definition of this property in the full version of the paper.

Theorem 4. *If* q-sdh *holds then Bingo satisfies secrecy.*

Finally, we prove the message, word, and round complexity of our protocol. We define asynchronous rounds following Canetti and Rabin [9], and define words as the basic objects (counters, indices, etc.) that make up a message, with cryptographic objects requiring $O(\lambda)$ words.

Theorem 5. *The* BingoShare *protocol requires $O(\lambda n^2)$ words and messages to be sent overall by all nonfaulty parties. Furthermore, if the bivariate and univariate PCSs satisfy correctness, interpolation binding, partial evaluation binding and evaluation binding, then every nonfaulty party completes the protocol in $O(1)$ rounds after the first nonfaulty party does so, and if the dealer is nonfaulty, all parties complete the protocol in $O(1)$ rounds. In addition, for every k, the* BingoReconstruct(k) *protocol requires $O(\lambda n^2)$ words and $O(n^2)$ messages to be sent overall by all nonfaulty parties, and takes $O(1)$ asynchronous rounds to complete.*

Corollary 2. *For any $m = \Omega(n)$, there exists a packed AVSS protocol sharing m secrets requiring $O(\lambda n^2 \cdot \frac{m}{n})$ words to be sent by nonfaulty parties in the sharing algorithm and $O(\lambda n^2)$ words to be sent while reconstructing any secret.*

Proof. Assume without loss of generality that $f = \frac{n-1}{3}$. The dealer can take the m secrets and partition them into $\left\lceil \frac{m}{f+1} \right\rceil = \Theta(\frac{m}{n})$ batches of no more than $f + 1$ secrets. The i-th secret s_i can be identified as the $(i \mod f + 1)$-th secret in the $\lfloor \frac{m}{f+1} \rfloor$-th batch. The dealer then shares each batch using BingoShare, yielding a communication complexity of $\Theta(\lambda n^2 \cdot \frac{m}{n})$. Reconstructing the secret entails calling BingoReconstruct once, yielding a word complexity of $O(\lambda n^2)$.

Remark 1. It is possible to share $m+1$ secrets with a polynomial of degree $f+m$ in X and f in Y, without changing the proofs. This yields rows of degree $f+m$ instead of degree $2f$.

Algorithm 4. $\mathsf{BingoReconstructSum}_i(\mathsf{dealers}, k)$ for $k \in [0, m]$

$\mathsf{shares}_{i,k} \leftarrow \emptyset$
$\forall i \in [n]\ \mathsf{cm}'_i \leftarrow \prod_{j \in \mathsf{dealers}} \mathsf{cm}_{i,j}$
$\mathsf{cm}' \leftarrow (\mathsf{cm}'_1, \ldots, \mathsf{cm}'_n)$
$v_{i,k}, \hat{v}_{i,k}, \pi_{i,k} \leftarrow \mathsf{Eval}(\sum_{j \in \mathsf{dealers}} \alpha_{i,j}, \sum_{j \in \mathsf{dealers}} \hat{\alpha}_{i,j}, \omega_{-k})$
send $\langle \text{“rec”}, k, v_{i,k}, \hat{v}_{i,k}, \pi_{i,k} \rangle$ to all parties
upon receiving the first $\langle \text{“rec”}, k, v_{j,k}, \hat{v}_{j,k}, \pi_{j,k} \rangle$ message from j, **do**
    if $\mathsf{Verify}(\mathsf{cm}', (-k, j), v_{j,k}, \hat{v}_{j,k}, \pi_{j,k}) = 1$ **then**
        $\mathsf{shares}_{i,k} \leftarrow \mathsf{shares}_{i,k} \cup \{(\omega_j, v_{j,k})\}$
        if $|\mathsf{shares}_{i,k}| = f + 1$ **then**
            $\beta_{-k} \leftarrow \mathsf{Interpolate}(\mathsf{shares}_{i,k})$
            output $\beta_{-k}(\omega_0)$ and **terminate**

4.3 Efficient Reconstruction

In this section, we highlight two ways to efficiently reconstruct secrets shared using BingoShare, namely how to reconstruct sums of secrets and how to batch-reconstruct multiple secrets.

First, we observe that sharing $O(n)$ secrets requires sending $O(\lambda n^2)$ words and reconstructing each secret requires $O(\lambda n^2)$ words. One way to leverage the efficient sharing protocol is by reconstructing significantly fewer secrets than the number of secrets shared. This can be done by using the fact that the KZG PCS is additively homomorphic, meaning if $\mathsf{cm}_1, \ldots, \mathsf{cm}_\ell$ are commitments to $(\phi_1, \hat{\phi}_1), \ldots, (\phi_\ell, \hat{\phi}_\ell)$ respectively, then $\prod_{i=1}^{\ell} \mathsf{cm}_i$ is a commitment to the polynomials $(\sum_{i=1}^{\ell} \phi_i, \sum_{i=1}^{\ell} \hat{\phi}_i)$. Therefore, let dealers be a set of dealers for which party i completed BingoShare, and set some $k \in [0, m]$. Then, if we define $r_{k,j}$ to be the k-th secret in the BingoShare invocation with j as dealer, parties can reconstruct $\sum_{j \in \mathsf{dealers}} r_{k,j}$. We provide the code for reconstructing the sum of several shared secrets in Algorithm 4 and highlight that $\alpha_{i,j}, \hat{\alpha}_{i,j}$ are the polynomials $\alpha_i, \hat{\alpha}_i$ set by party i when running BingoShare with j as dealer. Similarly, $\mathsf{cm}_{i,j}$ is the commitment cm_i in the BingoShare invocation with j as dealer.

It is also possible to batch-reconstruct all m secrets at once while sending only $O(\lambda n^2)$ words, as demonstrated in Algorithm 5. Observe that all secrets are values of the form $\phi(\omega_{-k}, \omega_0)$ for $k \in [0, m]$. This means that instead of reconstructing each secret by interpolating the polynomials $\phi(\omega_{-k}, Y)$ and evaluating them at ω_0, it is possible to interpolate the degree-$2f$ polynomial $\phi(X, \omega_0)$ in order to reconstruct all m secrets. This requires parties to send points on their β polynomials, and to provide adequate proofs. Seeing as those proofs need to be

Algorithm 5. $\mathsf{BingoReconstructBatch}_i()$

$\mathsf{shares}_i \leftarrow \emptyset$
$\mathsf{cm}_0 \leftarrow \mathsf{PartialEval}(\mathsf{CM}, \{\omega_0\})$ ▷ only compute partial for ω_0
$(y_0, \hat{y}_0, \pi_0) \leftarrow \mathsf{GetProofs}(\mathsf{proofs}_{\beta,i}, \{\omega_0\})$ ▷ only compute proof for ω_0
send ⟨"rec", $y_0, \hat{y}_0, \pi_0$⟩ to all parties
upon receiving the first ⟨"rec", $y_j, \hat{y}_j, \pi_j$⟩ message from j, **do**
    if $\mathsf{Verify}((\mathsf{cm}_0), (0, j), y_j, \hat{y}_j, \pi_j) = 1$ **then**
        $\mathsf{shares}_i \leftarrow \mathsf{shares}_i \cup \{(\omega_j, y_j)\}$
        if $|\mathsf{shares}_i| = n - f$ **then** ▷ reconstruct along 0'th row, use $\geq 2f+1$ shares
            $\alpha_0 \leftarrow \mathsf{Interpolate}(\mathsf{shares}_i)$
            output $(\alpha_0(\omega_0), \alpha_0(\omega_{-1}), \ldots, \alpha_0(\omega_{-m}))$ and **terminate**

interpolated and verified with respect to a commitment to $\phi(X, \omega_0), \hat{\phi}(X, \omega_0)$, we use PartialEval and GetProofs to compute those commitments and proofs.

In both BingoReconstructSum and BingoReconstructBatch, parties send a single message of the exact same size as the one sent in BingoReconstruct, resulting in identical complexity. The proofs that the BingoReconstructSum protocol and the BingoReconstructBatch protocol satisfy the required properties is identical to the proof of BingoReconstruct, using the commitments cm' and cm_0 respectively instead of cm, and is thus omitted. See the proofs of correctness and termination of BingoReconstruct for details.

5 From Bingo to ADKG

In this section we show how to use Bingo to achieve an adaptively secure asynchronous distributed key generation (ADKG) protocol that has $O(\lambda n^3)$ communication complexity of and produces a field element as a secret key. Our protocol can be used as a DKG for a low threshold of $f+1$, a high threshold of $2f+1$, or any threshold in between. This versatility enables setting up threshold signature schemes for different uses. For example, using a threshold of $f+1$ proves that at least one nonfaulty party signed a message, whereas using a threshold of $2f+1$ proves that a Byzantine quorum signed a message (which has an honest party in common with any other Byzantine quorum). The below description is consistent with an ADKG protocol with a threshold of $2f+1$, but the protocol can be adjusted to a general threshold of $f+m+1$ for $0 \leq m \leq f$ by having each dealer share only $m+1$ secrets.

In order to get to a DKG we use Bingo at two layers:

1. We use Bingo to get an adaptively secure *validated asynchronous Byzantine agreement* (VABA) protocol. The protocol, presented in the full version of the paper, allows proposals (inputs) of size $O(n)$ and requires $O(n^3)$ expected words.
2. Each party then uses Bingo to share a potential contribution to the DKG. Once the VABA protocol reaches agreement on a proposal, we use the ability of Bingo to reconstruct the sum of secrets. This sum is the secret key, however,

whereas the goal of the DKG is to generate the public key. We thus perform this reconstruction only in the exponent.

In more detail, we start by defining $\mathsf{CM}_j, \mathsf{proofs}_{\beta,i,j}$ as the values $\mathsf{CM}, \mathsf{proofs}_{\beta,i}$ in the invocation of $\mathsf{BingoShare}$ with j as dealer. Intuitively, our DKG protocol works as follows. First, each party j acts as the dealer for $f+1$ secrets, which we can think of as their 0-th row polynomial $\alpha_{0,j}$. Parties must then agree on a set of dealers whose secrets will contribute to the threshold public key g^s, where the corresponding secret key s is the polynomial $\alpha_{\sum} = \sum_{j \in \mathsf{dealers}} \alpha_{0,j}$ evaluated at ω_0. This agreement requires the use of a VABA protocol. Informally, a VABA protocol allows each party to input a value and output some agreed-upon value in a way that is *correct*, meaning all nonfaulty parties that complete the protocol output the same value, and *valid*, meaning that values output by nonfaulty parties satisfy some external validity function. For a formal definition of a VABA protocol, see the full version of the paper [44].

Once this set is agreed upon using the VABA protocol, parties act to reconstruct the g^s term, as well as their own secret share. For the set of agreed dealers $\mathsf{dealers}$, this latter value for party i is the sum of the column polynomials $\beta_{i,j}$ evaluated at ω_0, where $\beta_{i,j}$ is i's column polynomial in the $\mathsf{BingoShare}$ invocation with j as the dealer. Because $\beta_{i,j}(\omega_0) = \alpha_{0,j}(\omega_i)$, this is equivalent to evaluating α_{Σ} at ω_i. If enough parties share these evaluation points, they can thus interpolate α_{Σ} and evaluate it at ω_0 to reconstruct the secret key. Note that parties do not directly store their $\beta_{i,j}$ polynomials, so they must interpolate evaluations and proofs from their $\mathsf{proofs}_{\beta,i,j}$ sets. Similarly, parties do not compute a commitment to the 0-th row of the polynomial during $\mathsf{BingoShare}$, so they must compute it using CM_j for each dealer j.

We describe how to construct our VABA protocol in the full version of the paper, following closely the path of Abraham et al. [31], whose protocol structure is similar to ours but uses an aggregated PVSS transcript instead of $\mathsf{BingoShare}$. This means we use their Gather protocol and Bingo to build a *weak leader election* protocol, relying particularly on the ability in Bingo to reconstruct sums of secrets, as described in the previous section. From this weak leader election protocol, in which parties are guaranteed to elect the same nonfaulty party with only constant probability p, we build a *proposal election* protocol, and from that we build an adaptively secure VABA protocol. Our protocol has $O(\lambda n^3)$ word complexity and assumes the existence of a PKI and the setup required for the KZG polynomial commitment scheme [22].

Before describing our DKG based on this VABA protocol, we must first extend the $\mathsf{BingoReconstructSum}_i$ algorithm (Algorithm 4). Essentially, whereas $\mathsf{BingoReconstructSum}_i$ reconstructs the sum s of the k-th secrets across a given set of dealers, we need to be able to compute the public key g^s, which involves computing the sum in the exponent. The algorithm for party i, given in Algorithm 6, is similar to $\mathsf{BingoReconstructSum}_i$ but instead of sending y_i and $\hat{y}_i$ to other parties (the evaluations of $\sum_{j \in \mathsf{dealers}} \alpha_{i,j}$ and $\sum_{j \in \mathsf{dealers}} \hat{\alpha}_{i,j}$ at point 0 respectively) it sends $Y_i \leftarrow g^{y_i}$ and $\hat{Y}_i \leftarrow g^{\hat{y}_i}$ as well as proofs of knowledge of y_i and $\hat{y}_i$. We denote by $\pi \xleftarrow{\$} \mathsf{PoK.Prove}(Y, y)$ and $0/1 \leftarrow \mathsf{PoK.Verify}(Y, \pi)$ the respective algorithms for proving and verifying knowledge of y, and by Verify' the PCS algorithm that takes in $Y, \hat{Y}$ rather than $y, \hat{y}$, which is defined as follows.

- $0/1 \leftarrow \mathsf{Verify}'(\mathsf{cm}, \omega, Y, \hat{Y}, \pi)$ Output 1 if $e(\mathsf{cm} \cdot (Y \cdot \hat{Y})^{-1}, h) = e(\pi, h^{\tau-\omega})$, and otherwise output 0.

Finally, we denote by $Y_j \leftarrow \mathsf{IntEvalExp}(\{v_i, Y_i\}_{i=0}^{2f}, \omega_j)$ the algorithm that performs $\mathsf{EvalExp}(\omega_j, \mathsf{InterpolateExp}(\{v_i, Y_i\}_i))$; i.e., that interpolates the degree-$2f$ polynomial given $2f+1$ evaluations and then evaluates it at ω_j (all in the exponent).

With this subprotocol and our VABA in place, we construct our full DKG as shown in Algorithm 7. Once a party has completed BingoShare for at least $f+1$ dealers, it asks at least $f+1$ other parties to verify that those BingoShare sessions were indeed completed by sending the set of those dealers in a "proposal" message. After completing the BingoShare calls for all of these dealers, those parties reply with a signature on the set of $f+1$ dealers. All parties then agree on a set of $f+1$ dealers, dealers, and $f+1$ signatures, sigs, using the VABA protocol with an external validity function defined as follows:

$$\begin{aligned}\mathsf{checkValidity}(\mathsf{dealers}, \mathsf{sigs}) = (&|\mathsf{dealers}| \geq f+1 \ \wedge \ |\mathsf{sigs}| \geq f+1 \ \wedge \\ &\mathsf{Verify}(\mathsf{pk}_j, \sigma_j, \mathsf{dealers}) \ \forall (j, \sigma_j) \in \mathsf{sigs}).\end{aligned} \tag{1}$$

If this holds, meaning at least $f+1$ parties provided a signature for the set of dealers, then at least one nonfaulty party provided a signature. This nonfaulty party thus completed BingoShare, and by termination every nonfaulty party will eventually do so as well. Parties then wait to complete the $f+1$ BingoShare calls for the agreed set of dealers. Party i can then invoke $\mathsf{BingoSumExpAndRec}_i$ to output pk and sk_i.

Algorithm 6. $\mathsf{BingoSumExpAndRec}_i(\mathsf{dealers})$

$\mathsf{shares}_i \leftarrow \emptyset$
$\forall j \in \mathsf{dealers}\ \mathsf{cm}_{0,j} \leftarrow \mathsf{PartialEval}(\mathsf{CM}_j, \{\omega_0\})$
$\mathsf{cm}_0 \leftarrow \prod_{j \in \mathsf{dealers}} \mathsf{cm}_{0,j}$
$\forall j \in \mathsf{dealers}\ y_{i,j}, \hat{y}_{i,j}, \pi_{i,j} \leftarrow \mathsf{GetProofs}(\mathsf{proofs}_{\beta,i,j}, \{\omega_0\})$
$\mathsf{sk}_i \leftarrow \sum_{j \in \mathsf{dealers}} y_{i,j}, \hat{y}_i \leftarrow \sum_{j \in \mathsf{dealers}} \hat{y}_{i,j}, \pi_i \leftarrow \prod_{j \in \mathsf{dealers}} \pi_{i,j}$
$Y_i \leftarrow g^{\mathsf{sk}_i}, \pi \xleftarrow{\$} \mathsf{PoK.Prove}(Y_i, \mathsf{sk}_i)$
$\hat{Y}_i \leftarrow g^{\hat{y}_i}, \hat{\pi} \xleftarrow{\$} \mathsf{PoK.Prove}(Y_i, \hat{y}_i)$
send $\langle$"key share"$, Y_i, \hat{Y}_i, \pi_i, \pi, \hat{\pi}\rangle$ to all parties
upon receiving the first $\langle$"key share"$, Y_j, \hat{Y}_j, \pi_j, \pi, \hat{\pi}\rangle$ message from party j, **do**
    if $\mathsf{Verify}'(\mathsf{cm}_0, \omega_j, Y_j, \hat{Y}_j, \pi_j) = \mathsf{PoK.Verify}(Y_j, \pi) = \mathsf{PoK.Verify}(\hat{Y}_j, \hat{\pi}) = 1$ **then**
        $\mathsf{shares}_i \leftarrow \mathsf{shares}_i \cup \{(\omega_j, Y_j)\}$
        if $|\mathsf{shares}_i| = 2f+1$ **then**
            $\mathsf{pk} \leftarrow \mathsf{IntEvalExp}(\mathsf{shares}_i, \omega_0)$
            output $(\mathsf{pk}, \mathsf{sk}_i)$ and **terminate**

Algorithm 7. $\mathsf{ADKG}_i()$

$\mathsf{prop}_i \leftarrow \emptyset, \mathsf{dealers}_i \leftarrow \emptyset, \mathsf{sigs}_i \leftarrow \emptyset$
$s_0, \ldots, s_f \xleftarrow{\$} \mathbb{F}$
call BingoShare as dealer sharing $s_0, \ldots, s_f$
participate in BingoShare with j as dealer for every $j \in [n]$
upon completing BingoShare with j as dealer, **do**
    $\mathsf{dealers}_i \leftarrow \mathsf{dealers}_i \cup \{j\}$
    if $|\mathsf{dealers}_i| = f + 1$ **then** ▷ choose $f + 1$ dealers to propose
        $\mathsf{prop}_i \leftarrow \mathsf{dealers}_i$
        send $\langle$"proposal", $\mathsf{prop}_i\rangle$ to every $j \in [n]$
upon receiving the first $\langle$"proposal", $\mathsf{prop}_j\rangle$ message from party j, **do**
    upon completing BingoShare with k as leader for every $k \in \mathsf{prop}_j$, **do**
        send $\langle$"signature", $\mathsf{Sign}(\mathsf{sk}_i, \mathsf{prop}_j)\rangle$ to party j ▷ confirm share completion
upon receiving $\langle$"signature", $\sigma_j\rangle$ from j, **do**
    if $\mathsf{prop}_i \neq \emptyset$ and $\mathsf{Verify}(\mathsf{pk}_j, \mathsf{prop}_i, \sigma_j) = 1$ **then**
        $\mathsf{sigs}_i \leftarrow \mathsf{sigs}_i \cup \{(j, \sigma_j)\}$
        if $|\mathsf{sigs}_i| = f + 1$ **then**
            invoke VABA with input $(\mathsf{prop}_i, \mathsf{sigs}_i)$ and external validity function checkValidity ▷ agree on a set of dealers, at least one honest signature on proposal
upon VABA terminating with output (prop, sigs), **do**
    upon completing the BingoShare call with j as dealer for every $j \in$ prop, **do**
        invoke $\mathsf{BingoSumExpAndRec}_i$ with input prop ▷ reconstruct from agreed dealers
upon $\mathsf{BingoSumExpAndRec}_i$ terminating with output $(\mathsf{pk}, \mathsf{sk}_i)$, **do**
    output pk and **terminate**

In terms of the security of our DKG, we follow Gennaro et al. [34] in showing that it satisfies *robustness*, meaning that all honest parties agree on the same public key and that there exists an algorithm to allow parties to reconstruct the corresponding secret key.

Theorem 6. *If* Bingo *and the VABA protocol both satisfy correctness and termination, and the VABA protocol satisfies validity, then the ADKG in Algorithm 7 satisfies robustness against an adaptive adversary that can control f parties, where the total number of parties is $n > 3f$.*

We prove this formally in the full version of the paper. Intuitively, we already showed in the Bingo correctness proof that each iteration of BingoShare defines a polynomial and that when running BingoReconstruct each party can use only their share of this polynomial. In Bingo, reconstruction is done on the field element directly, but in the DKG we just need to show that it also holds when done in the exponent. This follows in a relatively straightforward way given that parties are also required to provide proofs of knowledge in their "key share" messages.

For secrecy, it is not clear how to satisfy the definition of Gennaro et al., as the Bingo secrecy definition guarantees the ability to simulate interactions in the BingoShare protocol but for a DKG we need to be able to continue simulating throughout reconstruction (albeit in the exponent) despite not knowing the underlying secret or polynomial. We instead prove that our protocol satisfies the notion of *oracle-aided algebraic simulatability*, as recently defined by Bacho and Loss [19, Definition 3.1]. This means that, following their results, our DKG can be used securely only in the context of threshold BLS signatures.

Definition 4 (Oracle-aided algebraic simulatability). [19] *A DKG protocol has* $(t, k, T_{\mathcal{A}}, T_{\mathsf{Sim}})$-oracle-aided algebraic simulatability *if for every adversary* $\mathcal{A}$ *that runs in time at most* $T_{\mathcal{A}}$ *and corrupts at most* t *parties, there exists an algebraic simulator* Sim *that runs in time at most* T_{Sim}*, makes* $k-1$ *queries to a discrete log oracle* $\mathsf{DL}(\cdot)$*, and satisfies the following properties:*

- *On input* $\xi \leftarrow (g^{z_1}, \dots, g^{z_k})$*,* Sim *simulates the role of the honest parties in an execution of the DKG. At the end of the simulation, Sim outputs the public key* $\mathsf{pk} = g^x$*.*
- *On input* $\xi \leftarrow (g^{z_1}, \dots, g^{z_k})$ *and for* $i \in [k-1]$*, let* g_i *denote the i-th query to* DL*. Let* $(\hat{a}_i, a_{i,1}, \dots, a_{i,k})$ *denote the corresponding algebraic coefficients, i.e. the values such that* $g_i = g^{\hat{a}_i} \cdot \prod_{j=1}^{k} (g^{z_j})^{a_{i,j}}$ *and denote by* $(\hat{a}, a_{0,1}, \dots, a_{0,k})$ *the algebraic coefficients corresponding to* pk*. Then the following matrix is invertible:*

$$L := \begin{pmatrix} a_{0,1} & a_{0,2} & \cdots & a_{0,k} \\ a_{1,1} & a_{1,2} & \cdots & a_{1,k} \\ \vdots & \vdots & & \vdots \\ a_{k-1,1} & a_{k-1,2} & \cdots & a_{k-1,k} \end{pmatrix}.$$

  Whenever Sim *completes a simulation of an execution of the DKG, we call* L *the* simulatability matrix *of* Sim *(for this particular simulation).*
- *Denote by* $\mathsf{view}_{\mathcal{A},y,\mathsf{DKG}}$ *the view of* $\mathcal{A}$ *in an execution of the DKG conditioned on all honest parties outputting* $\mathsf{pk} = y$*. Similarly, denote by* $\mathsf{view}_{\mathcal{A},\xi,y,\mathsf{Sim}}$ *the view of* $\mathcal{A}$ *when interacting with* Sim *on input* ξ*, conditioned on Sim outputting* $\mathsf{pk} = y$*. (For convenience,* Sim*'s final output* pk *is omitted from* $\mathsf{view}_{\mathcal{A},\xi,y,\mathsf{Sim}}$*). Then, for all* y *and all* ξ*,* $\mathsf{view}_{\mathcal{A},\xi,y,\mathsf{Sim}}$ *and* $\mathsf{view}_{\mathcal{A},y,\mathsf{DKG}}$ *are computationally indistinguishable.*

Intuitively, our DKG simulator follows the Bingo secrecy simulator during the BingoShare interactions and otherwise behaves honestly up until the point at which it has to send a "key share" message. It then uses the omdl challenges to define points on a polynomial and sends "key share" messages that are consistent with these points. Crucially, this polynomial is also consistent with the public key that the simulator needs to output, which it also chooses from its omdl challenge. If a party is corrupted after sending a "key share" message, the simulator can then create the appropriate state by calling its DL oracle. Access to the DL oracle is essential in doing this precisely because we need adaptive security and thus the simulator does not know in advance which parties will be corrupted.

Theorem 7. *If* Bingo *satisfies correctness and secrecy and the VABA satisfies correctness and external validity, then the ADKG in Algorithm 7 has* $(f, 2f+1)$*-oracle-aided algebraic security against an adaptive adversary that can control* f *parties, where the total number of parties is* $n > 3f$.

Proof. We begin by describing the simulator $\mathsf{Sim}_{\mathcal{A}}^{\mathsf{DL}(\cdot)}$, which takes in a generator g and $2f+1$ group elements $Z_0, Z_1, \ldots, Z_f, \hat{Z}_1, \ldots, \hat{Z}_f$. To simulate nonfaulty parties in the DKG protocol, Sim acts as the Bingo simulator during BingoShare interactions (this simulator is guaranteed to exist by secrecy, and is described in the proof of Theorem 4.) During all other parts of the DKG before line 20, the simulator behaves honestly; i.e. it honestly computes and sends "proposal" messages, responds with "signature" messages when it receives "proposal" messages, and invokes the VABA protocol once it has enough signatures.

When the first nonfaulty party completes the VABA protocol with output (dealers, sigs), Sim sets C to be the set of currently corrupted parties. From the correctness of the VABA protocol, all nonfaulty parties also output (dealers, sigs). In addition, from the external validity property, sigs contains at least $f+1$ signatures on the set dealers, which means that it includes at least one signature from a nonfaulty party. Nonfaulty parties only sign dealers if they have completed the BingoShare invocations with j as dealer for every $j \in$ dealers, and thus at least one nonfaulty party completed the protocol for each such dealer. As shown in Lemma 4, for every faulty dealer $j \in$ dealers, it is possible to extract polynomials $\phi_j, \hat{\phi}_j$ from the combined views of the nonfaulty parties, which Sim can do as it has these views and behaves completely honestly when the dealer is faulty. On the other hand, in the proof of Theorem 4, the simulator defines polynomials $\alpha_{i,j}, \hat{\alpha}_{i,j}, \beta_{i,j}, \hat{\beta}_{i,j}$ for every faulty i in the simulated BingoShare invocation with a nonfaulty j as dealer. Putting this together, Sim thus knows the polynomials $\alpha_{i,j}, \hat{\alpha}_{i,j}, \beta_{i,j}, \hat{\beta}_{i,j}$ for faulty dealers $j \in$ dealers and all parties i and the polynomials $\alpha_{i,j}, \hat{\alpha}_{i,j}, \beta_{i,j}, \hat{\beta}_{i,j}$ for nonfaulty dealers $j \in$ dealers and faulty parties i.

Let ℓ be the number of parties corrupted at the time the first nonfaulty party completes the VABA protocol, and let $C = \{i_1, \ldots, i_\ell\}$. Sim chooses $I = \{i_{\ell+1}, \ldots, i_f\} \subset [n]$ to be some subset of $[n]$ of size $f-k$ such that $C \cap I = \emptyset$ (for example, the $f-k$ minimal indices that aren't in C). Sim chooses an additional set $I' = \{i_{f+1}, \ldots, i_{2f}\}$[2] such that $I' \cap C = \emptyset$ and $I' \cap I = \emptyset$. Finally, let $i_{2f+1}, \ldots, i_n$ be the indices of the remaining parties, i.e. $\{i_{2f+1}, \ldots, i_n\} = [n] \setminus (C \cup I \cup I')$. Sim then defines $Z'_0 \leftarrow Z_0$ and $i_0 = 0$, as well as the following:

- For every $k \in [\ell]$, $Z'_{i_k} \leftarrow g^{\sum_{j \in \mathsf{dealers}} \beta_{i_k,j}(0)}$ and $\hat{Z}'_{i_k} \leftarrow \hat{g}^{\sum_{j \in \mathsf{dealers}} \hat{\beta}_{i_k,j}(0)}$.
- For every $k \in \{\ell+1, \ldots, f\}$, $Z'_{i_k} \leftarrow Z_k$ and $\hat{Z}'_{i_k} \leftarrow \hat{Z}_k$.
- For every $k \in \{f+1, \ldots, 2f\}$, Sim samples $z_{i_k}, \hat{z}_{i_k} \xleftarrow{\$} \mathbb{F}$ and sets $Z'_{i_k} \leftarrow g^{z_{i_k}}$ and $\hat{Z}_{i_k} \leftarrow \hat{g}^{\hat{z}_{i_k}}$.
- For every $k \in \{2f+1, \ldots, n\}$, $Z'_{i_k} \leftarrow \mathsf{IntEvalExp}(\{(\omega_{i_m}, Z'_{i_m})\}_{m=0}^{2f}, \omega_{i_k})$.

2 For a threshold of $f+m+1$, define $I' = \{i_{f+1}, \ldots, i_{f+m}\}$ instead.

The simulator then computes $Z'_\tau \leftarrow \mathsf{IntEvalExp}(\{(\omega_{i_m}, Z'_{i_m})\}_{m=0}^{2f}, \tau)$, as well as $\mathsf{cm}_0 \leftarrow \prod_{j\in\mathsf{dealers}} \mathsf{cm}_{0,j}$ (as computed in BingoSumExpAndRec), and $\hat{Z}'_\tau \leftarrow (\mathsf{cm}_0(Z'_\tau)^{-1})^{\frac{1}{x}}$. It computes $\hat{Z}'_{i_k} \leftarrow \mathsf{IntEvalExp}(\{(\omega_{i_m}, \hat{Z}'_{i_m})\}_{m\in[2f]} \cup \{(\tau, \hat{Z}'_\tau)\}, \omega_{i_k})$ for every $k \in \{2f+1, \ldots, n\}$. Finally, Sim calls its discrete log oracle 2ℓ times on $Z_{i_1}, \ldots, Z_{i_\ell}, \hat{Z}_{i_1}, \ldots, \hat{Z}_{i_\ell}$.

After computing these values, Sim is now ready to simulate nonfaulty parties in Algorithm 6. Whenever a nonfaulty party i should send a "key share" message, Sim computes $\pi_i \leftarrow (\mathsf{cm}_0 \cdot (Z'_i\hat{Z}'_i)^{-1})^{\frac{1}{\tau-\omega_i}}$ as well as simulated proofs of knowledge $\pi, \hat{\pi}$ for Z'_i and $\hat{Z}'_i$ respectively. Sim then adds messages to the buffer as if i sent the message $\langle$"key share"$Z'_i, \hat{Z}'_i, \pi_i, \pi, \hat{\pi}\rangle$ to all parties. If the adversary corrupts party i after this point and $i \notin \{i_{f+1}, \ldots, i_{2f}\}$, Sim calls its discrete log oracle twice to get $z_i = \mathsf{DL}(Z'_i), \hat{z}_i = \mathsf{DL}(\hat{Z}'_i)$. On the other hand, if the adversary corrupts party i and $i \in \{i_{f+1}, \ldots, i_{2f}\}$, it uses the previously sampled z_i and $\hat{z}_i$ instead and does not call its DL oracle. It then generates i's view following the Bingo simulator (described in the proof of secrecy) in all invocations of Bingo with honest dealers except for one nonfaulty dealer $j \in \mathsf{dealers}$, including generating appropriate α and β polynomials for i. For this dealer j, it uniformly samples a degree-f polynomial $\beta_{i,j}(Y)$ such that $\beta_{i,j}(0) = z_i - \sum_{k\in\mathsf{dealers}\setminus\{j\}} \beta_{i,k}(0)$ and $\alpha_{k,j}(\omega_i) = \beta_{i,j}(\omega_k)$ for all corrupted k. Similarly, it samples a degree-f polynomial $\hat{\beta}_{i,j}(Y)$ such that $\hat{\beta}_{i,j}(0) = \hat{z}_i - \sum_{k\in\mathsf{dealers}\setminus\{j\}} \hat{\beta}_{i,k}(0)$ and $\hat{\alpha}_{k,j}(\omega_i) = \hat{\beta}_{i,j}(\omega_k)$ for every corrupted k. Again following the Bingo simulator, Sim calls SimOpen to define $\alpha_{i,j}, \hat{\alpha}_{i,j}$ given the sampled $\beta_{i,j}, \hat{\beta}_{i,j}$, i.e. it computes $\alpha_{i,j}, \hat{\alpha}_{i,j} \xleftarrow{\$} \mathsf{SimOpen}(\tau_s, \mathsf{cm}_{i,j}, c_{i,j}, \{\omega_k, \beta_{k,j}(\omega_i), \hat{\beta}_{k,j}(\omega_i)\}_{k\in C})$, where C is the set of currently corrupted parties and $c_{i,j}$ is the auxiliary information computed by the Bingo simulator when running BingoShare with i as the dealer. Finally, in order to generate i's view as a dealer, Sim runs the Bingo simulator to generate the polynomials $\phi_i$and $\hat{\phi}_i$ and associated view. Sim then adds i to the set of corrupted parties and continues in the simulation. At the point at which some nonfaulty party completes the DKG protocol, let $j_{\ell+1}, \ldots, j_{\ell+m}$ be the indices of the parties corrupted after the first nonfaulty party completed the VABA protocol such that for every $k \in \{\ell+1, \ldots, \ell+m\}$, $j_k \notin I'$. Sim chooses indices $j_{\ell+m+1}, \ldots, j_f \notin I'$ of parties that weren't corrupted by the adversary and calls $\mathsf{DL}(Z'_{j_k})$ and $\mathsf{DL}(\hat{Z}'_{j_k})$ for every $k \in \{\ell+m+1, \ldots, f\}$. Finally, Sim outputs Z_0 as pk and terminates.

We must now argue that the simulator satisfies the requirements of oracle-aided algebraic security, namely that it correctly simulates interactions with honest parties and that the matrix containing its algebraic coefficients is invertible. For the first requirement, Theorem 4 tells us that the simulated runs of the BingoShare protocol are computationally indistinguishable from normal runs of the protocol. The simulator then runs the DKG protocol honestly up to line 20. In the non-simulated invocation of BingoSumExpAndRec, each nonfaulty party i sends a "key share" message with $Y_i = g^{\sum_{j\in\mathsf{dealers}} \beta_{i,j}(0)}$, $\hat{Y}_i = \hat{g}^{\sum_{j\in\mathsf{dealers}} \hat{\beta}_{i,j}(0)}$, π_i being the unique proof for which Verify$'$ verifies (once the other values have been fixed), and two proofs of knowledge. Importantly, the pair of polynomials $\phi_\Sigma = \sum_{j\in\mathsf{dealers}} \phi_j$ and $\hat{\phi}_\Sigma = \sum_{j\in\mathsf{dealers}} \hat{\phi}_j$ satisfy $\mathsf{cm}_0 = \mathsf{Commit}(\phi_\Sigma;\hat{\phi}_\Sigma)$. Note that $\sum_{j\in\mathsf{dealers}} \beta_{i,j}(0) = \sum_{j\in\mathsf{dealers}} \phi_j(\omega_i, 0)$ and similarly $\sum_{j\in\mathsf{dealers}} \hat{\beta}_{i,j}(0) = \sum_{j\in\mathsf{dealers}} \hat{\phi}_j(\omega_i, 0)$. From Theorem 4, before some nonfaulty party calls $\mathsf{BingoReconstruct}(0)$ on a value shared by a nonfaulty dealer, the value is entirely independent of the adversary's view. This is because the simulator could complete the run to correctly reconstruct any possible secret from that point on. Therefore, since the one nonfaulty dealer in $\mathsf{dealers}$ uniformly sampled its secrets, the sum is uniform and independent of the adversary's view. In the simulation, the nonfaulty parties also send messages with $Z'_i, \hat{Z}'_i$ such that their discrete logs lie on uniformly sampled polynomials of the same degree that are consistent with cm_0 and the points $\sum_{j\in\mathsf{dealers}} \phi_j(\omega_k, 0)$ and $\sum_{j\in\mathsf{dealers}} \hat{\phi}_j(\omega_k, 0)$ of faulty parties. In addition, the proof π is the unique proof for which Verify' verifies, and the proofs of knowledge are perfectly simulated. Finally, whenever a party i is corrupted during $\mathsf{BingoSumExpAndRec}$, its view is made consistent with $Z'_i, \hat{Z}'_i$ and the rest of the $\mathsf{BingoShare}$ simulation is identical to the simulation described in Theorem 4. Its view is thus sampled identically as well.

We now consider the matrix defined by the algebraic coefficients given by Sim when querying its DL oracle, with the goal of proving that it is invertible. For each $i \in [\ell]$, the algebraic representation for the oracle call $\mathsf{DL}(Z_i)$ is simply the indicator vector that equals 1 in the coordinate corresponding to the input element Z_i and 0 elsewhere. Similarly, for each $i \in [\ell]$, the algebraic representation for $DL(\hat{Z}_i)$ is the indicator vector for $\hat{Z}_i$, and the algebraic representation of $\mathsf{pk} = Z_0$ is the indicator vector for Z_0. We can thus rearrange the rows and columns of the matrix—which does not affect its invertibility—so that the first 2ℓ rows and columns are the indicator vectors corresponding to the elements $Z_1, \dots, Z_\ell, \hat{Z}_1, \dots, \hat{Z}_\ell$. The remaining algebraic expressions for each $\mathsf{DL}(Z'_i)$ call result from interpolating $Z'_0, Z'_1, \dots Z'_f$ and then evaluating at ω_i, both of which are linear functions. The algebraic expressions for $\hat{Z}'_i$ are computed in a similar fashion. The first set of elements were not used in forming any of the $Z'_i, \hat{Z}'_i$ group elements, and thus the rearranged matrix is a block matrix of the form $L = \begin{pmatrix} I & 0 \\ 0 & A \end{pmatrix}$, where I is the identity matrix of size $2\ell \times 2\ell$ and A is a matrix with the algebraic representation of the $\mathsf{DL}(Z'_i)$ and $\mathsf{DL}(\hat{Z}'_i)$ calls, as well as the algebraic representation of Z_0.

In order to show that L is invertible, it is enough to show that A is invertible, since I is trivially invertible. We do that by showing that the linear transformation defined by A is invertible. Let $j_{\ell+1}, \dots, j_f$ be defined as above. Then A represents some linear transformation from $Z_0, Z_{\ell+1}, \dots, Z_f, \hat{Z}_{\ell+1}, \dots, \hat{Z}_f$ to $\mathsf{pk}, Z'_{j_{\ell+1}}, \dots, Z'_{j_f}, \hat{Z}'_{j_{\ell+1}}, \dots, \hat{Z}'_{j_f}$. This function has the same size domain and range (since the number of elements is the same), so to prove that it is invertible it suffices to show that it is one-to-one. Assume that two sets of inputs $Z_0, Z_{\ell+1}, \dots, Z_f, \hat{Z}_{\ell+1}, \dots, \hat{Z}_f$ and $X_0, X_{\ell+1}, \dots, X_f, \hat{X}_{\ell+1}, \dots, \hat{X}_f$ yield the same output $\mathsf{pk}, Z'_{j_{\ell+1}}, \dots, Z'_{j_f}, \hat{Z}'_{j_{\ell+1}}, \dots, \hat{Z}'_{j_f}$. The discrete logs of

$Z'_0, Z'_1, \ldots, Z'_n$ and Z'_τ all lie on the same f-degree polynomial, and thus any $f+1$ such elements define the polynomial fully and the rest of the points. Therefore, the elements $Z'_0, Z'_{i_1}, \ldots, Z'_{i_\ell}, Z'_{j_{\ell+1}}, \ldots, Z'_{j_f}$ fully define the entire set $Z'_0, Z'_1, \ldots, Z'_n$. In this case, $Z'_0, Z'_{j_{\ell+1}}, \ldots, Z'_{j_f}$ are all parts of the output of the function, and $Z'_{i_1}, \ldots, Z'_{i_\ell}$ are constants computed directly by Sim. Therefore, the function's output uniquely defines $Z'_0, Z'_1, \ldots, Z'_n, Z'_\tau$. Note that by construction $Z'_0 = Z_0 = X_0$ and also $Z'_{i_k} = Z_k = X_k$ for every $k \in \{\ell+1, \ldots, f\}$, and thus the first half of the inputs is equal. In addition, $\hat{Z}'_\tau$ is uniquely defined given the previous values, and thus $\hat{Z}'_\tau, \hat{Z}'_{i_1}, \ldots, \hat{Z}'_{i_\ell}, \hat{Z}'_{j_{\ell+1}}, \ldots, \hat{Z}'_{j_f}$ define the group elements $\hat{Z}'_1, \ldots, \hat{Z}'_n$. Therefore, for similar reasons, $\hat{Z}'_{i_k} = \hat{Z}_k = \hat{X}_k$ for every $k \in \{\ell+1, \ldots, f\}$. In other words, all elements of the input must be equal, and thus the function is one-to-one. □

Acknowledgements. We would like to thank Alin Tomescu, Kobi Gurkan, Julian Loss, and Renas Bacho for many insightful discussions. Gilad Stern was supported by the HUJI Federmann Cyber Security Research Center in conjunction with the Israel National Cyber Directorate (INCD) in the Prime Minister's Office.

References

1. Cachin, C., Kursawe, K., Lysyanskaya, A., Strobl, R.: Asynchronous verifiable secret sharing and proactive cryptosystems. In: Proceedings of the 9th ACM Conference on Computer and Communications Security, CCS 2002, pp. 88–97 (2002)
2. Cachin, C., Kursawe, K., Shoup, V.: Random Oracles in Constantinople: practical asynchronous byzantine agreement using cryptography. J. Cryptol. **18**, 219–246 (2005)
3. Gurkan, K., Jovanovic, P., Maller, M., Meiklejohn, S., Stern, G., Tomescu, A.: Aggregatable distributed key generation. In: Canteaut, A., Standaert, F.-X. (eds.) EUROCRYPT 2021. LNCS, vol. 12696, pp. 147–176. Springer, Cham (2021). https://doi.org/10.1007/978-3-030-77870-5_6
4. Patra, A., Choudhury, A., Rangan, C.P.: Efficient Asynchronous verifiable secret sharing and multiparty computation. J. Cryptol. **28**(1), 49–109 (2015). https://doi.org/10.1007/s00145-013-9172-7
5. Syta, E., et al.: Scalable Bias-Resistant Distributed Randomness. In: 38th IEEE Symposium on Security and Privacy, San Jose, CA, May 2017
6. Chor, B., Goldwasser, S., Micali, S., Awerbuch, B.: Verifiable secret sharing and achieving simultaneity in the presence of faults (extended abstract). In: 26th Annual Symposium on Foundations of Computer Science, pp. 383–395 (1985)
7. Franklin, M.K., Yung, M.: Communication complexity of secure computation (extended abstract). In: Proceedings of the 24th Annual ACM Symposium on Theory of Computing, pp. 699–710. ACM (1992)
8. Ben-Or, M., Canetti, R., Goldreich, O.: Asynchronous secure computation. In: Proceedings of the Twenty-Fifth Annual ACM Symposium on Theory of Computing, pp. 52–61 (1993)
9. Canetti, R., Rabin, T.: Fast asynchronous Byzantine agreement with optimal resilience. In: Proceedings of the Twenty-Fifth Annual ACM Symposium on Theory of Computing, pp. 42–51 (1993)

10. Cramer, R., Damgård, I., Dziembowski, S., Hirt, M., Rabin, T.: Efficient multiparty computations secure against an adaptive adversary. In: Stern, J. (ed.) EUROCRYPT 1999. LNCS, vol. 1592, pp. 311–326. Springer, Heidelberg (1999). https://doi.org/10.1007/3-540-48910-X_22
11. Chopard, A., Hirt, M., Liu-Zhang, C.-D.: On communication-efficient asynchronous MPC with adaptive security. In: Nissim, K., Waters, B. (eds.) TCC 2021. LNCS, vol. 13043, pp. 35–65. Springer, Cham (2021). https://doi.org/10.1007/978-3-030-90453-1_2
12. Rabin, T., Ben-Or, M.: Verifiable secret sharing and multiparty protocols with honest majority (extended abstract). In: Proceedings of the 21st Annual ACM Symposium on Theory of Computing, pp. 73–85. ACM (1989)
13. Daian, P., et al.: Flash Boys 2.0: Frontrunning, Transaction Reordering, and Consensus Instability in Decentralized Exchanges. In: IEEE Symposium on Security and Privacy (2020)
14. Qin, K., Zhou, L., Gervais, A.: Quantifying blockchain extractable value: how dark is the forest? In: IEEE Symposium on Security and Privacy (2022)
15. Bowe, S., Gabizon, A., Miers, I.: Scalable Multi-party Computation for ZK-SNARK Parameters in the Random Beacon Model. Cryptology ePrint Archive, Paper 2017/1050 (2017)
16. Fuchsbauer, G., Kiltz, E., Loss, J.: The algebraic group model and its applications. In: Shacham, H., Boldyreva, A. (eds.) CRYPTO 2018. LNCS, vol. 10992, pp. 33–62. Springer, Cham (2018). https://doi.org/10.1007/978-3-319-96881-0_2
17. Kokoris Kogias, E., Malkhi, D., Spiegelman, A.: Asynchronous distributed key generation for computationally-secure randomness, consensus, and threshold signatures. In: CCS 2020: 2020 ACM SIGSAC Conference on Computer and Communications Security (2020)
18. Boneh, D., Lynn, B., Shacham, H.: Short signatures from the Weil pairing. J. Cryptol. **17**(4), 297–319 (2004)
19. Bacho, R., Loss, J.: On the adaptive security of the threshold BLS signature scheme. In: Proceedings of ACM CCS 2022 (2022)
20. Canetti, R., Gennaro, R., Jarecki, S., Krawczyk, H., Rabin, T.: Adaptive security for threshold cryptosystems. In: Wiener, M. (ed.) CRYPTO 1999. LNCS, vol. 1666, pp. 98–116. Springer, Heidelberg (1999). https://doi.org/10.1007/3-540-48405-1_7
21. Goldreich, O., Micali, S., Wigderson, A.: How to play any mental game or a completeness theorem for protocols with honest majority. In: Proceedings of the 19th Annual ACM Symposium on Theory of Computing, 1987, New York, New York, USA, pp. 218–229. ACM (1987)
22. Kate, A., Zaverucha, G.M., Goldberg. I.: Constant-size commitments to polynomials and their applications. In: Advances in Cryptology - ASIACRYPT 2010, pp. 177–194 (2010)
23. Kohlweiss, M., Maller, M., Siim, J., Volkhov, M.: Snarky ceremonies. In: Tibouchi, M., Wang, H. (eds.) ASIACRYPT 2021. LNCS, vol. 13092, pp. 98–127. Springer, Cham (2021). https://doi.org/10.1007/978-3-030-92078-4_4
24. Abraham, I., Asharov, G., Patil, S., Patra, A.: Asymptotically Free Broadcast in Constant Expected Time via Packed VSS. In: IACR Cryptol. ePrint Arch. (2022). https://eprint.iacr.org/2022/1266
25. Abraham, I., Asharov, G., Yanai, A.: Efficient perfectly secure computation with optimal resilience. J. Cryptol. **35**(4), 27 (2022)
26. Kate, A., Miller, A., Yurek, T.: Brief Note: Asynchronous Verifiable Secret Sharing with Optimal Resilience and Linear Amortized Overhead (2019). arXiv: 1902.06095 [cs.CR]

27. Backes, M., Datta, A., Kate, A.: Asynchronous computational VSS with reduced communication complexity. In: Topics in Cryptology – CT-RSA 2013, pp. 259–276 (2013)
28. AlHaddad, N., Varia, M., Zhang., H.: High-threshold AVSS with optimal communication complexity. In: Financial Cryptography and Data Security, pp. 479–498 (2021)
29. Yurek, T., Luo, L., Fairoze, J., Kate, A., Miller, A.K.: hbACSS: how to robustly share many secrets. In: Proceedings of the Network and Distributed System Security Symposium (NDSS) 2022 (2022)
30. Kate, A., Huang, Y., Goldberg, I.: Distributed key generation in the wild. In: Proceedings of ICDCS (2009)
31. Abraham, I., Jovanovic, P., Maller, M., Meiklejohn, S., Stern, G., Tomescu, A.: Reaching consensus for asynchronous distributed key generation. In: PODC 2021: ACM Symposium on Principles of Distributed Computing 2021, pp. 363–373 (2021)
32. Das, S., Yurek, T., Xiang, Z., Miller, A., Kokoris-Kogias, L., Ren, L.: Practical asynchronous distributed key generation. In: 2022 IEEE Symposium on Security and Privacy (SP), pp. 2518–2534 (2022)
33. Groth, J., Shoup, V.: Design and analysis of a distributed ECDSA signing service. In: Cryptology ePrint Archive (2022). https://eprint.iacr.org/2022/506
34. Gennaro, R., Jarecki, S., Krawczyk, H., Rabin, T.: Secure distributed key generation for discrete-log based cryptosystems. J. Cryptol. **20**(1), 51–83 (2007)
35. Feldman, P., Micali, S.: Optimal algorithms for byzantine agreement. In: Proceedings of the 20th Annual ACM Symposium on Theory of Computing, pp. 148–161. ACM (1988)
36. Ben-Sasson, E., Bentov, I., Horesh, Y., Riabzev, M.: Fast reed-solomon interactive oracle proofs of proximity. In: 45th International Colloquium on Automata, Languages, and Programming (ICALP 2018), pp. 14:1–14:17 (2018)
37. Ben-Sasson, E., Goldberg, L., Kopparty, S., Saraf, S.: DEEP-FRI: sampling outside the box improves soundness. In: 11th Innovations in Theoretical Computer Science Conference, ITCS, pp. 5:1–5:32 (2020)
38. Bootle, J., Cerulli, A., Chaidos, P., Groth, J., Petit, C.: Efficient zero-knowledge arguments for arithmetic circuits in the discrete log setting. In: Fischlin, M., Coron, J.-S. (eds.) EUROCRYPT 2016. LNCS, vol. 9666, pp. 327–357. Springer, Heidelberg (2016). https://doi.org/10.1007/978-3-662-49896-5_12
39. Bünz, B., Bootle, J., Boneh, D., Poelstra, A., Wuille, P., Maxwell, G.: Bulletproofs: short proofs for confidential transactions and more. In: 2018 IEEE Symposium on Security and Privacy, pp. 315–334 (2018)
40. Choudhury, A., Patra, A.: An efficient framework for unconditionally secure multiparty computation. IEEE Trans. Inf. Theory. **63**(1), 428–468 (2017). https://doi.org/10.1109/TIT.2016.2614685
41. Cascudo, I., David, B.: Scrape: scalable randomness attested by public entities. In: Gollmann, D., Miyaji, A., Kikuchi, H. (eds.) ACNS 2017. LNCS, vol. 10355, pp. 537–556. Springer, Cham (2017). https://doi.org/10.1007/978-3-319-61204-1_27
42. Cascudo, I., David, B.: ALBATROSS: publicly AttestabLe BATched randomness based on secret sharing. In: Moriai, S., Wang, H. (eds.) ASIACRYPT 2020. LNCS, vol. 12493, pp. 311–341. Springer, Cham (2020). https://doi.org/10.1007/978-3-030-64840-4_11
43. Das, S., Xiang, Z., Ren, L.: Asynchronous data dissemination and its applications. In: CCS 2021: 2021 ACM SIGSAC Conference on Computer and Communications Security, pp. 2705–2721 (2021)

44. Abraham, I., Jovanovic, P., Maller, M., Meiklejohn, S., Stern, G.: Bingo: Adaptivity and Asynchrony in Verifiable Secret Sharing and Distributed Key Generation (2022). https://eprint.iacr.org/2022/1759
45. Bellare, M., Rogaway, P.: The security of triple encryption and a framework for code-based game-playing proofs. In: Vaudenay, S. (ed.) EUROCRYPT 2006. LNCS, vol. 4004, pp. 409–426. Springer, Heidelberg (2006). https://doi.org/10.1007/11761679_25
46. Boneh, D., Boyen, X.: Short signatures without random oracles and the SDH assumption in bilinear groups. J. Cryptol. **21**(2), 149–177 (2008)
47. Bellare, M., Namprempre, C., Pointcheval, D., Semanko, M.: The one- more-RSA-inversion problems and the security of Chaum's blind signature scheme. J. Cryptol. **163** (2003)
48. von zur Gathen, J., Gerhard, J.: Modern Computer Algebra (3rd edn.) Cambridge University Press (2013). ISBN: 978-1-107-03903-2

Network-Agnostic Security Comes (Almost) for Free in DKG and MPC

Renas Bacho[1,2], Daniel Collins[3(✉)], Chen-Da Liu-Zhang[4,5], and Julian Loss[1]

[1] CISPA Helmholtz Center for Information Security, Saarbrücken, Germany
{renas.bacho,loss}@cispa.de
[2] Saarland University, Saarbrücken, Germany
[3] EPFL, Lausanne, Switzerland
daniel.collins@epfl.ch
[4] Luzern University of Applied Sciences and Arts, Lucerne, Switzerland
[5] Web3 Foundation, Houston, USA
chen-da.liuzhang@ntt-research.com

Abstract. Distributed key generation (DKG) protocols are an essential building block for threshold cryptosystems. Many DKG protocols tolerate up to $t_s < n/2$ corruptions assuming a well-behaved synchronous network, but become insecure as soon as the network delay becomes unstable. On the other hand, solutions in the asynchronous model operate under arbitrary network conditions, but only tolerate $t_a < n/3$ corruptions, even when the network is well-behaved.

In this work, we ask whether one can design a protocol that achieves security guarantees in either scenario. We show a complete characterization of *network-agnostic* DKG protocols, showing that the tight bound is $t_a + 2t_s < n$. As a second contribution, we provide an optimized version of the network-agnostic multi-party computation (MPC) protocol by Blum, Liu-Zhang and Loss [CRYPTO'20] which improves over the communication complexity of their protocol by a linear factor. Moreover, using our DKG protocol, we can instantiate our MPC protocol in the *plain PKI model*, i.e., without the need to assume an expensive trusted setup.

Our protocols incur comparable communication complexity as state-of-the-art DKG and MPC protocols with optimal resilience in their respective purely synchronous and asynchronous settings, thereby showing that network-agnostic security comes *(almost) for free.*

R. Bacho—The author was funded by the Deutsche Forschungsgemeinschaft (DFG, German Research Foundation) - 507237585.
D. Collins—This work was partially carried out while the author was visiting CISPA.
C.-D. Liu-Zhang—CMU and NTT Research and supported by the NSF award 1916939, DARPA SIEVE program, a gift from Ripple, a DoE NETL award, a JP Morgan Faculty Fellowship, a PNC center for financial services innovation award, and a Cylab seed funding award.

H. Handschuh and A. Lysyanskaya (Eds.): CRYPTO 2023, LNCS 14081, pp. 71–106, 2023.
https://doi.org/10.1007/978-3-031-38557-5_3

1 Introduction

The problem of *distributed key generation* (DKG) has been extensively studied in the cryptographic literature and is a fundamental building block for threshold cryptosystems. It allows a set of n parties to compute a uniform sharing of a secret key such that a sufficiently large threshold of $t + 1 < n$ parties must cooperate to reconstruct the secret or compute some function of it. As such, DKG has met several applications, including key escrow services, password-based authentication, threshold signing and encrypting, and many more.

Many existing protocols solve DKG for up to $t < n/2$ malicious corruptions, assuming that the network is *synchronous* [Ped91,GJKR99,SBKN21]. In the synchronous model, message delays are upper bounded by some known finite delay Δ and parties are assumed to have synchronized clocks. These protocols, however, provide no security guarantees when the network is *asynchronous*. Therefore, a more recent line of work has aimed at solving DKG in the asynchronous network model [KG09,AJM+21,DYX+22]. However, asynchronous protocols inherently tolerate at most $t < n/3$ malicious parties, even when the network is synchronous. This poses a vexing dilemma for a protocol designer who can not predict the behaviour of the network. On the one hand, she can choose a synchronous protocol that tolerates the maximum number of $t < n/2$ malicious parties. However, such a protocol might lose all security guarantees if the network ever becomes asynchronous. On the other hand, she can opt for an asynchronous protocol. While this type of protocol remains secure under arbitrary network conditions, it tolerates only $t < n/3$ corrupted parties *even if the network behaves synchronously.*

Motivated by the above discussion, we ask the following question: Is it possible to design a *network-agnostic* DKG protocol that achieves security guarantees in either scenario? Moreover, can we achieve network-agnostic security with no efficiency overhead, i.e., with the same efficiency as state-of-the-art purely synchronous and asynchronous DKG protocols?

We answer these questions in the affirmative. Our contributions are motivated by a series of recent works on network-agnostic protocols for various types of consensus [BKL19,BKL21] and multi-party computation [BLL20,ABKL22a, ACC22a] (MPC). Existing protocols, however, strongly rely on trusted setup, particularly in the form of threshold cryptosystems [BLL20,DHLZ21]. Thus, the import of our work lies within replacing this setup at essentially no cost. In more detail, we show the following results:

- We propose the first network-agnostic DKG protocol. Our protocol tolerates $n/3 < t_s < n/2$ corrupted parties in the synchronous model and $t_a < n/3$ parties in the asynchronous model where t_a and t_s can be chosen arbitrarily subject to $t_a + 2 \cdot t_s < n$. Our protocol is resilience-optimal since we also prove $t_a + 2 \cdot t_s < n$ is *necessary* for network-agnostic DKG. It works in the plain PKI model[1] and allows parties to agree on a *field element* x for public key

[1] In this model, the public keys of corrupted parties can be generated arbitrarily.

$y = g^x$ with only $O(\lambda n^3)$ communication complexity. This matches the best known results in synchrony [SBKN21] and asynchrony [DYX+22]. Thus, our DKG protocol can be used to efficiently bootstrap trusted key generation for network-agnostic consensus and MPC protocols.
- As a second contribution, we show an optimized version of network-agnostic MPC with communication complexity of $O(|C|n^2)$ field elements to evaluate a circuit C, that improves a linear factor over the state of the art (in the setting without the use of multiplicative-homomorphic encryption, see Sect. 1.4 for details). This protocol matches the most efficient purely asynchronous MPC protocol assuming the same setup in this setting, consisting of threshold linear-homomorphic encryption keys and a common reference string (CRS) for non-interactive zero-knowledge (NIZK) proofs. As an application of our DKG protocol, we also obtain the first network-agnostic MPC protocol with optimal resilience $t_a + 2 \cdot t_s < n$ in the plain PKI model, with communication complexity comparable to the previous most communication-efficient network-agnostic with this resilience (which required the usage of a trusted setup for linear-homomorphic threshold encryption keys and a CRS for NIZKs).

In summary, our protocols incur no additional setup assumptions or asymptotic overhead over state-of-the-art communication-efficient protocols for the synchronous and asynchronous network models. This shows that network-agnostic DKG and MPC essentially come 'for free'.

1.1 Background and Starting Point

We consider n parties $P_1, \ldots, P_n$ that communicate over pairwise authenticated channels. Moreover, we assume that parties share a public key infrastructure (PKI), and denote P_i's secret and public key as sk_i and pk_i, respectively. We do not make any assumption on the distributions of corrupted parties' keys and assume that they can be maliciously generated. Throughout, we fix thresholds $0 < t_a < \frac{n}{3} \leq t_s < \frac{n}{2}$ such that $t_a + 2 \cdot t_s < n$. Our model assumptions can now be characterized as follows:

- If the model is synchronous, parties are assumed to have synchronized clocks and messages sent by parties are delivered within some known finite upper bound Δ. At most t_s parties can be maliciously corrupted.
- Otherwise, if the network is asynchronous, messages can be arbitrarily delayed, as long as they are never dropped and are delivered within finite time. Moreover, parties' clocks can be arbitrarily out of synch. In this case, at most t_a parties may be maliciously corrupted. Note that the network can never become asynchronous once t_a or more parties have been corrupted.
- Parties do not know a priori how the network might behave.

Our goal is to design a distributed key generation (DKG) protocol for parties to securely distribute a uniform *field* element x corresponding to some public key $y = g^x$. Since parties cannot be sure whether the network is synchronous or not in general, we require that the secret reconstruction threshold be $\ell = t_s + 1$. With the aim of matching the best known DKG protocols for the synchronous and asynchronous model, we aim for our DKG to run in $O(\lambda n^3)$ communication complexity and be statically secure. In Table 1, we compare the existing state-of-the-art with our proposed DKG which, as we show, satisfies these aims.

Table 1. Comparison table of state-of-the-art DKG protocols. **Network** denotes the network model, which is synchronous (sync), asynchronous (async) or either synchronous or asynchronous (fallback). **Adv.** denotes the adversarial model, which is either static or adaptive. **Comm.** denotes communication complexity in bits. **Rounds** denotes the (expected) round complexity, where Shrestha et al. [SBKN21] provide a deterministic and a randomized protocol (deterministic/randomized). **Setup** denotes the setup assumptions, which include a bulletin board PKI (PKI), a random oracle (RO) or a common reference string (CRS). We note that [AJM+21] constructs a shared *group* element (rather than a *field* element), and [AJM+22] requires a powers-of-tau setup.

DKG Protocol	Network	Adv.	Comm.	Rounds	Setup
Shrestha et al. [SBKN21]	sync	Static	$O(\lambda n^3)$	$O(n)/O(1)$	PKI, RO, CRS
Das et al. [DYX+22]	async	Static	$O(\lambda n^3)$	$O(\log n)$	PKI, RO
Abraham et al. [AJM+21]	async	Static	$\tilde{O}(\lambda n^3)$	$O(1)$	PKI, CRS
Zhang et al. [ZDL+22]	async	Static	$O(\lambda n^4)$	$O(1)$	-
Abraham et al. [AJM+22]	async	Adaptive	$\tilde{O}(\lambda n^3)$	$O(1)$	PKI, CRS
This work (Sect. 5)	fallback	Static	$O(\lambda n^3)$	$O(n)$	PKI, RO, CRS

We stress that this goal cannot be achieved by simply running a generic, network-agnostic MPC protocol [BLL20, DHLZ21], since these protocols require trusted setup in the form of shared keys (which is exactly the goal we are trying to achieve).

Network-Agnostic Protocols: A Blueprint. To design an efficient network-agnostic DKG protocol, a natural approach is to follow the template of previous works [BKL19, BLL20, BKL21]. Here, the protocol is divided into two components, a synchronous component Π_s and an asynchronous component Π_a. Parties begin by running Π_s which performs securely, given that up to t_s parties are corrupted. In this case, parties pass the output v_s obtained from Π_s to Π_a. The final output of the protocol is the value v_a output by Π_a. Note, however, that Π_a achieves security only against t_a corruptions, as it is asynchronous. Thus, the key challenge is to prevent Π_a from simply overwriting the output v_s in a synchronous network, as this would degrade the overall corruption threshold of the protocol to t_a.

To prevent this outcome, the idea is to design Π_s and Π_a with two special properties. First, suppose that the network is synchronous and parties agree on the intermediate value v_s passed to the asynchronous component Π_a. In this case, Π_a should simply relay the correct output v_s (rather than recomputing it), *even* *if t_s parties are corrupted.* Second, if the network is asynchronous, Π_a should be able to compute the correct output v_a on its own in the presence of t_a corruptions. In addition to this, Π_s must prevent parties from computing a catastrophically incorrect intermediate output v_s that might violate the overall security properties of the protocol, given an asynchronous network with t_a corrupted parties.

Background: Synchronous DKG. The above discussion shows why naively running a synchronous DKG and then an asynchronous agreement protocol back-to-back would not produce a network-agnostic protocol. For the setting of DKG, this might lead to the resulting secret key not having enough 'contributions' from honest parties. Our starting point is the synchronous New-DKG protocol of Gennaro et al. [GJKR07], which we make amenable to our network model. Loosely speaking, New-DKG is divided into two phases as follows:

- **Sharing Phase.** In the first phase, each party performs verifiable secret sharing (VSS) using Pedersen's VSS scheme [Ped92] to share two random polynomials f and f' of the same degree. Parties then execute a public complaint management protocol, since some parties may try to misbehave and, e.g., not send (correct) shares to some parties. As a result, they agree on a set of parties Q that honestly executed Pedersen's VSS.
- **Reconstruction Phase.** In the second phase, parties then reconstruct their share of the final secret. To do so, they perform the reconstruction phase of Feldman's VSS [Fel87] from the sharing phase with respect to the polynomial f. The shares of misbehaving parties are reconstructed publicly to ensure termination.

By committing to a second polynomial f', Pedersen's VSS ensures that shared secrets are unconditionally hiding and parties can efficiently blindly evaluate f in the exponent to verify their shares. Then, Q is sufficiently large to ensure that at least one party must have honestly performed VSS. Thus, the adversary has no information about the secret when Q is decided.

One may be tempted to design a simpler and more efficient DKG protocol where parties, as in the so-called Joint-Feldman DKG [GJKR07], run Feldman's VSS in parallel. However, Gennaro et al. [GJKR07] highlighted that the adversary can bias the distribution of the public key by manipulating the set Q, thus precluding security. In general, a rushing adversary can choose to include or exclude the contributions of parties in the final secret which thus precludes any 'one-round' DKG protocol from outputting a uniformly random secret.[2]

In any case, it is not hard to see that the complaint management protocols in New-DKG fail in asynchrony. This is because the complaints of honest parties may be arbitrarily delayed on the network, precluding either correctness or liveness. Dealing with this issue creates additional challenges which we address in the following section.

---

[2] Note that a possibly biased secret can still be sufficient for applications like threshold signatures, as highlighted in [GJKR07, BL22].

1.2 Technical Overview: DKG

A natural idea is to replace Pedersen's VSS in the first phase with publicly verifiable secret sharing (PVSS) [CGMA85,Sta96]. The key property of PVSS is that all parties can *non-interactively* verify whether a given sharing is correct. We begin by presenting a secure, but excessively expensive strawman solution which will serve as our starting point.

A Strawman Solution. To ensure that parties agree on PVSS sharings, each party (acting as the dealer) would first synchronously broadcast their PVSS sharing. In the second phase, parties could then use the asynchronous common subset (ACS) protocol of Blum et al. [BKL21] to agree on a common subset of such sharings. In their protocol, each party provides an input v and the protocol lets them agree on a common subset of $n - t_a$ outputs, given t_a corruptions in an asynchronous network. In addition, their protocol guarantees that if all honest parties start with the *same* input v, then the protocol will remain secure for up to t_s corruptions and the output will be the singleton set $\{v\}$. These properties have made their protocol a staple building block in many network-agnostic protocols.

In our scenario, parties would input their common view of all sharings after the broadcast phase to ACS. Given that the synchronous phase succeeded (i.e., the network is synchronous), all parties would input the *same view* and hence ACS would allow them to (re-)agree on this view, given at most t_s corrupted parties. If parties have not obtained any output from the synchronous phase, they would simply input their PVSS dealing as an input to ACS directly. Even in case the network is asynchronous, parties would still be able to agree on a subset of $n - t_a$ dealings in this manner. From this, they could securely derive a common secret key[3].

Unfortunately, existing network-agnostic ACS protocols [BKL21, ABKL22b] execute n instances of binary consensus and consequently require $O(n)$ distributed coin flips, and adapting ACS to the network-agnostic setting without this requirement is an open problem. As the best known protocol to flip coins without trusted setup requires $O(\lambda n^3)$ communication complexity [GLL+21], this step alone incurs at least $O(\lambda n^4)$ overhead. In addition, the above solution requires all parties to broadcast $O(\lambda n)$-sized sets of ciphertexts containing the parties PVSS dealings. Using existing broadcast protocols, this step would incur an additional communication overhead of $O(\lambda^2 n^4)$. Towards building a network-agnostic DKG with $O(\lambda n^3)$ communication complexity, we introduce novel techniques to overcome the above challenges.

From ACS to Intrusion-Tolerant Consensus. Recall that under synchrony, all parties are guaranteed to output at least $n - t_s$ values from the parallel broadcast in our above strawman protocol. However, if the network is asynchronous, parties are not guaranteed agreement or termination of sufficiently many broadcast instances. To cope, our idea is to let parties execute an asynchronous agree-

[3] This discussion omits a minor technical detail: the adversary must not be able to broadcast incorrect messages on behalf of honest parties, even in asynchrony. Ensuring this, however, is easy using digital signatures.

ment protocol with an *intrusion tolerance* validity property [MR10]. Intrusion tolerance guarantees that a decided value is either one that is proposed by an honest party or a default value $\perp$. In addition, we will require that our agreement protocol satisfies a special *validity with termination property* for up to t_s corruptions. This property ensures that if all parties input the *same value* v to the protocol, they all terminate with this value. (This property was first formalized by Blum et al. [BKL19].) Given this building block, our high-level strategy (from the view of a party P) is as follows.

- If P correctly outputs in at least $n - t_s$ broadcasts, it inputs its set of values to the intrusion-tolerant consensus protocol Π_{IT}. Otherwise, it inputs a default value $\perp'$.
- If a set of values is decided upon by Π_{IT}, P continues with the protocol. Otherwise, P participates in an execution of an asynchronous DKG protocol with $O(\lambda n^3)$ complexity and reconstruction threshold of $t_s + 1$; the protocol of Das et al. [DYX+22] satisfies these requirements.

In synchrony, by the security of broadcast, all parties will propose the same set to Π_{IT} and, by the validity of consensus Π_{IT} under t_s corruptions, this set will be decided. In this case, parties do not fall back to the asynchronous path and can cheaply agree on a t_s-sharing of a field element x.

In asynchrony, the synchronous path might fail. In this case, however, agreement and intrusion tolerance of Π_{IT} ensure that all parties securely continue execution of the synchronous path with the same view or collectively fall back to asynchronous DKG. In case parties do not fall back, their common view on the protocol state allows them to securely emulate the synchronous protocol path. In either scenario, parties agree on a t_s-sharing of a field element x, *even if the network behaves asynchronously.* The following paragraphs describe how, for each phase of our protocol, we manage to keep communication below $O(\lambda n^3)$.

An Efficient Broadcast Protocol. The first ingredient we propose is an efficient multivalued synchronous broadcast protocol assuming $t < (1-\epsilon)\cdot n$ corruptions for any constant $\epsilon \in (0,1)$. Tsimos, Loss and Papamanthou [TLP22] propose an efficient *binary* broadcast protocol, $\mathsf{BulletinBC}$, that is statically secure. $\mathsf{BulletinBC}$ requires $O(\lambda^2 n^2)$ communication, and is very similar to the classic Dolev-Strong broadcast protocol [DS83] except to reduce communication complexity, parties *gossip* instead of *multicast* sets of signatures during the protocol. We modify this protocol and an extension protocol from Nayak et al. [NRS+20] in Sect. 3 to build a multivalued synchronous broadcast protocol with $O(n\ell + \lambda n^2)$ communication complexity where ℓ is the length of the input message. The best prior known protocol had a communication cost of $O(n\ell + n^3)$ and so this construction may be of independent interest. In Table 2, we compare our protocol to other synchronous broadcast protocols from the literature. We note that the extension protocol from Nayak et al. in combination with the Byzantine agreement protocol from Momose and Ren [MR21b] yields a synchronous broadcast protocol with quadratic communication complexity in the honest majority setting, but assumes trusted setup in the form of threshold signatures. In their paper, Momose and Ren also present a second efficient Byzantine agreement protocol that does not require trusted setup. However, that protocol only works with sub-optimal resilience $t < (\frac{1}{2} - \epsilon) \cdot n$.

Table 2. Comparison table of existing synchronous broadcast protocols. **Resil.** denotes the Byzantine corruption threshold as a fraction of the total number of parties, where $\epsilon \in (0, 1)$ is a constant. **Adaptive** denotes whether the adversary is adaptive or not. **Comm.** denotes communication complexity in bits for messages of length ℓ when relevant. **Rounds** denotes the round complexity. **Length** denotes whether the protocol is supports binary (Bin) input or is more general (MV, or multivalued). **Setup** denotes the setup assumption regarding the keys, either trusted or plain PKI.

Protocol	**Resil.**	**Adaptive**	**Comm.**	**Rounds**	**Len.**	**Setup**
Abraham et al. [ACD+19]	1/2	Yes	$\tilde{O}(\lambda n + \ell n)$	$O(1)$	MV	*Trusted*
Momose-Ren [MR21b]	1/2	Yes	$O(\lambda n^2)$	$O(n)$	Bin.	*Trusted*
Chan et al. [CPS20]	$1 - \epsilon$	Yes	$O(\lambda^2 n^2)$	$O(\lambda)$	Bin.	*Trusted*
Dolev-Strong [DS83]	1	Yes	$O(\lambda n^3 + \ell n)$	$O(n)$	MV	*Plain*
Momose-Ren [MR21b]	$1/2 - \epsilon$	Yes	$O(\lambda n^2)$	$O(n)$	Bin.	*Plain*
Tsimos et al. [TLP22]	$1 - \epsilon$	No	$O(\lambda^2 n^2)$	$O(n)$	Bin.	*Plain*
Our Protocol	$1 - \epsilon$	No	$O(n\ell + \lambda n^2)$	$O(n)$	MV	*Plain*

We use our extension protocol for the first phase of DKG. More precisely, each party P_i broadcasts (1) n Pedersen commitments corresponding to random polynomials f_i and f'_i, (2) n ciphertexts corresponding to each party P_j's share of P_i's secret, namely $f_i(j)$ and $f'_i(j)$, and (3) n NIZK proofs that proves ciphertext j, for each $j \in [1, n]$, contains encryptions of values $f_i(j)$ and $f'_i(j)$. This obviates the need for a complaint management protocol as each party can determine the well-formedness of each message broadcast themselves. With $O(\lambda)$-sized NIZKs [PHGR13, CGG+20], each party invokes broadcast with an $O(\lambda n)$-sized message, and consequently this step incurs $O(\lambda n^3)$ communication.

Our Intrusion-Tolerant Consensus Protocol. We adapt a multivalued Byzantine agreement protocol from Mostéfaoui and Raynal [MR17] to ensure intrusion tolerance and validity under t_s corruptions in synchrony. We show in Sect. 4 that the protocol has $O((\ell + \lambda)n^3 + \lambda n^3)$ communication complexity. As such, parties cannot simply propose their $O(\lambda n^2)$-sized set of sharings (recall that such a set contains $n - t_s$ sharings each of size $O(\lambda n)$) to consensus within DKG without incurring super-cubic complexity.

Efficiently Reconstructing the Final Output. To keep the communication complexity below $O(\lambda n^3)$, we observe that each party does not require the entire contents of the $O(\lambda n^2)$-sized set to reconstruct their share and the public key of the final secret. To this end, a party accumulates n 'personalised' values, one per party and each of size $O(\lambda n)$, into an accumulation value z that they propose to consensus. An accumulation value for party P_i contains a description of the qualified parties Q, the $|Q|$ ciphertexts P_i needs to reconstruct their share of the secret $\sum_{q\in Q} f_q(i)$ (alongside $\sum_{q\in Q} f'_q(i)$), and a Pedersen commitment corresponding to these two summations. By intrusion tolerance, if a non-trivial value is decided by consensus, the honest party (or parties) who proposed such a z can send the relevant part and proof of membership in z to each party. By using an accumulator with accumulation value z of size at most $O(\lambda)$ [BP97,Lip12], we thus achieve $O(\lambda n^3)$ complexity for this step. We emphasize that without the intrusion tolerance property it would be possible for parties to decide a value from consensus that does not correspond to an 'honest' accumulation value z. One could bypass intrusion tolerance using a consensus protocol with $O(n\ell+\lambda n^3)$ complexity that ensures *external validity* on decided values [CKPS01]. However, it appears difficult to design such a protocol using erasure codes (as is typical) as parties cannot feasibly evaluate an external validity function on a message until it is reconstructed.

From each party's personalized value, they can reconstruct their share of the secret key but not yet the public key. To reconstruct the public key, it is tempting to replace the reconstruction phase of New-DKG with another round of broadcast and agreement. However, this would allow an adversary to bias the distribution of the shared secret by deciding to fallback to asynchronous DKG depending on, e.g., the first bit of the reconstructed public key. We therefore avoid this by publicly reconstructing the public key using the approach of Shrestha et al. in [SBKN21]. More precisely, each party P_i computes and multicasts the value $G = g^{\sum_{q\in Q} f_q(i)}$ and their accumulation value that they prove is consistent with their Pedersen commitment via an efficient Fiat-Shamir based NIZK [CGJ+99, SBKN21]. Parties can thus collect $t_s + 1$ valid points in the exponent of g and then reconstruct the public key by Lagrange interpolation in the exponent and terminate.

1.3 Technical Overview: MPC

Our starting point is the protocol by Blum, Liu-Zhang and Loss [BLL20], which gave a network-agnostic MPC given an initial setup for threshold additive-homomorphic encryption. The protocol is composed of two parts. First, a synchronous MPC with t_s-full security when the network is synchronous, and achieves t_a-agreement on output (where the output can either be correct or $\bot$) when the network is asynchronous. Second, a purely asynchronous MPC with full security resilient to up to t_a corruptions. The bottleneck for the communication complexity lies in the first protocol, since it requires the usage of n network-agnostic Byzantine agreement (BA) protocols per multiplication gate. Given that the most efficient network-agnostic BA protocol [DHLZ21] incurs quadratic communication, the total communication amounts to $O(n^3|C|\lambda+\mathsf{poly}(n,\lambda))$ bits. However, the most communication-efficient MPC in the purely asynchronous setting (in the same setting, from additive-homomorphic encryption) incurs $O(n^2|C|\lambda + \mathsf{poly}(n,\lambda))$ communication.

In order to decrease a linear factor in the communication, we optimize the protocol using the well-known offline-online paradigm [Bea92]. The offline phase generates ℓ Beaver triples with network-agnostic security, where ℓ is the number of multiplication gates in the circuit: if the network is synchronous and there are up to t_s corruptions, all parties output the same ℓ encrypted random multiplication triples, with plaintexts unknown to the adversary; and if the network is asynchronous and there are up to t_a corruptions, each party outputs either ℓ triples as above, or $\bot$. With these triples, one can use standard techniques to achieve an online phase with quadratic communication, where each multiplication gate is reduced to two public reconstructions [Bea92]. The protocol makes use of a number of primitives, including 1) an efficient synchronous broadcast protocol for long messages with weak-validity and 2) a network-agnostic Byzantine agreement protocol. In a simplified form[4], the protocol works as follows:

- Each party P_i generates ℓ random encryptions $A_i^1, \ldots, A_i^\ell$, and broadcasts them using the broadcast for long messages.
- Parties agree on a subset S of parties that received the encryptions using n instances of network-agnostic BA. If the set has size less than $n - t_s$, output $\bot$ and terminate.
- The parties compute ℓ ciphertexts, where each ciphertext is the sum of all ciphertexts coming from parties in S, i.e. $A^j = \sum_{k \in S} A_k^j$.
- Each party P_i generates ℓ random encryptions $B_i^1, \ldots, B_i^\ell$, and ciphertexts $C_i^1, \ldots, C_i^\ell$ where $C_i^j = b_i^j \cdot A^i$ and b_i^j is the plaintext of B_i^j, and broadcasts all these values using the broadcast for long messages.
- Again, parties agree on a subset S' of parties that received the encryptions, as in Step 2.
- Compute $B^j = \sum_{k \in S'} B_k^j$ and $C^j = \sum_{k \in S'} C_k^j$.
- Output the triples (A^j, B^j, C^j) for $j = 1, \ldots, \ell$.

The communication complexity amounts to n instances of broadcast (note that the cost of the BA instances is independent of the number of multiplication gates). Since each broadcast incurs $O(n\ell + \lambda n^2)$ bits of communication, the total communication is $O(n^2\ell + \lambda n^3)$, or $O(n^2)$ per generated triple (ignoring additive terms). Intuitively, the protocol generates random triples because each component contains the contribution of at least an honest party. If the network is synchronous, all honest parties output the generated triples. However, if the network is asynchronous, some of the honest parties may not obtain the triples and output $\bot$. This will be enough in the online phase and is handled similarly as the protocol in [BLL20]. Finally, using the DKG protocol from above, and the observation that the NIZK proofs can be generated with no setup using the multi-string honest majority proof system by Groth and Ostrovsky [GO07], we can base our MPC protocol from plain PKI. This, however, incurs a blowup in the communication complexity, resulting in a communication complexity that is comparable to the state of the art of network-agnostic MPC.

[4] The simplified description tolerates only fail-stop corruptions. To achieve security against active adversaries, one needs NIZKs at appropriate steps of the protocol. See Sect. 6 for details.

1.4 Related Work

In [MR21a], Momose and Ren initiate the study of the network-agnostic setting where the thresholds for safety and liveness properties are considered separately, and construct corresponding state machine replication protocols.

Distributed Key Generation. Many synchronous DKG protocols assume the existence of broadcast channels, i.e., that essentially abstract away secure broadcast and consensus, including the seminal protocol of Gennaro et al. [GJKR07]. In a recent work, Shrestha et al. [SBKN21] consider when broadcast is no longer assumed (as in our work), and propose a protocol with $O(\lambda n^3)$ complexity which is the state-of-the-art. Canetti et al. [CGJ+99] propose an adaptively-secure DKG protocol, but almost all other work, including ours, consider static security.

Das et al. [DYX+22] propose an asynchronous DKG protocol with $O(\lambda n^3)$ communication complexity. In order to bypass the need for direct coin flipping (which incurs $O(\lambda n^3)$ overhead), they perform a clever reduction to n instances of binary consensus which uses $O(\lambda n^2)$ for coin flips from honest parties. Abraham et al. use a so-called aggregatable DKG protocol [GJM+21] to also build a protocol with $O(\lambda n^3)$ overhead that only requires an efficient Byzantine agreement primitive like [GLL+22]. However, the only efficient construction of aggregatable DKG we are aware of allows parties to agree on a shared *group* element as a secret which can thus be applied only to less standard cryptosystems. The DKG of Zhang et al. [ZDL+22] does not require a PKI, CRS or the ROM, but incurs $O(\lambda n^4)$ overhead. Recently, Abraham et al. construct asynchronous DKG with an adaptive security proof [AJM+22], although they require a powers-of-tau trusted setup which, using the best known asynchronous protocol [DXR22], implies $\tilde{O}(\lambda n^3)$ communication overhead overall.

Communication complexity in MPC. The literature in communication complexity is extensive, so we are only able to cover a part of it. In the synchronous model, solutions with linear communication, i.e. $O(\lambda n)$ bits per multiplication gate, have been known for a while (see e.g. [HN06, DI06, BTH08, BFO12, GLS19, GSZ20]), for several settings: $t < n/3$ without setup and $t < n/2$ with setup, as well as cryptographic and information-theoretic.

In the asynchronous model, information-theoretic solutions with optimal resilience $t < n/3$ were provided by Ben-Or et al. [BKR94], and later improved by Patra et al. [PCR10, PCR08] to $O(\lambda n^5)$ per multiplication, and by Choudhury [Cho20] to $O(\lambda n^4)$ per multiplication. Solutions with suboptimal resilience $t < n/4$ were achieved with linear communication $O(\lambda n)$ [SR00, PSR02, CHP13, PCR15]. For cryptographic security and optimal resilience $t < n/3$, current solutions require trusted setup, typically in the form of threshold cryptosystems. The works by [HNP05, HNP08, CHLZ21] make use of additive threshold homomorphic encryption, with the protocols [HNP08, CHLZ21] communicating $O(\lambda n^2)$ per multiplication. The work by Choudhury and Patra [CP15] achieves $O(\lambda n)$ per multiplication at the cost of using somewhat-homomorphic encryption, and the work by Cohen [Coh16] achieves communication independent of the circuit size using fully-homomorphic encryption.

In the setting with network-agnostic security, the protocols [BLL20, DHLZ21] achieve optimal resilience $t_a + 2 \cdot t_s < n$ and cryptographic security, with the first being more communication-efficient with $O(\lambda n^3)$ bits per multiplication gate (using the network-agnostic BA [DHLZ21]). These protocols make use of an additive threshold homomorphic encryption scheme, which is generally regarded as a more efficient primitive in practice than those that allow for multiplicative homomorphism. Further note that if one assumes for example threshold FHE, it is straightforward to achieve MPC in the network-agnostic setting with communication independent of the circuit size. [ACC22a] considers perfect security and achieves resilience $t_a + 3 \cdot t_s < n$ and communication complexity $O(\lambda n^4 |C|)$. Using the network-agnostic perfectly-secure message transmission protocol of [DLZ23], one can build network-agnostic MPC over a network with connectivity ℓ given $2 \cdot t_a + t_s < \ell$ also holds. Finally, [ACC22b] considers perfectly-secure MPC with respect to general adversary structures ($\mathcal{Q}^{(3)}$ and $\mathcal{Q}^{(4)}$ in synchrony and asynchrony, respectively) with complexity $\tilde{O}(\lambda n^5 |\mathcal{Z}_s|^3 c_m + n^6 |\mathcal{Z}_s|^2)$ bits for adversary structure $\mathcal{Z}_s$ and multiplication gate count c_m, and [AC23] very recently considers statistical security.

1.5 Paper Organisation

In Sect. 2, we define our model and relevant cryptographic and distributed primitives. In Sect. 3, we present our efficient broadcast protocols. In Sect. 4, we describe our intrusion-tolerant consensus protocol. In Sect. 5, we present our DKG protocol and argue for its security. In Sect. 6, we present our MPC protocol. In the full version of this paper [BCLZL22], we include deferred security definitions, sub-protocols for our intrusion-tolerant consensus protocol, a suitable threshold encryption scheme for MPC, full proofs and deferred figures.

2 Preliminaries and Definitions

Throughout the paper, we consider a network of n parties $P_1, \ldots, P_n$ that communicate over point-to-point authenticated channels. Some fraction of these parties are controlled by an adversary and may deviate arbitrarily from the protocol. We call the uncorrupted parties *honest* and the corrupted parties *dishonest*. When we say that a party *multicasts* a message, we mean that it sends it to all n parties in the network. We denote the security parameter by λ and the random variable X output by some probabilistic experiment Π by $X \leftarrow \Pi$. We denote the set of integers from a to b by $[a, b]$. For an element x in a set S, $x \leftarrow S$ denotes x being sampled from S uniformly at random. We sometimes use *maps* or key-value stores, which are data structures of the form $\mathsf{map}[k] = v$ for lookup key k which outputs value v.

We assume that global parameters $par = (\mathbb{G}, p, g, h)$ are fixed and known to all parties. Here, $\mathbb{G}$ is a cyclic group of prime order p with independent generators g and h. Given $(\mathbb{G}, p, g)$, we can choose h appropriately as, e.g., $H(1)$ where H is a random oracle of the form $H : \{0,1\}^* \rightarrow \mathbb{G}^* = \mathbb{G} \backslash \{1\}$.

Public Key Infrastructure. We assume that the parties have established a public key infrastructure before the protocol execution, which is a bulletin board or plain PKI. Namely, each party P_i has an encryption-decryption key pair $(\mathsf{ek}_i, \mathsf{dk}_i)$ for a public-key encryption scheme and a signing-verification key pair $(\mathsf{sk}_i, \mathsf{vk}_i)$ for a signature scheme, where ek_i and vk_i are known to all parties. We do not assume that these keys are computed in a trusted manner and instead we assume only that each party generates them locally and then makes the public components known to everybody using a public bulletin board. In particular, malicious parties may choose their keys arbitrarily, corrupt honest parties after seeing they generate their keys and choose keys maliciously based on keys registered by honest parties. We define the function $\mathcal{VK}(P')$ callable by each party which takes as input a sequence of parties $P' = (P_{i(1)}, \ldots, P_{i(k)})$ and outputs the corresponding registered verification keys as a sequence $(\mathsf{vk}_{i(1)}, \ldots, \mathsf{vk}_{i(k)})$.

Communication Model. Our network has two possible states, the synchronous and the asynchronous state. When the network is synchronous, all parties begin the protocol at the same time, the clocks of the parties progress at the same rate, and all messages are delivered within some known finite time $\Delta > 0$ (called the network delay) after being sent. In particular, messages of honest parties cannot be dropped from the network and are always delivered. Thus, we can consider protocols that execute in rounds of length Δ where parties start executing round r at time $(r-1)\Delta$. When the network is asynchronous, the adversary can delay messages arbitrarily as long as the messages exchanged between honest parties are eventually delivered. In contrast to the synchronous model, parties may start the protocol at different times in an asynchronous network, since their clocks and processing speeds are not necessarily synchronized. Finally, honest parties do not know a priori in which type of network they are in.

Adversarial Model. We assume a probabilistic polynomial-time (PPT) adversary that can corrupt up to t parties. The adversary may cause the corrupted parties to deviate from the protocol arbitrarily. Furthermore, we assume a rushing adversary who may obtain messages sent to it before choosing and sending messages of its own. Moreover, we assume a static adversary, who chooses which parties to corrupt before the execution of the protocol begins.

2.1 Cryptographic Primitives

Definitions and properties that we introduce hereafter are only required to hold with probability $1 - \mathsf{negl}(\lambda)$. We defer formal definitions of correctness and security alongside definitions of standard cryptographic primitives like public-key encryption to the full version [BCLZL22].

We begin by defining non-interactive zero-knowledge proofs (NIZKs). NIZKs enable a prover to non-interactively (i.e., generate a message that is then verified) to prove to a verifier the validity of a statement without revealing anything else.

Definition 1 (Non-interactive zero-knowledge proof (NIZK) [Gro06]**).** *Let R be an NP relation. For pairs $(X, \omega) \in R$ we call X the statement and ω the* *witness. Let L be the language consisting of statements in R. A non-interactive zero-knowledge proof is a tuple of PPT algorithms* $(\mathsf{Gen}, \mathsf{Prove}, \mathsf{Verify})$ *such that:*

- Gen*: This is a parameter generation algorithm that takes as input the security parameter λ. It outputs parameters par implicitly input to other algorithms.*
- Prove*: This is a probabilistic proving algorithm that takes as input a statement X to be proven and the corresponding witness ω where $(X, \omega) \in R$. It outputs a proof π, denoted as $\pi \leftarrow \mathsf{Prove}(X, \omega)$.*
- Verify*: This is a deterministic verification algorithm that takes as input a statement X and a proof π. It outputs an acceptance bit b, denoted as $b \leftarrow \mathsf{Verify}(X, \pi)$.*

We assume that NIZKs are of size $O(\lambda)$. The NIZKs that we use in our DKG construction can be constructed using efficient, Fiat-Shamir style proofs in the random oracle model [SBKN21,CGG+20]. Alternatively, one can use SNARKs with a common reference string setup [PHGR13].

We now define accumulators, a primitive that enables a party to accumulate several values from some set D into an accumulated value z. At this point, the party can generate (compact) proofs that verify that a given value is in D. A secure accumulator is in particular one where 'invalid' proofs are hard to forge.

Definition 2 (Cryptographic accumulator). *A cryptographic accumulator is a tuple of PPT algorithms* $(\mathsf{Gen}, \mathsf{Eval}, \mathsf{CreateWit}, \mathsf{Verify})$ *such that:*

- Gen*: This is an accumulator key generation algorithm that takes as input the security parameter λ and an accumulation threshold n. It outputs a (public) accumulator key ak.*
- Eval*: This is a deterministic evaluation algorithm that takes as input an accumulator key ak and a set $D = \{d_1, \ldots, d_n\}$ to be accumulated. It outputs an accumulation value z for D, denoted as $z \leftarrow \mathsf{Eval}(ak, D)$.*
- $\mathsf{CreateWit}$*: This is a probabilistic witness creation algorithm that takes as input an accumulator key ak, an accumulation value z for D, and a value d_i. It outputs $\perp$ if $d_i \notin D$, and a witness w_i otherwise, denoted as $w_i \leftarrow \mathsf{CreateWit}(ak, z, d_i)$.*
- Verify*: This takes as input an accumulator key ak, an accumulation value z for D, a witness w_i, and a value d_i. It outputs an acceptance bit b, denoted as $b \leftarrow \mathsf{Verify}(ak, z, w_i, d_i)$, where $b = 1$ when w_i proves that $d_i \in D$.*

The helper function $\mathsf{CreateWits}$*, denoted as* $(w_1, \ldots, w_n) \leftarrow \mathsf{CreateWits}(ak, z, D)$ *for set $D = \{d_1, \ldots, d_n\}$, is shorthand for the n calls* $(\mathsf{CreateWit}(ak, z, d_1), \ldots, \mathsf{CreateWit}(ak, z, d_n))$.

Note that the above definition does not consider updates or removals of elements from the accumulated value z, and so our definition is weaker than that of much of the literature. We require an accumulator with witnesses w and accumulation values z of size $O(\lambda)$. We also require that operations after ak was generated are *deterministic*. The classic RSA accumulator satisfies these requirements with trusted setup in the standard model [BP97]; without trusted setup, one can use, for instance, the accumulator from Lipmaa in [Lip12]. Looking ahead, it can be seen that our protocols can use vector commitments instead of accumulators, which can also be built without trusted setup with constant-sized openings [CF13].

Definition 3 (Linear erasure codes). *We use standard (b, n) Reed-Solomon codes. A Reed-Solomon (RS) code [RS60] is a linear error correction code in the finite field $\mathbb{F}_{2^a}$, parameterized by n and b with $n \leq 2^a - 1$, given by the tuple of algorithms* (Encode, Decode) *such that:*

- Encode*: This is an encoding algorithm that takes as input b data symbols $(m_1, \ldots, m_b) \in \mathbb{F}_{2^a}^b$ and outputs a codeword $(s_1, \ldots, s_n) \in \mathbb{F}_{2^a}^n$ of length n, denoted as $(s_1, \ldots, s_n) \leftarrow \mathsf{Encode}(m_1, \ldots, m_b)$. Knowledge of any b elements of the codeword uniquely determines the input message and the rest of the codeword.*
- Decode*: This is a decoding algorithm that takes as input a codeword $(s_1, \ldots, s_n)$ of length n and outputs b symbols $(m_1, \ldots, m_b) \in \mathbb{F}_{2^a}^b$, denoted as $(m_1, \ldots, m_b) \leftarrow \mathsf{Decode}(s_1, \ldots, s_n)$. It can tolerate up to c errors and d erasures in codewords $(s_1, \ldots, s_n)$ if and only if $n - b \geq 2c + d$.*

Our protocol that uses erasure codes will have $b = n - t$. Finally, we assume that parties have a threshold additively homomorphic encryption setup available. That is, it provides to each party P_i a global public key ek and a private key share dk_i.

Definition 4 (Threshold homomorphic encryption). *A threshold homomorphic encryption scheme is a tuple of PPT algorithms* (Keygen, TEnc, TDec) *such that:*

- Keygen*: This key generation algorithm takes as input integers (t, n) and outputs key pair $(\mathsf{ek}, \mathsf{dk})$, where ek is the public key, and $\mathsf{dk} = (\mathsf{dk}_1, \ldots, \mathsf{dk}_n)$ is the list of private keys, denoted as $(\mathsf{ek}, \mathsf{dk}) = \mathsf{Keygen}_{(t,n)}(1^\lambda)$.*
- TEnc*: This takes as input an encryption key ek and plaintext m and outputs an encryption $\mathsf{TEnc}_{\mathsf{ek}}(m)$ of m, which we denote explicitly.*
- TDec*: Given a ciphertext c and a secret key share dk_i, there is an algorithm that outputs $d_i = \mathsf{TDec}_{\mathsf{dk}_i}(c)$, such that $(d_1, \ldots, d_n)$ forms a t-out-of-n sharing of the plaintext $m = \mathsf{Dec}_{\mathsf{dk}}(c)$. Moreover, with $t + 1$ decryption shares $\{d_i\}$, one can reconstruct the plaintext $m = \mathsf{TRec}(\{d_i\})$.*

It further satisfies the following properties:

- Additively homomorphic*: Given ek and two encryptions $\mathsf{Enc}_{\mathsf{ek}}(a)$ and $\mathsf{TEnc}_{\mathsf{ek}}(b)$, one can efficiently compute an encryption $\mathsf{Enc}_{\mathsf{ek}}(a + b)$.*
- Multiplication by constant*: Given ek, a plaintext α and an encryption $\mathsf{Enc}_{\mathsf{ek}}(a)$, one can efficiently compute a random encryption $\mathsf{Enc}_{\mathsf{ek}}(\alpha a)$.*

In the full version [BCLZL22], we design a discrete logarithm-based additively homomorphic threshold encryption scheme based on the Elgamal cryptosystem [ElG84] which essentially is exponential ElGamal encryption where the message is encrypted bitwise. Looking ahead, it is thus directly compatible with our

DKG protocol. With trusted setup, a threshold encryption scheme can be based on, for example, the Paillier cryptosystem [Pai99].

2.2 Distributed Primitives

When relevant, our primitives take input from a value set V with $|V| \geq 2$; we assume that default value $\perp \notin V$. We distinguish between algorithms that *generate output* (generally called liveness), and algorithms that additionally *terminate.* In particular, an algorithm may be live but not terminating, since it may need to still remain online and send more messages to help other parties output. Our treatment of liveness and termination varies between the primitives we introduce below. Note that $\perp$ is considered as a valid output in each protocol.

We first introduce intrusion-tolerant Byzantine agreement and secure broadcast, the two main building blocks we use to build DKG. Byzantine agreement is a classic primitive that allows parties which each input a value to agree on a common output value. We define liveness (generating output) and termination in two separate properties below. We emphasise that our definition captures the standard Byzantine agreement problem.

Definition 5 (Byzantine agreement). *Let Π be a protocol executed by parties $P_1, \ldots, P_n$, where each party P_i begins holding input $v_i \in V$.*

- **Validity:** *Π is t-*valid *if the following holds whenever at most t parties are corrupted: if every honest party's input is equal to the same value v, then every honest party outputs v.*
- **Consistency:** *Π is t-*consistent *if whenever at most t parties are corrupted, every honest party that outputs a value outputs the same value v.*
- **Liveness:** *Π is t-*live *if whenever at most t parties are corrupted, every honest party outputs a value $v \in V \cup \{\perp\}$.*
- **Termination:** *Π is t-*terminating *if whenever at most t parties are corrupted, every honest party terminates.*
- **Intrusion tolerance:** *Π is t-*intrusion tolerant *if whenever at most t parties are corrupted, every honest party that outputs a value either outputs an honest party's input v or $\perp$.*
- **Validity with termination:** *Π is t-*valid with termination *if the following holds whenever at most t parties are corrupted: if every honest party's input is equal to the same value v, then every honest party outputs v and terminates.*

*If Π is t-valid, t-consistent, t-live, and t-terminating, we say it is t-*secure.[5] *If Π is t-secure and is t-intrusion tolerant, we say it is t-*secure with intrusion tolerance.

In secure broadcast (or just broadcast), parties aim to agree on a value which is either the value chosen by the designated sender or a default value (in case the sender is corrupted). Our definition handles termination directly, even in asynchrony (where we only guarantee weak validity). As for Byzantine agreement, the following captures the standard broadcast primitive.

[5] We emphasise that t-security does not imply t-intrusion tolerance.

Definition 6 (Secure broadcast (BC)). *Let Π be a protocol executed by parties $P_1, \ldots, P_n$, where a designated party P begins holding input $v \in V$.*

- **Validity:** *Π is t-*valid *if whenever at most t parties are corrupted: if party P is honest and inputs v, then all honest parties P_j output v.*
- **Consistency:** *Π is t-*consistent *if whenever at most t parties are corrupted, every honest party outputs the same value v'.*
- **Liveness:** *Π is t-*live *if whenever at most t parties are corrupted, every honest party outputs a value $v' \in V \cup \{\bot\}$.*
- **Termination:** *Π is t-*terminating *if whenever at most t parties are corrupted, every honest party terminates.*
- **External validity:** *Π is t-*externally valid *if the following holds whenever at most t parties are corrupted: if honest party P_i outputs v', then for validity predicate Q, $Q(v)$ is true.*
- **Weak validity:** *Π is t-*weakly valid *if whenever at most t parties are corrupted: if P is honest and inputs v, then all honest parties P_i output either v or $\bot$ and terminate upon generating output.*

*If Π is t-valid, t-consistent, t-live and t-terminating, we say it is t-*secure.

Note that weak validity was defined in [BKL19] and external validity was introduced in [CKPS01] for Byzantine agreement.

Following previous work, we introduce a property-based definition of distributed key generation (DKG) primitive. In DKG, a set of parties collaborates to share a uniformly random secret. Each party outputs the public key corresponding to the secret, their own secret share and a set of public shares that parties can use to prove ownership of their share. We restrict our definition to the case where parties share a uniform *field element* associated to some group generated by g, i.e., a public key $y = g^x$ and secret x; one can generalise or vary the definition to capture other settings.

Definition 7 (Distributed key generation (DKG)). *Let Π be a protocol executed by parties $P_1, \ldots, P_n$, where each party P_i outputs a secret key share ss_i, a vector of public key shares $(\mathsf{ps}_1, \ldots, \mathsf{ps}_n)$, a public key* pk *and parties terminate upon generating output.*

- **Correctness:** *Π is (t, d)-*correct *for $d > t$ if whenever at most t parties are corrupted, there exists a polynomial $f \in \mathbb{Z}_p[X]$ of degree $d - 1$ such that for all $i \in [1, n]$, $\mathsf{ss}_i = f(i)$ and $\mathsf{ps}_i = g^{\mathsf{ss}_i}$. Moreover, $\mathsf{pk} = g^{f(0)}$.*
- **Consistency:** *Π is t-*consistent *if whenever at most t parties are corrupted, all honest parties output the same public key* pk *and the same vector of public key shares $(\mathsf{ps}_1, \ldots, \mathsf{ps}_n)$.*
- **Secrecy:** *Π is t-*secret *if the following holds whenever at most t parties are corrupted: For every (PPT) adversary $\mathcal{A}$, there exists a (PPT) simulator $\mathcal{S}$ with the following property. On input an element $y \in \mathbb{G}$ and a set of corrupted parties B with $|B| \leq t$, $\mathcal{S}$ generates a transcript whose distribution is computationally indistinguishable from $\mathcal{A}$'s view of a run of Π with corrupted set B in which all honest parties output y as their public key.*

– **Uniformity:** *Π is t-*uniform *if the following holds whenever at most t parties are corrupted: Fix $y \in \mathbb{G}$. Then, for every (PPT) adversary $\mathcal{A}$, for every honest party that outputs public key* pk, $\mathsf{pk} = y$ *holds with probability negligibly close to $1/p$, where the probability is taken over $\mathcal{A}$'s randomness (and not the coins used in setup).*

*If Π is (t,d)-correct, t-consistent, t-secret, and t-uniform, we say it is (t,d)-*secure.

Our definition is adapted from that of Bacho and Loss [BL22] except we only require a standard secrecy notion akin to that of Gennaro et al. [GJKR07]. As we consider static security, our simulator is parametrised by the set of corrupted parties B chosen by the adversary. Apart from our additional uniformity property, the main difference is that we allow the secret threshold to be a value d that exceeds the number of corruptions t by more than 1. Looking forward, our DKG protocol will satisfy (t_s, d)-security in synchrony and (t_a, d)-security in asynchrony for $d = t_s + 1$. In particular, our protocol achieves t_a-secrecy in asynchrony. The definition of secrecy is not well-defined in asynchrony when considering more than t_a corruptions, because in particular not all parties may output y (or worse yet they may output different keys). One could define a variant of secrecy that guarantees 'secrecy with abort' but its usefulness is less clear given only a subset of honest parties could output a secret share.

2.3 Multi-party Computation

A multi-party computation (MPC) protocol allows n parties $P_1, \ldots, P_n$, where each party P_i has a private input x_i, to jointly compute a function over the inputs $f(x_1, \ldots, x_n)$ in such a way that nothing beyond the output is revealed.

Different levels of security guarantees have been considered in the MPC literature, such as guaranteed output delivery (a.k.a. full security), where honest parties are guaranteed to obtain the correct output, or security with selective abort [IOZ14,CL17], where the adversary can choose any subset of parties to receive $\bot$, instead of the correct output. In the case of *unanimous* abort [GMW87,FGH+02], the adversary can choose whether all honest parties receive the correct output or all honest parties receive $\bot$ as output.

When the network is asynchronous, it is provably impossible that the computed function takes into account all inputs from honest parties [BCG93, BKR94], since one cannot distinguish between a dishonest party not sending its input, or an honest party's input being delayed. Hence, we say that a protocol achieves L-output quality, if the output to be computed contains the inputs from at least L parties. This is modeled in the ideal functionality as allowing the ideal adversary to choose a subset S of L parties. The functionality then computes $f(x_1, \ldots, x_n)$, where $x_i = v_i$ is the input of P_i in the case that $P_i \in S$, and otherwise $x_i = \bot$.

We describe the ideal functionality $\mathcal{F}_{\mathsf{sfe}}^{\mathsf{sec},L}$ for MPC with full security and L-output quality below (Fig. 1). In addition, we denote the functionality $\mathcal{F}_{\mathsf{sfe}}^{\mathsf{sout},L}$

$\mathcal{F}_{\mathsf{sfe}}^{\mathtt{sec},L}$

- $\mathcal{F}_{\mathsf{sfe}}$ is parameterized by a set $\mathcal{P}$ of n parties and a function $f : (\{0,1\}^* \cup \{\perp\})^n \to (\{0,1\}^*)^n$. For each $P_i \in \mathcal{P}$, initialize the variables $x_i = y_i = \perp$. Set $S = \mathcal{P}$.
- On input (Input, v) from $P_i \in \mathcal{P}$, if $P_i \in S$, set $x_i = v$ and send a message (Input, P_i) to the adversary.
- On input $(\mathsf{OutputSet}, S')$ from the ideal adversary, where $S' \subseteq \mathcal{P}$ and $|S'| = L$, set $S = S'$ and $x_i = \perp$ for each $P_i \notin S$.
- Once all inputs from honest parties in S have been input, set each $y_i = f(x_1, \ldots, x_n)$.
- On input $(\mathsf{GetOutput})$ from P_i, output $(\mathsf{Output}, y_i, \mathsf{sid})$ to P_i.

Fig. 1. Secure Function Evaluation Functionality.

(resp. $\mathcal{F}_{\mathsf{sfe}}^{\mathtt{uout},L}$), the above functionality, where the adversary can selectively choose any subset of parties to obtain $\perp$ as the output (resp. choose that either all honest parties receive $f(x_1, \ldots, x_n)$ or $\perp$).

Definition 8. *A protocol π achieves full security (resp. selective abort; unanimous abort) with L output-quality if it UC-realizes functionality $\mathcal{F}_{\mathsf{sfe}}^{\mathtt{sec},L}$ ($\mathcal{F}_{\mathsf{sfe}}^{\mathtt{sout},L}$; $\mathcal{F}_{\mathsf{sfe}}^{\mathtt{uout},L}$).*

Since protocols run in a synchronous network typically achieve n-output quality, we implicitly assume that all synchronous protocols we discuss achieve n-output quality (unless otherwise specified).

Weak termination. In this work, similar to that of [BLL20], we consider protocols with the following weaker termination property: we say that a protocol has weak termination, if parties are guaranteed to terminate upon receiving an output different than $\perp$, but do not necessarily terminate if the output is $\perp$.

3 Communication-Efficient Synchronous Broadcast

In this section, we construct a synchronous secure broadcast protocol with $O(\ell n + \lambda n^2)$ communication complexity that tolerates $t < (1-\epsilon) \cdot n$ corruptions with $\epsilon \in (0,1)$ for messages of length ℓ. To do so, we adapt the extension protocol proposed by Nayak et al. [NRS+20]. Their protocol, however, relies on a λ-bit broadcast module with the same corruption tolerance and communication complexity $O(\lambda n^2)$. We therefore first construct such a protocol.

3.1 Short Message Broadcast Module

We present our protocol $\Pi_{\mathsf{BC}}^{t,\epsilon}$ in Fig. 2 that allows λ-bit messages to be broadcast with $O(\lambda n^2)$ communication complexity. We assume the existence of an aggregate signature scheme as. Let $R = O(\log n)$ and $q = O(1/\epsilon)$ be two constants that we use in the protocol and the proof in the full version [BCLZL22].

$\Pi_{\mathsf{BC}}^{t,\epsilon}(m^*)$

1. At time 0:
   - Set $\mathsf{sent}[m] = \mathsf{detect}[m] = \mathsf{false}$ for all $m \in M$ and $v = \bot$.
   - If $P_i = P^*$: set $\sigma^* \leftarrow \mathsf{as.Sign}(\mathsf{sk}_i, m^*)$ and $\mathsf{sent}[m^*] = \mathsf{detect}[m^*] = \mathsf{true}$, then multicast $(\sigma^*, \Sigma = (), \boldsymbol{P} = (), m^*)$.
2. For $r = 1, \ldots, t + R$: At time $r \cdot \Delta$: for each $m \in M$:
   - If received messages $(\sigma, \Sigma_1, \boldsymbol{P_1}, m), \ldots, (\sigma, \Sigma_j, \boldsymbol{P_j}, m)$ for distinct $\boldsymbol{P_1}, \ldots, \boldsymbol{P_j}$ from distinct parties such that for $\boldsymbol{P} = \cup_{k\in[1,j]} \boldsymbol{P_j}$
     (a) For each $k \in [1, j]$, $\mathsf{as.Verify}(\mathcal{VK}(\boldsymbol{P_k}), \Sigma_k, m) = 1$;
     (b) $\mathsf{as.Verify}(\mathcal{VK}(P^*), \sigma, m) = 1$;
     (c) $|\boldsymbol{P}| \geq \min\{r - 1, t\}$; and
     (d) $\{P_i, P^*\} \not\subseteq \boldsymbol{P}$:
     - If $\mathsf{sent}[m] = \mathsf{false}$ and $|\{m' \in M : \mathsf{sent}[m'] = \mathsf{true}\}| < 2$:
       * Set $\mathsf{sent}[m] = \mathsf{true}$.
       * Compute $\mathsf{as.Sign}(\mathsf{sk}_i, m) = \sigma$.
       * Compute $\mathsf{as.Combine}(\Sigma', VK', m) = \sigma'$, where $\Sigma' = (\Sigma_1, \ldots, \Sigma_j, \sigma)$ and $VK' = (\mathcal{VK}(\boldsymbol{P_1}), \ldots, \mathcal{VK}(\boldsymbol{P_j}), \mathsf{vk}_i)$.
       * For all $k \in [1, n]$, send $(\sigma_j, \sigma', \boldsymbol{P} \cup \{P_i\}, m)$ to P_k with probability q/n.
       * If $\mathsf{detect}[m] = \mathsf{false}$: set $\mathsf{detect}[m] = \mathsf{true}$ and multicast $(\sigma, (), (), m)$.
   - If received message $(\sigma, \cdot, \cdot, m)$ such that $\mathsf{as.Verify}(\mathcal{VK}(P^*), \sigma, m) = 1$:
     - If $\mathsf{detect}[m] = \mathsf{false}$ and $|\{m' \in M : \mathsf{detect}[m'] = \mathsf{true}\}| < 2$:
       * Set $\mathsf{detect}[m] = \mathsf{true}$ and multicast $(\sigma, (), (), m)$.
3. At time $(t + R + 1) \cdot \Delta$:
   - If $\mathsf{sent} = \mathsf{detect}$ and $|\{m' \in M : \mathsf{sent}[m'] = \mathsf{true}\}| = 1$: set $v = m'$. Output v and terminate.

Fig. 2. Synchronous broadcast (BC) protocol with sender P^* for $t < (1 - \epsilon) \cdot n$ and $\epsilon \in (0, 1)$ from the perspective of party P_i.

Our protocol is similar to BulletinBC ([TLP22], Figure 2), which in turn is similar to the well-known Dolev-Strong broadcast protocol. Whereas in Dolev-Strong signatures are multicast to all parties, in BulletinBC signatures are sent to each party only with probability q/n (the *gossiping* technique). We emphasise that gossiping does not require a common coin, but only a local source of randomness: parties each locally sample the set of parties to gossip messages to. To ensure security, BulletinBC thus requires an additional $R = O(\log n)$ rounds to ensure that the 'gossiped' message propagates to all parties except with negligible probability. Notably, we extend BulletinBC to support *multivalued* broadcast and improve upon the communication complexity by using an aggregate signature scheme $\mathsf{as} = (\mathsf{KeyGen}, \mathsf{Sign}, \mathsf{Combine}, \mathsf{Verify})$.

In $\Pi_{\mathsf{BC}}^{t,\epsilon}$, each party P_i manages two local maps $\mathsf{sent}, \mathsf{detect} : M \to \{\mathsf{false}, \mathsf{true}\}$ with initialization $\mathsf{sent}[m] = \mathsf{detect}[m] = \mathsf{false}$ for all $m \in M$ (where M denotes the message space). In the first step of the protocol, the sender P^* multicasts its signed input value m_i and sets $\mathsf{sent}[m_i] = \mathsf{detect}[m_i] = \mathsf{true}$. The protocol then runs $t + R$ rounds as follows. In rounds $1 \leq r \leq t + R$, for each $m \in M$, if P_i has 1) received a signature on m signed by the sender P^*; 2) can form a valid aggregate signature with $\min\{r - 1, t\}$ signers;[6] and 3) they have previously gossiped/multicast at most one message $m' \neq m$ (i.e. $|\{m' \in M : \mathsf{sent}[m'] = \mathsf{true}\}| \leq 1$, P_i sets $\mathsf{sent}[m] = \mathsf{true}$, computes an aggregate signature on it and sends this plus P^*'s signature to each party with probability q/n.

Note if we simply replace the (deterministic) multicast from Dolev-Strong with probabilistic sending, then consistency may not hold if P^* signs more than two messages above, since condition 3) above implies that honest parties do not relay all messages. To deal with this, parties keep track of P^*'s signatures separately. In particular, when P_i receives a signature σ of P^* on m, if $\mathsf{detect}[m] = \mathsf{false}$ and $|\{m' : \mathsf{detect}[m] = \mathsf{true}\}| < 2$, P_i *multicasts* (not gossips) m and σ and then sets $\mathsf{detect}[m] = \mathsf{true}$ so all parties receive it.[7]

Finally, in step 3 of the protocol in round $t+R+1$, if the maps sent and detect are equal and there is only one value $m' \in M$ such that $\mathsf{sent}[m'] = \mathsf{true}$, then P_i outputs this value and terminates; otherwise it outputs $\perp$ and terminates. Note if there are two or more messages m such that some honest party set $\mathsf{sent}[m] = \mathsf{true}$, then these honest parties will broadcast the signer's signature on each m which all honest parties will process and thus terminate with $|\mathsf{detect}| = 2$ and output $\perp$.

Communication Complexity. Each party gossips at most two messages of size $O(\lambda + n + \ell)$ and multicasts at most two messages of size $O(\lambda + \ell)$. Since $q = \Theta(\lambda)$, each party sends an expected $O(\lambda)$ messages in each gossip step. Thus, communication complexity is overall $O(\lambda n^2 + n\lambda^2 + \ell(\lambda + n^2))$ which, when $\ell = O(\lambda)$, is $O(\lambda n^2 + \lambda^2 n)$. For $n \geq \lambda$, we have $O(\lambda n^2 + \lambda^2 n) = O(\lambda n^2)$. For $n < \lambda$, there is a trivial solution to achieve $O(\lambda n^2)$ communication complexity. Namely, one can run standard Dolev-Strong broadcast [DS83] with multi-signatures which has communication complexity $O(n^3+\lambda n^2+\ell n^2)$. Since $n < \lambda$, we have $n^3 < \lambda n^2$, and since we have $\ell = O(\lambda)$, it follows that $O(n^3 + \lambda n^2 + \ell n^2) = O(\lambda n^2)$.

Theorem 1. *Let n, t be such that $t < (1 - \epsilon) \cdot n$ for some constant $\epsilon \in (0, 1)$. Then $\Pi_{\mathsf{BC}}^{t,\epsilon}$ (Fig. 2) is t-secure when run on a synchronous network and n-weakly valid when run on an asynchronous network.*

3.2 Broadcast Extension Protocol

Due to space constraints and its similarity to a protocol of Nayak et al. [NRS+20], we only provide a high-level overview of our synchronous broadcast extension protocol that achieves $O(\ell n/\epsilon + \lambda n^2)$ communication complexity for $t < (1 - \epsilon) \cdot n$; we elaborate in the full version [BCLZL22]. As in Nayak

6 For rounds $r \geq t + 1$ we only require $t + 1$ signatures including the sender's.

7 We conjecture that the protocol without these extra messages also satisfies consistency, but the protocol as written has the same asymptotic complexity and therefore we leave it as future work to prove it.

et al. (Figure 3 in [NRS+20]), the protocol is divided into two phases. In the first phase, the designated sender uses erasure codes to split their input message m into n equally-sized chunks, one per party. These are then accumulated into a constant-sized value z, which is broadcast using a suitably efficient protocol $\Pi_{\mathsf{BC}}^{t,\epsilon}$ (e.g., Fig. 2). The second phase broadly follows Dolev-Strong, except the sender first computes proofs of inclusion for each party's chunk in z and sends the chunk and proof to the relevant party. Then, as in Dolev-Strong, the sender signs a message and *multicasts* it. As in Fig. 2, in subsequent rounds parties will *gossip* their signed message instead of multicasting it in order to keep communication low. After this, all parties multicast their own chunk and (valid) proof if they receive one. Then (and at the end of each of the $O(n + \log n)$ rounds) parties who received enough valid chunks can reconstruct m' (where $m' = m$ if the sender is honest) and, given enough signatures, can add their signature and act as senders in the next round until $O(n + \log n)$ rounds have elapsed.

4 Multivalued Intrusion-Tolerant Consensus

In this section, we construct an intrusion-tolerant Byzantine agreement protocol with $O((\ell + \lambda)n^3)$ communication complexity from intrusion-tolerant *graded consensus* and a binary Byzantine agreement protocol. Graded consensus is a relaxation of Byzantine agreement/consensus where parties input a value v and output a value/grade pair (v, g) where $g \in \{0, 1, 2\}$ (other choices of the grade set are possible). Apart from validity, liveness and intrusion tolerance, graded consensus satisfies *graded consistency* which ensures that 1) the grades of all honest parties never differs by more than 1; and 2) all honest parties output the same v given they output grade $g \geq 1$ (note parties may output $(\bot, 0)$). In the full version [BCLZL22], we formally define and construct a graded consensus protocol with a high validity threshold and $O(\ell n^3)$ communication complexity. Our overall protocol is a modification Mostéfaoui and Raynal's asynchronous protocol for $t < n/3$ [MR17] which is not framed in terms of graded consensus.

Let $\Pi_{\mathsf{BA}}^{t_a,t_s}$ be a Byzantine agreement protocol with input domain $\{0, 1\}$ that is t_a-secure and t_s-valid with termination. In the full version [BCLZL22], we present a modified version of the protocol from [BKL19] with expected communication complexity $O(\lambda n^3)$ *without trusted setup* that satisfies these requirements. Let $\Pi_{\mathsf{GC}}^{t_a,t_s}$ be a t_a-secure and t_s-graded valid multivalued graded consensus protocol. We present intrusion-tolerant Byzantine agreement protocol $\Pi_{\mathsf{IT}}^{t_a,t_s}$ in Fig. 3.

We describe the protocol from the perspective of a party P_i with initial value $v_i \in V$. First, P_i runs the multivalued graded consensus protocol $\Pi_{\mathsf{GC}}^{t_a,t_s}$ on input v_i and outputs (v, g) (step 2). Then, if $g = 2$, P_i proposes 1 to $\Pi_{\mathsf{BA}}^{t_a,t_s}$ and otherwise proposes 0 (step 3). In particular, if an honest party P_i proposes 1, then by graded consistency, all honest parties output (v, g) from Π_{GC} with $g \in \{1, 2\}$, and so if bit 1 is decided in $\Pi_{\mathsf{BA}}^{t_a,t_s}$ then all parties can safely output v. Given this occurs, P_i then signs and multicasts the value v (received previously from the output of the graded consensus protocol) along with the signature, otherwise it multicasts $\bot$ together with a signature (step 4). In the final phase

$\Pi_{\mathsf{IT}}^{t_a,t_s}(v_i)$

1. Set $\mathsf{aux}_i = \bot, \mathsf{bp} = 0$.
2. Run $\Pi_{\mathsf{GC}}^{t_a,t_s}$ using input v_i.
3. Upon receiving output (v, g) from $\Pi_{\mathsf{GC}}^{t_a,t_s}$: set $\mathsf{aux}_i = v$. If $g = 2$, set $\mathsf{bp} = 1$. Run $\Pi_{\mathsf{BA}}^{t_a,t_s}$ using input bp.
4. Upon receiving output b from $\Pi_{\mathsf{BA}}^{t_a,t_s}$: if $b = 1$, then multicast $\langle \mathsf{commit}, \mathsf{aux}_i \rangle_i$. Otherwise, multicast $\langle \mathsf{commit}, \bot \rangle_i$.
5. Upon receiving $t_s + 1$ signatures of $(\mathsf{commit}, \mathsf{aux})$ from distinct parties: multicast $t_s + 1$ such signatures, output aux and terminate.

Fig. 3. Intrusion-tolerant multivalued Byzantine agreement from the perspective of party P_i.

of the protocol, P_i outputs a value aux (and terminates) if it received that value with at least $t_s + 1$ valid signatures, ensuring that at least one signature on aux is from an honest party (step 5).

Communication Complexity. $\Pi_{\mathsf{GC}}^{t_a,t_s}$ (step 2) has a communication complexity bounded by $O(\ell n^3)$ (note it is signature-free). $\Pi_{\mathsf{BA}}^{t_a,t_s}$ (step 3) has an expected complexity of $O(\lambda n^3)$. The multicast of commit messages in steps 4 and 5 an additional complexity of $O(\lambda n^3 + \ell n^2)$ using regular signatures or $O(n^3 + (\lambda + \ell)n^2)$ using aggregate signatures. Thus, the overall expected complexity of $\Pi_{\mathsf{IT}}^{t_a,t_s}$ is $O((\lambda + \ell)n^3)$.

Theorem 2. *Let n, t_s, t_a be such that $0 \le t_a < \frac{n}{3} \le t_s < \frac{n}{2}$ and $t_a + 2 \cdot t_s < n$. Then Byzantine agreement protocol $\Pi_{\mathsf{IT}}^{t_a,t_s}$ (Fig. 3) is t_s-valid and t_a-secure with intrusion tolerance.*

5 Communication-Efficient Network-Agnostic DKG

In this section, we construct our communication-efficient network-agnostic distributed key generation protocol $\Pi_{\mathsf{DKG}}^{t_a,t_s}$ with threshold $d = t_s + 1$. We prove it t_s-secure when run over a synchronous network and t_a-secure when run over an asynchronous network. We present Π_{DKG} in Fig. 4 which uses two helper functions that are defined in Fig. 5. We recall public parameters $par = (\mathbb{G}, p, g, h)$ introduced in Sect. 2, where g and h are independent generators of the cyclic group $\mathbb{G}$ of prime order p. Π_{DKG} relies on the following underlying protocols:

- Π_{ADKG}: an asynchronous DKG protocol. We assume that Π_{ADKG} is (t_a, d)-secure with threshold $d = t_s + 1$ and has $O(\lambda n^3)$ communication complexity. The protocol from Das et al. [DYX+22] satisfies these requirements.
- $\Pi_{\mathsf{BC\text{-}Ext}}$: a broadcast protocol with default value $\bot_{bc}$. We assume that $\Pi_{\mathsf{BC\text{-}Ext}}$ is t_s-secure when run on a synchronous network, t_a-weakly valid on an asynchronous network, and t_s-externally valid. For a message of length ℓ, we

$\Pi_{\mathsf{DKG}}^{t_a,t_s}$

1. Set $=$ $\mathsf{ready} = \mathsf{false}$. Choose two random polynomials f_i, f'_i over $\mathbb{Z}_p$ of degree t_s: $f_i(z) = a_{i0} + a_{i1}z + \ldots + a_{it_s}z^{t_s}$, $f'_i(z) = b_{i0} + b_{i1}z + \ldots + b_{it_s}z^{t_s}$. Let $z_i = a_{i0}$. Then:
   (a) For all $k \in [0, t_s]$, compute $C_{ik} = g^{a_{ik}}h^{b_{ik}}$.
   (b) For all $j \in [1, n]$, compute $s_{ij} = f_i(j)$, $u_{ij} = f'_i(j)$ and $c_{ij} = \mathsf{pke.Enc}(\mathsf{ek}_j, (s_{ij}, u_{ij}))$.
   (c) For all $j \in [1, n]$, compute $\pi_{ij} = \mathsf{nizk}_1.\mathsf{Prove}(X_1, \omega_1 = (s_{ij}, u_{ij}))$.
   Let $M_i = (C_i = (C_{i0}, \ldots, C_{it_s}), c_i = (c_{i1}, \ldots, c_{in}), \pi_i = (\pi_{i1}, \ldots, \pi_{in}))$. Run n instances of $\Pi_{\mathsf{BC\text{-}Ext}}^{t_s,\frac{1}{2}}$ with senders $P_1, \ldots, P_n$ using external validity predicate Valid with input M_i in instance i.
2. At time T: Let $(M'_1, \ldots, M'_n)$ be the output from the n instances of $\Pi_{\mathsf{BC\text{-}Ext}}^{t_s,\frac{1}{2}}$ where M'_j was output from instance $j \in [1, n]$:
   (a) If $\left|\{j \in [1, n] : M'_j \neq \bot_{bc}\}\right| \geq n - t_s$: Compute $(L_1, \ldots, L_n) = \mathsf{Split}(M'_1, \ldots, M'_n)$, $\mathsf{acc.Eval}(ak, (L_1, \ldots, L_n)) = z$ and $(w_1, \ldots, w_n) = \mathsf{acc.CreateWits}(ak, z, ((1, L_1), \ldots, (n, L_n)))$. Run $\Pi_{\mathsf{IT}}^{t_a,t_s}$ using input z.
   (b) Otherwise, run $\Pi_{\mathsf{IT}}^{t_a,t_s}$ using input $\bot_{dkg}$.
3. Upon receiving output z_{it} from $\Pi_{\mathsf{IT}}^{t_a,t_s}$: if $z_{it} \in \{\bot_{it}, \bot_{dkg}\}$, run Π_{ADKG}. Otherwise, set $=$ true.
4. Upon setting $=$ true: if $z = z_{it}$, for $j \in [1, n]$, send $(\mathsf{part}, L_j, w_j)$ to P_j.
5. Upon receiving $(\mathsf{part}, L_i = (c^*_i, C^*_i, Q), w_i)$: wait until $=$ true (never satisfied if Π_{ADKG} is invoked). Then, if $z_{it} \neq \bot$ and $\mathsf{acc.Verify}(ak, z_{it}, w_i, (i, L_i)) = 1$, set $\mathsf{ready} = \mathsf{true}$.
6. Upon setting $\mathsf{ready} = \mathsf{true}$: let $x_i = \sum_{j \in Q} s_{ji}$ and $x'_i = \sum_{j \in Q} u_{ji}$ where s_{ji} and u_{ji} are decrypted from c^*_i using $\mathsf{pke.Dec}$. Compute $D_i = g^{x_i}$, $C''_i = g^{x_i}h^{x'_i}$ and $\pi'_i = \mathsf{nizk}_2.\mathsf{Prove}(X_2, \omega_2 = (x_i, x'_i))$ where X_2 is defined with respect to $A = D_i$ and $B = C''_i$. Multicast $(\mathsf{recon}, D_i, \pi'_j, L_j = (c^*_j, C^*_j, Q), w_j)$.
7. Upon receiving $(\mathsf{recon}, D_j, \pi'_j, L_j = (c^*_j, C^*_j, Q), w_j)$ for $t_s + 1$ distinct values j with 1) $\mathsf{acc.Verify}(ak, z_{it}, w_j, (j, L_j)) = 1$ and 2) $\mathsf{nizk}_2.\mathsf{Verify}(X_2, \pi'_i) = 1$ using $A = D_j$ and $B = C^*_j$:
   (a) Wait until $\mathsf{ready} = \mathsf{true}$.
   (b) Consider $g^{F(x)}$, where $F(x)$ is the polynomial defined by Lagrange interpolation of the $t_s + 1$ distinct values $D_j = g^{x_j} = g^{F(j)}$ in the exponent. Compute $y = g^{F(0)}$. For $j \in [1, n]$, compute $\mathsf{ps}_j = g^{F(j)}$. Output $(x_i, (\mathsf{ps}_1, \ldots, \mathsf{ps}_n), y)$ and terminate.

Fig. 4. DKG protocol with threshold $d = t_s + 1$ from the perspective of party P_i. T denotes the time taken by $\Pi_{\mathsf{BC\text{-}Ext}}^{t_s,\frac{1}{2}}$ to terminate when run in synchrony. Note under synchrony that each step will be executed in sequence.

Helper functions for $\Pi_{\mathsf{DKG}}^{t_a,t_s}$

- $\underline{\mathsf{Valid}(M_j)}$: Return true if and only M_j can be parsed as $M_j = (C_i = (C_{j0}, \ldots, C_{jt_s}), c_j = (c_{j1}, \ldots, c_{jn}), \pi_j = (\pi_{j1}, \ldots, \pi_{jn}))$ and, for all $k \in [1, n]$, $\mathsf{nizk}_1.\mathsf{Verify}(X_1, \pi_{jk}) = 1$.
- $\underline{\mathsf{Split}(M_1, \ldots, M_n)}$: Let $Q = [q_1, \ldots, q_s] \subseteq [1, n]$ be the maximal set such that $M_j \neq \perp$. Then, for $j \in [1, n]$: let $c_j^* = (c_{q_1 j}, \ldots, c_{q_s j})$ and $C_j^* = \prod_{q \in Q} C_{j,q}^*$ where $C_{j,q}^* = \prod_{k=0}^{t_s} (C_{mk})^{j^k}$ for each $q \in Q$, and then let $L_j = (c_j^*, C_j^*, Q)$. Finally, output $(L_1, \ldots, L_n)$.

Fig. 5. DKG helper functions from the perspective of party P_i.

require that $\Pi_{\mathsf{BC\text{-}Ext}}$ has communication complexity $O(\ell n + \lambda n^2)$. Our extension protocol (formalised in [BCLZL22]) satisfies these requirements.
- Π_{IT}: a multivalued Byzantine agreement protocol with default value $\perp_{it}$. We assume that Π_{IT} is t_a-secure with intrusion tolerance and t_s-valid with termination, and has $O(\lambda n^3)$ communication complexity. The protocol Π_{IT} defined in Fig. 3 satisfies these requirements.

We also assume the existence of a public-key encryption scheme $\mathsf{pke} = (\mathsf{KeyGen}, \mathsf{Enc}, \mathsf{Dec})$, an accumulator acc, and a linear erasure coding scheme rs. Finally, we require two NIZK proof systems nizk_1 and nizk_2 which define the following relations:

- nizk_1: Statements X_1 and witnesses $(s_{ij}, u_{ij}) \in \mathbb{Z}_p^2$, where X_1 is the statement that $\prod_{k=0}^{t_s} (C_{ik})^{j^k} = g^{s_{ij}} h^{u_{ij}}$ and c_{ij} is an encryption of (s_{ij}, u_{ij}) under ek_j, where variables C_{ik} and c_{ij} are as defined in step 1 of Π_{DKG}.
- nizk_2: Statements X_2 and witnesses $(x_i, x_i') \in \mathbb{Z}_p^2$, where X_2 is the statement, given (public) values A and B, that $A = g^{x_i}$ and $B = g^{x_i} h^{x_i'}$.

In the following, we give a step-by-step description of Π_{DKG} (Fig. 4).

Step 1: Let P_i be an honest party executing Π_{DKG}. P_i chooses two random polynomials f_i, f_i' of degree t_s with coefficients a_{ik} and b_{ik} in $\mathbb{Z}_p$ for $k \in [0, t_s]$. In this step, P_i will share points $(j, f_i(j))$ and $(j, f_i'(j))$ with each party P_j, $j \in [1, n]$, using public-key encryption scheme pke. As in Pedersen's verifiable secret sharing scheme [Ped92], P_i will also compute Pedersen commitments $C_{ik} = g^{a_{ik}} h^{b_{ik}}$ that allow parties to evaluate the polynomials in the exponents g and h together. In particular, the inclusion of polynomial f' blinds f such that values that contribute to the final secret are hidden from the adversary until after it has been decided, preventing the adversary from biasing the secret. In order for all parties to verify that all parties have received correct sharings, P_i will further compute a NIZK π_{ij} via nizk_1 for each P_j that verifies that the encrypted values under P_j's key are exactly $f_i(j)$ and $f_i'(j)$. All n parties then invoke $\Pi_{\mathsf{BC\text{-}Ext}}$ (secure broadcast), inputting a message to the i-th instance containing these Pedersen commitments, encryptions for all n parties and the corresponding NIZK proofs.

Steps 2 and 3: If the network is synchronous, then by t_s-security of $\Pi_{\mathsf{BC\text{-}Ext}}$ and since at least $n - t_s$ honest parties broadcast, all parties will agree on the same set of values of size $\geq n - t_s$ once all instances of $\Pi_{\mathsf{BC\text{-}Ext}}$ terminate at the same time T. By t_s-external validity of $\Pi_{\mathsf{BC\text{-}Ext}}$, only messages that are Valid (Fig. 5) – namely, those which are well-formed and contain n valid NIZKs – can be output. Note in asynchrony that $\Pi_{\mathsf{BC\text{-}Ext}}$ does not satisfy consistency, so honest parties could output different messages. To resolve this, it would be natural for parties to execute consensus on the output of $\Pi_{\mathsf{BC\text{-}Ext}}$ that ensures t_s-validity in synchrony and t_a-security in asynchrony. However, not all parties may output $n - t_s$ values from $\Pi_{\mathsf{BC\text{-}Ext}}$, so parties require a mechanism to 'abort' if not enough values are obtained from consensus.

We use intrusion-tolerant consensus Π_{IT} to efficiently solve this problem. Rather than proposing the entire $O(\lambda n^2)$-sized output of $\Pi_{\mathsf{BC\text{-}Ext}}$ to consensus, P_i instead proposes an accumulated value z to Π_{IT}. Intuitively, z accumulates n values (one per party) each of size $O(\lambda n)$ corresponding to the information that each party 'needs' to eventually reconstruct their secret share and the common public key; we describe these values further below. If an honest party does not output enough values from $\Pi_{\mathsf{BC\text{-}Ext}}$, they instead propose $\bot_{dkg}$ to Π_{IT}. Π_{IT} guarantees that a decided value is either one proposed by an honest party or $\bot$. Consequently, if Π_{IT} outputs $v \in \{\bot, \bot_{dkg}\}$, all honest parties fallback to Π_{ADKG}. This will not occur in synchrony and may or may not occur in asynchrony. Otherwise, all honest parties output the same accumulated value z.

Steps 4 and 5: If $z \notin \{\bot, \bot_{dkg}\}$ is decided by Π_{IT}, then z must have been proposed by an honest party, say P_j. Assuming this is true, P_j (plus any other honest party that output z) sends each party their 'value' accumulated in z alongside a proof of membership. Party P_i obtains their value L_i this way, where L_i is computed using Split (Fig. 5). More precisely, L_i contains:

- The same Q for all n parties, corresponding to the 'qualified' set of parties of size $\geq n - t_s$ from which P_j received values from $\Pi_{\mathsf{BC\text{-}Ext}}$;
- $|Q|$ ciphertexts encrypting $f_q(i)$ and $f'_q(i)$ to P_i for all $q \in Q$; and
- Commitment $C^*_j = g^{\sum_{q \in Q} f_q(i)} h^{\sum_{q \in Q} f'_q(i)}$.

These messages allow each party to reconstruct a sharing of a secret $\sum_{q \in Q} f_q(0)$. After deciding z from Π_{IT}, P_j sends the relevant part message to all parties, which parties verify is correct with acc.Verify.

Steps 6 and 7: At this point, P_i has received a valid message of the form $(\mathsf{part}, L_i = (c^*_i, C^*_i, Q), w_i)$. By decrypting values in c^*_i, P_i can deduce its own secret share $x_i = \sum_{j \in Q} f_j(i)$ but not necessarily the corresponding public shares $g^{F(1)}, \ldots, g^{F(n)}$ and public key $g^{F(0)}$. Thus, parties will collaborate to compute

g^x by reconstructing the polynomial $F(\cdot) = \sum_{j \in Q} f_j(\cdot)$ in the exponent of g. To this end, parties will reveal their share g^{x_i} and then compute a proof with nizk_2 that shows that it is consistent with the sharings of polynomials $f_j(\cdot)$ and $f'_j(\cdot)$ in step 1 of the protocol (which were previously hidden). More precisely, P_i computes $D_i = g^{x_i}$, $x'_i = \sum_{j \in Q} f'_j(i)$ (by decryption of c^*_i), $C''_i = g^{x_i} h^{x'_i}$ and $\pi'_j = \mathsf{nizk}_2.\mathsf{Prove}(X_2, (x_i, x'_i))$. Then, P_i multicasts a reconstruction message recon containing D_i, the proof π'_j and P_i's value L_i alongside w_i, the proof of inclusion in z.

On receipt of a recon message from P_j, P_i can verify that 1) L_j was accumulated in z (using $\mathsf{acc.Verify}$), and 2) the NIZK π'_j is correct and, in particular, is consistent with the value $C^*_i = g^{x^*_i} h^{x'^*_i}$ contained in L_j. Because these checks pass, the value C^*_i must be of the form $g^{x_i} h^{x'_i}$ computed by a honest party that output z from Π_{IT}, and thus the value D_j contained in the recon message must be of the form $g^{\sum_{k \in Q} f_k(j)}$, i.e. it must be a valid share. When P_i receives $t_s + 1$ such values, P_i evaluates $F(0)$ in the exponent of g to derive public key g^x and $F(j)$ for $j \in [1, n]$ to derive the n public shares. At this point, P_i terminates.

Communication Complexity. At step 1, each party invokes secure broadcast with $O(\lambda n)$-sized input (assuming NIZKs are size $O(\lambda)$, each which costs $O(n\ell + \lambda n^2)$, so this step incurs $O(\lambda n^3)$ overhead. Apart from using generic NIZKs, one can instantiate nizk_1 with $O(\lambda)$-sized proofs in a suitable Paillier group under the decisional composite residuosity assumption [CGG+20]. At step 2, Π_{IT} takes $O(\lambda n^3)$ communication. If parties invoke Π_{ADKG}, then steps 4 to 7 are ignored, and Π_{ADKG} costs $O(\lambda n^3)$ itself. At step 4, $O(n)$ parties send n part messages, each of size $O(\lambda n)$, so this incurs $O(\lambda n^3)$ overhead. At step 5, $O(n)$ parties multicast a recon message of size $O(\lambda n)$, incurring $O(\lambda n^3)$ overhead, again assuming nizk_2 has $O(\lambda)$-sized proofs. nizk_2 can be instantiated using the efficient NIZK used in [SBKN21] in the random oracle model in any cryptographic group $\mathbb{G}$. Thus, Π_{DKG} has a communication complexity of $O(\lambda n^3)$.

Theorem 3. *Let n, t_s, t_a be such that $0 \le t_a < \frac{n}{3} \le t_s < \frac{n}{2}$ and $t_a + 2 \cdot t_s < n$, and let $d = t_s + 1$. Assuming a plain PKI, ROM and a CRS, the distributed key generation protocol $\Pi_{\mathsf{DKG}}^{t_a, t_s}$ (Figs. 4 and 5) is (t_s, d)-secure when run on a synchronous network and (t_a, d)-secure when run on an asynchronous network.*

Corruption Thresholds. Our construction shows that $t_a + 2 \cdot t_s < n$ corruptions are sufficient to ensure (t_s, d)-security in synchrony and (t_a, d)-security in asynchrony for $d = t_s + 1$. We note that it is also *necessary*:

Lemma 1. *Let n, t_a, t_s be such that $t_a + 2 \cdot t_s \ge n$. If DKG protocol Π is t_s-uniform in a synchronous network, then it cannot also be t_a-consistent in an asynchronous network.*

6 Multi-party Computation with Asynchronous Fallback

In this section, we describe an optimized version of the MPC protocol with fallback by Blum, Liu-Zhang and Loss [BLL20], with communication complexity

$O(n^2\lambda)$ bits per multiplication gate. This matches the asymptotic communication complexity of the current most efficient purely asynchronous MPC protocols [HNP08,CHLZ21] in the setting of optimal resilience $t < n/3$, without the use of multiplicative-homomorphic threshold encryption schemes.

The protocol makes use of a threshold additive homomorphic encryption scheme (Keygen, TEnc, TDec, TRec) (which may be generated with our DKG protocol), NIZKs, using standard relations detailed in the full version [BCLZL22], and a secure broadcast protocol $\Pi_{\mathsf{BC}}^{t_s,1/2}$ that achieves t_s-security when the network is synchronous and t_a-weak validity when the network is asynchronous and with communication complexity $O(n\ell + \mathsf{poly}(n,\lambda))$, where ℓ is the input size.

The protocol is divided into two phases: an offline and an online phase. The offline phase generates Beaver multiplication triples (in encrypted form) and can be executed without the knowledge of the inputs. In the online phase, parties distribute their inputs and process the circuit to evaluate in a gate-by-gate fashion, where addition gates are processed locally and multiplication gates are processed with the help of the Beaver triples, via two public reconstructions.

Triple Generation. In order to generate Beaver triples (c.f. the full version [BCLZL22]) we make use of a multi-valued broadcast protocol $\Pi_{\mathsf{BC}}^{t_s,1/2}$ that is t_s-secure when run on a synchronous network and t_a-weakly valid that terminates after T_{bc} rounds.

Communication Complexity. The communication complexity amounts to n parallel instances of secure broadcast with input size ℓ encryptions and non-interactive zero-knowledge proofs, and an additive term (independent of the number ℓ) corresponding to n parallel instances of BA. This incurs a total communication of $O(n^2\ell(|\mathtt{nizk}| + |\mathtt{ciph}|) + \mathsf{poly}(n,\lambda))$ bits, where $|\mathtt{nizk}|$ and $|\mathtt{ciph}|$ are the size of the proofs and ciphertexts in the protocol.

Lemma 2. *Let n, t_s, t_a be such that $t_a, t_s < n$. $\Pi_{\mathsf{triples}}^{t_a,t_s}(\ell)$ is an n-party protocol with communication complexity $O(n^2\ell(|\mathtt{nizk}|+|\mathtt{ciph}|)+\mathsf{poly}(n,\lambda))$, where $|\mathtt{nizk}|$ and $|\mathtt{ciph}|$ are the size of the proofs and ciphertexts in the protocol, achieving the following guarantees:*

- *When the network is synchronous and there are up to t_s corruptions, all parties output the same ℓ encrypted random multiplication triples, with the plaintexts unknown to the adversary.*
- *When the network is asynchronous and there are up to t_a corruptions, the output of each party P_i is either ℓ encrypted random multiplication triples with the plaintexts unknown to the adversary or $\perp$.*

Synchronous Protocol with Unanimous Output. We present the synchronous MPC protocol that achieves full security when the network is synchronous and there are t_s corruptions, but also achieves unanimous output up to t_a corruptions under an asynchronous network. The protocol is an optimized version of the one in [BLL20], where the multiplication gates are executed using

Beaver triples generated during an Offline Phase, and incurs a communication complexity of $O(n^2)$ field elements per multiplication gate. We defer the protocol description to the full version [BCLZL22], and only provide a high level description here.

The protocol closely follows the one by Blum, Liu-Zhang and Loss [BLL20], which uses a setup for threshold additive-homomorphic encryption. This approach was initially introduced by Cramer, Damgard and Nielsen [CDN01], and the idea is that parties keep threshold encryptions of the circuit wires and perform computations on a gate-by-gate fashion. First, the inputs are distributed in the form of a threshold encryption. Since the threshold encryption scheme is additively homomorphic, the addition gates can be performed locally by the parties. Multiplication gates are processed in a standard manner using Beaver triples. The only difference in the network-agnostic setting is that in some parts of the protocol (such as the input distribution, or the triples generation), in the case the network is asynchronous, there might be information missing (e.g. input ciphertexts or encrypted triples). For that, the protocol in [BLL20] makes use of an abort flag. As soon as a party detects that not enough information has arrived by a certain amount of time, it sets the flag to 1, and stops executing further steps of the protocol. This can only make the protocol stall, but will not compromise security. Before the output is decrypted, an agreement on a core-set sub-primitive also known as ACS (see [BLL20] for details on this primitive) is run to see whether parties must decrypt or not. This ensures that parties agree on whether the output was computed. If yes, they can jointly (and safely) decrypt the output ciphertext. If not, all parties output $\bot$.

Lemma 3. *Let* n, t_s, t_a *be such that* $0 \leq t_a < n/3 \leq t_s < n/2$ *and* $t_a + 2t_s < n$*. Protocol* $\Pi_{\mathsf{smpc}}^{t_s,t_a}$ *has communication complexity* $O(n^2|C|(|\mathtt{nizk}| + |\mathtt{ciph}|) + \mathsf{poly}(n, \lambda))$ *bits, where* C *is the circuit to evaluate,* $|\mathtt{nizk}|$ *and* $|\mathtt{ciph}|$ *are the size of the proofs and ciphertexts in the protocol, and satisfies:*

- *When run in a synchronous network, it achieves full security up to* t_s *corruptions.*
- *When run in an asynchronous network, it achieves unanimous output with weak termination up to* t_a *corruptions and has* $n - t_s$ *output quality.*

6.1 Protocol Compiler

In this section, we restate the protocol $\Pi_{\mathsf{mpc}}^{t_s,t_a}$ for secure function evaluation presented in [BLL20] which tolerates up to t_s (resp. t_a) corruptions when the network is synchronous (resp. asynchronous), for any $0 \leq t_a < \frac{n}{3} \leq t_s < \frac{n}{2}$ satisfying $t_a + 2t_s < n$. The protocol is based on two sub-protocols:

- $\Pi_{\mathsf{smpc}}^{t_s,t_a}$ is a secure function evaluation protocol which gives full security up to t_s corruptions when run in a synchronous network, and achieves unanimous output with weak termination up to t_a corruptions and has $n - t_s$ output quality when run in an asynchronous network.

- $\Pi^{t_a}_{\mathsf{ampc}}$ is a secure function evaluation protocol which gives full security up to t_a corruptions and has $n - t_a$ output quality when run in an asynchronous network.

Theorem 4 **([BLL20]).** *Let n, t_s, t_a be such that $0 \leq t_a < \frac{n}{3} \leq t_s < \frac{n}{2}$ and $t_a + 2t_s < n$. Given sub-protocols $\Pi^{t_s,t_a}_{\mathsf{smpc}}$ and $\Pi^{t_a}_{\mathsf{ampc}}$ with the guarantees described above, there is a protocol $\Pi^{t_s,t_a}_{\mathsf{mpc}}$ with communication complexity the sum of the communication of the two sub-protocols, satisfying the following properties:*

1. *When run in a synchronous network, it achieves full security up to t_s corruptions.*
2. *When run in an asynchronous network, it achieves full security up to t_a corruptions and has $n - t_s$ output quality.*

Assuming a setup for linear-homomorphic threshold encryption and a CRS for NIZKs, the size of the proofs and ciphertexts in $\Pi^{t_s,t_a}_{\mathsf{smpc}}$ are of size $O(\lambda)$. Using Lemma 3 and Theorem 4, and a quadratic asynchronous protocol (see e.g. [HNP08]) we obtain a protocol $\Pi^{t_s,t_a}_{\mathsf{mpc}}$ with communication complexity $O(n^2)$ field elements per multiplication gate. This improves over the communication complexity of the best previous network-agnostic MPC protocol by a linear factor and matches the current state of the art on purely asynchronous MPC protocols with the same setup.

Corollary 1. *Assuming a setup for linear-homomorphic threshold encryption and a CRS, there is an MPC protocol $\Pi^{t_s,t_a}_{\mathsf{mpc}}$ with communication complexity $O(n^2|C|\lambda + \mathsf{poly}(n, \lambda))$ bits, satisfying the following properties:*

1. *When run in a synchronous network, it achieves full security up to t_s corruptions.*
2. *When run in an asynchronous network, it achieves full security up to t_a corruptions and has $n - t_s$ output quality.*

Using Theorem 3 and multi-string NIZKs [GO07], we can base our protocol on a plain public-key infrastructure, obtaining the first network-agnostic MPC protocol based on plain PKI, and with communication complexity comparable with previous state of the art network-agnostic MPC.

Corollary 2. *Assuming a plain PKI, there is an MPC protocol $\Pi^{t_s,t_a}_{\mathsf{mpc}}$ with communication complexity $O(n^3|C|\mathsf{poly}(\lambda) + \mathsf{poly}(n, \lambda))$ bits, satisfying the following properties:*

1. *When run in a synchronous network, it achieves full security up to t_s corruptions.*
2. *When run in an asynchronous network, it achieves full security up to t_a corruptions and has $n - t_s$ output quality.*

Observe that our definition of DKG secrecy is simulation-based. Thus, when using our DKG protocol to replace the trusted setup to obtain the above results, in the proofs of the above results in the full version [BCLZL22], the MPC simulator will execute the DKG simulator to simulate its messages.

References

[ABKL22a] Alexandru, A.B., Blum, E., Katz, J., Loss, J.: State machine replication under changing network conditions. In: Agrawal, S., Lin, D. (eds.) ASIACRYPT 2022. LNCS, vol. 13791, pp. 681–710. Springer, Cham (2022). https://doi.org/10.1007/978-3-031-22963-3_23

[ABKL22b] Alexandru, A.B., Blum, E., Katz, J., Loss, J.: State machine replication under changing network conditions. Cryptology ePrint Archive, Paper 2022/698 (2022). https://eprint.iacr.org/2022/698

[AC23] Appan, A., Choudhury, A.: Network agnostic MPC with statistical security. Cryptology ePrint Archive, Paper 2023/820 (2023). https://eprint.iacr.org/2023/820

[ACC22a] Appan, A., Chandramouli, A., Choudhury, A.: Perfectly-secure synchronous MPC with asynchronous fallback guarantees. In: Proceedings of the 2022 ACM Symposium on Principles of Distributed Computing, PODC 2022, pp. 92–102. Association for Computing Machinery, New York (2022)

[ACC22b] Appan, A., Chandramouli, A., Choudhury, A.: Perfectly secure synchronous MPC with asynchronous fallback guarantees against general adversaries. Cryptology ePrint Archive, Paper 2022/1047 (2022). https://eprint.iacr.org/2022/1047

[ACD+19] Abraham, I., et al.: Communication complexity of byzantine agreement, revisited. In: Robinson, P., Ellen, F. (eds.) 38th ACM PODC, pp. 317–326. ACM, July/August 2019

[AJM+21] Abraham, I., Jovanovic, P., Maller, M., Meiklejohn, S., Stern, G., Tomescu, A.: Reaching consensus for asynchronous distributed key generation. In: Proceedings of the 2021 ACM Symposium on Principles of Distributed Computing, pp. 363–373 (2021)

[AJM+22] Abraham, I., Jovanovic, P., Maller, M., Meiklejohn, S., Stern, G.: Bingo: adaptively secure packed asynchronous verifiable secret sharing and asynchronous distributed key generation. Cryptology ePrint Archive, Paper 2022/1759 (2022). https://eprint.iacr.org/2022/1759

[BCG93] Ben-Or, M., Canetti, R., Goldreich, O.: Asynchronous secure computation. In: 25th ACM STOC, pp. 52–61. ACM Press, May 1993

[BCLZL22] Bacho, R., Collins, D., Liu-Zhang, C.-D., Loss, J.: Network-agnostic security comes (almost) for free in DKG and MPC. Cryptology ePrint Archive, Paper 2022/1369 (2022). https://eprint.iacr.org/2022/1369

[Bea92] Beaver, D.: Efficient multiparty protocols using circuit randomization. In: Feigenbaum, J. (ed.) CRYPTO 1991. LNCS, vol. 576, pp. 420–432. Springer, Heidelberg (1992). https://doi.org/10.1007/3-540-46766-1_34

[BFO12] Ben-Sasson, E., Fehr, S., Ostrovsky, R.: Near-linear unconditionally-secure multiparty computation with a dishonest minority. In: Safavi-Naini, R., Canetti, R. (eds.) CRYPTO 2012. LNCS, vol. 7417, pp. 663–680. Springer, Heidelberg (2012). https://doi.org/10.1007/978-3-642-32009-5_39

[BKL19] Blum, E., Katz, J., Loss, J.: Synchronous consensus with optimal asynchronous fallback guarantees. In: Hofheinz, D., Rosen, A. (eds.) TCC 2019, Part I. LNCS, vol. 11891, pp. 131–150. Springer, Cham (2019). https://doi.org/10.1007/978-3-030-36030-6_6

[BKL21] Blum, E., Katz, J., Loss, J.: TARDIGRADE: an atomic broadcast protocol for arbitrary network conditions. In: Tibouchi, M., Wang, H. (eds.) ASI-

ACRYPT 2021, Part II. LNCS, vol. 13091, pp. 547–572. Springer, Cham (2021). https://doi.org/10.1007/978-3-030-92075-3_19

[BKR94] Ben-Or, M., Kelmer, B., Rabin, T.: Asynchronous secure computations with optimal resilience (extended abstract). In: Anderson, J., Toueg, S. (eds.) 13th ACM PODC, pp. 183–192. ACM, August 1994

[BL22] Bacho, R., Loss, J.: On the adaptive security of the threshold BLS signature scheme. In: Proceedings of the 2022 ACM SIGSAC Conference on Computer and Communications Security, CCS 2022, pp. 193–207. Association for Computing Machinery, New York (2022)

[BLL20] Blum, E., Liu-Zhang, C.-D., Loss, J.: Always have a backup plan: fully secure synchronous MPC with asynchronous fallback. In: Micciancio, D., Ristenpart, T. (eds.) CRYPTO 2020, Part II. LNCS, vol. 12171, pp. 707–731. Springer, Cham (2020). https://doi.org/10.1007/978-3-030-56880-1_25

[BP97] Barić, N., Pfitzmann, B.: Collision-free accumulators and fail-stop signature schemes without trees. In: Fumy, W. (ed.) EUROCRYPT 1997. LNCS, vol. 1233, pp. 480–494. Springer, Heidelberg (1997). https://doi.org/10.1007/3-540-69053-0_33

[BTH08] Beerliová-Trubíniová, Z., Hirt, M.: Perfectly-secure MPC with linear communication complexity. In: Canetti, R. (ed.) TCC 2008. LNCS, vol. 4948, pp. 213–230. Springer, Heidelberg (2008). https://doi.org/10.1007/978-3-540-78524-8_13

[CDN01] Cramer, R., Damgård, I., Nielsen, J.B.: Multiparty computation from threshold homomorphic encryption. In: Pfitzmann, B. (ed.) EUROCRYPT 2001. LNCS, vol. 2045, pp. 280–300. Springer, Heidelberg (2001). https://doi.org/10.1007/3-540-44987-6_18

[CF13] Catalano, D., Fiore, D.: Vector commitments and their applications. In: Kurosawa, K., Hanaoka, G. (eds.) PKC 2013. LNCS, vol. 7778, pp. 55–72. Springer, Heidelberg (2013). https://doi.org/10.1007/978-3-642-36362-7_5

[CGG+20] Canetti, R., Gennaro, R., Goldfeder, S., Makriyannis, N., Peled, U.: UC non-interactive, proactive, threshold ECDSA with identifiable aborts. In: Ligatti, J., Ou, X., Katz, J., Vigna, G. (eds.) ACM CCS 2020, pp. 1769–1787. ACM Press, November 2020

[CGJ+99] Canetti, R., Gennaro, R., Jarecki, S., Krawczyk, H., Rabin, T.: Adaptive security for threshold cryptosystems. In: Wiener, M. (ed.) CRYPTO 1999. LNCS, vol. 1666, pp. 98–116. Springer, Heidelberg (1999). https://doi.org/10.1007/3-540-48405-1_7

[CGMA85] Chor, B., Goldwasser, S., Micali, S., Awerbuch, B.: Verifiable secret sharing and achieving simultaneity in the presence of faults. In: 26th Annual Symposium on Foundations of Computer Science (SFCS 1985), pp. 383–395. IEEE (1985)

[CHLZ21] Chopard, A., Hirt, M., Liu-Zhang, C.-D.: On communication-efficient asynchronous MPC with adaptive security. In: Nissim, K., Waters, B. (eds.) TCC 2021, Part II. LNCS, vol. 13043, pp. 35–65. Springer, Cham (2021). https://doi.org/10.1007/978-3-030-90453-1_2

[Cho20] Choudhury, A.: Optimally-resilient unconditionally-secure asynchronous multi-party computation revisited. Cryptology ePrint Archive, Report 2020/906 (2020). https://eprint.iacr.org/2020/906

[CHP13] Choudhury, A., Hirt, M., Patra, A.: Asynchronous multiparty computation with linear communication complexity. In: Afek, Y. (ed.) DISC 2013. LNCS, vol. 8205, pp. 388–402. Springer, Heidelberg (2013). https://doi.org/10.1007/978-3-642-41527-2_27

[CKPS01] Cachin, C., Kursawe, K., Petzold, F., Shoup, V.: Secure and efficient asynchronous broadcast protocols. In: Kilian, J. (ed.) CRYPTO 2001. LNCS, vol. 2139, pp. 524–541. Springer, Heidelberg (2001). https://doi.org/10.1007/3-540-44647-8_31

[CL17] Cohen, R., Lindell, Y.: Fairness versus guaranteed output delivery in secure multiparty computation. J. Cryptol. **30**(4), 1157–1186 (2017). https://doi.org/10.1007/s00145-016-9245-5

[Coh16] Cohen, R.: Asynchronous secure multiparty computation in constant time. In: Cheng, C.-M., Chung, K.-M., Persiano, G., Yang, B.-Y. (eds.) PKC 2016, Part II. LNCS, vol. 9615, pp. 183–207. Springer, Heidelberg (2016). https://doi.org/10.1007/978-3-662-49387-8_8

[CP15] Choudhury, A., Patra, A.: Optimally resilient asynchronous MPC with linear communication complexity. In: Proceedings of the 2015 International Conference on Distributed Computing and Networking, ICDCN 2015. Association for Computing Machinery, New York (2015)

[CPS20] Chan, T.-H.H., Pass, R., Shi, E.: Sublinear-round byzantine agreement under corrupt majority. In: Kiayias, A., Kohlweiss, M., Wallden, P., Zikas, V. (eds.) PKC 2020, Part II. LNCS, vol. 12111, pp. 246–265. Springer, Cham (2020). https://doi.org/10.1007/978-3-030-45388-6_9

[DHLZ21] Deligios, G., Hirt, M., Liu-Zhang, C.-D.: Round-efficient byzantine agreement and multi-party computation with asynchronous fallback. In: Nissim, K., Waters, B. (eds.) TCC 2021, Part I. LNCS, vol. 13042, pp. 623–653. Springer, Cham (2021). https://doi.org/10.1007/978-3-030-90459-3_21

[DI06] Damgård, I., Ishai, Y.: Scalable secure multiparty computation. In: Dwork, C. (ed.) CRYPTO 2006. LNCS, vol. 4117, pp. 501–520. Springer, Heidelberg (2006). https://doi.org/10.1007/11818175_30

[DLZ23] Deligios, G., Liu-Zhang, C.-D.: Synchronous perfectly secure message transmission with optimal asynchronous fallback guarantees. Financial Cryptography and Data Security (2023)

[DS83] Dolev, D., Strong, H.R.: Authenticated algorithms for byzantine agreement. SIAM J. Comput. **12**(4), 656–666 (1983)

[DXR22] Das, S., Xiang, Z., Ren, L.: Powers of tau in asynchrony. Cryptology ePrint Archive, Paper 2022/1683 (2022). https://eprint.iacr.org/2022/1683

[DYX+22] Das, S., Yurek, T., Xiang, Z., Miller, A., Kokoris-Kogias, L., Ren, L.: Practical asynchronous distributed key generation. In: 2022 IEEE Symposium on Security and Privacy (SP), pp. 2518–2534 (2022)

[ElG84] ElGamal, T.: A public key cryptosystem and a signature scheme based on discrete logarithms. In: Blakley, G.R., Chaum, D. (eds.) CRYPTO 1984. LNCS, vol. 196, pp. 10–18. Springer, Heidelberg (1985). https://doi.org/10.1007/3-540-39568-7_2

[Fel87] Feldman, P.: A practical scheme for non-interactive verifiable secret sharing. In: 28th Annual Symposium on Foundations of Computer Science (SFCS 1987), pp. 427–438. IEEE (1987)

[FGH+02] Fitzi, M., Gottesman, D., Hirt, M., Holenstein, T., Smith, A.: Detectable byzantine agreement secure against faulty majorities. In: Ricciardi, A. (ed.) 21st ACM PODC, pp. 118–126. ACM, July 2002

[GJKR99] Gennaro, R., Jarecki, S., Krawczyk, H., Rabin, T.: Secure distributed key generation for discrete-log based cryptosystems. In: Stern, J. (ed.) EUROCRYPT 1999. LNCS, vol. 1592, pp. 295–310. Springer, Heidelberg (1999). https://doi.org/10.1007/3-540-48910-X_21

[GJKR07] Gennaro, R., Jarecki, S., Krawczyk, H., Rabin, T.: Secure distributed key generation for discrete-log based cryptosystems. J. Cryptol. **20**(1), 51–83 (2007). https://doi.org/10.1007/s00145-006-0347-3

[GJM+21] Gurkan, K., Jovanovic, P., Maller, M., Meiklejohn, S., Stern, G., Tomescu, A.: Aggregatable distributed key generation. In: Canteaut, A., Standaert, F.-X. (eds.) EUROCRYPT 2021. LNCS, vol. 12696, pp. 147–176. Springer, Cham (2021). https://doi.org/10.1007/978-3-030-77870-5_6

[GLL+21] Gao, Y., Lu, Y., Lu, Z., Tang, Q., Xu, J., Zhang, Z.: Efficient asynchronous byzantine agreement without private setups. arXiv preprint arXiv:2106.07831 (2021)

[GLL+22] Gao, Y., Lu, Y., Lu, Z., Tang, Q., Xu, J., Zhang, Z.: Efficient asynchronous byzantine agreement without private setups. In: 42nd IEEE International Conference on Distributed Computing Systems, ICDCS 2022, Bologna, Italy, 10–13 July 2022, pp. 246–257. IEEE (2022)

[GLS19] Goyal, V., Liu, Y., Song, Y.: Communication-efficient unconditional MPC with guaranteed output delivery. In: Boldyreva, A., Micciancio, D. (eds.) CRYPTO 2019, Part II. LNCS, vol. 11693, pp. 85–114. Springer, Cham (2019). https://doi.org/10.1007/978-3-030-26951-7_4

[GMW87] Goldreich, O., Micali, S., Wigderson, A.: How to play any mental game or a completeness theorem for protocols with honest majority. In: Aho, A. (ed.) 19th ACM STOC, pp. 218–229. ACM Press, May 1987

[GO07] Groth, J., Ostrovsky, R.: Cryptography in the multi-string model. In: Menezes, A. (ed.) CRYPTO 2007. LNCS, vol. 4622, pp. 323–341. Springer, Heidelberg (2007). https://doi.org/10.1007/978-3-540-74143-5_18

[Gro06] Groth, J.: Simulation-sound NIZK proofs for a practical language and constant size group signatures. In: Lai, X., Chen, K. (eds.) ASIACRYPT 2006. LNCS, vol. 4284, pp. 444–459. Springer, Heidelberg (2006). https://doi.org/10.1007/11935230_29

[GSZ20] Goyal, V., Song, Y., Zhu, C.: Guaranteed Output Delivery Comes Free in Honest Majority MPC. In: Micciancio, D., Ristenpart, T. (eds.) CRYPTO 2020, Part II. LNCS, vol. 12171, pp. 618–646. Springer, Cham (2020). https://doi.org/10.1007/978-3-030-56880-1_22

[HN06] Hirt, M., Nielsen, J.B.: Robust multiparty computation with linear communication complexity. In: Dwork, C. (ed.) CRYPTO 2006. LNCS, vol. 4117, pp. 463–482. Springer, Heidelberg (2006). https://doi.org/10.1007/11818175_28

[HNP05] Hirt, M., Nielsen, J.B., Przydatek, B.: Cryptographic asynchronous multiparty computation with optimal resilience. In: Cramer, R. (ed.) EUROCRYPT 2005. LNCS, vol. 3494, pp. 322–340. Springer, Heidelberg (2005). https://doi.org/10.1007/11426639_19

[HNP08] Hirt, M., Nielsen, J.B., Przydatek, B.: Asynchronous multi-party computation with quadratic communication. In: Aceto, L., Damgård, I., Goldberg, L.A., Halldórsson, M.M., Ingólfsdóttir, A., Walukiewicz, I. (eds.) ICALP 2008, Part II. LNCS, vol. 5126, pp. 473–485. Springer, Heidelberg (2008). https://doi.org/10.1007/978-3-540-70583-3_39

[IOZ14] Ishai, Y., Ostrovsky, R., Zikas, V.: Secure multi-party computation with identifiable abort. In: Garay, J.A., Gennaro, R. (eds.) CRYPTO 2014, Part II. LNCS, vol. 8617, pp. 369–386. Springer, Heidelberg (2014). https://doi.org/10.1007/978-3-662-44381-1_21

[KG09] Kate, A., Goldberg, I.: Distributed key generation for the internet. In: 2009 29th IEEE International Conference on Distributed Computing Systems, pp. 119–128. IEEE (2009)

[Lip12] Lipmaa, H.: Secure accumulators from euclidean rings without trusted setup. In: Bao, F., Samarati, P., Zhou, J. (eds.) ACNS 2012. LNCS, vol. 7341, pp. 224–240. Springer, Heidelberg (2012). https://doi.org/10.1007/978-3-642-31284-7_14

[MR10] Mostéfaoui, A., Raynal, M.: Signature-free broadcast-based intrusion tolerance: never decide a byzantine value. In: Lu, C., Masuzawa, T., Mosbah, M. (eds.) OPODIS 2010. LNCS, vol. 6490, pp. 143–158. Springer, Heidelberg (2010). https://doi.org/10.1007/978-3-642-17653-1_13

[MR17] Mostéfaoui, A., Raynal, M.: Signature-free asynchronous byzantine systems: from multivalued to binary consensus with $t < n/3$, $O(n^2)$ messages, and constant time. Acta Informatica **54**(5), 501–520 (2017). https://doi.org/10.1007/s00236-016-0269-y

[MR21a] Momose, A., Ren, L.: Multi-threshold byzantine fault tolerance. In: Proceedings of the 2021 ACM SIGSAC Conference on Computer and Communications Security, pp. 1686–1699 (2021)

[MR21b] Momose, A., Ren, L.: Optimal communication complexity of authenticated byzantine agreement. In: Gilbert, S. (ed.) 35th International Symposium on Distributed Computing (DISC 2021), Volume 209 of Leibniz International Proceedings in Informatics (LIPIcs), Dagstuhl, Germany, pp. 32:1–32:16. Schloss Dagstuhl - Leibniz-Zentrum für Informatik (2021)

[NRS+20] Nayak, K., Ren, L., Shi, E., Vaidya, N.H., Xiang, Z.: Improved extension protocols for byzantine broadcast and agreement. In: Attiya, H. (ed.) 34th International Symposium on Distributed Computing (DISC 2020), Volume 179 of Leibniz International Proceedings in Informatics (LIPIcs), Dagstuhl, Germany, pp. 28:1–28:17. Schloss Dagstuhl-Leibniz-Zentrum für Informatik (2020)

[Pai99] Paillier, P.: Public-key cryptosystems based on composite degree residuosity classes. In: Stern, J. (ed.) EUROCRYPT 1999. LNCS, vol. 1592, pp. 223–238. Springer, Heidelberg (1999). https://doi.org/10.1007/3-540-48910-X_16

[PCR08] Patra, A., Choudhury, A., Rangan,C.P.: Efficient asynchronous multiparty computation with optimal resilience. Cryptology ePrint Archive, Report 2008/425 (2008). https://eprint.iacr.org/2008/425

[PCR10] Patra, A., Choudhary, A., Rangan, C.P.: Efficient statistical asynchronous verifiable secret sharing with optimal resilience. In: Kurosawa, K. (ed.) ICITS 2009. LNCS, vol. 5973, pp. 74–92. Springer, Heidelberg (2010). https://doi.org/10.1007/978-3-642-14496-7_7

[PCR15] Patra, A., Choudhury, A., Pandu Rangan, C.: Efficient asynchronous verifiable secret sharing and multiparty computation. J. Cryptol. **28**(1), 49–109 (2013). https://doi.org/10.1007/s00145-013-9172-7

[Ped91] Pedersen, T.P.: A threshold cryptosystem without a trusted party. In: Davies, D.W. (ed.) EUROCRYPT 1991. LNCS, vol. 547, pp. 522–526. Springer, Heidelberg (1991). https://doi.org/10.1007/3-540-46416-6_47

[Ped92] Pedersen, T.P.: Non-interactive and information-theoretic secure verifiable secret sharing. In: Feigenbaum, J. (ed.) CRYPTO 1991. LNCS, vol. 576, pp. 129–140. Springer, Heidelberg (1992). https://doi.org/10.1007/3-540-46766-1_9

[PHGR13] Parno, B., Howell, J., Gentry, C., Raykova, M.: Pinocchio: nearly practical verifiable computation. In: 2013 IEEE Symposium on Security and Privacy, pp. 238–252. IEEE Computer Society Press, May 2013

[PSR02] Prabhu, B., Srinathan, K., Rangan, C.P.: Asynchronous unconditionally secure computation: an efficiency improvement. In: Menezes, A., Sarkar, P. (eds.) INDOCRYPT 2002. LNCS, vol. 2551, pp. 93–107. Springer, Heidelberg (2002). https://doi.org/10.1007/3-540-36231-2_9

[RS60] Reed, I.S., Solomon, G.: Polynomial codes over certain finite fields. J. Soc. Ind. Appl. Math. **8**(2), 300–304 (1960)

[SBKN21] Shrestha, N., Bhat, A., Kate, A., Nayak, K.: Synchronous distributed key generation without broadcasts. Cryptology ePrint Archive, Paper 2021/1635 (2021). https://eprint.iacr.org/2021/1635

[SR00] Srinathan, K., Pandu Rangan, C.: Efficient asynchronous secure multiparty distributed computation. In: Roy, B., Okamoto, E. (eds.) INDOCRYPT 2000. LNCS, vol. 1977, pp. 117–129. Springer, Heidelberg (2000). https://doi.org/10.1007/3-540-44495-5_11

[Sta96] Stadler, M.: Publicly verifiable secret sharing. In: Maurer, U. (ed.) EUROCRYPT 1996. LNCS, vol. 1070, pp. 190–199. Springer, Heidelberg (1996). https://doi.org/10.1007/3-540-68339-9_17

[TLP22] Tsimos, G., Loss, J., Papamanthou, C.: Gossiping for communication-efficient broadcast. In: Dodis, Y., Shrimpton, T. (eds.) CRYPTO 2022. LNCS, vol. 13509, pp. 439–469. Springer, Cham (2022). https://doi.org/10.1007/978-3-031-15982-4_15

[ZDL+22] Zhang, H., et al.: Practical asynchronous distributed key generation: improved efficiency, weaker assumption, and standard model. Cryptology ePrint Archive, Paper 2022/1678 (2022). https://eprint.iacr.org/2022/1678

Practical Settlement Bounds for Longest-Chain Consensus

Peter Gaži[1], Ling Ren[2], and Alexander Russell[3](✉)

[1] IOG, Bratislava, Slovakia
peter.gazi@iohk.io
[2] University of Illinois at Urbana-Champaign, Urbana, IL, USA
renling@illinois.edu
[3] University of Connecticut and IOG, Storrs, CT, USA
acr@uconn.edu

Abstract. Nakamoto's longest-chain consensus paradigm now powers the bulk of the world's cryptocurrencies and distributed finance infrastructure. An emblematic property of longest-chain consensus is that it provides probabilistic settlement guarantees that strengthen over time. This makes the exact relationship between settlement error and settlement latency a critical aspect of the protocol that both users and system designers must understand to make informed decisions. A recent line of work has finally provided a satisfactory rigorous accounting of this relationship for proof-of-work longest-chain protocols, but those techniques do not appear to carry over to the proof-of-stake setting.

This article develops a new analytic approach for establishing such settlement guarantees that yields explicit, rigorous settlement bounds for proof-of-stake longest-chain protocols, placing them on equal footing with their proof-of-work counterparts. Our techniques apply with some adaptations to the proof-of-work setting where they provide improvements to the state-of-the-art settlement bounds for proof-of-work protocols.

1 Introduction

Satoshi Nakamoto introduced the longest-chain consensus paradigm in the 2008 Bitcoin whitepaper [21]. Since its original proposal, the framework has been extended and generalized, and variants of longest-chain protocols now support the bulk of the world's cryptocurrencies and decentralized finance infrastructure.

The fundamental dynamics of the algorithm—in particular, the rate at which participants converge to achieve consensus—depend primarily on three critical parameters: r_h, the rate at which honest players are elected to advance the system; r_a, the rate at which adversarial players are elected to advance the system; and Δ, the maximum network delay. Despite the visible prominence of the algorithm and over a decade of concerted effort by the research community, the relationship between these critical parameters and the resulting consensus guarantee is still not well understood.

The last few years have witnessed rapid progress on this question. In 2020, two independent articles [8,12] precisely determined the region of triples

H. Handschuh and A. Lysyanskaya (Eds.): CRYPTO 2023, LNCS 14081, pp. 107–138, 2023.
https://doi.org/10.1007/978-3-031-38557-5_4

(r_h, r_a, Δ) for which longest-chain consensus *eventually* provides consistency, which is to say that participants in the system eventually converge on a finite prefix of the ledger. These results apply to both proof-of-work and proof-of-stake longest-chain protocols and, somewhat surprisingly, prove that their fundamental "regime of security" is the same.

Practice, however, demands *explicit* settlement guarantees, as blockchain users in the real world must be able to determine when transactions in the ledger have in fact settled with known risk. Likewise, deployed systems must explicitly calibrate block production rate against (estimated) network delays to yield reasonable settlement latency. Such explicit settlement guarantees in the proof-of-work setting have been the subject of an active thread of research [13,19,20]. These works have succeeded in providing satisfactory results for proof-of-work systems with conservative parameters similar to those used in Bitcoin. But significant gaps still remain for more aggressive parameters such as those used in Ethereum (before its switch to proof of stake). Furthermore, very little is known about the proof-of-stake setting, where the only explicit result makes the unrealistic assumption that the network has zero delay ($\Delta = 0$) [16]. This is particularly concerning as it seems that in recent years we have been witnessing the sentiment of preference for PoS over PoW due to the environmental impact of PoW, and longest-chain PoS represents a fair share of PoS deployments.

The main purpose of this article is to develop a new analytic approach for rigorous settlement guarantees for longest-chain rule protocols in the presence of network delays. While the new approach is somewhat simpler than previous techniques, the chief advantage is that it provides estimates that are both tight enough to directly inform practice and can be explicitly calculated in time polynomial in the relevant parameters. Our new techniques provide improvements over the state-of-the-art settlement bounds for proof-of-work longest-chain protocols [13]; more importantly, they also yield the first concrete settlement bounds for proof-of-stake longest-chain, placing them on equal footing with their proof-of-work counterparts. Finally, our analysis in both cases is the first to apply to the entire security regime: in particular, if longest-chain consensus possesses eventual security for a triple of parameters (r_h, r_a, Δ), our approach provides explicit bounds of security that converge exponentially quickly.

Our techniques and results apply to a wide family of longest-chain protocols, including all proof-of-work protocols following Nakamoto's Bitcoin white paper [21] and all proof-of-stake protocols axiomatized in [16] (such as variants of Ouroboros [2,4,7,17] and Snow White [6]). Deployed systems based on these protocols include Bitcoin [21], Ethereum,[1] Dogecoin, Cardano,[2] Polkadot,[3] and Mina.[4]

[1] https://ethereum.org/, prior to its shift to PoS in September 2022. The analysis also applies to currently deployed Ethereum Classic (ETC) and PoW Ethereum (ETHW) blockchains. In the rest of the paper, we refer to all these three instances together as "PoW-based Ethereum," or simply Ethereum if no confusion can arise.

[2] https://cardano.org/.

[3] https://polkadot.network/.

[4] https://minaprotocol.com/.

Our Techniques. Our analysis provides a family of recurrence relations that determine, for a fixed transcript of the leader-election lotteries during the protocol's execution, a sufficient condition for transaction settlement in any execution with this sequence of lottery outcomes. Coupling this with the stochastic process that governs leader election yields an efficient procedure for computing explicit upper bounds on settlement failure probabilities. An analogous procedure can provide lower bounds on these probabilities which we use to demonstrate the tightness of our upper bounds.

It is most convenient to discuss our approach in the context of recent related works, viz. [8,12,13]. The main difficulty in the analysis arises from accounting for network delays, as honest players may fail to see each other's latest messages (blocks) and end up undermining each other's contributions. Tackling this requires analysis of the complex sequencing of honest and adversarial blocks when a sequence of elected leaders repeatedly fall within Δ time of a previous leader. The combinatorics and resulting stochastic process are particularly difficult during "close races," i.e., when the adversary possesses a private chain that is about as long as the public chain. In such circumstances, honest leaders may be manipulated to contribute to the adversary's (now revealed) chain. Roughly speaking, the articles that settled the security regime [8,12] did so by focusing on the more tractable case where the protocol is *not* in a close race, which is sufficient to characterize the asymptotic behavior of the protocol.

In more detail, [8] focuses on a special type of blocks they call "Nakamoto blocks." The definition of Nakamoto blocks depends on the indefinite future, making them a powerful tool to analyze asymptotic security. But the distribution of Nakamoto block instances is highly complicated (and self-correlated) and thus difficult to tightly estimate, making these appear unsuitable for our goal of exact analysis. Similarly, the analysis in [12], roughly speaking, accounts for the close-race situation by considering a sequence of about Δ^2 back-to-back sequences of Δ-long silence followed by a unique honest lottery success, an event with a constant yet extremely small probability. This is again sufficient for an asymptotic analysis but spoils any chance of obtaining concrete tight and practical bounds. Unfortunately, this looseness in the close-race analysis appears to be a necessary consequence of their approach where the execution is seen as a sequence of steps with potentially significant inter-step interactions.

The recent article [13] that achieved practical settlement estimates for the proof-of-work setting made progress on exactly this issue with a new method of "deferrals." Intuitively, time is divided into periods of Δ and message delivery is restricted to occur at the end of each Δ period. The adversary is allowed to either deliver a message at the end of a period or "defer" its delivery to the end of the next period. This significantly simplifies the analysis as it reduces the large space of adversarial strategies to a single choice per block: whether or not to defer it. Unfortunately, this method of deferrals is not applicable in the proof-of-stake setting because a proof-of-stake adversary can produce as many blocks as it wishes from a single leadership election success. In particular, an optimal deferral strategy may choose to defer *a part of* same-success adversarial

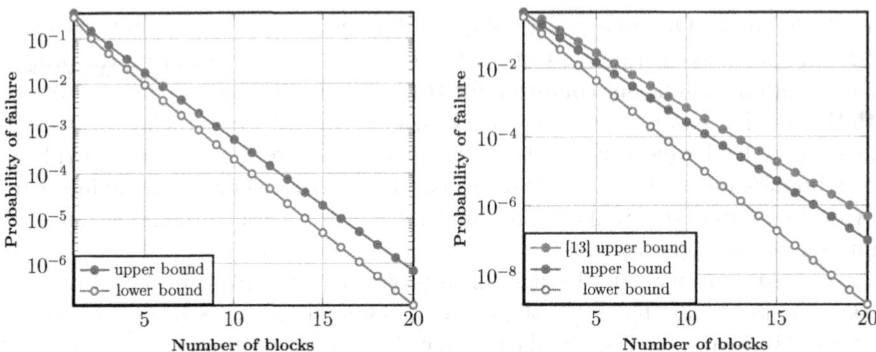

Fig. 1. Left: Cardano (PoS) block-based settlement failure for a 10% adversary and 2 seconds delay. **Right:** Ethereum (PoW) block-based settlement failure for a 10% adversary and 2 s delay, and results from [13] for comparison.

blocks, leading again to a large, complex strategy space that appears analytically intractable.

Our approach in this paper is, in some sense, the opposite of the deferral framework. Conceptually, our key idea is to divide time into judiciously defined periods—called *phases* in the rest of the paper—that are separated by Δ-long intervals of honest silence. Observe that when honest players carry out protocol execution in a given phase, they are aware of all honest messages (blocks) from all previous phases. From the perspective of the previous analysis of [12], this can be viewed as an aggressive expansion of the notion of a "step" so that they are long enough that troublesome inter-step interactions disappear. Indeed, it follows fairly easily that analysis of the protocol can be cleanly decomposed into a phase-by-phase analysis, without complicated interactions between phases. The natural concern with such an approach is that phases themselves are much more complex, both from a combinatorial perspective and in terms of the resulting stochastic process. Our principal contribution is to show that phases can be analyzed with high precision by examining certain *global properties* of the phase that were not available to analyses that operated on a "symbol-by-symbol" (or "step-by-step") level. For example, we show that a particular combinatorial quantity, "minimal honest depth," can capture most of the information necessary to characterize the relevant behavior of honest parties during the phase; this corresponds to the minimal possible maximal-chain growth in the phase over all blocktrees consistent with the phase; furthermore, this quantity gives rise to an analytically manageable stochastic process. These techniques significantly simplify the combinatorial treatment of longest chain rules and, aside from providing the first practical settlement bounds for the proof-of-stake setting, they also deliver improved guarantees in the proof-of-work case.

Example Results. Figure 1 shows some example results for both PoW-based Ethereum and Cardano (the largest longest-chain PoS blockchain at the time of writing). We assume an adversary that controls 10% of the total mining power or stake, and a network with maximum 2 s delay. The expected block interval in Ethereum and Cardano is around 13 s and 20 s, respectively. Our results for Cardano are within two confirmation blocks of optimality. Specifically, with a confirmation depth of 15 blocks, we can bound the settlement error probability at within 4.811×10^{-6} and 1.943×10^{-5}. Furthermore, the settlement error probability with 13 blocks is at least 2.143×10^{-5} (the lower bound), which is larger than the settlement error upper bound at 15 blocks. Similarly, our results for PoW-based Ethereum are within three or four confirmation blocks of optimality.

Additionally, our results allow us to compare for the first time the settlement speed of longest-chain protocols based on PoW versus PoS. We provide such comparison in Fig. 5 for Cardano's parametrization, quantifying the tradeoff between these two approaches.

2 Preliminaries and Model

Basic Notation. We use $\mathbb{N}$ to denote the set of natural numbers with zero, i.e., $\mathbb{N} = \{0, 1, 2, \ldots\}$. Throughout this paper, we use the symbol $\Delta \in \mathbb{N}$ to denote the maximum delay of a message, expressed in slots. Most of the notions defined below depend on Δ, but we keep this dependence implicit for the sake of lighter notation. When we want to refer to maximum delay expressed in *seconds* rather than slots, in line with previous work we use the symbol Δ_{r}, where "r" stands for "real".

2.1 Modeling Blockchains with Network Delay

Our modeling of the protocol and its execution environment adopts and extends the model from [12,13] and applies to both PoW and PoS. We summarize the model here for completeness.

A longest-chain protocol is carried out by a set of parties of two types: *honest* parties follow the protocol and *adversarial* parties may deviate arbitrarily. The execution timeline is divided into consecutive discrete short time intervals called *slots*. In each slot, each party evaluates a private lottery (implemented for example using a cryptographic hash function for PoW or a verifiable random function [5] for PoS) to determine whether she is eligible to act as a *slot leader* for that slot, which affords her the right to contribute to the ledger by creating block(s). We use a *characteristic string* to indicate a summary of the outcomes of the lottery in each slot.

More concretely, given an alphabet $\Sigma = \mathbb{N} \times \mathbb{N}$, a *characteristic string* $w = w_1 \ldots w_n \in \Sigma^n$ is a sequence of symbols over Σ. Intuitively, each symbol $w_i = (h_i, a_i) \in \Sigma$ indicates that h_i honest parties and a_i adversarial parties were eligible slot leaders for slot i, based on their private lotteries. For a characteristic string $w = w_1 \ldots w_n \in \Sigma^n$ where each $w_i = (h_i, a_i) \in \mathbb{N} \times \mathbb{N}$, we define $\#_{\mathsf{h}}(w) := \sum_{i=1}^{n} h_i$ and similarly $\#_{\mathsf{a}}(w) := \sum_{i=1}^{n} a_i$, i.e., the total number of honest and adversarial slot leaders over a sequence of slots corresponding to w. Moreover, we sometimes make use of a similar quantity $\#_{[a]}(w)$ that denotes the number of symbols in w with positive second coordinate, i.e.,

$$\#_{[a]}(w) := |\{i \in \{1, \ldots, n\} \mid w_i \notin \mathbb{N} \times \{0\}\}| \ .$$

A longest-chain protocol calls for parties to exchange *blockchains*, each of which is an ordered sequence of blocks beginning with a distinguished "genesis block," known to all parties. When an honest party becomes a slot leader, she always creates a single block, and follows the *longest-chain rule* which dictates that she adds her block to the longest blockchain she has observed thus far; she also broadcasts the new block(-chain) to all other parties. When an adversarial party becomes a slot leader, what he is allowed to do differs between PoW and PoS. Intuitively, in PoW an adversarial success allows for creating a single block that extends an arbitrary chain chosen by the adversary, while in PoS an adversarial success can be used to create any number of blocks and hence extend any number of previously existing chains by one block. Naturally, the adversary is not forced to immediately propagate his blocks, and can distribute them strategically.

More formally, let $\mathcal{C}_t$ denote the collection of all blockchains created by the end of slot t and let $H(\mathcal{C}_t)$ denote the subset of all chains in $\mathcal{C}_t$ whose last block was created by an honest party. Set $\mathcal{C}_0 = \{G\}$, where G denotes the unique chain consisting solely of the genesis block. The genesis block is considered "honest"; thus $H(\mathcal{C}_0) = \mathcal{C}_0$. It is convenient to adopt the convention that $\mathcal{C}_{-t} = H(\mathcal{C}_{-t}) = \{G\}$ for any negative integer $-t < 0$. Then the protocol execution proceeds as follows. For each slot $t = 1, 2, \ldots$:

- Initiate $\mathcal{C}_t := \mathcal{C}_{t-1}$ and $H(\mathcal{C}_t) := H(\mathcal{C}_{t-1})$.
- Given $w_t = (h, a)$ the following modifications are applied:
  - The adversary *must* perform the following *honest iteration* exactly h times: select any collection of chains $\mathcal{V}$ for which $H(\mathcal{C}_{t-1-\Delta}) \subseteq \mathcal{V} \subseteq \mathcal{C}_t$. This is the "view" of the honest slot leader, who applies the longest chain rule to $\mathcal{V}$, selects the longest chain $L \in \mathcal{V}$ (resp. $L \in \mathcal{V} \cap \mathcal{C}_{t-1}$ in PoS) where ties are broken by the adversary, and adds a new block to create a new chain L', which is added to $\mathcal{C}_t$ and also $H(\mathcal{C}_t)$.
  - If $a > 0$, the adversary *may* perform the following *adversarial iteration* at most a times for PoW or an arbitrary number of times for PoS: select a single blockchain C from $\mathcal{C}_t$ (in PoS, it must be from $\mathcal{C}_{t-1}$) and add a block to create a new chain C', which is added to $\mathcal{C}_t$. $H(\mathcal{C}_t)$ remains unchanged.

Note that the synchrony assumption is reflected in the description of the honest iteration: the adversary is obligated to deliver all chains produced by honest parties that are Δ slots old, i.e., the set of chains in $H(\mathcal{C}_{t-1-\Delta})$.

Also note that the model grants the adversary to power to break ties in the longest-chain rule. Considering that the adversary selects both the view $\mathcal{V}$ of each honest party and is empowered to break ties, the structure of the resulting sequence of chains (that is, the directed acyclic graph naturally formed by the blocks) is determined entirely by the adversary and the characteristic string.

We make several additional remarks. First, we permit the adversary to have full view of the characteristic string during this process. In reality, a PoS adversary can only predict its own lottery successes, not those of honest parties, while in PoW, neither successes are predictable. Hence our modeling here only makes the adversary stronger. (Looking ahead, this strengthening only affects our upper bounds, as we determine lower bounds via concrete attacks that can be performed by a realistic adversary, see Sect. 5.) Second, we have placed an implicit constraint on the adversary: the only means of producing a new chain is to append a block (containing a proof of a slot leadership) to an existing chain. In practice, this constraint is guaranteed with cryptographic hash functions. Third, we assume that the distribution of slot leaders is impervious to adversarial tampering and, as in previous treatments, is fixed throughout the analysis. This is motivated by the fact that settlement in deployed protocols takes place at much smaller time scales than shifts in mining power or stake distributions. Lastly, the model does not reflect attacks exploiting rational behaviors of parties, such as selfish-mining attacks [10], beyond simply considering such parties corrupt.

2.2 Ledger Consensus

In the context of ledger consensus protocols (also referred to as blockchain [11] or state machine replication [22] protocols), one is usually interested in preserving two properties, *consistency* and *liveness*, formulated in [11,18,22]. Consistency means that once a block (or equivalently, a transaction within it) is considered *settled* by some honest party, then it is present in the currently held chains of all parties, and remains that way forever. In this work we consider the *block-based settlement* rule for longest-chain consensus, where a party considers a block settled if it appears a particular number of blocks deep in the longest chain currently known to that party. Block-based settlement is adopted in practice, and is generally preferable to time-based settlement, as argued in [13].

To describe consistency and liveness concisely under the longest-chain rule, we define the set of *Δ-dominant* chains $\mathcal{D}_t \subseteq \mathcal{C}_t$ in each time step t. The set $\mathcal{D}_t \subseteq \mathcal{C}_t$ is determined entirely by $\mathcal{C}_t$ and $H(\mathcal{C}_{t-1-\Delta})$: namely, $\mathcal{D}_t$ is the set of all chains in $\mathcal{C}_t$ that are at least as long as the longest chain in $H(\mathcal{C}_{t-1-\Delta})$. The intuition behind this definition is that, in a time slot t, it is in principle possible for the adversary to manipulate an honest party into adopting any Δ-dominant chain, as the adversary is only obligated to deliver those chains in $H(\mathcal{C}_{t-1-\Delta})$ and the chains in $\mathcal{D}_t$ are at least as long as those in $H(\mathcal{C}_{t-1-\Delta})$.

Consistency for block-based settlement; with parameter k. A block B that is k blocks deep in some chain in $\mathcal{D}_t$ is contained in every chain $C \in \mathcal{D}_{t'}$ for all $t' \geq t$.

The goal of this paper is to bound (from both above and below) the probability that consistency is violated as a function of the parameter k.

For completeness, we also mention the liveness property [12], though it is not the focus of this paper.

Liveness; with parameter u. For any two slots $t_1, t_2 > 0$ with $t_1 + u \leq t_2$, and any chain $C \in \mathcal{D}_{t_2}$, there is a time $t' \in \{t_1, \ldots, t_1 + u\}$ and a chain $C' \in H(\mathcal{C}_{t'}) \setminus H(\mathcal{C}_{t'-1})$ such that C' is a prefix of C.

3 Proof-of-Work Settlement

In this section we first showcase our approach in the more familiar PoW setting, where it provides tighter results than state-of-the-art settlement bounds.

3.1 Proof-of-Work Blocktrees

We formally capture the above protocol dynamics by the combinatorial notion of a *PoW tree.* It is a variant of the "fork" concept first considered for the proof-of-stake case in [2,7,17] and more recently also employed for PoW-analysis [1,12, 13]. An example PoW tree is shown in Fig. 2, illustrating several of the concepts defined below.

Definition 1 (PoW tree). *Let $n \in \mathbb{N}$. A* PoW tree *for the string $w \in \Sigma^n$ is a directed, rooted tree $F = (V, E)$ with a pair of functions*

$$\mathsf{l}_{\#} : V \to \{0, \ldots, n\} \qquad \text{and} \qquad \mathsf{l}_{\mathsf{type}} : V \to \{\mathsf{h}, \mathsf{a}\}$$

satisfying the axioms below. Edges are directed "away from" the root so that there is a unique directed path from the root to any vertex. The value $\mathsf{l}_{\#}(v)$ is referred to as the label *of v. The value $\mathsf{l}_{\mathsf{type}}(v)$ is referred to as the* type *of the vertex: when $\mathsf{l}_{\mathsf{type}}(v) = \mathsf{h}$, we say that the vertex is* honest; *otherwise it is* adversarial.

(A1) the root $r \in V$ is honest and is the only vertex with label $\mathsf{l}_{\#}(r) = 0$;
(A2) for any pair of honest vertices v, w for which $\mathsf{l}_{\#}(v) + \Delta < \mathsf{l}_{\#}(w)$, $\mathsf{len}(v) < \mathsf{len}(w)$, where $\mathsf{len}()$ denotes the depth of the vertex;
(W3) the sequence of labels $\mathsf{l}_{\#}()$ along any directed path is non-decreasing;
(W4) if $w_i = (h_i, a_i)$ then there are exactly h_i honest vertices and at most a_i adversarial vertices in F with the label i.

We will refer to PoW trees simply as *trees* when the context is clear. Unless explicitly stated otherwise, throughout the paper we reserve the term "tree" for the above structure, as opposed to the underlying graph-theoretic notion.

A PoW tree abstracts a protocol execution with a simple but sufficiently descriptive discrete structure. Its vertices and edges stand for blocks and their connecting hash links (in reverse direction), respectively. The root represents the genesis block, and for each vertex v, $\mathsf{l}_{\#}(v)$ and $\mathsf{len}(v)$ denote the slot in which the corresponding block was created and the block's depth, respectively.

It is easy to see the correspondence between the above axioms and the constraints imposed in the protocol execution. In particular, (A1) corresponds to the trusted nature of the genesis block; (A2) reflects the fact that given sufficient time, as needed for block propagation in the network, an honest party will

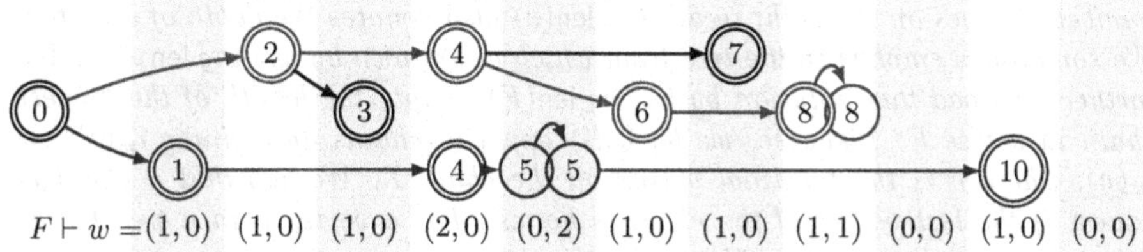

Fig. 2. A PoW tree F for the characteristic string w with $\Delta = 1$. Honest vertices are shown with double-struck boundaries, while adversarial vertices are simple circles. Vertices are labeled with $\mathsf{l}_{\#}(\cdot)$. The tree indicates a k-consistency violation for $k = 4$ —given by the red and blue chains—in a circumstance where the simple private-chain attack does not succeed: in particular, the tree constructs two alternate chains with disjoint suffixes of length 5, while only three adversarial proofs of work are discovered over this period. We remark that $F = F_{\lceil 1}$, since the last symbol of w is $(0, 0)$, and that $\overline{F_{\lceil 1}}$ is obtained by removing the adversarial vertex with label 8. Thus $\mathsf{len}(\overline{F_{\lceil 1}}) = 5$, this maximum length achieved by the blue chain. Note, then, that the two chains indicated in red and blue each have advantage equal to zero, and both are dominant. Considering that these chains share no vertices after the root, they witness $\beta_1(F) \geq 0$ for the tree F and hence $\beta_1(w) \geq 0$ for the characteristic string w. (Color figure online)

take into account the blocks produced by previous honest parties. Axiom (W3) reflects that the blocks' ordering in a chain must be consistent with the order of their creation and finally (W4) reflects that honest players produce exactly one block per PoW success, while the adversary might forgo a block-creation opportunity. Looking ahead, the labeling of the above axioms reflects that while (A1) and (A2) will apply universally to PoW and PoS alike, axioms (W3) and (W4) are specific to PoW, and will be replaced for PoS analysis by appropriate variations (S3) and (S4) in Sect. 4.

Definition 2 (PoW tree notation). *We write $F \vdash^{\mathsf{W}} w$ if F is a PoW tree for the characteristic string w. When the setting is clear from context or not germane to the discussion, we drop the superscript and simply write $F \vdash w$. If $F' \vdash w'$ for a prefix w' of w, we say that F' is a* subtree *of F if F contains F' as a consistently-labeled subgraph. A tree $F \vdash w$ is* public *if all leaves are honest. The trivial tree, consisting solely of a root vertex, is considered public. The* public core *of a tree F, denoted $\overline{F}$, is the maximal public subtree of F.*

An individual blockchain constructed during the protocol execution is represented by the notion of a *chain*, defined next.

Definition 3 (Chains). *A path in a tree F originating at the root is called a* chain *(note that a chain does not necessarily terminate at a leaf). As there is a one-to-one correspondence between directed paths from the root and vertices of a tree, we routinely overload notation so that it applies to both chains and vertices. Specifically, we let $\mathsf{len}(T)$ denote the* length *of the chain, equal to the* *number of edges on the path; recall that* $\mathsf{len}(v)$ *also denotes the depth of a vertex. We sometimes emphasize the tree from which* v *is drawn by writing* $\mathsf{len}_F(v)$. *We further overload this notation by letting* $\mathsf{len}(F)$ *denote the length of the longest chain in a tree* F. *Likewise, we let* $\mathsf{l}_\#(\cdot)$ *apply to chains by defining* $\mathsf{l}_\#(T) := \mathsf{l}_\#(v)$, *where* v *is the terminal vertex on the chain* T. *We say that a chain is* honest *if the last vertex of the chain is honest. For a vertex* v *in a tree* F, *we denote by* $F(v)$ *the chain in* F *terminating in* v.

Definition 4 (Branches). *For an integer* $\ell \geq 1$ *and for two chains* T *and* T' *of a tree* F, *we write* $T \sim_\ell T'$ *if the two chains share a vertex with a label greater than or equal to* ℓ. *The set of all chains* $T' \in F$ *such that* $T \sim_\ell T'$ *is called the* branch *of* T *in* F *and denoted* $\mathsf{B}_F(T;\ell)$; *when* ℓ *can be inferred from context, we write* $\mathsf{B}_F(T)$.

Intuitively, $T \sim_\ell T'$ guarantees that the respective blockchains agree on the state of the ledger up to time slot ℓ. Looking ahead, the adversary can make two honest parties disagree on the state of the ledger up to time ℓ only if she makes them hold two blockchains chains $T \not\sim_\ell T'$.

Definition 5 (Tree trimming; dominance). *For a string* $w = w_1 \ldots w_n$ *and some* $k \in \mathbb{N}$, *we let* $w_{\lceil k} = w_1 \ldots w_{n-k}$ *denote the string obtained by removing the last* k *symbols. For a tree* $F \vdash w_1 \ldots w_n$ *we let* $F_{\lceil k} \vdash w_{\lceil k}$ *denote the tree obtained by retaining only those vertices labeled from the set* $\{1, \ldots, n-k\}$. *For convenience, we sometimes prefer to emphasize the* remaining *length of the string (resp. tree), and denote by* $w_{m\rceil}$ *and* $F_{m\rceil}$ *the* m*-symbol prefix of* w *and the corresponding tree, formally* $w_{m\rceil} := w_{\lceil n-m}$ *and* $F_{m\rceil} := F_{\lceil n-m}$. *We say that a chain* T *in* F *is* dominant *if* $\mathsf{len}(T) \geq \mathsf{len}(\overline{F_{\lceil \Delta}})$.

Observe that honest chains appearing in $F_{\lceil \Delta}$ are those that are necessarily visible to honest players at a round just beyond the last one described by the characteristic string. Correspondingly, the notion of a dominant chain matches the use of this term in Sect. 2.1.

Looking ahead, our approach is to analyze phases that end with Δ consecutive slots with no honest successes. Hence, at the end of each phase the characteristic string has the form wx with $x \in (\{0\} \times \mathbb{N})^\Delta$. We note the following fact.

Fact 1. *For a characteristic string of the form* wx, *where* $x \in (\{0\} \times \mathbb{N})^\Delta$, *any tree* $F \vdash wx$ *has the property that* $\mathsf{len}(\overline{F_{\lceil \Delta}}) = \mathsf{len}(\overline{F})$ *and hence dominance follows simply from* $\mathsf{len}(T) \geq \mathsf{len}(\overline{F})$.

Definition 6 (Honest depth h_Δ**).** *For* $x \in \{0,1\}^*$, *we define* $h_\Delta(x)$ *inductively so that* $h_\Delta(\epsilon) = 0$, $h_\Delta(x0) = h_\Delta(x)$, *and* $h_\Delta(x1) = h_\Delta(x_{\lceil \Delta}) + 1$. *We often overload* h_Δ *to apply to strings from* $\Sigma^* = (\mathbb{N} \times \mathbb{N})^*$, *in which case symbols with non-zero first coordinate (i.e., from* $((\mathbb{N} \setminus \{0\}) \times \mathbb{N})^*$ *are counted as 1s, while symbols from* $(\{0\} \times \mathbb{N})^*$ *are treated as 0s.*

The honest depth $h_\Delta(x)$ of a string x captures the minimum growth of honest blockchains over a period of slots corresponding to x. More concretely, it is the minimum number of times during x that an honest slot leader must create a block at a higher depth because it is guaranteed to "see" an honest blockchain at one depth lower that was created at least Δ slots earlier.

3.2 PoW Characteristic Quantity: Margin (β_ℓ)

As shown in previous works [1,12,13], the core quantity useful for analyzing PoW longest-chain blockchains is *margin*, defined next.

Definition 7 (PoW Margin β_ℓ). *For a PoW tree $F \vdash^{\mathsf{W}} w$, we define the* advantage *of a chain $T \in F$ as*

$$\alpha_F(T) = \mathsf{len}(T) - \mathsf{len}(\overline{F_{\lceil \Delta}}) .$$

Observe that $\alpha_F(T) \geq 0$ if and only if T is dominant in F. For $\ell \geq 1$, we define the margin *of a tree F as*

$$\beta_\ell(F) = \max_{\substack{T_h \not\sim_\ell T_a \\ T_h \text{ is dominant}}} \alpha_F(T_a) ,$$

this maximum extended over all pairs of chains (T_h, T_a) where T_h is dominant and $T_a \not\sim_\ell T_h$. We call the pair (T_h, T_a) the witness chains *for F if the above conditions are satisfied; i.e., T_h is dominant, $T_h \not\sim_\ell T_a$, and $\beta_\ell(F) = \alpha_F(T_a)$. Note that there might exist multiple such pairs in F, but under the condition $\ell \geq 1$ there will always exist at least one such pair, as the trivial chain T_0 containing only the root vertex satisfies $T_0 \not\sim_\ell T$ for any T and $\ell \geq 1$, in particular $T_0 \not\sim_\ell T_0$. For this reason, we will always consider β_ℓ only for $\ell \geq 1$.*

We overload the notation and let

$$\beta_\ell(w) = \max_{F \vdash^{\mathsf{W}} w} \beta_\ell(F) .$$

We call a PoW tree $F \vdash^{\mathsf{W}} w$ a witness tree *for w if $\beta_\ell(w) = \beta_\ell(F)$; again many witness trees may exist for a string w.*

There is a known tight connection between margin and settlement, captured by the following lemma and motivating our effort to upper-bound β_ℓ.

Lemma 1 ([12,13]). *Consider an execution of a PoW blockchain for L slots as described above, resulting in a characteristic string $w = w_1 \ldots w_L$. Let B be a block produced in slot $\ell \in [L]$, and let $t > \ell$ be such that B is contained in some chain $C \in \mathcal{D}_t$. If for every $t' \in \{t, \ldots, L\}$ we have $\beta_\ell(w_1 \ldots w_{t'}) < 0$ then B is contained in every $C' \in \mathcal{D}_{t'}$ for all $t' \in \{t, \ldots, L\}$.*

Note that if a tree $F \vdash^{\mathsf{W}} w$ has $\beta_\ell(F) < 0$ then all chains T of length at least $\mathsf{len}(\overline{F_{\lceil \Delta}})$ belong to the same branch, which we call the main branch.

Definition 8 (Main branch, PoW). *Let $w \in \Sigma^n$, $\ell \geq 1$, and $F \vdash^{\mathsf{W}} w$ such that $\beta_\ell(F) < 0$. The unique branch of F that contains all chains of length at least $\mathsf{len}(\overline{F_{\lceil \Delta}})$ (and possibly other chains) is called the* main branch *of F and denoted $\mathsf{M}^{\mathsf{W}}(F)$.*

3.3 Main PoW Theorem

The goal of Sect. 3 is to provide recurrences that allow us to upper-bound the value of margin $\beta_\ell(w)$ for any PoW characteristic string w. As shown in Lemma 1, this allows us to upper-bound the probability of a settlement violation in any execution with leadership lottery outcomes captured by w.

We approach this challenge by splitting w into consecutive, non-overlapping substrings called *phases*, in a way that ensures the following property:

Phase property: any honest party producing a block in a particular phase is at that time necessarily aware of all honest blocks that have been produced in all previous phases.

To ensure this property, we determine phase boundaries in w so that two consecutive phases are separated by a Δ-long sequence of slots in which no honest successes occur. Notice that this clearly implies the phase property, as any honest block created in phase i will have been delivered to all honest parties within Δ slots, before the beginning of phase $i+1$.

More formally, we devise a recurrence determining the quantity $\beta_\ell(wsxt)$ based on the value $\beta_\ell(ws)$ and the suffix xt, where $w, x \in \Sigma^*$ are arbitrary characteristic strings, while $s, t \in (\{0\} \times \mathbb{N})^\Delta$ represent Δ-long periods with no honest successes. Together with the trivial initial condition $\beta_\ell(\varepsilon) = 0$ for the empty string ε, this gives us a phase-based inductive characterization of β_ℓ, where xt denotes the currently processed phase. Our main result in this section is the following theorem providing such a characterization.

Theorem 1 (The PoW Phase Recurrence). *Let $\ell \geq 1$, let $w, x \in (\mathbb{N} \times \mathbb{N})^*$ and $s, t \in (\{0\} \times \mathbb{N})^\Delta$ be characteristic strings. We have:*

Margin recurrence. $\beta_\ell(\varepsilon) = 0$. *Furthermore,*

$$\beta_\ell(wsxt) \begin{cases} = \beta_\ell(ws) + \#_{\mathsf{a}}(xt) - h_\Delta(x) & \text{if } \beta_\ell(ws) < -\#_{\mathsf{a}}(xt) \\ & \text{or } \beta_\ell(ws) > h_\Delta(x), \\ \leq \min\{0, \beta_\ell(ws)\} + \#_{\mathsf{a}}(xt) & \text{otherwise.} \end{cases}$$

Crossing zero. *If $|ws| \geq \ell - 1$ and $\beta_\ell(ws) = 0$ then $\beta_\ell(ws(1,0)(0,0)^\Delta) = -1$.*

Hot, cold, and critical regions. We establish the recurrences above over a sequence of lemmas. These lemmas consider β_ℓ in one of the regions that we informally call *hot*, *cold*, and *critical*. A quantity is said to be in the hot region if its value is sufficiently above zero, such that the currently considered phase cannot bring it down to zero. On the other hand, it is said to be in the cold region if it is sufficiently negative so that it won't climb to zero within the current phase. Finally, it is said to be in a critical region if it is close to zero as detailed below.

The critical region corresponds to the situation of a "close race" discussed in Sect. 1. This is the most difficult situation to analyze as special behaviors of the considered quantities (in this case β_ℓ) manifest here: most notably, it is possible in this region for a new honest success to make things worse for the honest players. For example, consider a situation where an honest player builds a new block B on a chain so that it is exactly one block longer than the best competing chain; now, an additional honest block produced by an honest player that has not seen B can be placed on the competing chain which "neutralizes" this one-block advantage. In contrast, in the hot and cold regions, this second honest block is merely wasted: it does not benefit the honest players but does not hurt either.

With the above discussion, Theorem 1 says that in both the hot and cold regions, β_ℓ exactly follows an ideal recurrence

$$\beta_\ell(wsxt) = \beta_\ell(ws) + \#_{\mathsf{a}}(xt) - h_\Delta(x) \tag{1}$$

where it increases by 1 for each adversarial success, and decreases by 1 whenever the pattern of honest successes enforces an increase in the honest depth h_Δ. In the critical region, $\beta_\ell(wsxt)$ can still be upper-bounded by both $\#_{\mathsf{a}}(xt)$ and $\beta_\ell(ws) + \#_{\mathsf{a}}(xt)$. Intuitively, this means that if $\beta_\ell(ws)$ is "close to zero" from the negative side, then the worst-case behavior observed in the subsequent phase xt is as if the ideal recurrence was applied but xt contained no honest successes, while if $\beta_\ell(ws)$ is "close to zero" from the positive side, $\beta_\ell(wsxt)$ is still upper-bounded by $\#_{\mathsf{a}}(xt)$. Finally, note that these rules by themselves would never permit β_ℓ to descend below zero; for this purpose we establish a separate statement that if $\beta_\ell(ws) = 0$, then a subsequent phase containing only a single success that is honest, brings margin into negative values.

We remark that the exact behavior near zero appears to be quite complicated, in part because there is no longer a clear optimal strategy for the adversary to neutralize honest successes. We identified the simplest and most common scenario, i.e., a single honest success followed by a Δ period of no success, that transitions the quantity from zero to negative. There might be other advanced patterns of honest successes that cannot be neutralized but we treat as thought they can. This is also why we give an upper bound rather than an exact recurrence in the critical region.

3.4 Existing Tools: Tree Compression and the PoW Restructuring Lemma

In our PoW arguments we make use of special honest vertices called *tight* that are, informally speaking, at the minimal depth that the preceding part of the tree allows without violating the axiom (A2). Here we define these vertices formally and summarize several useful properties they have. In particular, in Lemma 3 we show how a PoW tree that has a tight vertex at each possible depth (we call such trees *compressed*) allows for a complex restructuring operation that leads to a lower-bound on the margin of the underlying characteristic string.

Definition 9. *Let $F \vdash w \in \Sigma^n$. An honest vertex v of F is called* tight *if* $\mathsf{len}(v) = \mathsf{len}(\overline{F_{\lceil \#(v)-\Delta-1 \rceil}}) + 1$. *The tree F is said to be* compressed *if, for every depth $0 \leq d \leq \mathsf{len}(\overline{F})$, there is a tight honest vertex v of depth d.*

We recall two lemmas established in [12]. The first asserts that witness trees may be assumed to be compressed without loss of generality. The second identifies and analyses a restructuring operation in compressed trees. Proofs of both lemmas, adapted to our notation but following those of previous work, appear in the full version [14].

Lemma 2 **([12]).** *Let* $w \in (\mathbb{N} \times \mathbb{N})^*$ *and* $s \in (\{0\} \times \mathbb{N})^{\Delta}$*. Then there exists a witness tree* $F \vdash^{\mathsf{W}} ws$ *that is compressed.*

Lemma 3 (Restructuring lemma, [12]). *Let* $\ell \geq 1$*, let* $w \in \Sigma^*$ *be a characteristic string and* $F \vdash^{\mathsf{W}} w$ *be a compressed PoW tree for* w*; let* $T_1 \not\sim_\ell T_2$ *be arbitrary chains in* F*. For* $i \in \{1, 2\}$*, let* v_i *be an honest vertex on* T_i *and let* A_i *denote the set of all adversarial vertices on* T_i *deeper than* v_i*. If* $\mathsf{l}_\#(v_1) \leq \mathsf{l}_\#(v_2)$ *then*

$$\beta_\ell(w) \geq \alpha_F(v_1) + |A_1 \cup A_2| \; .$$

3.5 Outside of the Critical Region

We establish the ideal recurrence (1) outside of the critical region in a sequence of three lemmas: first, Lemma 4 shows that the recurrence gives a lower bound for β_ℓ, and then Lemmas 5 and 6 show that it is also an upper bound in the cold and the hot region, respectively.

Lemma 4 (Lower bound). *Let* $\ell \geq 1$*, let* $w, x \in (\mathbb{N} \times \mathbb{N})^*$ *and* $s, t \in (\{0\} \times \mathbb{N})^{\Delta}$ *be characteristic strings. Then*

$$\beta_\ell(wsxt) \geq \beta_\ell(ws) + \#_{\mathsf{a}}(xt) - h_\Delta(x) \; .$$

Proof. Let F be a witness PoW tree $F \vdash^{\mathsf{W}} ws$, and let (T_h, T_a) be a pair of witness chains in F, i.e., $T_h \not\sim_\ell T_a$, T_h is dominant in F, and $\alpha_F(T_a) = \beta_\ell(F) = \beta_\ell(ws)$.

We construct a tree $F' \vdash^{\mathsf{W}} wsxt$ such that $\beta_\ell(F') = \beta_\ell(F) + \#_{\mathsf{a}}(xt) - h_\Delta(x)$. Namely, we add $\#_{\mathsf{a}}(xt) + \#_{\mathsf{h}}(x)$ new vertices to F in two steps. First, we extend T_a by a path consisting of $\#_{\mathsf{a}}(xt)$ adversarial vertices that we label consistently with xt to satisfy axiom (W4), call the resulting chain T'_a. Second, we also add $\#_{\mathsf{h}}(x)$ honest vertices that form a subtree rooted in the terminating vertex of T_h, where each of these honest vertices is always put at the minimal depth allowed by axiom (A2), and labeling them consistently with x to again satisfy axiom (W4). Let T'_h denote a chain terminating in some maximum-depth newly added honest vertex. The resulting tree (call it F') is indeed a PoW tree: it is easy to observe that all axioms of a PoW tree are satisfied by construction. Note that $\mathsf{len}_{F'}(T'_a) = \mathsf{len}_F(T_a) + \#_{\mathsf{a}}(xt)$, $\mathsf{len}_{F'}(T'_h) = \mathsf{len}_F(T_h) + h_\Delta(x)$, and we have $T'_h \not\sim_\ell T'_a$ as these chains share no new vertices. Finally, T'_h is clearly dominant, and hence the pair (T'_h, T'_a) witnesses $\beta_\ell(F') = \beta_\ell(F) + \#_{\mathsf{a}}(xt) - h_\Delta(x)$ as desired. □

Lemma 5 (Cold region). *Let* $\ell \geq 1$*, let* $w, x \in (\mathbb{N} \times \mathbb{N})^*$ *and* $s, t \in (\{0\} \times \mathbb{N})^{\Delta}$ *be characteristic strings. If* $\beta_\ell(ws) < -\#_{\mathsf{a}}(xt)$ *then*

$$\beta_\ell(wsxt) \leq \beta_\ell(ws) + \#_{\mathsf{a}}(xt) - h_\Delta(x) \; .$$

The proof of Lemma 5 is an adaptation of the proof of Lemma 8 from [12] to our setting. Note that our new approach of processing the characteristic string by phases allows for a stronger statement: the ideal recurrence is shown to hold closer to the critical region. At the same time, the proof becomes simpler.

Proof. Let $w' := wsxt$ and let F' be a witness PoW tree $F' \vdash^{\mathsf{W}} w'$; let (T'_h, T'_a) be a pair of witness chains in F' such that $\mathsf{len}(T'_h) = \mathsf{len}(\overline{F'_{\lceil\Delta}})$. Furthermore, let $F := F'_{|ws|\rceil} \vdash^{\mathsf{W}} ws$ and define $T_h := (T'_h)_{|ws|\rceil}$ and $T_a := (T'_a)_{|ws|\rceil}$, i.e., T_h and T_a are the restrictions of T'_h and T'_a to vertices with labels at most $|ws|$; we have $T_h, T_a \in F$ by definition of F. Note that, as s, t contain no honest successes, we have $\overline{F_{\lceil\Delta}} = \overline{F}$ and $\overline{F'_{\lceil\Delta}} = \overline{F'}$, and

$$\mathsf{len}(\overline{F'_{\lceil\Delta}}) \geq \mathsf{len}(\overline{F_{\lceil\Delta}}) + h_\Delta(x) \; . \tag{2}$$

By our assumption of negative $\beta_\ell(ws)$, there is a well-defined main branch $\mathsf{M}^{\mathsf{W}}(F)$. We first establish that, intuitively speaking, any chains in F outside of $\mathsf{M}^{\mathsf{W}}(F)$ are, after ws, extended by adversarial vertices only.

Claim. Consider any chain $T \in F$ such that $T \notin \mathsf{M}^{\mathsf{W}}(F)$ and any $T' \in F'$ that extends T in F' so that $T = T'_{|ws|\rceil}$. Then the set of vertices $T' \setminus T$ contains no honest vertices.

To see this, observe that any honest vertex in F' with label greater than $|ws|$ must have depth at least $\mathsf{len}(\overline{F_{\lceil\Delta}}) + 1 = \mathsf{len}(\overline{F}) + 1$ by axiom (A2), hence all vertices in $T' \setminus T$ with depth at most $\mathsf{len}(\overline{F})$ must be adversarial. However, $\mathsf{len}(T) + \#_{\mathsf{a}}(xt) < \mathsf{len}(\overline{F})$. To see this, note that we have $\alpha_F(T) \leq \beta_\ell(ws)$ as $T \notin \mathsf{M}^{\mathsf{W}}(F)$ and hence again there exists some dominant chain in $\mathsf{M}^{\mathsf{W}}(F)$ that forms a witness pair with T. Moreover, $\beta_\ell(ws) < -\#_{\mathsf{a}}(xt)$ by assumption, and this together implies $\mathsf{len}(T) + \#_{\mathsf{a}}(xt) < \mathsf{len}(\overline{F})$ and hence $\mathsf{len}(T') < \mathsf{len}(\overline{F})$. This already shows that there are no honest vertices in $T' \setminus T$ and establishes Claim 3.5.

We now argue that $T_h \in \mathsf{M}^{\mathsf{W}}(F)$. Towards contradiction, assume that $T_h \notin \mathsf{M}^{\mathsf{W}}(F)$. Then Claim 3.5 applies to T_h and $T'_h \setminus T_h$ contains no honest vertices, hence

$$\mathsf{len}(T'_h) \leq \mathsf{len}(T_h) + \#_{\mathsf{a}}(xt) \; . \tag{3}$$

However, by assumption $\mathsf{len}(T_h) - \mathsf{len}(\overline{F}) = \alpha_F(T_h) \leq \beta_\ell(ws) < -\#_a(xt)$, where the first inequality holds as $T_h \notin \mathsf{M}^{\mathsf{W}}(F)$ and hence there exists some dominant chain in $\mathsf{M}^{\mathsf{W}}(F)$ that forms a witness pair with T_h. Hence $\mathsf{len}(T_h) < \mathsf{len}(\overline{F}) - \#_{\mathsf{a}}(xt)$, and using equations (3) and (2) gives us $\mathsf{len}(T'_h) < \mathsf{len}(\overline{F}) \leq \mathsf{len}(\overline{F'})$, a contradiction with the definition of T'_h. Therefore, $T_h \in \mathsf{M}^{\mathsf{W}}(F)$.

Since $T'_h \not\sim_\ell T'_a$, it also follows that $T_h \not\sim_\ell T_a$, and at most one of these chains belongs to $\mathsf{M}^{\mathsf{W}}(F)$, hence we have $T_a \notin \mathsf{M}^{\mathsf{W}}(F)$. By Claim 3.5, $T'_a \setminus T_a$ contains no honest vertices. Hence we have $\mathsf{len}(T'_a) \leq \mathsf{len}(T_a) + \#_{\mathsf{a}}(xt)$ and we can combine this with Eq. (2) to get

$$\begin{aligned}\beta_\ell(ws) &\geq \alpha_F(T_a) = \mathsf{len}(T_a) - \mathsf{len}(\overline{F}) \geq \mathsf{len}(T'_a) - \#_{\mathsf{a}}(xt) - \mathsf{len}(\overline{F'}) + h_\Delta(x) \\ &= \alpha_{F'}(T'_a) - \#_{\mathsf{a}}(xt) + h_\Delta(x) = \beta_\ell(w') - \#_{\mathsf{a}}(xt) + h_\Delta(x) \; ,\end{aligned}$$

where the first inequality is again justified by $T_a \notin \mathsf{M}^{\mathsf{W}}(F)$. This concludes the proof of Lemma 5. □

Lemma 6 (Hot region). *Let $\ell \geq 1$, let $w, x \in (\mathbb{N} \times \mathbb{N})^*$ and $s, t \in (\{0\} \times \mathbb{N})^{\Delta}$ be characteristic strings. If $\beta_\ell(ws) > h_\Delta(x)$ then*

$$\beta_\ell(wsxt) \leq \beta_\ell(ws) + \#_{\mathsf{a}}(xt) - h_\Delta(x) . \tag{4}$$

The proof of the above lemma employs as a crucial ingredient the tree compression concept and the restructuring lemma that we recalled in Sect. 3.4.

Proof of Lemma 6. As in the cold case, the proof begins with a witness tree F' for $wsxt$ and shows how to construct a tree $F^* \vdash ws$ for which $\beta_\ell(F^*) \geq \beta_\ell(wsxt) - \#_{\mathsf{a}}(xt) + h_\Delta(x)$; this completes the theorem as $\beta_\ell(ws) \geq \beta_\ell(F^*)$. To set down notation, define $F' \vdash wsxt$ to be a compressed witness tree with witness chains (T'_h, T'_a); we then consider the restriction $F \vdash ws$ of F' to the string ws and, in particular, the restrictions (T_h, T_a) of the witness chains (T'_h, T'_a) to F. To prepare for the main argument, we establish a few straightforward properties of these two trees. First, observe that the inequality

$$\mathsf{len}(\overline{F'_{\lceil\Delta}}) = \mathsf{len}(\overline{F'}) \geq \mathsf{len}(\overline{F}_{\lceil\Delta}) + h_\Delta(x) = \mathsf{len}(\overline{F}) + h_\Delta(x) \tag{5}$$

follows immediately from Fact 1, tree axiom (A2), the definition of honest height, and the fact that s and t contain no honest successes. We then establish that there are no honest vertices on T'_a with label exceeding $|ws|$; in other words, there are no honest vertices in $T'_a \setminus T_a$. Towards a contradiction, assume that there is an honest vertex in $T'_a \setminus T_a$ and let v'_{a} be such an honest vertex with maximum label (and hence maximum depth). Since $\mathsf{l}_\#(v'_{\mathsf{a}}) > |ws|$, all vertices u on T'_a with $\mathsf{len}(u) > \mathsf{len}(v'_{\mathsf{a}})$ also have $\mathsf{l}_\#(u) > \mathsf{l}_\#(v'_{\mathsf{a}}) > |ws|$ and, by maximality of v'_{a}, all these vertices are adversarial; hence there are at most $\#_{\mathsf{a}}(xt)$ subsequent vertices (on T'_h) by axiom (W4). However, as v'_{a} is honest we also have $\mathsf{len}(v'_{\mathsf{a}}) \leq \mathsf{len}(\overline{F'})$. Combining these, we conclude $\beta_\ell(wsxt) = \mathsf{len}(T'_a) - \mathsf{len}(\overline{F'}) \leq \mathsf{len}(T'_a) - \mathsf{len}(v'_{\mathsf{a}}) \leq \#_{\mathsf{a}}(xt)$. Combining this with the assumption $\beta_\ell(ws) > h_\Delta(x)$ yields a direct contradiction to Lemma 4, which asserts that $\beta_\ell(wsxt) \geq \beta_\ell(ws) + \#_{\mathsf{a}}(xt) - h_\Delta(x)$. We conclude that there are no honest vertices on $T'_a \setminus T_a$ and, in particular, that $\mathsf{len}(T'_a) - \mathsf{len}(T_a) \leq \#_{\mathsf{a}}(xt)$.

The last honest vertices on the chains T_h and T_a play a central role in the remainder of the analysis; these we denote v_h and v_a, respectively. We handle the two cases $\mathsf{l}_\#(v_h) \geq \mathsf{l}_\#(v_a)$ and $\mathsf{l}_\#(v_h) < \mathsf{l}_\#(v_a)$ separately, in either setting concluding the argument with an application of Lemma 3 to a vertex with minimal label.

The case $\mathsf{l}_\#(v_h) < \mathsf{l}_\#(v_a)$. We define the sets A_a and A'_a to consist of the adversarial vertices appearing after v_a on T_a in F and F', respectively; thus $A_a \subset A'_a$. We likewise define A_h and A'_h for the chain T_h and vertex v_h.

We first establish that

$$\mathsf{len}(v_a) \leq \mathsf{len}(v_h) + |A'_h| . \tag{6}$$

Recalling that T'_h is dominant, $\mathsf{len}(v_a) \le \mathsf{len}(\overline{F}) \le \mathsf{len}(\overline{F'}) = \mathsf{len}(\overline{F'_{\lceil\Delta}}) = \mathsf{len}(T'_h)$. In the case when all vertices of T'_h after v_h are adversarial, the inequality (6) follows immediately because $\mathsf{len}(T'_h) = \mathsf{len}(v_h) + |A'_h|$. Otherwise, there is a first honest vertex v'_h on T'_h that appears after v_h; by definition, this vertex does not lie in F and is labeled by an index in x. Considering that the quiet region s lies between the labels for v_a and v'_h, we must have $\mathsf{len}(v_a) < \mathsf{len}(v'_h)$ by axiom (A2). Combining this with the fact that $\mathsf{len}(v'_h) \le \mathsf{len}(v_h) + |A'_h| + 1$, the inequality (6) follows. We may then conclude that

$$\begin{aligned} \beta_\ell(wsxt) &= \alpha_{F'}(T'_a) = \mathsf{len}(T'_a) - \mathsf{len}(\overline{F'_{\lceil\Delta}}) = \mathsf{len}(T'_a) - \mathsf{len}(\overline{F'}) \\ &= \mathsf{len}(v_a) + |A'_a| - \mathsf{len}(\overline{F'}) \le \mathsf{len}(v_h) + |A'_a| + |A'_h| - \mathsf{len}(\overline{F'})\,. \end{aligned} \tag{7}$$

Now we invoke Lemma 3 with chains T_h, T_a and vertices v_h, v_a in F. By assumption $\mathsf{l}_\#(v_h) < \mathsf{l}_\#(v_a)$, and hence we obtain

$$\beta_\ell(ws) \ge \alpha_F(v_h) + |A_a \cup A_h| = \mathsf{len}(v_h) + |A_a| + |A_h| - \mathsf{len}(\overline{F}) \tag{8}$$

using the definition of α_F, Fact 1, and the observation that $\mathsf{l}_\#(v_h) < \mathsf{l}_\#(v_a)$ implies $v_h \ne v_a$ and together with the definition of v_h, v_a this means that $A_a \cap A_h = \emptyset$ and $|A_a \cup A_h| = |A_a| + |A_h|$. Combining (7) and (8), we conclude that

$$\begin{aligned} \beta_\ell(wsxt) - \beta_\ell(ws) &\le |A'_a| - |A_a| + |A'_h| - |A_h| - \big(\mathsf{len}(\overline{F'}) - \mathsf{len}(\overline{F})\big) \\ &\le \#_{\mathsf{a}}(xt) - h_\Delta(x) \end{aligned}$$

as desired. The last inequality follows from (5) and the fact that there are no more than $\#_{\mathsf{a}}(xt)$ adversarial vertices in F' that do not lie in F.

The case $\mathsf{l}_\#(v_h) \ge \mathsf{l}_\#(v_a)$. We remark that the tree F is compressed. To see this, note that any honest vertex v of F' labeled from the suffix xt must have height strictly larger than $\mathsf{len}(\overline{F_{\lceil\Delta}})$ by axiom (A2); on the other hand, in light of Fact 1 $\mathsf{len}(\overline{F_{\lceil\Delta}}) = \mathsf{len}(\overline{F})$ since ws ends with a quiet period and it follows that the removal of the honest vertices labeled by xs does not affect those of depth at most $\mathsf{len}(\overline{F})$. In particular, F still has an honest vertex of each relevant height and is compressed.

We now invoke Lemma 3 with the chains T_a, T_h and vertices v_a, v_h in F. Since $\mathsf{l}_\#(v_a) \le \mathsf{l}_\#(v_h)$, we obtain:

$$\begin{aligned} \beta_\ell(ws) &\ge \alpha_F(v_a) + |A_a| = \alpha_F(T_a) = \mathsf{len}_F(T_a) - \mathsf{len}(\overline{F_{\lceil\Delta}}) \\ &\ge \big(\mathsf{len}_{F'}(T'_a) - \#_{\mathsf{a}}(xt)\big) - \big(\mathsf{len}(\overline{F'}) - h_\Delta(x)\big) \qquad (9) \\ &= \alpha_{F'}(T'_a) - \#_{\mathsf{a}}(xt) + h_\Delta(x) = \beta_\ell(wsxt) - \#_{\mathsf{a}}(xt) + h_\Delta(x)\,, \end{aligned}$$

where the inequality in line (9) follows from (5). This concludes the proof. □

3.6 The Critical Region

Finally, it remains to tackle the behavior of β_ℓ in the critical region. We establish the two upper bounds mentioned in Sect. 3.3 in Lemmas 7 and 8, and show the crossing-zero property in Lemma 9.

Lemma 7. *Let $\ell \geq 1$, let $w, x \in (\mathbb{N}\times\mathbb{N})^*$ and $s, t \in (\{0\}\times\mathbb{N})^{\Delta}$ be characteristic strings. Then*

$$\beta_\ell(wsxt) \leq \beta_\ell(ws) + \#_{\mathsf{a}}(xt)\ .$$

Proof. As before, let $w' := wsxt$ and let F' be a witness PoW tree $F' \vdash^{\mathsf{W}} w'$; let (T'_h, T'_a) be a pair of witness chains in F' such that $\mathsf{len}(T'_h) = \mathsf{len}(\overline{F'_{\lceil \Delta}}) = \mathsf{len}(\overline{F'})$ (cf. Fact 1). Furthermore, let $F := F'_{|ws|\rceil} \vdash^{\mathsf{W}} ws$ and define $T_h := (T'_h)_{|ws|\rceil}$ and $T_a := (T'_a)_{|ws|\rceil}$, i.e., T_h and T_a are the restrictions of T'_h and T'_a to vertices with labels at most $|ws|$; we have $T_h, T_a \in F$ by definition of F. Moreover, let T_H be a chain in F such that $\mathsf{len}(T_H) = \mathsf{len}(\overline{F})$.

If $T_H \not\sim_\ell T_a$, we have $\beta_\ell(ws) \geq \alpha_F(T_a)$. Looking at the set of vertices $T'_a \setminus T_a$ in F', let $\mathcal{H} \subseteq T'_a \setminus T_a$ denote the set of those vertices $v \in T'_a \setminus T_a$ that satisfy $\mathsf{len}(\overline{F}) < \mathsf{len}(v) \leq \mathsf{len}(\overline{F'})$. Intuitively, $\mathcal{H}$ covers the vertices in the extension $T'_a \setminus T_a$ that have depths in which F' might contain honest vertices with labels greater than $|ws|$. Observe that therefore $|\mathcal{H}| \leq \mathsf{len}(\overline{F'}) - \mathsf{len}(\overline{F})$ and all vertices in $(T'_a \setminus T_a) \setminus \mathcal{H}$ are adversarial. This gives us

$$\begin{aligned}\beta_\ell(w') - \beta_\ell(ws) &\leq \big(\mathsf{len}(T'_a) - \mathsf{len}(\overline{F'})\big) - \big(\mathsf{len}(T_a) - \mathsf{len}(\overline{F})\big) \\ &= \big(\mathsf{len}(T'_a) - \mathsf{len}(T_a)\big) - \big(\mathsf{len}(\overline{F'}) - \mathsf{len}(\overline{F})\big) \\ &\leq \big(|\mathcal{H}| + \#_{\mathsf{a}}(xt)\big) - \big(\mathsf{len}(\overline{F'}) - \mathsf{len}(\overline{F})\big) \leq \#_{\mathsf{a}}(xt)\end{aligned}$$

as desired.

On the other hand, if $T_H \sim_\ell T_a$ then we have $T_H \not\sim_\ell T_h$, and

$$\begin{aligned}\beta_\ell(w') - \beta_\ell(ws) &\leq \big(\mathsf{len}(T'_a) - \mathsf{len}(\overline{F'})\big) - \big(\mathsf{len}(T_h) - \mathsf{len}(T_H)\big) \\ &\leq \big(\mathsf{len}(T'_a) - \mathsf{len}(\overline{F'})\big) + \big(\mathsf{len}(T_H) - \mathsf{len}(T_h)\big)\ .\end{aligned}$$

Observe that if $\mathsf{len}(T'_a) - \mathsf{len}(\overline{F'}) > 0$, all vertices on T'_a with depth greater than $\mathsf{len}(\overline{F'})$ must be adversarial by definition of $\overline{F'}$. Similarly, if $\mathsf{len}(T_H) - \mathsf{len}(T_h) > 0$, then all vertices on T'_h with depth d satisfying $\mathsf{len}(T_h) \leq d \leq \mathsf{len}(\overline{F}) = \mathsf{len}(T_H)$ must be adversarial, as the minimum depth at which honest vertices labeled from x can appear is $\mathsf{len}(\overline{F}) + 1$ due to axiom (A2) and the fact that s contains no honest successes. Putting these two facts together, we get $\mathsf{len}(T'_a) - \mathsf{len}(\overline{F'}) + \mathsf{len}(T_H) - \mathsf{len}(T_h) \leq \#_{\mathsf{a}}(xt)$, concluding the proof also for this case. □

Lemma 8. *Let $\ell \geq 1$, let $w, x \in (\mathbb{N}\times\mathbb{N})^*$ and $s, t \in (\{0\}\times\mathbb{N})^{\Delta}$ be characteristic strings. If $\beta_\ell(ws) \leq h_\Delta(x)$ then*

$$\beta_\ell(wsxt) \leq \#_{\mathsf{a}}(xt)\ .$$

Proof (sketch). The lemma can be established by an argument identical to the proof of Lemma 6, with a single exception.

Using the notation from that proof, in this case we do not prove that $T'_a \setminus T_a$ contains no honest vertices as before. Instead, we observe that if there actually *is* an honest vertex on $T'_a \setminus T_a$, then by definition of T_a this vertex has a label exceeding $|ws|$, and hence the deepest honest vertex in T'_a can only be followed by at most $\#_{\mathsf{a}}(xt)$ adversarial vertices. This directly implies $\beta_\ell(wsxt) \le \#_{\mathsf{a}}(xt)$ and proves the lemma for this case.

Otherwise we again have no honest vertices on $T'_a \setminus T_a$, and the rest of the argument is identical to the proof of Lemma 6 as it never again invokes the assumption about $\beta_\ell(ws)$. The argument gives us $\beta_\ell(wsxt) \le \beta_\ell(ws) + \#_{\mathsf{a}}(xt) - h_\Delta(x)$, and since here we assume $\beta_\ell(ws) \le h_\Delta(x)$ we can conclude $\beta_\ell(wsxt) \le \#_{\mathsf{a}}(xt)$ as desired. □

Lemma 9. *Let $\ell \ge 1$, let $w, x \in (\mathbb{N}\times\mathbb{N})^*$ and $s, t \in (\{0\}\times\mathbb{N})^\Delta$ be characteristic strings. If $|ws| \ge \ell - 1$ and $\beta_\ell(ws) = 0$ then*

$$\beta_\ell(ws(1,0)(0,0)^\Delta) \le -1 .$$

Proof. Let $w' := ws(1,0)(0,0)^\Delta$ and towards a contradiction, assume $\beta_\ell(w') \ge 0$. By definition of β_ℓ, there exists a witness PoW tree $F' \vdash^{\mathsf{W}} w'$ and two chains T'_1, T'_2 in F' such that $T'_1 \not\sim_\ell T'_2$, $\alpha_{F'}(T'_1) = 0$, $\alpha_{F'}(T'_2) \ge 0$, and T'_1 terminates with the unique (and honest) vertex with $\mathsf{l}_\#(v'_\mathsf{h}) = |ws| + 1$ prescribed by w'; let us call this vertex v'_h. (Note that (T'_1, T'_2) are not necessarily witness chains as we don't ask for $\alpha_{F'}(T'_2) = \beta_\ell(F')$, this allows us to require that T'_1 terminates in v'_h without loss of generality.) Denote $F := F'_{|ws|\rceil} \vdash^{\mathsf{W}} ws$ and note that F is in fact obtained from F' by just removing v'_h. As $\#_\mathsf{h}(s) = 0$ and $|s| = \Delta$, by axiom (A2) we have $\mathsf{len}_{F'}(v'_\mathsf{h}) > \mathsf{len}(\overline{F})$ and hence $\mathsf{len}(\overline{F'_{\lceil\Delta}}) = \mathsf{len}(\overline{F'}) > \mathsf{len}(\overline{F}) = \mathsf{len}(\overline{F_{\lceil\Delta}})$. Let $T_1 := (T'_1)_{|ws|\rceil}$. Note that as $T'_1 \not\sim_\ell T'_2$ and $|ws(1,0)| \ge \ell$, we must have $v'_\mathsf{h} \notin T'_2$ and $T'_1 \ne T'_2$, hence T'_2 also exists in F and $T_1 \not\sim_\ell T'_2$ in F. As $\mathsf{len}(\overline{F_{\lceil\Delta}}) < \mathsf{len}(\overline{F'_{\lceil\Delta}})$, we have $\alpha_F(T_1) \ge 0$ and $\alpha_F(T'_2) > 0$, resulting in $\beta_\ell(ws) \ge \beta_\ell(F) > 0$, a contradiction. □

4 Proof-of-Stake Settlement

4.1 Proof-of-Stake Blocktrees

The execution of a longest-chain PoS protocol is in principle similar to the execution of its PoW counterpart, with two notable differences, described in passing already in Sect. 2.1. Most importantly, the effect of an adversarial lottery success is different: it allows the adversary to create an arbitrary number of blocks for the corresponding slot, while in PoW a single lottery success only leads to a single block. Second, a valid PoS chain may only contain at most one block from any given slot, while in PoW the adversary can in principle use multiple adversarial blocks from the same slot to extend the same chain.

To model this behavior, we consider the same alphabet $\Sigma = \mathbb{N} \times \mathbb{N}$ for characteristic strings also in the PoS case. However, the notion of a tree needs to be adapted to capture the above differences. The resulting notion of a PoS tree conceptually matches the 'fork' notion from previous PoS works [2,7].

Definition 10 (PoS tree). *A* PoS tree *is defined exactly as a PoW tree (cf. Definition 1), except that axioms (W3) and (W4) are replaced by the following axioms:*

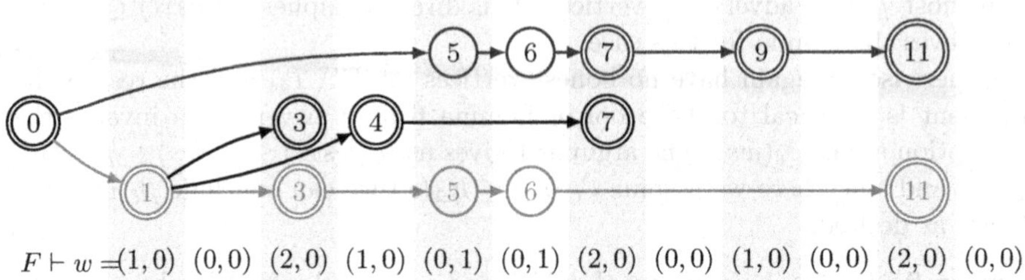

Fig. 3. A public PoS tree F for the characteristic string w with $\Delta = 1$, using the same graphical representation as Fig 2. The tree indicates a successful double spend attack given by the orange and blue chains and highlights a notable feature of the proof-of-stake setting: the adversary's ability to play multiple blocks in slots 5 and 6 permits a double spend attack in circumstances where there would be no attack in the proof-of-work case. We remark that $F = \overline{F} = F_{\lceil 1} = \overline{F_{\lceil 1}}$, since all leaves of F are honest and the last symbol of w is $(0, 0)$. Clearly $\mathsf{len}(\overline{F}_{\lceil 1}) = 5$. The two chains indicated in red and blue each have advantage equal to zero, and both are dominant. Considering that these chains share no vertices after the root, they witness $\mu_1(F) \geq 0$ for the tree F and hence for the characteristic string w. (Color figure online)

(S3) the sequence of labels $\mathsf{l}_\#()$ *along any directed path is strictly increasing;*

(S4) if $w_i = (h_i, a_i)$ *then there are exactly* h_i *honest vertices of* F *with the label* i *and if the number of adversarial vertices with label* i *is nonzero then* $a_i > 0$.

The two changes to tree axioms formally capture the two differences from the PoW setting, listed above. Note that the notation laid out in Definitions 2–6, as well as Fact 1, immediately apply also to the PoS case. An example PoS tree is depicted in Fig. 3.

4.2 PoS Characteristic Quantities: Reach (ρ) and Margin (μ_ℓ)

As established in an existing line of work on PoS protocols going back to [17], the dynamics of a PoS longest-chain protocol can be captured by a pair of quantities called *reach* and *margin*. Note that this is in contrast to the PoW case where a single quantity is sufficient (see Sect. 3), and represents the additional complexity in analyzing the PoS case. We recall the notions of reach and margin as generalized in [3], and adapt them to our notation. For consistency with these works, we refer to μ_ℓ as *margin*; no confusion should arise as it is always clear whether we consider the PoW or PoS margin.

Definition 11 (PoS reach, margin). *For a public PoS tree* $F \vdash^{\mathbf{s}} w$*, we define the* advantage *of a chain* $T \in F$ *exactly as in the PoW case in Definition 7. We define the* reserve *of a chain* T *in* F *to be the number of adversarial indices appearing in* w *after the last index in* T*; specifically, if* v *is the terminal vertex of* T*, we define*

$$\text{reserve}_F(T) := |\{i > \mathsf{l}_\#(v) \mid w_i = (h_i, a_i) \wedge a_i > 0\}| .$$

We then define

$$\text{reach}_F(T) := \alpha_F(T) + \text{reserve}_F(T) ,$$

$$\rho(F) := \max_{T \text{ in } F} \text{reach}_F(T) \qquad \textit{and} \qquad \rho(w) := \max_{\substack{F \vdash^{\mathsf{S}} w \\ F \text{ public}}} \rho(F) .$$

For a given w, we sometimes refer to a tree F and a chain T maximizing the above expressions as a witness tree *and a* witness chain, *respectively; note that these are not necessarily unique.*

For a public PoS tree $F \vdash^{\mathsf{S}} w$ we define the margin *of F, denoted $\mu_\ell(F)$, to be the "penultimate" reach taken over chains T_1, T_2 of F such that $T_1 \not\sim_\ell T_2$:*

$$\mu_\ell(F) := \max_{T_1 \not\sim_\ell T_2} \Big(\min\{\text{reach}_F(T_1), \text{reach}_F(T_2)\}\Big) .$$

There might exist multiple such pairs in F, but under the condition $\ell \geq 1$ there will always exist at least one such pair, as the trivial chain T_0 containing only the root vertex satisfies $T_0 \not\sim_\ell T$ for any T and $\ell \geq 1$, in particular $T_0 \not\sim_\ell T_0$. For this reason, we will always consider $\mu_\ell(\cdot)$ only for $\ell \geq 1$. We again overload the notation by defining

$$\mu_\ell(w) := \max_{\substack{F \vdash^{\mathsf{S}} w \\ F \text{ public}}} \mu_\ell(F) .$$

We use the terms witness tree and witness chains analogously also in the case of margin, it will be always clear from the context whether we are referring to witnesses with respect to reach or margin.

Intuitively, there is again a natural connection between margin and settlement: if w is a characteristic string capturing the execution of the PoS blockchain up to some current time t, and $\mu_\ell(w) < 0$ for some $\ell < t$, then any tree $F \vdash^{\mathsf{S}} w$ that resulted from the execution has $\mu_\ell(F) < 0$ and hence does not allow the adversary to make any honest party at time t adopt a blockchain that would not agree with its current chain up to the index ℓ. In other words, all chains with non-negative reach share their prefix up to slot ℓ, i.e., belong to the same branch. This connection was formally established for PoS in [7,17]; we summarize it for our setting in the following lemma. This will motivate our effort to upper-bound μ_ℓ.

Lemma 10 **([7,17]).** *Consider an execution of a PoS blockchain for L slots as described above, resulting in a characteristic string $w = w_1 \dots w_L$. Let B be a block produced in slot $\ell \in [L]$, and let $t > \ell$ be such that B is contained in some chain $C \in \mathcal{D}_t$. If for every $t' \in \{t, \dots, L\}$ we have $\mu_\ell(w_1 \dots w_{t'}) < 0$ then B is contained in every $C' \in \mathcal{D}_{t'}$ for all $t' \in \{t, \dots, L\}$.*

Similarly as before, if a PoS-tree $F \vdash^{\mathsf{S}} w$ has $\mu_\ell(F) < 0$ then all chains T with $\text{reach}_F(T) \geq 0$ at least $\mathsf{len}(\overline{F_{\lceil \Delta}})$ belong to the same branch. This justifies the following definition.

Definition 12 (Main branch, PoS). *Let* $w \in \Sigma^n$, $\ell \geq 1$, *and* $F \vdash^{\mathsf{S}} w$ *such that* $\mu_\ell(F) < 0$. *The unique branch of* F *that contains all chains with non-negative reach (and possibly other chains) is called the* main branch *of* F *and denoted* $\mathsf{M}^{\mathsf{S}}(F)$.

4.3 Main PoS Theorem

The main result of this section is the following theorem, which is an analogue of Theorem 1 for the PoS case.

Theorem 2 (The PoS Phase Recurrences). *Let* $\ell \geq 1$, *let* $w, x \in (\mathbb{N} \times \mathbb{N})^*$ *and* $s, t \in (\{0\} \times \mathbb{N})^\Delta$ *be characteristic strings. Then we have:*

Reach. $\rho(\varepsilon) = 0$. *Furthermore,*

$$\rho(wsxt) \begin{cases} = \rho(ws) + \#_{[\mathsf{a}]}(xt) - h_\Delta(x) & \text{if } \rho(ws) > h_\Delta(x), \\ \leq \#_{[\mathsf{a}]}(xt) & \text{otherwise.} \end{cases}$$

Margin. *If* $|wsxt| < \ell$ *then* $\mu_\ell(wsxt) = \rho(wsxt)$, *otherwise*

$$\mu_\ell(wsxt) \begin{cases} = \mu_\ell(ws) + \#_{[\mathsf{a}]}(xt) - h_\Delta(x) & \text{if } \mu_\ell(ws) < -\#_{[\mathsf{a}]}(xt), \\ \leq \rho(wsxt) & \text{otherwise.} \end{cases}$$

Crossing zero. *If* $|ws| \geq \ell - 1$ *and* $\rho(ws) = \mu_\ell(ws) = 0$ *then*

$$\mu_\ell(ws(1,0)(0,0)^\Delta) \leq -1\,.$$

Theorem 2 describes the characteristic PoS quantities ρ and μ_ℓ in terms of phase-based recurrences. Similarly to the PoW case, the quantities behave differently in the three regions. Recall that a quantity is informally said to be in the hot region if it is sufficiently positive, such that the currently considered phase cannot bring it down to zero; it is said to be in the cold region if it is sufficiently negative so that it won't climb to zero within the current phase; and finally, it is said to be in the critical region if it is so close to zero that the effects of the special behavior the quantity exhibits around zero are manifested within this phase.

Informally speaking, Theorem 2 states that the reach quantity, as long as it remains within the hot region, exactly performs an "ideal recurrence"

$$\rho(wsxt) = \rho(ws) + \#_{[\mathsf{a}]}(xt) - h_\Delta(x)\,, \tag{10}$$

where it increases by 1 for each adversarially-successful slot, and decreases by 1 whenever the pattern of honest successes enforces an increase in the honest depth h_Δ. Whenever reach approaches the critical region (recall that reach is never negative by definition), we only upper-bound it with the quantity $\#_{[\mathsf{a}]}(xt)$—note that this is analogous to the outcome of the ideal recurrence in a hypothetical case where the honest successes first bring ρ to zero where the remaining honest successes have no effect, while the remaining adversarial successes increase ρ back up to $\#_{[a]}(xt)$. As for margin, before slot ℓ it is identical to reach, and after slot ℓ it (again exactly) performs an analogue of the ideal recurrence (10) as long as it remains within the cold region, while outside of it we only make use of the trivial upper bound by ρ. Finally, we also establish a statement describing the crossing of zero, analogous to PoW.

4.4 Bounding Reach

The following lemma establishes the tightness of the ideal recurrence (10) for reach in the hot region.

Lemma 11 (Reach in the hot region). *Let $\ell \geq 1$, let $w, x \in (\mathbb{N} \times \mathbb{N})^*$ and $s, t \in (\{0\} \times \mathbb{N})^\Delta$ be PoS characteristic strings. If $\rho(ws) > h_\Delta(x)$ then*

$$\rho(wsxt) = \rho(ws) + \#_{[a]}(xt) - h_\Delta(x) .$$

Proof. Denote $w' := wsxt$. We first prove a lower bound on $\rho(w')$. Towards that, consider a public witness tree $G \vdash^{\mathsf{s}} ws$ for reach in wx, and let U be the witness chain achieving $\text{reach}_G(U) = \rho(ws)$. Let v_h be some maximum-depth honest vertex in G, i.e., $\mathsf{len}_G(v_h) = \mathsf{len}(G)$. Construct a labeled rooted tree G' from G by adding $\#_{\mathsf{h}}(x)$ honest vertices that form a subtree rooted in v_h, where each of these honest vertices is always put at the minimal depth allowed by axiom (A2), and labeling them consistently with x. Observe that by construction, G' is a valid public PoS-tree for w'. Using Fact 1 and the construction of G' we have $\mathsf{len}(\overline{G'_{\lceil\Delta}}) = \mathsf{len}(G') = \mathsf{len}(G) + h_\Delta(x)$, and hence

$$\begin{aligned}
\rho(w') &\geq \text{reach}_{G'}(U) = \alpha_{G'}(U) + \text{reserve}_{G'}(U) \\
&= (\alpha_G(U) - h_\Delta(x)) + \big(\text{reserve}_G(U) + \#_{[a]}(xt)\big) \\
&= \rho(ws) + \#_{[a]}(xt) - h_\Delta(x) > \#_{[a]}(xt) , \qquad (11)
\end{aligned}$$

where the last inequality follows by our assumption on $\rho(ws)$.

Towards an upper bound, let $F' \vdash^{\mathsf{s}} w'$ be a public witness tree for reach in w', and let T' be the witness chain for reach in F', i.e., $\text{reach}_{F'}(T') = \rho(w')$. Let $F := \overline{F'_{|ws|\rceil}} \vdash^{\mathsf{s}} ws$ and let T be the restriction of T' to F. Using Fact 1 and the fact that F and F' are by definition public, we have $\overline{F_{\lceil\Delta}} = F$, $\overline{F'_{\lceil\Delta}} = F'$, and $\mathsf{len}(\overline{F'_{\lceil\Delta}}) \geq \mathsf{len}(\overline{F_{\lceil\Delta}}) + h_\Delta(x)$.

We now establish that $T = T'$. Indeed, if that is not the case, let v' be the terminating honest vertex of T'. Since $\mathsf{l}_\#(v') > |ws|$, it must be $\text{reserve}(T') \leq \#_{[a]}(xt)$; and since v' is honest, we have $\rho(w') = \text{reach}_{F'}(T') \leq \#_{[a]}(xt)$. This would be a contradiction with (11), proving that $T = T'$.

Given the above, we have

$$\begin{aligned}
\rho(w') &= \text{reach}_{F'}(T') = \alpha_{F'}(T') + \text{reserve}_{F'}(T') \\
&\leq (\alpha_F(T) - h_\Delta(x)) + \big(\text{reserve}_F(T) + \#_{[a]}(xt)\big) \\
&= \text{reach}_F(T) + \#_{[a]}(xt) - h_\Delta(x) \leq \rho(ws) + \#_{[a]}(xt) - h_\Delta(x)
\end{aligned}$$

as desired. □

It remains to prove the upper bound for reach in the critical region, this is done in the following lemma.

Lemma 12 (Reach approaching zero). *Let $\ell \geq 1$, let $w, x \in (\mathbb{N} \times \mathbb{N})^*$ and $s, t \in (\{0\} \times \mathbb{N})^{\Delta}$ be PoS characteristic strings. If $\rho(ws) \leq h_{\Delta}(x)$ then*

$$\rho(wsxt) \leq \#_{[\mathsf{a}]}(xt) \,.$$

Proof. Let w', F', T', F, T be as in the proof of Lemma 11. We again have $\overline{F_{\lceil\Delta}} = F$, $\overline{F'_{\lceil\Delta}} = F'$, and $\mathsf{len}(\overline{F'_{\lceil\Delta}}) \geq \mathsf{len}(\overline{F_{\lceil\Delta}}) + h_{\Delta}(x)$.

Towards a contradiction, assume that $\rho(wsxt) = \text{reach}_{F'}(T') > \#_{[\mathsf{a}]}(xt)$. As F' is public, clearly T' is honest without loss of generality, and $\mathsf{len}_{F'}(T') \leq \mathsf{len}(F')$, hence we have $\text{reserve}_{F'}(T') > \#_{[\mathsf{a}]}(xt)$. However, this is only possible if $\text{reserve}_{F'}(T')$ accounts also for some indices i (where $w'_i = (h_i, a_i)$ and $a_i > 0$) that satisfy $i < |ws|$, i.e., some adversarial vertices labeled from ws, and hence $T' = T$. However, given that $\mathsf{len}(\overline{F'_{\lceil\Delta}}) \geq \mathsf{len}(\overline{F_{\lceil\Delta}}) + h_{\Delta}(x)$, this means that $\text{reach}_F(T) > h_{\Delta}(x)$ and therefore $\rho(w) > h_{\Delta}(x)$, contradicting our assumption and hence concluding the proof. □

4.5 Bounding Margin

Towards bounding the quantity $\mu_\ell(\cdot)$, first observe that its definition directly implies that $\mu_\ell(w) \leq \rho(w)$ for any $w \in \Sigma^*$. Moreover, for any w with $|w| < \ell$, we actually have $\mu_\ell(w) = \rho(w)$ as, recalling the definition of $\mu_\ell(F)$ and the relation $\not\sim_\ell$, notice that any chain T with $\mathsf{l}_\#(T) < \ell$ satisfies $T \not\sim_\ell T$, and hence the witness chains T_1, T_2 for $\mu_\ell(F)$ may satisfy $T_1 = T_2$.

We now proceed to prove a lower bound on μ_ℓ.

Lemma 13 (Margin lower bound). *Let $\ell \geq 1$, let $w, x \in (\mathbb{N} \times \mathbb{N})^*$ and $s, t \in (\{0\} \times \mathbb{N})^{\Delta}$ be characteristic strings. If $\mu_\ell(ws) < -\#_{[\mathsf{a}]}(xt)$ then*

$$\mu_\ell(wsxt) \geq \mu_\ell(ws) + \#_{[\mathsf{a}]}(xt) - h_{\Delta}(x) \,.$$

The proof of the above lemma uses the same approach as the proof of Lemma 4 in the PoW case, we give it in the full version [14] for completeness. Note that in the PoS case, the construction given in the proof only works under the assumption $\mu_\ell(ws) < -\#_{[\mathsf{a}]}(xt)$, which is however exactly the region we are interested in.

We now turn to upper-bounding μ_ℓ in the specific case $\mu_\ell(ws) < -\#_{[\mathsf{a}]}(xt)$. Given that as observed above, for any ws satisfying $|ws| < \ell$ we have $\mu_\ell(ws) = \rho(ws) \geq 0$, this bound is only applicable after $|ws| \geq \ell$.

Lemma 14 (Margin in the cold region). *Let $\ell \geq 1$, let $w, x \in (\mathbb{N} \times \mathbb{N})^*$ and $s, t \in (\{0\} \times \mathbb{N})^{\Delta}$ be PoS characteristic strings. If $\mu_\ell(ws) < -\#_{[\mathsf{a}]}(xt)$ then*

$$\mu_\ell(wsxt) \leq \mu_\ell(ws) + \#_{[\mathsf{a}]}(xt) - h_{\Delta}(x) \,.$$

The proof of Lemma 14 is an adaptation of the proof of Lemma 5 to the PoS setting, we give it in the full version [14] for completeness.

The previous two lemmas together establish that margin follows an analogue of the ideal recurrence (10) in the cold region.

4.6 Crossing Zero

Finally, we show that if after slot ℓ both quantities are equal to zero, margin can descend to negative values. The proof of Lemma 15 uses essentially the same reasoning as that of Lemma 9, we provide it in the full version.

Lemma 15. *Let $\ell \geq 1$, let $w, x \in (\mathbb{N}\times\mathbb{N})^*$ and $s, t \in (\{0\}\times\mathbb{N})^{\Delta}$ be characteristic strings. If $|ws| \geq \ell - 1$ and $\rho(ws) = \mu_\ell(ws) = 0$ then*

$$\mu_\ell(ws(1,0)(0,0)^{\Delta}) \leq -1 .$$

4.7 A Practical PoS Adversary

In order to evaluate the strength of our settlement bounds, we describe and analyze a natural practical adversary in the proof-of-stake setting. It is analogous to the conventional "private-chain attack" adversary in the PoW setting.

In general, the adversary maintains two chains (L, S) and a "public depth" p, equal to the current depth of the deepest honest block. We collect this data together, writing $(\{L, S\}, p)$, and use l and s to denote the lengths of the chains L and S. We adopt the convention that L is the longer and S is the shorter of the two chains, with ties broken arbitrarily. The adversary will maintain the invariant that $l \geq \max(p, s)$ and that L and S diverge after ℓ. Then it is clear that $l-p$ is a lower bound for reach and that $s-p$ is a lower bound on margin. Given a current adversarial state $(\{L, S\}, p)$, we describe how the adversary responds to a new phase corresponding to a characteristic string x for which $\#_{\mathsf{a}}(x) = a$ and $h_{\Delta}(x) = h$.

In preparation for the full description, we set some terminology. Consider a chain C in this context (which is to say that C is one of S and L). We define the *adversarial extension* to be the chain C_a obtained by adding a path of $\#_{\mathsf{a}}(x)$ adversarial vertices to the end of C; this chain extension is consistent with x. If the length of C is at least p, we additionally define the *honest extension* C_h as follows: Define T_h to be a tree, rooted at the unique vertex of C of depth p, that contains one vertex for each honest success in x arranged so that each vertex is at the minimal depth dictated by Δ delay. The depth of this tree is $h_{\Delta}(x)$. Then define C_h, the honest extension of C, to be any path in this tree of maximal depth (thus having depth $p + h_{\Delta}(x)$). Note that this honest extension C_h is consistent with the characteristic string x of the new phase.

Prior to ℓ, the adversary maintains the invariant that $L = S$. A new phase with characteristic string x is fielded by constructing both the adversarial and honest extensions of L, called L_a and L_h, respectively, and assigning L' to be the longer of these. The resulting state is L' (and $S' = L'$). In the case where this phase includes the slot ℓ, the resulting state is $(\{L_a, L_h\}, p + h)$; observe that these do not share a vertex with label ℓ or more.

After ℓ, there are two cases depending on $(\{L, S\}, p)$. If $s < p$, no honest blocks can be immediately placed on S. In this case, define $S' = S_a$, the adversarial extension of S and define L' be the longer of L_a and L_h, the adversarial and honest extensions of L. The resulting output state is $(\{L', S'\}, p+h)$. The second case arises when $s \geq p$: here we carry out the same procedure but reverse the roles of L and S: specifically, the honest spur is added to S rather than L, yielding two extensions of interest S_h and S_a. The longer of these is declared to be S'; L' is defined to be the simple adversarial extension of L. Note that while these rules are defined in terms of features of the entire phase, they can be carried out in an online fashion with no particular attention to placement of honest vertices (except that all blocks are delivered to honest parties with maximal delay). Note, furthermore, that the attack requires no tie breaking and can be thus carried out by an adversary that requires no capabilities beyond globally and uniformly delayed honest messages. (In contrast, it is not clear how to practically implement adaptive adversarial tie breaking.)

In terms of the recurrence relations (for μ_ℓ and ρ) that this yields, prior to ℓ we have $\mu_\ell = \rho$ by definition and $\rho' = \mu'_\ell = \max(0, \rho + a - h)$ by construction. After ℓ, reach continues to satisfy $\rho' = \max(0, \rho + a - h)$. If $\mu_\ell < 0$ it similarly satisfies $\mu'_\ell = \mu_\ell + a - h$. Otherwise, μ_ℓ is non-negative. We say that a configuration-input pair is "critical" if $\rho + a - h < 0$ (and $\mu_\ell \geq 0$). If the setting is critical, then margin satisfies $\mu'_\ell = \rho + a - h$. (Note that in this case, the two chains have switched roles.) Otherwise, set $\mu'_\ell = 0$ for convenience (as the exact value is not important to track).

5 Numerical Evaluation

In this section, we study explicit bounds provided by our analysis. We implement our analytical framework and make the code available at https://github.com/renling/LCanalysis/. We are interested in both PoW and PoS longest-chain consensus, and we pick one representative system for each. For PoW blockchains we study PoW-based Ethereum because its relatively short block interval presents a more challenging subject for analysis, while Bitcoin with its long block interval was already given fairly tight bounds [13,15]. For PoS blockchains we study Cardano, which implements the Ouroboros Praos protocol [7].

5.1 Modeling the Slot Leader Distribution

We assume the slot leader election is an ideal lottery. That is to say, the probability that any party (honest or adversary) becomes a leader in a slot is proportional to its hashing power (for PoW) or its stake[5] (for PoS), and this probability is independent of any other parties or any other slot. Thus, the total number of slot leaders in a given slot is given by a sum of Bernoulli random variables, one for each party. When there are sufficiently many parties, the sum of Bernoulli

[5] This is a slight simplification in the case of Ouroboros Praos, where the probability of a party that holds an s-fraction of stake (for $s \in [0, 1]$) becoming a slot leader is in fact $1-(1-f)^s$ for a constant f set to 1/20 in Cardano. We adopt this simplification for the sake of broader applicability of our bounds.

random variables can be approximated by a Poisson random variable. More concretely, we model the number of honest leaders in a single slot as a Poisson random variable of parameter r_h, and the number of adversarial leaders in a single slot as a Poisson random variable of parameter r_a. Then, $\frac{r_h}{r_h+r_a}$ (resp. $\frac{r_a}{r_h+r_a}$) is the fraction of honest (resp. adversarial) hashing power in PoW, or stake in PoS. Furthermore, $\frac{1}{r_h+r_a}$ is the expected time it takes for one slot leader to appear, which is the target inter-block time. The inter-block time of Ethereum is roughly 13 s; the inter-block time of Cardano is 20 s. We can then derive r_h and r_a from the target block interval of the blockchain systems, and the assumed adversarial fraction.

Next, we need to make an assumption on the network propagation delay (recall that we denote it Δ_{r} when denominated in seconds). The 90th percentile block propagation time for Ethereum has been measured to be around 2 s [9], hence we will use 2 s as one example value of Δ_{r}. We will also give results for $\Delta_{\mathsf{r}} = 5$ s as a more conservative estimate. We did not find public propagation delay measurements for Cardano, but since Cardano and Ethereum have very similar block sizes, we use the same estimated values of Δ_{r} (i.e., 2 s and 5 s) for Cardano as well.

5.2 Symbol Distribution in a Phase

As our recurrences from Sects. 3 and 4 work at the phase granularity, the first step of the numeric evaluation is to compute the distribution of symbols in a phase. We will use PoS as the example in this subsection. The treatment for PoW is very similar.

Let xt be the characteristic string corresponding to a phase where $x \in (\mathbb{N} \times \mathbb{N})^*$ and $t \in (\{0\} \times \mathbb{N})^{\Delta}$. There are three quantities our recurrences need for each phase:

- $\#_{\mathsf{h}}(x)$, the total number of honest successes in the phase,
- $\#_{[\mathsf{a}]}(xt)$, the total number of slots with adversarial successes in the phase, and
- $h_{\Delta}(x)$, the honest depth of the phase.

The latter two quantities are directly used in the recurrences, and we will explain the role of $\#_{\mathsf{h}}(x)$ in Sect. 5.3.

We now explain how we can compute the joint distribution of the above three quantities for a given slot. By definition, whenever there is a Δ period with no honest successes, the phase ends. We will process one honest success at a time, and at each step, update the joint probability density functions (pdf) of the three quantities of interest. This way makes it easy to compute the distribution of $\#_{\mathsf{h}}(x)$. Each step has a probability of ending the phase and the i-th step gives the probability of $\#_{\mathsf{h}}(x) = i$. To compute the distributions of the other two quantities, we introduce and keep track of the distributions of two additional random variables representing elapsed times:

- S: elapsed time since the beginning of the phase, and
- S_{h_Δ}: elapsed time since the last increase of honest depth.

Let T_h be the interarrival time between the current honest success and the previous honest success. T_h as an interarrival time in a Poisson point process follows an exponential distribution. With each new honest success, the distribution of S is updated by a simple convolution of T_h and the original S (which yields the pdf of the sum of two random variables). The distribution of S_{h_Δ} can be similarly updated except that we always have $S_{h_\Delta} < \Delta$, so the post-Δ portion of the resulting pdf (after convolution) is reset and added to the its pdf at 0 (i.e., probability of $S_{h_\Delta} = 0$). This post-Δ portion of the resulting pdf is also the probability that the new honest success increments the honest depth $h_\Delta(x)$, allowing us to compute the distribution of $h_\Delta(x)$. From here, we can also compute the distribution of the latest inter-honest-success time T_h conditioned on whether or not $h_\Delta(x)$ is incremented. We can then compute the distribution of adversarial successes during this latest T_h, again conditioned on whether or not $h_\Delta(x)$ is incremented. Lastly, we can update the distribution of $\#_{[\mathsf{a}]}(xt)$ and the joint distribution of all three quantities by convolving it with the above conditional pdfs.

5.3 Evaluating the Recurrence

Once we have the characteristic string distribution within a phase, it is relatively straightforward to numerically evaluate the recurrences. We again focus on the PoS case. The PoW case is similar (in fact, simpler, because there is only one quantity involved in the PoW recurrence).

Initially, we must settle on a distribution of (μ_ℓ, ρ) at time ℓ, which corresponds to the moment the transaction of interest appears in a block). While this does depend on ℓ, the distribution converges quickly to a geometric distribution for reasonably large ℓ. For this reason, we will use the stationary distribution of the initial (μ_ℓ, ρ) as its distribution at time ℓ. Also observe that before ℓ, the margin μ_ℓ was equal to reach ρ, making ρ the only quantity of interest. Intuitively, this initial distribution of ρ represents the number of private blocks that the adversary has on top of the longest public honest block when the transaction of interest enters the ledger.

Next, we need to evolve the recurrence until settlement happens. Unfortunately, we do not know when exactly settlement happens as that depends on the adversarial strategy and the initial value of ρ. Therefore, we instead evolve the recurrence until the *earliest possible* time that a settlement error could occur. Observe that a settlement error can occur only after $2k-s$ lottery successes have occurred since ℓ, where s is value of ρ at time ℓ and k is the settlement depth. This is because two chains of length k must exist for the adversary to cause a settlement error. (For example, if $\rho = 2k$ at time ℓ, an adversary can immediately activate the settlement of "buried by k blocks" and violate consistency.) To do so, we need the distribution of the total number of successes in each phase, which is also why we need the quantity $\#_{\mathsf{h}}(x)$ in the joint distribution of a phase.

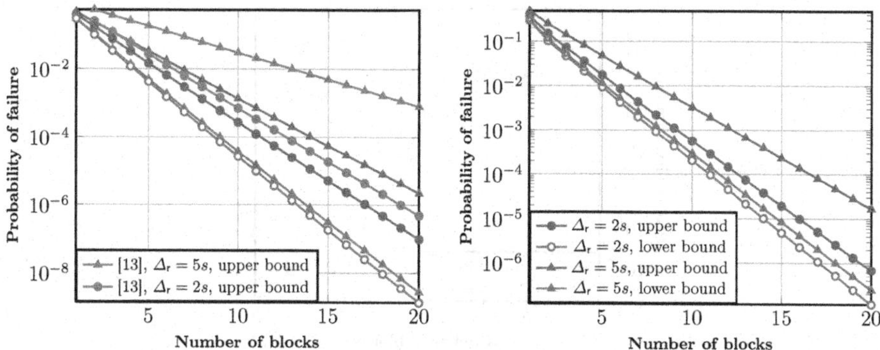

Fig. 4. Left: Ethereum (PoW) block-based settlement failure for a 10% adversary, results from [13] for comparison. **Right:** Cardano (PoS) block-based settlement failure for a 10% adversary. (The right-side legend applies to both figures.)

From here, we keep evolving the recurrence, but "freezing" any probability mass on positive values of the margin. We then evolve the system forward until the (exponentially decaying) contributions from further evolution are negligible.

The same approach can be used to numerically evaluate the concrete attack described in Sect. 4.7 to yield lower bounds on the settlement failure probability for PoS blockchains. The lower bounds for PoW blockchains are based on a simple private-mining attack.

5.4 Numerical Results

Figure 4 is a more detailed version of Fig. 1 from the introduction. It depicts our settlement bounds for Ethereum, compared to the best previous bounds for Ethereum [13]; as well as our new settlement bounds for Cardano. We provide more numerical results in the full version [14].

Our methods also enable a direct comparison between PoW and PoS blockchains in terms of settlement error and settlement delay. Figure 5 plots our settlement upper bound for Cardano and compares it against a hypothetical PoW blockchain with the same inter-block time as Cardano, and under the same network delay and adversarial ratio. We can see that given the same system parameters and at the same settlement depth, a PoS blockchain has a larger settlement error; equivalently, to obtain the same settlement error, a PoS blockchain needs a slightly higher settlement depth. This is an expected price being paid for avoiding the enormous energy consumption of PoW, and is caused by giving the adversary the extra power of creating as many blocks as it wishes using a single success. Our results allow this price to be precisely quantified for the first time.

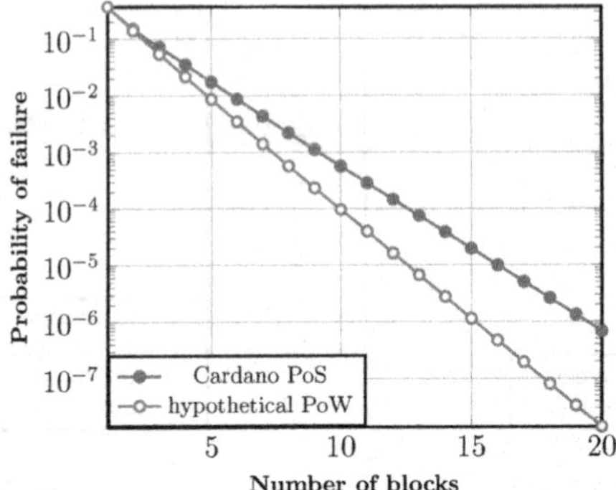

Fig. 5. Comparison of block-based settlement failure upper bounds for Cardano (PoS, 10% adversary, $\Delta_r = 2s$) and a hypothetical PoW protocol with the same parametrization.

6 Conclusions: Practical Relevance

The goal of our work is to provide concrete settlement bounds with practical applicability to deployed longest-chain protocols. We provide the first such bounds for longest-chain PoS, and along the way also derive the best existing settlement bounds for PoW.

We remark that in specific PoS systems there may be additional security factors that affect settlement times. For example, while the lottery in protocols such as Ouroboros [17] cannot be biased by an adversary, another class of protocols including Ouroboros Praos [7] and Snow White [6] allow for so-called grinding of the randomness beacon. While the results of this paper describe the intrinsic aspects of longest-chain rule and apply to both of these protocol classes, for the latter one an additional term accounting for grinding must be considered. Fortunately, these two sources of settlement failure can be studied independently and combined in a straightforward fashion.

While the concrete results we quote consider the parametrizations of Ethereum and Cardano, our methods can be directly applied to compute these statistics for any other choice of block interval, block propagation delay Δ_r, and assumed share of adversarial power. In each specific case, the value Δ_r can be estimated based on measurements, such as those we reference for Ethereum. Finally, estimating the fraction of adversarially controlled stake ultimately comes down to each user's belief about the state of stake distribution across the set of users; nonetheless our results allow each individual user to choose their settlement rule based on their own beliefs about the system and their acceptable failure probability (perhaps depending on the transacted amount).

Acknowledgements. This work is funded in part by National Science Foundation award 2143058.

References

1. Badertscher, C., Gaži, P., Kiayias, A., Russell, A., Zikas, V.: Consensus redux: distributed ledgers in the face of adversarial supremacy. Cryptology ePrint Archive, Report 2020/1021 (2020). https://eprint.iacr.org/2020/1021
2. Badertscher, C., Gazi, P., Kiayias, A., Russell, A., Zikas, V.: Ouroboros genesis: composable proof-of-stake blockchains with dynamic availability. In: Lie, D., Mannan, M., Backes, M., Wang, X. (eds.) ACM CCS 2018, pp. 913–930. ACM Press, October 2018. https://doi.org/10.1145/3243734.3243848
3. Blum, E., Kiayias, A., Moore, C., Quader, S., Russell, A.: The combinatorics of the longest-chain rule: linear consistency for proof-of-stake blockchains. In: Chawla, S. (ed.) 31st SODA, pp. 1135–1154. ACM-SIAM, January 2020. https://doi.org/10.1137/1.9781611975994.69
4. Bonneau, J., Meckler, I., Rao, V., Shapiro, E.: Coda: decentralized cryptocurrency at scale. Cryptology ePrint Archive, Report 2020/352 (2020). https://eprint.iacr.org/2020/352
5. Chen, J., Micali, S.: Algorand. arXiv preprint: arXiv:1607.01341 (2016)
6. Daian, P., Pass, R., Shi, E.: Snow White: robustly reconfigurable consensus and applications to provably secure proof of stake. In: Goldberg, I., Moore, T. (eds.) FC 2019. LNCS, vol. 11598, pp. 23–41. Springer, Cham (2019). https://doi.org/10.1007/978-3-030-32101-7_2
7. David, B., Gaži, P., Kiayias, A., Russell, A.: Ouroboros Praos: an adaptively-secure, semi-synchronous proof-of-stake blockchain. In: Nielsen, J.B., Rijmen, V. (eds.) EUROCRYPT 2018, Part II. LNCS, vol. 10821, pp. 66–98. Springer, Cham (2018). https://doi.org/10.1007/978-3-319-78375-8_3
8. Dembo, A., et al.: Everything is a race and Nakamoto always wins. In: Ligatti, J., Ou, X., Katz, J., Vigna, G. (eds.) ACM CCS 20, pp. 859–878. ACM Press, November 2020. https://doi.org/10.1145/3372297.3417290
9. Ethstats (2021). https://ethstats.net/
10. Eyal, I., Sirer, E.G.: Majority is not enough: Bitcoin mining is vulnerable. In: Christin, N., Safavi-Naini, R. (eds.) FC 2014. Lecture Notes in Computer Science(), vol. 8437, pp. 436–454. Springer, Berlin (2014). https://doi.org/10.1007/978-3-662-45472-5_28
11. Garay, J., Kiayias, A., Leonardos, N.: The bitcoin backbone protocol: analysis and applications. In: Oswald, E., Fischlin, M. (eds.) EUROCRYPT 2015, Part II. LNCS, vol. 9057, pp. 281–310. Springer, Heidelberg (2015). https://doi.org/10.1007/978-3-662-46803-6_10
12. Gazi, P., Kiayias, A., Russell, A.: Tight consistency bounds for bitcoin. In: Ligatti, J., Ou, X., Katz, J., Vigna, G. (eds.) ACM CCS 20, pp. 819–838. ACM Press, November 2020. https://doi.org/10.1145/3372297.3423365
13. Gazi, P., Ren, L., Russell, A.: Practical settlement bounds for proof-of-work blockchains. In: Proceedings of the 2022 ACM SIGSAC Conference on Computer and Communications Security, CCS 2022, pp. 1217–1230. Association for Computing Machinery, New York (2022). https://doi.org/10.1145/3548606.3559368
14. Gaži, P., Ren, L., Russell, A.: Practical settlement bounds for longest-chain consensus. Cryptology ePrint Archive, Paper 2022/1571 (2022). https://eprint.iacr.org/2022/1571
15. Guo, D., Ren, L.: Bitcoin's latency-security analysis made simple. In: Proceedings of the 4th ACM Conference on Advances in Financial Technologies (2022)

16. Kiayias, A., Quader, S., Russell, A.: Consistency of proof-of-stake blockchains with concurrent honest slot leaders. In: 40th IEEE International Conference on Distributed Computing Systems, ICDCS 2020, Singapore, November 29 - December 1, 2020, pp. 776–786. IEEE (2020). https://doi.org/10.1109/ICDCS47774.2020.00065
17. Kiayias, A., Russell, A., David, B., Oliynykov, R.: Ouroboros: a provably secure proof-of-stake blockchain protocol. In: Katz, J., Shacham, H. (eds.) CRYPTO 2017, Part I. LNCS, vol. 10401, pp. 357–388. Springer, Cham (2017). https://doi.org/10.1007/978-3-319-63688-7_12
18. Lamport, L.: The part-time parliament. In: Concurrency: the Works of Leslie Lamport, pp. 277–317 (2019)
19. Li, J., Guo, D.: On analysis of the bitcoin and prism backbone protocols in synchronous networks. In: 2019 57th Annual Allerton Conference on Communication, Control, and Computing (Allerton), pp. 17–24. IEEE (2019)
20. Li, J., Guo, D., Ren, L.: Close latency-security trade-off for the Nakamoto consensus. In: Proceedings of the 3rd ACM Conference on Advances in Financial Technologies, pp. 100–113 (2021)
21. Nakamoto, S.: Bitcoin: a peer-to-peer electronic cash system (2008)
22. Schneider, F.B.: Implementing fault-tolerant services using the state machine approach: a tutorial. ACM Comput. Surv. (CSUR) **22**(4), 299–319 (1990)

New Bounds on the Local Leakage Resilience of Shamir's Secret Sharing Scheme

Ohad Klein[1(✉)] and Ilan Komargodski[1,2]

[1] Hebrew University of Jerusalem, Jerusalem, Israel
ohadkel@gmail.com, ilank@cs.huji.ac.il
[2] NTT Research, Sunnyvale, USA

Abstract. We study the local leakage resilience of Shamir's secret sharing scheme. In Shamir's scheme, a random polynomial f of degree t is sampled over a field of size $p > n$, conditioned on $f(0) = s$ for a secret s. Any t shares $(i, f(i))$ can be used to fully recover f and thereby $f(0)$. But, any $t-1$ evaluations of f at non-zero coordinates are completely independent of $f(0)$. Recent works ask whether the secret remains hidden even if say only 1 bit of information is leaked from each share, independently. This question is well motivated due to the wide range of applications of Shamir's scheme. For instance, it is known that if Shamir's scheme is leakage resilient in some range of parameters, then known secure computation protocols are secure in a local leakage model.

Over characteristic-2 fields, the answer is known to be negative (e.g., Guruswami and Wootters, STOC '16). Benhamouda, Degwekar, Ishai, and Rabin (CRYPTO '18) were the first to give a positive answer assuming computation is done over prime-order fields. They showed that if $t \geq 0.907n$, then Shamir's scheme is leakage resilient. Since then, there has been extensive efforts to improve the above threshold and after a series of works, the current record shows leakage resilience for $t \geq 0.78n$ (Maji et al., ISIT '22). All existing analyses of Shamir's leakage resilience for general leakage functions follow a single framework for which there is a known barrier for any $t \leq 0.5n$.

In this work, we a develop a new analytical framework that allows us to significantly improve upon the previous record and obtain additional new results. Specifically, we show:

1. Shamir's scheme is leakage resilient for any $t \geq 0.69n$.
2. If the leakage functions are guaranteed to be "balanced" (i.e., splitting the domain of possible shares into 2 roughly equal-size parts), then Shamir's scheme is leakage resilient for any $t \geq 0.58n$.
3. If the leakage functions are guaranteed to be "unbalanced" (i.e., splitting the domain of possible shares into 2 parts of very different sizes), then Shamir's scheme is leakage resilient as long as $t \geq 0.01n$. Such a result is *provably* impossible to obtain using the previously known technique.

All of the above apply more generally to any MDS codes-based secret sharing scheme.

Confirming leakage resilience is most important in the range $t \leq n/2$, as in many applications, Shamir's scheme is used with thresholds $t \leq n/2$.

H. Handschuh and A. Lysyanskaya (Eds.): CRYPTO 2023, LNCS 14081, pp. 139–170, 2023.
https://doi.org/10.1007/978-3-031-38557-5_5

As opposed to the previous approach, ours does not seem to have a barrier at $t = n/2$, as demonstrated by our third contribution.

Keywords: Secret sharing · Shamir's scheme · local leakage resilience

1 Introduction

Secret sharing schemes, introduced by Shamir [35] and Blakley [6] are methods that enable a dealer, that holds a secret piece of information, to distribute this secret among n parties such that any subset of at least t parties can reconstruct the secret, while subsets that contain fewer than t parties learn nothing about it.

Secret sharing schemes are extremely useful in various applications across multiple sub-areas of computer science, including cryptography, complexity, and distributed computing and storage. Secret sharing schemes are also strongly related to error correcting codes. We name just a few concrete applications where secret sharing schemes are a fundamental building block: secure multiparty computation protocols [3,11,17], threshold cryptography schemes [13,16,34], and leakage-resilient circuit compilers [15,21,33].

At their basic use-case, secret sharing schemes have an "all-or-nothing"-style security guarantee, wherein an adversary is allowed to corrupt up to t parties but must know absolutely nothing about the others parties' shares. While this assumption is often made in an ideal world, it is a very strong assumption in many practical scenarios. Indeed, it has been long known that side-channel information is widely available [22,23].

Research then has focused on designing new leakage resilient cryptographic protocols in various models of leakage, for example, [2,7,14,30,31]. However, it is also worth understanding whether existing schemes are leakage resilient. Indeed, if an existing method is already leakage resilient, it alleviates the necessity to design, analyse, and deploy new schemes. In this work, we focus on the latter and continue the recent line of works studying the leakage resilience of Shamir's secret sharing scheme [1,5,25–28], the most well-known and useful secret sharing scheme.

(Local) Leakage Resilience of Shamir's Scheme. Shamir's scheme is very simple to describe: For a secret s, the dealer samples a random degree $t-1$ (univariate) polynomial f over a sufficiently large finite field $\mathbb{F}$, conditioned on $f(0) = s$. Then, the dealer gives party i the field element $f(i)$. Evaluations of f at t different points can be used to fully recover f and thereby $s = f(0)$. Also, it is known that any $< t$ evaluations of f (excluding $f(0)$) are completely uncorrelated with $f(0)$. This scheme is the most commonly used (threshold) secret sharing scheme, both in theory and in practice. This is mostly due to its simplicity, elegance, and various useful features it supports like additive homomorphism (i.e., linearity).

We consider local leakage attacks: In addition to fully learning some of the shares, the attacker can leak few bits of information about each other parties' share locally, independently of the other parties' state. That is, the adversary can specify $t' < t$ indices $i_1, \dots, i_{t'} \in [n]$ and n functions $f_1, \dots, f_n$ with a short output. Denoting the shares by $\pi_1, \dots, \pi_n$, it then receives back $\pi_{i_1} \dots, \pi_{i_{t'}}$ and $f_1(\pi_1), \dots, f_n(\pi_n)$, and it needs to guess (something about) $f(0)$.

The motivation of the problem comes from that if Shamir's scheme is leakage resilient, then some applications that use it are more secure than what they are currently known to be. For instance, the work of Benhamouda, Degwekar, Ishai, and Rabin [4,5] (who initiated the study of the problem that we consider) showed that Shamir's scheme leakage resilience implies that a minor variant of the Goldreich-Micali-Wigderson's [17] secure computation protocol is secure even in a local leakage model. Apart from its applications, understanding the leakage resilience of Shamir's scheme is a very natural question on its own right, especially due to its connection to error correcting codes, and more precisely to Reed-Solomon codes. (Shamir's scheme is in particular a Reed-Solomon code.)

State of the Art. The local leakage resilience of Shamir's scheme is far from being understood. Despite significant efforts, there is essentially only one method for analyzing it and for this method there are known barriers showing that it cannot lead to full resolution of the problem. This method, based on Fourier analysis over prime-order fields, was introduced by [4] and since then all works improving upon their bound, somewhat incrementally optimize various parts of the analysis.

For concreteness and simplicity of presentation, we focus on the most studied case where each leakage function (i.e., each f_i) outputs a single bit. Benhamouda et al.'s [4] original work showed that Shamir's scheme is leakage resilient as long as $t \geq 0.907n$. Then, Maji et al. [28] and Benhamouda et al. [5] independently lowered this threshold to $t \geq 0.8675n$ and $t \geq 0.85n$, respectively. The state of the art is due to Maji et al. [27] who showed that Shamir's scheme is leakage resilient as long as $t \geq 0.78n$.

All of the above works, use an analytic proxy (introduced already in [4]'s original work) for upper bounding the statistical distance between leakage distributions of different secrets. Maji et al. [28] showed an inherent barrier for this proof strategy: It is impossible to prove any meaningful result for any $t \leq 0.5n$ (which is required to, say, execute secure computation protocols in the honest majority setting). It is worth noting that Shamir's scheme is *not* leakage resilient if $t = O(n/\log n)$ [28,32].[1]

At a very high level, the analytical proxy bounds the statistical distance between certain distributions via direct expansion and summing up the distances at every point in the sample space. Then, a triangle inequality is performed so that each term in the summation could be analyzed and bound by itself.

[1] Shamir's scheme uses $t \cdot \log p$ bits of entropy if we work over a p-size field, and so intuitively, the total amount of entropy leaked should not exceed this number. If we leak just one bit from every share, then $n < t \cdot \log p$ is required for security. As mentioned, $\log p$ can be replaced by $\log n$.

This triangle inequality, however, is very lossy and causes the proof approach to provably fail whenever $t \leq 0.5n$ [28]. Since many of the applications of Shamir's scheme require $t < n/2$ or $t < n/3$ (for example, BGW [3] or GMW [17] with fairness) there is currently no path to handle them.

1.1 Our Results

In this work, we introduce a completely new analytical framework that, in particular, bypasses the barrier of the only previously known approach. We use our approach to prove several new results that were out of reach previously. At a very high level, we obtain our improvements because our analysis is roughly an ℓ_2 bound on the distance between the corresponding distributions, whereas the previous approach is an ℓ_1 bound. In particular, we never apply lossy triangle inequalities.

Using our new framework, we prove several new results for the leakage resilience of Shamir's scheme. In what follows, we assume that the leakage functions output a single bit, either -1 or 1. Further, we assume that the field size, p, is at most $2^{O(n)}$.[2]

1. We improve the previously best bound on the leakage resilience of Shamir's scheme from $0.78n$ to $0.69n$. That is, Shamir's scheme is leakage resilient as long as $t \geq 0.69n$.
2. We further improve the threshold to $0.58n$ for all "balanced" leakage functions. That is, assuming that the leakage functions satisfy $|\mathbb{E}[f_i]| \leq c$,[3] where $c > 0$ a universal constant, then Shamir's scheme is leakage resilient as long as $t \geq 0.58n$.
3. For the complementary case, where the leakage functions are unbalanced, we break the $t \geq 0.5n$ barrier. Specifically, we show that if the leakage functions satisfy $|\mathbb{E}[f_i]| \geq C$ with a specific constant $C < 1$, then Shamir's scheme is leakage resilient as long as $t \geq 0.01n$. We show that it is *provably* impossible to obtain such a result using the previously known technique.

All of the results above directly generalize to the setting where the adversary further obtains some of the shares in their entirety.[4] Also, we note that all of the above results apply to any MDS code-based secret sharing scheme (i.e., so called Massey secret sharing schemes [29]) of which Shamir's scheme is a special case obtained by using the Reed-Solomon code (see Sect. 2.1).

[2] Typically, Shamir's scheme is used with p proportional to n.

[3] The bias $\mathbb{E}[f_i]$ is the proportion of inputs for which f_i outputs 1 minus the proportion of inputs f_i outputs -1. Note that intuitively, the balanced case has the highest leakage of information.

[4] This is a standard reduction. The view of a distinguisher that sees t' of the n shares in their entirety, can be reduced to a distinguisher for a Shamir secret sharing scheme over $n - t'$ parties that sees none of the shares in their entirety.

Technical Highlight. Our analysis completely deviates from the previous approach that all works followed. In our view this is one of the highlights of this work and we believe that further improvements and results are achievable with our framework. We also believe that some of our intermediate technical transitions are of independent interest. We highlight some of the technical ideas behind our analysis in Sect. 1.3.

Paper Organization. In Sect. 1.2 we survey some related work. In Sect. 1.3 we highlight some of the main technical ideas underlying our analyses. In Sect. 2 we provide preliminary definitions and notation. The main analytical framework is given in Sect. 3. The improved bound for Shamir's scheme leakage resilience for $t \geq 0.69n$ is given in Sect. 4. The bound for $t \geq 0.58n$ and balanced leakage functions is given in Sect. 5. The bound for $t \geq 0.01n$ and unbalanced leakage functions is given in Sect. 6.

1.2 Related Work

While the notion of local leakage may seem rather weak, it can be quite powerful. In particular, it is not hard to see that if we work over a field $\mathbb{F}_{2^k}$ of characteristic 2, then a bit of the secret can be learnt by leaking just one bit from each share. (This is true for any linear secret sharing scheme.) Surprisingly, for Shamir's scheme and in some settings of parameters, Guruswami and Wooters [20] showed that full recovery of a multi-bit secret is possible by leaking only one bit from each share.

Benhamouda et al. [4] were the first to study the local leakage resilience of Shamir's scheme (over prime-order fields) showing that whenever $t \geq 0.907n$, Shamir's scheme is leakage resilient. Maji et al. [28] and Benhamouda et al. [5] independently lowered the threshold to $t \geq 0.8675n$ and $t \geq 0.85n$, respectively. Before the current work, the record was leakage resilience whenever $t \geq 0.78n$ due to Maji et al. [27]. Nielsen and Simkin [32] presented an attack that requires $m > t \log p/(n - t)$ bits of leakage from each secret share, where p is the field size, and then guesses the secret with probability $1/2$.

With the lack of progress in analyzing Shamir's scheme for general leakage functions, efforts have been made to analyze restricted classes of leakage functions or "random" constructions. Maji et al. [25] considered a leakage family that is only allowed to leak an arbitrary single bit from each share (given in their binary representation). This was later generalized to arbitrary bounded-size families of leakage functions by Maji et al. [26]. Maji et al. [28] also proved that a random (linear) secret sharing scheme is leakage resilient to one-bit local leakage when $t \geq 0.5n$. This was partially derandomized in [26,28] who studied the leakage resilience of Shamir's scheme with random evaluation points.

All of the above works essentially use the analytic proxy from [4]'s work for upper bounding the statistical distance between leakage distributions of different secrets. Maji et al. [28] showed that this technique cannot be used to go below threshold $t = n/2$ for general leakage functions.

New (Non-linear) Schemes. A large body of work focused on designing new leakage resilient secret sharing schemes from scratch. Such schemes were constructed for the first time by Dziembowski and Pietrzak [14]. Their scheme involved an interactive reconstruction procedure, which was needed for allowing the reconstruction to access only small part of the shares. Simpler constructions (without the latter efficiency feature) were proposed by Davì et al. [12]. In particular, they presented a simple two-party scheme based on any two-source extractor, such as the inner-product extractor. More general constructions of leakage-resilient secret-sharing schemes were given by Goyal and Kumar [18,19], Srinivasan and Vasudevan [36], Kumar, Meka, and Sahai [24], Chattopadhyay et al. [10], and Chandran et al. [8,9]. All of these works, design specialized secret sharing schemes that have strong leakage resilience properties and/or apply to more general access structures. It is noteworthy that in all of these works, the schemes are non-linear, making them less applicable.

1.3 Main Techniques

A Bound on the Statistical Distance. While the previous approaches directly bound the statistical distance between leakage distributions corresponding to different secrets via a point-by-point analysis, we rather take a more "average case" approach. As our starting point, we use the following inequality[5]. Consider two random variables X and Y, where X is uniform over a size p set and Y is arbitrary. Then for all x_1, x_2 we have

$$\mathsf{SD}(Y|X = x_1, Y|X = x_2) \leq p \cdot \sqrt{\mathop{\mathbb{E}}_{Y}\left[\|P(X|Y) - 1/p\|_2^2\right]}, \tag{1}$$

where $\mathsf{SD}(\cdot,\cdot)$ stands for statistical distance and $P(X|Y)$ is the length-p vector of probabilities of X conditioned on Y. (See Lemma 2.2 for the statement.) The proof of this inequality follows by applying a Pinsker inequality and then expanding via the definition of the Kullback-Leibler (KL) divergence.

In our use case, Y is the output of the leakage functions and X is the secret. The left hand side captures the advantage of an adversary in guessing which secret was used given the leakage. The lemma says that this advantage is upper bounded, roughly, by the average distance of the "distribution of the secret given the leakage" from random.

After reducing the problem to bounding the right-hand side, the analysis continues via (discrete) high-order Fourier analysis. We refer to Sect. 2.4 for an introduction and preliminaries. After several Fourier analytic manipulations, we obtain our main technical result "proxy" for analyzing the leakage resilience of Shamir's scheme, stated next.

Let $f_1, \ldots, f_n \colon \mathbb{F}_p \to \{\pm 1\}$ be arbitrary leakage functions. Further, assume that the secret sharing scheme generates shares π_i via linear functions $\ell_i \colon \mathbb{F}_p^t \to$

[5] We suspect that this inequality is well known, but we could not find it in the literature. Thus, we include a self contained proof.

$\mathbb{F}_p$. Since each ℓ_i is linear, we will sometimes view it as a vector which represents the function by performing inner product with the input. Let ℓ_0 be the function/vector that corresponds to the secret. Lastly, for a set $S \subseteq [n]$, let

$$f_S(x) := \prod_{i \in S} f_i(\ell_i(x)).$$

We show that the chance of guessing the secret correctly given the leakage via the f_i's is at most

$$2\left(p^3 \sum_{k \in \mathbb{F}\setminus\{0\}} \sum_{S \subseteq [n]} \left|\widehat{f_S}(k \cdot \ell_0)\right|^2\right)^{1/4}. \tag{2}$$

Here, $\widehat{f_S}(\alpha)$ is a Fourier coefficient of f_S corresponding to a frequency $\alpha \in \mathbb{F}_p^t$. (See Theorem 3.1 for the statement.)

Interpretation of Eq. (2). Let $S \subseteq [n]$. The attacker is able to compute $f_S(x)$ using the leakage information $f_i(\ell_i(x))$. The correlation between $f_S(x)$ and $\exp(2\pi\iota k\ell_0(x)/p)$ is by definition $\widehat{f_S}(k \cdot \ell_0)$. If the attacker arranges functions f_i (of his choice) with $|\widehat{f_S}(k \cdot \ell_0)|$ large, then by computing $f_S(x)$ the attacker ends up with significant statistical knowledge regarding the secret $\ell_0(x)$. Roughly speaking, the bound in Eq. (2) states that this attack is in some sense optimal – the advantage of the attacker is bounded by the aggregation (sum) of the advantages over all $S \subseteq [n]$ and $k \in \mathbb{F}_p$. We note that the additional p factors in the right hand side of Eq. (2) are presumably an artifact of our proof, and the (standard) choice to bound the left hand side of Eq. (1) rather than a more average-case measure of advantage, such as $\mathsf{SD}(\textbf{Secret}|\textbf{Leakage}, \text{Uniform}(\mathbb{F}_p))$.

General Case $t \geq 0.69n$. We proceed by bounding Eq. (2) in various ways. For instance, when $t \geq n/2$ and $S \subseteq n$, we show that

$$|\widehat{f_S}(\ell_0)| \leq O((2/\pi)^{2t-|S|}). \tag{3}$$

Plugging this in Eq. (2), and replacing ℓ_0 with $k \cdot \ell_0$, we get a geometric sum which is $\exp(-\Omega(n))$ as long as $t \geq 0.69n$ and $p \leq \exp(O(n))$, where the hidden term in the "O" is some fixed small constant. This confirms leakage resilience. In order to prove Eq. (3), we split S into half $S = L \cup R$ and consider

$$\widehat{f_S}(\ell_0) = \mathop{\mathbb{E}}_x \left[f_L(x) \cdot f_R(x) \cdot \exp\left(\frac{2\pi\iota\langle \ell_0, x\rangle}{p}\right)\right] \tag{4}$$

as an inner product of two functions. Using Plancherel's identity we move to Fourier representation. Since the ℓ_i's are MDS (that is, no short linear combination of the ℓ_i's is zero), and the Fourier spectrum of f_L is contained in $\text{span}\{\ell_i \colon i \in L\}$ (likewise for R), most summands vanish, being equal to 0 in one of the Fourier transforms, and allowing to obtain Eq. (3).

Balanced Case $t \geq 0.58n$. Assume the f_i are completely balanced, that is, $\mathbb{E}[f_i] = 0$. Then, $\{f_S\}_{S \subseteq [n] \setminus [n-t]}$ is an orthonormal set of functions. To see this, note that $f_S \cdot f_T = f_{S \Delta T}$ and that $|f_S| = 1$. It is hence sufficient to verify $\mathbb{E}[f_S] = 0$ whenever $S \neq \emptyset$. The premise of t-out-of-n secret sharing scheme implies that as $|S| \leq t$, there is no annihilating linear combination of $\{\ell_i\}_{i \in S}$, which yields that $\mathbb{E}[f_S] = \widehat{f_S}(0) = 0$ through discrete Fourier expansion.

Viewing Eq. (2) as a sum of squares of inner products, we use a variant of the classical Pythagorean theorem to leverage Eq. (3) to the bound

$$\sum_{S\colon S \cap [n-t] = I} \widehat{f_S}(\ell_0)^2 \leq O((2/\pi)^{2t-2|I|})$$

for any $I \subseteq [n-t]$ (see further details in Lemma 5.3). Finally, we use induction to relax this argument for quite (and not completely) balanced functions.

Unbalanced Case $t \geq 0.01n$. This is the simplest of the cases and it applies whenever the leakage functions f_i are sufficiently (but constantly) biased. We first reduce the problem to bounding $\widehat{g_{[n]}}(\ell_0)$ where $g_i = f_i - \mathbb{E}[f_i]$. Then we use that $\mathbb{E}[g_i^2] = \mathbb{E}[f_i^2] - \mathbb{E}[f_i]^2 = \epsilon_i$ with $\epsilon_i > 0$ small to proceed with a Cauchy-Schwarz argument.

2 Preliminaries

For a distribution X we denote by $x \leftarrow X$ the process of sampling a value x from the distribution X. For a set X, we denote by $x \leftarrow X$ the process of sampling a value x from the uniform distribution on X. The support of the distribution X is denoted $\mathsf{supp}(X)$. For an integer $n \in \mathbb{N}$ we denote by $[n]$ the set $\{1, 2, \ldots, n\}$.

2.1 Coding and Secret Sharing

Coding. Let $\mathbb{F}_p$ be a finite field of order p. A linear code C over $\mathbb{F}_p$ of length $n+1$ and rank t is a t-dimensional vector space of $\mathbb{F}_p^{n+1}$. It is often referred to as a $[n+1, t]_{\mathbb{F}_p}$-code. The generator matrix $\mathbf{G} \in \mathbb{F}_p^{t \times (n+1)}$ of C satisfies that for every $\overrightarrow{y} \in C$, there is $\overrightarrow{x} \in \mathbb{F}_p^t$ such that $\overrightarrow{x}\mathbf{G} = \overrightarrow{y}$. We say that a generator matrix $\mathbf{G}$ is in *standard form* if $\mathbf{G} = [\mathbf{I}_t \mid \mathbf{P}]$ where $\mathbf{I}_t \in \mathbb{F}_p^{t \times t}$ is the identity matrix and $\mathbf{P} \in \mathbb{F}_p^{t \times (n-t+1)}$ is the parity check matrix of C. We always assume that generating matrices are in standard form.

Secret Sharing. Secret sharing schemes allow a dealer to distribute a secret piece of information among several parties such that only qualified subsets of parties can reconstruct the secret. The most famous scheme is due to Shamir [35]. In this scheme, a secret is shared among n parties such that any $1 < t < n$ parties can recover the secret while any $t-1$ parties learn nothing about the secret. The scheme is often described as follows: the dealer chooses a random polynomial of degree $t-1$ conditioned on setting the free coefficient to be the secret, and gives the i-th party the evaluation of the polynomial at the point i (the computation is done over a field of size $p > n$). Another way to describe this scheme is by sampling a codeword from a Reed-Solomon code. In fact, any (linear) code gives rise to a secret sharing scheme, as we describe next.

Massey Secret Sharing. Let $C \subseteq \mathbb{F}_p^{n+1}$ be a code. Let $s \in \mathbb{F}_p$ be a secret that we wish to share among n parties. Sample a random codeword $(s_0, \dots, s_n) \in C$ conditioned on $s_0 = s$. Give party i the share s_i, for $i \in [n]$. If the code C is linear with associated generating matrix $\mathbf{G}$, this process can be done as follows. Pick $x_2, \dots, x_t \in \mathbb{F}_p$ uniformly at random and set $x_1 = s$ be the secret. Let $(y_0, \dots, y_n) = (x_1, x_2, \dots, x_t) \cdot \mathbf{G}$. The secret share of party i is y_i. Observe that since $\mathbf{G}$ is in standard form, $y_0 = s$. Since y_i is some linear function of $\{x_j\}_j$, we usually write $y_i = \ell_i(x)$ where $\ell_i \colon \mathbb{F}_p^t \to \mathbb{F}_p$ is a linear function.

2.2 Entropy and Distances

Given a random variable X supported in a finite set $\mathcal{X}$, its entropy is

$$H(X) = -\sum_{x \in \mathcal{X}} \Pr[X = x] \cdot \log \Pr[X = x].$$

The conditional entropy of a random variable Y supported in a finite set $\mathcal{Y}$ given that the value of another random variable X supported in a finite set $\mathcal{Y}$

$$H(Y \mid X) = -\sum_{x \in \mathcal{X}, y \in \mathcal{Y}} \Pr[X = x, Y = y] \cdot \log \frac{\Pr[X = x, Y = y]}{\Pr[X = x]}.$$

Let P and Q be two distributions over a finite set Ω. The statistical distance between P and Q is

$$\mathsf{SD}(P, Q) = \frac{1}{2} \sum_{x \in \Omega} |P(x) - Q(x)|.$$

We say that P and Q are ϵ-close if $\mathsf{SD}(P, Q) \le \epsilon$.
The KL-divergence between the distributions P and Q is defined to be

$$\mathsf{KL}(P \| Q) = \sum_{x \in \Omega} P(x) \cdot \log \frac{P(x)}{Q(x)} = H(P, Q) - H(P),$$

where and $H(P) = -\sum_{x \in \Omega} P(x) \cdot \log P(x)$ is the entropy of P and $H(P, Q) = -\sum_{x \in \Omega} P(x) \cdot \log Q(x)$ is the cross entropy of P and Q.

The well-known Pinsker inequality relates the statistical distance and the KL-divergence of P and Q.

Theorem 2.1 (Pinsker inequality).

$$\mathsf{SD}(P, Q) \le \sqrt{\frac{1}{2} \cdot \mathsf{KL}(P \| Q)}.$$

Using Pinsker's inequality, we prove the following useful inequality.

Lemma 2.2. *Let X, Y be (possibly dependent) random variables. Assume that X is uniformly distributed in a set $\mathcal{X}$ of size p. Then, for every $x_1, x_2 \in \mathcal{X}$, it holds that*

$$\mathsf{SD}(Y|X = x_1, Y|X = x_2) \le p \cdot \sqrt{\mathop{\mathbb{E}}_{Y}\left[\|P(X|Y) - P(X)\|_2^2\right]},$$

where $P(X)$ is the length-p vector of probabilities of X.

Proof. For X distributed uniformly over $\mathcal{X}$ and for every $x_1, x_2 \in \mathcal{X}$ (assuming $x_1 \neq x_2$), applying the triangle inequality, we have that

$$\begin{aligned}(\mathsf{SD}(Y|X = x_1, Y|X = x_2))^2 &\le \sum_{k=1}^{2} 2 \cdot (\mathsf{SD}(Y|X = x_k, Y))^2 \\ &\le \sum_{x \in \mathcal{X}} 2 \cdot (\mathsf{SD}(Y|X = x, Y))^2 .\end{aligned}$$

By Pinsker's inequality (Theorem 2.1), the above can be bounded by

$$\le \sum_{x \in \mathcal{X}} \mathsf{KL}\left(Y|X = x \| Y\right)$$

Let $\mathcal{Y}$ be the support of Y. By definition of KL divergence, we expand the above as

$$\begin{aligned}&= \sum_{x \in \mathcal{X}} \sum_{y \in \mathcal{Y}} \Pr[Y = y|X = x] \cdot \log \frac{\Pr[Y = y|X = x]}{\Pr[Y = y]} \\ &= \sum_{x \in \mathcal{X}} \sum_{y \in \mathcal{Y}} \Pr[X = x|Y = y] \cdot \frac{\Pr[Y = y]}{\Pr[X = x]} \cdot \log \frac{\Pr[X = x|Y = y]}{\Pr[X = x]} \\ &= p \cdot \sum_{x \in \mathcal{X}} \mathop{\mathrm{E}}_{y \leftarrow Y} \left[\Pr[X = x|Y = y] \cdot \log \frac{\Pr[X = x|Y = y]}{1/p}\right]\end{aligned}$$

Since $\log x \le x - 1$ and by linearity of expectation, we get

$$\begin{aligned}&\le p^2 \cdot \sum_{x \in \mathcal{X}} \mathop{\mathrm{E}}_{y \leftarrow Y} \left[\Pr[X = x|Y = y] \cdot \left(\Pr[X = x|Y = y] - \frac{1}{p}\right)\right] \\ &= p^2 \cdot \mathop{\mathrm{E}}_{y \leftarrow Y} \left[\sum_{x \in \mathcal{X}} \Pr[X = x|Y = y] \cdot \left(\Pr[X = x|Y = y] - \frac{1}{p}\right)\right] \\ &= p^2 \cdot \mathop{\mathbb{E}}_{Y}\left[\|P(X|Y) - P(X)\|_2^2\right],\end{aligned}$$

where the last equality holds since $\sum_{x \in \mathcal{X}} \Pr[Z = x](\Pr[Z = x] - 1/p) = \sum_{x \in \mathcal{X}} (\Pr[Z = x] - 1/p)^2$ for a random variable Z supported on a set $\mathcal{X}$ of size p. ◻

2.3 Leakage Resilient Secret Sharing

We consider the local leakage resilience notion, following Benhamounda et al. [4] and [5, Definition 4.1]. In this model, in addition to fully learning some of the shares, the attacker can leak few bits of information about each other parties' share locally and independently of the other parties' state.

Consider a t-out-of-n secret sharing scheme with shares ranging in a set $\mathcal{X}$ of size p. Denote by $\mathsf{Share}(s)$ the function that takes as input a secret s and outputs n shares $\pi_1, \ldots, \pi_n$ (fed with uniform randomness). We say that the scheme is (t', m, ϵ)-*local leakage resilient* if for any two secrets s_0, s_1, any $f_1, \ldots, f_n \colon \mathcal{X} \to \{-1, 1\}^m$ and any subset of parties $\Theta \subseteq [n]$ of size at most t', it holds that the distributions

$$(\{\pi_i\}_{i\in\Theta}, f_1(\pi_1), \ldots, f_n(\pi_n)) \quad | \quad \pi_1, \ldots, \pi_n \leftarrow \mathsf{Share}(s_0)$$

and

$$(\{\pi_i\}_{i\in\Theta}, f_1(\pi_1), \ldots, f_n(\pi_n)) \quad | \quad \pi_1, \ldots, \pi_n \leftarrow \mathsf{Share}(s_1)$$

are ϵ-close in statistical distance.

Assuming that $t' = 0$. Following all previous works in this area, in our technical part, we assume that $t' = 0$. This is justified since it can be made somewhat without loss of generality, up to a loss in parameters. Specifically, since we consider MDS code-based secret sharing schemes, once some t' shares are fully leaked, the rest behaves as an MDS code except on fewer parties. That is, if we fully leak t' shares, then we remain with an identical secret sharing scheme on $n - t'$ parties. So, if we prove $(0, m, \epsilon)$-leakage resilience for a t-out-of-n scheme, then it implies a (t', m, ϵ)-leakage resilience for a t-out-of-$(n - t')$ scheme.

2.4 Fourier Analysis

We introduce basic notation and recall facts from Fourier analysis. We interchangeably write $\mathbb{F}_p$ either for the field with p (prime) elements, or the group $\mathbb{Z}/p\mathbb{Z}$, or the set of numbers $\{0, 1, \ldots, p-1\}$ where the meaning is clear from the context.

The characters of the group $\mathbb{F}_p$ are the complex-valued functions $\chi_a \colon \mathbb{F}_p \to \mathbb{C}$, where a ranges over $\mathbb{F}_p$, defined as $\chi_a(x) = \exp(2\pi\iota a x/p)$. For a complex number $z \in \mathbb{C}$, we let $\overline{z}$ be its complex conjugate. The characters are an orthonormal basis with respect to the inner product $\langle f, g\rangle = \mathbb{E}_x[f(x) \cdot \overline{g(x)}]$ with x chosen uniformly from $\mathbb{F}_p$. The characters inherit the group structure: $\chi_a \cdot \chi_b = \chi_{a+b}$ and $\chi_a^{-1} = \overline{\chi_a} = \chi_{-a}$. Every function $f \colon \mathbb{F}_p \to \mathbb{C}$ can then be uniquely written as a linear combination $f = \sum_{a\in\mathbb{F}_p} \widehat{f}(a) \cdot \chi_a$ with the Fourier coefficients $\widehat{f}(a)$ given by $\widehat{f}(a) = \langle f, \chi_a\rangle = \mathbb{E}_x[f(x) \cdot \overline{\chi_a(x)}]$.

The L_2-norm of f is $\|f\|_2 = (\mathbb{E}_x[|f(x)|^2])^{1/2}$ and its L_∞ norm is $\|f\|_\infty = \max_x |f(x)|$. The ℓ_2 norm of $\widehat{f}$ is $\|\widehat{f}\|_2 = \sqrt{\sum_{\alpha\in\mathbb{F}_p} \left|\widehat{f}(\alpha)\right|^2}$. Parseval's identity is

$\|f\|_2^2 = \sum_{\alpha\in\mathbb{F}_p} \left|\widehat{f}(\alpha)\right|^2$. All of the above naturally extends to $\mathbb{F}_p^n$ by tensoring. Explicitly, a character of $\mathbb{F}_p^n$ associated with the frequency $\alpha \in \mathbb{F}_p^n$ is given by $\chi_\alpha(x) := \exp(2\pi\iota\langle\alpha, x\rangle/p)$, and the Fourier expansion of $f\colon \mathbb{F}_p^n \to \mathbb{C}$ is given by $f = \sum_{\alpha\in\mathbb{F}_p^n} \widehat{f}(\alpha)\chi_\alpha$ with $\widehat{f}(\alpha) \in \mathbb{C}$ satisfying $\widehat{f}(\alpha) = \mathbb{E}_x[f(x)\overline{\chi_\alpha(x)}]$, where $x \sim \mathbb{F}_p^n$ is uniformly distributed. In addition, α is interchangeably identified with the linear function $\alpha(x) = \langle\alpha, x\rangle$. Plancherel's identity gives $\mathbb{E}_x[f(x)\overline{g(x)}] = \sum_{\alpha\in\mathbb{F}_p^n} \widehat{f}(\alpha)\overline{\widehat{g}(\alpha)}$ where $g\colon \mathbb{F}_p^n \to \mathbb{C}$.

Euler's formula states that for any real number x, $\exp(ix) = \cos(x) + i\sin(x)$ and therefore $\mathsf{Re}(\exp(ix)) = \cos(x)$, where $\mathsf{Re}(z) = (z + \overline{z})/2$.

3 Main Analytical Framework

Let $\ell_0, \ldots, \ell_n\colon \mathbb{F}_p^t \to \mathbb{F}_p$ be linear functions (i.e., $\ell_i(x) = \sum_{j=1}^t \ell_{ij}x_j$), and let $f_1, \ldots, f_n\colon \mathbb{F}_p \to \{-1, 1\}$ be arbitrary functions. In applications, x is the internal randomness generating the secret sharing scheme, while $\ell_i(x)$ is the i'th share, with $\ell_0(x)$ the secret. We may sometimes view the ℓ_i's as functions and other times as vectors, depending on the context. We denote

$$\mathsf{leak}(x) := (f_1(\ell_1(x)), \ldots, f_n(\ell_n(x))).$$

Moreover, when ℓ_i are clear from the context, define the function $f_S\colon \mathbb{F}_p^t \to \{-1, 1\}$ as

$$f_S(x) := \prod_{i\in S} f_i(\ell_i(x)).$$

The main theorem of this section is stated next.

Theorem 3.1. *Let $\ell_0, \ldots, \ell_n\colon \mathbb{F}_p^t \to \mathbb{F}_p$ be $n+1$ nonzero linear functions. Let $f_1, \ldots, f_n\colon \mathbb{F}_p \to \{-1, 1\}$ be arbitrary functions. Then, for every $s_1, s_2 \in \mathbb{F}_p$, it holds that*

$$\mathsf{SD}(\mathsf{leak}(X)|\ell_0(X) = s_1, \mathsf{leak}(X)|\ell_0(X) = s_2) \\ \leq \\ 2\left(p^3 \sum_{k\in\mathbb{F}_p\setminus\{0\}} \sum_{S\subseteq[n]} \left|\widehat{f_S}(k\cdot\ell_0)\right|^2\right)^{1/4}, \tag{5}$$

where X is distributed uniformly over $\mathbb{F}_p^t$.

Proof. Let

$$(*) := \left(\mathsf{SD}(\mathsf{leak}(X)|\ell_0(X) = s_1, \mathsf{leak}(X)|\ell_0(X) = s_2)\right)^2.$$

For X distributed uniformly over $\mathbb{F}_p^t$ and for every $s_1, s_2 \in \mathbb{F}_p$, applying Lemma 2.2, we have that

$$(*) \leq p^2 \cdot \mathop{\mathbb{E}}_{b \leftarrow \mathsf{leak}(X)} \left[\| P(\ell_0(X) | \mathsf{leak}(X) = b) - P(\ell_0(X)) \|_2^2 \right].$$

For $b \in \{-1, 1\}^n$, let $D_b \colon \mathbb{F}_p \to \mathbb{R}$ be $D_b = P(\ell_0(X) | \mathsf{leak}(X) = b)$, that is

$$D_b(k) = \Pr_{X \leftarrow \mathbb{F}_p^t} [\ell_0(X) = k | \mathsf{leak}(X) = b].$$

Further, recall that ℓ_0 is some nonzero linear function from $\mathbb{F}_p^t$ to $\mathbb{F}_p$, and as such, it satisfies

$$\Pr[\ell_0(X) = k] = 1/p.$$

We immediately deduce that

$$(*) \leq p^2 \cdot \mathop{\mathbb{E}}_{b \leftarrow \mathsf{leak}(X)} \left[\sum_{k \in \mathbb{F}_p} |D_b(k) - 1/p|^2 \right].$$

Observe that for all b,

$$\widehat{D_b}(0) = \mathop{\mathbb{E}}_{k \leftarrow \mathbb{F}_p} [D_b(k)] = \frac{1}{p} \sum_{k \in \mathbb{F}_p} \Pr_{x \leftarrow \mathbb{F}_p^t} [\ell_0(x) = k | \mathsf{leak}(x) = b] = \frac{1}{p} \cdot 1.$$

Therefore, by Parseval's identity,

$$\sum_{k \in \mathbb{F}_p} |D_b(k) - 1/p|^2 = \sum_{k \in \mathbb{F}_p} |D_b(k) - \widehat{D_b}(0)|^2 = p \sum_{k \in \mathbb{F}_p \setminus \{0\}} \left| \widehat{D_b}(k) \right|^2.$$

Hence,

$$(*) \leq p^3 \cdot \mathop{\mathbb{E}}_{b \leftarrow \mathsf{leak}(X)} \left[\sum_{k \in \mathbb{F}_p \setminus \{0\}} \left| \widehat{D_b}(k) \right|^2 \right] \tag{6}$$

$$= p^3 \cdot \sum_{k \in \mathbb{F}_p \setminus \{0\}} \mathop{\mathbb{E}}_{b \leftarrow \mathsf{leak}(X)} \left[\left| \widehat{D_b}(k) \right|^2 \right] \tag{7}$$

For $b \in \{-1, 1\}^n$, let A_b be the set of x's with $\mathsf{leak}(x) = b$. Define $\mu(A_b) = |A_b|/p^t$ to be its density. For a set A, we let $\mathbf{1}_A(x)$ be the indicator function that outputs 1 if $x \in A$, and 0 otherwise. Likewise, for an event E, we denote $\mathbf{1}_E$ as the indicator that is 1 if E happens and 0 otherwise. For each $k \in \mathbb{F}_p$, it holds that

$$\begin{aligned}
\widehat{D_b}(k) = \langle D_b, \chi_k \rangle &= \frac{1}{p} \cdot \sum_{z \in \mathbb{F}_p} D_b(z) \cdot \overline{\chi_k(z)} \\
&= \frac{1}{p} \cdot \sum_{z \in \mathbb{F}_p} \Pr_{x \leftarrow \mathbb{F}_p^t} [\ell_0(x) = z | \mathsf{leak}(x) = b] \cdot \overline{\chi_k(z)} \\
&= \frac{1}{p} \cdot \sum_{z \in \mathbb{F}_p} \sum_{x \in \mathbb{F}_p^t} \frac{\mathbf{1}_{x \in A_b}}{\mu(A_b)} \cdot \frac{\mathbf{1}_{\ell_0(x)=z}}{p^t} \cdot \overline{\chi_k(z)} \\
&= \frac{1}{p \cdot \mu(A_b)} \sum_{x \in \mathbb{F}_p^t} \frac{1}{p^t} \cdot \mathbf{1}_{x \in A_b} \sum_{z \in \mathbb{F}_p} \mathbf{1}_{\ell_0(x)=z} \cdot \overline{\chi_k(z)} \\
&= \frac{1}{p \cdot \mu(A_b)} \sum_{x \in \mathbb{F}_p^t} \frac{1}{p^t} \cdot \mathbf{1}_{x \in A_b} \cdot \overline{\chi_k(\ell_0(x))} \\
&= \frac{1}{p \cdot \mu(A_b)} \mathop{\mathbb{E}}_{x \leftarrow \mathbb{F}_p^t} \left[\mathbf{1}_{A_b}(x) \cdot \overline{\chi_k(\ell_0(x))} \right] \\
&= \frac{\widehat{\mathbf{1}_{A_b}}(k \cdot \ell_0)}{p \cdot \mu(A_b)}.
\end{aligned}$$

In order to simplify $\widehat{\mathbf{1}_{A_b}}(k \cdot \ell_0)$, we denote $f_S(x) = \prod_{i \in S} f_i(\ell_i(x))$ and $b^S = \prod_{i \in S} b_i$, as well as $g_b(x) = 2^{-n} \sum_{S \subseteq [n]} \left(b^S \cdot f_S(x) \right)$. We prove $g_b = \mathbf{1}_{A_b}$:

$$\mathbf{1}_{A_b}(x) = \prod_{i=1}^{n} \mathbf{1}_{f_i(\ell_i(x))=b_i} = \prod_{i=1}^{n} \frac{1 + b_i \cdot f_i(\ell_i(x))}{2} = \frac{1}{2^n} \sum_{S \subseteq [n]} = g_b(x).$$

In particular,

$$\widehat{\mathbf{1}_{A_b}}(k \cdot \ell_0) = \widehat{g_b}(k \cdot \ell_0).$$

Plugging it back in (6) we get

$$\begin{aligned}
(*) &\le p^3 \cdot \sum_{k \in \mathbb{F}_p \setminus \{0\}} \mathop{\mathbb{E}}_{b \leftarrow \mathsf{leak}(X)} \left[\left| \widehat{D_b}(k) \right|^2 \right] \\
&= p \cdot \sum_{k \in \mathbb{F}_p \setminus \{0\}} \mathop{\mathbb{E}}_{b \leftarrow \mathsf{leak}(X)} \left[\left| \frac{\widehat{g_b}(k \cdot \ell_0)}{\mu(A_b)} \right|^2 \right] \\
&= p \cdot \sum_{k \in \mathbb{F}_p \setminus \{0\}} \sum_{\substack{b \in \{-1,1\}^n, \\ \mu(A_b) \neq 0}} \frac{|\widehat{g_b}(k \cdot \ell_0)|^2}{\mu(A_b)},
\end{aligned} \tag{8}$$

where the last equality holds since each $b \in \{-1, 1\}^n$ is attained as $\mathsf{leak}(X)$ with probability $\mu(A_b)$.

To bound the last term on (8), we separately bound the b's with $\mu(A_b) < C/2^n$, and b's with $\mu(A_b) \ge C/2^n$, where $C > 0$ is a parameter that will be optimized later. For the first type of summands, we note that always $|\widehat{g_b}(k \cdot \ell_0)| \le \mathbb{E}\,|g_b| = \mu(A_b)$, as $\widehat{g_b}(k \cdot \ell_0)$ is a Fourier coefficient of $g_b = \mathbf{1}_{A_b}$. Hence,

$|\widehat{g_b}(k\cdot\ell_0)|^2/\mu(A_b)$ is bounded by $\mu(A_b)$. For b's with $\mu(A_b) \geq C/2^n$, we are going to replace $\mu(A_b)$ in the denominator by $C/2^n$.

$$
\begin{aligned}
(*) &\leq p \cdot \sum_{k\in\mathbb{F}_p\setminus\{0\}} \sum_{\substack{b\in\{-1,1\}^n,\\ 0<\mu(A_b)<C/2^n}} \mu(A_b) + p\cdot \sum_{k\in\mathbb{F}_p\setminus\{0\}} \frac{2^n}{C} \cdot \sum_{\substack{b\in\{-1,1\}^n,\\ \mu(A_b)\geq C/2^n}} |\widehat{g_b}(k\cdot\ell_0)|^2 \\
&\leq p^2\cdot 2^n \cdot \frac{C}{2^n} + p\cdot \frac{\sum_{k\in\mathbb{F}_p\setminus\{0\}} \mathbb{E}_{b\leftarrow\{-1,1\}^n}\left[\left|\sum_{S\subseteq[n]} b^S\cdot \widehat{f_S}(k\cdot\ell_0)\right|^2\right]}{C} \\
&= p^2\cdot C + \frac{p\cdot\sum_{k\in\mathbb{F}_p\setminus\{0\}}\sum_{S\subseteq[n]}\left|\widehat{f_S}(k\cdot\ell_0)\right|^2}{C},
\end{aligned}
\tag{9}
$$

where the last inequality is Parseval's identity for functions over $\{-1,1\}^n$. Optimizing the value of C, we conclude

$$
(*) \leq 2\cdot\sqrt{p^3\sum_{k\in\mathbb{F}_p\setminus\{0\}}\sum_{S\subseteq[n]}\left|\widehat{f_S}(k\cdot\ell_0)\right|^2},
$$

finishing the proof (recall the definition of $(*)$). □

Remark 1 (Multi-bit output leakage). It is possible to extend the statement and analysis of Theorem 3.1 to the setting where each f_i outputs more than 1 bit. (Specifically, the definition of f_S would need to be adjusted). We leave this direction for future research.

4 Leakage Resilience for $t \geq 0.69n$

The main theorem we prove in this section is as follows.

Theorem 4.1. *Let $\ell_0,\ldots,\ell_n\colon \mathbb{F}_p^t \to \mathbb{F}_p$ be $n+1$ linear functions such that every t of them are linearly independent. Let $f_1,\ldots,f_n\colon \mathbb{F}_p \to \{-1,1\}$ be arbitrary functions. Let $f_S(x) = \prod_{i\in S} f_i(\ell_i(x))$. Then, for $t \geq 0.69n$, it holds that*

$$
\sum_{k\in\mathbb{F}_p\setminus\{0\}}\sum_{S\subseteq[n]}\left|\widehat{f_S}(k\cdot\ell_0)\right|^2 \leq (p-1)\cdot 2^{-\Omega(n)}.
$$

Theorem 4.1 is an implication of the following lemma:

Lemma 4.2. *Let $\ell_0,\ldots,\ell_n\colon \mathbb{F}_p^t \to \mathbb{F}_p$ be $n+1$ linear functions such that every t of them are linearly independent. Let $f_1,\ldots,f_n\colon \mathbb{F}_p \to \{-1,1\}$ be arbitrary functions. If $n \leq 2t$ and $p \geq n$, then*

$$
\left|\widehat{f_{[n]}}(\ell_0)\right| \leq O((2/\pi)^{2t-n}). \tag{10}
$$

To deduce Theorem 4.1 we plug in the above lemma with $[n]$ replaced by S. That is, because the assumptions of Lemma 4.2 apply to $\{\ell_i\}_{i\in S}$ and $\{f_i\}_{i\in S}$ from Theorem 4.1, we may deduce (10) with $[n]$ replaced by S, that is,

$$\left|\widehat{f_S}(\ell_0)\right| \leq O((2/\pi)^{2t-|S|}).$$

We note that once $|S| < t$ then in fact

$$\widehat{f_S}(\ell_0) = 0,$$

as the Fourier coefficients of f_S are supported on characters corresponding to functionals of the form $\sum_{i\in S} \alpha_i \ell_i$ with $\alpha_i \in \mathbb{F}_p$. However, non of these functionals is being ℓ_0, by assumption.

Proof (Proof of Theorem 4.1*).* For each $k \in \mathbb{F} \setminus \{0\}$ and $S \subseteq [n]$, we bound $\left|\widehat{f_S}(k\cdot\ell_0)\right|$ separately. Specifically, Lemma 4.2 implies that for every $k \in \mathbb{F}\setminus\{0\}$ and $S \subseteq [n]$, it holds that

$$\left|\widehat{f_S}(k\cdot\ell_0)\right|^2 \leq O\left((2/\pi)^{4t-2|S|}\right). \tag{11}$$

Hence,

$$\begin{aligned}\sum_{S\subseteq[n]} \left|\widehat{f_S}(k\cdot\ell_0)\right|^2 &\leq \sum_{z=0}^{n} \binom{n}{z} \cdot O\left((2/\pi)^{4t-2z}\right) \\ &= O\left((2/\pi)^{4t} \cdot \left((\pi/2)^2+1\right)^n\right).\end{aligned}$$

This last term is exponentially small in n as long as t/n is strictly larger than a constant C that we find next. The ratio of t/n in which the bound is $\exp(0\cdot n) = 1$ corresponds to $(2/\pi)^{4t} \cdot ((\pi/2)^2+1)^n = 1$, that is

$$4t\log(2/\pi) = -n\left(\log\left((\pi/2)^2+1\right)\right)$$

which means that

$$C = \frac{t}{n} = \frac{\log((\pi/2)^2+1)}{4\log(\pi/2)} \approx 0.688.$$

Since we assume $t \geq 0.69n$, then

$$\sum_{k\in\mathbb{F}_p\setminus\{0\}} \sum_{S\subseteq[n]} \left(\widehat{f_S}(k\cdot\ell_0)\right)^2 \leq (p-1)\cdot 2^{-\Omega(n)},$$

as required. □

We proceed with the proof of Lemma 4.2.

Notation. Let $g\colon \mathbb{F}_p \to \mathbb{R}$ be a function. We define the max-norm of its Fourier spectrum as

$$\|\widehat{g}\|_\infty := \max_{k\in\mathbb{F}_p} |\widehat{g}(k)|.$$

Lemma 4.3. *Let $t \le n \le 2t$ $\ell_0,\ldots,\ell_n\colon \mathbb{F}_p^t \to \mathbb{F}_p$ be linear functions, with every t of them being linearly independent. Let $A, B\colon \mathbb{F}_p^{n-t} \to \{-1,1\}$ and $C\colon \mathbb{F}_p^{2t-n} \to \{-1,1\}$ be any functions, write*

$$F(x) = A(\ell_1(x),\ldots,\ell_{n-t}(x)) \cdot C(\ell_{n-t+1}(x),\ldots,\ell_t(x)) \cdot B(\ell_{t+1}(x),\ldots,\ell_n(x)),$$

then

$$|\widehat{F}(\ell_0)| \le \|A\|_2 \, \|B\|_2 \left\|\widehat{C}\right\|_\infty \tag{12}$$

Corollary 4.4. *Let ℓ_i be as in Lemma 4.3 and let $g_1,\ldots,g_n\colon \mathbb{F}_p \to \mathbb{R}$ be arbitrary functions, and set $m = 2n - 2t$, then*

$$|\widehat{g_{[n]}}(\ell_0)| \le \prod_{i=1}^{m} \|g_i\|_2 \cdot \prod_{i=m+1}^{n} \|\widehat{g}_i\|_\infty \cdot \tag{13}$$

Proof. We get the result by applying Lemma 4.3 with

$$\begin{aligned} A(z_1,\ldots,z_{n-t}) &= g_1(z_1)\cdots g_{n-t}(z_{n-t}) \\ B(z_1,\ldots,z_{n-t}) &= g_{n-t+1}(z_1)\cdots g_{2n-2t}(z_{n-t}) \\ C(z_1,\ldots,z_{2t-n}) &= g_{2n-2t+1}(z_1)\cdots g_n(z_{2t-n}), \end{aligned}$$

Hence $F(x)$ from Lemma 4.3 is $g_{[n]}$. Moreover, note that ranging over the entire input space of A, the inputs to g_i in the definition of A are independent of each other (likewise for B and C). This implies that we have

$$\|A\|_2 = \prod_{i=1}^{n-t} \|g_i\|_2\,, \quad \|C\|_\infty = \prod_{i=n-t+1}^{t} \|g_i\|_\infty\,, \quad \|B\|_2 = \prod_{i=t+1}^{n} \|g_i\|_2\,,$$

which completes the proof. To see that indeed the inputs of the g_i's are independent random variables, recall that $n - t \le t$ (likewise $2t - n \le t$), and the assumption that any t of the ℓ_i's are linearly independent. □

Corollary 4.4 is insufficient for proving Lemma 4.2. It may give a poor upper bound of 1 when, say, $g_i \equiv 1$. Combining this lemma with the following claim, we can strengthen this estimate and deduce Lemma 4.2.

Claim 4.5. *Let $f\colon \mathbb{F}_p \to [-1,1]$ where $\mathbb{E}[f] = \mu$. Then, for all $k \ne 0$ we have*

$$|\widehat{f}(k)| \le \frac{2}{\pi}\cos\left(\frac{\pi}{2}\mu\right) + O(1/p^2). \tag{14}$$

For completeness we give the proof of the above claim in Appendix A.

At this point the essence of the proof of Lemma 4.2 is already available. Corollary 4.4 bounds the Fourier coefficient $\widehat{g}_{[n]}(\ell_0)$ with a product of $2t-n$ Fourier coefficients of g_i. In case that $|\mathbb{E}[g_i]| \leq 2/\pi$, Claim 4.5 gives that actually $\|\widehat{g}_i\| \lesssim 2/\pi$, which gives the required $|\widehat{g}_{[n]}(\ell_0)| \leq (2/\pi)^{2t-n}$. Hence, the following proof focuses on extending this to the case where some of the g_i's have $|\mathbb{E}[g_i]| > 2/\pi$.

Proof. (Proof of Lemma 4.2*).* For the proof, we go through the following generalization of Corollary 4.4.

Let n, t, m, g_i, ℓ_i be exactly as in Corollary 4.4. If additionally $M \geq m = 2n-2t$ satisfies that $|g_i| \leq 1$ for $i = 1 \ldots M$ and $\|g_i\|_2 \leq 1$ for $i = M+1 \ldots n$, then

$$|\widehat{g_{[n]}}(\ell_0)| \leq (2/\pi)^{M-m} \prod_{i=M+1}^{n} \|\widehat{g}_i\|_\infty . \tag{15}$$

We note that Eq. (15) interpolates between Corollary 4.4 ($M = m$) which we will prove later, and Lemma 4.2 ($M = n$) which is what we are trying to prove. The proof is by induction on M.

A minor detail that we omit is that the $2/\pi$ in Eq. (15) should be replaced by $2/\pi + O(1/p^2)$, where the error term stems from Eq. (14). Since we raise $2/\pi + O(1/p^2)$ to a power smaller than n, the ratio between the bounds we state, and the actual bounds we get is $1 + O(n/p^2)$. Though, as we assume $p \geq n$, the overall effect of this error term translates to a $1 + O(1/n)$ multiplicative factor appearing in the bound in Eq. (10).

Base Case. The $M = m$ case of Eq. (15) is already covered in Corollary 4.4.

Induction Step. To prove Eq. (15) for some values of n, t, M (with $M > 2n-2t$), we suppose it holds whenever M is replaced by smaller values (maybe with different n, t).

In the case where $\|\widehat{g_M}\|_\infty \leq 2/\pi + O(1/p^2)$ we immediately deduce Eq. (15) by applying it with $M' = M-1$ (and same n, t).

In the case where $\|\widehat{g_M}\|_\infty \geq 2/\pi$, we first deduce that $\mu := \mathbb{E}[g_M]$ satisfies $|\mu| > 2/\pi$, as Eq. (14) shows that regardless of the value of μ, we have all other Fourier coefficients of g_M smaller than $2/\pi$ (note that $|g_M| \leq 1$ by assumption). Plugging in

$$2/\pi \leq |\mu| \leq 1 \tag{16}$$

we see $g := g_M - \mu$ satisfies $\|\widehat{g}\|_\infty \leq \frac{2}{\pi}\cos(\frac{\pi}{2}\mu)$.

The decomposition $g_M = \mu + g$ translates to

$$\widehat{g_{[n]}}(\ell_0) = \mu(\widehat{g_{[n]\setminus\{M\}}})(\ell_0) + (\widehat{g \cdot g_{[n]\setminus\{M\}}})(\ell_0). \tag{17}$$

We henceforth bound each of the summands in Eq. (17) using the induction hypothesis, and deduce Eq. (15).

The bound on $\widehat{g_{[n]\setminus M} \cdot \mu}(\ell_0)$ is obtained by applying Eq. (15) with $(n', t', M') = (n-1, t, M-1)$ (note that $M' \geq 2n' - 2t'$ by the assumption $M > 2n - 2t$):

$$\begin{aligned}|\widehat{g_{[n]\setminus M} \cdot \mu}(\ell_0)| &\leq |\mu|(2/\pi)^{M'-(2n'-2t')} \prod_{i=M+1}^{n} \|\widehat{g_i}\|_\infty \\ &= |\mu|(2/\pi)^{M-m+1} \prod_{i=M+1}^{n} \|\widehat{g_i}\|_\infty . \end{aligned} \tag{18}$$

The bound on $\widehat{g_{[n]\setminus M} \cdot g}(\ell_0)$ is obtained by applying Eq. (15) with $(n'', t'', M'') = (n, t, M-1)$:

$$\begin{aligned}|\widehat{g_{[n]\setminus M} \cdot g}(\ell_0)| &\leq (2/\pi)^{M''-(2n''-2t'')} \|\widehat{g}\|_\infty \prod_{i=M+1}^{n} \|\widehat{g_i}\|_\infty \\ &= (2/\pi)^{M-m-1} \|\widehat{g}\|_\infty \prod_{i=M+1}^{n} \|\widehat{g_i}\|_\infty . \end{aligned} \tag{19}$$

Note that while $|g_M| \leq 1$ it is not necessary that $|g| \leq 1$. However, the application of Eq. (15) is valid as $\|g\|_2 \leq \|g_M\|_2 \leq 1$.

In order to combine the two estimates in Eqs. (18) and (19), and conclude with Eq. (15) we must show

$$\begin{aligned}|\mu|(2/\pi)^{M-m+1} \prod_{i=M+1}^{n} \|\widehat{g_i}\|_\infty + (2/\pi)^{M-m-1} \|\widehat{g}\|_\infty \prod_{i=M+1}^{n} \|\widehat{g_i}\|_\infty \\ \leq (2/\pi)^{M-m} \prod_{i=M+1}^{n} \|\widehat{g_i}\|_\infty .\end{aligned}$$

Dividing by the common factor $2^{M-m} \prod_{i=M+1}^{n} \|\widehat{g_i}\|_\infty$, our task boils down to verifying

$$\frac{2}{\pi}|\mu| + \frac{\pi}{2} \|\widehat{g}\|_\infty \leq 1.$$

Recall $\|\widehat{g}\|_\infty \leq \frac{2}{\pi}\cos(\frac{\pi}{2}\mu)$, so we only need to check

$$\frac{2}{\pi}|\mu| + \cos(\frac{\pi}{2}\mu) \leq 1.$$

This inequality is not true in general (witnessed by $\mu = \pm 1/4$), but in the present case $2/\pi \leq |\mu| \leq 1$ it does hold. To see that, notice $\cos(\frac{\pi}{2}\mu) = \sin(\frac{\pi}{2}(1-|\mu|)) \leq \frac{\pi}{2}(1-|\mu|)$, hence it is sufficient to check that

$$\frac{2}{\pi}|\mu| + \frac{\pi}{2} - \frac{\pi}{2}|\mu| \leq 1.$$

In the range of Eq. (16), this inequality is most tight at $|\mu| = \frac{2}{\pi}$, where it reads

$$0.98 \approx (\frac{2}{\pi} - \frac{\pi}{2})\frac{2}{\pi} + \frac{\pi}{2} \leq 1,$$

completing the proof. □

Proof. (Proof of Lemma 4.3*).* Set

$$I = \{1, \dots, n-t\},$$
$$K = \{n-t+1, \dots, t\},$$
$$J = \{t+1, \dots, n\},$$

and denote

$$A'(x) = A((\ell_i(x))_{i \in I}), \quad B'(x) = B((\ell_j(x))_{j \in J}), \quad C'(x) = C((\ell_k(x))_{k \in K})$$

As we are required in Eq. (12) to bound $|(\widehat{A' \cdot B' \cdot C'})(\ell_0)|$, we present

$$(\widehat{A' \cdot B' \cdot C'})(\ell_0) = \sum_{\alpha+\beta+\gamma=\ell_0} \widehat{A'}(\alpha)\widehat{B'}(\beta)\widehat{C'}(\gamma), \tag{20}$$

where $\alpha, \beta, \gamma \in \mathbb{F}_p^t$ correspond to Fourier characters.

Note that $\widehat{A'}(\alpha)$ may be nonzero only when $\alpha \in \text{span}\{\ell_i : i \in I\}$. This is because the Fourier expansion of a product, is the convolution of Fourier expansions, so that

$$\widehat{A'}(\alpha) = \sum_{\substack{a_i \in \mathbb{F}_p \\ \sum_{i \in I} a_i \ell_i = \alpha}} \prod_{i \in I} \widehat{g_i}(a_i).$$

The analogous claims hold also to $\widehat{B'}(\beta)$ and to $\widehat{C'}(\gamma)$. Hence, for $\widehat{B'}(\beta)\widehat{C'}(\gamma)$ to be non-zero we must have $\beta + \gamma \in \text{span}\{\ell_i : i \in J \cup K\}$. Since $|J \cup K| = t$, $\{\ell_i\}_{i \in J \cup K}$ are linearly independent, and so every α may have at most one pair of (β, γ) with $\alpha + \beta + \gamma = \ell_0$ and $\widehat{B'}(\beta)\widehat{C'}(\gamma) \neq 0$.

Since each of α and β appear at most once in any nonzero term of the sum in Eq. (20), we may find a matching $\alpha \sim \beta$, so that if α (or β) appears in a nonzero term, it must be the term indexed by $(\alpha, \beta, \ell_0 - \alpha - \beta)$. Hence, we may rewrite Eq. (20) as

$$A' \cdot B' \cdot C' = \sum_{\alpha \sim \beta} \widehat{A'}(\alpha)\widehat{B'}(\beta)\widehat{C'}(\ell_0 - \alpha - \beta).$$

We bound the $\widehat{C'}(\ell_0 - \alpha - \beta)$ term in the last equation by $\left\|\widehat{C'}\right\|_\infty$. Note that C depends on $\leq t$ indpendent variables $\{\ell_i(x)\}_{i \in K}$ and hence $\left\|\widehat{C'}\right\|_\infty = \left\|\widehat{C}\right\|_\infty$.

Hence,

$$\left|(\widehat{A' \cdot B' \cdot C'})(\ell_0)\right| \leq \sum_{\alpha \sim \beta} |\widehat{A'}(\alpha)||\widehat{B'}(\beta)| \cdot \|C'\|_\infty .$$

Therefore, it is sufficient to show that

$$\sum_{\alpha \sim \beta} |\widehat{A'}(\alpha)||\widehat{B'}(\beta)| \leq \|A\|_2 \cdot \|B\|_2 . \tag{21}$$

Cauchy-Schwarz inequality shows that

$$\sum_{\alpha\sim\beta} |\widehat{A'}(\alpha)||\widehat{B'}(\beta)| \leq \sqrt{\sum_{\alpha} |\widehat{A'}(\alpha)|^2} \cdot \sqrt{\sum_{\beta} |\widehat{B'}(\beta)|^2}.$$

Notice that we used that each of α and β appears exactly once in the sum. Plugging in Parseval's identity, we find

$$\sum_{\alpha\sim\beta} |\widehat{A'}(\alpha)||\widehat{B'}(\beta)| \leq \|A'\|_2 \|B'\|_2 .$$

However, since each t of the ℓ_i's are independent, and both A and B depend on $n-t \leq t$ variables, we have $\|A'\|_2 = \|A\|$ as well as $\|B'\|_2 = \|B\|$. Hence we deduce Eq. (21), as required. □

5 Balanced Leakage Resilience for $t \geq 0.58n$

It is intuitive that in order for an attacker to leak the most information from the shares, they should leak the most from each share, that is choose functions $f_i : \mathbb{F}_p \to \{-1, 1\}$ which are unbiased, that is $\Pr[f_i = 1] \approx 1/2$.

We do not know to formalize this intuition. All the more so, we show security in broader range of parameters when the functions are unbiased. We believe this 'unbiased' regime is instructive – first because almost all functions are unbiased, and second because our proxy Theorem 3.1 may (conceivably) be improved in the biased regime. Meanwhile, in the unbiased case, we expect even the most deleterious part in Theorem 3.1, that is (9), to be quite tight.

The main theorem we prove in this section is as follows.

Theorem 5.1. *Let $\ell_0, \ldots, \ell_n : \mathbb{F}_p^t \to \mathbb{F}_p$ be $n+1$ linear functions such that every t of them are linearly independent. Let $C > 0$ and let $f_1, \ldots, f_n : \mathbb{F}_p \to \mathbb{R}$ be functions satisfying*

- $\|f_i\|_2 \leq 1$,
- $\left\|\widehat{f_i}\right\|_\infty \leq \frac{2}{\pi} + O(1/p^2)$,
- $|\mathbb{E}[f_i]| \leq C$.

If $n \leq p$, then

$$\sum_{S\subseteq[n]} \left|\widehat{f_S}(\ell_0)\right|^2 \leq (1+\pi^2/4)^{n-t} e^{1.5Cn} \left(\frac{2}{\pi} + O\left(\frac{1}{p^2}\right)\right)^{2t}. \tag{22}$$

Corollary 5.2. *Let ℓ_i be as in Theorem 5.1 and let $f_1, \ldots, f_n : \mathbb{F}_p \to \{-1, 1\}$ be functions satisfying $|\mathbb{E}[f_i]| \leq 1/1000$. Then, for $t \geq 0.58n$, it holds that*

$$\sum_{k\in\mathbb{F}\setminus\{0\}} \sum_{S\subseteq[n]} \left|\widehat{f_S}(k\cdot\ell_0)\right|^2 \leq O(p)\cdot 2^{-\Omega(n)}. \tag{23}$$

Proof. The functions f_i satisfy the requirements in Theorem 5.1 by Claim 4.5, with $C = 1/1000$.

The bound (22) is exponentially small in n so long as

$$-(2t\log(2/\pi) + (n-t)\log(1+\pi^2/4) + 1.5Cn) \geq \Omega(n),$$

that is

$$t/n > \frac{\log(1+\pi^2/4) + 1.5C}{2\log(\pi/2) + \log(1+\pi^2/4)} \approx 0.57995.$$

As usual we omitted the $O(1/p^2)$ term, which contributes a $1 + O(n/p^2)$ multiplicative factor. Since we assume $t/n \geq 0.58$ the bound (22) is exponentially small in n.

Finally, ℓ_0 may be replaced by $k \cdot \ell_0$ for any $k \neq 0$, thus yielding the $O(p)$ factor in the right hand side of Eq. (23). □

In the proof, we use the following variant of the Pythagorean theorem:

Lemma 5.3. *Let $v = \sum_i v_i$ be a vector such that $\langle v_i, v_j\rangle = 0$ whenever $i \neq j$. Further let $\{u_j\}$ be a set of vectors satisfying $\langle v_i, u_j\rangle = 0$ whenever $i \neq j$. Further assume that $|\langle v_i, u_i\rangle| \leq \beta \|v_i\|$, then*

$$\sum_j |\langle v, u_j\rangle|^2 \leq \beta^2 \|v\|^2. \tag{24}$$

Proof (Proof of Lemma 5.3*).* By direct calculation:

$$\begin{aligned}\sum_j |\langle v, u_j\rangle|^2 &= \sum_j |\langle \sum_i v_i, u_j\rangle|^2 = \sum_j |\langle v_j, u_j\rangle|^2 \\ &\leq \sum_j \beta^2 \|v_j\|^2 = \beta^2 \|v\|^2,\end{aligned}$$

where the last equality is the Pythagorean theorem. □

We demonstrate the core of the proof of Theorem 5.1, by restricting ourselves to the case $\mathbb{E}[f_i] = 0$. Later, we will reduce to this case.

Lemma 5.4. *Theorem 5.1 holds if $C = 0$, that is, if $\mathbb{E}[f_i] = 0$ for all $i = 1 \ldots n$.*

Proof (Proof of Lemma 5.4*).* Let $I \subseteq [n-t]$. We will later show that Lemma 5.3 implies the following inequality:

$$\sum_{H \subseteq [n]\setminus[n-t]} |\widehat{f_{I \cup H}}(\ell_0)|^2 \leq \left(\frac{2}{\pi} + O(1/p^2)\right)^{2(t-|I|)}. \tag{25}$$

Using Eq. (25), we obtain

$$\begin{aligned}\sum_{S\subseteq[n]}\left|\widehat{f_S}(\ell_0)\right|^2 &= \sum_{I\subseteq[n-t]}\ \sum_{H\subseteq[n]\setminus[n-t]}\left|\widehat{f_{I\cup H}}(\ell_0)\right|^2\\ &\le \sum_{I\subseteq[n-t]}\left(\frac{2}{\pi}\right)^{2(t-|I|)}\cdot(1+O(1/p^2))^n\\ &= O\left(\sum_{i=0}^{n-t}\binom{n-t}{i}\left(\frac{2}{\pi}\right)^{2(t-i)}\right)\\ &= O\left(\left(\frac{2}{\pi}\right)^{2t}(1+\pi^2/4)^{n-t}\right).\end{aligned}$$

To derive Eq. (25), we consider the vector space of functions $\mathbb{F}_p^t \to \mathbb{C}$ associated with the inner product $\langle f,g\rangle = \mathbb{E}[f\bar{g}]$. Let

$$u_J(x) = f_J(x)\cdot\chi_{\ell_0}(x) = f_J(x)\cdot\exp\left(\frac{2\pi\iota\ell_0(x)}{p}\right)$$

for $J\subseteq[n]\setminus[n-t]$. Note that $\widehat{f\cdot f_H}(\ell_0) = \langle f, u_H\rangle$, and in particular

$$|\widehat{f_{I\cup H}}(\ell_0)|^2 = |\langle f_I, u_H\rangle|^2, \tag{26}$$

hence the bound from Eq. (24) is relevant for proving Eq. (25).

Let $v := f_I$, we apply Lemma 5.3 with v, u_J and with $\beta = \left(\frac{2}{\pi}+O(1/p^2)\right)^{t-|I|}$. For this we need to decompose $v=\sum_J v_J$ so that $\langle v_J, v_{J'}\rangle = 0$ whenever $J\neq J'$.

Since $\ell_{n-t+1},\ldots,\ell_n$ are linearly independent, each linear function $\alpha\colon\mathbb{F}_p^t\to\mathbb{F}_p$ can uniquely be written as $\alpha = \ell_0+\sum_{i=n-t+1}^{n}\alpha_i\ell_i$. We denote the *dual-support* by

$$\operatorname{supp}^*(\alpha) = \{i\in[n]\setminus[n-t]\colon \alpha_i\neq 0\}.$$

For $J\subseteq[n]\setminus[n-t]$ we write

$$v_J = \sum_{\alpha\colon\,\operatorname{supp}^*(\alpha)=J}\widehat{v}(\alpha)\chi_\alpha.$$

Since $\ell_{n-t+1},\ldots,\ell_n$ is a basis of linear functions, we have $v=\sum_J v_J$, as every linear function has some dual-support. Moreover, two distinct v_J's are orthogonal, because their Fourier spectrum are disjoint. Moreover, $\langle v_{J'}, u_J\rangle\neq 0$ only if $J'=J$. To see this, note the the Fourier-spectrum of $u_J=f_J$ is contained in $\ell_0+\sum_{j\in J}(\mathbb{F}_p\setminus\{0\})\ell_j$. This is the crucial place in which this proof requires that $\mathbb{E}[f_j]=0$ (for all $j\in[n]\setminus[n-t]$). This fact implies that the Fourier spectrum of $v_{J'}$ and u_J can intersect only if $J=J'$.

Finally, to apply Lemma 5.3 we need to verify

$$|\langle v_J, u_J\rangle| \le \beta\,\|v_J\|, \tag{27}$$

with $\beta = (2/\pi+O(1/p^2))^{t-|I|}$.

First, recall Eq. (26) that $\langle v_J, u_J\rangle = \widehat{v_J \cdot f_J}(\ell_0)$; hence we must bound $\widehat{v_J \cdot f_J}(\ell_0)$. Recall further that v_J constitutes only from a part of the Fourier decomposition of $v = f_I$. Since v depends only on $\{\ell_i(x)\}_{i\in I}$, also v_J is a function of these variables.

We split the proof of Eq. (27) into two cases.

Case $|J| < t - |I|$**.** Since $|I \cup J| < t$, $\{\ell_i\}_{i\in I\cup J\cup\{0\}}$ are linearly independent, therefore there is no vanishing linear combination of ℓ_i, $i \in I \cup J$, and the Fourier spectrum of $v = f_I$ is disjoint from that of u_J, hence $v_J = 0$ and in particular

$$|\langle v_J, u_J\rangle| = 0 \le \beta \|v_J\| .$$

Case $|J| > t - |I|$**.** In this case, we use Lemma 4.3 with the linear functions $\{\ell_i\}_{i\in\{0\}\cup I\cup J}$, namely $n' = |I| + |J|$ in that lemma. Specifically, we set $A((\ell_i)_{i\in I}) := v_J$. We arbitrarily split the product $u_J = \chi_{\ell_0}(x) \cdot \prod_{j\in J} f_j(\ell_j(x))$ and the associated linear functions between B and C, with B depending on $n'-t$ variables, and C on $2t - n'$. We get

$$|\langle v_J, u_J\rangle| = |\widehat{\overline{v_J} \cdot f_J}(\ell_0)| \le \|A\|_2 \|B\|_2 \left\|\widehat{C}\right\|_\infty .$$

Note that $\|A\|_2 = \|v_J\|$ as well as $\|B\| \le 1$ (recall the assumption $\|f_i\|_2 \le 1$). For $\left\|\widehat{C}\right\|_\infty$, we note that C is a product of $2t - n'$ functions. Since we assume $n' = |I| + |J| \ge t$, C is a product of at most t functions. Using again that every t ℓ_i's are linearly independent, and that $\mathbb{E}[f_i] = 0$, every Fourier coefficient of C is a product of $2t - n'$ Fourier coefficients of the corresponding f_i's. As $2t - n' = 2t - (|I| + |J|) \ge 2t - (|I| + t) = t - |I|$ functions with $\mathbb{E}[f_i] = 0$. Hence we have through Claim 4.5,

$$\left\|\widehat{C}\right\|_\infty \le \left(2/\pi + O(1/p^2)\right)^{t-|I|} .$$

We summarize

$$|\widehat{\overline{v_J} \cdot f_J}(\ell_0)| \le \left(\frac{2}{\pi} + O(1/p^2)\right)^{t-|I|} \|v_J\| ,$$

which proves Eq. (27), and concludes the proof. □

For the proof of Theorem 5.1 we need the following simple lemma, which, roughly speaking, reduces our attention to unbiased functions.

Definition 5. *Let* $\ell_0, \ldots, \ell_n \colon \mathbb{F}_p^t \to \mathbb{F}_p$ *be* $n+1$ *linear functions. For functions* $f_1, \ldots, f_n \colon \mathbb{F}_p \to \mathbb{R}$ *define*

$$B(f_1, \ldots, f_n) := \sum_{S\subseteq[n]} \left|\widehat{f_S}(\ell_0)\right|^2 .$$

Lemma 5.6. *Let ℓ_i and f_i be as in Definition 5. If $\mu := \mathbb{E}[f_1]$, then*

$$B(f_1, f_2, \ldots, f_n) \le (1 + |\mu| + \mu^2) B(f_1 - \mu, f_2, \ldots, f_n). \tag{28}$$

Note that B does not depend on the order of the f_i's, given that ℓ_i are ordered accordingly. Hence the index 1 is not special in Eq. (28).

Proof. Write $f'_i = f_i$ except when $i = 1$ in which case $f'_1 = f_1 - \mu$.

$$\begin{aligned} B(f_1, \ldots, f_n) &= \sum_{S \subseteq [n]} \left| \widehat{f_S}(\ell_0) \right|^2 \\ &= \sum_{1 \notin S} \left| \widehat{f_S}(\ell_0) \right|^2 + \sum_{1 \in S} \left| \widehat{f_S}(\ell_0) \right|^2 \\ &= \sum_{1 \notin S} \left| \widehat{f'_S}(\ell_0) \right|^2 + \sum_{1 \in S} \left| \widehat{f'_S}(\ell_0) + \mu \widehat{f'_{S \setminus \{1\}}}(\ell_0) \right|^2 . \end{aligned} \tag{29}$$

Note the final term has the form $|a + \mu b|^2$. It can be bounded as

$$|a + \mu b|^2 = |a|^2 + \mu^2 |b|^2 + 2\mu \mathrm{Re}(ab) \le (1 + |\mu|)|a|^2 + (|\mu| + \mu^2)|b|^2.$$

Plugging it back in Eq. (29), we get

$$\begin{aligned} B(f_1, \ldots, f_n) &\le \sum_{1 \notin S} \left| \widehat{f'_S}(\ell_0) \right|^2 + (1 + |\mu|) \sum_{1 \in S} \left| \widehat{f'_S}(\ell_0) \right|^2 + (|\mu| + \mu^2) \sum_{1 \notin S} \left| \widehat{f'_S}(\ell_0) \right|^2 \\ &= (1 + |\mu| + \mu^2) \sum_{1 \notin S} \left| \widehat{f'_S}(\ell_0) \right|^2 + (1 + |\mu|) \sum_{1 \in S} \left| \widehat{f'_S}(\ell_0) \right|^2 \\ &\le (1 + |\mu| + \mu^2) B(f'_1, \ldots, f'_n). \end{aligned}$$

□

Proof (Proof of Theorem 5.1*).* Given $f_1, \ldots, f_n$, we will show that

$$B(f_1, \ldots, f_n) \le (1 + \pi^2/4)^{n-t} e^{1.5Cn} \left(\frac{2}{\pi} + O\left(\frac{1}{p^2} \right) \right)^{2t} .$$

Using Lemma 5.6 repeatedly, we get that

$$B(f_1, \ldots, f_n) \le B(f_1 - \mu_1, \ldots, f_n - \mu_n) \cdot \prod_{i=1}^{n} (1 + |\mu_i| + \mu_i^2),$$

with $\mu_i := \mathbb{E}[f_i]$. Note that $(1 + |\mu_i| + \mu_i^2) \le \exp(1.5|\mu_i|)$, and because we assume $|\mu_i| \le C$ we get

$$B(f_1, \ldots, f_n) \le e^{1.5Cn} B(f_1 - \mu_1, \ldots, f_n - \mu_n). \tag{30}$$

Note that the functions $f_1 - \mu_1, \ldots, f_n - \mu_n$ satisfy the requirements of Lemma 5.4. Hence,

$$B(f_1 - \mu_1, \ldots, f_n - \mu_n) \le (1 + \pi^2/4)^{n-t} \left(\frac{2}{\pi} + O\left(\frac{1}{p^2} \right) \right)^{2t} . \tag{31}$$

The combination of Eq. (30) and Eq. (31) concludes the proof. □

6 Unbalanced Leakage Resilience for $t \geq 0.01n$

Contrast to the previous section, if the leakage functions are sufficiently biased, then the security of the scheme applies to an even broader regime of parameters Recall that we define $B(f_1, \ldots, f_n) := \sum_{S \subseteq [n]} \widehat{f_S}(\ell_0)^2$.

Theorem 6.1. *Let $\ell_0, \ldots, \ell_n \colon \mathbb{F}_p^t \to \mathbb{F}_p$ be $n+1$ linear functions such that every t of them are linearly independent. Let $C > 0$ and let $f_1, \ldots, f_n \colon \mathbb{F}_p \to \{-1, 1\}$ be functions satisfying*

$$|\mathbb{E}[f_i]| \geq C \qquad \text{for } i = 1 \ldots n.$$

Then,

$$B(f_1, \ldots, f_n) \leq 15^n \cdot \left(\frac{1 - C^2}{5}\right)^t. \tag{32}$$

Corollary 6.2. *In the setting of Theorem 6.1, if $|\mathbb{E}[f_i]| \geq 1 - 2/15^{n/t}$, then $B(f_1, \ldots, f_n) \leq (4/5)^t$, and consequently the advantage of an adversary to guess the secret is exponentially small given the leakage, assuming $p = 2^{o(n)}$.*

Proof. Setting $C = 1 - \alpha$ (for α defined below) in Theorem 6.1 we have

$$B(f_1, \ldots, f_n) \leq \left(15 \cdot \left(\frac{1 - C^2}{5}\right)^{t/n}\right)^n \leq \left(15 \cdot (2\alpha/5)^{t/n}\right)^n.$$

This bound is exponentially small in n as long as $\alpha < \frac{5}{2 \cdot 15^{n/t}}$. Hence, $\alpha = 2/15^{n/t}$ is sufficient. The result follows from Theorem 3.1. □

Example 3. Shamir's secret sharing scheme with $n \leq 100t$ and $p = 2^{o(n)}$ is resilient against binary leakage functions that each of them discloses at most $H(1/15^{100})$ bits of information (corresponding to $|\mathbb{E}[f_i]| \geq 1 - 2/15^{100}$). Here, $H(q) = -q \log_2(q) - (1 - q) \log_2(1 - q)$.

Proof (Proof of Theorem 6.1). Let $\mu_i := \mathbb{E}[f_i]$. Note that $|\mu_i| \leq 1$, hence repeated applications of Lemma 5.6 yield that

$$B(f_1, \ldots, f_n) \leq 3^n B(f_1 - \mu_i, \ldots, f_n - \mu_n). \tag{33}$$

Hence, we restrict our attention to bounding $B(g_1, \ldots, g_n) = \sum_{S \subseteq [n]} \widehat{g_S}(\ell_0)^2$ with $g_i = f_i - \mu_i$.

Recall the definition

$$\widehat{g_S}(\ell_0) = \mathop{\mathbb{E}}_{x}\left[\prod_{j \in S} g_j(x) \cdot \exp\left(\frac{-2\pi \iota \ell_0(x)}{p}\right)\right].$$

If $|S| < t$, the fact that ℓ_0 is not a linear combination of less that t of the other linear functions implies $\widehat{g_S}(\ell_0) = 0$, hence we consider $|S| \geq t$.

Splitting an S with $|S| \geq t$ as $S = U \sqcup V$ with $|U| = t$, the Cauchy-Schwarz inequality implies $|\widehat{g_S}(\ell_0)| \leq \|g_U\|_2 \|g_V\|_2$:

$$|\widehat{g_S}(\ell_0)| = |\langle g_U g_V, \chi_{\ell_0} \rangle| = |\langle g_U, \overline{g_V} \chi_{\ell_0} \rangle| \leq \|g_U\|_2 \|\overline{g_V} \cdot \chi_{\ell_0}\|_2 = \|g_U\|_2 \|g_V\|_2 .$$

In order to bound $\|g_V\|_2$, note that $\|g_i\|_\infty \leq \|f_i\|_\infty + |\mu_i| \leq 2$, hence

$$\|g_V\|_2 \leq \|g_V\|_\infty \leq 2^{|V|}.$$

In order to bound $\|g_U\|_2$, note that $\{\ell_i\}_{i \in U}$ are independent linear functions, hence

$$\|g_U\|_2 = \prod_{i \in U} \|g_i\|_2 .$$

However, Parseval's identity implies that

$$\|g_i\|_2^2 = \mathbb{E}[f_i^2] - \mathbb{E}[f_i]^2 \leq 1 - C^2,$$

and hence

$$\|g_U\|_2 \leq (1 - C^2)^{t/2}.$$

We deduce that $g_S(\ell_0)^2 \leq 2^{2(|S|-t)}(1 - C^2)^t$, and overall

$$B(g_1, \dots, g_n) \leq \sum_{k=0}^{n} \binom{n}{k} 2^{2(k-t)}(1 - C^2)^t \leq (1 - C^2)^t \cdot 5^{n-t}.$$

Combining with Eq. (33), we conclude with

$$B(f_1, \dots, f_n) \leq 15^n \cdot \left(\frac{1 - C^2}{5}\right)^t .$$

□

6.1 A Barrier of Previous Methods

It is already known that previous methods cannot prove local leakage resilience of Shamir's scheme for any $t \leq n/2$ for general leakage functions. Indeed, [28] showed a particular leakage function for which a proxy quantity in their analysis becomes too large. The leakage function is the quadratic-residue function. This leakage function is balanced and therefore cannot be used to claim that previous techniques cannot be used to derive a result similar to what we get in Example 3. We show an unbalanced variant of the quadratic-residue function for which a similar barrier for previous techniques can be shown. We refer to Appendix B for details.

Acknowledgements. Research supported in part by an Alon Young Faculty Fellowship, by a grant from the Israel Science Foundation (ISF Grant No. 1774/20), and by a grant from the US-Israel Binational Science Foundation and the US National Science Foundation (BSF-NSF Grant No. 2020643).

A Proof of Claim 4.5

Let $f\colon \mathbb{F}_p \to [-1,1]$ have $\mathbb{E}[f] = \mu$. Then, for all $k \neq 0$, we must show that

$$|\widehat{f}(k)| \leq \frac{2}{\pi} \cos\left(\frac{\pi}{2}\mu\right) + O(1/p^2). \tag{34}$$

Note $\widehat{f}(k)$ is a complex number, which we write as $\widehat{f}(k) = |\widehat{f}(k)| \cdot e^{i\theta}$ with $\theta \in [-\pi, \pi]$ and $|\widehat{f}(k)| \geq 0$ a positive real number. It is sufficient we prove

$$e^{-i\theta}\widehat{f}(k) = |\widehat{f}(k)| \leq \frac{2}{\pi} \cos\left(\frac{\pi}{2}\mu\right) + O(1/p^2).$$

Note that

$$\begin{aligned} e^{-i\theta}\widehat{f}(k) &= \mathrm{Re}(e^{-i\theta}\widehat{f}(k)) = \mathrm{Re}(e^{-i\theta} \mathop{\mathbb{E}}_{x\sim\mathbb{F}_p}[f(x)\exp(-2\pi kxi/p)]) \\ &= \mathop{\mathbb{E}}_{x\sim\mathbb{F}_p}[f(x)\mathrm{Re}(\exp(-(2\pi kx/p+\theta)i))] = \mathop{\mathbb{E}}_{x\sim\mathbb{F}_p}[f(x)\cos(2\pi kx/p+\theta)] \\ &= \mathop{\mathbb{E}}_{x\sim\mathbb{F}_p}[f(x/k)\cos(2\pi x/p+\theta)] \end{aligned}$$

We define the function $g\colon \mathbb{F}_p \to [-1,1]$ having $g(x) = f(x/k)$ which satisfies $\mathbb{E}[g] = \mathbb{E}[f] = \mu$ and

$$e^{-i\theta}\widehat{f}(k) = \underbrace{\mathop{\mathbb{E}}_{x\sim\mathbb{F}_p}[g(x)\cos(2\pi x/p+\theta)]}_{F(g)} \tag{35}$$

We now find a function g that maximizes $F(g)$ among functions satisfying $\mathbb{E}[g] = \mu$, and show this value is upper bounded by the right hand side of (34).

Intuitively, a g that maximizes $F(g)$ "should" have $g(x)$ larger as $\cos(2\pi x/p + \theta)$ is larger (among $x \in \{0, 1, \ldots, p-1\}$) and smaller when $\cos(2\pi x/p + \theta)$ is smaller. This intuition can be formalized as follows. Write $P(x) := \cos(2\pi x/p + \theta)$. If $P(y) \leq P(z)$ and both $-1 < g(y)$ and $g(z) < 1$, we may outflow a small quantity from $g(y)$ (thus decreasing it) while increasing $g(z)$, so that both $\mathbb{E}[g]$ is preserved and (35) grows. Specifically, letting $\nu = \min\{g(y)+1, 1-g(z)\}$ and defining $g'\colon \mathbb{F}_p \to [-1,1]$ as

$$g'(x) = g(x) + \nu(\mathbf{1}_{\{x=z\}} - \mathbf{1}_{\{x=y\}}),$$

has $|g'| \leq 1$ and $\mathbb{E}[g'] = \mathbb{E}[g] = \mu$ and

$$F(g', \theta) = F(g) + \nu(P(z) - P(y)) > F(g).$$

Hence, for all $\mu \in [-1,1]$ there is a function g_μ which maximizes $F(g_\mu, \theta)$ under the condition $\mathbb{E}[g_\mu] = \mu$, that has $|g(x)| = 1$ for all points $x \in \mathbb{F}_p$, except for at most one point x'. Moreover, $g_\mu(x)$ is monotonically non-decreasing in $P(x)$. We must show

$$F(g_\mu, \theta) \leq \frac{2}{\pi} \cos\left(\frac{\pi}{2}\mu\right) + O(1/p^2).$$

Consider first the case where $\mu = -1 + \frac{2}{p}t$, for some positive integer t. In this case, $g_\mu(x) = 1$ on t x's with largest $P(x)$, and $g_\mu(x) = -1$ on the remaining $p - t$ x's.

For the purpose of computing $F(g_\mu, \theta)$, these x's for which $g_\mu(x) = 1$ can be described as $m \leq x \leq m+t-1$ for some integer m. Using that $\sum_{x=0}^{p-1} \cos(2\pi x/p+\theta) = 0$, we see that

$$\left| \sum_{x:\, g_\mu(x)=1} \cos(2\pi x/p + \theta) \right| = \left| \sum_{x:\, g_\mu(x)=-1} \cos(2\pi x/p + \theta) \right|$$

and so

$$F(g) = \frac{2}{p} \sum_{x=m}^{m+t-1} \cos(2\pi x/p + \theta) = \frac{2}{p} \frac{\sin(\pi t/p)\cos((2m+t-1)\pi/p + \theta)}{\sin(\pi/p)} \tag{36}$$

where the last equality follows from an elementary trigonometric summation. Using that $|\cos| \leq 1$ and that $t = p/2(1+\mu)$ we get

$$F(g) \leq \left| \frac{2\sin((1+\mu)\pi/2)}{p\sin(\pi/p)} \right| \cdot 1 = \frac{2\cos(\pi\mu/2)}{p\sin(\pi/p)}. \tag{37}$$

Using that $1/\sin(\epsilon) = \frac{1}{\epsilon} + O(\epsilon)$ for $|\epsilon| \leq 1$ in Eq. (37), we get

$$F(g) = 2\cos\left(\frac{\pi}{2}\mu\right) \cdot (1/\pi + O(1/p^2)) = \frac{2}{\pi}\cos\left(\frac{\pi}{2}\mu\right) + O(1/p^2),$$

as required. For the case of general $\mu \in [-1, 1]$, it holds that $F(g_\mu)$ is a piecewise-linear function in μ. Thus, the almost-coincidence of $F(g_\mu)(1)$ with $\frac{2}{\pi}\cos(\frac{\pi}{2}\mu)$ on $\mu \in -1 + \frac{2}{p}\mathbb{Z}$, implies a similar $O(1/p^2)$ approximation for interpolated μ values, as $\frac{2}{\pi}\cos(\frac{\pi}{2}\mu)$ has bounded second derivative (Taylor-approximation type estimate).

B Details for a Barrier of Previous Methods

As pointed out in [28], previous studies of the leakage resilience of Shamir's secret sharing scheme aim at upper bounding some proxy quantity, which can be too large if $n \geq 2t$. Their analytic proxy is[6]

$$\sum_{c \in \ell^\perp \setminus \{0\}} \prod_{i=1}^{n} |\widetilde{f}_i(c_i)|, \qquad \text{with} \quad \widetilde{f}_i(c_i) = \begin{cases} \widehat{f}_i(c_i) & c_i \neq 0 \\ 1 & c_i = 0, \end{cases} \tag{38}$$

where $\ell^\perp$ is the set of all linear combinations $c \in \mathbb{F}_p^n$ for which the equation $\sum_{i=1}^{n} c_i \ell_i = 0$ holds. In particular, $|\ell^\perp| = p^{n-t}$. See Sect. 2.3 for the interpretation of what Eq. (38) bounds.

[6] The proxy found in [28, Section 5] is $\sum_{b \in \{-1,1\}^n} \sum_{c \in \ell^\perp \setminus \{0\}} \prod_{i=1}^{n} |\widehat{\frac{1+b_i f_i}{2}}(c_i)|$. However syntactially different from Eq. (38), it is identical.

In order to show that the quantity in Eq. (38) may be large if $n \geq 2t$, Maji et al. [28] presented the quadratic-residue function

$$f_i(s) = f(s) := \begin{cases} 1 & s = y^2 \pmod{p} \\ -1 & \text{otherwise} \end{cases}$$

which satisfies $|\widehat{f_i}(\alpha)| \sim \sqrt{1/p}$ for all $\alpha \in \mathbb{F}_p$. Hence, Eq. (38) is a sum of p^{n-t} terms, each of the order of $p^{-n/2}$, thus being > 1 if $n > 2t$.

In order to see the similar barrier in the case where the f_i's are constantly biased (that is, as in the setting of Example 3), consider some constant $\mu < 1$ (the bias), and set

$$g_i(s) = g(s) := (1-\mu)f_i(s) + \mu.$$

Note that the range of g is $[-1,1]$, unlike f whose range is $\{-1,1\}$. Anyways, it follows that $|\widehat{g}(\alpha)| \gtrsim (1-\mu)/\sqrt{p}$ for all α. Also, $\mathbb{E}[g] = \mu + (1-\mu)\,\mathbb{E}[f] \approx \mu$.

Substituting g_i in place of f_i in (38), we get p^{n-t} summands, each of the order of $(1-\mu)^n/p^{n/2}$, thus being

$$(1-\mu)^n p^{n/2-t}.$$

In case $t = (1/2 - \epsilon)n$, the sum in Eq. (38) is hence at least

$$(1-\mu)^n p^{\epsilon n} \gg 1, \tag{39}$$

for any constant $\epsilon > 0$. This gives a barrier on how effective Eq. (38) can be if $t = (1/2 - \epsilon)n$.

Note however that g does not strictly output a single bit. We sketch how to fix this issue (since this section only points out a barrier with previous approaches, we skip technical details.) Observe that g is an average of functions whose range is $\{-1,1\}$. Then, we notice that Eq. (38) is a convex function of the g_i's (as a composition of convex functions). If we hence choose g_i randomly (and independently across i's) from a distribution whose mean is g, we get in expectation a value larger than Eq. (39). Note that it is important to surely have g_i with mean $\approx \mu$. For this, we note that g is two-valued with values 1 and $2\mu - 1$. By rounding μ-fraction out of these s with $g(s) = 2\mu - 1$ to have $g_i(s) = 1$, and the rest with $g_i(s') = -1$, we guarantee $\mathbb{E}[g_i] = \mu$. That is, the number of s's we round to 1 is

$$\frac{p \cdot \mu \cdot (1 - \mathbb{E}[f])}{2}.$$

There is a fine net of μ's in $[-1,1]$ for which this quantity turns out an integer. We may choose any μ with that property.

References

1. Adams, D.Q., et al.: Lower bounds for leakage-resilient secret-sharing schemes against probing attacks. In: IEEE International Symposium on Information Theory, ISIT, pp. 976–981 (2021)

2. Akavia, A., Goldwasser, S., Vaikuntanathan, V.: Simultaneous hardcore bits and cryptography against memory attacks. In: TCC, pp. 474–495 (2009)
3. Ben-Or, M., Goldwasser, S., Wigderson, A.: Completeness theorems for non-cryptographic fault-tolerant distributed computation (extended abstract). In: STOC, pp. 1–10 (1988)
4. Benhamouda, F., Degwekar, A., Ishai, Y., Rabin, T.: On the local leakage resilience of linear secret sharing schemes. In: Shacham, H., Boldyreva, A. (eds.) CRYPTO 2018. LNCS, vol. 10991, pp. 531–561. Springer, Cham (2018). https://doi.org/10.1007/978-3-319-96884-1_18
5. Benhamouda, F., Degwekar, A., Ishai, Y., Rabin, T.: On the local leakage resilience of linear secret sharing schemes. J. Cryptol. **34**(2), 10 (2021)
6. Blakley, G.R.: Safeguarding cryptographic keys. In: Proceedings of the AFIPS National Computer Conference, vol. 22, pp. 313–317 (1979)
7. Boyle, E., Segev, G., Wichs, D.: Fully leakage-resilient signatures. J. Cryptol. **26**(3), 513–558 (2013)
8. Chandran, N., Kanukurthi, B., Obbattu, S.L.B., Sekar, S.: Adaptive extractors and their application to leakage resilient secret sharing. In: Malkin, T., Peikert, C. (eds.) CRYPTO 2021. LNCS, vol. 12827, pp. 595–624. Springer, Cham (2021). https://doi.org/10.1007/978-3-030-84252-9_20
9. Chandran, N., Kanukurthi, B., Obbattu, S.L.B., Sekar, S.: Short leakage resilient and non-malleable secret sharing schemes. In: Dodis, Y., Shrimpton, T. (eds.) CRYPTO 2022. LNCS, vol. 13507, pp. 178–207. Springer, Cham (2022). https://doi.org/10.1007/978-3-031-15802-5_7
10. Chattopadhyay, E., et al.: Extractors and secret sharing against bounded collusion protocols. In: FOCS, pp. 1226–1242 (2020)
11. Chaum, D., Crépeau, C., Damgård, I.: Multiparty unconditionally secure protocols (extended abstract). In: STOC, pp. 11–19 (1988)
12. Davì, F., Dziembowski, S., Venturi, D.: Leakage-resilient storage. In: SCN, pp. 121–137 (2010)
13. Desmedt, Y., Frankel, Y.: Threshold cryptosystems. In: Advances in Cryptology - CRYPTO, pp. 307–315 (1989)
14. Dziembowski, S., Pietrzak, K.: Leakage-resilient cryptography. In: FOCS, pp. 293–302 (2008)
15. Faust, S., Rabin, T., Reyzin, L., Tromer, E., Vaikuntanathan, V.: Protecting circuits from computationally bounded and noisy leakage. SIAM J. Comput. **43**(5), 1564–1614 (2014)
16. Frankel, Y.: A practical protocol for large group oriented networks. In: Quisquater, J.-J., Vandewalle, J. (eds.) EUROCRYPT 1989. LNCS, vol. 434, pp. 56–61. Springer, Heidelberg (1990). https://doi.org/10.1007/3-540-46885-4_8
17. Goldreich, O., Micali, S., Wigderson, A.: How to play any mental game or A completeness theorem for protocols with honest majority. In: STOC, pp. 218–229 (1987)
18. Goyal, V., Kumar, A.: Non-malleable secret sharing. In: STOC, pp. 685–698 (2018)
19. Goyal, V., Kumar, A.: Non-malleable secret sharing for general access structures. In: Shacham, H., Boldyreva, A. (eds.) CRYPTO 2018. LNCS, vol. 10991, pp. 501–530. Springer, Cham (2018). https://doi.org/10.1007/978-3-319-96884-1_17
20. Guruswami, V., Wootters, M.: Repairing Reed-Solomon codes. IEEE Trans. Inf. Theory **63**(9), 5684–5698 (2017)
21. Ishai, Y., Sahai, A., Wagner, D.: Private circuits: securing hardware against probing attacks. In: Boneh, D. (ed.) CRYPTO 2003. LNCS, vol. 2729, pp. 463–481. Springer, Heidelberg (2003). https://doi.org/10.1007/978-3-540-45146-4_27

22. Kocher, P.C.: Timing attacks on implementations of Diffie-Hellman, RSA, DSS, and other systems. In: Koblitz, N. (ed.) CRYPTO 1996. LNCS, vol. 1109, pp. 104–113. Springer, Heidelberg (1996). https://doi.org/10.1007/3-540-68697-5_9
23. Kocher, P., Jaffe, J., Jun, B.: Differential power analysis. In: Wiener, M. (ed.) CRYPTO 1999. LNCS, vol. 1666, pp. 388–397. Springer, Heidelberg (1999). https://doi.org/10.1007/3-540-48405-1_25
24. Kumar, A., Meka, R., Sahai, A.: Leakage-resilient secret sharing against colluding parties. In: FOCS, pp. 636–660 (2019)
25. Maji, H.K., Nguyen, H.H., Paskin-Cherniavsky, A., Suad, T., Wang, M.: Leakage-resilience of the Shamir secret-sharing scheme against physical-bit leakages. In: Canteaut, A., Standaert, F.-X. (eds.) EUROCRYPT 2021. LNCS, vol. 12697, pp. 344–374. Springer, Cham (2021). https://doi.org/10.1007/978-3-030-77886-6_12
26. Maji, H.K., et al.: Tight estimate of the local leakage resilience of the additive secret-sharing scheme & its consequences. In: Information-Theoretic Cryptography, ITC, pp. 16:1–16:19 (2022)
27. Maji, H.K., Nguyen, H.H., Paskin-Cherniavsky, A., Wang, M.: Improved bound on the local leakage-resilience of Shamir's secret sharing. In: IEEE International Symposium on Information Theory, ISIT, pp. 2678–2683 (2022)
28. Maji, H.K., Paskin-Cherniavsky, A., Suad, T., Wang, M.: Constructing locally leakage-resilient linear secret-sharing schemes. In: Malkin, T., Peikert, C. (eds.) CRYPTO 2021. LNCS, vol. 12827, pp. 779–808. Springer, Cham (2021). https://doi.org/10.1007/978-3-030-84252-9_26
29. Massey, J.L.: Some applications of source coding in cryptography. Eur. Trans. Telecommun. **5**(4), 421–430 (1994)
30. Micali, S., Reyzin, L.: Physically observable cryptography (extended abstract). In: TCC, pp. 278–296 (2004)
31. Naor, M., Segev, G.: Public-key cryptosystems resilient to key leakage. SIAM J. Comput. **41**(4), 772–814 (2012)
32. Nielsen, J.B., Simkin, M.: Lower bounds for leakage-resilient secret sharing. In: Canteaut, A., Ishai, Y. (eds.) EUROCRYPT 2020. LNCS, vol. 12105, pp. 556–577. Springer, Cham (2020). https://doi.org/10.1007/978-3-030-45721-1_20
33. Rothblum, G.N.: How to compute under $\mathcal{AC}^0$ leakage without secure hardware. In: Safavi-Naini, R., Canetti, R. (eds.) CRYPTO 2012. LNCS, vol. 7417, pp. 552–569. Springer, Heidelberg (2012). https://doi.org/10.1007/978-3-642-32009-5_32
34. Santis, A.D., Desmedt, Y., Frankel, Y., Yung, M.: How to share a function securely. In: STOC, pp. 522–533 (1994)
35. Shamir, A.: How to share a secret. Commun. ACM **22**(11), 612–613 (1979)
36. Srinivasan, A., Vasudevan, P.N.: Leakage resilient secret sharing and applications. In: Boldyreva, A., Micciancio, D. (eds.) CRYPTO 2019. LNCS, vol. 11693, pp. 480–509. Springer, Cham (2019). https://doi.org/10.1007/978-3-030-26951-7_17

Arithmetic Sketching

Dan Boneh[1(✉)], Elette Boyle[2,3], Henry Corrigan-Gibbs[4], Niv Gilboa[5], and Yuval Ishai[6]

[1] Stanford University, Stanford, USA
dabo@cs.stanford.edu
[2] Reichman University, Herzliya, Israel
eboyle@alum.mit.edu
[3] NTT Research, Sunnyvale, USA
[4] MIT, Cambridge, USA
henrycg@csail.mit.edu
[5] Ben-Gurion University, Beersheba, Israel
gilboan@bgu.ac.il
[6] Technion, Haifa, Israel
yuvali@cs.technion.ac.il

Abstract. This paper introduces *arithmetic sketching*, an abstraction of a primitive that several previous works use to achieve lightweight, low-communication zero-knowledge verification of secret-shared vectors. An arithmetic sketching scheme for a language $\mathcal{L} \subseteq \mathbb{F}^n$ consists of (1) a randomized linear function compressing a long input x to a short "sketch," and (2) a small arithmetic circuit that accepts the sketch if and only if $x \in \mathcal{L}$, up to some small error. If the language $\mathcal{L}$ has an arithmetic sketching scheme with short sketches, then it is possible to test membership in $\mathcal{L}$ using an arithmetic circuit with few multiplication gates. Since multiplications are the dominant cost in protocols for computation on secret-shared, encrypted, and committed data, arithmetic sketching schemes give rise to lightweight protocols in each of these settings.

Beyond the formalization of arithmetic sketching, our contributions are:

- A general framework for constructing arithmetic sketching schemes from algebraic varieties. This framework unifies schemes from prior work and gives rise to schemes for useful new languages and with improved soundness error.
- The first arithmetic sketching schemes for languages of *sparse* vectors: vectors with bounded Hamming weight, bounded L_1 norm, and vectors whose few non-zero values satisfy a given predicate.
- A method for "compiling" any arithmetic sketching scheme for a language $\mathcal{L}$ into a low-communication malicious-secure multi-server protocol for securely testing that a client-provided secret-shared vector is in $\mathcal{L}$.

We also prove the first nontrivial lower bounds showing limits on the sketch size for certain languages (e.g., vectors of Hamming-weight one) and proving the non-existence of arithmetic sketching schemes for others (e.g., the language of all vectors that contain a specific value).

H. Handschuh and A. Lysyanskaya (Eds.): CRYPTO 2023, LNCS 14081, pp. 171–202, 2023.
https://doi.org/10.1007/978-3-031-38557-5_6

1 Introduction

In many cryptographic protocols, a server holds an encoding of a large client-provided vector. To protect against client misbehavior, the server must test whether the vector satisfies a simple predicate. For example:

- In private ad measurement [24,37], an aggregation server holds a linearly homomorphic encryption of a client-provided vector; the server must test that the encrypted vector is zero everywhere except with a "1" at a single location.
- In PIR writing [34] and private messaging [1,15,21], a set of servers holds additive secret shares of a client-provided vector; the servers must test that the secret-shared vector is zero everywhere except that it contains an arbitrary value at a single location.
- In private-aggregation [9,14,18,29,35], a set of servers holds a secret-sharing of a large client-provided vector; the server must test whether the vector has bounded Hamming weight.
- In e-voting schemes [26], a tally server holds a linearly homomorphic encryption of a vector representing a ballot; the server must test that the vector has non-negative entries and bounded L_1 norm.
- In verifiable distributed multi-point functions [19], a set of servers holds (compressed) additive secret shares of a client-provided vector; the servers must test whether the vector has Hamming weight exactly w.
- In protocols for malicious-secure OT and MPC [17], a verifier holds a linearly homomorphic commitment to a prover-provided vector; the verifier must test whether the vector has bounded Hamming weight.

Each of these prior works gives a clever special-purpose protocol for its particular property-testing problem. And each scheme has the desirable feature that in the most important complexity measure–typically server-to-server communication or proof size—the server's cost is sublinear in the input size.

At the same time, each of the state-of-the-art schemes has at least one of three shortcomings: dependence on proofs, limited extensibility, and unclear optimality of their complexity measures. In particular, many of these protocols [9,14,15,17,21,26] require the client to provide some auxiliary information ("proof") about the vector to the servers/verifier to perform the validity check, or even require interaction with the client [8,17]. This dependence on the client precludes important use cases such as distributing the client, e.g. in an MPC protocol, or accepting the aggregate contribution of multiple clients. Also, in some applications, the servers must check a property on a subset of the vector that only the servers know [9]. So even if there is a single client, the client may not know what exactly it needs to prove. In addition, these protocols are purpose-built to test specific properties required for their applications, without necessarily considering extensions or generalizations. For example, testing that a vector has a single non-zero location is useful for different applications, but the set of authorized non-zero payloads might change between applications. Making these tools most broadly useful requires generalizing and unifying these constructions. Finally, in each of these protocols, it is not clear whether the known schemes are the best possible, in terms of the key complexity metrics.

In this work, we introduce arithmetic sketching schemes, giving a general framework for constructing protocols that enable testing simple properties on large vectors. Our schemes resolve the main shortcomings of those in prior work: they require no auxiliary "proof" information from the client in the secret-shared setting, they are extensible, and in certain cases they match new efficiency lower bounds that we prove. The general framework provides simple, concretely efficient protocols for each of the aforementioned applications.

Formalization of Arithmetic Sketching. The first contribution of this paper is the definition of arithmetic sketching schemes. The purpose of an arithmetic sketching scheme for a language of vectors $\mathcal{L} \subseteq \mathbb{F}^n$, over a finite field $\mathbb{F}$ and input size $n \in \mathbb{N}$, is to test whether a given input $x \in \mathbb{F}^n$ is in the language $\mathcal{L}$. Typically, the languages $\mathcal{L}$ we consider are "simple" ones, such as the language of vectors of Hamming-weight one, of bounded-L_1 norm, etc.

More precisely, an arithmetic sketching scheme for a language $\mathcal{L}$ is a pair of algorithms: a sketching algorithm and a decision algorithm.

- The *sketching algorithm* is a randomized procedure that outputs a matrix $Q \in \mathbb{F}^{\ell \times n}$. The number of rows in the matrix ℓ (the "sketch size") is typically small—constant in the input length n.
- The *decision algorithm*, takes as input ℓ values, corresponding to the matrix-vector product of the sketching matrix $Q \in \mathbb{F}^{\ell \times n}$ with the input vector $x \in \mathbb{F}^n$. The decision algorithm must accept all $x \in \mathcal{L}$ and, with high probability, reject all $x \notin \mathcal{L}$. Furthermore, the decision algorithm must be *arithmetic*, in the sense that it is computed by an arithmetic circuit over the field $\mathbb{F}$, with size independent of the field size $|\mathbb{F}|$ and the input length n.

We can think of the vector $(Q \cdot x) \in \mathbb{F}^\ell$ as a succinct "sketch" of the large input $x \in \mathbb{F}^n$, since these $\ell \ll n$ values contain enough information to decide whether or not $x \in \mathcal{L}$. While all of the algorithms we construct are computationally efficient, when defined relative to infinite families of languages $\{\mathcal{L}_n\}_{n=1}^{\infty}$, computational efficiency plays no role in our definitions—an arithmetic sketching scheme is a purely information-theoretic object.

While linear sketching is a staple of data-structure and algorithm design [2, 13,33], the key distinction here is the requirement for the decision predicate to be a small arithmetic circuit. Removing this arithmetic requirement trivializes the problem: as we discuss in Sect. 2.2, every sparse-enough language has a simple non-arithmetic sketching scheme with a small sketch size (albeit with a computationally inefficient decision procedure). Even if we require computational efficiency, the arithmetic requirement limits the power of the sketches we consider: they cannot, say, test predicates of very large algebraic degree. At the same time, as we now discuss, arithmetic sketching schemes are a natural fit for cryptographic applications.

Applications of Arithmetic Sketching. Whenever verifiers can inexpensively apply *linear functions* to a large input x, arithmetic sketches yield asymptotically and concretely efficient protocols for testing properties on the input x. For example, consider a set of verifiers who hold linear secret shares of a large vector x, as is the case in multiparty computations [5] and many practical protocols [1,8,9,14,15,18–21,34], and who want to test whether $x \in \mathcal{L}$. An arithmetic sketching scheme for $\mathcal{L}$ gives a very simple multiparty protocol for this problem: The verifiers can use shared randomness to generate the sketching matrix $Q \in \mathbb{F}^{\ell \times n}$ and can locally compute secret shares of the "sketch" $Q \cdot x \in \mathbb{F}^{\ell}$. Then, the verifiers can run the decision procedure on these ℓ values in a small multiparty computation to determine whether $x \in \mathcal{L}$. The fact that the decision procedure is arithmetic and of small size (independent of $|\mathbb{F}|$ and n) ensures that this last step is inexpensive, even in the multiparty setting.

Analogously, consider a server who holds the encryption of a client-provided vector $x \in \mathbb{F}^n$ under a linearly homomorphic encryption (or commitment) scheme $E(\cdot)$, as is the case in a number of protocols [17,24,26,35,37]. In this case, the server can unilaterally compute the sketch under encryption: $E(Q \cdot x)$ using random coins it shares with the client. The client can then convince the server that $x \in \mathcal{L}$ using a small zero-knowledge proof—again, whose size is independent of $\mathbb{F}$ and n. While general-purpose succinct zero-knowledge techniques [7] can of course achieve the same goal, arithmetic sketching schemes can yield simpler protocols under simpler assumptions.

Efficiency Metrics. When using arithmetic sketching schemes in cryptographic protocols, there are three main complexity metrics of interest:

- The *sketch size* dictates the computation required to evaluate the sketch. Since computing the sketch is the only part of the computation that depends on the (large) input length n, minimizing the sketch size—down to the constant—is crucial for concrete efficiency.
- The *algebraic degree* of the decision procedure dictates the round complexity of a multiparty computation for evaluating the sketch. Or, when s servers evaluate the sketch in a non-interactive multiparty computation, a sketch of degree d dictates the collusion threshold $t < s/d$—the number of colluding servers that the protocol can tolerate.
- The *number of multiplication gates* in the arithmetic circuit representing the decision procedure dictates the communication complexity of evaluating the sketch in a multiparty computation. Or, when the sketch is used to construct zero-knowledge proof, the gate count determines the size and time cost of generating and verifying the proof.

With an eye towards building the most concretely efficient multiparty protocols, our constructions aim to minimize these costs, which may each form a bottleneck in natural application scenarios.

1.1 Our Contributions

We now summarize our technical contributions.

New Framework for Sketching Weight-One Vectors. Our first contribution is a new framework for constructing arithmetic sketching schemes languages of vectors $\mathcal{L} \subseteq \mathbb{F}^n$ with at most one non-zero entry, where the non-zero entry must lie in a certain set $B \subseteq \mathbb{F}$. Such languages feature prominently in schemes for PIR writing [1,15,21,34], private ad-measurement systems [24,37] private telemetry applications [9,18], and two-party ORAM schemes [20]. Our new view of arithmetic sketching schemes for weight-one vectors yields the first arithmetic sketching schemes for weight-one vectors with $B = \mathbb{F}$ and $B = \{-1, 0, 1\}$ (for "like/abstain/dislike" voting), and also gives a clean derivation of existing schemes.

Our approach works in three steps:

1. In Sect. 3.1, we define *algebraic manipulation detection distributions* ("AMD distributions"), an object inspired by AMD codes [16], a primitive of independent interest. For $B \subseteq \mathbb{F}^\ell$, a B-multiplicative AMD distribution is a distribution $\mathcal{D}$ over codewords in $\mathbb{F}^\ell$, along with a verifier. For a word sampled from $\mathcal{D}$, verification succeeds if a "permitted" affine transformation $\mathbb{F}^\ell \to \mathbb{F}^\ell$ has been applied to the word, and verification fails (with high probability) otherwise. More precisely, the verifier must accept all words in the support of $\mathcal{D}$ scaled by any value in B. The verifier must reject, with high probability, all affine functions on words in the support of $\mathcal{D}$ that fall outside of this "permitted" set.
2. In Sect. 3.2, we show that any B-multiplicative AMD distribution gives a simple arithmetic sketching scheme for the language of vectors of weight at most one, whose non-zero element lies in B. The size ℓ of the sketch is equal to the length of codewords in the AMD distribution.
3. Finally, in Sect. 3.3, we show that pairs of polynomials over $\mathbb{F}$ whose zeros satisfy certain conditions yield AMD distributions.

Putting these three components together gives both a recipe for constructing new arithmetic sketching schemes for weight-one vectors, and a characterization of existing schemes for testing properties of weight-one vectors [12].

The First Arithmetic Sketching Schemes for Low-Weight Vectors. In Sect. 4, we use new techniques to construct arithmetic sketching schemes for vectors of various form with bounded weight.

First, in Sect. 4.2, we show how to repurpose existing algorithms for black-box testing of sparse polynomials [25] to construct an arithmetic sketching scheme for vectors in $\mathbb{F}^n$ of Hamming weight w, where the non-zero entries can be arbitrary in $\mathbb{F}$.

Our idea is to view the input vector $x \in \mathbb{F}^n$ as the coefficients of a polynomial $f_x \in \mathbb{F}[Z]$ of degree at most $n-1$. Now, the input x has Hamming weight w if and only if the polynomial f_x has w non-zero coefficients. Prior work [25] shows that $O(w)$ polynomial-evaluation queries are enough to test whether a polynomial has w non-zero coefficients. Furthermore the decision procedure for this test can be made arithmetic. With a single linear combination of the elements of x, of the form $(1, r, r^2, r^3, \ldots, r^{n-1}) \in \mathbb{F}^n$, we can compute an evaluation of f_x on r. So, we obtain an $O(w)$-size sketch for the language of weight-w vectors.

Next, in Sect. 4.3, we construct an arithmetic sketching scheme for vectors in $\mathbb{F}^n$ whose non-zero components are in the set $\{0, \ldots, w\}$ and sum to exactly w (i.e., the "L_1-norm" is w). This language comes up in voting applications, where a client may cast w votes for n candidates, and may vote multiple times for the same candidate. Our technical idea is to construct a low-degree multivariate polynomial whose coefficients are determined by the input vector $x \in \mathbb{F}^n$, such that the polynomial is (a) identically zero whenever the vector x has L_1-norm w and is (b) non-zero otherwise. We construct this polynomial via Newton's identities. Then, we show that it is possible to evaluate this polynomial at a random point using $w + 1$ queries to the input vector.

As a final arithmetic sketching scheme for the bounded-weight case, we show in Sect. 4.4 how to sketch for vectors $\mathbb{F}^n$ of weight w whose non-zero elements satisfy an arbitrary arithmetic circuit $C\colon \mathbb{F} \to \mathbb{F}$, where the size of C is independent of $\mathbb{F}$. To do so, we first use the aforementioned results to test that the input vector x has Hamming weight w. We next use linear queries to partition the input vector at random into w^2 chunks of size n/w^2, and to sum the values in each chunk. We then accept if either (a) the vector has Hamming weight $< w$, in which case two non-zero elements were hashed to the same chunk or (b) the sums all satisfy the circuit C, which happens whenever the vector is valid and there are no collisions. (By the birthday bound, the latter happens with constant probability.) This basic scheme has large correctness error, so we drive the correctness error down using a careful repetition of these steps.

We summarize our new sketch constructions in Table 1.

Table 1. Our new sketch constructions and their relation to prior work. Here, we assume that the sketch is over a finite field $\mathbb{F}$ of characteristic greater than two. The note "Requires proof" indicates that the scheme is a fully linear probabilistically checkable proof [8] (see Sect. 5), rather than an arithmetic sketching scheme.

Language	Our sketch				
	Result	Size	Deg	Muls	Notes
Weight at most one, non-zero value in B...					
...with $B = \{0, 1\}$	n/a	2	2	1	} *From BGI* [12]
...with $B = \{-1, 1\}$	n/a	2	2	1	
...with $B = \{1\}$	n/a	2	2	1	
...with $B = \mathbb{F}$	Theorem 13	3	2	2	*Requires proof* [12]
...with $B = \{-1, 0, 1\}$	"	2	3	2	" "
...with $B = \{0, 1\}$	Theorem 16	3	2	2	*Soundness err.* $O(\lvert\mathbb{F}\rvert^{-2})$
Weight at most w**, non-zero values in** B...					
...with $B = \mathbb{F}$	Corollary 22	$O(w^2)$	3	$O(w^4)$	*Requires proof* [17]
...with $B = \{0, 1\}$	Corollary 27	$O(w^2)$	3	$O(w^{2.81})$	" "
...with $B = \{0, \ldots, w\}$, entries sum to $\leq w$	Theorem 26	$w + 1$	$w + 2$	w^2	" "
Weight exactly w	Theorem 21	$2w + 1$	3	$O(w^{2.81})$	*Only for DPF* [19]

From Sketching to Malicious-Secure Client-Server Multiparty Protocols. As we have discussed, arithmetic sketching schemes naturally give rise to protocols that a set of servers can use to check that a client-provided secret-shared vector x lies in a language $\mathcal{L}$. In essentially all applications, $x \in \mathcal{L}$ if the client is honest, and $x \notin \mathcal{L}$ otherwise. To recall: the servers, each holding additive shares of x, use shared randomness to generate the sketching matrix, they compute shares of the sketch locally, and then run a multiparty computation to run the decision procedure on these answers.

This simple protocol is *not* maliciously secure: any one of the servers can shift their share of the input $x \in \mathbb{F}^n$ by an additive offset $\Delta \in \mathbb{F}^n$. If the client is honest ($x \in \mathcal{L}$), the sketch should always accept and the servers learn nothing about x apart from the fact that $x \in \mathcal{L}$. However, once the malicious server has shifted its input by Δ, the output of the decision procedure reveals whether $(x + \Delta) \in \mathcal{L}$, which could reveal one bit of information about x. (In an e-voting setting, for example, this bit could reveal which candidate the client voted for.)

In Sect. 5, we give a general method for augmenting sketch-based client-server protocols of this form with malicious security at minimal cost. So, we show that any good arithmetic sketching scheme for a language $\mathcal{L}$ yields a malicious-secure client-server protocol of this type for $\mathcal{L}$. The technique is to have the client provide a randomized encoding of its input to the servers, using a flavor of algebraic manipulation detection distributions (as in Sect. 3). Our construction generalizes beyond arithmetic sketching schemes to also provide malicious-secure client-server protocols for languages with "fully linear probabilistically checkable proofs" [8].

Limits of Arithmetic Sketching Schemes. Our final contributions are to give lower bounds on the efficiency and power of arithmetic sketching schemes.

In Sect. 6, we use an algebraic argument to show that any arithmetic sketching scheme for vectors in $\mathbb{F}^n$ of weight at most one ($B = \mathbb{F}$) with sketch size ℓ and a decision predicate of degree d has soundness error at least $\left((d+1)\,|\mathbb{F}|^{\ell-2}\right)^{-1}$. This establishes that our arithmetic sketching scheme of Sect. 3 with sketch size $\ell = 3$ is essentially optimal in terms of its sketch size, providing an unexpected separation from the case of unit vectors in $\mathbb{F}^n$ ($B = \{0, 1\}$), in which sketch size $\ell = 2$ is enough for $O(1/|\mathbb{F}|)$ soundness error.

In Sect. 7, we use lower bounds from communication complexity to show that certain languages cannot have arithmetic sketching schemes. For example, define the L_p-norm of $x = (x_1, \ldots, x_n) \in \mathbb{F}^n$, for p relatively prime to $|\mathbb{F}| - 1$, as the scalar $(x_1^p + \cdots + x_n^p)^{1/p} \in \mathbb{F}$. In Sect. 4, we give a arithmetic sketching scheme for the language of vectors of L_1 norm w, with entries in $\{0, \ldots, w\}$. It is something of a surprise then that, as we show, there are no analogous arithmetic sketching schemes the language of vectors with L_p-norm, for any $p > 1$. For any $B \subseteq \mathbb{F}$, we also rule out arithmetic sketching schemes for the language of vectors that are all zeros with a contiguous run of values in B of arbitrary length, and the language of vectors that contains one value in B and arbitrary values elsewhere.

1.2 Related Work

Boyle, Gilboa, and Ishai [12] implicitly constructed arithmetic sketching schemes for languages of vectors in $\mathbb{F}^n$ of Hamming weight one, where the non-zero element is in $B \subseteq \mathbb{F}$, for $B = \{0,1\}, \{-1,1\}, \{1\}$. They also presented a solution for the case of an unrestricted payload (i.e., $B = \mathbb{F}$), but their approaches required auxiliary proof information from the client. A variant of this construction that avoids the extra proof was given in the Blinder system [1].

Distributed point functions [12] (DPFs) give a compressed representation of additive secret shares of a weight-one vector in $\mathbb{F}^n$. A work of de Castro and Polychroniadou [19] gives a technique that two parties, each holding a DPF key, can use to verify that their keys together indeed represent a vector of Hamming-weight one ($B = \mathbb{F}$ in our notation). When their protocol applies, it is extremely efficient. However, their protocol only applies to a specific tree-based DPF construction, thus not applying to input vectors that are secret-shared directly or encrypted. Moreover, their protocol cannot check further properties of the non-zero element (i.e., $B = \{0,1\}$), which is critical for many applications.

Arithmetic sketching schemes are closely related to fully linear probabilistically checkable proofs [8] (FL-PCPs). Essentially an FL-PCP for a language $\mathcal{L} \subseteq \mathbb{F}^n$ is a Merlin-Arthur analogue of arithmetic sketching scheme. In an FL-PCP, the verifier's queries compute an inner product with the input x concatenated with a proof string π, whose length may grow with the input length n. (The number of queries is typically constant in n.) If $x \in \mathcal{L}$, there is a proof π that causes the verifier to accept. If $x \notin \mathcal{L}$ the verifier almost always rejects. Arithmetic sketching schemes are thus FL-PCPs with an empty proof string. FL-PCPs are more powerful than arithmetic sketching schemes—given a large enough proof, they can check whether the input satisfies an arbitrary arithmetic circuit. Yet FL-PCPs require additional proof, which can be costly in communication or infeasible when there is no one party that knows the full input.

Traditional sketching data structures [2,13,33], which summarize a large data stream in small space, inspire our approach. As we discuss in Sect. 2, the arithmetic nature of our sketches means that most traditional sketching techniques do not naturally apply in our setting.

Finally, the combination of secure computation and sketching was previously considered in the context of sublinear-communication secure computation protocols for approximations [22,27,28]. Since the focus of these works was on crude asymptotic efficiency rather than concrete efficiency, they could rely on traditional (non-arithmetic) linear sketching. Moreover, in contrast to the approximate sketching problems considered in these works, here we consider arithmetic sketching schemes that yield the exact output except with negligible failure probability.

Notation. For a finite set S, we use $x \xleftarrow{\text{R}} S$ to denote a uniformly random sample from S. We use $x \stackrel{\text{def}}{=} 3$ to note definition and $\langle \cdot, \cdot \rangle$ to denote inner product. For a finite field $\mathbb{F}$, when $|\mathbb{F}| > n$ we use $1, 2, 3, \ldots, n$ to denote distinct non-zero field elements.

2 A Formalization of Arithmetic Sketching Schemes

We characterize our goal by the following notion of an *arithmetic sketching* scheme. Our definition (Sect. 2.2) is roughly analogous to the definition of fully linear PCPs [8], with the role of the witness and prover removed.

2.1 Overview

We define arithmetic sketching schemes with respect to a finite field $\mathbb{F}$, a dimension $n \in \mathbb{N}$, and a language $\mathcal{L} \subseteq \mathbb{F}^n$. For a given input $x \in \mathbb{F}^n$, the task is to determine whether $x \in \mathcal{L}$ given only the output of a *linear function* applied to the input vector x. That is, in a arithmetic sketching scheme with sketch size ℓ, we consider a verifier who uses randomness to produce a sketching matrix $Q \in \mathbb{F}^{\ell \times n}$. The verifier receives the matrix-vector product of the sketching matrix Q with the input vector x: that is, $Q \cdot x \in \mathbb{F}^{\ell}$. The verifier decides whether to accept ($x \in \mathcal{L}$) or reject ($x \notin \mathcal{L}$) by running a decision algorithm D on the vector $Q \cdot x$.

All of the specific languages $\mathcal{L}$ we will consider in this work are simple, and can be decided in linear time in the input size. What makes constructing arithmetic sketching schemes non-trivial is that (1) the decision algorithm takes as input a small linear sketch of the (large) input vector and (2) the decision algorithm must be a small arithmetic circuit, as we discuss now.

Arithmetic Verifier. We will typically consider infinite families of languages $\mathcal{L}$, parameterized by the field $\mathbb{F}$ and input length n. For example, we could consider the family of all unit vectors in $\mathbb{F}^n$. We will require our arithmetic sketching constructions to have an *arithmetic verifier*: that is, the decision algorithm D applies an arithmetic circuit to the sketch, and accepts if and only if the circuit outputs the all-zeros vector in $\mathbb{F}$. Restricting the decision circuit to being arithmetic means that it is possible to compute with good concrete efficiency in a secure multi-party computation, as in our motivating applications. (Later, in Sect. 4.1, we will also consider relaxed arithmetic sketching schemes with partially arithmetic decision predicates.)

Universal Family of Sketching Schemes. We require by default that the family be *universal* in the sense that both the sketch size ℓ and the decision algorithm D are independent of the field $\mathbb{F}$ and input size n.

Complexity Measures. In our constructions, we will aim to minimize the *sketch size* ℓ (influencing the computation time), the algebraic *degree* of D (influencing the round complexity or security threshold), and the multiplicative *size* of D (number of multiplication gates, influencing communication complexity).

2.2 Formal Definitions

We now formalize the above discussion.

Definition 1 (Arithmetic sketching scheme: Syntax). *Let $\mathbb{F}$ be a finite field. A* arithmetic sketching *scheme for a language $\mathcal{L} \subseteq \mathbb{F}^n$ with sketch size $\ell \in \mathbb{N}$ consists of a pair of algorithms (S, D):*

- *$S() \to Q \in \mathbb{F}^{\ell \times n}$. The randomized sketching algorithm outputs a query matrix $Q \in \mathbb{F}^{\ell \times n}$. (We also refer to Q as the "sketching matrix.")*
- *$D(a) \to y \in \mathbb{F}^m$. The decision algorithm takes as input a sketch vector $a \in \mathbb{F}^\ell$ and outputs a vector $y \in \mathbb{F}^m$. (To enable stronger security, we will later allow the decision algorithm D to be randomized, taking random field elements $r_1, \ldots, r_k$ as additional inputs.)*

We assume by default that the decision algorithm D is implemented by an arithmetic circuit over $\mathbb{F}$, consisting of addition, subtraction and multiplication gates, as well as a unit gate outputting the constant $\mathbf{1} \in \mathbb{F}$. We measure the complexity of D by its algebraic degree *and* multiplicative size *(counting the number of multiplication gates).*

A arithmetic sketching scheme as above must satisfy the following properties.

Definition 2 (Completeness and soundness). *A arithmetic sketching scheme (S, D) for a language $\mathcal{L} \subseteq \mathbb{F}^n$ is*

- ***Complete** if, for all $x \in \mathcal{L}$, the verifier accepts:*

$$\Pr[D(Q \cdot x) = \mathbf{0}^m : Q \leftarrow S()] = 1.$$

  (If this probability is at least $1-\epsilon$, we say that the arithmetic sketching scheme has completeness error ϵ.)
- ***Sound** with soundness error ϵ if, for all $x \notin \mathcal{L}$, the acceptance probability, as in the completeness definition, is at most ϵ.*

A few remarks on the definition of arithmetic sketching schemes:

Linear Decision Not Interesting. The decision algorithm D must contain at least one multiplication gate. If not, the arithmetic sketching accepts the vectors in the kernel of a linear map and thus can only test linear predicates.

Non-arithmetic Sketching. We restrict the decision algorithm D to have low arithmetic complexity. Without this restriction, any language $\mathcal{L} \subseteq \mathbb{F}^n$ can be decided using a sketch of size $\ell = O(\log |\mathcal{L}|)$. The sketch, given input $x \in \mathbb{F}^n$, just computes a random linear combination $r \leftarrow R(x) \in \mathbb{F}^\ell$ of the input vector. The decision predicate searches—via brute-force search—for a value $x' \in \mathcal{L}$ such that $R(x') = r$ and accepts if, and only if, one exists. Since a random linear code has good distance, the sketch will be sound. When the decision predicate must be algebraic, constructing arithmetic sketching schemes is non-trivial, even in the information-theoretic setting.

2.3 Zero Knowledge

In the context of cryptographic applications, it is important that if $x \in \mathcal{L}$, then the sketching-based verification reveal nothing beyond the fact that $x \in \mathcal{L}$. For the above notion of arithmetic sketching, this *zero-knowledge* property is automatically guaranteed by the completeness requirement if we use a secure computation protocol to compute the output of the decision algorithm D. Indeed, for $x \in \mathcal{L}$, the output of D is always $\mathbf{0}^m$. However, some applications motivate a stronger notion of *two-sided zero knowledge*, requiring that the output of the decision algorithm D hides all information about the input x apart from whether $x \in \mathcal{L}$. To this end, we allow the decision algorithm D to be randomized, taking secret random field elements as additional inputs.

Definition 3 (Two-sided zero knowledge). *We say that an arithmetic sketching scheme has* δ-two-sided zero knowledge *if there exists a simulator* Sim *such that for all* $x \in \mathbb{F}^n$*, the following distributions are* δ*-close in statistical distance:*

$$\mathcal{D}_{\text{ideal}} = \mathsf{Sim}(\mathbb{1}\{x \in \mathcal{L}\}) \quad // \mathsf{Sim} \textit{ gets the bit indicating whether } x \in \mathcal{L}$$

$$\mathcal{D}_{\text{real}} = \left\{ \Big(Q, v\Big) : \begin{array}{c} Q \leftarrow S() \\ r \xleftarrow{\text{R}} \mathbb{F}^k \\ v \leftarrow D(Q \cdot x; r) \end{array} \right\}.$$

If $\delta = 0$*, we say that the scheme satisfies* perfect *zero knowledge.*

An arithmetic sketching scheme may not necessarily satisfy two-sided zero knowledge. In particular, if $x \notin \mathcal{L}$ the output of D could leak additional information about the input x. But the following generic transformation, whose proof we give in the full version of this paper, uses a standard random-linear-combination technique to modify any arithmetic sketching scheme into one with two-sided zero knowledge at a small additional cost:

Fact 4. *It is possible to modify any arithmetic sketching scheme over finite field* $\mathbb{F}$ *with decision predicate* $D\colon \mathbb{F}^\ell \times \mathbb{F}^k \to \mathbb{F}^m$ *to satisfy perfect two-sided zero knowledge by allowing* D *to use* m *secret random field elements. This modification increases the multiplicative size of* D *by* m*, the algebraic degree of* D *by 1, and the soundness error by* $1/|\mathbb{F}|$.

3 Sketching via Algebraic Manipulation Detection

We will be particularly interested in languages consisting of vectors whose Hamming weight is at most 1, possibly with additional restrictions on the nonzero entry. (For simplicity, in the following we will sometimes use "weight 1" to refer to weight *at most* 1.) In this section, we present a new framework for constructing arithmetic sketching schemes for such languages. The framework captures several existing ad-hoc constructions in a unified way and gives rise to efficient new constructions. The central tool is a new object that we call an *algebraic manipulation detection (AMD) distribution.* This notion is inspired by the notion of AMD codes of Cramer et al. [16], extending it to provide limited forms of *targeted malleability* [10].

Background: AMD Codes. An AMD code gives a (randomized) way to encode a message into a codeword in a way that allows detection of "additive tampering" of the encoded message. In particular, an AMD code consists of a randomized encoder $\mathsf{Enc}\colon \mathbb{F}^n \to \mathbb{F}^\ell$ and decoder $\mathsf{Dec}\colon \mathbb{F}^\ell \to \mathbb{F}^n$ such that:

- it is possible to recover the message from the codeword: for all messages $m \in \mathbb{F}^n$, $\Pr[m = \mathsf{Dec}(\mathsf{Enc}(m))] = 1$, and
- the codeword shifted by any additive offset either decodes to the correct message m or a failure symbol $\perp$: for all messages $m \in \mathbb{F}^n$ and $\Delta \in F^\ell$,

$$\Pr\big[\mathsf{Dec}(\mathsf{Enc}(m) + \Delta) \notin \{m, \perp\}\big] \le \epsilon,$$

  where the probability is taken over the randomness of Enc and ϵ is some small value $\epsilon \approx 1/|\mathbb{F}|$.

Our Notion: AMD Distributions. Our notion of AMD distributions differs from standard AMD codes in three ways:

1. First, there is no encoder and no message to be encoded. Instead we define a sampling algorithm S_{AMD} that outputs, effectively, a random codeword r.
2. Second, we demand that attempting to decode a codeword r that has been shifted by a non-zero additive offset results in a decoding failure with high probability. (In traditional AMD codes, a shifted codeword may decode to the failure symbol $\perp$ *or* to the original message.) This stronger AMD requirement appears in several works on secure computation [23].
3. Third, and most important, we demand that the manipulation-detection property of the coding scheme holds even for *affine* tampering: that is, taking r to $\beta r + \Delta$ for nonzero scalar β and vector Δ. (Traditional AMD codes detect only additive shifts.) In some cases, we allow decoding to succeed if the codeword r is multiplied by an "allowable" value $\beta \in B$, for some prespecified set $B \subseteq \mathbb{F}$. We call these "B-multiplicative" AMD distributions.

Looking ahead, we will show that any B-multiplicative AMD distribution yields a sketching scheme for the language of vectors of weight one whose payload is in the set B.

3.1 Definition

We now make our notion of AMD distributions formal.

Definition 5 (AMD Distribution). *An* algebraic manipulation detection (AMD) distribution *over finite field $\mathbb{F}$ with codeword length $\ell \in \mathbb{N}$ and error ϵ is given by a pair of procedures:*

- *$S_{\mathsf{AMD}}() \to r \in \mathbb{F}^\ell$. A randomized algorithm that samples a codeword r.*
- *$V_{\mathsf{AMD}}(r) \to y \in \mathbb{F}$. A verification algorithm, represented as an arithmetic circuit, that accepts a vector $r \in \mathbb{F}^\ell$ and outputs an element $y \in \mathbb{F}$. We interpret the output as accepting if $y = 0$ and rejecting otherwise.*

These procedures must satisfy the following properties:

- **Nontriviality:** *The distribution of* S_{AMD} *is supported by at least two vectors.*
- **Completeness:** *We have that:*

$$\Pr[V_{\mathsf{AMD}}(r) = 0 : r \leftarrow S_{\mathsf{AMD}}()] = 1.$$

- **Affine manipulation detection:** *For every scalar* $\beta \in \mathbb{F}$ *and additive offset* $\Delta \in \mathbb{F}^{\ell}$ *with* $\beta \neq 0$ *and* $\Delta \neq \mathbf{0}^{\ell}$, *it holds that*

$$\Pr[V_{\mathsf{AMD}}(\beta r + \Delta) = 0 : r \leftarrow S_{\mathsf{AMD}}()] \leq \epsilon.$$

Remark. In Sect. 3.5, we will consider a more refined notion of AMD distributions, requiring that the decoder detect any nontrivial linear combination of two or more (distinct) random samples from S_{AMD} with high probability.

For our applications, we will often need AMD distributions that satisfy forms of *targeted malleability.* That is, for some set $B \subseteq \mathbb{F}$, we would like the AMD decoder to accept codewords that have been scaled by a constant $\beta \in B$ and to reject, with high probability, all codewords scaled by constants $\beta' \in \mathbb{F} \setminus B$.

Note that the completeness requirement implies that $1 \in B$. In the context of the sketching application this is without loss of generality, since for any $\beta \in B \setminus \{0\}$ scaling the queries by β effectively converts B to $\beta^{-1} \cdot B$.

The following definition captures the above notion of targeted malleability:

Definition 6 (B-Multiplicative AMD Distribution). *Let* $\mathbb{F}$ *be a finite field and let* $B \subseteq \mathbb{F}$ *such that* $1 \in B$. *We say that an AMD distribution* $(S_{\mathsf{AMD}}, V_{\mathsf{AMD}})$ *over* $\mathbb{F}$ *and with error* ϵ *is* B-multiplicative *if it additionally satisfies the following properties:*

- *For every* $\beta \in B$, *it holds that* $\Pr[V_{\mathsf{AMD}}(\beta r) = 0 : r \leftarrow S_{\mathsf{AMD}}] = 1$.
- *For every* $\beta' \in \mathbb{F} \setminus B$, *it holds that* $\Pr[V_{\mathsf{AMD}}(\beta' r) = 0 : r \leftarrow S_{\mathsf{AMD}}] \leq \epsilon$.

We will need the following lemma, which we prove in the full version:

Lemma 7. *Let* $(S_{\mathsf{AMD}}, V_{\mathsf{AMD}})$ *be an AMD distribution with codeword length* ℓ *over finite field* $\mathbb{F}$, *where* $|\mathbb{F}| > 2$, *with error* ϵ. *Then for all* $r_0 \in \mathbb{F}^{\ell}$, *we have* $\Pr[S_{\mathsf{AMD}} = r_0] \leq \epsilon$.

3.2 From AMD Distributions to Sketching Schemes

We now use AMD distributions to construct arithmetic sketching schemes for the language of vectors of Hamming weight (at most) one, whose non-zero entry lies within a specific set B. For our discussion, the following notation will be useful:

Definition 8 (Language $\mathcal{L}_B$). *For a finite field* $\mathbb{F}$, *dimension* $n \in \mathbb{N}$, *and set* $B \subseteq F$, *we define the language* $\mathcal{L}_B$ *to be the set of* B*-multiples of unit vectors in* $\mathbb{F}^n$. *That is,* $\mathcal{L}_B = \{\beta \cdot \mathbf{e}_i \mid i \in [n], \beta \in B\}$, *where* $\mathbf{e}_i \in \mathbb{F}^n$ *is the vector of zeros with a single one at coordinate* i.

The following construction shows that B-multiplicative AMD distributions immediately give rise to arithmetic sketching schemes for the language $\mathcal{L}_B$.

Construction 9 (Sketch for Hamming-weight one from AMD distributions). *The construction is parameterized by a finite field $\mathbb{F}$, an input size $n \in \mathbb{N}$, a set $B \subseteq \mathbb{F}$ such that $1 \in B$, and a B-multiplicative AMD distribution $(S_{\mathsf{AMD}}, V_{\mathsf{AMD}})$ with codeword length $\ell \in \mathbb{N}$. The arithmetic sketching scheme (S, D) is over the field $\mathbb{F}$, has sketch size ℓ, and is defined as follows:*

- $S() \to Q \in \mathbb{F}^{\ell \times n}$.
  - *For $i \in [n]$, compute $r_i \xleftarrow{\text{R}} S_{\mathsf{AMD}}() \in \mathbb{F}^\ell$.*
  - *Output the matrix $Q \in \mathbb{F}^{\ell \times n}$ whose columns are $(r_1, \ldots, r_n)$.*
- $D(a) \to y \in \mathbb{F}^m$.
  - *Output $V_{\mathsf{AMD}}(a)$.*

Theorem 10. *If $(S_{\mathsf{AMD}}, V_{\mathsf{AMD}})$ is a B-multiplicative AMD distribution over finite field $\mathbb{F}$ ($|\mathbb{F}| > 2$) with codeword length ℓ and error ϵ then, for all $n \in \mathbb{N}$, Construction 9 instantiated with $(S_{\mathsf{AMD}}, V_{\mathsf{AMD}})$ is an arithmetic sketching scheme for the language $\mathcal{L}_B \subseteq \mathbb{F}^n$ (as in Definition 8) with soundness error 2ϵ.*

Proof. To show completeness: We can write any valid input $x \in \mathcal{L}_B$ as $x = \beta \boldsymbol{e}_i$ for some $\beta \in B$ and $i \in [n]$. Then, for sketching query matrix $Q \leftarrow S_{\mathsf{AMD}}()$, we have that $a = Q \cdot x = Q \cdot (\beta \boldsymbol{e}_i) \in \mathbb{F}^\ell$; i.e., the i-th column of the query matrix multiplied by the scalar β. By construction, the i-th column of the matrix Q is computed as $(r_{i1}, \ldots, r_{i\ell}) \leftarrow S_{\mathsf{AMD}}()$. So the sketch decision procedure outputs $D(\beta r_{i1}, \ldots, \beta r_{i\ell}) = V_{\mathsf{AMD}}(\beta r_{i1}, \ldots, \beta r_{i\ell})$. This value is always 0 by the B-multiplicative property of the AMD distribution $(S_{\mathsf{AMD}}, V_{\mathsf{AMD}})$, so the verifier always accepts.

To show soundness: Let $x' \notin \mathcal{L}_B$. There are two cases.

- Case 1: $x' = \beta' \boldsymbol{e}_i$ for some $i \in [n]$, $\beta' \notin B$.
  By the B-multiplicative property of the AMD distribution:

$$\begin{aligned} &\Pr\left[D(Q \cdot x') = \mathbf{0} \colon Q \leftarrow S()\right] \\ &= \Pr\left[V_{\mathsf{AMD}}(\beta' r_{i1}, \ldots, \beta' r_{i\ell}) = \mathbf{0} \colon (r_{i1}, \ldots, r_{i\ell}) \leftarrow S_{\mathsf{AMD}}()\right] \\ &\leq \epsilon. \end{aligned}$$

- Case 2: x' has Hamming weight $k \geq 2$. Letting Q be the random $\ell \times n$ query matrix, we can write the answer vector $a = Q \cdot x'$ as a linear combination of $k \geq 2$ independent samples r^i from the AMD distribution S_{AMD}. Namely, $a = \sum_{i=1}^k \beta_i r^i$ for nonzero $\beta_i \in \mathbb{F}$. Letting $\Delta = \sum_{i=2}^k \beta_i r^i$, we can now write:

$$\begin{aligned} \Pr\left[D(a) = 0\right] &= \Pr\left[V_{\mathsf{AMD}}(\beta_1 r^1 + \Delta) = 0\right] \\ &\leq \Pr\left[\Delta = 0\right] + \Pr\left[V_{\mathsf{AMD}}(\beta_1 r^1 + \Delta) = 0 \mid \Delta \neq 0\right] \\ &\leq \epsilon + \epsilon = 2\epsilon, \end{aligned}$$

  where the last inequality follows from Lemma 7 and the affine manipulation detection property of S_{AMD}. □

3.3 Constructing AMD Distributions from Algebraic Varieties

We now show how to construct AMD distributions based on algebraic varieties. These AMD distributions, via Theorem 10, give rise to practical arithmetic sketching schemes for useful instances of the Hamming-weight one languages $\mathcal{L}_B$ that minimize the relevant complexity measures.

Construction 11 (AMD distribution from varieties). *The construction is parameterized by a finite field $\mathbb{F}$, randomness complexity $k \in \mathbb{N}$, a codeword size $\ell \in \mathbb{N}$, an arithmetic AMD sampler, defined by a polynomial map $\mathbf{g}\colon \mathbb{F}^k \to \mathbb{F}^\ell$, and an AMD verifier, defined by a polynomial $f \in \mathbb{F}[R_1, \ldots, R_\ell]$. The construction is then:*

- $S_{\mathsf{AMD}}() \to r \in \mathbb{F}^\ell$:
  - *Sample a random vector* $(s_1, \ldots, s_k) \xleftarrow{R} \mathbb{F}^k$.
  - *Output* $r \leftarrow \mathbf{g}(s_1, \ldots, s_k) \in \mathbb{F}^\ell$.
- $V_{\mathsf{AMD}}(r_1, \ldots, r_\ell) \to y \in \mathbb{F}$: *Output* $y \leftarrow f(r_1, \ldots, r_\ell) \in \mathbb{F}$.

The following theorem follows almost immediately by construction:

Theorem 12. *When instantiated with a polynomial map $\mathbf{g}\colon \mathbb{F}^k \to \mathbb{F}^\ell$ with total degree $\deg \mathbf{g}$ and polynomial $f \in \mathbb{F}[R_1, \ldots, R_\ell]$ with total degree $\deg f$, Construction 11 is a B-multiplicative AMD distribution, in the sense of Definition 6, with soundness error $(\deg f \cdot \deg \mathbf{g})/|\mathbb{F}|$ when:*

(1) [for completeness] the polynomial $f \circ \mathbf{g} \equiv 0 \in \mathbb{F}[S_1, \ldots, S_k]$,
(2) [for AMD] for all non-zero $\beta \in \mathbb{F}$ and non-zero $\Delta \in \mathbb{F}^\ell$, the formal polynomial $f \circ (\beta\mathbf{g} + \Delta) \not\equiv 0 \in \mathbb{F}[S_1, \ldots, S_k]$, and
(3) [for B-multiplicativity] it holds that $f \circ \beta\mathbf{g} \equiv 0$ if and only if $\beta \in B$.

Proof. For completeness: By property (1), $V_{\mathsf{AMD}}(S_{\mathsf{AMD}}) = f(\mathbf{g}(s_1, \ldots, s_k)) = 0$.

For AMD: When at least one of $\beta \in \mathbb{F}$ and $\Delta \in \mathbb{F}^\ell$ is non-zero, we have:

$$\Pr[V_{\mathsf{AMD}}(\beta r + \Delta) = 0 \colon r \leftarrow S_{\mathsf{AMD}}()] = \Pr[f(\beta\mathbf{g}(s) + \Delta) \colon s \xleftarrow{R} \mathbb{F}^k].$$

By property (2), $f \circ (\beta\mathbf{g} + \Delta) \in \mathbb{F}[S_1, \ldots, S_k]$ is a non-zero polynomial, and its total degree is at most $\deg f \cdot \deg \mathbf{g}$. Then by the Schwartz-Zippel Lemma, the probability that a random point in $\mathbb{F}^k$ is a zero is at most $(\deg f \cdot \deg \mathbf{g})/|\mathbb{F}|$.

For B-multiplicativity: we invoke property (3). When $\beta \in B$, the argument is the same as for completeness. When $\beta \notin B$, the argument is the same as for AMD. □

If the pair $(f, \mathbf{g})$ satisfy properties (1) and (2) of Theorem 12, we can use the theorem to characterize the B-multiplicativity properties of the AMD distribution resulting from Construction 11. In particular, when f has monomials of only two degrees, we have the following:

- **One degree:** Suppose f is homogeneous; i.e., every monomial of f has the same total degree $d \geq 0$. Then the pair $(f, \mathbf{g})$ give a B-multiplicative AMD distribution for $B = \mathbb{F}$. That is because, since for all $\beta \in \mathbb{F}$,

$$f \circ \beta\mathbf{g} = \beta^d \cdot (f \circ \mathbf{g}) \equiv 0,$$

  where the final step holds by the completeness guarantee $f \circ \mathbf{g} \equiv 0$.
- **Two degrees:** Suppose $f(R_1, \dots, R_\ell) = f_1(R_1, \dots, R_\ell) + f_2(R_1, \dots, R_\ell)$, where $f_1, f_2 \not\equiv 0$ and every monomial of f_1 (respectively, f_2) has total degree $d_1 + d_2$ (resp, d_2), where $d_1 > 0, d_2 \geq 0$. Then

$$\begin{aligned} f \circ \beta\mathbf{g} &= f_1 \circ \beta\mathbf{g} + f_2 \circ \beta\mathbf{g} \\ &= \beta^{d_1+d_2} \cdot (f_1 \circ \mathbf{g}) + \beta^{d_2} \cdot (f_2 \circ \mathbf{g}) \\ &= \beta^{d_2}(1 - \beta^{d_1}) \cdot (f_2 \circ \mathbf{g}), \end{aligned}$$

  where the final step holds since $f_1 \circ \mathbf{g} \equiv -f_2 \circ \mathbf{g}$ by the completeness guarantee. Since $f_2 \not\equiv 0$, this polynomial is the zero polynomial precisely for values of β which annihilate the prefixed multiplicative term. Depending on the choices of d_1, d_2, this directly corresponds to the sets $B = \{1\}, \{0,1\}, \{-1,1\}, \{-1,0,1\}$.

3.4 New Sketching Schemes for Weight-One Vectors

We now consider several useful instantiations of Construction 11, including both new sketching schemes and abstractions of existing ones.

New Instantiations. Our characterization also yields useful new arithmetic sketching schemes for the case $\mathrm{char}(\mathbb{F}) > 2$:

$$\begin{aligned} &B = \{-1,0,1\}: \quad && f(r_1, r_2) = r_1^3 - r_2 \quad && \mathbf{g}(s) = (s, s^3) \\ &B = \mathbb{F}: \quad && f(r_1, r_2, r_3) = r_1 r_2 - r_3^2 \quad && \mathbf{g}(s_1, s_2) = (s_1^2, s_2^2, s_1 s_2). \end{aligned}$$

Constructions from [12]. The following sketching schemes from [12] fit directly into the characterization above, yielding a simple unified derivation based on Theorem 12:

$$\begin{aligned} &B = \{0,1\}: \quad && f(r_1, r_2, r_3) = r_3 - r_1 r_2 \quad && \mathbf{g}(s_1, s_2) = (s_1, s_2, s_1 s_2) \\ &B = \{0,1\}: \quad && f(r_1, r_2) = r_1^2 - r_2 \quad && \mathbf{g}(s) = (s, s^2) \\ &B = \{1\}: \quad && f(r_1, r_2) = (r_1 + 1)^2 - r_2 \quad && \mathbf{g}(s) = (s, (s+1)^2), \end{aligned}$$

where the last two schemes require $\mathrm{char}(\mathbb{F}) > 2$.
We illustrate checking the conditions of Theorem 12 for the case $B = \mathbb{F}$:

- Completeness: $f \circ \mathbf{g} = s_1^2 s_2^2 - (s_1 s_2)^2 \equiv 0$.
- AMD: for $\beta \in \mathbb{F}$ and $\Delta = (\Delta_1, \Delta_2, \Delta_3) \in \mathbb{F}^3$, we have $f \circ (\beta\mathbf{g} + \Delta)(s_1, s_2) = \beta\Delta_2 s_1^2 + \beta\Delta_1 s_2^2 - 2\beta\Delta_3 s_1 s_2 + (\Delta_1\Delta_2 - \Delta_3^2)$. For any non-zero β and non-zero Δ, this polynomial in (s_1, s_2) is not identically zero.

- B-multiplicative: Since f is homogeneous of degree two, it holds by the completeness property that $f \circ \beta \mathbf{g} \equiv 0$ for all $\beta \in \mathbb{F}$.

We summarize the above by the following theorem.

Theorem 13 (Arithmetic sketching with a single decision polynomial). *Let n be a positive integer and $\mathbb{F}$ be a finite field with char($\mathbb{F}$) > 2. There are arithmetic sketching schemes for the language $\mathcal{L}_B \subseteq \mathbb{F}^n$ (as in Definition 8), with soundness error $O(1/|\mathbb{F}|)$ and a single decision polynomial f, for the following choices of B.*

- $B = \{0, 1\}$*: sketch size* 2*, f of degree* 2 *and multiplicative size 1;*
- $B = \{1\}$*: sketch size* 2*, f of degree* 2 *and multiplicative size 1;*
- $B = \{-1, 0, 1\}$*: sketch size* 2*, f of degree* 3 *and multiplicative size 2;*
- $B = \mathbb{F}$*: sketch size* 3*, f of degree* 2 *and multiplicative size 2.*

Jumping ahead, in Theorem 29 we will show that the extra query required for the case $B = \mathbb{F}$ is not an artifact of our construction, and it is in fact necessary even if a decision algorithm D consisting of multiple decision polynomials f_i is allowed.

Remark (General $\mathcal{L}_B$). An arithmetic sketching scheme for $\mathcal{L}_B$ with an arbitrary $B \subset \mathbb{F}$ of size k can be reduced to the case of $\mathcal{L}_{\mathbb{F}}$ by adding the single additional query $q_0 = (1, 1, \ldots, 1)$ and another decision polynomial of degree k, checking that $a_0 = \langle x, q \rangle \in B$. However, this general solution is significantly less efficient than the sketching schemes from Theorem 13.

3.5 A Sketch with $1/|\mathbb{F}|^2$ Soundness for Binary Weight 1

In Sect. 3.2 we used AMD distributions to construct sketching schemes for the language $\mathcal{L}_B \subseteq \mathbb{F}^n$ (Definition 8) for certain sets $B \subseteq \mathbb{F}$. When char($\mathbb{F}$) > 2, the sketch from Sect. 3.2 for $\mathcal{L}_{\{0,1\}}$ contains two elements and has soundness error $O(1/|\mathbb{F}|)$.

In this section we construct a sketch for $\mathcal{L}_{\{0,1\}}$ that contains *three* elements and has soundness error $O(1/|\mathbb{F}|^2)$. One can repeat the sketch for $\mathcal{L}_{\{0,1\}}$ from Sect. 3.2 twice to obtain the same soundness level, however the resulting sketch would have length four, whereas our sketch has length three.

The previous notion of AMD distributions is insufficient for this purpose. First, the verification algorithm $V_{\mathsf{AMD}}(r)$ outputs only a single field element, which is insufficient to achieve soundness error $\epsilon < 1/|\mathbb{F}|$. More inherently, the failure probability ϵ must be bigger than the inverse of the support size of S_{AMD}, since a successful additive attack can be based on a guess of the codeword r. In the following, we will modify original notion of AMD distributions (Definition 5) to address both limitations. Concretely, the new notion allows $V_{\mathsf{AMD}}(r)$ to output multiple field elements, and requires detection of linear combinations of two or more *distinct* samples from S_{AMD}. Somewhat surprisingly, the latter requirement will allow us to break the inverse-support-size barrier.

Definition 14 (Low-Error AMD Distribution). *A low-error AMD distribution with error ϵ is defined similarly to a standard AMD distribution from Definition 5, with the following modified syntax and detection property.*

- **Syntax:** $V_{\mathsf{AMD}}(r) \to y \in \mathbb{F}^m$, *namely the verification circuit outputs m field elements. We interpret the all-0 output as accepting.*
- **Completeness:** $\Pr\left[V_{\mathsf{AMD}}(r) = 0^m \ : \ r \leftarrow S_{\mathsf{AMD}}()\right] = 1$.
- **Detection:** *Let S be the support size of S_{AMD} and let $n \in \mathbb{N}$ satisfy $2 \leq n < S$. Let $S_{\mathsf{AMD}}^{(n)}$ denote the probability distribution of n independent samples from S_{AMD},* conditioned on all samples being distinct. *Then for all $(\beta_1, \ldots, \beta_n)$ in $\mathbb{F}^n \setminus \mathcal{L}_{\{0,1\}}$ it holds that*

$$\Pr\left[V_{\mathsf{AMD}}(\beta_1 r^{(1)} + \ldots + \beta_k r^{(n)}) = 0^m : (r^{(1)}, \ldots, r^{(n)}) \leftarrow S_{\mathsf{AMD}}^{(n)}\right] \leq \epsilon. \quad (1)$$

A low-error AMD distribution as above naturally gives rise to an arithmetic sketching scheme detecting inputs in $\mathcal{L}_{\{0,1\}}$, as in Construction 9. The only difference is that instead of sampling the columns of the sketching matrix uniformly at random from S_{AMD}, their choice is now conditioned on the distinctness requirement. We next show how to instantiate this approach with S_{AMD} that samples powers of a random field element.

Construction 15 (A low-error AMD distribution). *The construction is parameterized by a codeword length $\ell \in \mathbb{N}$, a finite field $\mathbb{F}$, and a polynomial map $\mathbf{f} : \mathbb{F}^\ell \to \mathbb{F}^m$. The construction is then:*

- $S_{\mathsf{AMD}}() \to r \in \mathbb{F}^\ell$:
  - *Sample a random $s \xleftarrow{R} \mathbb{F}^*$.*
  - *Output $r \leftarrow (s, s^2, \ldots, s^\ell) \in \mathbb{F}^\ell$*
- $V_{\mathsf{AMD}}(r_1, \ldots, r_\ell) \to y \in \mathbb{F}$: *Output $\mathbf{f}(r_1, \ldots, r_\ell) \in \mathbb{F}^m$.*

The next theorem shows that instantiating this construction with $\ell = 3$, which implies a sketch of size three, gives a low-error AMD distribution with error $\epsilon = O(1/|\mathbb{F}|^2)$.

Theorem 16. *Let $n \in \mathbb{N}$ and let $\mathbb{F}$ be a field where $|\mathbb{F}| > n^2$. Then the S_{AMD} in Construction 15, instantiated with $\ell = 3$ and the polynomial map*

$$\mathbf{f}(r_1, r_2, r_3) = \left(r_1^2 - r_2, \quad r_3 - r_1 r_2\right) \in \mathbb{F}^2$$

is a low-error AMD distribution with error $\epsilon \leq 6e/(|\mathbb{F}|^2 - 3|\mathbb{F}|)$.

Proof idea. We give the full proof in the full version of this paper. Completeness follows directly from the construction. To prove the detection property defined in (1), we have two cases: First, suppose the input vector has weight 1 but that its non-zero element u is not in $\{0, 1\}$. Then $u^2 \neq u$ and therefore $(s_i u)^2 \neq s_i^2 u$ because $s_i \in \mathbb{F}^*$. This means that $z_1^2 - z_2 \neq 0$ as required. Second, suppose that the input vector β has weight w greater than one. Define the set $(\mathbb{F}_{\neq})^n$ as the set of all n-tuples in $(\mathbb{F}^*)^n$ whose elements are pairwise distinct. Then for the sketch to fail, the random vector $\mathbf{s} \in (\mathbb{F}_{\neq})^n$, whose elements are pairwise distinct, must lie on the intersection of the two n-variate polynomials

$$\langle \mathbf{X}, \beta \rangle^2 = \langle \mathbf{X}^2, \beta \rangle \qquad \text{and} \qquad \langle \mathbf{X}^3, \beta \rangle = \langle \mathbf{X}, \beta \rangle \cdot \langle \mathbf{X}^2, \beta \rangle. \tag{2}$$

For a fixed β of weight at least two, we will appeal to Bézout's theorem to argue that the intersection contains at most $6\,|\mathbb{F}|^{n-2}$ points $\mathbf{s} \in (\mathbb{F}_{\neq})^n$. Given that, we can bound the detection error as required. □

4 Sketching for Low-Weight Vectors

In this section, we construct sketching schemes for languages of vectors of low Hamming weight.

Throughout this section, when working with input vectors of dimension n, we assume that the finite field $\mathbb{F}$ over which we work contains an element of order at least n. If the field $\mathbb{F}$ is too small for such an element to exist, we can lift the input vector to an extension $\mathbb{K}/\mathbb{F}$ such that $|\mathbb{K}| \geq n$. When working with a secret-shared input vector, this lifting requires no communication between the verifiers. Using such an extension increases the communication cost, in terms of bits, by at most a multiplicative $\lceil \log_2 n \rceil$ factor.

4.1 Refined Definitions: Arithmetic sketching with Private Decision

In this section, we give refined definitions of arithmetic sketching schemes, which give more efficient constructions when implementing the decision predicate in a multiparty computation (as in many applications). In particular, we now split the decision predicate D into two parts: a *private predicate* D^{priv} and a *public predicate* D^{pub}:

- The private predicate, D^{priv}, operates on the verifier's sketch of the input vector x and evaluates a (typically small) randomized arithmetic circuit on the sketch. The output of D^{priv} is essentially a "sanitized" version of the sketch—the sanitized sketch leaks nothing about the input x, in a sense that we will define shortly. In applications, we will typically evaluate D^{priv} via secure multiparty computation.
- The public predicate, D^{pub}, takes the "sanitized" sketch as input and determines whether the verifier will accept or reject. The public predicate may compute a complicated high-degree function of its inputs. Since the inputs to D^{pub} leak nothing about the instance x, in applications, it is safe to publish these values and compute D^{pub} in the clear.

The refined syntax is then:

- $S() \to Q$. The sketching algorithm outputs a query matrix $Q \in \mathbb{F}^{\ell \times n}$.
- $D^{\mathsf{priv}}(a, (r_1, \dots, r_k)) \to y \in \mathbb{F}^m$. The private decision algorithm takes as input the sketch $a = Q \cdot x \in \mathbb{F}^\ell$ and random field elements $r_1, \dots, r_k$, and outputs a vector $y \in \mathbb{F}^m$.

– $D^{\text{pub}}(y) \rightarrow \{0,1\}$. The public decision algorithm takes as input a vector $y \in \mathbb{F}^m$ and outputs an accept/reject bit.

Completeness and soundness are as in the standard definition of arithmetic sketching schemes (Definition 2) with the combined decision algorithm $D^{\text{pub}} \circ D^{\text{priv}}$ replacing the single algorithm D. For zero knowledge, we require that the output of the *private* decision algorithm leak nothing about the input x apart from the fact that $x \in \mathcal{L}$.

Definition 17 (Zero knowledge with split decision predicate). *We say that an arithmetic sketching scheme* $(S, D^{\text{priv}}, D^{\text{pub}})$ *for a language* $\mathcal{L} \subseteq \mathbb{F}$ *satisfies* δ-*zero knowledge if there exists a simulator* Sim *such that for all* $x \in \mathcal{L}$, *the following distributions are* δ-*close in statistical distance:*

$$\mathcal{D}_{\text{ideal}} = \mathsf{Sim}()$$
$$\mathcal{D}_{\text{real}} = \left\{ \Big(Q,\ D^{priv}(Q \cdot x, r)\Big) : \begin{array}{c} Q \leftarrow S() \\ r \xleftarrow{\text{R}} \mathbb{F}^k \end{array} \right\}.$$

If an arithmetic sketching scheme has δ-*zero knowledge for* $\delta = 0$, *we say that the sketch has* perfect zero knowledge.

Our notion of zero knowledge is analogous to the notion of *strong* zero-knowledge in the setting of zero-knowledge proof systems on secret-shared data [8].

Fact 4 shows that when the decision algorithm is a single arithmetic circuit, it is easy to modify any arithmetic sketching scheme to satisfy the stronger notion of *two-sided* zero knowledge (Definition 3) by augmenting the decision algorithm with a bit of additional randomness. Since the decision routine here may have a non-algebraic (high-degree) public predicate, it is no longer always easy to add two-sided zero knowledge to such arithmetic sketching schemes.

4.2 Weight-w Vectors with Arbitrary Payload

We first give a linear sketch-verification scheme that recognizes vectors of Hamming weight w with arbitrary payload.

Given an input vector $x = (x_0, \ldots, x_{n-1}) \in \mathbb{F}^n$, we view the vector x as holding the coefficients of the polynomial $p(Z) = \sum_{i=0}^{n-1} x_i Z^i \in \mathbb{F}[Z]$. Notice that the number of non-zero coefficients of the polynomial p is exactly equal to the number of non-zero elements of the input vector x. Furthermore, for all $r \in \mathbb{F}$, it is possible to compute the evaluation of the polynomial p at the point r by taking a single linear combination of the elements of x, of the form $(1, r, r^2, \ldots, r^{n-1}) \in \mathbb{F}^n$. So, if we can test whether a polynomial p has w non-zero coefficients using ℓ polynomial-evaluation queries to p, we can test whether the input vector x has w non-zero coefficients using a linear sketch of size ℓ. By applying existing algorithms for testing whether a polynomial's coefficient vector is sparse [25], we thus construct linear sketch-verification schemes for low-weight vectors.

The sketch-verification schemes in this section rely on the following lemma, which appears in a similar form in the work of Grigorescu, Jung, and Rubinfeld [25]:

Lemma 18 (Ben-Or and Tiwari [6]). *Let $\mathbb{F}$ be a finite field, let $p \in \mathbb{F}[U]$ be a polynomial, and let ℓ be a non-negative integer. Then for any $u \in \mathbb{F}$, define the Hankel matrix $H_p(u)$ as:*

$$H_p(u) \stackrel{\text{def}}{=} \begin{pmatrix} p(1) & p(u) & p(u^2) & \dots & p(u^\ell) \\ p(u) & p(u^2) & p(u^3) & \dots & p(u^{\ell+1}) \\ p(u^2) & p(u^3) & p(u^4) & \dots & p(u^{\ell+2}) \\ \vdots & \vdots & & \ddots & \vdots \\ p(u^\ell) & p(u^{\ell+1}) & p(u^{\ell+2}) & \dots & p(u^{2\ell}) \end{pmatrix} \in \mathbb{F}^{(\ell+1)\times(\ell+1)}.$$

Then for a polynomial p with w non-zero coefficients,

- *if $w > \ell$, the determinant $\det(H_p(U))$ is a non-zero polynomial in U of degree at most $2\binom{\ell+1}{2}\deg(p)$, and*
- *if $w \le \ell$, the determinant $\det(H_p(U)) \equiv 0$, as a polynomial in U.*

In particular, if the polynomial p of Lemma 18 has more than ℓ non-zero coefficients, then for a random $u \xleftarrow{R} \mathbb{F}$, the matrix $H_p(u)$ will be full rank and its determinant $\det(H_p(u))$ will be non-zero with high probability. If the polynomial p has ℓ or fewer non-zero coefficients, the matrix $H_p(u)$ will be of rank w, with high probability over the a random choice of $u \xleftarrow{R} \mathbb{F}$.

We will also need the following standard fact, proven in the full version of this paper:

Fact 19. *Let $\mathbb{F}$ be a finite field and let n be a positive integer. Then the probability that a random matrix $R \xleftarrow{R} \mathbb{F}^{n\times n}$ is full rank is at least $\frac{1}{|\mathbb{F}|-1}$.*

Construction 20 (Sketching for Hamming weight w). *The construction is parameterized by a finite field $\mathbb{F}$, and integers w and n with $w < n < |\mathbb{F}|$. The sketch accepts the language of vectors in $\mathbb{F}^n$ of Hamming weight exactly w. The scheme has sketch size $\ell = 2w + 1$, completeness error $2/(|\mathbb{F}| - 1)$ soundness error $O(w^2 n/|\mathbb{F}|)$, and a decision algorithm implementable by an arithmetic circuit with $O(w^\alpha)$ multiplication gates, where $\alpha < 2.81$ is the (algebraic) matrix-multiplication constant.*

- $S() \to Q$.
  - *Sample a random value $u \xleftarrow{R} \mathbb{F}$.*
  - *Return*

$$Q = \begin{pmatrix} 1 & 1 & 1 & 1 & \dots & 1 \\ 1 & u & u^2 & u^3 & \dots & u^{(n-1)} \\ 1 & u^2 & u^4 & u^6 & \dots & u^{2(n-1)} \\ \vdots & \vdots & \vdots & \vdots & \ddots & \vdots \\ 1 & u^{\ell-1} & u^{2(\ell-1)} & u^{3(\ell-1)} & \dots & u^{(\ell-1)(n-1)} \end{pmatrix} \in \mathbb{F}^{\ell\times n}.$$

– $D^{\mathsf{priv}}(a,(r_1,\ldots,r_k)) \to y \in \mathbb{F}^m$.
 • *Use the sketch* $a \in \mathbb{F}^\ell$ *of size* $\ell = 2w+1$ *to form a Hankel matrix* H*:*

$$H = \begin{pmatrix} a_1 & a_2 & a_3 & \cdots & a_{w+1} \\ a_2 & a_3 & a_4 & \cdots & a_{w+2} \\ a_3 & a_4 & a_5 & \cdots & a_{w+3} \\ \vdots & \vdots & & \ddots & \vdots \\ a_{w+1} & a_{w+2} & a_{w+3} & \cdots & a_{2w+1} \end{pmatrix} \in \mathbb{F}^{(w+1)\times(w+1)}.$$

 • *Use the* $k = 2(w+1)^2$ *random values* $r_1,\ldots,r_k \in \mathbb{F}$ *given as input to sample two square matrices* $R_1, R_2 \in \mathbb{F}^{(w+1)\times(w+1)}$.
 • *Compute the matrix-matrix product* $R_1 \cdot H \cdot R_2 \in \mathbb{F}^{(w+1)\times(w+1)}$.
 • *Output this product as a vector of dimension* $m = (w+1)^2$.

– $D^{\mathsf{pub}}(y) \to \{0,1\}$. *Interpret the input* $y \in \mathbb{F}^m$ *as a matrix* Y *of dimension* $(w+1)\times(w+1)$. *Accept if and only if* $\mathrm{rank}(Y) = w$.

Theorem 21. *Construction 20 has completeness error* $\frac{2}{|\mathbb{F}|-1}$*, soundness error* $O(w^2 n/|\mathbb{F}|)$*, and perfect zero knowledge.*

Proof of Theorem 21. For completeness: By Lemma 18, when the input vector x has Hamming weight w, the matrix H will have rank w. Then provided that the random matrices R_1 and R_2 that D^{priv} samples are of full rank, the matrix $R_1 \cdot H \cdot R_2$ will have rank w and the verifier will accept. By Fact 19 and the union bound, the probability that either matrix fails to be invertible is $2/(|\mathbb{F}|-1)$.

For soundness: When the input vector x has Hamming weight $w' < w$, the matrix H has rank $w' < w$ (by Lemma 18), so the matrix $H \cdot R$ has rank at most w' and the verifier will always reject. When the input vector x has Hamming weight $w' > w$, again by Lemma 18, the determinant is a polynomial in u of degree $O(w^2 \deg p)$. So in this case the determinant is non-zero, and the verifier will accept with probability at most $O(w^2 \deg p)$.

For zero knowledge: The simulator outputs a random matrix in $\mathbb{F}^{(w+1)\times(w+1)}$ of rank w. To explain why the simulation is correct, if x has Hamming weight w, the matrix H always has rank w, by Lemma 18. Multiplying a rank-w matrix on the left and right by random invertible matrices yields a random rank-w matrix. □

Bounded Weight. Construction 20 accepts vectors of Hamming weight *exactly* w. In some applications, we want to accept the language $\mathcal{L}_B^{\times \leq w}$ of vectors of Hamming weight *at most* w. We prove the following in the full version of this paper:

Corollary 22. *There is an explicit arithmetic sketching scheme for the language of vectors in* $\mathbb{F}^n$ *of Hamming weight* at most w*. The scheme has sketch size* $O(w^2)$*, completeness error* $2/(|\mathbb{F}|-1)$ *soundness error* $O(w^2 n/|\mathbb{F}|)$*, perfect zero knowledge, and a single arithmetic decision circuit with* $O(w^4)$ *multiplication gates.*

4.3 Sketching for Vectors with L_1 Norm w

Let w and n be a positive integers, and let $\mathbb{F}$ be a finite field of characteristic greater than wn. In this section we give a linear sketch-verification scheme that recognizes vectors of a bounded L_1 norm, specifically the set

$$\mathcal{L}_1^{(=w)} \stackrel{\text{def}}{=} \left\{ (x_1, \ldots, x_n) \in \mathbb{F}^n \ : \ \sum_{i=1}^{n} x_i = w, \ \ x_i \in \{0, \ldots, w\} \right\}. \tag{3}$$

This sketch is useful for voting or private-telemetry applications in which each client casts w votes for n candidates, while allowing the client to vote for the same candidate multiple times.

To outline the main technical idea: given an input vector $x = (x_1, \ldots, x_n) \in \mathbb{F}^n$, the sketch chooses a random vector $(r_1, \ldots, r_n) \in \mathbb{F}^n$ and evaluates the power sums

$$p_j \stackrel{\text{def}}{=} \sum_{i=1}^{n} x_i \cdot r_i^j \in \mathbb{F}, \quad \text{for } j = 1, \ldots, w+1 \tag{4}$$

using a total of $w+1$ linear queries to x (i.e., using a sketch of size $w+1$). To decide whether or not to accept the vector x, we apply the Newton identities (Theorem 23) to the sketch $(p_1, \ldots, p_{w+1})$ to obtain the quantities e_w and e_{w+1} in $\mathbb{F}$. Then the decision algorithm accepts the instance x if $e_{w+1} = 0$ and $e_w \neq 0$.

The sketch can be adapted to test membership in $\mathcal{L}_1^{(\leq w)}$ where the equality in (3) is changed to $\sum_{i=1}^{n} x_i \leq w$. The only modification to the sketch is that x is accepted whenever $e_{w+1} = 0$ (we drop the check that $e_w \neq 0$).

To explain why this approach is sound, let us first review the Newton identities. For $w \geq 0$

- let $P_w(X_1, \ldots, X_n)$ be the w-th power sum polynomial defined as $P_w(X_1, \ldots, X_n) = \sum_{j=1}^{n} X_j^w$.
- Let $E_w(X_1, \ldots, X_n)$ be the w-th symmetric polynomial, defined as $E_w(X_1, \ldots, X_n) = \sum_{1 \leq j_1 < j_2 < \cdots < j_w \leq n} X_{j_1} X_{j_2} \cdots X_{j_w}$.

The Newton identities relate these two families via a recurrence relation.

Theorem 23 (Newton identities [32]). *For all finite fields $\mathbb{F}$ and integers $k, n \in \mathbb{N}$ with $k \leq n$:*

$$k \cdot E_k(X_1, \ldots, X_n) = \sum_{i=1}^{k} (-1)^{i-1} \cdot E_{k-i}(X_1, \ldots, X_n) \cdot P_i(X_1, \ldots, X_n).$$

The recurrence lets us express E_k purely in terms of $P_1, \ldots, P_k$. For example

$$E_1 = P_1, \qquad 2E_2 = P_1^2 - P_2, \qquad 6E_3 = P_1^3 - 3P_1P_2 + 2P_3, \tag{5}$$

and so on. In other words, for every $k > 0$ there is a polynomial N_k such that $E_k = N_k(P_1, \ldots, P_k)$. This N_k has total degree k.

Then observe that if the input vector x has L_1 norm greater than w, the polynomial $E_{w+1}(X_1, \ldots, X_n)$ will not be identically zero. Its evaluation at the point $(r_1, \ldots, r_n)$ then will be non-zero with high probability.

Construction 24 (Sketching for L_1 weight w). *The construction is parameterized by integers w and n and a finite field $\mathbb{F}$ of characteristic greater than nw. The sketch accepts the language of vectors $\mathcal{L}_1^{(=w)}$ in $\mathbb{F}^n$. The scheme has sketch size $w+1$, soundness error $O((w+1)/|\mathbb{F}|)$, and a decision predicate with $O(w^2)$ multiplication gates.*

- $S() \rightarrow (q_1, \dots, q_{w+1})$.
  - *Sample random values* $r_1, \dots, r_n \xleftarrow{R} \mathbb{F}$.
  - *Return*
$$Q = \begin{pmatrix} r_1 & r_2 & r_3 & r_4 & \cdots & r_n \\ r_1^2 & r_2^2 & r_3^2 & r_4^2 & \cdots & r_n^2 \\ \vdots & & \vdots & & \ddots & \vdots \\ r_1^\ell & r_2^\ell & r_3^\ell & r_4^\ell & \cdots & r_n^\ell \end{pmatrix} \in \mathbb{F}^{\ell \times n}.$$
- $D^{priv}((p_1, \dots, p_{w+1}), (d_1, d_2)) \rightarrow y \in \mathbb{F}^2$.
  - *Use the $\ell = w+1$ sketch values $(p_1, \dots, p_{w+1})$ to compute the quantities e_w and e_{w+1} using* (5)*, namely, $e_w = N_w(p_1, \dots, p_w)$ and $e_{w+1} = N_{w+1}(p_1, \dots, p_{w+1})$.*
  - *Use the two random values $d_1, d_2 \in \mathbb{F}^*$ to blind e_w and e_{w+1} by computing $\hat{e}_w = e_w \cdot d_1$ and $\hat{e}_{w+1} = e_{w+1} \cdot d_2$.*
  - *Output $y = (\hat{e}_w, \hat{e}_{w+1}) \in \mathbb{F}^2$.*
- $D^{pub}(y) \rightarrow \{0,1\}$. *Parse $y = (\hat{e}_w, \hat{e}_{w+1}) \in \mathbb{F}^2$. Accept if and only if $\hat{e}_w \neq 0$ and $\hat{e}_{w+1} = 0$.*

Theorem 25. *Construction 24 is complete, sound, and zero knowledge.*

Zero knowledge as in Definition 3 is immediate. The following theorem, which we prove in the full version of this paper, proves completeness and soundness of the construction.

Theorem 26. *Let $\mathbb{F}$ be a finite field of characteristic greater than nw. Then the following holds for all $x = (x_1, \dots, x_n) \in \mathbb{F}^n$. Sample a random $(r_1, \dots, r_n) \in \mathbb{F}^n$, compute the power sums $p_1, \dots, p_{w+1} \in \mathbb{F}$ as in* (4)*, and use* (5) *to compute $e_{w+1} \in \mathbb{F}$ as $e_{w+1} = N_{w+1}(p_1, \dots, p_{w+1})$. Then*

- *if $x \in \mathcal{L}_1^{(\leq w)}$ then* $\Pr[e_{w+1} = 0] = 1$,
- *if $x \notin \mathcal{L}_1^{(\leq w)}$ then* $\Pr[e_{w+1} = 0] \leq (w+1)/|\mathbb{F}|$.

Here the probability is over the random choice of $(r_1, \dots, r_n)$ in $\mathbb{F}^n$.

Note that Construction 24 uses Theorem 26 twice: once to prove that $x \in \mathcal{L}_1^{(\leq w)}$ and once to prove that $x \notin \mathcal{L}_1^{(\leq w-1)}$. Together this proves that x is in $\mathcal{L}_1^{(=w)}$.

Binary Vectors of Hamming Weight w. By combining Construction 20 and Construction 24 we obtain a sketch that accepts vectors $x \in \mathbb{F}^n$ that (i) have Hamming weight w and (ii) are in $\mathcal{L}_1^{(=w)}$. The only such vectors are vectors in $\{0,1\}^n$ that have Hamming weight w. We have:

Corollary 27. *There is an arithmetic sketch for binary vectors of Hamming weight w; the cost is that of running both Construction 20 and Construction 24.*

Vectors of Hamming Weight w with Equal Non-zero Entries. To test if a vector is of Hamming weight w with all non-zero entries equal to one another, the verifier can apply a sketch vector of the form $(1, 1, 1, \ldots, 1)$ to the input to compute the sum $\sigma \in \mathbb{F}$ of the entries of the input vector. If the input vector $x \in \mathbb{F}^n$ is well formed, then the value $\sigma w^{-1} \in \mathbb{F}$ is the value of the non-zero entries. Then the vector $(w \cdot \sigma^{-1})x \in \mathbb{F}^n$ is a binary vector of Hamming weight w if and only if $x \in \mathbb{F}^n$ is a vector of Hamming weight w with equal non-zero entries. The verifier can then test that the vector $(w \cdot \sigma^{-1})x \in \mathbb{F}^n$ is a binary vector of Hamming weight w. If so, the verifier can conclude that x is of Hamming weight w with equal non-zero entries.

More generally, the verifier can apply an arbitrary arithmetic circuit $C \colon \mathbb{F} \to \mathbb{F}$ to $\sigma w^{-1} \in \mathbb{F}$, such as a bounds check, to ensure that all of the non-zero entries are equal and satisfy circuit C.

4.4 Bounded-Weight Vectors with Arbitrarily Restricted Payloads

In the full version of this paper, we construct arithmetic sketching schemes for vectors in $\mathbb{F}^n$ with exactly w non-zero entries *and* where each non-zero entry satisfies a arithmetic circuit $C \colon \mathbb{F} \to \mathbb{F}$. (We assume that $C(0) \neq 0 \in \mathbb{F}$. Otherwise we can use the remark below to sketch for the language of vectors of Hamming weight at most w whose non-zero entries satisfy C.) We have:

Theorem 28. *For all $\lambda, w, n \in \mathbb{N}$ with $w \leq n < |\mathbb{F}|$, and arithmetic circuits $C \colon \mathbb{F} \to \mathbb{F}$ (with size independent of $\mathbb{F}$), there is a arithmetic sketching scheme for the language of vectors in $x \in \mathbb{F}^n$ of Hamming weight w such that each non-zero element satisfies C. The scheme (in the full version) has completeness error $\epsilon = 4/(|\mathbb{F}| - 1) + 2^{-\lambda}$, soundness error $O(w^2 n / |\mathbb{F}|)$, sketch size $O(w\lambda)$ and ϵ-zero knowledge.*

5 From Arithmetic Sketching to Client-Server Protocols

As discussed, a natural motivating application scenario of our arithmetic sketching schemes is in a client-server setting, where a client secret shares a sensitive vector across servers, and the servers must verify that the shared vector has a proper form. The linear nature of the sketching scheme enables the servers to individually compute shares of the sketch of the input. The low arithmetic complexity of the decision algorithm D means that servers can securely secure evaluate D on their shares of the sketch using a via multi-party computation (MPC). If the arithmetic sketching scheme satisfies the property of zero knowledge from Definition 17, then the corresponding client-server verification scheme further provides zero-knowledge guarantees against *semi-honest* servers. We refer the reader to prior work [8] for a detailed treatment of this transformation in the semi-honest model. Indeed, our arithmetic sketching schemes can be seen as a special case of *fully linear probabilistically checkable proofs* (FL-PCP) from prior work [8], without a Prover procedure.

However, note that the properties of the arithmetic sketching scheme do not directly give any guarantees against a potentially adversarial verifier. Indeed, in the solutions thus far, a *malicious* server may be able to reveal information about the input. In what follows, we analyze this more adversarial setting, and provide general techniques for achieving privacy against malicious verifiers.

We give the technical details on our client-server schemes in the full version of this paper, and we give an overview of the results here.

Auxiliary Client Information Required. We first observe that, in general, achieving security against a malicious verifier/server *requires* the client to send additional information to the servers, beyond simply its secret shared vector. In particular, without some form of auxiliary client information π, the scheme will inevitably be subject to a selective-failure attack. Consider, for example, the language $\mathcal{L}_{\{0,1\}} \subseteq \mathbb{F}^n$ of binary vectors of weight at most 1. Given only secret shares of x, a malicious server can learn whether x is the all-zero vector, by adding $+1$ offset to one position of his secret share, and seeing if the resulting vector is accepted (or whether the vector is any other particular unit vector, by analogous adjustments).

Given this state of affairs, we thus turn back to the more general notion of fully linear PCPs from [8], incorporating also a procedure for the client to generate auxiliary information to provide to the servers. We provide a formal definition in the full version of this paper. Note that in the definition of FL-PCP, queries are restricted to make linear access to both the input x *and* the auxiliary proof material π, i.e., in our notation the sketch is computed as $Q \cdot (x \| \pi)$ for sketching matrix Q over $\mathbb{F}$. Requiring the sketch to be a linear function of the proof π is not inherent, but will be convenient for us. In particular, the client can send the auxiliary information π to the servers in *additive secret-shared form*, meaning that we can include sensitive information within π to aid in authentication without revealing it to malicious servers.

Toward Malicious Security. We next observe that a malicious-secure protocol must enforce the correct execution of the sketching algorithm S and private decision algorithm D, even in the presence of malicious servers. We can achieve this using malicious-secure multiparty computation protocols. Given the low arithmetic complexity of the decision algorithm D, this resulting overhead will be minimal. In most cases, to run the sketching algorithm S in a multiparty computation, the verifiers may simply run a coin tossing protocol to sample the randomness for query generation.

Privacy Against Additive *Attacks.* At this point, only one attack surface remains: incorrectly performing query evaluation. Equivalently, the adversary's remaining power is to submit improper inputs to the secure computation protocol for the decision algorithm D. Recall the inputs to the execution of D are (allegedly) each server's additive share of the query answers. Since the verifiers only hold additive secret shares of both the input x and proof material π by design, the adversarially chosen input must be independent of these secret values; this corresponds to an arbitrary fixed *additive* offset attack on the combined value. That is, a malicious verifier can learn the output of D on the shifted vector $a + \Delta \in \mathbb{F}^\ell$ where $a \in \mathbb{F}^\ell$ is the honest sketch value and $\Delta \in \mathbb{F}^\ell$ is an adversarially chosen additive offset.

This kind of additive attack can reveal sensitive information, as the selective-failure attack discussed above demonstrates. Even with auxiliary proof material π, one must be careful. Suppose, for example, the value of π for x depends only on the product of two symbols $x_i x_j$ and not on the symbols themselves; a malicious verifier can then learn whether $x_i = 0$ for a secret input x by adding a garbage offset to his share of x_j and seeing if the value is still accepted.

We formulate a notion of *additive-attack privacy* for the FL-PCP, strengthening zero knowledge by requiring no information is revealed even in the face of additive attacks. Utilizing an FL-PCP with this extra property, together with MPC secure against malicious parties for jointly executing the sketching algorithm S and decision algorithm D suffices to yield a secure client-server protocol in the manner described above.

Privacy Against Additive Attacks via AMD Distributions. As the final step, we develop a general approach for obtaining this notion of additive-attack privacy. This will be done by once again making use of *algebraic manipulation detection (AMD) distributions*, as put forth in Sect. 3. We show that if the distribution of (honestly generated) FL-PCP query and answer values satisfies a form of AMD guarantee, then the FL-PCP indeed provides privacy against additive attacks. Then, we provide general transformations for "hardening" general FL-PCPs to ones providing this additional AMD property, with mild overhead.

In the general case, the additional authentication values introduced in our approach result in a constant multiplicative overhead above the secret sharing of the vector x. However, this approach is particularly useful for the setting of sparse vectors x (as is predominantly the focus of this paper), in which the cost of secret sharing the additional proof information adds little overhead beyond secret sharing the input itself. See also the discussion in the full version of this paper.

6 Lower Bound on Sketch Size

In this section we establish a lower bound on the sketch size of an arithmetic sketching scheme for weight-one vectors using an algebraic argument. We show that the soundness error of an arithmetic sketching scheme for this language depends on its sketch size. More precisely, the soundness error is at least $\frac{1}{(d+1)|\mathbb{F}|^{\ell-2}}$ if the sketch size is ℓ and the algebraic degree of the decision algorithm is d. Consequently, any arithmetic sketching scheme with sketch size only two has constant soundness error. This bound proves that the positive result of Sect. 3

constructing a scheme for weight-one vectors with sketch size $\ell = 3$ is optimal for any scheme with soundness error of the form $\frac{f(n)}{|\mathbb{F}|}$ for some function f.

In the rest of the section we slightly abuse the terminology and say that any scheme with soundness error larger than $\frac{f(n)}{|\mathbb{F}|}$ is not an arithmetic sketching scheme, instead of stating the exact error. Additional terminology and notation follow. Let $\mathcal{L}_{\mathbb{F}}$ be the language of vectors of weight at most 1 and length $n \geq 1$ over a field $\mathbb{F}$. That is, $\mathcal{L}_{\mathbb{F}} = \{\beta \boldsymbol{e}_i : i \in [n], \beta \in \mathbb{F}\} \subset \mathbb{F}^n$ for unit vectors $e_i \in \mathbb{F}^n$. Recall that the decision predicate $D : \mathbb{F}^\ell \to \mathbb{F}^m$ is arithmetic and therefore $D(a_1, \ldots, a_\ell) = (z_1, \ldots, z_m)$ can be represented as m polynomials $D_1, \ldots, D_m$ over $\mathbb{F}$ such that $D_j(a_1, \ldots, a_\ell) = z_j$.

Theorem 29 states the main result of this section, which bounds the soundness error of an arithmetic sketching scheme for $\mathcal{L}_{\mathbb{F}}$ as a function of its sketch size. We prove Theorem 29 in the full version of this paper.

Theorem 29. *Let (S, D) be a arithmetic sketching scheme for the language $\mathcal{L}_{\mathbb{F}}$. If the sketch size of the scheme is ℓ, and the algebraic degree of D is d then the soundness error of the scheme is at least $\frac{1}{(d+1)|\mathbb{F}|^{\ell-2}}$.*

Corollary 30. *Any scheme in our setting for $\mathcal{L}_{\mathbb{F}}$ with sketch size at most two has soundness error at least $\frac{1}{d+1}$. Therefore, any arithmetic sketching scheme for $\mathcal{L}_{\mathbb{F}}$ must have sketch size at least three.*

7 Languages Without Arithmetic Sketching Schemes

Consider two parties, one holding an input $x \in \mathbb{F}^n$, and the other holding an input $y \in \mathbb{F}^n$ who wish to determine if $(x, y) \in \mathcal{L}'$ for some language $\mathcal{L}' \subseteq (\mathbb{F}^n)^2$, using public coins. Let $R(\mathcal{L}')$ denote the minimal communication complexity to decide whether $(x, y) \in \mathcal{L}'$ for all x, y with probability bounded away from 1/2.

An arithmetic sketching scheme for the language $\mathcal{L} = \{x + y \mid (x, y) \in \mathcal{L}'\}$ induces an instance of a protocol that decides $\mathcal{L}'$ in two steps. First, the two parties derive the sketching matrix from the public random coins, and locally compute shares of the sketch on $x + y$ using linearity. Then, the parties use an interactive protocol to compute the decision on the sketch.

The communication complexity of this type of scheme depends only on the decision algorithm D. However, since the families of sketching schemes we consider are universal, D is independent of $\mathbb{F}$ and n, i.e. the communication complexity of the scheme is $O(1)$.

In this section, we use known lower bounds on the communication complexity of any protocol that computes a language $\mathcal{L}'$ to derive lower bounds on the size of a decision circuit D in an arithmetic sketching scheme for the associated language $\mathcal{L}$. Indeed, we show that several natural languages $\mathcal{L}$ do not have a universal family of arithmetic sketching scheme by proving that their decision circuits must depend on n or on $\mathbb{F}$.

The communication complexity lower bounds we use are on the problems of Set Disjointness (DISJ) and Greater Than (GT). In Set Disjointness the inputs

x, y are subsets of a universe $\{1, \ldots, n\}$, and the goal is to decide the language $\mathcal{L}^{DISJ} = \{(x, y) \subseteq \{1, \ldots, n\} \mid x \cap y = \emptyset\}$. A series of works [4,30,36] established that $R(DISJ) = \Theta(n)$. The inputs x, y in the problem of Greater Than are the binary representation of two non-negative integers, and the goal is to decide the language $\mathcal{L}^{GT} = \{(x, y) \mid x > y\}$. Viola [38] proved that $R(\mathcal{L}^{GT}) = \Omega(\log n)$.

7.1 L_p Norm

An arithmetic sketch for the language of vectors with L_1 norm equal to some w is presented in Sect. 4.3. It is natural to ask whether this construction can be generalized to an arithmetic sketch for L_p such that $p > 1$ is a constant integer. Even though L_p is not necessarily a norm over the field, computing it as a function is interesting and useful.

Previous work [3,31] on computing moments in the streaming model [2] with low space complexity is sufficient to establish that arithmetic sketching schemes for the L_p norm are impossible. In this model there are n real-valued changes to a given vector of real numbers, and the goal is estimate the L_p norm of the vector with small error and minimal space. Translating the bounds on space complexity from the streaming model to sketch size in an arithmetic sketching shows that $\ell = \Omega(\log n)$ for L_2 and $\ell = \Theta(n^{1-2/p} \log n)$ for $p > 2$. However, the streaming model accepts a decision algorithm that is not necessarily arithmetic.

In this section we show a tighter bound for arithmetic sketching schemes via a communication complexity argument. Specifically, we show that the decision algorithm for L_p, $p > 1$, is of multiplicative size $\Omega(n)$ via a reduction of a general protocol for DISJ to an arithmetic sketching for L_p.

More formally, for an integer $p \geq 2$ and a field $\mathbb{F}$ such that p and $|\mathbb{F}| - 1$ are co-prime let $\mathcal{L}_p^{(=w)} \overset{\text{def}}{=} \left\{(x_1, \ldots, x_n) \in \mathbb{F}^n \ : \ \left(\sum_{i=1}^n x_i^p\right)^{1/p} = w\right\}$. This definition of L_p restricts the field to ensure that a p-th root exists for every field element. For L_2, which is the most useful case of L_p, we also consider the norm squared, which can be defined for all fields. Define the language $\mathcal{L}_2^{2(=w)} \overset{\text{def}}{=} \left\{(x_1, \ldots, x_n) \in \mathbb{F}^n \ : \ \sum_{i=1}^n x_i^2 = w\right\}$.

The proof of the following theorem appears in the full version of this paper:

Theorem 31. *Let $n, p \geq 2$ be integers, $p \geq 2$, let $\mathbb{F}$ be a finite field such that $|\mathbb{F}| - 1$ and p are co-prime, and let $\mathbb{E}$ be a finite field, $|\mathbb{E}| > 2$. If $w_f \in \mathbb{F}$ and $w_e \in \mathbb{E}$ then the decision algorithm for any arithmetic sketching scheme for the languages $\mathcal{L}_p^{(=w_f)}$ over $\mathbb{F}$ or $\mathcal{L}_2^{2(=w_e)}$ over $\mathbb{E}$ is of multiplicative size $\Omega(n)$.*

7.2 Specified Value in Arbitrary Vector

In Sect. 3 we construct arithmetic sketching schemes for the language $\mathcal{L}_B$ of B-multiples of unit vectors, i.e. vectors in which all entries are 0, except for one entry which is in the set $B \subseteq \mathbb{F}$. It seems natural to ask whether there is an arithmetic sketching scheme for the language of all vectors in which one entry is in B, while all other entries are arbitrary elements in $\mathbb{F}$. The next theorem proves that this language, namely $\mathcal{L}_{B,\mathbb{F}} \stackrel{\text{def}}{=} \{(x_1,\ldots,x_n) \in \mathbb{F}^n \mid \exists i, x_i \in B\}$, has no arithmetic sketching scheme for B that is not too large, via a reduction from DISJ. We prove the following theorem in the full version of this paper:

Theorem 32. *Let $n \geq 2$ be an integer, let $\mathbb{F}$ be a field, and let $B \subseteq \mathbb{F}$ such that $\frac{|B|}{|\mathbb{F}|} \leq \frac{1}{3n}$. Then, the language $\mathcal{L}_{B,\mathbb{F}}$ has no arithmetic sketching scheme.*

7.3 Intervals

Shared vectors that are all zero, except for a secret interval $[a,b], 1 \leq a \leq b \leq n$ on which their value is some constant $\beta \in B$ have several different applications, e.g. [11,12]. Let

$$\mathcal{L}_{int,B} \stackrel{\text{def}}{=} \left\{ \begin{matrix} (x_1,\ldots,x_n) \in \mathbb{F}^n : \exists\, 1 \leq a \leq b \leq n, \exists \beta \in B\ \forall a \leq i \leq b\ x_i = \beta, \\ \forall\ (i < a \vee i > b)\ x_i = 0 \end{matrix} \right\}.$$

We prove the following theorem in the full version of this paper:

Theorem 33. *If $B = \{0,1\}$ then there does not exist an arithmetic sketching scheme for the language $\mathcal{L}_{int,B}$.*

8 Open Questions

Our results leave several natural open questions. A broad question is to obtain a tight understanding of the achievable tradeoffs between sketch size, decision degree, and soundness error for languages of interest. Even for the simple "weight-1" languages covered by Theorem 13, where our sketching schemes are optimal with respect to both sketch size and decision degree, the soundness error we obtain is only optimal up to a constant factor.

The gaps are bigger for more complex languages. For example, in the case of vectors of Hamming weight *at most* w, it is open whether our $O(w^2)$ sketch size (Corollary 22) can be improved to to match our $O(w)$ sketch size for the case of Hamming weight *exactly* w (Theorem 21).

Finally, it may be useful to extend the scope of arithmetic sketching to capture *approximate* computations, which are commonly considered in the algorithmic literature on (insecure) sketching and streaming.

Acknowledgements. D. Boneh is supported by NSF, the DARPA SIEVE program, the Simons Foundation, UBRI, and NTT Research. E. Boyle is supported by AFOSR Award FA9550-21-1-0046, ERC Project HSS (852952), and a Google Research Award. H. Corrigan-Gibbs is supported by Capital One, Facebook, Google, Mozilla, Seagate, MIT's FinTech@CSAIL Initiative, and NSF Award CNS-2054869. N. Gilboa is supported by ISF grant 2951/20, ERC grant 876110, and a grant by the BGU Cyber Center. Y. Ishai is supported by ERC Project NTSC (742754), BSF grant 2018393, and ISF grant 2774/20. Opinions, findings, and conclusions or recommendations expressed in this material are those of the authors and do not necessarily reflect the views of DARPA.

References

1. Abraham, I., Pinkas, B., Yanai, A.: Blinder: MPC based scalable and robust anonymous committed broadcast (2020)
2. Alon, N., Matias, Y., Szegedy, M.: The space complexity of approximating the frequency moments. In: STOC, pp. 20–29 (1996)
3. Andoni, A., Nguyen, H.L., Polyanskiy, Y., Wu, Y.: Tight lower bound for linear sketches of moments. In: Fomin, F.V., Freivalds, R., Kwiatkowska, M., Peleg, D. (eds.) ICALP 2013. LNCS, vol. 7965, pp. 25–32. Springer, Heidelberg (2013). https://doi.org/10.1007/978-3-642-39206-1_3
4. Bar-Yossef, Z., Jayram, T.S., Kumar, R., Sivakumar, D.: An information statistics approach to data stream and communication complexity. J. Comput. Syst. Sci. **68**(4), 702–732 (2004)
5. Ben-Or, M., Goldwasser, S., Wigderson, A.: Completeness theorems for noncryptographic fault-tolerant distributed computation. In: STOC (1988)
6. Ben-Or, M., Tiwari, P.: A deterministic algorithm for sparse multivariate polynomial interpolation. In: Proceedings of the Twentieth Annual ACM Symposium on Theory of Computing, pp. 301–309 (1988)
7. Bitansky, N., et al.: The hunting of the SNARK. J. Cryptol. **30**(4), 989–1066 (2017)
8. Boneh, D., Boyle, E., Corrigan-Gibbs, H., Gilboa, N., Ishai, Y.: Zero-knowledge proofs on secret-shared data via fully linear PCPs. In: Boldyreva, A., Micciancio, D. (eds.) CRYPTO 2019. LNCS, vol. 11694, pp. 67–97. Springer, Cham (2019). https://doi.org/10.1007/978-3-030-26954-8_3
9. Boneh, D., Boyle, E., Corrigan-Gibbs, H., Gilboa, N., Ishai, Y.: Lightweight techniques for private heavy hitters. In: IEEE Symposium on Security and Privacy. IEEE (2021)
10. Boneh, D., Segev, G., Waters, B.: Targeted malleability: homomorphic encryption for restricted computations. In: Goldwasser, S. (ed.) Innovations in Theoretical Computer Science 2012, Cambridge, MA, USA, 8–10 January 2012, pp. 350–366. ACM (2012)
11. Boyle, E., et al.: Function secret sharing for mixed-mode and fixed-point secure computation. In: Canteaut, A., Standaert, F.-X. (eds.) EUROCRYPT 2021. LNCS, vol. 12697, pp. 871–900. Springer, Cham (2021). https://doi.org/10.1007/978-3-030-77886-6_30
12. Boyle, E., Gilboa, N., Ishai, Y.: Function secret sharing: improvements and extensions. In: CCS (2016)
13. Cormode, G., Muthukrishnan, S.: An improved data stream summary: the count-min sketch and its applications. J. Algorithms **55**(1), 58–75 (2005)
14. Corrigan-Gibbs, H., Boneh, D.: Prio: private, robust, and scalable computation of aggregate statistics. In: NSDI, pp. 259–282 (2017)
15. Corrigan-Gibbs, H., Boneh, D., Mazières, D.: Riposte: an anonymous messaging system handling millions of users. In: IEEE Symposium on Security and Privacy (2015)
16. Cramer, R., Dodis, Y., Fehr, S., Padró, C., Wichs, D.: Detection of algebraic manipulation with applications to robust secret sharing and fuzzy extractors. In: Smart, N. (ed.) EUROCRYPT 2008. LNCS, vol. 4965, pp. 471–488. Springer, Heidelberg (2008). https://doi.org/10.1007/978-3-540-78967-3_27
17. Damgård, I., Luo, J., Oechsner, S., Scholl, P., Simkin, M.: Compact zero-knowledge proofs of small hamming weight. In: Abdalla, M., Dahab, R. (eds.) PKC 2018. LNCS, vol. 10770, pp. 530–560. Springer, Cham (2018). https://doi.org/10.1007/978-3-319-76581-5_18

18. Davis, H., Patton, C., Rosulek, M., Schoppmann, P.: Verifiable distributed aggregation functions. Cryptology ePrint Archive (2023)
19. de Castro, L., Polychroniadou, A.: Lightweight, maliciously secure verifiable function secret sharing. In: Dunkelman, O., Dziembowski, S. (eds.) EUROCRYPT 2022. LNCS, vol. 13275, pp. 150–179. Springer, Cham (2022). https://doi.org/10.1007/978-3-031-06944-4_6
20. Doerner, J., Shelat, A.: Scaling ORAM for secure computation. In: CCS (2017)
21. Eskandarian, S., Corrigan-Gibbs, H., Zaharia, M., Boneh, D.: Express: lowering the cost of metadata-hiding communication with cryptographic privacy. arXiv preprint arXiv:1911.09215 (2019)
22. Feigenbaum, J., Ishai, Y., Malkin, T., Nissim, K., Strauss, M.J., Wright, R.N.: Secure multiparty computation of approximations. ACM Trans. Algorithms **2**(3), 435–472 (2006)
23. Genkin, D., Ishai, Y., Prabhakaran, M.M., Sahai, A., Tromer, E.: Circuits resilient to additive attacks with applications to secure computation. In: Shmoys, D.B. (ed.) Symposium on Theory of Computing, STOC, pp. 495–504. ACM (2014)
24. Green, M., Ladd, W., Miers, I.: A protocol for privately reporting ad impressions at scale. In: CCS (2016)
25. Grigorescu, E., Jung, K., Rubinfeld, R.: A local decision test for sparse polynomials. Inf. Process. Lett. **110**(20), 898–901 (2010)
26. Groth, J.: Non-interactive zero-knowledge arguments for voting. In: Ioannidis, J., Keromytis, A., Yung, M. (eds.) ACNS 2005. LNCS, vol. 3531, pp. 467–482. Springer, Heidelberg (2005). https://doi.org/10.1007/11496137_32
27. Indyk, P., Woodruff, D.: Polylogarithmic private approximations and efficient matching. In: Halevi, S., Rabin, T. (eds.) TCC 2006. LNCS, vol. 3876, pp. 245–264. Springer, Heidelberg (2006). https://doi.org/10.1007/11681878_13
28. Ishai, Y., Malkin, T., Strauss, M.J., Wright, R.N.: Private multiparty sampling and approximation of vector combinations. Theor. Comput. Sci. **410**(18), 1730–1745 (2009)
29. Jansen, R., Johnson, A.: Safely measuring Tor. In: CCS, pp. 1553–1567 (2016)
30. Kalyanasundaram, B., Schintger, G.: The probabilistic communication complexity of set intersection. SIAM J. Discret. Math. **5**(4), 545–557 (1992)
31. Kane, D.M., Nelson, J., Woodruff, D.P.: On the exact space complexity of sketching and streaming small norms. In: Proceedings of the Twenty-First Annual ACM-SIAM Symposium on Discrete Algorithms, pp. 1161–1178. SIAM (2010)
32. Mead, D.G.: Newton's identities. Am. Math. Mon. **99**(8), 749–751 (1992)
33. Nelson, J.J.O.: Sketching and streaming high-dimensional vectors. Ph.D. thesis, Massachusetts Institute of Technology (2011)
34. Ostrovsky, R., Shoup, V.: Private information storage. In: Proceedings of the Twenty-Ninth Annual ACM Symposium on Theory of Computing, pp. 294–303 (1997)
35. Popa, R.A., Balakrishnan, H., Blumberg, A.J.: VPriv: protecting privacy in location-based vehicular services. In: USENIX Security, pp. 335–350 (2009)
36. Razborov, A.A.: On the distributional complexity of disjointness. In: Paterson, M.S. (ed.) ICALP 1990. LNCS, vol. 443, pp. 249–253. Springer, Heidelberg (1990). https://doi.org/10.1007/BFb0032036
37. Toubiana, V., Narayanan, A., Boneh, D., Nissenbaum, H., Barocas, S.: Adnostic: privacy preserving targeted advertising. In: NDSS (2010)
38. Viola, E.: The communication complexity of addition. Combinatorica **35**(6), 703–747 (2015). https://doi.org/10.1007/s00493-014-3078-3

Additive Randomized Encodings and Their Applications

Shai Halevi[1], Yuval Ishai[2(✉)], Eyal Kushilevitz[2], and Tal Rabin[3]

[1] Algorand, New York, USA
[2] Technion - Israel Institute of Technology, Haifa, Israel
yuval.ishai@gmail.com, eyalk@cs.technion.ac.il
[3] University of Pennsylvania, Philadelphia, USA
talr@seas.upenn.edu

Abstract. Addition of n inputs is often the easiest nontrivial function to compute securely. Motivated by several open questions, we ask what can be computed securely given only an oracle that computes the sum. Namely, what functions can be computed in a model where parties can only encode their input locally, then sum up the encodings over some Abelian group $\mathbb{G}$, and decode the result to get the function output.

An *additive randomized encoding* (ARE) of a function $f(x_1, \ldots, x_n)$ maps every input x_i independently into a randomized encoding $\hat{x}_i$, such that $\sum_{i=1}^{n} \hat{x}_i$ reveals $f(x_1, \ldots, x_n)$ and nothing else about the inputs. In a *robust* ARE, the sum of *any subset* of the $\hat{x}_i$ only reveals the *residual function* obtained by restricting the corresponding inputs.

We obtain positive and negative results on ARE. In particular:

- *Information-theoretic ARE.* We fully characterize the 2-party functions $f : X_1 \times X_2 \to \{0, 1\}$ admitting a perfectly secure ARE. For $n \geq 3$ parties, we show a useful "capped sum" function that separates statistical security from perfect security.
- *Computational ARE.* We present a general feasibility result, showing that *all functions* can be computed in this model, under a standard hardness assumption in bilinear groups. We also describe a heuristic lattice-based construction.
- *Robust ARE.* We present a similar feasibility result for *robust* computational ARE based on ideal obfuscation along with standard cryptographic assumptions.

We then describe several applications of ARE and the above results.

- Under a standard cryptographic assumption, our computational ARE schemes imply the feasibility of general non-interactive secure computation in the *shuffle model*, where messages from different parties are shuffled. This implies a general utility-preserving compiler from differential privacy in the central model to computational differential privacy in the (non-robust) shuffle model.
- The existence of information-theoretic *robust* ARE implies "best-possible" information-theoretic MPC protocols (Halevi et al., TCC 2018) and degree-2 multiparty randomized encodings (Applebaum et al., TCC 2018). This yields new positive results for specific functions in the former model, as well as a simple unifying barrier for obtaining negative results in both models.

H. Handschuh and A. Lysyanskaya (Eds.): CRYPTO 2023, LNCS 14081, pp. 203–235, 2023.
https://doi.org/10.1007/978-3-031-38557-5_7

1 Introduction

Secure multiparty computation (MPC) [14,17,23,35] enables n parties to evaluate a distributed function $f(x_1, \ldots, x_n)$ on their local inputs, while revealing nothing except the output of f. Most of the questions about the general *feasibility* of MPC in different models have already been settled, shifting the focus of most research in the area to improved *efficiency*. The current work is motivated by several remaining questions on the feasibility front. Unless stated otherwise, we consider here security in the presence of *semi-honest* parties, who send messages as instructed by the protocol.

- **Non-interactive MPC in the shuffle model** [32]. Is it possible to compute every function f securely (with either information-theoretic or computational security) by having the parties simultaneously send *anonymous* messages to an evaluator? The evaluator should be able to recover $f(x_1, \ldots, x_n)$ from the shuffled messages, but learn nothing else about the inputs.
- **Best-possible information-theoretic MPC** [27]. Does every function f admit an information-theoretic MPC protocol that offers security against $t < n/2$ corrupted parties while only revealing to $t \geq n/2$ corrupted parties the *residual function* of f obtained by fixing the inputs of honest parties?
- **Minimal complete primitive for MPC** [3,4]. Is it possible to compute every function f with information-theoretic security against any number of corrupted parties, by using a single call to a degree-2 function g, or alternatively parallel calls to functions $g_{i,j}$ that depend on only 2 inputs and make their outputs public?

When f is just the n-party addition function over a finite Abelian group, then the answer to all of the above questions is "yes." The addition function is also attractive from an (asymptotic and concrete) *efficiency* perspective, and several lines of works propose optimized protocols and applications of secure addition in the context of federated learning [15], private analytics [19], and more. In light of this, it is natural to ask:

What can be computed securely given only an oracle for addition?

Additive Randomized Encoding. We capture this question via the new notion of an *additive randomized encoding* (ARE). Given a function $f(x_1, \ldots, x_n)$ and an Abelian group $\mathbb{G}$, an ARE scheme for f over $\mathbb{G}$ is defined by n randomized local encoding functions Enc_i, mapping each input x_i to a group element $\hat{x}_i \in \mathbb{G}$, and a decoder $\mathsf{Dec}(\hat{y})$, mapping the sum of the encodings $\hat{y} = \sum_{i=1}^{n} \hat{x}_i$ (over $\mathbb{G}$) to an output y. It will sometimes be convenient to consider ARE as a non-interactive *protocol*, referring to $\hat{x}_i$ as the ARE message of party P_i.

An ARE as above should satisfy the following correctness and security requirements. The *correctness* requirement is that the above process results in $y = f(x_1, \ldots, x_n)$. The *security* requirement is that the sum $\hat{y}$ reveals nothing about the inputs except the output of f. This can be viewed as an instance of the standard notion of a randomized encoding (RE) of functions [7], where the encoding $\hat{f}$ of f is restricted to "adding up local randomized functions." See Sect. 1.3 for further discussion of the relation with RE and its multiparty variant from [4].

As a simple example, consider the following ARE for the OR of n input bits: given a group $\mathbb{G}$, an input $x_i = 0$ is encoded as $\hat{x}_i = 0$ and $x_i = 1$ is encoded as a uniformly random element of $\mathbb{G}$. If $\mathrm{OR}(\mathbf{x}) = 0$ then the sum $\hat{y}$ of encodings is 0, while if $\mathrm{OR}(\mathbf{x}) = 1$ then $\hat{y}$ is random in $\mathbb{G}$, so security is perfect. Correctness error occurs with probability $1/|\mathbb{G}|$, if $\mathrm{OR}(\mathbf{x}) = 1$ but the sum of the ARE messages turns out to be 0 by chance.

Robust ARE. The above notion of ARE is natural when the encoded output $\hat{y}$ is revealed to an external party, who does not collude with any of the n parties. For the case where $\hat{y}$ can be learned by a coalition $T \subseteq [n]$ of corrupted parties, we need to account for the fact that corrupted parties can learn the sum $\hat{y}_H$ of the encodings $\hat{x}_i$ generated by the set of honest parties $H = [n] \setminus T$. This allows them to compute the value $f(x_T^*, x_H)$ for any x_T^* of their choice. We say that an ARE is *robust* if this is the only information that can be deduced from $\hat{y}_H$. It is not hard to verify that the above ARE scheme for OR is robust in this sense.

1.1 Our Contribution

In this work we study the feasibility of ARE and robust ARE for general functions f, with perfect, statistical, and computational security, apply our positive results towards solutions for the first two motivating questions discussed above, and highlight ARE as a new barrier for obtaining negative answers to the last two motivating questions.

Information-theoretic ARE. In the information-theoretic setting, we obtain both positive and negative results. In particular, we fully characterize the 2-party functions $f : X_1 \times X_2 \to \{0,1\}$ admitting a *perfectly secure* (but possibly statistically correct) ARE. These are precisely the functions f that can be written as $g(f_1(x_1), f_2(x_1))$ for some Boolean functions f_1 and f_2. This means that, when insisting on perfect security, OR and XOR are the only two-party Boolean functions that can be realized (up to local preprocessing of inputs and postprocessing of the output).

For $n \geq 3$ parties, we consider a natural "capped sum" function that adds up integer-valued inputs and reveals the sum only if it is at most (alternatively, at least) some predetermined threshold θ. (Otherwise the only bit of information revealed is that the threshold has been met.) We also consider a variant that includes "payloads," that are revealed when the sum does not exceed the threshold. The capped sum functionality is motivated by applications related to anonymous communication. We present an ARE for capped sum (including the "payload" variant) in which both correctness and security are statistical, and apply this towards an ARE for multiplication modulo an arbitrary integer m. We prove that there is no perfectly secure ARE for capped sum, thus providing a provable separation between perfect and statistical security for ARE. All of our constructions of information-theoretic ARE schemes are in fact robust. We leave open the existence of *statistically secure* ARE for general (or even constant-size) functions, and describe a failed attempt in this direction in the full version [28].

Computational ARE. We present a general feasibility result, showing that *all* polynomial-time computable functions admit a computationally secure ARE, under a standard hardness assumption in bilinear groups. An optimized variant of this scheme is quite practical: each party needs to send only a constant number of group elements per input bit, and additionally one of the parties needs to generate and send a standard garbled circuit for f. We also describe a heuristic lattice-based construction that we conjecture to be secure. These constructions do *not* realize the stronger notion of *robust* ARE that we discuss next.

Robust Computational ARE. The necessity of revealing the *residual* function in robust ARE means that robust ARE for general functions (over large input domains) implies obfuscation. We show that the converse is in a sense also true. Using *resettable* MPC [24,25] (which can be based on standard cryptographic assumptions), we obtain a general feasibility result for robust ARE based on *ideal obfuscation.*[1] The ideal obfuscation model, which was used to establish several recent results in cryptography, is similar in spirit to other generic models, such as the random oracle model. A formal support for this view was recently given in [33]. To get a (heuristic) standard-model construction, the ideal obfuscation oracle can instantiated using indistinguishability obfuscation. Alternatively, our robust ARE can be provably realized (under standard assumptions) in the *pseudorandom oracle model* of [33].

Application 1: Non-interactive MPC in the shuffle model. The *shuffle model* assumes that parties can send anonymous messages which are effectively shuffled before arriving to their destination. (Each party may send multiple messages.) First studied in the context of MPC [32], the shuffle model is currently a popular model for distributed *differential privacy* [18,20], offering better privacy-utility tradeoffs than the distributed *local model* while requiring less trust than the *central model.*

An MPC protocols for *addition* in the shuffle model was given in [32] (see [10, 22] for a tighter analysis). Combining this protocol with our computational ARE constructions, we get the first general feasibility results for (computationally secure, non-interactive) MPC in the shuffle model. Depending on the kind of ARE used, one either gets a non-robust (and practical) protocol under a standard cryptographic assumption, or an optimally robust (but currently impractical) protocol under strong assumptions. The ARE-based protocols do not involve any setup, thus providing qualitative advantages over alternative models for non-interactive MPC such as the PSM model [21] or robust non-interactive MPC with public-key setup [26]. The non-robust variant of the protocol implies a

[1] A combination of resettable MPC and ideal obfuscation was informally proposed in [26] in the related context of non-interactive MPC (see Sect. 1.3). It was recently used in [9] in a very different context: constructing a counterexample to a dream version of Yao's XOR lemma.

general utility-preserving compiler from differential privacy in the central model to computational differential privacy in the (non-robust) shuffle model. We do not know how to usefully apply robust ARE towards differential privacy in the robust shuffle model, and leave this as an interesting open question.

Application 2: Best-possible Information-Theoretic MPC. The notion of Best-possible Information-Theoretic MPC (BIT-MPC), introduced in [27], considers a stronger variant of the standard notion of information-theoretic security for MPC, which is in a sense the best possible. In the standard notion of IT-MPC for f, there are $t < n/2$ corrupted parties, and the protocol should guarantee that corrupted parties learn nothing except the output. The notion of BIT-MPC makes the additional requirement that even a majority of t corrupted parties should not learn more than the *residual function* obtained from f by fixing the inputs of the honest parties. It was shown in [27] that this information must be leaked, hence BIT-MPC indeed provides the best possible security. The main question left open by [27] is whether *all* functions can be realized in this model, regardless of efficiency. We connect this question to ARE, by showing that any perfectly (resp., statistically) secure robust ARE for f implies a perfectly (resp., statistically) BIT-MPC protocol for f. This allows transferring our positive results, such as the ones for variants of capped-sum, into the BIT-MPC setting. Moreover, obtaining negative results for (robust) statistical ARE is a necessary condition, which may be viewed as a *barrier*, for ruling out BIT-MPC protocols for general functions.

Application 3: Barrier for Multiparty Randomized Encoding. Finally, we show that a (hypothetical) robust information-theoretic ARE would imply an optimal construction of *multiparty randomized encodings* (MPRE) [4] and thus, again, can be viewed as a barrier for settling a well-known open problem. In an MPRE for $f(x_1, \ldots, x_n)$, each input x_i can be preprocessed "for free" by a local encoder before feeding it into a global encoder $\hat{f}$ whose output is made public. MPRE requires that even from the point of view of *insiders*, the output of $\hat{f}$ must reveal no more information about the other inputs than what follows from their own inputs and the output of f. The (effective) *degree* of an MPRE is the algebraic degree of $\hat{f}$. ARE can be viewed as a variant of MPRE with degree 1, but where security is only guaranteed against an outsider who observes the output. Robust ARE also falls short of meeting the MPRE requirement because of the leakage of the residual function. However, we show that robust ARE can still be used to construct standard MPRE with degree 2. This should be contrasted with the best known information-theoretic MPRE constructions, which either have degree 3 [3,4] or alternatively have degree 2 but are only secure against $2n/3$ corrupted parties [6]. In fact, our transformation only requires a robust MPRE for a simple (and constant-size) 3-party function. Thus, a robust statistical ARE for such functions would settle the main open question in this area.

We note that while our computational construction of robust ARE implies *computational* degree-2 MPRE, such a result was already known based on the much weaker assumption that oblivious transfer exists [4]. The significance of the ARE-to-MPRE transformation is that it gives another barrier for ruling out degree-2 MPRE: such a negative result requires ruling out statistical robust ARE for a constant-size 3-party function. Another (23-year old) barrier for the MPRE question is ruling out standard statistically secure degree-2 RE for general functions [3,30]. While the two barriers seem technically incomparable (see Sect. 1.3 below for discussion), we believe that the ARE barrier may be easier to make progress on because of the simpler additive structure. For the BIT-MPC question, ARE give the first simple barrier for proving negative results: the degree-2 RE barrier does not seem to apply, since BIT-MPC protocols are not known to follow from degree-2 RE.

1.2 Open Questions

Our work leaves many questions about ARE open. The main open question is whether *all* functions admit a statistically secure (robust or non-robust) ARE. This is open even for very simple functions, such as equality of two inputs from the domain $\{0, 1, 2\}$, which can be shown to be complete for non-robust ARE (Theorem 5.9). We strongly conjecture that the answer is negative. However, we were not able to prove this conjecture, and document in the full version the closest we got: a negative result under an alternative security definition that replaces the standard l_1 (statistical) distance between distributions by l_2 distance.

Other questions for information-theoretic ARE include extending our full characterization for *perfectly* secure ARE beyond two parties, and ruling out an ARE for OR with perfect correctness.

For (non-robust) computational ARE, the main question is to better understand the required assumptions. Can we use other "public-key" assumptions, such as DDH or LWE? Is public-key cryptography even needed? Are there any general connections with other cryptographic primitives?

Finally, can we construct *robust* ARE (for constant-size functions) from iO and standard cryptographic assumptions, avoiding the use of ideal obfuscation?

1.3 Related Work

Randomized Encoding of Functions. It is often useful to replace a given function f by a "simpler" randomized function $\hat{f}$ whose output can be used to recover the output of f but reveals no additional information about the input. This was formalized by the abstract notion of *randomized encoding* (RE) of functions [7,30], which has found many applications in cryptography and beyond (see [2,29] for surveys). ARE can be viewed as an instance of RE where the notion of simplicity is "adding up local randomized functions."

The main open question about RE is the existence of *statistically secure* degree-2 RE for all (constant-size) functions. This question, first posed in [30], is open for over 20 years, and has been put forward as a barrier for solving other questions [3,5]. We note that the class of functions admitting (statistical) degree-2 RE seems incomparable to the class of functions admitting (statistical) ARE, even when restricting the ARE model to allow a single bit of input per party. On the one hand, the mod-2 inner product function trivially has a degree-2 RE whereas it is conjectured not to have ARE. (In the case of perfect security, this provably follows from our 2-party characterization.) On the other hand, the capped sum function has (statistical) ARE, but it seems reasonable to conjecture that it has no degree-2 RE. (A natural implementation of our ARE scheme in the RE setting would lead to a degree-3 RE.)

Multiparty Randomized Encoding. As discussed above, MPRE [4] is a natural extension of RE to the multi-party setting. Viewed as an MPRE, ARE maximizes the simplicity of the global encoder, but (inherently) does so at the expense of sacrificing full security against insiders. For standard (non-robust) ARE, the only security requirement is against an outsider who obtains the output of $\hat{f}$, whereas a robust ARE offers the best-possible security against insiders.

Non-interactive MPC. ARE serves as a natural tool for non-interactive MPC in different models. Unlike existing models for non-interactive MPC, including the well-studied PSM model [21] or its robust variants from [1,13,26], ARE does not require any form or correlated randomness or public-key setup.

Organization. In Sect. 2 we provide a technical overview of our results. A more detailed treatment can then be found in Sects. 3 (definitions), 4 (information-theoretic constructions and lower-bounds), 5 (computational constructions), and 6 (some applications). The construction of robust ARE from ideal obfuscation is described in the full version, as well as some of the proofs.

2 Overview of Techniques

In this section we give a detailed but informal overview of the technical ideas behind our main results.

2.1 Information-Theoretic ARE

Our positive results for information-theoretic AREs, consist of randomization techniques for the functions in question. We start by recalling the simple example of OR of n input bits described in the introduction: $x_i = 0$ is encoded as a 0, while $x_i = 1$ is encoded as a uniformly random value in $\mathbb{G}$. If $\mathrm{OR}(\mathbf{x}) = 0$ then the sum of encodings is 0 while if $\mathrm{OR}(\mathbf{x}) = 1$ then the sum of encodings is random in $\mathbb{G}$. Privacy is therefore perfect, and correctness error occurs with probability $1/|\mathbb{G}|$. Note that this is in fact a *robust* ARE, since the sum of a subset of the ARE messages only reveals the OR of the corresponding inputs, which coincides with the residual function restricted to these inputs.[2] This OR protocol can be

[2] In the following we will not refer to robustness, though all of our ARE constructions in the information-theoretic setting are in fact robust.

extended to compute the MAX function (maximum of n integers), though the communication complexity in this case scales exponentially with the bit-length of the inputs.

A more interesting example is the *capped-sum* function where the output is the sum of the inputs (over the integers), unless the sum exceeds some pre-set cap θ, in which case the output is just θ. Beyond being a natural example, it also serves as a building block for other constructions (such as ARE for product modulo m) and can be extended to a variant with payloads that can be motivated by anonymity-related applications. To get an ARE scheme for capped sum, each input x_i is encoded as a random $\theta \times \theta$ matrix with rank x_i, over a sufficiently large finite field. The observation is that up to θ, the rank of the sum is equal, with high probability, to the sum of the ranks: in that range, a sum of random matrices of ranks x_i is close to a random matrix of rank $\sum_i x_i$. And, of course, the rank can never exceed θ. In this case, both correctness and security of the ARE are statistical.

We also present several negative results for perfectly-secure information-theoretic AREs. Among other things, we show that the above capped sum function cannot have a perfectly-secure ARE, and the statistical security in our solution is necessary. In this overview, it is convenient to restrict attention to two-argument functions $f(x, y)$. The (randomized) encoding for every value of x is associated with some probability distribution p_x and, similarly, every y is associated with some probability distribution q_y. The sum of the two encodings for inputs (x, y) is therefore distributed according to the *convolution* of the two distributions, $p_x * q_y$. A convenient way to look at convolutions is by switching to the Fourier representation of the distributions. While each entry in $p_x * q_y$ (viewed as vectors) depends on all the entries of p_x and q_y, in the Fourier representation each entry depends only on the corresponding entries in the transforms of p_x and of q_y. Namely, $\widehat{p_x * q_y} = \widehat{p}_x \odot \widehat{q}_y$, where $\odot$ denotes entry-wise product and $\widehat{p}$ denotes the Fourier representation of p.

We then define a notion of a *Vector Multiplication Program* (VMP) for the function f. This is a collection of (complex) vectors v_x for each input value x, vectors w_y for each input value y, and distinct vectors u_z for each output value z, such that for all (x, y) we have $v_x \odot w_y = u_{f(x,y)}$. It follows from the above discussion that if there is a perfectly-secure ARE for $f(x, y)$ then there is also a VMP for f. Using the simplicity of the VMP framework, we are able to obtain, for example, an exact characterization of the two-argument Boolean functions that admit a perfectly-secure ARE. Concretely, this is exactly the set of functions $f(x, y)$ that can be expressed as $g(f_1(x), f_2(y))$, for Boolean f_1, f_2.

2.2 Computational ARE

Central to our treatment of computational ARE is the observation that the *two-party equality function* is complete in some sense, even over domains of fixed size (see below). We therefore begin by describing a pairing-based two-party ARE scheme for the equality function. The starting point for that scheme is considering the equation

$$(s_1 + s_2)(x_1 s_1 - x_2 s_2) \stackrel{?}{=} (x_1 s_1^2 - x_2 s_2^2)$$

and noting that the cross-terms $s_1 s_2$ are canceled out if and only if $x_1 = x_2$. This suggests a protocol where $P_1(x_1)$ sends $(s_1, x_1 s_1, x_1 s_1^2)$ for a random s_1, and $P_2(x_2)$ sends $(s_2, -x_2 s_2, -x_2 s_2^2)$ for a random s_2. If $x_1 = x_2 = x$, then the sum of these two vectors is of the form $(s_1 + s_2, x(s_1 - s_2), x(s_1^2 - s_2^2))$, and the evaluator can check that the last element equals the product of the first two. If $x_1 \neq x_2$ then the product of the first two will have additional terms that depend on the random s_1, s_2, so it will not be equal to the third term (except with a negligible probability).

Of course, sending the terms above "in the clear" will be insecure, in particular the evaluator can learn the difference $x_1 - x_2$. To avoid that, we encode those terms "in the exponent" and rely on DDH-like assumptions. Since evaluation requires computing the product, we use pairing-friendly groups that allow us to perform this multiplication in the exponent. More details are provided in Sect. 5.1. In the full version we also describe a heuristic construction that attempts to replicate this structure with a lattice-based construction.

Once we have a scheme for equality, we can build from it a scheme for all other boolean functions with small domains: Party $P_2(x_2)$ prepares a list of all the possible inputs x_1 such that $f(x_1, x_2) = 1$, then run an equality ARE for each one to see if P_1's input is any of them. To ensure security, P_2 needs to pad the list so as to always run the same number of equality tests, and shift it by a random amount to hide which of these instances matches. See Sect. 5.2.

Having access to ARE schemes for all boolean functions of small domains, we use it to get 1-out-of-2 oblivious-transfer (OT), and combine it with a standard garbling technique (e.g., [7]) to get a computational ARE for any multiparty function f. That is, one party (say P_1) will prepare a garbled circuit and send it to the evaluator, and will also engage in an OT instance with each other party for each bit of the input labels for that circuit. See Sect. 5.3. In the full version we also observe that the structure of the equality ARE scheme from Sect. 5.1 makes it easy to modify so as to get directly a scheme for OT, bypassing some of the generic transformations above. This optimization leads to a practical protocol in which the communication includes a standard garbled circuit along with a constant number of group elements per input bit.

2.3 Robust ARE

We note that general robust ARE over large input domains implies obfuscation. We therefore construct robust ARE using obfuscation. A natural approach is to start from a "sufficiently robust" interactive protocol, and obfuscate its next-message function. Of course, doing so means that the adversary can reset the honest parties, so the underlying interactive protocol must achieve best-possible security even with a resetting adversary.

A first attempt at getting a robust ARE for $f(x_1, \ldots, x_n)$ is therefore to start from a resettable-secure MPC protocol for f [24,25], then obfuscate its next message function (with the input and randomness of each party hard-wired). Of course, this does not use the summation oracle of ARE, and so (unsurprisingly) it is insecure. To see the problem, note that the adversary can reset *any subset of the honest parties*, then run the protocol with these parties fixed and the inputs to all other parties chosen arbitrarily. In other words, the adversary gets access to the *full residual function* of $f(x_1, \ldots, x_n)$, where it can substitute *any subset* of the inputs. In contrast, a robust ARE scheme can only leak the (standard) residual function, where the inputs of *all the honest parties* are fixed.

To do better, we extend the function f in a way that allows us to "lock" the inputs of the honest parties. To wit, we consider the extended function

$$g_f\big((x_1,\rho_1,\sigma_1),\ldots,(x_n,\rho_n,\sigma_n)\big) = \begin{cases} f(x_1,\ldots,x_n) & \text{if } \sigma_1 = \cdots = \sigma_n = \bigoplus_{i\in[n]} \rho_i, \\ \bot & \text{otherwise.} \end{cases}$$

Similarly to previous applications combining ideal obfuscation and resettable MPC [9,26], we use this mechanism to emulate an ideal access to the *full* residual function of g_f, enabling the adversary to fix the inputs of *any strict subset* of the parties. This is done by sending obfuscations of the next message functions of a resettable MPC protocol for g_f, where (similarly to [9]) the protocol works over broadcast channels and uses signatures to enforce in-order executions. In addition to the full residual function of g_f, the sum $\sigma = \rho_1 + \ldots + \rho_n$ is communicated to the evaluator via the ARE.

The key point is that given oracle access to the full residual function of g_f, the adversary cannot predict the sum of the ρ_i's of a strict subset of the honest parties. The only way for the adversary to get a matching σ is to use the one that the evaluator received. But this σ ties it also to the ρ_i's of all the other honest parties. Hence, if the adversary uses any inputs of the honest parties then it must use them all.

2.4 Applications

Application 1: MPC in the Shuffle Model. The shuffle model was discussed and motivated above. Here, we outline our construction of MPC protocols in this model. Such a protocol for a function f is based on two ingredients. The first is an ARE for f over some group $\mathbb{G}$. Using this ARE, our protocol starts by each party P_i locally encoding its input x_i into $\hat{x}_i$. Next, we would like to compute the encoded output $\hat{y}$ which is just $\sum_i \hat{x}_i$. This is done, using an addition protocol for the shuffle model from [32] (tightly analyzed in [10,22]). In this protocol, the messages of each party are an additive secret sharing (over $\mathbb{G}$) of its input. The value $\hat{y}$ is reconstructed by adding up the shuffled shares, and then the ARE decoder is applied to obtain $y = f(\mathbf{x})$.

Application 2: From ARE to Best-Possible Information-Theoretic MPC. The notion of Best-possible Information-Theoretic MPC (BIT-MPC), introduced in [27], considers protocols that provide best possible type of security, depending on the number of dishonest parties. Namely, it offers the standard notion of security against a corruption of a minority of parties and, additionally, offers residual security in case that the adversary corrupts a majority of the parties. The work of [27] provides BIT-MPC protocols for certain families of functions (such as OR, and deciding the solutions of a system of linear equations $Ax = b$) but rules out *efficient* BIT-MPC for all efficiently computable functions. They leave open the question of the possibility of non-efficient BIT-MPC for all functions, or BIT-MPC for all constant-size functions.

We show that information-theoretic robust ARE for a function f can be transformed into a BIT-MPC for f, hence enriching the set of functions for which such BIT-MPC protocols are known. Moreover, this also implies that proving negative results for BIT-MPC requires proving impossibility of statistical ARE, explaining our difficulty of proving such results.

Given such an ARE for f, we construct a BIT-MPC protocol for f as follows. Each party P_i first uses the ARE to (locally) encode its input x_i into $\hat{x}_i$. Then, the parties employ a simple n-secure addition protocol that computes an additive secret sharing of $\hat{y} = \sum_i \hat{x}_i$. Finally, they use a standard information-theoretic MPC protocol (such as the BGW protocol [14]), secure in the presence of honest majority, to compute the ARE decoder on the sum of additive shares, which results in the desired output $f(x_1, \ldots, x_n)$. To argue BIT security, note that if there is a honest majority, then nothing beyond the output is revealed. On the other hand, if there is a dishonest majority, then the adversary may learn $\hat{y}$. However, the robustness of the ARE, implies that no more than the residual function of the honest parties' inputs is leaked by $\hat{y}$.

Application 3: Barrier for Multiparty Randomized Encoding. To obtain degree-2 MPRE from robust ARE, our starting point is that every function g that can be written as the sum of 2-local functions $f_{ij}(x_i, x_j)$ admits a degree-2 MPRE. The main technical challenge is leveraging robust ARE towards constructing an MPRE of the above form for general functions.

A key difference between the robust ARE model and the MPRE model is that the former (inherently) has residual function leakage whereas the latter (by requirement) does not. To eliminate the residual function leakage, we convert $f(x_1, \ldots, x_n)$ into a new N-party function f', for $N = \binom{n}{2}$ "virtual parties," which applies a simple *constant-size* pairwise multiparty authentication for the inputs of f. Concretely, for each pair of parties $1 \leq i < j \leq n$, there is a virtual party P_{ij} whose input to f' is a pair $x^{i,j} = (x_i^{i,j}, x_j^{i,j})$. The function f' checks that all input pairs are consistent with some global input vector $(x_1, \ldots, x_n)$, outputting $f(x_1, \ldots, x_n)$ if it is and $\perp$ otherwise. Namely,

$$f'(x^{1,2}, \ldots, x^{n-1,n}) = \begin{cases} f(x_1, \ldots, x_n) & \text{if } \exists x_1, \ldots, x_n \text{ s.t. } \forall i, j, x^{i,j} = (x_i, x_j) \\ \perp & \text{otherwise} \end{cases}.$$

Note that if f has constant-size input domains then so does f'.

We now use a robust ARE for f' to define an MPRE for f in which the function g is a sum of 2-local functions, which (as noted above) suffices for our purposes. The function g takes from each party P_i the following inputs: its original input x_i, and additional inputs ρ_{ij} (for all $j \neq i$) that will be used to generate the ARE messages of virtual parties P_{ij}.

Letting $\Pi = (\mathsf{Enc}_{ij}, \mathsf{Dec})$ be a robust ARE for f' over a group $\mathbb{G}$, the function g is defined as:

$$g\left((x_1, (\rho_{1j})_{j\neq 1}), \ldots, (x_n, (\rho_{nj})_{j\neq n})\right) = \sum_{1\leq i<j\leq n} \mathsf{Enc}_{ij}((x_i, x_j); \rho_{ij} \oplus \rho_{ji})$$

where summation is over $\mathbb{G}$, and $\mathsf{Enc}_{ij}((x_i, x_j); \rho)$ denotes an ARE encoding for f' of input (x_i, x_j) (for virtual party P_{ij}) using randomness ρ. By construction, the function g is indeed a sum of 2-local functions, as required. The output of f can be recovered from the output of g by applying the ARE decoder Dec of Π. Intuitively, a set of corrupted parties can learn nothing (given their inputs, randomness, and the output of g) beyond the output of f because the honest parties contribute secret randomness to the ARE message of each virtual party that involves at least one honest party. Since the inputs of these virtual parties determine all inputs, the residual function of f' with these inputs fixed is determined by the output $f(x_1, \ldots, x_n)$. Finally, we note that by a known completeness results [3], applying the above transformation for to a constant-size 3-party function suffices.

3 Additive Randomized Encoding: Definitions and Properties

Here we define Additive Randomized Encoding (ARE), considering both information-theoretic and computational security, both with and without robustness. Below we define the ARE syntax in the most general case, where the function to compute and the group over which the encodings are added are parameterized by several parameters. In the sequel, not all the parameters will be relevant in all the settings, and we often omit some of them (e.g., in Sect. 4, we consider information-theoretic AREs, in which case setup algorithm, public parameters etc. are not needed, and functions are often defined over a finite domain).

Definition 3.1 (ARE Syntax). *Let $f : (\{0,1\}^*)^* \to \{0,1\}^*$ be a multiparty function. An ARE scheme for f is a triple of algorithms $\Pi = (\mathsf{Setup}, \mathsf{Enc}, \mathsf{Dec})$ with the following syntax:*

- $\mathsf{Setup}(1^\lambda, 1^n, 1^\ell) \to \mathsf{pp}$ *is a PPT* setup algorithm *that, given security parameter λ, number of parties n, and input length ℓ, generates public parameters* pp. *The public parameters include λ, n, ℓ, and an explicit description of an Abelian group $\mathbb{G}$. They can also include some randomness, such as random generators of $\mathbb{G}$ and/or a common reference string (CRS). We will sometimes eliminate* Setup *and consider $\mathbb{G}$ as being fixed.*
- $\mathsf{Enc}(\mathsf{pp}, i, x_i) \to \hat{x}_i$ *is a PPT* encoding algorithm *that maps an input x_i of party i to a group element from $\mathbb{G}$. We refer to $\hat{x}_i$ as the encoding of x_i, or the ARE message of party i.*

– $\mathsf{Dec}(\mathsf{pp}, \hat{y}) \to y$ *is a PPT* decoding algorithm *that maps a group element* $\hat{y} \in \mathbb{G}$ *to an output* y.

Π is correct, with a possible error of $\epsilon = \epsilon(\lambda)$, if for all λ, n, ℓ, and $x_1, \ldots, x_n \in \{0,1\}^\ell$:

$$\Pr\left[\begin{array}{l}\mathsf{pp} \leftarrow \mathsf{Setup}(1^\lambda, 1^n, 1^\ell);\\ \hat{x}_i \leftarrow \mathsf{Enc}(\mathsf{pp}, i, x_i);\\ \hat{y} = \sum_{i=1}^n \hat{x}_i\end{array} : \mathsf{Dec}(\mathsf{pp}, \hat{y}) = f(x_1, \ldots, x_n)\right] \geq 1 - \epsilon(\lambda),$$

where summation is taken over the group $\mathbb{G}$ specified by pp. *In the statistical and computational settings, we require by default that ϵ is negligible in the security parameter.*

We will often consider functions f for which n and/or ℓ are fixed. In such cases, these parameters will be omitted. Also, in some cases we do not need the setup procedure at all, and in the perfect security setting we do not have a security parameter.

Remark 3.2 (Sending messages to the evaluator). Note that the encoded input could be a vector, where we use different slots for different purposes. The ARE group in this case is the direct product of the groups in all the slots.

This syntax allows parties to directly send messages to the evaluator, by allocating a slot in the vector to one party, where that party puts the message and all other parties put zeros. We use the shorthand "party P_i sends $(x_i; y_i)$" to mean that x_i is added to the x'es of all the other parties, and y_i is sent directly to the evaluator.

3.1 ARE Security

Our basic security notion, without robustness, asserts that $\hat{y}$ can be simulated given access to $f(x_1, \ldots, x_n)$. For any λ, n, ℓ and $x_1, \ldots, x_n \in \{0,1\}^\ell$, let us denote by $\Pi(1^\lambda, x_1, \ldots, x_n)$ the output of the process:

$$\Pi(1^\lambda, x_1, \ldots, x_n) := \left\{\begin{array}{l}\mathsf{pp} \leftarrow \mathsf{Setup}(1^\lambda, 1^n, 1^\ell); \hat{x}_i \leftarrow \mathsf{Enc}(\mathsf{pp}, i, x_i); \hat{y} = \sum_{i=1}^n \hat{x}_i;\\ \text{output } (\mathsf{pp}, \hat{y})\end{array}\right\}.$$

We often omit some of these parameters, if they are irrelevant in a given context.

Definition 3.3 (ARE Security). *An ARE scheme $\Pi = (\mathsf{Setup}, \mathsf{Enc}, \mathsf{Dec})$ for $f : (\{0,1\}^*)^* \to \{0,1\}^*$ as in Definition 3.1, is said to be secure if there exists a randomized algorithm* Sim*, called a simulator, such that:*

Perfect security. *For all n, ℓ and $x_1, \ldots, x_n \in \{0,1\}^\ell$, $\mathsf{Sim}(1^n, 1^\ell, f(x_1, \ldots, x_n)) \equiv \Pi(x_1, \ldots, x_n)$.*

Statistical security. *For some negligible function $\delta(\cdot)$, it holds for all λ, n, ℓ and $x_1, \ldots, x_n \in \{0,1\}^\ell$, that*

$$SD\left(\mathsf{Sim}(1^\lambda, 1^n, 1^\ell, f(x_1, \ldots, x_n)),\ \Pi(1^\lambda, x_1, \ldots, x_n)\right) \leq \delta(\lambda),$$

where $SD(\cdot,\cdot)$ is the statistical distance.

Computational security. Sim *is a PPT algorithm, and for all* λ, n, ℓ *and* $x_1, \ldots, x_n \in \{0,1\}^\ell$, $\mathsf{Sim}(1^\lambda, 1^n, 1^\ell, f(x_1, \ldots, x_n))$ *and* $\Pi(1^\lambda, x_1, \ldots, x_n)$ *are computationally indistinguishable.*

Robustness. The above definition only considers security against the *external* evaluator who only sees the sum of the ARE encodings. When the evaluator may collude with a subset of the parties, we need a stronger notion of *robust ARE.*

It is easy to see that a collusion between the evaluator and some parties can get the sum of encodings of the other (honest) parties by subtracting out from $\hat{y}$ the encodings of the colluding parties. Below we denote, for any subset of honest parties $H \subset [n]$,

$$\Pi_H(1^\lambda, x_1, \ldots, x_n) := \left\{ \begin{matrix} \mathsf{pp} \leftarrow \mathsf{Setup}(1^\lambda, 1^n, 1^\ell); \hat{x}_i \leftarrow \mathsf{Enc}(\mathsf{pp}, i, x_i); \hat{y}_H = \sum_{i \in H} \hat{x}_i; \\ \text{output } (\mathsf{pp}, \hat{y}) \end{matrix} \right\}.$$

Clearly, a collusion of the evaluator with the parties in $[n] \setminus H$ necessarily gets access to the *residual function* of the honest parties in H. In the definition below for robust ARE, the simulator will therefore get access not just to $f(x_1, \ldots, x_n)$, but to the entire residual function.

For any n-party function f, subset $H \subset [n]$, and inputs $\mathbf{x} = (x_i : i \in H) \in (\{0,1\}^\ell)^{|H|}$, the residual function defined by $H, \mathbf{x}$ is the following function on $m = n - |H|$ inputs:

$$f_{H,\mathbf{x}}(w_1, \ldots, w_m) = f(z_1, \ldots, z_n), \text{ where } z_i = \begin{cases} x_i & \text{if } i \in H \\ w_{j_i} & \text{if } i \notin H \end{cases},$$

where j_i, for $i \notin H$, is the index of i in the set $[n] \setminus H$.

Definition 3.4 (Robust ARE). *An ARE scheme* $\Pi = (\mathsf{Setup}, \mathsf{Enc}, \mathsf{Dec})$ *for* $f : (\{0,1\}^*)^* \to \{0,1\}^*$ *as in Definition 3.1, is said to be* robust *if there exists a simulator* Sim *with access to a residual-function oracle, such that:*

Perfect robustness. *For all* n, ℓ, $H \subset [n]$, *and inputs* $\mathbf{x} = (x_i : i \in H)$, $\mathsf{Sim}^{f_{H,\mathbf{x}}}(1^n, H, 1^\ell) \equiv \Pi_H(\mathbf{x})$.

Statistical robustness. *For some negligible function* $\delta(\cdot)$, *it holds for all* λ, n, ℓ, $H \subset [n]$, *and inputs* $\mathbf{x} = (x_i : i \in H)$, *that*

$$SD\left(\mathsf{Sim}^{f_{H,\mathbf{x}}}(1^\lambda, 1^n, H, 1^\ell),\ \Pi_H(1^\lambda, \mathbf{x})\right) \leq \delta(\lambda),$$

where $SD(\cdot,\cdot)$ *is the statistical distance.*

Computational simulation-robustness. Sim *is a PPT algorithm, and for all* λ, n, ℓ, $H \subset [n]$, *and inputs* $\mathbf{x} = (x_i : i \in H)$, $\mathsf{Sim}^{f_{H,\mathbf{x}}}(1^\lambda, 1^n, H, 1^\ell)$ *and* $\Pi_H(1^\lambda, \mathbf{x})$ *are computationally indistinguishable. We will also consider the weaker notion of computational VBB-robustness, where the order of quantifiers is reversed: for every efficient Boolean distinguisher* $\mathcal{A}$ *there is an efficient simulator* Sim *such that* $\mathcal{A}$ *has a negligible advantage distinguishing between* $\mathsf{Sim}^{f_{H,\mathbf{x}}}$ *and* Π_H.

Indistinguishability robustness. Sim *is an unbounded algorithm, and for all* λ, n, ℓ, $H \subset [n]$, *and inputs* $\mathbf{x} = (x_i : i \in H)$, $\mathsf{Sim}^{f_{H,\mathbf{x}}}(1^\lambda, 1^n, H, 1^\ell)$ *and* $\Pi_H(1^\lambda, \mathbf{x})$ *are computationally indistinguishable.*

Note that the indistinguishability variant of robustness can be equivalently defined by requiring that for any H, if $\mathbf{x}$ and $\mathbf{x}'$ induce the same residual function (namely, $f_{H,\mathbf{x}} \equiv f_{H,\mathbf{x}'}$) then their partial sums $\sum_{i \in H} \hat{x}_i$ and $\sum_{i \in H} \hat{x}'_i$ are computationally indistinguishable, even given pp.

Remark 3.5 (On the different notions of robust computational ARE). In the 2-party case ($n = 2$), the different notions of robust ARE are analogous to corresponding notions of obfuscation. In fact, a robust ARE for a *universal* function f implies obfuscation of the corresponding function class. Similarly to obfuscation, the simulation and VBB variants are generally impossible to realize [12]. The VBB variant can potentially be realized for simple but nontrivial classes of functions, such as evasive functions [11]. In contrast, the simulation variant is only meaningful in idealized models, such as the ideal obfuscation model [33].

We will be particularly interested in "constant-size" functions f, for which both n and ℓ are bounded. While there is no meaningful notion of obfuscation for constant-size functions, here we get a meaningful notion, which is stronger than the non-robust notion. (This is similar to the robust non-interactive MPC model from [13].) For such constant-size f, all the above notions of robustness are equivalent, and we refer to the indistinguishability variant by default.

Remark 3.6 (On separating robust ARE from standard ARE). Let $f(x, y)$ be a constant function, for $x, y \in \{0, 1\}$. Consider the following ARE for f over $\mathbb{Z}_m$: input x is encoded by x itself, while y is encoded by $r \in_R \mathbb{Z}_m$. This ARE satisfies the standard notion of security, as the sum of encodings is random in $\mathbb{Z}_m$, but the evaluator together with the second party learn x (which they should not).

3.2 Basic Properties of ARE

We note that if we have ARE schemes for two functions f, f' defined over the same set of inputs, then we also have an ARE for the function $g(\mathbf{x}) = (f(\mathbf{x}), f'(\mathbf{x}))$. This is analogous to the standard concatenation property for randomized encoding of functions.

Claim (cf. [8], *Fact 3.3).* Let f, f' be two n-party function. If both functions have perfect (alternatively, statistical or computational) secure/robust ARE schemes, then the concatenation function $g = (f, f')$ also has an ARE of the same type.

Proof. An ARE Π'' for g, is obtained by concatenating the two ARE schemes for f, f': The public parameters are concatenated, and so are the encodings. The evaluator decodes each part separately. The various types of security are easy to verify.

ARE "over the Integers". It is sometimes convenient to convert an ARE for some function f from one group to another. For that purpose, it is convenient to talk about ARE schemes over the ring of integers $\mathbb{Z}$. While the syntax in Definition 3.1 requires a finite group, it is often easy to project $\mathbb{Z}$ down to some $\mathbb{Z}_t$ for large enough t, such that the summation of encodings (almost) never triggers modular reduction. We refer to such ARE scheme with no modular reduction as being "over the integers."

Conveniently, we can convert ARE over $\mathbb{Z}_m$ to one over the integers, using the standard technique of adding a sufficiently large random multiple of m.

Claim (cf. [8]*, Claim 5.3).* If f has a statistical/perfect secure ARE scheme over $\mathbb{Z}_m$, then it has a statistical ARE over the integers.

Proof. The scheme over the integers has $\mathsf{Enc}_i'(x_i) = \mathsf{Enc}_i(x_i) + r_i \cdot m$ (over the integers), where $r_i \in_R [0, \mu - 1]$ for some parameter μ.[3] The decoder just reduce everything modulo m and runs the original decoder. For security, we note that if the original scheme has n parties and statistical security upto δ, the new one will have statistical security upto at most $\delta + n/\mu$. Choosing μ sufficiently large gives what we need.

Note that the proof in fact uses only a finite portion of the integers, so we can again view the resulting scheme as being over some large enough $\mathbb{Z}_t$.

This can be useful for proving impossibility results: For example, suppose that we could rule out statistical ARE schemes for a certain function modulo any prime. Then we can use this to also rule out ARE over $\mathbb{Z}_m$ for non-prime moduli: if there were such a scheme over $\mathbb{Z}_m$, we could use this to convert it to an ARE over $\mathbb{Z}_t$ for a prime t sufficiently larger than m. (See for example the claim in Sect. 4.1.)

4 Information-Theoretic ARE

In the full version of this work [28] we describe in detail a few examples of information-theoretic AREs for some simple (but useful) functions. These are summarized in the following theorem:

Theorem 4.1. *There exist statistically-correct (over sufficiently large groups), perfectly-secure, robust AREs for the functions OR, MAX, Equal and* $Mult_p$*. Concretely, let* $\epsilon > 0$ *be the desired bound on the correctness error, then our ARE for OR requires a group* $\mathbb{G}$ *of size at least* $1/\epsilon$*, our ARE for MAX over the domain* $[M]$ *requires a group* $\mathbb{G} = (\mathbb{G}_0)^{M-1}$ *with* $\mathbb{G}_0$ *of size* $\Omega(M/\log 1/(1-\epsilon))$*, our ARE for Equal over the domain* $[M]$ *requires a group* $\mathbb{G} = (\mathbb{G}_0)^M$ *with* $\mathbb{G}_0$ *of size* $\Omega(M/\log 1/(1-\epsilon))$*, and our ARE for* $Mult_p$ *requires a group* $\mathbb{G} = \mathbb{Z}_m \times \mathbb{Z}_{p-1}$ *with* $m \geq 1/\epsilon$*.*

[3] In the context of information-theoretic AREs it is often convenient to replace the notation $\mathsf{Enc}(\mathsf{pp}, i, x_i)$ by $\mathsf{Enc}_i(x_i)$.

4.1 ARE for Capped Sum

In this section, we consider the capped-sum function that returns the sum of inputs $x_1, \ldots, x_n$, unless the sum is larger than some cap parameter θ, in which case the function returns θ. For simplicity, we assume in this section that the input domains are $D_i = \{0, 1\}$, though our results can be extended to larger domains (see Remark below). The special cases of $\theta = 1$ and $\theta = n$ are already covered by OR_n and SUM_n, respectively.

The capped-sum function has several motivations. On the technical side, it serves as a building block in the construction of other protocols (see below). However, it is also motivated as a stand-alone functionality. For example, consider a "whistle blowing" scenario in which n parties are given the opportunity to complain about something/somebody but, for privacy considerations, the number of complaints will be exposed only if it is above some threshold t. This can be achieved via a capped-sum protocols, where each party inputs 0 for "complain" and 1 for non-complain. The cap will be $\theta = n - t$. If there are at most t complaints then the output will be θ. However, if more than t complaints are cast then the output is some $y < \theta$ (which implies $n - y$ complaints).

Claim. Let $f : \{0,1\}^n \to \{0, 1, \ldots, \theta\}$ be the capped sum function with cap θ. Then, there exists a statistically-secure, robust ARE for f over $\mathbb{G} = (\mathbb{F}_p)^{\theta^2}$.

Proof. The encoding algorithm Enc_i on input $x_i = 0$ outputs an all-0 matrix M_i of dimension $\theta \times \theta$, and on input $x_i = 1$ it outputs M_i which is a random $\theta \times \theta$ rank-1 matrix, with entries in $\mathbb{F}_p$ (selected by choosing random, length θ vectors u_i, v_i over $\mathbb{F}_p$ and setting $M_i = u_i \times v_i^T$). Denote $M = \sum_{i=1}^n M_i$. The decoder on input M outputs $\mathrm{rank}_{\mathbb{F}_p}(M)$. The (simple) analysis of this scheme can be found in the full version of this work [28].

Remark 4.2. To deal with capped-sum over a larger domain $\{0, 1, \ldots, m\}$, we can choose M_i as a random matrix of rank x_i or, to make the analysis similar to the binary case, as the sum of x_i rank-1 random matrices.

Capped Sum with Payloads. Next, we describe an extension of the capped sum functionality, that we sometimes refer to as "capped sum with payloads". Concretely, each party has a pair of inputs (x_i, y_i). If the capped-sum of $\mathbf{x}$ is below the threshold θ then the ARE reveals this capped-sum along with $\sum_{i=1}^n y_i$, while if the capped-sum is at least θ then nothing about $\mathbf{y}$ is revealed. More generally, we can replace $\sum_{i=1}^n y_i$ by any function $f(y)$ for which an ARE over some $\mathbb{Z}_m$ exists; we denote this functionality CS_f.

Claim. Let f be a function with an ARE over $\mathbb{Z}_m$. Then, there is a statistical ARE for CS_f over $\mathbb{Z}_{m'}$, for sufficiently large m'.

Proof. The idea is to reduce this problem to the standard capped-sum, by increasing the range from $\{0, 1, \ldots \theta\}$ to $\{0, 1, \ldots \theta \cdot \beta\}$, where $\mathbb{Z}_\beta$ is the group to which we can transform the ARE for f, as described in Sect. 3.2, and is sufficiently large to make sure that there no modular reduction occurs. Specifically, each x_i is first multiplied by β and then we add to it $\mathsf{Enc}_i(y_i) \in \mathbb{Z}_\beta$ (where Enc_i is the encoder described in Sect. 3.2) to get a new input z_i for capped-sum (with cap $\theta \cdot \beta$).

If the sum of x_i's is at least θ then the sum of z_i's is at least $\theta \cdot \beta$ and so capped-sum reveals no additional information on the inputs. If the sum of x_i's is some $s < \theta$ then the sum of z_i's is $< \theta \cdot \beta$ and more precisely, it is $s \cdot \beta$ (from the x_i's) plus the sum of ARE encodings in $\mathbb{Z}_\beta$ (where here we use the property of this ARE that no modular reduction occurs). This allows for decoding s and, from the sum of encodings, decoding also the value $f(\mathbf{y})$ (but no other information about $\mathbf{y}$).

Example 4.3. **(ARE for Multiplication over $\mathbb{Z}_m$.)** Let $D_i = \mathbb{Z}_m$, for some integer m and let $Mult_m(\mathbf{x}) = \Pi_{i=1}^n x_i \bmod m$. Our ARE for $mult_p$ reduced multiplication to summation of $\log x_i$ (in the case that the product is not 0). While (discrete) log is defined in $\mathbb{Z}_p$ it is not defined in $\mathbb{Z}_m$, hence extra care is required.

We start with the case that $m = p^e$. We write each x_i as $x_i = p^{e_i} \cdot y_i$, where y_i co-prime with p, and encode it into the pair (e_i, b_i), where $b_i = \log_g y_i$ for g a generator of the multiplicative group $\mathbb{Z}_{p^e}^*$ (for convenience we view a 0 input as p^e). Let $e' = \sum_{i=1}^n e_i$. If $e' \geq e$ then $Mult_m(\mathbf{x}) = 0$; otherwise, it is $\Pi_{i=1}^n x_i = p^{e'} \cdot \Pi_{i=1}^n y_i = p^{e'} \cdot g^{\sum_{i=1}^n b_i}$. Note, that if $e' \geq e$ then its exact value should not be revealed. This is achieved by computing e' as the capped sum of $e_1, \ldots, e_n$. Moreover, if this capped sum equals e, the output is 0 and the ARE should not reveal $\sum_{i=1}^n b_i$. This is immediately solved via the capped sum with payloads ARE, described above (Claim 4.1).

Finally, we consider the case of general m; that is, $m = p_1^{e_1} \cdot p_2^{e_2} \cdots p_k^{e_k}$. In this case, the ARE is constructed by just applying, for each $i \in [k]$, the ARE for $Mult_{p_i^{e_i}}(\mathbf{x})$, which uniquely determine $Mult_m(\mathbf{x})$ via the Chinese Remainder Theorem (CRT). Whenever all the e_i's equal 1, we can use the much more efficient $Mult_{p_i}$ encodings.

4.2 Negative Results for Perfectly Secure ARE

In this section we present some impossibility results for Information-theoretic AREs. These results complement the positive results above, and should also be contrasted with the strong positive results in the *computational* case, presented in the next section.

Towards these negative results, we start by presenting some tools. We first review some facts about the Discrete Fourier Transform of functions representing probability distributions. Then we introduce a new notion that we call "Vector Multiplication Programs" (VMP) that is central to our negative results, and is motivated by the connection to Fourier Transform, and connect it to ARE. Finally we use this connection in to prove negative results for *perfect* information-theoretic ARE of various functions. Proving negative results for *statistical* AREs, remains as an intriguing open problem.

Discrete Fourier Transform for Distributions. The notion of ARE relies on distributions over $\mathbb{G}$, representing the randomized mappings from each input x_i to its encoding; intuitively, we ask that the two distributions $\sum \mathsf{Enc}(x_i)$ and $\sum \mathsf{Enc}(y_i)$ are "close" if $f(\mathbf{x}) = f(\mathbf{y})$ and are "far" if $f(\mathbf{x}) \neq f(\mathbf{y})$. To analyze such probability distributions, it is useful to view them as functions $p_{x_i} : \mathbb{G} \to \mathbb{R}$ (assigning to each element of the group $\mathbb{G}$ its probability to be chosen as the encoding of a certain value x_i), where the group $\mathbb{G}$ is assumed to be finite and Abelian.

The *Discrete Fourier Transform* (DFT) is a "change of basis" that gives a way to express each such function in an orthonormal basis that have convenient properties.

The DFT of any function $f : \mathbb{G} \to \mathbb{C}$ is defined, using a set of basis functions called *characters.* For groups of the form $\mathbb{Z}_m$, the standard characters are $\chi_j : \mathbb{Z}_m \to \mathbb{C}$, defined by $\chi_j(x) = \omega^{jx}$, where ω is the m-th root of unity and $j \in \{0, \ldots, m-1\}$. The change of basis from f to its Fourier representation $\widehat{f}$ can be obtained by viewing f as a length m vector and writing $\widehat{f} = V \cdot f$, where V is an $m \times m$ (normalized) Vandermonde matrix with $V_{i,j} = \omega^{ij}/\sqrt{m}$, for $0 \leq i, j < m$.[4] If $\mathbb{G} = \mathbb{Z}_m^n$ the characters are obtained by products of the above; that is, for $\alpha \in \{0, \ldots, m-1\}^n$, we have $\chi_\alpha : \mathbb{Z}_m^n \to \mathbb{C}$ defined by $\chi_\alpha(x) = \Pi_{j=1}^n \chi_{\alpha_j}(x_j)$. The general case, where the finite Abelian group $\mathbb{G}$ is expressed as a product of cyclic prime order groups, the characters are similarly obtained via product of characters of the corresponding cyclic groups.

If $p, q : \mathbb{G} \to \mathbb{R}$ represent two probability distributions, corresponding to two random variable X, Y over $\mathbb{G}$, then their *convolution*, denoted by $p * q$, represents the distribution of the random variable $X + Y$.[5] That is, for all $z \in \mathbb{G}$, we have $(p * q)(z) = \sum_{x \in \mathbb{G}} p(x) \cdot q(z - x)$.

The next theorem (see, e.g., [34, Thm 8.60]) is extremely useful, stating that in the Fourier representation, the coefficients of the convolution $p * q$ can be obtained simply by multiplying the corresponding coefficients of $\widehat{p}, \widehat{q}$

Proposition 4.4 (Convolution Theorem). *Let $p, q : \mathbb{G} \to \mathbb{R}$ be two distributions. Then, for all α, $\widehat{p * q}(\alpha) = \widehat{p}(\alpha) \cdot \widehat{q}(\alpha)$.*

Vector Multiplication Programs. In this section, we present a model that we term *Vector Multiplication Programs* (VMP), that we will use for proving our negative results for ARE. For intuition, consider a two-argument function $f : D_1 \times D_2 \to R$ and assume that we have an ARE over a group $\mathbb{G}$ for f. Then, we can associate with each value $x \in D_1$ a probability distribution $p_x : \mathbb{G} \to \mathbb{R}$,

---

[4] The notation $\widehat{f}$ is a standard notation for the Fourier representation of f and is used only in Sect. 4.2 of this paper. It is unrelated to the notation of encoding (e.g., $\hat{x}_i$ denotes the encoding of x_i) that we use in other parts of the paper, and is standard in the randomized-encoding literature.

[5] Actually, convolution can be defined not just for functions that correspond to distributions and also the theorem applies to the more general case, but in this paper we will only be interested in the restricted case of distributions.

induced by the encoder Enc_1 and, similarly, with each value $y \in D_2$ a probability distribution $q_y : \mathbb{G} \to \mathbb{R}$, induced by the encoder Enc_2. As explained above, the sum of these two random encodings, is distributed as the *convolution* $p_x * q_y$ and these distribution, over the different (x, y)'s should satisfy Correctness and Security, as required by the definition of ARE. Finally, we rely on the Convolution Theorem, that states that if we represent the probability distributions p_x, q_y using their Fourier representation $\widehat{p}_x, \widehat{q}_y$, then the Fourier representation of $p_x * q_y$ is simply the coordinate wise multiplication of $\widehat{p}_x, \widehat{q}_y$.

For convenience, we present a definition that corresponds to the simpler case of ARE with *perfect* security (but not necessarily perfect correctness). In this case, for any possible output $z \in R$, all inputs x, y such that $f(x, y) = z$ should have the *same* $p_x * q_y$ and hence $\widehat{p_x * q_y}$ is the same, and by the convolution theorem this is just $\widehat{p}_x \cdot \widehat{q}_y$. On the other hand, if $f(x, y) \neq f(x', y')$ then $p_x * q_y, p_{x'} * q_{y'}$ are "far" and $\widehat{p_x * q_y}, \widehat{p_{x'} * q_{y'}}$ are, at least, different. Formally,

Definition 4.5. *A* Vector Multiplication Program (VMP) *for a function $f : D_1 \times \ldots \times D_n \to R$ is a collection of vectors $\{v_{i,x_i}\}_{i \in [n], x_i \in D_i}$ from $\mathbb{C}^s$, for some length s, satisfying the following properties:*

- *Perfect security: If $\mathbf{x}, \mathbf{y}$ are such that $f(\mathbf{x}) = f(\mathbf{y})$ then $\odot_{i=1}^n v_{i,x_i} = \odot_{i=1}^n v_{i,y_i}$, where $\odot$ stands for coordinate-wise multiplication of the vectors.*
- *Weak correctness:*[6] *If $\mathbf{x}, \mathbf{y}$ satisfy $f(\mathbf{x}) \neq f(\mathbf{y})$ then $\odot_{i=1}^n v_{i,x_i} \neq \odot_{i=1}^n v_{i,y_i}$.*

In other words, there are distinct vectors $u_z \in \mathbb{C}^s$, corresponding to all possible output values $z \in R$, such that for all $\mathbf{x}$ such that $f(\mathbf{x}) = z$, we have $\odot_{i=1}^n v_{i,x_i} = u_z$.

The Relation Between VMPs and Perfectly Secure AREs. Next, we formalize the intuition presented in the previous section to show that if a function f admits a perfectly-secure ARE over $\mathbb{G}$ then it also has a VMP with corresponding parameters. Formally,

Theorem 4.6. *Let $\epsilon < 1/2$ and $f : D_1 \times \ldots \times D_n \to R$ be a function with an ϵ-correct, perfectly secure ARE over a group $\mathbb{G}$. Then, f admits a VMP, with vectors in $\mathbb{C}^{|\mathbb{G}|}$.*

Proof. Denote $s = |\mathbb{G}|$ and let $\mathsf{Enc}_1, \ldots, \mathsf{Enc}_n$ be the encoding algorithms of the ARE for f. Let $p_{i,x_i} : \mathbb{G} \to \mathbb{R}$ be the output distribution of $\mathsf{Enc}_i(x_i)$. Let $v_{i,x_i} = \widehat{p_{i,x_i}}$ in $\mathbb{C}^s$ be the Fourier representation of p_{i,x_i}. We next argue that these vectors form a VMP for f.

By perfect security of the ARE, we know that for all $\mathbf{x}$ where $f(\mathbf{x})$ is the same, say z, then $\sum_{i=1}^n \mathsf{Enc}_i(x_i)$ is identically distributed; denote this distribution by V_z and note that we can write V_z as the convolution $p_{1,x_1} * \ldots * p_{n,x_n}$. This implies, by the Convolution Theorem, that for all $\mathbf{x}$'s that are mapped to z we

[6] Since this definition is used for proving negative results, weakening the definition only makes the results stronger.

have the same $\widehat{p_{1,x_1}} \odot \ldots \odot \widehat{p_{n,x_n}}$, which implies, using the definition of the vectors v_{i,x_i} that for all the $\mathbf{x}$'s that are mapped to the same z we have that $\odot_{i=1}^{n} v_{i,x_i}$ is identical. A similar argument, using the ϵ-correctness of the ARE, shows that if $f(\mathbf{x}) \neq f(\mathbf{y})$ then $\odot_{i=1}^{n} v_{i,x_i}$ and $\odot_{i=1}^{n} v_{i,y_i}$ are different.

Remark 4.7. The ARE to VMP transformation above, is what we need for our negative results. Namely, we will show that certain VMPs do not exist and conclude that corresponding AREs cannot exist. It is possible to show certain transformations also from VMP to ARE. We note that, as far as we know, no such VMP to ARE transformation respects efficiency. To see this, consider the example of the two-party MAX function over $[M]$. A (perfectly correct) VMP for this function, can use vectors in $\{0,1\}^{M-1}$ as follows: for any $z \in [M]$ let $v_{1,z} = v_{2,z} = V_z = 0^{z-1}1^{M-z}$. For all x, y it follows that $v_{1,x} \odot v_{2,y} = V_{MAX(x,y)}$. On the other hand, the best ARE that we know for MAX (cf. Theorem 4.1) has exponential in M many encodings.

Functions Admitting VMP. We start by considering two-argument boolean functions f (i.e., functions with range $R = \{0,1\}$). If we also have that the domains are of size 2 (i.e., $|D_1| = |D_2| = 2$), then all boolean functions are either isomorphic to XOR, or isomorphic to OR or constant and hence all have AREs (XOR and the constant functions in a trivial way, and OR as in Theorem 4.1). Next, we consider boolean functions with larger domains and show that except for in degenerate cases, no such function admits a VMP.

Lemma 4.8. *Let $f : D_1 \times D_2 \to \{0,1\}$. Assume that $|D_1| \geq 2, |D_2| \geq 3$ (alternatively, that $|D_1| \geq 3, |D_2| \geq 2$) and that f is non-redundant (i.e., there are no x, x' such that $f(x,y) = f(x',y)$ for all y, and no y, y' such that $f(x,y) = f(x,y')$ for all x). Then, there is no VMP for f.*

Proof. Assume for contradiction, that $\{v_x\}_{x \in D_1}$ and $\{w_y\}_{y \in D_2}$ are vectors in $\mathbb{C}^s$, for some s, that form a VMP for f. Further, denote by u_0, u_1, the distinct vectors in $\mathbb{C}^s$ such that, for all (x,y), if $f(x,y) = b$, for $b \in \{0,1\}$ then $v_x \odot w_y = u_b$. Since $u_0 \neq u_1$ then, for some coordinate j, we have $u_0^j \neq u_1^j$.

Let $x \in D_1$ be such that $f(x,\cdot)$ is not constant (such x exists, as otherwise all rows are identical). Since, $|D_2| \geq 3$, there are $b \in \{0,1\}$ and $y_1, y_2, y_3 \in D_2$ such that $f(x,y_1) = f(x,y_2) = b$ and $f(x,y_3) = 1-b$. Hence, $v_x \odot w_{y_1} = v_x \odot w_{y_2} = u_b$ and, in particular,

$$v_x^j \cdot w_{y_1}^j = v_x^j \cdot w_{y_2}^j.$$

Since f is non-redundant, there is some $x' \in D_1$ such that $f(x',y_1) \neq f(x',y_2)$ which implies that $w_{y_1} \neq w_{y_2}$ and, moreover, since $u_0^j \neq u_1^j$, we have $w_{y_1}^j \neq w_{y_2}^j$. Combining this with the above equation, we get that $v_x^j = 0$. It follows that both u_0^j, u_1^j equal 0, contradicting the choice of j.

Combined with our ARE to VMP transformation, we get that no such function admits an ARE. This leads to characterization of two-party functions with IT-AREs as those that are "isomorphic" to a 2×2 boolean function:

Corollary 4.9. *Let $f : D_1 \times D_2 \to \{0,1\}$ be a Boolean function. Then, f has information theoretic perfectly-secure ARE iff $f(x,y) = g(f_1(x), f_2(y))$, where $f_1 : D_1 \to \{0,1\}, f_2 : D_2 \to \{0,1\}$ and $g : \{0,1\} \times \{0,1\} \to \{0,1\}$.*

Proof. Let f, g, f_1, f_2 be as in the claim. Use an ARE $(\mathsf{Enc}_1, \mathsf{Enc}_2, \mathsf{Dec})$ for g, that exist for all 2×2 Boolean functions. An ARE for f applies the encoder Enc_1 on $f_1(x)$, the encoder Enc_2 on $f_2(x)$, and uses Dec for decoding.

In the reverse direction, assume that there is an ARE for f. Then, there is an ARE for the non-redundant version of f, by using $f_1(x)$ to map every x to a canonical element of its equivalence class (say, the "first"), and similarly $f_2(y)$ to map every y to a canonical element of its equivalence class. By the above lemma, non-redundant Boolean functions have ARE only if $|D_1|, |D_2| \leq 2$. Hence f_1, f_2 are Boolean and f is of the desired form.

Next, we consider (multiparty) functions f with boolean inputs and outputs, and show a condition that rules outs the existence of a VMP for most such f's and, as a corollary, also perfectly-secure AREs for them. Clearly this condition does not hold for constant functions or functions isomorphic to either $XOR_{\leq n}$ or $OR_{\leq n}$.

Lemma 4.10. *Let $f : \{0,1\}^n \to \{0,1\}$. Assume that for some $i \in [n]$, some input value $b \in \{0,1\}$ for x_i and some output value $\alpha \in \{0,1\}$, there are $\mathbf{y}, \mathbf{y}', \mathbf{y}'' \in \{0,1\}^{n-1}$ (inputs for all other $n-1$ variables) such that*

$$f(b, \mathbf{y}) = \alpha, f(b, \mathbf{y}') = \alpha, f(b, \mathbf{y}'') = 1 - \alpha,$$

and

$$f(1-b, \mathbf{y}) = \alpha, f(1-b, \mathbf{y}') = 1 - \alpha, f(1-b, \mathbf{y}'') = 1 - \alpha,$$

Then, there is no VMP for f.

Proof. The proof follows similar ideas to the proof of the previous lemma. Let $u_0 \neq u_1 \in \mathbb{C}^s$ be the two target vectors that correspond to outputs 0 and 1, and let j be a coordinate where $u_0^j \neq u_1^j$.

Assume there is a VMP for f. Let $i, b, \alpha, \mathbf{y}, \mathbf{y}', \mathbf{y}''$, as guaranteed by the claim's assumption. It follows that $v_{i,b} \odot v_{\mathbf{y}} = v_{i,b} \odot v_{\mathbf{y}'}$ (where $v_{\mathbf{y}}$ stands for the product of the $n-1$ vectors corresponding to the bits of $\mathbf{y}$) and, in particular, $v_{i,b}^j \cdot v_{\mathbf{y}}^j = v_{i,b}^j \cdot v_{\mathbf{y}'}^j$. Moreover, $f(1-b, \mathbf{y}) \neq f(1-b, \mathbf{y}')$ and since $u_0^j \neq u_1^j$ we have $v_{\mathbf{y}}^j \neq v_{\mathbf{y}'}^j$ (as both are multiplied by the same $v_{i,1-b_i}^j$). It follows that $v_{i,b}^j = 0$. However, by a similar argument applied to $1-b, \mathbf{y}', \mathbf{y}''$ we will also get that $v_{i,1-b}^j = 0$ which (together with $v_{i,b}^j = 0$) contradicts the assumption that $f(b, \mathbf{y}') \neq f(1-b, \mathbf{y}')$.

Next, we turn to the case of the capped-sum function, which does admit a statistically secure ARE and rule out perfectly secure ARE for it. This follows directly from the following claim. In fact, we rule it out even in the case $n = 2$ and where the inputs come from a small domain.

Claim. There is no VMP for the two-argument capped-sum function $f(x, y)$ over the domain $\{0, 1, 2\}$ and with cap=2.[7]

Proof. Assume that such VMP exists, and denote the VMP vectors corresponding to x by v_0, v_1, v_2, the VMP vectors corresponding to y by w_0, w_1, w_2 and by u_0, u_1, u_2 the distinct target vectors corresponding to the outputs $0, 1, 2$ (respectively). Let j be such that $u_1^j \neq u_2^j$.

Following ideas from the above proofs, since $f(1, 1) = f(1, 2)$ but $f(0, 1) \neq f(0, 2)$ it follows that $v_1^j \cdot w_1^j = v_1^j \cdot w_2^j$ and $w_1^j \neq w_2^j$ and so $v_1^j = 0$. However, since $f(1, 0) \neq f(1, 1)$, we have $v_1 \odot w_0 \neq v_1 \odot w_1$, and by the choice of j this means $v_1^j \cdot w_0^j \neq v_1^j \odot w_1^j$. This contradict the conclusion that $v_1^j = 0$.

5 Computational ARE from Bilinear Maps

Next we show that under standard hardness assumptions, any multi-party function admits a computationally secure ARE scheme (without robustness). To that end we show:

1. A pairing-based ARE scheme for the two-party equality function (Sect. 5.1);
2. A reduction of any two-party boolean function over a polynomial-size domain to equality, with application to computing the two-party string-oblivious-transfer function (Sect. 5.2);
3. An ARE scheme for every efficiently-computable multi-party function, using the two-party string-oblivious-transfer function together with garbled circuits (Sect. 5.3).

5.1 A Pairing-Based Two-Party Equality Scheme

Background: Pairing Groups and Squaring XDH. To comply with our "additive RE" frame of mind, we use additive notations for our pairing-friendly groups. Otherwise, the notations below are similar to [16, Sec 3.1].

Parameters. A "Pairing parameter-generator" is an efficient (possibly randomized) procedure $\mathcal{G}$, taking as input the security parameter λ. It outputs a description of additive groups G_1, G_2, G_T of the same order q, distinguished generators $g_1 \in G_1$ and $g_2 \in G_2$, efficient addition/subtraction procedures for these groups, and an efficiently computable and nontrivial bilinear map $e : G_1 \times G_2 \to G_T$. A distinguished generator in G_T can be computed as $g_T := e(g_1, g_2)$.

We require that $q > 2^\lambda$, and assume below for simplicity that the order q of these groups is known and a prime (but our protocols can easily be adjusted to the unknown-order, non-prime case). Sampling random elements in these groups can be done by drawing $\rho \leftarrow \mathbb{Z}_q$ and computing $x := \rho \cdot g_*$. We denote $(q, G_1, G_2, G_T, g_1, g_2, g_T, e) \leftarrow \mathcal{G}(1^\lambda)$.

Also, our protocols work in either the symmetric case ($G_1 = G_2$) or the asymmetric case ($G_1 \neq G_2$). In the symmetric case we will still need to have $g_1 \neq g_2$, and we assume that it is hard to compute $DLOG_{g_1}(g_2)$.

[7] In fact, the proof rules out even the case with $D_1 = \{0, 1\}, D_2 = \{0, 1, 2\}$.

Squaring XDH. Recall that the XDH assumption (for the asymmetric case $G_1 \neq G_2$) simply asserts that the standard decision Diffie-Hellman hardness assumption holds in G_1. Similarly, squaring-XDH asserts that decision-squaring-DH holds in G_1.

Definition 5.1 (Squaring XDH). *The decision Squaring-XDH holds for a parameter-generator $\mathcal{G}$, if the following distribution ensembles are computationally indistinguishable: $SQ_\lambda := (\mathsf{pp}_\lambda,\ \rho{\cdot}g_1,\ \rho^2{\cdot}g_1)$, and $U_\lambda := (\mathsf{pp}_\lambda,\ \rho{\cdot}g_1,\ \rho'{\cdot}g_1)$, where $\mathsf{pp}_\lambda = (q, G_1, G_2, G_T, g_1, g_2, g_T, e) \leftarrow \mathcal{G}(1^\lambda)$ and $\rho, \rho' \leftarrow \mathbb{Z}_q$.*

We now describe our ARE scheme for two-party equality. Security of this scheme can be reduced to a hardness assumption in paring groups that we call ASDH, which is weaker than Squaring XDH. (ASDH is implied by Squaring SDH, but it could plausibly hold also in the symmetric setting $G_1 = G_2$, where Squaring XDH is easy.) The two-party equality function over domain D is

$$f_{eq} : D \times D \to \{0,1\}, \quad f_{eq}(x_1, x_2) = \begin{cases} 1 & \text{if } x_1 = x_2, \\ 0 & \text{otherwise.} \end{cases}$$

For our pairing-based protocol we let $D = \{0,1\}^\ell$, and use $\mathcal{G}(1^{\max(\lambda,\ell+1)})$ to ensure that the order q of the pairing groups is more than $2^{\ell+1}$. We then use an injective embedding function $\mathsf{emb} : \{0,1\}^\ell \to \left[1, \frac{q-1}{2}\right]$ to embed the parties' inputs as integers between 1 and $\frac{q-1}{2}$. For example, $\mathsf{emb}(s) = \mathsf{bin}(s) + 1$, with $\mathsf{bin}(s)$ is the integer whose ℓ-bit binary expansion is s. Since it is injective then $x_1 = x_2$ if and only if $\mathsf{emb}(x_1) = \mathsf{emb}(x_2)$, and since the range is $\left[1, \frac{q-1}{2}\right]$ then $\mathsf{emb}(x_1) + \mathsf{emb}(x_2) \neq 0 \pmod q$ for any $x_1, x_2 \in \{0,1\}^\ell$. The protocol is described in Fig. 1.

Correctness. Denote $\delta = \chi_1 - \chi_2$, so we have $e(y_1, y_2) = (\sigma_1 + \sigma_2)(\chi_1\sigma_1 - \chi_2\sigma_2) \cdot g_T = \left(\chi_1\sigma_1^2 - \chi_2\sigma_2^2 + (\chi_1 - \chi_2)\sigma_1\sigma_2\right) \cdot g_T = y_3 + \delta\sigma_1\sigma_2 \cdot g_T$. If $\delta \neq 0$ then equality only holds when $\sigma_1 = 0$ or $\sigma_2 = 0$, which happens with probability at most $2/q$.

Security. Note that regardless of the inputs χ_1, χ_2, the elements y_1, y_2 that the evaluator sees are uniform and independent in G_1, G_2, respectively. The reason is that $\chi_1 \neq -\chi_2$, and therefore $\sigma_1 + \sigma_2$ and $\chi_1\sigma_1 - \chi_2\sigma_2$ are two linearly independent equations in σ_1, σ_2.

It follows that for the case $\chi_1 = \chi_2$ we get information-theoretical security: In this case the evaluator's view is just $(\rho_1 g_1, \rho_2 g_2, \rho_1\rho_2 g_T)$ (for independent uniform $\rho_1, \rho_2 \in \mathbb{Z}_q$), regardless of the actual values χ_1, χ_2.

For the case $\chi_1 \neq \chi_2$ we only get computational indistinguishability, under a hardness assumption that we call additive-squaring-DH (ASDH).

Parameters: Parameter-generating procedure $\mathcal{G}$, security parameter λ, input length ℓ.
Setup$(1^\lambda, 1^\ell)$:

1. Let $\lambda' = \max(\lambda, \ell+1)$, set $\mathsf{pp} \leftarrow \mathcal{G}(1^{\lambda'})$ (recall that $q > 2^{\ell+1}$);
2. Let $\mathsf{emb} : \{0,1\}^\ell \to [1, \frac{q-1}{2}]$ be injective (e.g., $\mathsf{emb}(s) = \mathsf{bin}(s) + 1$).

Encoding, $\mathsf{Enc}(\mathsf{pp}, i, x_i)$:

3. Embed $\chi_i := \mathsf{emb}(x_i) \in [1, \frac{q-1}{2}]$;
4. Choose at random $\sigma_i \leftarrow Z_q$;
5. Send $\hat{x}_i = \left(\sigma_i \cdot g_1,\ (-1)^i \chi_i \sigma_i \cdot g_2,\ (-1)^i \chi_i \sigma_i^2 \cdot g_T\right)$.

Evaluation, $\mathsf{Dec}\big(\mathsf{pp},\ y_1 = (\sigma_1+\sigma_2)g_1,\ y_2 = (\chi_1\sigma_1 - \chi_2\sigma_2)g_2,\ y_3 = (\chi_1\sigma_1^2 - \chi_2\sigma_2^2)g_T\big)$:

6. If $e(y_1, y_2) = y_3$ output 1, otherwise output 0.

Fig. 1. Pairing-based computational ARE for equality

Definition 5.2 (Additive Squaring DH). *The decision ASDH holds for a parameter-generator $\mathcal{G}$, if for every efficiently computable $\eta = \eta(q) \in \mathbb{Z}_q^*$, the following two distribution ensembles are computationally indistinguishable:*

$$D[\eta]_\lambda := \left(\mathsf{pp}_\lambda,\ \rho_1 g_1,\ \rho_2 g_2,\ (\rho_1^2 + \eta\rho_2^2)g_T\right) \text{ and } R_\lambda := \left(\mathsf{pp}_\lambda,\ \rho_1 g_1,\ \rho_2 g_2,\ \rho_3 g_T\right), \tag{1}$$

where $\mathsf{pp}_\lambda = (q, G_1, G_2, G_T, g_1, g_2, g_T, e) \leftarrow \mathcal{G}(1^\lambda)$ *and* $\rho_1, \rho_2, \rho_3 \leftarrow \mathbb{Z}_q$.

In the full version we prove the following two lemmas:

Lemma 5.3. *Under ASDH, the scheme from Fig. 1 is a secure ARE scheme for the equality function.*

Lemma 5.4. *Any distinguisher for ASDH can be converted to a distinguisher for Squaring XDH with the same advantage.*

Remark 5.5 (A plain-model construction). As described above, the ASDH-based construction requires a trusted setup to choose the groups and their generators. We can get a setup-free construction by settling on a less standard (but equally believable) hardness assumption, where each value of λ is deterministically mapped into some groups and generators. (For example by derandomizing the usual setup, drawing the randomness from a hash function that can be modeled as a random oracle.)

5.2 From Equality to Any Small Function

We observe that for any boolean function f over a small domain, an ARE scheme for f can be obtained from an ARE for equality.

Lemma 5.6. *Let $f : D_1 \times D_2 \to \{0,1\}$ be a boolean function over finite domains D_1, D_2. Assume w.l.o.g. that $|D_1| \le |D_2|$, and let z be an arbitrary symbol, $z \notin D_1$. Then a secure ARE scheme $\mathcal{S}_{eq}$ for equality over the domain $D_1' = D_1 \cup \{z\}$ can be converted into a secure ARE scheme $\mathcal{S}_f$ for f, where the communication complexity of $\mathcal{S}_f$ is at most $|D_1|$ times larger than that of $\mathcal{S}_{eq}$.*

Proof. Consider the $|D_1| \times |D_2|$ truth table for f, and let $k \le |D_1|$ be (an upper bound on) the largest number of 1's in any column of this table.

The Scheme $\mathcal{S}_f$. On inputs x, y, the parties run in parallel k copies of the equality scheme $\mathcal{S}_{eq}$:

- Party 1 uses their input x in all these copies.
- For Party 2, consider the column corresponding to y in the truth table, and let $x_1, x_2, \ldots, x_{k'}$ be all the possible party-1 inputs for which $f(x_i, y) = 1$. (Recall that $k' \le k$). Party 2 concatenates $k - k'$ copies of the value $z \notin D_1$, yielding a sequence of length exactly k, $(x_1, \ldots, x_{k'}, z, \ldots, z) \in {D'_1}^k$.
  Party 2 also chooses a shift amount at random $\delta \leftarrow [1, k]$. Then in the i'th copy of the equality scheme, Party 2 uses the input $x_{i-\delta}$ if $i - \delta \le k'$, and the input z if $i - \delta > k'$ (with index arithmetic modulo k).

The evaluator gets k sums $y_1, \ldots, y_k$ from the k copies of $\mathcal{S}_{eq}$, and decodes them to get the k results $b_i = \mathsf{Dec}(\mathsf{pp}, y_i) \in \{0, 1\}$. It outputs 1 if there is any match $b_i = 1$, and outputs 0 if they are all 0 (i.e., no match).

Correctness. Since Party 1 uses $x \in D_1$ in all the copies of $\mathcal{S}_{eq}$ and Party 2 uses $k' \le k$ distinct inputs from D_1 and the value $z \notin D_1$, then at most one of them will be a match. Moreover, it can only be one of the x_i's for $i \le k'$ (since party 1 never inputs the value z). Thus, there is a match if and only if $x = x_i$ for some $i \le k'$, which means that $f(x, y) = f(x_i, y) = 1$.

Security. Since the underlying $\mathcal{S}_{eq}$ is a secure ARE scheme, then the transcripts of all the non-matching instances are indistinguishable from some distribution $\mathcal{D}$, whereas the matching instance (if it exists) has transcript indistinguishable from another distribution $\mathcal{D}'$. Moreover, due to the random shift amount δ, the location of the matching instance (if it exists) is random in $[1, k]$.

Therefore, for any x, y such that $f(x, y) = 0$ the evaluator's view is indistinguishable from $\mathcal{D}^k$, and for any x, y such that $f(x, y) = 1$ the evaluator's view is indistinguishable from $(\mathcal{D}^{\delta-1}, \mathcal{D}', \mathcal{D}^{k-\delta})$ for a uniform index $\delta \in [1, k]$.

5.3 Computational ARE for General Functions

Using Lemma 5.6, we can use ARE for equality to implement ARE for Oblivious-Transfer, and then extend it to general functions making a standard use of garbled circuits (see, e.g., [7]).

Lemma 5.7. *Let $f : (\{0,1\}^*)^* \to \{0,1\}^*$ be an n-party function as in Definition 3.1, and let $\{C_{\lambda,n,\ell}\}$ be a boolean circuit family that computes f. Given a secure ARE scheme $\mathcal{S}_{eq}$ for equality over domains of size three, and a secure PRG, one can construct a computationally secure ARE scheme $\mathcal{S}_f$ for f, with complexity at most $2\lambda\ell(n-1) \cdot \mathsf{complexity}(\mathcal{S}_{eq}) + O(\lambda \cdot |C_{\lambda,n,\ell}|)$.*

Proof. We build an ARE scheme for f from a garbling of $C_{\lambda,n,\ell}$ [35] (which can be implemented from any secure PRG), along with the two-party ARE scheme for string-OT that we can get from Lemma 5.6.

Given the public parameters $\mathsf{pp} \leftarrow \mathsf{Setup}(1^\lambda, 1^n, 1^\ell)$ and a description of the circuit $C_{\lambda,n,\ell}$, Party 1 will construct and send to the evaluator a garbling of $C_{\lambda,n,\ell}$, and will run with each other party ℓ instances of $\mathcal{S}_{sot}$ for strings of length λ, one for each of their input bits. In each instance, Party 1 will play the role of the sender (Party 2 from $\mathcal{S}_{sot}$) using as input the two labels for that input wire, and the other party will play the receiver (Party 1 from $\mathcal{S}_{sot}$) using the corresponding input bit as the OT choice bit. (Party 1 will also send to the evaluator the labels corresponding to its own input bits.) The evaluator will therefore receive the garbled circuit, along with one label for each input wire. It will then evaluate the garbled circuit and compute the output. Correctness and security follow from those of $\mathcal{S}_{sot}$ and the garbling scheme. For complexity, we have $\ell(n-1)$ instances of $\mathcal{S}_{sot}$, each of complexity $2\lambda \cdot \mathsf{complexity}(\mathcal{S}_{sot})$, and in addition sending the garbled circuit itself.

Theorem 5.8 (Computational ARE from ASDH). *Under the ASDH assumption, there exists a computationally secure ARE scheme for every polynomial-time computable multiparty function f.*

Proof. Follows directly from Lemmas 5.3 and 5.7, and the fact that ASDH implies a secure PRG.

Finally, we note that by using information-theoretic garbling (cf. [31]), one can obtain an unconditional variant of Lemma 5.7, as stated in the following completeness theorem.

Theorem 5.9 (Equality is complete). *If there is a statistical ARE for equality over domains of size three, then every function f admits a statistical ARE, with communication complexity polynomial in the branching-program size of f.*

6 From ARE to Multiparty Randomized Encoding

The notion of a multiparty randomized encoding (MPRE) [4] is a natural extension of the notion of randomized encoding of functions from [7,30] to the multiparty setting. We say that an n-party function f has a t-secure MPRE in a function class $\mathcal{G}$ if there is an n-party function $g \in \mathcal{G}$ such that f can be realized with security against at most t *semi-honest* parties by performing a local (randomized) computation on the inputs followed by a single call to g. Here we consider an *external-output* variant of MPRE, where the output of g is public. Namely, the output of g is delivered not only to the n parties but also to an external party, who should only learn the output of f. This stronger notion of MPRE will be more convenient for our purposes. We will refer to the usual notion of MPRE as *internal-output* MPRE. Finally, unless stated otherwise, we will assume a *full security* threshold of $t = n - 1$.

The power of randomized encoding comes from the implementation class $\mathcal{G}$ being "simpler" than the original function f. Two related notions of simplicity that were studied in the literature are *algebraic degree* (say, over $\mathbb{F}_2$), and *locality.* We say that an MPRE has locality d if each output bit of g depends on the inputs of at most d *parties.*

Note that any d-local external-output MPRE can be realized via parallel calls to a $(d+1)$-party "internal-output" functionality, by just using an additional party to receive the output.

The main open question about MPRE is whether every n-party function has a degree-2 (or 2-local) information-theoretic MPRE with *full security* (i.e., with $t = n-1$). Even in a computational setting, such a construction is only known based on (a non-black-box use of) oblivious transfer [4]. The best known construction of information-theoretic degree-2 MPRE [6] is t-secure only for $t < 2n/3$.[8]

Insisting on full security, the following results are known.

Lemma 6.1 (Fully secure 3-local, degree-3 MPRE). *[3, Theorem 6.4]. Every n-party function f admits a 3-local degree-3 fully secure external-output MPRE g that consists of multiple copies of the function*

$$\mathsf{3MULTPlus}((x_1, z_1), (x_2, z_2), (x_3, z_3)) = x_1 x_2 x_3 + z_1 + z_2 + z_3$$

(defined over $\mathbb{F}_2$) over different sets of inputs. Requiring the MPRE to be efficient, this holds either with information-theoretic security for f in NC^1 or with computational security for general polynomial-time f, assuming one-way functions.

By Lemma 6.1, to obtain a fully-secure 2-local, degree-2 MPRE for general functions, it suffices to obtain such an MPRE for the function $\mathsf{3MULTPlus}$. We will construct such an MPRE assuming the existence of *robust* ARE for a related (but still constant-size) 3-party function. Our proof relies on the following lemma, which is a simple generalization[9] of [3, Lemma 6.1].

Lemma 6.2 (2-local MPRE for sum of 2-local functions). *Let g be an n-party function of the form $g(x_1, \ldots, x_n) = \sum_{1 \le i < j \le n} g_{ij}(x_i, x_j)$, where addition is over some finite Abelian group. Then, g has a perfect 2-local MPRE.*

Remark 6.3 (Public parameters vs. plain model). For simplicity, in the computational setting we will assume that the ARE works in the "plain model" without any public parameters pp. If the ARE does have public parameters, then so will the resulting MPRE. Note, however, that the indistinguishability variant will suffice for our purposes. Hence, we can instantiate our resettable-MPC-based construction (in the full version) with a protocol in the plain model, which (when instantiating ideal obfuscation by iO) yields a candidate for general indistinguishability-robust ARE in the plain model.

---

[8] For standard internal-output MPRE, this can be improved to $t \le 2n/3$.

[9] The lemma from [3] applies to degree-2 polynomials. Here we replace each monomial by a 2-local function.

We now prove our main technical theorem, which implies a 2-local encoding for 3MULTPlus.

Theorem 6.4 (2-local MPRE from robust ARE: The constant-size case). *Suppose every 3-party function f with constant-size input domains admits an indistinguishability-robust computational ARE (resp., robust statistical ARE) in the plain model. Then, every such f admits a computationally (resp., statistically) secure 2-local (external-output) MPRE.*

Proof. (sketch) While the 3-party case suffices for our purposes, we will in fact prove the theorem for any n-party f with constant input size per party. Also, to simplify notation we will only consider here the statistical case. The computational case is similar.

By Lemma 6.2 and MPRE composition, it suffices to show that every function f as in the theorem statement admits an MPRE where g is a sum of 2-local functions. Since we assume that f has a robust ARE, then a first attempt is to use g that directly computes the sum of the ARE messages. (This is a degenerate special case, since each 1-local function is also 2-local.) However, even a robust ARE still allows the corrupted parties to learn the residual function induced by the inputs of the honest parties, which violates MPRE security.

To avoid leaking the residual function, we define a new N-party function f', for $N = \binom{n}{2}$ "virtual parties," which applies a simple *constant-size* pairwise multiparty authentication for the inputs of f. Concretely, for each pair of parties $1 \leq i < j \leq n$, there is a virtual party P_{ij} whose input to f' is a pair $x^{ij} = (x_i^{ij}, x_j^{ij})$. The function f' checks that all input pairs are consistent with some global input vector $(x_1, \ldots, x_n)$, outputting $f(x_1, \ldots, x_n)$ if it is and $\perp$ otherwise. Namely,

$$f'(x^{1,2}, \ldots, x^{n-1,n}) = \begin{cases} f(x_1, \ldots, x_n) & \text{if } \exists x_1, \ldots, x_n \text{ s.t. } \forall i, j, x^{i,j} = (x_i, x_j) \\ \perp & \text{otherwise} \end{cases}.$$

Note that if f has constant-size input domains then so does f'.

We now use a robust ARE for f' to define an MPRE for f in which the function g is a sum of 2-local functions. By Lemma 6.2, this suffices to get a 2-local MPRE for f. The function g takes from each party P_i the following inputs: its original input x_i, and additional inputs ρ_{ij} (for all $j \neq i$) that will be used to generate the ARE messages of virtual parties P_{ij}.

Letting $\Pi = (\mathsf{Enc}_{ij}, \mathsf{Dec})$ be a robust ARE for f', the function g is:

$$g\left((x_1, (\rho_{1j})_{j \neq 1}), \ldots, (x_n, (\rho_{nj})_{j \neq n})\right) = \sum_{1 \leq i < j \leq n} \mathsf{Enc}_{ij}((x_i, x_j); \rho_{ij} \oplus \rho_{ji})$$

where summation is over the ARE group, and $\mathsf{Enc}_{ij}((x_i, x_j); \rho)$ denotes an ARE encoding for f' of input (x_i, x_j) (for virtual party P_{ij}) using randomness ρ. By construction, the function g is indeed a sum of 2-local functions, as required. The output of f can be recovered from the output of g by applying the ARE decoder

Dec of Π. It remains to argue that a set of corrupted parties can learn nothing (given their inputs, randomness, and the output of g) beyond the output of f.

We refer to the ARE message of virtual party P_{ij} as being *fully-corrupted* if both i, j are corrupted and *partially-honest* otherwise. We now argue that, conditioned on the adversary's inputs and randomness, the extra information revealed by the output of g can be simulated given the sum of the partially-honest ARE messages. This follows because: (1) conditioned on the adversary's randomness, a partially-honest message is distributed as it should (since either ρ_{ij} or ρ_{ji} is unknown to the adversary), and (2) g outputs the sum of all ARE messages of virtual parties, where the fully-corrupted ones can be determined by the adversary.

It remains to argue that learning the sum of the partially-honest ARE messages reveals no more than the output of f. By the robust ARE security of Π, this sum only reveals the residual function of f' restricted to partially-honest inputs (x_i, x_j). Assuming at least one party is honest, every input x_k is included in at least one such partially-honest pair. Hence, by the definition of f', the residual function induced by the partially-honest inputs depends only on $f(x_1, \ldots, x_n)$, as required.

Since a 2-local MPRE implies a degree-2 MPRE [3], Theorem 6.4 can be viewed as a barrier for ruling out a degree-2 statistical MPRE for general functions. Indeed, this would require proving the same for robust statistical ARE. Such ARE look incomparable to degree-2 statistical randomized encodings [30], which are another barrier for ruling out degree-2 MPRE [3]. See Sect. 1.3 for further discussion.

Combining Theorem 6.4 with Lemma 6.1, using a natural composition property for MPRE, we get the following.

Corollary 6.5 (MPRE from robust ARE: The general case). *Suppose every constant-size 3-party function f admits an indistinguishability-robust (resp., statistically robust) ARE in the plain model. Then every n-party f admits a 2-local degree-2 (external-output) MPRE, or alternatively a non-interactive protocol using parallel invocations of a 3-party functionality.*

Requiring the MPRE to be efficient, this holds for computational security if one-way functions exist, and for statistical security if both f and the ARE encoding are in NC^1.

Acknowledgements. We thank Jonathan Ullman for helpful discussions on differential privacy in the shuffle model and the anonymous reviewers for their comments. Y. Ishai and E. Kushilevitz were supported by ISF grant 2774/20 and BSF grant 2018393. Y. Ishai was additionally supported by ERC Project NTSC (742754).

References

1. Agarwal, N., Anand, S., Prabhakaran, M.: Uncovering algebraic structures in the MPC landscape. In: Ishai, Y., Rijmen, V. (eds.) EUROCRYPT 2019, Part II. LNCS, vol. 11477, pp. 381–406. Springer, Cham (2019). https://doi.org/10.1007/978-3-030-17656-3_14
2. Applebaum, B.: Garbled circuits as randomized encodings of functions: a primer. In: Tutorials on the Foundations of Cryptography. ISC, pp. 1–44. Springer, Cham (2017). https://doi.org/10.1007/978-3-319-57048-8_1
3. Applebaum, B., Brakerski, Z., Garg, S., Ishai, Y., Srinivasan, A.: Separating two-round secure computation from oblivious transfer. In: Vidick, T. (ed.) 11th Innovations in Theoretical Computer Science Conference, ITCS 2020(January), pp. 12–14 (2020). Seattle, Washington, USA. LIPIcs, vol. 151, pp. 71:1–71:18. Schloss Dagstuhl - Leibniz-Zentrum für Informatik (2020). https://doi.org/10.4230/LIPIcs.ITCS.2020.71, https://eprint.iacr.org/2020/116.pdf
4. Applebaum, B., Brakerski, Z., Tsabary, R.: Perfect secure computation in two rounds. SIAM J. Comput. **50**(1), 68–97 (2021). https://doi.org/10.1137/19M1272044
5. Applebaum, B., Haramaty, N., Ishai, Y., Kushilevitz, E., Vaikuntanathan, V.: Low-complexity cryptographic hash functions. In: Papadimitriou, C.H. (ed.) 8th Innovations in Theoretical Computer Science Conference, ITCS 2017, 9–11 January 2017, Berkeley, CA, USA. LIPIcs, vol. 67, pp. 7:1–7:31. Schloss Dagstuhl - Leibniz-Zentrum für Informatik (2017). https://doi.org/10.4230/LIPIcs.ITCS.2017.7, https://doi.org/10.4230/LIPIcs.ITCS.2017.7
6. Applebaum, B., Ishai, Y., Karni, O., Patra, A.: Quadratic multiparty randomized encodings beyond honest majority and their applications. In: Dodis, Y., Shrimpton, T. (eds.) Advances in Cryptology - CRYPTO 2022–42nd Annual International Cryptology Conference, CRYPTO 2022, Santa Barbara, CA, USA, 15–18 August 2022, Proceedings, Part IV. LNCS, vol. 13510, pp. 453–482. Springer, Cham (2022). https://doi.org/10.1007/978-3-031-15985-5_16
7. Applebaum, B., Ishai, Y., Kushilevitz, E.: Cryptography in NC^0. SIAM J. Comput. **36**(4), 845–888 (2006). https://doi.org/10.1137/S0097539705446950
8. Applebaum, B., Ishai, Y., Kushilevitz, E.: How to garble arithmetic circuits. SIAM J. Comput. **43**(2), 905–929 (2014). https://doi.org/10.1137/120875193
9. Badrinarayanan, S., Ishai, Y., Khurana, D., Sahai, A., Wichs, D.: Refuting the dream XOR lemma via ideal obfuscation and resettable MPC. In: ITC 2022, LIPIcs, vol. 230, pp. 10:1–10:21 (2022)
10. Balle, B., Bell, J., Gascón, A., Nissim, K.: Private summation in the multi-message shuffle model. In: Ligatti, J., Ou, X., Katz, J., Vigna, G. (eds.) CCS 2020: 2020 ACM SIGSAC Conference on Computer and Communications Security, Virtual Event, USA, 9–13 November 2020, pp. 657–676. ACM (2020). https://doi.org/10.1145/3372297.3417242
11. Barak, B., Bitansky, N., Canetti, R., Kalai, Y.T., Paneth, O., Sahai, A.: Obfuscation for evasive functions. In: Lindell, Y. (ed.) TCC 2014. LNCS, vol. 8349, pp. 26–51. Springer, Heidelberg (2014). https://doi.org/10.1007/978-3-642-54242-8_2
12. Barak, B., et al.: On the (IM)possibility of obfuscating programs. J. ACM **59**(2), 6:1–6:48 (2012). https://doi.org/10.1145/2160158.2160159
13. Beimel, A., Gabizon, A., Ishai, Y., Kushilevitz, E., Meldgaard, S., Paskin-Cherniavsky, A.: Non-interactive secure multiparty computation. In: Garay, J.A., Gennaro, R. (eds.) CRYPTO 2014, Part II. LNCS, vol. 8617, pp. 387–404. Springer, Heidelberg (2014). https://doi.org/10.1007/978-3-662-44381-1_22

14. Ben-Or, M., Goldwasser, S., Wigderson, A.: Completeness theorems for non-cryptographic fault-tolerant distributed computation. In: Proceedings of the Twentieth Annual ACM Symposium on Theory of Computing, pp. 1–10 (1988)
15. Bonawitz, K.A., et al.: Practical secure aggregation for privacy-preserving machine learning. In: Thuraisingham, B., Evans, D., Malkin, T., Xu, D. (eds.) Proceedings of the 2017 ACM SIGSAC Conference on Computer and Communications Security, CCS 2017, Dallas, TX, USA, October 30–November 03, 2017. pp. 1175–1191. ACM (2017). https://doi.org/10.1145/3133956.3133982
16. Boneh, D., Franklin, M.: Identity-based encryption from the weil pairing. SIAM J. Comput. **32**(3), 586–615 (2003). https://doi.org/10.1137/S0097539701398521
17. Chaum, D., Crépeau, C., Damgård, I.: Multiparty unconditionally secure protocols (extended abstract). In: ACM STOC (1988)
18. Cheu, A., Smith, A., Ullman, J., Zeber, D., Zhilyaev, M.: Distributed differential privacy via shuffling. In: Ishai, Y., Rijmen, V. (eds.) EUROCRYPT 2019. LNCS, vol. 11476, pp. 375–403. Springer, Cham (2019). https://doi.org/10.1007/978-3-030-17653-2_13
19. Corrigan-Gibbs, H., Boneh, D.: Prio: private, robust, and scalable computation of aggregate statistics. In: Akella, A., Howell, J. (eds.) 14th USENIX Symposium on Networked Systems Design and Implementation, NSDI 2017, Boston, MA, USA, 27–29 March 2017, pp. 259–282. USENIX Association (2017). https://www.usenix.org/conference/nsdi17/technical-sessions/presentation/corrigan-gibbs
20. Erlingsson, Ú., et al.: Encode, shuffle, analyze privacy revisited: Formalizations and empirical evaluation. CoRR abs/2001.03618 (2020). https://arxiv.org/abs/2001.03618
21. Feige, U., Kilian, J., Naor, M.: A minimal model for secure computation (extended abstract). In: Leighton, F.T., Goodrich, M.T. (eds.) Proceedings of the Twenty-Sixth Annual ACM Symposium on Theory of Computing, 23–25 May 1994, Montréal, Québec, Canada, pp. 554–563. ACM (1994). https://doi.org/10.1145/195058.195408
22. Ghazi, B., Manurangsi, P., Pagh, R., Velingker, A.: Private aggregation from fewer anonymous messages. In: Canteaut, A., Ishai, Y. (eds.) EUROCRYPT 2020. LNCS, vol. 12106, pp. 798–827. Springer, Cham (2020). https://doi.org/10.1007/978-3-030-45724-2_27
23. Goldreich, O., Micali, S., Wigderson, A.: How to play any mental game, or a completeness theorem for protocols with honest majority. In: Providing Sound Foundations for Cryptography: On the Work of Shafi Goldwasser and Silvio Micali, pp. 307–328. ACM (2019)
24. Goyal, V., Maji, H.K.: Stateless cryptographic protocols. In: Ostrovsky, R. (ed.) IEEE 52nd Annual Symposium on Foundations of Computer Science, FOCS 2011. pp. 678–687. IEEE Computer Society (2011). https://doi.org/10.1109/FOCS.2011.74
25. Goyal, V., Sahai, A.: Resettably secure computation. In: Joux, A. (ed.) EUROCRYPT 2009. LNCS, vol. 5479, pp. 54–71. Springer, Heidelberg (2009). https://doi.org/10.1007/978-3-642-01001-9_3
26. Halevi, S., Ishai, Y., Jain, A., Komargodski, I., Sahai, A., Yogev, E.: Non-interactive multiparty computation without correlated randomness. In: Takagi, T., Peyrin, T. (eds.) ASIACRYPT 2017, Part III. LNCS, vol. 10626, pp. 181–211. Springer, Cham (2017). https://doi.org/10.1007/978-3-319-70700-6_7
27. Halevi, S., Ishai, Y., Kushilevitz, E., Rabin, T.: Best possible information-theoretic MPC. In: Beimel, A., Dziembowski, S. (eds.) TCC 2018. LNCS, vol. 11240, pp. 255–281. Springer, Cham (2018). https://doi.org/10.1007/978-3-030-03810-6_10

28. Halevi, S., Ishai, Y., Kushilevitz, E., Rabin, T.: Additive randomized encodings and their applications. IACR Cryptology ePrint Archive (2023). https://eprint.iacr.org/
29. Ishai, Y.: Randomization techniques for secure computation. In: Prabhakaran, M., Sahai, A. (eds.) Secure Multi-Party Computation, Cryptology and Information Security Series, vol. 10, pp. 222–248. IOS Press (2013). https://doi.org/10.3233/978-1-61499-169-4-222
30. Ishai, Y., Kushilevitz, E.: Randomizing polynomials: a new representation with applications to round-efficient secure computation. In: 41st Annual Symposium on Foundations of Computer Science, FOCS 2000, 12–14 November 2000, Redondo Beach, California, USA, pp. 294–304. IEEE Computer Society (2000). https://doi.org/10.1109/SFCS.2000.892118
31. Ishai, Y., Kushilevitz, E.: Perfect constant-round secure computation via perfect randomizing polynomials. In: Widmayer, P., Eidenbenz, S., Triguero, F., Morales, R., Conejo, R., Hennessy, M. (eds.) ICALP 2002. LNCS, vol. 2380, pp. 244–256. Springer, Heidelberg (2002). https://doi.org/10.1007/3-540-45465-9_22
32. Ishai, Y., Kushilevitz, E., Ostrovsky, R., Sahai, A.: Cryptography from anonymity. In: 47th Annual IEEE Symposium on Foundations of Computer Science (FOCS 2006), pp. 239–248. IEEE Computer Society (2006). https://doi.org/10.1109/FOCS.2006.25
33. Jain, A., Lin, H., Luo, J., Wichs, D.: The pseudorandom oracle model and ideal obfuscation. IACR Cryptol. ePrint Arch, p. 1204 (2022). https://eprint.iacr.org/2022/1204
34. O'Donnell, R.: Analysis of Boolean Functions. Cambridge University Press, Cambridge (2014). https://arxiv.org/abs/2105.10386
35. Yao, A.C.C.: How to generate and exchange secrets. In: 27th Annual Symposium on Foundations of Computer Science, pp. 162–167 (1986)

How to Recover a Secret with $O(n)$ Additions

Benny Applebaum[1(✉)], Oded Nir[1], and Benny Pinkas[2]

[1] Tel Aviv University, Tel Aviv, Israel
bennyap@post.tau.ac.il
[2] Aptos Labs and Bar Ilan University, Ramat Gan, Israel
benny@pinkas.net

Abstract. Threshold cryptography is typically based on the idea of secret-sharing a private-key $s \in F$ "in the exponent" of some cryptographic group G, or more generally, encoding s in some linearly homomorphic domain. In each invocation of the threshold system (e.g., for signing or decrypting) an "encoding" of the secret is being recovered and so the complexity, measured as the number of group multiplications over G, is equal to the number of F-additions that are needed to reconstruct the secret. Motivated by this scenario, we initiate the study of n-party secret-sharing schemes whose reconstruction algorithm makes a minimal number of *additions*. The complexity of existing schemes either scales linearly with $n \log |F|$ (e.g., Shamir, CACM'79) or, at least, quadratically with n independently of the size of the domain F (e.g., Cramer-Xing, EUROCRYPT '20). This leaves open the existence of a secret sharing whose recovery algorithm can be computed by performing only $O(n)$ additions.

We resolve the question in the affirmative and present such a near-threshold secret sharing scheme that provides privacy against unauthorized sets of density at most τ_p, and correctness for authorized sets of density at least τ_c, for any given arbitrarily close constants $\tau_p < \tau_c$. Reconstruction can be computed by making at most $O(n)$ additions and, in addition, (1) the share size is constant, (2) the sharing procedure also makes only $O(n)$ additions, and (3) the scheme is a blackbox secret-sharing scheme, i.e., the sharing and reconstruction algorithms work universally for all finite abelian groups F. Prior to our work, no such scheme was known even without features (1)–(3) and even for the ramp setting where τ_p and τ_c are far apart. As a by-product, we derive the first blackbox near-threshold secret-sharing scheme with linear-time sharing. We also present several concrete instantiations of our approach that seem practically efficient (e.g., for threshold discrete-log-based signatures).

Our constructions are combinatorial in nature. We combine graph-based erasure codes that support "peeling-based" decoding with a new randomness extraction method that is based on inner-product with

B. Applebaum and O. Nir are supported by ISF grant no. 2805/21 and by the European Union (ERC-2022-ADG) under grant agreement no.101097959 NFITSC.

H. Handschuh and A. Lysyanskaya (Eds.): CRYPTO 2023, LNCS 14081, pp. 236–262, 2023.
https://doi.org/10.1007/978-3-031-38557-5_8

a small-integer vector. We also introduce a general concatenation-like transform for secret-sharing schemes that allows us to arbitrarily shrink the privacy-correctness gap with a minor overhead. Our techniques enrich the secret-sharing toolbox and, in the context of blackbox secret sharing, provide a new alternative to existing number-theoretic approaches.

Keywords: Secret Sharing · Threshold Cryptography · Blackbox secret sharing

1 Introduction

1.1 Motivation

Threshold signatures and threshold cryptosystems [21,22] typically rely on linear secret sharing schemes [8,41] "over the exponent" of some abelian group $\mathbb{G}$. Specifically, each server i holds a share s_i of the secret key s, and, loosely speaking, the signing process (or decryption process in threshold encryption) has the following form: The client broadcasts to the servers a public value M (e.g., the hash of the message on which we want to sign) and each server i replies with M^{s_i}. The goal of the client is to compute the signature M^s. If the client gets enough responses, say at least $\tau_c n$ out of the n servers, she can compute the signature (or decrypt the ciphertext) by computing a linear combination of the shares "in the exponent", i.e., $\prod M^{\alpha_i s_i}$, where the coefficients α_i depend on the set T of servers that are available, and satisfy $\sum \alpha_i s_i = s$. The client computes $M^{\alpha_i s_i}$ by raising each M^{s_i} to the power of α_i. By using repeated squaring, this requires between $\log |\alpha_i|$ and $2 \log |\alpha_i|$ group multiplications, and so the overall complexity for $|T| = n$ is about $n \log |\alpha_i|$ multiplications.[1]

The cost of computing $\prod M^{\alpha_i s_i}$ can be quite large when there are many servers and when the group is large. For example, if one uses Shamir's secret sharing [41] the cost is $\Omega(n \log p)$ multiplications where p is the order of group $\mathbb{G}$, even without accounting for the cost of computing the Lagrange coefficients. Alternatively, by employing a blackbox secret sharing (BBSS) [17,22] that works "universally" over any ring (or even abelian group), the cost can be made independent of p. However, the best existing schemes [19] use relatively large coefficients of bit-length $\Omega(n \log n)$ and so the recovery in the exponent takes at least $\Omega(n^2 \log n)$ multiplications. Furthermore, this holds even for the ramp setting where the correctness τ_c threshold of the scheme is bounded away from the privacy threshold τ_p. (See Sect. 1.5 for more details about the cost of these two approaches and of other related works.)

Our goal in this paper is to design secret-sharing schemes in which the overall complexity of the recovery is linear in the number of parties. More precisely, we

[1] The overhead of computing $\prod M^{\alpha_i s_i}$ can be reduced by computing a multi-exponentiation, namely computing the final result directly rather than computing each $M^{\alpha_i s_i}$ separately and multiplying the results. This optimization, e.g. using Pippenger's algorithm [39], improves performance by a factor of $O(\log n)$, but when $\log n \ll |\alpha_i|$ (which is the typical case in the threshold setting) this optimization has a limited effect compared to our improvements.

would like to minimize the number of group multiplications that are performed during reconstructions. One should note that the question can (and will) be studied purely in terms of linear secret sharing schemes regardless of the encryption/signature system that is being used. Keeping in mind that every addition in $\mathbb{Z}_p$ translates into a multiplication over the group $\mathbb{G}$, we are interested in the following secret-sharing task:

> Design a secret sharing scheme over $\mathbb{Z}_p$ that supports secret-recovery with a small number of *additions*. Sepcifically, is it possible to achieve an asymptotic upper-bound of $O(n)$ additions?

1.2 Our Results

We initiate the study of Additive-Only Secret-Sharing Schemes (AOS) and settle the above question in the affirmative for *near-threshold* secret sharing schemes. Such schemes provide privacy against unauthorized sets of density at most τ_{p}, and correctness for authorized sets of density at least τ_{c}, given some arbitrarily-close constants $\tau_{\mathsf{p}} < \tau_{\mathsf{c}}$. We prove the following main theorem.

Theorem 1 (main theorem). *For every constants $0 < \tau_{\mathsf{p}} < \tau_{\mathsf{c}} < 1$ there exists an ensemble of $(\tau_{\mathsf{p}}, \tau_{\mathsf{c}})$ near-threshold secret sharing schemes whose recovery algorithm makes only $O(n)$ additions. Moreover, (1) the share size is constant, (2) the sharing also makes $O(n)$ additions, and (3) the scheme is a BBSS scheme and the sharing and reconstruction algorithms work universally for all finite abelian groups $\mathbb{G}$.*

A few comments are in place.

- (**Ensembles**) The term *ensemble* refers to the fact that the scheme is parameterized with reusable public parameters that are sampled during the randomized set-up of the system. It is guaranteed that, except with exponentially small failure probability over the choice of the parameters, the resulting scheme satisfies correctness and privacy for all sets of density at most τ_{c} and τ_{p}, respectively. That is, each choice of the public parameters defines a scheme, and for almost all choices of the public parameters, τ_{c}-correctness and τ_{p}-privacy hold. The public parameters can be placed in a public file and can be re-used. We can also completely remove the public parameters without affecting the asymptotic complexity of the scheme at the expense of introducing a negligible statistical error in the correctness and privacy. (See Remark 3.) In typical applications (e.g., threshold cryptography), this relaxation has a minor effect (if any) since the secret sharing scheme will be employed inside a computational system that can be broken anyway with a small probability.
- (**Main vs secondary features**) We view the "near-threshold" property as well as items (1–3) as "bonus" features. That is, even a weak theorem that, for every large prime p, promises a *ramp secret sharing scheme* that supports some concrete privacy and correctness thresholds $(\tau_{\mathsf{p}}, \tau_{\mathsf{c}})$ (e.g., $(1/3, 2/3)$) and achieves recovery with $O(n)$ additions and, say, quadratic sharing complexity

and super-constant share size, would be useful for many usage scenarios. Furthermore, to the best of our knowledge, even the existence of such a weak scheme was open prior to this work. We will later present such weak versions of the main theorem that have very good concrete complexity and are likely to be useful in practice. (See Sect. 1.4.)

- (**Some advantages of the secondary features**) The BBSS property is especially useful for RSA-based threshold cryptography (e.g., threshold RSA signatures such as in [42]). Moreover, as a by-product, Theorem 1 recovers some recent fundamental results about the complexity of secret-sharing schemes, such as the existence of BBSS near-threshold schemes with constant-size shares [19] and the existence of linear-time computable secret-sharing schemes [16,23]. (See Sect. 1.5). In fact, to the best of our knowledge, even if we ignore the complexity of recovery, our results are the first to obtain linear-time computable BBSS schemes for any ramp-secret sharing scheme.
- (**Application to LWE-based schemes**) Our result is also relevant in the context of LWE-based constructions (e.g., the threshold FHE of [9]). In this case, instead of placing the shares $s_i \in \mathbb{F}_p$ in the exponents, one releases "noisy" versions of the shares modulo a larger prime q, and recovery is applied over "noisy" shares. Large interpolation coefficients expand the noise magnitude by a large factor and lead to errors (e.g., bad threshold-decryption). To avoid this, one can encode separately each bit of the share, however, this means that, in the recovery, each party has to send $\log p$ noisy elements instead of a single one. Motivated by this problem, Ball et al. [2] studied the problem of secret-sharing with 0–1 reconstruction coefficients. (See Sect. 1.5.) We note that the binary-reconstruction requirement can be typically relaxed to the more liberal requirement of an *addition-only reconstruction algorithm with low depth* since the bit-length of the noise grows linearly with the "depth" of the algorithm. Indeed, all our constructions achieve an optimal depth of $O(\log n)$, which makes them valuable also in the LWE setting.

1.3 Technical Overview

Additive-only Erasure Codes. We begin by ignoring the privacy condition in an attempt to construct "non-private" additive-only τ_c-correct schemes with a recovery algorithm that performs only $O(n)$ operations. When privacy is removed, this is essentially equivalent to erasure codes that correct in the presence of $(1-\tau_c)$-fraction of erasures. (For now, we think of the secret as a vector of $\Theta(n)$ field elements.) Our first observation is that graph-theoretic codes, e.g., binary low-density parity-check (LDPC) codes [25] and their derivatives (e.g., [35]) admit an additive-only decoding algorithm.

Let us focus, for concreteness, on the LDPC case. An LDPC code that maps k-long information words to n-long codewords is described by a $(n-k)\times n$ binary parity-check matrix H which is *sparse*: i.e., each of its rows/columns contains a constant number of ones. The set of codewords is the right kernel of H, i.e., all vectors $v \in \mathbb{F}_2^n$ for which $Hv = 0^{n-k}$. We think of H as a constant-degree bipartite graph G (the Tanner graph of H) whose n left vertices correspond to the codeword and its right $n-k$ nodes correspond to constraints nodes. (In other words, each constraint corresponds to a row of H.) The constraint associated with a right node asserts that the sum of all the left nodes connected to it is 0. Given a partial codeword $y_T = (y_i)_{i \in T}$ we use the following peeling-based decoding algorithm: (1) For $i \in T$ assign y_i to the ith left vertex; (2) While possible, pick a right (constraint) vertex r that all its neighbors $i_1, \ldots, i_{d-1}$ have been assigned except for one neighbor i_d and set the value of the i_dth left-node to $0-(i_1+\ldots+i_{d-1})$. (The algorithm works with any subset of $d-1$ neighbors that have already been assigned values. To simplify the notation, we denoted these neighbors as $i_1, \ldots, i_{d-1}$.) It turns out that a proper choice of the graph (or the sparse matrix) guarantees that, if one starts with a sufficiently large set of un-erased symbols T, the decoding process never stops until all the codeword is recovered. In particular, such codes can achieve a constant rate $R = k/n$ and recover from a constant fraction of erasures. (In fact, one can get an almost optimal trade-off and, for any small $\varepsilon > 0$, design a sparse LDPC that recovers the codeword from $(R+\varepsilon)$ fraction of un-erased symbol, see e.g., [35,36].)

Observe that the above procedure works over any field, or even abelian group, $\mathbb{G}$. In particular, if the codeword is a vector that satisfies the equation $Hv = 0^{n-k}$ then the peeling-based decoder works properly.[2] Indeed, the success of the decoding is independent of the underlying domain and depends only on the *combinatorial properties* of the graph. The decoder performs at most m additions where $m = O(n)$ is the number of edges in the constant-degree graph. Let us further assume, for now, that the code also admits an encoder that maps k-long vectors to n-long codewords by making $O(n)$ blackbox additions. This assumption does not hold in general for LDPC codes, but it holds for other related codes that support similar peeling-based decoding with $O(n)$ additions, e.g., [35]. (We will also explain later how to generically rely on an arbitrary LDPC code that does not satisfy this additional requirement.)

From Additive-Only Codes to Additive-Only Secret-Sharing. It is well-known that secret-sharing schemes are closely related to erasure codes [14,37,41]. The literature contains two main approaches for deriving secret-sharing from codes. The first traditional approach of Massey [37] (which is also implicit in Shamir's work [41]) is algebraic in nature and relies on the dual-distance of the code. Roughly speaking, the idea is to sample a codeword $y = (s, y_1, \ldots, y_n)$ and deliver y_i as the share of the ith party. An authorized coalition of density τ_c can recover the secret, by using decoding under $(1-\tau_c)$-fraction of erasures. It can be proved that privacy holds for sets of density τ_p if the code has a dual distance of $\tau_p n + 1$. Unfortunately, the codes that are employed in our work (e.g., LDPC codes) fail to achieve this property.

A second, more modern, approach of Cramer et al. [16] is information-theoretic in nature. The idea is to encode a random information vector r into

[2] The condition $Hv = 0^{n-k}$ is well defined over any abelian group $\mathbb{G}$ by interpreting the multiplication of a group element by an integer as iterated addition over $\mathbb{G}$. See Sect. 2 for details.

a codeword $y = (y_1, \ldots, y_n)$ and deliver y_i as the share of the ith party. The main observation is that, for a privacy threshold τ_{p} that is strictly smaller from the code's rate R, a τ_{p}-fraction of the parties has a small amount of information about the information vector. Specifically, given their view, the information vector is distributed uniformly over a set of size exponential in $(R - \tau_{\mathsf{p}})n$. Thus, one can use pairwise independent hashing to extract from the information word r an element that is almost-uniform conditioned on the view of the adversary, and use this element to pad the secret. (In fact, $\Omega(n)$ secrets can be packed using this approach.) One can set the parameters so that the error is sufficiently small, and apply a union-bound over all un-authorized sets. This leads to a collection of ramp (or even near-threshold) secret sharing schemes. Furthermore, if the family of hash functions is linear, the resulting scheme is linear, and if the code and hash function are computable in linear-time then so is the secret sharing scheme. Unfortunately, while there are pairwise-independent hash functions that can be computed by a linear-size arithmetic circuit [3,23,30] we are not aware of any pairwise-independent hash functions that can be computed by a linear number of *additions* and we conjecture that such an object does not exist.

Our Approach. Our approach follows the approach of Cramer et al. [16] except that instead of applying the hash function we apply to the information vector r a random linear combination with small, constant-size integer coefficients. We replace the information-theoretic argument with a linear-algebraic argument and show that a random linear combination with small-integer coefficients "extracts" well from any source that is uniformly distributed over a "nice" low-dimensional subspace. Furthermore, this extraction works in a domain-independent way. In more detail, fix the generating matrix M of the code and a subset T, and consider a random "small" integer column vector $a \in \mathbb{N}^k$. We show that a extracts well in the following scenario: Fix an arbitrary group $\mathbb{G}$, and consider a random vector $r \stackrel{R}{\leftarrow} \mathbb{G}^k$, then $a \cdot r$ is almost surely uniform over $\mathbb{G}$ even conditioned on the T-restricted codeword $(Mr)_T$. Equivalently, in linear algebraic terms, for every prime p, the vector a almost surely falls out of the row span of M_T modulo p.

The actual statement depends on the magnitude of the integers in M and here the fact that the code has $O(n)$ additive complexity plays on our side. Roughly, the analysis, which uses elementary linear algebra and probability, treats separately each small prime and each prime larger than some $p_0 = O(n)$. This resembles the case analysis of BBSS of [19] with an important distinction: In [19] the authors design different schemes for each case and glue them together via CRT, and in our case the construction is uniform and the distinction between different primes happens only in the analysis. Indeed, conceptually, our approach exploits the combinatorial structure induced by graph-based codes and avoids the relatively complicated number theory that is employed by previous BBSS schemes.

Deriving Near-Threshold Schemes. The techniques introduced so far yield ramp secret sharing but they fall short of providing near-threshold BBSS schemes. (The main loss is due to the analysis over small primes.) To obtain the main theorem, we import the coding-theoretic paradigm of code concatenation to the domain of secret sharing. Specifically, by using a simple combinatorial object known as *sampler graph* that satisfies some expansion-like properties, we show that it is possible to generically combine a "fast" ramp secret sharing scheme over n parties with a "slow" near-threshold scheme over a constant number d of parties, and derive a new near-threshold scheme that is almost as efficient as the fast scheme. The efficiency degrades by a constant factor that depends on the complexity of the slow scheme applied to d parties.

In our case, the fast scheme is the ramp secret sharing with $O(n)$ additive complexity for sharing and recovering from the previous section. The slow scheme can be taken to be any BBSS near-threshold or even threshold scheme, such as the scheme of Benaloh and Leichter [7] that is based on monotone formulas for the threshold function. It should be emphasized that, in our setting, the concatenation maneuver cannot be applied at the code level since the bottleneck is not the code (i.e., the correctness properties) but the analysis of the BBSS that incurs a loss in the *privacy* threshold.

We note that this amplification approach is quite generic and can be applied to any natural efficiency measure as well as to robust secret-sharing schemes. Concatenation techniques (aka party virtualization) are commonly used in the context of secure computation and distributed computing [12,20,24,28,29,31] and also appear in protocols for verifiable secret sharing [1]. However, to the best of our knowledge, this technique was not used so far in the secret-sharing context. (Though it was implicitly used when concatenated codes were employed, e.g., by [16] who employed the code of [27].) We believe that secret-sharing concatenation forms a useful tool in the secret-sharing toolbox that is likely to lead to other applications and can probably simplify, in retrospect, previous constructions. As our concrete setting demonstrates, in some scenarios, secret-sharing concatenation cannot be replaced by concatenation in the code-level.

1.4 A Practical Instantiation

Theorem 1 mainly forms a feasibility result. However, our techniques give rise to potentially practical ramp secret-sharing schemes. Let us focus for concreteness on the problem of constructing threshold BLS-signatures [10] instantiated over, say, the commonly used BLS12-381 curve. In this case the signature is computed as $(H(m))^s$ in a subgroup of the curve, whose order r is a prime which is 255 bits long. The secret is s and secret sharing must be computed modulo r. In this case, we can focus on the prime $p = r$ of bit length 255 and design an LSS over the field $\mathbb{F}_p = \{0, \ldots, p-1\}$. (The following example works even for much smaller primes.) Let us assume that there are $n \geq 1000$ parties. Assume that we have an R-rate erasure code of codeword length n that can recover the information word given a fraction of $\tau_{\mathsf{c}} = (R + \varepsilon_{\mathsf{c}})$ un-erased symbols, by making $D \cdot n$ additions for decoding. Then, our basic construction (encode + extract via short inner-product) can be set to have a privacy threshold of $\tau_{\mathsf{p}} = (R - \varepsilon_{\mathsf{p}})$, except with statistical failure probability of 2^{-100}, so that recovering a secret costs $(D + (1.1/\varepsilon_{\mathsf{p}})n$ additions. (See Theorem 5) For $\varepsilon_{\mathsf{p}} = 0.1$ this adds an overhead of 11 operations per party. Next, we should decide which code to use. There are numerous options here and let us review some of them.

Using Capacity-Achieving LDPCs. We can use LDPC codes that almost achieve the capacity, i.e., $\tau_c = (R + \varepsilon_c)$ where ε_c can be arbitrarily small (the computational overhead D grows with $1/\varepsilon_c$). Such an ensemble of LDPC codes appears in [35,36,38]. However, these codes typically achieve a *weak correctness* property: For every authorized set T of density τ_c, a random code sampled from the ensemble can decode a T-partial codeword, except with probability which is inverse polynomial in the codeword length. Note that there are two issues here: (1) a non-negligible error probability and (2) the existence of "bad sets" for which decoding fails given a description of the code. The problem can be fully avoided by using other ensembles that achieve sub-optimal, yet constant, decoding capability and rate.[3] Regardless, we argue that even weakly-correct ensembles of secret-sharing schemes may be useful in some scenarios. First, observe that privacy remains "strong", that is, our construction ensures that, except for probability 2^{-100}, the scheme is private for *every* coalition of density τ_c. Keeping this in mind, we can think of the correctness threshold as a way to guarantee liveliness against random failures. In this case, the weak correctness guarantee promises that most of the time reconstruction succeeds. Furthermore, we can share the secret key independently also via some "slow" secret sharing scheme, e.g., Shamir. Whenever the fast scheme fails (due to a failure of the decoding algorithm to handle some authorized coalition T), we can use the slow track to generate a signature via Shamir's reconstruction.

Using Standard LDPCs. Suppose that the privacy and correctness threshold can be far apart. A typical example is the case where $\tau_p = 1/3$ and $\tau_c = 2/3$ which corresponds to the classical setting in MPC and byzantine agreement in which the adversary can corrupt up to $n/3$ of the parties. In this case, we can use a random $(3, 6)$ LDPC code whose binary parity-check matrix represents a random graph with left-degree of 3 and right degree of 6. (In fact, it is better to sub-sample the code from a sub-family of "expurgated codes"). Peeling-based decoding takes at most $3n$ additive operations and can correct up to 0.429-fraction of errors for sufficiently large lengths n (and is therefore well within the bounds $\tau_p = 1/3$ and $\tau_c = 2/3$). Concretely, for $n = 350$ (resp., 700 and 1225), decoding fails with probability smaller than 10^{-6} for erasure fractions of 0.3 (resp., 0.375 and 0.4), see [40, Figure 3.156]. The overall complexity of recovering a secret or computing a signature is less than $10n$ additions (since $\varepsilon_p = R - \tau_p = 1/2 - 1/3 = 1/6$).

Low Complexity Encoding. There are families of LDPC codes (and variants of them) that admit fast and even linear-time encoding (see [40]). In fact, in our context, there is a simple way to generically achieve this additional feature. Instead of generating a codeword in the Kernel of an LDPC matrix H, sample a

[3] In fact there are deterministic families of such codes and we employ them as part of the proof of Theorem 1.

truly random vector v and publish its syndrome $Hv = z$ as public information. The computation is fast (since H is sparse) and we can think about (H, z) as the specification of the code. The peeling-based algorithm works as before except that in each peeling step when looking at the ith constraint the right-hand side value is set to be v_i, which is whp non-zero. We abstract this idea via the notion of public shares/header and think of z as public information that is left in a public repository.

It is important to mention that this approach has a caveat. Whenever a secret is reconstructed, the public share which potentially contains large field elements should be combined in the computation (instead of only using 0's for right-hand side values). This means that a client who asks for a signature has to raise the hashed document to the power of the typically-large entries of the public share z. Still, this part of the computation can be pre-computed by the client non-interactively or while waiting for the servers' responses. Alternatively, we can partially delegate the work to the servers by asking each of them to locally raise the hashed document to the power of $(v_i : i \in S)$ for a constant-size set of indices that is determined pseudorandomly (e.g., by applying a hash function on the identity of the server). In a concrete example where $|v| = n/2$, if we ask each party to handle, say $C = 3$ random public entries, then $2n/3$ of the parties are expected to cover all but $n/2 \cdot e^{-4C/3} = n/2 \cdot e^{-12/3} \approx n/109$ of the public elements, and so the client is left with a small overhead. Of course, the whole problem can be avoided by using codes with linear additive encoding complexity (e.g., the cascade LDPC construction of [36]).

The above discussion covers only a few of the possible instantiations and other choices would likely lead to different efficiency trade-offs. We, therefore, present our constructions and proofs in a modular way that generically supports both weakly-correct ensembles and public shares/headers.

1.5 Related Work

There is a rich literature that tries to improve various efficiency measures of secret sharing schemes and most notably the share size (See Beimel's survey [5]). While we are not aware of previous works that studied the *additive complexity* of recovering secrets, let us mention some of the most relevant previous works.

Linear-Time Sharing. Druk and Ishai [23] constructed near-threshold linear secret sharing schemes (LSS) over constant-size fields in which one can share a secret by computing $O(n)$ arithmetic operations where multiplication is counted as a single operation. Cramer et al. [16] extended this result to the case where the secret is a vector of length $\Omega(n)$. It seems likely that these constructions generalize to larger fields $\mathbb{F}_p$. However, the recovery and sharing algorithms in this case use arbitrary field elements, which leads to $O(n \log p)$ additions. (Also note that, unlike [16], in our setting of threshold cryptography the secret is naturally interpreted as a *single element* in a large field or ring.)

BBSS Schemes. BBSS schemes were first introduced by Desmedt and Frankel [22] and were further developed by [17–19] (see also references therein).

Near-threshold BBSS with constant-size shares were recently constructed by [19]. Roughly speaking, they (1) glue together, via CRT, schemes that work individually for each prime $p < n$ and combine the result with (2) a scheme that works simultaneously for all large primes. Consequently, part (1) of the construction induces recovery coefficients whose order is of the order of nth primorial integer P_n (the product of the first n primes). Since the bit-length of P_n is $\Omega(n \log n)$ this means that recovering the secret under scheme (1) takes $\Omega(n^2 \log n)$ additions. Part (2) has also similar complexity since it employs "Reed-Solomon over the integers" where each entry is of magnitude $\Omega(n \log n)$, leading to $\Omega(n^2 \log n)$ addition during reconstruction.

Secret Sharing with Small Recovery Coefficients. Ball et al. [2] studied the related problem of designing threshold LSS in which the secret can be recovered by a 0–1 linear combination. Note that the existence of such a scheme with constant-size shares would also lead to recovery by $O(n)$ additions. Unfortunately, Ball et al. rule out this possibility by showing that if the recovery vector is a 0–1 vector, the share size must be $\Omega(n \log n)$ assuming that the field is of characteristic 2 or (for general fields) assuming that the scheme satisfies a natural uniform distribution requirement. Our results bypass this lower-bound by considering the more general recovery model of $O(n)$-size additive circuit and by allowing a gap between the privacy and correctness thresholds.[4]

On the positive side, it is observed in [2] that a "bit-decomposition" of Shamir's scheme gives rise to a secret sharing scheme in which each share contains $\log |\mathbb{F}|$ field elements for $|\mathbb{F}| > n$. Reconstruction can be applied by taking a 0–1 linear combination of the shares, and so the number of additions over $\mathbb{F}$ is $\Omega(n \log |\mathbb{F}|)$ for a linear threshold of $\Theta(n)$. From our perspective, this variant has no advantage over "standard" Shamir as the total number of additions remains the same, i.e., $\Omega(n \log |\mathbb{F}|)$.

As already mentioned, for the motivating application in [2] (i.e., slow-noise-growth in LWE-based construction), the binary-reconstruction requirement can be typically relaxed to the more liberal requirement of an addition-only reconstruction algorithm with low (e.g., $\log n$) depth. From this point of view, our solutions are valuable also in the LWE setting.

Recovering a Secret "in the Exponent", and the Cost of Computing the Interpolation Coefficients. Although the issue we discuss here is general, we focus on the motivating example from the introduction in which a secret key $s \in \mathbb{Z}_p$ is being shared among n servers, and a client broadcasts $M \in \mathbb{G}$ and wishes to compute the value M^s. The textbook solution, based on Shamir's secret sharing, is to ask each server respond with M^{s_i}, and, assuming that the client receives the shares of a sufficiently large coalition T of size at least $\tau_c n$ recover the secret in the exponent. This process consists of two steps:

1. Computing over $\mathbb{Z}_p$ the Lagrange coefficients $(\alpha_i)_{i \in T}$ such that $s = \sum_i \alpha_i s_i$.
2. Computing $\prod M^{\alpha_i s_i}$ where the product is over $\mathbb{G}$.

[4] We do not know whether both relaxations are needed.

The first stage is computed over $\mathbb{Z}_p$ and can be done naively by computing $O(n^2)$ additions and multiplications. It can also be implemented using FFT, as suggested in [11], and making only $O(n \log^2(n))$ additions and multiplications (and as shown in [44], this technique provides better performance, roughly from $n \approx 256$). The second stage consists of $O(n \log p)$ multiplications over the cryptographic group $\mathbb{G}$ which are typically more expensive than modular operations.

To capture the distinction between the above 2 steps, one could partition the cost of the secret-sharing recovery algorithm $\mathsf{Rec}(T, (s_i)_{i \in T \cup \{n+1\}})$ into two parts: (1) Given T the cost of generating an Addition-Only circuit Rec_T for recovering the secret given T-shares; and (2) The number of additions that Rec_T performs. Our definitional framework measures the total number of additions that are performed in both steps, and, even under this strict measure of complexity, our constructions achieve linear complexity. This is in contrast to Shamir, and all other existing schemes that achieve super-linear complexity even if we count only the complexity of Step (2).

Let us emphasize that the gain is even more significant when working over groups of unknown order. Specifically, the cost of computing Lagrange coefficients is extremely prohibitive for the case of RSA-based threshold cryptography, such as threshold RSA signatures as suggested in [42]. Indeed, since the order of the group $\mathbb{Z}_N^*$ is unknown, the interpolation coefficients must be computed over the integers. This leads to very large coefficients as they are the result of multiplying $O(n)$ integers. Subsequently, raising values to the power of these exponents modulo N can be quite inefficient.

An Alternative Interactive Solution. Deviating from the textbook solution, one can get a linear complexity via the following alternative route. The client can ask who is willing to participate in the recovery. Then, each available party broadcasts her name. Finally, once the coalition is known the coefficients are determined and each party can locally raise her share to the power of α_i and send the result to the client that just needs to multiply everything. This solution has two drawbacks: It adds interaction and it is not resilient to malicious parties or to simple failures. In contrast, our solution is non-interactive and can be easily adapted to malicious settings by assuming that the original shares are committed and that each "signature" share consists of a zero-knowledge proof of consistency. In the discrete-log setting, this can be done relatively cheaply.

2 Preliminaries

By default, all logarithms are taken to base 2. We let $h_2(\cdot)$ denote the *binary entropy function*, that maps a real number $\alpha \in (0,1)$ to $h_2(\alpha) = -\alpha \log \alpha - (1 - \alpha)\log(1-\alpha)$ and is set to zero for $\alpha \in \{0,1\}$. We use the following standard estimate for the binomial coefficients

$$\binom{n}{\alpha n} \leq 2^{h_2(\alpha)n}. \tag{1}$$

For a matrix M we let M_i and M^i denote the ith row and ith column of M, respectively. All vectors are column vectors by default. For two random variables X and Y, we say that $X \equiv Y$ if they are identically distributed.

2.1 Secret Sharing: Definitions

We begin by recalling the notion of a *partial access structures*, that defines authorized and unauthorized sets while allowing a gap between them. A *ramp access structures* is a partial access structures with two thresholds, where all sets smaller than the first threshold are unauthorized and all sets larger than the second threshold are authorized.

Definition 1 (partial access structure and ramp access structure). *A* partial access structure *over n parties is a pair $\Gamma = (\Gamma_0, \Gamma_1)$ where $\Gamma_0, \Gamma_1 \subseteq 2^{[n]}$ are non-empty collections of sets such that $B \not\subseteq A$ for every $A \in \Gamma_0, B \in \Gamma_1$. Sets in Γ_1 are called* authorized, *and sets in Γ_0 are called* unauthorized.

For $0 < \tau_{\mathsf{p}} < \tau_{\mathsf{c}} \leq 1$, the $(\tau_{\mathsf{p}}, \tau_{\mathsf{c}})$-ramp access structure over n parties $\Gamma = (\Gamma_0, \Gamma_1)$ is defined by letting Γ_0 be the collection of all subsets of size at most $\tau_{\mathsf{p}} n$ and letting Γ_1 be the collection of all subsets of size at least $\tau_{\mathsf{c}} n$.

We move on and define the semantics of secret-sharing schemes. Our definition is equivalent to standard definitions (e.g., [6,15]) though our syntax is slightly different. Notably, the dealing function, which distributes the shares, $(s_1, \ldots, s_n)$, of the secret s, is also allowed to generate an additional "public" share, s_{n+1} that is available to all parties.

Definition 2 (Secret-sharing schemes). *A pair of deterministic algorithms, $(\mathsf{Deal}, \mathsf{Rec})$ is a* secret-sharing scheme *that realizes a (possibly partial) access structure $\Gamma = (\Gamma_0, \Gamma_1)$ with domain of secrets S, domain of random strings R, and finite domains of shares $S_1, \ldots, S_n$ and S_{n+1} (the latter domain is for public shares) if the following hold:*

- *(Correctness): For any authorized set $T \in \Gamma_1$ and every secret $s \in S$, the following T-*correctness *property holds:*

$$\Pr[\mathsf{Rec}(T, (s_i)_{i \in T \cup \{n+1\}}) \neq s] = 0,$$

where $(s_1, \ldots, s_n, s_{n+1}) \xleftarrow{R} \mathsf{Deal}(s)$. (The latter notation means that r is selected uniformly at random from R, and $(s_1, \ldots, s_n, s_{n+1}) = \mathsf{Deal}(s; r)$.)
- *(Privacy): For any unauthorized set $T \in \Gamma_0$ and every secret $s \in S$, the following T-*privacy *property holds:*

$$(s_i)_{i \in T \cup \{n+1\}} \equiv (s'_i)_{i \in T \cup \{n+1\}}$$

where $(s_1, \ldots, s_n, s_{n+1}) \xleftarrow{R} \mathsf{Deal}(s)$ is a random s-sharing, and the vector $(s'_1, \ldots, s'_n, s'_{n+1}) \xleftarrow{R} \mathsf{Deal}(0)$ is a random 0-sharing for some fixed canonical element 0 in S.

Note that privacy is a property of the sharing algorithm Deal.

Ensembles of Secret Sharing. Let $\Gamma = \{\Gamma_n\}_{n\in\mathbb{N}}$ be a sequence of access structures where Γ_n is an n-party (possibly partial) access structure. A triple of efficient algorithms $(\mathsf{Setup}, \mathsf{Deal}, \mathsf{Rec})$ is a δ-ensemble of Γ secret sharing schemes if for every n, except with probability $1 - \delta(n)$ over the choice of $\mathsf{pp} \xleftarrow{R} \mathsf{Setup}(1^n)$, the n-party scheme $(\mathsf{Deal}_{\mathsf{pp}}, \mathsf{Rec}_{\mathsf{pp}})$ realizes Γ_n. We highlight the following properties of this definition.

- We refer to δ as the failure or error probability of the ensemble and take it by default to be negligible in n.
- We can use a relaxed version of *ε-weakly-correct δ-private* ensemble that requires *strong privacy* and *weak correctness*. Here strong privacy means that

$$\Pr_{\mathsf{pp} \xleftarrow{R} \mathsf{Setup}(1^n)} [\forall \text{ unauthorized } T, (\mathsf{Deal}_{\mathsf{pp}}, \mathsf{Rec}_{\mathsf{pp}}) \text{ is } T\text{-private}] \geq 1 - \delta(n),$$

  and weak correctness means that for every n and every authorized set T

$$\Pr_{\mathsf{pp} \xleftarrow{R} \mathsf{Setup}(1^n)} [(\mathsf{Deal}_{\mathsf{pp}}, \mathsf{Rec}_{\mathsf{pp}}) \text{ is } T\text{-correct}] \geq 1 - \varepsilon(n).$$

  By default, we set δ to be negligible in n and set ε to some, possibly non-negligible function, that converges to 0.
- One can define weakly-private ensembles analogously though we will not use this variant in the paper. That is, in this paper even for a ε weakly-correct ensemble, except with probability δ over the choice of the public parameters, privacy holds over all unauthorized sets.

All the following variants of secret sharing (e.g., additive-only secret-sharing) can be naturally generalized to the setting of secret sharing collections. Whenever possible, we keep this extension implicit.

Remark 1 (Boosting weakly-correct ensembles). It is possible to reduce the correctness error ε of any weakly-correct ensemble to a negligible error via standard repetition (e.g., exponential in n) by independently sampling $k = O(n/\log(\varepsilon))$ public parameters $\mathsf{pp}_1, \ldots, \mathsf{pp}_k$ and sharing the secret k times independently with respect to each public parameter pp_i. As long as ε is polynomially-bounded away from 1, i.e., $\varepsilon < 1 - 1/\mathrm{poly}(n)$, the overhead k is polynomial and so the privacy error remains negligible. Recovery can be achieved by applying the original recovery algorithm to each part until we find an instance for which recovery succeeds.[5] This increases the sharing complexity and share size by a factor of k, however we can keep the expected running time of recovery essentially unchanged by applying the original recovery algorithm on the ith copy for a randomly chosen $i \in [k]$ and re-try if recovery fails.

[5] Here we assume that given a pp, T and the shares of a T-subset, one can efficiently check whether the reconstruction succeeds or fail. This assumption always hold for linear schemes (since detecting a failure boils down to checking whether a system of equation is solvable) which are the main focus of this paper. It can also be enforced for general schemes with a relatively minor cost via standard authentication techniques.

Remark 2 (deterministic constructions, public parameters and public shares). When the Setup algorithm is deterministic, the ensemble is referred to simply as a secret-sharing scheme. We note that one can always turn an ensemble to a deterministic construction (with statistical error) by pushing the public parameters as part of the public share. However, there is a conceptual difference between the public parameters and public share since the former can be sampled once and for all (and re-used over repeated applications) whereas the latter should be freshly sampled together with secret.

2.2 Additive-Only Algorithms and BBSS

An additive algorithm A is an algorithm that receives two types of inputs, arithmetic data inputs $x = (x_1, \dots, x_k)$ and some binary meta-data information $T = (T_1, \dots, T_m)$. The algorithm A manipulates the arithmetic data by making queries to an addition/subtraction oracle that takes two arithmetic elements and returns their sum/difference. The binary meta-information can be manipulated arbitrarily. The algorithm generates arithmetic outputs $y = (y_1, \dots, y_\ell)$. In principle, we can allow also binary outputs though we will not need this extension in this paper. The additive complexity of A is the maximal number of additions and subtractions that it performs.[6] For simplicity, we will ignore the complexity of non-arithmetic operations. Indeed, in all our constructions, the arithmetic complexity dominates the binary complexity. For any fixing T of the binary inputs and any fixing of an Abelian group $\mathbb{G}$, the algorithm $A_T^{\mathbb{G}}(x) = A^{\mathbb{G}}(T, x)$ defines a mapping from $x \in \mathbb{G}^k$ to $y \in \mathbb{G}^\ell$. This mapping can be always described by an $\ell \times k$ integer matrix M such that, for every $i \in [m]$, it holds that $y_i = \sum_{j=1}^{k} M_{i,j} x_j$ where for a positive integer k (resp., negative integer) and group element $g \in \mathbb{G}$ we write $k \cdot g$ for k-iterated additions (resp., subtractions) of g and when $k = 0$ we let $k \cdot g$ be the neutral element of $\mathbb{G}$ which will be denoted by 0.

Additive-Only Secret Sharing: Syntax. We say that an (ensemble of) secret-sharing schemes is *Additive-Only* if both the distribution and recovery algorithms are additive-only algorithms. For the recovery algorithm Rec the arithmetic inputs are the shares and the binary inputs are the public parameters pp and the set of parties T that will be represented by an n-bit vector. For the distribution algorithm Deal, the vector of random elements $r = (r_1, \dots, r_k)$ and the secret s are treated as arithmetic inputs and the public-parameters pp are treated as binary inputs. As a result, the distribution algorithm can be always represented by an integer *distribution matrix* M whose rows are labeled by indices in $[n]$ such that the rows that are labeled by i correspond to the computation of the shares of the ith party. That is, for secret s and randomness $r = (r_1, \dots, r_k)$,

[6] One can always reduce the number of subtractions to 1 at the expense of doubling the number of addition by maintaining for each intermediate arithmetic value v a pair of values a, b such that $v = a - b$ and postpone the actual subtraction to the end. See [43, proof of Thm 2.11] for a similar statement for the case of division/multiplication operations.

the share that the ith party gets is all the entries $M_j \cdot \binom{s}{r}$ for which the row j is labeled by i. Throughout the paper, we will always assume that each party gets a single group element as a share and so we may assume that the ith share is computed by the ith row of M. We assume that the public share consists of ℓ group elements and is computed by the last ℓ rows of M so the distribution matrix is always an $(n+\ell) \times (1+k)$ integer matrix.

Additive-Only Secret Sharing: Semantics. We say that an additive-only secret-sharing scheme (AOS) $(\mathsf{Deal}, \mathsf{Rec})$ realizes an access structure Γ over an Abelian group $\mathbb{G}$ if $(\mathsf{Deal}^{\mathbb{G}}, \mathsf{Rec}^{\mathbb{G}})$ realizes Γ. We say that $(\mathsf{Deal}, \mathsf{Rec})$ is a black-box secret-sharing (BBSS) for Γ if $(\mathsf{Deal}^{\mathbb{G}}, \mathsf{Rec}^{\mathbb{G}})$ realizes Γ for *every* Abelian group $\mathbb{G}$. We say that an additive-only distribution algorithm Deal realizes Γ over $\mathbb{G}$ if there exists an additive-only reconstruction algorithm Rec such that $(\mathsf{Deal}, \mathsf{Rec})$ realize Γ over $\mathbb{G}$. Similarly, we say that Deal is a BBSS for Γ if there exists an additive-only reconstruction algorithm Rec such that $(\mathsf{Deal}, \mathsf{Rec})$ form a BBSS for Γ.

The following proposition follows from pioneering works about linear secret sharing and black-box secret sharing [4,17,32] and relates the correctness and privacy properties of an AOS to the properties of the distribution algorithm, and, more specifically, to the linear-algebraic properties of the distribution matrix M.

Proposition 1 (implicit in [4,17,32]). *An additive distribution algorithm* Deal *with an $(n+\ell) \times k$ integer distribution matrix M realizes an access structure Γ over $\mathbb{F}_p$ for a prime p if and only if:*

- *(correctness) For every authorized set $T \subset [n]$, the unit vector $e_1 = (10^{n-1})$ is spanned, modulo p, by the rows of matrix M_T that contain all the rows $M_i, i \in [T]$ and all the "public-share" rows $(M_{n+1}, \ldots, M_\ell)$.*
- *(privacy) For every unauthorized set $T \subset [n]$, the unit vector $e_1 = (10^{n-1})$ is not spanned, modulo p, by the rows of matrix M_T that contains all the rows $M_i, i \in T$ and all the "public-share" rows $(M_{n+1}, \ldots, M_\ell)$. Equivalently, there exists a* sweeping *(column) vector $v_T \in \mathbb{N}^n$ such that $M_T v_T = 0 \pmod{p}$ but $\langle e_1, v_T \rangle \neq 0 \pmod{p}$.*

Moreover, Deal *is a BBSS for Γ if the above holds for* every *prime p.*

The first part follows from the works of Karchmer and Wigderson [32] and Beimel [4] about the relation between linear secret sharing schemes over finite fields and span programs. The "Moreover" part implicitly follows from the work of Cramer and Fehr [17], and specifically, from Lemma 1 that asserts that an integer system over the integers is solvable if and only if it is solvable over any prime. (Indeed both the privacy and correctness conditions boils down to the solvability of an integer linear system).

2.3 Additive-Only Erasure Codes

A pair of deterministic encoder and decoder algorithms $(\mathsf{Enc}, \mathsf{Dec})$ forms an (n, k) erasure code over alphabet Σ with correctness capability of η erasures if Enc maps an information word in Σ^k to a codeword in Σ^n, and for every $(1-\eta)n$-subset T, and every information word $x \in \Sigma^k$ and T-partial codeword $y_T = (\mathsf{Enc}(x)_i)_{i\in T}$ the decoder $\mathsf{Dec}(T, y_T)$ returns x. We consider a non-standard notion of *codes with header* in which $\mathsf{Enc}(x)$ also outputs a public header $z \in \Sigma^m$ that is always fully available to the decoder and is *not* subject to erasures. (Jumping ahead public headers correspond to public shares.) If one stores the entire information word in the public header then erasures are trivial to correct. To avoid such trivialities, we require that the length of the information word, k, will be larger than the length m of the header. Furthermore, letting $\mu := m/n$ be the *header rate*, we define the rate R of the scheme to be $\frac{k}{n} - \mu = \frac{k-m}{n}$ and require a positive rate R. This definition matches the standard definition of rate when there is no public header (i.e., $m, \mu = 0$).

We say that $(\mathsf{Enc}, \mathsf{Dec})$ are additive-only erasure codes if the algorithms are additive-only algorithms, i.e., the information word, codeword and public header are all treated as vectors of arithmetic elements over a general abelian group $\mathbb{G}$ and the set T is treated as a binary input. We require that correctness holds over any instantiation of an abelian group $\mathbb{G}$.

Ensembles of erasure codes are defined in the natural way. A tuple $\mathcal{C} = (\mathsf{CG}, \mathsf{Enc}, \mathsf{Dec})$ is a δ-ensemble of additive erasure codes that corrects up to η erasures with a rate of R and public-information rate μ if, except with probability $1-\delta$ over the choice of $\mathsf{cp} \xleftarrow{R} \mathsf{CG}(1^n)$, it holds that $(\mathsf{Enc}_{\mathsf{cp}}, \mathsf{Dec}_{\mathsf{cp}})$ form an additive erasure-code with $k = (R+\mu)n$ long information word, n-long codewords, and μn-long public header, that corrects up to η erasures. The ensemble is δ-weakly correct if for every n and $(1-\eta)n$-subset T, except with probability $1-\delta$ over $\mathsf{cp} \xleftarrow{R} \mathsf{CG}(1^n)$, it holds that for every information word $x \in \Sigma^k$ and codeword $(y, z) = (\mathsf{Enc}(x))$ the decoder $\mathsf{Dec}(T, (y_i)_{i\in T}, z)$ returns x.

3 The Basic Construction

In the basic construction, the vector of shares is sampled as a random information word r, and the ith party receives the ith entry of the corresponding codeword. In addition, we sample a random vector a of coefficients that is as long as the information word. The public information includes the public part of the codeword (if it exists), the vector a, and the value $z_0 = s + \sum_i a_i r_i$, where s is the secret that is shared. If the information word r is reconstructed, then the secret s can be recovered from z_0. We also show below that an unauthorized set learns no information about the secret.

Construction 2 (from additive codes to AOS). *Let* $\mathcal{C} = (\mathsf{CG}, \mathsf{Enc}, \mathsf{Dec})$ *be a (possibly weak) δ-ensemble of additive erasure codes that corrects a fraction of* $1-\tau_{\mathsf{c}}$ *erasures with a rate of R and public-information rate μ. For a parameter* $c \in \mathbb{N}$, *define the AOS* $\mathsf{Sharing} = (\mathsf{Setup}, \mathsf{Deal}, \mathsf{Rec})$ *as follows:*

1. $\mathsf{Setup}(1^n)$: *Sample a code parameters via* $\mathsf{cp} \xleftarrow{R} \mathsf{CG}(1^n)$ *and sample an integer vector* $a \xleftarrow{R} \{0, \ldots, c-1\}^{(R+\mu)n}$, *output* $\mathsf{pp} = (1^n, \mathsf{cp}, a)$.

2. $\mathsf{Deal}_{\mathsf{pp}}(s)$: *Sample a random information codeword* $y \in \mathbb{G}^n$ *and a (possibly empty) public header* $z_1 \in \mathbb{G}^{\mu n}$ *by computing* $(y, z_1) = \mathsf{Enc}_{\mathsf{cp}}(r)$ *where* $r \xleftarrow{R} \mathbb{G}^{(R+\mu)n}$ *is a random information word. Set* y_i *to the share of the ith party, compute* $z_0 = s + \sum_i a_i r_i$, *and set the public share* $z = (z_0, z_1)$.
3. $\mathsf{Rec}_{\mathsf{pp}}(T, z, y_T)$: *For a set* T *of size at most* $\tau_{\mathsf{c}} n$, *recover the information word* $r \in \mathbb{G}^n$ *via the decoding-under-erasure algorithm* $\mathsf{Dec}_{\mathsf{cp}}(z_1, T, y_T)$, *and output* $s = z_0 - \sum_i a_i r_i$.

Let us demonstrate the construction using an example: Suppose that we wish to provide n shares, and use a code that has a public header of length $n/3$. Then, using the notation of Sect. 2.3 we have that the length of the information word is $k = n$, the header is of length $m = n/3$, the header rate is $\mu = 1/3$, and the rate is $R = k/n - \mu = 2/3$. The construction chooses in the setup phase a vector a of $(R+\mu)n = n$ coefficients. In the deal phase, it chooses a random vector r of length $(R+\mu)n = n$, sets $y = r$ and sets the public header z_1 of length $n/3$ to be the result of multiplying the generating matrix of the code by r. The recovery phase uses the code to recover r and output $s = z_0 - \sum_{i=1}^{n} a_i r_i$.

Analysis. The correctness of the scheme (over any group) follows trivially from the correctness of the erasure code. Also, if the code ensemble is only weakly-correct then so is the resulting secret-sharing ensemble. The additive complexity of sharing/recovering is exactly the complexity of encoding/decoding plus the complexity of recovering the secret from z_0, which is $(R+\mu)n\lceil\log(c-1)\rceil + (R+\mu)n \leq n\lceil\log(c-1)\rceil + n$. (The inequality holds since, by assumption, $R+\mu \leq 1$.) The parallel additive complexity is $\log\log c + \log n + \log(R+\mu) + 1 \leq \log\log c + \log n + 1$. The next sub-sections (Sects. 3.1 and 3.2) will be devoted to the privacy analysis and will focus on the case where the scheme is applied over $\mathbb{F}_p$ for a fixed prime.

3.1 Privacy Lemmas

To analyze the privacy of the scheme, we restrict our attention to a fixed prime and make use of the following simple claims.

Claim 3 (privacy from linear independence). *Fix the code parameters* cp, *a prime* p *and a set* $T \subset [n]$. *Let* G *denote the generating matrix of the code* $\mathsf{Enc}_{\mathsf{cp}}$ *and let* G_T *denote the sub-matrix of* G *that is obtained by keeping the rows that are indexed by the set* T *and the "public" part. Then, the secret-sharing scheme from Construction 2 indexed by* $\mathsf{pp} = (1^n, \mathsf{cp}, a)$ *is* T*-private over* $\mathbb{F}_p$ *if and only if the vector* a *is not in the row-span of* G_T *over* $\mathbb{F}_p$.

Proof. Let G be the $(n+\mu n) \times (Rn+\mu n)$ generating matrix of the code $\mathsf{Enc}_{\mathsf{cp}}$ whose last μn rows correspond to the public header of the encoding. The distribution matrix M of the scheme is the $((1+\mu)n+1) \times (1+(R+\mu)n)$ integer matrix $M = \begin{pmatrix} 0^{(1+\mu)n} & G \\ 1 & a \end{pmatrix}$. Let M_T denote the sub-matrix of M that contains the rows that are indexed by T and the last $\mu n + 1$ rows (that corresponds to the public share). By Proposition 1, privacy for a set T over $\mathbb{F}_p$ is equivalent to the requirement that M_T does not span the vector e_1 over $\mathbb{F}_p$ which happens, in our case, if and only if G_T does not span the vector a. □

The following claim shows that a random small-integer vector is likely to fall out of the span of a degenerate matrix.

Claim 4. *Let M be an $k \times \ell$ integer matrix with $k < \ell$, let p be a prime and c be a positive integer. Then the probability that a randomly chosen vector $a \in \{0, \dots, c-1\}^{\ell}$ is in the row-span of M computed modulo p, is at most $\alpha_{c,p}^{\ell-k} = 2^{-(\log(1/\alpha_{c,p}))(\ell-k)}$ where $\alpha_{c,p}$ equals to $1/c$ if $c \le p$ and to $\lceil c/p \rceil / c$ otherwise.*

Note that $\alpha_{c,p} < 1/c + 1/p$ for every c and p.

Proof. Denote the row span (modulo p) of M by V. The matrix M has $k' \le k$ independent columns $M^{i_1}, \dots, M^{i_{k'}}$ over $\mathbb{F}_p$. Let $I = \{i_1, \dots, i_{k'}\} \subset [\ell]$ denote the set of positions of these columns. Then, for every $j \notin I$, we can write the jth column M^j as $M^I \alpha_j$ for some coefficient (row) vector $\alpha_j \in \mathbb{F}_p^{k'}$, and therefore, every vector $v \in V$ is fully determined by its values over the I-coordinates, i.e., $v_j = \alpha_j \cdot v_I$ for every index $j \notin I$. Hence, we can write $\Pr_a[a \in V]$ as

$$\sum_{v \in V} \Pr_a[a = v] = \sum_{v \in V} \left(\Pr_a[a_I = v_I] \prod_{j \notin I} \Pr[a_j = \alpha_j \cdot v_I] \right)$$

$$\le \sum_{v \in V} \left(\Pr_a[a_I = v_I] \prod_{j \notin I} \alpha_{c,p} \right) \le \alpha_{c,p}^{(\ell - |I|)} \le 2^{-(\log 1/\alpha_{c,p})(\ell-k)},$$

where the first equality is due to the independence of the entries of a, and the second inequality holds since, for each j and each $b \in \{0, \dots, p-1\}$ the probability that $a_j = b \pmod p$ is at most $\alpha_{c,p}$. The claim follows. □

By combining the above claims, we derive the following lemma.

Lemma 1 (privacy for a fixed prime). *For every code parameter cp, parameter $c \in \mathbb{N}$, and prime p the following holds. For every set $T \subset [n]$ of size $t < Rn$, the secret-sharing scheme from Construction 2 with parameters $\mathsf{pp} = (1^n, \mathsf{cp}, a)$ is T-private over $\mathbb{F}_p$ with probability of $2^{-(\log \alpha_{c,p}^{-1})(Rn-t)} = (\alpha_{c,p})^{Rn-t}$ over the choice of a. Furthermore, for τ_p that satisfies $h_2(\tau_\mathsf{p}) < (R - \tau_\mathsf{p}) \log \alpha_{c,p}^{-1}$, the scheme is τ_p-private over $\mathbb{F}_p$ except with exponentially small probability of $2^{n(h_2(\tau_\mathsf{p}) - (R-\tau_\mathsf{p}) \log \alpha_{c,p}^{-1})} = 2^{-\Omega(n)}$ over the choice of a.*

Proof. Fix the code parameters cp, a prime p and a set $T \subset [n]$, and let G denote the generating matrix of the code $\mathsf{Enc}_{\mathsf{cp}}$, and G_T denote the sub-matrix of G that is obtained by keeping the rows that are indexed by the set T and the "public" part (as in Claim 3).

The first part follows from Claims 4 and 3 by recalling that G_T is a $(t + \mu n) \times (Rn + \mu n)$ matrix for $(t + \mu n) < (Rn + \mu n)$, and the "furthermore" part follows by a union-bound over all $\tau_p n$-size subsets of n and by using the standard inequality $\binom{n}{\tau_p n} \leq 2^{nh_2(\tau_p)}$. □

3.2 Immediate Corollaries

Let us record two useful corollaries.

Theorem 5 (AOS with optimal privacy for fixed large primes). *For every $\varepsilon > 0$, rate $R > 0$ and error parameter $\beta > 0$, take c to be a constant of bit length at least $(h_2(\tau_p) + \beta)/(R - \tau_p)$. Then, Construction 2 instantiated with the constant c and an δ-ensemble (resp., weak δ-ensemble) of R-rate $(1 - \tau_c)$-erasure codes yields an AOS-ensemble with the following properties:*

- *(Complexity) The additive complexity (resp., parallel additive complexity) of sharing/recovering is exactly the complexity of encoding/decoding plus* $n(\lceil \log(c-1) \rceil + 1)$ *(resp.,* $\log \log c + \log n + 1$*).*
- *(Correctness) Except with probability δ over the choice of the code parameters* cp *and for every choice of a, the scheme is τ_c-correct for every prime (resp., weakly τ_c-correct if the coding ensemble is weakly correct).*
- *(Privacy) For every* $\mathsf{cp} \in \mathsf{Setup}(1^n)$ *and every prime $p \geq c$, except with probability $2^{-\beta n}$ over the choice of a, the algorithm* $\mathsf{Deal}_{(1^n,\mathsf{cp},a)}$ *is $(\tau_p = R - \varepsilon)$-private.*

Proof. The choice of c guarantees that $\beta < \log c(R - \tau_p) - h_2(\tau_p)$. The theorem now follows from Lemma 1 by recalling that $\alpha_{c,p} = 1/c$ when $p \geq c$. □

Note that the privacy threshold is almost optimal: it can be arbitrarily close to R from below. Indeed, if the underlying code is near-optimal, i.e., decoding works even when we have only $\tau_c = (R+\varepsilon)n$ non-erased symbols for an arbitrarily small constant ε (given to the code-generation algorithm), we get a near-threshold AOS whose privacy-to-correctness gap, $\tau_c - \tau_p$, is 2ε. Furthermore, the concrete constants are relatively small! Assuming that the failure probability should be at most 2^{-n} (which makes sense if there are at least 100 parties), we can take $\beta = 1$ and use a constant c of bit length at most $2(R - \tau_p)^{-1}$. If the number of parties is $n \geq 1000$, then β can be taken to be 0.1 and the complexity is at most $1.1(R - \tau_p)^{-1}$.

If we do not care about the optimality of the privacy threshold, we can derive a scheme that works for every fixed prime (including small primes such as $p = 2$) with high probability.

Theorem 6 (AOS for small primes). *For every rate $R > 0$ there exists small constants τ_p, β such that Construction 2 instantiated with any constant $c \geq 2$ and δ-ensemble (resp., weak δ-ensemble) of R-rate $(1 - \tau_c)$-erasure codes yields an AOS-ensemble with the following properties:*

- *Correctness and complexity as in Theorem 5.*
- *(Privacy) For every* $\mathsf{cp} \in \mathsf{Setup}(1^n)$ *and every prime $p \geq 2$, except with probability $2^{-\beta n}$ over the choice of a, the algorithm* $\mathsf{Deal}_{(1^n,\mathsf{cp},a)}$ *is τ_p-private. Consequently, the ensemble is τ_p-private simultaneously for* all *primes smaller than, say, $2^{\beta n/2}$, except with probability $2^{-\beta n/2}$.*

Proof. First, observe that for every prime p and constant $c \geq 2$ it holds that $\alpha_{c,p} < 5/6$. Indeed, if $c = 2$, it holds that $\alpha_{2,p} = 1/p \leq 1/2$ for every prime $p \geq 2$; and if $c \geq 3$, we have $\alpha_{c,p} < 1/p + 1/c \leq 1/2 + 1/3 = 5/6$ for every prime $p \geq 2$. Next, take τ_{p} to be a sufficiently small constant for which $(R - \tau_{\mathsf{p}}) \log(6/5) - h_2(\tau_{\mathsf{p}})$ is positive and take $\beta < (R - \tau_{\mathsf{p}}) \log(6/5) - h_2(\tau_{\mathsf{p}})$. This guarantees that $\beta < ((R - \tau_{\mathsf{p}}) \log \alpha_{c,p}^{-1} - h_2(\tau_{\mathsf{p}}))$ and the main part of the theorem now follows from Lemma 1. The "Consequently" part follows by applying a union bound over all primes of size at most $2^{\beta n/2}$. □

4 Analyzing the Basic Construction over All Primes Simultaneously

The above theorems are not sufficiently strong to handle infinitely many primes simultaneously. For this purpose, we will have to apply a more refined argument that exploits the fact that our sharing algorithm makes a linear number of additions. Let us start with the following claim that will replace Claim 4. In the following, we say that an integer vector $v \in \mathbb{N}^\ell$ has an *additive complexity of* e if the mapping that takes an integer vector $x \in \mathbb{N}^\ell$ to $\langle v, x \rangle$ can be computed by applying at most e additions/subtractions.

Claim 7. *Let M be an $k \times \ell$ integer matrix where $k < \ell$ and assume that each row of M has an additive complexity of e.*[7] *Let b be an integer and c be a prime of size at least $2b$. Then, except with failure probability $b^{k-\ell}(2e+1)^k$ over the choice of $a \in \{0, \ldots, c-1\}^\ell$,*

$$\exists \text{ integer vector } v \in [\pm b]^\ell \text{ s.t. } \quad Mv = 0^k \quad \text{ and } \quad \langle v, a \rangle \neq 0, \qquad (2)$$

where arithmetic is over the integers. Consequently, whenever (2) happens, the vector a is not in the row span of M modulo p for every prime $p > 2(c-1)b\ell$.

Proof. Let $N := b^{\ell-k}/(2e+1)^k$ and let V denote the set of integer vectors $0 \neq v \in [\pm b]^\ell$ for which the equality $Mv = 0^k$ holds over the *integers*. We begin by showing that V is of size at least $N - 1$. To see this, consider the mapping ρ that takes $v \in [1..b]^\ell$ and sends it to Mv (computed over the integers). Observe that the i-th entry of Mv is an integer in the range $[-be, .., be]$ and therefore the image of ρ is of size at most $(2be+1)^k < b^k(2e+1)^k$. Since the domain of ρ is of size b^ℓ, by the pigeonhole principle, there exist a set of at least $N = b^{\ell-k}/(2e+1)^k$ distinct input vectors $v_0, \ldots, v_{N-1}$ that are all mapped to the same output. By the linearity of ρ, the $N-1$ vectors $\{v_i - v_0 | 1 \leq i \leq N-1\}$ are all non-zero vectors that are mapped by ρ to zero.

Let us further filter the set $V \subset [1-b, b-1]^\ell$ by choosing a maximal subset $V' \subset V$ of vectors that are linearly independent over $\mathbb{F}_c$. Denote the size of V' by N'. Observe that the mod-c projected set of vectors $\{v \bmod c : v \in V\}$ contains

[7] The hypothesis can be relaxed so that e only upper-bounds the average additive complexity of the rows in M.

N' distinct non-zero vectors since $V \subset [1-b, b-1]^\ell$ and since the length of the interval, $[1-b, b-1]$, is smaller than $2b < c$. Therefore, $c^{N'} - 1 \geq |V|$ and $N' \geq \log_c(|V|+1) \geq \log_c(N)$.

To complete the main argument, it suffices to show that, except with probability $c^{-N'} \leq 1/N$, there exists a vector $v \in V'$ for which $\langle v, a\rangle \neq 0 \pmod{c}$. To see this, consider the random variables

$$(\langle v, a\rangle \pmod{c})_{v \in V'}$$

induced by the choice of $a \in \{0, \ldots, c-1\}^n = \mathbb{F}_c^\ell$. These random variables are mutually independent (since the vectors in V' are linearly independent) and each of them is uniformly distributed over $\mathbb{F}_c$. Therefore, the probability that all of them simultaneously take the value zero is $c^{-N'} \leq 1/N$ as promised.

Finally, the "consequently" part follows, by noting that the integer $\langle v, a\rangle$ is in the interval $[\pm(c-1)b\ell]$ and so $\langle v, a\rangle \pmod{p} \neq 0$ for every prime $p > 2(c-1)b\ell$. Since $Mv = 0^k \pmod{p}$, v certifies that the vector a is not in the row-span of M over $\mathbb{F}_p$. □

In order to employ Claim 7, we will need a good upper-bound e on the complexity of each row of the generating matrix of the underlying erasure code. Let us refer to such a code as e-bounded. We note that every code whose encoding can be computed by a linear number of additions can be turned into an $O(1)$-bounded code.

Claim 8. *There exists an efficient transformation that takes a constant $\alpha \in [0,1]$ and an additive erasure code $\mathcal{C} = (\mathsf{CG}, \mathsf{Enc}, \mathsf{Dec})$ whose additive complexity is An and outputs an (A/α)-bounded additive erasure code $\mathcal{C}' = (\mathsf{CG}, \mathsf{Enc}', \mathsf{Dec}')$ whose parameters almost match the ones of $\mathcal{C}$. Specifically, $\mathcal{C}'$ has an additive complexity of An, public rate of at least $\mu - \alpha$, rate of $R - \alpha$ and it can correct up to $\eta - \alpha$ erasures where μ, R and η are the public rate, rate and erasure correction capability of $\mathcal{C}$. Furthermore, if $\mathcal{C}$ is a (possibly weak) δ-ensemble then so is $\mathcal{C}'$.*

Proof. Fix some $\mathsf{cp} \in \mathsf{CG}(1^n)$ and observe that the average complexity of a row in the generating matrix of $\mathsf{Enc}_{\mathsf{cp}}$ is at most $\frac{An}{(1+\mu)n} < A$. Let us remove an α-fraction of the outputs whose complexity is the largest and let $\mathsf{Enc}'_{\mathsf{cp}}$ denote the resulting code. By Markov's inequality the resulting code is (A/α)-bounded. Decoding can be performed by invoking $\mathsf{Dec}_{\mathsf{cp}}$ while treating the removed entries as additional erasures. The other properties of the code can be easily verified. □

Theorem 9 (AOS for all large primes). *For every constants $R, \mu > 0$, $e \in \mathbb{N}$, $\tau_{\mathsf{p}} \in (0, R)$, error parameter $\beta > 0$, and $b \in \mathbb{N}$ whose bit-length $\log b$ is at least $(\beta + h_2(\tau_{\mathsf{p}}) + (\log(e)+2)(\mu+\tau_{\mathsf{p}}))/(R-\tau_{\mathsf{p}})$ the following holds. Construction 2 instantiated with any prime $c \geq 2b$ and δ-ensemble (resp., weak δ-ensemble) e-bounded $(1-\tau_{\mathsf{c}})$-erasure codes with rate R and public rate μ yields an AOS-ensemble with the following properties:*

- *Correctness and efficiency as in Theorem 5.*

– *(Privacy) For every* $\mathsf{cp} \in \mathsf{Setup}(1^n)$*, except with probability* $2^{-\beta n}$ *over the choice of* a*, the algorithm* $\mathsf{Deal}_{(1^n,\mathsf{cp},a)}$ *is simultaneously* τ_p*-private for* all *primes* p *larger than* $c^2 n$ *(or even* $p \geq 2cb(\mu + R)n$*).*

Proof. Fix some prime $c > 2b$. Fix n and code parameters $\mathsf{cp} \in \mathsf{Setup}(1^n)$ and let G denote the $(n + \mu n) \times (Rn + \mu n)$ generating matrix of the code Enc_cp whose last μn rows correspond to the public header of the encoding. For a set T of size τ_p, let G_T denote the sub-matrix of G that is obtained by keeping the rows that are indexed by the set T and the "public" part (as in Claim 3). By Claim 3, it suffices to show that, except with probability $2^{-\beta n}$, the event (2) happens for G_T for every set T of size $\tau_\mathsf{p} n$. Recall that G_T has $k = (\mu + \tau_\mathsf{p})n$ rows and $\ell = (R + \mu)n$ columns and each of its rows has an additive complexity of e. Hence, by Claim 7, the event (2) happens for any fixed T, with probability at most $b^{k-\ell}(2e + 1)^k \leq 2^{-\eta n}$ where

$$\eta \geq (R - \tau_\mathsf{p})(\log b) - (\log(e) + 2)(\mu + \tau_\mathsf{p}).$$

When the bit length of b is larger than $(\beta + h_2(\tau) + (\log(e) + 2)(\mu + \tau_\mathsf{p}))/(R - \tau_\mathsf{p})$, we get that $\eta > \beta + h_2(\tau)$, which, by a union bound over all T's, yields the result. □

For example, for every fixing of constants $R > 0$, $e \in \mathbb{N}$, we can take $\tau_\mathsf{p} \in (0, R)$ to be arbitrarily close to R (up to any small constant), and get an arbitrary exponential small error probability for all primes larger than $c^2 n$ by taking a sufficiently large constant c. Alternatively, when the code has no public information ($\mu = 0$), for every fixed odd prime c, there exist some (small) constants $\tau_\mathsf{p} \in (0, R), \beta > 0$ for which the construction achieves τ_p-privacy except with exponentially small probability of $2^{-\beta n}$ simultaneously for all primes larger than $c^2 n$.

In any case, by combining the above theorem with Theorem 6 and Proposition 1, we derive the following theorem.

Theorem 10 (AOS for all primes). *For every rate* $R > 0$ *there exists constants* τ_p, β *and* c *such that Construction 2 instantiated with* c *and* δ*-ensemble (resp., weak* δ*-ensemble) of* R*-rate* $(1 - \tau_\mathsf{c})$*-erasure codes yields an AOS-ensemble with the following properties:*

– *Correctness and complexity as in Theorem 5.*
– *(Privacy) For every* $\mathsf{cp} \in \mathsf{Setup}(1^n)$ *and every prime* $p \geq 2$*, except with probability* $2^{-\beta n}$ *over the choice of* a*, the algorithm* $\mathsf{Deal}_{(1^n,\mathsf{cp},a)}$ *is* τ_p*-private simultaneously for* all *primes.*

There exists a (deterministic) construction of AOS erasure codes with linear complexity constant rate and constant erasure capability (e.g., by using the Capalbo et al. [13] unbalanced expanders in the cascade construction of Luby et al. [35]). Thus, by Proposition 1, we derive the following corollary.

Corollary 1. *For some constants $0 < \tau_{\mathsf{p}} < \tau_{\mathsf{c}} < 1$ there exists an $(\tau_{\mathsf{p}}, \tau_{\mathsf{c}})$-ramp ensemble of BBSS scheme with constant-size shares, and where the recovery and sharing algorithms make only $O(n)$ additions, and thee setup algorithm errs with probability $2^{-\Omega(n)}$. Furthermore, the public share is a single field element and so it can be completely removed (by appending it to each party's share).*

Remark 3 (compressing the ensemble parameters). Since the underlying code is computed the public parameters of the secret sharing ensemble contain only the vector a whose length is $O(n)$ bits. Following [16,34] this public information can be completely eliminated via information dispersal. Specifically, encode the vector a into a vector $A \in \{0,1\}^{O(n)}$ using some AOS-ensemble of erasure codes with linear complexity and hand A_i to the ith party. The share size remains constant and the additive complexity of sharing and recovering remains unchanged. Of course, this introduces a negligible error probability in the recovery algorithm and a negligible deviation in the privacy.

5 Deriving Near-Threshold Schemes

We will need the following proposition about the existence of *bipartite sampler graphs*.

Proposition 2 (efficient samplers [26,33]). *For every positive constants $\varepsilon > 0, \delta > 0$, there exists a constant $d = O(1/(\varepsilon^2\delta))$ and a* poly$(n, 1/\varepsilon, 1/\delta)$*-time algorithm that on input 1^n outputs an bipartite graph $G = ((L, R), E)$ with the the following properties:*

1. *$|L| = |R| = n$ and the right degree of G is d.*
2. *For every $S \subset L$, it holds that for at least $1 - \delta$ fraction of the vertices $r \in R$, it holds that*

$$\left| \frac{d_S(r)}{d} - \frac{|S|}{n} \right| \leq \varepsilon,$$

where $d_S(r)$ is the number of vertices in S that are connected to r.

*A graph that satisfies the above properties is called an $(n, d, \varepsilon, \delta)$-*sampler.

The following lemma takes an outer "fast" ramp scheme with "bad threshold" over n parties and near-threshold "slow" scheme over a constant $d = O(1)$ number of parties, and generates a new near-optimal scheme over n parties whose complexity (sharing, reconstruction and share size) are inherited from the fast scheme up to a constant multiplicative overhead that depends on d.

Lemma 2. *For every ε, δ, d and n and $(n, d, \varepsilon, \delta)$-sampler $G = ((L, R), E)$ the following holds for any $\varepsilon < \gamma < 1 - \varepsilon$. Let $(\mathsf{Deal}_{\mathsf{out}}, \mathsf{Rec}_{\mathsf{out}})$ be an "outer" $(\delta, 1 - \delta)$-ramp secret sharing scheme over n parties and let $(\mathsf{Deal}_{\mathsf{in}}, \mathsf{Rec}_{\mathsf{in}})$ be an "inner" $(\gamma - \varepsilon, \gamma + \varepsilon)$-ramp secret sharing scheme over d parties. Define a secret-sharing scheme $(\mathsf{Deal}, \mathsf{Rec})$ over the n parties in L as follows:*

1. $\mathsf{Deal}(s)$: *Generate n "virtual shares"* $(s'_r)_{r\in R} \stackrel{R}{\leftarrow} \mathsf{Deal}_{\mathsf{out}}(s)$. *For each* $r \in R$, *share each virtual share* s'_r *via* $(s_{r,\ell})_{\ell\in L(r)} \stackrel{R}{\leftarrow} \mathsf{Deal}_{\mathsf{in}}(s'_r)$ *where* $L(r) \subset L$ *is the set of left neighbors of a vertex* $r \in R$ *in the graph* G. *Set the share of the* $\ell \in L$ *party to be* $(s_{r,\ell})_{r\in R(\ell)}$ *where* $R(\ell) \subset R$ *is the set of right neighbors of a vertex* $\ell \in L$.
2. $\mathsf{Rec}(T, (s_i)_{i\in T})$: *For a left set* $T \subset L$ *denote by*

$$R_+(T) = \{r \in R : d_T(r) \geq (\gamma + \varepsilon)d\}$$

the set of right vertices r *that have at least* $(\gamma+\varepsilon)d$ *neighbors in* T. *Recover all the virtual secrets* (s'_r) *for* $r \in R_+(T)$ *by applying* $\mathsf{Rec}_{\mathsf{in}}((s'_{r,\ell})_{\ell\in L(r)\cap T})$ *and output the result of* $\mathsf{Rec}_{\mathsf{out}}((s'_r)_{r\in R_+(T)})$.

Then the secret-sharing scheme $(\mathsf{Deal}, \mathsf{Rec})$ *is a* $(\gamma - 2\varepsilon, \gamma + 2\varepsilon)$*-ramp secret sharing scheme.*

Proof. For correctness, consider a left set T of size at least $(\gamma + 2\varepsilon)n$. By the sampling properties of G, the set $R_+(T)$ is of size at least $(1-\delta)n$ and so, by the correctness of the inner scheme, at least $(1-\delta)n$ fraction of the virtual shares are recovered by the coalition T. Hence, correctness follows from the correctness of the outer secret-sharing schemes.

For privacy, consider a left set T of size at most $(\gamma - 2\varepsilon)n$ and let $R_-(T) = \{r \in R : d_T(r) \leq (\gamma - \varepsilon)d\}$ be the set of right vertices r that have at most $(\gamma-\varepsilon)d$ neighbors in T. By the sampling properties of G, the set $R_-(T)$ is of size at least $(1-\delta)n$ and so, by the privacy of the inner scheme, at least $1-\delta$ fraction of the virtual shares are perfectly hidden from the coalition T. Hence, privacy follows from the privacy of the outer secret-sharing schemes. □

We note that the above lemma naturally generalizes to the case where the graph is unbalanced. (We omit the details since this variant is not needed here).

For every constant $\varepsilon > 0$, we can instantiate the lemma with an outer $(\delta, 1-\delta)$-ramp AOS of linear additive complexity $O(n)$ (e.g., from Corollary 1) and an inner γd-threshold AOS over $d = O(1)$ parties of complexity polynomial in d (say based on the formula construction of [7]) and derive a near-threshold AOS with linear complexity as promised by the main theorem (restated here for the convenience of the reader).

Theorem 11 (Theorem 1 restated). *For every constants* $0 < \tau_{\mathsf{p}} < \tau_{\mathsf{c}} < 1$ *there exists an ensemble of* $(\tau_{\mathsf{p}}, \tau_{\mathsf{c}})$ *near-threshold ensemble of secret sharing schemes whose recovery algorithm makes only* $O(n)$ *additions. Moreover, (1) the share size is constant, (2) the sharing also makes* $O(n)$ *additions, and (3) the scheme is a BBSS scheme and the sharing and reconstruction algorithms work universally for all finite Abelian groups* $\mathbb{G}$.

Acknowledgements. We thank Amos Beimel for helpful discussions.

References

1. Applebaum, B., Kachlon, E., Patra, A.: Verifiable relation sharing and multi-verifier zero-knowledge in two rounds: trading nizks with honest majority - (extended abstract). In: Advances in Cryptology - CRYPTO 2022–42nd Annual International Cryptology Conference, CRYPTO 2022, Santa Barbara, CA, USA, August 15–18, 2022, Proceedings, Part IV, pp. 33–56 (2022). https://doi.org/10.1007/978-3-031-15985-5_2
2. Ball, M., Çakan, A., Malkin, T.: Linear threshold secret-sharing with binary reconstruction. In: Tessaro, S. (ed.) 2nd Conference on Information-Theoretic Cryptography, ITC 2021, 23–26 July 2021, Virtual Conference. LIPIcs, vol. 199, pp. 12:1–12:22. Schloss Dagstuhl - Leibniz-Zentrum für Informatik (2021)
3. Baron, J., Ishai, Y., Ostrovsky, R.: On linear-size pseudorandom generators and hardcore functions. Theor. Comput. Sci. **554**, 50–63 (2014)
4. Beimel, A.: Secure schemes for secret sharing and key distribution. Ph.D. thesis, Technion - Israel Institute of Technology, Israel (1996)
5. Beimel, A.: Secret-sharing schemes: a survey. In: Chee, Y.M., et al. (eds.) IWCC 2011. LNCS, vol. 6639, pp. 11–46. Springer, Heidelberg (2011). https://doi.org/10.1007/978-3-642-20901-7_2
6. Beimel, A., Chor, B.: Universally ideal secret-sharing schemes. IEEE Trans. Inf. Theory **40**(3), 786–794 (1994)
7. Benaloh, J., Leichter, J.: Generalized secret sharing and monotone functions. In: Goldwasser, S. (ed.) CRYPTO 1988. LNCS, vol. 403, pp. 27–35. Springer, New York (1990). https://doi.org/10.1007/0-387-34799-2_3
8. Blakley, G.R.: Safeguarding cryptographic keys. In: 1979 International Workshop on Managing Requirements Knowledge, MARK 1979, New York, NY, USA, 4–7 June 1979, pp. 313–318. IEEE (1979)
9. Boneh, D., et al.: Threshold cryptosystems from threshold fully homomorphic encryption. In: Shacham, H., Boldyreva, A. (eds.) CRYPTO 2018. LNCS, vol. 10991, pp. 565–596. Springer, Cham (2018). https://doi.org/10.1007/978-3-319-96884-1_19
10. Boneh, D., Lynn, B., Shacham, H.: Short signatures from the weil pairing. J. Cryptol. **17**(4), 297–319 (2004)
11. Borodin, A., Moenck, R.: Fast modular transforms. J. Comput. Syst. Sci. **8**(3), 366–386 (1974)
12. Bracha, G.: An asynchronous [(n-1)/3]-resilient consensus protocol. In: Proceedings of the Third Annual ACM Symposium on Principles of Distributed Computing (PODC), 1984. pp. 154–162 (1984)
13. Capalbo, M.R., Reingold, O., Vadhan, S.P., Wigderson, A.: Randomness conductors and constant-degree lossless expanders. In: Reif, J.H. (ed.) Proceedings on 34th Annual ACM Symposium on Theory of Computing, 19–21 May 2002, Montréal, Québec, Canada, pp. 659–668. ACM (2002)
14. Chen, H., Cramer, R., Goldwasser, S., de Haan, R., Vaikuntanathan, V.: Secure computation from random error correcting codes. In: Naor, M. (ed.) EUROCRYPT 2007. LNCS, vol. 4515, pp. 291–310. Springer, Heidelberg (2007). https://doi.org/10.1007/978-3-540-72540-4_17
15. Chor, B., Kushilevitz, E.: Secret sharing over infinite domains. J. Cryptology **6**(2), 87–95 (1993). https://doi.org/10.1007/BF02620136
16. Cramer, R., Damgård, I.B., Döttling, N., Fehr, S., Spini, G.: Linear secret sharing schemes from error correcting codes and universal hash functions. In: Oswald, E.,

Fischlin, M. (eds.) EUROCRYPT 2015. LNCS, vol. 9057, pp. 313–336. Springer, Heidelberg (2015). https://doi.org/10.1007/978-3-662-46803-6_11

17. Cramer, R., Fehr, S.: Optimal black-box secret sharing over arbitrary abelian groups. In: Yung, M. (ed.) CRYPTO 2002. LNCS, vol. 2442, pp. 272–287. Springer, Heidelberg (2002). https://doi.org/10.1007/3-540-45708-9_18
18. Cramer, R., Fehr, S., Stam, M.: Black-box secret sharing from primitive sets in algebraic number fields. In: Shoup, V. (ed.) CRYPTO 2005. LNCS, vol. 3621, pp. 344–360. Springer, Heidelberg (2005). https://doi.org/10.1007/11535218_21
19. Cramer, R., Xing, C.: Blackbox secret sharing revisited: a coding-theoretic approach with application to expansionless near-threshold schemes. In: Canteaut, A., Ishai, Y. (eds.) EUROCRYPT 2020. LNCS, vol. 12105, pp. 499–528. Springer, Cham (2020). https://doi.org/10.1007/978-3-030-45721-1_18
20. Damgård, I., Ishai, Y., Krøigaard, M., Nielsen, J.B., Smith, A.: Scalable multiparty computation with nearly optimal work and resilience. In: Wagner, D. (ed.) CRYPTO 2008. LNCS, vol. 5157, pp. 241–261. Springer, Heidelberg (2008). https://doi.org/10.1007/978-3-540-85174-5_14
21. Desmedt, Y.: Threshold cryptography. Eur. Trans. Telecommun. **5**(4), 449–458 (1994)
22. Desmedt, Y., Frankel, Y.: Threshold cryptosystems. In: Brassard, G. (ed.) CRYPTO 1989. LNCS, vol. 435, pp. 307–315. Springer, New York (1990). https://doi.org/10.1007/0-387-34805-0_28
23. Druk, E., Ishai, Y.: Linear-time encodable codes meeting the gilbert-varshamov bound and their cryptographic applications. In: Naor, M. (ed.) Innovations in Theoretical Computer Science, ITCS 2014, Princeton, NJ, USA, 12–14 January 2014, pp. 169–182. ACM (2014)
24. Fitzi, M., Franklin, M., Garay, J., Vardhan, S.H.: Towards optimal and efficient perfectly secure message transmission. In: Vadhan, S.P. (ed.) TCC 2007. LNCS, vol. 4392, pp. 311–322. Springer, Heidelberg (2007). https://doi.org/10.1007/978-3-540-70936-7_17
25. Gallager, R.G.: Low-density parity-check codes. IRE Trans. Inf. Theory **8**(1), 21–28 (1962)
26. Goldreich, O.: A sample of samplers: a computational perspective on sampling. In: Goldreich, O. (ed.) Studies in Complexity and Cryptography. Miscellanea on the Interplay between Randomness and Computation. LNCS, vol. 6650, pp. 302–332. Springer, Heidelberg (2011). https://doi.org/10.1007/978-3-642-22670-0_24
27. Guruswami, V., Indyk, P.: Linear-time encodable/decodable codes with near-optimal rate. IEEE Trans. Inf. Theory **51**(10), 3393–3400 (2005)
28. Harnik, D., Ishai, Y., Kushilevitz, E.: How many oblivious transfers are needed for secure multiparty computation? In: Menezes, A. (ed.) CRYPTO 2007. LNCS, vol. 4622, pp. 284–302. Springer, Heidelberg (2007). https://doi.org/10.1007/978-3-540-74143-5_16
29. Ishai, Y., Kushilevitz, E., Ostrovsky, R., Sahai, A.: Zero-knowledge from secure multiparty computation. In: Proceedings of the 39th Annual ACM Symposium on Theory of Computing, San Diego, California, USA, 11–13 June 2007, pp. 21–30 (2007)
30. Ishai, Y., Kushilevitz, E., Ostrovsky, R., Sahai, A.: Cryptography with constant computational overhead. In: Dwork, C. (ed.) Proceedings of the 40th Annual ACM Symposium on Theory of Computing, Victoria, British Columbia, Canada, 17–20 May 2008, pp. 433–442. ACM (2008)

31. Ishai, Y., Prabhakaran, M., Sahai, A.: Founding cryptography on oblivious transfer - efficiently. In: Advances in Cryptology - CRYPTO 2008, 28th Annual International Cryptology Conference, Santa Barbara, CA, USA, 17–21 August 2008. Proceedings. pp. 572–591 (2008)
32. Karchmer, M., Wigderson, A.: On span programs. In: Proceedings of the Eigth Annual Structure in Complexity Theory Conference, San Diego, CA, USA, 18–21 May 1993. pp. 102–111. IEEE Computer Society (1993)
33. Karp, R., Pippenger, N., Sipser, M.: A time-randomness tradeoff. In: AMS Conference on Probabilistic Computational Complexity, vol. 111 (1985)
34. Krawczyk, H.: Distributed fingerprints and secure information dispersal. In: Anderson, J., Toueg, S. (eds.) Proceedings of the Twelth Annual ACM Symposium on Principles of Distributed Computing, Ithaca, New York, USA, 15–18 August 1993, pp. 207–218. ACM (1993)
35. Luby, M., Mitzenmacher, M., Shokrollahi, M.A., Spielman, D.A.: Efficient erasure correcting codes. IEEE Trans. Inf. Theory **47**(2), 569–584 (2001)
36. Luby, M., Mitzenmacher, M., Shokrollahi, M.A., Spielman, D.A., Stemann, V.: Practical loss-resilient codes. In: Leighton, F.T., Shor, P.W. (eds.) Proceedings of the Twenty-Ninth Annual ACM Symposium on the Theory of Computing, El Paso, Texas, USA, 4–6 May 1997, pp. 150–159. ACM (1997)
37. Massey, J.L.: Some applications of source coding in cryptography. Eur. Trans. Telecommun. **5**(4), 421–430 (1994)
38. Oswald, P., Shokrollahi, A.: Capacity-achieving sequences for the erasure channel. IEEE Trans. Inf. Theory **48**(12), 3017–3028 (2002)
39. Pippenger, N.: On the evaluation of powers and monomials. SIAM J. Comput. **9**(2), 230–250 (1980)
40. Richardson, T.J., Urbanke, R.L.: Modern Coding Theory. Cambridge University Press, Cambridge (2008)
41. Shamir, A.: How to share a secret. Commun. ACM **22**(11), 612–613 (1979)
42. Shoup, V.: Practical threshold signatures. In: Preneel, B. (ed.) EUROCRYPT 2000. LNCS, vol. 1807, pp. 207–220. Springer, Heidelberg (2000). https://doi.org/10.1007/3-540-45539-6_15
43. Shpilka, A., Yehudayoff, A.: Arithmetic circuits: a survey of recent results and open questions. Found. Trends Theor. Comput. Sci. **5**(3–4), 207–388 (2010)
44. Tomescu, A., et al.: Towards scalable threshold cryptosystems. In: 2020 IEEE Symposium on Security and Privacy, SP 2020, San Francisco, CA, USA, 18–21 May 2020, pp. 877–893. IEEE (2020)

On Linear Communication Complexity for (Maximally) Fluid MPC

Alexander Bienstock[1(✉)], Daniel Escudero[2], and Antigoni Polychroniadou[2]

[1] New York University, New York, USA
abienstock@cs.nyu.edu
[2] J.P. Morgan AI Research & J.P. Morgan AlgoCRYPT CoE, New York, USA

Abstract. Secure multiparty computation protocols with dynamic parties, which assume that honest parties do not need to be online throughout the whole execution of the protocol, have recently gained a lot of traction for computations of *large scale* distributed protocols, such as blockchains. More specifically, in *Fluid* MPC, introduced in (Choudhuri *et al.* CRYPTO 2021), parties can dynamically join and leave the computation from round to round. The best known Fluid MPC protocol in the honest majority setting communicates $O(n^2)$ elements per gate where n is the number of parties online at a time. While Le Mans (Rachuri and Scholl, CRYPTO 2022) extends Fluid MPC to the dishonest majority setting with preprocessing, it still communicates $O(n^2)$ elements per gate.

In this work we present alternative Fluid MPC solutions that require $O(n)$ communication per gate for both the information-theoretic honest majority setting and the information-theoretic dishonest majority setting with preprocessing. Our solutions also achieve *maximal fluidity* where parties only need to be online for a single communication round. Additionally, we show that a protocol in the information-theoretic dishonest majority setting with sub-quadratic $o(n^2)$ overhead per gate requires for each of the N parties who may ever participate in the (later) execution phase, $\Omega(N)$ preprocessed data per gate.

1 Introduction

Secure multiparty computation (MPC) is a promising set of techniques that has been studied since the 80s [9,21,26], and aims at enabling a set of mutually distrustful parties to securely compute a given function on their private inputs, without leaking anything but the output of the function. This should hold even if an unknown subset of the parties is corrupted by an adversary which tries to compromise the privacy of the remaining honest parties.

A protocol may be designed to tolerate an arbitrary amount of corruptions, refereed to as the the *dishonest majority* setting, or this can be relaxed to only require security as long as a minority of the parties are corrupted, *honest majority* setting. Even though dishonest majority MPC protocols offer stronger security guarantees tolerating a higher corruption threshold, protocols in the honest

The full version [5] is available as entry 2023/839 in the IACR eprint archive.

H. Handschuh and A. Lysyanskaya (Eds.): CRYPTO 2023, LNCS 14081, pp. 263–294, 2023.
https://doi.org/10.1007/978-3-031-38557-5_9

majority setting do not require any computational assumptions and tend to be computationally more efficient than the cryptographic machinery required for the dishonest majority setting. Ever since the introduction of MPC, big efforts have been made at improving its efficiency, which has resulted in a rich and fruitful line of works, including [3,15] for the dishonest majority setting, and [6,10,14,16,18,22,23] for honest majority.

The narrow set of use-cases that MPC has seen in practice, in spite of the major push to improve its efficiency and the amount of prototype implementations available, may be a direct effect of some of the other limitations present in MPC which are not precisely related to efficiency metrics such as running times or communication complexities. MPC protocols are distributed interactions that obey a set of rules and, importantly, take place over a communication network, such as the internet. In the real world, networks are unstable, nodes join and leave, computers crash, software has bugs and messages take variable times to reach their destination—or they may even not arrive at all. Moreover, in the cloud setting, cloud resiliency is essential given that networks are dynamic and need to tolerate power and regional outages. Unfortunately, most MPC protocols are not designed to tolerate such unstable networking settings which appear in practice. One may argue that *actively* secure protocols do tolerate unstable environments, since, ultimately, they tolerate arbitrary behavior from the set of corrupted parties. This, however, is unsatisfactory: every MPC protocol has a limited amount of active corruptions it can tolerate, and treating genuinely honest parties as corrupt due to, say, networking or software errors is unacceptable. In particular, not only it reduces the amount of actual malicious corruptions the protocol can tolerate, but also deprives the flagged honest party from any security guarantee, since from a definitional point of view corrupt parties do not need any protection.

Fluid MPC. The limitations of MPC mentioned above have been already identified by several previous works [1,11,12,20,24,25]. These works aim at developing MPC solutions for more unstable settings where the parties or the network may fail to accommodate real world conditions. We discuss these in more detail in the related work section (Sect. 1.2). In this work we focus on the *Fluid MPC setting*, introduced in [11]. This approach aims at making MPC more suitable for practical settings by reducing the connectivity requirements that the set of computing parties need to have. Instead of requiring all parties to stay 100% online and with no failures during the whole duration of the computation (which, depending on the protocol, can range from a few minutes to hours, to a whole day), the fluid MPC model allows the parties to join only at parts of the computation, which can be made as "small" as required. More specifically, parties are called online to participate in a committee for a given set of communication rounds. Each committee computes over a specific number of rounds, and once the task is completed the parties in the committee need to *transfer* the state of the computation to the next committee in line, who continues with the computation.

In [11] it was shown how to instantiate fluid MPC in the *maximal fluidity setting* where parties only need to be online for a single communication round. The parties receive the previous state of the computation, advance one step, and transfer the new state to the next committee. This is done in the setting where the adversary corrupts at most a minority in each chosen committee, or in other words, each committee contains an honest majority. Later, in [25], it was shown how to obtain fluid MPC with maximal fluidity in the setting where each committee contains an arbitrary amount of corruptions, or put differently, the corruptions in each committee may constitute of a dishonest majority. The authors aim for an information-theoretic online phase and thus require to assume certain "global preprocessing" among the pool of all parties who will eventually form the different computation committees. The preprocessing is "consumed" at execution time in order to accelerate the computation and is independent of the inputs to the computation and the evaluation function. Both of these works make a noticeable step in making MPC more suitable for practical settings where participants do not need to guarantee stability for extended periods of time.

However, for both the protocols in [11,25], the fluidity feature comes at the expense of asymptotically increasing communication complexity with respect to state-of-the art solutions in the non-fluid setting, such as [3,15] for dishonest majority, and [6,10,14,16,18,22,23] for honest majority. Existing non-fluid techniques achieve *linear communication complexity*, which is to say that the communication complexity per party does not increase in the average as the set of computing parties increases. In contrast, the protocols from [11,25] require *quadratic* communication, which means the communication complexity per party grows linearly with the total number of parties. Such an overhead deprives the scalability of the protocols (*e.g.* if there are twice the amount of parties, then each party needs to send twice the amount of messages). In a way, it seems that achieving the flexibility of the fluid MPC setting comes at the expense of lowering the performance of the resulting protocol. That said, there is no known MPC protocol in the fluid setting which only requires constant communication overhead per party for any corruption threshold (for both honest and dishonest majority).

1.1 Our Contribution

In this work we aim at achieving the efficiency of the non-fluid MPC protocols (*i.e.* overall linear communication complexity), while simultaneously achieving maximal fluidity[1] where a participating party stays online for a single communication round of the secure computation. The goal is to achieve the best of both worlds: flexible enough computation that can somehow mitigate the instability of networks present in the real world without significantly degrading the communication complexity. In particular, we propose fluid MPC protocols with constant communication overhead per party in a committee of size n for any corruption threshold.

In the following we let C be a *layered* arithmetic circuit over a finite field $\mathbb{F}$ with $|C|$ multiplication gates and depth $\mathsf{depth}(C)$. A layered circuit is a type of arithmetic circuit comprised of input, output, addition, multiplication, and identity gates, where all output wires of a given layer go only to the immediately next layer. As is common in MPC protocols that achieve linear communication

[1] Note that even for fluidity $f \geq 2$ the works of [11,25] still only achieve communication complexity $\Omega(n^2 \cdot |C|/f)$; in particular quadratic if f is constant.

complexity (e.g., [13,14]), we assume that the width of all layers of considered circuits is at least proportional to n. We remark, however, that even with smaller widths, our result is a strict improvement over prior works.

- *Information-theoretic honest majority without preprocessing:* We show that, in the case where each committee contains an honest majority (*i.e.* the setting from [11]), the circuit C can be evaluated with maximal fluidity by using $(2\cdot\mathsf{depth}(C)+14)$ different committees in the execution stage with a total communication of $O(n|C|)$ for the largest n. The input and output stages require a small constant of committees. This protocol requires no preprocessing among the parties for the circuit computation and is information-theoretic.
- *Information-theoretic dishonest majority with preprocessing:* For the case where each committee may contain a dishonest majority (*i.e.* the setting from [25]), we show that the circuit C can be evaluated with maximal fluidity by using $(2\cdot\mathsf{depth}(C)+5)$ different committees during the execution stage, with a total communication of $O(n|C|)$ for the largest n. This is done starting from a global preprocessing among the pool of all parties that, crucially, does not assume knowledge of the committee assignments ahead of the computation. The online phase is information-theoretic. Similarly to the honest majority case, the input and output stages require a small constant of committees.
- *Lower bound on the amount of preprocessed data:* Finally, on the negative side, we prove a lower bound on the amount of preprocessing required in the information-theoretic dishonest majority setting in order to transfer the secret-shared execution state st from one committee to the next, which is a major building block used in fluid protocols. We show that, in order to achieve sub-quadratic communication for the transfer, it must be the case that each party in the global pool of parties has preprocessing whose size is proportional to $\Omega(N\cdot|\mathsf{st}|)$, where N is the total amount of parties in the global pool. In particular, if each committee computes the output of at most one circuit layer (possibly including multiplication gates) at a time, and each party may participate in a constant fraction of committees in the worst-case, then the total preprocessing per party must be $\Omega(N\cdot|C|)$. Such large preprocessing is not needed for the case in which quadratic communication suffices, since in this case the parties can perform a *resharing* step where each party secret-shares their share to each other party in the next committee, without making use of any preprocessing.
  This result shows that linear communication complexity in the dishonest majority setting comes at a price: if more parties join the global pool, the preprocessing held by each party must necessarily grow.[2]

[2] We remark however that, even in [25], the preprocessing per party grows as $\Omega(N)$, even when quadratic communication is achieved. This preprocessing is of a different nature though and is not related to resharing, as it comes in the form of pairwise products that are used to build multiplication triples once the exact committees are known. Our result implies that, even if multiplication triples are pre-distributed within each committee, transferring the state from one committee to the next will still require $\Omega(N)$ preprocessing, unless $O(n^2)$ communication is allowed. We discuss this in more detail in Sect. 5.

As in [11,25], both of our protocols are actively secure and offer security with abort (unanimous abort, if the clients have access to broadcast). A crucial property of the model for fluid computation is that each committee only knows the identities of the parties it is directly connected to on-the-fly without the need to commit to a specific online time way ahead of time. Both [11,25] provide ample motivation for this setting, which includes, for example, applications to computing via distributed systems such as blockchains.

We summarize our results in the following theorems. First some extra notation: given a layered circuit C, we let w_ℓ be the width of the ℓ-th layer in C and for some gate g in C, we let $\ell(g)$ be the index of the layer that g belongs to in C.

Theorem 1 (Informal). *For a layered arithmetic circuit C over a finite field $\mathbb{F}$, there exists an information-theoretic fluid MPC protocol with maximal fluidity which securely computes C in the presence of an active adversary controlling up to $t < n/2$ parties. The protocol uses $2 \cdot \mathsf{depth}(C) + 14$ n-party committees and the communication cost per gate g is $O(n^2/w_{\ell(g)})$ for the largest n. In particular, if the width of all layers is $w = \Omega(n)$, then the total cost is $O(n|C|)$ elements of communication for the largest n.*

Theorem 2 (Informal). *For an arithmetic circuit C over a finite field $\mathbb{F}$, there exists an information-theoretic fluid MPC protocol with maximal fluidity in the preprocessing model which securely computes C in the presence of an active adversary controlling up to $t \geq n/2$ parties. The protocol uses $(2 \cdot \mathsf{depth}(C) + 5)$ n-party committees in the execution stage and the communication cost per gate g is $O(n^2/w_{\ell(g)})$ for the largest n. In particular, if the width of all layers is $w = \Omega(n)$, then the total cost is $O(n|C|)$ elements of communication for the largest n.*

Theorem 3 (Informal). *A secure message transmission protocol for messages of length λ with two n-party committees that uses $o(n^2 \cdot \lambda)$ total communication must have $\Omega(N \cdot \lambda)$ preprocessed data.*

At the crux of our techniques for the protocols are methods to allow reconstruction and resharing of shares in the presence of an active adversary with linear communication in the fluid setting while dealing with the challenge of dynamic committees which are not known ahead of time and announced one by one on the fly. Paradoxically, we adapt the common "king" technique, originated in the non-fluid honest majority setting [14], to obtain our results in the dishonest majority setting. And at the same time, we start with the non-fluid SPDZ-like techniques (additive secret sharing and authenticated shares), originated in the non-fluid dishonest majority setting [15], to obtain our honest majority results without the need of preprocessing. Finally, we cast the problem of transferring the secret-shared execution state from one committee to the next into the secure message transmission setting and use information theoretic arguments to prove our lower bound.

1.2 Related Work

As mentioned above, our work expands on the work of [11,25] for MPC in the fluid model. There are several works that study other alternative models to Fluid MPC, that also aim at making MPC solutions more resilient to unstable networking settings. Early works like [17] study MPC in the setting where the adversary may "fail-stop" corrupt some parties, meaning these parties can crash upon an adversarial command, but they do not reveal their state to the adversary. Other models such as Lazy MPC [1] or sleepy MPC [24] aim at enabling dropouts, but they do so in different ways to Fluid MPC: in Lazy MPC the parties can drop but they cannot return to the computation, and in sleepy in MPC parties can return, but they are assumed to receive all messages sent to them while being offline. In the recent work of [12], a model is presented where the parties can return to the computation while enabling lost messages. Last but not least, the YOSO work of [19] splits the computation to committees where each committee passes the control of the computation to the next committee. However, their work requires all parties to be online at all times. Moreover, unlike [19], we have no restrictions on the size of committees nor the overlap between them. We refer the reader to the full version for a more thorough description of these works.

2 Technical Overview

We begin by presenting the general idea of our fluid dishonest majority protocol with linear communication complexity, in the preprocessing model. It turns out some of the ideas present in this part of our work will also be helpful for the construction of our fluid honest majority protocol. Due to space constraints, our main body contains our honest majority construction only, in Sect. 4. Our dishonest majority construction appears in the full version. We aim at compensating by presenting a thorough overview of our dishonest majority solution below, and having a shorter overview for the honest majority protocol in Sect. 2.3.

2.1 Our Starting Point: Le Mans [25]

We first present the high level ideas of the protocol from [25], which achieves fluid MPC in the dishonest majority setting with quadratic communication complexity. The overall idea is the following. The circuit at hand is considered to be a *layered circuit*. As in [11], the invariant that will be kept is that the parties in committee C_i will hold certain sharings of all the current intermediate values in layer i. Eventually, the last committee obtains shares of the outputs of the circuit, which are then transmitted to the clients. Unlike [11] however, Le Mans makes use of additive secret-sharing in contrast to Shamir's, due to the setting being dishonest majority in contrast to honest majority.

Resharing and Openings. To maintain the aforementioned invariant, Le Mans makes use of two major blocks. Let us denote by $[x]^{\mathcal{C}}$ additive shares held by committee $\mathcal{C}$ of some secret x. First, to preserve the invariant for addition and identity gates, the parties make use of a *resharing* procedure which enables the parties in committee $\mathcal{C}_i$ to transfer additive sharings of some given values $[x_1]^{\mathcal{C}_i}, \ldots, [x_m]^{\mathcal{C}_i}$ to committee $\mathcal{C}_{i+1}$ so that, as long as there is at least one honest party in each of these two committees, the adversary learns no information about the underlying secrets, and the parties in $\mathcal{C}_{i+1}$ obtain fresh-looking shares $[x_1]^{\mathcal{C}_{i+1}}, \ldots, [x_m]^{\mathcal{C}_{i+1}}$. As we will see later, this resharing can be achieved quite efficiently (in particular, with linear communication complexity) by preprocessing most of the shares that the receiving committee $\mathcal{C}_{i+1}$ should hold.

The second major block used in Le Mans is that of Beaver triples, which is preprocessed material of the form $([a]^{\mathcal{C}_i}, [b]^{\mathcal{C}_i}, [c]^{\mathcal{C}_i})$ where $c = a \cdot b$, held by a committee $\mathcal{C}_i$.[3] This enables sharings $[x]^{\mathcal{C}_i}, [y]^{\mathcal{C}_i}$ held by $\mathcal{C}_i$ to be "multiplied", so that committee $\mathcal{C}_{i+1}$ obtains sharings $[x \cdot y]^{\mathcal{C}_{i+1}}$. This is done by the parties in $\mathcal{C}_i$ locally computing $[x+a]^{\mathcal{C}_i}$ and $[y+b]^{\mathcal{C}_i}$, followed by *opening* these sharings towards $\mathcal{C}_{i+1}$ by each party in $\mathcal{C}_i$ revealing their shares to each party in $\mathcal{C}_{i+1}$. Notice that this takes quadratic communication, and in fact, opening shared values are in essence the exact quadratic bottleneck in Le Mans.

Let us assume temporarily that committee $\mathcal{C}_{i+1}$ has sharings of the same multiplication triple, that is, $([a]^{\mathcal{C}_{i+1}}, [b]^{\mathcal{C}_{i+1}}, [c]^{\mathcal{C}_{i+1}})$. After $\mathcal{C}_{i+1}$ receives $x+a$ and $y+b$, they can locally compute $[x \cdot y]^{\mathcal{C}_{i+1}} = (x+a)(y+b) - (y+b)[a]^{\mathcal{C}_{i+1}} - (x+a)[b]^{\mathcal{C}_{i+1}} + [c]^{\mathcal{C}_{i+1}}$, as required. Now, one way in which committee $\mathcal{C}_{i+1}$ could have obtained the multiplication triple is by assuming they obtain it from the preprocessing. However, notice that this triple has to coincide with the one held by $\mathcal{C}_i$, which is harder to achieve while maintaining the requirement of committee-agnostic preprocessing. Instead, in Le Mans the following approach is taken: the parties in $\mathcal{C}_i$ *reshare* their triple $([a]^{\mathcal{C}_i}, [b]^{\mathcal{C}_i}, [c]^{\mathcal{C}_i})$ to committee $\mathcal{C}_{i+1}$, which enables the latter committee to obtain $([a]^{\mathcal{C}_{i+1}}, [b]^{\mathcal{C}_{i+1}}, [c]^{\mathcal{C}_{i+1}})$. In principle, using the resharing method sketched above, this can be done with linear communication complexity. However, as we will discuss below, active security demands that besides additive sharings the parties also hold sharings of certain MACs. In Le Mans this is handled by using a different resharing method named key-switching, which makes use of openings and hence it suffers from quadratic communication.

Authenticated Sharings. To prevent a corrupt party from breaking security, Le Mans, as all of the dishonest majority MPC protocols, relies on the SPDZ paradigm [15] of adding authentication to every shared value. This consists of additive sharings of a global MAC key $[\Delta]$, and for each shared value $[x]$, additive

[3] Recall that a requirement in the fluid preprocessing model is that the correlations the parties receive have to be agnostic to the specific committee assignments. It may not be clear now, but it turns out multiplication triples are committee-agnostic, if the parties start with BeDOZa-style correlations [4]. This will be made clearer.

sharings of the MAC of this value, computed as $[\Delta \cdot x]$. In the fluid setting, each committee $\mathcal{C}_i$ who has shares of a value $[x]^{\mathcal{C}_i}$ must also have shares of its MAC $[\Delta_{\mathcal{C}_i} \cdot x]^{\mathcal{C}_i}$, together with shares of the global key $[\Delta_{\mathcal{C}_i}]^{\mathcal{C}_i}$.

The shared MAC key $[\Delta_{\mathcal{C}_i}]^{\mathcal{C}_i}$ can be preprocessed, but it may be different from committee to committee as a result of the committee-agnostic preprocessing condition. Due to this, if the first committee has sharings $([x]^{\mathcal{C}_i}, [\Delta_{\mathcal{C}_i} \cdot x]^{\mathcal{C}_i}, [\Delta_{\mathcal{C}_i}]^{\mathcal{C}_i})$, and the second committee $\mathcal{C}_{i+1}$ wants to obtain authenticated sharings $([x]^{\mathcal{C}_{i+1}}, [\Delta_{\mathcal{C}_{i+1}} \cdot x]^{\mathcal{C}_{i+1}}, [\Delta_{\mathcal{C}_{i+1}}]^{\mathcal{C}_{i+1}})$ under the different key $\Delta_{\mathcal{C}_{i+1}}$, this cannot be achieved with the simple resharing from before, given that the secret $\Delta_{\mathcal{C}_i} \cdot x$ changes to $\Delta_{\mathcal{C}_{i+1}} \cdot x$. This is addressed in Le Mans by using a key switching method (Protocol $\Pi_{\mathsf{Key\text{-}Switch}}$ in [25]) that enables an authenticated value under one committee's key to be transferred to the next committee so that it remains authenticated, but under the key of the next committee.

In a bit more detail, assume preprocessed sharings $([r]^{\mathcal{C}_i}, [\Delta_{\mathcal{C}_{i+1}} \cdot r]^{\mathcal{C}_{i+1}})$.[4] With this, given $[\Delta_{\mathcal{C}_i} \cdot x]^{\mathcal{C}_i}$, committee $\mathcal{C}_{i+1}$ can obtain $[\Delta_{\mathcal{C}_{i+1}} \cdot x]^{\mathcal{C}_{i+1}}$ by letting $\mathcal{C}_i$ first compute locally $[x-r]^{\mathcal{C}_i}$ and then *opening* this value towards committee $\mathcal{C}_{i+1}$. Then, committee $\mathcal{C}_{i+1}$ computes locally $[\Delta_{\mathcal{C}_{i+1}} \cdot x]^{\mathcal{C}_{i+1}} = (x-r) \cdot [\Delta_{\mathcal{C}_{i+1}}]^{\mathcal{C}_{i+1}} + [\Delta_{\mathcal{C}_{i+1}} \cdot r]^{\mathcal{C}_{i+1}}$. Again, because this requires opening shared values from one committee to another, the resulting communication complexity is quadratic.

2.2 The "King Idea" in the Fluid Setting

The reconstruction of a value d requires n^2 communication if all parties just send shares to each other, but it can be done with communication $O(n)$ based on the "king idea" from [14]. This is achieved as follows: in a first round, all share owners send their shares to a single party, a "king", who reconstructs d and sends this value to the intended receiving parties in a second round.

Given that, as we have highlighted above, opening shared values is the bottleneck in Le Mans, a natural approach to achieving linear communication complexity in that protocol is to replace all-to-all openings, which have quadratic communication complexity, by the king idea above. However, this imposes a major complication: all-to-all openings require quadratic communication, but only make use of *one single round*, while in contrast, the king idea has linear communication complexity but requires *two rounds*. As a result, using the king idea does not allow committee $\mathcal{C}_i$ to open shared values to committee $\mathcal{C}_{i+1}$, but rather, these can be opened towards a committee $\mathcal{C}_{i+2}$ (by making use of a king

[4] This form of preprocessing is not committee-agnostic, but a simpler form of it is, and the actual tuple required is obtained by adding an extra resharing step. This is not relevant for our discussion.

in $\mathcal{C}_{i+1}$). At first sight, one may think that the techniques from Le Mans carry over when using this king idea by simply using two committees per circuit layer, instead of one, to accommodate for the extra round required for the reconstruction of shared values. Unfortunately, as we will argue below, such approach is much more complicated than how it looks at a high level.

Problems with Key Switching. Recall the key switching protocol from Le Mans sketched above. In that protocol, the parties start with a pair $([r]^{\mathcal{C}_i}, [\Delta_{\mathcal{C}_{i+1}} \cdot r]^{\mathcal{C}_{i+1}})$, and this enables committee $\mathcal{C}_i$ to "transfer" shares of MACs $[\Delta_{\mathcal{C}_i} \cdot x]^{\mathcal{C}_i}$ to committee $\mathcal{C}_{i+1}$ so that the latter obtains $[\Delta_{\mathcal{C}_{i+1}} \cdot x]^{\mathcal{C}_{i+1}}$. This approach works for the one-round openings used in the key switching, but if instead we want to use two-round openings with a king, the king would have to be a member of $\mathcal{C}_{i+1}$ itself, and the key switching would have to be done towards committee $\mathcal{C}_{i+2}$ instead. This raises a number of complications. First, such approach would require an initial pair $([r]^{\mathcal{C}_i}, [\Delta_{\mathcal{C}_{i+2}} \cdot r]^{\mathcal{C}_{i+2}})$, but unfortunately such pair is not easily obtainable. The reason is that $[\Delta_{\mathcal{C}_{i+1}} \cdot r]^{\mathcal{C}_{i+1}}$ for the inefficient key-switch protocol is obtained in part by the parties of committee $\mathcal{C}_i$ using preprocessed "local MACs" of their shares of r under some keys that each party in committee $\mathcal{C}_{i+1}$ has. This is allowed in the fluid model, since committee $\mathcal{C}_i$ *does* learn the parties of committee $\mathcal{C}_{i+1}$ at some point (so that they know to whom to send their sharings of intermediate circuit values). However, committee $\mathcal{C}_i$ *never* learns the parties of committee $\mathcal{C}_{i+2}$, so we do not have the preprocessing required to obtain $[\Delta_{\mathcal{C}_{i+2}} \cdot r]^{\mathcal{C}_{i+2}}$.

Instead, our approach is to let committee $\mathcal{C}_{i+2}$ obtain sharings of the MAC of the secret x, but under a MAC key corresponding to the previous committee $\mathcal{C}_{i+1}$, that is, $[\Delta_{\mathcal{C}_{i+1}} \cdot x]^{\mathcal{C}_{i+2}}$. The Le Mans key switching protocol is naturally extended to achieve this by using the king of committee $\mathcal{C}_{i+1}$ to reconstruct $(x - r)$ to the parties of committee $\mathcal{C}_{i+2}$ and also having committee $\mathcal{C}_{i+1}$ reshare $[\Delta_{\mathcal{C}_{i+1}} \cdot r]^{\mathcal{C}_{i+1}}$ and $[\Delta_{\mathcal{C}_{i+1}}]^{\mathcal{C}_{i+1}}$ with committee $\mathcal{C}_{i+2}$. Committee $\mathcal{C}_{i+2}$ can then perform the same computation as committee $\mathcal{C}_{i+1}$ did before with these sharings to obtain $[\Delta_{\mathcal{C}_{i+1}} \cdot x]^{\mathcal{C}_{i+2}}$. However, with this key switching protocol, we need to take some extra care in our protocol to ensure that MACs of intermediate circuit values do not "fall behind".

In particular, we maintain the invariant that the inputs to the gates at the circuit layer which some committee $\mathcal{C}_i$ processes must be authenticated under the MAC key of committee $\mathcal{C}_{i-2}$. For example, $([x]^{\mathcal{C}_{i+2}}, [\Delta_{\mathcal{C}_i} \cdot x]^{\mathcal{C}_{i+2}})$. This is achieved by preprocessing a multiplication triple where the sharings of a and b are authenticated under the MAC keys of both committees $\mathcal{C}_{i-2}$ and $\mathcal{C}_{i-1}$. For example, the a sharing is of the form: $([a]^{\mathcal{C}_{i-2}}, [\Delta_{\mathcal{C}_{i-2}} \cdot a]^{\mathcal{C}_{i-2}}, [\Delta_{\mathcal{C}_{i-1}} \cdot a]^{\mathcal{C}_{i-1}})$.[5] Now, committee $\mathcal{C}_{i-2}$ can first reshare the triple that is authenticated under their MAC key Δ_{i-2} to committee $\mathcal{C}_{i-1}$, who can then reshare it to committee $\mathcal{C}_i$.

[5] This kind of triple authenticated under the MAC keys of both committees $\mathcal{C}_{i-2}$ and $\mathcal{C}_{i-1}$ can indeed still be computed from our actual committee-agnostic preprocessing.

Assuming the invariant holds for committee $\mathcal{C}_i$, it can then successfully compute authenticated sharings of $(x + a)$ and $(y + b)$ under MAC key Δ_{i-2} needed to multiply x and y. Also, from the above resharing by committee $\mathcal{C}_{i-2}$, and the MACs on the triple that committee $\mathcal{C}_{i-1}$ already holds, committee $\mathcal{C}_{i-1}$ obtains the triple authenticated under their MAC key Δ_{i-1}. Committee $\mathcal{C}_{i-1}$ can then key switch the triple with committee $\mathcal{C}_{i+1}$ using a king in committee $\mathcal{C}_i$. From this key switching, committee $\mathcal{C}_{i+1}$ receives the triple authenticated under the MAC key of committee $\mathcal{C}_i$, e.g., for the a part: $([a]^{\mathcal{C}_{i+1}}, [\Delta_{\mathcal{C}_i} \cdot a]^{\mathcal{C}_{i+1}})$. Committee $\mathcal{C}_{i+1}$ can then reshare this triple to committee $\mathcal{C}_{i+2}$, who can then use the above multiplication technique to obtain $([xy]^{\mathcal{C}_{i+2}}, [\Delta_{\mathcal{C}_i} \cdot (xy)]^{\mathcal{C}_{i+2}})$, also authenticated under the MAC key of committee $\mathcal{C}_i$. Thus the invariant is preserved.

Authenticating Multiplication Triples. There is a second and perhaps more subtle problem that arises when using an intermediate king for linear reconstruction. Note that the above preprocessed triples that we can obtain are such that the sharing $[c]^{\mathcal{C}_i}$ is *not* authenticated. This is addressed in Le Mans by letting committee $\mathcal{C}_i$ learn the authentication of $[c]^{\mathcal{C}_i}$, and in fact the whole multiplication triple, from the previous committee $\mathcal{C}_{i-1}$. In a bit more detail, $\mathcal{C}_{i-1}$ obtains $([a]^{\mathcal{C}_{i-1}}, [\Delta_{\mathcal{C}_{i-1}} \cdot a]^{\mathcal{C}_{i-1}}, [b]^{\mathcal{C}_{i-1}}, [\Delta_{\mathcal{C}_{i-1}} \cdot b]^{\mathcal{C}_{i-1}}, [c]^{\mathcal{C}_{i-1}})$ from the preprocessing, and they perform key switching so that committee $\mathcal{C}_i$ obtains the multiplication triple with the MAC shares of the factors, only missing the shares of the MAC of c. To obtain $[\Delta_{\mathcal{C}_i} \cdot c]^{\mathcal{C}_i}$, a pair $([v]^{\mathcal{C}_{i-1}}, [\Delta_{\mathcal{C}_i} \cdot v]^{\mathcal{C}_i})$ is generated using the key switch protocol on a preprocessed pair $([v]^{\mathcal{C}_{i-1}}, [\Delta_{\mathcal{C}_{i-1}} \cdot v]^{\mathcal{C}_{i-1}})$.[6] With the former pair at hand, the parties in $\mathcal{C}_{i-1}$ can open $[c - v]^{\mathcal{C}_{i-1}}$ to $\mathcal{C}_i$, who can then compute locally $[\Delta_{\mathcal{C}_i} \cdot c]^{\mathcal{C}_i} = (c - v) \cdot [\Delta_{\mathcal{C}_i}]^{\mathcal{C}_i} + [\Delta_{\mathcal{C}_i} \cdot v]^{\mathcal{C}_i}$.

We can easily enough tweak our multiplication procedure sketched above so that committee $\mathcal{C}_{i-2}$ instead uses a king in committee $\mathcal{C}_{i-1}$ to open $(c - v)$ to committee $\mathcal{C}_i$. However, recall that using our key-switch procedure, committee $\mathcal{C}_i$ can only obtain sharings from committee $\mathcal{C}_{i-2}$ that are authenticated under the MAC key of committee $\mathcal{C}_{i-1}$. But, we need c to be authenticated under the MAC key of committee $\mathcal{C}_i$ in order to preserve the invariant described above, since these shares of c are used to compute the shares of the output. Thus, we must wait until committee $\mathcal{C}_{i+1}$ to authenticate c under the key of committee $\mathcal{C}_i$. However, since $(x + a)$ and $(y + b)$ are opened to the (possibly corrupt) king of committee $\mathcal{C}_{i+1}$, the adversary could then add errors dependent on x and y to c while authenticating it. The adversary could thus mount a selective failure attack using these errors. To solve this we still use the king technique so that committee $\mathcal{C}_{i-2}$ can open $(c - v)$ to committee $\mathcal{C}_i$. We then have *only* some king in committee $\mathcal{C}_i$ (to preserve linear communication) again forward $(c - v)$ to committee $\mathcal{C}_{i+1}$, who can then authenticate c. To ensure that this king does not cheat as above, we also have the parties of committee $\mathcal{C}_i$ hash the received $(c - v)$ values for *all* multiplication gates at this circuit layer, using a universal hash function. Then the parties of committee $\mathcal{C}_i$ send these hashes to *each* party

[6] [25] uses 'l' instead of our 'v' here.

of $\mathcal{C}_{i+1}$, who use them to check consistency of their received openings. Since these hashes are short, in fact independent of the number of gates at this layer, communication is still efficient. We use a similar hashing technique as part of the procedure that checks the MACs of shared values.

2.3 Fluid Honest Majority MPC with Linear Communication

Here we comment briefly on how we obtain our results in the honest majority setting. We remark that, for the purpose of this overview, we present our results using as a starting point the previous discussion on dishonest majority, even though in the main body the honest majority appears first in Sect. 4. In this section, let us denote by $[x]_t^{\mathcal{C}}$ Shamir shares of degree t, held by the parties in committee $\mathcal{C}$. In the work of [11], honest majority fluid MPC is achieved by letting the parties in a given committee $\mathcal{C}_i$ hold *Shamir* sharings of the intermediate circuit values $[x_1]_t^{\mathcal{C}_i}, \ldots, [x_\ell]_t^{\mathcal{C}_i}$ in the i-th layer, where $t < n/2$. To preserve the invariant observe that, because of the multiplicative properties of Shamir secret-sharing, the parties in $\mathcal{C}_i$ can *locally* obtain sharings of every intermediate value $[y_1]_{t'_1}^{\mathcal{C}_i}, \ldots, [y_{\ell'}]_{t'_1}^{\mathcal{C}_i}$ in the next layer, where each degree t'_j is either equal to t (for addition and identity gates), or $2t$, which is less than n (for multiplication gates). At this point, the parties in $\mathcal{C}_i$ can *reshare* these shared values towards committee $\mathcal{C}_{i+1}$, who obtains $[y_1]_{t'_1}^{\mathcal{C}_{i+1}}, \ldots, [y_{\ell'}]_{t'_{\ell'}}^{\mathcal{C}_{i+1}}$, hence maintaining the invariant.

While in the dishonest majority setting resharing additively shared values (with no authentication) can be achieved with linear communication complexity assuming certain form of committee-agnostic preprocessing, such approach does not work in our current setting. Here, Shamir secret-sharing is used, and resharing in one round requires a quadratic amount of communication as it is done by each party in $\mathcal{C}_i$ distributing shares of their Shamir share to each party in $\mathcal{C}_{i+1}$, which can be aggregated to obtain Shamir shares of the underlying secret. This is indeed the approach taken in [11], and this is one of the fundamental reasons for the quadratic communication in that work. A second reason is also similar to the one in the dishonest majority setting, and it is related to the reconstruction of secret-shared values.

We can interpret our protocol in the honest majority setting as addressing the two issues highlighted above using some techniques from the dishonest majority case as a base, while adding other new ones, and for the purpose of this section, we describe our protocol in these terms. In a bit more detail, we overcome the issue of resharing with squared communication by, instead of using Shamir secret-sharing with degree $t < n/2$, using a larger degree $n - 1$, which is in essence equivalent to additive secret-sharing, as used in the dishonest majority setting. In principle, this would enable us to perform resharing with linear communication by using preprocessed data as sketched in Sect. 2.1. However, an important challenge in the honest majority setting is that we should not use any preprocessing whatsoever since, unlike the dishonest majority setting, it is not required.

Due to the above, our approach for resharing degree-$(n-1)$ Shamir sharings *without preprocessing* with linear communication is different. Assume committee

$\mathcal{C}_i$ has sharings $[x]_{n-1}^{\mathcal{C}_i}$, and the goal is for committee $\mathcal{C}_{i+1}$ to obtain $[x]_{n-1}^{\mathcal{C}_{i+1}}$. Let us write $\mathcal{C}_i = \{P_1, \dots, P_n\}$ and $\mathcal{C}_{i+1} = \{Q_1, \dots, Q_n\}$, and also $[x]_{n-1}^{\mathcal{C}_i} = (x_1, \dots, x_n)$. Assume the parties in $\mathcal{C}_i$ have preprocessed a sharing of zero $[0]_{n-1}^{\mathcal{C}_i} = (r_1, \dots, r_n)$.[7] Our resharing protocol is summarized as follows: each party P_j sends $x_j + r_j$ to Q_j, and committee $\mathcal{C}_{i+1}$ defines $[x]_{n-1}^{\mathcal{C}_{i+1}}$ to be these received shares. In words, shares are transferred in a "straight line fashion" (after randomizing with shares of zero), and the new sharings are exactly *the same* as the previous ones. This approach does not work in the dishonest majority setting: the adversary can corrupt, say, $P_1, \dots, P_{n-1}$ in the first committee, and by corrupting Q_n the adversary learns all shares. In contrast, in the honest majority setting, the adversary learns at most t shares in the first committee and t shares in the second, for a total of $\leq 2t < n$ shares, which maintain privacy of the underlying secret. This powerful observation turns out to be the enabling tool for linear communication.

Using degree-$(n-1)$ Shamir sharings means that the shares of the honest parties in a given committee do not determine the underlying secret anymore, which enables a corrupt party to cheat by modifying their share. Importantly, a similar issue was faced in the dishonest majority setting with additive secret-sharing, and fortunately we are able to take a similar approach here by using MACs in order to prevent cheating. We remark that these are not needed in [11], since they use Shamir sharings of low degree. We do not elaborate on how MACs are used in our protocol to prevent cheating, but we mention that the approach is in spirit similar to the one sketched in the dishonest majority overview.

The final details we comment on are related to the "preprocessing" required in our protocol. As we mentioned initially, it is imperative that our honest majority protocol does not make use of any preprocessing material. However, we already mentioned some form of preprocessing (namely, shares of zero $[0]_{n-1}^{\mathcal{C}_i}$), plus, several ideas from the dishonest majority protocol require preprocessing such as authenticated values $([r]_{n-1}^{\mathcal{C}_i}, [\Delta_{\mathcal{C}_i} \cdot r]_{n-1}^{\mathcal{C}_i}, [\Delta_{\mathcal{C}_i}]_{n-1}^{\mathcal{C}_i})$, or authenticated multiplication triples. Fortunately, in our work we are able to leverage once more the fact that we have an honest majority in order to let committee $\mathcal{C}_{i-1}$ generate the "preprocessing" for committee $\mathcal{C}_i$ *on the fly*. For correlations that are "linear" such as sharings of zero, the approach from [14] can be easily adapted, where the parties in committee $\mathcal{C}_{i-1}$ distribute sharings to $\mathcal{C}_i$, and the latter perform randomness extraction using a Vandermonde matrix. On the other hand, for correlations that include a multiplication, like multiplication triples or authenticated values $([r]_{n-1}^{\mathcal{C}_i}, [\Delta_{\mathcal{C}_i} \cdot r]_{n-1}^{\mathcal{C}_i}, [\Delta_{\mathcal{C}_i}]_{n-1}^{\mathcal{C}_i})$, the parties in $\mathcal{C}_{i-1}$ can obtain the linear part $([r]_t^{\mathcal{C}_{i-1}}, [\Delta_{\mathcal{C}_i}]_t^{\mathcal{C}_{i-1}})$ from $\mathcal{C}_{i-2}$ using the ideas we just described for linear correlations (notice the degree is $t < n/2$). Then, the parties in $\mathcal{C}_{i-1}$ locally multiply these sharings, to obtain $[\Delta_{\mathcal{C}_i} \cdot r]_{2t}^{\mathcal{C}_{i-1}}$. Finally, the parties in $\mathcal{C}_{i-1}$ perform the "straight-line" resharing from before so that $\mathcal{C}_i$ obtains $([r]_{n-1}^{\mathcal{C}_i}, [\Delta_{\mathcal{C}_i} \cdot r]_{n-1}^{\mathcal{C}_i}, [\Delta_{\mathcal{C}_i}]_{n-1}^{\mathcal{C}_i})$.

7 As we elaborate on below, this type of preprocessing can in fact be generated "on the fly" by the different committees, so it is not considered preprocessing as such.

2.4 Technical Overview of SMT Lower Bound

Now we provide an overview for the lower bound on the amount of preprocessed data, for the dishonest majority case. We do this in the context of secure message transmission (SMT). Assume we have some sender A who wants to send some secret value x to a receiver B through two committees that are not known ahead of time. This is related to fluid MPC: we can think of an identity function that is to be computed using two committees. That said, assume that between A and B, there are two (non-overlapping) committees $\mathcal{C}_1$ and $\mathcal{C}_2$, each of size n, that are chosen at random from the larger universe $\mathcal{U}$ of parties of size N. Furthermore, assume that some adversary $\mathcal{A}$ that is trying to learn x is able to (passively) corrupt all-but-one party in each of $\mathcal{C}_1$ and $\mathcal{C}_2$, as well as any other parties in $\mathcal{U}$. In such a setting, we also allow for some *global preprocessing protocol* that the parties of $\mathcal{U}$ can run amongst each other *before* the secret x or committees $\mathcal{C}_1$ and $\mathcal{C}_2$ are chosen. We show that if the size of each preprocessing state is $o(N \cdot |x|)$, then the total communication must be $\Omega(n^2 \cdot |x|)$. The intuition is as follows.

Suppose that $\mathcal{A}$ corrupts all but the first parties of each committee. Furthermore, suppose, towards contradiction, that the size of the message $c_{1,1}$ that the first party of $\mathcal{C}_1$ sends to the first party of $\mathcal{C}_2$ is small ($\ll |x|$). First, this means that $\mathcal{A}$ can guess this message with high probability. Now, suppose that the preprocessing $r_{1,1}$ of the first party of $\mathcal{C}_1$ is not anymore correlated with the preprocessing $r_{2,1}$ of the second party of $\mathcal{C}_2$, than the preprocessing of the rest of the corrupted parties of $\mathcal{C}_1$. This correlation is what the parties of $\mathcal{C}_1$ (perhaps, implicitly) use to construct messages that will eventually result in correct transmission to the receiver B. In particular, any possible preprocessing $r'_{2,1}$ that has non-zero probability weight conditioned on the preprocessing of the parties of $\mathcal{C}_1$, and thus by the above assumption, the corrupted parties of $\mathcal{C}_1$, must enable correct transmission. So, since the first party of $\mathcal{C}_2$ only uses $r_{2,1}$ along with the ciphertexts it receives to produce its message to the receiver B, $\mathcal{A}$ must be able to use a guess for $r_{2,1}$ conditioned on the preprocessing of corrupt parties of $\mathcal{C}_1$ to produce a valid such message. Together with the other messages to the receiver B from the corrupted parties of $\mathcal{C}_2$, $\mathcal{A}$ can reconstruct x with high probability.

So, it must in fact be that $r_{1,1}$ provides some unique information on the preprocessing of $r_{2,1}$ that the corrupted parties of $\mathcal{C}_1$ do not already provide. However, it is just as likely that some other party in $\mathcal{U}$ could have been chosen to be the first party of $\mathcal{C}_1$, in some other execution of the protocol. So, in fact *every* party outside of $\mathcal{C}_1$ and $\mathcal{C}_2$ must provide some unique information on the preprocessing of $r_{2,1}$. Since $\mathcal{A}$ can corrupt as many of these parties as it wishes, if $r_{2,1}$ is small enough (in particular, $o(N \cdot |x|)$), then $\mathcal{A}$ will eventually be able to reconstruct $r_{2,1}$ completely, guess (short) $c_{1,1}$ and thus again reconstruct x with high probability, as above. Therefore, a contradiction is reached, and the size of each (n^2 total) ciphertext $c_{i,j}$ must be $\Omega(|x|)$.

3 Security Model and Preliminaries

We present some of the preliminaries required in our work. First we discuss the fluid model in Sect. 3.1, and then in Sect. 3.2 we present our security model. We utilize the universal composability framework of [8].

3.1 Modelling Fluid MPC

We first recall at a high level the modelling of Fluid MPC from [11,25]. A more detailed description is given in the full version. We consider the *client-server* model, where there is a universe $\mathcal{U}$ of parties, that includes both the clients, who provide inputs, and servers, who perform computation. Computation is composed of an optional preprocessing stage among all clients and servers, an input phase where clients provide inputs, an execution stage where the servers compute the function, and an output phase where the clients receive output. The execution step is itself divided into *epochs*, where each epoch i runs among a fixed set of servers, or committee $\mathcal{C}_i$. An epoch contains two parts, the computation phase, where the committee performs some computation local to itself, followed by a hand-off phase, where the current committee securely transfers some current state to the next committee. We assume that all parties have access to only point-to-point channels. For simplicity, throughout the paper we may refer to the set of clients, $\mathcal{C}_{\mathsf{clnt}}$, as $\mathcal{C}_0$ (the 0-th committee) and $\mathcal{C}_\ell$ (the last committee).

Fluidity. This is defined as the minimum number of rounds in any given epoch of the execution stage. We say a protocol achieves *maximal fluidity* if each epoch i only lasts for one total round. In this paper, as in [11,25], we only consider maximal fluidity.

Committee Formation. The committees used in each epoch are chosen on-the-fly throughout the execution stage. See [11] for more motivation and details on committee selection. The model of [11] specifies the formation process via an ideal functionality that samples and broadcasts committees according to the desired mechanism. However, as in [25], we desire to divorce the study of committee selection from the actual MPC and simply require that all parties of the current committee $\mathcal{C}_i$ somehow agree on the next committee $\mathcal{C}_{i+1}$. Specifically, the parties of committee $\mathcal{C}_i$ during the hand-off phase of epoch i (and not before) are informed by the environment $\mathcal{Z}$ of its choice of committee $\mathcal{C}_{i+1}$ (i.e., it is a worst-case choice by $\mathcal{Z}$). We make no assumptions or restrictions on the size of committees nor the overlap between committees. In particular, committees may consist of a large number (possibly constant fraction) of parties in the entire universe, $\mathcal{U}$.

Corruptions. We study two different settings for the number of parties that may be corrupted for our model to still require security:

- For *honest majority*, the adversary $\mathcal{A}$ may only corrupt any minority of servers in the committee of each epoch.[8] This is the setting that [11] studies.

[8] All-but-one client could be corrupted, however.

- For *dishonest majority*, the adversary $\mathcal{A}$ may corrupt all-but-one client and all-but-one server in the committee of each epoch. This is the setting that [25] studies.

We consider a *malicious R-adaptive adversary* from [11] and used in [25]. In short, if there is a preprocessing stage, the adversary *statically* chooses some parties to corrupt beforehand. Then, the adversary *statically* chooses a set of clients to corrupt. During each epoch i of the execution phase, after learning which servers are in committee $\mathcal{C}_i$, the adversary *adaptively* chooses a subset of $\mathcal{C}_i$ to corrupt. Upon such a corruption, the adversary learns the server's entire past state and can send messages on its behalf in epoch i. Therefore, when counting the number of corruptions for some epoch i, we must retroactively include those servers in committee $\mathcal{C}_i$ that are corrupted in some later epoch $j > i$. Furthermore, if there is a preprocessing stage, we count a server in committee $\mathcal{C}_i$ as corrupted also if they were corrupted during the preprocessing phase.

3.2 Security Model

To model Fluid MPC, we adapt the dynamic arithmetic black box (DABB) ideal functionality $\mathcal{F}_{\mathsf{DABB}}$ of [25]. First, we note that our protocols, as written, achieve *security with selective abort* (same as [11,25]), where the adversary can prevent any clients of his or her choice from receiving output. However, similar to the protocol of [11] (c.f. Appendix A), our protocols can easily achieve *unanimous abort* (in which honest clients either all receive the output or all abort) if the clients have access to a broadcast channel in the last round or if they implement a broadcast over their point-to-point channels. The same applies to the protocol of [25]. Functionality $\mathcal{F}_{\mathsf{DABB}}$, presented below, is parameterized by a finite field $\mathbb{F}_p$, and supports addition and multiplication operations over the field. It keeps track of the current epoch number in a variable i and the committee of the current epoch i in a variable $\mathcal{C}_i$. The functionality receives the identity of the first committee from the clients via input **Init**. During the execution stage, where the current committee may change, the functionality receives the identity of the next committee from the currently active parties via input **Next-Committee** (if it receives inconsistent committees for either of these two inputs, we assume it aborts).

Functionality 1: $\mathcal{F}_{\mathsf{DABB}}$

Parameters: Finite field $\mathbb{F}_p$, universe $\mathcal{U}$ of parties, and set of clients $\mathcal{C}_{\mathsf{clnt}} \subseteq \mathcal{U}$. The functionality assumes that all parties have agreed upon public identifiers id_x, for each variable x used in the computation.

Init: On input $(\mathsf{Init}, \mathcal{C})$ from every party $P_j \in \mathcal{C}_{\mathsf{clnt}}$, where each P_j sends the same set $\mathcal{C} \subseteq \mathcal{U}$, initialize $i = 1$, $\mathcal{C}_1 = \mathcal{C}$ as the first active committee. Send $(\mathsf{Init}, \mathcal{C}_1)$ to $\mathcal{S}$.

Input: On input $(\mathsf{Input}, \mathsf{id}_x, x)$ from some $P_j \in \mathcal{C}_{\mathsf{clnt}}$, and $(\mathsf{Input}, \mathsf{id}_x)$ from all other parties in $\mathcal{C}_{\mathsf{clnt}}$, store the pair (id_x, x). Send $(\mathsf{Input}, \mathsf{id}_x)$ to $\mathcal{S}$.

Next-Committee: On input $(\mathsf{Next\text{-}Committee}, \mathcal{C})$ from every party $P_j \in \mathcal{C}_i$, where each P_j sends the same set $\mathcal{C} \subseteq \mathcal{U}$, update $i = i + 1$, $\mathcal{C}_i = \mathcal{C}$. Send $(\mathsf{Next\text{-}Committee}, \mathcal{C}_i)$ to $\mathcal{S}$.

Add: On input $(\mathsf{Add}, \mathsf{id}_z, \mathsf{id}_x, \mathsf{id}_y)$ from every party $P_j \in \mathcal{C}_i$, compute $z = x + y$ and store (id_z, z). Send $(\mathsf{Add}, \mathsf{id}_z, \mathsf{id}_x, \mathsf{id}_y)$ to $\mathcal{S}$.

Multiply: On input $(\mathsf{Mult}, \mathsf{id}_z, \mathsf{id}_x, \mathsf{id}_y)$ from every party $P_j \in \mathcal{C}_i$, compute $z = x \cdot y$ and store (id_z, z). Send $(\mathsf{Mult}, \mathsf{id}_z, \mathsf{id}_x, \mathsf{id}_y)$ to $\mathcal{S}$.

Output: On input $(\mathsf{Output}, \{\mathsf{id}_{z_m}\})$ from every party $P_j \in \mathcal{C}_{\mathsf{clnt}} \cup \mathcal{C}_i$, where a value z_m for each id_{z_m} has been stored previously, retrieve $\{(\mathsf{id}_{z_m}, z_m)\}$ and send $(\mathsf{Output}, \{(\mathsf{id}_{z_m}, z_m)\})$ to $\mathcal{S}$. Wait for input from $\mathcal{S}$, and if it is $\mathsf{Deliver}$, send the output to every $P_i \in \mathcal{C}_{\mathsf{clnt}}$. Otherwise, abort.

3.3 Preliminaries

Notation. We first note that we will often use $l \in \mathcal{C}_i$ as shorthand to refer to some party $P_l \in \mathcal{C}_{i+1}$. We use $x \leftarrow_{\$} \mathcal{X}$ to denote sampling x randomly from distribution $\mathcal{X}$.

Universal Hashing. We make use of universal hash function families in both our honest and dishonest majority protocols. A family of hash functions $\mathcal{H} = \{\mathcal{H}_s : \mathbb{F}_p^T \to \mathbb{F}_p\}$ is *universal* if for all $x \neq y \in \mathbb{F}_p^T$, $\Pr_s[\mathcal{H}_s(x) = \mathcal{H}_s(y)] \leq 1/p$.

Functionalities, Protocols and Procedures. In this work we denote functionalities by $\mathcal{F}$ and some subscript, and protocols by Π and some subscript. We also consider *procedures*, denoted by π and some subscript. These are similar to protocols except that (1) they act like "macros" that can be called within actual protocols and (2) they are not intended to instantiate a given functionality. Instead, security is proven in the protocol where they are used.

Layered Circuits. We refer the reader to [11] for a more precise description on layered circuits. In short, these are arithmetic circuits composed of addition, multiplication and identity gates. The circuit is divided in *layers*, and for each such layer, the inputs to each gate on the layer come directly from the layer above. Every circuit can be made layered by adding enough identity gates.

4 Honest Majority

We begin our technical description by presenting our protocol for fluid MPC with linear communication complexity and maximal fluidity in the honest majority setting, where each committee contains at most a minority of corrupt parties. The outline of this section is the following. First, in Sect. 4.1, we present a major building block, Procedure $\pi_{\mathsf{eff\text{-}reshare\text{-}hm}}$, which enables a given committee holding a sharing of a random value to efficiently reshare this secret to the next committee. As in the two previous fluid protocols [11,25], we make use of a randomized version of the circuit that aims at detecting cheating in multiplication gates, and we also draw inspiration from [25] and make use of a MAC check that accounts for the correctness of the openings throughout the computation, which is crucial in our case to achieve linear communication complexity. This is discussed in Sect. 4.2. Then, in Sect. 4.3 we show how the parties make progress through the computation by processing multiplication gates. Finally, these pieces are put together in Sect. 4.4 to obtain our final protocol, $\Pi_{\mathsf{main\text{-}hm}}$, for honest majority MPC in the fluid model with linear communication complexity and maximal fluidity.

Notation and Initial Building Blocks. We let $[x]_{t_i}^{\mathcal{C}_i}$ denote a Shamir secret-sharing of value x with degree-t_i among the parties of committee $\mathcal{C}_i$. A SPDZ sharing [15] of a value x among the parties of committee $\mathcal{C}$, $[\![x]\!]^{\mathcal{C}}$ contains a vector of degree-$2t$ Shamir shares $[\![x]\!]^{\mathcal{C}} := ([x]_{2t}, [\Delta]_{2t}, [\Delta \cdot x]_{2t})$.

We now describe some of the building blocks we will require for our final protocol. Some of these are fairly standard in the literature and implementing them in the fluid setting represents little challenge, so we postpone their detailed description and instantiation to the full version. For our main honest majority protocol, we will require the following functionalities. $\mathcal{F}_{\mathsf{rand}}$ provides degree-t_i sharings of a random value r to committee $\mathcal{C}_i$. $\mathcal{F}_{\mathsf{coin}}$ samples a random coin $c \in \mathbb{F}_p$ to the parties in committee $\mathcal{C}_i$. $\mathcal{F}_{\mathsf{double\text{-}rand}}$ distributes degree-t_i and degree-$2t_i$ sharings of the same random value r to $\mathcal{C}_i$. $\mathcal{F}_{\mathsf{zero}}$ distributes degree $2t_i$ shares of $o = 0$ to $\mathcal{C}_i$.

As we will later accomplish in $\Pi_{\mathsf{main\text{-}hm}}$, each committee will have a degree-t_i and degree-$2t_i$ double sharing of the global MAC key Δ. Therefore we will assume that all procedures presented below that are invoked by $\mathcal{C}_i$ will implicitly take these sharings as input.

We rely on the following procedure that enables the parties in a given committee $\mathcal{C}_i$ to obtain authenticated sharings of a uniformly random value $[\![r]\!]^{\mathcal{C}_i}$, assuming Shamir sharings of the key $([\Delta]_{t_i}^{\mathcal{C}_i}, [\Delta]_{2t_i}^{\mathcal{C}_i})$. This is described below. Observe that in the protocol the MAC sharings produced $[r \cdot \Delta]_{t_i}^{\mathcal{C}}$ are not uniformly random, but instead, they are a product $[r]_{t_i}^{\mathcal{C}_i} \cdot [\Delta]_{t_i}^{\mathcal{C}_i}$. These sharings will be randomized in the places we use them.

Procedure 1: $\pi_{\mathsf{get\text{-}rand\text{-}sharing}}$

Usage: Using double sharing $([\Delta]_{t_i}^{\mathcal{C}_i}, [\Delta]_{2t_i}^{\mathcal{C}_i})$ of the global MAC key, $\mathcal{C}_i$ outputs a random SPDZ sharing $[\![r]\!]^{\mathcal{C}_i}$.

1. All parties in $\mathcal{C}_i$ invoke $\mathcal{F}_{\mathsf{double\text{-}rand}}$ to get random double sharing $([r]_{t_i}^{\mathcal{C}_i}, [r]_{2t_i}^{\mathcal{C}_i})$.
2. Parties in $\mathcal{C}_i$ then locally obtain and output authenticated sharing $[\![r]\!]^{\mathcal{C}_i} = ([r]_{2t_i}^{\mathcal{C}_i}, [r]_{t_i}^{\mathcal{C}_i} \cdot [\Delta]_{t_i}^{\mathcal{C}_i}, [\Delta]_{2t_i}^{\mathcal{C}_i})$.

4.1 Efficient Resharing for Honest Majority

As we highlighted in Sect. 2, a fundamental reason why the protocol from [11] does not achieve linear communication complexity stems from the fact that the hand-off procedure from one committee to the next one consists of every party resharing their share towards the next committee, which requires quadratic communication. In our work, we address this limitation by making use of Procedure $\pi_{\mathsf{eff\text{-}reshare\text{-}hm}}$ below, which shows how to reshare a degree-$2t_i$ Shamir sharing from committee $\mathcal{C}_i$ to the next committee $\mathcal{C}_{i+1}$, while using only linear communication. The idea is in fact simple: assuming each committee has the same amount of parties n (the procedure below is more general), each party with index j in committee $\mathcal{C}_i$ will send (a re-randomized version of) their share to the party with index j in $\mathcal{C}_{i+1}$ directly. This is secure since the adversary learns in total at most $2t$ shares across the two committees, which is the degree of the polynomial used. As briefly mentioned above, the parties first re-randomize their shares using $\mathcal{F}_{\mathsf{zero}}$, which is done to prevent a new sharing from leaking the underlying secret when transmittted to the next committee.

Procedure 2: $\pi_{\mathsf{eff\text{-}reshare\text{-}hm}}$

Usage: $\mathcal{C}_i$ reshares re-randomized $[r]_{2t_i}^{\mathcal{C}_i}$ to $\mathcal{C}_{i+1}$. Assume that the parties in $\mathcal{C}_i$ are indexed from 1 to n_i and those in $\mathcal{C}_{i+1}$ are indexed from n_i+1 to n_i+n_{i+1}.

1. Let $[r]_{2t_i}^{\mathcal{C}_i}$ be the input shares.
2. $\mathcal{C}_i$ invokes $\mathcal{F}_{\mathsf{zero}}$ and receives a sharing of $o=0$, $[o]_{2t_i}^{\mathcal{C}_i}$.
3. All parties locally compute $[r']_{2t_i}^{\mathcal{C}_i} = [r]_{2t_i}^{i} + [o]_{2t_i}^{i}$, for $r' = r + 0 = r$.
4. Finally:
   - If $n_i < n_{i+1}$: Let $d = n_{i+1}/n_i$ (assuming $n_i | n_{i+1}$ for simplicity). Each $P_j \in \mathcal{C}_i$ samples $d-1$ random values r_l, sets $r_{j \cdot d} = (r')^j - \sum_{l=1}^{d-1} r_l$, where $(r')^j$ is their share of $[r']_{2t_i}^{\mathcal{C}_i}$, and sends each r_l for $l \in [d]$ to $P_{n_i+(j-1)\cdot d+l} \in \mathcal{C}_{i+1}$, who outputs this as their share of $[r']_{2t_{i+1}}^{\mathcal{C}_{i+1}}$.
   - Else: Let $d = n_i/n_{i+1}$ (assuming $n_{i+1}|n_i$ for simplicity). For l such that $(l-1)\cdot d < j \leq l \cdot d$, each $P_j \in \mathcal{C}_i$ sends their share r'^j to $P_{n_i+l} \in \mathcal{C}_{i+1}$, who outputs as their share of $[r']_{2t_{i+1}}^{\mathcal{C}_{i+1}}$, $\sum_j r'^j$ for each P_j it received from.

Lemma 1. *Assume that at most* $2t_i$ *shares of* $[r]_{2t_i}^{\mathcal{C}_i}$ *can be computed by* $\mathcal{A}$ *(and the rest are uniformly random to* $\mathcal{A}$*). Then procedure* $\pi_{\mathsf{eff\text{-}reshare\text{-}hm}}$*'s transcript is simulatable with random values and preserves the invariant that at most* $2t_{i+1}$ *shares of* $[r]_{2t_{i+1}}^{\mathcal{C}_{i+1}}$ *can be computed by* $\mathcal{A}$*, while the rest are uniformly random to* $\mathcal{A}$.

The proof appears in the full version.

Inefficient resharing. We will also need to reshare degree-t_i Shamir sharings across committees using Procedure $\pi_{\mathsf{ineff\text{-}reshare\text{-}hm}}$, below. This can only be done with $\Omega(n^2)$ communication, however, since it is only done once per committee, we can still achieve $O(n|C|)$ total communication if the width of circuit C is $\Omega(n)$.

Procedure 3: $\pi_{\mathsf{ineff\text{-}reshare\text{-}hm}}$

Usage $\mathcal{C}_i$ reshares $[r]_{t_i}^{\mathcal{C}_i}$ to $\mathcal{C}_{i+1}$.

1. Let r^j be P_j's share of $[r]_{t_i}^{\mathcal{C}_i}$. Each $P_j \in \mathcal{C}_i$ will create a random degree t_{i+1} Shamir secret sharing $\left[r^j\right]_{t_{i+1}}^{\mathcal{C}_i}$ of their share and distribute the corresponding shares to each $P_l \in \mathcal{C}_{i+1}$.
2. Finally, each $P_l \in \mathcal{C}_{i+1}$ will then compute $[r]_{t_{i+1}}^{\mathcal{C}_i} = \sum_{j \in \mathcal{C}_i} c_j \left[r^j\right]_{t_{i+1}}^{\mathcal{C}_i}$, where c_j is the Lagrange reconstruction coefficient for a degree-t_{i+1} polynomial.

Lemma 2. *Procedure* $\pi_{\mathsf{ineff\text{-}reshare\text{-}hm}}$*'s transcript is simulatable with random values.*

Proof. This follows easily from the fact that the shares of the honest parties of $\mathcal{C}_i$ are unknown to the adversary. So, by the security of Shamir secret sharing, the t_{i+1} shares of each honest party's share in $\mathcal{C}_i$ that the corrupt parties of $\mathcal{C}_{i+1}$ receive are uniformly random.

4.2 Incremental Checks

As in [11], we achieve active security by maintaining a few "accumulators" that somehow aggregate the potential errors that are introduced by each committee. These accumulators are updated by every other committee, and the current (possibly updated) version of the accumulator is transferred from one committee to the next. Finally, the final committees will use these accumulators to verify the integrity of the computation.

In our protocol, we make use of the "straightline" resharing procedure $\pi_{\mathsf{eff\text{-}reshare\text{-}hm}}$ that achieves linear communication complexity, but requires a larger threshold of $2t_i$ to achieve security. This means that the underlying secrets are not determined by the honest parties alone, and as a result a malicious adversary can in fact add errors to *any* value throughout the computation. A similar issue happens in the dishonest majority fluid protocol of [25], and we draw inspiration from such approach to address this attack in our protocol. The solution consists of using MACs, which are used to authenticate every intermediate value used throughout the computation and serve as additional redundancy on secret values that guarantees integrity. This is done by maintaining an accumulator that attests for the integrity of all of the reconstructions, which is built using the shared MACs and the claimed openings.

Succinctly maintaining this accumulator involves opening random challenges β to committees, who then use such β to compute random linear combinations that *compress* the verification of many MACs into one field element that should be 0. However, these challenges β should not be opened at the same time that the values whose MACs it checks are opened, for otherwise the adversary could cheat in the above linear combination. Thus, when the parties of $\mathcal{C}_i$ receive some openings and want to verify their MACs, they each hash together all of these openings and then send these hashes to each of the parties of $\mathcal{C}_{i+1}$. The challenge β is then opened to $\mathcal{C}_{i+1}$, and only P_1 of $\mathcal{C}_i$ forwards all of the openings to all of the parties of $\mathcal{C}_{i+1}$, in order to maintain linear communication. Since the hashes prevent P_1 from changing the openings, they cannot be dependent on β. Since the hashes are short, total communication will still be $O(n|C|)$ if the width of C is $\Omega(n)$.

Also note that it takes two committees to update the accumulator based on values opened to the first committee. However, since values are only opened to every other committee, there is no entanglement of updates. Details are given in Procedure $\pi_{\mathsf{MAC\text{-}check\text{-}hm}}$ below.

Procedure 4: $\pi_{\mathsf{MAC\text{-}check\text{-}hm}}$

Usage: Each committee $\mathcal{C}_i$ incrementally updates a MAC check state $[\sigma]_{2t_i}^{\mathcal{C}_i}$ based on the values opened to them, which the final committees at the end of the computation use to check that all openings throughout the protocol were performed correctly.

Init: Each Party P_i in committee $\mathcal{C}_4$ (the first to have values opened to it, since the first invocation of $\pi_{\mathsf{mult\text{-}hm}}$ is by $\mathcal{C}_2$ to create randomized versions of the circuit inputs) initially defines their share of $[\sigma]_{2t_4}^{\mathcal{C}_4}$ as $\sigma^i = 0$.

Update State: On input $(\mathsf{update}, \{(A_m, [\Delta \cdot A_m]_{2t_i}^{\mathcal{C}_i})\}_{m\in[T]}, [\Delta]_{2t_i}^{\mathcal{C}_i})$ from committee $\mathcal{C}_i$, where $\{A_m\}_{m\in[T]}$ were the values opened to $\mathcal{C}_i$:

1. First each party $P_j \in \mathcal{C}_i$ samples keys $s_{j,l}$ to the universal hash family $\mathcal{H} = \{\mathcal{H}_s : \mathbb{F}_p^T \to \mathbb{F}_p\}$ for each $P_l \in \mathcal{C}_{i+1}$ and computes $h_{j,l} = \mathcal{H}_{s_{j,l}}(\{A_m\}_{m\in[T]})$.
2. In parallel: (i) each party $P_j \in \mathcal{C}_i$ then sends to each $P_l \in \mathcal{C}_{i+1}$ the universal hash key and value $s_{j,l}, h_{j,l}$; (ii) only P_1 sends $\{A_m\}_{m\in[T]}$ to each $P_l \in \mathcal{C}_{i+1}$; and (iii) all of $\mathcal{C}_i$ invokes $\pi_{\mathsf{eff\text{-}reshare\text{-}hm}}$ on $[\sigma]_{2t_i}^{\mathcal{C}_i}, \{[\Delta \cdot A_m]_{2t_i}^{\mathcal{C}_i}\}_{m\in[T]}$.
3. Each P_l in Committee $\mathcal{C}_{i+1}$ first for each $P_j \in \mathcal{C}_i$ computes $h'_{j,l} = \mathcal{H}_{s_{j,l}}(\{A_m\}_{m\in[T]})$ and checks if $h'_{j,l} = h_{j,l}$. If not, it aborts; else continues.
4. $\mathcal{C}_{i+1}$ then invokes $\mathcal{F}_{\mathsf{coin}}$ to get a random challenge β.
5. Each $P_l \in \mathcal{C}_{i+1}$ next locally computes $A = \sum_{m=1}^{T} \beta^m \cdot A_m$ and $[\gamma]_{2t_{i+1}}^{\mathcal{C}_{i+1}} = \sum_{m=1}^{T} \beta^m \cdot [\Delta \cdot A_m]_{2t_{i+1}}^{\mathcal{C}_i}$.
6. It finally updates $[\sigma]_{2t_{i+1}}^{\mathcal{C}_{i+1}} = [\sigma]_{2t_{i+1}}^{\mathcal{C}_{i+1}} + [\gamma]_{2t_{i+1}}^{\mathcal{C}_{i+1}} - [\Delta]_{2t_{i+1}}^{\mathcal{C}_{i+1}} \cdot A$ and invokes $\pi_{\mathsf{eff\text{-}reshare\text{-}hm}}$ on $[\sigma]_{2t_{i+1}}^{\mathcal{C}_{i+1}}$.

Check State: On input check from committee $\mathcal{C}_i$:

1. Let σ^j be the share of the MAC check state $[\sigma]_{2t_i}^{\mathcal{C}_i}$ held by each $P_j \in \mathcal{C}_i$. Each P_j creates a random degree-t_{i+1} Shamir secret share $[\sigma^j]_{t_{i+1}}^{\mathcal{C}_{i+1}}$ of their share σ^j and distributes the corresponding shares to the parties of $\mathcal{C}_{i+1}$.
2. Then each party $P_l \in \mathcal{C}_{i+1}$ computes $[\sigma]_{t_{i+1}}^{\mathcal{C}_{i+1}} = \sum_{j\in\mathcal{C}_i} c_j \cdot [\sigma^j]_{t_{i+1}}^{\mathcal{C}_{i+1}}$, where c_j is the Lagrange reconstruction coefficient for a degree-$2t_i$ polynomial.

3. Finally, parties open the shares of $[\sigma]_{t_{i+1}}^{\mathcal{C}_{i+1}}$ to each party of $\mathcal{C}_{i+2}$, who reconstruct σ, and if successful, output Accept if $\sigma = 0$; else Reject.

Lemma 3. *Procedure $\pi_{\mathsf{MAC\text{-}check\text{-}hm}}$ is correct, i.e., it accepts if all the opened values A_m and the corresponding MACs are computed correctly. Moreover, it is sound, i.e., it rejects except with probability at most $(2 + \max_i T_i)/p$ in case at least one opened value is not correctly computed. Furthermore, the transcript of* ***Update State*** *is simulatable.*

The proof appears in the full version.

Unfortunately, this is not the only kind of error we need to account for. As in [25], the c parts of multiplication triples that are used in $\pi_{\mathsf{mult\text{-}hm}}$ are only authenticated "on the fly". This means that the adversary can inject additive errors into these c parts that $\pi_{\mathsf{MAC\text{-}check\text{-}hm}}$ will not catch (since the corresponding errors will be incorporated into the MACs, too). As a result, multiplications may not be computed correctly. To address this attack vector, we use similar ideas to [11,25], which have their roots in the techniques of [10], and consists of maintaining a randomized version of the circuit which can be used to verify multiplications. The associated accumulator is presented in Procedure $\pi_{\mathsf{mult\text{-}verify\text{-}hm}}$ below.[9]

Procedure 5: $\pi_{\mathsf{mult\text{-}verify\text{-}hm}}$

Usage: Each committee $\mathcal{C}_i$ that gets the output wires of the multiplication gates of some layer ℓ of the circuit incrementally updates a multiplication verification state $(\llbracket u' \rrbracket^{\mathcal{C}_{2t_i}}, \llbracket w' \rrbracket^{\mathcal{C}_{2t_i}})$, which the final committees at the end of the computation use to check that all multiplications throughout the protocol were performed correctly.

Init: Each Party P_i in committee $\mathcal{C}_4$ (the first to get output from $\pi_{\mathsf{mult\text{-}hm}}$, as a result of $\mathcal{C}_2$ creating randomized versions of the circuit inputs) initially defines their shares of $\llbracket u' \rrbracket^{\mathcal{C}_4}, \llbracket w' \rrbracket^{\mathcal{C}_4}$ as $(u')^i = (w')^i = 0$ (same for the MAC shares).

Update State: On input $(\mathsf{update}, \{(\llbracket z_m \rrbracket^{\mathcal{C}_i}, \llbracket r z_m \rrbracket^{\mathcal{C}_i}\}_{m \in [T]})$ from committee $\mathcal{C}_i$, where $\{(\llbracket z_m \rrbracket^{\mathcal{C}_i}, \llbracket r z_m \rrbracket^{\mathcal{C}_i}\}_{m \in [T]}$ were the output wires of multiplication gates computed by $\mathcal{C}_i$:

1. Each P_j in $\mathcal{C}_i$ invokes $\mathcal{F}_{\mathsf{coin}}$ to get random challenge α.
2. Parties P_j in $\mathcal{C}_i$ locally compute $\llbracket u \rrbracket^{\mathcal{C}_i} = \llbracket u \rrbracket^{\mathcal{C}_i} + \sum_{m=1}^{T} \alpha^m \cdot \llbracket r z_m \rrbracket^{\mathcal{C}_i}$ and $\llbracket w \rrbracket^{\mathcal{C}_i} = \llbracket w \rrbracket^{\mathcal{C}_i} + \sum_{m=1}^{T} \alpha^m \cdot \llbracket z_m \rrbracket^{\mathcal{C}_i}$.
3. Finally $\mathcal{C}_i$ invokes $\pi_{\mathsf{eff\text{-}reshare\text{-}hm}}$ on $\llbracket u \rrbracket^{\mathcal{C}_i}, \llbracket w \rrbracket^{\mathcal{C}_i}$.

Check State: On input check from the clients $\mathcal{C}_i$:

1. The parties of $\mathcal{C}_i$ first open $\llbracket r \rrbracket^{\mathcal{C}_i}$ to the parties of $\mathcal{C}_{i+1}$, who then check its MAC by running both phases of $\pi_{\mathsf{MAC\text{-}check\text{-}hm}}$ on it.

[9] Note that the invocations of $\pi_{\mathsf{MAC\text{-}check\text{-}hm}}$ in the **Check State** phase of $\pi_{\mathsf{mult\text{-}verify\text{-}hm}}$ can be condensed to 3 rounds, since only one value at a time is opened.

2. Then the parties of $\mathcal{C}_{i+4}$ ($\pi_{\mathsf{MAC\text{-}check\text{-}hm}}$ takes 4 rounds) all open ($[\![u]\!]^{\mathcal{C}_{\mathsf{clnt}}} - r \cdot [\![w]\!]^{\mathcal{C}_{\mathsf{clnt}}}$) to the parties of $\mathcal{C}_{i+5}$, who then check its MAC by running both phases of $\pi_{\mathsf{MAC\text{-}check\text{-}hm}}$ on it. If the opened value is 0, the parties of $\mathcal{C}_{i+8}$ ($\pi_{\mathsf{MAC\text{-}check\text{-}hm}}$ takes 4 rounds) output Accept; else Reject.

Lemma 4. *Procedure $\pi_{\mathsf{mult\text{-}verify\text{-}hm}}$ is correct, i.e., it accepts if all multiplications are computed correctly. Moreover, it is sound, i.e., it rejects except with probability at most $(1 + \max_i T_i)/p$ in case at least one multiplication is not correctly computed. Furthermore, the transcript of* ***Update State*** *is simulatable.*

The proof is given in the full version.

4.3 Secure Multiplication

Finally, before we discuss our ultimate protocol, we present Procedure $\pi_{\mathsf{mult\text{-}hm}}$ below which enables a given committee to make progress on the computation by securely processing multiplication gates. At a high level, this procedure makes use of multiplication triples [2] to reduce the task of securely multiplying two shared values, to that of reconstructing two secrets. Reconstruction is done by using the "king idea", originating from [14], which achieves linear communication complexity by first reconstructing to a single party who then sends the reconstruction to the other parties.

However, there are a couple of issues we need to deal with. First, using multiplication triples requires different committees to have access to the same multiplication triple. We indeed achieve this by making use of our resharing procedure $\pi_{\mathsf{eff\text{-}reshare\text{-}hm}}$ from Sect. 4.1. Second, a given committee can only obtain a *partially* authenticated multiplication triple ($[\![a]\!]^{\mathcal{C}}, [\![b]\!]^{\mathcal{C}}, [c]_{2t}^{\mathcal{C}}$), where the c part is not authenticated. Using an idea from [25], we authenticate the c part of each triple "on the fly". Intuitively, this is done by masking $[c]_{2t}^{\mathcal{C}}$ with a random, authenticated sharing $[\![v]\!]^{\mathcal{C}}$, reconstructing $(c+v)$, then creating unmasked, authenticated shares of c using $[\![v]\!]^{\mathcal{C}}$ (including its MAC). Reconstructing $(c+v)$ here is also done by using the "king idea". The details are presented below.

Procedure 6: $\pi_{\mathsf{mult\text{-}hm}}$

Usage: Using double sharing ($[\Delta]_{t_i}^{\mathcal{C}_i}, [\Delta]_{2t_i}^{\mathcal{C}_i}$) of the global MAC key, multiply $[\![x]\!]^{\mathcal{C}_i}$ and $[\![y]\!]^{\mathcal{C}_i}$ held by $\mathcal{C}_i$ so that $\mathcal{C}_{i+2}$ outputs $[\![x \cdot y]\!]^{\mathcal{C}_{i+2}}$.

1. All parties in $\mathcal{C}_{i-2}$ agree on a special party P_{king} in $\mathcal{C}_{i-1}$.
2. All parties in $\mathcal{C}_{i-2}$ invoke $\pi_{\mathsf{get\text{-}rand\text{-}sharing}}$ three times to get $[\![a]\!]^{\mathcal{C}_{i-2}}, [\![b]\!]^{\mathcal{C}_{i-2}}, [\![v]\!]^{\mathcal{C}_{i-2}}$ (they also save the sharings $[a]_{t_{i-2}}^{\mathcal{C}_{i-2}}, [b]_{t_{i-2}}^{\mathcal{C}_{i-2}}$ generated during this invocation).
3. $\mathcal{C}_{i-2}$ then locally obtains (unauthenticated) $[c]_{2t_{i-2}}^{\mathcal{C}_{i-2}} = [a]_{t_{i-2}}^{\mathcal{C}_{i-2}} \cdot [b]_{t_{i-2}}^{\mathcal{C}_{i-2}}$.

4. Finally, parties in $\mathcal{C}_{i-2}$ in parallel invoke $\pi_{\text{eff-reshare-hm}}$ on input $[\![a]\!]^{\mathcal{C}_{i-2}}, [\![b]\!]^{\mathcal{C}_{i-2}}, [\![v]\!]^{\mathcal{C}_{i-2}}$ and open $[c+v]_{2t_{i-2}}^{\mathcal{C}_{i-2}}$ to P_{king} in $\mathcal{C}_{i-1}$.
5. Then, while P_{king} distributes opened $(c+v)$ to the parties of $\mathcal{C}_i$, the rest of the parties in $\mathcal{C}_{i-1}$ in parallel invoke $\pi_{\text{eff-reshare-hm}}$ on input $[\![a]\!]^{\mathcal{C}_{i-1}}, [\![b]\!]^{\mathcal{C}_{i-1}}, [\![v]\!]^{\mathcal{C}_{i-1}}$.
6. Parties in $\mathcal{C}_i$ then use opened $(c+v)$ to compute authenticated $[\![c]\!]^{\mathcal{C}_i} = ((c+v) - [v]_{2t_i}^{\mathcal{C}_i}, [\Delta]_{2t_i}^{\mathcal{C}_i} \cdot (c+v) - [\Delta \cdot v]_{2t_i}^{\mathcal{C}_{i+2}}, [\Delta]_{2t_i}^{\mathcal{C}_i})$.
7. Parties in $\mathcal{C}_i$ agree on a special party P'_{king} in $\mathcal{C}_{i+1}$ and then compute $[\![x + a]\!]^{\mathcal{C}_i} = [\![x]\!]^{\mathcal{C}_i} + [\![a]\!]^{\mathcal{C}_i}$, and $[\![y]\!]^{\mathcal{C}_i} = [\![y]\!]^{\mathcal{C}_i} + [\![b]\!]^{\mathcal{C}_i}$.
8. Parties in $\mathcal{C}_i$ then in parallel open $[\![x+a]\!]^{\mathcal{C}_i}, [\![y+b]\!]^{\mathcal{C}_i}$ to P'_{king} in $\mathcal{C}_{i+1}$ and invoke $\pi_{\text{eff-reshare-hm}}$ on $[\![a]\!]^{\mathcal{C}_i}, [\![b]\!]^{\mathcal{C}_i}, [\![c]\!]^{\mathcal{C}_i}, [\Delta \cdot (x+a)]_{2t_i}^{\mathcal{C}_i}, [\Delta \cdot (y+b)]_{2t_i}^{\mathcal{C}_i}$.
9. Then while P'_{king} distributes opened $d = x + a$ and $e = y + b$ to the parties of $\mathcal{C}_{i+2}$, all parties in $\mathcal{C}_{i+1}$ invoke $\pi_{\text{eff-reshare-hm}}$ on input $[\![a]\!]^{\mathcal{C}_{i+1}}, [\![b]\!]^{\mathcal{C}_{i+1}}, [\![c]\!]^{\mathcal{C}_{i+1}}, [\Delta \cdot (x+a)]_{2t_{i+1}}^{\mathcal{C}_{i+1}}, [\Delta \cdot (y+b)]_{2t_{i+1}}^{\mathcal{C}_{i+1}}$.
10. $\mathcal{C}_{i+2}$ finally locally computes $[\![x \cdot y]\!]^{\mathcal{C}_{i+2}} = de - d[\![b]\!]^{\mathcal{C}_{i+2}} - e[\![a]\!]^{\mathcal{C}_{i+2}} + [\![c]\!]^{\mathcal{C}_{i+2}}$.
11. Parties in $\mathcal{C}_{i+2}$ will also invoke $\pi_{\text{MAC-check-hm}}$ on input $(\text{update}, \{((x_m + a_m, [\Delta \cdot (x_m + a_m)]_{2t_{i+2}}^{\mathcal{C}_{i+2}}), (y_m + b_m, [\Delta \cdot (y_m + b_m)]_{2t_{i+2}}^{\mathcal{C}_{i+2}}))\}_{m \in [T]})$ corresponding to all of the openings of the above form they receive for the multiplication gates at this layer of the circuit.

Lemma 5. *Procedure $\pi_{\text{mult-hm}}$'s transcript is simulatable.*

Proof. First, we know that $\pi_{\text{eff-reshare-hm}}$ is simulatable by random values from Lemma 1. Also, since a, b, v are uniformly random and unknown to the adversary by the security of $\mathcal{F}_{\text{double-rand}}$, openings $(c+v), (x+a), (y+b)$ are simulatable by random values. Finally, from Lemma 3, we know that $\pi_{\text{MAC-check-hm}}$'s transcript is indeed simulatable. □

4.4 Honest Majority Protocol

With all the previous tools into place, we are finally ready to present our full-fledged actively secure, honest majority MPC protocol in the fluid setting, achieving linear communication complexity and maximal fluidity. The clients first distribute double sharings $([x_i]_{t_1}^{\mathcal{C}_1}, [x_i]_{2t_1}^{\mathcal{C}_1})$ of their inputs to $\mathcal{C}_1$. Then $\mathcal{C}_1$ obtains a double sharing $([\Delta]_{t_1}^{\mathcal{C}_1}, [\Delta]_{2t_1}^{\mathcal{C}_1})$ of the global MAC key using $\mathcal{F}_{\text{double-rand}}$, and forms authenticated SPDZ sharings of the inputs using these sharings. The committees then proceed to compute both the regular and randomized version of the circuit on the authenticated inputs, using $\pi_{\text{mult-hm}}$ as well as addition and identity gate procedures that work similarly using the same "mask, open to king, and unmask" paradigm along with some local computation. The committees also make sure to update the accumulators of $\pi_{\text{MAC-check-hm}}$ and $\pi_{\text{mult-verify-hm}}$ along the way with each opening and multiplication, respectively. Finally, once all circuit layers have been computed, the final committees invoke the **Check State** phases of $\pi_{\text{MAC-check-hm}}$ and $\pi_{\text{mult-verify-hm}}$, then reconstruct the outputs to the clients. We note that, as it is remarked in the protocols of [11,25], if the clients indeed have access to a broadcast channel in the last round of the protocol, or implement a broadcast over their point-to-point channels, then security with unanimous abort can be achieved by having the clients broadcast "abort", if their check on their output fails.

Protocol 7: $\Pi_{\text{main-hm}}$

Input Phase: To form a SPDZ sharing of an input x_i possessed by $P_i \in \mathcal{C}_{\text{clnt}}$:

1. P_i samples random degree-t_1 and degree-$2t_1$ Shamir sharings of x_i and distributes the corresponding shares to all parties in $\mathcal{C}_1$.
2. $\mathcal{C}_1$ then invokes $\mathcal{F}_{\text{double-rand}}$ to get random double sharings of the global MAC key $([\Delta]_{t_1}^{\mathcal{C}_1}, [\Delta]_{2t_1}^{\mathcal{C}_1})$.
3. Next, parties in $\mathcal{C}_1$ locally obtain authenticated sharing $[\![x_i]\!]^{\mathcal{C}_1} = ([x_i]_{2t_1}^{\mathcal{C}_1}, [x_i]_{t_1}^{\mathcal{C}_1} \cdot [\Delta]_{t_1}^{\mathcal{C}_1}, [\Delta]_{2t_1}^{\mathcal{C}_1})$ and invoke $\pi_{\text{ineff-reshare-hm}}$ on input $[\Delta]_{t_1}^{\mathcal{C}_1}$ and $\pi_{\text{eff-reshare-hm}}$ on input $[\![x_i]\!]^{\mathcal{C}_1}$.[a]
4. Parties in $\mathcal{C}_2$ then invoke $\pi_{\text{get-rand-sharing}}$ to get $[\![r]\!]^{\mathcal{C}_2}$ and invoke $\pi_{\text{mult-hm}}$ on input $[\![x_i]\!]^{\mathcal{C}_2}$ and $[\![r]\!]^{\mathcal{C}_2}$, as well as the identity gate procedure (below) on $[\![x_i]\!]^{\mathcal{C}_2}$ so that $\mathcal{C}_4$ gets $[\![x_i]\!]^{\mathcal{C}_4}, [\![rx_i]\!]^{\mathcal{C}_4}$.
5. Finally, $\mathcal{C}_4$ invokes $\pi_{\text{mult-verify-hm}}$ on input $(\text{update}, \{([\![x_i]\!]^{\mathcal{C}_4}, [\![rx_i]\!]^{\mathcal{C}_4})\}_{i \in [|\mathcal{C}_{\text{clnt}}|]})$, corresponding to each input.

Execution Phase:

1. Each Committee $\mathcal{C}_i$ of the execution phase will first of all invoke $\pi_{\text{ineff-reshare-hm}}$ on input $[\Delta]_{t_i}^{\mathcal{C}_i}$ and $\pi_{\text{eff-reshare-hm}}$ on input $[\![r]\!]^{\mathcal{C}_i}$ and $[\Delta]_{2t_i}^{\mathcal{C}_i}$.
2. In parallel, every other committee (with the help of the others) will compute the gates at each layer of the circuit as below:

Addition: To perform addition on $[\![x]\!]^{\mathcal{C}_i}$ and $[\![y]\!]^{\mathcal{C}_i}$ (and identically for $[\![rx]\!]^{\mathcal{C}_i}$ and $[\![ry]\!]^{\mathcal{C}_i}$):

1. All parties in $\mathcal{C}_i$ agree on a special party P_{king} in $\mathcal{C}_{i+1}$ then invoke $\pi_{\text{get-rand-sharing}}$ to get $[\![s]\!]^{\mathcal{C}_i}$.
2. Then, parties in $\mathcal{C}_i$ locally obtain $[\![x+y+s]\!]^{\mathcal{C}_i}$ and open it to P_{king} while invoking $\pi_{\text{eff-reshare-hm}}$ on input $[\![s]\!]^{\mathcal{C}_i}$.
3. While P_{king} distributes opened $x+y+s$ to the parties of $\mathcal{C}_{i+2}$, all parties in $\mathcal{C}_{i+1}$ invoke $\pi_{\text{eff-reshare-hm}}$ on $[\![s]\!]^{\mathcal{C}_{i+1}}$.
4. Parties in $\mathcal{C}_{i+2}$ finally locally compute $[\![x+y]\!]^{\mathcal{C}_{i+2}} = (x+y+s) - [\![s]\!]^{\mathcal{C}_{i+2}}$.
5. Parties in $\mathcal{C}_{i+2}$ will also invoke $\pi_{\text{MAC-check-hm}}$ on input $(\text{update}, \{(x_m + y_m + s_m, [\Delta \cdot (x_m + y_m + s_m)]_{2t_{i+2}}^{\mathcal{C}_{i+2}})\}_{m \in [T]})$ corresponding to all of the openings of the above form they receive for the addition gates at this layer of the circuit.[b]

Identity Gates: $\mathcal{C}_i$ forwards $[\![x]\!]^{\mathcal{C}_i}, [\![rx]\!]^{\mathcal{C}_i}$ to $\mathcal{C}_{i+2}$ in a similar fashion as addition above.

Multiplication: To multiply $[\![x]\!]^{\mathcal{C}_i}$ and $[\![y]\!]^{\mathcal{C}_i}$, invoke $\pi_{\text{mult-hm}}$ on them (and identically for $[\![rx]\!]^{\mathcal{C}_i}$ and $[\![y]\!]^{\mathcal{C}_i}$). Then invoke $\pi_{\text{mult-verify-hm}}$ on input (update, $\{([\![x_m y_m]\!]^{\mathcal{C}_{i+2}}, [\![(rx)_m y_m]\!]^{\mathcal{C}_{i+2}})\}_{m \in [T_i]}$), corresponding to each multiplication performed at this layer of the circuit.

Output Phase:

1. Parties in the last committee $\mathcal{C}_\ell$ who compute the shares of the output gates then invoke $\pi_{\mathsf{MAC\text{-}check\text{-}hm}}$ on check. If it outputs Reject, then abort; else, continue.
2. Parties in $\mathcal{C}_{\ell+2}$ (check of $\pi_{\mathsf{MAC\text{-}check\text{-}hm}}$ takes 3 rounds) then invoke $\pi_{\mathsf{mult\text{-}verify\text{-}hm}}$ on check. If it outputs Reject, then abort; else, continue.
3. Next, for Party P_j in $\mathcal{C}_{\ell+9}$ (check of $\pi_{\mathsf{mult\text{-}verify\text{-}hm}}$ takes 8 rounds), let $z^j, (\Delta \cdot z)^j$ be their respective shares of output wire $[z]_{2t_{\ell+9}}^{\mathcal{C}_{\ell+9}}$ and MAC $[\Delta \cdot z]_{2t_{\ell+9}}^{\mathcal{C}_{\ell+9}}$. Each P_j creates random degree-$t_{\ell+10}$ Shamir secret sharings $\left[z^j\right]_{t_{\ell+10}}^{\mathcal{C}_{\ell+10}}, \left[(\Delta \cdot z)^j\right]_{t_{\ell+10}}^{\mathcal{C}_{\ell+10}}$ and distributes the corresponding shares to the parties of $\mathcal{C}_{\ell+10}$.
4. Then each party $P_l \in \mathcal{C}_{\ell+10}$ computes $[z]_{t_{\ell+10}}^{\mathcal{C}_{\ell+10}} = \sum_{j \in \mathcal{C}_{\ell+9}} c_j \cdot \left[z^j\right]_{t_{\ell+10}}^{\mathcal{C}_{\ell+10}}$, and similarly for $[\Delta \cdot z]_{t_{\ell+10}}^{\mathcal{C}_{\ell+10}}$, where c_j is the Lagrange reconstruction coefficient for a degree-$2t_{\ell+9}$ polynomial.
5. Finally, the parties of $\mathcal{C}_{\ell+10}$ open the shares of each $[z]_{t_{\ell+10}}^{\mathcal{C}_{\ell+10}}$, $[\Delta]_{t_{\ell+10}}^{\mathcal{C}_{\ell+10}}$, and $[\Delta \cdot z]_{t_{\ell+10}}^{\mathcal{C}_{\ell+10}}$ to the clients, who attempt to reconstruct them and check that indeed the product of the former two values equal the last value. If so, they output each z; else, they abort.

[a] Note that the computed MAC for $[\![x_i]\!]^{\mathcal{C}_1}$ is re-randomized with a fresh 0-sharing in $\pi_{\mathsf{eff\text{-}reshare\text{-}hm}}$.

[b] This invocation can be combined with that of the multiplication gates for this circuit layer.

Theorem 4. *Let $\mathcal{A}$ be an* R*-adaptive adversary in $\Pi_{\mathsf{main\text{-}hm}}$. Then the protocol UC-securely computes $\mathcal{F}_{\mathsf{DABB}}$ in the presence of $\mathcal{A}$ in the $(\mathcal{F}_{\mathsf{rand}}, \mathcal{F}_{\mathsf{coin}}, \mathcal{F}_{\mathsf{double\text{-}rand}}, \mathcal{F}_{\mathsf{zero}})$-hybrid model.*

The proof is given in the full version.

5 Dishonest Majority Preprocessing Size Is Tight

In this section, we show that the per-party size of the preprocessing produced in our dishonest majority protocol $\Pi_{\mathsf{main\text{-}dm}}$ is tight in the following sense. *Any* protocol that uses more than one committee to compute some function must have per-party size of preprocessing proportional to N, i.e. the size of the entire server universe, $\mathcal{U}$.

To show this, we intuitively reduce the problem of MPC in the Fluid Model with more than two committees to the problem of simply resharing state securely. Indeed, for any such MPC protocol, after one committee finishes their step of the computation, they must securely reshare some sort of state to the next committee, since the next committee has no information about the current state of the computation (e.g., including the original inputs).

More formally, we show a lower bound on the per-party preprocessing size for Secure Message Transmission (SMT) with two committees. In such an SMT setting, there is a sender A who wishes to send some (possibly uniformly random) message x to a receiver B, but first must send some private representation of x through two committees, $\mathcal{C}_1$ and $\mathcal{C}_2$ that are not known ahead of time. Informally, this corresponds to the "resharing" argument in the Fluid MPC model above, since the transmitted x corresponds to the state that is being reshared by the first committee to the next.

In the full version we present some standard notation and definitions from probability and information theory.

5.1 Secure Message Transmission with Two Committees

Now we formally define SMT with two committees. In this definition, we will demand that a uniformly random message x of length λ, i.e., $x \leftarrow_\$ \{0,1\}^\lambda$, will be transmitted from A to B, after passing through committees $\mathcal{C}_1$ and $\mathcal{C}_2$. The two committees $\mathcal{C}_1$ and $\mathcal{C}_2$ can be arbitrarily chosen from a larger universe $\mathcal{U} = \{P_1, \ldots, P_N\}$ of size N. We will allow for a *preprocessing phase* to be performed *before* the input x and committees $\mathcal{C}_1$ and $\mathcal{C}_2$ are chosen. First we present the syntax:

- Algorithm $\{r_i\}_{P_i \in \mathcal{U}} \leftarrow_\$ \mathsf{SMT\text{-}Prep}(\mathcal{U})$ takes as input the set of parties in $\mathcal{U}$ and outputs a preprocessing state, r_i, for each $P_i \in \mathcal{U}$.
- The sender will use algorithm $\{A_i\}_{P_i \in \mathcal{C}_1} \leftarrow_\$ \mathsf{SMT\text{-}A\text{-}Send}(x, \mathcal{C}_1)$ to send messages A_i for each P_i in $\mathcal{C}_1$, based on chosen $x \in \{0,1\}^\lambda$.
- Each $P_i \in \mathcal{C}_1$ will then use $\{c_{i,j}\}_{P_j \in \mathcal{C}_2} \leftarrow_\$ \mathsf{SMT\text{-}}\mathcal{C}_1\mathsf{\text{-}Send}(r_i, A_i, \mathcal{C}_2)$ to send message $c_{i,j}$ to each P_j in $\mathcal{C}_2$.
- Next, each $P_j \in \mathcal{C}_2$ will use algorithm $B_j \leftarrow_\$ \mathsf{SMT\text{-}}\mathcal{C}_2\mathsf{\text{-}Send}(r_j, \{c_{i,j}\}_{P_i \in \mathcal{C}_1}, \mathcal{C}_1)$ to send message B_j to the receiver.
- Finally, the receiver will use algorithm $x \leftarrow \mathsf{SMT\text{-}B\text{-}Rcv}(\{B_j\}_{P_j \in \mathcal{C}_2})$ to output the message x.

Since we are in the dishonest majority setting, we will consider any *unbounded* adversary $\mathcal{A}$ that corrupts all-but-one party in each committee, *only* during the online phase. That is, using the same notation as earlier in the paper, the sizes of corruption sets $\mathcal{T}_{\mathcal{C}_1}$ and $\mathcal{T}_{\mathcal{C}_2}$ satisfy $t_1 < n_1$ and $t_2 < n_2$, respectively. Now, we are ready for the definition:

Definition 1 (Secure Message Transmission with Two Committees.). *A* Secure Message Transmission with Two Committees *protocol* Π_{SMT} *is* perfectly-correct *if for any choice of committees* $\mathcal{C}_1, \mathcal{C}_2 \subseteq \mathcal{U}$,

$$\Pr\Big[x \leftarrow \mathsf{SMT\text{-}B\text{-}Rcv}(\{B_j\}_{P_j \in \mathcal{C}_2}) : x \leftarrow_\$ \{0,1\}^\lambda, \{r_l\}_{P_l \in \mathcal{U}} \leftarrow_\$ \mathsf{SMT\text{-}Prep}(\mathcal{U}),$$

$$\{A_i\}_{P_i \in \mathcal{C}_1} \leftarrow_\$ \mathsf{SMT\text{-}A\text{-}Send}(x, \mathcal{C}_1), \forall P_i \in \mathcal{C}_1, \{c_{i,j}\}_{P_j \in \mathcal{C}_2} \leftarrow_\$ \mathsf{SMT\text{-}}\mathcal{C}_1\mathsf{\text{-}Send}(r_i, A_i, \mathcal{C}_2),$$

$$\forall P_j \in \mathcal{C}_2, B_j \leftarrow_\$ \mathsf{SMT}\text{-}\mathcal{C}_2\text{-}\mathsf{Send}(r_j, \{c_{i,j}\}_{P_i \in \mathcal{C}_1}, \mathcal{C}_1)] = 1.$$

Moreover, Π_{SMT} *is* statistically-secure *if for any choice of committees* $\mathcal{C}_1, \mathcal{C}_2 \subseteq \mathcal{U}$*, and any choice of corruptions* $\mathcal{T}_{\mathcal{C}_1} \subseteq \mathcal{C}_1, \mathcal{T}_{\mathcal{C}_2} \subseteq \mathcal{C}_2$ *satisfying* $t_1 < n_1$ *and* $t_2 < n_2$*, respectively,*

$$\Pr\Big[x \leftarrow \mathcal{A}(\{(r_i, A_i)\}_{P_i \in \mathcal{T}_{\mathcal{C}_1}}, \{(r_j, \{c_{l,j}\}_{P_l \in \mathcal{C}_1})\}_{P_j \in \mathcal{T}_{\mathcal{C}_2}}) : x \leftarrow_\$ \{0,1\}^\lambda,$$

$$\{r_l\}_{P_l \in \mathcal{U}} \leftarrow_\$ \mathsf{SMT}\text{-}\mathsf{Prep}(\mathcal{U}), \{A_i\}_{P_i \in \mathcal{C}_1} \leftarrow_\$ \mathsf{SMT}\text{-}\mathsf{A}\text{-}\mathsf{Send}(x, \mathcal{C}_1),$$

$$\forall P_i \in \mathcal{C}_1, \{c_{i,j}\}_{P_j \in \mathcal{C}_2} \leftarrow_\$ \mathsf{SMT}\text{-}\mathcal{C}_1\text{-}\mathsf{Send}(r_i, A_i, \mathcal{C}_2),$$

$$\forall P_j \in \mathcal{C}_2, B_j \leftarrow_\$ \mathsf{SMT}\text{-}\mathcal{C}_2\text{-}\mathsf{Send}(r_j, \{c_{i,j}\}_{P_i \in \mathcal{C}_1}, \mathcal{C}_1)\Big] \leq 2^{-\lambda}.$$

In the rest of the section, we will assume for simplicity that the two committees, $\mathcal{C}_1$ and $\mathcal{C}_2$, will each be of the same size $n_1 = n_2 = n$. Without loss of generality, we may refer to the two committees as $\mathcal{C}_1 = \{P_1, \ldots, P_n\}$ and $\mathcal{C}_2 = \{P_{n+1}, \ldots, P_{2n}\}$.

Communication Complexity. We will in part be concerned by the size of communication needed for a correct and secure SMT protocol. Towards this end, let $\mathsf{Comm} = \sum_{i \in \mathcal{C}_1, j \in \mathcal{C}_2} |c_{i,j}|$ be the total communication from some particular execution of an SMT protocol Π_{SMT}.

5.2 Lower Bound on Per-Party Preprocessing for Linear SMT

We will now prove the following lower bound which informally states that in order for an SMT protocol Π_{SMT} to have, in expectation over the choice of committees $\mathcal{C}_1, \mathcal{C}_2$ and any randomness of the algorithms, $o(n^2 \cdot \lambda)$ total communication Comm, the expected size of each preprocessing state must be $\Omega(N \cdot \lambda)$:

Theorem 5. *For any perfectly-secure SMT protocol* Π_{SMT} *for two committees* $\mathcal{C}_1, \mathcal{C}_2$ *of size* n*, if* $\mathcal{C}_1, \mathcal{C}_2$ *are sampled uniformly at random from the universe* $\mathcal{U}$ *of size* N*, such that* $\mathcal{C}_1 \cap \mathcal{C}_2 \neq \emptyset$*, and* $\mathbb{E}_{P_i \in \mathcal{U}}[|r_i|] \leq (N - 2n + 1) \cdot \lambda/8$*, then* $\mathbb{E}_{\mathcal{C}_1, \mathcal{C}_2}[\mathsf{Comm}] \geq n^2 \cdot \lambda/4$.

First, we provide the following lemma that will help us in proving the above theorem. Assume w.l.o.g. that the smallest ciphertext in a given execution is $c_{1,n+1}$. Also, assume that the adversary corrupts (at least) every party in the two committees except for P_1 and P_{n+1}. In particular, this gives the adversary preprocessing states $R = r_2, \ldots, r_n, r_{n+2}, \ldots, r_{2n}$, ciphertexts $\{c_{i,n+1}\}_{i \in [2,n]}$ sent by the corrupted parties of $\mathcal{C}_1$ to P_{n+1}, and ciphertexts $B_{n+2}, \ldots, B_{2n}$ sent to the receiver by the corrupted parties of $\mathcal{C}_2$. So, the adversary is just missing the message B_{n+1} used by the receiver B in the protocol to reconstruct x. To produce this message B_{n+1}, the adversary in addition to ciphertexts $\{c_{i,n+1}\}_{i \in [2,n]}$ it has, only needs to learn $c_{1,n+1}$ and r_{n+1}. What this Lemma intuitively shows is that if $|c_{1,n+1}| < \lambda/2$ (so that the adversary can guess it with high enough probability), then the preprocessing r_1 *must* provide some additional, non-trivial correlation with r_{n+1} that the corrupted preprocessing states, R, do not provide on their own. If this were not the case, then the adversary could simply sample r_{n+1} conditioned on R. This preprocessing would then be "close enough" to what the correlations in the entire protocol execution indicate it should be so that, by correctness, it should also work, together with the ciphertexts $\{c_{i,n+1}\}_{i\in[n]}$, to produce the missing B_{n+1}.

In the following, we use notation R_J to represent the set of preprocessing states $\{r_j\}_{j\in J}$, where $J \subseteq [N]$.

Lemma 6. *Assume that the two committees $\mathcal{C}_1, \mathcal{C}_2$, each of size n, are chosen uniformly at random from the universe $\mathcal{U}$ of size N, such that $\mathcal{C}_1 \cap \mathcal{C}_2 = \emptyset$. Also, let J be some random (fixed-size) subset of $[N]$ such that $|J| \geq 2n-2$. If $\Pr_{\mathcal{C}_1,\mathcal{C}_2,i,j}[|c_{i,j}| < \lambda/2] > 1/2$, then for random $i' \neq j' \in \mathcal{U} \setminus J$, we have: $\mathbb{E}_{J,i',j'}[\mathrm{I}(r_{j'}|R_J; r_{i'})] \geq \lambda/4$.*

Proof. We start with the following inequality, where the randomness is over the choice of $J \cup \{i', j'\} \subseteq [N]$, as well as the actual generated preprocessing state $r_{i'}$:

$$\mathbb{E}_{J,i',j',r_{i'}}[\mathsf{SD}((r_{j'}|R_J \cup \{r_{i'}\}), (r_{j'}|R_J))] \leq$$

$$\mathbb{E}_{J,i',j'r_{i'}}\left[1 - \frac{1}{2}\exp(-D_{\mathrm{KL}}((r_{j'}|R_J \cup \{r_{i'}\})||(r_{j'}|R_J)))\right] \leq$$

$$1 - \frac{1}{2}\exp(-\mathbb{E}_{J,i',j',r_{i'}}[D_{\mathrm{KL}}((r_{j'}|R_J \cup \{r_{i'}\})||(r_{j'}|R_J))]) =$$

$$1 - \frac{1}{2}\exp(-\mathbb{E}_{J,i',j'}[\mathrm{I}(r_{j'}|R_J; r_{i'})]).$$

The first inequality follows from the Bretagnolle-Huber inequality [7], and the second inequality from Jensen's inequality, since $f(x) = e^{-x}$ is convex, while the last equality is a well-known identity.

Thus, if we assume towards contradiction that $\mathbb{E}_{J,i',j'}[\mathrm{I}(r_{j'}|R_J; r_{i'})] < \lambda/4$, this means that $\mathbb{E}_{J,i',j',r_{i'}}[\mathsf{SD}((r_{j'}|R_J), (r_{j'}|R_J \cup \{r_{i'}\}))] < 1 - \frac{1}{2}\exp(-\lambda/4)$.

Now, it could be the case that some $2n-2$ randomly sampled indices in J correspond exactly to the first $n-1$ parties of $\mathcal{C}_1$ and $\mathcal{C}_2$ in a given protocol execution, and further that $P_{i'}$ is the last party chosen for $\mathcal{C}_1$, and $P_{j'}$ is the last party chosen for $\mathcal{C}_2$. Also, from correctness, we know that for any $r_{j'}$ that is produced by the preprocessing phase for $P_{j'}$ with non-zero probability, the SMT protocol must successfully transmit the secret x. Based on this and the above inequality, we describe the following attack: The adversary $\mathcal{A}$ corrupts the set of preprocessing states R_J and then samples guess $r'_{j'}$ for $r_{j'}$ conditioned on the states in R_j, and samples (uniformly) guess $c'_{i',j'}$ for $c_{i',j'}$. Using the guessed $r'_{j'}$ and $c'_{i,j'}$ along with the learned $\{c_{i,j'}\}_{i\in[n]\setminus\{i'\}}$ via corruptions, invoke SMT-$\mathcal{C}_2$-Send to produce $B_{j'}$. Finally, using $\{B_j\}_{j\in[n+1,2n]}$, invoke SMT-B-Rcv to produce x.

Now, let us analyze the success probability of this attack. First, we have from $\Pr_{\mathcal{C}_1,\mathcal{C}_2,i,j}[|c_{i,j}| < \lambda/2] > 1/2$, that $\Pr[c'_{j',j} = c_{j',j}] > 2^{-\lambda/2-1}$. Next, consider the event in which $\mathcal{A}$ samples some $r'_{j'}$ conditioned on R_J that has weight-0 in the distribution of $r_{j'}$ conditioned on $R_J \cup \{r_{i'}\}$. We call such an $r'_{j'}$ a *bad* sample. From the above inequality, such an $r'_{j'}$ is sampled with probability less than $1 - \frac{1}{2}\exp(-\lambda/4)$, in expectation. In particular, this means that in expectation, $\mathcal{A}$ samples a *good* $r'_{j'}$ with probability at least $\frac{1}{2}\exp(-\lambda/4)$. Such an $r'_{j'}$ is *good* because by correctness, the protocol must successfully transmit the secret x if in fact $r'_{j'}$ were the actual preprocessing of $P_{j'}$.

Therefore, in expectation over the choice of committee members and the preprocessing $r_{i'}$, the attack by $\mathcal{A}$ succeeds with probability greater than $1/2^{\lambda}$. □

Now we can prove Theorem 5 using Lemma 6. The intuition stems from the fact that the protocol does not *a priori* know which parties will be in the committees. So, we can use Lemma 6 to show that in fact *many* parties outside of the two committees must in expectation provide some unique correlation with r_{n+1} (the receiver of small message $c_{1,n+1}$), in case they were actually the first party of $\mathcal{C}_1$ sending this small ciphertext. As a result, if the state r_{n+1} is small enough, we can completely recover it, guess $c_{1,n+1}$, then recover x with high enough probability.

Proof (of Theorem 5). Assume towards contradiction that $\Pr_{\mathcal{C}_1,\mathcal{C}_2,i,j}[|c_{i,j}| < \lambda/2] > 1/2$. Also assume that some adversary $\mathcal{A}$ in a given execution of some Π_{SMT} first corrupts every party in $\mathcal{C}_1$ and $\mathcal{C}_2$ except randomly chosen P_i of $\mathcal{C}_1$ and randomly chosen P_j of $\mathcal{C}_2$. In particular, this means that the set of indices J of corrupt parties is some random subset of $[N]$ of size $2n-2$, and index j is some random other index outside of J. Now, the adversary will one by one sample $M = (N - 2n + 1)/2$ indices $i_1, \ldots, i_M$ from $\mathcal{U}$ that are not already part of J, and add them to J. Let J' be the final such set. From Lemma 6, we know that under the above assumption on message size, for any random, fixed-size subset $J \subseteq [N]$ of size $|J| \geq 2n-2$, and random index $j' \notin J$, if we pick another random index $i_l \notin J$, $\mathbb{E}_{J,i_l,j'}[\mathrm{I}(r_{j'}|R_J; r_{i_l})] \geq \lambda/4$. Thus, recalling that $\mathrm{I}(r_{j'}|R_J; r_{i_l}) = \mathrm{H}(r_{j'}|R_j) - \mathrm{H}(r_{j'}|R, r_{i_l})$, we can write

$$\mathbb{E}_{J',j}[\mathrm{I}(r_j; R_{J'})] = \mathbb{E}_{J',j}[\mathrm{H}(r_j) - \mathrm{H}(r_j|R_{J'})] =$$

$$\mathbb{E}_j[\mathrm{H}(r_j)] + \mathbb{E}_{J',j,i_M}[-\mathrm{H}(r_j|R_{J'}) + \mathrm{H}(r_j|R_{J'} \setminus \{r_{i_M}\})]$$

$$+\mathbb{E}_{J',j,i_M,i_{M-1}}[-\mathrm{H}(r_j|R_{J'} \setminus \{r_{i_M}\}) + \mathrm{H}(r_j|R_{J'} \setminus \{r_{i_M}, r_{i_{M-1}}\})]$$

$$\ldots$$

$$+\mathbb{E}_{J',j,i_M,\ldots,i_1}[-\mathrm{H}(r_j|R_{J'} \setminus \{r_{i_l}\}_{l\in[2,M]}) + \mathrm{H}(r_j|R_{J'} \setminus \{r_{i_l}\}_{l\in[M]})]$$

$$-\mathbb{E}_{J',j,i_M,\ldots,i_1}[\mathrm{H}(r_j|R_{J'} \setminus \{r_{i_l}\}_{l\in[M]}])]$$

$$\geq M \cdot \lambda/4 + \mathbb{E}_{J',j,i_M,\ldots,i_1}[\mathrm{H}(r_j) - \mathrm{H}(r_j|R_{J'} \setminus \{r_{i_l}\}_{l\in[M]}) \geq M \cdot \lambda/4.$$

Now, these indices J' will correspond to the parties that $\mathcal{A}$ will corrupt in the execution. However, if some randomly chosen index i_l is indeed the index i corresponding to the only honest party P_i of $\mathcal{C}_1$, the attack will fail, as $\mathcal{A}$ cannot corrupt P_i. Yet, the probability that this happens corresponds to the probability that if we pick M items at random from $N-2n+1$ total items, i is not one of them, which is equal to: $\frac{\binom{N-2n}{M}}{\binom{N-2n+1}{M}} = 1 - \frac{M}{N-2n+1} = 1/2$, since we choose $M = (N-2n+1)/2$.

So, if $\mathbb{E}[|r_j|] \leq (N-2n+1)\cdot\lambda/8$ as in the Theorem statement, in expectation, $\mathcal{A}$ can sample r_j conditioned on $R_{J'}$ correctly (i.e., with probability 1) and guess $c_{i,j}$ with probability greater than $2^{-\lambda/2-1}$. Using the guessed r_j and $c_{i,j}$ along with the learned $\{c_{i',j}\}_{i'\in[n]\setminus\{i\}}$ via corruptions, we can reconstruct B_j. Finally, using $\{B_j\}_{j\in[n+1,2n]}$, we can successfully reconstruct x.

Thus, it cannot be true that $\Pr_{\mathcal{C}_1,\mathcal{C}_2,i,j}[|c_{i,j}| < \lambda/2] > 1/2$. By the law of total probability, it must therefore be that: $\mathbb{E}_{\mathcal{C}_1,\mathcal{C}_2}[\mathsf{Comm}] = \sum_{i,j}\mathbb{E}_{\mathcal{C}_1,\mathcal{C}_2}[|c_{i,j}|] \geq \sum_{i,j}\lambda/2\cdot\Pr_{\mathcal{C}_1,\mathcal{C}_2}[|c_{i,j}|\geq\lambda/2] = \lambda/2\cdot\sum_{i,j}\Pr_{\mathcal{C}_1,\mathcal{C}_2}[|c_{i,j}|\geq\lambda/2] \geq \frac{n^2\cdot\lambda}{4}$. □

Acknowledgments. This paper was prepared in part for information purposes by the Artificial Intelligence Research group of JPMorgan Chase & Co and its affiliates ("JP Morgan"), and is not a product of the Research Department of JP Morgan. JP Morgan makes no representation and warranty whatsoever and disclaims all liability, for the completeness, accuracy or reliability of the information contained herein. This document is not intended as investment research or investment advice, or a recommendation, offer or solicitation for the purchase or sale of any security, financial instrument, financial product or service, or to be used in any way for evaluating the merits of participating in any transaction, and shall not constitute a solicitation under any jurisdiction or to any person, if such solicitation under such jurisdiction or to such person would be unlawful.

References

1. Badrinarayanan, S., Jain, A., Manohar, N., Sahai, A.: Secure MPC: laziness leads to GOD. In: Moriai, S., Wang, H. (eds.) ASIACRYPT 2020. LNCS, vol. 12493, pp. 120–150. Springer, Cham (2020). https://doi.org/10.1007/978-3-030-64840-4_5
2. Beaver, D.: Efficient multiparty protocols using circuit randomization. In: Feigenbaum, J. (ed.) CRYPTO 1991. LNCS, vol. 576, pp. 420–432. Springer, Heidelberg (1992). https://doi.org/10.1007/3-540-46766-1_34
3. Ben-Efraim, A., Nielsen, M., Omri, E.: Turbospeedz: double your online SPDZ! Improving SPDZ using function dependent preprocessing. In: Deng, R.H., Gauthier-Umaña, V., Ochoa, M., Yung, M. (eds.) ACNS 2019. LNCS, vol. 11464, pp. 530–549. Springer, Cham (2019). https://doi.org/10.1007/978-3-030-21568-2_26
4. Bendlin, R., Damgård, I., Orlandi, C., Zakarias, S.: Semi-homomorphic encryption and multiparty computation. In: Paterson, K.G. (ed.) EUROCRYPT 2011. LNCS, vol. 6632, pp. 169–188. Springer, Heidelberg (2011). https://doi.org/10.1007/978-3-642-20465-4_11
5. Bienstock, A., Escudero, D., Polychroniadou, A.: On linear communication complexity for (maximally) fluid MPC. Cryptology ePrint Archive, Report 2023/839 (2023). https://eprint.iacr.org/2023/839
6. Boyle, E., Gilboa, N., Ishai, Y., Nof, A.: Efficient fully secure computation via distributed zero-knowledge proofs. In: Moriai, S., Wang, H. (eds.) ASIACRYPT 2020. LNCS, vol. 12493, pp. 244–276. Springer, Cham (2020). https://doi.org/10.1007/978-3-030-64840-4_9

7. Bretagnolle, J., Huber, C.: Estimation des densités : Risque minimax. In: Dellacherie, C., Meyer, P.A., Weil, M. (eds.), Séminaire de Probabilités XII, pp. 342–363. Berlin, Heidelberg (1978)
8. Canetti, R.: Universally composable security: a new paradigm for cryptographic protocols. In: FOCS 2001, 14–17 October 2001, Las Vegas, Nevada, USA, pp. 136–145. IEEE Computer Society (2001)
9. Chaum, D., Crépeau, C., Damgård, I.: Multiparty unconditionally secure protocols (abstract). In: Advances in Cryptology - CRYPTO 1987, A Conference on the Theory and Applications of Cryptographic Techniques, Santa Barbara, California, USA, 16–20 August 1987, Proceedings, p. 462 (1987)
10. Chida, K., et al.: Fast large-scale honest-majority MPC for malicious adversaries. In: Shacham, H., Boldyreva, A. (eds.) CRYPTO 2018. LNCS, vol. 10993, pp. 34–64. Springer, Cham (2018). https://doi.org/10.1007/978-3-319-96878-0_2
11. Choudhuri, A.R., Goel, A., Green, M., Jain, A., Kaptchuk, G.: Fluid MPC: secure multiparty computation with dynamic participants. In: Malkin, T., Peikert, C. (eds.) CRYPTO 2021. LNCS, vol. 12826, pp. 94–123. Springer, Cham (2021). https://doi.org/10.1007/978-3-030-84245-1_4
12. Damgård, I., Escudero, D., Polychroniadou, A.: Phoenix: secure computation in an unstable network with dropouts and comebacks. Cryptology ePrint Archive (2021)
13. Damgård, I., Ishai, Y., Krøigaard, M.: Perfectly secure multiparty computation and the computational overhead of cryptography. In: Gilbert, H. (ed.) EUROCRYPT 2010. LNCS, vol. 6110, pp. 445–465. Springer, Heidelberg (2010). https://doi.org/10.1007/978-3-642-13190-5_23
14. Damgård, I., Nielsen, J.B.: Scalable and unconditionally secure multiparty computation. In: Menezes, A. (ed.) CRYPTO 2007. LNCS, vol. 4622, pp. 572–590. Springer, Heidelberg (2007). https://doi.org/10.1007/978-3-540-74143-5_32
15. Damgård, I., Pastro, V., Smart, N., Zakarias, S.: Multiparty computation from somewhat homomorphic encryption. In: Safavi-Naini, R., Canetti, R. (eds.) CRYPTO 2012. LNCS, vol. 7417, pp. 643–662. Springer, Heidelberg (2012). https://doi.org/10.1007/978-3-642-32009-5_38
16. Escudero, D., Goyal, V., Polychroniadou, A., Song, Y.: Turbopack: honest majority MPC with constant online communication. In: ACM Conference on Computer and Communications Security (CCS) (2022)
17. Fitzi, M., Hirt, M., Maurer, U.: Trading correctness for privacy in unconditional multi-party computation. In: Krawczyk, H. (ed.) CRYPTO 1998. LNCS, vol. 1462, pp. 121–136. Springer, Heidelberg (1998). https://doi.org/10.1007/BFb0055724
18. Genkin, D., Ishai, Y., Prabhakaran, M.M., Sahai, A., Tromer, E.: Circuits resilient to additive attacks with applications to secure computation. In: Proceedings of the Forty-sixth Annual ACM Symposium on Theory of Computing, STOC 2014, pp. 495–504, New York, NY, USA, ACM (2014)
19. Gentry, C., et al.: YOSO: you only speak once. In: Malkin, T., Peikert, C. (eds.) CRYPTO 2021. LNCS, vol. 12826, pp. 64–93. Springer, Cham (2021). https://doi.org/10.1007/978-3-030-84245-1_3
20. Gentry, C., et al.: YOSO: you only speak once - secure MPC with stateless ephemeral roles. In: CRYPTO 2021 (2021)
21. Goldreich, O., Micali, S., Wigderson, A.: How to play any mental game or a completeness theorem for protocols with honest majority. In: Proceedings of the 19th Annual ACM Symposium on Theory of Computing, 1987, New York, New York, USA, pp. 218–229 (1987)

22. Goyal, V., Li, H., Ostrovsky, R., Polychroniadou, A., Song, Y.: ATLAS: efficient and scalable MPC in the honest majority setting. In: Malkin, T., Peikert, C. (eds.) CRYPTO 2021. LNCS, vol. 12826, pp. 244–274. Springer, Cham (2021). https://doi.org/10.1007/978-3-030-84245-1_9
23. Goyal, V., Song, Y.: Malicious security comes free in honest-majority MPC. Cryptology ePrint Archive, Report 2020/134 (2020). https://eprint.iacr.org/2020/134
24. Guo, Y., Pass, R., Shi, E.: Synchronous, with a chance of partition tolerance. In: Boldyreva, A., Micciancio, D. (eds.) CRYPTO 2019. LNCS, vol. 11692, pp. 499–529. Springer, Cham (2019). https://doi.org/10.1007/978-3-030-26948-7_18
25. Rachuri, R., Scholl, P.: Le mans: dynamic and fluid MPC for dishonest majority. In: CRYPTO (2022)
26. Yao, A.C.: How to generate and exchange secrets (extended abstract). In: 27th Annual Symposium on Foundations of Computer Science, Toronto, Canada, 27–29 October 1986, pp. 162–167 (1986)

Cryptography with Weights: MPC, Encryption and Signatures

Sanjam Garg[1(✉)], Abhishek Jain[2], Pratyay Mukherjee[3], Rohit Sinha[4], Mingyuan Wang[5], and Yinuo Zhang[5]

[1] UC Berkeley and NTT Research, Berkeley, USA
sanjamg@berkeley.edu
[2] John Hopkins University, Baltimore, USA
abhishek@cs.jhu.edu
[3] Supra Research, Kelowna, Canada
[4] Swirlds Labs, Dallas, USA
[5] UC Berkeley, Berkeley, USA
{mingyuan,yinuo}@berkeley.edu

Abstract. The security of many powerful cryptographic systems such as secure multiparty computation, threshold encryption, and threshold signatures rests on trust assumptions about the parties. The de-facto model treats all parties equally and requires that a certain fraction of the parties are honest. While this paradigm of one-person-one-vote has been very successful over the years, current and emerging practical use cases suggest that it is outdated.

In this work, we consider *weighted* cryptosystems where every party is assigned a certain weight and the trust assumption is that a certain fraction of the total weight is honest. This setting can be translated to the standard setting (where each party has a unit weight) via virtualization. However, this method is quite expensive, incurring a multiplicative overhead in the weight.

We present new weighted cryptosystems with significantly better efficiency: our proposed schemes incur only an *additive* overhead in weights.

- We first present a weighted ramp secret-sharing scheme (WRSS) where the size of a secret share is $O(w)$ (where w corresponds to the weight). In comparison, Shamir's secret sharing with virtualization requires secret shares of size $w \cdot \lambda$, where $\lambda = \log |\mathbb{F}|$ is the security parameter.

S. Garg, M. Wang, and Y. Zhang–Were supported in part by DARPA under Agreement No. HR00112020026, AFOSR Award FA9550-19-1-0200, NSF CNS Award 1936826, and research grants by the Sloan Foundation, and Visa Inc. The second author was supported in part by NSF CNS-1814919, NSF CAREER 1942789, Johns Hopkins University Catalyst award, AFOSR Award FA9550-19-1-0200, JP Morgan Faculty Award, and research gifts from Ethereum, Stellar and Cisco. Any opinions, findings and conclusions, or recommendations in this material are those of the authors and do not necessarily reflect the views of the United States Government or DARPA.

H. Handschuh and A. Lysyanskaya (Eds.): CRYPTO 2023, LNCS 14081, pp. 295–327, 2023.
https://doi.org/10.1007/978-3-031-38557-5_10

– Next, we use our WRSS to construct weighted versions of (semi-honest) secure multiparty computation (MPC), threshold encryption, and threshold signatures. All these schemes inherit the efficiency of our WRSS and incur only an additive overhead in weights.

Our WRSS is based on the Chinese remainder theorem-based secret-sharing scheme. Interestingly, this secret-sharing scheme is *non-linear* and only achieves statistical privacy. These distinct features introduce several technical hurdles in applications to MPC and threshold cryptosystems. We resolve these challenges by developing several new ideas.

Keywords: Weighted cryptography · Secret-sharing · Secure multiparty computation · Threshold cryptography

1 Introduction

Cryptography enables mutually distrusting parties to accomplish various tasks as long as a certain subset of the parties are honest. For example, a secure multiparty computation protocol (MPC) [26,43] allows a group of parties to jointly compute a public function over their private inputs such that nothing beyond the function output is revealed if a subset of the participants are honest. Specific instances such as threshold signatures (resp., encryption) [19,20] work by distributing a secret signing (resp. decryption) key among multiple parties such that it is possible to sign a message (resp., decrypt a ciphertext) if and only if a threshold number of parties participate honestly.

This paradigm of trust has been immensely successful over the years. Threshold cryptosystems have seen widespread use in recent years, especially within the blockchain ecosystem [40]. Furthermore, efforts to standardize threshold cryptosystems have already begun [37]. MPC protocols have also started seeing increased adoption due to recent dramatic improvements in their efficiency.

Traditionally, in such systems, parties are considered as *equals*. For instance, it is assumed that all parties are equally motivated to participate in the protocol actively; or that it is equally hard for an adversary to corrupt any party. However, the "everyone is equal" paradigm does not suffice for many emerging applications. For instance, in stake-based blockchains [32], parties are associated with stakes that are not necessarily binary. Similarly, in oracle networks [14,21], parties have reputation scores with high variance. In these scenarios, parties in the system are naturally asymmetrical and unequal. Therefore, it is appropriate to consider a *weighted* setting where every party is associated with a weight: the adversarial capability (i.e., privacy threshold) is modeled in terms of the total weight that can be compromised, and a successful protocol execution requires a sufficiently weighted set of participants (i.e., reconstruction threshold). Naturally, the reconstruction threshold is strictly larger than the privacy threshold.

Despite being a natural problem, essentially, the only general approach in the literature [31,38] to realize weighted cryptography is via *virtualization*. That is, a party with assigned weight w is treated as w virtual parties, and then a standard unweighted system is used for all the virtual parties. This straightforward solution, however, is extremely inefficient: a party with weight w has to bear w times the amount of computation and/or communication cost that one does in the unweighted setting. When the weights are large, this multiplicative overhead in efficiency can be prohibitive.

In this work, we ask the following question:

Can we realize weighted cryptography with better efficiency?
Specifically, could the efficiency degradation depend additively on the weights?

Summary of this Work. Our work answers this question positively. Our first contribution is an *efficient* weighted secret sharing scheme (WRSS) where the size of the secret share of a party with weight w is only $O(w)$. We obtain this result in the ramp setting [13], where there is a gap between the privacy and reconstruction thresholds. In comparison, the virtualized version of Shamir's secret sharing requires a share of size $w \cdot \log |\mathbb{F}|$, where $\mathbb{F}$ is the underlying field. We obtain our result by lifting secret-sharing schemes based on the Chinese Remainder Theorem (CRT) [5,27,35] to the weighted setting and leveraging the ramp structure to achieve our desired efficiency.

Building on our efficient WRSS scheme, we construct several efficient distributed cryptographic protocols: a secure (semi-honest) MPC protocol for general functionalities, a threshold (public-key) encryption scheme, and a threshold signature scheme. In all of these schemes, the computation/communication cost of the parties only degrades *additively* in their weights. Interestingly, as our WRSS scheme is both *non-linear* and *imperfect* (i.e., it only achieves statistical privacy in contrast with Shamir's, which achieves perfect privacy), several new technical ideas are required for each application.

1.1 Our Contribution

Secret Sharing. Our first contribution is a construction of a weighted ramp secret-sharing with *succinct* share sizes. Recall that a ramp secret sharing scheme is parameterized by two thresholds: a reconstruction threshold T and a privacy threshold t. Any collection of parties with cumulative weights $\geqslant T$ should be able to reconstruct the secret; any collection of parties with cumulative weights $\leqslant t$ should not learn anything about the secret (see Definition 1).

We prove the following theorem.

Theorem 1 (Efficient WRSS). *Let $(w_1, \ldots, w_n, T, t)$ define a weighted access structure, where w_i are weights and T and t are reconstruction and privacy thresholds, respectively. Assume $T - t = \Theta(\lambda)$. There exists a weighted ramp secret sharing scheme realizing $(w_1, \ldots, w_n, T, t)$ such that*

- *The share size of a party with weight w is $O(w)$.*[1]

[1] In all theorems, the size and the communication complexity are measured by bits.

- *It has perfect correctness.*
- *It is $2^{-\lambda}$-statistically private.*

Our WRSS scheme is built upon CRT-based secret sharing scheme previously studied by [5,27,35]. Our contribution lies in identifying that by relaxing the "sharp" threshold setting (i.e., $T = t+1$) to the ramp setting (i.e., $T-t = \Theta(\lambda)$), it is possible to achieve significant efficiency improvement.

While the ramp structure has been previously used to obtain more efficient secret-sharing schemes (and their applications), our specific application to the weighted setting is novel. Indeed, as we discuss in Sect. 1.2, leveraging the ramp structure with Shamir-style secret-sharing schemes does not seem to offer significant benefits in the weighted setting. In contrast, by exploiting the ramp setting in CRT-based secret-sharing, we obtain our desired efficiency while also preserving the algebraic structure of the secret. This enables our applications to MPC and threshold cryptosystems.

Weighted Secure Multiparty Computation. Next, we consider weighted MPC where every party is assigned a weight. We aim for information-theoretic security in the honest majority setting, where the cumulative weight of the malicious parties is less than half of the total weight.

Using our new WRSS scheme, we construct a weighted MPC protocol following the BGW framework [11]. Our result is summarized as follows.

Theorem 2 (Efficient Weighted MPC). *Let C be an arithmetic circuit over a field $\mathbb{F}$ with depth d. There exists a weighted MPC protocol for n parties with weights $w_1, \ldots, w_n$ and total weight W for computing C satisfying the following:*

- *The round complexity is $d + O(1)$.*
- *In the pre-processing phase, the communication cost per party per gate is $O(W)$.*
- *In the online phase, the communication cost per gate for party P_i with weight w_i is $O(w_i)$.*
- *For any semi-honest (computationally unbounded) adversary who may corrupt a total weight of t, this protocol is $\exp(-\lambda)$-secure given $W - 2t = \Theta(\lambda)$.*

In comparison, the BGW protocol based on Shamir's secret sharing with virtualization would require a communication cost $W \cdot \log|\mathbb{F}|$ and $w_i \cdot \log|\mathbb{F}|$ in the preprocessing and online phase, respectively.

While MPC protocols provide a generic solution to threshold cryptography, it would incur a large overhead if one needs to transform group operations into an arithmetic circuit over $\mathbb{F}$. Therefore, our next objectives are to construct efficient weighted threshold encryption and signature schemes.

Weighted (Ramp) Threshold Encryption. We construct a weighted threshold encryption scheme based on the ElGamal cryptosystem. As typical in the literature, we aim for a scheme with *one-round* threshold decryption and a reusable setup. Our result is summarized as follows.

Theorem 3. *For any privacy threshold t and decryption threshold T such that $T - t = \Theta(\lambda)$, there is a weighted (ramp) threshold ElGamal encryption satisfying:*

- *Assume all weights are sufficiently large*[2] *(in particular, $\geqslant \log^2(\lambda)$), it is CPA-secure against any adversary that corrupts any subset of parties with cumulative weights $\leqslant t$.*
- *Any subset of parties with cumulative weight T could decrypt the ciphertext. The computation work for the party with weight w is $O(w) + \mathsf{poly}(\lambda)$.*

In contrast, a virtualization approach to existing threshold encryption schemes that use Shamir's secret sharing would require a computation cost of $O(w)$ *group operations* (in contrast to bit operations).

The communication cost in our scheme is only λ as partial decryption only consists of one group element. This is identical to the Shamir-based approach (See Remark 1).

Weighted (Ramp) Threshold Signature. Finally, we construct a weighted threshold signature scheme based on the ECDSA signature. In particular, building on our weighted MPC protocol, we construct a special protocol for ECDSA signing functionality summarized as follows.

Theorem 4. *For any privacy threshold t, reconstruction threshold T, and total weight W such that $T - t = \Theta(\lambda)$ and $W - 2t = \Theta(\lambda)$, there is a weighted MPC protocol realizing ECDSA signing functionality such that:*

- *It has a semi-honestly secure two-round pre-signing protocol in which all the parties participate. The communication/computation cost per party is $O(W + \lambda)$.*
- *It has a non-interactive signing phase where each party i broadcasts a partial signature. The communication/computation cost per party is $O(w_i)$. As long as the cumulative weight of parties who send their partial signature is $\geqslant T$, one could correctly aggregate the signature.*

1.2 Related Work

Weighted Secret-sharing. The notion of weighted secret-sharing was proposed in the original work of Shamir [38]. It is well-known that the maximum weight for the worst weighted threshold function is $O(n^n)$ [10]. Beimel and Weinreb [10] studied the share size of weighted secret sharing in both the information-theoretic and computational settings. In more detail, for any access structure given by a set of (potentially exponentially large) weights, [10] constructs a circuit of polynomial size and logarithmic depth that computes this access structure. Given such a circuit, one can generically transform it into a secret-sharing scheme in the information-theoretic or computational setting. In the information-theoretic setting, applying the compiler on [10] yields a secret sharing scheme with the

[2] This can always be achieved by multiplying all weights by a large enough factor.

share size $n^{\log n}$. This is worse than our scheme for any weights $< n^{\log n}$, but better than ours for even higher weights. In the computational setting, they use techniques similar to Yao's garbling to garble the circuit that computes the access structure. This compiler is explicitly written in [42], which states that the share size resulting from this compiler depends (linearly) on the number of fan-out gates in the circuit. It is, thus, unclear what polynomial describes the share size of the computational scheme and how it compares to our scheme when the weights are polynomially large. When the weight is super-polynomially large, their computational scheme will have a smaller share size than ours. However, we stress that the computational secret-sharing scheme completely breaks the algebraic structure; hence, it is not clear if one could apply it to threshold cryptography and MPC.

The works of [9,36] studied the information rate of the weighted threshold access structure. In a secret-sharing scheme, the information rate is the ratio between the secret size and the (maximum) share size. A secret sharing scheme is called "ideal" if its information rate is 1. [9,36] asked when the weighted threshold access structure admits an ideal secret sharing scheme. In particular, they gave a characterization for such weighted threshold access structures. These works, however, do not give constructions for weighted secret sharing.

Also, it should be mentioned that any secret sharing schemes for general access structure also realize weighted secret sharing. The state-of-the-art construction [3] achieves a share size of 1.5^n. This is worse than virtualization for any polynomially large weights.

CRT-based Secret-sharing. The Chinese remainder theorem-based secret-sharing was first proposed by Mignotte [35] and Asmuth and Bloom [5]. Subsequently, Iftene and Boureanu [31] (also see [29]) proposed an extension of Mignotte's construction to the weighted setting. However, their approach essentially applies the naïve virtualization technique[3] to CRT-based secret sharing. This is as inefficient (if not more) as the scheme obtained by applying virtualization to Shamir's secret sharing. Zou et al. [44] also investigated the problem of weighted secret sharing using CRT-based secret sharing. Experimentally, they showed that their scheme could be more efficient than the virtualization approach.

We emphasize, however, that *none of the above works provide any formal proof of security.*[4] As we show in this paper, the efficiency of CRT-based secret-sharing is closely related to its security parameter. Hence, without formal security analysis, it is not at all clear what efficiency they achieve. Moreover, in the (sharp) threshold setting considered in the above works (as opposed to the ramp setting), it is unclear if any efficiency improvement (over the naïve virtualization) is even *possible.* Based on our formal security analysis (see Theorem 6), we identify that efficiency can be improved in the ramp setting instead.

[3] Their scheme is described informally on Page-6, after Remark 1. See the online version at https://core.ac.uk/download/pdf/147979029.pdf of the paper [31].

[4] To our best knowledge, the only formal security analysis for CRT-based secret sharing appears in [27], where they studied how to error-correct CRT-based *codes.*

Ramp Secret-sharing. Ramp secret-sharing was first introduced by Blakley and Meadows [13]. Historically, the ramp structure has been used to improve the share size and achieve features such as *packing* [23] that have found significant applications over the years in the design of efficient MPC protocols (see, e.g., [17, 18, 23]) and other primitives such as broadcast encryption [41]. We observe that packed secret-sharing [23] based on Shamir's secret-sharing to obtain slightly improved weighted secret-sharing, but with significant caveats. Specifically, one can treat the secret $s \in \mathbb{F}$ as a binary string $(s^{(1)}, s^{(2)}, \ldots, s^{(\lambda)})$, where each $s^{(i)}$ is treated as a field element of some small field $\mathbb{F}'$. Next, one uses packed secret-sharing (over $\mathbb{F}'$) to share the λ secrets $(s^{(1)}, s^{(2)}, \ldots, s^{(\lambda)})$ among the W virtual parties. This scheme can be proven secure with t-privacy and $(t+\lambda)$-reconstruction. Furthermore, a party with weight w has share size $w \cdot \log|\mathbb{F}'|$ (which is smaller than the share size $w \cdot \log|\mathbb{F}|$ obtained by naïve virtualization).

However, there are several issues with this approach. First, the size of $\mathbb{F}'$ cannot be too small. In particular, $\mathbb{F}'$ needs to contain $> W$ elements to share it among W (virtual) parties, which means that the share size is at least $w \cdot \log W$ (compared to just w in our construction). Second, and more crucially, this approach entirely *breaks* the algebraic structure of the secrets. In particular, one cannot hope to locally compute the secret share of $x + y \in \mathbb{F}$, given secret shares of both x and y.

Additionally, we note that, if there are multiple secrets and we are considering the *amortized cost* of storing all such secrets, then packed secret sharing (over the original field $\mathbb{F}$) does provide efficiency gains similar to our improvement. Indeed, many recent works on multiparty computation [7, 22, 28] take advantage of this to improve the communication complexity of the MPC protocol. Compared to our work, these MPC protocols either only applies to circuits with specific topological structure (e.g., SIMD) or requires an expensive one-time compilation step, which introduces additional overheads.

Concurrent Work. Recently, Benhamouda, Halevi, and Stambler [12] also studied weighted ramp secret sharing schemes. They considered a ramp setting with reconstruction threshold $T = \beta \cdot W$ and privacy threshold $t = \alpha \cdot W$, where $0 < \alpha < \beta < 1$ are constants. They present two schemes based on different techniques. The first scheme, based on rounding techniques, has share size $\frac{n}{\beta-\alpha} \cdot \log|\mathbb{F}|$. The second scheme, based on wiretap channel techniques, has share size $f(\alpha, \beta)$, where f is a fixed function depending on the employed wiretap channel techniques.[5]

Our work, in comparison, considers a more "fine-grained" ramp setting, where we only require $T - t = \Theta(\lambda)$. In contrast, their results only work when both T and t are a constant fraction of the total weights. Furthermore, the share size in their rounding-based scheme depends on the number of parties, which might be undesirable in some scenarios (e.g., imagine a threshold signature scheme among 1000 parties with weights $0 < w_i \leqslant 50$). The share size in their wiretap-channel-

[5] For instance, if the wiretap channel in use is the binary symmetric channel, the share size is $\Theta\left(\frac{1}{(\alpha-\beta)^2}\right)$. We refer the readers to their paper for details.

based scheme is independent of both the weight w_i and n. However, this scheme breaks the algebraic structure of the secret; hence, it is not clear how one could apply this scheme to MPC and threshold cryptosystems.[6]

Other Work. A standard way of reducing the dependence on the number of (virtual) parties is to rely on small committees. In this approach, a small number of parties are selected as committee members to perform the task on behalf of all parties. This approach has been considered both in the MPC setting [16,25] and threshold signature schemes [15]. This approach, however, is not generally preferable because it incurs high costs for specific parties, and is typically vulnerable to adaptive corruption attacks.

2 Technical Overview

The secret-sharing scheme is essential to any threshold cryptosystem. To build any efficient weighted threshold primitive, an efficient weighted secret-sharing scheme is usually the first objective. Hence, we start our discussion with weighted secret-sharing.

Linear Secret-sharing.[7] We first observe that it is not clear if an efficient linear weighted secret-sharing scheme exists. For a particular set of weights (for instance, if all the weights are the same), one might be able to construct a linear secret with a small overhead. However, to construct a general linear scheme that works an arbitrary set of weights, it seems inevitable that the secret share of a party with weight w contains at least $\Omega(w)$ field elements.[8] Therefore, in order to obtain a more efficient weighted secret-sharing scheme, we have to resort to non-linear schemes.

Non-linear Secret-sharing. Compared to linear secret-sharing schemes, non-linear secret-sharing schemes are much less well-understood. Most of the non-linear secret-sharing schemes that have been studied are either for specialized access structures [8] or for general access structures [1,2,34]. These schemes

6 To elaborate, in their scheme, the secret s is viewed as a binary string and encoded using some binary error-correcting code $\mathsf{Enc}(s)$ padded with n instances of noises $\rho_1, \rho_2, \ldots, \rho_n$, i.e., $\mathsf{Enc}(s) \oplus \rho_1 \oplus \cdots \oplus \rho_n$. The noisy encoding is public, while the secret share of party i is ρ_i, Intuitively, one could reconstruct the secret by canceling the noise in noisy encoding with the secret shares. If one gets sufficient many secret shares, one could reconstruct the secret; if one has few secret shares, the encoding is noisy enough to hide s. Clearly, one could not locally compute a secret sharing of, for instance, $x + y \in \mathbb{F}$ given the secret shares of both x and y.

7 We consider linear scheme over the natural field $\mathbb{F}$ that the secret lives in. In particular, the discussion here does not include the linear ramp scheme that we discussed in Sect. 1.2, which is over some unnatural field $\mathbb{F}'$ that breaks the algebraic structure of the secret.

8 Unless one could generically transform a set of weight $\{w_i\}$ to another set of weights $\{w_i'\}$ that are significantly smaller (i.e., $w_i' = o(w_i)$), but define the same access structure. However, this seems extremely challenging, if at all possible.

either cannot realize the weighted threshold structure or have an exponential-size secret share. The only exception of a non-linear secret sharing scheme for threshold structure is the Chinese remainder theorem-based secret sharing scheme [5,27,35]. Indeed, as we explain later, CRT-based secret-sharing can help construct efficient weighted secret-sharing schemes.

CRT-Based Secret-sharing. Let us first recall the (unweighted) CRT-based secret-sharing. Let p_0 be the order of the field $\mathbb{F}$. In CRT-based secret-sharing, parties are associated with distinct integers $p_1, \ldots, p_n$, where $p_0, p_1, \ldots, p_n$ are required to be *coprime*. To share a secret $s \in \mathbb{F}_{p_0}$, one picks a random integer

$$S = s + u \cdot p_0,$$

where the operations are over the integer and u is uniform over some range $\{1, 2, \ldots, L\}$. The choice of L will become clear as we proceed to discuss the correctness and security. Now, the ith party shall get

$$s_i = S \mod p_i$$

as its secret share. For an authorized set A of parties, one may reconstruct the field element s by finding the unique integer S such that

$$0 \leqslant S \leqslant P_A - 1 \qquad \text{and} \qquad \forall i \in A,\ S = s_i \mod p_i,$$

where $P_A = \prod_{i \in A} p_i$. Once one finds S, s can be reconstructed by computing $s = S \mod p_0$. Therefore, to ensure perfect correctness, it must hold that $(p_0 + 1) \cdot L \leqslant P_A - 1$ for all authorized set A. On the other hand, for privacy, consider an unauthorized set $\overline{A}$. The adversary's view is equivalent to

$$\{S \mod p_i\}_{i \in \overline{A}} \qquad \Longleftrightarrow \qquad S \mod P_{\overline{A}}.$$

Hence, it suffices to prove that $S \mod P_{\overline{A}}$ is statistically close to the uniform distribution. This is indeed the case as long as $P_{\overline{A}}/L$ is exponentially small (see Claim 1). To summarize, we can construct a CRT-based secret sharing as long as we can pick L such that

$$\max_{\overline{A}} P_{\overline{A}} \ll L \leqslant \min_{A} P_A/2^{\lambda}.$$

For example, for a threshold secret sharing with reconstruction threshold T. One may pick p_i as n distinct primes with length 2λ. Then, $\max_{\overline{A}} P_{\overline{A}}$ and $\min_A P_A$ are approximately $2^{2\lambda(T-1)}$ and $2^{2\lambda \cdot T}$, respectively. Consequently, letting L to be $2^{2\lambda \cdot T - \lambda}$ satisfies the constraint above.

Note that one could again use virtualization to realize weighted secret-sharing through (unweighted) CRT-based secret-sharing (as done by [31]). This approach will result in a secret share of length $\Theta(w \cdot \lambda)$ for a party with weight w, similar to Shamir's secret sharing.

Main Idea: Weighted Ramp Secret-sharing can be Efficient. In this work, we observe that in the *ramp* setting, where there is a gap between the privacy and reconstruction threshold, one could construct an extremely efficient weighted secret sharing based on CRT secret sharing. Let w_i be the weight of the ith party. One may pick the associated number p_i to be of length $c \cdot w_i$ (as opposed to the aforementioned share size of $\Theta(w \cdot \lambda)$). Here, the same constant c is picked for all parties. Then, the constraint naturally transforms into

$$\max_{\overline{A}} 2^{\sum_{i \in \overline{A}} c \cdot w_i} \ll L \leqslant \min_{A} 2^{\sum_{i \in A} c \cdot w_i} / 2^{\lambda}.$$

In a threshold setting, where $\max_{\overline{A}}(\sum_{i \in \overline{A}} w_i)$ can be as high as $T-1$ and $\min_A(\sum_{i \in A} w_i)$ can be as low as T, one has to pick c to be $\Theta(\lambda)$. However, if we consider a ramp secret-sharing with a privacy threshold t and reconstruction threshold T, it suffices to pick c such that $c \cdot (T-t) = \Theta(\lambda)$. In particular, in the case where $T - t = \Theta(\lambda)$, one may pick $c = 1$. In other words, we observe

There is a natural trade-off between the gap of privacy and reconstruction threshold and the efficiency for CRT-based secret sharing.

Indeed, for the applications that we envision, it is often reasonable to assume a large gap between the privacy and reconstruction threshold. For instance, one may assume that $\leqslant 1/3$ fraction of the weights are corrupted and $\geqslant 1/2$ fraction of the weights will come online during reconstruction. In this scenario, as long as the total weight $\sum_{i=1}^{n} w_i$ is $\Theta(\lambda)$, the large gap is guaranteed.

2.1 Challenges in Using the WRSS Scheme

Our ultimate goal is to use the efficient WRSS to realize weighted cryptosystems with efficient communication/computation costs. Now, although the WRSS is well-suited for efficient weighted secret-sharing, it comes with several critical challenges. We shall discuss them next.

1. **Non-linearity.** One prominent feature of the WRSS is its non-linearity. Given secret shares $s_1, \ldots, s_n$, one needs to reconstruct the secret through a *non-linear function* as

$$\Big((\lambda_1 \cdot s_1 + \lambda_2 \cdot s_2 + \cdots + \lambda_n \cdot s_n) \mod P \Big) \mod p_0,$$

where $P = p_1 p_2 \cdots p_n$. Similar to Lagrange coefficients, here, λ_i is the integer satisfying[9]

$$\lambda_i \mod p_i = 1 \quad \text{and} \quad \forall j \neq i,\ \lambda_i \mod p_j = 0.$$

Now, imagine we want to reconstruct g^s for some generator g from the group $\mathbb{G}$ of order p_0. In Shamir's secret sharing, parties may simply broadcast g^{s_i},

[9] We note that λ_i could be efficiently computed. Refer to Remark 2.

and later one can use Lagrange interpolation to find g^s. In WRSS scheme, however, interpolation using group elements g^{s_i} will only give $g^{\lambda_1 \cdot s_1 + \cdots + \lambda_n \cdot s_n}$, whose exponent is effectively equal to

$$\left(\lambda_1 \cdot s_1 + \lambda_2 \cdot s_2 + \cdots + \lambda_n \cdot s_n\right) \mod p_0,$$

which is not necessarily equal to s. Evidently, the non-linearity poses a challenge to correctness.

2. **Integer Growing Problem.** Although the reconstruction procedure of the WRSS is non-linear, it does preserve the algebraic structure and support local computations similar to Shamir's secret sharing. For instance, suppose x and y are secret shared. Intuitively, parties can locally compute $x_i + y_i \mod p_i$ as a secret share of the secret $x+y$. This, however, is not always correct. The issue is that the associated integer might grow out of range. Recall that x is re-randomized as some integer $X = x + u \cdot p_0$ and y as $Y = y + u' \cdot p_0$. For any authorized set A and the product P_A, the correctness guarantees that both X and Y is $< P_A$. Nonetheless, it is not guaranteed that $X + Y < P_A$. Therefore, when parties use secret shares $x_i + y_i \mod p_i$ to reconstruct $x+y$, they are trying to reconstruct the secret integer $X + Y$ first. And they can only correctly reconstruct $X + Y$ when $X + Y < P_A$.
   Similar issues arise when one wants to locally compute the secret shares of $-x$, $x \cdot y$, and scalar multiplication $c \cdot x$ for some constant c. Therefore, one must be careful with correctness when trying to do local computations.
3. **Challenges for Simulation.** Consider a secret-sharing-based MPC protocol. At the end of the protocol, parties typically broadcast the secret share s_i of the output wire to allow reconstruction of the output s. A simulator, given the output s, needs to simulate all the secret shares of the honest parties. This is usually not an issue for linear secret sharing schemes as, at each wire s, it is maintained that s_i's are identically distributed as freshly sampled secret sharing of s (and, hence, simulatable). However, consider a WRSS secret sharing of x and y. Observe that the secret shares of $x_i + y_i \mod p_i$ is *not* identically distributed as a fresh secret sharing of $x+y$.[10] Therefore, given the output $x + y$, it is not clear how to simulate the broadcast secret shares. One may hope to resolve this issue by masking the secret shares with a fresh secret sharing of 0. However, note that we are essentially trying to mask an integer $X + Y$ over integer operations (instead of over a field). Consequently, extra care is required for this to go through.

Next, we discuss how we address these issues in different settings.

2.2 Weighted Threshold Encryption

For expository purposes, we start with a threshold encryption scheme. Recall that we aim for a scheme with one-round threshold decryption. Typically, this is

[10] In fact, their statistical distance is quite far. In particular, the distribution of the integer $X + Y$, where $X = x + u \cdot p_0$ and $Y = y + u' \cdot p_0$ is very different from the integer $(x + y) + u'' \cdot p_0$.

done by combining a PKE scheme with a secret sharing scheme, where the secret key is shared among parties. In this work, we consider the ElGamal encryption scheme for the underlying PKE scheme. Let us recall it first. In the ElGamal encryption scheme, a group $\mathbb{G}$ with order p_0 and generator g is sampled. The secret key sk and public key pk are sampled as s and g^s where $s \leftarrow \mathbb{F}_p$. To encrypt a message msg, one sample a random $r \leftarrow \mathbb{F}_p$, and the ciphertext is defined as $(\mathsf{msg} \cdot \mathsf{pk}^r, g^r)$. Given a ciphertext (c_1, c_2), one could decrypt it as $c_1 \cdot c_2^{-\mathsf{sk}}$. This encryption scheme is semantically secure as long as DDH is hard.

Now, suppose we sample a public key and secret key (g^s, s) from ElGamal and secret share s using our WRSS scheme. Given a ciphertext $(\mathsf{msg} \cdot g^{r \cdot s}, g^r)$, what should parties send as a partial decryption? As we discussed earlier, if parties simply send $g^{r \cdot s_i}$, one cannot correctly aggregate it to obtain $g^{r \cdot s}$.

Towards resolving this challenge, we first observe that the reconstruction of CRT-based secret sharing can be rewritten as

$$\Big(\big((\lambda_1 \cdot s_1 \mod P) + (\lambda_2 \cdot s_2 \mod P) + \cdots + (\lambda_n \cdot s_n \mod P)\big) \mod P\Big) \mod p_0.$$

For simplicity, let us write $(\lambda_i \cdot s_i \mod P)$ as α_i. There are several benefits to writing the reconstruction as above. First, parties can locally compute α_i. Second, given $\alpha_1, \alpha_2, \ldots, \alpha_n$, we know that the secret s is of the form

$$s = (\alpha_1 + \alpha_2 + \cdots + \alpha_n - \Delta \cdot P) \mod p_0, \qquad \text{where } \Delta \in \{0, 1, \ldots, n-1\}.$$

Crucially, the overflow number Δ has only polynomially many possibilities. Therefore, given the partial decryption $g^{r \cdot \alpha_i}$, one knows that the one-time pad g^{rs} is one of the following

$$g^{r \cdot (\sum_i \alpha_i)}, g^{r \cdot (\sum_i \alpha_i) - r \cdot P}, \ldots, g^{r \cdot (\sum_i \alpha_i) - r \cdot (n-1) \cdot P}.$$

To get statistical correctness, we shall ask the encryptor to include a hash of the encapsulated key $H(g^{r \cdot s})$ (using, for example, a universal hash function). Consequently, the decryptor could check all possibilities of the encapsulated key against the hash $H(g^{r \cdot s})$ to find $g^{r \cdot s}$. Finally, since $H(g^{r \cdot s})$ leaks information about $g^{r \cdot s}$, we shall add a randomness extractor Ext to extract uniform randomness from $g^{r \cdot s}$. Overall, the ciphertext would be

$$\mathsf{msg} \cdot \mathsf{Ext}(\mathsf{seed}, g^{r \cdot s}), \ \mathsf{seed}, \ g^r, \ H(g^{r \cdot s}).$$

This presents the main ideas behind our efficient weight threshold decryption scheme. To prove the security, we need the additional guarantee that the weights cannot be too small (for example, a constant). Indeed, if the weight w_i is too small, one could use an exhaustive search to find party P_i's secret share using its partial decryption output. We refer the readers to Sect. 6 for more details.

Remark 1 (Raise hand setting). We note that our scheme is in the "raise hand" setting. That is, parties need to know what authorized set will participate in the partial decryption process. This is because the Lagrange coefficient λ_i depends on this information. In contrast, Shamir's secret sharing-based scheme does not need this information for partial decryption. Indeed, parties could directly send g^{s_i} and the aggregator could do Lagrange interpolation over the group elements.

However, we note that, even for Shamir's secret sharing, "raise hand" might be preferable in the weighted setting as the communication cost is much lower compared to the non-raise-hand setting. Indeed, a party with weight w would need to broadcast w many group elements in the non-raise-hand setting; while in the "raise hand" setting, parties aggregate the partial decryption locally first and only need to broadcast one group element.

2.3 Weighted MPC

Next, we consider weighted MPC. In a weighted MPC protocol, every party is assigned some weights. And it is assumed that the cumulative weight of the corrupted parties is upper-bounded by a certain fraction. In this work, we restrict to the information-theoretic honest majority setting and semi-honest adversaries. Crucially, the communication/computation cost (per party i and gate) should be $O(w_i) + \lambda$.

On a high level, our protocol adopts the secret-sharing-based MPC framework (e.g., BGW protocol [11]), where we shall use the WRSS scheme as the underlying secret sharing scheme. Consequently, the efficiency of the WRSS scheme will determine the efficiency of the weighted MPC protocol. As we have mentioned, this approach involves several issues. We discuss how to address these issues next.

Multiplication. We consider the multiplication gate first. Let $W = w_1 + \cdots + w_n$ be the total weight and assume that the adversary may corrupt parties with weight at most t. The security of the WRSS requires that: if the value x of a wire is secret shared, it must be the case that the random integer $X = x + u \cdot p_0$ is sampled from $u \leftarrow \{1, \ldots, L\}$ with $L \gg 2^t$ (e.g., $L = 2^{t+\lambda}$). Therefore, the integer X associated with every wire x is (approximately) of size $2^{t+2\lambda}$. Now, suppose we want to compute the product $x \cdot y$. The corresponding integer $X \cdot Y$ may be as large as $2^{2t+4\lambda}$. This integer XY (henceforth, the secret xy) could only be reconstructed if the total weight W satisfies $2^W \geqslant 2^{2t+4\lambda}$. Therefore, our protocol only works in the setting where there is an honest majority and a large enough gap (i.e., $\Theta(\lambda)$) between the corruption threshold t and half of the total weight $W/2$.

Although the secret could be reconstructed after one multiplication gate, one cannot let the integer grow indefinitely. Therefore, after every multiplication gate, one has to use a "degree reduction" protocol[11] to reduce the integer Z associated with $z = xy$ to a smaller range. Our degree reduction protocol follows

[11] We call this a degree reduction protocol as it is reminiscent of the degree reduction protocol in the BGW protocol based on Shamir's secret sharing. In Shamir's secret sharing, the product of two secrets shared by a degree-t polynomial is shared by a degree-$2t$ polynomial. A degree reduction protocol in this case brings down the degree of the polynomial back to t.

the standard approach in the MPC literature. In particular, in the preprocessing phase, we ask parties to generate two secret shares $[r]^0$ and $[r]^1$ of a random value r. Here, in the share $[r]^0$, r is re-randomized as some integer over the small range $L = 2^{t+\lambda}$; while in the share $[r]^1$, r is re-randomized as some integer over the large range $L = 2^{2t+4\lambda}$. The idea is that parties will use the secret shares of $[r]^1$ to reconstruct $r + xy$ in the clear. Afterward, they may locally subtract $r + xy$ from $[r]^0$ to obtain a secret share of xy with a small integer range.

However, there is one crucial issue here. One has to guarantee that the reconstruction of $r+xy$ leaks only the value $r+xy$ and nothing else. While this comes for free in Shamir's secret sharing, it is not the case here. Indeed, the secret shares of $r + xy$ reveal its associated integer, whose distribution may not be indistinguishable from a *fresh* secret sharing of the secret $r + xy$. We defer the discussion of this issue to the discussion on the output reconstruction procedure.

Addition. Similarly to the multiplication gate, the addition gate also has integer growing issues. One might think if we can handle the multiplication gate, we can certainly handle the addition gate in the same way. While this is true, we do not want to invoke a degree reduction protocol for addition gates, which incurs additional interactions and consumes correlations.

Instead, we observe that the growth of the integer for addition gates is very slow. In particular, if a circuit has size $\mathsf{poly}(\lambda)$, the integer associated with a wire, which is a sum of several other wires, is upper-bounded by $\mathsf{poly}(\lambda) \cdot 2^{t+2\lambda} \ll 2^W$. Hence, reconstructing the sum of wires is not an issue. However, it becomes problematic when we want to reconstruct $x \cdot y$, where x and y are the sums of several wires. Indeed, both X and Y are now upper-bounded by $\mathsf{poly}(\lambda) \cdot 2^{t+2\lambda}$ and $X \cdot Y$ might be $\geqslant 2^W$ if $W \approx 2t + 4\lambda$. However, this is not an issue as long as W is large enough (e.g., $W \geqslant 2t + 5\lambda$). In other words, if the total weight is large enough, the integer growing for the addition gates is not an issue.

Output Reconstruction. As we have mentioned, unlike Shamir's secret sharing, it is not clear if parties could broadcast the secret shares of the output wire for reconstruction. To resolve this issue, we shall use a freshly sampled secret share $[0]$ to mask the secret shares $[\mathsf{out}]$ of the output wire. Parties will reconstruct $\mathsf{out} + 0$ as the output of the protocol. Again, here, we need to argue that the secret shares of $\mathsf{out}+0$ leak only $\mathsf{out}+0$. In particular, the integer associated with the secret $\mathsf{out}+0$ should only depend on $\mathsf{out}+0$. We observe that if the integer associated with out is (arbitrarily) distributed over some range $\{1, \ldots, L\}$, it suffices to sample the integer associated with 0 uniformly randomly from an exponentially large range $\{1, \ldots, L \cdot 2^\lambda\}$. The sum of these two integers will be exponentially close to a freshly sampled secret share of $0 + \mathsf{out}$ from the range $\{1, \ldots, L \cdot 2^\lambda\}$. We formally prove this by our integer masking lemma (Lemma 1).

2.4 Weighted Threshold Signature

Lastly, we consider the threshold signature protocol. In particular, we consider a weighted multiparty signing protocol based on the ECDSA signatures.

Let us first recall the signing functionality of the ECDSA signature. Let sk be the signing key, G be the curve base point, H be a cryptographic hash function and m be the message. To sign message m with sk, one computes the following:

1. **(Pre-signing Phase)** Generate a secret random value $k \leftarrow \mathbb{F}_q$, and then compute (public) group element $k \times G$.
2. **(Signing Phase)** Parse $k \times G$ as curve point (r_x, r_y). Then compute $\sigma = k^{-1} \cdot (H(m) + r_x \cdot \mathsf{sk})$.
3. Output the signature (r_x, σ).

Note that we could generically use our MPC protocol to compute all the field operations. However, parties do need to construct the group element $k \times G$ in the clear. We further note that parties need to agree on the exact value of $k \times G$ in order to proceed in the signing phase (i.e., step 2). Hence, our ideas from the threshold encryption section, where parties agree that $k \times G$ is one of n possibilities, are not applicable.

However, note that our task at hand is significantly simpler compared to the threshold encryption setting. In the pre-signing phase, we simply need all parties to collectively sample a random group element $k \times G$ while also obtaining a secret sharing of k. This is different from the threshold encryption setting, where parties start with a secret share of k. And later in the online phase, they need to reconstruct $(g')^k$ for some random group element g'.

To collectively sample $k \times G$ and the secret shares $[k]$, we simply ask party P_i sample a random k_i and (i) secret share $[k_i]$ among all the parties; (ii) broadcast the group element $k_i \times G$. Afterward, parties could locally reconstruct $k \times G$ as $\sum_i (k_i \times G)$. Party P_i locally computes the secret share of k by computing $\sum_j [k_j]_i$. This is secure simply because $k_i \times G$ forms an additive secret share of $k \times G$ and could be simulated given only $k \times G$.

Finally, by standard techniques in ECDSA, one could prepare the secret shares of the correlated values $[k^{-1}]$ and $[r_x \cdot \mathsf{sk}]$ in the pre-signing protocol, which leads to a one-round signing phase. We refer the readers to Sect. 7 for details.

3 Preliminaries

We use λ for the security parameter. Let $\mathsf{negl}(\lambda)$ denote a negligible function. That is, for all polynomial $p(\lambda)$, it holds that $\mathsf{negl}(\lambda) < 1/p(\lambda)$ for large enough λ. For any two distributions A, B over the finite universe Ω, the statistical distance between A and B is defined as $\mathsf{SD}(A, B) = \frac{1}{2}\sum_{\omega \in \Omega} |\Pr[A = \omega] - \Pr[B = \omega]|$. For an integer n, we shall use $[n]$ for the set $\{1, 2, \ldots, n\}$. For an integer M, we also use U_M for the uniform distribution over $\{0, 1, \ldots, M-1\}$.

Next, we define secret-sharing schemes.

Definition 1 (Secret-sharing Scheme). *The access structure of the secret-sharing scheme consists of two subsets $\mathcal{A}, \overline{\mathcal{A}} \subseteq 2^{[n]}$, where $\mathcal{A}$ consists of all authorized subsets of parties and $\overline{\mathcal{A}}$ consists of all unauthorized subsets of parties.*

A secret-sharing scheme among n parties for access structure $(\mathcal{A}, \overline{\mathcal{A}})$ *consists of two algorithms* (Share, Reconst)*, which satisfies the following.*

- ***Perfect Correctness.*** *For all secret s and authorized set* $A \in \mathcal{A}$*, it holds*

$$\Pr\left[s' = s \ : \ \begin{array}{c} (s_1, s_2, \ldots, s_n) \leftarrow \mathsf{Share}(s) \\ s' = \mathsf{Reconst}\left(\{s_i\}_{i \in A}\right) \end{array}\right] = 1.$$

- ***ε-Statistical Security.*** *For any unauthorized set* $\overline{A} \in \overline{\mathcal{A}}$ *and two secrets* s, s'*, it holds that the following two distributions are ε-statistically close.*

$$\left\{ \begin{array}{c} (s_1, s_2, \ldots, s_n) \leftarrow \mathsf{Share}(s) \\ Output \ \{s_i\}_{i \in \overline{A}} \end{array} \right\} \approx \left\{ \begin{array}{c} (s'_1, s'_2, \ldots, s'_n) \leftarrow \mathsf{Share}(s') \\ Output \ \{s'_i\}_{i \in \overline{A}} \end{array} \right\}.$$

In particular, for a weighted ramp secret sharing scheme with privacy threshold t *and reconstruction threshold* T*, each party is associated with a weight* w_i *and the authorized* $\mathcal{A}$ *and unauthorized* $\overline{\mathcal{A}}$ *set are defined as Fig. 2.*

The security of CRT-based secret sharing relies heavily on the following claim.

Claim 1 ([27])**.** *Let* $M < L$ *be arbitrary integers. Let* p *be an arbitrary integer that is coprime with* M*. Let* s *be any integer. We have*

$$\mathsf{SD}\left((s + p \cdot U_L) \mod M \quad , \quad U_M \right) < M/L.$$

Intuitively, this claim states the following. Suppose we have a secret $s \in \mathbb{F}$, where the order of $\mathbb{F}$ is p. If we pick a sufficiently random[12] integer $S = s + p \cdot U_L$, it is guaranteed that $S \mod M$ is statistically close to uniformly random. This claim is crucial in proving the security of the CRT-based secret-sharing scheme. We defer the formal proof to the full version of this paper.

4 Efficient Weighted Ramp Secret-Sharing Scheme

In this section, we show how to construct an efficient weighted ramp secret-sharing (WRSS) scheme. Our scheme is based on the Chinese Remainder Theorem-based (CRT-based) secret-sharing scheme. This scheme is introduced by [5,27,35] in the unweighted setting. Let us recall their scheme and formally present its security. Next, we show how to transform this scheme to the weighted setting, where the size of the secret share is small.

4.1 Unweighted CRT-Based Secret-Sharing

Let $\mathbb{F}_{p_0}$ be a field, where $p_0 \approx 2^\lambda$. Suppose we want to secret share a secret $s \in \mathbb{F}_{p_0}$. Unlike Shamir's secret-sharing scheme, the CRT-based scheme is non-linear. In particular, the secret shares are not elements from $\mathbb{F}_{p_0}$. Instead, for all $i \in [n]$, the ith party is associated with an integer p_i and its secret share shall be an integer s_i such that $0 \leqslant s_i < p_i - 1$. Formally, the CRT-based secret-sharing scheme among n parties is constructed as follows.

[12] Measured by the parameter L.

- **Access Structure.** Let $\mathcal{A}$ be the set of authorized subsets and $\overline{\mathcal{A}}$ be the set of unauthorized subsets.
- **Parameters.** The scheme is parametrized by a set of integers $p_1, p_2, \ldots, p_n$ and an additional integer L. It is required that all the p_i's (including p_0) are *coprime* with each other. These parameters implicitly define the following two products. (Note that $P_{\mathsf{max}} < P_{\mathsf{min}}$.)

$$P_{\mathsf{max}} = \max_{\overline{A} \in \overline{\mathcal{A}}} \left(\prod_{i \in \overline{A}} p_i \right) \qquad \text{and} \qquad P_{\mathsf{min}} = \min_{A \in \mathcal{A}} \left(\prod_{i \in A} p_i \right).$$

- **Share the secret.** To share a secret s, one picks a *random integer*

$$S = s + p_0 \cdot U_L.$$

Recall that U_L is uniformly distributed over $[L]$. We will refer to the integer S as the lifting of s and write the above step as $S = \mathsf{Lift}(s, U_L)$. When it is clear from the text, we also write $S = \mathsf{Lift}(s)$. The secret share of the ith party shall be

$$s_i = S \mod p_i.$$

- **Reconstruct the secret.** For an authorized set $A \in \mathcal{A}$, parties in A reconstruct the secret as follows. Using Chinese remainder theorem, they can find a set of Lagrange coefficients $\{\lambda_i\}_{i \in A}$ such that $S = \sum_{i \in A} \lambda_i \cdot s_i \bmod P$. Then they can reconstruct the secret s as

$$s = S \mod p_0.$$

Fig. 1. A generic CRT-based Secret-sharing Scheme

Remark 2. The Lagrange coefficient λ_i here are integers such that

$$\lambda_i \mod p_i = 1 \qquad \text{and} \qquad \forall j \neq i,\ \lambda_i \mod p_j = 0.$$

We note that the Lagrange coefficients λ_i could be efficiently computed as follows. Let $Q = \prod_{j \neq i} P_j$ be the product of p_j's except for p_i. Then,

$$\lambda_i = Q \cdot Q^{-1},$$

where Q^{-1} is the inverse of Q modulo p_i. That is, $Q \cdot Q^{-1} \mod p_i = 1$.

Theorem 5. *The secret-sharing scheme in Fig. 1 satisfies the following.*

- ***Correctness.*** *The scheme is perfectly correct if* $(L+1) \cdot p_0 < P_{\mathsf{min}}$.
- ***Security.*** *The insecurity of scheme is* $\leqslant P_{\mathsf{max}}/L$. *That is, for any unauthorized set, the statistical distance between the distributions of its secret shares for any two distinct secrets is at most* P_{max}/L.

Proof. Suppose $(L+1) \cdot p_0 < P_{\mathsf{min}}$. For any authorized set A and secret s, observe the following. The random integer $S = s + p_0 \cdot U_L$ always satisfies

$$S \leqslant (L+1) \cdot p_0 < P_{\mathsf{min}} \leqslant \prod_{i \in A} p_i.$$

Consequently, given the secret shares s_i for $i \in A$, parties can always correctly recover the integer S and, consequently, correctly reconstruct the secret $s = S \mod p_0$.

Next, we argue the security. For any unauthorized set $\overline{A}$ and any secret s, observe the following. Let $P = \prod_{i \in \overline{A}} p_i$. By the Chinese remainder theorem, there is a bijection between the secret shares $\{s_i\}_{i \in \overline{A}}$ and the integer in $\{0, 1, \ldots, P-1\}$. Therefore, instead of considering the distribution of the secret shares, i.e.,

$$\{s + p_0 \cdot U_L \mod p_i\}_{i \in \overline{A}},$$

we shall equivalently consider the distribution of the following integer

$$s + p_0 \cdot U_L \mod P.$$

By Claim 1, for any secret s, this distribution is (P/L)-close to the uniform distribution over U_P. Therefore, for any unauthorized set $\overline{A}$, the insecurity is $\leqslant (\prod_{i \in \overline{A}} p_i)/L$ and, by definition, the insecurity of the whole scheme is $\leqslant P_{\mathsf{max}}/L$.

Threshold Secret-sharing. As a representative example, we illustrate how one can implement a t-threshold secret-sharing using the CRT-based scheme. The parameters can be set up as follows. Pick $p_1, \ldots, p_n$ as n distinct prime numbers of length 2λ. By definition, P_{max} is the maximum product of $t-1$ integers, which is approximately $P_{\mathsf{max}} \approx 2^{(2\lambda)\cdot(t-1)}$; P_{min} is the minimum product of t integers, which is approximately $P_{\mathsf{min}} \approx 2^{(2\lambda)\cdot t}$. Then, if one picks L to be $L \approx 2^{2t\lambda - \lambda}$, one can verify by Theorem 5 that the scheme is a threshold secret-sharing with perfect correctness and $2^{-\lambda}$-insecurity.

4.2 Realizing Efficient WRSS Using CRT-Based Secret-Sharing

Weighted Secret-Sharing. In a weighted secret-sharing among n parties, every party i is associated with a weight $w_i \in \mathbb{N}$. We consider *the ramp secret-sharing* setting. That is, there is a reconstruction threshold T and also a privacy threshold t. A set of parties is authorized if their collective weight is $\geqslant T$; a set of parties is unauthorized if their collective weight is $\leqslant t$. In a ramp scheme, a set of parties with collective weight $\in (t, T)$ may learn partial information about the secret.

- Reconstruction threshold T. A set $A \in \mathcal{A}$ is authorized if $\sum_{i \in A} w_i \geqslant T$.
- Privacy threshold t. A set $\overline{A} \in \overline{\mathcal{A}}$ is unauthorized if $\sum_{i \in B} w_i \leqslant t$.

Fig. 2. The access structure of the weighted ramp secret-sharing scheme.

Naïve Construction with Large Share Size: Shamir's Secret-sharing with Virtual Parties. It is not hard to see that one can construct the (threshold) weighted secret-sharing scheme using Shamir's secret-sharing scheme. In particular, one thinks of the ith party with weight w_i as w_i *virtual parties*. That is, one can use the standard Shamir's secret-sharing scheme with $w_1 + w_2 + \cdots + w_n$

parties. Afterward, the ith party shall get w_i secret shares as its secret share. In words, the ith party represents w_i virtual parties in this secret-sharing scheme with $w_1 + \cdots + w_n$ virtual parties.
However, the size of the secret share in this naïve construction is quite large. In particular, party with weight w_i shall get w_i field elements $\in \mathbb{F}_{p_0}$ as its secret share. Therefore, the total length of the secret share is $w_i \cdot \lambda$.

CRT-based Construction with Small Share Size. To realize the access structure of the weighted secret-sharing scheme, we shall pick each p_i to be an integer of w_i length.[13] In particular, we shall pick p_i in the range $2^{w_i}/(1+1/n) \leqslant p_i < 2^{w_i}$.[14] By definition,

$$P_{\mathsf{max}} = \max_{A \in \overline{\mathcal{A}}} \left(\prod_{i \in \overline{A}} p_i \right) < \max_{A \in \overline{\mathcal{A}}} \left(\prod_{i \in \overline{A}} 2^{w_i} \right) \leqslant 2^t.$$

On the other hand,

$$P_{\mathsf{min}} = \min_{A \in \mathcal{A}} \left(\prod_{i \in A} p_i \right) \geqslant \max_{A \in \mathcal{A}} \left(\prod_{i \in A} 2^{w_i}/(1+1/n) \right) \geqslant 2^T/(1+1/n)^n = 2^{T-O(1)}.$$

Therefore, if one picks the parameter L to be $2^{t+\lambda}$. One may verify by Theorem 5 that this secret-sharing scheme is $O(2^{-\lambda})$-insecure and is perfectly correct as long as $T \geqslant t+2\lambda+\Theta(1)$. Furthermore, observe that the secret shares of the ith party is simply an integer between 0 and p_i. Therefore, the total length of the ith secret share is w_i. In conclusion, this construction gives rise to the following theorem.

Theorem 6. *Assume $T \geqslant t + 2\lambda + \Theta(1)$, the CRT-based secret-sharing scheme described above realizes the access structure in Fig. 2 with perfect correctness and $2^{-\lambda}$ insecurity. Furthermore, the length of the secret share with weight w_i is w_i.*

Observe that, if the gap $T - t$ could always be amplified at the cost of efficiency. In particular, for any integer c, the access structure of parties with weights $c \cdot w_1, c \cdot w_2, \ldots, c \cdot w_n$ and reconstruction (resp. privacy) threshold $c \cdot T$ (resp. $c \cdot t$) is identical to the original access structure. Hence, this gives us the following corollary.

Corollary 1 (Efficient WRSS). *For any integer c such that $c \cdot (T-t) \geqslant 2\lambda + \Theta(1)$, the weighted ramp secret-sharing scheme described above realizes the access structure in Fig. 2 with perfect correctness and $2^{-\lambda}$ insecurity. Furthermore, the length of the secret share with weight w_i is $c \cdot w_i$.*

---

[13] To ensure they are coprime, we may pick p_i to be a distinct prime of length w_i.

[14] There are $2^{w_i}/(n+1)$ many integers between $2^{w_i}/(1+1/n)$ and 2^{w_i}, among which, there are asymptotically $2^{w_i}/((n+1) \cdot w_i)$ many primes numbers. Therefore, as long as w_i is large enough, e.g., $\mathsf{polylog}(\lambda)$, one could always pick a p_i for all parties. Even if the smallest w_i is a small constant, one could always multiply every weight by some small factor to enable this.

In particular, as long as $T - t = \Omega(\lambda)$, we can construct a weighted ramp secret sharing scheme with share size $O(w_i)$.

5 Efficient Weighted MPC

In this section, we shall present a weighted MPC protocol against semi-honest adversaries. Moreover, we consider an honest majority in the weighted setting[15] and information-theoretic security. Let us first define security. We follow the definition in [4] with appropriate adaptation to the weighted setting.

Definition 2 (Semi-honestly Security). *Let* $\mathbf{W} = (w_1, \ldots, w_n)$ *be the weights of a total of* n *parties. Let* $C : \mathcal{X}_1 \times \mathcal{X}_2 \times \cdots \times \mathcal{X}_n \to \mathcal{Y}$ *be an arithmetic circuit over* $\mathbb{F}_{p_0}$. *We say that a protocol* π ε*-securely realized* C *with corruption threshold* t *in the weighted setting if the following holds. For any input* $\vec{x}$ *and any subset* $I \subset [n]$ *such that* $\sum_{i \in I} w_i \leqslant t$, *there exists an efficient simulator* $\mathcal{S}$ *such that*

$$\mathsf{SD}\left(\left(\mathcal{S}(I, \vec{x}_I, C(\vec{x})_I), C(\vec{x})\right), \left(\mathsf{View}_I^\pi(\vec{x}), \mathsf{Output}^\pi(\vec{x})\right)\right) \leqslant \varepsilon.$$

Notations. We use the following notations for the WRSS in our weighted MPC protocol. Let $\mathbf{W} = (w_1, \ldots, w_n)$ be the weights of a total of n parties, $\mathbf{P} = (p_0, p_1, \ldots, p_n)$ be the corresponding bases and let (T, t) be the reconstruction and privacy threshold. In the MPC case, the reconstruction threshold $T = W$ is the total weight of all parties. We denote the weighted ramp secret sharing of some secret s by $\{[s]_i\}_{i \in [n]} \leftarrow \mathsf{Share}(\mathbf{P}, T, t, s)$, where $[s]_i$ is party P_i's share of the secret s. Furthermore, we express the associated lifting of s as $S = \mathsf{Lift}(s)$ where the randomness U_L is implicit. Correspondingly we let $S = \mathsf{Reconstruct}(\{[s]_i\}_{i \in [n]})$ be the reconstructed integer $\mathsf{Lift}(s)$ value. For every secret s, we have $s = S \mod p_0$.

Overview of the Protocol. For every input wire s, we secret share the value s using our WRSS where the parameter L is $2^{t+\lambda}$. Therefore, $\mathsf{Lift}(s)$ is of size at most $(2^{t+\lambda}+1) \cdot p_0 \leqslant 2^{t+2\lambda}$. Throughout the MPC protocol, we shall maintain the invariant that the for every wire s, the secret integer $S = \mathsf{Lift}(s)$ associated with the secret share of s is upper-bounded by some $\mathsf{poly}(\lambda) \cdot 2^{t+2\lambda}$. Intuitively, this invariant is maintained for each addition gate. However, after each multiplication gate (including scalar multiplication where the scalar is superpolynomial in λ), this invariant is broken. Hence, we shall employ a degree reduction protocol to re-establish this invariant. For degree reduction, in the preprocessing phase, every party shall generate two secret shares of a random value r, denoted by $[r]^0$ and $[r]^1$. The instance $[r]^0$ is sampled where the corresponding parameter L is $2^{t+\lambda}$; while the instance $[r]^1$ is sampled where the corresponding parameter L is $2^{2t+5\lambda}$. Parties shall use $[r]^1$ as a mask to reconstruct the value $r + s$ in the clear and then deduct it from the secret share $[r]^0$ locally. To successfully reconstruct

[15] I.e., the cumulative weight of the corrupted party is less than half of the total weight.

the value $r + s$, which corresponds to an integer of size at most $2^{2t+5\lambda} \cdot p_0$, we need the total weights to satisfy $W \geqslant 2t + 6\lambda + \Theta(1)$. Therefore, as long as $W - 2t = \Theta(\lambda)$, we have the following theorem.

Theorem 7. *Let C be an arithmetic circuit over $\mathbb{F}$ with depth d. There is a weighted MPC protocol realizing C with the following property.*

- *The round complexity is $d + O(1)$.*
- *In the online phase, the communication/computation cost per party per gate is $O(w_i)$.*
- *In the preprocessing phase, the communication/computation cost per party per gate is $O(W)$.*
- *For any semi-honest adversary who may corrupt a total weight of t, this protocol is $\exp(-\lambda)$-secure given $W - 2t = \Theta(\lambda)$.*

We next describe our protocol in detail.

5.1 Generating Shares of Random Value F_{Random}

In this sub-protocol, parties generate a secret sharing of a random value. Observe that the communication cost per party is $O(W)$ as it sends $O(w_i)$ bits to the ith party.

- For all $i \in [n]$, the ith party samples a random value $r_i \in \mathbb{F}$. It secret shares $r_i : \{[r_i]_j\}_{j\in[n]} \leftarrow \mathsf{Share}(\mathbf{P}, W, t, r_i)$ and sends the shares to each party.
- For all $i \in [n]$, the ith party locally computes $[r]_i = \Big([r_1]_i + [r_2]_i + \cdots + [r_n]_i\Big)$ mod p_i as its secret share of the random field element $r = r_1 + \cdots + r_n \in \mathbb{F}$.

We note that the threshold parameter L in generating the WRSS secret shares is either $2^{t+\lambda}$ or $2^{2t+5\lambda}$.

Furthermore, we also use this protocol for generating secret shares of the value 0 among all the parties. The only difference is that parties sample a fresh secret share of 0 instead of a random r_i. The threshold L is generating the secret sharing of 0 is $2^{t+3\lambda}$.

We will sometimes refer to the above protocol as $F_{\mathsf{Random}}(r = \sum_{i\in[n]} r_i)$ to specify the individual randomness r_i from each party.

5.2 Degree Reduction Protocol F_{deg}

In this sub-protocol, parties re-sample the secret share of some wire x such that the corresponding integer $\mathsf{Lift}(x)$ is small enough. Observe that the communication cost per party is $O(w_i)$.

- **Input.** Parties hold the secret shares $[x]$ of some wire x. Additionally, parties hold two secret shares (i.e., $\{[r]_i^0\}_{i\in[n]}$ and $\{[r]_i^1\}_{i\in[n]}$) of a random r. Both $[r]^0$ and $[r]^1$ are sampled using the F_{Random} protocol, where the threshold parameters are $2^{t+\lambda}$ and $2^{2t+5\lambda}$, respectively.
- Party P_i locally computes and broadcasts $\left([x]_i + [r]_i^1\right) \mod p_i$ as the secret shares of $x + r$.
- Given all the secret shares, parties locally reconstruct $x + r \in \mathbb{F}$ and subtract $(x + r) \mod p_i$ from the secret shares $\{[r]_i^0\}_{i\in[n]}$.

5.3 Opening Secret Shares F_{open}

In this sub-protocol, parties open the value of the output wire. Observe that the communication cost per party is $O(w_i)$

- **Input.** Parties hold a secret share $[\mathsf{out}]$ of the output wire. Parties also hold a secret sharing of $[0]$ generated similarly as in the F_{Random} sub-protocol.
- Party P_i locally computes and broadcasts $\left([0]_i + [\mathsf{out}]_i\right) \mod p_i$ as the secret shares of $0 + \mathsf{out}$.
- Parties locally reconstruct $0 + \mathsf{out}$ as the value of out.

5.4 Realizing Negation Gate F_{neg}

In this (non-interactive) sub-protocol, parties switch the secret shares $[x]$ of x to the secret shares of $[-x]$. Negation gate usually comes for free in the Shamir secret share-based MPC. However, in our scheme, it requires some special care. Observe that if parties simply invert their secret share from $[x]_i$ to $p_i - [x]_i$. The lifted integer goes from $\mathsf{Lift}(x)$ to $P - \mathsf{Lift}(x)$, where P is the product of p_i. Crucially, note that

$$\mathsf{Lift}(x) = x \mod p_0 \quad \not\Rightarrow \quad P - \mathsf{Lift}(x) = -x \mod p_0$$

as P is not a multiple of p_0. Therefore, this approach has a correctness issue. We realize negation by the following protocol.

- **Input.** Parties hold WRSS of some secret x.
- Parties (locally) identify a bound $B \cdot p_0$ on the integer $\mathsf{Lift}(x)$. For example, if x is an input wire, $\mathsf{Lift}(x)$ is at most $(2^{t+\lambda}+1)\cdot p_0$. Hence, one set $B = 2^{t+\lambda}+1$. If x is the secret share of the sum of two input wires, the corresponding bound B will be $2 \cdot (2^{t+\lambda} + 1)$. If x is the output of a degree reduction protocol, the maximum value of $\mathsf{Lift}(x)$ is reset to be $(2^{t+\lambda} + 1) \cdot p_0$. Hence, one could again pick $B = 2^{t+\lambda} + 1$. Consequently, this bound B only depends on the topology of the circuit, and parties could identify the same bound B without interaction.
- Party P_i locally computes $[-x]_i = (B \cdot p_0 - [x]_i) \mod p_i$.

Observe that the lifting integer of the secret shares $[-x]_i$ is now the integer $B \cdot p_0 - \mathsf{Lift}(x)$ and we have $(B \cdot p_0 - \mathsf{Lift}(x)) = -x \mod p_0$. Therefore, this sub-protocol correctly realizes the negation gate.

- **Preprocessing Phase.**
  - Parties generate $|C|$ fresh samples of $[r]^0, [r]^1$ (as described in F_{Random}).
  - Parties generate samples of the secret sharing $[0]$ of 0 (as described in F_{Random}). The number of instances equals to the number of output wires of C.
- **Online Phase.**
  - Parties sample a WRSS of their inputs and send it to all parties. The threshold parameter L in generating the secret shares is $2^{t+\lambda}$.
  - Addition Gate $x + y$: Parties locally compute $([x]_i + [y]_i) \mod p_i$ as the secret share of $x + y$.
  - Multiplication Gate $x \cdot y$: Parties locally compute $([x]_i \cdot [y]_i) \mod p_i$ as the secret share of $x \cdot y$. They then employ a degree reduction protocol F_{deg} and obtain $[z]_i$ as the new share where $z = x \cdot y$. In subsequent sections we will refer to this as F_{Mult}.
  - Negation Gate $-x$: Parties use the sub-protocol F_{neg}.
  - Scalar Multiplication Gate $c \cdot x$: Parties locally compute $(c \cdot [x]_i) \mod p_i$ as the secret share of $c \cdot x$. They then employ a degree reduction protocol F_{deg} and obtain $[z]_i$ as the new share where $z = c \cdot x$. In subsequent sections we will refer to this as F_{sMult}.
- **Reconstruct the Output.** For each output wire out, parties use the F_{Open} with input [out] to reconstruct the value out.

Fig. 3. Our Efficient Weighted MPC Protocol

5.5 Our Protocol

We are now ready to state our protocol in Fig. 3. The correctness is straightforward as the reconstruction of the secret is correct for each sub-protocol.
For security, the following lemma is helpful. We defer the formal proof to the full version of this paper.

Lemma 1 (Integer Masking Lemma). *Let p and $0 \leqslant r_1, r_2 < p$ be any integers. Let $M < N$ also be arbitrary integers. Let D be an arbitrary distribution over the universe $\{r_1, p + r_1, 2p + r_1, \ldots\} \cap [M]$. Then,*

$$\mathsf{SD}\left(\left(D + U_N \,\middle|\, U_N \mod p = r_2\right), \left(U_N \,\middle|\, U_N \mod p = r_1 + r_2\right)\right) \leqslant M/N + 2p/N,$$

where the addition is over the integers.

We provide some intuition about this lemma and why it is relevant to the security of the MPC protocol. Take the multiplication sub-protocol as an example. We need to argue that the reconstructed integer $[x] \cdot [y] + [r]^1$ could be simulated. Here, the integer corresponds to $[x] \cdot [y]$ is the distribution D and the integer corresponds to $[r]^1$ is the distribution U_N. The conditioning on $U_N \mod p$ is because of the adversary's secret share of $[r]^1$. That is, it knows that the remainder of U_N modulo some product of p_i. Now, this lemma states that as long as the range of the integer $[r]^1$ is sampled from a much larger domain (measured by N) compared to the maximum value of $[x] \cdot [y]$ (measured by M), one may simply sample the integer corresponds to $[x] \cdot [y] + [r]^1$ as a uniformly random one (given that it is consistent with the adversary's secret share).[16]

Security. The security proof essentially follows from the security of the WRSS and Lemma 1. Due to space constraints, we defer the formal proof to the full version of this paper.

6 Efficient Weighted Threshold Encryption Scheme

In this section, we will demonstrate the utility of our secret-sharing scheme by constructing a weighted threshold encryption scheme, where the size of the secret-key shares is small. Let us first define the primitive.

Definition 3. *A public-key encryption scheme with weighted threshold decryption consists of a tuple of PPT algorithms* (Gen, Enc, PartialDec, Reconstruct).

- $(\mathsf{pk}, \{\mathsf{sk}_i\}_{i=1}^n) \leftarrow \mathsf{Gen}(1^\lambda, \{w_1\}_{i=1}^n, T, t)$: *The* Gen *algorithm takes the security parameter* 1^λ *as input and a weighted access structure with privacy threshold* t *and reconstruction threshold* T *as inputs. It outputs a public key* pk *and a set of secret-key shares* $\{sk_i\}_{i=1}^n$, *where* sk_i *is given to the* i^{th} *party.*
- $c \leftarrow \mathsf{Enc}(\mathsf{pk}, m)$: *The* Enc *algorithm takes as input the public key* pk, *a message* m, *and outputs a ciphertext* c.
- $\mu \leftarrow \mathsf{PartialDec}(S, \mathsf{sk}', c)$: *The* PartialDec *algorithm takes as input a subset* $S \subseteq [n]$, *secret-key share* sk', *ciphertext* c, *and outputs partial decryption* μ.
- $m \leftarrow \mathsf{Reconstruct}(\{\mu_i\}_{i \in S}, c)$: *The* Reconstruct *is a deterministic algorithm that takes as input a set of partial decryptions* $\{\mu_i\}_{i\in S}$ *from a subset* S *of parties, a ciphertext* c, *and outputs a message* m. *When fails, it outputs* $\perp$.

It shall satisfy the following guarantees.

- ***Statistical Correctness.*** *For any weighted access structure* $(\{w_i\}_{i=1}^n, T, t)$, *authorized subset* $S \subseteq [n]$, *and message* m, *it holds that*

$$\Pr\left[m^* = m \; : \; \begin{array}{c} (\mathsf{pk}, \{\mathsf{sk}_i\}_{i=1}^n) \leftarrow \mathsf{Gen}(1^\lambda, \{w_1\}_{i=1}^N, T, t) \\ c \leftarrow \mathsf{Enc}(\mathsf{pk}, m) \\ \forall i \in S \; : \; \mu_i \leftarrow \mathsf{PartialDec}(S, \mathsf{sk}_i, c) \\ m^* \leftarrow \mathsf{Reconstruct}(\{\mu_i\}_{i\in S}, c) \end{array} \right] \geqslant 1 - \mathsf{negl}(\lambda).$$

[16] The term p/N will always be small since p is the product of the adversary's p_i, which is at most 2^t. The WRSS scheme requires that whenever we pick a random lift integer, we shall always pick a domain much larger than 2^t.

- ***ε-Strong CPA Security.*** *For any PPT adversary A, any weighted access structure $(\{w_i\}_{i=1}^n, T, t)$, and any unauthorized subset $S \subseteq [n]$, it holds that*

$$\Pr\left[b^* = b \ : \ \begin{array}{c} (\mathsf{pk}, \{\mathsf{sk}_i\}_{i=1}^n) \leftarrow \mathsf{Gen}(1^\lambda, \{w_1\}_{i=1}^N, T, t) \\ (m_0, m_1) \leftarrow A^{\mathcal{O}(\cdot)}(\mathsf{pk}, \{\mathsf{sk}\}_{i\in S}) \\ b \leftarrow \{0,1\};\ c \leftarrow \mathsf{Enc}(\mathsf{pk}, m_b) \\ b^* \leftarrow A^{\mathcal{O}(\cdot)}(\mathsf{pk}, \{\mathsf{sk}_i\}_{i\in S}, m_0, m_1, c) \end{array} \right] \leqslant 1/2 + \varepsilon.$$

Here, the oracle $\mathcal{O}(A, B, m)$ takes as input an authorized set A and a subset B such that $B \cup S$ is unauthorized, and a message m. Its outputs are sampled from the following distribution

$$\left\{ \begin{array}{c} c \leftarrow \mathsf{Enc}(\mathsf{pk}, m), \quad \forall i \in B,\ \mu_i = \mathsf{PartialDec}(A, \mathsf{sk}_i, c) \\ \textit{Output}\ (c, \{\mu_i\}_{i\in B}) \end{array} \right\}.$$

In other words, the adversary is given access to the partial decryption oracle on honestly sampled *ciphertexts.*

Remark 3. We notice that, in the threshold setting, the plain CPA security (where the adversary does not have any access to partial decryption) is trivial to achieve. For instance, consider the following trivial scheme. Take any CPA-secure PKE scheme and any secret-sharing scheme. Sample the public key and secret key pair from the underlying PKE scheme and secret share the secret key with all parties. Now, the partial decryption algorithm simply outputs the secret share. Observe that even this scheme satisfies the plain CPA security.
Due to this observation, we consider a stronger definition, where the adversary has access to partial decryption on ciphertexts that are honestly sampled. This stronger CPA-security definition excludes the trivial construction above.

6.1 Building Blocks

ElGamal Encryption. Our construction is based on the ElGamal encryption system. Let us recall it. In the ElGamal encryption scheme, a group $\mathbb{G}$ with order p and generator g is sampled as $(\mathbb{G}, g) \leftarrow \mathsf{Setup}(1^\lambda)$. The secret key sk and public key pk are sampled as s and g^s where $s \leftarrow \mathbb{F}_p$. To encrypt a message m, one sample a random $r \leftarrow \mathbb{F}_p$, and the ciphertext is defined as $(m \cdot \mathsf{pk}^r, g^r)$. Given a ciphertext (c_1, c_2), one could decrypt it as $c_1 \cdot c_2^{-\mathsf{sk}}$. This encryption scheme is semantically secure as long as the Decisional Diffie-Hellman (DDH) problem is hard in $\mathbb{G}$, which states that the following two distributions are computationally indistinguishable

$$(g, g^a, g^b, g^{ab}) \approx (g, g^a, g^b, g^c),$$

where $a, b, c \leftarrow \mathbb{F}_p$.
We need the following definitions regarding min-entropy and randomness extractor. For a distribution X, its min-entropy is defined as

$$H_\infty(X) = -\log\left(\max_x \Pr[X = x]\right).$$

Definition 4 (Randomness Extractor). *A function* $\mathsf{Ext}\colon \{0,1\}^n \times \{0,1\}^d \to \{0,1\}^m$ *is called a* (k,ε)-strong randomness extractor *if, for all distributions* X *over* $\{0,1\}^n$ *such that* $H_\infty(X) \geqslant k$, *we have*

$$\mathsf{SD}\left(\ (s, \mathsf{Ext}(X,s))\ ;\ (U_{\{0,1\}^d}, U_{\{0,1\}^m})\ \right) \leqslant \varepsilon,$$

where the seed s *is chosen uniformly at random from* $\{0,1\}^d$.

For our purpose, we may use the *leftover hash lemma* [30] as a concrete instantiation of the randomness extractor.

Definition 5 (Universal Hashing). *A family of hash function* $\{h_k : \{0,1\}^\lambda \to \{0,1\}^\alpha\}_k$, *where* $k \in \{0,1\}^\beta$ *is called a universal hashing function family if, for any two distinct inputs* $x, y \in \{0,1\}^\lambda$, *it holds that*

$$\Pr_{k \leftarrow \{0,1\}^\beta}\left[h_k(x) = h_k(y)\right] = 1/2^\alpha.$$

Instantiation. We provide a simple instantiation as follows. Given a message space $\{0,1\}^\lambda$, one picks $\alpha = \lambda/2$ and $\beta = \lambda$. A message $x \in \{0,1\}^\lambda$ is treated as a vector $(x_1, x_2) \in \mathbb{F}_{2^\alpha} \times \mathbb{F}_{2^\alpha}$. Similarly, the index of the hash function $k \in \{0,1\}^\lambda$ is also treated as $(k_1, k_2) \in \mathbb{F}_{2^\alpha} \times \mathbb{F}_{2^\alpha}$. Define the hash function output as

$$h_{k_1,k_2}(x_1, x_2) = k_1 \cdot x_1 + k_2 \cdot x_2,$$

where the operations are over $\mathbb{F}_{2^\alpha}$. One may verify that it is indeed a universal hash function.

For our purpose, observe that for any key $(k_1, k_2) \neq (0,0)$ and any hash output $\sigma \in \{0,1\}^{\lambda/2}$, it holds that

$$H_\infty\left(U_{\{0,1\}^\lambda}\ \middle|\ (k_1,k_2),\ h_{k_1,k_2}\left(U_{\{0,1\}^\lambda}\right) = \sigma\right) = \lambda/2.$$

That is, a uniformly sampled message has at least $\lambda/2$ bits of entropy after being conditioned on the hash function output.

6.2 Our Construction

Our construction based on the ElGamal encryption scheme is in Fig. 4.

Efficiency. The efficiency of our threshold encryption scheme inherits the efficiency of the WRSS scheme as the size of the secret key share is $O(w_i)$. Moreover, the partial decryption and reconstruction time is $O(W) + \mathsf{poly}(\lambda)$, where W is the total weights $\sum_{i\in S} w_i$. This is because every party is computing an $O(W)$-bit integer, i.e., $\mathsf{sk}_i \cdot \lambda_i \bmod P_S$, which takes $O(W)$ time and the rest of the reconstruction time is independent of the weight and takes $\mathsf{poly}(\lambda)$ time.

In comparison, if one uses Shamir's secret sharing with the virtualization approach, every party needs to interpolate a degree-$(W-1)$ polynomial and evaluate it at 0. This needs at least $W \log W$ field operations based on fast Fourier transform techniques, which takes at least $O(W \cdot \lambda)$ time.

Correctness. Observe that the decryption is correct as long as it finds the correct index j^*. Furthermore, it might not find the correct j^* if and only if there is a collision for the universal hash function h_k. By the property of the universal hash function, for any $j \neq j^*$, the probability of the collision between j and j^* is $\exp(-\lambda)$. Therefore, by union bound, the probability of incorrectness is upper-bounded by $n \cdot \exp(-\lambda)$.

We note that, with a slight modification, we can achieve perfect correctness. That is, the encryptor can ensure the decryption is correct by picking a "good" universal hash function.

$\underline{\mathsf{Gen}(1^\lambda, \{w_1\}_{i=1}^n, T, t)}$. The public key and secret keys are set up as follows.

- Sample $(\mathbb{G}, g) \leftarrow \mathsf{Setup}(1^\lambda)$ and $s \leftarrow \mathbb{F}_p$.
- Set $\mathsf{pk} = s$. Use the WRSS scheme with access structure $(\{w_1\}_{i=1}^n, T, t)$ to secret share s as $s_1, \ldots, s_n$. Set $\mathsf{sk}_i = s_i$.

$\underline{\mathsf{Enc}(\mathsf{pk}, m)}$. To encrypt a message m, one computes:

- Sample a random exponent $r \leftarrow \mathbb{F}_p$, a hash function $k \leftarrow \{0,1\}^\beta$, and a seed for the randomness extractor $\mathsf{sd} \leftarrow \{0,1\}^d$.
- The ciphertext is defined as

$$m \oplus \mathsf{Ext}(\mathsf{sd}, \mathsf{pk}^r),\ \mathsf{sd},\ g^r,\ k,\ h_k(\mathsf{pk}^r).$$

$\underline{\mu \leftarrow \mathsf{PartialDec}(S, \mathsf{sk}', c)}$. The partial decryption is defined as follows. Note that the authorized set S implicitly defined $P_S = \prod_{i \in S} p_i$ and also the Lagrange coefficients λ_i. That is, the unique integer λ_i that satisfies

$$\lambda_i = 1 \mod p_i \qquad \text{and} \qquad \forall j \in S \setminus \{i\},\ \lambda_i = 0 \mod p_j.$$

Parse the ciphertext c as above and the partial decryption outputs

$$(g^r)^{\left(\mathsf{sk}' \cdot \lambda_i \mod P_S\right)}.$$

$\underline{m \leftarrow \mathsf{Reconstruct}(\{\mu_i\}_{i \in S}, c)}$. Given all the partial decryptions $\{\mu_i\}_{i \in S}$, the reconstruction does the following. It set $\mu = \prod_{i \in S} \mu_i$ and computes

$$\mu,\ \mu \cdot (g^r)^{-P_S},\ \ldots,\ \mu \cdot (g^r)^{-(|S|-1) \cdot P_S}.$$

It checks if there exists an j such that

$$h_k\left(\mu \cdot (g^r)^{-j \cdot P_S}\right) = h_k(\mathsf{pk}^r).$$

If such an j does not exist, it output $\perp$; otherwise, it finds any such j^* and outputs

$$c \oplus \mathsf{Ext}\left(\mathsf{sd}, \mu \cdot (g^r)^{-j^* \cdot P_S}\right).$$

Fig. 4. Our Efficient Threshold Encryption Scheme

Security. We now show the CPA security of our weighted public-key threshold encryption scheme. In particular, in the generic group model [39], we shall prove that our scheme satisfies ε-strong CPA-security where $\varepsilon = \mathsf{poly}(\lambda)/p_{\mathsf{min}}$ where $p_{\mathsf{min}} = \min_i p_i$. Therefore, as long as the minimum weight is large enough, e.g., $w_{\mathsf{min}} \geqslant \log^2 \lambda$, our threshold encryption scheme satisfies the $\mathsf{negl}(\lambda)$-strong CPA security.

We briefly explain why p_{min} needs to be large, and we need the generic group model (instead of DDH). Note that if w_i is small, the total possibility of the secret share of party P_i is also small $2^{O(w_i)}$. Therefore, given the partial decryption output of P_i, one could use an exhaustive search (in time p_i) to find the exact s_i. Therefore, it is inevitable that the security depends on the minimum w_i.

Next, our proof relies on the generic group model as our WRSS is non-linear. In particular, for a linear partial decryption, given g^{s_i}, one could easily simulate $(g^r, (g^{s_i})^r)$, where $r \leftarrow \mathbb{F}_p$. However, in our case, given g^{s_i}, it is not clear how to simulate $(g^r, (g^r)^{(s_i \cdot \lambda_i \bmod N)})$. Therefore, we have to rely on the generic group to argue that this distribution is indistinguishable from two random group elements. Due to space constraints, the full proof is deferred to the full version of this paper.

7 Efficient Weighted Threshold Signature

ECDSA Signature Scheme

Let G be the elliptic curve base point which generates a subgroup of some prime order q. Let $H(\cdot)$ be a cryptographic hash function. We use $a \times G$ to denote the multiplication of curve point G by a scalar a.

- $\mathsf{Gen}(1^\lambda)$: Sample signing key as $\mathsf{sk} \leftarrow \mathbb{F}_q$ and then set verification key as $\mathsf{vk} = \mathsf{sk} \times G$.
- $\mathsf{Sign}(\mathsf{sk}, m)$: Sample random element $k \leftarrow \mathbb{F}_q$. Compute curve point $(r_x, r_y) = k \times G$ and let $r = r_x$. Then set $\sigma = k^{-1} \cdot (H(m) + r \cdot \mathsf{sk})$. Output (r, σ).
- $\mathsf{Verify}(\mathsf{vk}, m, (r, \sigma))$: Compute $(r_x, r_y) = \sigma^{-1} \cdot H(m) \times G + \sigma^{-1} \cdot r \times \mathsf{vk}$. Then, output 1 if and only if $r_x = r$.

Fig. 5. ECDSA Signature

We show how to apply our weighted MPC protocol in the context of threshold signatures. More specifically, we show how to construct a weighted multiparty signing protocol for ECDSA signatures. Such protocol is also known as weighted threshold signature.

7.1 ECDSA Signatures

We first briefly recall the ECDSA signature scheme in Fig. 5.

Following the same general framework as previous approaches [24,33], our weighted threshold ECDSA signature scheme starts with a WRSS of the secret signing key sk among all parties. We described this step next.

Weighted Threshold ECDSA Key Generation Functionality $\mathcal{F}_{\mathsf{Gen}}(1^\lambda, T, t)$:

$\mathcal{F}_{\mathsf{Gen}}$ takes as input the security parameter 1^λ and CRT-based weighted (Ramp) secret-sharing scheme with respect to reconstruction threshold T and privacy threshold t. Then it does the following:

1. Sample a secret signing key $\mathsf{sk} \leftarrow \mathbb{F}_q$. Then it sets verification key as $\mathsf{vk} = \mathsf{sk} \times G$.
2. Generate a WRSS of sk : $\{[\mathsf{sk}]_i\} \leftarrow \mathsf{Share}(\mathbf{P}, T, t, \mathsf{sk})$. Then send $(\mathsf{vk}, \{[\mathsf{sk}]_i\})$ to each party i.

In order to build a weighted multiparty signing protocol for ECDSA signing functionality, we begin by describing the ideal signing functionality, step by step as follows:

ECDSA Signing Functionality F_{Sign}

1. Generate a secret random value $k \leftarrow \mathbb{F}_q$, and then compute (public) group element $k \times G$.
2. Parse $k \times G$ as curve point (r_x, r_y).
3. Compute multiplication between inverse of secret random value k and secret signing key sk. We denote this by $s = k^{-1} \cdot \mathsf{sk}$.
4. Compute two scalar multiplications: $k^{-1} \cdot H(m)$ and $r_x \cdot s$.
5. Add up the above two values and obtain σ.

Our weighted MPC protocol will proceed as follows: For the first step of signing, the secret random value k shall be contributed by all parties. More specifically, each party i will sample its own secret random value k_i, broadcast the group element $k_i \times G$, and then distribute the WRSS of k_i among all parties. This allows each party to obtain a share of the combined random value $k = \sum_{i \in [n]} k_i$ as well as the group element $k \times G = \sum_{i \in [n]} k_i \times G$. The subsequent steps naturally fit into our MPC protocol: step 2 only incurs public operations, and step 5 only incurs addition, both of which can be computed locally by every party. Step 3 involves first computing the inversion k^{-1} and then multiplying it with sk. Using the inversion protocol as suggested in [6], these operations can be handled via F_{Mult} and F_{Open}. Finally, step 4 involves scalar multiplications. While in our weighted MPC protocol parties need to run degree reduction to keep the integer value of share small for subsequent multiplications; here each party can perform scalar multiplication locally since there are no multiplications afterward.

We describe our weighted multiparty ECDSA signing protocol which realizes the ideal ECDSA signing functionality in Fig. 6. We split our signing protocol into two phases: a pre-signing protocol which only depends on the shares of the signing key, followed by a non-interactive signing protocol which depends on the actual message.

Correctness and Security. Both correctness and security of our weighted multiparty ECDSA signing protocol follow from these of weighted MPC protocol. The only catch is that we also need to simulate the value $k_i \times G$ sent by each honest party. However, since those values form an additive sharing of $k \times G$, they can be simulated given only $k \times G$.

Weighted Threshold ECDSA Signing Protocol

Let there be a total of n parties where each party i has base p_i, its secret input $[\mathsf{sk}]_i$, public input vk and m. Let $S \subseteq [n]$ be the subset of parties participating in the weighted threshold ECDSA signing protocol and let W be the total weight of these parties. We will rely on the following protocols: $(F_{\mathsf{Random}}, F_{\mathsf{Mult}}, F_{\mathsf{Open}})$.

Pre-signing Phase

1. Parties generate CRT shares of random values $\{[\gamma]_i\}_{i \in S} \leftarrow F_{\mathsf{Random}}(\gamma = \sum_{i \in S} \gamma_i)$, and $\{[k]_i\}_{i \in S} \leftarrow F_{\mathsf{Random}}(k = \sum_{i \in S} k_i)$. Each party i also broadcasts $k_i \times G$.
2. Parties compute $\{[\delta]_i\}_{i \in S} = F_{\mathsf{Mult}}(\{[\gamma]_i\}_{i \in S}, \{[k]_i\}_{i \in S})$, and $\{[\theta]_i\}_{i \in S} = F_{\mathsf{Mult}}(\{[\gamma]_i\}_{i \in S}, \{[\mathsf{sk}]_i\}_{i \in S})$.
3. Parties compute $\delta = F_{\mathsf{Open}}(\{[\delta]_i\}_{i \in S}))$. Then they compute $R = \sum_{i \in S} k_i \times G$ and set curve point $R = (r_x, r_y)$
4. Each party i computes $[\sigma^0]_i = \delta^{-1} \cdot [\gamma]_i$ and $[\sigma^1]_i = r_x \cdot \delta^{-1} \cdot [\theta]$. Note that $[\sigma^0]_i$ is a share of k^{-1} and $[\sigma^1]_i$ is a share of $k^{-1} \cdot \mathsf{sk}$.
5. Each party i saves the values $(r_x, [\sigma^0]_i, [\sigma^1]_i)$.

Signing Phase

1. Each party i locally computes $[\sigma]_i = H(m) \cdot [\sigma^0]_i + [\sigma^1]_i$.
2. Parties compute $\sigma = F_{\mathsf{Open}}(\{[\sigma]_i\}_{i \in S}))$. The signature of m is (σ, r_x).

Fig. 6. Weighted Threshold ECDSA Signing

Efficiency. The aforementioned pre-signing phase involves three rounds. However, instead of having the parties perform a multiplication protocol on $[\gamma]_i \cdot [k]_i$ and then open the result, we can directly let the parties open the multiplication of their local shares, thus bringing the pre-signing phase to two rounds. The communication cost per party in the pre-signing phase is $O(W + \lambda)$.
The online signing phase is non-interactive. Each party i broadcasts a share of final signature $[\sigma]_i$ which has size $O(w_i)$.

References

1. Applebaum, B., Beimel, A., Farràs, O., Nir, O., Peter, N.: Secret-sharing schemes for general and uniform access structures. In: Ishai, Y., Rijmen, V. (eds.) EUROCRYPT 2019, Part III. LNCS, vol. 11478, pp. 441–471. Springer, Cham (2019). https://doi.org/10.1007/978-3-030-17659-4_15
2. Applebaum, B., Beimel, A., Nir, O., Peter, N.: Better secret sharing via robust conditional disclosure of secrets. In: Makarychev, K., Makarychev, Y., Tulsiani, M., Kamath, G., Chuzhoy, J. (eds.), 52nd ACM STOC, pp. 280–293. ACM Press, June 2020
3. Applebaum, B., Nir, O.: Upslices, downslices, and secret-sharing with complexity of 1.5^n. In: Malkin, T., Peikert, C. (eds.) CRYPTO 2021, Part III. LNCS, vol. 12827, pp. 627–655. Springer, Cham (2021). https://doi.org/10.1007/978-3-030-84252-9_21
4. Asharov, G., Lindell, Y.: A full proof of the BGW protocol for perfectly secure multiparty computation. J. Cryptology **30**(1), 58–151 (2017)

5. Asmuth, C., Bloom, J.: A modular approach to key safeguarding. IEEE Trans. Inf. Theory **29**(2), 208–210 (1983)
6. Beaver, D.: Efficient multiparty protocols using circuit randomization. In: Feigenbaum, J. (ed.) CRYPTO 1991. LNCS, vol. 576, pp. 420–432. Springer, Heidelberg (1992). https://doi.org/10.1007/3-540-46766-1_34
7. Beck, G., Goel, A., Jain, A., Kaptchuk, G.: Order-c secure multiparty computation for highly repetitive circuits. In: Canteaut, A., Standaert, F.-X. (eds.) EUROCRYPT 2021, Part II. LNCS, vol. 12697, pp. 663–693. Springer, Cham (2021). https://doi.org/10.1007/978-3-030-77886-6_23
8. Beimel, A., Ishai, Y.: On the power of nonlinear secret-sharing. IACR Cryptol. ePrint Arch., p. 30 (2001)
9. Beimel, A., Tassa, T., Weinreb, E.: Characterizing ideal weighted threshold secret sharing. In: Kilian, J. (ed.) TCC 2005. LNCS, vol. 3378, pp. 600–619. Springer, Heidelberg (2005). https://doi.org/10.1007/978-3-540-30576-7_32
10. Beimel, A., Weinreb, E.: Monotone circuits for monotone weighted threshold functions. Inf. Process. Lett. **97**(1), 12–18 (2006)
11. Ben-Or, M., Goldwasser, S., Wigderson, A.: Completeness theorems for non-cryptographic fault-tolerant distributed computation (extended abstract). In: 20th ACM STOC, pp. 1–10. ACM Press, May 1988
12. Benhamouda, F., Halevi, S., Stambler, L.: Weighted secret sharing from wiretap channels. In: ITC (2023)
13. Blakley, G.R., Meadows, C.: Security of ramp schemes. In: Blakley, G.R., Chaum, D. (eds.) CRYPTO 1984. LNCS, vol. 196, pp. 242–268. Springer, Heidelberg (1985). https://doi.org/10.1007/3-540-39568-7_20
14. Breidenbach, L., et al.: Chainlink 2.0: next steps in the evolution of decentralized oracle networks. Chainlink Labs (2021)
15. Chaidos, P., Kiayias, A.: Mithril: stake-based threshold multisignatures. Cryptology ePrint Archive, Report 2021/916 (2021). https://eprint.iacr.org/2021/916
16. Choudhuri, A.R., Goel, A., Green, M., Jain, A., Kaptchuk, G.: Fluid MPC: secure multiparty computation with dynamic participants. In: Malkin, T., Peikert, C. (eds.) CRYPTO 2021, Part II. LNCS, vol. 12826, pp. 94–123. Springer, Cham (2021). https://doi.org/10.1007/978-3-030-84245-1_4
17. Damgård, I., Ishai, Y., Krøigaard, M.: Perfectly secure multiparty computation and the computational overhead of cryptography. In: Gilbert, H. (ed.) EUROCRYPT 2010. LNCS, vol. 6110, pp. 445–465. Springer, Heidelberg (2010). https://doi.org/10.1007/978-3-642-13190-5_23
18. Damgård, I., Ishai, Y., Krøigaard, M., Nielsen, J.B., Smith, A.: Scalable multiparty computation with nearly optimal work and resilience. In: Wagner, D. (ed.) CRYPTO 2008. LNCS, vol. 5157, pp. 241–261. Springer, Heidelberg (2008). https://doi.org/10.1007/978-3-540-85174-5_14
19. Desmedt, Y.: Society and group oriented cryptography: a new concept. In: Pomerance, C. (ed.) CRYPTO 1987. LNCS, vol. 293, pp. 120–127. Springer, Heidelberg (1988). https://doi.org/10.1007/3-540-48184-2_8
20. Desmedt, Y., Frankel, Y.: Threshold cryptosystems. In: Brassard, G. (ed.) CRYPTO 1989. LNCS, vol. 435, pp. 307–315. Springer, New York (1990). https://doi.org/10.1007/0-387-34805-0_28
21. Ellis, S., Juels, A., Nazarov, S.: Chainlink: a decentralized oracle network. Retrieved March **11**(2018), 1 (2017)
22. Escudero, D., Goyal, V., Polychroniadou, A., Song, Y.: TurboPack: honest majority MPC with constant online communication. In: Yin, H., Stavrou, A., Cremers, C., Shi, E. (eds.), ACM CCS 2022, pp. 951–964. ACM Press, November 2022

23. Franklin, M.K., Yung, M.: Communication complexity of secure computation (extended abstract). In: 24th ACM STOC, pp. 699–710. ACM Press, May 1992
24. Gennaro, R., Goldfeder, S.: Fast multiparty threshold ECDSA with fast trustless setup. In: Lie, D., Mannan, M., Backes, M., Wang, X.F. (eds.), ACM CCS 2018, pp. 1179–1194. ACM Press, October 2018
25. Gentry, C., et al.: YOSO: you only speak once. In: Malkin, T., Peikert, C. (eds.) CRYPTO 2021, Part II. LNCS, vol. 12826, pp. 64–93. Springer, Cham (2021). https://doi.org/10.1007/978-3-030-84245-1_3
26. Goldreich, O., Micali, S., Wigderson, A.: How to play any mental game or a completeness theorem for protocols with honest majority. In: Aho, A. (ed.), 19th ACM STOC, pp. 218–229. ACM Press, May 1987
27. Goldreich, O., Ron, D., Sudan, M.: Chinese remaindering with errors. In: 31st ACM STOC, pp. 225–234. ACM Press, May 1999
28. Goyal, V., Polychroniadou, A., Song, Y.: Unconditional communication-efficient MPC via hall's marriage theorem. In: Malkin, T., Peikert, C. (eds.) CRYPTO 2021, Part II. LNCS, vol. 12826, pp. 275–304. Springer, Cham (2021). https://doi.org/10.1007/978-3-030-84245-1_10
29. Harn, L., Miao, F.: Weighted secret sharing based on the Chinese remainder theorem. Int. J. Netw. Secur. **16**(6), 420–425 (2014)
30. Håstad, J., Impagliazzo, R., Levin, L.A., Luby, M.: A pseudorandom generator from any one-way function. SIAM J. Comput. **28**(4), 1364–1396 (1999)
31. Iftene, S., Boureanu, I.: Weighted threshold secret sharing based on the Chinese remainder theorem. Sci. Ann. Cuza Univ. **15**, 161–172 (2005)
32. Kiayias, A., Russell, A., David, B., Oliynykov, R.: Ouroboros: a provably secure proof-of-stake blockchain protocol. In: Katz, J., Shacham, H. (eds.) CRYPTO 2017. LNCS, vol. 10401, pp. 357–388. Springer, Cham (2017). https://doi.org/10.1007/978-3-319-63688-7_12
33. Lindell, Y., Nof, A.: Fast secure multiparty ECDSA with practical distributed key generation and applications to cryptocurrency custody. In: Lie, D., Mannan, M., Backes, M., Wang, X. (eds.), ACM CCS 2018, pp. 1837–1854. ACM Press, October 2018
34. Liu, T., Vaikuntanathan, V.: Breaking the circuit-size barrier in secret sharing. In: Diakonikolas, I., Kempe, D., Henzinger, M. (eds.), 50th ACM STOC, pp. 699–708. ACM Press, June 2018
35. Mignotte, M.: How to share a secret. In: Beth, T. (ed.) EUROCRYPT 1982. LNCS, vol. 149, pp. 371–375. Springer, Heidelberg (1983). https://doi.org/10.1007/3-540-39466-4_27
36. Morillo, P., Padró, C., Sáez, G., Villar, J.L.: Weighted threshold secret sharing schemes. Inf. Process. Lett. **70**(5), 211–216 (1999)
37. National institute of standards and technology. Multi-party threshold cryptography (2018)
38. Shamir, A.: How to share a secret. Commun. Assoc. Comput. Mach. **22**(11), 612–613 (1979)
39. Shoup, V.: Lower bounds for discrete logarithms and related problems. In: Fumy, W. (ed.) EUROCRYPT 1997. LNCS, vol. 1233, pp. 256–266. Springer, Heidelberg (1997). https://doi.org/10.1007/3-540-69053-0_18
40. Stathakopoulous, C., Cachin, C.: Threshold signatures for blockchain systems. Swiss Federal Institute of Technology, vol. 30 (2017)
41. Stinson, D.R., Wei, R.: An application of ramp schemes to broadcast encryption. Inf. Process. Lett. **69**(3), 131–135 (1999)

42. Vinod, V., Narayanan, A., Srinathan, K., Rangan, C.P., Kim, K.: On the power of computational secret sharing. In: Johansson, T., Maitra, S. (eds.) INDOCRYPT 2003. LNCS, vol. 2904, pp. 162–176. Springer, Heidelberg (2003). https://doi.org/10.1007/978-3-540-24582-7_12
43. Yao, A.C.C.: How to generate and exchange secrets (extended abstract). In: 27th FOCS, pp. 162–167. IEEE Computer Society Press, October 1986
44. Zou, X., Maino, F., Bertino, E., Sui, Y., Wang, K., Li, F.: A new approach to weighted multi-secret sharing. In: Wang, H., Li, J., Rouskas, G.N., Zhou, X. (eds.), Proceedings of 20th International Conference on Computer Communications and Networks, ICCCN 2011, Maui, Hawaii, USA, July 31–August 4, 2011, pp. 1–6. IEEE (2011)

Best of Both Worlds
Revisiting the Spymasters Double Agent Problem

Anasuya Acharya[1(✉)], Carmit Hazay[1], Oxana Poburinnaya[1,2], and Muthuramakrishnan Venkitasubramaniam[2]

[1] Bar-Ilan University, Ramat Gan, Israel
{acharya,carmit.hazay}@biu.ac.il, oxanapob@bu.edu
[2] Georgetown University, Washington D.C., District of Columbia, USA
mv783@georgetown.edu

Abstract. This work introduces the notion of secure multiparty computation: MPC with fall-back security. Fall-back security for an n-party protocol is defined with respect to an adversary structure $\mathcal{Z}$ wherein security is guaranteed in the presence of both a computationally unbounded adversary with adversary structure $\mathcal{Z}$, and a computationally bounded adversary corrupting an arbitrarily large subset of the parties. This notion was considered in the work of Chaum (Crypto 89) via the Spymaster's double agent problem where he showed a semi-honest secure protocol for the honest majority adversary structure.

Our first main result is a compiler that can transform any n-party protocol that is semi-honestly secure with statistical security tolerating an adversary structure $\mathcal{Z}$ to one that (additionally) provides semi-honest fall-back security w.r.t $\mathcal{Z}$. The resulting protocol has optimal round complexity, up to a constant factor, and is optimal in assumptions and the adversary structure. Our second result fully characterizes when malicious fall-back security is feasible. More precisely, we show that malicious fall-back secure protocol w.r.t $\mathcal{Z}$ exists if and only if $\mathcal{Z}$ admits unconditional MPC against a semi-honest adversary (namely, iff $\mathcal{Z} \in \mathcal{Q}^2$).

Keywords: MPC with Fall-back Security · Best of Both Worlds · MPC Protocols Compiler

1 Introduction

The problem of secure multiparty computation (MPC) considers a set of parties with private inputs that wish to jointly compute some function of their inputs while preserving certain security properties, like privacy (nothing but the output is learned), and correctness (output is computed correctly according to the specified function). These properties are required to hold in the presence of an adversary that controls a subset of the parties and launches an attack on the protocol in an attempt to breach its security (e.g., to learn more than it should about the honest parties' inputs).

H. Handschuh and A. Lysyanskaya (Eds.): CRYPTO 2023, LNCS 14081, pp. 328–359, 2023.
https://doi.org/10.1007/978-3-031-38557-5_11

A standard classification distinguishes adversaries that are *computationally unbounded* from those that are *computationally bounded* (i.e. probabilistic polynomial time algorithms). MPC protocols secure against the former can be designed only when the adversary corrupts fewer than half of the parties but *unconditionally*, whereas, MPC protocols secure against the latter can be designed for arbitrary corruptions (i.e. up to all-but-one of the parties) but require making *cryptographic assumptions* (such as the hardness of factoring or discrete logarithm). In this work, we revisit the question of achieving the "best of both worlds", as considered in the work of Chaum [5] motivated by the following scenarios:

1. **Bringing people of different beliefs.** Is it possible to design an MPC protocol where some of the parties want unconditional security while some parties demand security against arbitrary collusion?
2. **Resistance to future attacks.** Can we design an MPC protocol with security against arbitrary collusion that offers some security even when the underlying cryptographic assumption is broken? For example, can we build an MPC based on *quantum un-safe* primitives that can offer some protection should quantum computers become feasible?
3. **David versus many Goliaths.** Can we design an n party MPC protocol where a single (designated) party can be unconditionally protected against an (unbounded) adversary colluding with the rest of the world (i.e. remaining $n-1$ parties)?

We answer all these questions in the affirmative by studying MPC protocols that offer *best of both worlds* security, namely, unconditional security against minority collusion and computational security against arbitrary collusion.

Chaum in [5] motivated this notion of security via the "Spymasters double agent problem" where a set of countries are willing to perform an MPC to identify "double agents". The main concern for spymasters is that a majority of the countries could collude or a minority of them could break the cryptosystem to uncover secrets. In the same work, Chaum designed an "optimal" n-party MPC protocol in the passive (semi-honest) setting, namely, security holds unconditionally against fewer than $n/2$ corruptions whereas computational security holds against arbitrary corruptions in the presence of a passive adversary. In the active setting, Chaum constructed a protocol with unconditional security against fewer than $n/3$ corruptions and computational security against fewer than $n/2$ corruptions. However, this protocol was subsumed by later results that provided a stronger security guarantee, namely, unconditional security against fewer than $n/2$ corruptions. Thus, the main challenge of designing an MPC protocol with best-of-both-worlds security against an active adversary still remains open. More precisely, we investigate in this work the following question:

Under what circumstances can we achieve best of both worlds security against an active adversary?

1.1 Our Contributions

In this work, we completely characterize when best of both worlds security is feasible. Roughly speaking, any adversary structure that admits an information-theoretically secure MPC against a passive adversary can be compiled into one that simultaneously provides information-theoretically security against an active adversary w.r.t the same adversary structure and additionally provides computational security against arbitrary corruptions. In fact, for this reason, we call our best-of-both-worlds security notion as *fall-back security.*

MPC WITH FALL-BACK SECURITY. We introduce a new notion of secure multiparty computation: MPC with fall-back security. Fall-back security for an n-party protocol is defined with respect to an adversary structure $\mathcal{Z}_\mathsf{S}$ wherein security is guaranteed in the presence of both a computationally unbounded adversary with adversary structure $\mathcal{Z}_\mathsf{S}$, and a computationally bounded adversary corrupting an arbitrary subset of the parties. We consider this definition in the context of semi-honest and malicious adversaries.

FALL-BACK SECURITY W.R.T SEMI-HONEST ADVERSARIES. We show that for any adversary structure $\mathcal{Z}_\mathsf{S}$ that admits an MPC protocol with unconditional security in the presence of a passive adversary, we can compile it to another MPC protocol that additionally provides computational security w.r.t arbitrary corruption of parties (again with a passive adversary). We build our compiler in two steps:

- First, we design an MPC protocol for a specific adversary structure. In fact, this will correspond to the"David vs many Goliaths" setting. More precisely, consider the adversary structure $\mathcal{Z}$ over n parties such that one designated party can never be corrupted. We describe an n-party protocol that can compute any functionality with semi-honest fall-back security tolerating $\mathcal{Z}$.
- Let Π_stat be an n-party protocol that is secure in the presence of a semi-honest unbounded adversary with adversary structure $\mathcal{Z}_\mathsf{S}$. We use the protocol designed in the first step as a building block to compile Π_stat into a protocol with semi-honest fall-back security tolerating $\mathcal{Z}_\mathsf{S}$.

More precisely, we achieve the following theorem:

Theorem (Informal) 1. *Assuming the existence of an r_{OT}-round oblivious transfer (OT) protocol with one-sided statistical security (i.e. statistical sender security or statistical receiver security) against a passive adversary. Then, any n-party function that can be securely implemented via an r-round n-party protocol Π_stat, that is secure in the presence of an unbounded semi-honest adversary w.r.t adversary structure $\mathcal{Z}_\mathsf{S}$, can be compiled to an $O(r \cdot r_{OT})$-round n-party protocol for the same functionality with semi-honest fall-back security tolerating $\mathcal{Z}_\mathsf{S}$.*

We remark that the existence of OT with one-sided statistical security is necessary and therefore minimal assumption. This result re-establishes the result of Chaum [5] for threshold adversary structures. The main difference is that our construction is round optimal up to a constant factor, relies on the underlying assumption in a black-box manner, and generalizes to arbitrary adversary structures. Moreover, we achieve optimality in terms of adversary structures since we can compile any information-theoretic MPC for $\mathcal{Z}_\mathsf{S}$ to one with fall-back security. Recalling from [11] that an MPC protocol is feasible in the semi-honest setting iff the adversary structure $\mathcal{Z}_\mathsf{S} \in \mathcal{Q}^2$ where $\mathcal{Z}_\mathsf{S} \in \mathcal{Q}^2$ if for any two $Z_1, Z_2 \in \mathcal{Z}_\mathsf{S}$, it holds that $Z_1 \cup Z_2 \neq \{1, \ldots, n\}$. Thus, we have the corollary:

Corollary 2. *We can securely compute any functionality with semi-honest fall-back security w.r.t* $\mathcal{Z}_\mathsf{S}$ *if and only if* $\mathcal{Z}_\mathsf{S} \in \mathcal{Q}^2$.

FALL-BACK SECURITY W.R.T MALICIOUS ADVERSARIES. Next, we construct a protocol that can compute any functionality with maliciously secure fall-back security tolerating any possible adversary structure for statistical security. We use the SPDZ-type paradigm [7], where we first generate authenticated Beaver triples and then use that to securely compute a function. Since the SPDZ online phase is essentially information-theoretically secure against arbitrary corruption by an unbounded adversary, it will suffice to design an MPC protocol with fall-back security with respect to malicious parties, for the authenticated Beaver triples functionality. We use a variant of the [10] compiler (which, in turn, is a variant of [13]) that "generically" compiles semi-honest protocols to malicious ones in a "modular" way. Formally, we prove the following theorem:

Theorem (Informal) 3. *Assume the existence of an OT protocol with one-sided statistical security against semi-honest adversaries. Then if the authenticated Beaver triples functionality can be securely implemented via a n-party protocol* Π_stat *secure in the presence of an unbounded semi-honest adversary w.r.t adversary structure* $\mathcal{Z}_\mathsf{S}$, *then any function can be compiled to an n-party protocol that computes the same functionality with malicious fall-back security tolerating* $\mathcal{Z}_\mathsf{S}$.

We remark that our result is optimal in terms of adversary structure and assumptions. Since any MPC protocol that is malicious fall-back secure w.r.t $\mathcal{Z}_\mathsf{S}$ is also information-theoretically secure w.r.t $\mathcal{Z}_\mathsf{S}$ against a passive adversary and as alluded before, implies OT with one-sided statistical security. Therefore, both assumptions are necessary. Thus, we have the following corollary.

Corollary 4. *We can securely compute any functionality with malicious fall-back security w.r.t* $\mathcal{Z}_\mathsf{S}$ *if and only if* $\mathcal{Z}_\mathsf{S} \in \mathcal{Q}^2$.

We remark here that [11] showed that malicious security in the information-theoretic setting is achievable iff $\mathcal{Z}_\mathsf{S} \in \mathcal{Q}^3$. Our result does not violate this since we only achieve security w.r.t abort in both the information-theoretic and computational settings.

1.2 Related Work

Several variants of best-of-both-worlds notions have been considered in the literature. The works of [12,14] consider achieving *full security* and is closest to our security notion. In these works, the authors consider an MPC protocol that provides guaranteed output delivery when there is an honest majority and security with abort against arbitrary corruption. They identify the necessary conditions for feasibility and design a protocol that offers only computational security in both corruption scenarios. Our work, in contrast, does not offer guaranteed output delivery but achieves unconditional security when a minority of the parties are corrupted.

In [16], Khurana and Mughees studied the round complexity of designing a 2PC protocol that offers unconditional security against one party and computational against the other (which is optimal as we cannot achieve statistical security against both parties). They showed that 4 rounds are sufficient to design such a protocol where the output is delivered to one designated party and 5 rounds if both parties receive output. This is optimal as previous works have shown matching lower bounds that hold even for the standard computational security against both parties [9,15]. This work has been improved more recently by [1] showing a wide variety of assumptions to design such a protocol. Our work can be viewed as a generalization of their work from two-party to multiparty where even feasibility was previously unknown.

The work of Chaum et al. [6] shows how to construct a protocol in the dishonest majority setting where one designated party's view is unconditionally hidden from the rest of the parties. Their protocol solves our third motivating question of David versus many Goliaths, however, their protocol is based on a specific assumption and proceeds in a round-robin fashion. Our protocol is optimal in round complexity up to a constant factor, and can be based on the minimal assumption of existence of oblivious transfer with one-sided statistical security.

1.3 Technical Overview

We define our notion of MPC with fall-back security. We also construct protocols that satisfy this in the presence of semi-honest and malicious adversaries.

FALL-BACK SECURITY. For an n-party functionality $\mathcal{F}$, we define the notion of Fall-Back security with respect to an adversary structure $\mathcal{Z}_{\mathsf{S}}$. Let $\mathcal{P}$ be the set of n parties executing a protocol to realize this functionality. We say that the protocol achieves fall-back security if it is secure in the presence of a computationally unbounded adversary corrupting any subset of parties $Z \in \mathcal{Z}_{\mathsf{S}}$. The protocol is additionally secure in the presence of a PPT adversary corrupting any $Z \subset \mathcal{P}$. We state formally two flavours of fall-back security, one in the presence of semi-honest adversaries and one in the presence of malicious adversaries in Sect. 3.

Protocols with Fall-Back Security: the 2PC Case. Before describing our n-party protocol that achieves fall-back security, let us examine the toy case of the 2-party setting. Recall that the standard 2-party Yao's Garbled circuit protocol where one party, referred to as the garbler, creates a garbled circuit computing the function and gives this to the other party, referred to as the evaluator, along with the input labels corresponding to its inputs. Then both parties engage in multiple instances of oblivious transfer (OT) through which the evaluator securely learns input labels corresponding to its inputs. The evaluator evaluates the garbled circuit and shares the output with the garbler.

In this protocol, suppose we instantiate the OT protocol with one that is secure in the presence of a semi-honest unbounded corrupt sender, then the view of the garbler contains the garbled circuit and input labels corresponding to its inputs (which are both independent of the evaluator's inputs) and the messages in the OT protocol that statistically secure against the sender. Therefore, we can argue that this protocol is secure against a semi-honest unbounded adversary corrupting the garbler and computational security against the evaluator, thus fall-back secure. We extend this to the multiparty setting for the "David and multiple Goliaths" case.

Warmup: Solving the David and Multiple Goliaths Problem. Let $\mathcal{P} = \{P_i\}_{i\in[n]}$ be a set of n-parties and let $\mathcal{Z}$ be an adversary structure containing all subsets of $\mathcal{P}$ that do not include P_n. We describe an n-party protocol that can compute any function with semi-honest fall-back security tolerating $\mathcal{Z}$. We remark that the work of [6] solves this using a specific assumption and proceeds in a round-robin manner. Here, we describe a protocol that proceeds in $O(r)$-rounds, assuming an r-round OT protocol with one-sided statistical security, that is optimal in rounds and assumptions.

The protocol designates the first $n-1$ parties as garblers and P_n as the evaluator. First, the parties in $\{P_i\}_{i\in[n-1]}$ jointly compute a garbled circuit for the computed function using a distributed garbling protocol such as [3] and hand it to P_n. This computation also produces certain 'masking bits' such that each party can XOR its inputs and masking bits to create a 'masked input' that reveals no information about the input itself. Each garbler then gives its masked input to P_n, which engages in multiple instances of oblivious transfer as the receiver, with each garbler being the sender. After these executions, P_n has received the input labels corresponding to all the masked inputs from each garbler. Finally, it uses these input labels to evaluate the garbling and sends the output to all the other parties.

The protocol is secure in the presence of a semi-honest unbounded adversary corrupting any subset of the garbling parties. This follows from the fact that a simulator for such an adversary would just need to honestly participate in the garbling, the oblivious transfer is secure in the presence of an unbounded sender and, since the adversary does not corrupt P_n, it never gets to see the masked inputs or input labels used for evaluation. The protocol is also secure in the presence of a semi-honest PPT adversary corrupting an arbitrary subset of $\mathcal{P}$.

Hence any n-party function can be computed with semi-honest fall-back security tolerating $\mathcal{Z}$. Details for this protocol can be found in Sect. 3.1.

COMPILING TO SEMI-HONEST FALL-BACK SECURITY. The protocol above can be used as a building-block to construct a compiler that can convert any n-party protocol Π_{stat} that satisfies semi-honest security in the presence of an unbounded adversary tolerating an adversary structure $\mathcal{Z}_{\mathsf{S}}$, to a protocol Π_{in} that satisfies semi-honest fall-back security tolerating the same adversary structure $\mathcal{Z}_{\mathsf{S}}$.

The idea is to first parse Π_{stat} as a sequence of next-message functions, one for each party i in round j. For each such function, we define a functionality that receives as input from n parties corresponding to the *shares* of the view of party i, reconstructs this view, computes the next-message function, and shares the output among n parties using n-out-of-n secret-sharing.

Our compiler works by first having each party $P_i \in \mathcal{P}$ secret-share its inputs to Π_{stat}, to all other parties using n-out-of-n secret-sharing. Then for each next-message function for the ith party in Π_{stat}, we use the protocol Π_{DG} from the "David and multiple Goliaths" setting outlined above to compute the corresponding functionality with party P_i as David, i.e. the designated evaluator. Once this has been executed for all next-message functions, all parties have a share of the output of every party in protocol Π_{stat}. Then, all parties (except P_i) give the shares of the ith party in Π_{stat} to P_i. Each P_i reconstructs and obtains the output of the protocol.

We argue the security of the protocol in the presence of computational and unbounded adversaries. The computational setting follows directly as the next-message functions of Π_{stat} can be viewed as a functionality that computes the same functionality as the target functionality on secret shares and we rely on our warm-up protocol that offers security in the dishonest majority setting to implement each step in Π_{in}. Thus, essentially by composition, we obtain that every internal computation and message in the emulation of Π_{stat} remains hidden to any subset of the parties.

To argue security against a semi-honest unbounded adversary tolerating $\mathcal{Z}_{\mathsf{S}}$, we analyze the case when the adversary corrupts a subset $Z \in \mathcal{Z}_{\mathsf{S}}$. For every $i \notin Z$, it holds that the next-message computations of the virtual party S_i in Π_{in} has P_i as the Evaluator when executed via our warmup protocol. We have that the evaluator P_i is not corrupted by the adversary, and the security of the warmup protocol guarantees that the view of the virtual party S_i will be statistically hidden from Z (as Z does not include P_i). However, when $i \in Z$, an unbounded adversary controls P_i, and the warmup protocol is secure only if an unbounded adversary corrupts everyone but P_i. Since we are in the passive setting, we can conclude that each of these instances of the warmup protocol will proceed correctly. Still, an unbounded adversary can obtain the entire view of the virtual party S_i. This amounts to corrupting all parties indexed $i \in Z$ in the virtual protocol. We conclude from the statistical security of the virtual protocol Π_{in} against Z that the compiled protocol will also offer statistical security with respect to Z.

MALICIOUSLY SECURE FALL-BACK SECURITY. Next, we describe our protocol that achieves malicious fall-back security with respect to an adversary structure $\mathcal{Z}_\mathsf{S}$. The classical GMW paradigm is to rely on coin-tossing and distributed zero-knowledge proofs to compile a semi-honest secure protocol to a malicious one. Such an approach will require designing distributed commit-and-prove protocols with fall-back security with respect to $\mathcal{Z}_\mathsf{S}$ and typically results in a non-black-box construction in the underlying primitives. Instead, we will pursue another approach pioneered by Ishai, Prabhakaran, and Sahai [13] that is based on player virtualization and allows compiling a "semi-honest" protocol to malicious in a modular way. This will have the benefit of not relying on distributed zero-knowledge proofs. We will use a slight variant of the compiler designed by Hazay et al. [10], which is based on the IPS compiler.

In slightly more detail, we will rely on the offline-online paradigm refined in the SPDZ line of works [7], where the parties first generate so-called *authenticated Beaver triples* in an offline input-independent phase and then consume them in an online phase. The main feature of this protocol relevant to our setting is that once the offline protocol is executed, the online protocol is unconditionally secure, assuming commitment schemes. Therefore, designing a malicious protocol with fall-back security reduces to designing a malicious fall-back secure protocol for the authenticated Beaver triples functionality and distributed commitment scheme with fall-back security. For our protocol to realize the authenticated triples functionality, we will need the following ingredients:

1. Fall-back secure extractable commitment scheme: We need a scheme where a single committer commits a value v to the $n-1$ parties that is unconditionally secure against $\mathcal{Z}_\mathsf{S}$, and computationally secure against arbitrary collusion. We will additionally need the commitment to be extractable.
2. Fall-back secure coin-tossing and coin-tossing-in-the-well protocols. We can use standard applications of $\mathcal{F}_\mathsf{Com}$ to obtain these protocols.
3. Semi-honest fall-back secure protocol for a simple functionality (closely related to the authenticated Beaver triples functionality).

REALIZING $\mathcal{F}_\mathsf{Com}$. In the fall-back setting, the committer and (any one of) the receivers could be corrupted by an unbounded adversary (depending on $\mathcal{Z}_\mathsf{S}$). Recall that it is impossible to design a commitment scheme that is simultaneously unconditionally hiding and binding. Instead, we will rely on both a statistically hiding commitment Com_SH and a statistically binding commitment Com_SB. Additionally, we will need a secret-sharing scheme with respect to adversary structure $\mathcal{Z}_\mathsf{S}$. First, we design a fall-back secure extractable commitment scheme and then compile it to a protocol that realizes $\mathcal{F}_\mathsf{Com}$.

The committer takes its value v, secret shares it to $v_1, \ldots, v_n$, and commits to v_i, with P_i being the receiver, using a statistically binding scheme, and commits to v using a statistically hiding commitment scheme. This scheme is hiding against a dishonest majority as both commitments are hiding against a computational adversary. This is statistically hiding against an unbounded adversary since it can only break the statistically-binding commitment scheme and learn secret shares of v that statistically hid it against corruption in $\mathcal{Z}_{\mathsf{S}}$. This commitment is binding in the dishonest majority setting because the committer uses a statistically hiding commitment scheme to commit v to every party. When an unbounded adversary corrupts in $\mathcal{Z}_{\mathsf{S}}$ (that includes the committer), the values of the secret shares committed to the honest parties and the statistically binding commitment statistically bind the value v. To make the scheme extractable, the committer uses computational zero-knowledge proof-of-knowledge (cZKPOK) to prove the knowledge of the values committed within $\mathsf{Com}_{\mathsf{SB}}$ and a statistical zero-knowledge argument-of-knowledge (sZKAOK) to prove the knowledge of the values committed via $\mathsf{Com}_{\mathsf{SH}}$. The simulator invokes the extractor of the sZKAOK in order to extract the inputs in the dishonest majority case and that of the cZKPOK to extract the input shares in the statistical case.

Next, to realize $\mathcal{F}_{\mathsf{Com}}$, we will rely on the lookahead trapdoor commitment scheme of [17]. Roughly speaking, in this commitment scheme, the committer, instead of committing to a bit σ, commits to κ 2×2-matrices

$$\begin{pmatrix} \eta_i & \eta_i \oplus \sigma \\ \eta_i & \eta_i \oplus \sigma \end{pmatrix}$$

where κ is the statistical security parameter and η_i's are chosen uniformly at random. Then the receiver provides a random κ-bit challenge to determine which columns in each of the κ matrices should be decommitted by the committer. The receiver accepts the commitment if the decommitment values in each column are equal. In the decommit phase, the committer picks a random row in each matrix and decommits the remaining value. This commitment can be made "equivocal" by having the receiver commit to its challenge before the committer's first commitment. This allows a simulator to "look ahead" the challenge and rewind to provide an equivocal commitment. Namely, each matrix will have identical values in the opened column and different bits in the unopened column so that in the decommitment phase, the simulator can choose the right opening depending on what value it needs to decommit to.

In our setting, we can essentially rely on this protocol, where in the first round, we have $n-1$ parties commit to a random string which it will decommit to in the third round, and the challenge will be the XOR of all strings. Next, the committer will use the weak-extractable commitment described above to commit to each entry of the matrices. The weak extractability suffices to extract the value, and the lookahead trapdoor property will help to equivocate.

Fall-back Secure Coin-Tossing and Coin-Tossing in the Well. Once we have a commitment scheme, we can rely on the standard mechanisms to design coin-tossing and coin-tossing-in-the-well schemes.

Putting it Together. In the IPS-type compiler, the parties emulate a virtual "outer" malicious information theoretic MPC protocol among m parties (also denoted by servers) by maintaining each party's view in a secret-shared state and securely computing the next message functions via semi-honest "inner" protocol.

In this work, we will rely on a vanilla outer protocol (such as BGW [4]), whereas the inner protocol is instantiated using our semi-honest fall-back secure protocol. Since we are only implementing the authenticated Beaver triples functionality with a small depth, we can consider an outer protocol where the parties do not communicate with each other (i.e., all computations are local). This is not necessary for our compiler but simplifies our description and analysis.

On a high-level, our protocol proceeds in the following phases:

- Phase 1: The parties commit to a coin-tossing (by simply having each party commit to a random string) that will be opened in Phase 5.
- Phase 2: The parties secretly share their inputs for the m virtual parties and then commit to the shares using our fall-back extractable commitment scheme.
- Phase 3: The parties execute a coin-tossing-in-the-well protocol to generate randomness for the m virtual parties.
- Phase 4: All parties engage in m execuctions of the semi-honest fall-back secure protocol to emulate the m virtual parties.
- Phase 5: The parties open the coin-tossing and sample t of the m virtual parties where all parties open the randomness and inputs used for emulating those t parties.

The security proof follows a similar approach to [10,13]. We remark that (similar to [13]), we will need the inner protocol to meet some adaptive security guarantees. We describe our protocol assuming this property but later argue that we can use an inner protocol without additional assumptions.

In more detail, in Phase 1, the simulator executes the coin-tossing honestly but extracts the outcome of the coin-toss and identifies the virtual servers whose views will be opened (referred to as watched executions) in the cut-and-choose phase (Phase 5 above). In Phase 2, the simulator extracts the adversary's inputs, sends the adversary's triples shares to the ideal functionality, and receives the offset as the output. Before discussing Phase 3, we mention that the idea for simulating Phase 4 is to have the simulator simulate the messages for the honest parties in the watched virtual parties honestly and rely on a simulation of the semi-honest fall-back secure protocol for the unwatched sessions. Since the outputs of the watched sessions are fixed, the simulator first generates the outputs for all of the remaining virtual parties in the outer protocol so that it is consistent with the output received from the ideal functionality and the output of the watched sessions. Next, it runs the semi-honest fall-back secure protocol simulator for the unwatched sessions to determine the randomness of the parties corrupted by the adversary in the unwatched sessions. Now, it proceeds with simulation, where in Phase 3, it will manipulate the coin-tossing-in-the-well protocol to fix the adversary's random tape in the unwatched sessions corresponding to the simulated views. Next, it will simulate Phase 5, hoping the adversary will not deviate in the unwatched sessions. If the adversary does indeed deviate in the emulation of one of the virtual parties, the simulator will invoke the adaptive simulation for that instance.

We will consider an outer protocol that is t private with $t/2$ sessions to watch. This will allow the simulator to generate inputs of the virtual parties (by simply sampling them uniformly at random) for up to $t/2$ more sessions where the adversary deviates. If it deviates in more than $t/2$ unwatched sessions, the simulator fails (where this will happen only with negligible probability due to the cut-and-choose check).

As with the analysis in [13], proving security additionally requires the "inner" protocol, i.e. the semi-honest fall-back secure protocol to be adaptively secure where an adversary can eventually corrupt all parties. However, our semi-honest fall-back security does not satisfy this guarantee. Nevertheless, the full version contains an explanation as to how the adaptive security requirement can be weakened, and a slight variant of the semi-honest protocol (without requiring any additional assumptions) will meet that requirement.

2 Preliminaries

We denote by κ a computational security parameter and s a statistical security parameter that captures a statistical error of up to 2^{-s}. We assume $s \leq \kappa$. We denote by $\mathsf{SS}_{t,m} = (\mathsf{Share}_{t,m}, \mathsf{Recon}_{t,m})$ a t-out-of-m threshold secret-sharing scheme [18] where up to t shares *do not* reveal information about the secret. We refer the reader to the full version for additional preliminaries.

Secure Multiparty Computation. Let $\mathcal{P} = \{P_i\}_{i\in[n]}$ be a set of n parties. MPC involves the computation of a random process that maps a tuple of inputs to a tuple of outputs (one for each party). This random process is referred to as a functionality $f : \{0,1\}^* \times \cdots \times \{0,1\}^* \to \{0,1\}^* \times \cdots \times \{0,1\}^*$ where $f = (f_1, \ldots, f_n)$. Each party P_i has input x_i. For simplicity and without loss of generality, we work over functionalities for which $x_i \in \{0,1\}$. For every tuple of inputs $\vec{x} = (x_i, \ldots, x_n)$, the vector output by f is a random variable $(f_1(\vec{x}), \ldots, f_n(\vec{x}))$ ranging over tuples of strings where P_i receives $f_i(\vec{x})$. The following notation describes a functionality:

$$(x_1, \ldots, x_n) \mapsto (f_1(\vec{x}), \ldots, f_n(\vec{x}))$$

We prove the security of our MPC protocols in the presence of semi-honest and malicious adversaries in the dishonest majority setting.

In the semi-honest setting, an adversary can control a subset of the participating parties and always follows the protocol specification but may try to learn additional information from the transcript of messages received and its internal state. Let $f = (f_1, \ldots, f_n)$ be a multiparty functionality and Π be an n-party protocol computing f in t rounds. The view of party P_i in an execution of Π on inputs $\vec{x} = (x_1, \ldots, x_n)$ is,

$$\mathbf{View}_{\Pi,i}(\kappa, \vec{x}) = (\kappa, x_i, r_i, \{m^j_{k\to i}\}_{j\in[t],k\neq i\in[n]})$$

where κ is the security parameter, r_i is the content of P_i's internal random tape, and each $m^j_{k\to i}$ represents the message received from party P_k in round

j. The output of P_i in an execution of Π on $\vec{x}$ is denoted $\mathsf{output}_{\Pi,i}(\vec{x})$ and can be computed from $\mathbf{View}_{\Pi,i}(\kappa, \vec{x})$. The set of corrupted parties is denoted by $Z \subset \mathcal{P}$ and the set of honest parties by $\overline{Z}$. We extend the view notation to capture any subset of parties, denoting by $\mathbf{View}_{\Pi,T}(\kappa, \vec{x})$ the joint view of all parties in $T \subseteq \mathcal{P}$ on $(\kappa, \vec{x})$.

Definition 5. *Let f and Π be as above, and let $\mathcal{Z}_{\mathsf{C}} \subseteq 2^{\mathcal{P}}$ be an adversary structure. The protocol Π is said to securely compute f in the presence of a* ***PPT semi-honest adversary*** *tolerating adversary structure $\mathcal{Z}_{\mathsf{C}}$ if there exists a PPT simulator* Sim *such that for every $Z \in \mathcal{Z}_{\mathsf{C}}$,*

$$\left\{\mathsf{Sim}(1^\kappa, Z, \{x_i, f_i(\vec{x})\}_{i \in Z}), \{f_i(\vec{x})\}_{i \notin Z}\right\}_{\kappa \in \mathbb{N}, \vec{x} \in \{0,1\}^*}$$
$$\stackrel{\mathrm{c}}{\equiv} \left\{\mathbf{View}_{\Pi,Z}(\kappa, \vec{x}), \mathsf{output}_{\Pi,\overline{Z}}(\kappa, \vec{x})\right\}_{\kappa \in \mathbb{N}, \vec{x} \in \{0,1\}^*}$$

where κ is the computational security parameter. The distribution is considered over the randomness of the simulator and random tapes of parties in the protocol.

Definition 6. *Let f and Π be as above, and let $\mathcal{Z}_{\mathsf{S}} \subseteq 2^{\mathcal{P}}$ be an adversary structure. The protocol Π is said to securely compute f in the presence of an* ***unbounded semi-honest adversary*** *tolerating adversary structure $\mathcal{Z}_{\mathsf{S}}$ if there exists a PPT simulator* Sim *such that for every $Z \in \mathcal{Z}_{\mathsf{S}}$,*

$$\left\{\mathsf{Sim}(1^s, Z, \{x_i, f_i(\vec{x})\}_{i \in Z}), \{f_i(\vec{x})\}_{i \notin Z}\right\}_{s \in \mathbb{N}, \vec{x} \in \{0,1\}^*}$$
$$\stackrel{\mathrm{s}}{\equiv} \left\{\mathbf{View}_{\Pi,Z}(s, \vec{x}), \mathsf{output}_{\Pi,\overline{Z}}(s, \vec{x})\right\}_{s \in \mathbb{N}, \vec{x} \in \{0,1\}^*}$$

where s is the statistical security parameter. The distribution is considered over the simulator's randomness and the parties' random tapes in the protocol.

In the malicious setting, an adversary controlling a subset of the participating parties can have them deviate arbitrarily from the protocol specification. Security in this setting is defined by a comparison between an execution of the functionality in an ideal model and an execution of the protocol in the real model.

Execution in the Ideal Model. An ideal execution is an interaction between all the parties in $\mathcal{P}$ and a trusted party $\mathcal{F}$, wherein the parties submit their input to the trusted party that computes the output and returns it. An honest party receives input for the computation and forwards it to the trusted party. In contrast, a corrupt party can replace its input with an arbitrary value of the same length. On receiving these, $\mathcal{F}$ computes the output and first sends the outputs of the corrupt parties to the adversary. The adversary then decides whether the honest parties will receive their outputs from $\mathcal{F}$ or an abort symbol $\perp$. For a multiparty functionality $f = (f_1, \ldots, f_n)$, let $\mathcal{A}$ be a non-uniform probabilistic machine and $Z \subset \mathcal{P}$ be the set of corrupted parties. Then the ideal execution of f on inputs $(\kappa, \vec{x})$, auxiliary input z to $\mathcal{A}$ and security parameter κ is defined as the output tuple of the honest parties and the adversary from this execution and is denoted as $\mathbf{IDEAL}_{f,\mathcal{A}(z),Z}(\kappa, \vec{x})$.

Execution in the Real Model. This is an interaction directly among the parties in $\mathcal{P}$ wherein the honest parties follow the instructions in the protocol Π. The adversary $\mathcal{A}$ sends all messages in place of the corrupted parties and may follow any arbitrary strategy. Letting Π be a protocol that computes f as above, $\mathcal{A}$ be a non-uniform probabilistic machine, and let $Z \subset \mathcal{P}$ be the set of corrupted parties, the real execution of Π on inputs $(\kappa, \vec{x})$, auxiliary input z to $\mathcal{A}$ and security parameter κ is defined as the output tuple of the honest parties and the adversary from this execution and is denoted as $\mathbf{REAL}_{\Pi,\mathcal{A}(z),Z}(\kappa, \vec{x})$.

Definition 7. *Let f and Π be as above, and let $\mathcal{Z}_\mathsf{C} \subseteq 2^\mathcal{P}$ be an adversary structure. The protocol Π is said to securely compute f with abort in the presence of* ***PPT malicious adversaries*** *tolerating adversary structure $\mathcal{Z}_\mathsf{C}$ if there exists a PPT adversary* Sim *in the ideal model such that for every PPT $\mathcal{A}$ in the real model and $Z \in \mathcal{Z}_\mathsf{C}$,*

$$\left\{\mathbf{IDEAL}_{f,\mathsf{Sim}(z),Z}(\kappa, \vec{x})\right\}_{\kappa\in\mathbb{N},\vec{x},z\in\{0,1\}^*} \stackrel{\mathsf{c}}{\equiv} \left\{\mathbf{REAL}_{\Pi,\mathcal{A}(z),Z}(\kappa, \vec{x})\right\}_{\kappa\in\mathbb{N},\vec{x},z\in\{0,1\}^*}$$

where κ is the computational security parameter. The distribution is considered over the adversaries' randomness and all the parties' random tapes.

Definition 8. *Let f and Π be as above, and let $\mathcal{Z}_\mathsf{S} \subseteq 2^\mathcal{P}$ be an adversary structure. The protocol Π is said to securely compute f with abort in the presence of* ***unbounded malicious adversaries*** *tolerating adversary structure $\mathcal{Z}_\mathsf{S}$ if there exists an adversary* Sim *in the ideal model such that for every computationally unbounded $\mathcal{A}$ in the real model and every $Z \in \mathcal{Z}_\mathsf{S}$,*

$$\left\{\mathbf{IDEAL}_{f,\mathsf{Sim}(z),Z}(s, \vec{x})\right\}_{s\in\mathbb{N},\vec{x},z\in\{0,1\}^*} \stackrel{\mathsf{s}}{\equiv} \left\{\mathbf{REAL}_{\Pi,\mathcal{A}(z),Z}(s, \vec{x})\right\}_{s\in\mathbb{N},\vec{x},z\in\{0,1\}^*}$$

where s is the computational security parameter. The distribution is considered over the adversaries' randomness and all the parties' random tapes.

Multi-Party Garbling. For a function $f : \{0,1\}^n \rightarrow \{0,1\}^m$, let $\mathbf{C}$ be its circuit representation. Let q be the number of gates in $\mathbf{C}$. Each gate $g \in [q]$ is defined by a gate functionality $f_g \in \{\mathsf{AND}, \mathsf{XOR}\}$, two input wires A, B and an output wire g where, $A, B, g \in [n+q]$ and topological ordering holds: $A, B < g$.

A multi-party garbling protocol is one in which a set of parties use their combined randomness to create a garbled representation of a function. In such a protocol, it should hold that even when all-but-one of the garblers collude, no information about the randomness contributed by the non-colluding party is

Distributed Garbling

Setting: Let f be a function with input $x = \{x_i\}_{i \in [n]}$ and circuit representation **C**. Let $\kappa = \ell$ be a security parameter and $\mathcal{P}_{\mathsf{N}} = \{P_i\}_{i \in [\mathsf{N}]}$ be the set of garblers where $\mathcal{P}_{\mathsf{N}} \subseteq \mathcal{P} = \{P_i\}_{i \in [n]}$. Let $\mathsf{PRF} : \{0,1\}^\kappa \times \{0,1\}^\kappa \times \{0,1\}^{\log q + \log \mathsf{N}} \rightarrow \{0,1\}^{\kappa+1}$ be a pseudo-random function. The functionality $\mathcal{F}_{\mathsf{GS}}$ operates as follows:

- **Inputs:** Each party $P_i \in \mathcal{P}_{\mathsf{N}}$ has the following inputs:
  - for each input wire $w \in [n]$, if $w = i$ or $w \notin [\mathsf{N}]$, then $\lambda_w^i \leftarrow \{0,1\}$; else $\lambda_w^i = 0$
  - for each gate output wire $w \in [q]$, sample $\lambda_w^i \leftarrow \{0,1\}$
  - for each wire $w \in [n+q]$, sample labels $k_{w,0}^i, k_{w,1}^i \leftarrow \{0,1\}^\ell$
  - for all $j \in [\mathsf{N}], (a,b) \in \{0,1\}^2$ and gate $g \in [q]$ with inputs A and B,

$$F_{a,b}^{i,j,g} = \mathsf{PRF}_{k_{A,a}^i, k_{B,b}^i}(g||j)$$

  $\mathcal{F}_{\mathsf{GS}}$ gets from P_i:

$$\{\lambda_w^i, k_{w,0}^i, k_{w,1}^i\}_{w \in [n+q]}, \{F_{a,b}^{i,j,g}\}_{g \in [q], j \in [\mathsf{N}], (a,b) \in \{0,1\}^2}$$

  Each party $P_i \in \mathcal{P} - \mathcal{P}_{\mathsf{N}}$ does not provide any input.
- **Computation:** The functionality $\mathcal{F}_{\mathsf{GS}}$ computes for all gate $g \in [q]$ with functionality f_g, $\forall (a,b) \in \{0,1\}^2, \forall j \in [\mathsf{N}]$:

$$G_{a,b}^j = \left(\bigoplus_{i=1}^{\mathsf{N}} F_{a,b}^{i,j,g} \right) \oplus ((\lambda_w \oplus f_g(a,b)) || k_{w,f_g(a,b)}^j)$$

- **Outputs:** $\mathcal{F}_{\mathsf{GS}}$ gives to all parties $P_i \in \mathcal{P}$:
  - The garbling

$$\{G_{a,b}^j\}_{j \in [\mathsf{N}], g \in [q], (a,b) \in \{0,1\}^2}$$

  - For each circuit output wire $w \in [n+q-m, n+q]$, $\lambda_w = \bigoplus_{i=1}^{\mathsf{N}} \lambda_w^i$

  Each party $P_i \in \mathcal{P} - \mathcal{P}_{\mathsf{N}}$ gets for input wire $w = i$, $\lambda_w = \bigoplus_{i=1}^{\mathsf{N}} \lambda_w^i$
  Each garbler $P_i \in \mathcal{P}_{\mathsf{N}}$ sets for input wire $w = i$, $\lambda_w = \lambda_w^i$

Fig. 1. Distributed Garbling

revealed beyond what can be deduced from the final garbling. There exist protocols in the literature [2,3] that compute this for an n-party garbling protocol in the presence of a semi-honest corruption of any $n-1$ parties. In our construction, we require a multi-party garbling functionality that operates as in Fig. 1. Our protocols use a multi-party garbling protocol that implements the functionality $\mathcal{F}_{\mathsf{GS}}$ (Fig. 1) as a sub-protocol where $\mathsf{N} = n - 1$ parties participate in the joint garbling process. We require one such protocol that is secure in the presence of PPT semi-honest adversaries.

3 MPC with Fall-Back Security

We define a new notion of multi-party computation: MPC with fall-back security. Informally, a multi-party protocol satisfies fall-back security if it is secure when certain subsets of parties are corrupted by a computationally unbounded adversary. However, if more parties than that are corrupted, computational security is still guaranteed.

Definition 9. (Semi-Honest Fall-Back Security). *For a set of parties $\mathcal{P} = \{P_i\}_{i\in[n]}$ where P_i has input x_i, let $\Pi = \langle\mathcal{P}\rangle$ be an n-party protocol computing a function f with input $\vec{x} = \{x_i\}_{i\in[n]}$. Let $\mathcal{Z}_{\mathsf{C}} = 2^{\mathcal{P}}$ and $\mathcal{Z}_{\mathsf{S}} \subseteq \mathcal{Z}_{\mathsf{C}}$ be adversary structures for PPT and unbounded semi-honest adversaries, respectively. The protocol Π satisfies* ***fall-back security in the semi-honest setting tolerating*** *$\mathcal{Z}_{\mathsf{S}}$ if there exists a PPT* Sim *such that for every $Z \in \mathcal{Z}_{\mathsf{C}}$,*

$$\left\{\mathsf{Sim}(1^\kappa, Z, \{x_i, f_i(\vec{x})\}_{i\in Z}), \{f_i(\vec{x})\}_{i\notin Z}\right\}_{\kappa\in\mathbb{N},\vec{x}\in\{0,1\}^*}$$
$$\stackrel{c}{\equiv}\left\{\mathbf{View}_{\Pi,Z}(\kappa,\vec{x}), \mathsf{output}_{\Pi,\overline{Z}}(\kappa,\vec{x})\right\}_{\kappa\in\mathbb{N},\vec{x}\in\{0,1\}^*}$$

where κ is the computational security parameter; and there exists a PPT simulator Sim *such that for every $Z \in \mathcal{Z}_{\mathsf{S}}$,*

$$\left\{\mathsf{Sim}(1^s, Z, \{x_i, f_i(\vec{x})\}_{i\in Z}), \{f_i(\vec{x})\}_{i\notin Z}\right\}_{s\in\mathbb{N},\vec{x}\in\{0,1\}^*}$$
$$\stackrel{s}{\equiv}\left\{\mathbf{View}_{\Pi,Z}(s,\vec{x}), \mathsf{output}_{\Pi,\overline{Z}}(s,\vec{x})\right\}_{s\in\mathbb{N},\vec{x}\in\{0,1\}^*}$$

where s is the statistical security parameter. The distribution is considered over the randomness of the simulator and all random tapes of parties in the protocol.

Malicious Fall-Back Security. Fall-back security can be similarly defined also in the malicious setting.

Definition 10. (Malicious Fall-Back Security). *For a set of parties $\mathcal{P} = \{P_i\}_{i\in[n]}$ where P_i has input x_i, let $\Pi = \langle\mathcal{P}\rangle$ be an n-party protocol computing a function f with input $\vec{x} = \{x_i\}_{i\in[n]}$. Let $\mathcal{Z}_{\mathsf{C}} = 2^{\mathcal{P}}$ and $\mathcal{Z}_{\mathsf{S}} \subseteq \mathcal{Z}_{\mathsf{C}}$ be adversary structures for PPT and computationally unbounded malicious adversaries, respectively. The protocol Π satisfies* ***fall-back security in the malicious setting tolerating*** *$\mathcal{Z}_{\mathsf{S}}$ if there exists a PPT adversary* Sim *in the ideal model such that for every PPT $\mathcal{A}$ in the real model and every $Z \in \mathcal{Z}_{\mathsf{C}}$,*

$$\left\{\mathbf{IDEAL}_{f,\mathsf{Sim}(z),Z}(\kappa,\vec{x})\right\}_{\kappa\in\mathbb{N},\vec{x},z\in\{0,1\}^*} \stackrel{c}{\equiv} \left\{\mathbf{REAL}_{\Pi,\mathcal{A}(z),Z}(\kappa,\vec{x})\right\}_{\kappa\in\mathbb{N},\vec{x},z\in\{0,1\}^*}$$

where κ *is the computational security parameter; and there exists an adversary* Sim *in the ideal model such that for every computationally unbounded* $\mathcal{A}$ *in the real model and every* $Z \in \mathcal{Z}_{\mathsf{S}}$*,*

$$\left\{\mathbf{IDEAL}_{f,\mathsf{Sim}(z),Z}(s,\vec{x})\right\}_{s\in\mathbb{N},\vec{x},z\in\{0,1\}^*} \stackrel{s}{\equiv} \left\{\mathbf{REAL}_{\Pi,\mathcal{A}(z),Z}(s,\vec{x})\right\}_{s\in\mathbb{N},\vec{x},z\in\{0,1\}^*}$$

where s *is the statistical security parameter. The distribution is considered over the randomness of the simulator and all random tapes of parties in the protocol.*

3.1 Example Protocol with Semi-Honest Fall-Back Security

The protocol in Fig. 2 is an n-party protocol Π in the $(\mathcal{F}_{OT}, \mathcal{F}_{\mathsf{GS}})$-hybrid that can compute any function f. In the protocol, out of the set of parties $\mathcal{P} = \{P_i\}_{i\in[n]}$, the parties $\{P_i\}_{i\in[n-1]}$ are designated the garblers and P_n is the evaluator. The garblers collectively create a garbled circuit F for the function f. This garbled circuit F and the output decoding information d are given to P_n. The evaluator P_n also receives from each garbling party P_i a 'masked value' Λ_i that hides its private input x_i. It then engages as a receiver in an OT protocol with each garbling party P_i as the sender and receives the active labels corresponding to all the masked values. P_n, with all the active labels, evaluates the garbled circuit to derive the output $f(\vec{x})$. It then sends $f(\vec{x})$ to all the other parties.

Figure 2 is a protocol with fall-back security against an unbounded adversary corrupting any subset of $\mathcal{P}_{\mathsf{N}}$ and a PPT adversary corrupting any subset of parties in $\mathcal{P}$. This also holds in the plain model when $\mathcal{F}_{\mathsf{OT}}$ is replaced with a semi-honest secure OT protocol that is secure against an unbounded sender and PPT receiver [8]; and when $\mathcal{F}_{\mathsf{GS}}$ is replaced by a multiparty garbling protocol [3] that involves only the parties in $\mathcal{P}_{\mathsf{N}}$ for garbling the circuit.

Lemma 11. *Let* $\mathcal{Z}_{\mathsf{S}}$ *be the set of all subsets of* $\{P_i\}_{i\in[n-1]}$.

- *Let* Π_{GS} *be an* n*-party protocol computing* $\mathcal{F}_{\mathsf{GS}}$ *that is secure against a semi-honest PPT adversary corrupting any subset of* $n-1$ *parties, with* $\mathcal{P}_{\mathsf{N}} = \{P_i\}_{i\in[n-1]}$ *as the set of garblers.*
- *Let* Π_{OT} *be a protocol computing* $\mathcal{F}_{OT}$ *that is secure against a semi-honest unbounded sender and a semi-honest PPT receiver.*

Then Fig. 2 securely computes any function f *with fall-back security (Definition 9) tolerating* $\mathcal{Z}_{\mathsf{S}}$ *for semi-honest adversaries in the plain model when the functionalities* $\mathcal{F}_{OT}$ *and* $\mathcal{F}_{\mathsf{GS}}$ *are replaced by* Π_{OT} *and* Π_{GS} *respectively.*

The complete proof for this can be found in the full version.

4 Compiling to Semi-Honest Fall-Back Security

In this section, we will describe an MPC protocol for general functionalities that satisfies semi-honest fall-back security for $\mathcal{Z}_{\mathsf{S}}$ containing any subset of less than

Semi-honest Fall-Back Secure Protocol

Setting: Let $\mathcal{P} = \{P_i\}_{i\in[n]}$ be such that P_i has input x_i. Let f be a function, $\vec{x} = \{x_i\}_{i\in[n]}$ be its input and the protocol outputs $f(\vec{x})$ to all parties in $\mathcal{P}$.

1. **Garbling Phase:** Letting the garblers be $\mathcal{P}_\mathsf{N} = \{P_i\}_{i\in[n-1]}$, $\mathcal{P}$ invokes the garbling functionality $\mathcal{F}_\mathsf{GS}$ as in Figure 1 for $\mathsf{N} = n-1$.
   - Each $P_i \in \mathcal{P}_\mathsf{N}$ inputs to $\mathcal{F}_\mathsf{GS}$:
     - for each wire $w \in [n+q]$, values $\lambda_w^i, k_{w,0}^i, k_{w,1}^i$
     - $\forall j \in [\mathsf{N}], (a,b) \in \{0,1\}^2$, $g \in [q]$, $F_{a,b}^{i,j,g} = \mathsf{PRF}_{k^i_{A,a},k^i_{B,b}}(g||j)$
   - All $P_i \in \mathcal{P}$ get output from $\mathcal{F}_\mathsf{GS}$:
     - the garbled circuit $\{G_{a,b}^j\}_{j\in[\mathsf{N}],g\in[q],(a,b)\in\{0,1\}^2}$
     - colour bit for each output wire $\{\lambda_w\}_{w\in[n+q-m,n+q]}$
     - for input wire i, colour bit λ_i
2. **OT Phase:**
   - Each party $P_i \in \mathcal{P}_\mathsf{N}$ sends $\Lambda_i = x_i \oplus \lambda_i$ to P_n
   - P_n computes $\Lambda_n = x_n \oplus \lambda_n$
   - $\forall i \in [n], j \in [\mathsf{N}]$, $\mathcal{F}_\mathsf{OT}$ is invoked where P_n is the receiver with input Λ_i and P_j is the sender with inputs $(k_{i,0}^j, k_{i,1}^j)$
   - After all $\mathcal{F}_\mathsf{OT}$ calls, P_n receives $\{k_{i,\Lambda_i}^j\}_{j\in[n-1],i\in[n]}$
3. **Evaluation Phase:** P_n evaluates the garbled circuit:
   - for each gate $g \in [q]$ in topological order, and public values a and b on the input wires A and B, for all $j \in [\mathsf{N}]$, compute

$$c||k_{g,c}^j = G_{a,b}^j \oplus \left(\bigoplus_{i=1}^{n-1} \mathsf{PRF}_{k^i_{A,a},k^i_{B,b}}(g||j) \right)$$

   - for each output wire w with value Λ_w, compute actual value $\Lambda_w \oplus \lambda_w$
   - P_n sends $f(\vec{x})$ to all parties

Fig. 2. Semi-honest Fall-Back Secure Protocol

$\frac{n}{2}$ parties. At the heart of this protocol is a compiler that we construct that can upgrade any MPC protocol that is secure against semi-honest unbounded adversaries with an adversary structure $\mathcal{Z}_\mathsf{S}$ to a protocol with semi-honest fall-back security for $\mathcal{Z}_\mathsf{S}$. The final protocol combines two components: a 'virtual protocol' that is secure in the presence of semi-honest unbounded adversaries; and a 'real protocol' compiling this into a protocol with fall-back security.

VIRTUAL PROTOCOL. Let $\mathcal{V} = \{V_i\}_{i\in[n]}$ be a set of n virtual parties. Let Π_stat be an n-party protocol executed among $\mathcal{V}$ with security against a semi-honest unbounded adversary corrupting $< \frac{n}{2}$ of the parties in $\mathcal{V}$. For any function f there exists such a protocol [4] that computes it. For a party $V_i \in \mathcal{V}$, we refer to its complete view in Π_stat as $\mathbf{View}_{\Pi_\mathsf{stat},i}$ and by $\mathbf{View}^j_{\Pi_\mathsf{stat},i}$, we refer to the partial view of V_i in the protocol up to round j. This includes the security parameter κ, the input x_i, contents of the random tape r_i, and all the messages received from all parties in $\mathcal{V}$ up to round j.

$$\mathbf{View}^{j}_{\Pi_{\mathsf{stat}},i} = (\kappa, x_i, r_i, \{m^{j'}_{k\to i}\}_{j'\in[j],k\neq i\in[n]})$$

Here $m^{j'}_{k\to i}$ is the message that party V_k sends V_i in round j'. Let NxtMsg be the next message function such that,

$$\mathsf{NxtMsg}^{j}_{i}(\mathbf{View}^{j-1}_{\Pi_{\mathsf{stat}},i}) = \{m^{j}_{i\to k}\}_{k\neq i\in[n]}$$

This function is parameterized by $i \in [n]$ that indexes the virtual party $V_i \in \mathcal{V}$. It takes as input the view up to round $j-1$ and creates all the messages to be delivered to all the parties in round j. Note that after each round,

$$\mathbf{View}^{j}_{\Pi_{\mathsf{stat}},i} = \mathbf{View}^{j-1}_{\Pi_{\mathsf{stat}},i} \cup \{m^{j}_{k\to i}\}_{k\neq i\in[n]}$$

Letting r be the number of rounds in Π_{stat}, the complete protocol Π_{stat} itself can be described as a set of the next message functions,

$$\Pi_{\mathsf{stat}} = \{\mathsf{NxtMsg}^{j}_{i}(\mathbf{View}^{j-1}_{\Pi_{\mathsf{stat}},i})\}_{i\in[n],j\in[r]}$$

Finally, for any subset of parties $Z \subseteq \mathcal{V}$ we denote by $\mathbf{View}_{\Pi_{\mathsf{stat}},Z}$ the combined view of Π_{stat} for all the parties in Z and similarly, we denote by $\mathbf{View}^{j}_{\Pi_{\mathsf{stat}},Z}$ the combined view up to round j in the protocol.

Real Protocol. Let $\mathcal{P} = \{P_i\}_{i\in[n]}$ be n parties that need to compute a multi-party function f on $\vec{x} = \{x_i\}_{i\in[n]}$. Each party $P_i \in \mathcal{P}$ has input x_i. Let Π_{stat} be an n-party protocol for the function f defined as follows:

- Each party $V_i \in \mathcal{V}$ has the input bit x_i and this is given to $\mathcal{F}$.
- $\mathcal{F}$ uses $\vec{x} = \{x_i\}_{i\in[n]}$ to compute $f(\vec{x})$ and gives it to each party $V_i \in \mathcal{V}$.

This protocol Π_{stat} can be re-written as a set of next message functions $\Pi_{\mathsf{stat}} = \{\mathsf{NxtMsg}^{j}_{i}\}_{i\in[n],j\in[r]}$. Let $\mathsf{SS}_{n,n} = (\mathsf{Share}_{n,n}, \mathsf{Recon}_{n,n})$ be an n-out-of-n secret-sharing scheme. For each $i \in [n], j \in [r]$ let $\mathcal{F}_{\mathsf{NxtMsg}^{j}_{i}}$ be a functionality as in Fig. 3.

Note that $\mathcal{F}_{\mathsf{NxtMsg}^{j}_{i}}$ is a functionality whose output is symmetric. Let Π be a protocol that computes any functionality exactly as in Fig. 2. For each $i \in [n]$, let Π_i denote the protocol Π with party P_i playing the role of the evaluator and all other parties as the garbler. Let $\Pi_{\mathsf{NxtMsg}^{j}_{i}}$ denote a protocol Π_i executed to compute the functionality $\mathcal{F}_{\mathsf{NxtMsg}^{j}_{i}}$. That is, it is an n-party protocol with $n-1$ garblers and one evaluator that is secure against the corruption of any subset of the garblers by a semi-honest unbounded adversary, and the corruption of any subset of parties by a PPT semi-honest adversary. The protocol $\Pi_{\mathsf{NxtMsg}^{j}_{i}}$ is executed by the parties $\mathcal{P} = \{P_k\}_{k\in[n]}$ and the party P_i is designated as the evaluator, while all other parties are the garblers.

Combined Protocol. The complete protocol Π_{in} is the set of all the protocols $\{\Pi_{\mathsf{NxtMsg}^{j}_{i}}\}_{i\in[n],j\in[r]}$ for any virtual protocol Π_{stat} with r rounds computing $\mathcal{F}$. It is formally described in Fig. 4.

Next Message Functionality $\mathcal{F}_{\mathsf{NxtMsg}_i^j}$

Setting: Let $\mathcal{P} = \{P_i\}_{i\in[n]}$ be n parties. Let $\mathsf{SS}_{n,n} = (\mathsf{Share}_{n,n}, \mathsf{Recon}_{n,n})$ be an n-out-of-n secret-sharing scheme. For a protocol Π_{stat} computing $\mathcal{F}$ let

$$\mathsf{NxtMsg}_i^j(\mathbf{View}_{\Pi_{\mathsf{stat}},i}^{j-1}) = \{m_{i\to k}^j\}_{k\neq i\in[n]}$$

be the next message function for party V_i in round j. The n-party functionality $\mathcal{F}_{\mathsf{NxtMsg}_i^j}$ operates as follows:

- **Inputs:** Each party $P_k \in \mathcal{P}$ has:
  - Let $\ell' = |\{[m_{i\to i'}^j]_k\}_{i'\neq i\in[n]}|$. Sample a random mask $M_k \leftarrow \{0,1\}^{\ell'}$.
  - Share of the view of V_i until round $(j-1)$ in Π_{stat},

$$[\mathbf{View}_{\Pi_{\mathsf{stat}},i}^{j-1}]_k = \left(\kappa, [x_i]_k, [r_i]_k, \{[m_{i'\to i}^{j'}]_k\}_{j'\in[j-1],i'\neq i\in[n]}\right)$$

  P_k gives to $\mathcal{F}_{\mathsf{NxtMsg}_i^j}$ the inputs,

$$[\mathbf{View}_{\Pi_{\mathsf{stat}},i}^{j-1}]_k, M_k$$

- **Computation:** The functionality $\mathcal{F}_{\mathsf{NxtMsg}_i^j}$ computes:

$$\begin{aligned} \mathbf{View}_{\Pi_{\mathsf{stat}},i}^{j-1} &\leftarrow \mathsf{Recon}_{n,n}(\{[\mathbf{View}_{\Pi_{\mathsf{stat}},i}^{j-1}]_k\}_{k\in[n]}) \\ \{m_{i\to i'}^j\}_{i'\neq i\in[n]} &= \mathsf{NxtMsg}_i^j(\mathbf{View}_{\Pi_{\mathsf{stat}},i}^{j-1}) \\ \forall i'\neq i\in[n], \quad \{[m_{i\to i'}^j]_k\}_{k\in[n]} &\leftarrow \mathsf{Share}_{n,n}(m_{i\to i'}^j) \\ \vec{c} &= \{c_k = M_k \oplus \{[m_{i\to i'}^j]_k\}_{i'\neq i\in[n]}\}_{k\in[n]} \end{aligned}$$

- **Output:** $\mathcal{F}_{\mathsf{NxtMsg}_i^j}$ gives $\vec{c}$ to each $P_k \in \mathcal{P}$.

Fig. 3. Next Message Functionality

Theorem 12. *Let Π_{stat} be a n-party protocol that securely computes a function f in the presence of an unbounded semi-honest adversary with adversary structure $\mathcal{Z}_{\mathsf{S}}$. Assuming protocol Π is an n-party protocol that computes any function with fall-back security with respect to $\mathcal{Z}_{\mathsf{S}}' = \{Z \subseteq \{P_i\}_{i\in[n-1]}\}$, the protocol in Fig. 4 securely compiles Π_{stat} to compute f with fall-back security (Definition 9) tolerating $\mathcal{Z}_{\mathsf{S}}$ in the presence of semi-honest adversaries.*

A detailed proof for this can be found in the full version.

Corollary 13. *Let Π_{stat} be a n-party protocol that securely computes a function f in the presence of an unbounded semi-honest adversary with adversary structure $\mathcal{Z}_{\mathsf{S}}$. For each $i \in [n]$, let Π_i be an n-party protocol that can compute any functionality with semi-honest fall-back security with respect to the adversary structure $\mathcal{Z}_{\mathsf{S}}^i = \{Z : Z \in \mathcal{Z}_{\mathsf{S}}, P_i \notin Z\}$. Then Fig. 4 securely compiles Π_{stat}*

Compiler for Semi-honest Fall-Back Security

Setting: For function f on $\vec{x} = \{x_i\}_{i\in[n]}$, let $\Pi_{\mathsf{stat}} = \{\mathsf{NxtMsg}_i^j\}_{i\in[n],j\in[r]}$ be a protocol computing the functionality $\mathcal{F}$ among $\mathcal{V} = \{V_i\}_{i\in[n]}$. Π_{stat} securely computes $\mathcal{F}$ against a semi-honest unbounded adversary corrupting $< \frac{n}{2}$ parties. Let $\mathcal{P} = \{P_i\}_{i\in[n]}$ be the set of real parties where P_i has input x_i.

1. **Initialize shared state.** Each party $P_i \in \mathcal{P}$ does the following:
   - Compute $\mathsf{Share}_{n,n}(x_i) \to \{[x_i]_{i'}\}_{i'\in[n]}$
   - Sample $r_i \leftarrow \mathcal{R}(\kappa)$ and compute $\mathsf{Share}_{n,n}(r_i) \to \{[r_i]_{i'}\}_{i'\in[n]}$
   - $\forall i' \neq i \in [n]$, send $([x_i]_{i'}, [r_i]_{i'})$ to $P_{i'}$
   - $\forall k \in [n]$, set the share of the initial state of virtual party $V_k \in \mathcal{V}$ as,
   $$[\mathbf{View}^0_{\Pi_{\mathsf{stat}},k}]_i = ([x_k]_i, [r_k]_i)$$
2. **Compute virtual protocol.** For each $\mathsf{NxtMsg}_i^j \in \Pi_{\mathsf{stat}}$, let $\Pi_{\mathsf{NxtMsg}_i^j}$ be an n-party protocol as in Figure 2 with P_i as the evaluator and $\mathcal{P}_{\mathsf{N}} = \mathcal{P} - \{P_i\}$ as the garblers. Each party $P_{i'} \in \mathcal{P}$ does the following:
   - $P_{i'}$ has input $[\mathbf{View}^{j-1}_{\Pi_{\mathsf{stat}},i}]_{i'}$ and samples $M_{i'} \leftarrow \{0,1\}^{\ell'}$
   - $P_{i'}$ participates in an execution of $\Pi_{\mathsf{NxtMsg}_i^j}$ with input
   $$[\mathbf{View}^{j-1}_{\Pi_{\mathsf{stat}},i}]_{i'}, M_{i'}$$
   Let $\mathbf{View}_{\mathsf{NxtMsg}_i^j,i'}$ be the view of $P_{i'}$ in this protocol.
   - $P_{i'}$ gets the output $\vec{c} = \{c_k = M_k \oplus \{[m^j_{i\to k'}]_k\}_{k'\neq i\in[n]}\}_{k\in[n]}$
   - $P_{i'}$ extracts $\{[m^j_{i\to k'}]_{i'}\}_{k'\neq i\in[n]} = c_{i'} \oplus M_{i'}$
   - $P_{i'}$ updates the view for each virtual party $V_k \in \mathcal{V} - \{V_i\}$,
   $$[\mathbf{View}^j_{\Pi_{\mathsf{stat}},k}]_{i'} = [\mathbf{View}^j_{\Pi_{\mathsf{stat}},k}]_{i'} \cup \{[\mathbf{View}^{j-1}_{\Pi_{\mathsf{stat}},k}]_{i'}, [m^j_{i\to k}]_{i'}\}$$
   $\Pi_{\mathsf{NxtMsg}_i^j}$ is computed for all $V_i \in \mathcal{V}$ and rounds indexed $j \in [r]$ in Π_{stat}
3. **Derive the output.** After the complete virtual protocol is computed, each party $P_i \in \mathcal{P}$ has a share of the view of each virtual party,
   $$\{[\mathbf{View}_{\Pi_{\mathsf{stat}},j}]_i\}_{j\in[n]}$$
   - Each party $P_i \in \mathcal{P}$ extracts the shares of the output:
   $$\{[f_j(\vec{x})]_i\}_{j\in[n]} \leftarrow \{[\mathbf{View}_{\Pi_{\mathsf{stat}},j}]_i\}_{j\in[n]}$$
   - P_i sends $[f_j(\vec{x})]_i$ to $P_j \in \mathcal{P}$
   - On receiving $\{[f_i(\vec{x})]_j\}_{j\in[n]}$, P_i reconstructs the output $f_i(\vec{x}) = f(\vec{x})$

Fig. 4. Compiler for Semi-honest Fall-Back Security

to compute f with fall-back security (Definition 9) with respect to $\mathcal{Z}_{\mathsf{S}}$ and in the presence of semi-honest adversaries.

5 MPC with Fall-Back Security – Malicious Security

This section will describe an MPC protocol for general functionalities that satisfies malicious fall-back security. Let $\mathcal{Z}_\mathsf{S}$ be any adversary structure for which there exists a protocol for computing any functionality in the presence of a malicious unbounded adversary tolerating $\mathcal{Z}_\mathsf{S}$ [11]. We construct a protocol that is maliciously fall-back secure with respect to $\mathcal{Z}_\mathsf{S}$.

Our protocol works in the offline-online paradigm with a function-and-input-independent pre-processing phase based on [10]. This phase has an n-party protocol computing the authenticated triples functionality $\mathcal{F}_{\mathsf{AuthTriples}}$ as given in Fig. 5 with malicious fall-back security tolerating $\mathcal{Z}_\mathsf{S}$. Then, given the output of this phase, we use a protocol in the online phase, based on that in [7], that computes any function f with malicious fall-back security. Our focus here is on designing the protocol for the pre-processing phase and providing a construction for the commitment scheme used in the online phase.

Pre-Processing. This phase contains an n-party protocol for computing authenticated multiplication triples with malicious fall-back security tolerating $\mathcal{Z}_\mathsf{S}$. The protocol conceptually contains three main components:

- **Authenticated Triples Generation Functionality.** Our starting point is the Authenticated Triples functionality $\mathcal{F}_{\mathsf{AuthTriples}}$ as given in Fig. 5. This is the n-party functionality that the pre-processing phase aims to realize. Details can be found in Sect. 5.1.
- **Semi-honest adaptively secure protocol with fall-back security.** We require a protocol realizing $\mathcal{F}_{\mathsf{AuthTriples}}$ that is fall-back secure tolerating $\mathcal{Z}_\mathsf{S}$ in the presence of semi-honest adaptive adversaries. Our starting point for this is an n-client-m-server protocol realizing $\mathcal{F}_{\mathsf{AuthTriples}}$ in the presence of an unbounded semi-honest adversary that can corrupt any number of the clients and up to a threshold t of the servers (Protocol 14). In this protocol, each server works by receiving inputs from all the clients, performing local computation, and giving outputs to these clients. As such, the actions of each server can be abstracted into a functionality $\mathcal{F}_S$ (Fig. 6). The final semi-honest fall-back secure protocol for $\mathcal{F}_{\mathsf{AuthTriples}}$ that we need works by having all the n parties act as the clients and also jointly compute $\mathcal{F}_S$ for each of the m servers. This computation of $\mathcal{F}_S$ is done by a semi-honest fall-back secure protocol that is secure in the presence of adaptive adversaries. This is discussed in detail in Sect. 5.2.
- **Compiling to maliciously secure fall-back security.** The adaptively secure protocol with semi-honest fall-back security as described above is then lifted to provide malicious fall-back security tolerating the same adversary structure $\mathcal{Z}_\mathsf{S}$. This is done using an n-party commitment protocol with fall-back security tolerating $\mathcal{Z}_\mathsf{S}$ as a building block. The construction for this is discussed in Sect. 5.3. The details of the final pre-processing protocol can be found in Sect. 5.4.

Online Phase. Given the output of the pre-processing phase, our online protocol follows the online phase closely in [7] that can compute any functionality in the presence of an unbounded malicious adversary corrupting any subset of the parties in the $\mathcal{F}_{\mathsf{Com}}$-hybrid, with $\mathcal{F}_{\mathsf{Com}}$ being an n-party commitment functionality. We describe our protocol in the plain model, instantiating $\mathcal{F}_{\mathsf{Com}}$ with a commitment protocol with fall-back security tolerating $\mathcal{Z}_{\mathsf{S}}$.

5.1 Authenticated Triples Generation

We describe an n-party Authenticated Triples Generation functionality $\mathcal{F}_{\mathsf{AuthTriples}}$ (Fig. 5). Let f be a function and $\vec{x}$ be its input. Let $\mathcal{P} = \{P_i\}_{i\in[n]}$ where each party P_i has private input $x_i \in \vec{x}$ such that $x_i \in \{0,1\}$. Let $\mathbf{C}$ be a circuit representing f using only binary addition and multiplication gates. Let $\mathsf{T} \in \mathbb{N}$ be the number of multiplication gates in $\mathbf{C}$. The functionality $\mathcal{F}_{\mathsf{AuthTriples}}$ creates an n-out-of-n additive sharing of T random multiplication triples of the form $\{a^j, b^j, c^j = (a^j \cdot b^j)\}_{j\in[\mathsf{T}]}$ and gives one share to each party. Additionally, it additively secret-shares a MAC key Δ and MACs on the multiplication triples $\{\mathsf{MAC}(a^j) = (a^j \cdot \Delta),\ \mathsf{MAC}(b^j) = (b^j \cdot \Delta),\ \mathsf{MAC}(c^j) = (c^j \cdot \Delta)\}_{j\in[\mathsf{T}]}$ among the parties. Finally, for each input bit x_i, it samples a random number r_i and gives it to P_i. It distributes among all parties a sharing of r_i and $\mathsf{MAC}(r^i) = (r^i \cdot \Delta)$. The functionality first allows corrupted parties to sample their own shares and then samples shares for the honest parties, setting the shares of a designated party P_1 such that the constraints are met.

5.2 Authenticated Triples with Semi-Honest Fall-Back Security

In this section, we describe the protocol computing $\mathcal{F}_{\mathsf{AuthTriples}}$ with semi-honest fall-back security tolerating $\mathcal{Z}_{\mathsf{S}}$ for adaptive corruption. This is the starting point from which we lift semi-honest to malicious security. However, before discussing the fall-back secure protocol, consider the semi-honest protocol as in Protocol 14.

For a security parameter κ, let $t = \kappa$ be a threshold and set $m = 16t$. Protocol 14 is a semi-honest secure protocol for computing $\mathcal{F}_{\mathsf{AuthTriples}}$ among n clients $\mathcal{P} = \{P_i\}_{i\in[n]}$ and m virtual servers $\mathcal{S} = \{S_j\}_{j\in[m]}$. In this protocol, the clients have the inputs and receive the outputs of the functionality and the servers only aid in computation. The protocol works by having each client sample its inputs and use t-out-of-m threshold secret-sharing to share it among the servers. Then each server performs some symmetric local computation to produce shares of the outputs of the functionality. The actions of each server can be captured by an n-party functionality $\mathcal{F}_{\mathcal{S}}$ (Fig. 6). Each server then gives these shares to the respective clients and each client reconstructs its outputs.

Protocol 14. *For a security parameter κ, let $t = \kappa$ be a threshold and for $m > 16t$, let $\mathcal{S} = \{S_i\}_{i\in[m]}$ be a set of m virtual servers. Let $\mathsf{SS}_{t,m} = (\mathsf{Share}_{t,m}, \mathsf{Recon}_{t,m})$ be a t-out-of-m threshold secret-sharing scheme [18]. Let $\mathcal{V} = \{V_i\}_{i\in[n]}$ be a set of n virtual parties.*

Authenticated Triples Generation $\mathcal{F}_{\mathsf{AuthTriples}}$

Setting: Let $\mathcal{P} = \{P_i\}_{i\in[n]}$ be a set of parties. Let f be a function and $\vec{x} \in \{0,1\}^n$ be its input such that each party $P_i \in \mathcal{P}$ has input $x_i \in \vec{x}$. Let $\mathbb{F}$ be a field and $\mathsf{T} \in \mathbb{N}$ be the number of multiplication gates in a circuit $\mathbf{C}$ representing f. Let $Z \subset \mathcal{P}$ be the corrupt parties. The functionality $\mathcal{F}_{\mathsf{AuthTriples}}$ operates as follows:

- **Inputs:** Each corrupt party $P_i \in Z$ samples:
  - $\forall j \in [\mathsf{T}]$, triples shares $a_i^j, b_i^j, c_i^j, \mathsf{MAC}_i(a^j), \mathsf{MAC}_i(b^j), \mathsf{MAC}_i(c^j) \in \mathbb{F}$
  - $\forall k \in [n]$, input mask shares $r_i^k, \mathsf{MAC}_i(r^k) \in \mathbb{F}$
  - key share $\Delta_i \in \mathbb{F}$
- **Computation:** The functionality $\mathcal{F}_{\mathsf{AuthTriples}}$ computes,
  - $\forall P_i \in \mathcal{P} - Z$, sample

$$\Delta_i \leftarrow \mathbb{F}, \{r_i^k, \mathsf{MAC}_i(r^k) \leftarrow \mathbb{F}\}_{k\in[n]}$$
$$\{a_i^j, b_i^j, c_i^j, \mathsf{MAC}_i(a^j), \mathsf{MAC}_i(b^j), \mathsf{MAC}_i(c^j) \leftarrow \mathbb{F}\}_{j\in[\mathsf{T}]}$$

  - Compute,

$$\forall k \in [n], \qquad r^k = \sum_{i\in[n]} r_i^k$$
$$\mathsf{MAC}'(r^k) = (\sum_{i\in[n]} r_i^k) \cdot (\sum_{i\in[n]} \Delta_i) - (\sum_{i\in[n]} \mathsf{MAC}_i(r^k))$$
$$\forall j \in [\mathsf{T}], \qquad c'^j = (\sum_{i\in[n]} a_i^j) \cdot (\sum_{i\in[n]} b_i^j) - (\sum_{i\in[n]} c_i^j)$$
$$\mathsf{MAC}'(a^j) = (\sum_{i\in[n]} a_i^j) \cdot (\sum_{i\in[n]} \Delta_i) - (\sum_{i\in[n]} \mathsf{MAC}_i(a^j))$$
$$\mathsf{MAC}'(b^j) = (\sum_{i\in[n]} b_i^j) \cdot (\sum_{i\in[n]} \Delta_i) - (\sum_{i\in[n]} \mathsf{MAC}_i(b^j))$$
$$\mathsf{MAC}'(c^j) = (\sum_{i\in[n]} a_i^j) \cdot (\sum_{i\in[n]} b_i^j) \cdot (\sum_{i\in[n]} \Delta_i) - (\sum_{i\in[n]} \mathsf{MAC}_i(c^j))$$

- **Outputs:** $\mathcal{F}_{\mathsf{AuthTriples}}$ gives to each $P_i \neq P_1 \in \mathcal{P}$,

$$\Delta_i, r^i, \{r_i^k, \mathsf{MAC}_i(r^k)\}_{k\in[n]}, \{a_i^j, b_i^j, c_i^j, \mathsf{MAC}_i(a^j), \mathsf{MAC}_i(b^j), \mathsf{MAC}_i(c^j)\}_{j\in[\mathsf{T}]}$$

  $\mathcal{F}_{\mathsf{AuthTriples}}$ gives to P_1,

$$\Delta_1, r^1, \{r_1^k, \mathsf{MAC}_1(r^k) = \mathsf{MAC}_1(r^k) + \mathsf{MAC}'(r^k)\}_{k\in[n]},$$
$$\{a_1^j, b_1^j, c_1^j = c_1^j + c'^j, \mathsf{MAC}_1(a^j) = \mathsf{MAC}_1(a^j) + \mathsf{MAC}'(a^j),$$
$$\mathsf{MAC}_1(b^j) = \mathsf{MAC}_1(b^j) + \mathsf{MAC}'(b^j), \mathsf{MAC}_1(c^j) = \mathsf{MAC}_1(c^j) + \mathsf{MAC}'(c^j)\}_{j\in[\mathsf{T}]}$$

Fig. 5. Authenticated Triples Generation

- *Each party $V_i \in \mathcal{V}$ first samples,*

$$\Delta_i \leftarrow \mathbb{F}, \{r_i^k, \mathsf{MAC}_i(r^k) \leftarrow \mathbb{F}\}_{k\in[n]}$$
$$\{a_i^j, b_i^j, c_i^j, \mathsf{MAC}_i(a^j), \mathsf{MAC}_i(b^j), \mathsf{MAC}_i(c^j) \leftarrow \mathbb{F}\}_{j\in[\mathsf{T}]}$$

It then computes a 3t-out-of-m threshold secret-sharing of each element in $\{\mathsf{MAC}_i(c^j)\}_{j\in[\mathsf{T}]}$ *and a t-out-of-m threshold secret-sharing of all other elements.*

- *Each party* $V_i \in \mathcal{V}$ *gives to server* $S_j \in \mathcal{S}$ *the shares,*

$$[\Delta_i]_j, \{[r_i^k]_j, [\mathsf{MAC}_i(r^k)]_j\}_{k\in[n]}$$

$$\{[a_i^{j'}]_j, [b_i^{j'}]_j, [c_i^{j'}]_j, [\mathsf{MAC}_i(a^{j'})]_j, [\mathsf{MAC}_i(b^{j'})]_j, [\mathsf{MAC}_i(c^{j'})]_j\}_{j'\in[\mathsf{T}]}$$

- *Each server* $S_j \in \mathcal{S}$ *computes the functionality* $\mathcal{F}_{\mathcal{S}}$ *(Fig. 6). It gives to party* $V_1 \in \mathcal{V}$ *the values,*

$$[r^1]_j, \{[\mathsf{MAC}'(r^k)]_j\}_{k\in[n]}, \{[c'^{j'}]_j, [\mathsf{MAC}'(a^{j'})]_j, [\mathsf{MAC}'(b^{j'})]_j, [\mathsf{MAC}'(c^{j'})]_j\}_{j'\in[\mathsf{T}]}$$

  It gives each party $V_i \in \mathcal{V}$ *the share* $[r^i]_j$.
- *The party* V_1 *reconstructs,*

$$\Delta_1, r^1, \{r_1^k, \mathsf{MAC}_1(r^k) = \mathsf{MAC}_1(r^k) + \mathsf{MAC}'(r^k)\}_{k\in[n]},$$
$$\{a_1^j, b_1^j, c_1^j = c_1^j + c'^j, \mathsf{MAC}_1(a^j) = \mathsf{MAC}_1(a^j) + \mathsf{MAC}'(a^j),$$
$$\mathsf{MAC}_1(b^j) = \mathsf{MAC}_1(b^j) + \mathsf{MAC}'(b^j), \mathsf{MAC}_1(c^j) = \mathsf{MAC}_1(c^j) + \mathsf{MAC}'(c^j)\}_{j\in[\mathsf{T}]}$$

- *Each* $V_i \neq V_1$ *reconstructs* r^i.

Lemma 15. *Protocol 14 securely realizes functionality* $\mathcal{F}_{\mathsf{AuthTriples}}$ *(Fig. 5) in the presence of an unbounded semi-honest adversary corrupting all-but-one parties in* $\mathcal{V}$ *and any subset of t servers in* $\mathcal{S}$.

The semi-honest secure Protocol 14 is secure in the presence of a semi-honest unbounded adversary corrupting all-but-one of the clients and up to t servers. We define a protocol Π_S to be an n-party protocol realizing $\mathcal{F}_{\mathcal{S}}$ (Fig. 6) with semi-honest fall-back security tolerating $\mathcal{Z}_\mathsf{S}$ in the presence of adaptive corruptions. Given such a protocol, we can define a protocol $\Pi_{\mathsf{AuthTriples}}$ that realizes $\mathcal{F}_{\mathsf{AuthTriples}}$ with semi-honest fall-back security tolerating $\mathcal{Z}_\mathsf{S}$ for adaptive adversaries. This protocol would work by first having each of the n parties generate their inputs and create t-out-of-m threshold secret-shares. Then execute m instances of Π_S, each with a different set of shares as input. The output of these executions is reconstructed to get the output of $\mathcal{F}_{\mathsf{AuthTriples}}$.

5.3 Commitment Protocols with Fall-Back Security

Both the pre-processing and online phases require commitment schemes that are maliciously fall-back secure tolerating $\mathcal{Z}_\mathsf{S}$. In this subsection we first describe an n-party commitment protocol (Fig. 8 – excluding the steps marked in gray) between one committer and $n-1$ viewers that preserves fall-back security. This protocol operates in a commit phase and a decommit phase. It uses as its building-blocks a 2-party statistically binding commitment scheme, a statistically hiding commitment scheme, and an n-party secret-sharing scheme for which a secret cannot be reconstructed for adversary structure $\mathcal{Z}_\mathsf{S}$.

Virtual Server Functionality $\mathcal{F}_S$

Setting: Let κ be a computational security parameter, $\mathsf{T} \in \mathbb{N}$ and $\mathbb{F}$ be a field. Let $\mathcal{V} = \{V_i\}_{i\in[n]}$ be a set of parties. The functionality $\mathcal{F}_S$ operates as follows:

- **Inputs:** Each party $V_i \in \mathcal{V}$ has:

$$[\Delta_i]_j, \{[r_i^k]_j, [\mathsf{MAC}_i(r^k)]_j\}_{k\in[n]}$$

$$\{[a_i^{j'}]_j, [b_i^{j'}]_j, [c_i^{j'}]_j, [\mathsf{MAC}_i(a^{j'})]_j, [\mathsf{MAC}_i(b^{j'})]_j, [\mathsf{MAC}_i(c^{j'})]_j\}_{j'\in[\mathsf{T}]}$$

  as in Protocol 14.
- **Computation:** The functionality $\mathcal{F}_S$ computes,

$$\forall k \in [n], \quad [r^k]_j = \sum_{i\in[n]} [r_i^k]_j$$

$$[\mathsf{MAC}'(r^k)]_j = (\sum_{i\in[n]} [r_i^k]_j) \cdot (\sum_{i\in[n]} [\Delta_i]_j) - (\sum_{i\in[n]} [\mathsf{MAC}_i(r^k)]_j)$$

$$\forall j' \in [\mathsf{T}], \quad [c'^{j'}]_j = (\sum_{i\in[n]} [a_i^{j'}]_j) \cdot (\sum_{i\in[n]} [b_i^{j'}]_j) - (\sum_{i\in[n]} [c_i^{j'}]_j)$$

$$[\mathsf{MAC}'(a^{j'})]_j = (\sum_{i\in[n]} [a_i^{j'}]_j) \cdot (\sum_{i\in[n]} [\Delta_i]_j) - (\sum_{i\in[n]} [\mathsf{MAC}_i(a^{j'})]_j)$$

$$[\mathsf{MAC}'(b^{j'})]_j = (\sum_{i\in[n]} [b_i^{j'}]_j) \cdot (\sum_{i\in[n]} [\Delta_i]_j) - (\sum_{i\in[n]} [\mathsf{MAC}_i(b^{j'})]_j)$$

$$[\mathsf{MAC}'(c^{j'})]_j = (\sum_{i\in[n]} [a_i^{j'}]_j) \cdot (\sum_{i\in[n]} [b_i^{j'}]_j) \cdot (\sum_{i\in[n]} [\Delta_i]_j) - (\sum_{i\in[n]} [\mathsf{MAC}_i(c^{j'})]_j)$$

- **Outputs:** $\mathcal{F}_S$ gives to V_1:

$$[r^1]_j, \{[\mathsf{MAC}'(r^k)]_j\}_{k\in[n]}\{[c'^{j'}]_j, [\mathsf{MAC}'(a^{j'})]_j, [\mathsf{MAC}'(b^{j'})]_j, [\mathsf{MAC}'(c^{j'})]_j\}_{j'\in[\mathsf{T}]}$$

  It gives $[r^i]_j$ to each $V_i \neq V_1 \in \mathcal{V}$.

Fig. 6. Virtual Server Functionality

Commitment Functionality $\mathcal{F}_{\mathsf{Com}}$

Setting: Let $\mathcal{P} = \{P_i\}_{i\in[n]}$ be a set of parties. Let $C \in \mathcal{P}$ be the committer with input $x \in \mathcal{X}$. The functionality $\mathcal{F}_{\mathsf{Com}}$ operates as follows:

- **Inputs:** C has input x. All other parties have no input.
- **Commit Phase:** C gives x or $\perp$ to $\mathcal{F}_{\mathsf{Com}}$.
- **Decommit Phase:** $\mathcal{F}_{\mathsf{Com}}$ gives x to all parties in $\mathcal{P}$ if input is not $\perp$.

Fig. 7. n-party Commitment Functionality

We also require another variant (Fig. 8) that is extractable: there exists a PPT extractor that can extract the value committed to while playing the role of one

Extractable Commitment with Fall-Back Security

Setting: Let $\mathcal{P} = \{P_i\}_{i\in[n]}$ and $\mathcal{Z}_S \subset 2^{\mathcal{P}}$. Let $C \in \mathcal{P}$ be the committer with input $x \in \mathcal{X}$. There exist secure point-to-point and broadcast channels for all parties. Let $\mathsf{Com}_{\mathsf{SB}}$ be a statistically binding commitment. For the adversary structure $\mathcal{Z}_S$ let $\mathsf{SS}_{\mathcal{Z}_S} = (\mathsf{Share}_{\mathcal{Z}_S}, \mathsf{Recon}_{\mathcal{Z}_S})$ be a secret-sharing scheme over $\mathcal{X}$. Let $\mathsf{Com}_{\mathsf{SH}}$ be a statistically hiding commitment and let SZKAoK be a statistical zero-knowledge argument of knowledge protocol for the statement:

$$\exists x, r \text{ s.t. } c_{\mathsf{Com}_{\mathsf{SH}}} = \mathsf{Com}_{\mathsf{SH}}(x; r)$$

For each $k \in [n]$, let ZKPoK be a zero-knowledge proof of knowledge for the statements of the form:

$$\exists [x]_k, r^k_{\mathsf{Com}} \text{ s.t. } c^k_{\mathsf{Com}_{\mathsf{SB}}} = \mathsf{Com}_{\mathsf{SB}}([x]_k; r^k_{\mathsf{Com}})$$

The protocol operates as follows:

1. **Commit Phase.**
   - C computes shares $\{[x]_k\}_{k\in[n]} \leftarrow \mathsf{Share}_{\mathcal{Z}_S}(x)$.
   - For each $P_k \in \mathcal{P}$ such that $P_k \neq C$, C samples randomness r^k_{Com} and computes $c^k_{\mathsf{Com}_{\mathsf{SB}}} = \mathsf{Com}_{\mathsf{SB}}([x]_k; r^k_{\mathsf{Com}})$.
   - For each $P_k \in \mathcal{P}$ such that $P_k \neq C$, C executes ZKPoK as the prover and P_k as the verifier.
   - C samples $r_{\mathsf{Com}_{\mathsf{SH}}}$ and broadcasts $c_{\mathsf{Com}_{\mathsf{SH}}} = \mathsf{Com}_{\mathsf{SH}}(x; r_{\mathsf{Com}_{\mathsf{SH}}})$.
   - C executes SZKAoK as the prover with all other parties as verifiers.
2. **De-commit Phase.**
   - C sends r^k_{Com} to each $P_k \in \mathcal{P}$ and broadcasts $(r_{\mathsf{Com}_{\mathsf{SH}}}, x, \{[x]_k\}_{k\in[n]})$.
   - Each party $P_k \neq C \in \mathcal{P}$, checks if

$$x == \mathsf{Recon}_{\mathcal{Z}_S}(\{[x]_k\}_{k\in[n]})$$
$$c_{\mathsf{Com}_{\mathsf{SH}}} == \mathsf{Com}_{\mathsf{SH}}(x; r_{\mathsf{Com}_{\mathsf{SH}}})$$
$$c^k_{\mathsf{Com}_{\mathsf{SB}}} == \mathsf{Com}_{\mathsf{SB}}([x]_k; r^k_{\mathsf{Com}})$$

   If this holds, accept x as output.

Fig. 8. Extractable Commitment with Fall-Back Security

of the viewers. We rely on a statistical zero-knowledge argument of knowledge and a computational zero-knowledge proof of knowledge to achieve extraction.

n-Party Commitment with Fall-Back Security. Given the two fall-back secure protocols described above, we construct in Fig. 9 a protocol that realizes $\mathcal{F}_{\mathsf{Com}}$ (Fig. 7) with malicious fall-back security. This protocol realizes the required functionality but only for binary inputs in $\{0, 1\}$. For it to work for any input domain, we convert the required input into a binary string and bit-wise

n-party protocol realizing $\mathcal{F}_{\mathsf{Com}}$

Setting: Let $\mathcal{P} = \{P_i\}_{i\in[n]}$ and $\mathcal{Z}_\mathsf{S} \subset 2^{\mathcal{P}}$. Let $C \in \mathcal{P}$ be the committer with input $x \in \{0,1\}$. There exist secure point-to-point and broadcast channels for all parties. Let Com be a fall-back secure commitment protocol and ECom (Figure 8) be an extractable fall-back secure commitment protocol tolerating $\mathcal{Z}_\mathsf{S}$. Let κ be a security parameter.
The commitment protocol Π_{Com} operates as follows:

1. **Commit Phase.**
   - Each party $P_i \in \mathcal{P}$ such that $P_i \neq C$ samples a string $r_i \in \{0,1\}^\kappa$ and executes the 'commit phase' of Com with this as input.
   - For each $j \in [\kappa]$, C samples ν_j and creates a matrix:
   $$M_j = \begin{bmatrix} \nu_j, \nu_j + x \\ \nu_j, \nu_j + x \end{bmatrix}$$
   Execute the 'commit phase' of ECom with each element of M_j as input.
   - For each party $P_i \in \mathcal{P}$ such that $P_i \neq C$ the 'decommit phase' of Com is executed and all parties learn r_i.
   - C can compute $r = \sum_{P_i \neq C \in \mathcal{P}} r_i$. For each $j \in [\kappa]$, For the $r[j]^{th}$ column in M_j, the 'decommit phase' of ECom is executed and all parties learn (ν_j^*, ν_j^{**}).
   - For each $P_i \in \mathcal{P}$ where $P_i \neq C$, for each $j \in [\kappa]$, P_i checks if $\nu_j^* == \nu_j^{**}$. If all checks pass, it accepts $\{M_j\}_{j\in[\kappa]}$ as the commitment to x.
2. **De-commit Phase.**
   - For each $j \in [\kappa]$, C samples $b_j \leftarrow \{0,1\}$ at random and executes the 'decommit phase' of ECom for the commitment in the b_j^{th} row of the $(\neg r[j])^{th}$ column. All parties learn ν_j' and compute $x_j' = \nu_j^* - \nu_j'$.
   - If $\forall j \in [\kappa]$, x_j' is equal to the same value x, accept x as the output.

Fig. 9. Realizing $\mathcal{F}_{\mathsf{Com}}$ with malicious fall-back security

commit to the complete string. In our final construction, we denote by Π_{Com} this commitment protocol for an arbitrary input domain.

5.4 Malicious Fall-Back Secure Protocol for Authenticated Triples

We compile $\Pi_{\mathsf{AuthTriples}}$ as given in Sect. 5.2 to provide malicious fall-back security tolerating $\mathcal{Z}_\mathsf{S}$. This requires putting mechanisms in place that ensure that all the parties execute the protocol $\Pi_{\mathsf{AuthTriples}}$ in a semi-honest manner. This is done in three steps.

1. **Randomness Generation.** For each of the n parties and each of the m executions of Π_S, all the parties execute a coin-tossing in-the-well protocol to sample uniformly the random tape to be used by a party in the execution of Π_S. In each such execution, a designated party receives the random tape and

all other parties receive a commitment to this randomness. This is done in a way that preserves malicious fall-back security tolerating $\mathcal{Z}_\mathsf{S}$ and uses the commitment and extractable commitment protocols described in Sect. 5.3. Executing $n \cdot m$ such protocols determines all the randomness to be used in the execution of $\Pi_{\mathsf{AuthTriples}}$, with the exception of the randomness involved in secret-sharing the inputs of each party to create the inputs for each Π_S.
2. **Input Commitment.** Each of the n parties sample their inputs to $\Pi_{\mathsf{AuthTriples}}$ and creates a t-out-of-m threshold-secret-sharing of each of these values as given in Protocol 14. The party then uses the fall-back secure extractable commitment protocol to commit to these shares to all other parties.
3. **Consistency Checks.** Intuitively, compiling the semi-honest protocol to malicious security involves first having all the parties commit to all their inputs and randomness and then executing the protocol with the values committed. Owing to the t-out-of-m secret sharing, the semi-honest protocol $\Pi_{\mathsf{AuthTriples}}$ is secure in the presence of up to t failed executions of Π_S. So an adversary corrupting too few of these executions cannot affect security. First, a degree-test needs to be conducted to ensure that the inputs to all the instances of Π_S when looked at collectively are indeed a t-out-of-m secret sharing of the inputs of $\Pi_{\mathsf{AuthTriples}}$.
Next, for malicious security, $\frac{t}{2}$ out of the m instances of the Π_S executions are chosen at random, and all the parties need to decommit to the inputs and randomness used for these executions. All parties then check if these have been computed correctly where security in the presence of a malicious adversary is based on the fact that if the adversary deviates in the protocol in more than t of the instances, it would, with overwhelming probability, be detected within the opened executions.

Protocol 16 describes the final pre-processing protocol realizing $\mathcal{F}_{\mathsf{AuthTriples}}$.

Protocol 16. *Let $\mathcal{P} = \{P_i\}_{i\in[n]}$ and $\mathcal{Z}_\mathsf{S} \subset 2^{\mathcal{P}}$. Let f be function and $\vec{x} \in \{0,1\}^n$ be the input such that $P_i \in \mathcal{P}$ has input $x_i \in \vec{x}$. Let $\mathbb{F}$ be a field and $\mathsf{T} \in \mathbb{N}$ be the number of multiplication gates in circuit $\mathbf{C}$ representing f. There exist secure point-to-point and broadcast channels for all parties.*
Let κ be a security parameter, $t = \kappa$ and $m \geq 16t$. Let $\Pi_{\mathsf{AuthTriples}}$ be a semi-honest fall-back secure protocol tolerating $\mathcal{Z}_\mathsf{S}$ for adaptive adversaries. For each $j \in [m]$, let Π_S^j denote the jth instance of Π_S in $\Pi_{\mathsf{AuthTriples}}$. Let Π_{Com} (Fig. 9) be a protocol realizing $\mathcal{F}_{\mathsf{Com}}$ with fall-back security for any input domain.

1. ***Coin Toss Phase.*** *Execute the commit phase of a coin-tossing protocol. Let $\mathcal{R}_t = \{0,1\}^s$ where $s = \frac{t}{2}\log m$. Let $\vec{r} \in \mathcal{R}_t$ be a vector containing $\frac{t}{2}$ elements $\vec{r} = \{j \in \{0,1\}^{\log m}\}$*
   - ***Inputs:*** *Each $P_i \in \mathcal{P}$ generates randomness $\vec{r_i} \leftarrow \mathcal{R}_t$.*
   - ***Protocol Π_{coin} – Commit Phase:***
     - *Sequentially for each $P_i \in \mathcal{P}$, execute the **commit phase** of Π_{Com} with P_i as the committer and input $\vec{r_i}$.*
     - *Let $\mathbf{View}^{i,k}_{\mathsf{Com},r}$ denote the view of party $P_k \neq P_i$ in this execution.*

– ***Outputs:*** *Every* $P_i \in \mathcal{P}$ *accepts* $\{\mathbf{View}^{k,i}_{\mathsf{Com},r}\}_{k\in[n]}$.

Let $\mathbb{F}^{2n+6\mathsf{T}+1}$ *be the space of inputs of each party* P_i *to* Π^j_S. *Execute the* ***commit phase*** *of* Π_{coin} *as above:*

– ***Inputs:*** *Each* $P_i \in \mathcal{P}$ *samples* $\vec{d_i} \leftarrow \mathbb{F}^{2n+6\mathsf{T}+3}$.

– ***Outputs:*** *Every* $P_i \in \mathcal{P}$ *accepts* $\{\mathbf{View}^{k,i}_{\mathsf{Com},d}\}_{k\in[n]}$.

2. ***Input Commitment Phase.*** $\forall i \in [n]$, P_i *commits to its inputs in* $\Pi_{\mathsf{AuthTriples}}$.
   – ***Inputs:*** P_i *generates a vector* $\vec{v_i}$ *containing the random elements,*

$$\Delta_i \leftarrow \mathbb{F}, \{r^k_i, \mathsf{MAC}_i(r^k) \leftarrow \mathbb{F}\}_{k\in[n]}$$

$$\{a^j_i, b^j_i, c^j_i, \mathsf{MAC}_i(a^j), \mathsf{MAC}_i(b^j), \mathsf{MAC}_i(c^j) \leftarrow \mathbb{F}\}_{j\in[\mathsf{T}]}$$

   – ***Protocol*** Π^i_{Com} ***– Commit Phase:***
     - P_i *computes for each* $v \in \vec{v_i}$ *the shares* $\{[v]_j\}_{j\in[m]} \leftarrow \mathsf{Share}_{t,m}(v)$. *Let* $\vec{v^j_i} = \{[v]_j\}_{v\in\vec{v_i}}$ *be* P_i*'s inputs to* Π^j_S.
     - *Sequentially for each* $j \in [m]$, *execute the* ***commit phase*** *of* Π_{Com} *where* P_i *is the committer with input* $\vec{v^j_i}$. *Let* $\mathbf{View}^{i,k}_{\mathsf{Com},j,v}$ *be the view of each* $P_k \neq P_i$ *in this execution.*

   – ***Outputs:***
     - *Every* $P_k \neq P_i$ *accepts* $\{\mathbf{View}^{k,i}_{\mathsf{Com},j,v}\}_{j\in[m]}$.
     - P_i *sets for each* $j \in [m]$, *the input to* Π^j_S *the vector* $\vec{v^j_i}$ *of the form,*

$$\vec{v^j_i} = \big([\Delta_i]_j, \{[r^k_i]_j, [\mathsf{MAC}_i(r^k)]_j\}_{k\in[n]}, \{[a^{j'}_i]_j, [b^{j'}_i]_j, [c^{j'}_i]_j, [\mathsf{MAC}_i(a^{j'})]_j, [\mathsf{MAC}_i(b^{j'})]_j, [\mathsf{MAC}_i(c^{j'})]_j\}_{j'\in[\mathsf{T}]}\big)$$

3. ***Randomness Generation Phase.*** *Sequentially* $\forall i \in [n], j \in [m]$, *the commit phase of a coin-tossing-in-the-well protocol* $\Pi^{i,j}_{\mathsf{CTW}}$ *is executed.*
   Let $P_i \in \mathcal{P}$ *be the receiver,* $\mathcal{R}$ *be the space of random tapes.*
   – ***Inputs:*** *Each* $P_k \in \mathcal{P}$ *generates randomness* $r^k_{i,j} \leftarrow \mathcal{R}$.
   – ***Protocol*** $\Pi^{i,j}_{\mathsf{CTW}}$ ***– Commit Phase:***
     - *Sequentially for each* $P_k \in \mathcal{P}$, *execute the* ***commit phase*** *of* Π_{Com} *where* P_k *is the committer with input* $r^k_{i,j}$. *Let* $\mathbf{View}^{k,k',i,j}_{\mathsf{Com}}$ *be the view of each* $P_{k'} \neq P_k$.
     - $\forall P_k \neq P_i$, *execute* ***decommit phase*** *of* Π_{Com} *with committer* P_k.

   – ***Outputs:***
     - P_i *sets* $r_{i,j} = \sum_{k\in[n]} r^k_{i,j}$ *as its randomness for* Π^j_S.
     - *Every* $P_k \neq P_i$ *accepts* $(\mathbf{View}^{i,k,i,j}_{\mathsf{Com}}, \{r^k_{i,j}\}_{P_k \neq P_i \in \mathcal{P}})$.
4. ***Compute Phase.*** $\forall j \in [m]$, *execute* Π^j_S *(functionality* $\mathcal{F}_S$ *– Fig. 6).*
   – ***Inputs:*** *Each* $P_i \in \mathcal{P}$ *uses* $\vec{v^j_i}$ *as the input to* Π^j_S.
   – ***Outputs:*** *Party* $P_i \in \mathcal{P}$ *gets the output vector* $\vec{s^j_i}$.

   Each $P_i \in \mathcal{P}$ *computes* $\vec{s_i} \leftarrow \mathsf{Recon}_{4t,m}(\{\vec{s^j_i}\}_{j\in[m]})$.
5. ***Check Phase.*** *Perform consistency checks on the execution of* $\Pi_{\mathsf{AuthTriples}}$.

(a) ***Degree Test:***

- *Each* $P_i \in \mathcal{P}$ *samples* $z_0, z_1 \leftarrow \mathbb{F}$.
  It computes $\vec{z_0} \leftarrow \mathsf{Share}_{t,m}(z_0)$ *and* $\vec{z_1} \leftarrow \mathsf{Share}_{t,m}(z_1)$.
- *Complete the 'reveal phase' of* Π_{coin} *with domain* $\mathbb{F}^{2n+6\mathsf{T}+1}$*:*
  - *Sequentially for each* $P_i \in \mathcal{P}$*, execute the* ***decommit phase*** *of* Π_{Com} *where* P_i *is the committer and receive* $\vec{d_i}$.

  Every party $P_i \in \mathcal{P}$ *accepts* $\vec{d} = \sum_{k\in[n]} \vec{d_k} \in \mathbb{F}^{2n+6\mathsf{T}+3}$.
- $\forall j \in [m]$, $P_i \in \mathcal{P}$ *broadcast* $d_{i,j} = \langle \vec{d}, \vec{s^i_j} \rangle$ *where* $\vec{s^i_j} = (z_0[j], z_1[j], \vec{v^i_j})$.
- *All parties check* $\exists i \in [n], \mathsf{Recon}_{t,m}(\{d_{i,j}\}_{j\in[m]}) == \perp$ *then ABORT.*

(b) ***Watch-list:***

- *Complete the 'reveal phase' of* Π_{coin} *with domain* $\mathcal{R}_t$*:*
  - *Sequentially for each* $P_i \in \mathcal{P}$*, execute the* ***decommit phase*** *of* Π_{Com} *where* P_i *is the committer and receive* $\vec{r_i}$.
  - *Each party* $P_i \in \mathcal{P}$ *accepts* $\vec{r} = \sum_{k\in[n]} \vec{r_k}$.
- *For each* $j \in \vec{r}$, $\forall P_i \in \mathcal{P}$*, execute the 'reveal phase' of* $\Pi^{i,j}_{\mathsf{CTW}}$*:*
  - *Execute the* ***decommit phase*** *of* Π_{Com} *where* P_i *is the committer and receive* $r^i_{i,j}$.
  - *Each* $P_k \neq P_i$ *accepts* $r_{i,j} = \sum_{k'\in[n]} r^{k'}_{i,j}$.
- *For each* $j \in \vec{r}$, $\forall P_i \in \mathcal{P}$*, reveal the input commitments in* Π^i_{Com}*:*
  - *Broadcast* $z_0[j]$ *and* $z_1[j]$ *and execute the* ***decommit phase*** *of* Π_{Com} *where* P_i *is the committer and receive* $\vec{v^j_i}$.
- $\forall j \in \vec{r}$*, check if the view of the execution of* Π^j_S *in the* ***Compute Phase*** *equals the view produced on computing* Π^j_S *with inputs* $\{\vec{v^j_i}\}_{i\in[n]}$ *and randomness* $\{r_{i,j}\}_{i\in[n]}$*. Also for each* $i \in [n]$*, check if* $d_{i,j} == \langle \vec{d}, \vec{s^i_j} \rangle$*. If the check fails, ABORT.*

Theorem 17. *For a set of n parties* $\mathcal{P} = \{P_i\}_{i\in[n]}$*, let* $\mathcal{Z}_{\mathsf{S}} \subset 2^{\mathcal{P}}$ *be an adversary structure for unbounded malicious adversaries.*

- *Let* $\Pi_{\mathsf{AuthTriples}}$ *be an n-party protocol that realizes* $\mathcal{F}_{\mathsf{AuthTriples}}$ *(Fig. 5) with semi-honest fall-back security tolerating* $\mathcal{Z}_{\mathsf{S}}$ *for adaptive adversaries.*
- *Let* Π_{online} *be an n-party protocol that can compute* $\mathcal{F}$ *with malicious fall-back security tolerating* $\mathcal{Z}_{\mathsf{S}}$*, in the* $\mathcal{F}_{\mathsf{AuthTriples}}$*-hybrid.*

Then Protocol 16 and Π_{online} *can compute any function f with malicious fall-back security (Definition 10) tolerating* $\mathcal{Z}_{\mathsf{S}}$.

The complete proof for this can be found in the full version.

Acknowledgments. Anasuya Acharya and Carmit Hazay are supported by ISF grant No. 1316/18. Carmit Hazay is also supported by the Algorand Centres of Excellence programme managed by Algorand Foundation. Any opinions, findings, and conclusions or recommendations expressed in this material are those of the author(s) and do not necessarily reflect the views of Algorand Foundation. The fourth author was supported by a JPMorgan Chase Faculty Research Award, Technology, and Humanity Fund from the McCourt School of Public Policy at Georgetown University, and a Google Research Award.

References

1. Badrinarayanan, S., Patranabis, S., Sarkar, P.: Statistical security in two-party computation revisited. In: Kiltz, E., Vaikuntanathan, V. (eds.) Theory of Cryptography. TCC 2022, LNCS, vol. 13748, pp. 181–210. Springer, Cham (2022). https://doi.org/10.1007/978-3-031-22365-5_7
2. Beaver, D., Micali, S., Rogaway, P.: The round complexity of secure protocols (extended abstract). In: ACM, pp. 503–513 (1990)
3. Ben-Efraim, A., Lindell, Y., Omri, E.: Optimizing semi-honest secure multiparty computation for the internet. In: ACM SIGSAC, pp. 578–590 (2016)
4. Ben-Or, M., Goldwasser, S., Wigderson, A.: Completeness theorems for non-cryptographic fault-tolerant distributed computation (extended abstract). In: Proceedings of the 20th Annual ACM Symposium on Theory of Computing, pp. 1–10 (1988)
5. Chaum, David: The spymasters double-agent problem. In: Brassard, Gilles (ed.) CRYPTO 1989. LNCS, vol. 435, pp. 591–602. Springer, New York (1990). https://doi.org/10.1007/0-387-34805-0_52
6. Chaum, David, Damgård, Ivan B.., van de Graaf, Jeroen: Multiparty computations ensuring privacy of each party's input and correctness of the result. In: Pomerance, Carl (ed.) CRYPTO 1987. LNCS, vol. 293, pp. 87–119. Springer, Heidelberg (1988). https://doi.org/10.1007/3-540-48184-2_7
7. Damgård, I., Pastro, V., Smart, N., Zakarias, S.: Multiparty computation from somewhat homomorphic encryption. In: Safavi-Naini, R., Canetti, R. (eds.) CRYPTO 2012. LNCS, vol. 7417, pp. 643–662. Springer, Heidelberg (2012). https://doi.org/10.1007/978-3-642-32009-5_38
8. Even, S., Goldreich, O., Lempel, A.: A randomized protocol for signing contracts. CRYPTO **1982**, 205–210 (1982)
9. Garg, S., Mukherjee, P., Pandey, O., Polychroniadou, A.: The exact round complexity of secure computation. In: Fischlin, M., Coron, J.-S. (eds.) EUROCRYPT 2016. LNCS, vol. 9666, pp. 448–476. Springer, Heidelberg (2016). https://doi.org/10.1007/978-3-662-49896-5_16
10. Hazay, C., Venkitasubramaniam, M., Weiss, M.: The price of active security in cryptographic protocols. In: Canteaut, A., Ishai, Y. (eds.) EUROCRYPT 2020. LNCS, vol. 12106, pp. 184–215. Springer, Cham (2020). https://doi.org/10.1007/978-3-030-45724-2_7
11. Hirt, M., Maurer, U.M.: Complete characterization of adversaries tolerable in secure multi-party computation (extended abstract). PODC **1997**, 25–34 (1997)
12. Ishai, Y., Katz, J., Kushilevitz, E., Lindell, Y., Petrank, E.: On achieving the "best of both worlds" in secure multiparty computation. SIAM J. Comput. **40**(1), 122–141 (2011)
13. Ishai, Y., Prabhakaran, M., Sahai, A.: Founding cryptography on oblivious transfer - efficiently. CRYPTO **2008**, 572–591 (2008)
14. Katz, J.: On achieving the "best of both worlds" in secure multiparty computation. ACM STOC **2007**, 11–20 (2007)
15. Katz, J., Ostrovsky, R.: Round-optimal secure two-party computation. In: Franklin, M. (ed.) CRYPTO 2004. LNCS, vol. 3152, pp. 335–354. Springer, Heidelberg (2004). https://doi.org/10.1007/978-3-540-28628-8_21
16. Khurana, D., Mughees, M.H.: On statistical security in two-party computation. In: Pass, R., Pietrzak, K. (eds.) TCC 2020. LNCS, vol. 12551, pp. 532–561. Springer, Cham (2020). https://doi.org/10.1007/978-3-030-64378-2_19

17. Pass, R., Wee, H.: Black-box constructions of two-party protocols from one-way functions. In: Reingold, O. (ed.) TCC 2009. LNCS, vol. 5444, pp. 403–418. Springer, Heidelberg (2009). https://doi.org/10.1007/978-3-642-00457-5_24
18. Shamir, A.: How to share a secret. Commun. ACM **22**(11), 612–613 (1979)

Perfect MPC over Layered Graphs

Bernardo David[1(✉)], Giovanni Deligios[2], Aarushi Goel[3], Yuval Ishai[4], Anders Konring[1], Eyal Kushilevitz[4], Chen-Da Liu-Zhang[3], and Varun Narayanan[4]

[1] IT University of Copenhagen, Copenhagen, Denmark
beda@itu.dk
[2] ETH Zurich, Zürich, Switzerland
[3] NTT Research, Sunnyvale, USA
[4] Technion - Israel Institute of Technology, Haifa, Israel

Abstract. The classical "BGW protocol" (Ben-Or, Goldwasser, and Wigderson, STOC 1988) shows that secure multiparty computation (MPC) among n parties can be realized with *perfect full security* if $t < n/3$ parties are corrupted. This holds against malicious adversaries in the "standard" model for MPC, where a fixed set of n parties is involved in the full execution of the protocol. However, the picture is less clear in the mobile adversary setting of Ostrovsky and Yung (PODC 1991), where the adversary may periodically "move" by uncorrupting parties and corrupting a new set of t parties. In this setting, it is unclear if full security can be achieved against an adversary that is maximally mobile, *i.e.,* moves after every round. The question is further motivated by the "You Only Speak Once" (YOSO) setting of Gentry *et al.* (Crypto 2021), where not only the adversary is mobile but also each round is executed by a disjoint set of parties. Previous positive results in this model do not achieve perfect security, and either assume probabilistic corruption and a nonstandard communication model, or only realize the weaker goal of security-with-abort. The question of matching the BGW result in these settings remained open.

In this work, we tackle the above two challenges simultaneously. We consider a *layered MPC* model, a simplified variant of the fluid MPC model of Choudhuri *et al.* (Crypto 2021). Layered MPC is an instance of standard MPC where the interaction pattern is defined by a layered graph of width n, allowing each party to send secret messages and broadcast messages only to parties in the next layer. We require perfect security against a malicious adversary who may corrupt at most t parties in each layer. Our main result is a perfect, fully secure layered MPC protocol with an optimal corruption threshold of $t < n/3$, thus extending the BGW feasibility result to the layered setting. This implies perfectly secure MPC protocols against a maximally mobile adversary.

1 Introduction

The goal of classic Secure Multiparty Computation (MPC) protocols is for a set of n mutually distrusting parties to jointly compute a function on their secret

This paper is a merged version of the papers [19,20].

H. Handschuh and A. Lysyanskaya (Eds.): CRYPTO 2023, LNCS 14081, pp. 360–392, 2023.
https://doi.org/10.1007/978-3-031-38557-5_12

inputs without revealing anything but the output of the function. The protocols are typically run in the presence of an adversary and security is guaranteed if no more than t out of the n parties in the system are compromised for the duration of the *entire protocol.* In this setting, the well known result by Ben-or, Goldwasser and Wigderson [4] (BGW) shows that it is possible to achieve *perfect full security* when $t < n/3$, *i.e.* security against an unbounded active adaptive adversary corrupting $t < n/3$ parties with guaranteed output delivery (G.O.D.).

Inspired by real-world scenarios with long-running computations where parties may recover from corruptions, Ostrovsky and Yung [41] put forward a notion of a mobile adversary that is able to compromise all parties *eventually,* but is limited to a threshold of t out of n parties at any given time. In this setting, an execution is divided in rounds that are grouped into epochs. The adversary can "move" at the onset of every epoch by choosing a new set of parties to corrupt and remains static for the remainder of the epoch. Former corrupted parties are "rebooted" into a clean initial state (or, equivalently, update their internal state and securely erase past state). In [41], it is proven that there exists a fully secure proactive MPC protocol in the presence an active mobile adversary but allowing only a small constant fraction of corrupted parties. Subsequent works [2,3,22,34] explored more efficient protocols with other security guarantees under further restrictions on the mobile adversary, but still fell short of 1-round epochs or achieving the optimal corruption threshold ($t < n/3$) of BGW.

Departing from player replaceability[1] and anonymous committees of distributed ledgers, the notion of You Only Speak Once (YOSO) MPC (introduced in [28]) takes proactive security one step further, by having a freshly elected anonymous committee of parties execute each round of the protocol. As an extra restriction, parties are only allowed to send messages once (*i.e.* when they execute their role in the protocol). However, YOSO assumes parties can use ideal *target-anonymous channels* to send messages to parties who are elected to execute a role in any future round without learning their identities. The fact that each round is executed by anonymous parties elected at random, makes the corruption model probabilistic: even though an adaptive adversary may corrupt any party at any time (up to a corruption threshold t), it only successfully corrupts a party executing a certain round with some small constant probability (given that committees are large enough). In this setting, it was shown [28] that statistically secure MPC with G.O.D. is possible when the adversary corrupts $t < n/2$ parties, albeit not for constant n due to probabilistic corruptions. Fluid MPC [13] is a variant of this model without target-anonymous channels, where parties may act in more than one round before being substituted, but the results presented in [13] fall short of full security, as they do not achieve G.O.D. Another variation was shown in SCALES [1], which allows for special clients who provide an input and receive an output to act in more than one round (while server committees may only act once), focusing on protocols with computational security.

---

[1] A term from [30] for protocols where a new set of parties executes each round.

Inspired by the original mobile adversary characterized by [41] and the recent line of work on MPC with dynamic committees [1,13,28], we ask again the question originally settled in BGW [4] but now in a more challenging setting:

Is it possible to construct MPC with dynamic committees achieving perfect full security against an adaptive rushing adversary and with optimal corruption threshold?

1.1 Our Contributions

Layered MPC. We first define layered MPC, which captures the most stringent setting in the intersection of the mobile adversary and the YOSO models. In layered MPC, parties communicate through a directed layered graph of d layers corresponding to each protocol round. Each round is executed by a unique set of n parties sitting at a layer, which is disjoint from all other sets of parties in other layers. Parties in one layer can only receive messages from parties in the immediately previous layer and send messages to the parties in the immediately next layer. We consider an active, adaptive, rushing adversary that corrupts up to t out of n parties in each layer. We write (n, t, d)-layered MPC as shorthand for a layered MPC protocol with d layers (*i.e.* rounds) of n parties out of which t may be corrupted. We provide a formalization of this model and show that layered MPC protocols can be analyzed within well established frameworks such as the real/ideal world paradigm [8,31] and Universal Composability [9].

Layered MPC is similar to maximally-Fluid MPC [13] with parties only executing one round. We show that a secure layered MPC protocol is also secure against a maximally mobile adversary [41], that moves after every round. In comparison to YOSO [28], layered MPC imposes stronger restrictions on honest parties, who cannot receive a message from a party in an arbitrary past committee or send a message to a party in an arbitrary future committee. Moreover, similar to Fluid MPC, the adversary is not restricted to probabilistic corruptions but is limited to corrupting t out n parties in each layer, allowing for threshold-optimal protocols.

Main Results. In Sect. 3 we construct basic primitives that help realize layered VSS based on CNF[2] (replicated) secret sharing. We present a nontrivial adaptation of a VSS protocol of Gennaro et al. [27] to the layered setting. The main challenge is to eliminate the repeated interaction between the parties and the dealer, which is not possible in the layered setting. While CNF-based protocols scale exponentially with n, they are simpler than their Shamir-based counterparts that we will present next, and can have efficiency advantages for small values of n, especially when settling for computational security.

Theorem 1 (CNF-Based Layered VSS). *For any n, t such that $t < n/3$, and $d \geq 5$, there exists an (n, t, d)-layered MPC protocol realizing CNF-VSS. For*

[2] In CNF-based secret sharing, the secret is first split into $\binom{n}{t}$ additive shares–a share r_T for each set $T \subset [n]$ of size t–and party i receives all shares r_T such that $i \notin T$.

$d = O(1)$ and secrets of length ℓ, the protocol requires $\ell \cdot 2^{O(n)}$ bits of communication, counting both point-to-point messages and broadcast. When settling for computational *security with perfect correctness and using a black-box PRG with seed length λ, there is a protocol with $\lambda \cdot 2^{O(n)} + O(n\ell)$ bits of communication.*

In Sect. 4 we build on the above VSS protocol to obtain a *general* layered MPC protocol based on CNF secret sharing. The protocol applies to layered arithmetic circuits, in which each layer of the circuit only takes inputs from the previous layer. Every circuit of depth D can be converted to a layered circuit with D layers, incurring at most a quadratic but typically (nearly) linear overhead to the circuit size. Building on a constant-round protocol from [17], in the full version of this paper [19] we describe how to amortize the overhead of CNF secret sharing by settling for computational security.

Theorem 2 (CNF-Based Layered MPC). *Let f be an n-party functionality computed by a layered arithmetic circuit C over a finite ring, with D layers and M gates. Then, for any $t < n/3$, there is an $(n, t, O(D))$-layered MPC protocol for f. The communication consists of $2^{O(n)} \cdot M$ ring elements. Alternatively, settling for* computational *security with perfect correctness and using a black-box PRG with seed length λ, there is a $(n, t, O(1))$-layered MPC protocol for a Boolean circuit (i.e., the ring is $\mathbb{F}_2$) with M gates with $\lambda \cdot 2^{O(n)} + O(n^5 \cdot M)$ bits of communication.*

While the CNF-based protocols are relatively simple and have concrete efficiency benefits for small values of n, they do not yield a general feasibility result that scales polynomially with n. In Sect. 5 we establish such a result using (the bivariate version of) Shamir's secret-sharing scheme.

Theorem 3 (Efficient Layered MPC). *Let f be an n-party functionality computed by a layered arithmetic circuit C over a finite field $\mathbb{F}$, with D layers and M gates. Then, for any $t < n/3$, there is a polynomial-time $(n, t, O(D))$-layered MPC protocol for f. More concretely, the communication consists of $M \cdot O(n^9)$ field elements.*

Further, in Sect. 6, we present a computationally secure, efficient layered protocol that achieves G.O.D. against adversaries who can corrupt $t < n/2$ parties in each layer.

Theorem 4 (Efficient Layered MPC for $t < n/2$). *Let f be an n-party functionality computed by a layered arithmetic circuit C over a finite field $\mathbb{F}$, with D levels and M gates. Then, for any $t < n/2$, there is an $(n, t, O(D))$-layered MPC protocol for f assuming non-interactive linearly-homomorphic equivocal commitments. The communication complexity is $M \cdot O(n^9)$ field elements over the point-to-point channels and $M \cdot O(n^5)$ field elements + $M \cdot O(n^{10} \cdot \lambda)$ bits over the broadcast channels, where λ is the security parameter.*

Proactive MPC. The original concept of proactive MPC put forward by [41] considered an adversary that has the ability to corrupt a fresh set of parties in *every* round of the protocol. We refer to such an adversary as maximally mobile. This notion is formally defined in the full version of the paper [19], while protocols that can thwart such an adversary are called maximally proactive. We show that a secure layered MPC protocol is a maximally proactively secure protocol. We also remark on an alternate and stronger notion of maximal adversary in the full version [19, Remark 2], against which perfectly secure VSS and MPC are impossible with the optimal threshold of $t < n/3$ corruptions in each layer. This allows us to extend our security analysis from the layered to the proactive setting. The full version [19] defines maximally Proactive Secret Sharing and MPC and we obtain the following threshold-optimal result by combining Theorem 3 and [19, Lemma 1].

Corollary 1 (Perfectly Secure Maximally Proactive MPC). *Let f be an n-party functionality computed by a layered circuit C over a field $\mathbb{F}$, with D layers. Then, for $t < n/3$, there is an efficient maximally proactive MPC protocol computing f in $r = O(D)$ rounds.*

Secure Message Transmission and Broadcast. Sending a message to a party that acts in an arbitrary future round is a recurring problem in settings such as layered MPC. In YOSO [28] it is circumvented by assuming target-anonymous channels, an ideal resource that allows a party in round r to send a message to a party who is elected to perform a certain role in round $r' > r + 1$ without learning its identity. We take steps to obtain a similar primitive (although without anonymity guarantees) by relying only on the parties in the layered graph to carry the message forward, despite our much more restrictive interaction pattern that precludes such communication. In Sect. 3.1 we provide a thorough analysis of an important primitive in layered MPC called *Future Messaging*. The functionality f_{FM} is described in Sect. 3.1 and presented in [19, Figure 3.1]. Future Messaging takes as input a message m from a sender in $\mathcal{L}_0$ and, if the sender is honest, the message m arrives at the recipient. In the context of layered MPC this primitive is close to an instance of 1-way Secure Message Transmission (SMT) over a directed graph. We show that it is possible to self-compose this primitive to carry a message from a sender in $\mathcal{L}_0$ to a designated receiver in $\mathcal{L}_d$ for $d > 1$. The following theorem characterizes our construction.

Theorem 5 (Restatement of Theorem 7). *For any $d > 0$, any n and t where $t < n/3$, and message domain M, there exists a protocol Π_{FM} that realizes f_{FM} from $\mathcal{L}_0$ to $\mathcal{L}_d$ with perfect t-security and communication complexity $O(n^{\lceil \log d \rceil} \log |M|)$.*

Using the layered protocol for Shamir VSS and resharing, which we construct building on Future Messaging, we can make the dependence of the communication cost of Future Messaging on d linear. This is achieved by having the sender verifiably secret the message using VSS and then reshare it repeatedly until reaching the layer previous to that of the receiver, at which point the shareholders of the value can reveal the message to the receiver by transferring all its shares. Communication cost of VSS and of resharing across a constant number of layers is $\mathsf{poly}(n)$, making the communication of Future Messaging linear in d.

The layered model allows for layer-to-layer broadcast: any party in $\mathcal{L}_a$ may broadcast to parties in $\mathcal{L}_{a+1}$. It turns out that this assumption is necessary, since we prove that deterministic broadcast in the setting of layered MPC is possible only if $t = 0$. Our analysis is shown in the full version [19], where we cast the result of [26] to the setting of layered MPC and obtain the following result.

Theorem 6. *Deterministic perfect Broadcast in the setting of layered MPC is possible iff* $t = 0$.

This limitation can be overcome by the use of randomization. Several works achieve broadcast in the honest-majority setting with overwhelming probability after a number of rounds that is linear in the security parameter, without setup tolerating $t < n/3$ corruptions [23], and with different types of setup tolerating $t < n/2$ corruptions [24,25,29,36].

These protocols can be ported to the layered setting at the cost of decreasing the corruption threshold by a factor that is linear in the security parameter. This is done by naively porting the protocol to the layered setting after ensuring that the parties 'persist' across all the layers by simply forwarding the view of each party to their counterpart in the next layer. When the adversary corrupts t' parties in each layer, by the end of the protocol, the adversary would corrupt at most $t = t' \cdot O(\kappa)$ parties executing different party roles, for security parameter κ. If the total number of corruptions that the original protocol tolerates is bounded by $t < n/3$ (resp. $t < n/2$), we have that the ported protocol remains secure. Obtaining the optimal corruption threshold $t' < n/3$ without setup, or $t' < n/2$ with setup, for broadcast is beyond the scope of this paper.

1.2 Related Work

We summarize the relationship between previous works in similar settings and our results in Table 1. We discuss further related works below.

Proactive Secret Sharing (PSS). PSS protocols aim at solving the problem that shares learned by the adversary are compromised forever by resharing the secret periodically. The *static group* setting where resharing is done among the same set of parties is considered in [2,3,11,34]. However, this is often insufficient since it assumes a world where a server never fails to the extend that it cannot recover again. The setting of *dynamic groups* where resharing is done towards a different (possibly disjoint) set of parties is considered in [21,22,44]. Finally, proactive techniques in asynchronous settings have been treated in [7,43].

Permissionless Networks. In the context of permissionless networks where parties are allowed to join and leave as they wish, the *dynamic group* property has taken on a new meaning. The notion of player replaceability (where the set of parties get replaced in every round) has previously been studied in the context of consensus primitives [6,12,40,42]. The recent focus on this setting spurred new interest in (dynamic) proactive techniques [32,38]. Particularly interesting, is the

Table 1. Protocols realizing primitives in the most extreme proactive settings. (*protocol security relies on the adversary only doing probabilistic corruption, †assumes access to ideal target-anonymous channels for future messaging)

Results for Maximally Proactive MPC with Dynamic Committees					
Functionality	Reference	Level	Security	Complexity	Threshold
Future Messaging	Section 3.1	perfect	full	$\mathsf{poly}(n)$	$t < n/3$
VSS	[5]	computational	full	$\mathsf{poly}(n)$	$t < n/4^*$
	Section 4.2	perfect	full	$2^{O(n)}$	$t < n/3$
	Section 5	perfect	full	$\mathsf{poly}(n)$	$t < n/3$
MPC	[28] (YOSO)	statistical	full (w/setup†)	$\mathsf{poly}(n)$	$t < n/2^*$
	[13] (Fluid)	statistical	w/abort	$\mathsf{poly}(n)$	$t < n/2$
	[41]	perfect	full	$\mathsf{poly}(n)$	$t < n/d$
	Section 4.4	perfect	full	$2^{O(n)}$	$t < n/3$
	Section 5	perfect	full	$\mathsf{poly}(n)$	$t < n/3$
	Section 6	computational	full	$\mathsf{poly}(n)$	$t < n/2$

definition of evolving committee secret sharing [5] that places the responsibility of keeping a tolerable corruption threshold on the protocol designer.

Maximally PSS and MPC with Dynamic Committees. Recently, a number of works [1,13,28,30] have considered extreme settings with dynamic committees, where each round of a protocol is executed by a new set of parties considering maximally mobile (or even adaptive) adversaries. In YOSO [28], an ideal mechanism guarantees that a set of anonymous parties is selected at random to execute each round, effectively limiting the adversary to probabilistic corruptions. Hence, YOSO is incompatible with settings where n and t are constant. Moreover, parties have access to ideal target-anonymous channels allowing for communication to *any* party in the future. Hence, results in the YOSO model do not directly translate to our setting even if we settle for non-optimal corruption thresholds, as YOSO protocols may crucially rely on the ability to send messages across many layers. For example, in the information theoretical signature protocol of [28, Section 3.3], a cut-and-choose mechanism is realized assuming that a sender can commit to a set of message authentication codes (MACs) by sending them directly to a receiver, after which verifiers broadcast random subsets of keys, which the receiver uses to check these MACs. The security of this technique crucially relies on the fact that using ideal target-anonymous channels guarantees that the sender cannot changes the MACs sent to the user *after* the verifiers announce the checking keys. This technique does not work in the layered MPC setting with our weaker Future Messaging protocol, which does not commit a corrupted sender to the messages it transmits to future layers.

Closest to layered MPC is Fluid MPC [13] in its most extreme configuration (fully fluid), where parties can execute a single round of the protocol and immediately leave but are not necessarily selected anonymously and at random. Curiously, one of the goals of Fluid MPC is maintaining a small state complexity. In particular, the computation and communication of each committee in Fluid

MPC is independent of the size of the circuit. While this is attractive, we do not make any such claims and we also only consider already layered circuits[3]. Finally, a crucial difference is that the known protocols for Fluid MPC only enjoy security-with-abort while we aim for full security.

While the use of an arbitrary interaction pattern in layered MPC is similar to [33], our focus is on a specific interaction pattern capturing extreme cases of MPC with dynamic committees and a maximally mobile adversary.

1.3 Technical Overview

The goal of this paper is to build a layered MPC protocol that takes inputs from a set of clients in the input layer and securely delivers a function of the inputs to a set of output clients in a later layer. For $t < n/3$, we present two layered protocols for general MPC with t-security: a simple but inefficient construction based on CNF secret sharing and a more complex but efficient construction based on Shamir secret sharing.

Owing to a highly restrictive communication pattern and the presence of a very powerful adversary, implementing layered MPC with optimal corruption threshold presents several interesting challenges. The most apparent is the complete prohibition of interaction, as parties executing the protocol do not persist. We emulate a limited kind of interaction by having a party who wants to speak a second time hide all possible messages it may want to convey in a future layer and selectively reveal the appropriate message to the next layer. In such cases, it is imperative to the security of the party that only the appropriate message is revealed while the other messages are effectively destroyed. Interestingly, realizing this limited form of interaction takes us a long way in implementing layered MPC. This leads us to the first primitive we construct in this presentation:

Future Messaging. Future messaging allows a party (sender) to securely send a message to another party (receiver) situated in a later layer. To send a message two layers down, the sender can secret share the message onto the next layer using any t-secure secret sharing scheme; parties in the next layer can then forward these shares to the receiver who can recover the message by robust reconstruction of the received shares. We extend this intuition to allow a sender to securely send a message to a designated receiver in any future layer. This protocol is non-commiting; hence, a corrupt sender can choose the message to deliver to the receiver based on the adversary's view until the layer in which the receiver is situated. Effectively, future messaging allows rushing till the receiver's layer! Future messaging allows a sender to distribute a secret sharing of a value onto a future layer; parties in this layer can disclose this value to a receiver (or broadcast it to all parties) in the next layer based on a unanimous decision (potentially depending on computation that was carried out in an intermediate

[3] The inherent issue with state complexity originates from a common misconception (see fx [18]) that *any* general arithmetic circuit can be transformed into a layered circuit with same depth and only linear overhead in width.

layer). In this manner, we emulate the aforementioned (limited) interaction by the sender.

MPC using CNF Shares. Equipped with a protocol for future messaging, we set out to build a layered protocol for verifiable secret sharing (VSS). We will then follow the standard approach for secure function evaluation, where a layered arithmetic circuit computing the function is evaluated by progressively and securely computing secret shares of the value on the output wire of each gate using the secret shares of the values on the input wires, finally revealing the values on the output wires of the circuit to the output clients.

Verifiable CNF Secret Sharing. To achieve verifiable CNF secret sharing, it suffices to implement a seemingly simpler primitive, namely future multicast, which allows a dealer to securely send a message to a designated subset of receivers in a later output layer with the guarantee that all receivers get the same message even if the sender is corrupt. Verifiable CNF secret sharing is achieved by having the dealer split the secret into $\binom{n}{t}$ additive shares (a share r_T for each $n-t$ sized set $T \subset [n]$) and multicast r_T to all output clients in T.

While implementing multicast, we encounter many challenges inherent to layered MPC. When realizing multicast, the sender sends the same message to a (sub)set of parties in the next layer, who raise a complaint if they receive distinct messages, in which case the sender publicly discloses the message. Clearly, this sequence of interactions is non-trivial to realize in a layered network, where the sender cannot speak a second time and the parties in a layer cannot communicate with each other. Hence, we use a weak notion of secure addition (See Sect. 3.2) to allow the receiving parties to securely reveal the difference between the values they received to all parties two layers down. If the difference is non-zero for any pair of values, the layer that learns this difference collectively decides to disclose the sender's message using the trick we previously outlined.

Having implemented verifiable CNF secret sharing, we proceed to secure computation of arithmetic gates. Since the secret sharing is linear, addition and multiplication-by-constant gates can be computed by local processing, which leaves us with the secure computation of the multiplication gate that takes the secret shares of two values and computes a secret sharing of their product.

Multiplication. Our layered protocol for multiplication is built by porting the classic protocol for secure multiplication in the standard (non-layered) setting. In this process, we face all the challenges we encountered while realizing future multicast. Suppose a value is secret shared on a layer and is also required in another layer. Naively replicating the same share in the later layer is insecure since the adversary can reconstruct the secret by corrupting t parties in each of these layers and obtaining $2t$ shares. We get around this problem with a simple trick that avoids using a full-fledged protocol for resharing CNF shares.

We realize secure computation by evaluating a layered arithmetic circuit using the protocols we constructed so far. To properly process the layered circuit, we rely on the invariant that the secret shares of the values on all the input wires to any layer of the circuit are simultaneously available on the same layer of the layered network. However, secret shares of the output of a linear gate (addition or multiplication-by-constant) can be computed locally while those of a multiplication gate using our protocol consume several layers. To keep the invariant, we need the outputs of the linear gates to be available on the output layer of multiplication. Once again, the shares of the outputs cannot be naively secret shared. Instead, we attach a multiplication gate to the output wire of linear gate that takes identity as the other input; this ensures that the shares of the values on all output wires are available simultaneously on the same layer.

Composability of Layered Protocols. We use simpler layered protocols as subroutines for building more complex ones. For example, the multiplication protocol uses a protocol for verifiable secret sharing (among others) as a subroutine. Hence, it is necessary that the concurrent execution of layered protocols preserve their security guarantees under concurrent composition. We refrain from first proving UC security of our building blocks and then using modular composition theorems since such an analysis will be cumbersome over a synchronous layered graph. Instead, we prove the security of our protocols by constructing simulators and carefully arguing their security. We establish game based properties of layered protocols that are preserved when they are used as subroutines and prove the security using hybrid arguments that exploit these properties. Finally, a few of our constructions make exclusively sequential (non-concurrent) calls to subroutines that have been proven to be standalone secure; in such instances, we use the sequential composition theorem of Canetti [8] to argue security (see the security proofs for future messaging and secure function evaluation protocols).

Efficient MPC using Shamir Secret Sharing. We build layered protocols whose communication complexity scales polynomially with the number of parties per layer. This is achieved by porting the cannonical secure function evaluation protocol using Shamir secret shares into the layered model. To achieve this, we first develop a layered protocol for verifiable Shamir secret sharing.

Verifiable Shamir Secret Sharing. We "port" the classic protocol for VSS in the standard setting to the layered setting using the tools we developed in the previous sections along the way to tackle the usual challenges faced in the process. At the end of this process, the parties in the layer right after the input layer hold the purported shares of the dealer's secret and parties 5 layers down publicly hold the updates to the purported shares such that, they together form a valid secret sharing. The parties cannot transfer these shares to the shareholders in the output layer without causing duplication. To get around this, the dealer secret shares coefficients of a random degree-t polynomial they wish to use for Shamir secret sharing; the evaluation of the polynomial at distinct points is computed using linear operations and securely delivered to the shareholders in the output layer. This ensures privacy of the secret when the dealer is honest.

Equipped with a layered protocol for Shamir VSS, we use known techniques to realize resharing which allows a layer holding valid shares of a value to securely deliver fresh shares of the same value to a later layer. Using VSS and resharing, porting protocols for secure multiplication and then secure function evaluation into the layered setting is relatively straightforward. We depart form the protocol for general MPC provided in [16]. The protocol uses a form of reinforced secret sharing where the shares of a secret are further secret shared among the shareholders, which is straightforward to implement using VSS and resharing.

2 Preliminaries

2.1 Layered MPC

A layered MPC protocol can be viewed as a special case of standard MPC with a general adversary structure, specialized in the following way: (1) the interaction pattern is defined by a layered graph; (2) the adversary can corrupt at most t parties in each layer. This is illustrated in full version [19, Fig. 1] and formalized below.

Definition 1 (Layered MPC). *Let n, t, d be positive integers. An (n, t, d)-* layered protocol *is a synchronous protocol Π over secure point-to-point channels and a broadcast channel, with the following special features.*

- **Parties.** *There are $N = n(d+1)$ parties partitioned into $d+1$ layers $\mathcal{L}_i$, $0 \leq i \leq d$, where $|\mathcal{L}_i| = n$. Parties in the first layer $\mathcal{L}_0$ and the last layer $\mathcal{L}_d$ are referred to as* input clients *and* output clients, *respectively.*
- **Interaction pattern.** *The interaction consists of d rounds, where in round i parties in $\mathcal{L}_{i-1}$ may send messages to parties in $\mathcal{L}_i$ over secure point-to-point channels. By default, we additionally allow each party in $\mathcal{L}_{i-1}$ to send a broadcast message to all parties in $\mathcal{L}_i$.*
- **Functionalities.** *We consider functionalities f that take inputs from input clients and deliver outputs to output clients.*
- **Adversaries.** *We consider adversaries who may corrupt any number of input and output clients, and additionally corrupt t parties in each intermediate layer $\mathcal{L}_i$, $0 < i < d$. We consider active, rushing, adaptive*[4] *adversaries.*

We say that a protocol Π is a layered MPC protocol for f *if it realizes f in the standard sense of (standalone) secure MPC with general adversary structures [8, 31, 35]. We require* perfect full security *(with guaranteed output delivery).*

Remark 1 (Generalized layered MPC). The above definition is meant to give the simplest formalization of the core problem we study. It can be naturally extended to allow a different number of parties n_i and a different corruption threshold t_i in each layer (our main feasibility result extends to the case where $t_i < n_i/3$), and to allow inputs and outputs from parties in intermediate layers. Our strict notion of perfect full security can also be relaxed in the natural ways. In some cases, we will present efficiency improvements that achieve *computational* (full) security with perfect correctness, meaning that the effect of a computationally unbounded adversary on the outputs of honest parties can be perfectly simulated.

[4] In the coming sections our security analysis is with respect to non-adaptive adversaries for simplicity. In Sect. 2.2 we justify this leap appealing to the work of [10].

The Need for Ideal Broadcast: In the full version [19, Appendix 3] we show that broadcast for layered MPC is impossible if $t > 0$. Hence, we must assume ideal broadcast.

Layered MPC Implies Proactive Security: In the [19, Section 2.2] we precisely define maximally proactive security and prove that it is implied by layered MPC. Also see Remark 2 in the section that addresses a natural and stronger notion of maximally proactive security.

2.2 Adaptivity and Composability in Layered MPC

Let Π_g be a layered protocol realizing functionality g with standalone t-security, and let Π_f be another layered protocol in which Π_g is used as a subroutine to implement g. Suppose the layers where g is computed using Π_g do not execute any other protocol in parallel; i.e., only a single invocation of Π_g is made in such layers. Then, to prove the security of Π_f, it is sufficient to show that Π_f is t-secure in the so called g-hybrid model, where the calls to the sub routine Π_g is replaced with calls to the functionality g itself. This allows for a modular construction and analysis of protocols.

Formally, the g-hybrid model involves a communication protocol as well as calls to functionality g. Suppose l is the designated output layer of g. In a protocol Π_f in g-hybrid model, parties in layer $i-1$ can send their inputs to functionality g in round i. The functionality will deliver the output of g to receivers in the output layer l in round l which may be used by the parties in executing Π_f.

The following proposition adapts the sequential composability theorem of [8] to the layered setting. The proposition holds simply because a layered protocol with d layers and n parties per layer is essentially a nd party protocol with communication between a pair of adjacent layers in every round.

Proposition 1 (Sequential Composability for layered protocols). *Suppose a (n, t, d)-layered protocol Θ implements a functionality g with perfect standalone t-security [8,31]. Suppose a layered protocol Π with input layer $\mathcal{L}_0$ and output layer $\mathcal{L}'_d, d' > d$ invokes Θ as a subroutine from $\mathcal{L}_a$ to $\mathcal{L}_{a+d}$, where $0 \leq a < a + d \leq d'$. Π making subroutine calls to Θ is t-secure if it is t-secure in the g-hybrid model.*

Universal Composability. As discussed in Definition 1, we are interested in realizing functionalities f that take input from the input clients in layer $\mathcal{L}_0$ by default and deliver outputs to the output clients in the last layer (layer $\mathcal{L}_d$) of a layered network. We develop a protocol for computing general functionalities in the stand-alone model showing perfect security by means of a straight-line black-box simulator and, thus, we can invoke Theorem 1.2 in [37] and argue that the protocol is, in fact, secure under the definition of universal composability[5].

[5] While we can meaningfully argue that the final protocol for computing general functionalities is UC-secure, we do not treat individual components of this protocol in a UC manner. This would require a significant modelling effort of communication and synchronization for layered MPC and would be counterproductive in our effort to present layered MPC as a simple special case of secure MPC as in [8,31].

On Adaptive Adversaries. In Definition 1, we define layered MPC in the presence of a *rushing* and *adaptive* adversary. Clearly, this extra power for the adversary separates layered MPC from maximally proactive MPC and shows that layered MPC is strictly stronger. Looking forward, we will, however, only analyze the layered protocols with respect to static (and rushing) adversaries. To argue adaptive security, we need to be able to simulate even when the real world adversary corrupts a party midway through the protocol. [10] showed an exotic example of a perfectly secure protocol with static security against malicious adversaries but without adaptive security. Fortunately, all our protocols are based on linear secret sharing which makes extending our analysis to layered (*and* adaptive) MPC significantly easier.

As an example, consider a simulator's job when a set of parties $\mathcal{C}$ is already corrupted during a protocol execution and a new party P_i has just been added to this set. First, the simulator needs to construct a complete view (including the input) of the honest P_i that is consistent with all messages exchanged with the ideal functionality and communication with parties in $\mathcal{C}$. Secondly, the simulator's state needs to be "extended" with this new information. Concretely, the state should be as if P_i has been corrupted from the start of the protocol but behaved honestly until this point. In our protocols for perfect layered MPC, we let the simulator handle this challenge using conditional sampling. Since parties in $\mathcal{C}$ will only hold shares of a linear secret sharing scheme, even if the newly corrupted P_i is the dealer of such shares we can simulate the randomness used in the sharing algorithm. This is feasible since as long as the shares of $n-t$ honest parties are fixing the secret, the simulator is free to change the randomness to be consistent with the shares of parties in $\mathcal{C}$. Finally we note that when referring to computationally secure (PRG-based) protocols, we either need to settle for non-adaptive security or implement the PRG in the random oracle model.

3 Basic Primitives

We introduce the basic primitives Future Messaging (f_{FM}) and Multiparty Addition (f_{add}) that serve as building blocks for later constructions. In the layered model, Future Messaging is a primitive which allows an input client S to securely send a message m to an output client R in a later layer. Multiparty Addition allows a subset of parties in a layer to broadcast the sum of their inputs to all parties in a later layer.

3.1 Future Messaging

Future Messaging emulates a *secure channel* between a sender S and a receiver R in a future layer. As such, the primitive is similar[6] to Secure Message Transmission (SMT) over the specific directed and layered network where intermediate nodes may take part in the protocol and not merely forward messages from adjacent nodes. The functionality is formalized in full version [19, Figure 3.1].

[6] The instance of Future Messaging with honest sender in $\mathcal{L}_0$ and honest receiver in $\mathcal{L}_2$ is equivalent to perfect 1-way SMT.

Parallel Composition. Functionality f_{FM} delivers a message from a sender to a receiver in a later layer $\mathcal{L}_d$. However, when our protocol implementing f_{FM} is composed in parallel, the resulting functionality is not the natural parallel composition of f_{FM} which takes the input from each sender to each receiver and delivers them.

In fact, this functionality is impossible to realize even in the trivial case of messaging from one layer to the very next using the provided secure communication link. As an example, suppose communication from $\mathsf{S}_1 \in \mathcal{L}_0$ to $\mathsf{R}_1 \in \mathcal{L}_1$ and from $\mathsf{S}_2 \in \mathcal{L}_0$ to $\mathsf{R}_2 \in \mathcal{L}_1$ are composed in parallel. Now, a rushing adversary corrupting S_1 and R_2 can collect the message from S_2 to R_2 and set this as the message from S_1 to R_1. Interestingly, this limitation persists when parallely composing our protocol for realizing f_{FM} from $\mathcal{L}_0$ to $\mathcal{L}_d$ (even for $d > 1$) with t-security for $t < n/3$. See the full version [19] for more details.

We capture the functionality realized by parallel execution of our future messaging protocol using a corruption aware functionality in Fig. 3.1.

Figure 3.1 (Corruption-aware parallel Future Messaging functionality f^n_{FM})

PUBLIC PARAMETERS: Senders $\mathsf{S}_1, \dots, \mathsf{S}_n \in \mathcal{L}_0$, receivers $\mathsf{R}_1, \dots, \mathsf{R}_n \in \mathcal{L}_d$ where $d > 0$. The domain $M_{i,j}$ of message from S_i to R_j.
SECRET INPUTS: Each S_i wants to send each R_j a message $m_{(i,j)} \in M_{i,j}$.
ADDITIONAL INPUT TO FUNCTIONALITY: Set of corrupted parties $\mathcal{I}_0 \subseteq \mathcal{L}_0$ and corrupted receivers $\mathcal{I}_d \subseteq \mathcal{L}_d$.

1. For each honest $\mathsf{S}_i \notin \mathcal{I}_0$ and each $\mathsf{R}_j \in \mathcal{L}_d$, f^n_{FM} receives message $m_{(i,j)}$ from S_i to R_j.
2. For each honest $\mathsf{S}_i \notin \mathcal{I}_0$ and corrupt $\mathsf{R}_j \in \mathcal{I}_d$, f^n_{FM} forwards $m_{(i,j)}$ to the (ideal) adversary.
3. For each corrupt $\mathsf{S}_i \in \mathcal{I}_0$ and each $\mathsf{R}_j \in \mathcal{L}_d$, f^n_{FM} receives from the (ideal) adversary the message $m_{(i,j)}$ that S_i wants to send to R_j.
4. For each $\mathsf{S}_i \in \mathcal{L}_0$ and $\mathsf{R}_j \in \mathcal{L}_d$, f^n_{FM} sends $m_{(i,j)}$ to R_j as message from S_i.

A Protocol for Future Messaging. Realizing Future Messaging from a sender in $\mathcal{L}_0$ to a receiver in $\mathcal{L}_1$ is trivial since there is a secure communication link between any such pair.

A $(n, t, 2)$-layered protocol for Future Messaging from a sender in $\mathcal{L}_0$ to a receiver in $\mathcal{L}_2$ can be achieved as follows. Sender $\mathsf{S} \in \mathcal{L}_0$ shares the message m among the parties in $\mathcal{L}_1$ using a t-secure robust secret sharing scheme. The parties in $\mathcal{L}_1$ forward their shares to the receiver $\mathsf{R} \in \mathcal{L}_2$ who uses the reconstruction algorithm on the received shares to recover the message. By t-security of the secret sharing scheme, an adversary corrupting at most t parties in $\mathcal{L}_1$ learns nothing about the message. However, since the secret sharing scheme is t-robust, R correctly reconstructs m even if at most t corrupt parties send incorrect shares.

This idea can be generalized to construct Future Messaging from $\mathcal{L}_0$ to $\mathcal{L}_d$ for any $d > 2$ using the secure (n, t, ℓ)-layered protocol for Future Messaging from $\mathcal{L}_0$ to $\mathcal{L}_\ell$ and then from $\mathcal{L}_\ell$ to $\mathcal{L}_d$. Here, ℓ is any number such that $0 < \ell < d$; specifically, we can take $\ell = \lfloor \frac{d}{2} \rfloor$. This is achieved as follows. The sender $\mathsf{S} \in \mathcal{L}_0$ produces shares $(s_1, \ldots, s_n)$ of its message m, and sends the share s_i to the i-th party (P_i^ℓ) in $\mathcal{L}_\ell$ using Future Messaging from $\mathcal{L}_0$ to $\mathcal{L}_\ell$. Each party in level ℓ forwards its share to the receiver using Future Messaging from $\mathcal{L}_\ell$ to $\mathcal{L}_d$.

This protocol can be executed in parallel, for each sender in $\mathcal{L}_0$ and receiver in $\mathcal{L}_d$, in order to realize the corruption aware (parallel) functionality f^n_{FM} (Fig. 3.1) from $\mathcal{L}_0$ to $\mathcal{L}_d$ using f^n_{FM} from $\mathcal{L}_0$ to $\mathcal{L}_\ell$ and from $\mathcal{L}_\ell$ to $\mathcal{L}_d$. The protocol is formally described in Fig. 3.2.

Figure 3.2 (Π^n_{FM}, an (n, t, d)-layered protocol realizing f^n_{FM})

PUBLIC PARAMETERS: Senders $\mathsf{S}_1, \ldots, \mathsf{S}_n \in \mathcal{L}_0$, receivers $\mathsf{R}_1, \ldots, \mathsf{R}_n \in \mathcal{L}_d$ where $d > 1$.
SECRET INPUTS: Each S_i wants to send $m_{(i,j)} \in M$ to a each receiver R_j.
RESOURCES: f^n_{FM} (with message domain M^n) from $\mathcal{L}_0$ to $\mathcal{L}_\ell$ and $\mathcal{L}_\ell$ to $\mathcal{L}_d$.

1. Each $\mathsf{S}_i, i \in [n]$ samples $(s_{(i,j),1}, \ldots, s_{(i,j),n}) \leftarrow \mathsf{Sh}(m_{(i,j)})$ for each $j \in [n]$.
2. For $k \in [n]$, S_i sets the message to $\mathsf{P}^\ell_k \in \mathcal{L}_\ell$ in f^n_{FM} from $\mathcal{L}_0$ to $\mathcal{L}_\ell$ to $(s_{(i,1),k}, \ldots, s_{(i,n),k})$.
3. Each party $\mathsf{P}^\ell_k : k \in [n]$ receives $(\hat{s}_{(i,1),k}, \ldots, \hat{s}_{(i,n),k})$ from $\mathsf{S}_i, i \in [n]$ (delivered by f^n_{FM}).
4. $\mathsf{P}^\ell_k, k \in [n]$ sets the message to $\mathsf{R}_j \in \mathcal{L}_d$ in f^n_{FM} from $\mathcal{L}_\ell$ to $\mathcal{L}_d$ to $(\hat{s}_{(1,j),k}, \ldots, \hat{s}_{(n,j),k})$.
5. Each receiver $\mathsf{R}_j : j \in [n]$ computes the message from $\mathsf{S}_i : i \in [n]$ as $\mathsf{Rec}(\hat{s}_{(i,j),1}, \ldots, \hat{s}_{(i,j),n})$.

Lemma 1 (Layered protocol for f^n_{FM}). *Let* $(\mathsf{Sh}, \mathsf{Rec})$ *be a robust* (t, n) *secret-sharing scheme [19, Definition 6], the* (n, t, d)*-layered protocol in Fig. 3.2 realizes the functionality* f^n_{FM} *in Fig. 3.1 with perfect security for* $t < n/3$.

We formally describe the simulator and provide a formal proof in the full version [19].

Going forward, we will focus on the (non-parallel) Future Messaging functionality f_{FM} [19, Figure 3.1] from a designated sender in a layer to a designated receiver in a later layer. This is, indeed, a special case of f^n_{FM} $(n = 1)$ and a protocol was outlined informally in the beginning of this section.

Theorem 7. *For any* $d > 0$, *and message domain* M, *there exists an* (n, t, d)*-layered protocol* Π_{FM} *that realizes* f_{FM} *from a sender in* $\mathcal{L}_0$ *to a receiver in* $\mathcal{L}_d$ *with communication complexity* $O(n^{\lceil \log d \rceil} \log |M|)$.

Proof. For $d = 1$, there is a trivial protocol that realizes f_{FM} in which the sender sends the message (from a domain M) directly to the receiver using the provided secure communication link. The communication complexity of realizing this is simply $\log |M|$.

Suppose $d > 1$ and $\ell = \lfloor \frac{d}{2} \rfloor$. Consider protocols Π and Π' that realize functionalities f^n_{FM} from $\mathcal{L}_0$ to $\mathcal{L}_\ell$ and from $\mathcal{L}_\ell$ to $\mathcal{L}_d$, respectively for message domain M^n. In the protocol in Fig. 3.2, the f^n_{FM} from $\mathcal{L}_0$ to $\mathcal{L}_\ell$ and f^n_{FM} from $\mathcal{L}_\ell$ to $\mathcal{L}_d$ are called, sequentially. Hence, by the sequential modular composition theorem for layered protocols in Proposition 1, the protocol obtained by replacing these oracle calls with subroutine calls to Π and Π', is secure against any layered adversary that corrupts at most t parties in layers 1 to $\ell - 1$ and $\ell + 1$ to $d - 1$ in addition to corrupting at most t parties in layer ℓ. The communication complexity of the resulting protocol is the sum of communication complexity of Π and Π'. The statement of the theorem is obtained by recursion using this observation and the existence of the trivial protocol for realizing f_{FM} from $\mathcal{L}_0$ to $\mathcal{L}_1$. □

Corollary 2. *Suppose Π_{FM} is a (n, t, d)-layered protocol realizing f_{FM} from a sender $\mathsf{S} \in \mathcal{L}_0$ to a receiver $\mathsf{R} \in \mathcal{L}_d$. The following statements hold when Π_{FM} is executed in the presence of any adversary $\mathcal{A}$ described in Definition 1:*

(a) If S is honest, R correctly recovers the input of S at the end of Π_{FM}.
(b) When S and R are honest, and for any pair of inputs $m, m' \in M$,

$$\mathrm{ADVR}_{\Pi_{\mathsf{FM}},\mathcal{A}}(m) \equiv \mathrm{ADVR}_{\Pi_{\mathsf{FM}},\mathcal{A}}(m').$$

3.2 Multiparty Addition

The Multiparty Addition functionality f_{add} takes inputs from a set of input clients and delivers the sum of the inputs to all output clients in $\mathcal{L}_2$. However, f_{add} allows the adversary to choose the inputs of corrupt input clients after learning the sum of the inputs of the honest clients. Hence, if at least one party with input to f_{add} is corrupt, the adversary can choose the value that f_{add} outputs. Note that, this necessarily makes f_{add} a corruption aware functionality. The functionality is formally defined in [19, Figure 3.4] and can be realized by an $(n, t, 2)$-layered protocol as outlined below.

Each party in $\mathsf{S}_i \in S$ secret shares its input x_i to the parties in next layer using a t-robust linear secret sharing scheme. Parties in $\mathcal{L}_1$ broadcasts the sum of their respective shares for each of the inputs. Each party in $\mathcal{L}_2$ recovers the output by running the reconstruction algorithm on the received sum of shares. A formal description of the protocol is presented in the full version [19]. Clearly, all honest parties output the same value at the end of the protocol, irrespective of the number of corruption in S. If all parties in S are honest, each party in $\mathcal{L}_2$ receives a share of $\sum_{\mathsf{S}_i \in S} x_i$ for each party in $\mathcal{L}_1$. Although corrupt parties in $\mathcal{L}_1$ can potentially send invalid shares, by t-robustness of the secret sharing scheme all honest parties in $\mathcal{L}_2$ correctly reconstruct the sum of the inputs. Finally, the adversary who corrupts a non-empty set of parties in $\mathcal{L}_2$ only learns the sum of the shares of the honest parties' inputs. Since the secret sharing scheme is linear, this would only reveal the sum of the honest parties' inputs.

The following lemma formally states the game based security guarantees of any (n, t, d)-layered protocol realizing Multiparty Addition as per above.

Lemma 2. *The following statements hold when an (n, t, d)-layered protocol realizing f_{add} is executed in the presence of any adversary $\mathcal{A}$ described in Definition 1:*

1. *All honest clients output the same value at the end of Π_{add}. If all input clients are honest, this value coincides with the sum of the inputs.*
2. *The view of $\mathcal{A}$ only reveals the sum of the inputs of the honest parties.*

4 Layered MPC Based on CNF Secret Sharing

In this section, we start by building a protocol for Future Multicast based on primitives from Sect. 3. The protocol is then used in a simple way to obtain VSS using CNF-shares. We will build on this VSS protocol in order to realize secure multiplication and, finally, a protocol for layered MPC for *any* function.

4.1 Future Multicast

Future Multicast f_{FMcast} allows a sender S to send a secret to a set of receivers R located in a later layer. It guarantees that all honest receivers output the same value even if the sender is corrupt; if the sender is honest, this value coincides with the sender's input. Finally, if all receivers (and the sender) are honest, the secret remains hidden from the adversary. This primitive will be the backbone of our layered VSS protocol. Standard (Secure) Multicast is often described as the simplest non-trivial example of secure computation. Also, in layered MPC, Future Multicast generalizes Future Messaging and Future Broadcast[7] but is substantially harder to realize. The functionality is described in [19, Figure 4.1].

A Protocol for Future Multicast. As a first step towards realizing f_{FMcast}, we construct a protocol that achieves a weaker notion of Future Multicast. In this protocol, sender S in layer $\mathcal{L}_0$ sends a share to a set of intermediaries $U_T = \{\mathsf{P}_i^1 : i \in T\} \subset \mathcal{L}_1$, in the next layer, who communicate it to the receivers $R \subseteq \mathcal{L}_5$. The protocol for *weak Future Multicast* provides the following guarantees which are formally stated in Lemma 3.

1. (*Agreement*). If a majority of the intermediaries are honest, all honest receivers output the same value at the end of the protocol even if S is corrupt; if the sender is honest, this value coincides with the sender's input.
2. (*Security*). If the sender, all the intermediaries in U_T and all the receivers are honest, a layered adversary does not learn the sender's secret.

[7] Here, we refer to the primitive in the setting of layered MPC that ensures termination, validity and agreement among all parties located in some layer $d > 1$. Not Future Broadcast as defined in [28].

Observe that, when $t < n/3$, each subset U_T of $n - t$ parties in $\mathcal{L}_1$ contains a strict minority of corrupt parties. Furthermore, there is at least one such set that contains only honest parties. Given these observations, realizing f_{FMcast} from the weaker notion is straight forward: For each set $U_T \subset \mathcal{L}_1$ of $n - t$ parties, S sends r_T to the receivers using parties in U_T as intermediaries, where r_T for all possible T, form an additive secret sharing of the sender's secret. When the sender is honest and each set of intermediaries has an honest majority, by (1), all r_T reach the receivers correctly. Furthermore, for one set of intermediaries U_{T^*}, by (2), r_{T^*} remains hidden from the adversary. Thus, receivers can compute the sum of r_T for distinct sets T to obtain the secret, which will remain hidden from the layered adversary if all receivers are honest. Finally, by (1), the outputs of all honest receivers are consistent even if the sender is corrupt.

Weak Future Multicast. With the aid of a set of intermediaries $U_T = \{\mathsf{P}_i^1 : i \in T\} \subset \mathcal{L}_1$, weak Future Multicast can be achieved as follows: S sends the message r_T to every party in U_T. In addition, S distributes a robust secret sharing of r_T among the parties in $\mathcal{L}_3$ using Future Messaging. Every pair of intermediaries broadcasts the difference between the values they received to all parties in $\mathcal{L}_3$ using a protocol for the f_{add} functionality. Additionally, each intermediary distributes a secret sharing of the value they received among the parties in $\mathcal{L}_4$. If the difference comes out non-zero for any pair, the parties in $\mathcal{L}_3$ effectively reveals r_T to all parties in $\mathcal{L}_4$ by broadcasting the shares of r_T that S distributed. Parties in $\mathcal{L}_4$ then forwards (using layer-to-layer broadcast) r_T to all the receivers in R. By robustness of the secret sharing scheme, parties in $\mathcal{L}_4$ recover r_T if it was secret shared properly by the sender; moreover, even if S sent invalid shares, all honest parties recover the same value. Hence, receivers recover r_T from this because at most $t < n/3$ parties in $\mathcal{L}_4$ are corrupt. If the difference is zero for every pair of intermediaries, each party in $\mathcal{L}_4$ reveals the share sent to them by every intermediary to all the receiver in R. Using these shares, each receiver reconstructs the value that was shared by each intermediary. If the difference was zero for every pair of intermediaries, then all honest intermediaries must have received the same value from S (which is r_T if S is honest). Hence, a majority of the values recovered by every receiver coincides with this value. This ensures (1). If S and all intermediaries are honest, r_T is not revealed to parties in $\mathcal{L}_4$, and, hence, is disclosed only to the receivers ensuring (2).

An $(n, t, 5)$-layered protocol for Future Multicast Π_{FMcast} is formally described in the full version [19]. Importantly, it includes the sub-protocol for weak Future Multicast $\Pi_{\mathsf{weak\text{-}FMcast}}$. We identify two important properties of Π_{FMcast} that will be used going forward. The properties are stated in Lemma 3 and a formal proof is provided in [19].

Lemma 3. *For any $T \in \mathcal{T}$, the following properties hold for any weak future multicast protocol with U_T as intermediaries when executed in the presence of any adversary $\mathcal{A}$:*

(a) There exists $\hat{r}$ such that all honest receivers in R output $\hat{r}$ at the end of the protocol. Furthermore, if S is honest, $\hat{r} = r$.

(b) If S*, and all intermediaries and receivers are honest, for any* $r, r' \in M$*,*

$$\mathrm{ADVR}_{\Pi,\mathcal{A}}(r) \equiv \mathrm{ADVR}_{\Pi,\mathcal{A}}(r').$$

Theorem 8. *There is a secure* $(n, t, 5)$*-layered protocol realizing future multicast with input client* S *and output clients in* R*.*

Proof. Let $\Pi_{\mathsf{weak\text{-}FMcast}}$ be a protocol realizing weak future multicast. By statement (a) in Lemma 3, for every set of intermediaries $\{\mathsf{P}_i^1 : i \in T\}$, there exists $\hat{r}_T$ such that all honest receivers in R output $\hat{r}_T$ at the end of $\Pi_{\mathsf{weak\text{-}FMcast}}$. Furthermore, if S is honest, $\hat{r}_T = r_T$, for each $T \in \mathcal{T}$. Hence, at the end of the future multicast protocol, say Π_{FMcast}, the outputs of all receivers are the same and coincides with the input of an honest S.

It remains to show that if the sender and all receivers are honest, $\mathcal{A}$ does not learn the sender's input. We sketch the intuition: Consider $T^* \in \mathcal{T}$ such that the parties U_{T^*} are all honest; such a set exists because there are at most t corruptions in each layer. By statement (b) in Lemma 3, view of $\mathcal{A}$ interacting with $\Pi_{\mathsf{weak\text{-}FMcast}}$ with intermediaries in U_{T^*} is independent of the input r_{T^*} of S. But then, the view of $\mathcal{A}$ in the entire protocol Π_{FMcast} does not depend on m since $(r_T, T \in \mathcal{T})$ is an additive secret sharing of m. We formally prove security of Π_{FMcast} by demonstrating a simulator $\mathcal{S}$ in the full version [19].

4.2 Verifiable Secret Sharing

Using future multicast presented in Sect. 4.1, realizing verifiable secret sharing (VSS) is relatively straight-forward. The sender distributes the additive shares of the secret to each set of receivers using Future Multicast. The protocol in Fig. 4.1 realizes VSS from a dealer in $\mathcal{L}_0$ to shareholders in $\mathcal{L}_5$.

Figure 4.1 (Π_{VSS}, an $(n, t, 5)$-layered protocol for f_{VSS})

PUBLIC PARAMETERS: Sender $\mathsf{S} \in \mathcal{L}_0$, shareholders $\mathcal{L}_5$.
DEFINITIONS: Let $\mathcal{T} = \{T \subset [n] : |T| = n - t\}$.
SECRET INPUTS: S has input $m \in M$.
SUBROUTINES: Protocol Π_{FMcast} realizing f_{FMcast} functionality.

Layer $\mathcal{L}_0$:
1. S samples $(r_T)_{T \in \mathcal{T}}$ as additive secret sharing of m.
2. For each $T \in \mathcal{T}$, execute Π_{FMcast} with S as sender with input r_T and $\{\mathsf{P}_i^5 : i \in T\}$ as receivers.

Layer $\mathcal{L}_5$:
1. Each party $\mathsf{P}_i^5, i \in [n]$ recovers r_T as the output of Π_{FMcast} with S as sender if $i \in T$. P_i^5 outputs $(r_T)_{i \in T}$ as its share.

The protocol described in Fig. 4.1 is a $(n, t, 5)$-layered protocol realizing VSS. This follows from the definition of Future Multicast. The following theorem proves a stronger result: Suppose n protocols are executed in parallel with P_i^0 as dealer and $\mathcal{L}_5$ as shareholders for each $i \in [n]$, then we achieve a parallel $(n, t, 5)$-layered protocol for VSS functionality for $t < n/3$. The parallel VSS fuctionality is formally described below.

Figure 4.2 (Parallel VSS functionality $f_{\mathsf{parallel\text{-}VSS}}$)

PUBLIC PARAMETERS: Senders $\mathsf{S}_1, \ldots, \mathsf{S}_n \in \mathcal{L}_0$, shareholders $\mathsf{R}_1, \ldots, \mathsf{R}_n \in \mathcal{L}_5$. The domain M of secrets.

DEFINITIONS: Let $\mathcal{T} = \{T \subset [n] : |T| = n - t\}$.

1. Each $\mathsf{S}_i, i \in [n]$ sends $(r_T^i)_{T \in \mathcal{T}}$ to the functionality.
2. For each $i \in [n]$ and $T \in \mathcal{T}$, functionality sends (i, T, r_T^i) to $\{\mathsf{P}_j^5 : j \in T\}$.

Theorem 9. *The protocol in Fig. 4.1 executed in parallel realizes $f_{\mathsf{parallel\text{-}VSS}}$ with perfect t-security for $t < n/3$ by consuming 5 layers, and by communicating $\binom{n}{t}^3 \cdot O(n^2)$ field elements over the point-to-point channels and over the broadcast channels for each secret.*

Proof. The VSS protocol is essentially several multicast protocols executed in parallel. The security of the construction follows from the security of the multicast protocol, once we ensure that the adversary cannot correlate the shares of the corrupt parties with those of the honest parties across parallel executions of multicast protocols. The simulator for multicast extracts the input of a corrupt sender in $\mathcal{L}_0$ from the view of the honest parties in the protocol up to $\mathcal{L}_4$. This allows the simulator we build for parallel VSS to extract the shares of the corrupt dealers after simulating the protocol till $\mathcal{L}_4$ and provide them to $f_{\mathsf{parallel\text{-}VSS}}$. Whereas, a multicast from an honest sender to a set of receivers, potentially containing corrupt receivers, does not reveal the sent message to the corrupt parties until $\mathcal{L}_4$. Hence, the adversary chooses shares for corrupt parties before getting to see the shares chosen by the honest parties. This guarantees that the adversary cannot correlate the shares of the corrupted parties with the shares of the honest parties. We show a simulator and full proof in the full version of the paper [19]. □

Addition and Multiplication-by-Constant for CNF Shares. The CNF secret sharing scheme is linear; hence, parties holding valid CNF shares of a value s can locally transform it into a valid secret sharing of αs when α is a publicly known constant. In detail, let s_i be the share of s held by party i. Then, there exist $(\delta_T)_{T \in \mathcal{T}}$ such that $\sum_{T \in \mathcal{T}} \delta_T = s$, and $s_i = (\delta_T)_{T: i \in T}$ for each $i \in [n]$. Then $s'_1, \ldots, s'_n$ such that $s'_i = (\alpha \delta_T)_{T: i \in T}$ is a CNF secret sharing of αs. Additionally, suppose a value r is secret shared as $(r_1, \ldots, r_n)$ where $r_i = (\gamma_T)_{T: i \in T}$ for each $i \in [n]$, and $\sum_{T \in \mathcal{T}} \gamma_T = r$. Then, $s''_1, \ldots, s''_n$ such that $s''_i = (\delta_T + \gamma_T)_{T: i \in T}$ is a CNF secret sharing of $r + s$. In conclusion, addition and multiplication by constant of CNF shares can be computed locally.

4.3 Multiplication

The multiplication functionality f_{mult} (presented in [19, Figure 4.5]) takes valid CNF secret shares of two values r and s and computes fresh CNF secret shares of rs. This functionality requires that the input clients hold valid CNF secret sharing of the individual values to be multiplied, and that at most t input clients are corrupt. In contrast, by default, a layered adversary is allowed to corrupt arbitrarily many input and output clients.

Implementing f_{mult}. Suppose $r_1, \ldots, r_n$ and $s_1, \ldots, s_n$ are CNF secret shares of two values r and s, respectively. Recall that, when $\mathcal{T} = \{T_1, \ldots, T_N\} = \{T \subset [n] : |T| = n - t\}$, for each $i \in [n]$, $r_i = (\gamma_j)_{j:i \in T_j}$ and $s_i = (\lambda_j)_{j:i \in T_j}$, where $\sum_{i=1}^{N} \gamma_j = r$ and $\sum_{i=1}^{N} \lambda_j = s$. To compute a secret sharing of rs, it suffices to compute the secret sharing of $\gamma_i \lambda_j$ for every $i, j \in [N]$; secret shares of rs can be computed as the sum of these secret shares, which can be obtained by local computations. This follows from the fact that, $rs = \sum_{i=1}^{N} \sum_{j=1}^{N} \gamma_i \lambda_j$.

The main challenge in implementing multiplication is in obtaining correct secret shares of $\gamma_i \lambda_j$, for all $i, j \in [N]$. In the non-layered setting, classic protocols tackle this by having all parties who have access to γ_i and λ_j secret share their product. The parties then compute the difference between the values shared as purported product $\gamma_i \lambda_j$ by securely computing their differences. If all differences come out to be 0, since at least one of the parties secret sharing the product is honest, all the remaining parties must also have correctly shared the secret. Hence, one of these CNF-shares can be taken as a valid secret sharing of $\lambda_i \gamma_j$. Whenever the difference is non-zero, both γ_i and λ_j are publicly revealed, and a trivial secret sharing of $\gamma_i \lambda_j$ is taken instead of the ones submitted by the parties. Finally, these shares are 'added' together to get a secret sharing of rs.

The above protocol is clearly correct. The security of the protocol follows from the fact that, whenever all the parties submitting shares of $\gamma_i \lambda_j$ for some i, j are honest, the protocol never reaches the public reveal phase. A formal description of the protocol in the standard setting as constructed in [39] is provided in [19, Figure C.1]. Our multiplication protocol is a porting of the above protocol to the layered setting. In the process, we face two main challenges.

Firstly, when the public check of equality between purported shares of $\gamma_j \cdot \lambda_{j'}$ provided by a pair of parties fails in step 2, γ_j and $\lambda_{j'}$ need to be revealed by every party (in the input layer) with access to these values. This is tackled exactly as in the Future Multicast protocol. Using Future Messaging, all parties in the input layer secret share each γ_i and λ_i they hold to the layer where the equality check is made; the parties in this layer then selectively reveal the additive shares for which any of the equality checks fails.

The second challenge is less straightforward to handle. If the protocol is naively ported to the layered model, VSS of $\gamma_j \cdot \lambda_{j'}$ will be available in two different layers: once in the layer that initiates the equality check, and then again in the final layer that computes the VSS of $r \cdot t$ as the sum of VSS of $\gamma_j \cdot \lambda_{j'}$ for all $j, j' \in [N]$. But then, the adversary can corrupt t parties in both these layers, and recover $\gamma_j \cdot \lambda_{j'}$ for each (j, j'). This is overcome as follows: For each j, j', consider the special party whose share of $\gamma_j \cdot \lambda_{j'}$ will be chosen in the final addition (if the all equality checks for $\gamma_j \cdot \lambda_{j'}$ succeeds). This party samples $(\delta_k)_{k\in[N]}$ as additive secret shares of $\gamma_j\lambda_{j'}$, and verifiable secret share each δ_k instead of directly secret sharing $\gamma_j \cdot \lambda_{j'}$. The equality check is now carried out to check if $\sum_k \delta_k$ shared by the special party equals the value shared by every other party. Finally, parties in the output layer receive a VSS of $\gamma_j \cdot \lambda_{j'}$ in which the ith share is $(\delta_k)_{k:i\in T_k}$. This avoids reuse of the same VSS in two layers. The protocol is presented in [19, Figure 4.6].

We first establish properties of the subroutine $\Pi_{j,j'}$ that computes CNF shares of $\gamma_j \cdot \lambda_{j'}$ for each $j, j' \in [N]$. in the lemma below, proven in the full version of the paper [19, Section C.5].

Lemma 4. *For any $j, j' \in [N]$, the following properties hold for $\Pi_{j,j'}$ when executed in the presence of an adversary $\mathcal{A}$:*

(a) There exists $(\delta_k)_{k\in[N]}$ such that $\sum_{k=1}^{N} \delta_k = \lambda_j\gamma_{j'}$, and each honest party $\mathsf{P}_i^7, i \in [N]$ outputs $(\delta_k)_{k:i\in T_k}$ at the end of $\Pi_{j,j'}$.
(b) Suppose parties $\mathsf{P}_i^0, i \in H$ are honest, then for any a, b, a', b',

$$\mathrm{ADVR}_{\Pi_{j,j'},\mathcal{A}}(\gamma_j = a, \lambda_{j'} = b) \equiv \mathrm{ADVR}_{\Pi_{j,j'},\mathcal{A}}(\gamma_j = a', \lambda_{j'} = b').$$

By statement (a) in Lemma 4, for each $j, j' \in [N]$, parties in the output layer correctly receive a CNF secret sharing of $\gamma_j\lambda_{j'}$. Hence, the output of the parties at the end of the protocol is a CNF secret sharing of $\sum_{j=1}^{N}\sum_{j'=1}^{N} \gamma_j\lambda_{j'} = rs$. By statement (b) in Lemma 4, if $\lambda_{j'}$ or γ_j is not known to the adversary, the output of $\Pi_{j,j'}$ does not reveal $\gamma_j\lambda_{j'}$. This ensures that the protocol is secure. We obtain the following theorem.

Theorem 10. *There is an $(n, t, 7)$-layered protocol realizing f_{mult}, for $t < n/3$.*

Executing the above protocol in parallel realizes a parallel multiplication functionality.

4.4 Realizing MPC from Layered Multiplication and Addition

In this section, we construct a secure (n, t, d)-layered protocol for computing any given function f by evaluating an layered arithmetic circuit computing the function. Suppose each party $\mathsf{P}_i^0, i \in [n]$ in the input layer has $x_i \in \mathbb{F}$ as input, and each party in the output layer (specified later) wants to compute $f(x_1, \ldots, x_n)$. The secure computation of f proceeds in three phases: an input sharing phase, a circuit evaluation phase and an output reconstruction phase.

In the input sharing phase, each input client verifiably CNF secret shares their input. In the circuit evaluation phase, the layered protocol traverses the layered circuit that evaluates f and evaluates every gate in the circuit. Evaluating a gate amounts to securely computing a CNF secret sharing of the value on the output wire of each gate using the CNF secret sharing of the values on its input wires. Finally, in the output reconstruction phase, the secret sharing of the value on the output wire is revealed to the output clients.

We elaborate on the circuit emulation phase below. Let C be a layered arithmetic circuit over a field $\mathbb{F}$ with D layers that computes f. At the end of the input phase, the values on the input wires of all gates in layer one of C are simultaneously made available on the same layer of the protocol graph. In the circuit evaluation phase, the protocol keeps the invariant that, if a layer $i \in [D]$ of C is processed, then the values on all the output wires from layer i of C are simultaneously available of a specific layer of the protocol graph. The protocol can then process all gates in layer $i+1$ of C preserving the invariant.

Recall that every gate in C is either a multiplication-by-constant gate, an addition gate or a multiplication gate. Given a CNF secret sharing of the value on the input wire(s) of a multiplication-by-constant gate or an addition gate, a secret sharing of the value on the output wire can be computed by locally processing the share. That is, the value on the output wire of the gate is available on the same layer (of the protocol graph) on which the values on the input wires have been secret shared. However, for a multiplication gate, computing a CNF secret sharing of the product of the values on the input wires using a t-secure protocol for multiplication consumes 7 layers. This poses a challenge when ensuring the invariant that the values on the output wires of all gates in a layer (of C) are made available on the same layer of the protocol graph. We get around this obstacle as follows: for a multiplication-by-constant or an addition gate G, after locally computing the secret sharing of the value on the output wire, we further compute a multiplication gate with value on the output wire of G as one input and the other input value being fixed to one (identity). This is achieved by using a trivial secret sharing of one as the other input and executing the layered protocol for multiplication which consumes $d = 7$ layers. Hence, we ensure the invariant we require.

The protocol is formally described in the full version [19, Figure 4.7]. We get the following result.

Theorem 11. *Let f be an n-party functionality computed by a layered arithmetic circuit C over a finite field $\mathbb{F}$ and gates partitioned into layers $L_1, \ldots, L_D$. Then, for any $t < n/3$, there is an $(n, t, 6 + 7D)$-layered MPC protocol for f.*

5 Efficient Layered MPC

In this section, we present an *efficient* implementation of perfectly t-secure layered MPC when $t < n/3$. To achieve this, we first build verifiable Shamir secret sharing. As in our previous implementation of MPC, the only non-trivial step in developing a protocol for general MPC after implementing VSS is that of achieving perfectly secure multiplication of two values that are secret shared. We build the multiplication protocol by porting a multiplication protocol of [15,16] from the standard setting to the layered setting. For want of space, we present the formal constructions and proofs of their security in the appendix. The security of the protocols is argued along the lines of our previous constructions, albeit, with slightly more complex proofs.

5.1 Verifiable Shamir Secret Sharing

In this section, we implement verifiable Shamir secret sharing in the layered setting with perfect t-security for $t < n/3$. This is realized by porting a protocol from the standard setting to the layered setting. We mostly face the same set of challenges that we encountered while implementing future multicast in the previous section. Recall that (t, n)-Shamir secret sharing of a secret s in a field $\mathbb{F}$ involves sampling a random polynomial $q(x)$ of degree at most t under the constraint $q(0) = s$ and setting the ith share to be $q(i)$. We consider an equivalent functionality $f_{\mathsf{ShamirVSS}}$ that allows a dealer to distribute the evaluation of a degree (at most) t polynomial on distinct non-zero points. A formal description of the parallel $f_{\mathsf{ShamirVSS}}$ functionality is given in [19, Figure 5.1].

Implementing $f_{\mathsf{ShamirVSS}}$. The layered protocol realizing $f_{\mathsf{ShamirVSS}}$ is provided in the full version [19, Figure 5.2]. We sketch the outline and the intuition behind its construction.

The classic protocol for Shamir VSS in the standard setting proceeds as follows. Suppose the dealer wants to share a secret s from a field $\mathbb{F}$ such that $|\mathbb{F}| > n$ with t-security for $t < n/3$. The dealer samples a random bi-variate polynomial $S(x, y)$ of degree at most t in both the variables such that $S(0, 0) = s$, and transfers $f_i(x) = S(x, i)$ and $g_i(y) = S(i, y)$ to party P_i. If the polynomials were appropriately sampled, $f_i(j) = S(i, j) = g_j(i)$ for every i, j. Each pair of parties P_i, P_j check if $f_i(j) = g_j(i)$ and $f_j(i) = g_i(j)$; P_i raises a complaint by broadcasting $(i, j, f_i(j), g_i(j))$ if this check fails for P_j. The dealer addresses every valid complaint–a complaint of the form (i, j, u, v) such that $u \neq f_i(j)$ or $v \neq g_i(j)$–and broadcasts (f_i, g_i); otherwise, the dealer dismisses that complaint. This is followed by parties casting votes to accept or disqualify the dealer. P_i votes to accept the dealer if all the following conditions are met: dealer addressed one of every inconsistent mutual complaint–*i.e.*, a pair of complaints (i, j, u, v) and (j, i, u', v') such that $u \neq u'$ or $v \neq v'$; P_i itself did not issue a complaint; and for each broadcasted (f_j, g_j), $f_i(j) = g_j(i)$ and $g_i(j) = f_j(i)$. If the dealer receives less than $n - t$ votes, it is declared to be corrupt. Otherwise, each P_i updates (f_i, g_i) if it was broadcasted by the dealer and sets $f_i(0)$ as their share.

Using selective reveal in future messaging and checking equality using f_{add} as done in future multicast, we can port the above protocol into the layered setting. The protocol obtained in this manner is used as sub-protocol Π in our final construction [19, Figure 5.2]. Interestingly, this construction by itself is not a layered protocol for verifiable secret sharing. However, Π guarantees the following: Let $H_1 \subseteq [n]$ such that P_i^1 is honest iff $i \in H_1$; parties in $\mathcal{L}_5$ hold a secret sharing of a value $\hat{s}_i$ such that, all such $\hat{s}_i$ (there are at least $n - t$ of them) define a valid secret sharing of a value $\hat{s}$. Further, if the dealer is honest, $\hat{s} = s$ and $\hat{s}_i$ is the same as the value that the dealer transferred to P_i^1. This is formally stated in Lemma 5.

Lemma 5. *The following properties hold for an execution of Π in the presence of a layered adversary $\mathcal{A}$:*

(a) Let $G \subseteq [n]$ such that P_i^1 is honest if and only if $i \in H_1$. There exist polynomials $\hat{g}(x)$ and $\hat{g}_i(x), i \in H_1$, each of degree at most t, such that

$\hat{g}_i(0) = \hat{g}(i)$ *and* α_i^k *output by each honest party* P_k^5 *coincides with* $\hat{g}_i(k)$. *Furthermore, if* S *is honest,* $\hat{g}(x) = F(x, 0)$.

(b) If S *is honest, for any* $r, r' \in \mathbb{F}$,

$$\text{ADVR}_{\Pi,\mathcal{A}}(r) \equiv \text{ADVR}_{\Pi,\mathcal{A}}(r').$$

Using Π as a subroutine, verifiable secret sharing is achieved as follows (described in [19, Figure 5.2]). Let $q(x) = c_0 + c_1 x + \ldots c_t x^t$ be the polynomial that the dealer wants to secret share. For each $0 \leq l \leq t$, dealer S executes Π with c_i as its input. When $\mathsf{P}_i^5, i \in H_5$ are the set of honest parties in $\mathcal{L}_5$. By Lemma 5, for each $0 \leq l \leq t$, there exist polynomials $\hat{g}_l(x)$ and $\{\hat{g}_{l,i}(x)\}_{i \in H_1}$ of degree at most t such that, $\hat{g}_{l,i}(0) = \hat{g}_l(i)$, and for all $k \in H_5$ and $l \in H_1$, P_5^k holds $\alpha_{l,i}^k = \hat{g}_{l,i}(k)$. Since $|H_5| \geq n - t$, each $\mathsf{P}_j^6, j \in [n]$ recovers $\gamma_{i,j} = \mathsf{Rec}(\alpha_{l,j}^1, \ldots, \alpha_{l,j}^n) = \sum_{l=0}^t \hat{g}_l(i) j^l$ for all $i \in H_1$. Hence, $\gamma_j = \mathsf{Rec}(\gamma_{1,j}, \ldots, \gamma_{n,j}) = \sum_{l=0}^t \hat{g}_l(0) j^l$. Defining $\hat{q}(x) = \hat{g}_l(0) x^l$, we conclude that each P_j^6 receives $\hat{q}(j)$ as required in verifiable Shamir secret sharing. When S is honest, by Lemma 5 (a), $\hat{g}_l(0) = c_l$ for each $0 \leq l \leq t$. Hence, $\hat{q}(x) = q(x)$.

We next argue that, when S is honest, the view of the adversary is identical irrespective of the value of $q(0)$. Assume that the guarantee in Lemma 5 (b) is preserved when Π is executed concurrently as in the protocol. Then, the view of the adversary till $\mathcal{L}_5$ are identically distributed in the protocol irrespective of the values of $(c_l)_{0 \leq l \leq t}$. Hence, the view of the adversary in the protocol only reveals $q(i)$ for $i \in C_6$, where $\mathsf{P}_i^6, i \in C_6$ are the set of corrupt parties in $\mathcal{L}_6$.

In Protocol [19, Figure 5.2], the polynomial secret shared in $\mathcal{L}_6$ is exclusively determined by $\alpha_{l,i}^k$, for $i \in [n]$ and $0 \leq l \leq t$ stored by the honest parties P_k^5. In other words, the dealer is committed to polynomial $\hat{g}_l(x), 0 \leq l \leq t$ (as described in Lemma 5) when all the honest parties in $\mathcal{L}_5$ finish receiving messages from their predecessors. Furthermore, by Lemma 5, when S is honest, view of the layered adversary is identically distributed irrespective of input of S in each invocation of Π. This ensures that, when the protocol for verifiable secret sharing is executed in parallel, the polynomial being secret shared by a corrupt dealer cannot be correlated with that shared by an honest dealer. In the following theorem, we state this stronger result: when n verifiable secret sharing protocols are executed in parallel with $\mathsf{P}_i^0, i \in [n]$ as dealer and $\mathcal{L}_6$ as shareholders, we realize a parallel VSS functionality with t-security.

Theorem 12. *There is an* $(n, t, 6)$*-layered protocol which, when executed in parallel, realizes parallel Shamir-VSS for* $t < n/3$ *by communicating* $O(n^6)$ *field elements over the point-to-point channels and* $O(n^4)$ *field elements over the broadcast channels for each secret.*

Employing the layered protocol for VSS, we proceed to port the protocol for secure computation in [16] to the layered setting. An important functionality we use extensively for this transformation is *resharing*, which allows parties in $\mathcal{L}_a$ with (a valid) secret sharing of a secret s to "handover" the secret to parties in $\mathcal{L}_b$, for any $b > a$, by providing a fresh secret sharing of s. Using parallel invocation of VSS, realizing resharing is straight forward: secret shares of uniformly random secrets $c_l, 1 \leq l \leq t$ are made available on the input layer. Then, the secret s is reshared by distributing $f(i)$ to shareholder i in the output layer; here $f(x) = s + \sum_{l=1}^{t} c_l x^l$. Distributing secret shares of a uniformly random secret is achieved by having $t+1$ parties in a previous layer secret share random secrets and the parties locally computing the shares of their sum (See functionality in [19, Figure D.1] and its implementation in [19, Figure D.2]). The resharing functionality is formally defined in [19, Figure D.3], and it is implemented as outlined above in [19, Figure D.4].

5.2 Multiplication

The main challenge in realizing general MPC is securely implementing a multiplication protocol that computes a secret sharing of the product of two values using their shares. Following the outline of the MPC implementation in [16], we first realize a simpler primitive, namely multiplication with helper, where the input clients hold secret sharing of a pair of values, and a special input client called the helper holds both values. This primitive allows the helper to verifiably secret share of the product of these values onto the output clients. The helper will be disqualified if the value secret shared is not the product.

Implementing Multiplication with Helper. We realize this functionality by porting a modified version of the implementation of the same in standard setting as presented in [16]. The protocol in the standard setting works as follows: When α, β are the values to be multiplied, helper samples polynomials $f(x)$ and $g(x)$ of degree at most t conditioned on $f(0) = \alpha$ and $g(0) = \beta$. It then computes $h(x) = f(x)g(x)$; clearly, $h(0) = \alpha\beta$. It then verifiably secret shares $(\alpha_l)_{l\in[t]}, (\beta_l)_{l\in[t]}$ and $(\gamma_l)_{0\leq l\leq 2t}$, where $f(x) = \alpha + \sum_{l=1}^{t} \alpha_l x^l, g(x) = \beta + \sum_{l=1}^{t} \beta_l x^l$, and $h(x) = \sum_{l=0}^{2t} \gamma_l x^l$. The parties now enter a verification phase in which $f(i), g(i)$ and $h(i)$ are revealed to P_i for each $i \in [n]$. P_i is to verify if $f(i)g(i) = h(i)$ and raise a complaint otherwise. For each complaint, $f(i), g(i)$ and $h(i)$ are publicly revealed; parties unanimously disqualify the helper if any of the complaint is valid. If all complaints turn out to be bogus, then $h(x)$ is verified to be $f(x)g(x)$ and $\gamma = \alpha\beta$. The parties now store the secret shares of γ as the shares of the product.

Our layered protocol follows the same logic with one notable difference. The helper in $\mathcal{L}_0$ secret shares the coefficients of $f(x), g(x)$ and $h(x)$ to $\mathcal{L}_6$ using the VSS protocol, with the exception of α and β. Recall that α and β are secret shared on $\mathcal{L}_0$; it is imperative to the correctness of the protocol that the secret shares of α and β provided to $\mathcal{L}_6$ are valid. But, this can be easily ensured by having α and β in $\mathcal{L}_0$ reshared to $\mathcal{L}_6$. In the standard setting, this is realized by "transferring" the secret sharing of α and β to the helper; resharing ensures the same guarantees. By taking appropriate linear combinations of the coefficients of the polynomials, parties in $\mathcal{L}_6$ then reveal $f(i), g(i)$ and $h(i)$ to each $\mathsf{P}_i^7, i \in [n]$. Each P_i^7 raises a complaint if $f(i)g(i) \neq h(i)$ to $\mathcal{L}_8$. For each $i \in [n]$ with a complaint, parties in $\mathcal{L}_8$ selectively reveal $f(i), g(i)$ and $h(i)$ to all parties in $\mathcal{L}_9$. This is achieved by the trick we used in VSS as well as multicast and multiplication in the previous section. Finally, γ secret shared by the helper onto $\mathcal{L}_6$ is reshared to $\mathcal{L}_9$ and is used as the secret sharing of $\alpha\beta$ if the parties in $\mathcal{L}_8$ has not (unanimously) disqualified the helper.

When the helper is honest, throughout the protocol, the adversary only sees at most t shares of α, β, the evaluation of f, g and h on at most t points, and at most t shares of a sharing and resharing of γ. This ensures that the view of the adversary is identically distributed irrespective of the values of α and β. A corrupt helper is disqualified by the parties in $\mathcal{L}_8$ if and only if $h(x) \neq f(x)g(x)$. As we observed while analyzing the protocol for VSS, the sender commits to these coefficients by $\mathcal{L}_5$ as part of the VSS protocol. Hence, when this protocol is executed in parallel, a corrupt helper is unable to correlate the event of their getting disqualified with the secret sharing of the product achieved in another parallel execution with an honest helper. Thus, the protocol remains secure under parallel composition. The protocol is formally described in [19, Figure D.8].

Theorem 13. *There is a layered protocol that realizes multiplication with helper functionality with perfect t-security for $t < n/3$.*

Multiplication. We proceed to the main primitive required to implement MPC–secure processing of the multiplication gate. Suppose two values α, β are Shamir secret shared using polynomials $f(x)$ and $g(x)$. Since $f(x)g(x)$ is a polynomial of degree at most $2t$, given $f(i)g(i)$ for at least $2t+1$ distinct $i \in [n]$, there exists a linear transformation that computes $f(0)g(0) = \alpha\beta$. For each $i \in [n]$, suppose we execute the multiplication with helper protocol from the previous section to verifiably secret shares the product $f(i)g(i)$ with the help of the party holding $f(i)$ and $g(i)$. The protocol guarantees that the secret sharing of the product is accepted (and the helper is not disqualified) whenever the helper adheres to the protocol; whereas, if the helper secret shares a value other than the product then the helper is disqualified. Since at least $n - t$ parties are corrupt, we obtain the correct secret sharing of $f(i)g(i)$ for $n - t \geq 2t + 1$ distinct values of i, which can be locally transformed using the aforementioned linear transformation to obtain a secret sharing of $\alpha\beta$.

The above proposal has a clear flaw: to multiply $f(i)$ and $g(i)$ held by a helper, both these values need to be secret shared in the same layer. Hence, we need each $f(i)$ and $g(i)$ to be further secret shared onto the input layer. We refer to the 'data structure' where each share of a value is further verifiably secret shared as reinforced secret sharing (formally descrived in [19, Definition 10]). The multiplication functionality takes *reinforced secret shares* of two values as input; to promote sequential processing of multiplication, we also ensure that the output of the functionality is a reinforced secret sharing of the product of the input values.

It remains to convert the Shamir secret sharing to a reinforced secret sharing of the product. This is realized by executing a protocol for reinforced resharing, which takes valid Shamir shares of a value from the input clients and distributes a randomly sampled reinforced secret sharing of the same value. This functionality is formally described in [19, Figure D.6], and implemented (along the lines of Shamir resharing) in [19, Figure 5.4].

The protocol inherits security from the security of protocols implementing (parallel) multiplication with helper and reinforced resharing since the protocol exclusively uses these protocols in parallel. Indeed, the protocol remains secure under parallel composition because both the subroutines remain secure under parallel composition.

Theorem 14. *There is a layered protocol that realizes multiplication functionality with perfect t-security for $t < n/3$.*

5.3 MPC

In this section, we construct an efficient t-secure protocol for securely computing any given function f by evaluating a layered arithmetic circuit C computing the function. Suppose each party $\mathsf{P}_i^0, i \in [n]$ in the input layer has $z_i \in \mathbb{F}$ as input, and each party in the output layer (specified later) wants to compute $f(z_1, \ldots, z_n)$. Similar to our CNF secret sharing based construction, the secure computation of f proceeds in three phases: an input sharing phase, a circuit evaluation phase and an output reconstruction phase.

In the input sharing phase, each input client secret shares their input using reinforced secret sharing. In the circuit evaluation phase, the protocol keeps the invariant that, if a layer i of C is processed, then the values on all the output wires outgoing from layer i of C are simultaneously available of a specific layer of the protocol graph. Given a reinforced secret sharing of the value on the input wire(s) of a multiplication-by-constant gate or an addition gate, a secret sharing of the value on the output wire can be computed by locally processing the share. However, for a multiplication gate, computing a Shamir secret sharing of the product of the values on the input wires using a t-secure protocol for multiplication consumes 10 layers. Hence, we once again face the challenge of ensuring the invariant that the values on the output wires of all gates in a layer (of C) are made available on the same layer of the protocol graph. We get around this obstacle the same way we did in our previous construction: for a multiplication-by-constant or an addition gate G, after locally computing the reinforced secret sharing of the value on the output wire, we further compute a multiplication gate with value on the output wire of G as one output and the other value being fixed to one. This is achieved by taking a trivial secret sharing of one as the other input and executing the t-secure protocol for multiplication which consumes 10 layers. In this manner, we preserve the invariant we require. The protocol is formally described in [19, Figure 5.5].

Theorem 15. *Let f be an n-party functionality computed by a layered arithmetic circuit C over a finite field $\mathbb{F}$, with D levels and M gates. Then, for any*

$t < n/3$, there is an $(n, t, 8+10D)$-layered MPC protocol for f in which the communication consists of $M \cdot O(n^9)$ field elements over the point-to-point channels and $M \cdot O(n^7)$ field elements over the broadcast channels.

6 Computational Efficient Layered MPC for $t < n/2$

We introduce a computationally-secure layered MPC protocol with guaranteed output delivery, based on (non-interactive) equivocal linearly homomorphic commitments. We give a high-level overview and defer details to the full version [20].

Future Messaging. The primitive is achieved similarly as its perfectly-secure counterpart, but to tolerate $t < n/2$ corruptions, we cannot rely on plain error correction. Instead, parties broadcast commitments to (coefficients of) the polynomials used to share their values to the future layers. Every time a party wishes to re-share an intermediate value, they re-use the commitment to the constant coefficient, thereby ensuring that the proper value is being re-shared.

Distributed Commitments. This primitive (also referred to as *weak* secret sharing [27]) allows a dealer $\mathsf{D} \in \mathcal{L}_c$ to commit to a value s towards a future layer $\mathcal{L}_{c'}$, and later open the original value towards another further layer $\mathcal{L}_{c''}$. If D is honest, the opened value is s, and no information about s is revealed before the opening phase. Moreover, even if D is corrupted, the commit phase uniquely determines value s', such that the opening phase can only output s' or $\perp$.

The dealer $\mathsf{D} \in \mathcal{L}_c$ samples random degree-t polynomials $f(x), r(x)$, such that $f(0) = s$, computes a commitment to each coefficient in f using the coefficients in r as randomness and broadcasts these commitments to the future layers. The dealer then sends the evaluation points $(s(i), r(i))$ using future messaging to party $P_i^{c'}$. To reconstruct, layer $\mathcal{L}_{c'}$ broadcast these pairs to the future layers, and each party $P_i^{c''} \in \mathcal{L}_{c''}$ checks for each received pair whether it is consistent with the corresponding commitment. If there are more than t consistent pairs, interpolate a degree-t polynomial $f'(x)$ and output $f'(0)$. Otherwise, output $\perp$.

Remark 2. We can achieve a distributed commitment that allows to commit *to the same value* towards separate layers $\mathcal{L}_{c'}$ and $\mathcal{L}_{c''}$, such that even if P_d^c is corrupted, there exists a unique value s' such that the value that is opened by either layer is s' or $\perp$: let the dealer P_d^c execute the above protocol towards layers $\mathcal{L}_{c'}$ and $\mathcal{L}_{c''}$ with polynomials $f(x)$ and $f'(x)$ such that $f(0) = s = f'(0)$, but using *the same* commitment for the constant coefficient.

Verifiable Secret Sharing. For VSS, the dealer $\mathsf{D} \in \mathcal{L}_c$ with input s, samples random degree-t polynomial $f(x)$ with $f(0) = s$, and (duplicate) commits to each coefficient of f towards layers $\mathcal{L}_{c_1}$ and $\mathcal{L}_{c'}$ using the distributed commitment. This results in a matrix $\mathbf{M} = [{,}_{i,j}]_{0 \leq i,j \leq t}$ of public commitments, where ${,}_{i,j}$ is a commitment to the j-th coefficient of the polynomial used to share f_i: by linearity of the commitment, parties implicitly hold commitments to each evaluation $f(i)$. Using future messaging, the dealer D sends $s_i = f(i)$ and its opening information to $P_i^{c_1}$. Party $P_i^{c_1}$ can check that the received information is consistent with the published commitments, and broadcast to future layers a complaint if the check does not succeed. If the check succeeds, $P_i^{c_1}$ commits to s_i towards layer $\mathcal{L}_{c'}$; to ensure that $P_i^{c_1}$ commits to the value they received from P_c^d, the party uses the commitment to the constant term that is implicit from the published commitments in $\mathbf{M}$. If a complaint was raised by $P_i^{c_1}$, parties in layer $\mathcal{L}_{c'}$ publicly open s_i (and if the opened value is $\perp$, the dealer is disqualified). To reconstruct: for each index i corresponding to a party that did not complain, parties jointly reconstruct s_i. The final layer $\mathcal{L}_{c''}$ then uses any $t+1$ reconstructed shares to interpolate the secret. Moreover, as in Remark 2, by having both D and parties in layer $\mathcal{L}_{c_1}$ duplicate distribute commitments of s_i for all $i \in [1,n]$ towards layers $\mathcal{L}_{c'}$ and $\mathcal{L}_{\tilde{c}}$ for some $\tilde{c} \geq c'$, one guarantees that if D is not disqualified, then both $\mathcal{L}_{c'}$ and $\mathcal{L}_{\tilde{c}}$ hold sharings of the *same* value.

2-Level Verifiable Secret Sharing. To simplify the description of the MPC protocol, it is helpful that each party holds as part of their state a Shamir share of each wire value. For that, we modify the VSS as follows: the dealer D uses the above duplicate VSS to distribute shares of coefficients of f towards layers $\mathcal{L}_{c_1}$ and $\mathcal{L}_{c'}$, where $f(x)$ is a random degree-t polynomial with $f(0) = s$. Then, each party in $\mathcal{L}_{c_1}$ (privately) reconstructs towards party $P_i^{c'}$ the value $s_i = f(i)$. Notice that layer $\mathcal{L}_{c'}$ also holds sharings of all values $f(j)$ for $j \in [1,n]$ thanks to linearity of our VSS. This version of VSS can also be similarly duplicated.

Circuit Evaluation. Input parties use 2-level VSS to distribute their inputs towards a future layer. For each computation gate we maintain the invariant that layer $\mathcal{L}_c$ holds sharings (resulting from the 2-level VSS) of the input wire values x and y, and some future layer $\mathcal{L}_{c'}$ for $c' \geq c+6$ holds a sharing of the output wire value z. Addition gates are processed locally, exploiting the linearity of 2-level-VSS. Multiplication gates are processed by adapting a well-known protocol of Cramer et al. [14]: each party $P_i^c \in \mathcal{L}_c$ holds (as part of their 2-level VSS states to x and y) Shamir shares x_i and y_i of each value, and computes a 2-level VSS for x_i, y_i (but using the already known sharing to the constant coefficient of the used polynomial) and a fresh 2-level VSS for $z_i = x_i \cdot y_i$ towards a future layer. Finally, each party carries out a distributed *multiplication proof* (adapted from [14]) to prove that indeed $z_i = x_i \cdot y_i$: if this proof fails, parties jointly reconstruct (and adopt a standard sharing of) x_i and y_i to continue the computation.

Theorem 16. *Let f be an n-party functionality computed by a layered arithmetic circuit C over a finite field $\mathbb{F}$, with D levels and M gates. Then, for any $t < n/2$, there is an $(n, t, 4+6D)$-layered MPC protocol for f assuming non-interactive linearly-homomorphic equivocal commitments. The communication complexity is $M \cdot O(n^9)$ field elements over the point-to-point channels and $M \cdot O(n^5)$ field elements + $M \cdot O(n^{10} \cdot \lambda)$ bits over the broadcast channels, where λ is the security parameter.*

Acknowledgement. We thank the anonymous reviewers for helpful comments. B. David was supported by the Independent Research Fund Denmark (IRFD) grants number 9040-00399B (TrA^{2}C), 9131-00075B (PUMA) and 0165-00079B. A. Konring was supported by IRFD (TrA^{2}C) and by the Otto Mønsted Foundation in a joint program with Innovation Center Denmark - Israel. Y. Ishai, E. Kushilevitz, and V.

Narayanan were supported by ISF grant 2774/20 and BSF grant 2018393. Y. Ishai and V. Narayanan were also supported by ERC Project NTSC (742754).

References

1. Acharya, A., Hazay, C., Kolesnikov, V., Prabhakaran, M.: SCALES - MPC with small clients and larger ephemeral servers. In: Kiltz, E., Vaikuntanathan, V. (eds.) TCC 2022, Part II. LNCS, vol. 13748, pp. 502–531. Springer, Heidelberg (2022). https://doi.org/10.1007/978-3-031-22365-5_18
2. Almansa, J.F., Damgård, I., Nielsen, J.B.: Simplified threshold RSA with adaptive and proactive security. In: Vaudenay, S. (ed.) EUROCRYPT 2006. LNCS, vol. 4004, pp. 593–611. Springer, Heidelberg (2006). https://doi.org/10.1007/11761679_35
3. Baron, J., Defrawy, K.E., Lampkins, J., Ostrovsky, R.: Communication-optimal proactive secret sharing for dynamic groups. In: Malkin, T., Kolesnikov, V., Lewko, A.B., Polychronakis, M. (eds.) ACNS 2015. LNCS, vol. 9092, pp. 23–41. Springer, Cham (2015). https://doi.org/10.1007/978-3-319-28166-7_2
4. Ben-Or, M., Goldwasser, S., Wigderson, A.: Completeness theorems for non-cryptographic fault-tolerant distributed computation (extended abstract). In: 20th ACM STOC, pp. 1–10. ACM Press, May 1988
5. Benhamouda, F., et al.: Can a public blockchain keep a secret? In: Pass, R., Pietrzak, K. (eds.) TCC 2020. LNCS, vol. 12550, pp. 260–290. Springer, Cham (2020). https://doi.org/10.1007/978-3-030-64375-1_10
6. Blum, E., Katz, J., Liu-Zhang, C.-D., Loss, J.: Asynchronous byzantine agreement with subquadratic communication. In: Pass, R., Pietrzak, K. (eds.) TCC 2020. LNCS, vol. 12550, pp. 353–380. Springer, Cham (2020). https://doi.org/10.1007/978-3-030-64375-1_13
7. Cachin, C., Kursawe, K., Lysyanskaya, A., Strobl, R.: Asynchronous verifiable secret sharing and proactive cryptosystems. In: Proceedings of the 9th ACM Conference on Computer and Communications Security, pp. 88–97 (2002)
8. Canetti, R.: Security and composition of multiparty cryptographic protocols. J. CRYPTOLOGY **13**(1), 143–202 (2000)
9. Canetti, R.: Universally composable security: a new paradigm for cryptographic protocols. In: 42nd FOCS. pp. 136–145. IEEE Computer Society Press, October 2001
10. Canetti, R., Damgard, I., Dziembowski, S., Ishai, Y., Malkin, T.: Adaptive versus non-adaptive security of multi-party protocols. J. Cryptology **17**, 153–207 (2004)
11. Canetti, R., Herzberg, A.: Maintaining security in the presence of transient faults. In: Desmedt, Y.G. (ed.) CRYPTO 1994. LNCS, vol. 839, pp. 425–438. Springer, Heidelberg (1994). https://doi.org/10.1007/3-540-48658-5_38
12. Chen, J., Micali, S.: Algorand: a secure and efficient distributed ledger. Theor. Comput. Sci. **777**, 155–183 (2019)
13. Choudhuri, A.R., Goel, A., Green, M., Jain, A., Kaptchuk, G.: Fluid MPC: secure multiparty computation with dynamic participants. In: Malkin, T., Peikert, C. (eds.) CRYPTO 2021. LNCS, vol. 12826, pp. 94–123. Springer, Cham (2021). https://doi.org/10.1007/978-3-030-84245-1_4
14. Cramer, R., Damgård, I., Dziembowski, S., Hirt, M., Rabin, T.: Efficient multiparty computations secure against an adaptive adversary. In: Stern, J. (ed.) EUROCRYPT 1999. LNCS, vol. 1592, pp. 311–326. Springer, Heidelberg (1999). https://doi.org/10.1007/3-540-48910-X_22

15. Cramer, R., Damgård, I., Maurer, U.: General secure multi-party computation from any linear secret-sharing scheme. In: Preneel, B. (ed.) EUROCRYPT 2000. LNCS, vol. 1807, pp. 316–334. Springer, Heidelberg (2000). https://doi.org/10.1007/3-540-45539-6_22
16. Cramer, R., Damgård, I., Nielsen, J.B.: Secure Multiparty Computation and Secret Sharing. Cambridge University Press, Cambridge (2015). https://www.cambridge.org/de/academic/subjects/computer-science/cryptography-cryptology-and-coding/secure-multiparty-computation-and-secret-sharing?format=HB&isbn=9781107043053
17. Damgård, I., Ishai, Y.: Constant-round multiparty computation using a black-box pseudorandom generator. In: Shoup, V. (ed.) CRYPTO 2005. LNCS, vol. 3621, pp. 378–394. Springer, Heidelberg (2005). https://doi.org/10.1007/11535218_23
18. Damgård, I., Escudero, D., Polychroniadou, A.: Phoenix: secure computation in an unstable network with dropouts and comebacks. Cryptology ePrint Archive, Paper 2021/1376 (2021), https://eprint.iacr.org/2021/1376
19. David, B., Konring, A., Ishai, Y., Kushilevitz, E., Narayanan, V.: Perfect MPC over layered graphs. Cryptology ePrint Archive, Paper 2023/330 (2023). https://eprint.iacr.org/2023/330
20. Deligios, G., Goel, A., Liu-Zhang, C.D.: Maximally-fluid MPC with guaranteed output delivery. Cryptology ePrint Archive, Paper 2023/415 (2023). https://eprint.iacr.org/2023/415
21. Desmedt, Y., Jajodia, S.: Redistributing secret shares to new access structures and its applications. Technical Report, Citeseer (1997)
22. Eldefrawy, K., Lepoint, T., Leroux, A.: Communication-efficient proactive secret sharing for dynamic groups with dishonest majorities. In: Conti, M., Zhou, J., Casalicchio, E., Spognardi, A. (eds.) ACNS 2020. LNCS, vol. 12146, pp. 3–23. Springer, Cham (2020). https://doi.org/10.1007/978-3-030-57808-4_1
23. Feldman, P., Micali, S.: Byzantine agreement in constant expected time (and trusting no one). In: 26th FOCS, pp. 267–276. IEEE Computer Society Press, October 1985
24. Fitzi, M., Garay, J.A.: Efficient player-optimal protocols for strong and differential consensus. In: Borowsky, E., Rajsbaum, S. (eds.) 22nd ACM PODC. pp. 211–220. ACM, July 2003
25. Fitzi, M., Liu-Zhang, C.D., Loss, J.: A new way to achieve round-efficient byzantine agreement. In: Proceedings of the 2021 ACM Symposium on Principles of Distributed Computing, pp. 355–362 (2021)
26. Garay, J.A.: Reaching (and maintaining) agreement in the presence of mobile faults. In: Tel, G., Vitányi, P. (eds.) WDAG 1994. LNCS, vol. 857, pp. 253–264. Springer, Heidelberg (1994). https://doi.org/10.1007/BFb0020438
27. Gennaro, R., Ishai, Y., Kushilevitz, E., Rabin, T.: The round complexity of verifiable secret sharing and secure multicast. In: 33rd ACM STOC, pp. 580–589. ACM Press, July 2001
28. Gentry, C., et al.: YOSO: You Only Speak Once. In: Malkin, T., Peikert, C. (eds.) CRYPTO 2021. LNCS, vol. 12826, pp. 64–93. Springer, Cham (2021). https://doi.org/10.1007/978-3-030-84245-1_3
29. Ghinea, D., Goyal, V., Liu-Zhang, C.D.: Round-optimal byzantine agreement. In: Dunkelman, O., Dziembowski, S. (eds.) EUROCRYPT 2022, Part I. LNCS, vol. 13275, pp. 96–119. Springer, Heidelberg (May / Jun (2022). https://doi.org/10.1007/978-3-031-06944-4_4

30. Gilad, Y., Hemo, R., Micali, S., Vlachos, G., Zeldovich, N.: Algorand: scaling byzantine agreements for cryptocurrencies. In: Proceedings of the 26th Symposium on Operating Systems Principles, pp. 51–68 (2017)
31. Goldreich, O.: Foundations of Cryptography: volume 2, Basic Applications. Cambridge University Press, Cambridge (2009)
32. Goyal, V., Kothapalli, A., Masserova, E., Parno, B., Song, Y.: Storing and retrieving secrets on a blockchain. In: Hanaoka, G., Shikata, J., Watanabe, Y. (eds.) PKC 2022, Part I. LNCS, vol. 13177, pp. 252–282. Springer, Heidelberg (Mar (2022)
33. Halevi, S., Ishai, Y., Jain, A., Kushilevitz, E., Rabin, T.: Secure multiparty computation with general interaction patterns. In: Sudan, M. (ed.) ITCS 2016, pp. 157–168. ACM, January 2016
34. Herzberg, A., Jarecki, S., Krawczyk, H., Yung, M.: Proactive secret sharing or: how to cope with perpetual leakage. In: Coppersmith, D. (ed.) CRYPTO 1995. LNCS, vol. 963, pp. 339–352. Springer, Heidelberg (1995). https://doi.org/10.1007/3-540-44750-4_27
35. Hirt, M., Maurer, U.M.: Player simulation and general adversary structures in perfect multiparty computation. J. Cryptol. **13**(1), 31–60 (2000), https://doi.org/10.1007/s001459910003
36. Katz, J., Koo, C.-Y.: On expected constant-round protocols for byzantine agreement. In: Dwork, C. (ed.) CRYPTO 2006. LNCS, vol. 4117, pp. 445–462. Springer, Heidelberg (2006). https://doi.org/10.1007/11818175_27
37. Kushilevitz, E., Lindell, Y., Rabin, T.: Information-theoretically secure protocols and security under composition. SIAM J. Comput. **39**(5), 2090–2112 (2010). https://doi.org/10.1137/090755886
38. Maram, S.K.D., et al.: CHURP: dynamic-committee proactive secret sharing. In: Cavallaro, L., Kinder, J., Wang, X., Katz, J. (eds.) ACM CCS 2019, pp. 2369–2386. ACM Press, November 2019
39. Maurer, U.: Secure multi-party computation made simple. Discrete Appl. Math. **154**(2), 370–381 (2006)
40. Micali, S.: Very simple and efficient byzantine agreement. In: Papadimitriou, C.H. (ed.) ITCS 2017, vol. 4266, pp. 6:1–6:1. LIPIcs, 67, January 2017
41. Ostrovsky, R., Yung, M.: How to withstand mobile virus attacks (extended abstract). In: Logrippo, L. (ed.) 10th ACM PODC, pp. 51–59. ACM, August 1991
42. Pass, R., Shi, E.: The sleepy model of consensus. In: Takagi, T., Peyrin, T. (eds.) ASIACRYPT 2017. LNCS, vol. 10625, pp. 380–409. Springer, Cham (2017). https://doi.org/10.1007/978-3-319-70697-9_14
43. Schultz, D., Liskov, B., Liskov, M.: Mpss: mobile proactive secret sharing. ACM Trans. Inf. Syst. Secur. (TISSEC) **13**(4), 1–32 (2010)
44. Wong, T.M., Wang, C., Wing, J.M.: Verifiable secret redistribution for archive systems. In: First International IEEE Security in Storage Workshop, 2002. Proceedings, pp. 94–105. IEEE (2002)

Round-Optimal Black-Box MPC in the Plain Model

Yuval Ishai[1(✉)], Dakshita Khurana[2], Amit Sahai[3], and Akshayaram Srinivasan[4]

[1] Technion, Haifa, Israel
yuvali@cs.technion.ac.il
[2] UIUC, Champaign, USA
[3] UCLA, Los Angeles, USA
[4] Tata Institute of Fundamental Research, Bengaluru, India

Abstract. We give the first construction of a (fully) black-box round-optimal secure multiparty computation protocol in the plain model. Our protocol makes black-box use of a sub-exponentially secure two-message statistical sender private oblivious transfer (SSP-OT), which in turn can be based on (sub-exponential variants of) most of the standard cryptographic assumptions known to imply public-key cryptography.

1 Introduction

The exact round complexity of secure computation has been a focus of research in cryptography over the past two decades. This has been especially well-studied in the synchronous setting in the plain model, with up to all-but-one static malicious corruptions. It is known that general-purpose secure multiparty computation (MPC) protocols in this setting admitting a *black-box simulator* require at least 4 rounds of simultaneous exchange [GK96b,KO04,GMPP16].[1] In this work we focus on MPC with black-box simulation. On the positive side, there has been a long sequence of works [GMPP16,BHP17,ACJ17,KS17,BGI+17, BGJ+18,CCG+20] improving the round complexity, culminating in a round-optimal construction that relies on the minimal assumption that a 4-round malicious-secure OT protocol exists [CCG+20].

Black-Box Use of Cryptography. Notably, all MPC protocols discussed above make non-black-box use of cryptography, which is typically associated with significant overheads in efficiency. It is interesting, from both a theoretical and a practical perspective, to realize *fully black-box protocols* [RTV04] where not only does the simulator make black-box use of an adversary, but also the construction itself can be fully specified given just oracle access to the input-output relation of the underlying cryptographic primitives, and without being given any explicit

[1] By simultaneous message exchange we mean that in each round, every party can send a message over a broadcast channel. However, we allow the adversarial parties to be rushing, meaning that they can wait until they receive all the honest party messages in each round before sending their own messages.

H. Handschuh and A. Lysyanskaya (Eds.): CRYPTO 2023, LNCS 14081, pp. 393–426, 2023.
https://doi.org/10.1007/978-3-031-38557-5_13

representation of these primitives. In the following, we refer to this standard notion of fully black-box protocols as simply *black-box protocols*. The focus of this work is on the following natural question:

What is the round complexity of black-box MPC in the plain model?

It was only recently that the *concrete* round complexity of black-box MPC in the plain model was studied. Ishai et al. [IKSS21] obtained a *five-round* MPC protocol making only black-box use of a public-key encryption scheme with pseudorandom public keys, along with any 2-message OT protocol satisfying semi-malicious security. They also gave 4-round protocols for a restricted class of functionalities that consist of parallel copies of "sender-receiver" two-party functionalities. While significantly improving over prior works, which required more than 15 rounds, it did not generally match the known 4-round lower bound. Indeed, round-optimal black-box protocols are not known even for the restricted case of two-sided 2PC, where both parties receive the output at the end of the protocol execution. Furthermore, [IKSS21] highlighted significant barriers in extending their techniques to obtain a round-optimal construction.

Our Results. In this work, we overcome these barriers to obtain a 4-round black-box MPC, thereby obtaining the first round-optimal fully-black-box MPC in the plain model for general functions. Our construction makes black-box use of any sub-exponential secure two-message OT, that satisfies a well-studied "statistical sender privacy" (SSP-OT) property. This essentially requires that the sender input remain statistically hidden from an unbounded malicious receiver. Such an OT protocol can be instantiated based on (sub-exponential variants) of standard cryptographic assumptions such as DDH/QR/N^{th} Residuosity/LWE [NP01, AIR01, Kal05, HK12, BD18, DGI+19]. This covers most of the standard cryptographic assumptions known to imply public-key cryptography, with LPN being the most notable exception[2]

On the Role of Subexponentially Secure OT. We stress that even though we rely on sub-exponentially secure OT, our final simulator still runs in expected polynomial time. This itself may seem counter-intuitive, and indeed we see it as a highlight of our technique and work. Very roughly, the reason why subexponentially secure OT is helpful to us for achieving *polynomial-time* simulation is that we design a protocol that admits *two separate* means for extracting the adversary's input. One is an "optimistic" extraction that runs in expected polynomial time, and the other is a super-polynomial extraction that achieves stronger properties. We use the super-polynomial extraction to essentially "bootstrap" and allow the optimistic extraction to succeed for the purposes of simulation. (See Technical Overview below for more details.) We believe this technique is of independent interest and may inspire progress in other settings where standard polynomial simulation is desired, but there is a need to reduce round complexity

[2] Recently, SSP-OT was constructed from low-noise LPN and a standard derandomization assumption [BF22] (building on [DGH+20]). However, this construction is only secure against quasi-polynomial sized adversaries.

beyond a barrier that arises from the need for some component of the protocol to achieve simulation security.

Finally, we note that the 4-round lower bound [GK96b,KO04,GMPP16] holds even when considering protocols that rely on sub-exponential hardness assumptions as long as the simulator runs in (expected) polynomial time.

1.1 Related Work

The black-box round-complexity of general purpose secure computation as well as for specific tasks such as oblivious transfer, zero-knowledge, non-malleable commitments etc., has a long and rich history.

General Purpose MPC. Haitner et al. [HIK+11] gave the first construction of a malicious-secure black-box MPC protocol in the plain model based on any semi-honest secure oblivious transfer. However, the round complexity of this construction grew linearly in the number of parties (denoted by n) even if one starts with a constant round semi-honest OT protocol. A later work of Wee [Wee10] gave a $O(\log^* n)$ black-box protocol by relying on stronger cryptographic assumptions such as dense cryptosystems, or homomorphic encryption, or lossy encryption. This was later improved by Goyal [Goy11] to give a constant round protocol under similar assumptions. Unfortunately, this constant was more than 15 which is a far cry from the lower bound of 4. A recent work of Ishai et al. [IKSS21] gave a black-box five-round protocol based on any PKE with pseudorandom public keys and any two-message OT protocol with semi-malicious security.

Special Secure Computation Tasks. For the case of oblivious transfer, Ostrovsky et al. [ORS15] gave a round-optimal (i.e., a four-round) construction that made black-box use of enhanced trapdoor permutations. Friolo et al. [FMV19] gave a round-optimal black-box construction of OT based on any public key encryption with pseudorandom public keys. Other black-box constructions of four-round OT from lower level primitives were given in [CCG+21,MOSV22].

Ishai et al. [IKSS21] extended these results to the multiparty setting and gave a round-optimal protocol for pairwise oblivious transfer functionality. In the pairwise OT setting, each ordered pair of parties, namely, P_i and P_j execute an OT instance with P_i acting as the sender and P_j acting as the receiver. This can be extended to parallel instances of general two-party sender-receiver functionalities.

Hazay and Venkitasubramanian [HV18] and Khurana et al. [KOS18] gave round-optimal black-box constructions of zero-knowledge arguments based on injective one-way functions. Hazay et al. [HPV20] showed that unless the polynomial hierarchy collapses, all of NP cannot have a black-box zero-knowledge argument based on one-way functions.

Goyal et al. [GLOV12] gave the first constant-round black-box construction of non-malleable commitments based on one-way functions. A latter work of Goyal et al. [GPR16] gave a three-round (which is round-optimal) black-box construction that is secure against a weaker class of synchronizing adversaries assuming the existence of injective one-way functions.

2 Technical Overview

In this section, we give an overview of the main techniques used in our construction of a round-optimal black-box secure multiparty computation protocol.

Starting Point. The starting point of our work is the recent result of Ishai et al. [IKSS21] who gave a construction of a five-round MPC protocol that makes black-box use of any public-key encryption scheme with pseudorandom public keys and any two-message semi-malicious OT protocol.[3] Their protocol is obtained via a round-efficient implementation of the IPS compiler [IPS08] in the plain model.

We note a key component that was used in their instantiation: a four-round black-box protocol that securely implements the *watchlist functionality.* Informally speaking, the watchlist functionality is an n-party functionality where each ordered pair of parties (P_i, P_j) where $i, j \in [n]$ are involved in a k-out-of-m OT instance with P_i acting as the sender and P_j acting as the receiver. Using this four-round watchlist protocol, Ishai et al. [IKSS21] showed that with an additional round of interaction, it is possible to securely compute any multiparty functionality. Furthermore, the resulting protocol only made black-box use of cryptographic primitives.

Going Below Five Rounds. In the same work, Ishai et al. [IKSS21] also observed that to get a four-round protocol (which is round-optimal) in the plain model by making use of the IPS compiler, one needs a three-round watchlist protocol. However, such a protocol cannot satisfy the standard simulation based security definition w.r.t. a simulator that only makes black-box use of the adversary. This is because such a simulation-secure watchlist protocol almost directly implies a three-round protocol for oblivious transfer that satisfies standard simulation security. We know that such a protocol is impossible to construct (even with non-black-box use of cryptography) if the simulator uses the adversary in a black-box manner [KO04]. Furthermore, to make matters more complicated, the proof of security of the overall compiler given in [IKSS21] crucially relied on the watchlist protocol to satisfy the standard simulation-style definition. Therefore, to go below five rounds and obtain a round-optimal construction, we need to come up with a new set of techniques.

Our Approach in a Nutshell. In this work, we show how to instantiate the IPS compiler using a weaker notion of watchlists, that we call *watchlists with promise security.* As one of our main contributions, we give a construction of a three-round watchlist protocol that satisfies promise security. In Sect. 2.1, we motivate the definition of this weaker watchlist protocol and show how it can be used to instantiate the IPS compiler and in Sect. 2.2, we give the main ideas in constructing such a watchlist protocol.

[3] Recall that semi-malicious adversaries are stronger than the standard semi-honest adversaries and are allowed to fix the random tape of adversarial parties to arbitrary values. However, like in the semi-honest setting, they are forced to follow the protocol specification.

2.1 Instantiating the IPS Compiler with Three-Round Watchlist

What Security can be achieved in Three Rounds? The work of Ishai et al. [IKSS21] gave a round-preserving compiler that transforms any two-party computation protocol that satisfies certain additional properties (which we will ignore for the moment) to a watchlist protocol. To understand what security properties can be achieved by a three-round watchlist protocol, let us first try to understand what type of security can be achieved by a three-round 2PC protocol.

Recall that in the standard two-party protocol setting, there is a receiver who holds an input x and there is a sender who holds an input y. At the end of the protocol, the receiver obtains the output of $f(x, y)$ for some pre-determined functionality f. If we consider three-round protocols for the above task, then the first and the third round messages in the protocol are sent by the sender and the second round message is sent by the receiver.[4] As the sender is tasked with sending both the first and the third round message, a simulator could potentially rewind the second and the third round messages in the protocol and extract the effective private input from an adversarial sender. In other words, a three-round 2PC protocol could satisfy standard simulation-based security definition against malicious senders. However, the receiver in this protocol is only sending a single message, namely, the second round message. In fact, it is impossible to design a black-box PPT simulator that could extract the effective private input from an adversarial receiver.

The key observation is that if we allow the simulator against malicious receivers to run in *super-polynomial* time, then such a simulator can extract the effective receiver input and provide security against malicious receivers. Therefore, in the three-round setting, we can hope to construct a two-party protocol that satisfies standard simulation based security against malicious senders and super-polynomial time simulation security against malicious receivers. Indeed, as we explain later, we give a construction of such a three-round protocol that makes black-box use of a sub-exponentially hard two-message OT protocol with statistical sender security. Such an OT protocol is known from the (sub-exponential variant) of standard cryptographic hardness assumptions such as DDH/N^{th} residuosity/LWE/QR [AIR01,NP01,Kal05,HK12,BD18,DGI+19].

Instantiating the IPS Compiler with the Three-Round Watchlist. Given the two-party protocol above, we could hope to obtain a three-round watchlist satisfying "semi-SPS" security by following ideas in prior work [IKSS21]. If this were possible, could we directly get a four-round MPC protocol by instantiating the IPS compiler with this "semi-SPS" three-round watchlist protocol? Unfortunately, this is not quite possible, as we now explain. To understand this better, we give a brief overview of the IPS compiler which is simplified and tailored to constructing a four-round protocol. The IPS compiler makes use of the following components:

[4] We note that any protocol, even one in the bidirectional communication model, can be reduced to this setting.

- A two-round client-server MPC protocol that is secure against a malicious adversary that corrupts an arbitrary number of clients and a constant fraction of the servers. This is called as the outer protocol. Such an outer protocol was constructed by Ishai et al. [IKP10,Pas12] by making black-box use of any PRG.
- A four-round inner protocol that satisfies the following robustness property. Specifically, even if the adversary behaves maliciously and deviates arbitrarily from the protocol specification in the first three rounds, it cannot learn any information about the inputs of the honest parties. Furthermore, if the adversary is able to produce an input, random tape that correctly explains that the messages sent by it in the first three rounds, then the last round message from the honest parties only reveals the output of the functionality.[5]
- A three-round watchlist protocol that satisfies the standard extraction of the adversarial sender inputs and super-polynomial time extraction of the adversarial receiver inputs.

In the compiled protocol, each party plays the role of a client in the outer protocol and computation done by the servers are emulated by the inner protocol. To ensure that the adversary only cheats in at most a small number of these inner protocol executions, we make use of the *watchlist protocol*. Specifically, each party acting as the receiver in the watchlist protocol chooses a random subset of k executions as part of its secret watchlist. Every other party acting as the sender uses the input, randomness used in each of the inner protocol executions as the sender inputs. This watchlist protocol is run in parallel with the first three rounds of the inner protocol. At the end of the third round, each party checks if the input, randomness pair provided by every other party corresponding to its watched executions are consistent. If it detects any inconsistency, then it aborts. Using standard probabilistic arguments, it is possible to show that if the honest parties have not aborted at the end of their watchlist check, then the adversary only deviates in a tiny constant fraction of the inner protocol executions. These deviations can be directly mapped to the corresponding server corruptions in the outer protocol. Since the outer protocol is secure against a constant fraction of the server corruptions, security of the overall protocol follows.

While the above intuition seems sound, we encounter a major issue while formalizing it. In particular, recall that we are aiming for standard polynomial security for our 4-round protocol, but we are relying on super-polynomial time extraction as an ingredient. Thus, we are only able to show that this protocol satisfies security via a super-polynomial time simulator. The "super-polynomial" part in this simulator is needed to extract the receiver inputs used by the adversarial parties in the watchlist protocol. Recall that in the watchlist protocol, the

[5] For technical reasons, we actually need the inner protocol to run in three rounds instead of four rounds. However, to keep the exposition simple, we will ignore this in the overview. In the main body, we give a black-box construction of such a three-round inner protocol based on two-round semi-malicious OT protocol (which is implied by two-round SSP OT). This construction builds on the protocols given in [GS18,PS21].

adversarial receiver inputs correspond to the set of watched executions of the corrupted parties. We need to extract this information in order to invoke the security of the outer protocol.[6] Further, the simulator also needs to additionally extract the adversarial sender inputs. As mentioned earlier, we cannot hope to simultaneously achieve efficient polynomial time extraction of both the sender and the receiver inputs.

Our Solution: "Promise-Style" Extraction. In order to get around this issue, we use a "promise-style" extraction technique that is inspired by the notion of Promise Zero-Knowledge [BGJ+18]. Specifically, we seek to devise an alternative polynomial-time extraction system that guarantees extraction of the adversarial receiver inputs only against those adversaries that send a valid third round message in the watchlist protocol (with non-negligible probability). For all other adversaries, we do not provide any guarantees. Let us now explain how this weaker extraction guarantee is sufficient to instantiate the IPS compiler.

The simulator of the compiled protocol starts generating the first-round messages of the outer protocol using some default inputs for the honest parties. Note that these first round messages correspond to the inputs to the inner protocol executions. The simulator uses these "dummy" inputs to the inner protocol and starts interacting with the adversary for the first three rounds. If the adversary aborts during this interaction, or fails to send a valid third round message in the watchlist protocol, then the simulator simply outputs the view of this adversary. On the other hand, if the adversary sends a valid third round message in the watchlist protocol, then the simulator uses the "promise-style" extractor to extract the set of watched executions. This information is then used by the simulator to simulate the messages in the main thread (using Goldreich-Kahan simulation technique [GK96a]).

A subtle point to note here is that the third round message in the watchlist protocol is sent by the adversary only after it receives the third round message from the honest parties (as we are considering rushing adversaries). However, the third round message of the watchlist protocol delivers the input, randomness used by the honest parties corresponding to the adversarial watched executions. Recall that the simulator described above uses "dummy" inputs in the inner protocol executions and tries to extract the adversarial watched executions. This will succeed only if the distribution of the messages generated by the simulator is computationally indistinguishable to the messages in the real protocol. Specifically, to prove this indistinguishability, we need to make sure that the output of the watchlist protocol when using the real inputs is indistinguishable to the case when the simulator uses default inputs.

To argue this, we rely on the security of the outer protocol. Recall that the inputs given to the inner protocol executions correspond to the messages sent by the clients to the servers. By corrupting the servers corresponding to the

[6] Specifically, the set of watched executions of the adversarial parties correspond to a subset of the corrupted servers in the outer protocol. To invoke the security of the outer protocol, we need to extract this information from the watchlist messages.

adversarial watched executions, we are guaranteed that the first round message sent to these servers reveals no information about the inputs of the honest clients. To give a bit more details, this is realized by first relying on the SPS security of the watchlist protocol against adversarial receivers to extract the adversarial watched executions, and then switch the input to a default value by relying the security of the outer protocol, and then switch back to an honest watchlist execution using the default inputs.

Another point to note here is that we cannot guarantee perfect extraction of the adversarial receiver inputs even if it sends a valid third round message with non-negligible probability. Due to technical reasons, we can only guarantee "almost" perfect extraction. By this, we mean that whenever the output received by the adversarial receiver is not $\perp$, the output of the promise extractor is identical to the SPS extractor. In other cases, there are no guarantees about the extracted value. We show that this weaker property is sufficient to instantiate the IPS compiler. Roughly, this is because if the output of the watchlist protocol is provided to the adversary is $\perp$, the adversary learns no information about the input, randomness for any inner protocol execution. Hence, if the promise extractor "over-extracts" the adversarial watched executions, this does not create any trouble with the simulation.

2.2 Constructing Three-Round Watchlists with Promise Extraction

A core ingredient of our black-box MPC protocol is a three-round "watchlist" protocol with promise-style extraction guarantees. For every $i \in [n], j \in [n] \setminus \{i\}$, this functionality enables P_i to choose a (private) subset $K \subseteq [m]$ of protocol executions of size k, and obtain the input and randomness used by P_j in all executions in the set K, while all other input and randomness values of P_j remain hidden from P_i.

Our first goal is to develop a three round protocol that realizes the watchlist functionality in the plain model in the presence of *malicious* corruptions, with super-polynomial simulation and (polynomial) promise-style extraction. Following [IKSS21], we observe that it would suffice to implement "sender non-malleable" OTs with super-polynomial simulation-based "real/ideal" security and with promise-style polynomial extraction; where in the (i, j)-th execution for $i \in [n], j \in [n] \setminus \{i\}$, P_i is the receiver and P_j is the sender. P_j's input to the OT will be the input and randomness it used in each of the m instances of the inner protocol, and P_i's input is a random subset K of $[m]$ of size k. By sender non-malleability, we mean that the adversarial parties cannot maul the sender messages in an OT execution with an honest party to obtain a "related" sender inputs in an OT execution with an honest receiver.

The work of [IKSS21] showed how to implement such sender non-malleable OT in four rounds from any *four-round simulation-secure two-party computation protocol* with certain additional properties (which we ignore for the momemt). Since we need three-round watchlists, we would need to begin with three-round two-party computation, which is impossible to realize with black-box polynomial-time simulation security. Nevertheless, we show that it is possible to realize such two-party computation with super-polynomial simulation and promise-style extraction, which is one of our key technical contributions. We describe this in the next subsection; here we discuss how such a two-party protocol can be compiled into 3-round non-malleable OT.

Our overall approach builds on [IKSS21], but also diverges in some key technical aspects. Like [IKSS21], our construction relies on a secure two-party protocol between a sender and a receiver realizing a special functionality $\mathcal{F}$ (described in Fig. 1). Unlike [IKSS21], we must develop a *three-round* compiler instead of a four round one.

In the [IKSS21] compiler, the sender $\mathcal{S}$ on input $(\mathsf{m}_0, \mathsf{m}_1)$ first encodes these messages using an appropriate 2-split-state non-malleable code $(\mathsf{enc}, \mathsf{dec})$.[7] For technical reasons pertaining to the use of watchlists in our final protocol, we require our watchlists to satisfy 1-*rewinding security*, i.e., no adversary should be able to distinguish *the joint distribution* of a main and a rewinding thread (with common prefix) from the real distribution, from those sampled according to the simulated distribution. This was not needed by [IKSS21], but this requirement in our setting necessitates deviating from the [IKSS21] template, relying on (a special type of) 3-split-state non-malleable code – specifically one that is also a 3-out-of-3 secret sharing scheme – instead of 2-split-state non-malleable codes.

Specifically, our sender encodes m_0 into $\mathsf{L}_0, \mathsf{M}_0, \mathsf{R}_0$ and encodes m_1 into $\mathsf{L}_1, \mathsf{M}_1, \mathsf{R}_1$. The receiver obtains input a choice bit $b \in \{0,1\}$, and additionally samples a uniformly random $c \in \{0,1,2\}$. $\mathcal{S}$ and $\mathcal{R}$ invoke a two-party secure protocol Π to compute functionality $\mathcal{F}$, described in Fig. 1.

Sender Inputs: $\mathsf{m}_0, \mathsf{L}_0, \mathsf{M}_0, \mathsf{R}_0, \mathsf{m}_1, \mathsf{L}_1, \mathsf{M}_1, \mathsf{R}_1$, **Receiver Inputs:** b, c
The functionality $\mathcal{F}$ is defined as follows.

1. Check if $\mathsf{L}_0, \mathsf{M}_0, \mathsf{R}_0$ is a valid encoding of m_0 and if not, output $\perp$.
2. Check if $\mathsf{L}_1, \mathsf{M}_1, \mathsf{R}_1$ is a valid encoding of m_1 and if not, output $\perp$.
3. If $c = 0$, output $(\mathsf{m}_b, \mathsf{L}_0, \mathsf{L}_1)$.
4. If $c = 1$, output $(\mathsf{m}_b, \mathsf{M}_0, \mathsf{M}_1)$.
5. If $c = 2$, output $(\mathsf{m}_b, \mathsf{R}_0, \mathsf{R}_1)$.

Fig. 1. The functionality $\mathcal{F}$

We note that the ideal functionality $\mathcal{F}$ only reveals m_b to the receiver, and statistically hides m_{1-b}. This is because the receiver obtains *only one of* L_{1-b}, M_{1-b} and R_{1-b}, and secrecy follows from the security of the secret sharing scheme. Thus, given one of the states the message m_{1-b} is information-theoretically hidden. Further, even given two executions of the ideal functionality on the *same*

[7] Recall that a split-state non-malleable code $(\mathsf{enc}, \mathsf{dec})$ encodes any message m into multiple states, such that the distribution of the tampered message obtained by tampering the each state individually is independent of m.

sender inputs, same receiver input b, and different receiver challenges c, the receiver only obtains m_b and two out of L_{1-b}, M_{1-b} and R_{1-b}. Given two out of these three shares, m_{1-b} is again statistically hidden. Indeed, when $\mathcal{F}$ is realized via a secure protocol Π, m_{1-b} continues to be computationally hidden even given a main and rewinding thread (with same inputs $\mathsf{m}_0, \mathsf{m}_1, b$). This protocol Π makes only black-box use of cryptography, and can be based on black-box access to our three-round two-party computation protocol that additionally satisfies certain amount of rewinding security, which we discuss in the next subsection.

Proving Sender Non-malleability. We must prove that running this protocol Π between every pair of parties in parallel securely realizes the watchlist functionality. We model the adversary as a man-in-the-middle, which acts as a receiver in "left" sessions and as sender in "right" sessions. We require that there is a simulator-extractor Sim-Ext that given the inputs of all honest receivers (in all right sessions), is able to extract all the implicit inputs used by the man-in-the-middle in all its right sessions. Crucially, Sim-Ext *does not* have access to the inputs of honest senders. Since the underlying protocol Π may be susceptible to arbitrary mauling attacks, achieving this property is non-trivial, as we discuss next.

Similar to [IKSS21], we use the specific way that sender inputs are encoded to introduce an *alternate* extraction mechanism. Specifically, one could imagine rewinding the second and the third round message of Π twice, with first round message fixed, and using inputs $c = 0$, $c = 1$ and $c = 2$ on behalf of the honest receiver in the real and rewinding threads, respectively. Our two-party computation protocol will be developed in such a way that fixing the first round message will fix all other inputs $\mathsf{m}_0, \mathsf{m}_1, b$ in all left and right sessions. Let us make the simplifying assumption that our adversary does not abort. Therefore, we expect to obtain outputs $(\widetilde{\mathsf{L}}_0, \widetilde{\mathsf{L}}_1)$, $(\widetilde{\mathsf{M}}_0, \widetilde{\mathsf{M}}_1)$ and $(\widetilde{\mathsf{R}}_0, \widetilde{\mathsf{R}}_1)$ in the right session in the real and rewinding threads respectively. At this point, we can use the decoder of the non-malleable code to obtain $(\widetilde{\mathsf{m}}_0, \widetilde{\mathsf{m}}_1)$, which, by correctness of the two-party protocol, should correspond to the implicit inputs of the MIM in the right session.

The Need for 2-Rewinding Security. Before we can rely on non-malleable codes to formally argue security, we need to replace the two-party protocol Π with its *simulated version.* At the same time, we need to argue that the joint distribution of values extracted from the strategy above (via extracting $(\widetilde{\mathsf{L}}_0, \widetilde{\mathsf{L}}_1)$, $(\widetilde{\mathsf{M}}_0, \widetilde{\mathsf{M}}_1)$ and $(\widetilde{\mathsf{R}}_0, \widetilde{\mathsf{R}}_1)$) from the simulated two-party protocol, matches the distribution in the real protocol. This requires the two-party protocol Π to satisfy a stronger security property, that we call 2-rewind sender security. This roughly means that any adversarial receiver/MIM that rewinds the honest sender one time in the third and fourth rounds, with its input $\widetilde{c}$ set to a possibly different value, does not learn more than the output of $\mathcal{F}$ on (fixed) inputs $(\mathsf{m}_0, \mathsf{m}_1, \mathsf{L}_0, \mathsf{L}_1, \mathsf{M}_0, \mathsf{M}_1, \mathsf{R}_0, \mathsf{R}_1, \widetilde{b}, \widetilde{c} = 0)$, $(\mathsf{m}_0, \mathsf{m}_1, \mathsf{L}_0, \mathsf{L}_1, \mathsf{R}_0, \mathsf{R}_1, \widetilde{b}, \widetilde{c} = 1)$ and $(\mathsf{m}_0, \mathsf{m}_1, \mathsf{L}_0, \mathsf{L}_1, \mathsf{R}_0, \mathsf{R}_1, \widetilde{b}, \widetilde{c} = 2)$. This can be formalized by demonstrating the existence of a simulator that simulates the receiver's view in the real and rewinding threads, given only $(\mathsf{m}_{\widetilde{b}}, \mathsf{L}_0, \mathsf{L}_1)$ in the main thread, and $(\mathsf{m}_{\widetilde{b}}, \mathsf{M}_0, \mathsf{M}_1)$,

$(\mathsf{m}_{\tilde{b}}, \mathsf{R}_0, \mathsf{R}_1)$ respectively in each of the rewinding threads (w.l.o.g.). Now, it may seem like the sum total of this information could essentially allow the receiver to recover $\mathsf{m}_{1-\tilde{b}}$. Yet, we show that if Π satisfies this property, it becomes possible to replace $\mathsf{m}_{1-\tilde{b}}$ with an arbitrary value (say 0^λ). Here we make use of the fact that the different states of the non-malleable code are available to the MIM in separate (i.e. real and rewinding) executions, which allows us to rely on the security guarantees provided by non-malleable codes, by arguing that each of these states are essentially tampered by *independent* functions.

Finally, we note that just as in [IKSS21], we require these codes to satisfy *many-many* non-malleability. At a high level, these are codes that are secure against multiple tamperings of a codeword [CGL16]. We note that a construction of 3-out-of-3 non-malleable secret sharing from [GSZ21] satisfies all the required properties (if instantiated with the CGL non-malleable code). Also following [IKSS21], to deal with adversaries who might abort, we will modify the protocol and functionality $\mathcal{F}$ so that instead of encoding (m_0, m_1) a single time, the sender generates λ (where λ is the security parameter) fresh encodings $\{(\mathsf{L}^i_b, \mathsf{M}^i_b, \mathsf{R}^i_b)\}_{i\in[\lambda],b\in\{0,1\}}$ of m_0 and m_1. The receiver picks λ choice bits $c_1, \ldots, c_\lambda$ instead of a single bit c. The functionality $\mathcal{F}$ checks if for every $i \in [n], \mathsf{b} \in \{0,1\}$, $\{(\mathsf{L}^i_b, \mathsf{M}^i_b, \mathsf{R}^i_b)\}_{i\in[\lambda],b\in\{0,1\}}$ encode m_b. If the check fails, $\mathcal{F}$ outputs $\bot$. If it passes, then for every $i \in [n]$, it outputs $(\mathsf{L}^i_0, \mathsf{L}^i_1)$ if $c_i = 0$, $(\mathsf{M}^i_0, \mathsf{M}^i_1)$ if $c_i = 1$, and otherwise, outputs $(\mathsf{R}^i_0, \mathsf{R}^i_1)$. We also recall that our watchlists need to satisfy super-polynomial simulation with "promise-style" extraction, but we note that these properties in fact carry over from the underlying special two-party computation protocol.

2.3 Constructing Three-Round 2PC with Special Extraction

In this subsection, we explain the key ideas behind our construction of a three-round 2PC that satisfies the "promise-style" extraction guarantee and "2-rewinding" sender security.

3-Round OT Protocol. As a first step, we construct a three-round black-box OT protocol that satisfies standard simulation-based security against malicious senders and super-polynomial time simulation security against malicious receivers. For this purpose, we rely on a (sub-exponentially hard) two-round OT protocol that has super-polynomial time simulation security against malicious receivers. To enable polynomial time extraction of the malicious sender input, we additionally require the sender to generate an extractable commitment to its input. To ensure the consistency of inputs used in the extractable commitment and the ones used in the OT protocol, we rely on the IPS compiler. Specifically, we use the 1-out-of-2 SPS OT to construct a k-out-of-m SPS OT protocol (using Yao's garbled circuits) and use this as the watchlist protocol. We show that this watchlist protocol is sufficient to instantiate the IPS compiler when we only require SPS security against malicious receivers.

3-Round 2PC. As a next step, we use the above OT protocol to construct a three-round 2PC protocol that satisfies standard simulation security against malicious senders and SPS security against malicious receivers. This step involves standard tools and closely follows the construction given in [IKSS21]. Additionally, we also show how to add 2-rewinding sender security to this protocol. Specifically, we show that if the underlying 3-round OT is 2-rewinding sender secure and we also have a 2-rewinding secure extractable commitment scheme (which was constructed in [BGJ+18]), we get a 2-rewinding sender secure 2PC protocol. Further, we note that 2-rewinding sender security of our 3-round OT protocol just boils down to instantiating the underling extractable commitment on the sender side (as explained earlier) with a 2-rewinding secure one, and we instantiate this with the construction given in [BGJ+18].

3-Round 2PC with Special Extraction. We then use the above 3-round 2PC protocol to construct a protocol that additionally satisfies the "promise-style" extraction guarantee. To achieve this, we require the receiver to commit to its input (as well as the randomness) used in the 2PC protocol via a three-round extractable commitment. Again, as in the case of OT protocol, we need to make sure that the inputs committed via the extractable commitment is consistent with the inputs used in the 2PC protocol. As before, we rely on the IPS compiler but we observe that we do not need the "full-blown" watchlist protocol. Instead, we require the sender in the second round to send a set of executions to be opened in the *clear* and the receiver in the final round opens the extractable commitment corresponding to these executions. The sender then checks whether the input, randomness committed via the extractable commitment is consistent with the messages sent in the 2PC protocol. If they are consistent for randomly opened set of executions, then by standard statistical argument, we can show that they are consistent for a majority of the executions with overwhelming probability. This allows us to rewind and extract the receiver's input via the extractable commitment. We note that we are only able to guarantee "almost" perfect extraction due to the existence of a "small" set of inconsistent executions. Specifically, the "small" set of inconsistent executions could force the output of the watchlist protocol to be $\perp$, but even in this case, our polynomial time extract could extract some receiver input. But as explained earlier, this is not problematic and is sufficient to instantiate the IPS compiler. We also note that if the underlying 2PC protocol is 2-rewinding sender secure then this property is inherited by the 2PC protocol with special extraction as well.

Organization. Due to lack of space, we only present the watchlist protocol and defer the other constructions and their proof of security to the full version.

3 Preliminaries

We recall some standard cryptographic definitions in this section.

Split-State Non-malleable Codes We will use non-malleable codes in the split-state model that are one-many secure and satisfy a special augmented non-malleability [AAG+16] property, as discussed below.

Definition 1 (One-many augmented split-state non-malleable codes). *Fix any polynomials $\ell(\cdot), p(\cdot)$. An $\ell(\cdot)$-augmented non-malleable code with error $\epsilon(\cdot)$ for messages $m \in \{0,1\}^{p(\lambda)}$ consists of algorithms* $\mathsf{NM.Code}, \mathsf{NM.Decode}$ *where*

- $\mathsf{NM.Code}(m) \to (L, M, R)$ *where $L \in \mathcal{L}$, $M \in \mathcal{M}$ and $R \in \mathcal{R}$ (we will assume that $\mathcal{L} = \mathcal{M} = \mathcal{R}$) are a three-out-of-three secret sharing of the message,*
- *For every $m \in \{0,1\}^{p(\lambda)}$,*

$$\mathsf{NM.Decode}(\mathsf{NM.Code}(m)) = m, \text{ and}$$

- *For every set of functions $f = (f_1, f_2, \ldots f_{\ell(\lambda)}), g = (g_1, g_2, \ldots g_{\ell(\lambda)}), h = (h_1, h_2, \ldots h_{\ell(\lambda)})$ and every set of permutations $\{\sigma_i\}_{i \in [\ell(\lambda)]}, \sigma'$ on (L, M, R) there exists a random variable $\mathcal{D}_{f,g,h,\sigma,\sigma'}$ on $\mathcal{R} \times \{\{0,1\}^{p(\lambda)} \cup \mathsf{same}^*\}^{\ell(\lambda)}$ which is independent of the randomness in* $\mathsf{NM.Code}$ *such that for all messages $m \in \{0,1\}^{p(\lambda)}$ it holds that the statistical distance between the distributions*

$$\sigma'(\mathsf{L}), \sigma'(\mathsf{M}), \{\mathsf{NM.Decode}\big(f_i(\sigma_i(\mathsf{L})), g_i(\sigma_i(\mathsf{M})), h_i(\sigma_i(\mathsf{R}))\big)\}_{i \in [\ell(\lambda)]}$$

$$\text{and } (\mathsf{replace}(\mathcal{D}_{f,g,h,\sigma,\sigma'}, m)) \text{ where } (\mathsf{L}, \mathsf{M}, \mathsf{R} \leftarrow \mathsf{NM.Code}(m))$$

is at most $\epsilon(\lambda)$, where the function $\mathsf{replace} : \{0,1\}^* \times \{0,1\}^* \to \{0,1\}$ *replaces all occurrences of* same^* *in its first input with its second input, and outputs the result.*

We note that the construction of non-malleable secret sharing in [GSZ21] can be proven to satisfy this definition. This is already implicit in [GSZ21] for the case of single tampering but extension of their proof to the case of multiple tamperings follows directly if we use a strong two-source non-malleable extractors that is multi-tamperable [CGL16]. Thus, we have the following:

Lemma 1. *[GSZ21] For every polynomial $\ell(\cdot)$, there exists a polynomial $q(\cdot)$ such that for every $\lambda \in \mathbb{N}$, there exists an explicit ℓ-augmented, split-state non-malleable code satisfying Definition 1 with efficient encoding and decoding algorithms with code length $q(\lambda)$, rate $q(\lambda)^{-\Omega(1)}$ and error $2^{-q(\lambda)^{\Omega(1)}}$.*

Low-Depth Proofs. Any computation performed by a family of polynomial sized ciruits can be transformed into a proof that is verifiable by a family of circuits in NC1. We refer to the transformation as a low-depth proof, and we require such a proof to satisfy the following definition.

Definition 2 (Low-Depth Non-interactive Proofs). *A low-depth non-interactive proof with perfect completeness and soundness for a relation R consists of an (efficient) prover P and a verifier V that satisfy:*

- **Perfect completeness.** *A proof system is perfectly complete if an honest provers can always convince an honest verifier. For all* $x \in L$ *we have*

$$\Pr[V(\pi) = 1 | \pi \leftarrow P(x)] = 1$$

- **Perfect soundness.** *A proof system is perfectly sound if it is infeasible to convince an honest verifier when the statement is false. For all* $x \notin L$ *and all (even unbounded) adversaries* $\mathcal{A}$ *we have*

$$Pr[V(x, \pi) = 1 | \pi \leftarrow \mathcal{A}(x)] = 0.$$

- **Low Depth.** *The verifier* V *can be implemented in* $\mathsf{NC1}$.

It is shown in [IKSS21] building on [GGH+13] how such a non-interactive proof can be constructed in a simple way. Looking ahead, our construction of watchlists makes use of a (malleable) two-party computation protocol for $\mathsf{NC1}$ that must verify validity of a non-malleable code. We rely on low-depth proofs to ensure that the two-party computation protocol only performs $\mathsf{NC1}$ computations.

3.1 3-Round Two-Party Computation Protocol with Special Extraction

The watchlist protocol requires a special two-party computation protocol. We give a construction of this protocol in the full version and present the definition here.

Syntax. A three-round protocol $\Pi = (\Pi_1, \Pi_2, \Pi_3, \mathsf{out}_\Pi)$ between a sender and a receiver proceeds as follows. In each round $r \in [3]$, the sender runs Π_r on its identity, the transcript, its input and randomness to generate msg_r^S. Similarly, in round r, the receiver runs Π_r on its identity, the transcript, its input and randomness to generate msg_r^R. The sender sends msg_r^S to the receiver and the receiver sends msg_r^R to the sender and these messages are then added to the transcript. At the end of the protocol, the receiver run out_Π on its identity, transcript, its input and randomness to compute the output which is a string z or $\perp$. The sender runs out_Π on its identity and the first round message from the receiver, the second round message from the sender and third round message from the receiver and outputs either $\mathsf{accept/reject}$. We note that while the output computation of the receiver requires access to its private random tape, the output of the sender is publicly computable.

Definition 3. *A three-round two-party protocol* $\Pi = (\Pi_1, \Pi_2, \Pi_3, \mathsf{out}_\Pi)$ *for computing a function* f *is said to satisfy* k*-special extraction if:*

- ***Public Coin Second Round Messages.*** *The second round messages from the sender and the receiver are both public coin.*

- ***Security against Malicious Senders.*** *There exists an expected PPT machine* Sim_S *such that for every non-uniform* $\mathcal{A}$ *the corrupts the sender and for every receiver's input* $x \in \{0,1\}^n$*, we have:*

$$\left\{(\mathsf{View}_{\mathcal{A}}(\langle R(1^\lambda, x), \mathcal{A}(1^\lambda)\rangle), \mathsf{out}_R(\langle R(1^\lambda, x), \mathcal{A}(1^\lambda)\rangle))\right\} \approx_c$$
$$\left\{(\mathsf{View}_{\mathcal{A}}, f(x,y)) : (\mathsf{View}_{\mathcal{A}}, y) \leftarrow (\mathsf{Sim}_S)^{\mathcal{A}}(1^\lambda)\right\}$$

In the above definition, we note that if y *output by* Sim_S *is the special symbol* $\perp$*, then the output of* f *is also* $\perp$*. We additionally need the existence of a straight-line SPS simulator* SPSim_S *that has the same guarantees as* Sim_S*.*
- ***Super-Polynomial Time Simulation Security against Malicious Receivers.*** *There exists a super-polynomial time machine* $\mathsf{SPSim}_R = (\mathsf{SPSim}_R^1, \mathsf{SPExt}_R, \mathsf{SPSim}_R^2, \mathsf{SPSim}_R^3)$ *such that for every adversary* $\mathcal{A}$ *corrupting the receiver and for every sender's input* $y \in \{0,1\}^n$*, we have:*

$$\left\{\mathsf{View}_{\mathcal{A}}(\langle \mathcal{A}(1^\lambda), S(1^\lambda, y)\rangle)\right\} \approx_c \mathsf{Ideal}_R(1^\lambda, y, \mathcal{A}, \mathsf{SPSim}_R)$$

where the experiment Ideal_R *is described in Fig. 2.*
- ***2-Rewinding Sender Security against Sub-Exponential Adversaries.*** *We require that this protocol to be secure against any malicious sub-exponential time receiver that could rewind an honest sender twice by giving possibly different second round messages in each rewind.*
- ***Special Extraction of the Malicious Receiver Input.*** *There exists a super-polynomial time extractor* $\mathsf{SPSpecExt}_R$ *such that for any adversary* $\mathcal{A}$ *corrupting the receiver and for any sender input* $y \in \{0,1\}^n$*, the probability the following experiment outputs 1 is negligible:*
  1. *Sample a transcript* $\mathbb{T}$ *from* $\mathsf{Ideal}_R(1^\lambda, y, \mathcal{A}, \mathsf{SPSim}_R)$*.*
  2. *If the output of the sender* S *in the transcript* $\mathbb{T}$ *is* reject*, then output of the experiment is* 0*.*
  3. *Run* $\mathsf{SPExt}_R(\mathsf{msg}_R^1)$ *(where* $\mathsf{msg}_R^1 \in \mathbb{T}$*) to obtain* x*. If* $x = \perp$*, output of the experiment is* 0*.*
  4. *Else, run* $\mathsf{SPSpecExt}(\mathbb{T})$ *to obtain* x'*.*
  5. *The output of the experiment is* 1 *if and only if* $x \neq x'$*.*
- ***Existence of*** k ***accepting Transcript Extractor.*** *There exists a polynomial time machine* Ext_R *that on input any* k *transcripts* $\mathbb{T}_1, \ldots, \mathbb{T}_k$ *such that in each of the transcript the output of the sender is* accept *outputs* $\overline{x}$ *such that* $\overline{x} = \mathsf{SPSpecExt}(\mathbb{T}_1)$ *with overwhelming probability.*
- ***Delayed Function Selection.*** *The function to be computed can be chosen by the sender in the third round.*

4 The Watchlist Protocol

In this section, we formally construct and prove security of three-round watchlist protocol. Recall that in the watchlist protocol, each ordered pair of parties P_i

- Run $\mathsf{SPSim}^1_R(1^\lambda)$ to obtain $(\mathsf{msg}^S_1, \mathsf{st})$ and send msg^S_1 to $\mathcal{A}$. Receive msg^R_1 from $\mathcal{A}$.
- Run $\mathsf{SPExt}_R(\mathsf{msg}^R_1)$ to obtain x, st'.
- Sample $(\mathsf{msg}^S_2, \mathsf{st}'')$ from $\mathsf{SPSim}^2_R(\mathsf{st}, \mathsf{st}')$ and send msg^S_2 to $\mathcal{A}$.
- Receive msg^R_2 from $\mathcal{A}$.
- Run $\mathsf{SPSim}^3_R(\mathsf{st}'', f(x,y), \mathsf{msg}^R_1, \mathsf{msg}^R_2, \mathsf{msg}^S_2)$ to obtain msg^S_3 and send this to $\mathcal{A}$.
- Receive msg^R_3 from $\mathcal{A}$.
- Output view of $\mathcal{A}$.

Fig. 2. Description of Ideal_R.

and P_j invoke a ℓ-out-of-m OT functionality where P_i acts as the receiver and P_j acts as the sender. Specifically, the private input of party P_j in this OT instance consists of of $\mathbf{x}_j$ which is the vector of sender inputs of dimension m and the private input of party P_i is K_i which is a subset of $[m]$ of size ℓ. The output to party P_i consists of $\{\mathbf{x}_{j,k}\}_{k \in K_i}$. We note that in the watchlist protocol, every honest party P_i uses the same K_i in each instance of the OT functionality when acting as the receiver and same $\mathbf{x}_i$ in each instance when acting as the sender. However, the corrupted party P_i may choose different K_i and $\mathbf{x}_i$ for each instance when acting as the receiver and the sender respectively. For ease of notation, whenever we use K_i as the receiver input of a corrupted party P_i, we actually mean a set of subsets $\{K_{i,j}\}_{j \in H}$. Similarly, whenever we use $\mathbf{x}_j$ as the sender input of a corrupted party P_j, we actually mean set of vectors, one for each honest party.

4.1 Definitions

Before we proceed to the formal definition of the watchlist protocol, we give an informal overview of the various properties that the protocol needs to satisfy.

1. The first requirement is the existence of a straight-line super-polynomial time simulator $\mathsf{Sim}_{\mathsf{WL}}$ that has oracle access to the watchlist functionality and produces a view of the adversary that is computationally indistinguishable to the real world. This requirement is same as standard SPS security. Here, it is crucial that the simulator is straight-line i.e., it does not rewind the adversary.
2. The second property is about the existence of an "alternate" extraction mechanism of the malicious receiver inputs. Specifically, we require that if the output of all the honest parties when acting as the sender is not $\bot$ in the protocol, then there exists an alternate super-polynomial time extractor $\mathsf{SPExt}_{\mathsf{WL},R}$ that extracts the adversarial receiver inputs using the accepting transcript. Further, for each corrupted party, these inputs are the same as the ones extracted by $\mathsf{Sim}_{\mathsf{WL}}$ except in the case that it is $\bot$.

3. The third property is about the existence of polynomial-time rewinding extractor (that rewinds the adversary until it obtains k accepting transcripts) and outputs the malicious receiver inputs that is identical to the one output by $\mathsf{SPExt}_{\mathsf{WL},R}$. For technical reasons, we need to separate out the existence of a polynomial time rewinding extractor and super-polynomial time extractor in the alternate extraction mechanism.
4. The fourth property is about the one-rewinding sender non-malleability. Roughly speaking, it requires that adversarial sender inputs cannot depend on the honest party sender inputs even if the adversary is allowed to rewind the second and third round message of the protocol once.

Definition 4. (Extractable (n, m, ℓ)-Watchlists). *Fix any polynomials $n = n(\lambda), m = m(\lambda), \ell = \ell(\lambda)$. An extractable (n, m, ℓ)-watchlist is a protocol that achieves the simultaneous n-party m-choose-ℓ OT functionality with the following security guarantees:*

1. ***Real-Ideal Security with Straight-line SPS simulator.*** *There exists a (stateful) straight-line super-polynomial time simulator $\mathsf{Sim}_{\mathsf{WL}}$ such that for any (stateful) adversary $\mathcal{A}$ that is corrupting an arbitrary subset M of the parties and for any choice of honest party inputs $\{\mathbf{x}_j, K_j\}_{j\in H}$ (where H denotes the set of honest parties, $\mathbf{x}_j$'s denote the sender inputs of party j, and K_j's denote the set of executions that player j watches), we have the following two distributions are computationally indistinguishable:*
   (a) View of the adversary and the output of all the honest parties H in the real execution of the protocol.
   (b) $\mathsf{Ideal}_{SPS}(1^\lambda, M, \mathcal{A}, \mathsf{Sim}_{\mathsf{WL}})$ where Ideal_{SPS} is given in Fig. 3.
   Furthermore, the distribution of the messages generated by $\mathsf{Sim}_{\mathsf{WL}}$ on behalf of honest receivers is identically distributed to the real receiver messages with dummy inputs.
2. ***Special Extraction of the Malicious Receiver Input.*** *There exists a super-polynomial time extractor $\mathsf{SPExt}_{\mathsf{WL},R}$ such that for any adversary $\mathcal{A}$ corrupting a subset M of the parties and for any choice of honest party inputs $\{\mathbf{x}_j, K_j\}_{j\in H}$, the probability that the following experiment outputs 1 is negligible:*
   (a) Sample a transcript $\mathbb{T}$ from Ideal_{SPS} experiment and let $\{\sigma_j\}_{j\in H}$ be the output of the honest parties.
   (b) If $\sigma_j = \bot$ for each $j \in H$ in Ideal_{SPS} experiment, then output of the experiment is 0.
   (c) Else, run $\mathsf{Sim}_{\mathsf{WL}}(\{\mathsf{msg}_1^i\}_{i\in M})$ (where $\{\mathsf{msg}_1^i\}_{i\in M} \in \mathbb{T}$) to obtain $(\{K_i\}_{i\in M}, \mathsf{st})$.
   (d) Run $\mathsf{SPExt}_{\mathsf{WL},R}(\mathbb{T})$ to obtain $\{K_i'\}_{i\in M}$.
   (e) The output of the experiment is 1 if and only if there exists an $i \in H$ such that $K_i' \neq K_i$ whenever $K_i \neq \bot$.
3. ***Existence of k accepting Transcript Extractor.*** *There exists a polynomial time machine $\mathsf{Ext}_{\mathsf{WL},R}$ such that on input any k transcripts $\mathbb{T}_1, \ldots, \mathbb{T}_k$ with common first message such that in each of the transcript the output of the honest parties is not $\bot$ outputs $\{\overline{K}_j\}_{j\in H}$ such that $\{\overline{K}_j\}_{j\in H} = \mathsf{SPExt}_{\mathsf{WL},R}(\mathbb{T}_1)$ with overwhelming probability.*

4. ***One-Rewinding Sender Non-Malleability.*** *We require the existence of an (expected) PPT algorithm* $\mathsf{Ext}_{\mathsf{WL},S}$ *such that for any 1-rewinding adversary* $\mathcal{A}$ *corrupting any set* M *of the parties (by 1-rewinding, we refer to an adversary that is allowed to rewind the second and third round message of the protocol once) and for any choice of honest party inputs* $\{\mathbf{x}_j, K_j\}_{j\in H}$ *such that the following two distributions are computationally indistinguishable against adversaries that run in time which is polynomial in the running time of* $\mathsf{SPSim}_{\mathsf{WL},R}$*:*
   (a) *Consider the* Ideal_{SPS} *experiment in Fig. 3 with the 1-rewinding adversary* $\mathcal{A}$ *(i.e., step-4 in the experiment is repeated once more). Let us denote the first execution with the adversary as the main thread and the rewinding execution with* $\mathcal{A}$ *as the rewind thread. After step-4, run* $\mathsf{Sim}_{\mathsf{WL}}$ *on the messages generated in the main thread to compute* $\{\mathbf{x}_i\}_{i\in M}$*. Output the view of the adversary* $\mathcal{A}$ *and* $\{\mathbf{x}_i\}_{i\in M}$*.*
   (b) *Sample uniform random tape* $\{r_j\}_{j\in H}$ *and execute the protocol honestly with the 1-rewinding adversary* $\mathcal{A}$ *using the honest inputs* $\{K_j, \mathbf{x}_j\}_{j\in H}$ *with the above random tape. Run* $\mathsf{Ext}_{\mathsf{WL},S}(1^\lambda, \{K_j, \mathbf{x}_j, r_j\}_{j\in H})$ *to obtain* $\{\mathbf{x}_i\}_{i\in M}$*. Output view of the adversary in the above honest execution along with* $\{\mathbf{x}_i\}_{i\in M}$*.*

1. Run $\mathsf{Sim}_{\mathsf{WL}}(1^\lambda, M)$ to obtain $\{\mathsf{msg}_1^j\}_{j\in H}$ and send this to $\mathcal{A}$. Receive $\{\mathsf{msg}_1^i\}_{i\in M}$ from $\mathcal{A}$.
2. Run $\mathsf{Sim}_{\mathsf{WL}}(\{\mathsf{msg}_1^i\}_{i\in M})$ to obtain $(\{K_i\}_{i\in M}, \mathsf{st})$.
3. Compute the output of the watchlist received by the parties in M when the honest sender inputs are $\{\mathbf{x}_j\}_{j\in H}$ and the malicious receiver inputs are $\{K_i\}_{i\in M}$. Let $\{\sigma_i\}_{i\in M}$ be this output.
4. For each $r \in \{2, 3\}$:
   (a) Run $\mathsf{Sim}_{\mathsf{WL}}(\{\sigma_i\}_{i\in M}, \mathsf{st}, \{\mathsf{msg}_k^i\}_{k\in[r-1], i\in M})$ to obtain $\{\mathsf{msg}_r^j\}_{j\in H}$ and send this to $\mathcal{A}$. Receive $\{\mathsf{msg}_r^i\}_{i\in M}$ from $\mathcal{A}$.
5. Run $\mathsf{Sim}_{\mathsf{WL}}(\{\mathsf{msg}_k^i\}_{i\in M, k\in[3]})$ to obtain $\{\mathbf{x}_i\}_{i\in M}$.
6. Compute the output of the watchlist received by the parties in H when the honest receiver inputs are $\{K_j\}_{j\in H}$ and the malicious sender inputs are $\{\mathbf{x}_i\}_{i\in M}$. Let $\{\sigma_j\}_{j\in H}$ be this output.
7. Output view of $\mathcal{A}$ and $\{\sigma_j\}_{j\in H}$.

Fig. 3. Description of Ideal_{SPS}.

4.2 Construction

Our construction is described in Fig. 4, and makes use of the following ingredients:

- A 3 round two-party secure computation protocol Π satisfying Definition 3 with delayed-function selection for NC^1 circuits and 2-rewinding sender security.
- An information-theoretic $m(\lambda) \cdot \ell(\lambda)$ non-malleable coding scheme satisfying Definition 1.
- A low-depth proof for P according to Definition 2.
- An existentially unforgetable signature scheme with algorithms denoted by $\mathsf{Signature.Setup}$, $\mathsf{Signature.Sign}$ and $\mathsf{Signature.Verify}$.

We describe our protocol formally in Fig. 4. The correctness of this protocol follows from correctness of the underlying oblivious transfer, non-malleable codes and signature scheme. In what follows, we formally prove security according to Definition 4.

Theorem 1. *Let λ denote the security parameter, and $m = m(\lambda), k = k(\lambda), \ell = \ell(\lambda)$ be arbitrary polynomials. There exists a 3 round ℓ non-malleable $\binom{m}{k}$ oblivious transfer protocol satisfying Definition 4 that makes black-box use of any 3 round two-party secure computation protocol Π satisfying Definition 3 with 2-rewinding sender security, and any existentially unforgeable signature scheme.*

Proof of Theorem 1. We observe that properties 2 and 3 carry over from the properties of the underlying two-party computation protocol, and 1 is implied by 4 together with SPS security of the two-party protocol against malicious adversaries (following [IKSS21]). Our key goal is to prove that the protocol satisfies property 4. To keep exposition simple, we prove this property against polynomial time distinguishers. We note that indistinguishability against distinguishers running in time which is polynomial in the running time of $\mathsf{SPExt}_{\mathsf{WL},R}$ follows directly from the 2-rewinding sender security of the underlying 2PC protocol against such distinguishers.

We now consider a man-in-the-middle adversary that participates as an OT receiver in upto $\ell(\lambda)$ executions of this protocol on the right, and participates as an OT sender in upto $\ell(\lambda)$ executions on the left. Towards proving that our protocol satisfies property 1, we will prove that there exists a PPT algorithm $\mathsf{Sim\text{-}Ext}$, that with black-box access to the MIM, and to ℓ copies of the ideal OT functionality $\mathbf{OT} = \{\mathsf{OT}_j(\{\mathsf{m}_{i,j}\}_{i\in[m]}, \cdot)\}_{j\in[\ell]}$ and with input $\{K_j\}_{j\in[\ell]}$, simulates an execution of the protocol with the MIM and extracts all the inputs $\{(\{\widetilde{\mathsf{m}}_{i,j}\}_{i\in[m]})\}_{j\in[\ell]}$ used by the MIM in the executions where the MIM is sender. We will prove that the 1-rewinding view output by $\mathsf{Sim\text{-}Ext}$, that we denote by $\mathsf{Ideal}_{\mathsf{MIM}}(\{\mathsf{m}_{i,j}\}_{i\in[m],j\in[\ell]}, \{K_j\}_{j\in[\ell]})$ will be such that

$$\mathsf{Real}_{\mathsf{MIM}}\langle\{\mathcal{S}_j(\{\mathsf{m}_{i,j}\}_{i\in[m]})\}_{j\in[\ell]}, \{\mathcal{R}_j(K_j)\}_{j\in[\ell]}\rangle \approx_c \mathsf{Ideal}_{\mathsf{MIM}}(\{\mathsf{m}_{i,j}\}_{i\in[m],j\in[\ell]}, \{K_j\}_{j\in[\ell]})$$

where the expression on the left denotes the joint distribution of the view and messages committed by a 1-rewinding adversary in an interaction where honest senders $\mathcal{S}_j$ have inputs $\{\mathsf{m}_{i,j}\}_{i\in[m]}$, and honest receivers $\mathcal{R}_j$ have inputs K_j.

Inputs: Sender $\mathcal{S}$ has inputs $\{\mathsf{m}_j\}_{j \in m}$ and receiver $\mathcal{R}$ has input a set $K \subseteq [m]$ where $|K| = k$.

Protocol: $\mathcal{S}$ and $\mathcal{R}$ do the following.

1. $\mathcal{S}$ samples $(vk, sk) \leftarrow \mathsf{Signature.Setup}(1^\lambda)$, then does the following.
   - For each $i \in [\lambda], j \in [m]$, pick uniform randomness $r_{i,j}$ and compute
   $$(\mathsf{L}_{i,j}, \mathsf{M}_{i,j}, \mathsf{R}_{i,j}) = \mathsf{NM.Code}((vk|\mathsf{m}_j); r_{i,j}).$$
   - Set instance $x = (vk, \{(\mathsf{L}_{i,j}, \mathsf{M}_{i,j}, \mathsf{R}_{i,j}, \mathsf{m}_j)\}_{i\in[\lambda],j\in[m]})$ and language
   $$\mathcal{L} = \{(vk, \{(\mathsf{L}_{i,j}, \mathsf{M}_{i,j}, \mathsf{R}_{i,j}, \mathsf{m}_j)\}_{i\in[\lambda],j\in[m]}) : \\ \forall i \in [\lambda], j \in [m], \mathsf{NM.Decode}(\mathsf{L}_{i,j}, \mathsf{M}_{i,j}, \mathsf{R}_{i,j}) = (vk|\mathsf{m}_j)\}.$$

   Compute $\mathsf{ldp} = \mathsf{LDP.Prove}(x, \mathcal{L})$.
2. For each $i \in [\lambda]$, $\mathcal{R}$ picks $\mathsf{c}_i \leftarrow \{0, 1, 2\}$.
3. Both parties engage in the protocol Π to compute functionality $\mathcal{F}$ where:
   - $\mathcal{R}$ plays the receiver with input K committed in round 1 and delayed function $(\mathsf{c}_1, \ldots, \mathsf{c}_\lambda)$ chosen in round 2.
   - $\mathcal{S}$ plays the sender with input (x, ldp), where x is parsed as $(vk, \{\mathsf{m}_j, (\mathsf{L}_{i,j}, \mathsf{M}_{i,j}, \mathsf{R}_{i,j})\}_{i\in[\lambda],j\in[m]}$.
   - The functionality $\mathcal{F}$ on input $(vk, \{\mathsf{m}_j, \mathsf{L}_{i,j}, \mathsf{M}_{i,j}, \mathsf{R}_{i,j}\}_{i\in[\lambda],j\in[m]}, K, \{\mathsf{c}_i\}_{i\in[\lambda]})$ generates an output as follows:
     - If $\mathsf{LDP.Verify}(x, \mathsf{ldp}) \neq 1$, output $\perp$. Otherwise set $\mathsf{out} = vk, \{\mathsf{m}_j\}_{j\in K}$.
     - Additionally, for every $i \in [\lambda]$, if $c_i = 0$, append $(\{\mathsf{L}_{i,j}\}_{j\in[m]})$ to out, if $c_i = 1$, append $(\{\mathsf{M}_{i,j}\}_{j\in[m]})$ to out, else append $(\{\mathsf{R}_{i,j}\}_{j\in[m]})$ to out.
     - Output out.

   Additionally, $\mathcal{S}$ signs messages generated according to Π, denoted by (Π_1, Π_3). It sets $\sigma_1 = \mathsf{Signature.Sign}(\Pi_1, \mathsf{id}_\mathcal{S}, sk)$, $\sigma_3 = \mathsf{Signature.Sign}(\Pi_3, \mathsf{id}_\mathcal{S}, sk)$ where $\mathsf{id}_\mathcal{S}$ is the identity of the sender. It sends (σ_1, σ_3) to $\mathcal{R}$.
4. $\mathcal{R}$ obtains output out and parses $\mathsf{out} = (vk, \{\mathsf{m}_j\}_{j\in K}, \cdot)$. It outputs $\{\mathsf{m}_j\}_{j\in K}$ iff $\mathsf{Signature.Verify}(\sigma_1, \Pi_1, \mathsf{id}_\mathcal{S} vk) \wedge \mathsf{Signature.Verify}(\sigma_3, \Pi_3, \mathsf{id}_\mathcal{S}, vk) = 1$, otherwise outputs $\perp$.

Fig. 4. $\ell(\lambda)$ Non-Malleable $m(\lambda)$-choose-$k(\lambda)$ Oblivious Transfer

To prove indistinguishability, we define a sequence of hybrid experiments, where the first one outputs the distribution $\mathsf{Real}_{\mathsf{MIM}}\langle\{\mathcal{S}_j(\{\mathsf{m}_{i,j}\}_{i\in[m]})\}_{j\in[\ell]}, \{\mathcal{R}_j(K_j)\}_{j\in[\ell]}$ and the final one outputs the distribution $\mathsf{Ideal}_{\mathsf{MIM}}(\{\mathsf{m}_{i,j}\}_{i\in[m],j\in[\ell]}, \{K_j\}_{j\in[\ell]})$. Formally, these hybrids are defined as follows:

Hyb_0 : This corresponds to an execution of the MIM with ℓ honest senders $\{\mathcal{S}_j\}_{j\in[\ell]}$ on the left, each using inputs $\{\mathsf{m}_{i,j}\}_{i\in[m]}$ respectively and ℓ honest receivers on the right with inputs $(\{K_j\}_{j\in[\ell]})$ respectively. The output of this hybrid is $\mathsf{Real}_{\mathsf{MIM}}\langle\{\mathcal{S}_j(\{\mathsf{m}_{i,j}\}_{i\in[m]})\}_{j\in[\ell]}, \{\mathcal{R}_j(K_j)\}_{j\in[\ell]}$.

Hyb_1 : This experiment modifies Hyb_1 by introducing an additional abort condition. Specifically, the experiment first executes the complete protocol corresponding to the real execution of the MIM exactly as in Hyb_0 (including rewinding the MIM once) to obtain the distribution $\mathsf{Real}_{\mathsf{MIM}}\langle\{\mathcal{S}_j(\{\mathsf{m}_{i,j}\}_{i\in[m]})\}_{j\in[\ell]}, \{\mathcal{R}_j(K_j)\}_{j\in[\ell]}\rangle$.

Let $p(\lambda)$ denote the probability that the MIM completes this execution without aborting. Set $\gamma(\lambda) = \max\left(\lambda, p^{-2}(\lambda)\right)$. With the first two rounds of the transcript fixed, the rewind the right execution up to $\gamma^2(\lambda)$ times, picking inputs $(\mathsf{c}_1^j, \ldots, \mathsf{c}_\lambda^j)$ for each of the ℓ receivers $\{\mathcal{R}_j\}_{j\in[\ell]}$ independently and uniformly at random in every run. If there exist two rewinding threads where the MIM completes the protocol execution, denote the inputs chosen by the challenger on behalf of the honest receiver in these rewinding threads by $(\mathsf{c'}_1^j, \ldots, \mathsf{c'}_\lambda^j)$ and $(\mathsf{c''}_1^j, \ldots, \mathsf{c''}_\lambda^j)$ respectively. For every $j \in [\ell]$, let index $\alpha_j \in [\lambda]$ be such that $\mathsf{c}_{\alpha_j}^j = 0, \mathsf{c'}_{\alpha_j}^j = 1, \mathsf{c''}_{\alpha_j}^j = 2$.

Additionally for every $j \in [\ell], i \in [m]$, use $(\widetilde{\mathsf{L}}_{\alpha_j,i}^j, \widetilde{\mathsf{M}}_{\alpha_j,i}^j, \widetilde{\mathsf{R}}_{\alpha_j,i}^j)$ obtained as output from the main and rewinding executions respectively to compute $\widetilde{\mathsf{m}}_i^j = \mathsf{NM.Decode}(\widetilde{\mathsf{L}}_{\alpha_j,i}^j, \widetilde{\mathsf{M}}_{\alpha_j,i}^j, \widetilde{\mathsf{R}}_{\alpha_j,i}^j)$.

If no such rewinding thread exists, or if there exists $j \in [\ell]$ for which there does not exist $\alpha \in [\lambda]$ such that $\mathsf{c}_\alpha^j = 0, \mathsf{c'}_\alpha^j = 1, \mathsf{c''}_\alpha^j = 2$, then set $\widetilde{\mathsf{m}}_i^j = \perp$ for all $i \in [m]$. Now, the output of this hybrid is the joint distribution

$$\mathsf{View}_{\mathsf{MIM}}\langle\{\mathcal{S}_j(\{\mathsf{m}_i^j\}_{i\in[m]})\}_{j\in[\ell]}, \{\mathcal{R}^j(K^j)\}_{j\in[\ell]}\rangle, \{\widetilde{\mathsf{m}}_i^j\}_{j\in[\ell],i\in[m]}.$$

Lemma 2. *For every unbounded distinguisher $\mathcal{D}$ and large enough $\lambda \in \mathbb{N}$,*

$$\left|\Pr[\mathcal{D}(\mathsf{Hyb}_0) = 1] - \Pr[\mathcal{D}(\mathsf{Hyb}_1) = 1]\right| = \mathsf{negl}(\lambda)$$

Proof. Since the MIM's inputs $\{\widetilde{\mathsf{m}}_i^j\}_{j\in[\ell]}$ are committed in round 1 of the protocol, then conditioned on the adversary providing a non-aborting transcript in rewinding executions in Hyb_1, by simulation security of the 2pc, $\{(\widetilde{\mathsf{m}}_i^j\}_{j\in[\ell]}$ are correctly extracted.

Therefore, to prove this lemma it suffices to show that two rewinding executions (with a non-aborting transcript) can be found within $\gamma^2(\lambda)$ attempts, except with probability $\mathsf{negl}(\lambda)$. To see this, we observe that the probability of a non-aborting transcript is $p(\lambda)$, and therefore, the probability that $\gamma^2(\lambda) - 1$ out of the $\gamma^2(\lambda)$ trials abort is $\mathsf{negl}(\lambda)$.

Hyb_2: This experiment modifies Hyb_1 to execute the superpolynomial simulator of Π in all sessions where the MIM is a receiver. Specifically, in these executions, instead of the honest sender strategy with input $\{\mathsf{m}_i^j\}_{i\in[m],j\in[\ell]}$, we execute the superpolynomial simulator $\mathsf{Sim\text{-}2PC}_{\mathsf{Sen}}^{\mathsf{MIM},\mathcal{F}(\mathsf{inp}_{\mathcal{S}^j},\cdot)}$ where

$$\mathsf{inp}_{\mathcal{S}^j} = (\{\mathsf{m}_i^j, \mathsf{L}_{1,i}^j, \ldots, \mathsf{L}_{\lambda,i}^j, \mathsf{M}_{1,i}^j, \ldots, \mathsf{M}_{\lambda,i}^j, \mathsf{R}_{1,i}^j, \ldots, \mathsf{R}_{\lambda,i}^j\}_{i\in[m]}).$$

$\mathsf{Sim\text{-}2PC}_{\mathsf{Sen}}$ expects round 1 and round 2 messages from the MIM, and the MIM in turn expects corresponding messages from the receiver in the right execution. Receiver messages for the right execution are generated using honest receiver strategy with inputs K^j fixed, and inputs $c_1^j, \ldots, c_\lambda^j$ chosen uniformly at random, exactly as in Hyb_1. Denote the view of the MIM by

$$\mathsf{View}_{\mathsf{Sim}^{\{\mathcal{F}(\mathsf{inp}_{\mathcal{S}^j},\cdot)\}_{j\in[\ell]}}}\langle\{\mathcal{R}^j(K^j)\}_{j\in[\ell]}\rangle,$$

where for every $j \in [\ell]$, $\mathsf{inp}_{\mathcal{S}^j}$ is as defined above.

Next, with the first round of the transcript fixed, the challenger rewinds the right execution up to $\gamma^2(\lambda)$ times, picking inputs $(\mathsf{c}_1^j, \ldots, \mathsf{c}_\lambda^j)$ for $\mathcal{R}^j$ independently and uniformly at random in every run, and generating messages in the left execution by running the simulator $\mathsf{Sim\text{-}2PC}_{\mathsf{Sen}}$ each time.

If there exist two rewinding executions where the MIM completes the protocol, denote the inputs chosen by the challenger on behalf of the honest receiver in this rewinding thread by $(\mathsf{c'}_1^j, \ldots, \mathsf{c'}_\lambda^j)$ and $(\mathsf{c''}_1^j, \ldots, \mathsf{c''}_\lambda^j)$ respectively. For every $j \in [\ell]$, let index $\alpha_j \in [\lambda]$ be such that $\mathsf{c}_{\alpha_j}^j = 0, \mathsf{c'}_{\alpha_j}^j = 1, \mathsf{c''}_{\alpha_j}^j = 2$. Additionally for every $j \in [\ell], i \in [m]$, use $(\widetilde{\mathsf{L}}_{\alpha_j,i}^j, \widetilde{\mathsf{M}}_{\alpha_j,i}^j, \widetilde{\mathsf{R}}_{\alpha_j,i}^j)$ obtained as output from the main and the two rewinding executions respectively to compute $\widetilde{\mathsf{m}}_i^j = \mathsf{NM.Decode}(\widetilde{\mathsf{L}}_{\alpha_j,i}^j, \widetilde{\mathsf{M}}_{\alpha_j,i}^j, \widetilde{\mathsf{R}}_{\alpha_j,i}^j)$. If no such rewinding thread exists, or if there exists $j \in [\ell]$ for which there does not exist $\alpha \in [\lambda]$ such that $\mathsf{c}_\alpha^j = 0, \mathsf{c'}_\alpha^j = 1, \mathsf{c''}_\alpha^j = 2$, then abort.

The output of this hybrid is the joint distribution:

$$\mathsf{View}_{\mathsf{Sim}^{\{\mathcal{F}(\mathsf{inp}_{\mathcal{S}^j},\cdot)\}_{j\in[\ell]}}}\langle\{\mathcal{R}^j(K^j)\}_{j\in[\ell]}\rangle, \{\widetilde{\mathsf{m}}_i^j\}_{j\in[\ell],i\in[m]},$$

where for every $j \in [\ell]$, $\mathsf{inp}_{\mathcal{S}^j}$ is as defined above.

Lemma 3. *Assuming 2-rewinding secure two party computation according to Definition 3, for every PPT distinguisher $\mathcal{D}$ and large enough $\lambda \in \mathbb{N}$,*

$$\Big|\Pr[\mathcal{D}(\mathsf{Hyb}_1) = 1] - \Pr[\mathcal{D}(\mathsf{Hyb}_2) = 1]\Big| = \mathsf{negl}(\lambda)$$

Proof. We consider a sequence of sub-hybrids $\mathsf{Hyb}_{1,0}, \mathsf{Hyb}_{1,1}, \ldots \mathsf{Hyb}_{1,\ell}$ where for every $j \in [\ell]$, $\mathsf{Hyb}_{1,j}$ is identical to $\mathsf{Hyb}_{1,j-1}$, except that instead of executing the honest sender strategy using honest sender inputs $\{m_i^j\}_{i\in[m]}$, we execute the simulator in the jth left execution, where $\mathsf{Sim\text{-}2PC}_{\mathsf{Sen}}^{\mathsf{MIM},\mathcal{F}(\mathsf{inp}_{\mathcal{S}^j},\cdot)}$ where

$$\mathsf{inp}_{\mathcal{S}^j} = (\{\mathsf{m}_i^j, \mathsf{L}_{1,i}^j, \ldots, \mathsf{L}_{\lambda,i}^j, \mathsf{M}_{1,i}^j, \ldots, \mathsf{M}_{\lambda,i}^j, \mathsf{R}_{1,i}^j, \ldots, \mathsf{R}_{\lambda,i}^j\}_{i\in[m]})$$

Suppose the lemma is not true. Then for every large enough $\lambda \in \mathbb{N}$ there exists $j^*(\lambda) \in [\ell(\lambda)]$, a polynomial $p(\cdot)$ and a distinguisher $\mathcal{D}$ such that for infinitely many $\lambda \in \mathbb{N}$,

$$\Big|\Pr[\mathcal{D}(\mathsf{Hyb}_{1,j^*-1}) = 1] - \Pr[\mathcal{D}(\mathsf{Hyb}_{1,j^*}) = 1]\Big| = \frac{1}{q(\lambda)}$$

We derive a contradiction by building a reduction $\mathcal{A}$ that on input λ, obtains $j^*(\lambda)$ as advice and with black-box access to the MIM and to $\mathcal{D}$ contradicts 2-rewinding security of the two party computation protocol. $\mathcal{A}$ proceeds as follows:

- $\mathcal{A}$ first creates receiver $\mathcal{R}'$ that interacts with the external challenger as follows.
  - Obtain the first round sender message from the 2pc challenger, and forward this to the MIM as $\mathcal{S}^{j^*}$'s message in the j^{*th} left execution. In addition, generate the first round messages according to receiver strategy with inputs $\{K^j\}_{j\in[\ell]}$ for the right execution. Obtain the first round message from the MIM, which includes a (malicious) sender message for the right execution and a (malicious) receiver message for the left execution. Output the MIM's receiver message in the j^{*th} left execution to the challenger of the 2pc.
  - Generate the second round message for the right execution according to honest receiver strategy, and obtain the second round message for the left execution from the challenger. Forward the MIM's message in left session j^* to the challenger.
  - Obtain the third round message for the left execution externally from the challenger, and forward this to the MIM as $\mathcal{S}$'s message in the j^{*th} left execution. Generate messages for the right executions using honest receiver strategy. Obtain the third round message from the MIM for the right execution.
- Next, $\mathcal{A}$ rewinds $\mathcal{R}'$ twice with fixed first round, and obtains MIM outputs as follows.
  - Run the second round with honest receiver strategy on the right, and obtain challenger messages on the left. Obtain the second round message from the MIM, and output the MIM's message in session j^* to the challenger.
  - Obtain the third round message for the left execution externally from the challenger, and forward this to the MIM as $\mathcal{S}$'s message in the j^{*th} left execution. Obtain the third round messages from the MIM.
- If none of the executions abort, for every $j \in [\ell]$, find $\alpha_j \in [\lambda]$ such that $\mathsf{c}^j_{\alpha_j} = 0, \mathsf{c'}^j_{\alpha_j} = 1, \mathsf{c''}^j_{\alpha_j} = 2$. If these do not exist, abort. Otherwise use the outputs of the two-party computation protocol to compute $\widetilde{\mathsf{m}}^j_i = \mathsf{NM.Decode}(\widetilde{\mathsf{L}}^j_{\alpha_j,i}, \widetilde{\mathsf{M}}^j_{\alpha_j,i}, \widetilde{\mathsf{R}}^j_{\alpha_j,i})$ for $i \in [m], j \in [\ell]$. Else, set $\widetilde{\mathsf{m}}^j_i = \bot$ for $i \in [m], j \in [\ell]$
- $\mathcal{A}$ outputs the entire view of $\mathcal{R}'$ together with $\{\widetilde{\mathsf{m}}^j_i\}_{i\in[m],j\in[\ell]}$. If the challenger used honest sender messages, we denote the distribution output by $\mathcal{A}$ in this experiment by Dist_1 and if the challenger used simulated messages, we denote the distribution output by $\mathcal{A}$ in this experiment by Dist_2.

If the challenger's messages correspond to the real sender $\mathcal{S}$, then the distribution output by $\mathcal{A}$ conditioned on not aborting corresponds to Hyb_1, and if the challenger's messages correspond to $\mathsf{Sim\text{-}2PC}_{\mathsf{Sen}}$, then the distribution output by $\mathcal{A}$ conditioned on not aborting corresponds to Hyb_2.

By assumption, for infinitely many $\lambda \in \mathbb{N}$,

$$\left|\Pr[\mathcal{D}(\mathsf{Hyb}_1) = 1] - \Pr[\mathcal{D}(\mathsf{Hyb}_2) = 1]\right| = \frac{1}{q(\lambda)}$$

Since the MIM completes any run of the protocol without aborting with probability at least $p(\lambda)$, and because aborts are independent of the distinguishing advantage, for infinitely many $\lambda \in \mathbb{N}$:

$$\left|\Pr[\mathcal{D} = 1 \ \wedge \ \neg\mathsf{abort}|\mathsf{Hyb}_1] - \Pr[\mathcal{D} = 1 \ \wedge \ \neg\mathsf{abort}|\mathsf{Hyb}_2]\right| \geq \frac{1}{p^2(\lambda) \cdot q(\lambda)}$$

where $\neg\mathsf{abort}$ denotes the event that an execution that is completed in the main thread, is also completed without aborting in one rewinding execution.

This implies that for infinitely many $\lambda \in \mathbb{N}$:

$$\left|\Pr[\mathcal{D}(\mathsf{Dist}_1) = 1] - \Pr[\mathcal{D}(\mathsf{Dist}_2) = 1]\right| \geq \frac{1}{p^2(\lambda) \cdot q(\lambda)},$$

where Dist_1 and Dist_2 denote the real and ideal distributions of the underlying 2-party computation protocol under 2-rewinding security. This implies that $\mathcal{D}$ contradicts 2-rewinding security of the two party computation protocol.

Hyb_3: This hybrid is the same as Hyb_2 except whenever the challenger obtains as output a verification key in one of the right sessions that is identical to a verification key used in one of the left sessions, the hybrid outputs $\perp$. By existential unforgeability of the signature scheme, given any PPT adversary MIM, Hyb_2 and Hyb_3 are computationally indistinguishable.

Hyb_4: This hybrid is the same as Hyb_3 except that $\mathsf{inp}_{\mathcal{S}^j}$ is set differently. Specifically, for every $j \in [\ell], i \in [m]$ and $\alpha \in [\lambda]$, we set $(\mathsf{L}^j_{\alpha,i}, \mathsf{M}^j_{\alpha,i}, \mathsf{R}^j_{\alpha,i}) \leftarrow \mathsf{NM.Sim}(1^{p(\lambda)})$, and set

$$\mathsf{inp}_{\mathcal{S}^j} = (\{\mathsf{m}^j_i, \mathsf{L}^j_{1,i}, \ldots, \mathsf{L}^j_{\lambda,i}, \mathsf{M}^j_{1,i}, \ldots, \mathsf{M}^j_{\lambda,i}, \mathsf{R}^j_{1,i}, \ldots, \mathsf{R}^j_{\lambda,i}\}_{i\in[m]}).$$

We note that at this point, the functionality $\{\mathcal{F}(\mathsf{inp}_{\mathcal{S}^j}, \cdot)\}_{j\in[\ell]}$ can be perfectly simulated with access to the ideal functionality $\{\mathsf{OT}^j(\mathsf{m}^j_i, \mathsf{m}^j_i, \cdot)\}_{j\in[\ell]}$. Moreover, this hybrid runs the super-polynomial simulator of the two-party computation protocol, which can be split into a straight-line simulator that extracts adversarial receiver input from the first round, and then a rewinding-based expected polynomial-time simulator that extracts adversarial sender input. The latter can also be replaced by a straight-line superpolynomial simulator that extracts the adversarial sender-input by running the straight-line superpolynomial simulator of the two-party computation protocol. Finally, as long as the underlying two-party computation protocol has its ideal distribution be identical to an honest execution with dummy inputs, the same is true for our protocol. Therefore, the output of this hybrid is identical to the ideal distribution $\mathsf{Ideal}_{\mathsf{MIM}}(\{\mathsf{m}^j_i\}_{i\in[m],j\in[\ell]}, \{K^j\}_{j\in[\ell]})$.

Lemma 4. *Assuming $m(\lambda) \cdot \ell(\lambda)$ symmetric non-malleable codes satisfying Definition 1, for every unbounded distinguisher $\mathcal{D}$ and large enough $\lambda \in \mathbb{N}$,*

$$\left|\Pr[\mathcal{D}(\mathsf{Hyb}_4) = 1] - \Pr[\mathcal{D}(\mathsf{Hyb}_3) = 1]\right| = \mathsf{negl}(\lambda)$$

Proof. We prove indistinguishability between Hyb_3 and Hyb_4 by considering a sequence of sub-hybrids, $\{\mathsf{Hyb}_{3,i,j,k}\}_{i\in[1,m],j\in[1,\ell],k\in[0,\lambda]}$ where:

- $\mathsf{Hyb}_3 = \mathsf{Hyb}_{3,0,\ell,\lambda}$, $\mathsf{Hyb}_4 = \mathsf{Hyb}_{3,m,\ell,\lambda}$,
- for $i \in [m]$, $\mathsf{Hyb}_{3,i-1,\ell,\lambda} = \mathsf{Hyb}_{3,i,1,0}$
- for $j \in [\ell]$, $\mathsf{Hyb}_{3,i,j-1,\lambda} = \mathsf{Hyb}_{3,i,j,0}$,
- for every $i \in [m], j \in [\ell], k \in [\lambda]$, $\mathsf{Hyb}_{3,i,j,k}$ is identical to $\mathsf{Hyb}_{3,i,j,k-1}$ except that $\mathsf{Hyb}_{3,i,j,k}$ samples $(\mathsf{L}^j_{k,i}, \mathsf{M}^j_{k,i}, \mathsf{R}^j_{k,i}) \leftarrow \mathsf{NM.Code}(0)$.

Suppose the lemma is not true. Then there exists $i^* \in [m], j^* \in [\ell], k^* \in [\lambda]$, an unbounded distinguisher $\mathcal{D}$ and a polynomial $p(\cdot)$ such that for large enough $\lambda \in \mathbb{N}$,

$$\left|\Pr[\mathcal{D}(\mathsf{Hyb}_{3,i^*,j^*,k^*}) = 1] - \Pr[\mathcal{D}(\mathsf{Hyb}_{3,i^*,j^*,k^*-1}) = 1]\right| = \frac{1}{p(\lambda)} \tag{1}$$

We now define a set of tampering functions $(f_{\mathsf{MIM}}, g_{\mathsf{MIM}}, h_{\mathsf{MIM}})$, and a set of additional functions $(w_{\mathsf{MIM}}, y_{\mathsf{MIM}}, z_{\mathsf{MIM}})$. Before defining them, we define a shared state for these functions, that is generated as follows:

- Execute $\mathsf{Sim\text{-}2PC}^{\mathsf{MIM}}_{\mathsf{Sen}}$, using honest $\mathcal{R}$ strategy in the right executions with input $\{K^j\}_{j\in[\ell]}$ and uniformly chosen $\{c^j_1, \dots c^j_\lambda\}_{j\in[\ell]}$, until $\mathsf{Sim\text{-}2PC}_{\mathsf{Sen}}$ generates a query to the ideal functionality $\mathcal{F}$ at the end of round 2.
- At this point, $\mathsf{Sim\text{-}2PC}^{\mathsf{MIM}}_{\mathsf{Sen}}$ outputs a view and transcript of the MIM until the third round, as well as $\{\widetilde{K}^j\}_{j\in[\ell]}$ that correspond to the receiver's inputs in the left execution.
- Rewind the second round twice with uniformly and independently chosen $\{\mathsf{c}'^j_1, \dots, \mathsf{c}'^j_\lambda\}_{j\in[\ell]}$ and $\{\mathsf{c}''^j_1, \dots, \mathsf{c}''^j_\lambda\}_{j\in[\ell]}$ respectively in each rewind. If for every $j \in [\ell(\lambda)]$, there exists $\alpha_j \in [\lambda]$ such that $\mathsf{c}^j_{\alpha_j} = 0, \mathsf{c}'^j_{\alpha_j} = 1, \mathsf{c}''^j_{\alpha_j} = 2$, continue, otherwise abort.
- Obtain the rewinding message of the adversary in the second round (with the same first round prefix), as well as $(\overline{\mathsf{c}}_1, \dots, \overline{\mathsf{c}}_n)$ and $(\widehat{\mathsf{c}}_1, \dots, \widehat{\mathsf{c}}_n)$ that correspond to the receiver's chosen functions in the j^*th left session in this rewinding execution.
- If $\widetilde{\mathsf{c}}_{k^*}, \overline{\mathsf{c}}_{k^*}$ and $\widehat{\mathsf{c}}_{k^*}$ are all different, continue. Otherwise, abort.
- Generate $(\mathsf{L}^j_{k,i}, \mathsf{M}^j_{k,i}, \mathsf{R}^j_{k,i})$ for every $(i, j, k) \in [m] \times [\ell] \times [\lambda] \setminus \{i^*, j^*, k^*\}$ according to $\mathsf{Hyb}_{3,i^*,j^*,k^*-1}$ (this is identical to setting them according to $\mathsf{Hyb}_{3,i^*,j^*,k^*}$).
- Output the view of the MIM until round 2 in the main the rewinding threads, and also output (i^*, j^*, k^*), and the values $(\mathsf{L}^j_{k,i}, \mathsf{M}^j_{k,i}, \mathsf{R}^j_{k,i})_{(i,j,k)\in[m]\times[\ell]\times[\lambda]\setminus\{i^*,j^*,k^*\}}$.

- Additionally, output the receiver's inputs $\{\widetilde{K}^j, \widetilde{c}_1^j, \ldots, \widetilde{c}_\lambda^j\}_{j\in[\ell]}$ and also output the sender's inputs $\{sk^j, vk^j, \{\mathsf{m}_i^j\}_{i\in[m]}\}_{j\in[\ell]}$, along with randomness r.

The functions $f_{\mathsf{MIM},i,j}, g_{\mathsf{MIM},i,j}$ and $h_{\mathsf{MIM},i,j}$ correspond to tampering functions, and are defined as follows.

- The deterministic function $f_{\mathsf{MIM},i,j}$ on input L, sets $\mathsf{L}_{k^*,i^*}^{j^*} = \mathsf{L}, \mathsf{M}_{k^*,i^*}^{j^*} = 0, \mathsf{R}_{k^*,i^*}^{j^*} = 0$.
  Now, using hardwired values $\{vk^j, \{\mathsf{m}_i^j\}_{i\in[m]}\}_{j\in[\ell]}$, $\{\widetilde{K}^j, \widetilde{c}_1^j, \ldots, \widetilde{c}_\lambda^j\}_{j\in[\ell]}$ as well as the values $(\mathsf{L}_{k,i}^j, \mathsf{M}_{k,i}^j, \mathsf{R}_{k,i}^j)_{(i,j,k)\in[m]\times[\ell]\times[\lambda]\setminus\{i^*,j^*,k^*\}}$, it computes
  $$\mathsf{out} = \{\mathcal{F}^j(vk^j, \{\mathsf{m}_i, \mathsf{L}_{k,i}^j, \mathsf{M}_{k,i}^j, \mathsf{R}_{k,i}^j\}_{i\in[m],k\in[\lambda]}, \widetilde{K}^j, \{\widetilde{c}_k^j\}_{k\in[\lambda]})\}_{j\in[\ell]}.$$
  It then invokes $\mathsf{Sim\text{-}2PC_{Sen}}$ using randomness r on out to generate the third round message of the protocol transcript in the thread corresponding to the receiver challenge being 0. It outputs the value $\mathsf{L}_{\alpha_j,i}^j$ or $\mathsf{M}_{\alpha_j,i}^j$ or $\mathsf{R}_{\alpha_j,i}^j$ obtained from the MIM.
- The function $g_{\mathsf{MIM},i,j}$ on input M, sets $\mathsf{M}_{k^*,i^*}^{j^*} = \mathsf{M}, \mathsf{R}_{k^*,i^*}^{j^*} = \mathsf{L}_{k^*,i^*}^{j^*} = 0$.
  Now, using hardwired values $\{vk^j, \{\mathsf{m}_i^j\}_{i\in[m]}\}_{j\in[\ell]}$, $\{\widetilde{K}^j, \widetilde{c}_1^j, \ldots, \widetilde{c}_\lambda^j\}_{j\in[\ell]}$ as well as the values $(\mathsf{L}_{k,i}^j, \mathsf{M}_{k,i}^j, \mathsf{R}_{k,i}^j)_{(i,j,k)\in[m]\times[\ell]\times[\lambda]\setminus\{i^*,j^*,k^*\}}$, it computes
  $$\mathsf{out} = \{\mathcal{F}^j(vk^j, \{\mathsf{m}_i, \mathsf{L}_{k,i}^j, \mathsf{M}_{k,i}^j, \mathsf{R}_{k,i}^j\}_{i\in[m],k\in[\lambda]}, \widetilde{K}^j, \{\widetilde{c}_k^j\}_{k\in[\lambda]})\}_{j\in[\ell]}.$$
  It then invokes $\mathsf{Sim\text{-}2PC_{Sen}}$ using randomness r on out to generate the third round message of the protocol transcript in the thread corresponding to the receiver challenge being 1. It outputs the value $\mathsf{L}_{\alpha_j,i}^j$ or $\mathsf{M}_{\alpha_j,i}^j$ or $\mathsf{R}_{\alpha_j,i}^j$ obtained from the MIM.
- The function $h_{\mathsf{MIM},i,j}$ on input R, sets $\mathsf{R}_{k^*,i^*}^{j^*} = \mathsf{R}, \mathsf{M}_{k^*,i^*}^{j^*} = \mathsf{L}_{k^*,i^*}^{j^*} = 0$.
  Now, using hardwired values $\{vk^j, \{\mathsf{m}_i^j\}_{i\in[m]}\}_{j\in[\ell]}$, $\{\widetilde{K}^j, \widetilde{c}_1^j, \ldots, \widetilde{c}_\lambda^j\}_{j\in[\ell]}$ as well as the values $(\mathsf{L}_{k,i}^j, \mathsf{M}_{k,i}^j, \mathsf{R}_{k,i}^j)_{(i,j,k)\in[m]\times[\ell]\times[\lambda]\setminus\{i^*,j^*,k^*\}}$, it computes
  $$\mathsf{out} = \{\mathcal{F}^j(vk^j, \{\mathsf{m}_i, \mathsf{L}_{k,i}^j, \mathsf{M}_{k,i}^j, \mathsf{R}_{k,i}^j\}_{i\in[m],k\in[\lambda]}, \widetilde{K}^j, \{\widetilde{c}_k^j\}_{k\in[\lambda]})\}_{j\in[\ell]}.$$
  It then invokes $\mathsf{Sim\text{-}2PC_{Sen}}$ using randomness r on out to generate the third round message of the protocol transcript in the thread corresponding to the receiver challenge being 2. It outputs the value $\mathsf{L}_{\alpha_j,i}^j$ or $\mathsf{M}_{\alpha_j,i}^j$ or $\mathsf{R}_{\alpha_j,i}^j$ obtained from the MIM.

The functions $w_{\mathsf{MIM}}, y_{\mathsf{MIM}}, z_{\mathsf{MIM}}$ generate the threads themselves and are defined as follows.

- Next, the function w_{MIM} on input L, sets $\mathsf{L}_{k^*,i^*}^{j^*} = \mathsf{L}, \mathsf{M}_{k^*,i^*}^{j^*} = 0, \mathsf{R}_{k^*,i^*}^{j^*} = 0$.
  Now, using hardwired values $\{vk^j, \{\mathsf{m}_i^j\}_{i\in[m]}\}_{j\in[\ell]}$, $\{\widetilde{K}^j, \widetilde{c}_1^j, \ldots, \widetilde{c}_\lambda^j\}_{j\in[\ell]}$ as well as the values $(\mathsf{L}_{k,i}^j, \mathsf{M}_{k,i}^j, \mathsf{R}_{k,i}^j)_{(i,j,k)\in[m]\times[\ell]\times[\lambda]\setminus\{i^*,j^*,k^*\}}$, it computes
  $$\mathsf{out} = \{\mathcal{F}^j(vk^j, \{\mathsf{m}_i, \mathsf{L}_{k,i}^j, \mathsf{R}_{k,i}^j\}_{i\in[m],k\in[\lambda]}, \widetilde{K}^j, \{\widetilde{c}_k^j\}_{k\in[\lambda]})\}_{j\in[\ell]}.$$

It then invokes $\mathsf{Sim\text{-}2PC_{Sen}}$ on out to generate the third round message of the protocol transcript in the thread corresponding to receiver left challenge being 0. It outputs the resulting transcript as one thread in the view of the MIM.

– Next, the function y_{MIM} on input M, sets $\mathsf{L}^{j^*}_{k^*,i^*} = 0, \mathsf{M}^{j^*}_{k^*,i^*} = \mathsf{M}, \mathsf{R}^{j^*}_{k^*,i^*} = 0$. Now, using hardwired values $\{vk^j, \{\mathsf{m}^j_i\}_{i\in[m]}\}_{j\in[\ell]}$, $\{\widetilde{K}^j, \widetilde{\mathsf{c}}^j_1, \ldots, \widetilde{\mathsf{c}}^j_\lambda\}_{j\in[\ell]}$ as well as the values $(\mathsf{L}^j_{k,i}, \mathsf{M}^j_{k,i}, \mathsf{R}^j_{k,i})_{(i,j,k)\in[m]\times[\ell]\times[\lambda]\setminus\{i^*,j^*,k^*\}}$, it computes

$$\mathsf{out} = \{\mathcal{F}^j(vk^j, \{\mathsf{m}_i, \mathsf{L}^j_{k,i}, \mathsf{R}^j_{k,i}\}_{i\in[m],k\in[\lambda]}, \widetilde{K}^j, \{\widetilde{\mathsf{c}}^j_k\}_{k\in[\lambda]})\}_{j\in[\ell]}.$$

It then invokes $\mathsf{Sim\text{-}2PC_{Sen}}$ on out to generate the third round message of the protocol transcript in the thread corresponding to receiver left challenge being 1. It outputs the resulting transcript as another thread in the view of the MIM.

– Next, the function z_{MIM} on input R, sets $\mathsf{L}^{j^*}_{k^*,i^*} = 0, \mathsf{M}^{j^*}_{k^*,i^*} = 0, \mathsf{R}^{j^*}_{k^*,i^*} = \mathsf{R}$. Now, using hardwired values $\{vk^j, \{\mathsf{m}^j_i\}_{i\in[m]}\}_{j\in[\ell]}$, $\{\widetilde{K}^j, \widetilde{\mathsf{c}}^j_1, \ldots, \widetilde{\mathsf{c}}^j_\lambda\}_{j\in[\ell]}$ as well as the values $(\mathsf{L}^j_{k,i}, \mathsf{M}^j_{k,i}, \mathsf{R}^j_{k,i})_{(i,j,k)\in[m]\times[\ell]\times[\lambda]\setminus\{i^*,j^*,k^*\}}$, it computes

$$\mathsf{out} = \{\mathcal{F}^j(vk^j, \{\mathsf{m}_i, \mathsf{L}^j_{k,i}, \mathsf{R}^j_{k,i}\}_{i\in[m],k\in[\lambda]}, \widetilde{K}^j, \{\widetilde{\mathsf{c}}^j_k\}_{k\in[\lambda]})\}_{j\in[\ell]}.$$

It then invokes $\mathsf{Sim\text{-}2PC_{Sen}}$ on out to generate the third round message of the protocol transcript in the thread corresponding to receiver left challenge being 2. It outputs the resulting transcript as another thread in the view of the MIM.

Note that there is a fixed set of permutations $\sigma_{i,j}$ such that $f_{\mathsf{MIM},i,j}$, $g_{\mathsf{MIM},i,j}$, $h_{\mathsf{MIM},i,j}$ can be relabeled as functions $F_{i,j}, G_{i,j}, H_{i,j}$ such that $F_{i,j}$ outputs $\widetilde{L}$ values, $G_{i,j}$ outputs $\widetilde{M}$ values, and $H_{i,j}$ outputs $\widetilde{R}$ values.

By Definition 1 of ℓ augmented non-malleable codes, we have that for every permutation σ and σ' on $\mathsf{L}, \mathsf{M}, \mathsf{R}$, and every $F_{i,j}, G_{i,j}$ and $H_{i,j}$,

$$\Big(\sigma'(\mathsf{L}), \sigma'(\mathsf{M}), \{\mathsf{NM.Decode}\big(F_{i,j}(\sigma_{i,j}(\mathsf{L})), G_{i,j}(\sigma_{i,j}(\mathsf{M})), H_{i,j}(\sigma_{i,j}(\mathsf{R}))\big)\}_{i,j} \,\Big|\, \mathsf{L}, \mathsf{M}, \mathsf{R} \leftarrow \mathsf{NM.Code}(\mathsf{m}^{j^*}_{i^*})\Big) \approx_\epsilon$$

$$\Big(\sigma'(\mathsf{L}), \sigma'(\mathsf{M}), \{\mathsf{NM.Decode}\big(F_{i,j}(\sigma_{i,j}(\mathsf{L})), G_{i,j}(\sigma_{i,j}(\mathsf{M})), H_{i,j}(\sigma_{i,j}(\mathsf{R}))\big)\}_{i,j} \,\Big|\, \mathsf{L}, \mathsf{M}, \mathsf{R} \leftarrow \mathsf{NM.Code}(0)\Big)$$

But these distributions upon post-processing (via the functions w_{MIM}, y_{MIM}, z_{MIM}) exactly correspond to the outputs of $\mathsf{Hyb}_{3,i^*,j^*,k^*-1}$ and $\mathsf{Hyb}_{3,i^*,j^*,k^*}$ respectively, whenever $\widetilde{c}^{j^*}_{k^*}, \widetilde{c}^{j^*}_{k^*}$ and $\widetilde{c}^{j^*}_{k^*}$ are all different. On the other hand, when any two of the three values $\widetilde{c}^{j^*}_{k^*}, \widetilde{c}^{j^*}_{k^*}$ and $\widetilde{c}^{j^*}_{k^*}$ are identical, the distributions $\mathsf{Hyb}_{3,i^*,j^*,k^*-1}$ and $\mathsf{Hyb}_{3,i^*,j^*,k^*}$ are statistically indistinguishable because of the two-out-of-three secret sharing property of the code, i.e. they jointly do not depend on all three of the shares, L, R and M. Since $\epsilon(\lambda) = \mathsf{negl}(\lambda)$, this contradicts Eq. (1), as desired.

Finally, this proof also extends to show that security of the watchlist protocol holds against sub-exponential adversaries that run in time less than or equal to T, where T denotes the running time of adversaries against which the underlying two-party computation protocol is 2-rewinding sender secure.

5 4-Round Black-Box MPC Protocol

In this section, we give our construction of a four-round black-box MPC protocol from any two-message OT protocol that has super-polynomial time security against malicious receivers and sub-exponential indistinguishability-based security against malicious senders. Specifically, we prove the following theorem.

Theorem 2. *For some $\epsilon > 0$, assume black-box access to a two-round oblivious transfer protocol with super-polynomial time simulation security against malicious receivers and $(2^{\lambda^\epsilon}, 2^{-\lambda^\epsilon})$-indistinguishability-based security against malicious senders. Then, there exists a four-round protocol for computing general functions.*

5.1 Building Blocks

The construction makes use of the following building blocks:

1. A three-round watchlist protocol $\mathsf{WL} = (\mathsf{WL}_1, \mathsf{WL}_2, \mathsf{WL}_3, \mathsf{out}_{\mathsf{WL}})$ satisfying Definition 4. Let $T_1(\lambda)$ (abbreviated as T_1) be the running time of $\mathsf{Sim}_{\mathsf{WL}}$ (which is the SPS simulator for the watchlist protocol). Let $T_2(\lambda)$ (abbreviated as T_2) to be the running time of $\mathsf{Sim}_{\mathsf{WL},R}$ (which is the special SPS extractor that over extracts the receiver inputs).
2. A two-round n-client, m-server MPC protocol $\Phi = (\Phi_1, \Phi_2, \mathsf{out}_\Phi)$ that satisfies $((T_1 + T_2) \cdot \mathsf{poly}(\cdot), \mathsf{negl})$-privacy with knowledge of outputs property against any adversary corrupting upto t servers and an arbitrary number of clients. By (T, ϵ)-security, we require ϵ distinguishing advantage against any adversary that runs in time T. By privacy with knowledge of outputs [IKP10], we consider a weaker notion of security (when compared to standard malicious security in the real/ideal paradigm), wherein the adversary has the additional power to determine the outputs of the honest parties. This is modelled by the ideal functionality getting an output to be delivered to the honest parties from the adversary. We call this protocol as the outer protocol. We set $t = 2\lambda n^2$ and $m = 3t+1$. We need this protocol to additionally satisfy the property that the first round message generated by the simulator on behalf of the honest clients to the corrupted servers is identically distributed to the first round messages generated by honest clients on some default input. We note that [IKP10, Pas12] constructed such a protocol making black-box use of

a $((T_1+T_2)\cdot\mathsf{poly}(\cdot), \mathsf{negl})$-secure PRG. As noted in [IKSS21], we can delegate the PRG computations done by the servers to the clients and ensure that the computations done by the servers are information-theoretic.

3. For each $h \in [m]$, a three-round inner protocol $\Pi_h = (\Pi_{h,1}, \Pi_{h,2}, \Pi_{h,3}, \mathsf{out}_{\Pi_h})$ for computing the functionality of the h-th server in the outer protocol. We require this protocol to satisfy Definition 5 (discussed below) against adversaries running in time $(T_1 + T_2) \cdot \mathsf{poly}(\lambda)$ and the distinguishing advantage being $\mathsf{negl}(\lambda)$.

Syntax. The three-round inner protocol computing a function f is given by a tuple of algorithms $(\Pi_1, \Pi_2, \Pi_3, \mathsf{out}_\Pi)$ with the following syntax. For each round $r \in [3]$, the i-th party in the protocol runs Π_r on 1^λ, the index i, the private input x_i and the transcript of the protocol in the first $(r-1)$ rounds to obtain π_r^i. It sends π_r^i to every other party via a broadcast channel. We use $\pi(r)$ to denote the transcript of Π in the first r rounds. At the end of the interaction, parties run the public decoder $\mathsf{out}_\Pi(\pi(3))$ to compute the output.

Definition 5 (*[IKSS21]*)**.** *The protocol Π is said to be an inner protocol for computing a function f if it satisfies the following properties.*

- ***Correctness.*** *The protocol Π correctly computes a function f if for every choice of inputs x_i for party P_i,*

$$\Pr[\mathsf{out}_\Pi(\pi(3)) = f(x_1, \ldots, x_n)] = 1$$

  where $\pi(3)$ denotes the transcript of the protocol Π when the input of P_i is x_i.
- ***Security.*** *Let $\mathcal{A}$ be an adversary corrupting a subset of the parties indexed by the set M and let H be the set of indices denoting the honest parties. We require the existence of a simulator Sim_Π such that for any choice of honest parties inputs $\{x_i\}_{i\in H}$, we have:*

$$\mathit{Real}(\mathcal{A}, \{x_i, r_i\}_{i\in H}) \approx_c \mathit{Ideal}(\mathcal{A}, \mathsf{Sim}_\Pi, \{x_i\}_{i\in H})$$

  where the real and ideal experiments are described as in [IKSS21] (details deferred to the full version due to lack of space).

Given these building blocks, our construction is described in Fig. 5.

Due to space constraints, the full proof of security of this construction is deferred to the full version.

- **Round-1:** In the first round, the party P_i with input χ_i does the following:
  1. It chooses a random MAC key $k_i \leftarrow \{0,1\}^*$ and sets $z_i := (\chi_i, k_i)$.
  2. It computes $(\phi_1^{i\to 1}, \ldots, \phi_1^{i\to m}) \leftarrow \Phi_1(1^\lambda, i, z_i)$.
  3. It chooses a random subset $K_i \subset [m]$ of size λ and sets $x_{i,j} = K_i$ for every $j \in [n] \setminus \{i\}$.
  4. It chooses a random string $r_{i,h} \leftarrow \{0,1\}^*$ for every $h \in [m]$ and sets $y_{i,j} = \{r_{i,h}, \phi_1^{i\to h}\}_{h\in[m]}$ for every $j \in [n] \setminus \{i\}$.
  5. It computes $\mathsf{WL}_1^i \leftarrow \mathsf{WL}_1(1^\lambda, i, \{x_{i,j}, y_{i,j}\}_{j\in[n]\setminus\{i\}})$.
  6. It broadcasts WL_1^i.
- **Round-2:** In the second round, P_i does the following:
  1. For each $h \in [m]$, it computes $\pi_{h,1}^i := \Pi_{h,1}(1^\lambda, i, \phi_1^{i\to h}; r_{i,h})$.
  2. It computes $\mathsf{WL}_2^i \leftarrow \mathsf{WL}_2(1^\lambda, i, \{x_{i,j}, y_{i,j}\}_{j\in[n]\setminus\{i\}}, \mathsf{WL}(1))$. (Here, $\mathsf{WL}(r)$ denotes the transcript in the first r rounds of WL.)
  3. It broadcasts $\{\pi_{h,1}^i\}_{h\in[m]}, \mathsf{WL}_2^i$.
- **Round-3:** In the third round, P_i does the following:
  1. For every $h \in [m]$, it computes $\pi_{h,2}^i := \Pi_{h,2}(1^\lambda, i, \phi_1^{i\to h}, \pi_h(1); r_{i,h})$. (Here, $\pi_h(r)$ denotes the transcript in the first r rounds of Π_h.)
  2. It computes $\mathsf{WL}_3^i \leftarrow \mathsf{WL}_3(1^\lambda, i, \{x_{i,j}, y_{i,j}\}_{j\in[n]\setminus\{i\}}, \mathsf{WL}(2))$.
  3. It broadcasts $\{\pi_{h,2}^i\}_{h\in[m]}, \mathsf{WL}_3^i$.
- **Round-4:** In the fourth round, P_i does the following:
  1. It runs $\mathsf{out}_{\mathsf{WL}}$ on i, $\{x_{i,j}, y_{i,j}\}_{j\in[n]\setminus\{i\}}$, the random tape used to generate the messages in WL and $\mathsf{WL}(3)$ to obtain $\{r_{j,h}, \phi_1^{j\to h}\}_{j\in[n]\setminus\{i\}, h\in K_i}$.
  2. For each $j \in [n] \setminus \{i\}$ and $h \in K_i$, it checks:
     (a) If the PRG computations in $\phi_1^{j\to h}$ are correct.
     (b) For each $\ell \in [2]$, whether $\pi_{h,\ell}^j := \Pi_{h,\ell}(1^\lambda, j, \phi_1^{j\to h}, \pi_h(\ell-1); r_{j,h})$ where $\pi_h(0)$ is set to be the null string.
  3. If any of the above checks fail, then it aborts.
  4. Else, for each $h \in [m]$, it computes $\pi_{h,3}^i := \Pi_{h,3}(1^\lambda, i, \phi_1^{i\to h}, \pi_h(2); r_{i,h})$.
  5. It broadcasts $\{\pi_{h,3}^i\}_{h\in[m]}$ to every party.
- **Output Computation.** To compute the output, P_i does the following:
  1. If a party has aborted before sending the fourth round message, output $\perp$.
  2. For every $h \in [m]$, it computes $\phi_2^h := \mathsf{out}_{\Pi_h}(i, \pi_h(3))$.
  3. It runs out_Φ on $(\{\phi_2^h\}_{h\in[m]})$ to recover $(y, \sigma_1, \ldots, \sigma_n)$.
  4. It checks if σ_i is a valid tag on y using the key k_i. If yes, it outputs y and otherwise, it aborts.

Fig. 5. Description of the Four-Round MPC Protocol

Acknowledgment. Y. Ishai was supported in part by ERC Project NTSC (742754), BSF grant 2018393, ISF grant 2774/20, and a Google Faculty Research Award. D. Khurana was supported in part by NSF CAREER CNS-2238718 and DARPA SIEVE. A. Sahai was supported in part from a Simons Investigator Award, DARPA SIEVE award, NTT Research, NSF Frontier Award 1413955, BSF grant 2012378, a Xerox Faculty Research Award, a Google Faculty Research Award, and an Okawa Foundation Research

Grant. This material is based upon work supported by the Defense Advanced Research Projects Agency through Award HR00112020024. A. Srinivasan was supported in part by a SERB startup grant and Google India Research Award.

References

[AAG+16] Aggarwal, D., Agrawal, S., Gupta, D., Maji, H.K., Pandey, O., Prabhakaran, M.: Optimal computational split-state non-malleable codes. In: Kushilevitz, E., Malkin, T. (eds.) TCC 2016. LNCS, vol. 9563, pp. 393–417. Springer, Heidelberg (2016). https://doi.org/10.1007/978-3-662-49099-0_15

[ACJ17] Ananth, P., Choudhuri, A.R., Jain, A.: A new approach to round-optimal secure multiparty computation. In: Katz, J., Shacham, H. (eds.) CRYPTO 2017. LNCS, vol. 10401, pp. 468–499. Springer, Cham (2017). https://doi.org/10.1007/978-3-319-63688-7_16

[AIR01] Aiello, B., Ishai, Y., Reingold, O.: Priced oblivious transfer: how to sell digital goods. In: Pfitzmann, B. (ed.) EUROCRYPT 2001. LNCS, vol. 2045, pp. 119–135. Springer, Heidelberg (2001). https://doi.org/10.1007/3-540-44987-6_8

[BD18] Brakerski, Z., Döttling, N.: Two-message statistically sender-private OT from LWE. In: Beimel, A., Dziembowski, S. (eds.) TCC 2018. LNCS, vol. 11240, pp. 370–390. Springer, Cham (2018). https://doi.org/10.1007/978-3-030-03810-6_14

[BF22] Bitansky, N., Freizeit, S.: Statistically sender-private ot from LPN and derandomization. In: Dodis, Y., Shrimpton, T. (eds.) Advances in Cryptology, CRYPTO 2022. CRYPTO 2022. LNCS, vol. 13509. Springer, Cham (2022). https://doi.org/10.1007/978-3-031-15982-4_21

[BGI+17] Badrinarayanan, S., Garg, S., Ishai, Y., Sahai, A., Wadia, A.: Two-message witness indistinguishability and secure computation in the plain model from new assumptions. In: Takagi, T., Peyrin, T. (eds.) ASIACRYPT 2017. LNCS, vol. 10626, pp. 275–303. Springer, Cham (2017). https://doi.org/10.1007/978-3-319-70700-6_10

[BGJ+18] Badrinarayanan, S., Goyal, V., Jain, A., Kalai, Y.T., Khurana, D., Sahai, A.: Promise zero knowledge and its applications to round optimal MPC. In: Shacham, H., Boldyreva, A. (eds.) CRYPTO 2018. LNCS, vol. 10992, pp. 459–487. Springer, Cham (2018). https://doi.org/10.1007/978-3-319-96881-0_16

[BHP17] Brakerski, Z., Halevi, S., Polychroniadou, A.: Four round secure computation without setup. In: Kalai, Y., Reyzin, L. (eds.) TCC 2017. LNCS, vol. 10677, pp. 645–677. Springer, Cham (2017). https://doi.org/10.1007/978-3-319-70500-2_22

[CCG+20] Rai Choudhuri, A., Ciampi, M., Goyal, V., Jain, A., Ostrovsky, R.: Round optimal secure multiparty computation from minimal assumptions. In: Pass, R., Pietrzak, K. (eds.) TCC 2020. LNCS, vol. 12551, pp. 291–319. Springer, Cham (2020). https://doi.org/10.1007/978-3-030-64378-2_11

[CCG+21] Choudhuri, A.R., Ciampi, M., Goyal, V., Jain, A., Ostrovsky, R.: Oblivious transfer from trapdoor permutations in minimal rounds. In: Nissim, K., Waters, B. (eds.) TCC 2021. LNCS, vol. 13043, pp. 518–549. Springer, Cham (2021). https://doi.org/10.1007/978-3-030-90453-1_18

[CGL16] Chattopadhyay, E., Goyal, V., Li, X.: Non-malleable extractors and codes, with their many tampered extensions. In: Wichs, D., Mansour, Y. (eds.), 48th ACM STOC, pp. 285–298, Cambridge, MA, USA, 18–21 June 2016. ACM Press

[DGH+20] Döttling, N., Garg, S., Hajiabadi, M., Masny, D., Wichs, D.: Two-round oblivious transfer from CDH or LPN. In: Canteaut, A., Ishai, Y. (eds.) EUROCRYPT 2020. LNCS, vol. 12106, pp. 768–797. Springer, Cham (2020). https://doi.org/10.1007/978-3-030-45724-2_26

[DGI+19] Döttling, N., Garg, S., Ishai, Y., Malavolta, G., Mour, T., Ostrovsky, R.: Trapdoor hash functions and their applications. In: Boldyreva, A., Micciancio, D. (eds.) CRYPTO 2019. LNCS, vol. 11694, pp. 3–32. Springer, Cham (2019). https://doi.org/10.1007/978-3-030-26954-8_1

[FMV19] Friolo, D., Masny, D., Venturi, D.: A black-box construction of fully-simulatable, round-optimal oblivious transfer from strongly uniform key agreement. In: Hofheinz, D., Rosen, A. (eds.) TCC 2019. LNCS, vol. 11891, pp. 111–130. Springer, Cham (2019). https://doi.org/10.1007/978-3-030-36030-6_5

[GGH+13] Garg, S., Gentry, C., Halevi, S., Raykova, M., Sahai, A., Waters. B.: Candidate indistinguishability obfuscation and functional encryption for all circuits. In: 54th FOCS, pp. 40–49, Berkeley, CA, USA, 26–29 October 2013. IEEE Computer Society Press

[GK96a] Goldreich, O., Kahan, A.: How to construct constant-round zero-knowledge proof systems for NP. J. Cryptol. **9**(3), 167–189 (1996). https://doi.org/10.1007/BF00208001

[GK96b] Goldreich, O., Krawczyk, H.: On the composition of zero-knowledge proof systems. SIAM J. Comput. **25**(1), 169–192 (1996)

[GLOV12] Goyal, V., Lee, C.K., Ostrovsky, R., Visconti, I.: Constructing non-malleable commitments: a black-box approach. In: 53rd FOCS, pp. 51–60, New Brunswick, NJ, USA, 20–23 October 2012. IEEE Computer Society Press

[GMPP16] Garg, S., Mukherjee, P., Pandey, O., Polychroniadou, A.: The exact round complexity of secure computation. In: Fischlin, M., Coron, J.-S. (eds.) EUROCRYPT 2016. LNCS, vol. 9666, pp. 448–476. Springer, Heidelberg (2016). https://doi.org/10.1007/978-3-662-49896-5_16

[Goy11] Goyal. V.: Constant round non-malleable protocols using one way functions. In: Fortnow, L., Vadhan, S.P. (eds.) 43rd ACM STOC, pp. 695–704, San Jose, CA, USA, 6–8 June 2011. ACM Press

[GPR16] Goyal, V., Pandey, O., Richelson, S.: Textbook non-malleable commitments. In: Wichs, D., Mansour, Y. (eds.) 48th ACM STOC, pp. 1128–1141, Cambridge, MA, USA, 18–21 June 2016. ACM Press

[GS18] Garg, S., Srinivasan, A.: Two-round multiparty secure computation from minimal assumptions. In: Nielsen, J.B., Rijmen, V. (eds.) EUROCRYPT 2018. LNCS, vol. 10821, pp. 468–499. Springer, Cham (2018). https://doi.org/10.1007/978-3-319-78375-8_16

[GSZ21] Goyal, V., Srinivasan, A., Zhu, C.: Multi-source non-malleable extractors and applications. In: Canteaut, A., Standaert, F.-X. (eds.) EUROCRYPT 2021. LNCS, vol. 12697, pp. 468–497. Springer, Cham (2021). https://doi.org/10.1007/978-3-030-77886-6_16

[HIK+11] Haitner, I., Ishai, Y., Kushilevitz, E., Lindell, Y., Petrank, E.: Black-box constructions of protocols for secure computation. SIAM J. Comput. **40**(2), 225–266 (2011)

[HK12] Halevi, S., Tauman Kalai, Y.: Smooth projective hashing and two-message oblivious transfer. J. Cryptol. **25**(1), 158–193 (2012)

[HPV20] Hazay, C., Pass, R., Venkitasubramaniam, M.: Which languages have 4-round fully black-box zero-knowledge arguments from one-way functions? In: Canteaut, A., Ishai, Y. (eds.) EUROCRYPT 2020. LNCS, vol. 12107, pp. 599–619. Springer, Cham (2020). https://doi.org/10.1007/978-3-030-45727-3_20

[HV18] Hazay, C., Venkitasubramaniam, M.: Round-optimal fully black-box zero-knowledge arguments from one-way permutations. In: TCC 2018. Part I, LNCS, pp. 263–285. Springer, Heidelberg, (2018)

[IKP10] Ishai, Y., Kushilevitz, E., Paskin, A.: Secure multiparty computation with minimal interaction. In: Rabin, T. (ed.) CRYPTO 2010. LNCS, vol. 6223, pp. 577–594. Springer, Heidelberg (2010). https://doi.org/10.1007/978-3-642-14623-7_31

[IKSS21] Ishai, Y., Khurana, D., Sahai, A., Srinivasan, A.: On the round complexity of black-box secure MPC. In: Malkin, T., Peikert, C. (eds.) CRYPTO 2021. LNCS, vol. 12826, pp. 214–243. Springer, Cham (2021). https://doi.org/10.1007/978-3-030-84245-1_8

[IPS08] Ishai, Y., Prabhakaran, M., Sahai, A.: Founding cryptography on oblivious transfer – efficiently. In: Wagner, D. (ed.) CRYPTO 2008. LNCS, vol. 5157, pp. 572–591. Springer, Heidelberg (2008). https://doi.org/10.1007/978-3-540-85174-5_32

[Kal05] Kalai, Y.T.: Smooth projective hashing and two-message oblivious transfer. In: Cramer, R. (ed.) EUROCRYPT 2005. LNCS, vol. 3494, pp. 78–95. Springer, Heidelberg (2005). https://doi.org/10.1007/11426639_5

[KO04] Katz, J., Ostrovsky, R.: Round-optimal secure two-party computation. In: Franklin, M. (ed.) CRYPTO 2004. LNCS, vol. 3152, pp. 335–354. Springer, Heidelberg (2004). https://doi.org/10.1007/978-3-540-28628-8_21

[KOS18] Kiyoshima, S.: Round-optimal black-box commit-and-prove with succinct communication. In: Micciancio, D., Ristenpart, T. (eds.) CRYPTO 2020. LNCS, vol. 12171, pp. 533–561. Springer, Cham (2020). https://doi.org/10.1007/978-3-030-56880-1_19

[KS17] Khurana, D., Sahai, A.: Two-message non-malleable commitments from standard sub-exponential assumptions. IACR Cryptology ePrint Archive **2017**, 291 (2017)

[MOSV22] Madathil, V., Orsini, C., Scafuro, A., Venturi. D.: From privacy-only to simulatable OT: black-box, round-optimal, information-theoretic. In: ITC 2022, vol. 230, pp.5:1–5:20 (2022)

[NP01] Naor, M., Pinkas. B.: Efficient oblivious transfer protocols. In: Rao Kosaraju, S. (ed.) Proceedings of the Twelfth Annual Symposium on Discrete Algorithms, 7–9 January 2001, Washington, DC, USA., pp. 448–457. ACM/SIAM (2001)

[ORS15] Ostrovsky, R., Richelson, S., Scafuro, A.: Round-optimal black-box two-party computation. In: Gennaro, R., Robshaw, M. (eds.) CRYPTO 2015. LNCS, vol. 9216, pp. 339–358. Springer, Heidelberg (2015). https://doi.org/10.1007/978-3-662-48000-7_17

[Pas12] Paskin-Cherniavsky. A.: Secure computation with minimal interaction. Ph.D. thesis, Technion, 2012. http://www.cs.technion.ac.il/users/wwwb/cgi-bin/tr-get.cgi/2012/PHD/PHD-2012-16.pdf

[PS21] Patra, A., Srinivasan, A.: Three-round secure multiparty computation from black-box two-round oblivious transfer. In: Malkin, T., Peikert, C. (eds.) CRYPTO 2021. LNCS, vol. 12826, pp. 185–213. Springer, Cham (2021). https://doi.org/10.1007/978-3-030-84245-1_7

[RTV04] Reingold, O., Trevisan, L., Vadhan, S.: Notions of reducibility between cryptographic primitives. In: Naor, M. (ed.) TCC 2004. LNCS, vol. 2951, pp. 1–20. Springer, Heidelberg (2004). https://doi.org/10.1007/978-3-540-24638-1_1

[Wee10] Wee. H.: Black-box, round-efficient secure computation via non-malleability amplification. In: 51st FOCS, pp. 531–540, Las Vegas, NV, USA, October 23–26, 2010. IEEE Computer Society Press

Reusable Secure Computation in the Plain Model

Vipul Goyal[1,2(✉)], Akshayaram Srinivasan[3], and Mingyuan Wang[4]

[1] NTT Research, Sunnyvale, USA
[2] CMU, Pittsburgh, USA
vipul@cmu.edu
[3] Tata Institute of Fundamental Research, Mumbai, India
akshayaram.srinivasan@tifr.res.in
[4] UC Berkeley, Berkeley, USA
mingyuan@berkeley.edu

Abstract. Consider the standard setting of two-party computation where the sender has a secret function f and the receiver has a secret input x and the output $f(x)$ is delivered to the receiver at the end of the protocol. Let us consider the unidirectional message model where only one party speaks in each round. In this setting, Katz and Ostrovsky (Crypto 2004) showed that at least four rounds of interaction between the parties are needed in the plain model (i.e., no trusted setup) if the simulator uses the adversary in a black-box way (a.k.a. black-box simulation). Suppose the sender and the receiver would like to run multiple sequential iterations of the secure computation protocol on possibly different inputs. For each of these iterations, do the parties need to start the protocol from scratch and exchange four messages?

In this work, we explore the possibility of *amortizing* the round complexity or in other words, *reusing* a certain number of rounds of the secure computation protocol in the plain model. We obtain the following results.

- Under standard cryptographic assumptions, we construct a four-round two-party computation protocol where (i) the first three rounds of the protocol could be reused an unbounded number of times if the receiver input remains the same and only the sender input changes, and (ii) the first two rounds of the protocol could be reused an unbounded number of times if the receiver input needs to change as well. In other words, the sender sends a single additional message if only its input changes, and in the other case, we need one message each from the receiver and the sender. The number of additional messages needed in each of the above two modes is optimal and, additionally, our protocol allows arbitrary interleaving of these two modes.

A. Srinivasan was supported in part by a SERB startup grant and Google India Research Award. M. Wang was supported in part by DARPA under Agreement No. HR00112020026, AFOSR Award FA9550-19-1-0200, NSF CNS Award 1936826, and research grants by the Sloan Foundation, and Visa Inc. Any opinions, findings and conclusions, or recommendations in this material are those of the authors and do not necessarily reflect the views of the United States Government or DARPA. This work was partly done when M. Wang was an intern at CMU.

H. Handschuh and A. Lysyanskaya (Eds.): CRYPTO 2023, LNCS 14081, pp. 427–458, 2023.
https://doi.org/10.1007/978-3-031-38557-5_14

– We also extend these results to the multiparty setting (in the simultaneous message exchange model) and give round-optimal protocols such that (i) the first two rounds could be reused an unbounded number of times if the inputs of the parties need to change and (ii) the first three rounds could be reused an unbounded number of times if the inputs remain the same but the functionality to be computed changes. As in the two-party setting, we allow arbitrary interleaving of the above two modes of operation.

Keywords: Reusable secure computation · plain model · round optimal · reusable zero-knowledge · reusable oblivious transfer · 2PC · MPC

1 Introduction

Secure computation [21,31] is a fundamental cryptographic primitive with numerous applications. A secure computation protocol allows a set of parties to compute a joint function of their private inputs while hiding everything about their inputs except the output of the functionality. This property is required to hold even against a centralized adversary that might corrupt any subset of the participating parties and instruct them to deviate arbitrarily from the protocol specification (known as malicious adversaries). In this work, we focus on constructing secure computation protocols that provide security against malicious adversaries in the *plain model* (i.e., without assuming any trusted setup).

Round Complexity of Secure Computation. Consider the standard setting of two-party computation where a sender and receiver are computing a certain function on their private inputs. Specifically, the receiver has a private input x and the sender has a secret function f. At the end of the protocol, the receiver learns $f(x)$. We consider the unidirectional message model where, in each round of the protocol, a single party speaks. In this setting, Katz and Ostrovsky [27] showed that we need at least four rounds of communication in order to compute general functions if the simulator uses the adversary in a black-box way (i.e., black-box simulation). In the case of multiple parties, Garg et al. [19] showed a four-round lower bound in the simultaneous message exchange model where every party may speak in each round.

A long line of works, starting from the seminal works of Yao [31] and Beaver, Micali, Rogaway [7] have led to constructions of secure computation protocols that have minimal round complexity. Currently, we know of round-optimal malicious-secure protocols in the plain model in both the two-party and the multiparty setting under the minimal cryptographic hardness assumptions [1,4,10,12–14,18–20,23,25–27,30].

Reusability of Rounds. Let us consider a setting where the sender and the receiver are not just interested in computing a single secure computation instance, but are interested in computing several instances sequentially possibly on different inputs. For example, say two banks collaborate on detecting if a large transaction is fraudulent. The banks might have an evolving database of past transactions. In this case, the parties participating in the 2PC remain the same while their input changes consistently. We ask the question of whether it is necessary for the sender and the receiver to start the protocol from scratch in each of these iterations and exchange four messages. Or, can they reuse some of the rounds of the protocol?

In this work, we begin the systematic study of reusable secure computation protocols in the plain model. Specifically, we study the possibility of constructing protocols where some of the rounds could be reused if the parties need to change either their private inputs or change the functionality to be securely computed. Prior to our work, reusable secure computation protocols were considered only in the common random string (CRS) model [2,3,5,6,9,11], or in the plain model satisfying the weaker notion of super-polynomial simulation security [17].

1.1 Our Results

In this work, we give round-optimal (i.e., four-round) constructions of two-party protocol (in the unidirectional message exchange model) and multiparty protocol (in the simultaneous message exchange model) for computing general functions where an *optimal* number of rounds could be reused an unbounded number of times.

Reusable 2PC. In the case of 2PC, we give a construction of a four-round protocol where (i) the first three rounds of the protocol can be reused an unbounded number of times if the receiver input remains the same and only the sender input changes and (ii) the first two rounds of the protocol can be reused an unbounded of times if the receiver input needs to change as well. We observe that the number of additional messages needed in each mode of reuse is optimal. First, any 2PC protocol in the unidirectional message model requires at least four rounds (w.r.t. black-box simulation) [27]. Furthermore, it is easy to see that, for every new sender input, at least one additional round is needed. Finally, if the receiver input needs to change, then we need at least two rounds of interaction. Otherwise, if there is only one more additional round, a semi-honest receiver could launch the so-called *residual attack* [24] by evaluating it multiple times with different choices of her input. Further, we allow the parties to interleave the above two modes of operation arbitrarily.[1] We prove the following theorem.

Theorem 1 (Reusable 2PC). *Assume either DDH or QR assumption holds and the existence of a ZAP protocol. There exists a construction of a four-round reusable 2PC protocol with security against malicious adversaries.*

[1] In particular, we refer to every new third-round message the receiver sends using a new input as a new *reuse session*. Within each reuse session, the sender could send multiple fourth-round messages using different inputs. By interleaving the two modes of reusability arbitrarily, we mean that the protocol execution could switch between reuse sessions (or create new reuse sessions) in an arbitrary manner. In fact, our protocol remains secure even if the adversary *adaptively* chooses which reuse session to execute next. We refer the reader to Sect. 3.1 for the formal definition of a reusable 2PC.

We remark that in our model the sender maintains some state across each reuse session (i.e., in the sessions where the receiver's private input changes). This is used to ensure that the receiver's third-round messages across different reuse sessions are consistent. We argue that (refer to the technical overview) this is necessary for the unidirectional message model; without this, it is not possible to achieve even simple functionalities such as the zero-knowledge argument of knowledge.

Reusable MPC. In the case of multiple parties, we give a four-round protocol (in the simultaneous message exchange model) where (i) the first two rounds of the protocol can be reused an unbounded number of times if the parties need to change their private inputs and (ii) the first three rounds of the protocol can be reused an unbounded number of times if the private inputs remain the same but only the functionality to be computed changes. Again, as in the case of 2PC, we allow arbitrary interleaving of these two modes and observe that the number of additional messages needed in each reuse mode is optimal. We refer the reader to Sect. 3.2 for the formal definition of a reusable MPC. We prove the following theorem.

Theorem 2 (Reusable MPC). *Assuming the existence of a four-round reusable 2PC protocol, a two-round semi-malicious reusable MPC protocol, and ZAPs. Then, there exists a construction of a four-round reusable MPC protocol with security against malicious adversaries.*

We can instantiate the two-round semi-malicious reusable MPC protocol under the DDH assumption [5], SXDH assumption on asymmetric bilinear maps [11], LWE assumption [2,3,9], and the LPN assumption [6].

Other Contributions. Along the way to obtaining our final results, we also construct a reusable zero-knowledge argument of knowledge (Sect. 4) and a reusable oblivious transfer (Sect. 5) in this paper. As far as we know, our work is the first to consider these reusable primitives in the plain model.

Alternate View of Our Results. Our protocols in the two-party and the multiparty setting have the following two-phase structure: in the first phase, we run a "mini" protocol to establish a reusable setup and in the second phase, we run a secure computation protocol that uses this setup. The number of rounds in the first and second phases depends on whether the private inputs of the parties change, or whether the functionality to be computed changes. In both settings, the number of rounds in the setup phase is at most 3. This must be contrasted with a naïve way of generating this setup which is to use a coin-tossing protocol to establish a CRS and then run a reusable 2PC/MPC in the CRS model. As shown in the works of Katz-Ostrovsky [27] and Garg et al. [19], such a coin-tossing protocol requires four rounds, and hence, this setup phase requires at least four rounds. In contrast, our approach leads to construction where at most 3 fixed and reusable rounds are required. In cases where only the function changes, we require 1 fresh round per execution. If the input of the parties also changes, we require 2 fresh rounds per execution. In addition, since our ultimate goal is to obtain a construction in the plain model, our constructions are arguably cleaner and simpler when compared to the coin-tossing-based approach.

2 Technical Overview

In this section, we give the key technical ideas behind our construction of a reusable two-party (in Sect. 2.1) and multiparty secure computation protocol (in Sect. 2.2).

2.1 Reusable Two-Party Computation

As mentioned before, our goal is to construct a round-optimal (i.e., a four-round) two-party computation protocol where (i) the first three rounds of the protocol could be reused an unbounded number of times if the receiver input is fixed and only the sender input needs to change, and (ii) the first two rounds of the protocol could be reused an unbounded number of times if the receiver input needs to change as well.

The starting point of our construction is the (non-reusable) canonical two-party computation protocol in the plain model based on garbled circuits [31]. Specifically, we consider Yao's 2PC protocol where the semi-honest oblivious transfer (OT) is replaced with a four-round malicious secure OT and the sender additionally uses a zero-knowledge argument of knowledge (ZK-AoK) to prove that the garbled circuit is generated correctly. The security of this protocol against malicious receivers follows directly from the zero-knowledge property of the underlying proof system, the security of the OT, and the security of garbled circuits. To give a bit more details, (i) we first use the simulator for the zero-knowledge proof to show that the proof gives no information about the witness (which is the secret randomness used to generate garbled circuits and the sender OT messages), (ii) we then use the simulator for the underlying OT protocol to extract the effective receiver input x, and (ii) finally, we use the security of garbled circuits to show that only the output $f(x)$ is revealed. The security against malicious sender follows from the proof of knowledge property that allows the simulator to rewind and extract a witness proving that the garbled circuit was correctly generated. This witness is used to extract the effective sender input which is given to the ideal functionality.

We run into several roadblocks when we try to make this protocol reusable. The first issue is that the zero-knowledge property of the proof system might be completely compromised if the first three rounds of the protocol are reused for proving different statements. The second issue is that the receiver security of the OT protocol could be compromised if the first two rounds are reused (in the case when the receiver inputs need to change) and the sender security could be compromised if the first three rounds are reused (in the case when the sender inputs need to change). To get around these bottlenecks, we give constructions of round-optimal ZK-AoK and oblivious transfer protocol secure against malicious adversaries with the desired reusability properties. This forms the crux of our main technical contribution. Moreover, we show that the 2PC protocol constructed above inherits the reusability features of the underlying building blocks.

Reusable Zero-Knowledge Argument of Knowledge Let us first try to construct a ZK-AoK protocol that runs in four rounds and the first three rounds of the protocol could be reused an unbounded number of times to prove different statements. This means that for each new statement, the prover needs to send a single message to the verifier and the verifier can check if the proof is accepting or rejecting. Zero-knowledge arguments for NP without this additional reusability feature are known from one-way functions [8]. However, if we additionally require this reusability feature, then such a protocol can be shown to imply a pre-processing NIZK if the proof is not publicly verifiable and a designated prover NIZK when the proof is publicly verifiable. Indeed, the first three rounds of the protocol could be fixed as part of the CRS and the secret randomness used to generate the respective messages could be given to the prover and the verifier respectively as the proving and verifying keys. Now, the prover could use this key to generate proofs for an unbounded number of NP statements which could be verified by the verifier using the verifying key. All known constructions of pre-processing or designated prover NIZKs rely on assumptions stronger than one-way functions and, hence, it is likely that we need stronger assumptions to construct such a zero-knowledge protocol.

Our construction of reusable zero-knowledge builds on the FLS trapdoor paradigm [16]. In this protocol, the first three rounds are used to generate a trapdoor between the verifier and the prover. In parallel, the prover and the verifier in rounds 2–4, run a delayed-input WI-PoK showing that either the statement is in the NP language or the prover knows the trapdoor. The trapdoor generation phase has the property that a cheating prover cannot extract a trapdoor whereas a rewinding simulator can extract it and use it to complete the WI argument. This allows us to argue PoK as well as zero-knowledge property. Unfortunately, this protocol as such is not reusable as the witness indistinguishability property of the WI protocol could completely break down if the first two rounds of the protocol are reused. This is indeed the case for the FLS delayed-input WI proof.

Our Solution. Our idea is to replace this delayed-input WI proof with a ZAP protocol [15]. ZAP is a two-round WI protocol between a verifier and a prover where the verifier's first-round message is a random string. Importantly, for our purposes, the same random string could be reused by the prover to prove multiple statements. Therefore, we can modify the above protocol so that the verifier in the third round also sends the first round message of a ZAP scheme. The prover in the final round proves via the ZAP that either the statement is true or it knows the trapdoor. This construction can be shown to be reusable zero-knowledge, meaning that the zero-knowledge property holds even if the first three rounds are reused. Unfortunately, it is not clear how to prove the soundness of this construction as ZAPs are not proofs of knowledge. To fix this, we additionally ask the prover to send an extractable commitment and show using ZAP that either statement is true or this extractable commitment is a valid commitment to the trapdoor. While this modification is sufficient to prove soundness, it is still not sufficient to show proof of knowledge property as ZAP does not allow extracting a valid witness from a malicious prover. To get around this problem, we ask the prover to send an additional extractable commitment to the witness and show via ZAP that either the first extractable commitment is a commitment to the trapdoor or the second extractable commitment is a commitment to a valid witness. An astute reader might have noticed that the extractable commitment to the witness must have the delayed-input property (meaning that the message is not determined until the end of the third round) and also have the first two rounds reusable. This means that using the same first two rounds of messages, a committer must be able to commit to a priori unbounded number of messages while maintaining the hiding property against a malicious receiver. We give a construction of such a commitment scheme in the main body. At a high level, the committer commits to a key of an SKE using a standard extractable commitment and sends an encryption of the message to be committed under the key in the final round. With this modification, we can show that the above protocol satisfies both reusable zero-knowledge (where the first three rounds are reused) as well as satisfies proof of knowledge property. We refer the reader to Sect. 4 for the details.

On the Possibility of Two-Round Reusable ZK-AoK. A natural question to ask is whether we can construct a round-optimal ZK-AoK protocol where the first two rounds are reused and the verifier can send arbitrary third-round messages in each reuse session. Indeed, if this ZK-AoK has to be used in our 2PC construction, then in each reuse session where the receiver's inputs change, a malicious receiver could choose an arbitrary third-round message and ask the prover to use this message to generate the final round proof. Unfortunately, we argue that such a ZK-AoK (with black-box simulators and extractors) cannot exist. This is because a malicious verifier could use the same strategy as that of the black-box extractor and generate multiple third-round messages and use the honest prover responses to extract a valid witness. The same argument also rules out the existence of a 2PC protocol for general functions where the receiver can choose arbitrary third-round messages. To get around this issue, we let the sender in the 2PC protocol maintain some state across the reuse sessions. Specifically, the sender could check if the third round message of the ZK-AoK protocol in each of the subsequent reuse sessions is the same as the ones used before. If this check does not pass, then the sender aborts. This check is necessary to get around the above-mentioned roadblock.

Reusable Oblivious Transfer Protocol. We now highlight the main technical challenges in constructing a reusable oblivious transfer protocol and explain how we overcome them. Recall that our goal is to construct a four-round (round-optimal) oblivious transfer protocol in the plain model that is secure against malicious adversaries and has first two round reusability (in case the receiver inputs need to change) and first three round reusability (in case only the sender inputs need to change).

We first observe that it is sufficient to construct an OT protocol with the above reusability features and satisfies standard simulation security against malicious receivers but only has indistinguishability-based security against malicious senders. Specifically, we require the view of a malicious sender to be computationally independent of the receiver's choice bits. Once we have such a protocol, we can upgrade its security by additionally asking the sender to give a ZK-AoK that it generated its OT messages correctly. If we rely on the ZK-AoK constructed in the previous subsection, then one could use the proof of knowledge extractor to extract the malicious sender inputs and thereby, show simulation security against corrupted senders. The zero-knowledge property of the proof system protects an honest sender against a malicious receiver. Additionally, this transformation preserves the desired reusability features of the underlying OT protocol. Hence, in the rest of this subsection, we focus on constructing a four-round OT protocol that has simulation security against malicious receivers and indistinguishability-based security against malicious senders.

Key Technical Challenge. The key technical challenge we face in constructing such an OT protocol is in designing an extractor that could extract the effective choice bit from a malicious receiver. This task is further complicated because (i) it must be accomplished within the first three rounds and hence, we cannot use any ZK-AoK to extract this information, and (ii) more importantly, we need the first two rounds of the protocol to be reusable an unbounded number of times. This means the honest receiver's input in each iteration must be hidden even if the first two round messages are fixed.

Starting Point. The starting point of our construction, as in the previous works [18,27,30], is a two-round semi-honest oblivious transfer from a special public-key encryption scheme. This special public-key encryption has the property that randomly sampled public keys are computationally indistinguishable from random strings (i.e., they are pseudorandom). Given such public-key encryption, the construction of a semi-honest oblivious transfer is as follows. The receiver chooses a valid public key pk_b (where b is its choice bit) and chooses a random string pk_{1-b} and sends (pk_0, pk_1) to the sender. The sender encrypts m_0 and m_1 under pk_0 and pk_1 respectively and sends it to the receiver. The receiver can now use the secret key sk_b corresponding to pk_b to decrypt and obtain m_b. In the semi-honest setting, we can set pk_{1-b} to be the same as the public key obtained from an external challenger and hence, one can use the semantic security of PKE to show that m_{1-b} is hidden. To make this construction secure against malicious receivers, the prior works [18,27,30] used a special kind of three-round commitment scheme called 1-out-of-2 binding commitments. Specifically, in their construction, the receiver commits to two random strings via a standard extractable commitment. Let us call these two instances of the extractable commitment as $(\mathsf{Ecom}_0, \mathsf{Ecom}_1)$. In the second round, the sender sends a random string s. The receiver, in the third round, sends two strings (s_0, s_1) and proves using a WI proof that one of these strings is the same as the one that is committed in

Ecom_0 or Ecom_1. The honest receiver chooses s_{1-b} to be the same as the string committed in Ecom_0 and chooses $s_b = s \oplus pk$ where pk is a randomly sampled public key for which it knows the corresponding secret key. It completes the WI proof using s_{1-b} and the randomness used to generate Ecom_0 as the witness. The sender in the fourth round of the protocol sends encryptions of m_0 and m_1 under the public keys $s \oplus s_0$ and $s \oplus s_1$ respectively and the receiver can use the corresponding secret key to extract m_b.

To argue security against malicious receivers, we first observe that, from the soundness of the WI proof system, there exists some b such that s_{1-b} is the same as the value that was committed. The simulator first rewinds and extracts s_0, s_1 from the extractable commitment. It then sets s such that $s \oplus s_{1-b}$ is the public key obtained from the external challenger.[2] This allows us to argue that m_{1-b} is hidden and formally proves security against malicious receivers. Indistinguishability against malicious senders is shown via a careful hybrid argument.

Challenges in the Reusable Setting. Unfortunately, the above construction is completely insecure in the reusable setting. Namely, even if the first two messages of the protocol are reused once, then a corrupt sender can look at the two strings sent by the honest receiver in the third round and figure out if the choice bits used in the two iterations are the same or different. To get around this issue, we could try to use a delayed-input extractable commitment where the first two messages are reusable and the message to be committed is known only in the third round (see the previous discussion for such a construction). In this case, the construction becomes trivially insecure against a malicious receiver. This is because the sender sends s in the second round and this is fixed in all the executions. Therefore, the receiver could choose (s_0, s_1) such that it knows the corresponding secret keys for both $s \oplus s_0$ and $s \oplus s_1$ and break the sender's privacy.

Our Solution. Observe that in the non-reusable version, security against corrupted receivers crucially relied on sampling the string s uniformly after the receiver sent the commitments. However, in the reusable setting, the string s is "chosen once for all" and fixed in all the subsequent executions. Thus, to make the above template reusable secure, we need to come up with a mechanism wherein we can "derandomize" the choice of s so that *a single fixed s works for every execution.* Towards this purpose, we do the following:

1. Let us start with the flawed approach discussed earlier where s_0, s_1 are committed using a reusable delayed-input extractable commitment. In this case, the receiver can trivially break the security by choosing s_0 and s_1 such that $s \oplus s_c$ for $c \in \{0, 1\}$ is a valid public key for which it knows the corresponding secret key. In hindsight, the insecurity of this construction stems from the fact that the receiver has complete control in choosing the public keys for

[2] Here, the simulator needs to first guess the value of the malicious receiver's choice bit b and set s accordingly. In the third round, it checks if the guessed value is correct and proceeds only in that case.

both branches 0 and 1. As a first step, we modify the construction so that the receiver has full power to choose the public keys for one of the branches (namely, the branch corresponding to its choice bit b) but the possible choices of the public keys for the other branch are restricted, meaning that the number of possible choices of the string s_{1-b} that a corrupt receiver can choose is exponentially small.

2. Though the first step makes progress in restricting the power of a malicious receiver, we are still not done. This is because if the receiver is able to find a valid public key pk such that $pk \oplus s$ is in the restricted set, then it can use it to recover both the sender inputs. For instance, if the set of valid public keys is dense (as in the case of El-Gamal encryption), then the receiver can still break the security of the OT protocol. Hence, our next step is to use public-key encryption that has pseudorandom public keys, and additionally, the set of valid public keys is sparse. For security, we require that if a message is encrypted under an invalid public key, then it is statistically hidden. In the technical section (Sect. 5.1), we give constructions of such public-key encryption from standard assumptions such as DDH and QR. Given such public-key encryption, we can argue the security of our OT protocol against malicious receivers as follows. Since the number of possible choices of s_{1-b} is exponentially small and since the set of valid public keys is sparse, the set of possible values of s such that $s = s_{1-b} \oplus pk$ is exponentially small. Therefore, a randomly chosen s with overwhelming probability does not belong to this bad set and thus, can be fixed once and for all.

We now explain both the steps in a bit more detail. The approach we take in step-1 is inspired by Naor's commitments [28]. Specifically, we use an extractable commitment to commit to two random strings as before, but instead of showing that one of (s_0, s_1) is the same as the value committed in Ecom_0 or Ecom_1, we show that one of (s_0, s_1) is equal to a PRG applied on the value that is committed in Ecom_0 or Ecom_1. Since the set of valid public keys is sparse, with overwhelming probability a randomly chosen s has the property that the set $\{s \oplus \mathsf{PRG}(\cdot)\}$ has zero intersection with the set of valid public keys (if the PRG has a sufficiently large stretch). This allows us to argue that even if the receiver has the power to choose the value inside the extractable commitment after seeing s, it cannot break the sender's privacy. Furthermore, we observe that a similar extraction strategy as explained earlier allows us to extract the effective choice bit from the malicious receiver and prove simulation security.

To argue receiver privacy, we design a careful hybrid argument wherein we use the security of the underlying primitives. Specifically, we first switch s_b to also be the output of a PRG on a randomly chosen seed r_b by relying on the pseudorandomness of the public keys and that of the PRG. We commit to r_b in Ecom_1 and then switch the WI proof to using the randomness corresponding to Ecom_1 and r_b as the witness. We then switch Ecom_0 to be a commitment of r_b and switch $s_{1-b} = s \oplus pk$ for a randomly chosen pk. We now reverse the WI proof to use the randomness in Ecom_0 as the witness and switch Ecom_1 to be a commitment of a random seed. The final hybrid corresponds to an honest execution where the receiver's choice bit is $1 - b$.

Getting 3-Round Reusability. The above approach allows us to construct an oblivious transfer protocol where the first two rounds could be reused an unbounded number of times if the receiver inputs need to change. To make the first three rounds of the protocol to be reusable, we do the following. Instead of using (m_0, m_1) as the sender OT inputs, we sample two random keys (k_0, k_1) of an SKE scheme and use them as the sender OT inputs. In the final round, we send encryption of m_0 under k_0 and encryption of m_1 under k_1. If the receiver input b remains the same, then in each iteration, the receiver only learns k_b and k_{1-b} is hidden. It now follows from the security of the SKE scheme that m_{1-b} in each iteration is hidden and hence, this modification can be shown to have the desired reusability features.

2.2 Reusable MPC

In a recent work, Choudhuri et al. [13] constructed a four-round malicious-secure MPC protocol from the minimal assumption that a four-round malicious-secure OT protocol exists. In particular, their protocol makes use of several building blocks such as a four-round OT protocol, a rewind-secure WI proof, a rewind-secure semi-malicious four-round MPC protocol, etc. Via a careful parallelization of these building blocks, they show how to obtain a four-round malicious-secure MPC protocol.

Similar to the reusable 2PC case, we observe that if we instantiate every building block with a variant that supports reusability, then the protocol shall also be reusable. In particular, we shall instantiate the four-round OT protocol with the reusable OT protocol that we constructed earlier. The rewind-secure WI proof shall be replaced by the ZAP protocol (which naturally satisfies rewinding security). Moreover, we instantiate the four-round semi-malicious MPC protocol with the two-round reusable semi-malicious MPC protocol [2,3,5,9,11] where the first round message could be fixed and one can evaluate multiple functions by sending a single final round message. We prove that by using these reusable variants of the building blocks, the construction of Choudhuri et al. [13] is reusable. We refer the reader to Sect. 7 for the formal description.

3 Preliminaries

Let λ be the security parameter. We use $\mathsf{negl}(\lambda)$ to denote a negligible function. That is, for all polynomial $p(\lambda)$, it holds that $\mathsf{negl}(\lambda) < 1/p(\lambda)$ for large enough λ. For a randomized function f, we use $f(x; r)$ to denote the evaluation of f with input x and randomness r. For any distribution A, we use $a \leftarrow A$ to denote that a is drawn according to distribution A. For any two distributions A and B, we use $A \overset{c}{\approx} B$ to denote that any PPT distinguisher $\mathcal{D}$ cannot distinguish A and B with non-negligible advantage, i.e., $|\Pr[\mathcal{D}(1^\lambda, A) = 1] - \Pr[\mathcal{D}(1^\lambda, B) = 1]| = \mathsf{negl}(\lambda)$. For any positive integer n, we use $[n]$ to denote the set $\{1, 2, \ldots, n\}$.

3.1 Reusable Secure Two-Party Computation Protocol

We consider the standard setting of two-party computation in the unidirectional message model. Specifically, the receiver has a private input a string x and the sender has a private input a function f. At the end of the protocol, the receiver learns $f(x)$ and the sender gets no output. By the unidirectional message model, we refer to the setting where only one party speaks in each round of the protocol. We are interested in constructing round-optimal (i.e., four-round) protocols for this task.

Syntax. A four round reusable secure two-party computation protocol is given by a set of algorithms $\Pi = (\Pi_1, \Pi_2, \Pi_3, \Pi_4, \mathsf{out}_\Pi)$ with the following syntax.

- $\Pi_1(1^\lambda, 1^{|x|})$: It is a PPT algorithm that is run by the receiver and it outputs the first round message π_1 and a secret receiver state st_R.
- $\Pi_2(1^\lambda, \pi_1, 1^{|f|})$: It is a PPT algorithm that is run by the sender and outputs the second round message π_2 and a secret sender state st_S.
- $\Pi_3(1^\lambda, \pi_2, x, \mathsf{st}_R)$: It is a PPT algorithm that is run by the receiver and outputs the third round message π_3.
- $\Pi_4(1^\lambda, \pi_3, f, \mathsf{st}_S)$: It is a PPT algorithm that is run by the sender and outputs the final round message π_4 and outputs the updated sender state st_S.
- $\mathsf{out}_\Pi(\pi_3, \pi_4, x, \mathsf{st}_R)$: It is a deterministic algorithm that is run by the receiver and provides the output y.

Remark 1. As mentioned, for the unidirectional message model, it is necessary that Π_4 outputs an updated sender state to get around the impossibility of constructing reusable ZK-AoK w.r.t. black-box simulator and extractor.

Definition 1 (Reusable Security against Corrupted Receivers). *We say that the protocol Π satisfies reusable security against corrupted receivers if for every non-uniform (stateful) PPT adversary $\mathcal{A}$ that is corrupting the receiver, there exists an expected PPT (stateful) simulator* Sim *such that for all $\ell = \mathsf{poly}(\lambda)$ and for all non-uniform (stateful) PPT distinguishers D, the output of the real and ideal executions defined below are computationally indistinguishable.*

- ***Real Execution:***
  1. *$\mathcal{A}$ on input $(1^\lambda, 1^\ell)$ executes the first two rounds of the protocol with the honest sender.*
  2. *In the i-th reuse session:*
     (a) *$\mathcal{A}$ either sends a fresh third round message which is forwarded to the sender or asks the sender to reuse a prior third round message.*
     (b) *D on input the current view of $\mathcal{A}$ outputs the honest sender input $f^{(i)}$ for this session.*
     (c) *The honest sender generates the final round message in the protocol using the input $f^{(i)}$ and the adversarially chosen third round message (which is either fresh or reused from a prior session). This final round message is forwarded to the adversary.*

   3. *The output of the real execution corresponds to the final output of D which is given the view of $\mathcal{A}$ at the end of the ℓ-th reuse session.*
- ***Ideal Execution:***
   1. Sim *on input* $(1^\lambda, 1^\ell)$ *and oracle access to the adversary* $\mathcal{A}$ *generates the view of the adversary at the end of the first two rounds and outputs this view.*
   2. *The ideal execution starts by initializing the adversary* $\mathcal{A}$ *with this view and continues with the rest of the execution as follows.*
   3. *In the i-th reuse session:*
      (a) $\mathcal{A}$ *either sends a fresh third round message or asks the sender to reuse a prior third round message.*
      (b) *D on input the current view of* $\mathcal{A}$ *outputs the honest sender input* $f^{(i)}$ *for this session.*
      (c) *The simulator on input the relevant third round message from the adversary outputs* $x^{(i)}$.
      (d) *The simulator is provided with* $f^{(i)}(x^{(i)})$ *and uses it to generate the final round message in the protocol. This message is forwarded to the adversary.*
   4. *The output of the ideal execution corresponds to the final output of D which is given the view of* $\mathcal{A}$ *at the end of the* ℓ*-th reuse session.*

Definition 2 (Reusable Security against Corrupted Senders). *We say that the protocol* Π *satisfies reusable security against corrupted senders if for every non-uniform (stateful) PPT adversary* $\mathcal{A}$ *that is corrupting the sender there exists an expected PPT (stateful) simulator* Sim *such that for any* $\ell = \mathsf{poly}(\lambda)$ *and for all non-uniform (stateful) PPT distinguishers D, the output of the real and ideal executions defined below are computationally indistinguishable.*

- ***Real Execution:***
   1. $\mathcal{A}$ *on input* $(1^\lambda, 1^\ell)$ *executes the first two rounds of the protocol with the honest receiver.*
   2. *In the i-th reuse session:*
      (a) $\mathcal{A}$ *either asks the honest receiver to reuse the third round message in the j-th reuse session (for some* $j < i$*) or asks it to generate a fresh third round message.*
      (b) *In the case where a fresh message is requested, D on input the current view of* $\mathcal{A}$ *outputs* $x^{(i)}$*. This input is used by the honest receiver to sample a fresh third-round message.*
      (c) *The adversary generates a final round message in the protocol. The honest receiver computes the output of the protocol and this output is forwarded to the adversary.*
   3. *The output of the real execution corresponds to the final output of D which is given the view of* $\mathcal{A}$ *at the end of the* ℓ*-th reuse session.*
- ***Ideal Execution:***
   1. Sim *on input* $(1^\lambda, 1^\ell)$ *and oracle access to the adversary* $\mathcal{A}$ *generates the view of the adversary at the end of the first two rounds and outputs this view.*

2. *The ideal execution starts by initializing the adversary $\mathcal{A}$ with this view and continues with the rest of the execution as follows.*
3. *In the i-th reuse session:*
   (a) *$\mathcal{A}$ either asks to reuse the third round message in j-th reuse session or asks to sample a fresh third round message. In the former case, we reset $x^{(i)} = x^{(j)}$. In the latter case, D on input the current view of $\mathcal{A}$ outputs $x^{(i)}$.*
   (b) *Depending on $\mathcal{A}$'s request,* Sim *either reuses the third round message in the j-th session or samples a fresh third round message (without the knowledge of $x^{(i)}$).*
   (c) *The adversary generates a final round message in the protocol which is forwarded to the simulator. The simulator either provides $f^{(i)}$ which is forwarded to the trusted functionality or instructs the trusted functionality to output $\bot$. In the former case, the output of the honest receiver is set to $f^{(i)}(x^{(i)})$ and in the latter case, it is set to $\bot$. This output is forwarded to the adversary.*
4. *The output of the ideal execution corresponds to the final output of D which is given the view of $\mathcal{A}$ at the end of the ℓ-th reuse session.*

3.2 Reusable Secure Multiparty Computation

We consider the setting of multiparty computation in the bidirectional message model. Specifically, all parties hold an input x_i. Given a function f to compute, at the end of the protocol, all parties learn $f(x_1, \ldots, x_n)$. By bidirectional message model, we refer to the setting where all parties speak in each round of the protocol. We are interested in constructing round-optimal (i.e., four-round) protocols for this task.

Syntax. A four round reusable secure multiparty computation protocol is given by a set of algorithms $\Pi = (\Pi_1, \Pi_2, \Pi_3, \Pi_4, \mathsf{out}_\Pi)$ with the following syntax.

- $\Pi_1(1^\lambda, 1^{|x|})$: It is a PPT algorithm that is run by the party to generate the first round message π_1 and a secret state st.
- $\Pi_2(1^\lambda, \pi_1, 1^{|f|}, \mathsf{st})$: It is a PPT algorithm that is run by the party to generate the second round message π_2 and an updated state st.
- $\Pi_3(1^\lambda, \pi_2, x, \mathsf{st})$: It is a PPT algorithm that is run by the party to generate the third round message π_3.
- $\Pi_4(1^\lambda, \pi_3, f, \mathsf{st})$: It is a PPT algorithm that is run by the party to generate the final round message π_4 and an updated state st.
- $\mathsf{out}_\Pi(\pi_3, \pi_4, x, \mathsf{st})$: It is a deterministic algorithm that is run by the party and provides the output y.

Definition 3 (Reusable Security). *We say that the protocol Π satisfies reusable security if for every non-uniform (stateful) PPT adversary $\mathcal{A}$ that is corrupting a subset of parties $\mathcal{I} \subset [n]$ (let $\mathcal{H}$ be the set of honest parties), there exists an expected PPT (stateful) simulator* Sim *such that for all $\ell = \mathsf{poly}(\lambda)$ and for all non-uniform (stateful) PPT distinguishers D, the output of the real and ideal executions defined below are computationally indistinguishable.*

- ***Real Execution:***
  1. *$\mathcal{A}$ on input $(1^\lambda, 1^\ell)$ executes the first two rounds of the protocol with the honest parties.*
  2. *In the i-th reuse session:*
     (a) *$\mathcal{A}$ either asks the honest parties to reuse the third round message in the j-th reuse session (for some $j < i$) or requests to compute a new reuse session.*
     (b) *In the case where a fresh session is requested, D on input the current view of $\mathcal{A}$ outputs the honest input $\{x_k^{(i)}\}_{k \in \mathcal{H}}$ for the honest parties. $\mathcal{A}$ and the honest parties with this input execute the third round of the protocol.*
     (c) *D, on input the current view of the adversary, output a function $f^{(i)}$ to be computed in the fourth round. $\mathcal{A}$ executes the final round message with the honest parties computing the function $f^{(i)}$. The output of the honest parties is forwarded to $\mathcal{A}$.*
  3. *The output of the real execution corresponds to the final output of D which is given the view of $\mathcal{A}$ at the end of the ℓ-th reuse session.*
- ***Ideal Execution:***
  1. Sim *on input $(1^\lambda, 1^\ell)$ and oracle access to the adversary $\mathcal{A}$ generates the view of the adversary at the end of the first two rounds and outputs this view.*
  2. *The ideal execution starts by initializing the adversary $\mathcal{A}$ with this view and continues with the rest of the execution as follows.*
  3. *In the i-th reuse session:*
     (a) *$\mathcal{A}$ either asks to reuse the third round message in j-th reuse session or asks to sample a fresh third round message. In the former case, the party's input is reset as $x_k^{(i)} = x_k^{(j)}$ for each $k \in \mathcal{H}$. In the latter case, D on input the current view of $\mathcal{A}$ outputs the party's input $\{x_k^{(i)}\}_{k \in \mathcal{H}}$. On receiving the third round message from $\mathcal{A}$,* Sim *outputs $\{x_k^{(i)}\}_{k \in \mathcal{I}}$.*
     (b) *Depending on $\mathcal{A}$'s request,* Sim *either reuses the third round message in the j-th session or samples a fresh view for the third round (without the knowledge of $x^{(i)}$).*
     (c) *The distinguisher D on the current view of the adversary outputs a function $f^{(i)}$ to compute. The simulator outputs $(f^{(i)}, \{x_k^{(i)}\}_{k \in \mathcal{I}})$ which is forwarded to the trusted functionality. The trusted functionality replies with $f^{(i)}(x_1^{(i)}, \ldots, x_n^{(i)})$. The simulator instructs the trusted functionality to deliver $\bot$ or the output to the honest parties. In the latter case, the output of the honest party is set to $f^{(i)}(x_1^{(i)}, \ldots, x_n^{(i)})$ and in the former case, it is set to $\bot$. The output of the honest parties is forwarded to $\mathcal{A}$.*
  4. *The output of the ideal execution corresponds to the final output of D which is given the view of $\mathcal{A}$ at the end of the ℓ-th reuse session.*

Due to space constraints, the definitions of standard cryptographic primitives are deferred to the full version.

4 Reusable Zero-Knowledge Argument of Knowledge

In this section, we give a construction of a round-optimal reusable zero-knowledge argument of knowledge (ZK-AoK) protocol where the first three rounds of the protocol could be reused an unbounded number of times to prove different statements. Specifically, the prover and the verifier execute the first three rounds of the protocol once. Afterward, given any language $\mathcal{L}$ in NP and $(\mathsf{st}, w) \in \mathcal{R}_{\mathcal{L}}$, the prover could send the fourth round of the protocol to convince the verifier that the statement st is in the language $\mathcal{L}$. The fourth round could be re-executed for an unbounded number of times. We require the proof to be zero-knowledge and, additionally, the existence of a knowledge extractor. We start with the syntax and give the formal definition.

Syntax. A four-round reusable zero-knowledge argument of knowledge protocol consists of a tuple of algorithms $(\mathsf{rZK}_1, \mathsf{rZK}_2, \mathsf{rZK}_3, \mathsf{rZK}_4, \mathsf{out}_{\mathcal{V}})$. To generate the messages of the protocol in the first three rounds, the Prover $\mathcal{P}$ uses randomness $r_{\mathcal{P}}$ and the verifier uses randomness $r_{\mathcal{V}}$. That is, the verifier sends $\mathsf{rzk}_1 = \mathsf{rZK}_1(1^\lambda; r_{\mathcal{V}})$; the prover sends $\mathsf{rzk}_2 = \mathsf{rZK}_2(1^\lambda, \mathsf{rzk}_1; r_{\mathcal{P}})$; the verifier sends $\mathsf{rzk}_3 = \mathsf{rZK}_3(1^\lambda, \mathsf{rzk}_2; r_{\mathcal{V}})$.

In the ith reuse session, the prover with input $(\mathsf{st}^{(i)}, w^{(i)}) \in \mathcal{R}_{\mathcal{L}^{(i)}}$ sends the proof $\pi^{(i)} \leftarrow \mathsf{rZK}_4(\mathsf{rzk}_1, \mathsf{rzk}_3, r_{\mathcal{P}}, \mathsf{st}^{(i)}, w^{(i)})$.[3] The verifier with input $\mathsf{st}^{(i)}$ verifies the validity of the proof using $\mathsf{out}_{\mathcal{V}}(\mathsf{rZK}_1, \mathsf{rzk}_2, \mathsf{rzk}_3, \mathsf{st}^{(i)}, \pi^{(i)})$.[4]

Definition 4. *A four-round protocol* rZK *between a prover and a verifier is a reusable zero-knowledge argument of knowledge if it satisfies the following.*

- **Completeness.** *In honest execution, the verifier always accepts the proof.*
- **Zero-knowledge.** *For any malicious stateful PPT verifier $\mathcal{V}^*$, there exists a stateful (expected) PPT simulator* Sim *such that, for all $\ell = \mathsf{poly}(\lambda)$ and for any non-uniform (stateful) PPT distinguisher D, the real and the ideal executions described below are computationally indistinguishable.*
    - ***Real Execution.***
        - *The honest prover and the verifier $\mathcal{V}^*$ (which is given $1^\lambda, 1^\ell$) execute the first three rounds of the protocol. Let $r_{\mathcal{P}}$ denote the random tape used by the prover to generate the first three rounds and let $(\mathsf{rzk}_1, \mathsf{rzk}_2, \mathsf{rzk}_3)$ be the transcript.*
        - *For the i-th reuse session:*
            - *The distinguisher D on input the current view of $\mathcal{V}^*$ outputs $(\mathsf{st}^{(i)}, w^{(i)})$. If $(\mathsf{st}^{(i)}, w^{(i)}) \in \mathcal{R}_{\mathcal{L}^{(i)}}$, then the prover generates $\pi^{(i)} \leftarrow \mathsf{rZK}_4(\mathsf{rzk}_1, \mathsf{rzk}_3, r_{\mathcal{P}}, \mathsf{st}^{(i)}, w^{(i)})$ and otherwise, it sets $\pi^{(i)} = \bot$. It sends $\pi^{(i)}$ to the verifier $\mathcal{V}^*$.*
        - *The output of the real execution corresponds to the final output of D that is given as input the view of $\mathcal{V}^*$ at the end of the ℓ-th reuse session.*

[3] $r_{\mathcal{P}}$ is only the secret state of the prover. The prover has access to fresh randomness.

[4] Note that the verifier does not hold any secret state. Hence, given the first three rounds, the proof is publicly verifiable.

- ***Ideal Execution.***
  - ∗ *The simulator* Sim *on input* $(1^\lambda, 1^\ell)$ *and oracle access to* $\mathcal{V}^*$ *generates the view of* $\mathcal{V}^*$ *at the end of the third round and outputs it.*
  - ∗ *The ideal execution initializes* $\mathcal{V}^*$ *with this view and continues with the rest of the execution as follows.*
  - ∗ *In the i-th reuse session:*
    - · *The distinguisher D on input the current view of* $\mathcal{V}^*$ *outputs* $(\mathsf{st}^{(i)}, w^{(i)})$.
    - · *If* $(\mathsf{st}^{(i)}, w^{(i)}) \in \mathcal{R}_{\mathcal{L}^{(i)}}$, Sim *on input* $\mathsf{st}^{(i)}$ *generates* $\pi^{(i)}$*. Else, we set* $\pi^{(i)} = \bot$*. We send* $\pi^{(i)}$ *to the verifier* $\mathcal{V}^*$*.*

  The output of the ideal execution corresponds to the final output of D that is given as input the view of $\mathcal{V}^*$ *at the end of the* ℓ*-th reuse session.*

- **Knowledge Extraction.** *For any malicious prover* $\mathcal{P}^*$*, there exists an (expected) PPT knowledge extractor* E *such that, for all statement* $\mathsf{st}^{(i)}$*, it holds that*

$$\Pr\left[\left(\mathsf{st}^{(i)}\ ,\ \mathsf{E}^{\mathcal{P}^*}(\mathsf{st}^{(i)})\right) \in \mathcal{R}_{\mathcal{L}^{(i)}}\right] \geqslant \Pr\left[\mathsf{Accept}^{(i)}\right] - \mathsf{negl}(\lambda),$$

if $\Pr\left[\mathsf{Accept}^{(i)}\right]$ *is non-negligible where* $\mathsf{Accept}^{(i)}$ *denotes the event that the honest verifier accepts the proof in the* i^{th} *reuse session when interacting with the malicious prover* $\mathcal{P}^*$*.*

4.1 Construction

In Fig. 1, we present our construction with the following building blocks. Refer to the full version for the definitions of the respective primitives.

- A delayed-input reusable extractable commitment scheme $(\mathsf{rEcom}_1, \mathsf{rEcom}_2, \mathsf{rEcom}_3)$.
- A delayed-input extractable commitment scheme $(\mathsf{Ecom}_1, \mathsf{Ecom}_2, \mathsf{Ecom}_3)$.
- A trapdoor generation protocol $(\mathsf{TDGen}_1, \mathsf{TDGen}_2, \mathsf{TDGen}_3, \mathsf{TDOut}, \mathsf{TDValid})$.
- A ZAP scheme $(\mathsf{ZAP}_1, \mathsf{ZAP}_2)$.

- **Language** $\widehat{\mathcal{L}^{(i)}}$**.** Fix the transcript for the first three rounds. A statement

$$\widehat{\mathsf{st}^{(i)}} = \left((\mathsf{recom}_1, \mathsf{recom}_2, \mathsf{recom}_3^{(i)}), (\mathsf{ecom}_1, \mathsf{ecom}_2, \mathsf{ecom}_3), \mathsf{st}^{(i)}\right)$$

  is in language $\widehat{\mathcal{L}^{(i)}}$ with witness $(w^{(i)}, r_{\mathsf{recom}}, t, r_{\mathsf{ecom}})$ if either one of the following holds.
  - **Valid Witness.** $(\mathsf{recom}_1, \mathsf{recom}_2, \mathsf{recom}_3^{(i)})$ is an honest commitment of $w^{(i)}$ with randomness r_{recom} and $(\mathsf{st}^{(i)}, w^{(i)}) \in \mathcal{R}_{\mathcal{L}^{(i)}}$.
  - **Valid Trapdoor.** $\mathsf{TDValid}(t, \mathsf{td}_1) = 1$ and $(\mathsf{ecom}_1, \mathsf{ecom}_2, \mathsf{ecom}_3)$ is an honest commitment of t with randomness r_{ecom}.
- **Protocol description.**
  1. **Round-1:** The verifier sends $\mathsf{td}_1 \leftarrow \mathsf{TDGen}_1(r_{\mathsf{td}})$.

2. **Round-2:** The prover samples the following $\mathsf{td}_2 \leftarrow \mathsf{TDGen}_2$, $\mathsf{recom}_1 \leftarrow \mathsf{rEcom}_1(r_{\mathsf{recom}})$, and $\mathsf{ecom}_1 \leftarrow \mathsf{Ecom}_1(r_{\mathsf{ecom}})$. The prover sends td_2, recom_1, and ecom_1.
3. **Round-3:** The verifier samples the following $\mathsf{td}_3 = \mathsf{TDGen}_3(r_{\mathsf{td}}, \mathsf{td}_2)$, $\mathsf{recom}_2 \leftarrow \mathsf{rEcom}_2$, $\mathsf{ecom}_2 \leftarrow \mathsf{Ecom}_2$, and $\mathsf{zap}_1 \leftarrow \mathsf{ZAP}_1$. The verifier sends td_3, recom_2, ecom_2, and zap_1.
4. **Round-4:** For the ith reuse session, prover does the following.
   - The prover checks that the trapdoor generation is successful, i.e., $\mathsf{TDOut}(\mathsf{td}_1, \mathsf{td}_2, \mathsf{td}_3) = 1$. If not, the prover aborts. Otherwise, the prover continues to sample:
   $\mathsf{recom}_3^{(i)} = \mathsf{rEcom}_3(\mathsf{recom}_2, r_{\mathsf{recom}}, w^{(i)})$,
   $\mathsf{ecom}_3 = \mathsf{Ecom}_3(\mathsf{ecom}_2, r_{\mathsf{ecom}}, 0^\lambda)$,
   $\mathsf{zap}_2^{(i)} \leftarrow \mathsf{ZAP}_2(\mathsf{zap}_1, \widehat{\mathsf{st}^{(i)}}, (w^{(i)}, r_{\mathsf{recom}}, \bot, \bot))$ proving that $\widehat{\mathsf{st}^{(i)}} = ((\mathsf{recom}_1, \mathsf{recom}_2, \mathsf{recom}_3^{(i)}), (\mathsf{ecom}_1, \mathsf{ecom}_2, \mathsf{ecom}_3), \mathsf{st}^{(i)}) \in \widehat{\mathcal{L}^{(i)}}$ with witness $(w^{(i)}, r_{\mathsf{recom}}, \bot, \bot)$. The prover sends $\mathsf{recom}_3^{(i)}$, ecom_3, and $\mathsf{zap}_2^{(i)}$.
5. **Verifier Output.** The verifier accepts the proof if both $(\mathsf{recom}_1, \mathsf{recom}_2, \mathsf{recom}_3^{(i)})$ and $(\mathsf{ecom}_1, \mathsf{ecom}_2, \mathsf{ecom}_3)$ are accepting transcripts, and $(\mathsf{zap}_1, \mathsf{zap}_2)$ is a valid proof of the statement $\widehat{\mathsf{st}^{(i)}}$.

Fig. 1. Our four-round reusable ZK-AoK

We shall prove the following theorem. The completeness follows immediately. The proof of reusable zero-knowledge and knowledge extraction property are deferred to the full version.

Theorem 3. *Assuming the security of the reusable extractable commitment scheme, the extractable commitment scheme, the trapdoor generation protocol, and the ZAP, the protocol described in Fig. 1 is a reusable ZK-AoK (see Definition 4).*

5 Reusable Oblivious Transfer Protocol

In this section, we give a construction of a reusable four-round oblivious transfer protocol. That is, the sender and receiver shall only execute the first two rounds once. Afterward, given a new choice bit as input, the receiver could send a new third-round message. As for the sender, on fixing the first three rounds, the sender could send multiple fourth-round messages given different pairs of messages as inputs.

We first make the following observation on how to transform any OT protocol into one where the first three rounds of protocol could be reused an unbounded number of times.

Remark 2 (Any OT is sender reusable). Given any four-round OT protocol, one could transform it into a new four-round OT protocol such that the first three rounds are reusable. Specifically, the sender could execute the original OT protocol with two keys k_0 and k_1 as his inputs. To reuse the first three rounds with different sender's input m_0 and m_1, the sender could simply append the fourth round message with a public-coin symmetric key encryption of m_0 and m_1 using k_0 and k_1 respectively. The sender's privacy for the original OT protocol implies its privacy for the reusable OT protocol. Furthermore, this transformation preserves receiver reusability.

In light of this observation, we shall only focus on the reusability of the first two rounds where the receiver's choice bit may change.

As a first step, we shall construct a reusable oblivious transfer protocol that provides indistinguishability security against a malicious sender and simulation security against a malicious receiver, which we define below. In the next section, we use this protocol as our main building block and construct a reusable 2PC protocol.

Syntax. A four-round reusable OT protocol consists of the following algorithms $(\mathsf{rOT}_1, \mathsf{rOT}_2, \mathsf{rOT}_3, \mathsf{rOT}_4, \mathsf{out}_{\mathsf{rOT}})$. Let $r_{\mathcal{S}}$ and $r_{\mathcal{R}}$ denote the sender's and receiver's private randomness in the first two rounds. The receiver sends $\mathsf{ot}_1 = \mathsf{rOT}_1(1^\lambda; r_{\mathcal{R}})$ in the first round. The sender sends $\mathsf{ot}_2 \leftarrow \mathsf{rOT}_2(1^\lambda, \mathsf{ot}_1; r_{\mathcal{S}})$ in the second round. For the ith reuse session, let us denote the receiver's choice bit by $b^{(i)}$ and the sender's messages by $m_0^{(i)}, m_1^{(i)}$. Receiver shall send $\mathsf{ot}_3^{(i)} = \mathsf{rOT}_3(1^\lambda, \mathsf{ot}_2, r_{\mathcal{R}}, b^{(i)})$ as the third round message. The sender shall send $\mathsf{ot}_4^{(i)} = \mathsf{rOT}_4(1^\lambda, \mathsf{ot}_1, \mathsf{ot}_3^{(i)}, m_0^{(i)}, m_1^{(i)}, r_{\mathcal{S}})$ as the fourth round message.[5] The receiver finally runs $\mathsf{out}_{\mathsf{rOT}}$ on the transcript of the protocol and its entire random tape to compute the output.

Definition 5. *We say that* rOT *is a four-round reusable oblivious transfer protocol with simulation security against corrupted receivers and indistinguishability security against corrupted senders if:*

- **Correctness.** *For all i, the receiver's output for the ith session is $m_{b^{(i)}}^{(i)}$.*
- **Indistinguishability against the malicious sender.** *For any PPT adversary $\mathcal{S}^*$ and for any $\ell = \mathsf{poly}(\lambda)$, let $\mathsf{View}_{\mathcal{S}^*}\langle \mathcal{S}^*, \mathcal{R}(b^{(1)}, b^{(2)}, \ldots, b^{(\ell)})\rangle$ denote the view of the adversary when it interacts with an honest receiver with inputs $b^{(1)}, b^{(2)}, \ldots, b^{(\ell)}$ (where $b^{(i)}$ denotes the input used by $\mathcal{R}$ in the i-th reuse session). It holds that*

$$\mathsf{View}_{\mathcal{S}^*}\langle \mathcal{S}^*, \mathcal{R}(b^{(1)}, b^{(2)}, \ldots, b^{(\ell)})\rangle \overset{c}{\approx} \mathsf{View}_{\mathcal{S}^*}\langle \mathcal{S}^*, \mathcal{R}(0, 0, \ldots, 0)\rangle.$$

- **Simulation security against the malicious receiver.** *Same as Definition 3 adapted to the case of oblivious transfer.*

[5] We remark that the receiver (resp., sender) has access to fresh randomness for every third (resp., fourth) round message. $r_{\mathcal{R}}$ (resp., $r_{\mathcal{S}}$) is simply her secret state for the first two messages.

5.1 A Building Block

Our construction utilizes a special PKE scheme defined as follows.

Definition 6. *We consider a public-key encryption scheme* $(\mathsf{Gen}, \mathsf{Enc}, \mathsf{Dec})$ *such that the following hold.*

- **Correctness.** *For any message* m*, it holds that*

$$\Pr\left[\begin{array}{c}(\mathsf{pk}, \mathsf{sk}) \leftarrow \mathsf{Gen}(1^\lambda),\ \mathsf{ct} = \mathsf{Enc}(\mathsf{pk}, m)\\ m' = \mathsf{Dec}(\mathsf{ct}, \mathsf{sk})\end{array} : m' = m\right] = 1.$$

- **Semantic Security.** *For all PPT adversary* $\mathcal{A}$*, it holds that*

$$|\Pr\left[\begin{array}{c}(\mathsf{pk}, \mathsf{sk}) \leftarrow \mathsf{Gen}(1^\lambda),\ (m_0, m_1) \leftarrow \mathcal{A}(\mathsf{pk})\\ b \leftarrow \{0,1\},\ \mathsf{ct} = \mathsf{Enc}(\mathsf{pk}, m_b),\ b' \leftarrow \mathcal{A}(\mathsf{pk}, \mathsf{ct})\end{array} : b' = b\right] - \frac{1}{2}| = \mathsf{negl}(\lambda).$$

- **Valid public keys are (exponentially) sparse and pseudorandom.** *Let* $\mathcal{PK}$ *denote the set of all strings in the co-domain of* $\mathsf{Gen}(1^\lambda)$*. Let* $\mathcal{PK}'$ *be the set of valid public keys, i.e., those public keys in the support of* $\mathsf{Gen}(1^\lambda)$*. It holds that*
  - $|\mathcal{PK}'|/|\mathcal{PK}| = 2^{-\mathsf{poly}(\lambda)}$,
  - *For any PPT distinguisher* $\mathcal{D}$, $|\Pr[\mathcal{D}(\mathsf{pk}) = 1] - \Pr[\mathcal{D}(U) = 1]| = \mathsf{negl}(\lambda)$, *where* $(\mathsf{pk}, \mathsf{sk}) \leftarrow \mathsf{Gen}(1^\lambda)$ *and* U *is sampled uniformly from* $\mathcal{PK}$.
- **Invalid public keys statistically hide the message.**[6] *For any* $\mathsf{pk} \notin \mathcal{PK}'$*, it holds, for all messages* m_0 *and* m_1*, that* $\mathsf{Enc}(\mathsf{pk}, m_0)$ *and* $\mathsf{Enc}(\mathsf{pk}, m_1)$ *are statistically close.*

We provide instantiations of this primitive from a list of assumptions below.

- **DDH.** Such PKE can be constructed from the Decisional Diffie-Hellman assumption (DDH) similar to [29]. In particular, $\mathsf{Gen}(1^\lambda)$ samples a group $\mathbb{G}$ of order p and a generator g. pk and sk are sampled to be $\begin{pmatrix} g & g^a \\ g^b & g^{ab}\end{pmatrix}$ and (a, b) for randomly chosen a and b. The universe $\mathcal{PK}$ is $\begin{pmatrix} g & g^a \\ g^b & g^{c}\end{pmatrix}$ for all a, b, and c. To encrypt a message $m \in \mathbb{G}$, one sends $g^u \cdot (g^a)^v$ and $m \cdot (g^b)^u \cdot (g^c)^v$. If $c = ab$, then one can decrypt the message correctly. However, if $c \neq ab$, $g^u \cdot (g^a)^v$ and $m \cdot (g^b)^u \cdot (g^c)^v$ statistically hides m. This construction satisfies all the properties above.
- **SSP-OT.** In general, it can be constructed from any two-round OT protocol $(\mathsf{OT}_1, \mathsf{OT}_2)$ that satisfies (1) statistical sender privacy (a.k.a. SSP-OT) and (2) that the first round message is pseudorandom. In particular, we

[6] We note that computational security also works for our construction. We state the statistical security as all of our instantiations enjoys this stronger notion.

could sample the public key to be $(\mathsf{OT}_1(0; r_1), \ldots, \mathsf{OT}_1(0; r_\lambda))$ with independent randomness $r_1, \ldots, r_\lambda$. To encrypt a message m, one first samples $m_1, \ldots, m_\lambda$ that additively secret shares m. The ciphertext shall be $\{\mathsf{OT}_2(\mathsf{ot}_{i,1}, (m_i, \bot))\}_{i=1}^{\lambda}$, where $\mathsf{ot}_{i,1}$ stands for $\mathsf{OT}_1(0; r_i)$.
  The valid public key is pseudorandom as the first round message of the OT protocol is pseudorandom. Valid public keys are $2^{-\lambda}$ sparse if we assume the support of the first-round message with choice bit 0 is smaller than that with choice bit 1. Without loss of generality, we may assume this as, otherwise, we could simply switch the valid public keys to be $(\mathsf{OT}_1(1; r_1), \ldots, \mathsf{OT}_1(1; r_\lambda))$. Finally, invalid public keys statistically hide the message since the OT protocol enjoys statistical sender privacy.
  The construction we describe above is a particular case of this general construction using the statistical sender private OT from DDH [29].
- **QR.** Recall the PKE scheme [22] from the quadratic residuosity problem. Suppose N is a Blum integer $N = p \cdot q$. A random quadratic non-residue x, whose Jacobi symbol $\left(\frac{x}{N}\right)$ is 1, is sampled as the public key. To encrypt a bit b, one samples a random y, which is coprime to N, and encrypt it as $\mathsf{ct} = y^2 \cdot x^b$. The decryption algorithm uses p and q to check if ct is a quadratic residue or not, which, in turn, determines if b is 0 or 1.
  This PKE already satisfies several requirements. Valid public key x (i.e., quadratic non-residue with Jacobi symbol 1) is indistinguishable from a random integer with Jacobi symbol 1, hence, is pseudorandom.[7] Invalid public keys statistically hide the message as, if x is a quadratic residue, ct is simply a random quadratic residue, and all information regarding b is lost. The only issue is that the valid public keys are not sparse enough; they are only 1/2-sparse. We use our ideas above again. We sample λ public keys $x_1, \ldots, x_\lambda$. When one encrypts a bit b, one first additively secret shares b as $b_1, \ldots, b_\lambda$ and encrypts b_i with x_i. This ensures that the valid public keys are $2^{-\lambda}$-sparse.

5.2 Our Construction

Our protocol is formally presented in Fig. 2 using the following building blocks. Refer to the full version for the definitions of the respective primitives.

- $(\mathsf{rEcom}_1, \mathsf{rEcom}_2, \mathsf{rEcom}_3)$ is a delayed-input reusable extractable commitment scheme.
- $(\mathsf{ZAP}_1, \mathsf{ZAP}_2)$ is a ZAP scheme.

[7] Our OT protocol is written assuming pk is pseudorandom over binary strings and, hence, all the operations are over $\mathbb{F}_2$. If we plug the QR-based construction into our OT protocol, the operation will be over the multiplicative group $\mathbb{J}$, i.e., the set of integers with Jacobi 1. Additionally, we need a (deterministic) mapping from a random binary string to a random element from $\mathbb{J}$ (since the PRG outputs are binary strings). For instance, this mapping can be chosen to be any randomized process of picking random elements from $\mathbb{J}$ (i.e., the process uses the input as its randomness to pick elements from $\mathbb{J}$).

- (Gen, Enc, Dec) is a PKE scheme defined in Sect. 5.1.
- PRG is a pseudorandom generator with a sufficiently large stretch[8]

- **Inputs:** Suppose there are ℓ reuse sessions (where ℓ is not a priori fixed). Sender holds the input $\{m_0^{(i)}, m_1^{(i)}\}_{i\in[\ell]}$. Receiver holds the input $b^{(1)}, b^{(2)}, \ldots, b^{(\ell)}$.
- **Language $\mathcal{L}$:** Fix $(\mathsf{recom}_{1,1}, \mathsf{recom}_{1,2})$ and $(\mathsf{recom}_{2,1}, \mathsf{recom}_{2,2})$. A statement

$$\left(\mathsf{recom}_{1,3}^{(i)}, \mathsf{recom}_{2,3}^{(i)}, r_0^{(i)}, r_1^{(i)}\right)$$

  is in language $\mathcal{L}$ if there exists a witness $(\alpha^{(i)}, c, \tau)$ such that
  - $\left(\mathsf{recom}_{c,1}, \mathsf{recom}_{c,2}, \mathsf{recom}_{c,3}^{(i)}\right)$ is an honest commitment of $\alpha^{(i)}$ with randomness τ;
  - And either $r_0^{(i)}$ or $r_1^{(i)}$ equals to $\mathsf{PRG}(\alpha^{(i)})$.
- **Protocol description:**
  1. Receiver initiates two instances of the delayed-input reusable extractable commitment $\mathsf{recom}_{1,1} \leftarrow \mathsf{rEcom}_1(1^\lambda; \tau_1)$ and $\mathsf{recom}_{2,1} \leftarrow \mathsf{rEcom}_1(1^\lambda; \tau_2)$. Receiver sends $\mathsf{recom}_{1,1}, \mathsf{recom}_{2,1}$.
  2. Sender samples $\mathsf{recom}_{1,2} \leftarrow \mathsf{rEcom}_2$, $\mathsf{recom}_{2,2} \leftarrow \mathsf{rEcom}_2$, $\mathsf{zap}_1 \leftarrow \mathsf{ZAP}_1$, and a random string s. Sender sends $(\mathsf{recom}_{1,2}, \mathsf{recom}_{2,2}, s, \mathsf{zap}_1)$.
  - For the ith reuse session,

    i-3: Receiver samples random $\alpha^{(i)}$ and $(\mathsf{pk}^{(i)}, \mathsf{sk}^{(i)}) \leftarrow \mathsf{Gen}(1^\lambda)$. Set

$$r_{b^{(i)}}^{(i)} = s \oplus \mathsf{pk}^{(i)} \qquad r_{1-b^{(i)}}^{(i)} = \mathsf{PRG}\left(\alpha^{(i)}\right).$$

    The receiver commits to $\alpha^{(i)}$ in the first instance of the reusable commitment and junk in the second instance. That is,

$$\mathsf{recom}_{1,3}^{(i)} = \mathsf{rEcom}_3(\tau_1, \mathsf{recom}_{1,2}, \alpha^{(i)}),$$
$$\mathsf{recom}_{2,3}^{(i)} = \mathsf{rEcom}_3(\tau_2, \mathsf{recom}_{2,2}, \bot).$$

    The receiver samples $\mathsf{zap}_2^{(i)}$ which uses the witness $(\alpha^{(i)}, 1, \tau_1)$ to prove

$$(\mathsf{recom}_{1,3}^{(i)}, \mathsf{recom}_{2,3}^{(i)}, r_0^{(i)}, r_1^{(i)}) \in \mathcal{L}.$$

    Receiver sends $\left(\mathsf{recom}_{1,3}^{(i)}, \mathsf{recom}_{2,3}^{(i)}, r_0^{(i)}, r_1^{(i)}, \mathsf{zap}_2^{(i)}\right)$ to the sender.

[8] The stretch we need depends on how sparse the valid public keys are. Looking forward, our proof relies on the fact that strings of the form $\mathsf{pk} \oplus \mathsf{PRG}(s)$ (for all possible valid public keys pk and seed s) are also (exponentially) sparse in the universe. Therefore, if the valid public keys are, for instance, $2^{-\lambda}$ sparse, it suffices to have a PRG of seed length $\leqslant \lambda/2$ and, consequently, of stretch $\geqslant \log|\mathcal{PK}|/(\lambda/2)$.

i-4: Sender verifies that $(\mathsf{recom}_{1,1}, \mathsf{recom}_{1,2}, \mathsf{recom}_{1,3})$, $(\mathsf{recom}_{2,1}, \mathsf{recom}_{2,2}, \mathsf{recom}_{2,3})$, and $\mathsf{zap}_1, \mathsf{zap}_2^{(i)}$ are all accepting. If the verification fails, the sender aborts. For both $j \in \{0,1\}$, set $\mathsf{pk}_j^{(i)} = s \oplus r_j^{(i)}$ and $\mathsf{ct}_j^{(i)} = \mathsf{Enc}(\mathsf{pk}_j^{(i)}, m_j^{(i)})$. Sender sends $\left(\mathsf{ct}_0^{(i)}, \mathsf{ct}_1^{(i)}\right)$ to the receiver.

- **Receiver Output.** The receiver recovers message $m_{b^{(i)}}^{(i)} = \mathsf{Dec}(\mathsf{sk}^{(i)}, \mathsf{ct}_{b^{(i)}}^{(i)})$.

Fig. 2. Our four-round reusable OT

We shall prove the following theorem.

Theorem 4. *Assuming the security of the reusable extractable commitment scheme, the ZAP scheme, the pseudorandom generator, and the PKE scheme, the protocol defined in Fig. 2 is a reusable four-round oblivious transfer protocol with simulation security against malicious receivers and indistinguishability security against malicious senders (see Definition 5).*

The correctness of protocol follows the correctness of the PKE scheme.

Due to space constraints, we defer the proofs of the reusable security to the full version.

6 Reusable 2PC Protocol

In this section, we shall use our reusable OT protocol and the reusable zero-knowledge protocol to construct a reusable 2PC protocol. We consider the uni-directional message setting. That is, for every round, only one party shall send messages to the other party. In this setting, we consider a four-round reusable 2PC protocol, where only one party receives the output of the protocol.[9] In our protocol, the first two rounds shall only be executed once. In the third round, the receiver shall send a message depending on his input x. In the last round, the sender sends one message depending on her function f. Parties could either reuse the first two rounds, where both the input x and the function f could change, or reuse the first three rounds, where only the function f could change.

Our protocol follows the standard 2PC protocol based on Yao's garbled circuit. That is, a four-round oblivious transfer protocol is run and in the last round, the sender shall generate a garbled circuit and send the receiver his labels using the OT protocol. Since our OT protocol supports reusing its first two rounds with different receiver's choice bits, our 2PC protocol also supports reusing the first two rounds with different receiver's inputs. Additionally, we parallel this with our ZK-AoK protocol where the sender proves that the garbled circuits and OT messages are generated honestly. Crucially, we also rely on that the

[9] This is optimal as Katz and Ostrovsky [27] proved that five rounds are needed if both parties shall receive the output of the protocol.

zero-knowledge protocol is reusable so that the sender could prove a different statement in every fourth round message.

Our protocol is formally presented in Fig. 3 with the following blocks.

- $(\mathsf{rOT}_1, \mathsf{rOT}_2, \mathsf{rOT}_3, \mathsf{rOT}_4)$ is a four-round reusable OT from Sect. 5.
- $(\mathsf{rZK}_1, \mathsf{rZK}_2, \mathsf{rZK}_3, \mathsf{rZK}_4)$ is a four-round reusable ZK-AoK from Sect. 4.
- $(\mathsf{Garble}, \mathsf{Eval})$ is a garbling scheme.

We use C for the universal circuit that takes the input a function f and an input x and outputs $f(x)$.

Remark 3. As we discussed in the technical overview, it is necessary that the sender maintains (and updates) a secret state across different reuse sessions. Otherwise, a malicious receiver could employ the same strategy as the (black-box) simulator to effectively "rewind" the sender across multiple reuse sessions and, hence, extract the input of the sender.

- **Language $\mathcal{L}^{(i)}$.** Fix the first three rounds $(\mathsf{rot}_1, \mathsf{rot}_2, \mathsf{rot}_3^{(i)})$ and $(\mathsf{rzk}_1, \mathsf{rzk}_2, \mathsf{rzk}_3)$. A statement

$$\mathsf{st}^{(i)} = \left(\widehat{C},\ \{\mathsf{lab}_{w, f_w^{(i)}}\}_{w \in \mathcal{S}},\ \mathsf{rot}_4^{(i)}\right)$$

  is in the language $\mathcal{L}^{(i)}$ with witness $(f^{(i)}, r^{(i)}, r_{\mathcal{S},\mathsf{rot}}, r_{\mathcal{S},\mathsf{rot}}^{(i)})$ if both the following conditions are satisfied.
  - $\widehat{C}$ an honest garbling of $\mathsf{Garble}(C; r^{(i)})$ and $\{\mathsf{lab}_{w, f_w^{(i)}}\}_{w \in \mathcal{S}}$ is the correct labels corresponding to the sender's input $f^{(i)}$.
  - $\mathsf{rot}_4^{(i)}$ is honestly generated with the partial transcript $(\mathsf{rot}_1, \mathsf{rot}_2, \mathsf{rot}_3^{(i)})$ and the receiver's input labels as the input messages using randomness $(r_{\mathcal{S},\mathsf{rot}}, r_{\mathcal{S},\mathsf{rot}}^{(i)})$.
- **Protocol Description.**
  1. The receiver sends $\mathsf{rot}_1 \leftarrow \mathsf{rOT}_1(1^\lambda; r_{\mathcal{R},\mathsf{rot}})$ and $\mathsf{rzk}_1 \leftarrow \mathsf{rZK}_1(1^\lambda; r_{\mathcal{R},\mathsf{rzk}})$.
  2. The sender sends $\mathsf{rot}_2 \leftarrow \mathsf{rOT}_2(1^\lambda; r_{\mathcal{S},\mathsf{rot}}$ and $\mathsf{rzk}_2 \leftarrow \mathsf{rZK}_2(1^\lambda; r_{\mathcal{S},\mathsf{rzk}})$.
  - Suppose the sender and receiver are going to execute a new reuse session with $f^{(i)}$ and $x^{(i)}$ as their inputs, respectively.

    i-3. The receiver samples $\mathsf{rot}_3^{(i)} \leftarrow \mathsf{rOT}_3(\mathsf{rot}_2, x^{(i)}, r_{\mathcal{R},\mathsf{rot}},)$. That is, the receiver computes the third-round message of the reusable OT with $x^{(i)}$ as his choice bits. The receiver computes $\mathsf{rzk}_3 \leftarrow \mathsf{rZK}_3(\mathsf{rzk}_2, r_{\mathcal{R},\mathsf{rzk}})$. It sends $\mathsf{rot}_3^{(i)}$ and rzk_3.

    i-4. **Secret state updates.** The sender maintains a secret state ω, which is initially set to be an empty string. If ω is empty, it updates ω to be rzk_3, i.e., this is the first time the sender receives the third round message rzk_3. If ω is not empty and $\omega \neq \mathsf{rzk}_3$, the sender aborts, i.e., the new rzk_3 message the sender receives is different from the ones it receives from previous reuse sessions. The sender samples $(\widehat{C}, \{\mathsf{lab}_{w,b}\}_{w,b}) \leftarrow \mathsf{Garble}(C; r^{(i)})$ and

$\mathsf{rot}_4^{(i)} = \mathsf{rOT}_4(\mathsf{rot}_1, \mathsf{rot}_3^{(i)}, \{\mathsf{lab}_{w,0}\}_{w\in\mathcal{R}}, \{\mathsf{lab}_{w,1}\}_{w\in\mathcal{R}}, r_{\mathcal{S},\mathsf{rot}}; r_{\mathcal{S},\mathsf{rot}}^{(i)})$. That is, she samples the fourth OT message with the labels for the receiver's input wire as her messages. She samples $\mathsf{rzk}_4^{(i)} \leftarrow \mathsf{rZK}_4(\mathsf{rzk}_3, r_{\mathcal{S},r_{\mathsf{rzk}}}, \mathsf{st}^{(i)}, (f^{(i)}, r^{(i)}), r_{\mathcal{S},\mathsf{rot}}, r_{\mathcal{S},\mathsf{rot}}^{(i)})$, where $\mathsf{st}^{(i)} = (\widehat{C}, \{\mathsf{lab}_{w,f_w^{(i)}}\}_{w\in\mathcal{S}}, \mathsf{rot}_4^{(i)})$ and $(f^{(i)}, r^{(i)}, r_{\mathcal{S},\mathsf{rot}}, r_{\mathcal{S},\mathsf{rot}}^{(i)})$ is the witness. The sender sends $\widehat{C}$, $\{\mathsf{lab}_{w,f_w^{(i)}}\}_{w\in\mathcal{S}}$, $\mathsf{rot}_4^{(i)}$, and $\mathsf{rzk}_4^{(i)}$.

- Suppose the sender and receiver are going to use an old reuse session. In this case, only the sender needs to compute and send a new fourth-round message (w.r.t. a new input function f'). The sender does exactly the same as in i-4 except that she does not need to do the "secret state update" step.

- **The receiver output.** It verifies that $(\mathsf{rzk}_1, \mathsf{rzk}_2, \mathsf{rzk}_3, \mathsf{rzk}_4^{(i)})$ is an accepting proof of the statement $\mathsf{st}^{(i)}$. If not, it aborts. Otherwise, it recovers $\{\mathsf{lab}_{w,x_w^{(i)}}\}_{w\in\mathcal{R}}$ from the reusable OT. Then, it evaluates $z^{(i)} = \mathsf{Eval}(\widehat{C}, \{\mathsf{lab}_{w,b}\}_{w,b})$. It outputs $z^{(i)}$ as $C(f^{(i)}, x^{(i)})$.

Fig. 3. Our reusable 2PC protocol in the unidirectional message model

We shall prove the following. Due to space constraints, the proof is deferred to the full version.

Theorem 5. *Assuming the security of the reusable OT, the reusable ZK-AoK, and the garbling scheme, the protocol in Fig. 3 is a simulation-secure reusable 2PC protocol.*

7 Reusable MPC Protocol

In this section, we shall use our reusable oblivious transfer protocol to construct a four-round reusable MPC protocol. That is, the first two rounds of the protocol are executed once. Afterward, given every new input $\vec{x}$, parties execute the third round in a new reuse session. Finally, given any function f for a reuse session, parties execute the fourth round to evaluate $f(\vec{x})$.

Recently, Choudhuri et al. [13] constructed a four-round MPC protocol using any four-round OT protocol. Our protocol adapts their protocol appropriately to make it reusable. In particular, we instantiate the building blocks in their protocol using appropriate reusable variants. For instance, we instantiate the four-round OT in their protocol with the reusable four-round OT that we construct in Sect. 5.

Intuitively, Choudhuri et al. [13] prove the security of their protocol through a sequence of hybrids, where the indistinguishability among the hybrids reduces to the security of the underlying building blocks. We observe that, as long as each building block supports reusable security, their proof also works to prove the reusable security of the protocol by the same reduction.

We present the protocol in Sect. 7.1. We refer the readers to the full version for the description of the simulator and formal security proofs.

7.1 Our Protocol

Our protocol uses the following building blocks. Refer to the full version for the definitions of the respective primitives.

- $(\mathsf{rREcom}_1, \mathsf{rREcom}_2, \mathsf{rREcom}_3)$: This is a reusable rewind-secure extractable commitment scheme.
- $(\mathsf{Ncom}_1, \mathsf{Ncom}_2, \mathsf{Ncom}_3)$: This is the non-malleable commitment scheme.
- $(\mathsf{rMPC}_1, \mathsf{rMPC}_2)$: This the two-round semi-malicious MPC protocol.
- $(\mathsf{TDGen}_1, \mathsf{TDGen}_2, \mathsf{TDGen}_3)$: This is a *one-rewind secure* trapdoor generation protocol.[10]
- $(\mathsf{ZAP}_1, \mathsf{ZAP}_2)$: The is the ZAP protocol. Recall that ZAP is both delayed-input and also unbounded rewind-secure.
- $(\mathsf{rOT}_1, \mathsf{rOT}_2, \mathsf{rOT}_3, \mathsf{rOT}_4)$: This is the reusable OT protocol we constructed in Sect. 5.
- $(\mathsf{Garble}, \mathsf{Eval})$: This is a garbling scheme.

High-level Summary. Figure 4 presents a high-level sketch of the protocol. On a basic level, parties shall execute the 2-round semi-malicious MPC in the third and fourth rounds to compute any function f. To ensure honest behavior, however, the following blocks are also added. First, parties shall commit to their input using the reusable delayed-input commitment scheme rREcom. Second, a three-round trapdoor generation protocol TDGen and a three-round non-malleable commitment scheme are executed in the first three rounds. Now, parties are supposed to prove their honest behavior in the third round by the first instance of the ZAP protocol $\mathsf{zap}_{1,a}, \mathsf{zap}_{2,a}$.[11] However, this proof is not sent in the clear but used as choice bits for another OT protocol. Since the proof $\mathsf{zap}_{2,a}$ is not sent in the clear, parties cannot verify the honesty of other parties before the fourth round. Therefore, parties cannot send their message rMPC_2 in the clear as well. Instead, it will compute a garbled circuit that will spit out this message rMPC_2 after it verifies all the $\mathsf{zap}_{2,a}$ proofs. The labels of this garbled circuit are used as the sender's message in the OT protocol. Finally, another instance of the ZAP protocol is executed to prove the honest behavior of the last round. We refer the readers to the technical overview of [13] for a more detailed overview.

A formal description of our protocol is in Fig. 5.

---

[10] We note that the specific trapdoor generation protocol construction [13] (based on the signature scheme) satisfies the *unique last round message* property. That is, given the first two rounds of the protocol, there is a unique last-round message that is accepting. In terms of reusing the protocol, this means that the sender in the trapdoor generation protocol will always send the same message in the third message of every reuse session.

[11] ZAP proves that either the party is generating all the messages correctly, or the non-malleable commitment commits to a valid trapdoor.

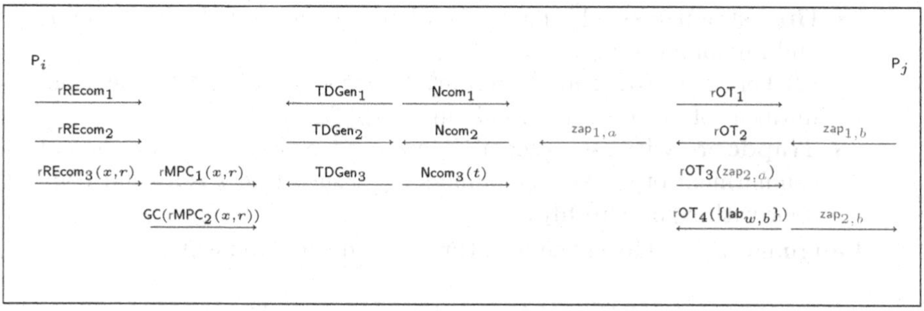

P_i P_j

rREcom$_1$ TDGen$_1$ Ncom$_1$ rOT$_1$

rREcom$_2$ TDGen$_2$ Ncom$_2$ zap$_{1,a}$ rOT$_2$ zap$_{1,b}$

rREcom$_3(x,r)$ rMPC$_1(x,r)$ TDGen$_3$ Ncom$_3(t)$ rOT$_3$(zap$_{2,a}$)

GC(rMPC$_2(x,r)$) rOT$_4$({lab$_{w,b}$}) zap$_{2,b}$

Fig. 4. A pictorial view of the messages exchanged between party i and j. Every row corresponds to one round. The red part indicates where we make appropriate modifications to [13]. The OT protocol is instantiated with a reusable OT protocol; the (bounded) rewind-secure WI proofs are instantiated with ZAP; the MPC is instantiated with a two-round reusable MPC.

Intuition for Reusability. [13] proves that their protocol is secure in the standalone setting. However, when one reuses the first two rounds of the protocol, this might cause issues as each reuse session shares the same first two rounds. In particular, in the security proof, when we try to reduce the indistinguishability between hybrids to the security of a particular building block, we might rely on the external challenger to send us the messages belonging to that building block for *all reuse sessions*. Therefore, it is crucial that all building blocks individually are reusable. And, indeed, as long as each building blocks are reusable, one can use the same proof as [13] to prove the reuse security. In particular, the indistinguishability between hybrids shall reduce to the *reusable* security of specific building blocks. Due to space constraints, the proof is deferred to the full version.

Theorem 6. *Assuming the reusable security of the building blocks, the protocol in Fig. 5 is a four-round reusable MPC protocol.*

For ease of presentation, we omit the $(\cdot)$ superscript indicating the reuse sessions.

– **Language $\mathcal{L}_a^{i\to j}$.** Given the first two rounds, a statement

$$\mathsf{st}_a^{i\to j} := \left(\mathsf{rmpc}_{i,1}, \left\{\mathsf{rrecom}_3^{i\to k}\right\}_k, \mathsf{ncom}_3^{i\to j}\right)$$

is in the language $\mathcal{L}_a^{i\to j}$ with witness

$$w_a^{i\to j} := \left(x_i, r_i, \left\{r_{\mathsf{rrecom}}^{i\to k}\right\}_k, r_{\mathsf{ncom}}^{i\to j}, t\right)$$

if either one of the following is true.

- **Honest witness.** (1) $\mathsf{rmpc}_{i,1}$ is a honestly generated with input x_i and randomness r_i;
  (2) For all k, $(\mathsf{rrecom}_1^{i\to k}, \mathsf{rrecom}_2^{k\to i}, \mathsf{rrecom}_3^{i\to k})$ is an honest commitment of (x_i, r_i) using randomness $r_{\mathsf{rrecom}}^{i\to k}$.
- **Trapdoor witness.** $(\mathsf{ncom}_1^{i\to j}, \mathsf{ncom}_2^{i\to j}, \mathsf{ncom}_3^{i\to j})$ is an honest commitment of t with randomness $r_{\mathsf{ncom}}^{i\to j}$ such that t is a valid trapdoor with respect to $\mathsf{td}_{1,j}$.

– **Language $\mathcal{L}_b^{i\to j}$.** Given the first three rounds, a statement

$$\mathsf{st}_b^{i\to j} := \left(\left\{\mathsf{rot}_4^{i\to k}\right\}_k, \widehat{C_i}, \mathsf{ncom}_3^{i\to j}\right)$$

is in the language $\mathcal{L}_b^{i\to j}$ with witness

$$w_b^{i\to j} := \left(x_i, r_i, \mathsf{rmpc}_{2,i}, \left\{r_{\mathsf{rrecom}}^{i\to k}, r_{\mathsf{rot}}^{i\to k}\right\}_k, r_{\mathsf{gc},i}, r_{\mathsf{ncom}}^{i\to j}, t\right)$$

if either one of the following is true.

- **Honest witness.** (1) $(\mathsf{rmpc}_{i,1}, \mathsf{rmpc}_{i,2})$ is honestly generated with input x_i and randomness r_i; (2) for all k, $(\mathsf{rrecom}_1^{i\to k}, \mathsf{rrecom}_2^{k\to i}, \mathsf{rrecom}_3^{i\to k})$ is an honest commitment of (x_i, r_i) using randomness $r_{\mathsf{rrecom}}^{i\to k}$; (3) $(\widehat{C_i}, \{\mathsf{lab}_{w,b}\}_{w,b})$ is an honest garbling of C_i with randomness $r_{\mathsf{gc},i}$; (4) for all k, $\mathsf{rot}_4^{i\to k}$ is honestly generated with randomness $r_{\mathsf{rot}}^{i\to k}$ and messages $\{\mathsf{lab}_{w,b}\}_{w\in \mathsf{P}_k,b}$.
- **Trapdoor witness.** $(\mathsf{ncom}_1^{i\to j}, \mathsf{ncom}_2^{i\to j}, \mathsf{ncom}_3^{i\to j})$ is an honest commitment of t with randomness $r_{\mathsf{ncom}}^{i\to j}$ such that t is a valid trapdoor with respect to $\mathsf{td}_{1,j}$.

– **Circuit.** The circuit C_i does the following.

- **Hardwired Inputs.** $\mathsf{rmpc}_{2,i}$, $\left\{\mathsf{st}_a^{j\to i}\right\}_j$, and $\left\{\mathsf{zap}_{1,a}^{i\to j}\right\}_j$
- **Inputs.** $\left\{\mathsf{zap}_{2,a}^{j\to i}\right\}_j$
- **Computation.** If for all j, $\left(\mathsf{zap}_{1,a}^{i\to j}, \mathsf{zap}_{2,a}^{j\to i}\right)$ is a valid proof of the statement $\mathsf{st}_a^{j\to i}$, output $\mathsf{rmpc}_{2,i}$. Otherwise, output $\perp$.

– **Protocol Description.**

1. P_i computes/broadcasts the following:
   - Trapdoor generation protocol: $\mathsf{td}_{1,i} \leftarrow \mathsf{TDGen}_1(r_{\mathsf{td},i})$

   For every $j \neq i$,
   - All Commitments:
     * $\mathsf{rrecom}_1^{i\to j} \leftarrow \mathsf{rREcom}_1(r_{\mathsf{rrecom}}^{i\to j})$
     * $\mathsf{ncom}_1^{i\to j} \leftarrow \mathsf{Ncom}_1(r_{\mathsf{ncom}}^{i\to j})$
   - Reusable OT: $\mathsf{rot}_1^{i\to j} \leftarrow \mathsf{rOT}_1(r_{\mathsf{rot}}^{i\to j})$
2. P_i computes/broadcasts the following. For every $j \neq i$:
   - Trapdoor generation protocol: $\mathsf{td}_2^{i\to j} \leftarrow \mathsf{TDGen}_2$
   - ZAP: $\mathsf{zap}_{1,a}^{i\to j} \leftarrow \mathsf{ZAP}_1$, $\mathsf{zap}_{1,b}^{i\to j} \leftarrow \mathsf{ZAP}_1$
   - All Commitments:
     * $\mathsf{rrecom}_2^{i\to j} \leftarrow \mathsf{rREcom}_2$

  * $\mathsf{ncom}_2^{i \to j} \leftarrow \mathsf{Ncom}_2$
- Reusable OT: $\mathsf{rot}_2^{i \to j} \leftarrow \mathsf{rOT}_2$

For the kth reuse session, computes the following.

3. P_i computes/broadcasts the following.
   - Reusable MPC: $\mathsf{rmpc}_{1,i} \leftarrow \mathsf{rMPC}_1(x_i, r_i)$. Here, x_i is P_i's input.
   - Let $\mathsf{td}_{2,i}$ be the concatenation of $\mathsf{td}_2^{j \to i}$ for all $j \neq i$.
     Trapdoor generation protocol: $\mathsf{td}_{3,i} \leftarrow \mathsf{TDGen}_3(\mathsf{td}_{1,i}, \mathsf{td}_{2,i}, r_{\mathsf{td},i})$.

   For every $j \neq i$:
   - All commitments.
     * $\mathsf{rrecom}_3^{i \to j} \leftarrow \mathsf{rREcom}_3((x_i, r_i), r_{\mathsf{rrecom}})$ commits to input x_i and randomness r_i used for the semi-malicious protocol.
     * $\mathsf{ncom}_3^{i \to j} \leftarrow \mathsf{Ncom}_3(t, r_{\mathsf{ncom}})$ commits to a random string t. (Note that parties keep committing to a new string t for each reuse session until the first reuse session where the third round messages do not cause an abort. In this case, this non-malleable commitment is fixed and shall be sent in all future reuse session as the third round message of the non-malleable commitment protocol.)
   - Sample $\mathsf{zap}_{2,a}^{i \to j} \leftarrow \mathsf{ZAP}_2$ such that $(\mathsf{zap}_{1,a}^{j \to i}, \mathsf{zap}_{2,a}^{i \to j})$ proves the statement $\mathsf{st}_a^{i \to j}$ using the honest witness. Note that $\mathsf{zap}_{2,a}^{i \to j}$ will not be sent.
   - $\mathsf{rot}_3^{i \to j} \leftarrow \mathsf{rOT}_3(\mathsf{zap}_{2,a}^{i \to j}, r_{\mathsf{rot}}^{i \to j})$. Here, P_i is the receiver in the OT protocol with choice bits $\mathsf{zap}_{2,a}^{i \to j}$.
4. P_i computes/broadcasts the following.
   - Check Trapdoor validity: if there exists j such that $(\mathsf{td}_{1,j}, \mathsf{td}_{2,j}, \mathsf{td}_{3,j})$ is invalid, abort.
   - Reusable rewind-secure MPC: $\mathsf{rmpc}_{2,i} \leftarrow \mathsf{rMPC}_2(x_i, r_i)$. Note that $\mathsf{rmpc}_{2,i}$ will not be sent.
   - Garbled Circuits: $\widehat{C_i}$, where $(\widehat{C_i}, \{\mathsf{lab}_{w,b}\}_{w,b}) \leftarrow \mathsf{Garble}(C_i, r_{\mathsf{gc},i})$.

   For every $j \neq i$:
   - OT messages: $\mathsf{rot}_4^{i \to j} \leftarrow \mathsf{rOT}_4(\{\mathsf{lab}_{w,b}\}_{w \in \mathsf{P}_j, b}, r_{\mathsf{rot}}^{i \to j})$. That is, P_i is the sender in the OT protocol with party j's input labels as its messages.
   - In order to facilitate other parties to recover the input labels corresponding to P_i for the garbled circuit $\widehat{C_j}$, P_i shall send its secret state to other parties.
     However, instead of broadcasting $r_{\mathsf{rot}}^{i \to j}$ as did in [13], parties shall broadcast the secret-key for decrypting the ciphertext of the last round.
     This change is necessary as the rOT is no longer reusable if the entire secret state $r_{\mathsf{rot}}^{i \to j}$ is revealed.
   - Sample $\mathsf{zap}_{2,b}^{i \to j} \leftarrow \mathsf{ZAP}_2$ such that $(\mathsf{zap}_{1,b}^{j \to i}, \mathsf{zap}_{2,b}^{i \to j})$ proves the statement $\mathsf{st}_b^{i \to j}$ using the honest witness.

– **Output Computation.** Party P_i computes the following.

- Verify that $(\mathsf{zap}_{1,b}^{j\to i}, \mathsf{zap}_{2,b}^{i\to j})$ is a valid proof of the statement $\mathsf{st}_b^{i\to j}$.
- Extract the OT messages: for all $j \neq i$, and for all $k \neq j$, extract $\{\mathsf{lab}_{w,b}\}_{w\in \mathsf{P}_k}$ from $\mathsf{rot}_4^{j\to k}$. This is feasible since P_k broadcasts the decryption key for the rOT messages it receives.
- Evaluate the garbled circuits: for all $j \neq i$, $\mathsf{rmpc}_{2,j} = \mathsf{Eval}(\widehat{C_j}, \{\mathsf{lab}_{w,b}\}_w)$.
- Given all the messages $\{\mathsf{rmpc}_{i,j}\}_{i\in[2],j\in[n]}$ of the semi-malicious MPC protocol, evaluate the output of the protocol.

Fig. 5. A formal description of our reusable MPC protocol

References

1. Ananth, P., Choudhuri, A.R., Jain, A.: A new approach to round-optimal secure multiparty computation. In: Katz, J., Shacham, H. (eds.) CRYPTO 2017, Part I. LNCS, vol. 10401, pp. 468–499. Springer, Cham (2017). https://doi.org/10.1007/978-3-319-63688-7_16
2. Ananth, P., Jain, A., Jin, Z., Malavolta, G.: Multi-key fully-homomorphic encryption in the plain model. In: Pass, R., Pietrzak, K. (eds.) TCC 2020, Part I. LNCS, vol. 12550, pp. 28–57. Springer, Cham (2020). https://doi.org/10.1007/978-3-030-64375-1_2
3. Ananth, P., Jain, A., Jin, Z., Malavolta, G.: Unbounded multi-party computation from learning with errors. In: Canteaut, A., Standaert, F.-X. (eds.) EUROCRYPT 2021, Part II. LNCS, vol. 12697, pp. 754–781. Springer, Cham (2021). https://doi.org/10.1007/978-3-030-77886-6_26
4. Badrinarayanan, S., Goyal, V., Jain, A., Kalai, Y.T., Khurana, D., Sahai, A.: Promise zero knowledge and its applications to round optimal MPC. In: Shacham, H., Boldyreva, A. (eds.) CRYPTO 2018, Part II. LNCS, vol. 10992, pp. 459–487. Springer, Cham (2018). https://doi.org/10.1007/978-3-319-96881-0_16
5. Bartusek, J., Garg, S., Masny, D., Mukherjee, P.: Reusable two-round MPC from DDH. In: Pass, R., Pietrzak, K. (eds.) TCC 2020, Part II. LNCS, vol. 12551, pp. 320–348. Springer, Cham (2020). https://doi.org/10.1007/978-3-030-64378-2_12
6. Bartusek, J., Garg, S., Srinivasan, A., Zhang, Y.: Reusable two-round MPC from LPN. In: Hanaoka, G., Shikata, J., Watanabe, Y. (eds.) PKC 2022, Part I. LNCS, vol. 13177, pp. 165–193. Springer, Cham (2022). https://doi.org/10.1007/978-3-030-97121-2_7
7. Beaver, D., Micali, S., Rogaway, P.: The round complexity of secure protocols (extended abstract). In: 22nd ACM STOC, pp. 503–513. ACM Press (1990)
8. Bellare, M., Jakobsson, M., Yung, M.: Round-optimal zero-knowledge arguments based on any one-way function. In: Fumy, W. (ed.) EUROCRYPT 1997. LNCS, vol. 1233, pp. 280–305. Springer, Heidelberg (1997). https://doi.org/10.1007/3-540-69053-0_20
9. Benhamouda, F., Jain, A., Komargodski, I., Lin, H.: Multiparty reusable non-interactive secure computation from LWE. In: Canteaut, A., Standaert, F.-X. (eds.) EUROCRYPT 2021, Part II. LNCS, vol. 12697, pp. 724–753. Springer, Cham (2021). https://doi.org/10.1007/978-3-030-77886-6_25

10. Benhamouda, F., Lin, H.: k-round multiparty computation from k-round oblivious transfer via garbled interactive circuits. In: Nielsen, J.B., Rijmen, V. (eds.) EUROCRYPT 2018, Part II. LNCS, vol. 10821, pp. 500–532. Springer, Cham (2018). https://doi.org/10.1007/978-3-319-78375-8_17
11. Benhamouda, F., Lin, H.: Mr NISC: multiparty reusable non-interactive secure computation. In: Pass, R., Pietrzak, K. (eds.) TCC 2020, Part II. LNCS, vol. 12551, pp. 349–378. Springer, Cham (2020). https://doi.org/10.1007/978-3-030-64378-2_13
12. Brakerski, Z., Halevi, S., Polychroniadou, A.: Four round secure computation without setup. In: Kalai, Y., Reyzin, L. (eds.) TCC 2017, Part I. LNCS, vol. 10677, pp. 645–677. Springer, Cham (2017). https://doi.org/10.1007/978-3-319-70500-2_22
13. Rai Choudhuri, A., Ciampi, M., Goyal, V., Jain, A., Ostrovsky, R.: Round optimal secure multiparty computation from minimal assumptions. In: Pass, R., Pietrzak, K. (eds.) TCC 2020, Part II. LNCS, vol. 12551, pp. 291–319. Springer, Cham (2020). https://doi.org/10.1007/978-3-030-64378-2_11
14. Choudhuri, A.R., Ciampi, M., Goyal, V., Jain, A., Ostrovsky, R.: Oblivious transfer from trapdoor permutations in minimal rounds. In: Nissim, K., Waters, B. (eds.) TCC 2021, Part II. LNCS, vol. 13043, pp. 518–549. Springer, Cham (2021). https://doi.org/10.1007/978-3-030-90453-1_18
15. Dwork, C., Naor, M.: Zaps and their applications. In: 41st FOCS, pp. 283–293. IEEE Computer Society Press (2000)
16. Feige, U., Lapidot, D., Shamir, A.: Multiple non-interactive zero knowledge proofs based on a single random string (extended abstract). In: 31st FOCS, pp. 308–317. IEEE Computer Society Press (1990)
17. Fernando, R., Jain, A., Komargodski, I.: Maliciously-secure MrNISC in the plain model. Cryptology ePrint Archive, Report 2021/1319 (2021). https://eprint.iacr.org/2021/1319
18. Friolo, D., Masny, D., Venturi, D.: A black-box construction of fully-simulatable, round-optimal oblivious transfer from strongly uniform key agreement. In: Hofheinz, D., Rosen, A. (eds.) TCC 2019, Part I. LNCS, vol. 11891, pp. 111–130. Springer, Cham (2019). https://doi.org/10.1007/978-3-030-36030-6_5
19. Garg, S., Mukherjee, P., Pandey, O., Polychroniadou, A.: The exact round complexity of secure computation. In: Fischlin, M., Coron, J.-S. (eds.) EUROCRYPT 2016, Part II. LNCS, vol. 9666, pp. 448–476. Springer, Heidelberg (2016). https://doi.org/10.1007/978-3-662-49896-5_16
20. Garg, S., Srinivasan, A.: Two-round multiparty secure computation from minimal assumptions. In: Nielsen, J.B., Rijmen, V. (eds.) EUROCRYPT 2018, Part II. LNCS, vol. 10821, pp. 468–499. Springer, Cham (2018). https://doi.org/10.1007/978-3-319-78375-8_16
21. Goldreich, O., Micali, S., Wigderson, A.: How to play any mental game or A completeness theorem for protocols with honest majority. In: Aho, A. (ed.) 19th ACM STOC, pp. 218–229. ACM Press (1987)
22. Goldwasser, S., Micali, S.: Probabilistic encryption and how to play mental poker keeping secret all partial information. In: 14th ACM STOC, pp. 365–377. ACM Press (1982)
23. Halevi, S., Hazay, C., Polychroniadou, A., Venkitasubramaniam, M.: Round-optimal secure multi-party computation. In: Shacham, H., Boldyreva, A. (eds.) CRYPTO 2018, Part II. LNCS, vol. 10992, pp. 488–520. Springer, Cham (2018). https://doi.org/10.1007/978-3-319-96881-0_17

24. Halevi, S., Lindell, Y., Pinkas, B.: Secure computation on the web: computing without simultaneous interaction. In: Rogaway, P. (ed.) CRYPTO 2011. LNCS, vol. 6841, pp. 132–150. Springer, Heidelberg (2011). https://doi.org/10.1007/978-3-642-22792-9_8
25. Ishai, Y., Kushilevitz, E., Ostrovsky, R., Prabhakaran, M., Sahai, A.: Efficient non-interactive secure computation. In: Paterson, K.G. (ed.) EUROCRYPT 2011. LNCS, vol. 6632, pp. 406–425. Springer, Heidelberg (2011). https://doi.org/10.1007/978-3-642-20465-4_23
26. Ishai, Y., Prabhakaran, M., Sahai, A.: Founding cryptography on oblivious transfer – efficiently. In: Wagner, D. (ed.) CRYPTO 2008. LNCS, vol. 5157, pp. 572–591. Springer, Heidelberg (2008). https://doi.org/10.1007/978-3-540-85174-5_32
27. Katz, J., Ostrovsky, R.: Round-optimal secure two-party computation. In: Franklin, M. (ed.) CRYPTO 2004. LNCS, vol. 3152, pp. 335–354. Springer, Heidelberg (2004). https://doi.org/10.1007/978-3-540-28628-8_21
28. Naor, M.: Bit commitment using pseudorandomness. J. Cryptol. **4**(2), 151–158 (1991). https://doi.org/10.1007/BF00196774
29. Naor, M., Pinkas, B.: Efficient oblivious transfer protocols. In: Rao Kosaraju, S. (ed.) 12th SODA, pp. 448–457. ACM-SIAM (2001)
30. Ostrovsky, R., Richelson, S., Scafuro, A.: Round-optimal black-box two-party computation. In: Gennaro, R., Robshaw, M. (eds.) CRYPTO 2015, Part II. LNCS, vol. 9216, pp. 339–358. Springer, Heidelberg (2015). https://doi.org/10.1007/978-3-662-48000-7_17
31. Yao, A.C.-C.: How to generate and exchange secrets (extended abstract). In: 27th FOCS, pp. 162–167. IEEE Computer Society Press (1986)

List Oblivious Transfer and Applications to Round-Optimal Black-Box Multiparty Coin Tossing

Michele Ciampi[1(✉)], Rafail Ostrovsky[2], Luisa Siniscalchi[3], and Hendrik Waldner[4,5]

[1] The University of Edinburgh, Edinburgh, UK
mciampi@ed.ac.uk

[2] University of California, Los Angeles, USA
rafail@cs.ucla.edu

[3] Danish Technical University, Copenhagen, Denmark
luisi@dtu.dk

[4] University of Maryland, College Park, USA
hwaldner@umd.edu

[5] Max Planck Institute for Security and Privacy, Bochum, Germany

Abstract. In this work we study the problem of minimizing the round complexity for securely evaluating multiparty functionalities while making black-box use of polynomial time assumptions. In Eurocrypt 2016, Garg et al. showed that assuming all parties have access to a broadcast channel, then at least four rounds of communication are required to securely realize non-trivial functionalities in the plain model.

A sequence of works follow-up the result of Garg et al. matching this lower bound under a variety of assumptions. Unfortunately, none of these works make black-box use of the underlying cryptographic primitives. In Crypto 2021, Ishai, Khurana, Sahai, and Srinivasan came closer to matching the four-round lower bound, obtaining a five-round protocol that makes black-box use of oblivious transfer and PKE with pseudorandom public keys.

In this work, we show how to realize any input-less functionality (e.g., coin-tossing, generation of key-pairs, and so on) in *four rounds* while making black-box use of two-round oblivious transfer. As an additional result, we construct the first four-round MPC protocol for generic functionalities that makes black-box use of the underlying primitives, achieving security against non-aborting adversaries.

Our protocols are based on a new primitive called *list two-party computation*. This primitive offers relaxed security compared to the standard notion of secure two-party computation. Despite this relaxation, we argue that this tool suffices for our applications. List two-party computation is of independent interest, as we argue it can also be used for the generation of setups, like oblivious transfer correlated randomness, in three rounds. Prior to our work, generating such a setup required at least four rounds of interactions or a trusted third party.

H. Handschuh and A. Lysyanskaya (Eds.): CRYPTO 2023, LNCS 14081, pp. 459–488, 2023.
https://doi.org/10.1007/978-3-031-38557-5_15

1 Introduction

Secure multi-party computation (MPC) [11,29] allows a group of mutually distrustful parties to jointly evaluate any function over their private inputs in such a way that no one learns anything beyond the output of the function. Since its introduction, MPC has been extensively studied in terms of assumptions, complexity, security definitions, and execution models [2,4,6,8–12,18,20,21,23,25,26,28]. In [10], Garg et al. established that *four rounds* are necessary to securely realize non-trivial functionalities (e.g., coin tossing) in the plain model with static corruption and black-box simulation[1] in the dishonest majority setting. A sequence of works tried to match this lower bound for the multi-party setting [2,6], and finally [3,14] showed the first four-round protocols based on polynomial time number theoretic assumptions. This result was later improved in [7] proposing a four-round scheme based on malicious secure oblivious transfer (OT).

Unfortunately, all these round-optimal protocols make non-black-box use of the underlying primitives. Recently, Ishai, Khurana, Sahai, and Srinivasan [17] came close to closing this gap, proposing a five-round protocol that makes black-box use of oblivious transfer and public-key encryption (PKE) with pseudorandom public keys. Prior to their work, MPC protocols that use the underlying primitives in a black-box way needed more than 15 rounds [12,18,28]. This leaves open the following questions:

> *What is the best-possible round complexity for securely evaluating any multi-party functionality in the plain model when the majority of the parties are corrupted while using the underlying cryptographic primitives in a black-box way?*

1.1 Our Contribution

In this work, we partially answer the above question by constructing the first round-optimal MPC protocol for computing any input-less functionality (e.g., coin tossing), while making black-box use of any perfect correct two-round private OT protocol. The notion of private OT, introduced in [1,24], requires that the receiver's only message is computationally indistinguishable between the cases where its input bit b is equal to 0 or 1. Moreover, regardless of the receiver's first message, the sender's message hides at least one of its inputs (denoted by s_0 and s_1). Private OT can be obtained from LWE [5], or number theoretic assumptions such as DDH [1,24] and DCR [19]. As an additional contribution, we show how to securely realize *any* efficiently computable functionality in four rounds, while relying on the same assumptions, against a weaker form of adversaries that promises to not abort during the computation with some unknown non-negligible probability. We will refer to this type of adversary as *sometimes aborting*. In summary, we prove the following theorems.

---

[1] All the results discussed and presented in this paper are with respect to black-box simulation. Hence, we will not specify this in the remainder of the paper.

Theorem 1 *(informal). Assuming two-round private OTs, then there exists a 4-round MPC protocol that realizes any multi-party input-less functionality with black-box use of the underlying primitives.*

Theorem 2 *(informal). Assuming two-round private OTs, then there exists a 4-round MPC protocol that realizes any multi-party functionality with black-box use of the underlying primitives in the presence of sometimes aborting adversaries.*

Our protocols are based on a new primitive called *list two-party computation.* This notion is an extension of the definition of list coin-tossing introduced in [3]. List coin tossing relaxes the standard simulation-based security definition, by allowing the adversary (hence, the simulator) to query the ideal functionality multiple times, thus obtaining multiple outputs (uniform random strings in this case). The adversary can then force the output of the honest parties to be one of the strings received from the ideal functionality.

List two-party computation (2PC) extends the notion of list coin-tossing to generic functionalities. In particular, we start by considering the *list OT functionality.* In this setting, for a corrupted receiver, the ideal world is formalized as follows: the adversary provides its input b and a parameter κ to the ideal functionality. The ideal functionality then samples κ random pairs $(s_0^i, s_1^i)_{i\in\kappa}$ uniformly at random, and provides $(s_b^i)_{i\in k}$ to the adversary. The adversary now picks an index $j \in [\kappa]$ and sends it to the ideal functionality, who delivers (s_0^j, s_1^j) to the sender in the ideal world. In summary, we allow the adversarial receiver to slightly bias the output of the computation. In [3], the authors observe that list coin-tossing suffices to generate a common random setup (e.g., for non-interactive zero-knowledge arguments). Similarly, we can argue that list-OT is sufficient for the generation of correlated OT randomness.

As previously mentioned, we propose a notion that is generic for any two-party functionality f. Suppose that only one party receives the output, so we can distinguish between a sender S and a receiver R, and let us assume that R is corrupted. The ideal functionality, upon receiving the input of the corrupted party x_R and κ, samples for each $i \in [\kappa]$ an input (according to some distribution by which the ideal world is parametrized) from the input domain of the sender, obtaining x_S^i. Afterwards, it computes $y^i \leftarrow f(x_R^i, x_S^i)$ and delivers $\{y^i\}_{i\in[k]}$ to the adversary. Upon receiving j from the adversary, the functionality returns (x_R^j) to the ideal world sender.

We show how to instantiate a list two-party protocol in just three rounds, where, in each round, both of the parties speak at the same time (this communication model is often referred to as the simultaneous message model), while making black-box use of the underlying cryptographic primitives. This tool will form the basis to instantiate our 3-round list-simulatable non-malleable OT protocol, which we will then plug into the MPC protocol proposed in [17] to obtain the first 4-round MPC protocol for input-less functionalities. We give more details on this in the next section. Additionally, we also show that a slight modification of this protocol yields the first round-optimal MPC protocol that realizes any functionality against sometimes aborting adversaries. We finally note that our list-OT protocol can be used to generate OT-correlated randomness in just three rounds. Prior results, required the execution of a four-round protocol or needed to rely on a trusted party for generating this type of setup. Closing the gap completely, and showing how to obtain a round optimal MPC protocol for generic functionalities from polynomial time assumptions while making black-box use of the underlying primitives, remains an important open question.

1.2 Technical Overview

List Oblivious Transfer. The first tool we construct, which will form the base of our three-round 2PC protocol, is a list OT protocol. Our protocol is based on a two-round private OT protocol which we denote with $\mathsf{OT}^{\mathsf{priv}}$. Our list OT protocol, which we denote with $\mathsf{OT}^{\mathsf{list}}$, works as follows: the sender and receiver run an OT combiner[2] on two instances of $\mathsf{OT}^{\mathsf{priv}}$. In the second round, the sender tosses a random coin c and asks the receiver to send a valid defence[3] for the c-th execution of $\mathsf{OT}^{\mathsf{priv}}$. The receiver sends the defence to the sender, which accepts if the defence is valid. The security of the combiner guarantees that the input choice of the receiver remains protected, even if the randomness of one of the OT instances is leaked. Hence, the obtained protocol preserves the privacy of the receiver's input. To prove that the protocol is list simulatable against corrupted receivers, we construct a simulator that rewinds the second round by sending a new coin $c' \neq c$. Upon receiving the defence for the remaining OT protocol, the simulator is able to reconstruct the input of the receiver.

There are many aspects that have not been taken into account in this high level description. For example, the list simulator needs to receive a valid third round to complete the simulation. If the corrupted receiver is rushing, then the simulator needs to complete an entire execution of the protocol before starting the extraction procedure. To do this, the simulator uses random inputs, during the main thread and the rewinding threads, and behaves as an honest sender would. After the extraction is performed, the simulator can query the ideal functionality with the choice bit of the receiver b and obtains as a reply s_b, which can then be used in the simulation. In more detail, the simulator rewinds the adversary and uses the input (s_b, s_b) to execute the OT combiner as the honest sender would. This approach is still unsatisfactory since it encounters the same issue as observed in [17]. Indeed, it may be that the receiver aborts when receiving the output s_b, whereas it did not abort in the main thread (where the simulator may have used $s'_b \neq s_b$). This is the reason why Badrinarayanan et al. [3] considered a relaxed ideal functionality, that returns many possible outputs to the adversary (and the simulator), which gives the simulator multiple opportunities to force the output to the receiver.

[2] We recall that an OT combiner allows combining two (or more) OT instances to obtain a new OT instance, that is guaranteed to be secure, as long as one of the input instances is not compromise. We refer to [16] for more details on OT combiners. Moreover, for our formal constructions we will not rely on a combiner in a black-box way, we will instead use techniques similar to those proposed in [16] to properly combine our OT protocols.

[3] A defence of a protocol execution is represented by the randomness and input that explain the generated transcript.

There are two main aspects left to clarify. The protocol just described works under the assumption that the input of the sender is sampled uniformly at random from a sampling space of exponential size (or at least with high min-entropy). This condition is necessary to prove the security of all the list-protocols we propose in this work. We also note that the protocol just described is still not secure. A receiver could decide to complete the protocol when $c = 0$ and abort when $c = 1$. Against such an adversary the simulator clearly fails. To solve this problem, the sender performs an n-out-of-n (where n is polynomial in the security parameter) secret sharing of its two inputs, thus obtaining $(s_0^1, \dots, s_0^n)$, $(s_1^1, \dots, s_1^n)$. Then, the sender and the receiver engage in n repetitions of the described protocol, where the sender uses as its input to the i-th combiner the values (s_0^i, s_1^i), and the receiver uses its bit b. We can now argue that the simulator will successfully extract from at least one of the executions after (expected) polynomially many rewinds. We highlight that if the corrupted receiver uses different inputs in different executions of the combiner, the receiver will not obtain enough shares to reconstruct neither s_0 nor s_1.

Unfortunately, we are only able to prove the property of list simulation against an adversary that does not abort in the third round. If a corrupted receiver does abort, then there is no hope of extracting its input. We can still argue that, in this case, the privacy of the sender's input remains, in the same way as for $\mathsf{OT}^{\mathsf{priv}}$.

Another crucial property we require from our OT protocol is B*-rewind security* (we elaborate more on the reason why we require it later in this section). This property guarantees that all the parties' inputs remain protected even if the adversary is able to rewind the receiver B times, thus getting multiple valid third rounds computed with respect to $B + 1$ different second rounds. Our protocol $\mathsf{OT}^{\mathsf{list}}$ trivially does not achieve this property in the case of a corrupted sender (i.e., a corrupted sender could act as the list-simulator and extract the receiver's input). To achieve 1-rewind security, we iterate the idea of the combiners twice. More precisely, in each of the n iterations, we consider four executions of $\mathsf{OT}^{\mathsf{priv}}$ (let us denote each instance as *leaf*), and apply a combiner on the first two leaves, therefore obtaining a new OT protocol (which we call *left node*). We do the same for the second two leaves thus obtaining a new OT protocol (denoted by *right node*). Afterwards, we apply a combiner on the two nodes (obtaining the root). The sender now sends a challenge $c \in \{0, 1\}^2$ that determines how to navigate the constructed tree. In more detail, the first bit of c selects the node, and the last bit selects the leaf. For the selected leaf, the receiver will provide the defence. Now, even if a corrupted sender rewinds the receiver, the best it can achieve is to extract 2 out of 4 defenses among the four different executions of $\mathsf{OT}^{\mathsf{priv}}$, and the security achieved by the combiners protects the input of the receiver. To increase the rewind security of the protocol, we can iterate the above approach recursively.

To construct a list protocol for generic functionalities, we use the 1-out-of-2 OT protocol just described, and a (B-rewind secure) k-out-of-n list OT protocol. To obtain such a protocol, we devise a compiler inspired by [27] that turns our 1-out-of-2 OT protocol into a k-out-of-n OT protocol while preserving the round complexity and all the security properties of the underlying 1-out-of-2 protocol.

In the remainder of this section, we denote by $\mathsf{OT}_{1,2}^{\mathsf{ListRew}}$ and $\mathsf{OT}_{k,n}^{\mathsf{ListRew}}$ the 1-out-of-2 and the k-out-of-n list-oblivious transfer B-rewind secure protocols, respectively.

List Two-Party Computation. The main structure of our two-party protocol is the same as the one proposed in [17]. The protocol of [17] can be seen as being composed of two main components: a four-round oblivious transfer protocol, and an application of the IPS [18] compiler that uses the OT to perform a cut-and-choose (this is often referred as the watchlist mechanism). The main reason why the 2PC protocol of [17] requires four-rounds is due to the use of a simulation based secure oblivious transfer protocol. Indeed, to obtain such an OT protocol, four rounds of communication are necessary.

At a very high level, to obtain our three-round protocol, we replace the 4-round OT protocol with a 3-round OT protocol, that is simulation based secure against corrupted senders, and list simulatable against corrupted receivers. Our main contribution is to construct such a 3-round OT protocol. We now give a sketch of this protocol.[4]

To achieve our goal, we need to enhance the security of $\mathsf{OT}_{1,2}^{\mathsf{ListRew}}$, and make it simulation based secure against corrupted senders, while preserving the list simulatability against corrupted receivers. To do that, we need a way to force the sender to compute its messages honestly and employ a mechanism that allows the extraction of the sender's inputs. The general idea to achieve this is the following: we let the sender and the receiver engage in multiple executions of $\mathsf{OT}_{1,2}^{\mathsf{ListRew}}$, and run a cut-and-choose to check that the sender is behaving correctly in a big portion of the OT executions (for this to work, the input of the sender needs to be properly secret shared among the executions. For simplicity, we will ignore this aspect in this overview). Unfortunately, this approach does not work in our case, because we only have a total of three rounds, and the first message of the sender of $\mathsf{OT}_{1,2}^{\mathsf{ListRew}}$ appears in the second round. Hence, there is no room for the cut-and-choose (if the receiver sends the challenge in the first or the second round the sender can adaptively decide which execution to perform correctly and which to perform incorrectly). To solve this problem we hide the challenge of the cut-and-choose using our k-out-of-n OT protocol $\mathsf{OT}_{k,n}^{\mathsf{ListRew}}$. The protocol to hide the challenge is run in parallel with the executions of $\mathsf{OT}_{1,2}^{\mathsf{ListRew}}$. In this protocol, the receiver inputs a random set of indices denoted with K, where $|K| = k$ (with k being a parameter that depends on the cut-and-choose), and the sender uses as its input the n defences for the executions of $\mathsf{OT}_{1,2}^{\mathsf{ListRew}}$. At the end of the protocol, the receiver accepts the output only if all the k defences obtained from $\mathsf{OT}_{k,n}^{\mathsf{ListRew}}$ are valid. Intuitively, this approach should guarantee that a big portion of the 1-out-of-2 OT executions are correct. Unfortunately, it is not clear how this can be formally argued. Indeed, one would like to claim that if this does not hold (i.e., the majority of the 1-out-of-2 OTs are not correct), then we can construct a reduction that breaks the receiver privacy of $\mathsf{OT}_{k,n}^{\mathsf{ListRew}}$.

[4] Our formal construction directly uses $\mathsf{OT}^{\mathsf{list}}$ to obtain a 3-round list 2PC protocol, so we do not need an intermediate step where we instantiate this special OT protocol, which is instead implicit in our 2PC protocol.

The reason why this is non-trivial is that the reduction would need to check in which of the $\mathsf{OT}_{1,2}^{\mathsf{ListRew}}$ executions the sender is behaving correctly, and this would reveal information about what input is used by the challenger (which is acting as the receiver) of $\mathsf{OT}_{k,n}^{\mathsf{ListRew}}$ in the reduction. For example, if we could detect that the sender's messages in the i-th execution of $\mathsf{OT}_{1,2}^{\mathsf{ListRew}}$ are not well-formed, then we know that $i \notin K$ with some non-negligible probability. The problem is that the reduction cannot efficiently check which executions are correct and which executions are not. To enable an efficient check, we modify the protocol requiring the sender to commit to the defence via a three-round extractable commitment scheme. We also require the sender, to input to the $\mathsf{OT}_{k,n}^{\mathsf{ListRew}}$ the randomness used to compute the extractable commitments. Hence, the honest receiver accepts the output if the randomness obtained via $\mathsf{OT}_{k,n}^{\mathsf{ListRew}}$ is valid with respect to the extractable commitments, and, moreover, the messages committed are valid defences for k executions of $\mathsf{OT}_{1,2}^{\mathsf{ListRew}}$. The reduction to the receiver security of $\mathsf{OT}_{k,n}^{\mathsf{ListRew}}$ can now extract from the extractable commitments, and check which $\mathsf{OT}_{1,2}^{\mathsf{ListRew}}$ executions are executed honestly by the sender. This information can then be used by the reduction to infer what value K is used by the challenger, thus reaching a contradiction. We note that this reduction crucially relies on the rewind security of $\mathsf{OT}_{k,n}^{\mathsf{ListRew}}$. Indeed, we need to make sure that we can extract from the extractable commitments while not perturbing the reduction to the receiver security of $\mathsf{OT}_{k,n}^{\mathsf{ListRew}}$. The addition of the extractable commitments helps us also in designing the simulator, allowing the simulator to extract the sender's input using the extractable commitments.

Now, we have constructed a three-round protocol that is simulation based secure against corrupted senders. We further need to make sure that this protocol is list-simulatable against corrupted receivers. At a high level, the list simulator runs the list simulators for $\mathsf{OT}_{k,n}^{\mathsf{ListRew}}$ and $\mathsf{OT}_{1,2}^{\mathsf{ListRew}}$, where the input extracted by the simulator of $\mathsf{OT}_{1,2}^{\mathsf{ListRew}}$ defines the choice bit of the receiver, and the values returned by the simulator of $\mathsf{OT}_{k,n}^{\mathsf{ListRew}}$ help to program which of the extractable commitments must contain a valid defence, and which commitments instead should contain a dummy value (e.g., the all-zero string). There are two subtleties in this simulation strategy. First, once K is extracted, the extractable commitments need to be programmed accordingly. Unfortunately, this is not possible if the extractable commitments are binding in the first round. This problem can be easily solved by using a delayed-input extractable commitment scheme. The other problem is related to the fact that, in the security proof, we need to rely on the hiding of the extractable commitments. In particular, we would need to rely on the hiding property while we are running the simulator of $\mathsf{OT}_{1,2}^{\mathsf{ListRew}}$, hence, we need an extractable commitment that is secure against rewinds. This creates a circularity, since we already require $\mathsf{OT}_{1,2}^{\mathsf{ListRew}}$ to be 1-rewind secure, but 1-rewind security is already sufficient to extract from the extractable commitment. Furthermore, we want to extract the input by rewinding $\mathsf{OT}_{1,2}^{\mathsf{ListRew}}$ while maintaining the hiding of the extractable commitment. To break this circularity, we rely on an extractable commitment that has a simulatable third round [15]. In a nutshell, this property allows to simulate a third round of the extractable commitment without knowing the randomness used to compute the first message. This property breaks the circularity, but it inherently makes the commitment extractable with over-extraction, hence, some effort is needed to show that all the arguments we have summarized in this section still hold.

Unfortunately, our 2PC has a limitation. The proof against corrupted receivers crucially relies on the fact that the value K can be extracted. This indicates which defences of the executions of $\mathsf{OT}_{1,2}^{\mathsf{ListRew}}$ the adversary will not obtain, and allows us to rely on the sender security of $\mathsf{OT}_{1,2}^{\mathsf{ListRew}}$. If a corrupted sender aborts in the third round, the extraction of K is not possible, which results in the simulator being stuck. For this reason, we prove that our 2PC enjoys a relaxed form of security, which guarantees that the simulation succeeds only when the corrupted sender provides an accepting transcript in the main-thread. Despite this limitation, we show that our 2PC suffices for our main applications.

List Non-malleable OT. The notion of non-malleable oblivious transfer has been introduced in [17]. In this notion, there is a man-in-the-middle adversary MiM that acts as a receiver in a subset of OT sessions (referred to as the *left sessions*) and as a sender in a different subset of OT sessions (referred to as the *right sessions*). A non-malleable OT requires the input used by the MiM acting as the sender being independent of the input used by the honest senders in the left sessions. This is formalized by requiring the existence of a simulator-extractor, that, given the inputs of all honest receivers participating in the right sessions, is able to extract all the implicit inputs used by the MiM in its right sessions. Note that the simulator does not have access to the inputs of the senders in the left session.

We recall how the Ishai et al. (four-round) construction, which we denote by $\mathsf{OT}^{\mathsf{NM}}$, works and then explain how we squeeze it into three rounds allowing us to obtain a list simulatable version of the protocol. The 1-out-of-2 NM-OT protocol of [17], uses a 4-round simulation secure two-party computation protocol Π that enjoys some special properties (we will elaborate more on this later) and a two split-state non-malleable code $\mathsf{NM} = (\mathsf{Code}, \mathsf{Decode})$.[5] The sender of $\mathsf{OT}^{\mathsf{NM}}$ uses inputs L_0, R_0 and L_1, R_1 which are obtained by running Code on s_0 and s_1 respectively (where s_0 and s_1 represent the inputs of the OT sender). The receiver of $\mathsf{OT}^{\mathsf{NM}}$ uses as its input the choice bit b. Then sender and receiver execute Π for the functionality f_c, where c is a random bit chosen by the receiver in the third round. f_c takes as its input $L_0, R_0, L_1, R_1, s_0, s_1, c, b$ and returns m_b, L_0, L_1 if $c = 0$ and m_b, R_0, R_1 otherwise.

The authors of [17] require that Π has the following properties: (1) the receiver input b is committed in the first round and security holds even if the

[5] A split state non-malleable code has an encoding algorithm Code that, on input a message m returns two codewords L and R. The security of the non-malleable code guarantees that there are no tampering functions f and g, that taking as an input L and R, respectively, return $\tilde{L}$ and $\tilde{R}$, such that the decoding of these tampered codewords has a relation with the message m.

receiver can adaptively select the function to be computed (i.e., the parameter c) in the third round; (2) the inputs of the sender are committed in the 2nd round; (3) Π is 1-rewinding sender secure. To argue that non-malleability holds, Ishai et.al. rely on an extractor, that can compute all the codewords of the MiM acting as senders in the right sessions, by sending different values of c through multiple rewinds.

In our approach, we follow a similar blueprint but use our three-round two-party computation protocol Π that satisfies the notion of list simulatability. We can prove that our 2PC also satisfies properties (1) and (3) mentioned above. However, the input of the sender in Π is fixed in the last round. Hence, the inputs of the sender can change during the rewinds executed to extract from MiM. Therefore, we modify the non-malleable OT protocols as follows: we require the sender to commit via a non-interactive commitment scheme to each codeword. We then modify the function computed by the 2PC protocol in such a way that when $c = 0$, the opening of the commitment for the left state codewords is sent as an additional output of the 2PC, and, if $c = 1$, the opening of the commitment for the right state codeword is sent. Unfortunately, forcing the sender to commit to their inputs causes problems in the list simulation proof. In particular, we have the same issue we had when designing the 2PC. That is, the list-simulator needs to use random inputs during the extraction phase but, if we commit to the codewords, we are implicitly committing to the sender's input in the first round. This prevents the simulator from changing those values after the extraction. To solve this issue, we do not commit to the codeword, instead, we commit to a share of each codeword and output the other share in the clear in the second round. Now, even if the input of the sender is specified in the second round, we have the advantage that the extractor can collect the openings of all the commitments via rewinds. The opened value can then be combined with the shares sent in the clear in the second round of the main thread to finally reconstruct the codewords used by the MiM (in the main thread).

There still remains a single issue. We recall that the receiver specifies the c value in the second round, hence, the MiM could adaptively commit to an invalid codeword by sending a random share instead of the correct codeword share in the third round. We prevent this by hiding the c values as follows: the receiver sends $c \oplus k$, where k is an input given to the 2PC protocol. Hence, the 2PC protocol can compute c and return either the opening of the commitment for the left codeword or the opening of the commitment for the right codeword, but the sender does not know what c has been used by the receiver. We recall that our 2PC protocol Π does not provide any protection of the sender's input if the receiver is aborting. This limitation is inherited by our non-malleable OT protocol. For more details on how our non-malleable OT protocol works, we refer to the technical section of this work.

Four-Round Multi-party Computation. Also in this last step, we follow the approach proposed in [17], which, in turn, is based on the IPS compiler [18].

This compiler combines an information-theoretic MPC protocol Φ (called *outer protocol*), secure in the honest majority setting, and a semi-honest protocol secure against a dishonest majority Π_h called *inner protocol.* The inner protocol is used to emulate an execution of Φ, which guarantees that the messages of Φ are generated honestly, as long as the parties running Π_h behave semi-honestly. To guarantee security in the malicious setting, the IPS compiler requires to perform a cut-and-choose to check that the majority of the parties are running Π_h honestly. This cut-and-choose is performed by relying on correlated OT randomness. In [17] the authors manage to make this paradigm work in just 5 rounds, using a 4-round inner protocol, and a 4-round non-malleable OT protocol for the generation of the correlated randomness.

In this work, we follow the same approach by relying on our three-round non-malleable OT protocol, and on a three-round semi-honest MPC protocol to realize the inner protocol. The main difference is that we are able to prove the security of the MPC protocol only against non-aborting adversaries. But, as mentioned before, this still suffices to securely realize any input-less functionality with standard simulation based security. Furthermore, our inner-protocol also needs to achieve our special security notion in which the inputs of the honest parties are sampled from a certain distribution by the ideal functionality in a similar fashion as in our list-2PC definition. This modification, with respect to the inner-protocol of [17], is needed to allow for later equivocality of the simulator to ensure that the overall protocol can be simulated in four-rounds.

2 Preliminaries

We assume familiarity with the notions of secret sharing, commitment, pseudorandom functions, CPA security, and multi-party computation. In this section, we introduce the core notions needed for our constructions and refer to the full version for the formal definitions of all the primitives involved.

Notation. We let $\mathrm{View}^{B}_{\Pi,A}(\lambda, x, y)$ be the random variable corresponding to the *view* of A in an execution of Π with B where A uses x as its input and B uses y as its input. If an algorithm A outputs a transcript τ, then we call the input d that explains the output, i.e. $\tau = A(d)$, its defense. We denote the security parameter with $\lambda \in \mathbb{N}$. A randomized algorithm $\mathcal{A}$ is running in *probabilistic polynomial time* (PPT) if there exists a polynomial $p(\cdot)$ such that for every input x the running time of $\mathcal{A}(x)$ is bounded by $p(|x|)$. We use "=" to check equality of two different elements (i.e. $a = b$ then...) and ":=" as the assigning operator (e.g. to assign to a the value of b we write $a := b$). A randomized assignment is denoted with $a \leftarrow A$, where A is a randomized algorithm. If the randomness is explicit we write $a := A(x; r)$ where x is the input and r is the randomness. When it is clear from the context, to not overburden the notation, we do not specify the randomness used in the algorithms unless needed for other purposes.

Rewind Secure Extractable Commitment Scheme. We propose, in Fig. 2.1, a delayed-input, 1-rewind secure 3-extractable 3-round commitment scheme ExtCom. A 3-round commitment scheme is: delayed-input if the sender uses its input only to compute the last round of the protocol; 3-extractable, if there exists an extractor that upon receiving three accepting transcripts computed with respect to the same first round but different second rounds, returns the committed message (we refer to the full version for the formal definitions). This commitment scheme is inspired by [13,22]. We prove the 3-extractability property as follows.

Figure 2.1: Rewind secure Extractable Commitment.

Public parameters: Prime $q > \lambda$.
Senders' private input: message $m \in \mathbb{F}_q$ (available to the sender only in the third round).

1) Sender. Sample $r, s, m_0 \leftarrow \mathbb{F}_q$, compute and send $, \leftarrow \mathsf{Com}(m_0||r||s)$.
2) Receiver. Sample and send $\alpha \leftarrow \mathbb{F}_q$.
3) Sender Compute $m_1 \leftarrow m + m_0$ and $a \leftarrow m + \alpha r + \alpha^2 s$, and send (a, m_1).

ExtCom also enjoys the property of *simulatability* [14]. The simulatability property requires that no adversarial receiver can distinguish whether a third round of the protocol is computed correctly, or with respect to a random input. We refer to the full version for the formal definition and all the proofs.

Private Two-Message Oblivious Transfer. A two-message oblivious transfer protocol consists of a tuple PPT algorithm $\mathsf{OT} = (\mathsf{OT}_1, \mathsf{OT}_2, \mathsf{OT}_3)$ with the following syntax.

- $\mathsf{OT}_1(1^\lambda, \beta)$ takes the security parameter λ and a selection bit β and outputs a message ot_1 and secret state st.
- $\mathsf{OT}_2(1^\lambda, (\nu_0, \nu_1), \mathsf{ot}_1)$ takes the security parameter λ and two inputs $(\nu_0, \nu_1) \in \{0,1\}^{\mathsf{len}}$ (where len is a parameter of the scheme) and a message ot_1. It outputs a message ot_2.
- $\mathsf{OT}_3(1^\lambda, \mathsf{st}, \mathsf{ot}_2, \beta)$ takes the security parameter, the bit β, secret state st and message ot_2 and outputs $\nu_\beta \in \{0,1\}^{\mathsf{len}}$.

Definition 2.1 ([5]). *A tuple PPT algorithm* $\mathsf{OT} = (\mathsf{OT}_1, \mathsf{OT}_2, \mathsf{OT}_3)$ *is a private-OT scheme if the following hold.*

Correctness: *For all* $\lambda, \beta, \nu_0, \nu_1$, *letting* $(\mathsf{ot}_1, \mathsf{st}) = \mathsf{OT}_1(1^\lambda, \beta)$, $\mathsf{ot}_2 = \mathsf{OT}_2(1^\lambda, (\nu_0, \nu_1), \mathsf{ot}_1)$, $\nu' = \mathsf{OT}_3(1^\lambda, \mathsf{st}, \mathsf{ot}_2, \beta)$, *it holds that* $\nu' = \nu_\beta$ *with probability 1.*

Receiver Privacy: *Consider the distribution* $\mathcal{D}_\beta(\lambda)$ *defined by running* $(\mathsf{ot}_1, \mathsf{st}) = \mathsf{OT}_1(1^\lambda, \beta)$ *and outputting* ot_1. *Then* $\mathcal{D}_0, \mathcal{D}_1$ *are computationally indistinguishable.*

Sender Privacy: *There exists an extractor* OTExt *s.t. for any sequence of messages* $\mathsf{ot}_1 = \mathsf{ot}_1(\lambda)$ *and inputs* $(\nu_0, \nu_1) = (\nu_0(\lambda), \nu_1(\lambda))$, *the distribution ensembles* $\mathsf{OT}_2(1^\lambda, (\nu_0, \nu_1), \mathsf{ot}_1)$ *and* $\mathsf{OT}_2(1^\lambda, (\nu_{\beta'}, \nu_{\beta'}), \mathsf{ot}_1)$, *where* $\beta' = \mathsf{OTExt}(\mathsf{ot}_1)$, *are statistically indistinguishable.*

Bounded Rewind Secure OT. A bounded rewind secure OT is defined as a standard OT protocol, with the difference that the corrupted party can receive multiple, in our case, third rounds of the protocol while still preserving the security for the honest party's input. In other words, we say that a protocol is B-rewind secure if security is maintained even when the malicious party (either sender or receiver) is allowed to obtain $B+1$ third-round messages with respect to $B+1$ different second rounds. We refer to the full version for a formal definition.

Non-malleable Codes. A non-malleable code consists of an encoding algorithm Enc and a decoding algorithm Dec. When a message m is encoded, then the resulting codeword consists of two parts L and R. Taking both of theses parts of the codeword, the decoding algorithm Dec allows to reconstruct the message m. The security property of the non-malleable code guarantees that for every pair of tampering functions (f, g), without any fixed points, the distribution of $m' \leftarrow \mathsf{Enc}(f(L), g(R))$, with $(L, R) \leftarrow \mathsf{Enc}(m)$ is independent of m. The formal definition of this primitive can be found in the full version.

Low-Depth Proofs. A low-depth proof is defined as a standard proof achieving completeness (a proof generated using a correct witness is valid) and soundness (it is not possible to generate a proof for an invalid statement). Furthermore, we require that a proof can be verified using an $\mathsf{NC1}$ circuit, which is the low-depth property. We provide the formal definitions in the full version.

3 Bounded-Rewind Secure List 2-Party Computation

In this section, we introduce the notion of bounded-rewind secure list 2-party computation. Let f be the function that the two parties P_0 and P_1 want to compute. $f : X^0 \times X^1 \to Y$ is a function that takes two inputs and returns two outputs (one for each party). We denote with $\mathcal{X}^d$ a PPT sampler for X^d for each $d \in \{0, 1\}$.

The notion of list 2PC differs from the standard notion of 2PC as follows: let us say that the party P_0 is corrupted and P_1 is honest. In the ideal world experiment, the adversary sends its input $x^0 \in \mathcal{X}^0$ to the ideal functionality, which we denote with $\mathcal{F}^{\mathcal{X}^1}$, together with an integer k. The ideal functionality does not wait to receive the input from the honest party, instead, it samples k inputs uniformly at random from the input domain of the honest party $x_1^1, \ldots, x_k^1 \leftarrow \mathcal{X}^1$, and, for each $j \in [k]$ computes $(\mathsf{out}_j^0, \mathsf{out}_j^1) \leftarrow f(x^0, x_j^1)$. Then the values $(\mathsf{out}_1^0, \ldots, \mathsf{out}_k^0)$ are given to the adversary. The adversary now sends an index $i \in [k]$ to the ideal functionality, which then sends $(x_i^1, \mathsf{out}_i^1)$ to the ideal-world honest party.

In our work, we focus on constructing and studying 3-round list 2PC protocols, where in each round both parties speak at the same time. We study our notion in a stronger adversarial setting where the adversary can ask the honest party to receive multiple third rounds for multiple second rounds. A protocol that is proven secure in this setting is usually said to be B-rewind secure, which means that the adversary can send $B+1$ second rounds and receive $B+1$ third rounds (one for each second round). We propose the formal definition of the real and the ideal world in Fig. 3.1, where the party P^d is assumed to be corrupted with $d \in \{0,1\}$. To make a protocol that satisfies our definition usable as a sub-routine of other protocols, we need to make sure that the distinguisher has somehow access to the inputs of the honest parties. In the ideal world, we do that by explicitly giving this input to the adversary together with the second round of the protocol. In the ideal world experiment, we do something similar by allowing sending to the adversary the input of the honest parties upon request of the simulator. More precisely, if the simulator sends a message to the adversary (π, j), then the ideal-world experiment would forward to the adversary the message (π, x_j^{1-d}). This guarantees that the distinguisher will get access to the honest party's input, while the simulator does not (this is exactly what makes our definition non-trivial to realize). We refer to Fig. 3.1 for the formal specification of real and ideal world and state the following.

Definition 3.1 (B-rewind secure list 2PC). *We say that a protocol Π is a B-rewind secure List 2PC if for every malicious PPT P_{1-d}, with $d \in \{0,1\}$, there exists a (expected) PPT simulator* $\mathsf{Sim} = \{\mathsf{Sim}_1, \mathsf{Sim}_2\}$ *such that* $\{\mathsf{Real}_{\mathcal{A},\Pi}(1^\lambda, 1^B)\}_{\lambda,B} \approx_c \{\mathsf{Ideal}_{\mathsf{Sim},\mathcal{F}^{\mathcal{X}^d}}(1^\lambda, 1^B)\}_{\lambda,B}$, *where $\lambda, B \in \mathbb{N}$.*

Figure 3.1: Real and ideal world

$\mathsf{Real}_{\mathcal{A},\Pi}(1^\lambda, 1^B)$:

1. Sample $x_d \leftarrow \mathcal{X}^d$, and compute the first round π_1^d of Π as the honest P_d would do on input x_d and the randomness $r \leftarrow \{0,1\}^\lambda$ and send π_1^d to $\mathcal{A}$.
2. Upon receiving π_1^{1-d} from $\mathcal{A}$, compute the second round π_2^d of Π as the honest party P_d on input (r, x_d) would do and send (π_2^d, x_d) to $\mathcal{A}$.
3. Upon receiving $\{\pi_{2,i}^{1-d}\}_{i\in[B]}$ from $\mathcal{A}$, for each $i \in [B]$, compute $\pi_{3,i}^d$ as the honest party P_d would do having on input $(\pi_1^{1-d}, \pi_{2,i}^{1-d}, r, x_d)$.
4. Send $\{\pi_{3,i}^d\}_{i\in[B]}$ to $\mathcal{A}$.
5. Upon receiving π_3^{1-d}, compute the output out as P_d would do, and return the view of $\mathcal{A}$.

$\mathsf{Ideal}_{\mathsf{Sim},\mathcal{F}^{\mathcal{X}^d}}(1^\lambda, 1^B)$:

1. $(x^{1-d}, 1^k, z) \leftarrow \mathsf{Sim}_1^{\mathcal{A}}(1^\lambda, 1^B)$
2. Send x^{1-d} to the ideal functionality $\mathcal{F}^{\mathcal{X}^d}$ which computes $\{\mathsf{out}_j^0, \mathsf{out}_j^1\}_{j\in[k]}$ as described using the sampled inputs $\{x_j^d\}_{j\in[k]}$.
3. Whenever $\mathsf{Sim}_2^{\mathcal{A}}$ queries $\mathcal{A}$ with a message (π, j), replace the query with (π, x_j^d) and forward the pair to $\mathcal{A}$.
4. $(i, \mathrm{View}) \leftarrow \mathsf{Sim}_2^{\mathcal{A}}(\mathsf{out}_1^{1-d}, \ldots, \mathsf{out}_k^{1-d}, z)$ with $i \in [k] \cup \{\bot\}$.
5. Send i to the ideal functionality, or abort if $i = \bot$ to instruct the honest party to abort, and return View.

List Oblivious Transfer. One of the main tools we construct is a protocol that realizes the OT functionality $\mathcal{F}_{\mathsf{OT}}$ with list simulation against corrupted sometimes aborting receivers. Then we show how to use such an OT to construct a 2PC protocol (where only one party gets the output) that is list simulatable against a corrupted sender, and list simulatable against sometimes aborting receivers. We then use the 2PC protocol to obtain a non-malleable OT protocol, which retains the same security as the 2PC protocol.

3.1 List 2PC with Delayed-Input Function Selection

Definition 3.2 (Adapted from [17]). *Let $\Pi = ((\Pi_1^S, \Pi_1^R), (\Pi_2^S, \Pi_2^R), (\Pi_3^S, \Pi_3^R), (\Pi_4^S, \Pi_4^R), \mathsf{out})$ be a 3-round protocol (in the simultaneous message model) between a receiver R and a sender S with the receiver computing the output at the end of the third round. We say that Π is 1-rewinding secure list-simulatable with delayed function selection for NC^1 circuits if it satisfies the following:*

Delayed function Selection. *The first message functions Π_1^S, Π_1^R and the second message function of the sender Π_2^S take as input the size of the function $f \in \mathsf{NC}^1$ to be securely computed and are otherwise, independent of the function description. The second round message from R contains the explicit description of the function f to be computed.*

1-Rewind receiver security. *For every malicious PPT adversary $\mathcal{A}$ that corrupts the sender, there exists an expected polynomial (black-box) simulator $\mathsf{Sim}_S = (\mathsf{Sim}_S^1, \mathsf{Sim}_S^2)$ such that for all choices of honest receiver input x_R and the function $f \in \mathsf{NC}^1$ the joint distribution of the view of $\mathcal{A}$ and R's output in the real execution is computationally indistinguishable from the output of the ideal experiment described in Fig. 3.2.*

Figure 3.2: 1-*Rewind receiver security*

$\mathsf{Real}(\mathcal{A}, \Pi, x_R)$:	$\mathsf{Ideal}(\mathcal{A}, \mathsf{Sim}_R, x_R)$:
1. *Initialize $\mathcal{A}$ with a uniform random tape s.* 2. *Compute $\pi_1^R \leftarrow \Pi_1^R(x_R)$ and send it to $\mathcal{A}$.* 3. *Upon receiving π_1^S, use it to run Π_2^R thus obtaining π_2^R, and send it to $\mathcal{A}$.* 4. *Upon receiving $(\pi_2^S[0], \pi_2^S[1])$ from $\mathcal{A}$ use Π_2^R to compute the third round $\pi_3^R[b]$ for each $b \in \{0,1\}$ and send $(\pi_3^R[0], \pi_3^R[1])$ to $\mathcal{A}$.* 5. *Output whatever $\mathcal{A}$ outputs.*	1. *Initialize $\mathcal{A}$ with a uniform random tape s.* 2. $(x^S, z) \leftarrow \mathsf{Sim}_R^1(1^\lambda)$. 3. *Send (x^S) to the ideal functionality which returns* $\mathsf{out} \leftarrow f(x^S, x^R)$. 4. $(\mathsf{abort}, \mathrm{View}) \leftarrow \mathsf{Sim}_R^2(\mathsf{out}, z)$. 5. *If* $\mathsf{abort} = 1$ *then return* abort *to the ideal functionality, else return* continue. 6. *Return* View.

1-Rewind sender security. *As in the definition of list-simulation security, ideal and real world are parametrized by a distribution $\mathcal{X}_S$. The input of the sender is sampled from $\mathcal{X}_S$ in the real-world experiment and used to execute Π. The real-world experiment is exactly the same as the one of Definition 3.1, with the difference that the ideal functionality, in addition to the input of the corrupted receiver x_R and 1^k, receives two functions (f_0, f_1). The ideal functionality then, for each $i \in [k]$ samples $x_S \leftarrow \mathcal{X}_S$ and computes $\mathsf{out}_i^0 \leftarrow f_0(x_S, x_R)$, $\mathsf{out}_i^1 \leftarrow f_1(x_S, x_R)$. Then the ideal functionality returns $\{\mathsf{out}_i^0, \mathsf{out}_i^1\}_{i \in [k]}$. We provide the formal description of the ideal and real-world in Fig. 3.3, and we say that a protocol Π is 1-rewind sender secure if for every malicious adversary $\mathcal{A}$ corrupting the receiver which is non-aborting in the last round, there exists an expected polynomial time simulator $\mathsf{Sim}_S = (\mathsf{Sim}_R^1, \mathsf{Sim}_R^2)$ such that, given $\mathcal{X}_S$ we have $\{\mathsf{Real}(\mathcal{A}, \Pi, \mathcal{X}_S)\} \approx \{\mathsf{Ideal}(\mathcal{A}, \mathsf{Sim}_S, \mathcal{X}_S)\}$.*

Figure 3.3: 1-*Rewind sender security.*

$\mathsf{Real}(\mathcal{A}, \Pi, \mathcal{X}_S)$:

1. *Initialize* $\mathcal{A}$ *with a uniform random tape* s, *and sample* $x_S \leftarrow \mathcal{X}_S$.
2. *Compute* $\pi_1^S \leftarrow \Pi_1^S(x_S)$ *and send it to* $\mathcal{A}$.
3. *Upon receiving* π_1^R, *use it to run* Π_2^S *thus obtaining* π_2^S, *and send* (π_2^S, x_S) *to* $\mathcal{A}$.
4. *Upon receiving* $(f_0, f_1, \pi_2^R[0], \pi_2^R[1])$ *from* $\mathcal{A}$ *use* $(f_b, \pi_2^R[b])$ *to compute the third round* $\pi_3^S[b]$ *for each* $b \in \{0,1\}$ *and send* $\pi_3^S[0], \pi_3^S[1]$ *to* $\mathcal{A}$.
5. *Output whatever* $\mathcal{A}$ *outputs.*

$\mathsf{Ideal}(\mathcal{A}, \mathsf{Sim}_S, \mathcal{X}_S)$:

1. *Initialize* $\mathcal{A}$ *with a uniform random tape* s.
2. $(x^R, f_0, f_1, 1^k, z) \leftarrow \mathsf{Sim}_S^{1\mathcal{A}}(1^\lambda, 1^B)$
3. *Send* (x^R, f_0, f_1) *to the ideal functionality* $\mathcal{F}^{\mathcal{X}^S}$ *which returns* $\{\mathsf{out}_j^0, \mathsf{out}_j^1\}_{j\in[k]}$ *computed as described using the sampled inputs* $\{x_j^S\}_{j\in k}$.
4. *Whenever* $\mathsf{Sim}_S^{2\mathcal{A}}$ *queries* $\mathcal{A}$ *with a message* (π, j), *replace the query with* (π, x_j^d).
5. $(i, \mathrm{View}) \leftarrow \mathsf{Sim}_S^2((\mathsf{out}_1^0, \mathsf{out}_1^1), \ldots, (\mathsf{out}_k^0, \mathsf{out}_k^0), z)$ *with* $i \in [k] \cup \{\bot\}$.
6. *Send* i *to the ideal functionality, or* abort *if* $i = \bot$ *to instruct the honest party to abort, and return* View.

Sometimes Aborting Adversaries. As previously mentioned, we consider the notion of sometimes aborting adversaries. This notion is the same as the list simulation notion, but it requires the list simulator to provide a simulated transcript with overwhelming probability, conditioned on the adversary providing an accepting transcript in the main thread. We still provide no security requirements (unless otherwise specified), in the case the adversary aborts with overwhelming probability, or it does not provide an accepting transcript in the main thread.

4 Sender List Simulatable OT

In this section, we construct a three-round OT protocol that is sender side list simulatable against sometimes aborting, and sender private otherwise. As an intermediate step, we propose a 3-round oblivious transfer protocol in the alternating message model that is not rewind-secure. This protocol consists of the following algorithms $\mathsf{OT}' = (\mathsf{OT}'_1, \mathsf{OT}'_2, \mathsf{OT}'_3, (\mathsf{OT}'^S_4, \mathsf{OT}'^R_4))$ where OT'^R_4 is the procedure used to compute the output of the OT protocol by the receiver and OT'^S_4 is the procedure run by the sender to decide whether to abort or not. We present the formal description of the protocol in Fig. 4.1, and refer the reader to the introductory part of the paper for an informal description of the scheme.

4.1 Construction

The only tool that we need for this construction is a maliciously private two-round OT protocol denoted as $\mathsf{OT} = (\mathsf{OT}_1, \mathsf{OT}_2, \mathsf{OT}_3)$ (Definition 2.1), where OT_3 is the procedure used by the receiver to compute the output of the OT protocol. We describe our first transformation in Fig. 4.1. We describe the final protocol in the next section.

Figure 4.1: 3-round sender list simulatable and receiver private OT OT'

Initialization: The receiver uses as its input a bit b and the sender has input s_0, s_1. The parties also receive a common parameter $m = \text{poly}(\lambda)$ as an input.

Round 1 (Receiver).

1. Sample $b_i \leftarrow \{0,1\}$ and compute $d_i = b_i \oplus b$ for all $i \in [m]$.
2. Generate $\mathsf{ot}_{1,i} := \mathsf{OT}_1(1^\lambda, b_i; r_i)$ and $\mathsf{ot}'_{1,i} := \mathsf{OT}_1(1^\lambda, d_i; r'_i)$ with $r_i, r'_i \leftarrow \{0,1\}^\lambda$ for all $i \in [m]$.
3. Send $\{\mathsf{ot}_{1,i}, \mathsf{ot}'_{1,i}\}_{i\in[m]}$ to S.

Round 2 (Sender).

1. Sample $\mathsf{k}^i_c, s_{c,j} \leftarrow \{0,1\}^\lambda$ for all $i \in [m], j \in [m-1], c \in \{0,1\}$. Set $s_{c,m} := s_c \oplus s_{c,1} \oplus \cdots \oplus s_{c,m-1}$ for both $c \in \{0,1\}$.
2. Compute $\mathsf{ct}^{0,i}_c := \mathsf{k}^i_c \oplus s_{c,i}$ and $\mathsf{ct}^{1,i}_c := \mathsf{k}^i_{1\oplus c} \oplus s_{c,i}$ for all $i \in [m], c \in \{0,1\}$.
3. Generate $\mathsf{ot}_{2,i} \leftarrow \mathsf{OT}_2(\mathsf{ot}_{1,i}, (\mathsf{k}^i_0, \mathsf{k}^i_1))$ and $\mathsf{ot}'_{2,i} \leftarrow \mathsf{OT}_2(\mathsf{ot}'_{1,i}, ((\mathsf{ct}^{0,i}_0, \mathsf{ct}^{0,i}_1), (\mathsf{ct}^{1,i}_0, \mathsf{ct}^{1,i}_1)))$ for all $i \in [m]$.
4. Sample $\mathcal{I} \leftarrow \{0,1\}^m$.
5. Send $\{\mathsf{ot}_{2,i}, \mathsf{ot}'_{2,i}\}_{i\in[m]}$ and $\mathcal{I}$ to R.

Round 3 (Receiver).

1. Send $\{b_i, r_i\}_{i\in[m]:\mathcal{I}_i=1}$ and $\{d_i, r'_i\}_{i\in[m]:\mathcal{I}_i=0}$ to S.

Offline computation.

Sender:

1. Check that $\mathsf{ot}_{1,i} := \mathsf{OT}_1(1^\lambda, b_i; r_i)$ for all $i \in [m]$ where $\mathcal{I}_i = 1$ and $\mathsf{ot}'_{1,i} := \mathsf{OT}_1(1^\lambda, d_i; r'_i)$ for all $i \in [m]$ where $\mathcal{I}_i = 0$.
2. If the previous check does not succeed output $\perp$.

Receiver:

1. Obtain $\mathsf{k}^i_{b_i} := \mathsf{OT}_3(\mathsf{ot}_{1,i}, \mathsf{ot}_{2,i})$ and $(\mathsf{ct}^{d_i,i}_0, \mathsf{ct}^{d_i,i}_1) := \mathsf{OT}_3(\mathsf{ot}_{1,i}, \mathsf{ot}_{2,i})$ for all $i \in [m]$.
2. Compute $s'_{b,i} := \mathsf{k}^i_{b_i} \oplus \mathsf{ct}^{d_i,i}_b$ for all $i \in [m]$ and output $s'_b := \bigoplus_{i\in[m]} s'_{b,i}$.

Theorem 4.1. *Let X be a high min-entropy random variable defined by a probability distribution $\mathcal{D}$ and let OT be a two round maliciously private OT protocol, then the OT protocol OT' described in Fig. 4.1 is a three-round sender list simulatable OT against sometimes aborting malicious receivers for the functionality $\mathcal{F}^{\mathcal{D}}_{\mathsf{OT}}$ (accordingly to Definition 3.1) and sender private OT otherwise (accordingly to Definition 2.1). Moreover, OT' is receiver private (accordingly to Definition 2.1). OT' makes black-box use of OT.*

The security proof for this construction, as well as for all following constructions, can be found in the full version.

5 Sender List Simulatable and Rewind-Secure Receiver Private OT

In this section, we present a transformation that turns a three-round oblivious transfer (OT) protocol, that is receiver private and sender list simulatable, in the alternating message model into a three-round OT protocol that is still sender side list simulatable in the same model but, moreover, is B-rewind receiver-private.

The transformation makes use of the oblivious transfer protocol $\mathsf{OT}' = (\mathsf{OT}'_1, \mathsf{OT}'_2, \mathsf{OT}'_3, (\mathsf{OT}'^S_4, \mathsf{OT}'^R_4))$ described in Fig. 4.1 (where we consider a single execution of the scheme without repetition).

Figure 5.1: 3-round sender list-simulatable OT and B-rewind receiver private $\mathsf{OT}^{\mathsf{ListRew}}$

Initialization: The sender's input is s_0, s_1. The receiver uses as its input a bit b. The parties also receive a common parameter $m := \text{poly}(\lambda)$.

Round 1 (Receiver).

1. Sample $b_i \leftarrow \{0,1\}$ and compute $d_i = b_i \oplus b$ for all $i \in [m]$.
2. For all $i \in [m]$ generate $\mathsf{ot}^0_{1,i} := \mathsf{OT}'_1(1^\lambda, b_i)$ and $\mathsf{ot}^1_{1,i}. := \mathsf{OT}'_1(1^\lambda, d_i)$;
3. Send $\{\mathsf{ot}^0_{1,i}, \mathsf{ot}^1_{1,i}\}_{i\in[m]}$ to S.

Round 2 (Sender).

1. Sample $\mathsf{k}^i_c, s_c, s_{c,j} \leftarrow \{0,1\}^\lambda$ for all $i \in [m], j \in [m-1], c \in \{0,1\}$. Set $s_{c,m} := s_c \oplus s_{c,1} \oplus \cdots \oplus s_{c,m-1}$ for both $c \in \{0,1\}$.
2. Compute $\mathsf{ct}^{0,i}_c := \mathsf{k}^i_c \oplus s_{c,i}$ and $\mathsf{ct}^{1,i}_c := \mathsf{k}^i_{1\oplus c} \oplus s_{c,i}$ for all $i \in [m], c \in \{0,1\}$.
3. Generate $\mathsf{ot}^0_{2,i} \leftarrow \mathsf{OT}'_2(\mathsf{ot}'_{1,i}, (\mathsf{k}^i_0, \mathsf{k}^i_1))$ and $\mathsf{ot}^1_{2,i} \leftarrow \mathsf{OT}'_2(\mathsf{ot}_{1,i}, ((\mathsf{ct}^{0,i}_0, \mathsf{ct}^{0,i}_1), (\mathsf{ct}^{1,i}_0, \mathsf{ct}^{1,i}_1)))$ for all $i \in [m]$.
4. Sample $\mathcal{I} \leftarrow \{0,1\}^m$.
5. Send $\{\mathsf{ot}^0_{2,i}, \mathsf{ot}^1_{2,i}\}_{i\in[m]}, \mathcal{I}$ to R.

Round 3 (Receiver).

1. For all $i \in [m]$, if $\mathcal{I}_i = 0$, compute $\mathsf{ot}^0_{3,i} \leftarrow \mathsf{OT}'_3(\mathsf{ot}^0_{1,i}, \mathsf{ot}^0_{2,i})$; otherwise compute $\mathsf{ot}^1_{3,i} \leftarrow \mathsf{OT}'_3(\mathsf{ot}^1_{1,i}, \mathsf{ot}^1_{2,i})$.
2. Send $\{\mathsf{ot}^{\mathcal{I}_i}_{3,i}\}_{i\in[m]}$ to S.

Offline computation.

Sender:

1. For all $i \in [m]$, if $\mathcal{I}_i = 0$, check that $\bot \neq \mathsf{OT}'^S_4(\mathsf{ot}^0_{1,i}, \mathsf{ot}^0_{2,i}, \mathsf{ot}^0_{3,i})$ otherwise check that $\bot \neq \mathsf{OT}'^S_4(\mathsf{ot}^1_{1,i}, \mathsf{ot}^1_{2,i}, \mathsf{ot}^1_{3,i})$.
2. If the previous checks do not succeed output $\bot$; otherwise output s_0, s_1.

Receiver:

1. Obtain $\mathsf{k}^i_{b_i} := \mathsf{OT}'^R_4(\mathsf{ot}^0_{1,i}, \mathsf{ot}^0_{2,i})$ and $(\mathsf{ct}^{d_i,i}_0, \mathsf{ct}^{d_i,i}_1) := \mathsf{OT}'^R_4(\mathsf{ot}^1_{1,i}, \mathsf{ot}^1_{2,i})$ for all $i \in [m]$.
2. Compute $s'_{b,i} := \mathsf{k}^i_{b_i} \oplus \mathsf{ct}^{d_i,i}_b$ for all $i \in [m]$ and output $s'_b := \bigoplus_{i\in[m]} s'_{b,i}$.

Theorem 5.1. *Let X be a high min-entropy random variable defined by a probability distribution $\mathcal{D}$ and let OT' be the three-round OT protocol described in Fig. 4.1 for the functionality $\mathcal{F}_{\mathsf{OT}}^{\mathcal{U}}$ (where $\mathcal{U}$ is the uniform distribution), then the OT protocol $\mathsf{OT}^{\mathsf{ListRew}}$ described in Fig. 5.1 is a three-round sender list simulatable OT against malicious sometimes aborting receivers for the functionality $\mathcal{F}_{\mathsf{OT}}^{\mathcal{D}}$ (accordingly to Definition 3.1) otherwise, $\mathsf{OT}^{\mathsf{ListRew}}$ is sender private (accordingly to Definition 2.1). Moreover $\mathsf{OT}^{\mathsf{ListRew}}$ is a B-rewind receiver private OT, with $B = 2$. $\mathsf{OT}^{\mathsf{ListRew}}$ makes black-box use of OT'.*

5.1 Enhancing B-Rewind Security of $\mathsf{OT}^{\mathsf{ListRew}}$

In Sect. 5 we described a 1-out-of-two OT $\mathsf{OT}^{\mathsf{ListRew}}$ which is sender list simulatable and B-rewind receiver private, where $B = 2$. The construction is described in Fig. 5.1, and it uses as a building block a 1-out-of-2 OT OT' which is sender list simulatable and only receiver private.

We note that it is possible to construct a 1-out-of-2 OT $\mathsf{OT}_{B'}^{\mathsf{ListRew}}$ which is sender list simulatable and B'-rewind receiver private, for a constant $B' = 6$ using the construction described in Fig. 5.1, where the underlying OT used as a building block is already B-rewind receiver private. In more detail, the sender and receiver of $\mathsf{OT}_{B'}^{\mathsf{ListRew}}$ act exactly as described in Fig. 5.1 but using the algorithms of $\mathsf{OT}^{\mathsf{ListRew}}$ instead of OT'.

This observation leads to the following theorem.

Theorem 5.2. *Let X be a high min-entropy random variable defined by a probability distribution $\mathcal{D}$ and let $\mathsf{OT}^{\mathsf{ListRew}}$ the 1-out-of-two OT described in Fig. 5.1 for the functionality $\mathcal{F}_{\mathsf{OT}}^{\mathcal{U}}$ (which is 3-rewind receiver private), then the OT protocol $\mathsf{OT}_{B'}^{\mathsf{ListRew}}$ described above is a three-round sender list simulatable OT against sometimes aborting malicious receivers for the functionality $\mathcal{F}_{\mathsf{OT}}^{\mathcal{D}}$ (accordingly to Definition 3.1) otherwise, $\mathsf{OT}^{\mathsf{ListRew}}$ is sender private (accordingly to Definition 2.1). Moreover $\mathsf{OT}_{B'}^{\mathsf{ListRew}}$ is a B'-rewind receiver private OT protocol, with $B' = 6$ and $\mathsf{OT}_{B'}^{\mathsf{ListRew}}$ makes black-box use of $\mathsf{OT}^{\mathsf{ListRew}}$.*

The proof follows similar to the proof of Theorem 5.1. Besides being B-rewind secure, the presented OT protocol is also parallel composable. The parallel composability is important to construct the k-out-of-n OT protocol. In the full version we prove that our protocol is composable in parallel, and we show how to use it to construct a k-out-of-n OT protocol. We refer the reader to the full version for the formal description and proof of the protocol.

6 Two-Party Computation

In this section, we construct a three-round (in the simultaneous message model) 2-party computation protocol Π^{2PC} that is 1-rewinding secure list-simulatable with delayed function selection for NC_1 circuits (we refer to Definition 3.2 for a formal definition). To construct our protocol, we make use of the following tools:

- A two-round information-theoretic two client, m server MPC protocol $\Phi = (\Phi_1, \{\Phi_{2,i}\}_{i\in[m]})$[6] for computing NC^1 circuits, that satisfies security with selective abort against a malicious, adaptive adversary corrupting a single client and at most $t = (m-1)/3$. Here, we fix $m = 8\lambda$. We need the protocol to satisfy two additional properties:
  - We require the first round message of the protocol to be independent of the function description and only depend on its size.
  - Given a first round message from the clients, the servers in the second round, are given descriptions of two functions f_0, f_1 and should be able to generate the second-round message corresponding to these two functions on the same first-round message from the client. In other words, we require the protocol's first round message to be reusable once.

  In [17] the authors argue how to obtain such a scheme.
- A PRF $\mathsf{PRF} : \{0,1\}^\lambda \times \{0,1\}^* \to \{0,1\}^*$.
- A symmetric encryption scheme $\mathsf{SE} = (\mathsf{Enc}, \mathsf{Dec})$.
- The commitment scheme $\mathsf{ExtCom} = (\mathsf{ExtCom}_1, \mathsf{ExtCom}_2, \mathsf{ExtCom}_3)$ proposed in Sect. 2.
- A three-round list simulatable against sometimes aborting adversaries λ-out-of-m OT protocol $\mathsf{OT}^{\lambda,m} := (\mathsf{OT}_1^{\lambda,m}, \mathsf{OT}_2^{\lambda,m}, \mathsf{OT}_3^{\lambda,m}, \mathsf{OT}_{\mathsf{out}}^{\lambda,m})$. We require the protocol to be $B^{\mathsf{ot}} = 6$-rewind secure against corrupted receivers for the uniform distribution $\mathcal{U}$, i.e. for the functionality $\mathcal{F}_{\mathsf{OT}}^{\mathcal{U}}$. In more detail, the uniform distribution $\mathcal{U}$ here samples m random strings of length λ each that act as the randomness s_i for all $i \in [m]$ used for the commitment generated in the first round of the protocol.
- A three-round list simulatable against sometimes aborting corrupted receivers, and private against corrupted sender 1-out-of-2 OT protocol $\mathsf{OT}^{1,2} := (\mathsf{OT}_1^{1,2}, \mathsf{OT}_2^{1,2}, \mathsf{OT}_3^{1,2}, \mathsf{OT}_{\mathsf{out}}^{1,2})$ that is $B^{\mathsf{ot}} = 6$ rewind secure against corrupted receiver for the uniform distribution $\mathcal{U}$, i.e. for the functionality $\mathcal{F}_{\mathsf{OT}}^{\mathcal{U}'}$. In more detail, the uniform distribution $\mathcal{U}'$ here samples two random strings of length λ each that act as the secret keys $(\mathsf{sk}_0^{i,j,k}, \mathsf{sk}_1^{i,j,k})$ used for the ciphertexts generated in the third round of the protocol.
- A garbling scheme $\mathsf{GC} = (\mathsf{Garble}, \mathsf{Eval})$.

We propose the formal construction of our protocol in Fig. 6.1, and refer to the introduction for an informal description of the protocol.

Figure 6.1: The three rounds of the 2PC protocol Π^{2PC}

Initialization: The sender S has input y and the receiver R has input x.

Round 1.

Sender:

1. Compute $,_1^i := \mathsf{ExtCom}_1(1^\lambda; s_i)$ with $s_i \leftarrow \{0,1\}^\lambda$ for all $i \in [m]$.

[6] Here, $\Phi_{2,i}$ is the function that takes $\{y_{i,j}\}_{j\in[\ell]}$ and $\{x_{i,j,k}\}_{j\in[\ell],k\in[\lambda]}$ as inputs and first reconstructs $\{x_{i,j}\}_{j\in[\ell]}$ and then applies the function computed by the i-th server in the outer protocol Φ on $f, \{x_{i,j}, y_{i,j}\}_{j\in[\ell]}$.

2. Send $(\{{,}^{i}_{1}\}_{i\in[m]})$ to R.

Receiver:

1. Compute $(x_1,\ldots,x_m) \leftarrow \Phi_1(x)$. We assume that $x_i \in \{0,1\}^{\ell}$ and we denote by $x_{i,j}$ the j-th bit of x_i fo r all $j \in [\ell]$.
2. Sample $x_{i,j,1},\ldots,x_{i,j,\lambda-1} \leftarrow \{0,1\}$ and set $x_{i,j,\lambda-1} := x_{i,j} \bigoplus_{k\in[\lambda-1]} x_{i,j,k}$ for all $i \in [m], j \in [\ell]$.
3. Choose a random subset $K \subset [m]$.
4. For all $i \in [m], j \in [\ell], k \in [\lambda]$ sample $r_{i,j,k} \leftarrow \{0,1\}^{\lambda}$ and compute $\mathsf{ot}_1^{i,j,k} \leftarrow \mathsf{OT}_1^{1,2}(1^{\lambda}, x_{i,j,k})$. Sample $r \leftarrow \{0,1\}^{\lambda}$ and compute $\mathsf{ot}_1 \leftarrow \mathsf{OT}_1^{\lambda,m}(1^{\lambda}, K; r)$.
5. Send ot_1^{i} and $\{\mathsf{ot}_1^{i,j,k}\}_{i\in[m],j\in[\ell],k\in[\lambda]}$ to S.

Round 2.

Sender:

1. Sample $\mathsf{sk}_0^{i,j,k}, \mathsf{sk}_1^{i,j,k} \leftarrow \{0,1\}^{\lambda}$ for all $i \in [m], j \in [\ell]$ and $k \in [\lambda]$.
2. Sample $\rho^{i,j,k}$ and compute $\mathsf{ot}_2^{i,j,k} \leftarrow \mathsf{OT}_2^{1,2}(\mathsf{ot}_1^{i,j,k}, (\mathsf{sk}_0^{i,j,k}, \mathsf{sk}_1^{i,j,k}); \rho^{i,j,k})$ for all $i \in [m], j \in [\ell]$ and $k \in [\lambda]$.
3. Compute $\mathsf{ot}_2 \leftarrow \mathsf{OT}_2^{\lambda,m}(\mathsf{ot}_1, \{s_j\}_{j\in[m]})$.
4. Send ot_2 and $\{\mathsf{ot}_2^{i,j,k}\}_{i\in[m],j\in[\ell],k\in[\lambda]}$ to R.

Receiver:

1. Compute ${,}^{i}_{2} \leftarrow \mathsf{ExtCom}_2({,}^{i}_{1})$ for all $i \in [m]$.
2. Send $(\{{,}^{i}_{2}\}_{i\in[m]}, f)$ to S.

Round 3.

Sender:

1. Sample $\mathsf{k}_i \leftarrow \{0,1\}^{\lambda}$ for all $i \in [m]$.
2. Compute $(y_1,\ldots,y_m) \leftarrow \Phi(y)$. We assume that $y_i \in \{0,1\}^{\ell}$ and we denote by $y_{i,j}$ the j-th bit of y_i for all $j \in [\ell]$.
3. Compute ${,}^{i}_{3} := \mathsf{ExtCom}_3(1^{\lambda}, y_i, \mathsf{k}_i, \{\mathsf{sk}_0^{i,j,k}, \mathsf{sk}_1^{i,j,k}, \rho^{i,j,k}\}_{j\in[\ell],k\in[\lambda]}; s_i)$ for all $i \in [m]$.
4. Compute $r_i := \mathsf{PRF}(\mathsf{k}_i, f)$ and use it to generate $(\tilde{\Phi}_i, \{\overline{\mathsf{lab}}_0^{i,j}, \overline{\mathsf{lab}}_1^{i,j}\}_{i\in[m],j\in[\ell]}, \{\mathsf{lab}_0^{i,j,k}, \mathsf{lab}_1^{i,j,k}\}_{i\in[m],j\in[\ell],k\in[\lambda]}) \leftarrow \mathsf{Garble}(1^{\lambda}, \Phi_{2,i}, r_i)$ for all $i \in [m]$ where $\{\overline{\mathsf{lab}}_0^{i,j}, \overline{\mathsf{lab}}_1^{i,j}\}_{i\in[m],j\in[\ell]}$ are the input labels for the sender and $\{\mathsf{lab}_0^{i,j,k}, \mathsf{lab}_1^{i,j,k}\}_{i\in[m],j\in[\ell],k\in[\lambda]}$ are the input labels for the receiver.
5. Sample $\mathsf{k}_0^{i,j,k}, \mathsf{k}_1^{i,j,k} \leftarrow \{0,1\}^{*}$ and generate $\mathsf{ct}_b^{i,j,k} := \mathsf{Enc}(\mathsf{sk}_b^{i,j,k}, \mathsf{lab}_b^{i,j,k}; \mathsf{PRF}(\mathsf{k}_b^{i,j,k}, f))$ for all $b \in \{0,1\}, i \in [m], j \in [\ell]$ and $k \in [\lambda]$.
6. Send $\{{,}^{i}_{3}, \tilde{\Phi}_i\}_{i\in[m]}$ and $\{\mathsf{ct}_0^{i,j,k}, \mathsf{ct}_1^{i,j,k}, \overline{\mathsf{lab}}_{y_{i,j}}^{i,j}\}_{i\in[m],j\in[\ell],k\in[\lambda]}$ to R.

Receiver:

1. Compute $\mathsf{ot}_3^{i,j,k} \leftarrow \mathsf{OT}_3^{1,2}(\mathsf{ot}_2^{i,j,k}; r^{i,j,k})$ for all $i \in [m], j \in [\ell]$ and $k \in [\lambda]$.

2. Compute $\mathsf{ot}_3 \leftarrow \mathsf{OT}_3^{\lambda,m}(\mathsf{ot}_2; r)$.
3. Send ot_3 and $\{\mathsf{ot}_3^{i,j,k}\}_{i\in[m],j\in[\ell],k\in[\lambda]}$ to S.

Figure 6.2: The output computation of the 2PC protocol Π^{2PC}.

Output Computation.

Sender:

1. Verify that all the OTs are accepting, and reject if this is not the case.

Receiver:

1. Compute $\{s_i\}_{i\in K} := \mathsf{OT}_{\mathsf{out}}^{\lambda,m}(\mathsf{ot}_2; r)$
2. Compute $\mathsf{sk}_{x_{i,j,k}}^{i,j,k} := \mathsf{OT}_{\mathsf{out}}^{1,2}(\mathsf{ot}_2^{i,j,k}; r^{i,j,k})$ and $\mathsf{lab}_{x_{i,j,k}}^{i,j,k} := \mathsf{Dec}(\mathsf{sk}_{x_{i,j,k}}^{i,j,k}, \mathsf{ct}_{x_{i,j,k}}^{i,j,k})$ for all $i \in [m], j \in [\ell], k \in [\lambda]$.
3. For all $i \in K$:
   (a) Compute $(y_i, \mathsf{k}_i, \{sk_0^{\prime i,j,k}, sk_1^{\prime i,j,k}\}_{j\in[\ell]})$ from $,^{i}_{1}, ,^{i}_{3}$ and randomness s_i.
   (b) Compute $r := \mathsf{PRF}(\mathsf{k}_i, f)$.
   (c) Compute $\tilde{\Phi}_i, \{\widetilde{\mathsf{lab}}_0^{i,j}, \widetilde{\mathsf{lab}}_1^{i,j}\}_{j\in[\ell]}, \{\mathsf{lab}_0^{\prime i,j,k}, \mathsf{lab}_1^{\prime i,j,k}\}_{j\in[\ell]} := \mathsf{Garble}(1^\lambda, \Phi_{2,i}; r_i)$.
   (d) Check if $\tilde{\Phi}_i$ that is received in the third round is the same as the one computed above.
   (e) Check that $\overline{\mathsf{lab}}_{y_{i,j}}^{i,j} = \widetilde{\mathsf{lab}}_{y_{i,j}}^{i,j}$ for all $j \in [\ell]$.
   (f) Check that $\mathsf{sk}_{x_{i,j,k}}^{i,j,k} = \mathsf{sk}_{x_{i,j,k}}^{\prime i,j,k}$ for all $j \in [\ell], k \in [\lambda]$
   (g) Compute $\mathsf{lab}_{1-x_{i,j,k}}^{i,j,k} := \mathsf{Dec}(\mathsf{sk}_{1-x_{i,j,k}}^{\prime i,j,k}, \mathsf{ct}_{1-x_{i,j,k}}^{i,j,k})$ for all $j \in [\ell], k \in [\lambda]$.
   (h) Check that $\mathsf{lab}_b^{i,j,k} = \mathsf{lab}_b^{\prime i,j,k}$ for all $j \in [\ell], k \in [\lambda]$ and $b \in \{0,1\}$.
   (i) Check that $\mathsf{ot}_2^{i,j,k} = \mathsf{OT}_2^{1,2}(\mathsf{ot}_1^{i,j,k}, (\mathsf{sk}_0^{i,j,k}, \mathsf{sk}_1^{i,j,k}); \rho^{i,j,k})$ for all $j \in [\ell], k \in [\lambda]$
4. If any of the above checks fails, output $\perp$.
5. For all $i \in [m]$, compute $z_i := \mathsf{Eval}(\tilde{\Phi}_i, \{\overline{\mathsf{lab}}_{y_{i,j}}^{i,j}\}_{j\in[\ell]}, \{\mathsf{lab}_{x_{i,j,k}}^{i,j,k}\}_{j\in[\ell],k\in[\lambda]})$.
6. Compute the output by running out_Φ on $\{z_i\}_{i\in[m]}$, the input x and the random tape used for generating $(x_1, \ldots, x_m)$.

Theorem 6.1. *Let X_S be a high min-entropy random variable defined by a probability distribution $\mathcal{X}_S$, the protocol Π^{2PC} (Fig. 6.1) is* 1*-rewinding secure list-simulatable against sometimes aborting adversaries with delayed function selection for NC_1 circuits for the ideal functionality $\mathcal{F}^{\mathcal{X}_S}$ (accordingly to Definition 3.2), that makes block box use of $\mathsf{OT}^{1,2}, \mathsf{OT}^{k,\lambda}$, ExtCom, PRF, SE, and GC.*

7 List Non-malleable OT

In this section, we present our list non-malleable k-out-of-m oblivious transfer protocol.

7.1 Definition ℓ-Non-malleable k-Out-of-m Oblivious Transfer

In this section, we give the definition of list non-malleable k-out-of-m Oblivious Transfer. Roughly speaking, we consider an adversary (denoted by MIM) that interacts with up to ℓ senders $S_1, \ldots, S_\ell$ on the left, and up to ℓ receivers $R_1, \ldots, R_\ell$ on the right. The guarantee of non-malleability ensures that the inputs that the adversary uses in the right sessions (as a sender) are unrelated to the one used by $S_1, \ldots, S_\ell$. This is formalized by the existence of a simulator S which interacts with MIM as senders in the left sessions and as honest receivers in the right sessions. S having access to the list-simulatable ideal OT functionality $\mathcal{F}_{\mathsf{OT}}^{\mathsf{list}}$, is able to simulate $S_1, \ldots, S_\ell$. Specifically, $\mathcal{F}_{\mathsf{OT}}^{\mathsf{list}}$ will take as input the inputs of the corrupted receiver, i.e. the set of indices $\tilde{K}_j$ (with $j \in [\ell]$) and samples d inputs uniformly at random from the input domain of the honest parties $x_{j,i}^1, \ldots, x_{j,i}^d \leftarrow \mathcal{X}$ for all $i \in \tilde{K}_j$ and $j \in [\ell]$.

This definition is very close in spirit to the one described in [17], but adapted to our list simulatability paradigm.

Definition 7.1 (ℓ-Non-Malleable k-out-of-m Oblivious Transfer). *An ℓ-non-malleable Oblivious Transfer protocol is a protocol between a sender S with inputs $\{x_i\}_{i\in[m]}$ from a the domain $\mathcal{X}$ and a receiver R with input $K \subset [m]$ where $|K| = k$, that satisfies the following properties:*

Correctness: *For every $i \in [m], x_i \in \{0,1\}^\lambda$ and $K \subset [m]$ such that $|K| = k, \mathsf{out}_R\langle S(\{x_i\}_{i\in[m]}, R(K))\rangle = \{x_i\}_{i\in K}$*

Receiver Security (under Parallel Composition with Fixed Roles): *For every PPT sender S^* and every pair K, K' of k-sized subsets of $[m]$, we require $\mathrm{View}_{S^*}\langle S^*, R(K)\rangle \approx_c \mathrm{View}_{S^*}\langle S^*, R(K')\rangle$. Additionally, we require that there exists a PPT extractor $S.\mathsf{Ext}$ that on input any transcript τ and with black-box access to any PPT sender S^* in the j'th session of τ (if any input is not well-defined, it outputs $\bot$ in its place).*

List Non-Malleability: *Consider any PPT adversary (denoted by MIM) that interacts with up to ℓ senders $S_1, \ldots, S_\ell$ on the left, where for every $j \in [\ell]$, S_j has input $\{x_{i,j} \in \mathcal{X}\}_{i\in[m]}$, and up to ℓ receivers $R_1, \ldots, R_\ell$ on the right, where for every $j \in [\ell], R_j$ has input K_j. We denote by $\mathrm{View}_{\mathsf{MIM}}\langle\{S_j(\{x_{i,j}\}_{i\in[m]})\}_{j\in[\ell]}, \{R_j(K_j)\}_{j\in[\ell]}\rangle$ the view of the MIM in this interaction, and denote the i'th implicit input used by the MIM in the j'th right session by $x'_{i,j}$. We denote by $\mathrm{Real}_{\mathsf{MIM}}\langle\{S_j(\{x_{i,j}\}_{i\in[m]})\}_{j\in[\ell]}, \{R_j(K_j)\}_{j\in[\ell]}\rangle$ the joint distribution of $\{(x'_{i,j})\}_{i\in[m],j\in[\ell]}$ and $\mathrm{View}_{\mathsf{MIM}}\langle\{S_j(\{x_{i,j}\}_{i\in[m]})\}_{j\in[\ell]}, \{R_j(K_j)\}_{j\in[\ell]}\rangle$. Then, we require that there exists a two-step simulator, $(\mathsf{Sim}_1, \mathsf{Sim}_2)$ that outputs $(\mathsf{st}, \mathsf{trans}^{(1)}, \{\tilde{K}_j\}_{j\in[\ell]}) \leftarrow \mathsf{Sim}_1^{\mathsf{MIM}}(\{K_j\}_{j\in[\ell]})$ and $\mathrm{Ideal}_{\mathsf{MIM}}(\{x_{i,j}^k\}_{i\in[m],j\in[\ell]}, \{K_j\}_{j\in[\ell]}) \leftarrow \mathsf{Sim}_2^{\mathsf{MIM}, \mathcal{F}_{\mathsf{OT}}^{\mathsf{list},\mathcal{X}}(\cdot,\cdot)}(\mathsf{st}, \{\tilde{K}_j\}_{j\in[\ell]})$, with*

$k \in [d]$ and where $\mathsf{trans}^{(1)}$ *denotes the first round messages in a transcript generated by the* MIM *in its interaction with* Sim_1*, and* st *denotes the state of the simulator* Sim_1*. Furthermore,* $\mathcal{F}_{\mathsf{OT}}^{\mathsf{list},\mathcal{X}}$ *denotes the list-simulatable ideal OT functionality that takes as an input* $\{\tilde{K}_j\}_{j\in[\ell]}$ *and* 1^d *and outputs* $\{x_{i,j}^k\}_{i\in[m],j\in[\ell],k\in[d]}$*, where* $x_{i,j}^k$ *are sampled at random from* $\mathcal{X}$ *for all* $i \in [m], j \in [\ell], k \in [d]$*. We require that the adversary's "view" in the ideal world, which is part of the distribution* $\mathrm{Ideal}_{\mathsf{MIM}}(\{x_{i,j}\}_{i\in[m],j\in[\ell]}, \{K_j\}_{j\in[\ell]})$ *contains a transcript that has* $\mathsf{trans}^{(1)}$ *as the first message, and that for all honest inputs* $\{x_{i,j}\}_{i\in[m],j\in[\ell]}, \{K_j\}_{j\in[\ell]}$*, To achieve list non-malleability, we require that:* $\mathrm{Real}_{\mathsf{MIM}}\langle\{S_j(\{x_{i,j}^k\}_{i\in[m]})\}_{j\in[\ell]}, \{R_j(K_j)\}_{j\in[\ell]} \approx_c \mathrm{Ideal}_{\mathsf{MIM}}(\{x_{i,j}^k\}_{i\in[m],j\in[\ell]}, \{K_j\}_{j\in[\ell]})$*, for a* $k \in [d]$.

Our construction is similar to the one presented in [17], the crucial difference is that we use our three-round two-party computation protocol Π, which satisfies the notion of list simulatability against sometimes aborting, instead of a simulation secure two-party computation protocol. To construct our 3-round non-malleable OT protocol we make use of the following tools.

- A three-round list simulatable, against sometimes aborting adversaries, two-party computation protocol Π according to Definition 3.2 for NC^1 circuits (constructed in Sect. 6). Π implements the function $f_{\mathsf{NM-OT}}$ described in Fig. 7.1, the corresponding ideal list functionality parametrized by the distribution $\mathcal{D}_{\mathsf{NM-OT}}$ defined over the sender's inputs, i.e. the distribution induced by the digital signature scheme, the non-interactive commitment scheme, the non-malleable code, as well as the uniform distribution. More formally, this distribution is defined by the distributions derived from DS.Setup, $2 \cdot \lambda \cdot m$ random values, $\lambda \cdot m$ codewords generatd by NM.Code as well as $2 \cdot \lambda \cdot m$ commitments and decommitments generated by NICom.
- An information-theoretic $m(\lambda) \cdot \ell(\lambda)$ non-malleable coding scheme/split-state non-malleable code NM = (Code, Decode).
- A low-depth proof ldp = (Prove, Verify) for P.
- An existentially unforgeable signature scheme DS = (Setup, Sign, Verify).
- A non-interactive statistically binding commitment scheme $\mathit{\Pi}_,$ = (NICom, NIDec).

We propose the formal description of our k-out-of-m NM-OT protocol in Fig. 7.2 and refer the reader to the introductory section for an informal discussion on how the protocol works.

Theorem 7.2. *Let $\mathcal{X}$ be a high min-entropy random variable defined by a probability distribution $\mathcal{D}$, then the k-out-of-m OT* NM-OT *described in 7.2 satisfies Definition 7.1 for the functionality* $\mathcal{F}_{\mathsf{OT}}^{\mathsf{list},\mathcal{X}}$*, against sometimes aborting adversaries. Moreover* NM-OT *makes black-box use of* Π, $\mathit{\Pi}_,$, NM *and* DS.

Figure 7.1: Function $f_{\mathsf{NM\text{-}OT}}$ parametrized with $(c_1, \ldots, c_\lambda)$

$\underline{f_{\mathsf{NM\text{-}OT}}}$.

S's input: (x, ldp) with $x = (\mathsf{vk}, \{(s'_{L,i,j}, s'_{R,i,j}), (L_{i,j}, R_{i,j}, x_j), (\mathsf{dec}_{L,i,j}, s_{L,i,j}), (\mathsf{dec}_{R,i,j}, s_{R,i,j})\}_{i\in[\lambda],j\in[m]})$. R's input: indices K and $\{\mathsf{k}_i\}_{i\in[\lambda]}$.
The function $f_{\mathsf{NM-OT}}$ upon receiving the inputs defined above does the following.

1. Set $x' = (\mathsf{vk}, \{(s'_{L,i,j}, s_{L,i,j}, s'_{R,i,j}, s_{R,i,j}), (L_{i,j}, R_{i,j}, x_j)\}_{i\in[\lambda],j\in[m]})$.
2. If $\mathsf{LDP.Verify}(x', \mathsf{ldp}) \neq 1$, output $\perp$.
3. Otherwise set $\mathsf{out} = (\mathsf{vk}, \{x_j\}_{j\in K})$. Additionally, for every $i \in [\lambda]$, if $c_i \oplus \mathsf{k}_i = 0$, append $\{(\mathsf{dec}_{L,i,j}, s_{L,i,j})\}_{j\in[m]}$ to out and if $c_i \oplus \mathsf{k}_i = 1$, append $\{(\mathsf{dec}_{R,i,j}, s_{R,i,j})\}_{j\in[m]}$ to out.
4. Append $\{m_j\}_{j\in K}$ and $\{s'_{R,i,j}, s'_{L,i,j}\}_{i\in\lambda,j\in[m]}$ to out.
5. Output out.

Figure 7.2: Our $\ell(\lambda)$ Non-Malleable k-out-of-m OT protocol.

Initialization: The sender S has inputs $\{x_j\}_{j\in[m]}$ and the receiver R uses as its input a set $K \subseteq [m]$ where $|K| = k$
Protocol: S and R interact in the following way:

1. S generates $(\mathsf{vk}, \mathsf{sk}) \leftarrow \mathsf{DS.Setup}(1^\lambda)$ and does the following:
   - For each $i \in [\lambda], j \in [m]$, sample $r_{i,j} \leftarrow \{0,1\}^*$ and compute $(L_{i,j}, R_{i,j}) := \mathsf{NM.Code}((\mathsf{vk}\|x_j); r_{i,j})$.
   - For each $i \in [\lambda], j \in [m]$:
     - Sample $s_{L,i,j} \leftarrow \{0,1\}^*$ and compute $,_{L,i,j}, \mathsf{dec}_{L,i,j}$ running NICom on input $s_{L,i,j}$.
     - Sample $s_{R,i} \leftarrow \{0,1\}^*$ and compute $,_{R,i,j}, \mathsf{dec}_{R,i,j}$ running NICom on input $s_{R,i,j}$.
     - Set $s'_{L,i,j} = L_{i,j} \oplus s_{L,i,j}$ and $s'_{R,i,j} = R_{i,j} \oplus s_{R,i,j}$.
   - Set $x' = (\mathsf{vk}, \{(s'_{L,i,j}, s_{L,i,j}, s'_{R,i,j}, s_{R,i,j}), (L_{i,j}, R_{i,j}, x_j)\}_{i\in[\lambda],j\in[m]})$ and
   $\mathcal{L} = \{(\mathsf{vk}, \{(s'_{L,i,j}, s_{L,i,j}, s'_{R,i,j}, s_{R,i,j}), (L_{i,j}, R_{i,j}, x_j)\}_{i\in[\lambda],j\in[m]}) : \forall i \in [\lambda], j \in [m], L_{i,j} = s'_{L,i,j} \oplus s_{L,i,j}, R_{i,j} = s'_{R,i,j} \oplus s_{R,i,j}, \mathsf{NM.Decode}(L_{i,j}, R_{i,j}) = (\mathsf{vk}\|x_j)\}$. Then compute $\mathsf{ldp} = \mathsf{LDP.Prove}(x', \mathcal{L})$.
2. Both parties engage in a run of the two-party protocol Π where:
   - R acts as the receiver using as its private input K and $(\mathsf{k}_1, \ldots, \mathsf{k}_\lambda)$, and parametrizing the delayed function with $(c_1, \ldots, c_\lambda)$, where $\mathsf{k}_i, c_i \leftarrow \{0,1\}$ for all $i \in [\lambda]$.
   - S acts as the sender using (x, ldp) as its input where $x = (\mathsf{vk}, \{(s'_{L,i,j}, s'_{R,i,j}), (L_{i,j}, R_{i,j}, x_j), (\mathsf{dec}_{L,i,j}, s_{L,i,j}), (\mathsf{dec}_{R,i,j}, s_{R,i,j})\}_{i\in[\lambda],j\in[m]})$.

In addition, in the first round, S sends $\{,_{L,i,j}\ ,,_{R,i,j}\ \}_{i\in[\lambda],j\in[m]}$ and in the second round sends $\{s'_{L,i,j}, s'_{R,i,j}\}_{i\in[\lambda],j\in[m]}$. Additionally, S signs the messages generated from Π, denoted by (Π_1, Π_2, Π_3). It sets $\sigma_i \leftarrow \mathsf{DS.Sign}(\mathsf{sk}, \Pi_i)$ for all $i \in [3]$ and sends it to R.

3. R parses $\mathsf{out} = (\mathsf{vk}, \{(\mathsf{dec}_{i,j}, s_{i,j})\}_{j\in[m]}, \{x_j\}_{j\in K}, \{\overline{s'}_{L,i,j}, \overline{s'}_{R,i,j}\}_{i\in[\lambda],j\in[m]})$. It outputs $\{x_j\}_{j\in K}$ if and only if the following conditions hold
   (a) $\mathsf{DS.Verify}(\mathsf{vk}, \Pi_i, \sigma_i)$ for all $i \in [3]$
   (b) For each $i \in [\lambda]$ compute $c_i \oplus k_i = \gamma_1$. If $\gamma_i = 0$ then $\{(\mathsf{dec}_{i,j}, s_{i,j})\}_{j\in[m]}$ (contained in out) are valid decommitment information for $\{,_{L,i,j}\ \}_{i\in[\lambda],j\in[m]}$, else $\{(\mathsf{dec}_{i,j}, s_{i,j})\}_{j\in[m]}$ are valid decommitment information for $\{,_{R,i,j}\ \}_{i\in[\lambda],j\in[m]}$.
   (c) The values $\{s'_{L,i,j}, s'_{R,i,j}\}_{i\in[\lambda],j\in[m]}$ sent in the second round from the sender are equal to the values $\overline{s'}_{R,i,j}\}_{i\in[\lambda],j\in[m]})$ received as part of out.

Multiparty Simultaneous OT. The definition of list multiparty simultaneous OT, which is an adaption of the definition of multiparty simultaneous OT in the same way as the notion of non-malleable OT has been adapted, can be found in the full version. The realization of list multiparty simultaneous OT is straightforward and taken almost verbatim from [17]. The idea to realize the watchlist protocol is to let each pair of parties interact in the execution tow non-malleable OTs where in one of the executions one party acts as the sender and in the other execution the other party acts as a sender. This allows each party to get an OT correlation (both as a sender and as a receiver). We refer to the full-version for a formal treatment.

8 Four-Round Multi-party Computation

In this section, we present our MPC protocol. This is essentially an instantiation of the IPS compiler [18], following the approach of [17]. In a nutshell, the IPS compiler works as follows: a client-server protocol Φ, with a security threshold of $1/3$ is being executed to evaluate the function f that should be computed by the MPC protocol, this protocol is usually termed the outer protocol. To emulate the servers in this setting, additionally another semi-malicious MPC protocol, the inner-protocol Π_h, is executed in parallel to take over the role of the servers in the client-server protocol Φ. Due to the fact that the executed inner protocol is not maliciously secure, the overall protocol also does not achieve malicious security. To achieve full malicious security, we apply a cut-and-choose protocol. In more detail, we execute multiple instances of the inner protocol Π_h and run a cut-and-choose protocol over these instances, which prevents and adversary from the malicious generation of messages. The cut-and-choose is realized using a watchlist protocol as described in the previous section,

Now, we describe this construction more formally. It makes use of the following building blocks.

- A MAC scheme MAC.
- A list-simulatable secure Watchlist Protocol $\mathsf{WL} = (\mathsf{WL}_1, \mathsf{WL}_2, \mathsf{WL}_3)$ as realized in Sect. 7 for the functionality $\mathcal{F}_{\mathsf{OT}}^{\mathsf{list},\mathcal{X}}$ where $\mathcal{X}$ is the distribution induced by the uniform distribution, as well as the distribution of the outer protocol Φ introduced below. Here, we denote by $\mathsf{wl}(r)$ the transcript in the first r rounds of WL.
- The Inner Protocol $\Pi_h = (\Pi_{h,1}, \Pi_{h,2}, \Pi_{h,3})$. This protocol is semi-malicious and equivocal secure. We highlight that also this security definition is parameterized using a distribution $\mathcal{D}$ from which the inputs of the (honest) parties are sampled in the security game. Here, we denote by $\pi(r)$ the transcript in the first r rounds of Π_h. $\pi(0)$ is set to be the null string. The full details of this protocol can be found in the full version.
- The Outer Protocol $\Phi = (\Phi_1, \Phi_2)$, a 2-round, n-client, m-server MPC protocol achieving privacy with knowledge of outputs against a malicious, adaptive adversary corrupting up to $n-1$ clients and $t = (m-1)/3$ servers. We also need the protocol to be equipped with a simulator that works in two phases. In the first phase, it simulates the client messages using the same procedure the honest clients would use, using a default input. In the second phase, it generates the messages of the honest servers and returns the shares received by the corrupted servers from the honest clients. The full details of this protocol can be found in the full version.

Figure 8.1: MPC

Initialization: Each party P_i uses x_i as its input.

Round 1.

1. Choose a random MAC key $\mathsf{k}_i \leftarrow \{0,1\}^*$ and sets $z_i := (x_i, \mathsf{k}_i)$.
2. Compute $(\phi_1^{i\to 1}, \ldots, \phi_1^{i\to m}) \leftarrow \Phi_1(1^\lambda, i, z_i)$.
3. Sample a random subset $K_I \subset [m]$ of size λ and set $x_{i,j} := K_i$ for all $j \in [n] \setminus \{i\}$.
4. Sample $r_{i,h} \leftarrow \{0,1\}^*$ for all $h \in [m]$ and set $y_{i,j} := \{r_{i,h}, \phi_1^{i\to h}\}$ for all $j \in [n] \setminus \{i\}$.
5. Compute $\mathsf{wl}_1^i \leftarrow \mathsf{WL}_1(1^\lambda, i, \{x_{i,j}, y_{i,j}\}_{j\in[n]\setminus\{i\}}, \mathsf{wl}(0))$.
6. Broadcast wl_1^i.

Round 2.

1. Compute $\mathsf{wl}_2^i \leftarrow \mathsf{WL}_2(1^\lambda, i, \{x_{i,j}, y_{i,j}\}_{j\in[n]\setminus\{i\}}, \mathsf{wl}(1))$.
2. Compute $\pi_{h,1}^i := \Pi_{h,1}(1^\lambda, i, \phi_1^{i\to h}; r_{i,h})$ for all $h \in [m]$.
3. Broadcast $\mathsf{wl}_2^i, \{\pi_{h,1}^i\}_{h\in[m]}$.

Round 3.

1. Compute $\mathsf{wl}_3^i \leftarrow \mathsf{WL}_3(1^\lambda, i, \{x_{i,j}, y_{i,j}\}_{j\in[n]\setminus\{i\}}, \mathsf{wl}(2))$.
2. Compute $\pi_{h,2}^i := \Pi_{h,2}(1^\lambda, i, \phi_1^{i\to h}, \pi_h(1); r_{i,h})$ for all $h \in [m]$.
3. Broadcast $\mathsf{wl}_3^i, \{\pi_{h,2}^i\}_{h\in[m]}$.

Round 4.

1. Run $\mathsf{out}_{\mathsf{WL}}$ on $(i, \{x_{i,j}, y_{i,j}\}_{j\in[n]\setminus\{i\}})$, the random tape and $\mathsf{wl}(4)$ to obtain $\{r_{j,h}, \phi_1^{j\to h}\}_{j\in[n]\setminus\{i\}, h\in K_i}$.

2. For all $j \in [n] \setminus \{i\}$ and $h \in K_i$, check that:
   - The PRG computations in $\phi_1^{j \to h}$ are correct.
   - For all $\ell \in [2]$, whether $\pi_{h,\ell}^j = \Pi_{h,\ell}(1^\lambda, j, \phi_1^{j \to h}, \pi_h(\ell - 1); r_{j,h})$.
3. If any of the above checks fail, output $\perp$.
4. For all $h \in [m]$, compute $\pi_{h,3}^i := \Pi_{h,3}(1^\lambda, i, \phi_1^{i \to h}, \pi_h(2); r_{i,h})$.
5. Broadcast $\{\pi_{h,3}^i\}_{h \in [m]}$.

Output Computation.

1. Compute $\phi_2^h := \mathsf{out}_{\Pi_h}(i, \pi(3))$ for all $h \in [m]$.
2. Compute $(y, \sigma_1, \ldots, \sigma_n) := \mathsf{out}_\Phi(\{\phi_2^h\}_{h \in [m]})$.
3. Check if σ_i is a valid tag on y using the key k_i. If the check is successful output y, otherwise output $\perp$.

Figure 8.2: Circuit C computed by Φ

On input (x_i, k_i) from party P_i, with a MAC key k_i do the following:

1. Compute $y = f(x_1, \ldots, x_n)$
2. Output $(y, \mathsf{MAC}(\mathsf{k}_1, y), \ldots, \mathsf{MAC}(\mathsf{k}_n, y))$ to all P_i's.

Figure 8.3: Circuit C' computed by the inner-protocol Π_h

The i'th instance of the inner-protocol $\Pi_i = (\Pi_{i,1}, \ldots, \Pi_{i,3}, \mathsf{out}_{\Pi_i})$ implements the computation done by the i'th server in the outer protocol and the watchlist protocol.

Theorem 8.1. *Let* wl *be the watchlist protocol for the distribution* $\mathcal{X}$ *defined above that samples randomly from* Φ_1 *and* $\{0,1\}^\lambda$, *let* Π_h *be a secure inner-protocol,* Φ *a secure outer protocol and* MAC *a secure MAC scheme, then the protocol* Π *is secure against sometimes aborting adversaries.*

We can now claim the following corollary.

Corollary 8.2. *Let* wl *be the watchlist protocol for the distribution* $\mathcal{X}$ *defined above that samples randomly from* Φ_1 *and* $\{0,1\}^\lambda$, *let* Π_h *be a secure inner-protocol,* Φ *a secure outer protocol and* MAC *a secure MAC scheme, then* Π *realizes any input-less functionality with black-box use of the primitives against any PPT adversaries.*

To argue that our corollary holds, we observe the following. A malicious adversary is able to perform two types of attacks: it can learn the inputs of the honest parties and it can force wrong outputs on the honest parties. In the case of input-less functionalities, there is nothing to learn about the honest parties' inputs. Hence, we need to make sure that the adversary cannot force an incorrect output. If an adversary forces the honest parties to produce a wrong output, then it must be that these honest parties have received an accepting transcript (i.e., no abort was triggered). Therefore, by Theorem 8.1 (and by the definition of sometimes aborting security), there exists a simulator, which directly results in the claim of Corollary 8.2. Note that this implication may not hold if we assume security against non-aborting adversaries (i.e., adversaries that abort with negligible probability only).

Acknowledgements. This work is supported in part by DARPA under Cooperative Agreement HR0011-20-2-0025, the Algorand Centers of Excellence programme managed by Algorand Foundation, NSF grants CNS-2246355, CCF-2220450 and CNS-2001096, US-Israel BSF grant 2015782, Amazon Faculty Award, Cisco Research Award and Sunday Group. Any views, opinions, findings, conclusions or recommendations contained herein are those of the author(s) and should not be interpreted as necessarily representing the official policies, either expressed or implied, of DARPA, the Department of Defense, the Algorand Foundation, or the U.S. Government. The U.S. Government is authorized to reproduce and distribute reprints for governmental purposes not withstanding any copyright annotation therein.

References

1. Aiello, B., Ishai, Y., Reingold, O.: Priced oblivious transfer: how to sell digital goods. In: Pfitzmann, B. (ed.) EUROCRYPT 2001. LNCS, vol. 2045, pp. 119–135. Springer, Heidelberg (2001). https://doi.org/10.1007/3-540-44987-6_8
2. Ananth, P., Choudhuri, A.R., Jain, A.: A new approach to round-optimal secure multiparty computation. In: Katz, J., Shacham, H. (eds.) CRYPTO 2017, Part I. LNCS, vol. 10401, pp. 468–499. Springer, Cham (2017). https://doi.org/10.1007/978-3-319-63688-7_16
3. Badrinarayanan, S., Goyal, V., Jain, A., Kalai, Y.T., Khurana, D., Sahai, A.: Promise zero knowledge and its applications to round optimal MPC. In: Shacham, H., Boldyreva, A. (eds.) CRYPTO 2018, Part II. LNCS, vol. 10992, pp. 459–487. Springer, Cham (2018). https://doi.org/10.1007/978-3-319-96881-0_16
4. Beaver, D., Micali, S., Rogaway, P.: The round complexity of secure protocols (extended abstract). In: 22nd Annual ACM Symposium on Theory of Computing, Baltimore, MD, USA, 14–16 May 1990, pp. 503–513. ACM Press (1990). https://doi.org/10.1145/100216.100287
5. Brakerski, Z., Döttling, N.: Two-message statistically sender-private OT from LWE. In: Beimel, A., Dziembowski, S. (eds.) TCC 2018, Part II. LNCS, vol. 11240, pp. 370–390. Springer, Cham (2018). https://doi.org/10.1007/978-3-030-03810-6_14
6. Brakerski, Z., Halevi, S., Polychroniadou, A.: Four round secure computation without setup. In: Kalai, Y., Reyzin, L. (eds.) TCC 2017, Part I. LNCS, vol. 10677, pp. 645–677. Springer, Cham (2017). https://doi.org/10.1007/978-3-319-70500-2_22
7. Rai Choudhuri, A., Ciampi, M., Goyal, V., Jain, A., Ostrovsky, R.: Round optimal secure multiparty computation from minimal assumptions. In: Pass, R., Pietrzak, K. (eds.) TCC 2020, Part II. LNCS, vol. 12551, pp. 291–319. Springer, Cham (2020). https://doi.org/10.1007/978-3-030-64378-2_11
8. Ciampi, M., Ostrovsky, R., Waldner, H., Zikas, V.: Round-optimal and communication-efficient multiparty computation. In: Dunkelman, O., Dziembowski, S. (eds.) EUROCRYPT 2022, Part I. LNCS, vol. 13275, pp. 65–95. Springer, Heidelberg (2022). https://doi.org/10.1007/978-3-031-06944-4_3

9. Ciampi, M., Ravi, D., Siniscalchi, L., Waldner, H.: Round-optimal multi-party computation with identifiable abort. In: Dunkelman, O., Dziembowski, S. (eds.) EUROCRYPT 2022, Part I. LNCS, vol. 13275, pp. 335–364. Springer, Heidelberg (2022). https://doi.org/10.1007/978-3-031-06944-4_12
10. Garg, S., Mukherjee, P., Pandey, O., Polychroniadou, A.: The exact round complexity of secure computation. In: Fischlin, M., Coron, J.-S. (eds.) EUROCRYPT 2016, Part II. LNCS, vol. 9666, pp. 448–476. Springer, Heidelberg (2016). https://doi.org/10.1007/978-3-662-49896-5_16
11. Goldreich, O., Micali, S., Wigderson, A.: How to play any mental game or A completeness theorem for protocols with honest majority. In: Aho, A. (ed.) 19th Annual ACM Symposium on Theory of Computing, New York City, NY, USA, 25–27 May 1987, pp. 218–229. ACM Press (1987). https://doi.org/10.1145/28395.28420
12. Goyal, V.: Constant round non-malleable protocols using one way functions. In: Fortnow, L., Vadhan, S.P. (eds.) 43rd Annual ACM Symposium on Theory of Computing, San Jose, CA, USA, 6–8 June 2011, pp. 695–704. ACM Press (2011). https://doi.org/10.1145/1993636.1993729
13. Goyal, V., Richelson, S., Rosen, A., Vald, M.: An algebraic approach to non-malleability. In: 55th Annual Symposium on Foundations of Computer Science, Philadelphia, PA, USA, 18–21 October 2014, pp. 41–50. IEEE Computer Society Press (2014). https://doi.org/10.1109/FOCS.2014.13
14. Halevi, S., Hazay, C., Polychroniadou, A., Venkitasubramaniam, M.: Round-optimal secure multi-party computation. In: Shacham, H., Boldyreva, A. (eds.) CRYPTO 2018, Part II. LNCS, vol. 10992, pp. 488–520. Springer, Cham (2018). https://doi.org/10.1007/978-3-319-96881-0_17
15. Halevi, S., Hazay, C., Polychroniadou, A., Venkitasubramaniam, M.: Round-optimal secure multi-party computation. J. Cryptol. **34**(3), 1–63 (2021). https://doi.org/10.1007/s00145-021-09382-3
16. Harnik, D., Kilian, J., Naor, M., Reingold, O., Rosen, A.: On robust combiners for oblivious transfer and other primitives. In: Cramer, R. (ed.) EUROCRYPT 2005. LNCS, vol. 3494, pp. 96–113. Springer, Heidelberg (2005). https://doi.org/10.1007/11426639_6
17. Ishai, Y., Khurana, D., Sahai, A., Srinivasan, A.: On the round complexity of black-box secure MPC. In: Malkin, T., Peikert, C. (eds.) CRYPTO 2021, Part II. LNCS, vol. 12826, pp. 214–243. Springer, Cham (2021). https://doi.org/10.1007/978-3-030-84245-1_8
18. Ishai, Y., Prabhakaran, M., Sahai, A.: Founding cryptography on oblivious transfer – efficiently. In: Wagner, D. (ed.) CRYPTO 2008. LNCS, vol. 5157, pp. 572–591. Springer, Heidelberg (2008). https://doi.org/10.1007/978-3-540-85174-5_32
19. Kalai, Y.T.: Smooth projective hashing and two-message oblivious transfer. In: Cramer, R. (ed.) EUROCRYPT 2005. LNCS, vol. 3494, pp. 78–95. Springer, Heidelberg (2005). https://doi.org/10.1007/11426639_5
20. Katz, J., Ostrovsky, R.: Round-optimal secure two-party computation. In: Franklin, M. (ed.) CRYPTO 2004. LNCS, vol. 3152, pp. 335–354. Springer, Heidelberg (2004). https://doi.org/10.1007/978-3-540-28628-8_21
21. Katz, J., Ostrovsky, R., Smith, A.: Round efficiency of multi-party computation with a dishonest majority. In: Biham, E. (ed.) EUROCRYPT 2003. LNCS, vol. 2656, pp. 578–595. Springer, Heidelberg (2003). https://doi.org/10.1007/3-540-39200-9_36

22. Khurana, D., Ostrovsky, R., Srinivasan, A.: Round optimal black-box "commit-and-prove". In: Beimel, A., Dziembowski, S. (eds.) TCC 2018, Part I. LNCS, vol. 11239, pp. 286–313. Springer, Cham (2018). https://doi.org/10.1007/978-3-030-03807-6_11
23. Kilian, J.: Founding cryptography on oblivious transfer. In: 20th Annual ACM Symposium on Theory of Computing, Chicago, IL, USA, 2–4 May 1988, pp. 20–31. ACM Press (1988). https://doi.org/10.1145/62212.62215
24. Naor, M., Pinkas, B.: Efficient oblivious transfer protocols. In: Kosaraju, S.R. (ed.) 12th Annual ACM-SIAM Symposium on Discrete Algorithms, Washington, DC, USA, 7–9 January 2001, pp. 448–457. ACM-SIAM (2001)
25. Pass, R.: Bounded-concurrent secure multi-party computation with a dishonest majority. In: Babai, L. (ed.) 36th Annual ACM Symposium on Theory of Computing, Chicago, IL, USA, 13–16 June 2004, pp. 232–241. ACM Press (2004). https://doi.org/10.1145/1007352.1007393
26. Pass, R., Wee, H.: Constant-round non-malleable commitments from sub-exponential one-way functions. In: Gilbert, H. (ed.) EUROCRYPT 2010. LNCS, vol. 6110, pp. 638–655. Springer, Heidelberg (2010). https://doi.org/10.1007/978-3-642-13190-5_32
27. Shankar, B., Srinathan, K., Rangan, C.P.: Alternative protocols for generalized oblivious transfer. In: Rao, S., Chatterjee, M., Jayanti, P., Murthy, C.S.R., Saha, S.K. (eds.) ICDCN 2008. LNCS, vol. 4904, pp. 304–309. Springer, Heidelberg (2007). https://doi.org/10.1007/978-3-540-77444-0_31
28. Wee, H.: Black-box, round-efficient secure computation via non-malleability amplification. In: 51st Annual Symposium on Foundations of Computer Science, Las Vegas, NV, USA, 23–26 October 2010, pp. 531–540. IEEE Computer Society Press (2010). https://doi.org/10.1109/FOCS.2010.87
29. Yao, A.C.C.: How to generate and exchange secrets (extended abstract). In: 27th Annual Symposium on Foundations of Computer Science, Toronto, Ontario, Canada, 27–29 October 1986, pp. 162–167. IEEE Computer Society Press (1986). https://doi.org/10.1109/SFCS.1986.25

Security-Preserving Distributed Samplers: How to Generate Any CRS in One Round Without Random Oracles

Damiano Abram[1(✉)], Brent Waters[2,3], and Mark Zhandry[3]

[1] Aarhus University, Aarhus, Denmark
damiano.abram@cs.au.dk
[2] University of Texas at Austin, Austin, USA
bwaters@cs.utexas.edu
[3] NTT Research, Tokyo, Japan

Abstract. A distributed sampler is a way for several mutually distrusting parties to non-interactively generate a common reference string (CRS) that all parties trust. Previous work constructs distributed samplers in the random oracle model, or in the standard model with very limited security guarantees. This is no accident, as standard model distributed samplers with full security were shown impossible.

In this work, we provide new definitions for distributed samplers which we show achieve meaningful security guarantees in the standard model. In particular, our notion implies that the hardness of a wide range of security games is preserved when the CRS is replaced with a distributed sampler. We also show how to realize our notion of distributed samplers. A core technical tool enabling our construction is a new notion of single-message zero knowledge.

1 Introduction

Many protocols require a common reference string to be generated by a third party in order to securely run the protocol. Importantly, the security of the protocol requires that the any secrets revealed during setup are hidden from the parties of the protocol. For example, if the protocol relies on a public RSA modulus for a reference string, the parties of the protocol must not know the prime factors. Such a structured common reference string requires placing enormous trust in the third party, and naturally leads to the question:

What happens if the trusted third party is actually not trustworthy?

Digging deeper, there may be many potential third parties who are willing to run the setup: maybe certain state organizations (e.g. NIST) as well and independent organizations (e.g. EFF). Some participants in the protocol may trust some third parties, while some participants only trust other third parties, and there may be no overlap between the trusted parties. How can we ensure that all protocol participants trust the reference string?

H. Handschuh and A. Lysyanskaya (Eds.): CRYPTO 2023, LNCS 14081, pp. 489–514, 2023.
https://doi.org/10.1007/978-3-031-38557-5_16

An obvious solution is for all potential third parties to run an MPC protocol to generate the reference string. Then, as long as each participant trusts a single third party, they will trust the reference string (CRS). However, engaging in an MPC protocol can be a logistical burden for these third parties. For comparison, in a situation where the CRS is generated by a single trusted third party, that party can simply post the reference string they produce to some public domain. In contrast, if many third parties are engaging in an MPC protocol to compute the reference string, this requires the many third parties to send several messages back-and-forth between each other.

Another issue is the difficulty of updating the CRS if we want to expand the number of involved trusted parties. For example, suppose third parties A, B, C engaged in an MPC protocol to generate a CRS such as an RSA modulus N. At some later date, users u, v wish to engage in a protocol using an RSA modulus, but user u only trusts a new third party D and not A, B, C. Meanwhile v does not trust D since it is new. Unfortunately, this would require A, B, C to come back online and interact with D to create a new modulus N'. A, B, C may be unable or unwilling to do so, as it would be an unreasonable burden to re-run the MPC any time a trusted setup was requested with a new third party.

Solution: Distributed Samplers. Abram, Scholl, and Yakoubov [ASY22] proposed the notion of a *distributed sampler*. Here, parties A, B, C each individually run their own setup algorithm locally, arriving at messages U_A, U_B, U_C, which they post to some public domain. Now when a set of users want a CRS generated by A, B, C, they look up U_A, U_B, U_C, and run a procedure which deterministically extracts a CRS from U_A, U_B, U_C. Because the process of computing the CRS from U_A, U_B, U_C is deterministic, all parties can compute it from U_A, U_B, U_C for themselves, and therefore do not require any additional interaction. Thus, the tuple U_A, U_B, U_C now acts as the common reference string, which is simply the concatenation of the individual messages of the various third parties. Informally, as long as a user trusts at least one of the third parties, then they trust the CRS derived from the list of strings that includes that party.

When a set of users wishes to incorporate a new third party D, all they need is for D to generate and post its own U_D. Now the parties can derive a new CRS from U_A, U_B, U_C, U_D. Importantly the original parties A, B, C do not need to do anything to add a new third party. In the follow-up work of [AOS23], a construction is given that maintains security in such a scenario.

Limitations of Existing Work. The work of [ASY22] constructs two kinds of distributed samplers both utilizing indistinguishability obfuscation. The first achieves semi-honest security, where the third parties *honestly* generate their messages but wish to then break a protocol using the generated CRS. Unfortunately, this notion of security is rather limited, since a truly malicious adversary could try to generate their messages dishonestly in order to influence the generated CRS. Such influence over the CRS offers much greater flexibility in breaking the protocol. For example, if the CRS is for a statistically sound proof system, a malicious adversary may try to influence the CRS into a "bad" one where false proofs exist.

The second distributed sampler achieves full malicious security in the UC model. However, the construction requires the random oracle model, and worse requires the full power of programming the random oracle.

Thus, the existing work either requires the full power of the random oracle model, or achieves only a very limited notion of security. This is no accident: as shown by [AOS23], full standard model malicious security is in fact *impossible*. So the question becomes: what kind of malicious security can be meaningfully achieved in the standard model?

1.1 Our Work

In this work, we address the above limitations of prior work, by giving new definitions for distributed samplers that avoid the above impossibility while still guaranteeing meaningful security against malicious adversaries, and providing a new instantiation of distributed samplers satisfying this definition. As a crucial step toward this goal, we also investigate single message zero knowledge proofs in the standard model, and provide new constructions with novel features. A summary of our main results follows.

Defining Distributed Samplers. Our first contribution is to define new security notions for distributed samplers. We describe a notion of *security preserving* distributed samplers, which implies that, for any game-based protocol using a reference string, security is preserved by the distributed sampler. That is, if the protocol is secure under a reference string generated by a single trusted third party, then it is also secure when the reference string is generated via a distributed sampler, as long as *at least one* of the parties involved is trusted. We also give some technical definitions of security for distributed samplers that are easier to reason about, and we show that these notions imply adequate notions of security preservation. See Sects. 5 and 6 of the full version of this paper [AWZ23] for details.

Constructing Distributed Samplers. Next, we show how to construct distributed samplers meeting our new definition. We obtain two flavours of the primitive: a CRS-less distributed sampler with security against uniform adversaries and a construction achieving security against non-uniform adversaries by relying on a short, reusable and unstructured CRS.

Our construction uses [ASY22] as a starting basis. However, we need to make several key changes. Critically, we face the following challenge: in order to justify that the reference string is "as good as" an honestly generated one, the reduction needs to be able to embed an actual honestly generated reference string N into the honest third party's message, and somehow force the adversary to generate their own messages in a way that makes the derived reference string equal to N. But in the case of malicious adversaries, whatever strategy the reduction uses, the adversary can seemingly use as well to force the derived reference string to be their own, maliciously generated, N'.

Extractable 1-message zero knowledge. Resolving the above problem requires many tools. One of the main ones is a new 1-message zero knowledge proof, which crucially does not need a CRS. Now, such an object is normally considered impossible, but it can be possible if the simulator is allowed to be non-uniform while the adversary is required to be uniform. Such 1-message zero knowledge leveraging non-uniformity was considered before [BP04]. However, our use of zero knowledge requires several features, such as the ability for the reduction to extract the original proof from the sender's message, that were not present in existing 1-message zero knowledge. We therefore develop a new 1-message zero knowledge proof system with several useful features that we crucially leverage to achieve our notion of distributed samplers.

Updatability. The distributed samplers presented in this work assume that the set of participants is a-priori given. As a consequence, our constructions tolerate inactive parties (their distributed sampler messages can be generated using default randomness), but when new participants join, the protocol needs to restart.

Applications. A direct implication of our results is the existence of a 3-round OT protocol in the plain model (no CRS) with security against active, *uniform* adversaries and non-uniform simulation. This is achieved by directly applying our CRS-less distributed sampler to [PVW08]. More in general, our distributed samplers imply 3-round active MPC in the plain model (no CRS) with security against uniform adversaries and non-uniform simulation [BL18a].

Our distributed samplers can also be used to compile extractable NIZKs into 2-round zero-knowledge proofs of knowledge[1]. The resulting constructions either rely on a short, unstructured CRS or no CRS at all, depending on whether we aim for security against non-uniform adversaries or not. Furthermore, the 2-round protocols satisfy automatically concurrent security, independently of the properties of the original NIZKs.

2 Technical Overview

We present a technical overview of our work. For the details, we refer to the full version of this paper [AWZ23].

2.1 New Notions of Distributed Sampler

Full Malicious Security, and Its Impossibility. We first recall an informal description of the notion of malicious security obtained by [ASY22], which follows the real/ideal paradigm as shown in Fig. 1 (We use $\mathcal{D}$ to denote the distribution of honestly generated CRSs. Such distribution can be private-coin). In the real world, the adversary is given the messages of the honest third parties, and then

[1] Our techniques do not apply to non-extractable NIZKs. This is due to the challenger of the soundness game being not efficient.

subsequently generates the messages of the malicious third parties. The challenger then derives the CRS from the combined messages of third parties, and gives it to the adversary. In the ideal world, the honest third party message is instead generated by a simulator (which depends on the adversary), and the simulator is given as input a CRS generated honestly from $\mathcal{D}$. The adversary is then given the simulated message and the honestly generated CRS. Security dictates that the two worlds are indistinguishable, which in particular implies that the derived CRS is equal to the provided honest CRS in the ideal world.

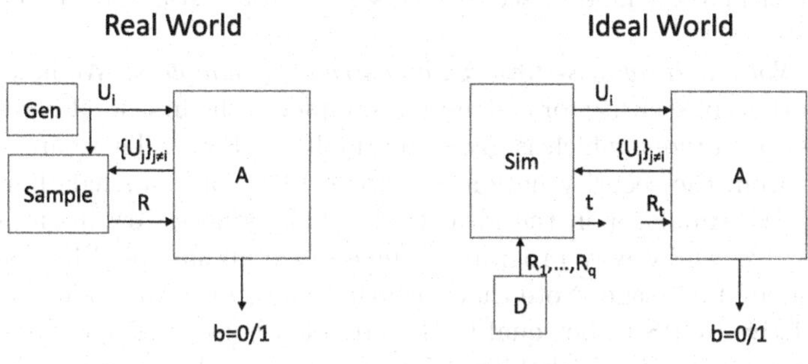

$$| \Pr[b = 1|\text{Real World}] - \Pr[b = 1|\text{Ideal World}] | < \mathsf{negl}$$

Fig. 1. An informal explanation of malicious security for distributed samplers. Here, Gen is the algorithm for honestly generating the third party messages U_j and Sample is the algorithm that combines the messages into the derived CRS R. i is the honest user, t is the simulator's choice of which of the honest CRS samples $R_1, \ldots, R_q$ to use.

This brief description is obviously impossible, however. Indeed, a malicious adversary could be *rushing*: *after* seeing the honest party's message, it could generate several sets of malicious third party messages (but even generate them honestly), compute the derived CRSs, and then select the set of third party messages that give a CRS most advantageous to the adversary. This means it is impossible for the simulator to guarantee that any single provided honest CRS is used by the adversary. To capture this ability of rushing adversaries, the definition actually gives the simulator a polynomial number of honestly generated potential CRSs, and the simulator can then choose which one gets sent to the adversary.

The above described notion of security is *still* impossible, as shown by [AOS23]. One basic reason is the following: the simulator has to produce a message U_i, whose length is fixed by the protocol. However, the sequence of honest CRSs provided to the simulator can be arbitrary long, since an arbitrary polynomial-time adversary can generate arbitrarily many sets of third party messages, thereby allowing them to select from an arbitrary polynomial number of CRSs. This means there is no way for a single U_i to embed all of the CRSs. [AOS23] formalize an impossibility, and it seems rather robust, since although their results apply only to the UC model with dishonest majority, different security settings such as standalone security, superpolynomial simulation, honest majority, or having the protocol depend itself on a CRS do not seem to solve the problem. The positive results of [ASY22, AOS23] therefore employ a random oracle. This avoids the impossibility, since the simulator can now program the random oracle with the various CRSs, instead of programming them into U_i. However, it requires the full power of programming the random oracle, and it is unclear what kind of security this gives in the standard model.

Our First Notion: Hardness-Preserving Distributed Samplers. We now describe our new notions of security for distributed samplers. The first we describe is that of *hardness preserving*, which is given informally in Fig. 2. There are two main differences from the security notion described. First, only a single honest CRS is given to the simulator in the ideal world. This is necessary in the standard model, as there is no way to program an unbounded number of CRSs into a fixed length simulated message. Note that with this change we can no longer hope to force the derived CRS to be equal to the provided honest CRS, except possibly with inverse polynomial probability. This means an adversary can distinguish real from ideal in the majority of cases. So the second change is to relax indistinguishability to the following. We only require that if the adversary outputs 1 in the real world with non-negligible probability ϵ_1, then it also outputs 1 in the ideal world with non-negligible probability ϵ_2. But ϵ_1 and ϵ_2 do not need to be close, and ϵ_2 can be far lower than ϵ_1.

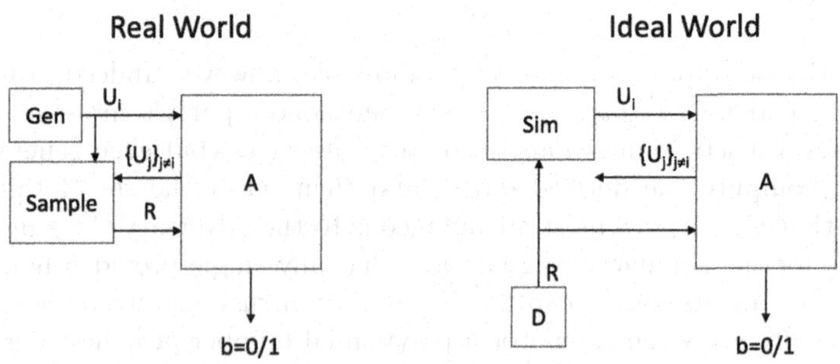

$$\Pr[b = 1|\text{Ideal World}] < \mathsf{negl} \Rightarrow \Pr[b = 1|\text{Real World}] < \mathsf{negl}$$

Fig. 2. An informal explanation of hardness-preserving security for distributed samplers. It is the same as Fig. 1, except that there is only a single honest CRS in the ideal world, and the relation between success probabilities in the two worlds is relaxed.

The obvious question is then: what kind of guarantees does such a relaxed definition provide? We show that hardness preserving distributed samplers are good for guaranteeing security for various *search* tasks. These are tasks where the adversary's goal is to output some value with non-negligible probability (as opposed to distinguishing tasks, where the goal is to output a value with probability non-negligibly larger than 1/2).

More precisely, we consider a general search game between a challenger and adversary, where at some step the challenger is provided with an honestly generated CRS, which it uses in its own internal logic but also sends to the adversary. We can compile such a game into one where the CRS is generated via distributed samplers, and the adversary controls all but one of the trusted third parties. A diagram of such a game and its compilation is given in Fig. 3. We show the following:

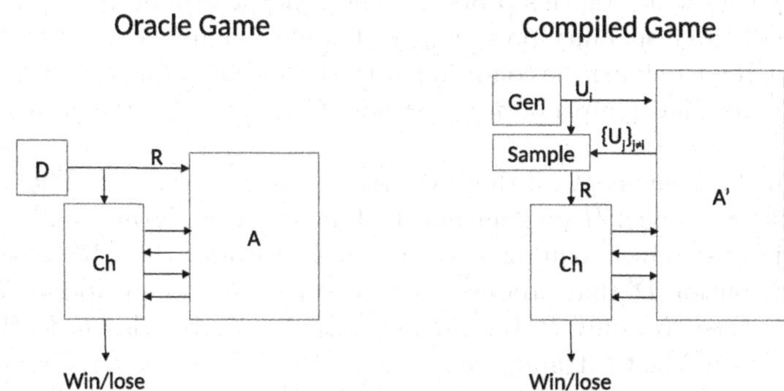

Fig. 3. Search games and their compilations. The figure on the left is a search game utilizing an honest CRS, while the figure on the right is the compiled game using a distributed sampler to generate the CRS.

Theorem 1 (informal). *If a distributed sampler is hardness-preserving and the search game is hard, then the compiled search game is also hard.*

Notice that there exists a non-negligible security loss between the original search game and the compiled version. Furthermore, the loss depends on the running time of the adversary. This is unavoidable: a rushing adversary can regenerate the corrupted party distributed sampler messages in its head many times, looking for an output that gives a higher chance of solving the search problem. The advantage will therefore degrade proportionally to the number of such trials, which is proportional to the running time.

Our second notion: indistinguishability-preserving distributed samplers. Hardness-preserving distributed samplers achieve a somewhat limited form of security against active adversaries. For starters, if the game is an indistinguishability game, the notion gives no guarantees. But a more subtle issue is the following. Consider a protocol like a NIZK with CRS. The definition of zero knowledge says that there exists a simulator which simulates both the CRS *and* the proof. Perhaps it generates the CRS such that it knows a certain trapdoor, which allows it to generate a proof without knowing a witness. When using a distributed sampler, we would like the ideal world to reflect this simulated CRS and proof. But this is not a simple matter of plugging in the existing simulated CRS into the simulator for the distributed sampler, as there is no way for the distributed sampler simulator to then use the CRS trapdoor to help generate the proof. In the language of protocols and functionalities, this means that for a protocol Π with CRS which implements a functionality $\mathcal{F}$, the compiled protocol Π' using the distributed sampler to generate the CRS might no longer implement $\mathcal{F}$.

The second distributed sampler notion we introduce, called *indistinguishability -preserving*, tries to tackle this problem. The concept is informally described in Fig. 4: an indistinguishability-preserving distributed sampler compiles any protocol Π with CRS satisfying the condition at the top of Fig. 4 for some functionality $\mathcal{F}$ and simulator Sim_Π, into a protocol without CRS satisfying the property at the bottom.

We focus for a moment on the property at the top of Fig. 4. The condition states that the protocol Π implements the functionality $\mathcal{F}$. However, it actually gives a strictly stronger requirement: in the ideal world, the CRS is simulated using a distribution $\mathcal{D}'$ that produces both a sample R and a trapdoor T. While the adversary receives only R, the simulator Sim_Π receives also T. In the NIZK example, $\mathcal{D}'$ would be the trapdoored CRS, and T is the trapdoor. An important point is that the simulated CRS is independent of any information known to the functionality. Not all protocols have this kind of simulation. For example, the HSS construction of [OSY21] satisfies the property: the CRS is a large RSA modulus distributed identically to the protocol and simulated before interacting with the functionality. On the other hand, imagine a protocol where the CRS consists of an RSA modulus N. Suppose that the protocol allows, e.g., generic MPC modulo N and N is chosen by the functionality (notice that the CRS is given by the functionality). If we use an indistinguishability-preserving distributed sampler to generate N, the compiled protocol will not implement the functionality anymore. This is because, in the simulation, we cannot ensure that the output of the distributed sampler is the modulus N chosen by the functionality.

Moving on to the bottom of Fig. 4, we observe that, in the ideal world, the sampling algorithm of the distributed sampler has been substituted with a new algorithm called $\mathsf{Trapdoor}$. The latter has the purpose of extracting the trapdoors from the outputs of the simulated distributed sampler. The resulting values are then given to Sim_Π. Observe that the property at the bottom implies that the compiled protocol implements $\mathcal{F}$.

Theorem 2 (informal). *If a distributed sampler is indistinguishability-preserving and the protocol Π implements the functionality $\mathcal{F}$ as in the top of Fig. 4, then the compiled protocol also implements $\mathcal{F}$.*

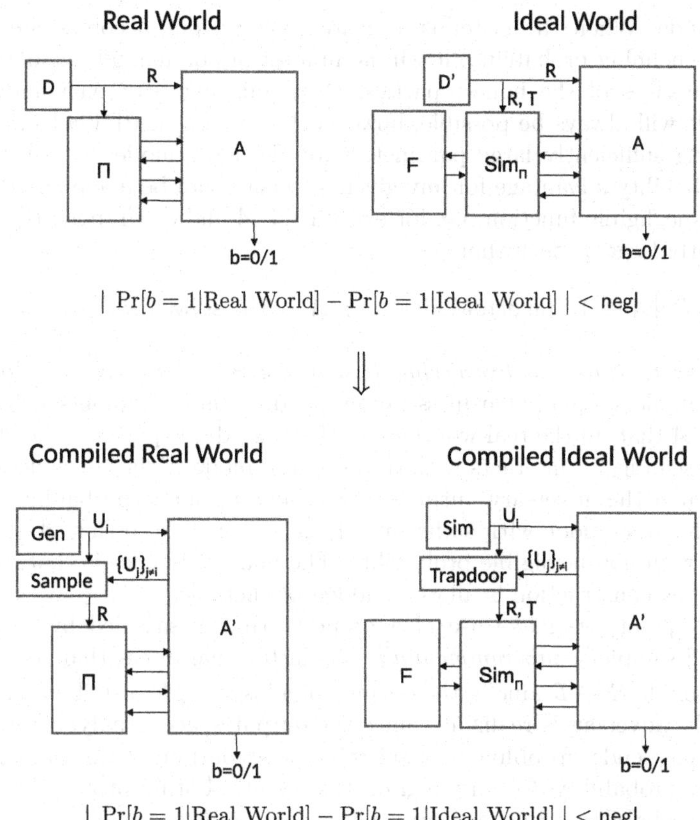

Fig. 4. An informal explanation of indistinguishability-preserving security for distributed samplers.

The definition of indistinguishability-preserving distributed sampler is actually more general than what we outlined here: it provides security guarantees even when the sample from $\mathcal{D}$ is not given as a CRS but as an "oracle sample" revealed halfway through the execution of the protocol. It is still possible to compile this kind of protocol using a distributed sampler: instead of executing it at the beginning, the parties will run it at a later stage. Sometimes, when the first round of the protocol Π is independent of the CRS, this fact allows us to compile Π without adding rounds of interaction. For more details, check Sect. 5 of the full version of this paper [AWZ23].

Lossy Distributed Samplers. In the paper, we introduce one last notion: *lossy distributed samplers.* This will be a convenient technical notion that will help us realize our notions of distributed samplers from above. Such a lossy sampler consists of two modes of operation: in addition to a standard mode, in which the output remains unpredictable as long as one party is honest, there exists a lossy mode. When the latter is activated, the output becomes predictable: with overwhelming probability, it will lie in a set of polynomial size determined by the messages of the honest parties. Distinguishing between standard and lossy mode will always be possible, however, for any given PPT adversary. But by choosing sufficiently large parameters for the lossy mode, we ask that the distinguishability advantage for any given adversary can be made an arbitrarily small non-negligible function, i.e. for every PPT $\mathcal{A}$ and $\delta = 1/\mathsf{poly}$, there exists a sufficiently large q[2] such that

$$\left|\Pr\left[\mathcal{A} \to 1 \middle| \mathsf{StandardMode}\right] - \Pr\left[\mathcal{A} \to 1 \middle| \mathsf{LossyMode}(q)\right]\right| \leq \delta.$$

From Lossy to Hardness-Preserving Distributed Samplers. We use lossy distributed samplers to build hardness-preserving distributed samplers. Consider an adversary $\mathcal{A}$ that, in the real-world game of the hardness-preserving distributed samplers (see Fig. 2), interacts with the standard mode of the construction. The idea is that if the adversary outputs 1 with non-negligible probability, we can activate the lossy mode with sufficiently large parameters so that $\mathcal{A}$ keeps outputting 1 with non-negligible probability. The main difference is that, now, the output of the construction is all of a sudden predictable.

At this point, we make use of a property that is satisfied by some lossy distributed samplers: *programmability.* The latter guarantees that we can hide an ideal sample $\hat{R} \xleftarrow{\$} \mathcal{D}$ among the outputs of a lossy-mode distributed samplers without the adversary's realizing. Since the output space is polynomial in size, the adversary ends up obliviously selecting $\hat{R}$ as output of the protocol with $p = 1/\mathsf{poly}$ probability. Conditioned on this event, $\mathcal{A}$ still outputs 1 with non-negligible probability ϵ. In conclusion, in the ideal world, the challenger just needs to send lossy-mode messages. The adversary will output 1 with probability at least $p \cdot \epsilon$.

Theorem 3 (Informal). *Any programmable, lossy distributed sampler is hardness-preserving.*

2.2 Building Lossy Distributed Samplers

We explain how to build programmable, lossy distributed samplers using, among other tools, indistinguishability obfuscation [GGH+13], multi-key FHE [AJJM20], extremely lossy functions (ELFs) [Zha16] and a new primitive called *almost everywhere extractable NIZKs.* We make extensive use of subexponentially secure primitives. The resulting lossy distributed sampler makes use of a short (polynomial in λ, but independent of $\mathcal{D}$), unstructured and reusable CRS (the construction is secure even if the CRS is reused in multiple concurrent instantiations of the protocol, potentially involving different subsets of parties). Our construction originates from the semi-honest distributed sampler of [ASY22]. We briefly recall it.

[2] q is a polynomial that upper bounds the size of the output space.

The encryption program. In [ASY22], a distributed sampler message consists of two obfuscated programs. Adapting the terminology to this paper, we call them the *encryption program* and the *decryption program.*

The encryption program of party P_i takes care of generating a multi-key FHE encryption of a random string s_i under a fresh key pk_i. The output of the construction will be obtained by adding the n random strings $s_1, \dots, s_n$ and feeding the result as randomness for $\mathcal{D}$, i.e. the output sample is $R := \mathcal{D}(\mathbb{1}^n; s_1 \oplus \cdots \oplus s_n)$. Observe that thanks to the homomorphic properties of multi-key FHE, given the encryptions of the random strings, everybody is able to derive an encryption of R[3]. The issue is that nobody is able to decrypt it: the output of the multi-key FHE evaluation is encrypted under a "joint key". In order to decrypt, the parties usually need to collaborate: each of them performs a partial decryption of the joint ciphertext and publishes the result. By pooling together the partial plaintexts, everybody can reconstruct the hidden message.

The decryption program. Usually, a multi-key FHE decryption requires interaction. In the distributed samplers of [ASY22], however, the decryption program takes care of everything without needing additional rounds of interaction.

Formally, the decryption program of party P_i takes as input the encryption programs of all the parties and evaluates them. After receiving the encryption of s_j for every $j \in [n]$, the program retrieves an encryption of the output R by applying homomorphic operations on the ciphertexts. Observe that all the decryption programs derive the same joint ciphertext C. The execution terminates by performing a partial decryption of C using the private counterpart of pk_i. The program outputs the resulting partial plaintext.

Observe that by evaluating all the decryption programs, the parties are able to retrieve all the partial decryptions of C. At that point, reconstructing R is immediate.

Counteracting the residual function attack. A common issue of all 1-round MPC protocols is that an adversary can rerun the protocol in its head many times changing a subset of the messages. The outputs of all these executions are correlated with the inputs of the honest parties. For particular functionalities, this could leak enough information to reconstruct the input of the honest parties.

In distributed samplers, there are no private inputs but we still need to be careful: we need to make sure that, in every distributed sampler execution, the encryption programs use independent looking random strings $s_1, \dots, s_n$. If that was not the case, the adversary might use the residual function attack to learn information about the randomness used in the main execution of the protocol.

In [ASY22], the authors ensure this by feeding the encryption program of each party with the hash of the encryption programs of the other players (notice that inputting the program themselves would not be possible for a matter of sizes). The encryption program generates the randomness for the multi-key FHE key

[3] The fact that the ciphertexts are encrypted under different keys does not constitute a problem.

EProg[K_i]

Hard-coded. The PPRF key K_i.
Input. A digest y.

1. $(s_i, r_i, r'_i) \leftarrow F(K_i, y)$
2. $(\mathsf{pk}_i, \mathsf{sk}_i) \leftarrow \mathsf{mkFHE.Gen}(1\!\!1^\lambda; r_i)$
3. $c_i \leftarrow \mathsf{mkFHE.Enc}(\mathsf{pk}_i, s_i; r'_i)$
4. Output (pk_i, c_i).

Fig. 5. A sketch of the unobfuscated encryption program of party P_i

DProg[$K_i, \mathsf{EP}_i, \sigma, (\mathsf{id}_j)_{j\neq i}$]

Hard-coded. The PPRF key K_i, the encryption program EP_i, the CRS for a NIZK σ, the identities of the other parties $(\mathsf{id}_j)_{j\neq i}$.
Input. Set of $n-1$ tuples $(\mathsf{EP}_j, \pi_j)_{j\neq i}$ where EP_j is the encryption program of party P_j and π_j is a NIZK proving its well-formedness.

1. $\forall j \neq i: \quad b_j \leftarrow \mathsf{NIZK.Verify}(\sigma, \mathsf{id}_j, \pi_j, \mathsf{EP}_j)$
2. If $\exists j \neq i$ such that $b_j = 0$, output $\bot$
3. $\forall j \in [n]: \quad y_j \leftarrow \mathsf{Hash}\big((\mathsf{EP}_l)_{l\neq j}\big)$
4. $\forall j \in [n]: \quad (\mathsf{pk}_j, c_j) \leftarrow \mathsf{EP}_j(y_j)$
5. $C \leftarrow \mathsf{mkFHE.Eval}\big(\mathcal{D}, c_1, \ldots, c_n\big)$
6. $(s_i, r_i, r'_i) \leftarrow F(K_i, y_i)$
7. $(\mathsf{pk}_i, \mathsf{sk}_i) \leftarrow \mathsf{mkFHE.Gen}(1\!\!1^\lambda; r_i)$
8. $d_i \leftarrow \mathsf{mkFHE.PartDec}(C, \mathsf{sk}_i)$
9. Output d_i

Fig. 6. A sketch of the unobfuscated decryption program of party P_i

pk_i and the string s_i by inputting the hash into a puncturable PRF. Observe that if any adversary reruns the distributed sampler in its head modifying any of the other messages, the hash fed in the encryption program changes. As a consequence, the program will use an independent looking s_i (and an independent looking multi-key FHE key pair).

In our lossy distributed sampler, the encryption program will remain the same as in [ASY22]. We sketch its code in Fig. 5.

Adding extractable NIZKs. The main change we bring to the construction is to add non-interactive zero knowledge (NIZK) proofs of the well-formedness of the encryption programs. These proofs will be inputted into the decryption programs. When any of the proofs do not verify, the decryption program will output $\bot$. We sketch their code in Fig. 6.

$\mathsf{EProg}_{\mathsf{Ls}}[K_i]$

Hard-coded. The PPRF key K_i.
Input. A digest y.

1. $(\eta_i, \eta'_i) \leftarrow F'(K_i, y)$
2. $(\phi, \mathsf{pk}_i, c_i) \leftarrow \mathsf{mkFHE.Sim}_1(1\!\!1^\lambda; \eta_i)$
3. Output (pk_i, c_i).

Fig. 7. A sketch of the unobfuscated encryption program for the lossy mode

In order to describe the lossy mode of the distributed sampler, we assume that the NIZK is *extractable*, which means there is a special trapdoor that allows for extracting from any proof the witness used to generate the proof. We defer the discussion of the exact properties needed until later in this overview.

The lossy mode of the distributed sampler tweaks the programs of one of the honest parties as follows. The encryption program will generate simulated public keys and ciphertexts. The decryption program, instead of verifying the NIZKs, will extract the witnesses from them using the extraction property of the NIZK. From the latter, it will derive the randomness used to generate the multi-keys FHE keys and ciphertexts of the other players. At that point, similarly to [HIJ+17], it simulates the partial decryption instead of directly performing it. We recall that the simulator for the partial decryption takes as input a targeted plaintext R' [AJJM20]. Such value might differ for the actual message hidden in the joint ciphertext C, however, the output of the decryption is still guaranteed to be R'.

Decreasing the Size of the Output Space Using an ELF. In the lossy mode, the output of the protocol is decided by the party that sends the lossy-mode programs (those that simulate the multi-key FHE operations). How can we restrict the output space to a set of polynomial size without the adversary's immediate detecting the small output space? After all, the adversary could keep generating outputs, hoping to find a collision. After only a polynomial number of outputs, the adversary would expect to find such a collision in the lossy mode.

To rectify this issue, we have the size of the lossy output space be a polynomial that grows with the adversary's run time and success probability, making sure it is a sufficiently large polynomial that the adversary cannot detect it in the time give.

At a lower level, we use extremely lossy functions (ELFs) [Zha16]. These are randomized algorithms generating deterministic functions with large domain. The primitive has two modes of operations: injective mode and lossy mode. When the first mode is activated, the function is injective. In the other case, the image of the function has size smaller than q, where q is a polynomial parameterizing the lossy mode. The two modes will be always distinguishable with non-negligible advantage. ELFs guarantee that, for any adversary $\mathcal{A}$ and

$\mathsf{DProg}_{\mathsf{Ls}}[K_i, \mathsf{EP}_i, \sigma, (\tau_e^j)_{j\neq i}, K, f]$

Hard-coded. The PPRF key K_i, the encryption program EP_i, the CRS for the almost everywhere extractable NIZK σ, the extraction trapdoors $(\tau_e^j)_{j\neq i}$, a PPRF key K, an ELF f.
Input. Set of $n-1$ tuples $(\mathsf{EP}_j, \pi_j)_{j\neq i}$ where EP_j is the encryption program of party P_j and π_j is an almost everywhere extractable NIZK proving its well-formedness.

1. $\forall j \neq i: \quad K_j \leftarrow \mathsf{NIZK.Extract}(\tau_e^j, \pi_j, \mathsf{EP}_j)$
2. If $\exists j \neq i$ such that $K_j = \bot$, output $\bot$
3. $\forall j \in [n]: \quad y_j \leftarrow \mathsf{Hash}\big((\mathsf{EP}_l)_{l\neq j}\big)$
4. $\forall j \neq i: \quad (s_j, r_j, r_j') \leftarrow F(K_j, y_j)$
5. $z \leftarrow f(\mathsf{EP}_1, \ldots, \mathsf{EP}_n)$
6. $s \leftarrow F(K, z)$
7. $R' \leftarrow \mathcal{D}(1\!\!1^\lambda;\ s)$
8. $(\eta_i, \eta_i') \leftarrow F'(K_i, y_i)$
9. $(\phi, \mathsf{pk}_i, c_i) \leftarrow \mathsf{mkFHE.Sim}_1(1\!\!1^\lambda;\ \eta_i)$
10. $d_i \leftarrow \mathsf{mkFHE.Sim}_2\Big(\phi, \mathcal{D}, R', (s_j, r_j, r_j')_{j\neq i};\ \eta_i'\Big)$
11. Output d_i

Fig. 8. A sketch of the unobfuscated decryption program for the lossy mode

inverse-polynomial δ, by choosing a sufficiently large polynomial q, it is possible to make the distinguishability advantage between the injective mode and the lossy mode smaller than δ.

In our construction, we generate the value R' input in the partial decryption simulator by applying an ELF on the concatenation of the encryption programs of the n parties. The result is then fed in a puncturable PRF. Its output is used as randomness for $\mathcal{D}(1\!\!1^\lambda)$. In this way, when the ELF has a small image, the distributed sampler will have a small output space. We sketch the code of the lossy-mode programs in Fig. 7 and Fig. 8.

Programmability. It is easy to see that our candidate distributed sampler is programmable: in order to hide an ideal sample $\hat{R}$ in the output space, we can just pick a random value $\hat{z}$ in the image of the ELF f and input $\hat{R}$ into the partial decryption simulator whenever $f(\mathsf{EP}_1, \ldots, \mathsf{EP}_n) = \hat{z}$. By the security of puncturable PRFs, the changes cannot be detected by the adversary. Furthermore, if the ELF satisfies an additional property called *regularity* [Zha16], it is guaranteed that the event $f(\mathsf{EP}_1, \ldots, \mathsf{EP}_n) = \hat{z}$ occurs with inverse-polynomial probability.

2.3 Security Proof Challenge 1: Simultaneous Extraction and Statistical Soundness

At this point, we can try to prove the security of the candidate lossy distributed sampler. However, there are some challenges that need to be overcome.

The first challenge is the following. In the lossy mode, we need to be able to extract witnesses from valid proofs. However, zero knowledge implies that there are false proofs that contain no witnesses. The existence of these false proofs presents a problem for proving security using indistinguishability obfuscation.

More generally, consider the following general setup. There is a program C_0 receiving n values $x_1, \dots, x_n$ as inputs from n parties along with n NIZKs proving their validity. The program C_0 outputs $\bot$ whenever any of the NIZKs does not verify. In the other cases, it outputs $C(x_1, \dots, x_n)$ where C is some circuit. There also a second program C_1 that, instead of verifying the NIZKs, it tries to extract the witnesses hidden in them (C_1 outputs $\bot$ if the extraction of any witness fails). Then it uses the extracted witnesses to attempt to simulate the same behavior as C_0. The goal is to have obfuscations of C_0 and C_1 be indistinguishable.

The Problem of Differing Inputs. The main issue is that C_0 and C_1 have differing inputs: the zero-knowledge property of the NIZKs guarantees the existence of proofs for which the witness cannot be extracted despite verification succeeds. On these inputs, the behavior of C_0 and C_1 can be easily told apart. In order to apply indistinguishability obfuscation, however, we need C_0 and C_1 to be equivalent programs.

Fortunately, finding these differing inputs is hard. Therefore the natural tool to achieve indistinguishability between obfuscations of C_0 and C_1 would be differing-input obfuscation [BGI+01]. The existence of such primitive is, however, controversial due to some results suggesting its impossibility [GGHW14,BSW16]. In [HIJ+17], Halevi *et al.* faced a problem similar to ours. They solved it by designing NIZKs that can be simulated only for statements hidden in the CRS. Since there is a small number of problematic statements, it is easy to take care of the corresponding executions of C_0 and C_1 using just indistinguishability obfuscation. The solution of Halevi *et al.*, however, compromises the reusability of the CRS and makes it grow with the size of the statements. Since we want to keep the CRS as simple as possible, we follow a different approach.

Indistinguishability Obfuscation is Enough. We rely solely on indistinguishability obfuscation. In [BCP14], Boyle, Chung and Pass showed that, if two programs have a polynomial number of differing inputs and finding any of them is hard, then iO is enough to hide which program was obfuscated. In our application, the number of differing inputs is of course superpolynomial, however, we notice that the result of [BCP14] can be generalized: assume that all differing inputs have a prefix in a set S. If finding an element in S is hard even for adversaries running in time $\mathsf{poly}(\lambda, |S|)$, subexponentially secure iO is sufficient to hide which program was obfuscated.

To leverage this observation, we introduce the notion of *almost everywhere extractable NIZKs*. Such NIZKs are designed so that the prefix of all the valid proofs for which the witness cannot be extracted lies in a set S. Finding an element in S is hard even for adversaries running in time $\mathsf{poly}(\lambda, |S|)$ that are provided with the extraction trapdoor. By using almost everywhere extractable NIZKs together with the generalization of [BCP14], we can show that P_0 and P_1 are hard to distinguish despite the existence of differing-inputs. We discuss building such NIZKs later in this overview.

2.4 Security Proof Challenge 2: More Differing Inputs

Decreasing the Entropy of the Encryption Programs. At this point, we can try to prove the security of the candidate lossy distributed sampler. The strategy is the following: using the properties of the almost everywhere extractable NIZKs followed by an input-by-input iO argument, we show that, if the ELF is in injective mode, the lossy-mode programs are indistinguishable from the usual ones. By switching to a lossy ELF, we can then argue that the distinguishability advantage between the modes of the distributed sampler can be made an arbitrarily small inverse-polynomial function.

There is only one problem that hinders this plan: beyond the differing-inputs caused by the NIZK extraction (which are taken care by the almost everywhere extractable NIZKs), there exist other inputs for which the lossy-mode programs have a clearly distinguishable behaviour. Consider indeed two tuples of encryption programs $(\mathsf{EP}_j)_{j \neq i}$ and $(\mathsf{EP}'_j)_{j \neq i}$ having colliding hashes. When these tuples are used along with normal programs for party P_i, the outputs of the protocol will be correlated: in both executions, the programs of P_i use the same random string s_i (see how s_i is generated in Fig. 5). If instead P_i sent lossy-mode programs, the outputs will look independent of each other (see how $\hat{R}$ is generated in Fig. 8).

Even if these problematic inputs are hard to find, this time we do not use the trick by Boyle, Chung and Pass [BCP14]. To work around the issue, we decrease the entropy of the encryption programs: we require that they are generated using the randomness produced by a PRG with a small λ-bit seed. The almost everywhere extractable NIZKs will guarantee that the adversary does not break this rule. On the other hand, the lossy-mode programs will use full-entropy randomness. In this way, the total number of valid encryption programs for the corrupted parties becomes smaller than $(2^\lambda)^{n-1}$. By adopting a subexponentially collision-resistant hash function, we can make sure that, with overwhelming probability, there exist no collisions among these $(2^\lambda)^{n-1}$ elements. Moreover, the digests will still be small enough to fit into the encryption programs.

This technique solves also circular dependencies between subexponentially secure primitives: the input-by-input iO argument requires us to work with a number of hybrids that is proportional to the number of valid encryption programs. In each of these hybrids, we need to rely on the security of multi-key FHE. In order for the proof to go through, the size of the multi-key FHE keys therefore needs to increase logarithmically with the number of hybrids. If we used full-entropy encryption programs, the size of the keys would be so large that they would not even fit in the encryption programs anymore. By forcing valid encryption programs to have low entropy, we can hybrid over only the valid programs instead of all possible encryption programs, thereby eliminating the circular dependency. The properties of the NIZK guarantee not only that the adversary cannot find non-valid encryption programs, but that they do not even exist.

With these challenges overcome, we prove the following:

Theorem 4 (Informal). *Assuming almost everywhere extractable NIZKs, subexponential iO, subexponential multi-key FHE, subexponentially collision-resistant hash functions and regular extremely lossy functions, the distributed sampler sketched above is lossy and programmable.*

2.5 Building Indistinguishability-Preserving Distributed Samplers

A lossy distributed sampler is not necessarily indistinguishability-preserving. We show, however, that the construction described above actually is:

Theorem 5 (Informal). *Assuming almost everywhere extractable NIZKs, subexponential iO, subexponential multi-key FHE, subexponentially collision-resistant hash functions and regular extremely lossy functions, the distributed sampler sketched above is indistinguishability-preserving.*

We start by considering a protocol Π that relies on a CRS sampled from the distribution $\mathcal{D}$. We suppose that Π implements a functionality $\mathcal{F}$ as described at the top of Fig. 4. In particular, in the ideal world, the CRS is simulated using a distribution $\mathcal{D}'$ that outputs a trapdoor T along with the sample R.

A sketch of the proof. We use a hybrid argument beginning from the compilation of the real world using the standard mode of our lossy distributed sampler and ending with the compilation of the ideal world using a simulated mode (see the bottom of Fig. 4). We prove that the compiled worlds are computationally indistinguishable.

As a first step, we switch the distributed sampler to lossy mode. This already introduces some non-negligible distinguishability advantage in the proof, we will explain later why this does not constitute a problem. On the other hand, the lossy mode allows us to move to a sample space of polynomial size.

Next, we gradually change the distribution of the outputs of the distributed sampler, switching from $\mathcal{D}$ to $\mathcal{D}'$. The technique here is rather simple: we just rely on the security of puncturable PRFs similarly to what we did to argue programmability. Along the way, we gradually switch from the execution of Π, to the execution of the simulator Sim_Π. In particular, there will some subhybrids in which some of the distributed sampler outputs come from $\mathcal{D}$ and some from $\mathcal{D}'$. We run Sim_Π only when the adversary chooses an execution where the sample comes from $\mathcal{D}'$. In these cases, we can retrieve the trapdoor by using the puncturable PRF key K and the ELF hidden in the lossy-mode programs (see Fig. 8).

Observe that, since the sample space is small, switching from $\mathcal{D}$ to $\mathcal{D}'$ needs only a polynomial number of subhybrids. As a consequence, we do not need that $\mathcal{D}$ and $\mathcal{D}'$ are subexponentially indistinguishable, nor that Π implements $\mathcal{F}$ with subexponential security.

In the last hybrid, we switch the ELF in the lossy-mode programs back to injective mode. Once again, the operation introduces a non-negligible distinguishability advantage. However, it allows us to move to a large sample space where all the elements are trapdoored.

The Compiled Games are Indistinguishable. We finally argue why the non-negligible advantage introduced in the first and the last hybrid does not constitute a problem: by contradiction, suppose that there exists an adversary $\mathcal{A}$ that distinguishes between the initial and the final stage with non-negligible advantage ϵ. By choosing sufficiently large parameters for the lossy mode of the ELF (which is used only in the intermediate hybrids, but not in the real and the ideal world), we can ensure that the advantage of $\mathcal{A}$ in the first and the last steps of the proof are both bounded by $\epsilon/4$. The total advantage of $\mathcal{A}$ against the compiled games would therefore be strictly smaller than ϵ, reaching a contradiction.

On the Reusability of the CRS of Our Distributed Samplers. It is easy to see that the CRS of a hardness-preserving distributed sampler is always reusable across multiple concurrent executions of the protocol. Indeed, the hardness of the search problem is not affected by the concurrent executions as the latter are always simulatable. On the other hand, the security of an indistinguishability-preserving distributed sampler can be affected by the concurrent executions. The construction presented in this paper, however, does not suffer from this issue.

2.6 Building Almost Everywhere Extractable NIZKs

We obtain almost everywhere extractable NIZKs in the CRS model using perfectly sound NIWIs, subexponentially secure injective one-way functions, perfectly binding commitments and perfectly correct identity-based encryption (IBE).

Why Consider Distributed Samplers that Need a CRS? It may seem strange to have a distributed sampler — whose purpose is to generate a CRS — in turn rely on a CRS. What is the advantage of generating a CRS using a distributed sampler if the latter still needs a CRS? There are several reasons why a distributed sampler using a CRS can be useful: the CRS of the distributed sampler might be reused multiple times, allowing the production of many samples. The CRS of the distributed sampler protocol can also be simple to generate, perhaps because it is short or because it is unstructured (i.e. a uniform string of bits).

Our Construction. The CRS consists of an IBE master public key and a one-way function challenge v. The proofs are associated to the identity of the party that issues them. Each of them consists of a commitment c_0, an IBE encryption of the witness c_1 under the party's identity and a NIWI guaranteeing that either

c_1 contains the witness or c_0 contains the preimage of v. In order to extract the witness, it is sufficient to decrypt c_1.

Observe that, in all valid proofs for which extraction fails, the prefix is a commitment to the preimage of v. Since the one-way function is injective, the number of such prefixes depends only on the size of the randomness of the commitment scheme. As the one-way function is subexponentially secure, we can make v hard to invert even for $\mathsf{poly}(\lambda, |S|)$-time adversaries that have enough power to brute-force the commitment to retrieve the hidden value. This ensures the property we need.

Why to Use Identity-Based Encryption? In many applications of almost everywhere extractable NIZKs, we would like to argue that the programs C_0 and C_1 are indistinguishable even if we simulate the NIZKs of the honest parties (clearly, in these situations, C_1 will try to extract the witnesses only from the NIZKs of the corrupted players). The issue is that the NIZK described in the previous paragraph is not simulation-almost everywhere extractable, i.e. leaking simulated proofs may allow distinguishing between C_0 and C_1. On the other hand, disclosing C_1 might compromise the zero-knowledge property of the NIZKs due to the extraction trapdoor hidden into it.

Identity-based encryption allows us to work around the problem: to extract the witness from a NIZK proven under the identity id, we do not need the IBE master secret key, but just the private key associated to id. In other words, if we equip C_1 only with the decryption keys associated to the identities of the corrupted players, we are still able to simulate the proofs of the honest parties. The identities associated with the NIZKs guarantee that no corrupted party can publish one of the simulated proofs as it was its own.

Note that some IBE schemes such as [BF01] have uniformly random public keys. If we also use a one-way *permutation* to generate v, then the CRS is actually uniformly random. As such, our resulting distributed samplers will take a uniformly random CRS, and can be used to generate any arbitrarily structured CRS.

Theorem 6 (Informal). *Assuming perfectly correct IBE, perfectly binding non-interactive commitments, perfectly sound NIWIs and subexponential OWFs, the NIZK sketched above is almost everywhere extractable.*

2.7 CRS-less NIZKs in the Uniform Setting

All the distributed samplers we described so far make use of a CRS. The latter, needed by the NIZKs in the construction, is short, reusable and unstructured, however, is it possible to completely remove it? For indistinguishability-preserving distributed samplers, this is too much to hope for: if that was not the case, we would obtain a 3-round OT protocol with active security by compiling any 2-round OT protocol with CRS such as [PVW08]. It is known that active OT requires at least 4 rounds [HV16]. We show, however, that, if we restrict to security against uniform adversaries, we can remove the CRS from all our primitives. We obtain this by constructing CRS-less NIZKs that can be plugged in our distributed samplers.

NIZKs Against Uniform Adversaries. The fact that NIZKs do not need CRSs if we restrict to security against uniform adversaries has been known for almost two decades: the fact was proven by Barak and Pass in [BP04] by building a CRS-less NIZK in the stand-alone model. In [BL18b], Bitansky and Lin studied a related question. They designed CRS-less NIZKs with a weak security guarantee against non-uniform adversaries: the number of false statements that can be proven is proportional to the non-uniformity of the adversary. Although this notion does not imply full soundness against uniform adversaries, it is easy to see that their constructions achieve the result. In this way, they indirectly obtain a CRS-less NIZK satisfying a weak form of simulation-soundness: a uniform adversary cannot generate proofs for false statements even if it has oracle access to the NIZK simulator that can be queried only with true statements (in the standard definition of simulation soundness, the simulator can be queried even with false statements).

Beyond these works, the topic remains rather unexplored. In this paper, we show how to construct CRS-less NIZKs achieving full simulation-soundness, simulation extractability and almost-everywhere extractability against uniform adversaries. All our constructions rely on the same trick: in order to simulate a proof, we need to use a trapdoor. Such trapdoor will be infeasible to compute for every uniform adversary but not for the simulator as it will be non-uniform.

Uniform-DDH and Uniform-LWE. We start by introducing natural variations of the DDH and LWE assumptions that we believe to hold against uniform adversaries.

Consider a uniform deterministic algorithm DDHGen that outputs the description of a cyclic group $\mathbb{G}$ along with two elements $g, h \in \mathbb{G}$ such that no uniform adversary can find the value α such that $h = g^{\alpha}$. A heuristic instantiation of this algorithm is to use a SHA hash function, or the digits of π, to generate g and h. The uniform-DDH assumption states that no uniform adversary can distinguish between pairs (g^r, h^r) and pairs (g^r, h^s) where r and s are uniformly random elements. Clearly, the assumption cannot hold against non-uniform adversaries: a non-uniform adversary can receive α as part of its non-uniform advice, at that point, distinguishing is trivial. Even uniform quantum adversaries can trivially distinguish by recovering α using Shor's algorithm. We however believe that it is possible to instantiate the assumption so that all uniform, classical PPT adversaries have subexponentially small advantage.

The uniform-LWE assumption follows a similar blueprint: we use a uniform deterministic algorithm LWEGen to generate the matrix $A \in \mathbb{Z}_q^{m\times n}$ describing a lattice. We then assume that no uniform PPT adversary can distinguish $A^{\intercal}\cdot s+x$ (where s is uniform in $\mathbb{Z}_q^n$ and x is a short vector in $\mathbb{Z}_q^m$) from a random element in $\mathbb{Z}_q^m$. Once again, we cannot hope to achieve security against non-uniform adversaries: if they receive a small vector u such that $A \cdot u = 0$ as part of their non-uniform advice, they can easily break the assumption. We however believe that every uniform, classical or quantum PPT adversary has a subexponentially small advantage.

The First Simulation-Sound NIZKs. We obtain simulation-sound NIZKs without CRS using two different approaches. We now describe the first one.

Challengeless One-Way Functions. The first NIZK makes use of challengeless one-way functions (COWFs): a one-way function in which the challenge is deterministically generated by a uniform algorithm. The guarantee is that no uniform PPT adversary can find a preimage of the challenge.

We actually need two COWFs that are *independently hard*: finding preimages for any of them remains hard even when we are given a preimage for the other one. Uniform-DDH and uniform-LWE easily give a pair of independently hard one-way functions: thanks to the subexponential security of the primitive, we can make sure that, for classical adversaries, breaking uniform-DDH is strictly harder than uniform-LWE (this is achieved by making an appropriate choice of the parameters of the assumptions). On the other hand, in a post-quantum world, uniform-DDH is broken, while uniform-LWE retains its security. If breaking any of the challengeless one-way functions allows an adversary to break the other one, one of these two facts would be contradicted.

The First Approach. The construction follows the blueprint of [BP04]. The proof consists of two commitments c_0 and c_1 along with a signature and a CRS-less NIWI [BOV03, GOS06a, GOS06b]. The NIZKs prove that either the statement lies in the language or one of the commitments hides a preimage for one of the independently hard challengeless one-way functions COWF_0 and COWF_1. These preimages will be used as trapdoors.

In order to achieve simulation-soundness, we need to ensure that the proof is non-malleable. We therefore generate c_0 and c_1 using a non-interactive CCA commitment without CRS [KS17, LPS17, BL18b, KK19, GKLW21]: each commitment is associated with a tag. The primitive guarantees that, given a commitment, no adversary can derive a commitment to a correlated value under a different tag. In our NIZK, similarly to [GO07], the tag will be a one-time signature verification key. Such key will be used to sign the proof. This ensures that, in order to produce a NIZK for a false statement, the adversary cannot reuse the commitments in the simulated proofs: it needs to at least change the tag (otherwise, it would need to forge a signature). The CCA security of the commitments guarantees the hardness of this task. Therefore, if the adversary manages to prove a false statement is because it discovered one of the trapdoors.

Why do We Need Two Challengeless One-Way Functions? The reason is that we need to argue that the NIWIs in the simulated proofs leak no information about the trapdoors. When the statement for a simulated proof lies in the language, it is guaranteed that the NIWI does not leak the trapdoor. If that was not the case, by witness indistinguishability, the trapdoor would have been leaked even if the NIWI was generated using the witness for our statement. This contradicts the fact that the trapdoor is hard to compute. What instead if the statement does not lie in the language? In this case, the NIWI does not allow us to tell which trapdoor was used for its generation, however, it might leak some generic information about them, e.g. the minimal trapdoor according to the lexicographical order.

Using two independently hard, challengeless one-way function, we avoid this problem: by the independent hardness, if we use the COWF_0 trapdoors for the simulated proofs, the NIWIs cannot leak any COWF_1 trapdoor and vice-versa. By witness indistinguishability, we conclude that the NIWIs do not leak any of the trapdoors.

Theorem 7 (Informal). *Assuming subexponential independently secure COWFs, non-interactive CCA-commitments without CRS, subexponential CRS-less NIWIs and strong one-time signatures, the CRS-less NIZK sketched above is simulation-sound against uniform adversaries.*

The Second Simulation-Sound NIZK. We describe the second approach to build simulation-sound NIZKs without CRS.

Labelled, Challengeless One-Way Functions (LOWF). Our second simulation-sound NIZK makes instead use of *labelled, challengeless one-way functions* CLOWF: on input any label id, a uniform algorithm deterministically generates a one-way function challenge. The primitive guarantees that no uniform PPT adversary can invert any challenge even given the preimages associated with some of the other labels. A heuristic instantiation of this primitive can use a SHA hash function to generate the verification key for a deterministic signature scheme. In this case, the preimage associated with a label id consists of a signature on id.

The Second Approach. Building simulation-sound NIZKs with the second approach is perhaps even easier: each proof consists of a commitment c, a CRS-less NIWI, a signature and the relative verification key vk. The NIWI is used to prove that either the statement belongs to the language or c hides a preimage for CLOWF where the label is vk. Such preimage acts as a trapdoor.

We use a signature over the whole proof to ensure that, if the adversary manages to prove a false statement, it uses a fresh verification key (otherwise, it would have succeeded in forging a signature). That means that the adversary needs to find a preimage relative to a fresh label of CLOWF. The trapdoors used in the simulated proof do not help in this task. We can therefore achieve simulation-soundness even with malleable commitments.

Theorem 8 (Informal). *Assuming subexponential LOWF, perfectly binding non-interactive commitments, CRS-less NIWIs and strong one-time signatures, the CRS-less NIZK sketched above is simulation-sound against uniform adversaries.*

CRS-less Simulation-Extractable NIZK. In order to build simulation-extractable NIZKs, we introduce CRS-less non-interactive extractable commitment schemes. Observe that the primitive can exist only if we restrict to security against uniform adversaries. We build two schemes. The first one is based on uniform-DDH, the second one on uniform-LWE. A commitment consists of an encryption of the value using the public keys deterministically produced by either DDHGen or LWEGen. In the first case, we use ElGamal, in the second case, we use dual-LWE. To extract the value, it is sufficient to perform a decryption (the extractor will be a non-uniform algorithm). The operation is however infeasible for the adversary as the secret key is hard to compute in uniform polynomial-time.

In order to obtain a simulation-extractable NIZK, we simply generate an extractable commitment c to the witness for the statement we want to prove. We then use a simulation-sound NIZK to prove that c is indeed what we claim it to be.

Theorem 9 (Informal). *Assuming CRS-less simulation-sound NIZKs and subexponential CRS-less non-interactive extractable commitments, the CRS-less NIZK sketched above is simulation-extractable against uniform adversaries.*

CRS-less Almost Everywhere Extractable NIZK. We finally present a CRS-less almost everywhere extractable NIZK with security against uniform adversaries. Differently from the construction described in Sect. 2.2, this NIZK will use a single extraction trapdoor for every prover's identity. On the other hand, the scheme will remain almost everywhere extractable even if we provide oracle access to the zero-knowledge simulator (we call the property *simulation-almost everywhere extractability*). This ensures that the obfuscated programs P_0 and P_1 remain indistinguishable even if the proofs of the honest parties are simulated (we recall that P_0 is a program that verifies the NIZKs proving the well-formedness of its inputs, while P_1 instead tries to extract the witnesses from them).

Independently Secure Labelled One-Way Functions and Extractable Commitments. The construction makes use of a labelled challengeless one-way function CLOWF and a non-interactive extractable commitment. The two primitives need to be independently secure: they need to retain their security properties even when we leak the other primitive's trapdoor. We can for instance ensure this using the same trick we adopted for simulation-sound NIZKs: we use a post-quantum extractable commitment (which can be obtained from uniform-LWE) and a quantumly-broken labelled, challengeless one-way function (heuristically, we can obtain it from any DLOG-based deterministic signature).

The reason why we need independently secure primitives is that almost everywhere extractability always requires that the simulation trapdoor (i.e. the trapdoor for CLOWF) is hard to compute in uniform polynomial time even if we leak the extraction trapdoor (i.e. the trapdoor for the extractable commitment). On the other hand, in our construction, the proof of zero-knowledge would require the symmetric relation. Independent security allows us to satisfy both conditions simultaneously.

The Simulation-Almost Everywhere Extractable NIZK Without CRS. A proof consists of two commitments c_0 and c_1, where c_1 is extractable, along with a CRS-less NIWI. The latter proves that either c_1 hides a witness for the statement we want to prove or c_0 hides a preimage for CLOWF where the label is the identity of the prover. In all the proofs where extraction fails, c_0 will therefore satisfy this second condition.

We select CLOWF so that the preimage for any given label is unique. In this way, the number of prefixes of problematic NIZKs for a given prover identity depends only on the size of the randomness of the commitment scheme. Since CLOWF is subexponentially secure, we can ensure that finding the right CLOWF preimage is infeasible even for $\mathsf{poly}(\lambda, |S|)$-time adversaries ($S$ denotes the set of problematic prefixes) that have enough computational power to recover the value hidden in c_0. Finding elements in S is therefore hard even for $\mathsf{poly}(\lambda, |S|)$-time algorithms. Learning simulated proofs under other provers' indentities does not help the adversary in the task.

Theorem 10 (Informal). *Assume the existence of a subexponential injective LOWF and a CRS-less non-interactive extractable commitment that are independently secure. Assume perfectly binding non-interactive commitments and CRS-less NIWIs. Then, the CRS-less NIZK sketched above is simulation-almost everywhere extractable against uniform adversaries.*

Acknowledgements. Damiano Abram thanks *Speedy's Tacos* for their delicious burritos and quesadillas. He also thanks the Aarhus Crypto Group and the people at NTT Research for being amazing humans (independently of their success in research). The work of Damiano Abram was carried out during an internship funded by NTT Research.

References

[AJJM20] Ananth, P., Jain, A., Jin, Z., Malavolta, G.: Multi-key fully-homomorphic encryption in the plain model. In: Pass, R., Pietrzak, K. (eds.) TCC 2020. Part I, volume 12550 of LNCS, pp. 28–57. Springer, Heidelberg (2020)

[AOS23] Abram, D., Obremski, M., Scholl, P.: On the (Im)possibility of Distributed Samplers: Lower Bounds and Party-Dynamic Constructions. Cryptology ePrint Archive, 2023/863 (2023)

[ASY22] Abram, D., Scholl, P., Yakoubov, S.: Distributed (Correlation) samplers: how to remove a trusted dealer in one round. In: Dunkelman, O., Dziembowski, S. (eds) Advances in Cryptology–EUROCRYPT 2022. EUROCRYPT 2022. LNCS, vol. 13275, pp. 790–820. Springer, Cham (2022). https://doi.org/10.1007/978-3-031-06944-4_27

[AWZ23] Abram, D., Waters, B., Zhandry, M.: Security-Preserving Distributed Samplers: How to Generate any CRS in One Round without Random Oracles. Cryptology ePrint Archive, 2023/860, 2023

[BCP14] Boyle, E., Chung, K.-M., Pass, R.: On extractability obfuscation. In: Lindell, Y. (ed.) TCC 2014. LNCS, vol. 8349, pp. 52–73. Springer, Heidelberg (2014)

[BF01] Boneh, D., Franklin, M.K.: Identity-based encryption from the Weil pairing. In: Kilian, J. (ed.) CRYPTO 2001. LNCS, vol. 2139, pp. 213–229. Springer, Heidelberg (2001)

[BGI+01] Barak, B., Goldreich, O., Impagliazzo, R., Rudich, S., Sahai, A., Vadhan, S.P., Yang, K.: On the (im)possibility of obfuscating programs. In: Kilian, J. (ed.) CRYPTO 2001. LNCS, vol. 2139, pp. 1–18. Springer, Heidelberg (2001)

[BL18a] Benhamouda, F., Lin, H.: k-Round Multiparty Computation from k-Round Oblivious Transfer via Garbled Interactive Circuits. In: Nielsen, J.B., Rijmen, V. (eds.) EUROCRYPT 2018. LNCS, vol. 10821, pp. 500–532. Springer, Cham (2018). https://doi.org/10.1007/978-3-319-78375-8_17

[BL18b] Bitansky, N., Lin, H.: One-message zero knowledge and non-malleable commitments. In: Beimel, A., Dziembowski, S. (eds.) TCC 2018. Part I, volume 11239 of LNCS, pp. 209–234. Springer, Heidelberg (2018)

[BOV03] Barak, B.: Shien Jin Ong, and Salil P. Vadhan. Derandomization in cryptography. In: Boneh, D. (ed.) CRYPTO 2003. LNCS, vol. 2729, pp. 299–315. Springer, Heidelberg (2003)

[BP04] Barak, B., Pass, R.: On the possibility of one-message weak zero-knowledge. In: Naor, M. (ed.) TCC 2004. LNCS, vol. 2951, pp. 121–132. Springer, Heidelberg (2004)

[BSW16] Bellare, M., Stepanovs, I., Waters, B.: New negative results on differing-inputs obfuscation. In: Fischlin, M., Coron, J.-S. (eds.) EUROCRYPT 2016. Part II, volume 9666 of LNCS, pp. 792–821. Springer, Heidelberg (2016)

[GGH+13] Garg, S., Gentry, C., Halevi, S., Raykova, M., Sahai, A., Waters, B.: Candidate indistinguishability obfuscation and functional encryption for all circuits. In: 54th FOCS, pp. 40–49. IEEE Computer Society Press, October 2013

[GGHW14] Garg, S., Gentry, C., Halevi, S., Wichs, D.: On the implausibility of differing-inputs obfuscation and extractable witness encryption with auxiliary input. In: Garay, J.A., Gennaro, R. (eds.) CRYPTO 2014. Part I, volume 8616 of LNCS, pp. 518–535. Springer, Heidelberg (2014)

[GKLW21] Garg, R., Khurana, D., George, L., Waters, B.: Black-box non-interactive non-malleable commitments. In: Canteaut, A., Standaert, F.-X. (eds.) EUROCRYPT 2021. Part III, volume 12698 of LNCS, pp. 159–185. Springer, Heidelberg (2021)

[GO07] Groth, J., Ostrovsky, R.: Cryptography in the multi-string model. In: Menezes, A. (ed.) CRYPTO 2007. LNCS, vol. 4622, pp. 323–341. Springer, Heidelberg (2007)

[GOS06a] Groth, J., Ostrovsky, R., Sahai, A.: Non-interactive zaps and new techniques for NIZK. In: Dwork, C. (ed.) CRYPTO 2006. LNCS, vol. 4117, pp. 97–111. Springer, Heidelberg (2006)

[GOS06b] Groth, J., Ostrovsky, R., Sahai, A.: Perfect Non-interactive Zero Knowledge for NP. In: Vaudenay, S. (ed.) EUROCRYPT 2006. LNCS, vol. 4004, pp. 339–358. Springer, Heidelberg (2006). https://doi.org/10.1007/11761679_21

[HIJ+17] Halevi, S., Ishai, Y., Jain, A., Komargodski, I., Sahai, A., Yogev, E.: Non-interactive multiparty computation without correlated randomness. In: Takagi, T., Peyrin, T. (eds.) ASIACRYPT 2017. Part III, volume 10626 of LNCS, pp. 181–211. Springer, Heidelberg (2017)

[HV16] Hazay, C., Venkitasubramaniam, M.: What Security Can We Achieve Within 4 Rounds? In: Zikas, V., De Prisco, R. (eds.) SCN 2016. LNCS, vol. 9841, pp. 486–505. Springer, Cham (2016). https://doi.org/10.1007/978-3-319-44618-9_26

[KK19] Kalai, Y.T., Khurana, D.: Non-interactive non-malleability from quantum supremacy. In: Boldyreva, A., Micciancio, D. (eds.) CRYPTO 2019. LNCS, vol. 11694, pp. 552–582. Springer, Cham (2019). https://doi.org/10.1007/978-3-030-26954-8_18

[KS17] Khurana, D., Sahai, A.: How to achieve non-malleability in one or two rounds. In: Umans, C., (ed.) 58th FOCS, pp. 564–575. IEEE Computer Society Press (2017)

[LPS17] Lin, H., Pass, R., Soni, P.: Two-round and non-interactive concurrent non-malleable commitments from time-lock puzzles. In: Umans, C., (ed.) 58th FOCS, pp. 576–587. IEEE Computer Society Press, October 2017

[OSY21] Orlandi, C., Scholl, P., Yakoubov, S.: The rise of paillier: Homomorphic secret sharing and public-key silent OT. In: Canteaut, A., Standaert, F.-X. (eds.) EUROCRYPT 2021. Part I, volume 12696 of LNCS, pp. 678–708. Springer, Heidelberg (2021)

[PVW08] Peikert, C., Vaikuntanathan, V., Waters, B.: A framework for efficient and composable oblivious transfer. In: Wagner, D. (ed.) CRYPTO 2008. LNCS, vol. 5157, pp. 554–571. Springer, Heidelberg (2008)

[Zha16] Zhandry, M.: The magic of ELFs. In: Robshaw, M., Katz, J. (eds.) CRYPTO 2016. Part I, volume 9814 of LNCS, pp. 479–508. Springer, Heidelberg (2016)

One-Message Secure Reductions: On the Cost of Converting Correlations

Yuval Ishai[1], Mahimna Kelkar[2,3(✉)], Varun Narayanan[1], and Liav Zafar[1]

[1] Technion, Haifa, Israel
yuvali@cs.technion.ac.il
[2] Cornell University, Ithaca, USA
[3] Cornell Tech, New York, USA
mahimna@cs.cornell.edu

Abstract. Correlated secret randomness is a useful resource for secure computation protocols, often enabling dramatic speedups compared to protocols in the plain model. This has motivated a line of work on identifying and securely generating useful correlations.

Different kinds of correlations can vary greatly in terms of usefulness and ease of generation. While there has been major progress on efficiently generating *oblivious transfer* (OT) correlations, other useful kinds of correlations are much more costly to generate. Thus, it is highly desirable to develop efficient techniques for securely *converting* copies of a given source correlation into copies of a given target correlation, especially when the former are cheaper to generate than the latter.

In this work, we initiate a systematic study of such conversions that only involve a single uni-directional message. We refer to such a conversion as a *one-message secure reduction* (OMSR). Recent works (Agarwal et al., Eurocrypt 2022; Khorasgani et al., Eurocrypt 2022) studied a similar problem when no communication is allowed; this setting is quite restrictive, however, with few non-trivial conversions being feasible. The OMSR setting substantially expands the scope of feasible results, allowing for direct applications to existing MPC protocols.

We obtain the following positive and negative results.

- **OMSR constructions.** We present a general rejection-sampling based technique for OMSR with OT source correlations. We apply it to substantially improve in the communication complexity of optimized protocols for distributed symmetric cryptography (Dinur et al., Crypto 2021).
- **OMSR lower bounds.** We develop general techniques for proving lower bounds on the communication complexity of OMSR, matching our positive results up to small constant factors.

1 Introduction

Secure multiparty computation [30,48] (MPC) is a fundamental cryptographic primitive that enables mutually distrusting parties to collaboratively compute a function over their combined data while keeping their local data secret. While MPC is a general tool, it can be quite heavyweight in terms of both computation

H. Handschuh and A. Lysyanskaya (Eds.): CRYPTO 2023, LNCS 14081, pp. 515–547, 2023.
https://doi.org/10.1007/978-3-031-38557-5_17

and communication compared to a non-secure evaluation. To minimize this cost, a common paradigm is to use preprocessing in the following way. Before the inputs are known, the parties run an *offline protocol* to generate some input-independent local information. The latter then serves as a resource for speeding up the *online protocol*, which is executed once the inputs are known. A qualitative advantage of this paradigm is that expensive cryptographic operations can be pushed to the offline phase, resulting in a simple and lightweight online protocol.

Abstractly, in the offline phase, the parties securely generate instances of *correlated randomness* or *correlations* that are independent of the protocol inputs, and can therefore be processed in advance. Examples for standard correlations include *oblivious transfer* (OT) correlations, which serve as a natural basis for MPC protocols for Boolean circuits [30,34,38,48], and *multiplication triples* [6,7,21], which serve as a basis for MPC for arithmetic circuits.

While the above standard correlations are universal, in the sense that they suffice for any online computation, in many cases it is more efficient to use a specially crafted correlation geared towards the particular function being evaluated. Moreover, while recent techniques support generation of n (pseudorandom) copies of any correlation with $o(n)$ communication cost [15,16], they are concretely efficient only for a few standard correlations, and therefore are not practical for most other useful correlations.

This motivates the central theme of our work: the study of efficiently and securely *deriving one type of correlation (the target) from another (the source)*; of particular relevance is when the source correlation can be generated very cheaply using known techniques. As an upshot, this allows us to broaden the class of correlations which can be concretely efficiently generated. We will restrict our attention to two-party protocols in this paper, and focus mainly on target correlations that are useful for secure computation in the *semi-honest* model.

Converting Between Correlations. A recent line of work [1,31,36,37,39] introduces secure "non-interactive" reductions/simulations (SNIR/SNIS) for securely converting one type of correlation to another. Here "non-interactive" refers to the strict notion of having *no communication at all.* This can be viewed as a secure analog of (non-secure) non-interactive simulations of joint distributions (NIS), which have been extensively studied in the information theory literature (see [42] for a recent survey). The SNIR/SNIS model, however, is highly restrictive. As intuition perhaps suggests, very few conversions between correlations are feasible, and many conversions are provably impossible. In fact, the model remains highly restrictive even when the security condition is dropped. As a result, there are no examples for nontrivial applications of SNIR/SNIS towards generating useful correlations for MPC.

One-Message Secure Reductions. Motivated by these limitations of the zero-interaction setting, we take the next natural step and study the same secure conversion problem in a setting where only one-way communication is allowed. In particular, denoting the two parties by the sender S and the receiver R, we allow for a single message to be sent from S to R. We refer to a conversion protocol in this model as a *one-message secure reduction* (OMSR). This relaxation of SNIR/SNIS dramatically changes the landscape, since in the OMSR setting many source correlations are *universal* in the sense that they can be converted into every target correlation [27]. Such source correlations include the string-OT correlation, which can be generated cheaply and "silently" (i.e., locally) using recent techniques [15]. This directly confirms the wide applicability of OMSR for generating correlations relevant for MPC, but leaves open the asymptotic and concrete *efficiency* of such reductions.

Limiting communication to be one-directional also comes with its own qualitative advantages which have motivated widely-studied models like non-interactive zero-knowledge (NIZK) [9], wiretap coding [45] and one-way secure computation (OWSC) [27]. Our OMSR model inherits these advantages. Finally, the simplicity of the OMSR model makes it more tractable for analysis and lower bound proofs than the fully interactive setting, while still permitting conversions that can make existing MPC protocols more efficient.

Non-trivial OMSR constructions for generating specific types of correlations can be implicitly found in a recent work by Dinur et al. [24], although there was no concrete objective to restrict to only single message protocols. The OMSRs were used in the context of concretely efficient distributed protocols for MPC-friendly symmetric-key cryptography that mixed together linear functions over different small moduli. They also serve as a starting point for us; our work defines the formalism for OMSR, generalizes the constructions used by [24], as well as provides substantial improvements. This directly translates to concrete efficiency gains in a number of settings including oblivious pseudorandom function (OPRF) evaluation, the MPC-in-the-head paradigm for signatures, and the distributed generation of keys for function secret sharing (FSS) with applications to privacy-preserving machine learning.

1.1 Our Contributions

OMSR **formalism (Sect.** 4**).** We start by formalizing the notion of an OMSR, for securely converting from m copies of a source correlation (X, Y) to n copies of a target correlation (U, V). We also consider relaxed flavors of OMSR that are useful towards our positive and negative results: a "Las Vegas" variant, which allows rejection without leaking information, and OMR, which forgoes the security requirement. We primarily focus on two concrete efficiency metrics: the number of *bits of communication* from the sender to the receiver, and the number of source copies $m(n)$ required for the conversion. In practice, the latter also captures *computation* cost to generate the initial source copies.

Efficient OMSRs **from OT-Correlations (Sect.** 5**).** We construct several OMSR protocols for converting from some type of OT source correlation to useful classes of target correlations; the use of OT as a source correlation is strongly motivated by a recent line of work on fast and "silent" generation of OT correlations [13,15,16,19,46].

We show OMSRs for generating two concrete correlations from OT: The first is the (t, q)-correlation (where $t < q$) which is the sharing of a random value r over both $\mathbb{Z}_t$ and $\mathbb{Z}_q$. This prepossessing is useful for the online conversion of a mod-t

shared secret value to a mod-q sharing of the same value, and provides efficiency gains in protocols which work over different rings (e.g., [23]). Our second OMSR is for the $(3, 2)$-correlation which was used in [24] to convert between a mod-3 sharing of secret x to a mod-2 sharing of x mod 2.

The former generalizes $(2, 3)$-correlations which along with $(3, 2)$-correlations were instrumental within [24] in building concretely efficient distributed protocols for candidate MPC-friendly weak-PRF and PRG constructions that mixed linear operations over $\mathbb{Z}_2$ and $\mathbb{Z}_3$. Our new OMSR constructions concretely improve the communication cost by more than 2x over the (already heavily optimized) protocols from [24] (The improvement is orthogonal to the single-message feature, and applies even when comparing to protocols that use an arbitrary number of rounds.). The same kind of improvement is expected to apply to future designs of symmetric primitives based on the same alternating moduli paradigm.

Applications (Sect. 5.4**).** Our improved OMSRs translate to improvements in all of the application scenarios considered in [24]: post-quantum oblivious PRF, fully distributed MPC protocols for PRF evaluation, signatures based on the MPC-in-the-head paradigm, and distributed generation for function secret sharing (FSS) keys. The latter is particularly motivated by applications to privacy-preserving machine learning, where FSS is an increasingly popular building block for fast offline-online secure protocols for ReLU and other nonlinear activation functions [11,17,40,41,43]. The PRG candidates from [24] serve as an attractive choice for MPC-friendly PRGs in such contexts, and were recently used in the FssNN system to optimize the distributed generation of FSS keys [47]. Our new OMSR protocols for $(2, 3)$ and $(3, 2)$ correlations would lead to significant improvement in the concrete communication cost of the protocol from [47] and similar protocols. We leave an optimized implementation and benchmarking to future work.

Lower Bounds (Sect. 6**).** We start by proving new lower bounds for (insecure) OMR. While the notion of OMR is meaningless in the presence of common randomness (which is cheap to generate in a cryptographic setting), we will later argue that OMR lower bounds without common randomness can be lifted to OMSR lower bounds that apply even in the presence of common randomness.

When a so-called S* measure (see Definition 1) of the source correlation is strictly smaller than that of the target, Theorem 8 shows that the communication cost of OMR is necessarily linear. This result strictly strengthens an impossibility result for non-interactive simulation [5]. A more precise analysis yields concrete lower bounds (Corollaries 3 and 5) on the amortized communication cost of OMR between specific source and target correlations from our positive results. Theorem 9 shows that deriving n-bit unit vector correlations for large enough n from almost any correlation requires linear communication even *with interaction*. In fact, the result applies to other target correlation families too (See Remark 7). This result can be thought of as a generalization of a result in [18] which is a similar result for deriving common randomness from noisy common randomness.

Role of Common Randomness (Sect. 7**).** Finally, in Theorem 10, we show that common randomness does not aid in OMSR; i.e., given an OMSR with common randomness we can derive an OMSR without common randomness with comparable error. Our proof relies on a convergence theorem for Markov chains. In contrast, with a sufficiently large amount of common randomness, any correlation can be non-securely derived without any communication.

A question that arises from the above discussion is whether OMSR is strictly harder to realize than OMR. The costs of OMSR and OMR trivially coincide for any pair of correlations that permit secure *non-interactive* reductions. In other non-trivial cases, our lower bound for both OMR and upper bound for OMSR are only tight up to a constant, hence, we do not know whether they match. However, security makes a big difference when augmenting nontrivial source correlations (such as OT correlations) with public randomness. This trivializes the notion of OMR, but keeps our lower bounds for OMSR unchanged (Theorem 10). While our results imply separations between the two notions, we do not know of any explicit non-trivial instances where the two notions provably do not match, although intuition suggests that OMR is an easier primitive than OMSR to realize.

1.2 Related Work

As mentioned above, we are motivated by the question of efficiently and securely deriving one type of correlation from another. A recent line of work [1,8,36,37] introduced secure non-interactive simulation/reduction which studied the problem of deriving a correlation from another without any communication and with information theoretic security. The non-secure variant of this problem, namely non-interactive simulation (NIS), has attracted a lot of attention from both computer science and information theory [5,22,29,35,42]. Generating correlations with *computational* security and low communication cost has been studied in a recent line of work on pseudorandom correlation generators (PCGs) [12,15]. A (two-party) PCG is a local deterministic algorithm that stretches a pair of short, correlated seeds into many copies of a correlation, while ensuring that each seed does not reveal more than necessary about the other output. A large body of work in this area [13–15,19,46] has focused on generating OT-correlations extremely cheaply in practice; this makes OT very suitable as a source correlation. However, other useful correlations, such as OLE and multiplication triples [16], are much more expensive to generate, and many other useful correlations do not admit a concretely efficient PCG. This is a primary motivation for our work.

One-way secure computation (OWSC), introduced in [27] and subsequently studied in [2,3], is closely related to OMSR. Here, a sender and a receiver securely implement a target channel with only one-way communication over a given source channel. Known results about OWSC can be used to realize limited forms of OMSR. In the other direction, OMSR implies OWSC whenever the induced channel of the target correlation allows a *random self reduction.* This is because after realizing OMSR, a random self reduction can be applied with one-directional communication to go from a random sample in the target correlation to the the given input to the sender. However, there is still a separation in terms of efficiency. The completeness of the string-OT correlation for OWSC, which in turn builds on information-theoretic analogs of garbled circuits [33,49], implies an OMSR converting string-OT correlations to any target correlation. A similar result can be based on the simpler bit-OT correlation, though requiring a much bigger number of copies and inevitably introducing an inverse-polynomial security error in the number of copies [2]. These generic constructions are typically very inefficient. Another drawback is that they entangle communication cost with the number of copies of the source correlation used. Our objective in this paper is to reduce the number of bits transmitted while possibly burning up more copies of the source correlation. Owing to this, the lower bounds in the OWSC model do not provide interesting insights for our model.

All our lower bounds apply more generally to (the non-secure variant) OMR; however, in the presence of common randomness they are only meaningful in the more restrictive OMSR setting. The problem of deriving common randomness from correlations has been extensively studied. The zero-communication version of this problem was studied in [26,44], which led way to the NIS model we previously described. Generalizing this, in [4], Ahlswede and Csiszar studied the rate of generating common randomness per use of correlation when communication is limited. Several works in computer science [10,18,28,32] considered a related problem of agreement distillation, where parties have unlimited access to a source of noisy common randomness and want to derive common randomness while minimizing communication. Our lower bounds use techniques developed in both these areas of work. To the best of our knowledge, deriving a target correlation given unlimited access to a source correlation is not studied in information theory or theoretical computer science.

2 Technical Overview

We now present an overview of our main technical contributions. We split this into two parts: in the first (Sect. 2.1), we provide an overview for our concrete OMSR protocols; in the second (Sects. 2.2 and 2.3), we present an overview of our lower bound results.

2.1 Concrete OMSR Protocols

OMSR **formalism.** Abstractly, in the OMSR model, we consider two parties: a sender S and a receiver R. The parties are given access to m copies of a *source* correlation (X, Y) jointly distributed according to p_{XY}, with the goal being for them to securely generate n copies of a *target* correlation (U, V) which is jointly distributed according to p_{UV}. To accomplish this task, S is only allowed to send a single message to R; no communication from R is allowed. Intuitively, the security of an OMSR is now defined as neither party learning anything about the other party. In other words, S's view u of the target correlation does not leak anything about R's view v and vice versa.

We focus on two concrete efficiency metrics: the primary one being the (expected) number of bits l communicated, and a secondary one being the number of source correlations $m(n)$ used to generate n target correlations (in the most general case, we allow access to an unlimited number of source correlations).

General OMSR **Protocols from Rejection Sampling.** For our concrete constructions, we study OMSRs in the ρ-Las-Vegas model; here, the output must be correct whenever it is produced but the protocol is also allowed (with probability $\leq \rho$) to return a failure symbol in which case correctness is not guaranteed.

We build general protocols in this model using the following approach: Suppose that the sender's and receiver's views of the source correlation are $\hat{X}$ and $\hat{Y}$. Often, by conditioning this on some variable C (dependent only on the private randomness of the sender), both parties can locally convert to the required target correlation. Equivalently, the sender computes some function $f(\hat{X}; r)$ for some private randomness r such that whenever $f(\cdot) = 1$ is communicated to the receiver, both parties can locally produce the required target correlation. Note that here, the sender only needs to send a single *accept* symbol to indicate whether the conversion can be done. We refer to this as an *accept-reject* protocol with parameter ρ denoting the accept probability (i.e., the probability that the sender produces an accept message).

General OMSR protocols with efficient asymptotic communication can be built using accept-reject protocols through rejection sampling. The intuitive idea is to consider k source copies together instead of one and send an accept message only when all k copies can be successfully converted locally. While this improves communication cost conditioned on an "accept" message, it exponentially reduces the probability of accepting. To get around this, the sender can now instead look at *batches* of k copies and send the *index* of the first batch where all k copies are accepting. This results in an efficient OMSR in the Las Vegas model. We show the following informal result for our general transformation.

Theorem 1 (Informal). *A secure accept-reject protocol with probability ρ can be turned into a secure Las Vegas* OMSR *with asymptotic communication* $\log(1/\rho)$.

Concrete OMSR **Protocol for** (t, q) **and** $(3, 2)$**-correlations.** We use the above general transformation to construct efficient OMSR protocols for (t, q) and $(3, 2)$-correlations. In a (t, q)-correlation (where $t < q$), the two parties are given (x_0, r_0) and (x_1, r_1) respectively where $x_i \in \mathbb{Z}_t$ and $r_i \in \mathbb{Z}_q$ such that $x_0 + x_1 \bmod t = r_0 + r_1 \bmod q$. The (t, q)-correlation generalizes the $(2, 3)$-correlation defined in [24].

We show an accept-reject protocol to generate a (t, q)-correlation using as the source correlation, a 1-out-of-t OT correlation over $\mathbb{Z}_q$ (we formally define this as well as other correlations we use in Sect. 4.3). For this source correlation, the sender is given a vector $\mathbf{v} = (v_0, \ldots, v_{t-1})$ with each $v_i \in \mathbb{Z}_q$, while the receiver is given (b, v_b) for a random $b \in \mathbb{Z}_t$.

The protocol has accept probability $\frac{tq}{q^t}$ and intuitively works as follows: given $\mathbf{v}$, the sender S checks if there is some (x, r) such that $(x + i) \bmod t = (r + v_i) \bmod q$ for all i. If this is the case, S can output (x, r) and send an accept symbol to R who then can just output its original OT source (b, v_b); this results in a (t, q)-correlation since by construction, regardless of b, $x + b \mod t = r + v_b \mod q$. We can now use the earlier general transformation (Theorem 1) to get an OMSR for (t, q)-correlations with communication of $\log(q^t/tq)$.

For $(3, 2)$-correlations, we first show that they are isomorphic to non-zero OLE correlations (see Sect. 4.3 and Lemma 1), following which we can use the above approach to construct an OMSR for them.

2.2 Lower Bounds

We prove linear lower bounds on the communication cost of OMSR for a large family of conversions. These lower bounds also hold more generally for non-secure one message reductions (OMR). For the specific conversions considered in the previous section, the lower bounds we obtain by applying these techniques justify the cost of their OMSR protocols.

Linear Lower Bound for One-Message Reductions. Our first result in this section can be stated informally as follows:

Theorem 2 (Informal). *The amortized communication cost of OMR converting a correlation (X, Y) to (U, V) is linear if $\mathrm{S}^*(X, Y) < \mathrm{S}^*(U, V)$.*

Here, S^* (see Definition 1) of a correlation (X, Y) is defined as $\sup_U \frac{I(U;Y)}{I(U;X)}$ where the supremum is taken over all U that is generated from X (conditionally independent of Y); The connection of this quantity with several other information theoretic measures is outlined in [5]. To prove Theorem 2, we first show that the amortized communication complexity of OMR converting (X, Y) to common randomness is exactly $1 - \mathrm{S}^*(X, Y)$. For this, we use a seminal result [4] from information theory which characterized the so called common randomness capacity of any correlation with limited communication. For communication rate $R \geq 0$, common randomness capacity $C(R)$ of a correlation (X, Y) is the asymptotic rate at which common randomness can be derived per use of (X, Y) by parties (S and R) using only one-way communication (from S to R) with rate limited to R. OMR converting (X, Y) to common randomness differs from this model in that the usage of correlation (X, Y) is not limited. Intuitively, the optimal communication cost of OMR converting (X, Y) to common randomness should be the smallest ratio between R to $C(R)$ as R tends to zero. Although, this observation is referenced in several works [32,42,50], to the best of our knowledge this is not formally proved. Revisiting the proof of common randomness capacity region in [4] and using a careful analysis, we prove this fact.

Now, suppose agreeing on n bits of common randomness using (arbitrarily many copies of) (X, Y) requires at least $n \cdot c$ bits of communication. Whereas, only $c' \cdot n$ (where $c' < c$) bits of communication is sufficient to agree on n bits of common randomness using $k \cdot n$ copies of (U, V). Then, OMR converting (X, Y) to (U, V) ought to have a communication complexity of at least $(c - c')/k$. Otherwise, the parties can generate $k \cdot n$ copies of (U, V) correlation with $(c - c')n$

bits of communication and then convert it to n bits of common randomness using less than $c' \cdot n$ bits of communication leading to a contradiction. Hence, we prove the theorem by showing that when $\mathrm{S}^*(X, Y) < \mathrm{S}^*(U, V)$, there is a sufficiently large k and $c' < \mathrm{S}^*(U, V)$, such that two parties can agree on n bits of common randomness using $k \cdot n$ copies of (U, V) and $c' \cdot n$ bits of communication. We then exactly compute S^* of several correlations and use the above technique to obtain concrete linear lower bounds. In Corollary 3 we show a lower bound on the communication cost of converting 1-out-of-2 OT to $(2, 3)$ correlation that is half of what our construction achieves; in Corollary 5 we show a lower bound for converting 1-out-of-3 OT to $(3, 2)$ correlation that is a third of what our construction achieves.

Linear Lower Bound for Interactive Reductions. We demonstrate much stronger lower bounds on communication costs when the target correlation of interest is "close" to common randomness. Consider an n-bit unit vector correlation in which the parties receive an additive secret sharing of an n-bit unit vector (a string of Hamming weight 1). This correlation is close to n-bits of common randomness in that the two strings are uniformly distributed and differ on exactly one (random) index. Another correlation that is close to common randomness is a 1-out-of-k n-bit string OT, where one party's uncertainty about the other party's part of the correlation is just $1/k$. Our next result shows that, deriving such correlations using any correlation (other than correlations with inherent common randomness) requires linear communication even using an *interactive protocol*. We state the result specifically for unit vector correlations.

Theorem 3 (Informal). *If a source correlation (X, Y) lacks common randomness, then any interactive protocol generating an n-bit unit vector correlation requires $\Omega(n)$ communication.*

In [18], Canonne et al. showed that a protocol in which parties with unlimited access to a source of noisy common randomness derive common randomness with ℓ bits of interactive communication can be converted into a zero communication protocol for deriving common randomness from the same source with $(2^{-O(\ell)})$ success probability. We observe that a similar approach can be used to convert an interactive protocol for deriving an n-bit unit vector correlation using a correlation (X, Y) with ℓ bits of interactive communication into a zero communication protocol for deriving the n-bits of common randomness from the same source with about $2^{-O(\ell)}$ success probability. For this, we only use the fact that n-bit unit vector correlation can be converted (with zero-communication) to n bits of common randomness with success probability $1/n$ by having one party simply flipping one of the n bits at random in their share of the correlation.

In the other direction, we show the success probability for agreeing on n bits is $2^{-\Omega(n)}$. Bogdanov and Mossel's result from [10] which showed that deriving n bits of common randomness using a source of noisy common randomness and zero communication succeeds only with $2^{-\Omega(n)}$ probability. The authors show this using hypercontractive inequality. We generalize this result to show that if correlation (X, Y) has no common randomness, then an analogous condition holds. The proof of the statement uses generalized hypercontractive inequality as defined in [35] and Holder's inequality. The lower bound follows from the above observations.

2.3 Role of Common Randomness in OMSR

In general, common randomness does not aid in OMSR. This is in line with the intuition that common randomness available to both parties cannot be used to achieve security. Note that this is in contrast with OMR where any correlation can be generated from common randomness with zero communication. The main result of this section is as follows:

Theorem 4 (Informal). *Suppose correlation (U, V) lacks common randomness. Given an OMSR converting a correlation (X, Y) to (U, V) using common randomness we can construct an OMSR for the same conversion without common randomness.*

All (target) correlations considered in this work lack inherent common randomness; more generally, this holds for most correlations with cryptographic applications because, intuitively, common information does not enable cryptographic tasks. In the case of OMSR with perfect security, an OMSR without common randomness can be obtained by simply conditioning on any of its realizations. Such an approach is used to the ineffectiveness of common randomness in statistical NISR [1]; but this approach fails for statistical OMSR. This is because the conversion amplifies the security error by a factor that is inversely proportional to the smallest probability assigned by the correlation to any member in the support. In OMSR, the conversion is to several copies of the target correlation which makes the error in the conversion increase exponentially.

We use a different approach. Consider an ϵ-secure OMSR using common randomness for converting a given source to n copies of the target correlation. By a Markov bound, there exists a realization of common randomness conditioned on which privacy against both parties is guaranteed with at most $\sqrt{\epsilon}$ error. Hence, on average, conditioned on sender's output, the receiver's output is distributed as prescribed by the target distribution, and vice versa. Since the conditional distribution on outputs is correct on average, it is sufficient to show that the marginal distribution of, say, the sender's output is correct. To show this, we consider two experiments; in the first one, we sample the receiver's output conditioned on sender's output and then sample back the receiver's output conditioned on the receiver's output according to conditional distributions prescribed by the output distribution of the OMSR. In the second, we do the same sampling but according to conditional distributions prescribed by the target correlation. These are Markov processes with the stationary distributions being the sender's output distribution and marginal distribution at the sender in the target distribution, respectively. We then use the closeness of the two Markov processes to show that stationary processes are close in total variation distance. This proves the theorem.

3 Preliminaries

Notation. We use calligraphic letters (e.g., $\mathcal{X}$, $\mathcal{Y}$) to denote finite sets or alphabets; the corresponding small letter x is used for members in $\mathcal{X}$, while the capital letter X is used for a random variable with values in $\mathcal{X}$. The distribution induced by X is denoted by p_X, while $X \sim \mu$ means that X follows the distribution μ.

For random variables X, and X' over the same domain $\mathcal{X}$, the total variation (aka statistical) distance TVD between their distributions is defined as:

$$\mathsf{TVD}(p_X, p_{X'}) = \frac{1}{2} \sum_{x \in \mathcal{X}} \left| \Pr[X = x] - \Pr[X' = x] \right|$$

For ease of exposition, without loss of generality, we may also often use the notation $\mathsf{TVD}(X, X')$; this will be equivalent to using $\mathsf{TVD}(p_X, p_{X'})$. For any $\epsilon \geq 0$, $X \approx^{\epsilon} X'$ denotes that $\mathsf{TVD}(p_X, p_{X'}) \leq \epsilon$.

We write $(X_i)_{i \in [n]} \overset{\text{i.i.d.}}{\sim} p_X$ to mean that $X_1, \ldots, X_n$ are i.i.d. according to p_X. A sequence of random variables $(X_1, \ldots, X_n)$ will be succinctly represented as X^n; similarly, joint random variables (X_1, Y_1) to (X_n, Y_n) will be represented as (X^n, Y^n).

Random variables (X, Y, Z) satisfy the Markov chain $X \leftrightarrow Y \leftrightarrow Z$ if X and Z are conditionally independent conditioned on Y; i.e., for all x, y, z.

$$\Pr[X = x | Y = y, Z = z] = \Pr[X = x | Y = y].$$

The unit vector with 1 at the ith position is denoted by e_i. The elements of the field $\mathbb{F}_4$ are represented by $\{0, 1, \alpha, \beta\}$ where $\alpha + 1 = \beta$.

Useful Quantities. We recall some basic information-theoretic quantities (see [20] for a primer).

The Shannon entropy of X, denoted by $\mathsf{H}(X)$, is defined as $\sum_{x \in \mathcal{X}} \Pr[X = x] \log\left(\frac{1}{\Pr[X=x]}\right)$. The binary entropy function for parameter $\rho \in [0, 1]$ is defined as $\mathsf{H}_b(\rho) = -\rho \log(\rho) - (1 - \rho) \log(1 - \rho)$.

The mutual information of (X, Y), denoted by $I(X; Y)$ is defined as $\mathsf{H}(X, Y) - \mathsf{H}(X|Y) - \mathsf{H}(Y|X)$.

Correlations. The central objects of interest in this work are pairwise joint distributions or correlations. We will often write "correlation (X, Y)" to refer to the correlation p_{XY} induced by (X, Y). We write "parties A and B receive/possess correlation $(X, Y) \sim p_{XY}$" to mean that A and B receive/possess random variables X and Y, respectively, where (X, Y) are jointly distributed according to the distribution p_{XY}.

Definition 1 (S* value of a correlation [5]**).** For a correlation (X, Y), the quantity $\mathrm{S}^*(X, Y)$ is defined as

$$\sup_U \frac{I(U; Y)}{I(U; X)},$$

where the supremum is taken over all random variables generated from X; i.e., (U, X, Y) satisfy the Markov chain $U \leftrightarrow X \leftrightarrow Y$ (See Notations in Sect. 3). Observe that S^* is not necessarily symmetric.

Definition 2 (Geometric Random Variable). *A geometric random variable X with success probability $0 \leq \rho \leq 1$, denoted by $X \sim \mathsf{Geo}(\rho)$ is defined by $\Pr[X = k] = (1 - \rho)^k \rho$, for every $k = 0, 1, 2, \ldots$.*

Fact 1 *If $X \sim \mathsf{Geo}(\rho)$ then $\mathsf{H}(X) = \frac{\mathsf{H}_b(\rho)}{\rho}$.*

4 One-Message Secure Reductions

We now formally introduce one-message secure reductions, or OMSRs. Abstractly, an OMSR is a secure protocol for converting copies of a source correlation (X, Y) to copies of a target correlation (U, V) by using only a single (uni-directional) message. Later, in Sect. 4.3, we also define several simple but useful correlations considered by our protocols.

4.1 OMR and OMSR Definitions

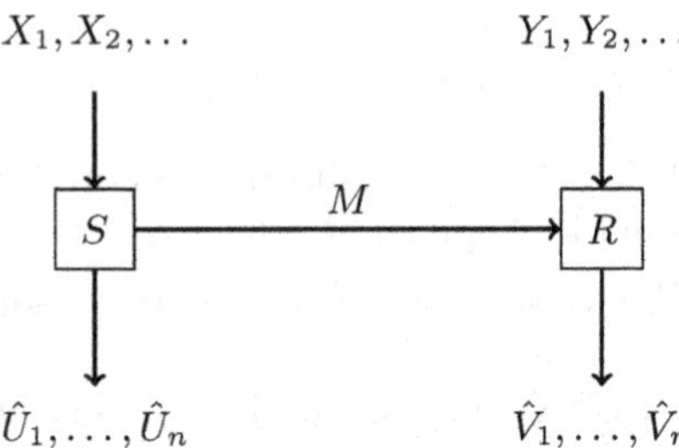

Fig. 1. The random variables involved in an OMSR converting p_{XY} into p_{UV}. Parties receive, $(X_1, Y_1), (X_2, Y_2) \ldots$, which are i.i.d. according to correlation p_{XY}. M denotes the single message sent from S to R. Parties output $(\hat{U}_1, \hat{V}_n), \ldots, (\hat{U}^n, \hat{V}^n)$ which are (close to being) i.i.d. according to correlation (U, V).

Basic Model. In an OMSR protocol, there are two parties: a sender S and receiver R. Consider two distributions (correlations) p_{XY} and p_{UV} referred to as the *source correlation* and the *target correlation* respectively. S and R are given an unbounded number of independent copies of correlation p_{XY}; i.e., for $i = 1, 2, \ldots$, S gets X_i and R gets Y_i, where (X_i, Y_i) are i.i.d. according to p_{XY}.

The goal now is for S and R to generate n independent copies of the target correlation (U, V). Based on its copies of the source correlation, S will be allowed to send a single message to R. Following this message, S and R compute the required copies target correlations based on their local views. Of particular interest to us are two efficiency metrics: the (expected) number of instances

$m = m(n)$ of X needed to generate n instances of Y, and the (expected) length $l = l(n)$ of the message from S to R. Hence, we define the expected amortized communication cost as $\limsup_n E[l(n)]/n$ and the worst case amortized communication cost as $\limsup_n \max(l(n))/n$.

Before detailing the security properties of OMSRs, we first introduce its non-secure counterpart—the one-message reduction (OMR).

Definition 3 (One-Message Reduction (OMR)**).** *An* ϵ*-error* one-message reduction *(*ϵ-OMR*) over* $(m, p_{XY}, n, p_{UV}, l)$ *is a pair of randomized algorithms* $\langle S, R\rangle$ *for (non-securely) converting* m *copies of a source correlation* p_{XY} *(over the domain* $\mathcal{X}\times\mathcal{Y}$*) to* n *copies of target correlation* p_{UV} *(over the domain* $\mathcal{U}\times\mathcal{V}$*) using* l *bits of communication.*

Let the private randomness of the sender and receiver be uniformly distributed in arbitrary finite domains $\mathcal{Q}$ *and* $\mathcal{Q}'$*, respectively. The algorithms are defined as* $S : \mathcal{X}^m \times \mathcal{Q} \to \mathcal{U}^n \times \{0,1\}^l$ *and* $R : \{0,1\}^l \times \mathcal{Y}^m \times \mathcal{Q}' \to \mathcal{V}^n$ *and they satisfy the following correctness condition:*

Correctness. *Let* $(X_i, Y_i)_{i\in[m]} \overset{i.i.d.}{\sim} p_{XY}$*, and* $(U_i, V_i)_{i\in[n]} \overset{i.i.d.}{\sim} p_{UV}$*. Let* Q, Q' *be uniformly distributed in* $\mathcal{Q}, \mathcal{Q}'$*, respectively. Then,* $(\hat{U}^n, M) \leftarrow S(X^m, Q)$ *and* $\hat{V}^n \leftarrow R(M, Y^m, Q')$ *are such that:*

$$\left(\hat{U}^n, \hat{V}^n\right) \approx^{\epsilon} (U^n, V^n) \tag{1}$$

We say that an OMR *is* perfect *if* $\epsilon = 0$*. When* m *is omitted (or* $m = \infty$*), the* OMR *will be given an unbounded number of copies of the source correlation. We also allow for* m *and* l *to be randomized functions of the* n*, in which case we will look at the expected number of source correlations used and the expected number of bits communicated as our efficiency metrics.*

OMSR **security.** An OMSR is an OMR where the conversion is also done *securely*. Informally, we define security as neither party learning more about the output of the other party than it should. We formalize this in Definition 4.

Definition 4 (One-Message Secure Reduction (OMSR)**).** *An* ϵ*-error one-message secure reduction (*ϵ-OMSR*) over* $(m, p_{XY}, n, p_{UV}, l)$ *is an* ϵ-OMR $\langle S, R\rangle$ *(for converting* m *copies of the source correlation* p_{XY} *to* n *copies of the target correlation* p_{UV} *using* l *bits of communication) which also satisfies the following security properties:*

Privacy against S*. Let* $X^m, Y^m, Q, Q', M, \hat{U}^n, \hat{V}^n$ *be as defined in Definition 3. Then,*

$$\mathbb{E}_{X^m,Q}\left[\mathit{TVD}\left(\left(\hat{V}^n \middle| X^m, Q\right), \left(\hat{V}^n \middle| \hat{U}^n\right)\right)\right] \leq \epsilon. \tag{2}$$

Privacy against R*. For* $X^m, Y^m, \hat{U}^n, \hat{V}^n$ *and* M *as defined above,*

$$\mathbb{E}_{Y^m,M,Q}\left[\mathit{TVD}\left(\left(\hat{U}^n \middle| M, Y^m, Q'\right), \left(\hat{U}^n \middle| \hat{V}^n\right)\right)\right] \leq \epsilon. \tag{3}$$

We say that an OMSR *is perfect if* $\epsilon = 0$.

We define simulation-based security for OMSR in the full version and prove that both definitions are equivalent with a comparable error.

Statistical OM(S)R. For a function $\epsilon : \mathbb{N} \to \mathbb{R}_{\geq 0}$, we say there is an $\epsilon(n)$-statistical one-message (secure) reduction converting p_{XY} to p_{UV} if, for each n, there exists an $\epsilon(n)$-OM(S)R converting (arbitrarily many copies of) p_{XY} to n copies of p_{UV} using $l(n)$ bits of communication. The communication cost for the OM(S)R is computed as $\limsup_n l(n)/n$. If $\epsilon(n)$ is a negligible function, we call the reduction an OM(S)R with negligible error.

The lower bounds we develop in this paper apply to statistical OMSR, in fact, more generally to statistical OMR. Note that the lower bounds also apply to OM(S)R with expected communication cost with variable message length and perfect correctness (and privacy). This can be seen as follows: suppose the OM(S)R has an expected communication cost of ℓ. Suppose the scheme is run n times independently, and let ℓ_i be the length of the message in the i-th execution of the scheme. The amortized length of the combined message is $(\ell_1 + \ldots + \ell_n)/n$; to combine messages we crucially use the fact that they are prefix-free. Fix $\epsilon > 0$; by the law of large numbers, for any $\delta > 0$, there exists a large enough n such that the amortized length is $\ell + \epsilon$ with probability $1 - \delta$. Hence, by aborting (sending $\perp$) whenever the amortized length is more than $\ell + \epsilon$, we obtain a statistical OM(S)R with a communication cost of $\ell + \epsilon$. Thus, a lower bound on the communication cost of statistical OM(S)R implies a lower bound on the expected amortized communication cost of OM(S)R.

OMSR for Distribution Families. In many cases, we are also interested in generating families of correlations starting from a given source correlation. Here, a *family* $\mathfrak{F}$ of correlations is a sequence of correlations parameterized by $n \in \mathbb{N}$, i.e., $\mathfrak{F} = \{(U_n, V_n)\}_{n \in \mathbb{N}}$. Generating correlation families are of practical interest. Examples include, the unit vector correlation family–a sequence of n-bit unit vector correlations for $n \in \mathbb{N}$, the string-OT correlation family–a sequence of n-bit 1-out-of-2 OT correlations for $n \in \mathbb{N}$, etc.

Note that, in Definition 3 and Definition 4, the correlations families of interest are $\mathfrak{F} = \{(U_n, V_n)\}_{n \in \mathbb{N}}$, where (U_n, V_n) is a sequence of n i.i.d. copies of a target distribution. Hence, the definitions for OMR and OMSR in Definition 3 and Definition 4 naturally extend to correlation families. We provide a formal definition of OMSR for distribution families in the full version.

4.2 OMSR in the Las Vegas Model

The Las Vegas model of computation requires algorithms or protocols to always output the correct result whenever some result is produced but allows for the output of a special failure symbol $\perp$, in which case no guarantees are made about correctness. In the Las Vegas model, the runtime may also depend on the input (and randomness). Many of our concrete constructions use this Las Vegas model; we formally define OMSR in this model below.

Definition 5 (OMSR in the Las Vegas Model). *A* OMSR *in the ρ-Las-Vegas model is the same as a perfect (i.e., with $\epsilon = 0$)* OMSR *from Definition*

4 over the parameters $(m, p_{XY}, n, p_{UV}, l)$ except for the property that the parties are additionally allowed to output a failure symbol $\perp$ (with probability $\leq \rho$). The correctness and security properties are exactly the same as Definition 4 except that now they are conditioned on the output not being $\perp$.

Las-Vegas OMSR is a stronger notation than statistical OMSR. Hence, we use this notion in our constructions. The lower bounds we develop for statistical OMSR naturally applies to Las-Vegas OMSR as well.

The Accept-Reject Paradigm. To build OMSR protocols in the Las Vegas model, we find it useful to define a simpler primitive where only a *single symbol* is sent from the sender to the receiver, after which both parties produce an output. Informally, this symbol represents an "accept" indication which signals that a target correlation can be realized based on the sender's view of the source correlation. Following this, the receiver can locally convert its view of the source correlation to the target correlation. If there is no communication, both parties output the failure symbol $\perp$ in which case no instance of the target correlation is produced. We refer to this as the accept-reject paradigm.

More formally, a probability ρ (secure) accept-reject protocol ρ-$\mathsf{Acc\text{-}Rej}$ from a source correlation (X, Y) to a target correlation (U, V) is an OMSR in the Las Vegas model over the parameters $(m, p_{XY}, n = 1, p_{UV}, l = 1)$ where S sends an "accept" symbol to R with probability ρ (taken over the the source correlations X^m). The goal is to generate just a single instance of the target correlation (as opposed to the general Las Vegas model). We often use the terminology that the sender's view is *accepting* if it results in an accept message being sent. While we denote $l = 1$, note that only a single symbol (rather than a bit) needs to be transmitted when accepting while nothing is communicated when rejecting.

4.3 Useful Correlations

We now define several simple but useful (2-party) correlations that are widely applicable for building efficient secure computation protocols. Several of our OMSR protocols will involve securely converting between these correlations.

Oblivious Transfer (OT) Correlation. A 1-out-of-k OT correlation over group $\mathbb{G}$ is a tuple $(\mathbf{r}, (b, r_b))$ where $\mathbf{r} = (r_0, \ldots, r_{k-1})$ is uniform over $\mathbb{G}^k$ and b is uniform over $\mathbb{Z}_k$.

Oblivious Linear Evaluation (OLE) Correlation. OLE can be viewed as an arithmetic extension of 1-out-of-2 OT. Specifically, an OLE correlation over a field $\mathbb{F}$ is a tuple $((a, s), (b, r))$ where a, b, s are uniform over $\mathbb{F}$ and $r = ab + s$.

Non-zero OLE Correlation. An nzOLE correlation is simply an OLE correlation that is conditioned on the event that $a, b \neq 0$.

(t, q)-Correlation for $t < q$. A (t, q)-correlation where $t < q$ is the tuple $((x_0, r_0), (x_1, r_1))$ where we choose $x_0, x_1 \in \mathbb{Z}_t$ and $r_0, r_1 \in \mathbb{Z}_q$ at random under the constraint that $x_0 + x_1 \pmod{t} = r_0 + r_1 \pmod{q}$. This generalizes the $(2, 3)$-correlation used by Dinur et al. [24] to securely convert an additively shared bit over $\mathbb{F}_2$ to an additive sharing of the same bit over $\mathbb{F}_3$.

(3, 2)-Correlation. A (3, 2)-correlation is the tuple $((x_0, u_0, v_0), (x_1, u_1, v_1))$ where we choose $x_i \in \mathbb{Z}_3$, $u_i, v_i \in \mathbb{Z}_2$ at random under the following constraints: x_0, u_0, v_0, x_1 are uniformly random and independent. Define $x = x_0 + x_1 \bmod 3, u = u_0 + u_1 \bmod 2, v = v_0 + v_1 \bmod 2$. Then we require that $u = x \bmod 2$ and $v = (x + 1 \bmod 3) \bmod 2$. This correlation was used in [24] to securely convert a mod-3 sharing of x to a mod-2 sharing of x mod 2. Perhaps surprisingly, we show that the (3, 2)-correlation is also isomorphic to a non-zero OLE over $\mathbb{F}_4$.

***n*-Bit Unit Vector (*n*-UV) Correlation.** An n-UV correlation is a tuple (u_0, u_1) where $u_0, u_1 \in \mathbb{F}_2^n$ and $u_0 + u_1$ is a random unit vector.

Additive Correlation. We will say a correlation (X, Y) is an additive correlation if there exists a distribution ψ over an abelian group $\mathbb{G}$ such that $X+Y \sim \psi$ and X and Y are both uniform over the group. Note that this generalizes several correlations, including n-UV and the (2, 3)-correlation.

5 Concrete OMSR Protocols

In this section, we provide concrete one-message secure reductions for converting from a source correlation (X, Y) to a target correlation (U, V). As mentioned earlier, we find it useful to build accept-reject protocols as a stepping stone to building Las Vegas OMSRs. We start with a general transformation that enables us to, in many cases, work with simpler accept-reject protocols.

Theorem 5. *Suppose that there exists a secure accept-reject protocol π from source correlation (X, Y) to target correlation (U, V) with accept probability ρ. Then, for every $\epsilon > 0$, there exists a perfect* OMSR *converting from (X, Y) to (U, V) with an expected amortized communication cost smaller than* $\log(1/\rho) + \epsilon$.

Proof. Suppose that the protocol π has an accept probability ρ. We show how to use this in a black-box way to construct an OMSR; the key idea is to process source correlations in batches of size km (where m in the number of correlations used by π) before sending a message.

Concretely, suppose that π involves the sender S looking at m source correlations, and based on some (possibly randomized) function computation $f(X^m; r)$ with private randomness r resulting in 1, decides on whether to send an accept symbol to R. For the OMSR model, recall that we always want to produce the target correlation (instead of e.g., with probability ρ). To achieve this, the basic idea is to have S send the *index* of the first set of correlations for which π would result in an accept message.

It turns out that we can substantially bring down the asymptotic cost by considering batches of size km. Notice as a first step that we can directly get an accept-reject protocol to generate k target copies; for this, S will look at km copies of the source correlation (as k batches X_i^m each of size m) and send a single-bit accept message only when $f(X_i^m; r_i) = 1$ is true for all $i \in \{1, \dots, k\}$. This however results in accept probability ρ^k, i.e., exponentially decreasing in

k. Now, to convert this into an OMSR, we can let S look at its source copies in batches of size km, and now send the index of the first batch where all the k instances in the batch would result in an accept message in π. Upon receiving this index, the receiver R can use its corresponding set of source correlations; this generates k copies of the target correlation. We denote this protocol by π_k^*.

Observe that the message from S is now a geometric random variable with success probability ρ^k. We can compress this message down to its entropy and achieve an expected amortized communication cost of $\frac{(1/\rho)^k \cdot \mathsf{H}_b(\rho^k)}{k}$. Notice that by taking a larger k, the communication cost is reduced at the cost of consuming more source copies. Since the limit of the function as $k \to \infty$ is $\log(1/\rho)$, for any $\epsilon > 0$, we can choose an appropriate k such that the expected amortized communication cost is smaller than $\log(1/\rho) + \epsilon$.

To complete the proof, we now show the privacy of π_k^*. This is easy to see intuitively: all of the copies of the correlation are independent, the output is only dependent on the utilized batch of the km source correlations, and the message from S doesn't reveal any more information than the message in π. Therefore, since π is secure, π_k^* should also be secure.

More formally, let us prove the privacy against R. Let $M = i$ be the message sent, Y^{ki} that was used by R and $\hat{V}^n$ the output of the protocol. We will denote by $\pi(Y)$ the output of R when an accept message was sent.

$$
\begin{aligned}
(\hat{U}^n | \hat{V}^n, Y^{ki}, M = i) &\equiv ((\pi(Y_{k(i-1)+1}), \ldots, \pi(Y_{k(i-1)+k})) | Y^{ki}, M = i) \\
&\equiv ((\pi(Y_1), \ldots, \pi(Y_k)) | Y^k, M = i) \\
&\equiv ((\pi(Y_1), \ldots, \pi(Y_k)) | Y^k) \\
&\equiv (U^n | V^n)
\end{aligned}
$$

The distributions are equivalent for every message and copies of the source correlation used, and thus in expectation over M and copies of the source, their total variation distance will be 0.

The proof of privacy against S proceeds in a similar manner; Let $M = i$ be the message sent, X^{ki} that was used by S and $\hat{U}^n$ the output of the protocol. Note that in this case we know that the first $(i-1)$ k-tuples will be rejected, and the last one will be accepted. We will denote by $\pi(X)$ the output of S when an accept message was sent.

$$
\begin{aligned}
(\hat{V}^n | X^{ki}, M = i) &\equiv ((\pi(X_{k(i-1)+1}), \ldots, \pi(X_{k(i-1)+k})) | X^{ki}, M = i) \\
&\equiv ((\pi(X_1), \ldots, \pi(X_k)) | X^k, M = i) \\
&\equiv ((\pi(X_1), \ldots, \pi(X_k)) | X^k) \\
&\equiv (V^n | U^n)
\end{aligned}
$$

The distributions are equivalent for every message, copies of the source correlation used and the output and thus in expectation over them, the total variation distance between the distributions will be 0.

Remark 1 (Extensions). In Sect. 5.3, we further optimize the above transformation for better concrete efficiency in a number of metrics. We also present a modified construction for which we can bound the worst-case communication (as opposed to the expected communication); this can be done within the Las Vegas model by outputting a failure symbol with only negligible probability.

5.1 Efficient OMSR for (t, q)-correlations

In this section, we show efficient OMSR protocols for generating (t, q)-correlations from OT-correlations. This provides concrete improvements as well as generalizes the protocol from [24, Protocol 5.2] for generating $(2, 3)$-correlations.

Theorem 6. *There exists a secure accept-reject protocol π for source 1-out-of-t OT correlation over $\mathbb{Z}_q$ and target (t, q)-correlation with accept probability $\frac{tq}{q^t}$. In particular, for $(2, 3)$-correlations, the accept probability is $\frac{2}{3}$.*

Proof. Recall that in a 1-out-of-t OT correlation over $\mathbb{Z}_q$, the sender S is given a tuple $\mathbf{r} = (r_0, \dots, r_{t-1})$ that is uniform over $\mathbb{Z}_q^t$, and the receiver R is given (b, r_b) where b is a uniformly random over $\mathbb{Z}_t$ and r_b is its corresponding element in $\mathbf{r}$.

Now, define a function $f_{r,s}(x) : \mathbb{Z}_t \to \mathbb{Z}_q$, parameterized by $r \in \mathbb{Z}_t$ and $s \in \mathbb{Z}_q$ as $f_{r,s}(x) = w$ where $w \in \mathbb{Z}_q$ is such that $(r + x) \bmod t = (s + w) \bmod q$. In other words, the output w is such that $((r, s), (x, w))$ is a valid (t, q)-correlation. Note that the function $f_{(r,s)}$ is distinct for distinct (r, s).

Now, for each (r, s), define the vector $\mathbf{a}_{(r,s)} = (f_{(r,s)}(0), \dots, f_{(r,s)}(t-1))$, i.e., defined by evaluating $f_{(r,s)}$ at each $i \in \mathbb{Z}_t$. Denote by Φ, the set of all possible vectors $\mathbf{r} \in \mathbb{Z}_q^t$ for which there exist some (r, s) such that $\mathbf{a}_{(r,s)} = \mathbf{r}$. Intuitively, Φ denotes the accept set for the conversion—when the OT source correlation $\mathbf{r}$ given to S is in Φ, then it will send an "accept" message after which both parties will compute the target (t, q) correlation by local computation; when $\mathbf{r} \notin \Phi$, then both parties will abort.

Now, given $\mathbf{r} \in \Phi$, to generate required the (t, q) correlation, S will find the (r, s) such that $\mathbf{r} = \mathbf{a}_{(r,s)}$ and output it; the receiver R will simply output (b, r_b).

Notice that this results in a valid (t, q)-correlation since $f_{(r,s)}(b) = r_b$, and therefore $r + b \bmod t = s + r_b \bmod q$.

Observe that there are tq valid tuples (r, s), each corresponding to a unique "accepting" $\mathbf{r}$ as given above. Therefore, over a random $\mathbf{r} \in \mathbb{Z}_q^t$, the probability that $\mathbf{r} \in \Phi$ will be $\frac{tq}{q^t}$; this is exactly the accept probability of the accept-reject protocol. Notice that this protocol works best when t is a small number.

It is easy to see that both parties don't learn any additional information about the other's output; The sender doesn't know which value of b the receiver has. The receiver's view consists of only b, r_b and he doesn't know which r, s were consistent with the sender's part of the correlation.

Corollary 1. *For every $\epsilon > 0$, there exists an* OMSR *for converting from 1-out-of-2 OT over $\mathbb{Z}_3$ to $(2, 3)$-correlations with an expected amortized communication cost smaller than* $\log(3/2) + \epsilon$.

Proof. This is a direct consequence of Theorems 5 and 6.

Remark 2. Our protocol provides concrete improvements in generating $(2,3)$-correlations compared to the protocol from [24]. In particular, the protocol from [24] has an expected communication cost of $1.5 \cdot \mathsf{H}_b(1/3) \approx 1.377$ bits to generate one $(2,3)$-correlation instance; our protocol brings this cost down to just $\log(3/2) + \epsilon \approx 0.585 + \epsilon$ for any $\epsilon > 0$—an over 2x improvement to an already optimized protocol.

Remark 3. In the lower bounds section, we show a lower bound of $\log(q/2)/2$ for any OMR converting OT to $(2,q)$ correlation, exactly a half of our upper bound (Corollary 3). In addition, we also show that an optimal OMR converting OT correlation to $(2,3)$ correlation would be with 1-out-of-2 OT (Corollary 4).

5.2 Efficient OMSR for $(3,2)$-correlations

We now show efficient OMSR protocols for generating $(3,2)$-correlations from OT. An interesting result we show is that $(3,2)$-correlations are isomorphic to non-zero OLE correlations. The proofs are given in the full version of this paper.

Lemma 1. *The non-zero OLE (*nzOLE*) over $\mathbb{F}_4$ is isomorphic to the $(3,2)$-correlation. In other words, there is a secure no-communication reduction (i.e., an SNIR) between the two correlations (in both directions).*

Theorem 7. *There exists a secure accept-reject protocol π for source 1-out-of-3 OT over $\mathbb{F}_4$ and target $(3,2)$-correlation with accept probability $\frac{3}{16}$.*

Corollary 2. *For any $\epsilon > 0$, there exists an* OMSR *for converting 1-out-of-3 OT over $\mathbb{F}_4$ to $(3,2)$-correlations with expected amortized communication cost of $\log(\frac{16}{3}) + \epsilon$.*

Proof. This is a direct consequence of Theorems 5 and 7.

Remark 4. Our protocol provides concrete improvements in generating $(3,2)$-correlations compared to the protocol from [24]. In particular, the protocol from [24] has a communication cost of 6 bits to generate one $(3,2)$-correlation instance; our protocol brings this cost down to just $\log(16/3) + \epsilon \approx 2.415 + \epsilon$ for any $\epsilon > 0$—an over 2x improvement.

Remark 5. In Sect. 6, we show a lower bound of $\log(16/3)/3$ for any OMR (i.e., even without security) for converting 1-out-of-3 OT to a $(3,2)$ correlation—exactly a third of our upper bound (Corollary 5).

5.3 Efficiency Metrics and Optimizations

In this section, we present several optimizations for our generic transformation (Theorem 5) from accept-reject protocols to OMSRs in the Las Vegas model.

Number of Source Correlation Copies Used. In the context of Theorem 5, the number of copies of the source correlation used grows exponentially with k. We now show how to use fewer copies of an OT source correlation while keeping communication the same by using long *string* OT-correlations instead of OT correlations over a small group. This technique is highly useful in practice since string OT-correlations are equally easy to produce as regular OTs—a trivial use of a PRG can extend short random strings to long pseudo-random strings.

For the optimization, first notice that the decision for whether to accept or reject a k-tuple of the source correlation is only based on the view of the sender S. We exploit this observation in the following way: Consider the source correlation to be a long string-OT. S proceeds to "cut" the long string into small segments according the size of the original OT correlation required (for example, if the source correlation in the original protocol was OT over $\mathbb{F}_4$ then each segment will be of length of two bits). Now, S just needs to send the index of the first batch of k segments where the underling accept-reject protocol would send an accept message. This results in the same communication as before since the message here again is the same geometric random variable; note that it also does not decrease the computation required in terms of bits that the sender has to read. Still, the upshot of this technique now is that it only requires 1 string-OT correlation to generate k instances of the target correlation.

Optimizing Computation. While the optimization using string-OT reduces the number of source correlations required, the computation required in terms of the number of bits read does not decrease; it is still exponential in k. More specifically, for an accept-reject protocol with probability ρ, the computation per instance of the target correlation generated is proportional to $(1/\rho)^k$. We will now show how to optimize the number of source copies in the original protocol, thereby also reducing the computation required by the parties.

As a specific illustrative example, we focus on the protocol to generate $(3, 2)$-correlations. Recall that for $k = 1$, using the notation from Theorem 7, the sender will first check whether its view $\mathbf{r} = (r_0, r_1, r_2)$ of the OT correlation is of the form $(f_{a,s}(1), f_{a,s}(\alpha), f_{a,s}(\beta))$ for some $a \in \mathbb{F}_4 \setminus \{0\}; s \in \mathbb{F}_4$ where $\mathbb{F}_4$ is written as $\{0, 1, \alpha, \beta = \alpha + 1\}$. The protocol accepts if the sender's OT correlation is of the correct form, following which both parties can locally compute the target $(3, 2)$-correlation. It is easy to see that there are $3 \times 4 = 12$ distinct valid OT-correlations that will result in an accept message; equivalently, for a particular (r_0, r_1), there is exactly 1 r' such that (r_0, r_1, r') results in an accept message. This happens only with probability $1/4$ over a random source correlation, which makes the probability of the accept-reject protocol $\frac{12}{16} \cdot \frac{1}{4} = \frac{3}{16}$. In turn, this affects the communication and the source copies used (i.e., computation) of the compiled Las Vegas OMSR protocol.

We use a simple optimization trick here—instead of hoping for r_2 in (r_0, r_1, r_2) to be of the correct form, the sender can simply force it to be so by sending the $\mathbb{F}_4$ element r^* such that $(r_0, r_1, r_2 + r^*)$ will result in an accepting execution. This results in an extra 2 bits of communication from the sender. But since it increases the accept probability by a factor of 4, there is no change in the communication cost. Still, the upshot is that it decreases the number of source correlation copies used from $(\frac{16}{3})^k$ to $(\frac{4}{3})^k$, i.e., an improvement by a factor of 4^k. Such optimization can therefore exponentially improve the computation cost of the protocol.

Table 1. Trade-off between the communication (in bits) and the computation (in terms of the expected number of original source copies to be read) per instance of the target correlation generated as the value of k increases.

Correlation	Efficiency	k value					
		1	2	5	10	15	∞
$(2,3)$-correlation	comm. (bits)	1.377	1.114	0.853	0.727	0.681	0.585
	computation	1.5	2.25	7.59	57.66	437.8	∞
$(3,2)$-correlation (optimized)	comm. (bits)	3.08	2.87	2.66	2.55	2.51	2.415
	computation	1.33	1.77	4.21	17.75	74.83	∞

We point out that this optimization is quite general. Whenever the sender correlation is (u, v) and conditioned on u, there is only one accepting v, acceptance can be forced by sending an appropriate v' such that $(u, v + v')$ is now accepting. Such an optimization can drastically improve the computation cost.

Computation vs Communication Trade-off. Following our string-OT optimization, a trade-off between computation and communication is uncovered as we increase the value of k; while the use of string-OT allows reducing the number of instances of the source correlation used, the number of bits read (or in other words, the computation required) is still exponential in k. In particular, observe that as $k \to \infty$, while the amortized communication tends to $\log(1/\rho)$ where ρ is the accept probability of the underlying protocol, the amortized computation required grows exponentially. Despite this, we find that we can choose k to be fairly small and still achieve a substantial reduction in the communication cost. This is illustrated in Table 1 for the $(2, 3)$ and $(3, 2)$-correlations.

Expected to Worst-Case. So far, for the general protocol (Theorem 5), we only looked at the *expected* communication and computation cost; the worst case cost is unbounded, of course with exponentially decreasing probability. We now show that in the Las Vegas model, by allowing a negligible (in n) failure probability, we can bound even the *worst case* cost of the protocol; notably, this worst case bound is only slightly worse than the expected cost of the original protocol.

Consider t mk-tuples of the source correlation copies. Let B be the event that among the t tuples, the number of accepted ones is smaller than $\frac{n}{k}$. We now want to bound the probability of the event B.

Let $\{I_i\}_{i=1}^t$ be indicator variables for whether the i-th mk-tuple is accepted and μ denote the expected number of total tuples accepted. The indicators are all i.i.d. and binomially distributed with probability ρ^k. Observe also that

$\mathbb{E}[\sum_{i=1}^{t} I_i] = \mu = \rho^k t$. Define $\delta = 1 - \frac{n/k-1}{\mu}$. Now,

$$\Pr[B] = \Pr[\sum_{i=1}^{t} I_i \leq n/k - 1] = \Pr[\sum_{i=1}^{t} I_i \leq (1-\delta)\cdot\mu] \leq 2^{-\Omega((1-\frac{n/k-1}{\mu})^2\mu)}$$

where the inequality is by using the Chernoff bound.

Therefore, for $\mu \geq (1+\epsilon)(n/k-1)$ (which can be achieved with $t = \lceil(1+\epsilon)\cdot\frac{n/k}{\rho^k}\rceil$), it holds that $\Pr[B] \leq 2^{-\Omega(n\epsilon^2/k)}$. Thus by using $\epsilon m(n/\rho^k)$ more copies of the source correlation and with all but negligible probability, the OMSR will succeed and we can bound the worst-case complexity for the number of source correlations used. In order to achieve a worst case bound on the amortized communication cost, we cannot use compression like in Theorem 5; note however, that we can encode the indices of the batches that we accepted using $\frac{n}{k}\log(t) = \frac{n}{k}(\log(1+\epsilon)+k\log(1/\rho)+\log(n/k))$ bits and achieve an amortized communication cost of $\log(1/\rho)$ as $k \to \infty$ and thus achieve the same asymptotic communication cost. An implicit point to be noted here is that in order for the probability of the event B to be negligible using the Chernoff bound, it must be that $k = o(n)$; for instance, we can use $k = \sqrt{n}$.

5.4 Concrete Improvements for Existing Applications

We now show how our OMSR protocols for $(2,3)$ and $(3,2)$-correlations lead to concrete efficiency improvements for existing applications. As mentioned earlier, a primary motivation for our study of $(2,3)$ and $(3,2)$-correlations was their importance in recent work by Dinur et al. [24]; we significantly improve over their optimized constructions for these types of correlations.

In particular, [24] proposes candidate constructions in the so called *alternating moduli* paradigm for symmetric-key primitives like weak-PRFs, OWFs, and PRGs; the key idea here being that by mixing linear functions over different moduli (e.g., 2 and 3), resistance to known cryptanalysis techniques can be argued. At the same time, this leads to highly efficient evaluations particularly in distributed settings since most parts of the construction involve linear operations which are cheap to perform. The only non-linear operations required in these constructions were conversions of secret shared values from $\mathbb{Z}_2$ to $\mathbb{Z}_3$ and vice versa. Both the $(2,3)$ and $(3,2)$-correlations were introduced in this context to enable more efficient online protocols; optimized ways to generate these correlations from OT were also constructed.

Our OMSR protocols show further improvements to the generation of these useful correlations; This directly translates to significant improvements in the distributed protocols, which were shown to already be competitive compared to prior work. Table 2 shows a 2x improvement across the board for the prepossessing cost associated with 2PC distributed protocols for all constructions studied in [24]. Concrete applications of our efficiency gains include:

- (Oblivious PRFs). The $(2,3)$-weak-PRF was shown to have significantly better performance (4-5x faster) in the *oblivious* evaluation setting compared

Table 2. Concrete comparison of our OMSRs vs [24] in the context of the cost for different MPC-friendly constructions in the distributed 2PC setting. All numbers in the table are in bits. The parameters (η, υ, τ) denote the length of the input, the length of the intermediate layer, and the length of the output in the constructions. Concrete parameters were chosen in [24] based on cryptanalysis.

MPC-Friendly Constructions [24]	Parameters (η, υ, τ)	Offline comm.		Online comm. (for both)
		[24]	This work	
(2, 3)-wPRF	(256, 256, 81)	353	150	1536
LPN-wPRF	(256, 256, 128)	1889	768	2860
(2, 3)-OWF	(128, 452, 81)	623	265	904
LPN-PRG	(128, 512, 256)	3249	1312	1880

to existing algebraic OPRFs at the cost of requiring some prepossessing; our optimizations provide the same performance while reducing the client's offline communication by roughly 33%.

- (MPC-in-the-head signatures). The (2, 3)-OWF, when used to generate signatures through the MPC-in-the-head paradigm, resulted in roughly 10% smaller signatures sizes than using the LowMC blockcipher; our optimizations would result in even smaller signature sizes.
- (Function secret sharing and applications). The LPN-PRG is useful for several distributed applications that require length-doubling PRGs with the same input and output space. Of particular relevance are the distributed generation of function secret sharing (FSS) keys, distributed point functions (DPF), and distributed comparison functions (DCF); the core operation here is the distributed evaluation of the PRG, which is significantly more communication efficient through an MPC-friendly PRG than e.g., using AES. For all these applications, our optimizations provide further efficiency by reducing the preprocessing cost of the LPN-PRG by roughly 2.5x.

  FSS has also found applications in privacy-preserving machine learning for dealing with non-linear functions, which arguably contribute to the bulk of the cost in the secure computation setting. In this vein, the usefulness of an MPC-friendly PRG was recently demonstrated by [47] to build a DCF for neural network training (each ReLU activation function involves a DCF evaluation which translates to n distributed PRG evaluations when the data values are over $\mathbb{Z}_{2^n}$) . Prior work either required distributed evaluation of a PRG that was not MPC-friendly which led to high communication cost, or used a technique by Doerner-shelat [25] which requires computation exponential in the input size and therefore is useful only for small input domains ($< 2^{16}$). In contrast, [47] used the LPN-PRG from [24] to efficiently support large input domains of size 2^{32}. Concretely, given inputs in $\mathbb{Z}_{2^{32}}$, each ReLU evaluation requires 32 PRG evaluations; therefore, for each non-linear ReLU layer, as earlier, our optimizations translate to roughly 2.5x smaller offline and 1.6x smaller total communication.

6 Lower Bounds

We now prove lower bounds on the communication cost of (non-secure) OMRs.

6.1 Linear Lower Bound for One-Message Reductions

Theorem 8 proves a constant lower bound on amortized communication cost of statistical OMR converting a target correlation to another with larger S^* value. In Corollaries 3 to 5, we use a more fine-grained analysis to prove concrete lower bounds for the correlations we considered in the previous section.

Theorem 8. *Amortized communication cost of statistical OMR converting a correlation* (X, Y) *to* (U, V) *is strictly positive if* $\mathrm{S}^*(X, Y) < \mathrm{S}^*(U, V)$.

We will assume that the sender's algorithm is a deterministic function of their part of the correlation and that of the receiver is a deterministic function of the received message and their part of the correlation. This is without loss of generality because the protocol can keep aside sufficiently many copies of the source correlation for both sender and receiver to extract private randomness from. Our lower bounds allow the parties to use arbitrarily many copies of source correlation. We first state Lemmas 2 to 4 which together imply the theorem.

Lemma 2. *Amortized communication cost of OMR converting a correlation* (X, Y) *to common randomness is lower bounded by* $1 - \mathrm{S}^*(X, Y)$.

We will show that any achievable amortized communication cost c of OMR converting a correlation (X, Y) to common randomness satisfies

$$c \geq 1 - \sup_{U : U \leftrightarrow X \leftrightarrow Y} \frac{I(U;Y)}{I(U;X)},$$

where U is any random variable that is generated from X, i.e., it satisfies Markov chain $U \leftrightarrow X \leftrightarrow Y$. Since $\mathrm{S}^*(X, Y)$ is defined as the expression in the RHS, the lemma follows. In order to prove the above inequality, we revisit the problem of common randomness capacity of a correlation which was studied by Ahlswede and Csiszar in [4]. For communication rate $R \geq 0$, common randomness capacity $C(R)$ of a correlation (X, Y) is the asymptotic rate at which common randomness can be derived *per use* of (X, Y) using only one-way communication (from S to R) with rate limited to R. By retracing the proof of converse for common randomness capacity, we show that the amortized communication cost of statistical OMR converting (X, Y) to common randomness cannot be lower than the smallest ratio between R to $C(R)$ as R tends to zero. Our proof closely follows the aforementioned converse; this is provided in the full version.

Lemma 3. *For any correlation* (U, V) *and* $c > 1 - \mathrm{S}^*(U, V)$, *there exists a constant* $\lambda > 0$ *such that, for each* $\epsilon > 0$ *and for all sufficiently large* n, *there are functions* $S : \mathcal{U}^n \to [\lfloor 2^{n/\lambda} \rfloor] \times [\lceil 2^{c \cdot n/\lambda} \rceil]$ *and* $R : \mathcal{V}^n \times [\lceil 2^{c \cdot n/\lambda} \rceil] \to [\lfloor 2^{n/\lambda} \rfloor]$ *such* *that, when* (U_i, V_i) *is i.i.d. according to* p_{UV} *for all* $i \in [n]$, $(K, M) \leftarrow S(U^n)$ *and* $L \leftarrow R(V^n, M)$,

$$\Pr[K \neq L] \leq \epsilon, \tag{4}$$

$$\sum_{k \in [\lfloor 2^{n/\lambda} \rfloor]} \left| \Pr[K = k] - \frac{1}{\lfloor 2^{n/\lambda} \rfloor} \right| \leq \epsilon. \tag{5}$$

Proof. To prove this lemma, we once again invoke a result from [4]. The common randomness capacity $C(r)$ of correlation (U, V) for communication rate of $r \geq 0$ from sender to receiver is defined as the supremum of all $s \geq 0$ such that for each $\epsilon > 0$ and all sufficiently large n, there exist functions $S : \mathcal{U}^n \to [\lfloor 2^{s \cdot n} \rfloor] \times [\lceil 2^{r \cdot n} \rceil]$ and $R : \mathcal{V}^n \times [2^{r \cdot n}] \to [\lfloor 2^{s \cdot n} \rfloor]$ such that, Eqs. (4) to (5) are satisfied for $\lambda = \frac{1}{s}$. [50, Theorem 3] showed that

$$\lim_{r \downarrow 0} \frac{C(r)}{r} = \inf_{p(u|x)} \frac{I(U; X)}{I(U; X) - I(U; Y)} = \frac{1}{1 - \mathrm{S}^*(U, V)}. \tag{6}$$

Hence, by basic real analysis, for any $c > 1 - \mathrm{S}^*(U, V)$, there exists $r > 0$ such that $\frac{C(r)}{r} > \frac{1}{c}$.

Define $s = \frac{r}{c}$; since $C(r) > s$, by definition of $C(r)$, for each $\epsilon > 0$ and all sufficiently large n, there exist functions $S : \mathcal{U}^n \to [\lfloor 2^{s \cdot n} \rfloor] \times [\lceil 2^{c \cdot s \cdot n} \rceil]$ and $R : \mathcal{V}^n \times [2^{c \cdot s \cdot n}] \to [\lfloor 2^{s \cdot n} \rfloor]$ such that, Eqs. (4) to (5) are satisfied for $\lambda = \frac{1}{s}$. The proof follows by taking $\lambda = \frac{1}{s}$.

Lemma 4. *For any correlation* (U, V)*, suppose* $\lambda > 0$ *and* $c > 0$ *are such that, for each* $\epsilon > 0$ *and for all sufficiently large* n*, there are functions* $S : \mathcal{U}^n \to [\lfloor 2^{n/\lambda} \rfloor] \times [\lceil 2^{c \cdot n/\lambda} \rceil]$ *and* $R : \mathcal{V}^n \times [\lceil 2^{c \cdot n/\lambda} \rceil] \to [\lfloor 2^{n/\lambda} \rfloor]$ *such that, when* (U_i, V_i) *is i.i.d according to* p_{UV} *for all* $i \in [n]$, $(K, M) \leftarrow S(U^n)$ *and* $L \leftarrow R(V^n, M)$,

$$\Pr[K \neq L] \leq \epsilon, \tag{7}$$

$$\sum_{k \in [\lfloor 2^{n/\lambda} \rfloor]} \left| \Pr[K = k] - \frac{1}{\lfloor 2^{n/\lambda} \rfloor} \right| \leq \epsilon. \tag{8}$$

If $c < 1 - \mathrm{S}^*(X, Y)$*, then the amortized communication cost of OMR converting* (X, Y) *to* (U, V) *is at least* $\frac{1}{\lambda}(1 - \mathrm{S}^*(X, Y) - c)$.

Proof. Suppose an amortized communication cost $c' > 0$ is achievable for OMR converting (X, Y) to (U, V). Then, for each $i \in \mathbb{N}$, there exist functions $S'_i : \mathcal{X}^{m_i} \to \mathcal{U}^{n_i} \times [2^{c \cdot n_i}]$ and $R'_i : \mathcal{Y}^{m_i} \times [2^{c \cdot n_i}] \to \mathcal{V}^{n_i}$ such that, for each i, when (X^{m_i}, Y^{m_i}) is i.i.d. according to p_{XY}, (U^{n_i}, V^{n_i}) is i.i.d. according to p_{UV}, $(\hat{U}^{n_i}, M) \leftarrow S'_i(X^{m_i})$ and $\hat{V}^{n_i} \leftarrow R'_i(V^{n_i}, M)$,

$$\left(\hat{U}^{n_i}, \hat{V}^{n_i}\right) \approx^{\epsilon_i} (U^{n_i}, V^{n_i}), \tag{9}$$

where, $\epsilon_i \to 0$ as $i \to \infty$.

We can choose i such that 1) S'_i, R'_i in the aforementioned sequence satisfies Eq. (9) with $\epsilon_i \leq \epsilon$, and 2) there exist $S_i : \mathcal{U}^{n_i} \to [\lfloor 2^{n_i/\lambda} \rfloor] \times [\lceil 2^{c \cdot n_i/\lambda} \rceil]$ and

$R_i : \mathcal{V}^{n_i} \times [\lceil 2^{c \cdot n_i/\lambda} \rceil] \rightarrow [\lfloor 2^{n_i/\lambda} \rfloor]$ such that, Eqs. (7) to (8) are satisfied for $n = n_i$.

We construct an OMR converting (X, Y) to common randomness as follows:

1. Using (X^{m_i}, Y^{m_i}) and $c' \cdot n_i$ bits of communication, generate $(\hat{U}^{n_i}, \hat{V}^{n_i})$, where $(\hat{U}^{n_i}, M) \leftarrow S_i'(X^{m_i})$ and $\hat{V}^{n_i} \leftarrow R_i'(V^{n_i}, M)$.
2. Using $(\hat{U}^{n_i}, \hat{V}^{n_i})$ and $c \cdot n_i/\lambda$ bits of communication, generate (K, L), where $(K, M) \leftarrow S(U^n)$ and $L \leftarrow R(V^n, M)$.

By Eqs. (8) to (9) and the data processing inequality of total variation distance,

$$\Pr[K \neq L] \leq \epsilon + \epsilon_i \leq 2\epsilon,$$

$$\sum_{k \in [\lfloor 2^{n_i/\lambda} \rfloor]} \left| \Pr[K = k] - \frac{1}{\lfloor 2^{n_i/\lambda} \rfloor} \right| \leq \epsilon + \epsilon_i \leq 2\epsilon.$$

Thus, we have established that, there is a 2ϵ-OMR converting m_i copies of (X, Y) to $n_i/\lambda - 1$ bits of common randomness using $n_i(c'/\lambda + c) + 1$ bits of communication. Hence, an amortized communication cost of $c + \lambda c'$ is achievable for OMR converting (X, Y) to common randomness. But then, by Lemma 2,

$$c + \lambda c' \geq 1 - \mathrm{S}^*(X, Y) \implies c' \geq \frac{1}{\lambda}(1 - \mathrm{S}^*(X, Y) - c).$$

This proves the lemma.

Proof of Theorem 8. Choose c such that $1 - \mathrm{S}^*(U, V) < c < 1 - \mathrm{S}^*(X, Y)$. Invoking Lemma 3, we get λ that satisfies the conditions in Lemma 4. Hence, by Lemma 4, since $c < 1 - \mathrm{S}^*(X, Y)$, the amortized communication cost of OMR converting (X, Y) to (U, V) is at least $\frac{1}{\lambda}(1 - \mathrm{S}^*(X, Y) - c)$. This proves the theorem.

The above approach for lower bound can be used to get concrete lower bounds for OMR between specific correlations. For this, we first calculate S^* of some correlations of interest.

Lemma 5. *For any finite group* $\mathbb{G}$ *and* $k \in \mathbb{N}$, S^* *of* 1*-out-of-*k *OT correlation over* $\mathbb{G}$ *is* $\frac{1}{k}$.

Using an information theoretic argument, we prove that $I(U; Y)/I(U; X) \leq \frac{1}{k}$ for any U generated from X. Taking $U = X$ we achieve this upper bound implying the lemma. A full proof of this lemma is provided in the full version.

In a similar manner, we prove (in the full version) the next lemma.

Lemma 6. *For any finite field* $\mathbb{F}$, S^* *of OLE correlation over* $\mathbb{F}$ *is* $\frac{1}{2}$.

Using the above characterizations of S^* and Lemma 4, we get the following lower bounds on statistical OMR which justify our constructions in Sect. 5.

Corollary 3 (Corollary of Lemma *4* and Lemma *5*). *The amortized communication cost of statistical OMR converting* 1*-out-of-*k *OT correlation over any group* $\mathbb{G}$ *to* $(2, q)$ *correlation is at least* $\log(\frac{q}{2})/2$.

We can construct a simple OMR converting $(2,q)$ correlation to CR, by simply sending x_0, and both outputting $x_0||r_0$. Thus we achieve the following functions $S:\mathcal{U}^n \to [\lfloor 2^{n/\lambda}\rfloor] \times [\lceil 2^{c \cdot n/\lambda}\rceil]$ and $R:\mathcal{V}^n \times [\lceil 2^{c \cdot n/\lambda}\rceil] \to [\lfloor 2^{n/\lambda}\rfloor]$ with $\lambda = c = \frac{1}{\log(2q)}$. Now, Lemma 4 with $\mathrm{S}^*(X,Y) = \frac{1}{k}$ gives us the lower bound of $\frac{k-1}{k}\log(2q) - 1$. This is an increasing function of k. Plugging $k=2$, will give us the desirable $\log(\frac{q}{2})/2$ lower bound.

Remark 6. The same lower bound can be given for source correlation OLE due to Lemma 6.

Corollary 4. *The optimal (in terms of amortized communication cost) protocol for* $(2,3)$ *correlation using OT will be with* 1*-out-of-*2 *OT.*

From the proof of Corollary 3, we know that the amortized communication cost using source correlation 1-out-of-k OT, with $k \geq 3$, we get a lower bound of $\frac{2}{3}\log(6) - 1 \approx 0.72$. Since in Corollary 1 we achieve an OMSR with amortized communication cost $\log(3/2) < 0.72$ using 1-out-of-2 OT, we can infer that the optimal OMSR will also need to have the source correlation 1-out-of-2 OT.

Corollary 5 (Corollary of Lemma *4* and Lemma *5*). *The amortized communication cost of OMR converting* 1*-out-of-*3 *OT correlation over any group* $\mathbb{G}$ *to* $(3,2)$ *correlation is at least* $\log(\frac{16}{3})/3$.

We can construct a simple OMR converting (3,2) correlation to CR, by simply sending x_0, and both outputting $x_0||u_0||v_0$. In a similar manner as in Corollary 3 we will achieve a lower bound of $\log(16/3)/3$.

Corollary 6 (Corollary of Theorem *8* and Lemma *5*). *The amortized communication cost of OMR converting* 1*-out-of-*2 *OT (or OLE) correlation over any group* $\mathbb{G}_1$ *to an additive correlation over a group* $\mathbb{G}_2$ *where* $H(\psi) < \frac{\log|\mathbb{G}|_2}{2}$ *(where* ψ *is as described in the definition of additive correlation in Sect. 4.3) is strictly greater than* 0.

This simple corollary is due to the fact that S^* of the additive correlation is strictly greater than $\frac{1}{2}$.

6.2 Linear Lower Bound for Interactive Reductions

Our next result establishes a much more general lower bound albeit for a more restricted class of correlations. We show that generating an n-bit vector correlation using any correlation (X,Y) such that $\mathrm{S}^*(X,Y) < 1$ requires $\Omega(n)$ bits of *interactive communication*. We note that, as intuition suggests, $\mathrm{S}^*(X,Y) < 1$ if and only if the correlation lacks common randomness. We refer to the full version for a detailed discussion.

Observe that we are interested in generating a single copy of a correlation of length n from a class of correlations (for increasing value of n). As n approaches infinity, S^* of n-bit vector correlation approaches 1; hence, in the case of OMR, the linear lower bound on communication cost is intuitively implied by our previous result. The following theorem makes a strictly stronger claim.

Theorem 9. *Let π be an interactive protocol between S and R using (arbitrarily many copies of) correlation (X, Y) and ℓ bits of communication which computes n-bit unit vector correlation with $\epsilon \leq \frac{1}{6}$ error. That is, S and R output $\hat{U}$ and $\hat{V}$, respectively, where $(\hat{U}, \hat{V})$ is ϵ far from being an n-bit unit vector correlation in total variation distance. If $\mathrm{S}^*(X, Y) < 1$, there exists $1 < q < p$ that depend only on the description of distribution p_{XY} such that $\ell \geq \frac{n}{2}(\frac{p-q}{pq}) - \frac{1}{2}\log(n) - 1$.*

We state a couple of lemmas that will be used to prove the theorem.

Lemma 7. *Let π be an interactive protocol between S and R using correlation (X, Y) and ℓ bits of communication in which S and R output $\hat{U}$ and $\hat{V}$, respectively, where $\hat{U}$ and $\hat{V}$ are uniformly distributed over $\{0,1\}^n$ and $(\hat{U}, \hat{V}) \approx^{\epsilon} (U, V)$, where (U, V) is an n-bit unit vector correlation.*

Using π, we can construct $f : \mathcal{X} \to \{0,1\}^n$ and $g : \mathcal{Y} \to \{0,1\}^n$ such that, $f(X)$ and $g(Y)$ are uniformly distributed over $\{0,1\}^n$, and

$$\Pr\left[f(X) = g(Y)\right] \geq \frac{4^{-\ell}}{32n}(1 - \epsilon)^3.$$

Lemma 8. *Let (X_i, Y_i) be i.i.d. p_{XY} for each $i \in [m]$. Let $f : \mathcal{X} \to \{0,1\}^n$ and $g : \mathcal{Y} \to \{0,1\}^n$ be any pair of functions such that $f(X)$ and $g(Y)$ are uniformly distributed over $\{0,1\}^n$. If $\mathrm{S}^*(X, Y) < 1$, there exist $1 < q < p$ that depend only on the description of p_{XY} such that*

$$\Pr\left[f(X) = g(Y)\right] \leq 2^{-n(\frac{p-q}{pq})}.$$

Proof of Lemma 7 follows the same blueprint as the proof of [18, Theorem 2.6]. We provide the proof in the full version. Before proving Lemma 8, we show how they imply the theorem.

Proof of Theorem 9. If $\hat{U}$ and $\hat{V}$ are not uniformly distributed over $\{0,1\}^n$, we transform π into π' which outputs correlation $(\tilde{U}, \tilde{V})$ with uniform marginals as follows: Let $Sup \subset \{0,1\}^n$, where $u \in Sup$ if $\Pr\left[\hat{U} = u\right] < \frac{1}{2^n}$. Let W be a random variable over the domain Sup s.t. $\Pr\left[W = u\right]$ is proportional to $\frac{1}{2^n} - \Pr\left[\hat{U} = u\right]$. Now, S on receiving $u \notin Sup$, w.p. $\frac{1}{\Pr\left[\hat{U}=u\right]}\frac{1}{2^n}$, S outputs u, and with the remainder probability, he outputs a sample from W. R outputs $\tilde{V}$ sampled analogously. It is easy to see that $\tilde{U}$ and $\tilde{V}$ are distributed uniformly over $\{0,1\}^n$. Since $(\hat{U}, \hat{V})$ is ϵ far from n-bit unit vector correlation in TVD,

$$\sum_{u \in \{0,1\}^n, \Pr\left[\hat{U}=u\right] > \frac{1}{2^n}} \Pr\left[\hat{U} = u\right] - \frac{1}{2^n} \leq \epsilon.$$

A similar condition holds for $\hat{V}$. By a union bound, $\Pr\left[\tilde{U} = \hat{U}, \tilde{V} = \hat{V}\right] \geq 1 - 2\epsilon$. From this it follows that, when (U, V) is distributed according to n-bit unit vector correlation,

$$\mathsf{TVD}\left((\tilde{U}, \tilde{V}), (U, V)\right) \leq (1 - 2\epsilon)\mathsf{TVD}\left((\hat{U}, \hat{V}), (U, V)\right) + 2\epsilon \leq 3\epsilon.$$

Since $(\tilde{U}, \tilde{V})$ has uniform marginals, invoking Lemma 7 with π', we obtain f, g such that $f(X^m)$ and $g(Y^m)$ are uniform in $\{0,1\}^n$ and

$$\Pr\left[f(X^m) = g(Y^m)\right] \geq \frac{4^{-\ell}}{32n}(1 - 3\epsilon)^3.$$

However, by Lemma 8, it holds that $\Pr\left[f(X^m) = g(Y^m)\right] \leq 2^{-n\left(\frac{p-q}{pq}\right)}$.

The two inequalities together imply that $2(\ell + 1) \geq n(\frac{p-q}{pq}) - \log(n)$ when $\epsilon < \frac{1}{6}$, proving the theorem. We conclude by proving Lemma 8.

Proof (Proof of Lemma 8). This lemma is proved along the lines of [10, Theorem 1]. Bogdanov and Mossel's showed in [10, Theorem 1] that deriving n bits of common randomness using a source of noisy common randomness and zero communication succeeds only with $2^{-\Omega(n)}$ probability. A noisy common randomness correlation with ϵ crossover probability is one in which the sender gets a random bit and the receiver gets the same bit with probability $1 - \epsilon$ and its complement with the remaining probability. Their approach used a version of hypercontractive inequality for noisy common randomness distribution. The following argument is a generalization of their argument. For every $z \in \{0,1\}^n$, define $f_z : \mathcal{X}^m \to \{0,1\}$ and $g_z : \mathcal{Y}^m \to \{0,1\}$ as

$$f_z(x^m) = \begin{cases} 1, \text{if } f(x^m) = z \\ 0, \text{otherwise,} \end{cases} \qquad g_z(y^m) = \begin{cases} 1, \text{if } g(y^m) = z \\ 0, \text{otherwise.} \end{cases}$$

Then,

$$\begin{aligned} \Pr\left[f(X^m) = g(Y^m)\right] &= \sum_{z \in \{0,1\}^n} \Pr\left[f(X^m) = z \wedge g(Y^m) = z\right] \\ &= \sum_{z \in \{0,1\}^n} \mathbb{E}_{X^m, Y^m}[f_z(X^m) \cdot g_z(Y^m)]. \end{aligned} \tag{10}$$

If $\mathrm{S}^*(X,Y) < 1$, there exist $1 < q < p$ such that, defining $p' = \frac{p}{p-1}$, for any pair of functions $f : \mathcal{X}^n \to \mathbb{R}$ and $g : \mathcal{Y}^n \to \mathbb{R}$,

$$\mathbb{E}_{X^m, Y^m}[f(X^m) \cdot g(Y^m)] \leq \left(\mathbb{E}_{X^m}[f^{p'}(X^m)]\right)^{\frac{1}{p'}} \left(\mathbb{E}_{Y^m}[g^q(Y^m)]\right)^{\frac{1}{q}}.$$

This follows almost immediately from known results; a formal proof is provided in the full version.

Using this in Eq. (10), and noting that f_z and g_z are Boolean functions,

$$\begin{aligned} &\sum_{z \in \{0,1\}^n} \mathbb{E}_{X^m, Y^m}[f_z(X^m) \cdot g_z(Y^m)] \\ &\leq \sum_{z \in \{0,1\}^n} \left(\mathbb{E}_{X^m}[f_z(X^m)]\right)^{\frac{1}{p'}} \left(\mathbb{E}_{Y^m}[g_z(Y^m)]\right)^{\frac{1}{q}} \\ &\leq \left(\sum_{z \in \{0,1\}^n} \left(\mathbb{E}_{X^m}[f_z(X^m)]\right)^{\frac{p'}{p'}}\right)^{\frac{1}{p'}} \left(\sum_{z \in \{0,1\}^n} \left(\mathbb{E}_{Y^m}[g_z(Y^m)]\right)^{\frac{p}{q}}\right)^{\frac{1}{p}}. \end{aligned} \tag{11}$$

Here, the last inequality used Holder's inequality:

$$\sum_{i=1}^{k} |a_i| \cdot |b_i| \leq \left(\sum_{i=1}^{k} |a_i|^{p'}\right)^{\frac{1}{p'}} \left(\sum_{i=1}^{k} |b_i|^{p}\right)^{\frac{1}{p}}.$$

Since $f(X^m)$ and $g(Y^m)$ are uniform over $\{0,1\}^n$, for all $z \in \{0,1\}^n$,

$$\mathbb{E}_{X^m}[f_z(X^m)] = 2^{-n} \qquad \mathbb{E}_{Y^m}[g(Y^m)] = 2^{-n}.$$

Hence, $\sum_{z\in\{0,1\}^n} (\mathbb{E}_{X^m}[f_z(X^m)]) = 1$, and since $p > q$,

$$\sum_{z\in\{0,1\}^n} (\mathbb{E}_{Y^m}[g_z(Y^m)])^{\frac{p}{q}} = \sum_{z\in\{0,1\}^n} 2^{-n} (\mathbb{E}_{Y^m}[g_z(Y^m)])^{\frac{p}{q}-1} = 2^{-n(\frac{p}{q}-1)}.$$

Using these observations in Eq. (11), we get $\Pr[f(X^m) = g(Y^m)] \leq 2^{-n(\frac{p-q}{pq})}$.

Remark 7. It is clear from the proof of Lemma 7 that n-bit unit vector correlation can be replaced by any correlation that can be converted to common randomness with n-bits of common randomness with success probability that is inverse polynomial in n. Hence, the result in Theorem 9 holds more generally for families of correlations with this property; this includes 1-out-of-$k(n)$ OT correlations of string length n when $k(n)$ is polynomial in n.

7 Role of Common Randomness in OMSR

In general, common randomness does not aid in OMSR whenever the target correlation does not have inherent common randomness. Correlation (U, V) is said to have non-trivial common randomness if it can be represented as $((W, U'), (W, V'))$ where W has non-zero entropy. In other words, there are deterministic functions f and g such that $f(U) = g(V)$ with probability 1 and $H(f(U)) > 0$. All (target) correlations considered in this work lack common information; more generally, this holds for most correlations with cryptographic applications because, intuitively, common information does not enable cryptographic tasks. In the case of perfect OMSR, by simply conditioning on any realization of common randomness we get a perfect OMSR without common randomness setup. However, for statistical OMSR, such a restriction need not necessarily be secure. The following theorem is proved by showing the existence of a realization of common randomness such that, restricted to this realization the OMSR still guarantees comparable security. A concrete consequence of the following theorem is that common randomness does not aid in statistical OMSR with negligible error for target correlations without common randomness. A proof of the theorem is provided in the full version.

Theorem 10. *Suppose there exists an ϵ-OMSR $\langle S, R\rangle$ converting a correlation (X, Y) to n copies of a target correlation (U, V) using common randomness Q. If (U, V) lacks common information, there exists an $O(n\epsilon)$-OMSR converting correlation (X, Y) to n copies of a target correlation (U, V) with the same cost without using common randomness.*

Acknowledgments. We thank the anonymous reviewers for helpful comments. M. Kelkar was partially supported by a Technion research scholarship. Y. Ishai and V. Narayanan were supported by ERC Project NTSC (742754), and ISF grant 2774/20. Y. Ishai was additionally supported by BSF grant 2018393.

References

1. Agarwal, P., Narayanan, V., Pathak, S., Prabhakaran, M., Prabhakaran, V.M., Rehan, M.A.: Secure Non-interactive reduction and spectral analysis of correlations. In: Dunkelman, O., Dziembowski, S. (eds.) Advances in Cryptology–EUROCRYPT 2022. LNCS, vol. 13277, pp. 797–827. Springer, Cham (2022). https://doi.org/10.1007/978-3-031-07082-2_28
2. Agrawal, S., et al.: Cryptography from one-way communication: on completeness of finite channels. In: Moriai, S., Wang, H. (eds.) ASIACRYPT 2020, Part III. LNCS, vol. 12493, pp. 653–685. Springer, Cham (2020). https://doi.org/10.1007/978-3-030-64840-4_22
3. Agrawal, S., et al.: Secure computation from one-way noisy communication, or: anti-correlation via anti-concentration. In: Malkin, T., Peikert, C. (eds.) CRYPTO 2021, Part II. LNCS, vol. 12826, pp. 124–154. Springer, Cham (2021). https://doi.org/10.1007/978-3-030-84245-1_5
4. Ahlswede, R., Csiszar, I.: Common randomness in information theory and cryptography. II CR capacity. IEEE Trans. Inf. Theory **44**(1), 225–240 (1998)
5. Anantharam, V., Gohari, A.A., Kamath, S., Nair, C.: On maximal correlation, hypercontractivity, and the data processing inequality studied by Erkip and Cover. CoRR abs/1304.6133 (2013). https://arxiv.org/abs/1304.6133
6. Beaver, D.: Efficient multiparty protocols using circuit randomization. In: Feigenbaum, J. (ed.) CRYPTO 1991. LNCS, vol. 576, pp. 420–432. Springer, Heidelberg (1992). https://doi.org/10.1007/3-540-46766-1_34
7. Bendlin, R., Damgård, I., Orlandi, C., Zakarias, S.: Semi-homomorphic encryption and multiparty computation. Cryptology ePrint Archive, Paper 2010/514 (2010)
8. Bhushan, K., Misra, A.K., Narayanan, V., Prabhakaran, M.: Secure non-interactive reducibility is decidable. In: TCC (2022)
9. Blum, M., Feldman, P., Micali, S.: Non-interactive zero-knowledge and its applications (extended abstract). In: STOC, pp. 103–112 (1988)
10. Bogdanov, A., Mossel, E.: On extracting common random bits from correlated sources. IEEE Trans. Inf. Theory **57**(10), 6351–6355 (2011)
11. Boyle, E., et al.: Function secret sharing for mixed-mode and fixed-point secure computation. In: Canteaut, A., Standaert, F.-X. (eds.) EUROCRYPT 2021, Part II. LNCS, vol. 12697, pp. 871–900. Springer, Cham (2021). https://doi.org/10.1007/978-3-030-77886-6_30
12. Boyle, E., Couteau, G., Gilboa, N., Ishai, Y.: Compressing vector OLE. In: ACM CCS, pp. 896–912 (2018)
13. Boyle, E., et al.: Correlated pseudorandomness from expand-accumulate codes. In: Dodis, Y., Shrimpton, T. (eds.) Advances in Cryptology–CRYPTO 2022. CRYPTO 2022. LNCS, vol. 13508, pp. pp. 603–633. Springer, Cham (2022). https://doi.org/10.1007/978-3-031-15979-4_21
14. Boyle, E., et al.: Efficient two-round OT extension and silent non-interactive secure computation. In: ACM CCS, pp. 291–308 (2019)

15. Boyle, E., Couteau, G., Gilboa, N., Ishai, Y., Kohl, L., Scholl, P.: Efficient pseudorandom correlation generators: silent OT extension and more. In: Boldyreva, A., Micciancio, D. (eds.) CRYPTO 2019, Part III. LNCS, vol. 11694, pp. 489–518. Springer, Cham (2019). https://doi.org/10.1007/978-3-030-26954-8_16
16. Boyle, E., Couteau, G., Gilboa, N., Ishai, Y., Kohl, L., Scholl, P.: Efficient pseudorandom correlation generators from ring-LPN. In: Micciancio, D., Ristenpart, T. (eds.) CRYPTO 2020, Part II. LNCS, vol. 12171, pp. 387–416. Springer, Cham (2020). https://doi.org/10.1007/978-3-030-56880-1_14
17. Boyle, E., Gilboa, N., Ishai, Y.: Secure computation with preprocessing via function secret sharing. In: Hofheinz, D., Rosen, A. (eds.) TCC 2019, Part I. LNCS, vol. 11891, pp. 341–371. Springer, Cham (2019). https://doi.org/10.1007/978-3-030-36030-6_14
18. Canonne, C.L., Guruswami, V., Meka, R., Sudan, M.: Communication with imperfectly shared randomness. In: ITCS, pp. 257–262 (2015)
19. Couteau, G., Rindal, P., Raghuraman, S.: Silver: silent VOLE and oblivious transfer from hardness of decoding structured LDPC codes. In: Malkin, T., Peikert, C. (eds.) CRYPTO 2021, Part III. LNCS, vol. 12827, pp. 502–534. Springer, Cham (2021). https://doi.org/10.1007/978-3-030-84252-9_17
20. Cover, T.M., Thomas, J.A.: Elements of Information Theory. Wiley-Interscience (2006)
21. Damgård, I., Pastro, V., Smart, N., Zakarias, S.: Multiparty computation from somewhat homomorphic encryption. In: Safavi-Naini, R., Canetti, R. (eds.) CRYPTO 2012. LNCS, vol. 7417, pp. 643–662. Springer, Heidelberg (2012). https://doi.org/10.1007/978-3-642-32009-5_38
22. De, A., Mossel, E., Neeman, J.: Non interactive simulation of correlated distributions is decidable. In: SODA, pp. 2728–2746 (2018)
23. Demmler, D., Schneider, T., Zohner, M.: ABY - A framework for efficient mixed-protocol secure two-party computation. In: NDSS 2015 (2015)
24. Dinur, I., et al.: MPC-friendly symmetric cryptography from alternating moduli: candidates, protocols, and applications. In: Malkin, T., Peikert, C. (eds.) CRYPTO 2021, Part IV. LNCS, vol. 12828, pp. 517–547. Springer, Cham (2021). https://doi.org/10.1007/978-3-030-84259-8_18
25. Doerner, J., Shelat, A.: Scaling ORAM for secure computation. In: ACM CCS, pp. 523–535 (2017)
26. Gács, P., Körner, J.: Common information is far less than mutual information. Probl. Control Inf. Theory **2**(2), 149–162 (1973)
27. Garg, S., Ishai, Y., Kushilevitz, E., Ostrovsky, R., Sahai, A.: Cryptography with one-way communication. In: Gennaro, R., Robshaw, M. (eds.) CRYPTO 2015, Part II. LNCS, vol. 9216, pp. 191–208. Springer, Heidelberg (2015). https://doi.org/10.1007/978-3-662-48000-7_10
28. Ghazi, B., Jayram, T.S.: Resource-efficient common randomness and secret-key schemes. In: SODA, pp. 1834–1853 (2018)
29. Ghazi, B., Kamath, P., Sudan, M.: Decidability of non-interactive simulation of joint distributions. In: FOCS, pp. 545–554 (2016)
30. Goldreich, O., Micali, S., Wigderson, A.: How to play any mental game. In: STOC, pp. 218–229 (1987)
31. Goyal, S., Narayanan, V., Prabhakaran, M.: Oblivious-transfer complexity of noisy coin-toss via secure zero communication reductions. In: TCC, pp. 89–118 (2022)
32. Guruswami, V., Radhakrishnan, J.: Tight bounds for communication-assisted agreement distillation. In: CCC, pp. 1–17 (2016)

33. Ishai, Y., Kushilevitz, E.: Randomizing polynomials: a new representation with applications to round-efficient secure computation. In: FOCS, pp. 294–304 (2000)
34. Ishai, Y., Prabhakaran, M., Sahai, A.: Founding cryptography on oblivious transfer – efficiently. In: Wagner, D. (ed.) CRYPTO 2008. LNCS, vol. 5157, pp. 572–591. Springer, Heidelberg (2008). https://doi.org/10.1007/978-3-540-85174-5_32
35. Kamath, S., Anantharam, V.: On non-interactive simulation of joint distributions. IEEE Trans. Inf. Theory **62**(6), 3419–3435 (2016)
36. Khorasgani, H.A., Maji, H.K., Nguyen, H.H.: Secure non-interactive simulation: feasibility and rate. In: Dunkelman, O., Dziembowski, S. (eds.) Advances in Cryptology–EUROCRYPT 2022. LNCS, vol. 13277, pp. 767–796. Springer, Cham (2022). https://doi.org/10.1007/978-3-031-07082-2_27
37. Khorasgani, H.A., Maji, H.K., Nguyen, H.H.: Secure non-interactive simulation from arbitrary joint distributions. In: TCC, pp. 378–407 (2022)
38. Kilian, J.: Founding crytpography on oblivious transfer. In: STOC, pp. 20–31 (1988)
39. Narayanan, V., Prabhakaran, M., Prabhakaran, V.M.: Zero-communication reductions. In: TCC, pp. 274–304 (2020)
40. Ryffel, T., Tholoniat, P., Pointcheval, D., Bach, F.R.: Ariann: low-interaction privacy-preserving deep learning via function secret sharing. Proc. Priv. Enhanc. Technol. **2022**(1), 291–316 (2022)
41. Storrier, K., Vadapalli, A., Lyons, A., Henry, R.: Grotto: screaming fast $(2+1)$-pc for $\mathbb{Z}_{2^n}$ via (2, 2)-DPFs. Cryptology ePrint Archive, Paper 2023/108 (2023). https://eprint.iacr.org/2023/108
42. Sudan, M., Tyagi, H., Watanabe, S.: Communication for generating correlation: a unifying survey. IEEE Trans. Inf. Theory **66**(1), 5–37 (2020)
43. Wagh, S.: PIKA: secure computation using function secret sharing over rings. Proc. Priv. Enhanc. Technol. **2022**(4), 351–377 (2022)
44. Witsenhausen, H.S.: On sequences of pairs of dependent random variables. SIAM J. Appl. Math. **28**(1), 100–113 (1975)
45. Wyner, A.D.: The wire-tap channel. Bell Syst. Tech. J. **54**(8), 1355–1387 (1975)
46. Yang, K., Weng, C., Lan, X., Zhang, J., Wang, X.: Ferret: Fast extension for correlated OT with small communication. In: CCS, pp. 1607–1626 (2020)
47. Yang, P., et al.: FssNN: communication-efficient secure neural network training via function secret sharing. Cryptology ePrint Archive, Paper 2023/073 (2023). https://eprint.iacr.org/2023/073
48. Yao, A.C.: Protocols for secure computations. In: SFCS, pp. 160–164 (1982)
49. Yao, A.C.: How to generate and exchange secrets. In: SFCS, pp. 162–167 (1986)
50. Zhao, L., Chia, Y.K.: The efficiency of common randomness generation. In: Allerton, pp. 944–950 (2011)

A Framework for Statistically Sender Private OT with Optimal Rate

Pedro Branco[1(✉)], Nico Döttling[2], and Akshayaram Srinivasan[3]

[1] Max Planck Institute for Security and Privacy, Bochum, Germany
pedrodemelobranco@gmail.com
[2] Helmholtz Center for Information Security (CISPA), Saarbrücken, Germany
[3] Tata Institute of Fundamental Research, Mumbai, India

Abstract. Statistical sender privacy (SSP) is the strongest achievable security notion for two-message oblivious transfer (OT) in the standard model, providing statistical security against malicious receivers and computational security against semi-honest senders. In this work we provide a novel construction of SSP OT from the Decisional Diffie-Hellman (DDH) and the Learning Parity with Noise (LPN) assumptions achieving (asymptotically) optimal amortized communication complexity, i.e. it achieves rate 1. Concretely, the total communication complexity for k OT instances is $2k(1 + o(1))$, which (asymptotically) approaches the information-theoretic lower bound. Previously, it was only known how to realize this primitive using heavy rate-1 FHE techniques [Brakerski et al., Gentry and Halevi TCC'19].

At the heart of our construction is a primitive called statistical co-PIR, essentially a a public key encryption scheme which statistically erases bits of the message in a few hidden locations. Our scheme achieves nearly optimal ciphertext size and provides statistical security against malicious receivers. Computational security against semi-honest senders holds under the DDH assumption.

1 Introduction

Oblivious Transfer. Oblivious transfer (OT) [46] is one of the central objects of study in secure computation: OT is complete for secure two- and multiparty computation in the sense that given a secure OT protocol, any distributed function can be computed securely. In its basic form, OT is a protocol between a receiver, holding a bit $b \in \{0,1\}$ and a sender holding two bits $m_0, m_1 \in \{0,1\}$. It allows the receiver to retrieve the bit m_b in such a way that the sender learns nothing about b, while the receiver learns nothing about m_{1-b}.

In the two party setting, OT protocols[1] cannot be information-theoretically secure against both parties, hence a cryptographic communication overhead of size $\mathsf{poly}(\lambda)$ is necessary. To amortize this overhead, one of the protocol parameters has to grow polynomially. In string-OT, the sender transfers (potentially) long message strings $\mathbf{m}_0, \mathbf{m}_1 \in \{0,1\}^{\mathsf{poly}(\lambda)}$.

[1] without the help of additional trust assumptions such as e.g. secure hardware.

H. Handschuh and A. Lysyanskaya (Eds.): CRYPTO 2023, LNCS 14081, pp. 548–576, 2023.
https://doi.org/10.1007/978-3-031-38557-5_18

The batch-setting offers a different angle on amortization: Rather than increasing the length of the messages to size $\mathsf{poly}(\lambda)$, one can bundle the joint execution of many (say, k) OT-instances into a single protocol.

Oblivious Transfer with High Rate. Minimizing the communication overhead of OT in the string and batch setting has received considerable attention in recent years [1,9–13,22,23,25,31]. This line of research has culminated in constructions of OT protocols from several hardness assumptions [18,20,26] achieving optimal communication of $2k(1+o(1))$, which approaches the information theoretic lower-bound $2k$.[2] The rate of an OT protocol in the batch setting is defined as the ratio between the information-theoretic lower bound and the overall communication of a given protocol, hence protocols with communication $2k(1+o(1))$ have rate $1/(1+o(1)) = 1 - o(1)$ which approaches 1.

Compared to "low-rate" OT protocols, say protocols with rate $\leq 1/2$, such high-rate OT protocols have been notoriously hard to build and there is a fundamental reason for this. Achieving communication seems to involve a *phase-transition* and should be viewed as more than a *constant factor* improvement. For example, (two-message) OT with download-rate beyond this threshold implies the existence of lossy trapdoor functions [23][3] or succinct two-round protocols for branching program evaluation and PIR schemes [23,35].

The techniques developed in this context found surprising applications, and where instrumental in several constructions of correlation-intractable hash functions, which gave rise to non-interactive zero-knowledge protocols [21,36] or batch arguments [39] from weaker assumptions.

The goal of this paper is to study what is the strongest notion of security we can achieve for OT in the plain model (i.e., without any trusted setup assumptions) while preserving optimal communication.

Statistical Sender Privacy. The standard (simulation-based) security definition of OT is given with respect to semi-honest adversaries. To achieve simulation-based security against malicious parties, one has to either rely on trusted setup assumptions (or random oracles), or increase the round complexity of the protocol. Statistical sender privacy provides a meaningful relaxation to the standard notion of malicious security and has been shown to be achievable with *two-message protocols without making use of setup assumptions* [2,43]. Since then, SSP OT was built from several assumptions such as DDH [1,2,43], QR (or DCR) [30], lattice based assumptions [19,42], or LPN together with a derandomization assumption [8].

SSP OT protocols provide security against a computationally bounded sender, but a strong statistical security notion against malicious and unbounded receivers. In essence, this notion requires the existence of an *unbounded* simulator which extracts the receiver's choice bit b^* from his (potentially malformed)

[2] The communication complexity of any, even insecure, OT is at least $2k$. We can achieve this by sacrificing sender's security (the sender sends both (m_0, m_1)) or receiver's security (the receiver sends b and obtains m_b from the sender).

[3] This is the main reason for why one could expect such a protocol to inherently be heavier on public-key operations.

protocol message, and simulates the response of an honest sender given only the message m_{b^*} the receiver is supposed to obtain.

SSP OT has been the critical ingredient in the construction of several strong primitives, most notably the construction of malicious circuit-private FHE [44], two-round statistical zaps [5,6,29,37,38], non-malleable commitments [41] or two-party computation with statistical security [7,40].

SSP OT with Rate 1. The rate-1 and SSP properties are not *orthogonal*, but intricately connected. Specifically, SSP OT can be constructed from any rate 1 OT [6,23]. The catch is, however, that this transformation (and in fact any such generic transformation) does not preserve rate 1, but necessarily makes the rate drop below 1/2.

Further note that rate 1 (batch or string) OT is by no means automatically SSP. For string OT a malicious receiver might learn half of the bits of $\mathbf{m}_0$ and $\mathbf{m}_1$, whereas for batch OT a malicious receiver might learn both message bits m_0 and m_1 for some of the batch instances. Indeed, with no safeguards against such attacks in place, it is relatively straightforward to construct malformed receiver messages to implement this attack e.g. against the scheme of Brakerski et al. [18].

One may thus raise the question whether rate 1 and SSP security can actually be achieved simultaneously. Indeed, this question was answered affirmatively by Brakerski et al. [20] and by Gentry and Halevi [26] under the LWE assumption, whose constructions of rate-1 statistically circuit private FHE give rise to rate-1 SSP OT, both in the string OT and the batch OT setting.

Their constructions, however, relies on heavy FHE machinery and on specifics of the LWE problem which allow for *ciphertext compression*. As a consequence, their result should be seen as a feasibility result. Furthermore, due to its heavy reliance on FHE-specific (non-black-box) techniques their result does not provide a recipe on how to construct high-rate SSP OT from a wider range of assumptions, or how to realize this primitive with concrete efficiency. This is unsatisfactory both from a theoretical and an applied perspective: the foundation of rate 1 SSP OT is as narrow as that of FHE, and the heavy non-black-box machinery in their construction constitutes a serious roadblock for actually using this primitive.

More recently, in the string OT setting, Aggarwal et al [1] showed that *download* rate-1 SSP string OT (for asymptotically long strings) can be achieved from the standard DDH assumption via a fully black box construction.

However, in the setting of rate-1 SSP batch OT, the FHE-based constructions of [20,26] are currently the only candidates.

1.1 Our Results

A Framework for SSP OT with Optimal Rate. Our main result is a new framework for the construction of SSP batch OT schemes with optimal communication complexity in the plain model (i.e., no random oracles or common reference string).

Statistical co-PIR. Our framework is a refinement of the blueprint of [18]. One of the key tools in [18] is a primitive called co-PIR. On a high level, a co-PIR scheme can be seen as a rate-1 public key encryption scheme (for long messages) which erases some bits of the sender's message in a way such that they are not recoverable by the receiver.

We identify the construction of co-PIR in [18] as one of the main bottlenecks towards an SSP secure rate 1 batch OT construction. The main reason is that their construction is only computationally secure, and the *lost bits* of the sender's message are only computationally hidden from the receiver.

Our first contribution is a statistically secure construction of co-PIR, which guarantees that the lost bits of the sender's message are *statistically hidden* from the receiver. As such, a statistical co-PIR scheme can be seen *somewhere statistically hiding* encryption scheme.

Theorem 1 (Informal). *There exists a co-PIR scheme that is statistically secure against malicious receivers and computationally secure against semi-honest senders assuming the DDH assumption. Additionally, the scheme fulfills the following efficiency properties:*

- *The sender's computational complexity is subquadratic in the size of the database,* $|\mathbf{D}|^{1+\varepsilon} \cdot t \cdot \mathsf{poly}(\lambda)$ *where* $\mathbf{D}$ *represents the input of the sender and* t *represents the size of the receiver's input and* $1 > \varepsilon > 0$*. The receiver's computational complexity is* $|\mathbf{D}| \cdot t \cdot \mathsf{poly}(\lambda)$*.*
- *The size of the sender's message is* $|\mathbf{D}| + o(|\mathbf{D}|)$ *when* $t = o(|\mathbf{D}|)$*.*

We further provide a generic construction of a co-PIR scheme from any (statistically sender private) rate-1 block-PIR scheme, i.e. a PIR scheme which transfers large blocks. Such rate-1 block PIR schemes can be constructed from the DDH assumption [1]. A comparison between different co-PIR schemes is presented in Table 1.

Rate-1 SSP batch OT from DDH and LPN. We provide instantiations of the primitives of our framework from the DDH assumption. We thus obtain a rate-1 SSP batch OT scheme from the DDH and LPN (with inverse polynomial noise rate) assumptions. Specifically, to execute k independent OTs, the overall communication complexity required by our protocol is $2k(1 + o(1))$.

Theorem 2 (Informal). *There exists a SSP OT scheme with optimal rate where security for the receiver holds assuming both DDH and LPN (with inverse polynomial noise-rate) assumptions.*

Our result improves upon Brakerski et al. [18] (henceforth, denoted as BBDP scheme) in terms of security: Our work achieves a stronger notion of security, namely we prove security against unbounded malicious receivers whereas the BBDP scheme achieves only computational security against semi-honest receivers. We stress that, although the BBPD scheme achieves download rate 1, it

Table 1. Comparison between existing co-PIR schemes. Here, $\mathbf{D}$ represents the input of the sender (i.e., the database), t represents the size of the receiver's input (i.e., how many indices will be erased) and $1 > \varepsilon > 0$. SSP stands for statistical sender privacy. All schemes achieve (asymptotic) download-rate 1 and the receiver's message is of size $\mathsf{poly}(t, \lambda) \cdot \mathsf{polylog}(|\mathbf{D}|)$. For all schemes, the receiver's computational complexity is $|\mathbf{D}| \cdot t \cdot \mathsf{poly}(\lambda)$.

	Security	Hardness Assumption	Sender's Work
[18]	Semi-honest	DDH, QR, LWE	$\|\mathbf{D}\| \cdot t \cdot \mathsf{poly}(\lambda)$
This work	SSP	DDH	$\|\mathbf{D}\|^{1+\varepsilon} \cdot t \cdot \mathsf{poly}(\lambda)$
This work (Full version)	SSP	Rate-1 PIR	$\|\mathbf{D}\|^2 \cdot t \cdot \mathsf{poly}(\lambda)$

only provides *computational* (instead of statistical) security against semi-honest receivers. This is because a computationally unbounded semi-honest receiver has enough information to break a subset of the OTs. A comparison with BBDP is given in Table 2

Table 2. Comparison between existing optimal-rate OT schemes. Here, k represents the number of OT executions, and $1 > \varepsilon_0, \varepsilon_1 > 0$. SSP stands for statistical sender privacy. For all schemes, the receiver's computational complexity is slightly superlinear $k^{1+\varepsilon} \cdot \mathsf{poly}(\lambda)$.

	Security	Hardness Assumption	Sender's Work
[18]	Semi-honest	$\left\{\begin{matrix}\text{DDH, QR,}\\ \text{LWE}\end{matrix}\right\}$ + LPN	$k^{1+\varepsilon_0} \cdot \mathsf{poly}(\lambda)$
This work Sect. 10	SSP	DDH + LPN	$k^{1+\varepsilon_1} \cdot \mathsf{poly}(\lambda)$

Communication-Efficient 2PC. As an application of main result, we give a construction of a 2PC protocol that has statistical security against one of the parties and has constant communication overhead. We obtain this protocol by instantiating the GMW protocol [28] using our SSP OT scheme. An informal statement of this result is given below.

Theorem 3 (Informal). *There exists a two-party secure computation scheme with communication complexity of $\mathcal{O}(|C|) + |x| + |y| + \mathsf{poly}(\lambda)$ where C is the circuit being computed and x, y are the inputs of the parties. The scheme achieves statistical security against one of the parties and computational security against the other one (assuming both DDH and LPN assumptions) in the semi-honest setting.*

Previously, 2PC protocols for general circuits with constant overhead in the size of the circuit (or, better) and which provide semi-honest statistical security against one of the parties were known either from circuit-private FHE [44] or SSP OT along with PRGs in NC^0 [34].

2 Technical Overview

Throughout this technical overview, we refer to the ratio between the size of the receiver's protocol message and the size of the receiver's input as the *upload rate*, and the ratio between the size of the sender's protocol message and the size of the receiver's output as the *download rate*.

2.1 Optimal-Rate OT Secure Against Semi-honest Adversaries

Our starting point is the recent construction of *semi-honestly secure* rate-1 batch OT by Brakerski et al. [18]. In their construction semi-honest security against both senders and receivers holds computationally.

The core idea in [18] is the following: The receiver encrypts his choice-bits under a specific rate-1 private key encryption scheme, and encrypts the (short) keys under a linearly homomorphic public-key encryption (LHE) scheme. The private-key encryption scheme has the feature that approximate decryption is a linear operation. This allows the sender to decrypt the private-key ciphertext *under the hood* of the LHE an thus obtain a noisy LHE encryption of the receiver's choice. The actual OT function $f(\mathbf{x}) = (\mathbf{m}_1 - \mathbf{m}_0) \odot \mathbf{x} + \mathbf{m}_0$ (where $(\mathbf{m}_0, \mathbf{m}_1)$ is the sender's input) can now be evaluated homomorphically on the receiver's choice bits[4]. Here, $\odot$ denotes the component-wise multiplication.

Given that the LHE scheme supports *post-evaluation ciphertext compression*, the ciphertext thus generated can be compressed into a rate-1 ciphertext, which is then sent to the receiver.

In [18], the private-key scheme is instantiated from the LPN assumption and the LHE with post-evaluation compression mechanism using decisional Diffie-Hellman (DDH), quadratic residuosity (QR) or learning with errors (LWE) by adapting the ciphertext compression techniques from [15,17,18,23].

Co-private Information Retrieval. While the basic outline of the above scheme intuitively makes sense, there is a subtle issue we have glossed over: the decryption of the private key scheme is only approximate. Consequently, this will lead to a correctness error which causes the receiver to learn outputs he was not supposed to learn.

[4] For subtle technical reasons, the decryption and OT functions are combined into a single linear function.

More concretely, the private-key encryption scheme in [18] is realized as a basic LPN encryption scheme, where $\mathbf{A} \leftarrow_{\$} \mathbb{F}_2^{n\times m}$ is a public random matrix, $\mathbf{s} \in \mathbb{F}_2^n$ is the secret key, and ciphertexts are of the form $\mathbf{c} = \mathbf{sA} + \mathbf{e} + \mathbf{b}$, where $\mathbf{e} \in \mathbb{F}_2^m$ is a sparse random noise term, and $\mathbf{b}$ is the vector of choice bits . The noisy plaintext can be recovered by computing $\mathbf{c} - \mathbf{sA} = \mathbf{b} + \mathbf{e}$.

Consequently, in positions i where $\mathbf{e}_i = 1$, the receiver will obtain the wrong OT output, namely $\vec{m}_{1-\vec{b}_{1,i}}$. Note that this does not just constitute a correctness issue, but a security issue as the receiver is not supposed to learn this value.

To address this issue, [18] introduced a new primitive called co-Private Information Retrieval (co-PIR). A co-PIR scheme allows a receiver to retrieve a database from a sender with the guarantee that some positions (unknown to the sender) are erased. More precisely, in a co-PIR scheme, the receiver starts by choosing a subset of indices $S \subset [m]$ and computes a first message copir_1. S denotes the set of indices that the receiver wants to be erased. The sender, with input a database $\mathbf{D} \in \{0,1\}^m$, computes a second message copir_2 that allows the receiver to retrieve a database $\tilde{\mathbf{D}}$. The correctness property guarantees that $\mathbf{D}$ and $\tilde{\mathbf{D}}$ coincide for all the locations $[m] \setminus S$. For security, we require that the sender obtains no information about the receiver's input and the receiver in turn learns nothing about the positions $\mathbf{D}_i$ for $i \in S$.[5] In terms of efficiency, we require that the size of the receiver's message copir_1 to only grow polylogarithmically in the size of the database m and polynomially on the size of S. Moreover, the size of sender's message copir_2 should be $\mathbf{D} + o(\mathbf{D})$ and we call such a co-PIR scheme to have near optimal download rate.

[18] provided a computationally secure construction of co-PIR from punc-turable pseudorandom functions and PIR, or alternatively GGM PRFs [27] and (low-rate) OT following [10] (also known as punctured OT [16]). Moreover, these constructions achieve near optimal download rate. From a technical perspective, these constructions are *inherently* limited to computational security due to the way they use puncturable PRFs.

The above-mentioned issue can now be addressed as follows using both co-PIR and a (sender-private) PIR: The receiver generates a co-PIR message which erases all the locations corresponding to LPN errors (note that the error-locations are known to the receiver). Furthermore, he generates PIR instances which retrieve information at the locations corresponding to LPN errors. The sender will now transmit the compressed LHE ciphertext using the co-PIR, and use the PIR scheme to transmit the correct outputs at the erased positions.

2.2 Towards Statistical Sender Privacy

In order to adapt the BBDP-framework to the setting of statistical sender privacy *while preserving rate-1*, we encounter the following challenges.

[5] Co-PIR can be seen as the opposite of PIR: In a PIR the receiver retrieves the positions of the database that it is asking for, whereas in a co-PIR it gets the entire database except for those positions.

1. **Statistical co-PIR.** Clearly, the biggest issue with the BBDP construction with respect to SSP security lies in the fact that their co-PIR scheme offers only computational security, *even against semi-honest receiver.* Hence it seems inevitable that we have to take a different route to construct statistical co-PIR. Additionally, we need this statistical secure co-PIR scheme to have near optimal download rate.
2. **Consistency of Inputs.** We need the input set S sent by the receiver as part of PIR and co-PIR messages to be the same. Otherwise, a malicious receiver can cheat and learn both messages $m_{0,i}$ and $m_{1,i}$ for some position i and thus, breaking the sender security of OT.
3. **Well-formedness of ciphertexts.** The protocol described above assumes that the ciphertext ct (encrypting the LPN secret) generated by the receiver is well-formed. Namely, this ciphertext should encrypt bits and have a special structure that allows for packing of ciphertexts.

In the following, we will outline our approach to deal with these issues.

2.3 Statistical Co-PIR

Our main challenge is to construct a co-PIR scheme that provides statistical security against malicious receivers and has near optimal download rate. We build such a co-PIR scheme in a sequence of steps:

1. We start by building a one-query statistical semi-honest co-PIR, which erases only a single block of bits and provides semi-honest security for both the receiver and the sender.
2. We then show how to achieve a one-query statistical semi-honest co-PIR that erases a single bit (instead of an entire block).
3. In the next transformation, we show how to bootstrap a co-PIR that only allows to erase one bit into one where multiple bits are erased.
4. Finally, we show how to achieve statistical sender privacy.

One-Query Statistical Semi-honest Co-PIR. We first tackle the simpler task of constructing a statistical co-PIR which only erases one position of the database and the security is required to hold only against semi-honest adversaries. We will call this primitive a one-query semi-honest co-PIR.

One-Query Semi-honest co-PIR from PIR. One-query semi-honest co-PIR can be constructed in a generic way from PIR. The receiver's input to the PIR corresponds to the position that it wants to be erased. The sender's input to the PIR corresponds to vectors $\hat{\mathbf{D}}_1, \ldots, \hat{\mathbf{D}}_m$ where each $\hat{\mathbf{D}}_i$ corresponds to the database $\mathbf{D}$ with the i-th position erased. By the correctness of the PIR, the receiver obtains $\hat{\mathbf{D}}_i$.

For the resulting co-PIR scheme to be rate-1 and provide statistical security for the sender, we need that the underlying PIR to fulfill these requirements. Such a PIR scheme was recently constructed in the work of Aggarwal et al. [1].

However, a drawback of this construction is that the sender's work is proportional to $|\mathbf{D}|^2$, which is the size of the sender's input to the PIR, whereas the receiver's work is proportional to $|\mathbf{D}|$. We now explain how to build a co-PIR scheme which achieves better efficiency for the sender.

All-But-One Lossiness. Our first observation is that a one-query statistical co-PIR resembles a primitive called *all-but-one trapdoor lossy function* (ABO-TDF) [45]. Loosely speaking, an ABO-TDF is a function parametrized by some public key and which is invertible everywhere except for some specified one branch where it loses information. Crucially, the public key should not reveal about the lossy branch.

Peikert and Waters provide a simple construction of ABO-TDF from a linear homomorphic scheme LHE such as El Gamal: to generate an ABO-TDF public key which is lossy on a branch i^*, one first generates $(\mathsf{pk}, \mathsf{sk}) \leftarrow \mathsf{LHE.KeyGen}(1^\lambda)$ and encrypts $\mathsf{ct} \leftarrow \mathsf{LHE.Enc}(\mathsf{pk}, i^*)$. The new ABO-TDF public key is composed by $(\mathsf{pk}, \mathsf{ct})$. To encrypt a message $m \in \mathbb{Z}_2$ under index i, we homomorphically compute the function $f(x) = (i - x) \cdot m$ and obtain a new ciphertext $\tilde{\mathsf{ct}}$.

It is easy to see that for all $i \neq i^*$, decryption can recover $m = \mathsf{LHE.Dec}(\mathsf{sk}, \tilde{\mathsf{ct}}) \cdot (i - i^*)^{-1}$. However, when $i = i^*$ all information about m is statistically hidden, assuming that LHE is function private.

A Simple Statistical co-PIR with Large Computation. In the following, let p be the order of a DDH group and LHE be a function private LHE scheme over a smaller field $\mathbb{Z}_q$ for $q = \mathsf{poly}(\lambda)$, such as the one presented in [18]. Let $\mathbf{D} \in \mathbb{Z}_q^m$ be the database of the sender, where q will be later defined. As a first approach consider the following protocol for co-PIR:

- The receiver creates a pair of public/secret keys $(\mathsf{pk}, \mathsf{sk}) \leftarrow \mathsf{LHE.KeyGen}(1^\lambda)$ and encrypts $\mathsf{ct} \leftarrow \mathsf{LHE.Enc}(\mathsf{pk}, i^*)$ for $i^* \in [m]$.
- For all $i \in [m]$ the sender homomorphically computes $f_i(x) = (i - x) \cdot \mathbf{D}_i$ over ct and obtains ciphertexts $\tilde{\mathsf{ct}}_1, \ldots, \tilde{\mathsf{ct}}_m$.
- For all $i \neq i^*$ the receiver obtains $\mathbf{D}_i \leftarrow \mathsf{LHE.Dec}(\mathsf{sk}, \tilde{\mathsf{ct}}_i)$.

It is easy to see that correctness holds for all $i \neq i^*$. Semi-honest security for the receiver follows from the IND-CPA of LHE and semi-honest statistical security for the sender follows from the statistical function privacy of LHE and from the fact that $(i^* - i^*) \cdot m = 0 \cdot m = 0$.

In terms of efficiency, the receiver's message is composed by a public key and an encryption and hence its size is independent of $|\mathbf{D}|$. However, the sender's message is composed by m uncompressed ciphertexts. So the scheme does not achieve near optimal download rate.

To achieve near optimal download rate, we will use the ciphertext compression technique for El Gamal presented in [18] (which is itself based on previous works [15,17,23]). These techniques are specially designed for packed El Gamal and to use these packing techniques, we need the following two conditions to hold.

1. The receiver's message needs to encrypt a matrix rather than a single value i^*, in order for packing to be possible. That is, $\mathsf{ct} \leftarrow \mathsf{LHE.Enc}(\mathsf{pk}, i^* \cdot \mathbf{I})$ where $\mathbf{I}$ is the identity matrix of size k.
2. We need $\mathbf{D}_i$ to be in $\mathbb{Z}_q^k$ for large enough k in order to amortize the size of the ciphertext for a single block. Moreover, we need that $q > m$. The latter condition comes from the fact that the operation $(i - i^*)$ needs to be performed over a modulus greater than m. If that was not the case, then it might happen that $(i - i^*) = 0 \mod q$ for $i \neq i^*$ over the integers and we will loose correctness.

This gives us a statistical semi-honest one-query co-PIR for databases of size $\mathbf{D} = (\mathbf{D}_1, \ldots, \mathbf{D}_m)$ where each $\mathbf{D}_i \in \mathbb{Z}_q^k$ for $q > m$.

In terms of computation, the scheme still incurs a quadratic blowup for both the sender and the receiver. All ciphertext compression mechanisms for DDH [15,17,18,23] have computational complexity scaling with q for both the sender and the receiver. Since $q > m$, for each block, both parties have to spend computational work proportional to m. Since there are m blocks, we end up with computational complexity proportional to at least m^2. Thus, we have not achieved any significant gains over the simple solution from PIR.

An Efficient Statistical co-PIR. To improve the computational complexity of the protocol, we need a way to make the complexity of encrypting and decrypting each block independent of m. Towards this goal, we use a standard trick of embedding the underlying messages in an extension field.

To be a bit more specific, our idea is to parse the database $\mathbf{D}$ as a vector over an extension field $\mathbb{F}_{2^\mu}$ where $\mu = \lceil \log m \rceil$. That is, we parse $\mathbf{D} = (\mathbf{D}_1, \ldots, \mathbf{D}_m) \in \mathbb{F}_{2^\mu}^{k \cdot m}$ where each $\mathbf{D}_i \in \mathbb{F}_{2^\mu}^k$.

We rely on the fact that for any two elements $\hat{x}, \hat{a} \in \mathbb{F}_{2^\mu}$, where $\hat{x} = x_1 + x_2\alpha + \cdots + x_\mu \alpha^{\mu-1}$ for some symbol α, each coefficient of the product $\hat{x} \cdot \hat{a}$ can be expressed as a linear function depending only on $\hat{a}$. That is,

$$\hat{x} \cdot \hat{a} = f_{1,\hat{a}}(\mathbf{x}) + f_{2,\hat{a}}(\mathbf{x})\alpha + \cdots + f_{\mu,\hat{a}}(\mathbf{x})\alpha^{\mu-1}$$

where $\mathbf{x} = (x_1, \ldots, x_\mu)$ and each $f_{i,\hat{a}}$ is a $\mathbb{Z}_2$-linear function that depends solely on $\hat{a}$.

Given this, the new scheme with improved computational complexity can be obtained as follows:

- Given an index $i^* \in [m]$, the receiver first decomposes it into its binary decomposition $\mathbf{i}^* = (i_1^*, \ldots, i_\mu^*)$. Then, it creates $(\mathsf{pk}, \mathsf{sk}) \leftarrow \mathsf{LHE.KeyGen}(1^\lambda)$ and encrypts each i_1^*, that is, $\mathsf{ct}_j \leftarrow \mathsf{LHE.Enc}(\mathsf{pk}, i_j^* \cdot \mathbf{I})$ where $\mathbf{I}$ is the identity matrix of size k. It sends pk and the ciphertexts ct_j to the sender.
- The sender parses $\mathbf{D} = (\mathbf{D}_1, \ldots, \mathbf{D}_m) \in \mathbb{F}_{2^\mu}^{k \cdot m}$ where each $\mathbf{D}_i \in \mathbb{F}_{2^\mu}^k$. For each $\ell \in [m]$ it evaluates the function $f_i(\hat{\mathbf{X}}) = (\hat{\ell} \cdot \mathbf{I} - \hat{\mathbf{X}}) \cdot \mathbf{D}_\ell$ over $\mathbb{F}_{2^\mu}$ where $\hat{\ell}$ is the embbeding of ℓ in $\mathbb{F}_{2^\mu}$ (by first converting into its binary decomposition and then interpreting it as a $\mathbb{F}_{2^\mu}$ element). As we have seen, f_i can be expressed as a $\mathbb{Z}_2$-linear function. Let $\tilde{\mathsf{ct}}_\ell$ be the resulting ciphertexts. It compresses the ciphertexts $\tilde{\mathsf{ct}}_\ell$ to make them rate 1.

– Finally, the receiver decrypts each $\tilde{\mathsf{ct}}_\ell$ for $\ell \neq i^*$, interprets the result as a $\mathbb{F}_{2^\mu}^k$ vector $\mathbf{u}$ and computes $\tilde{\mathbf{D}}_\ell = (\hat{\ell} - \hat{i}^*)^{-1} \cdot \mathbf{u}$ over $\mathbb{F}_{2^\mu}$.

Correctness, semi-honest security for the receiver and semi-honest statistical sender security hold as in the protocol above.

Computational Complexity. Unlike the previous protocol, the sender needs to compress m ciphertexts of size $\mu \cdot k$. However, now all ciphertexts encrypt bits instead of messages over a larger modulus. Hence, the sender's computational complexity grows only linearly with the size $m \cdot k \cdot \mu$ of the database. Similarly, the receiver needs to decrypt the ciphertexts (encrypting bits) sent by the sender, hence the computational complexity for the receiver grows only linearly with the size of the database

Full-Fledged Statistical Co-PIR. Until now we have discussed how to obtain a semi-honest statistical one-query co-PIR. However, for our OT application, the co-PIR needs to i) provide statistical security against a malicious receiver, and ii) support more than one query. Additionally, to obtain a bit-OT, we need our co-PIR to erase a single bit of the database whereas the construction presented above only works for large erased blocks.

Bit co-PIR from Block co-PIR. We start by the simplest task of turning a co-PIR which erases an entire block, or block co-PIR, into one that erases a single bit, or bit co-PIR.

Assume that the receiver wants to erase the j^* bit of the i^* block. We show that a bit co-PIR can be built from a block co-PIR by additionally assuming the existence of a PIR scheme. The block co-PIR will erase an entire block $\mathbf{D}_{i^*} = (D_{i^*,1}, \ldots, D_{i^*,k})$. The remaining positions $D_{i^*,j}$ for $j \neq j^*$ can be sent to the receiver via a PIR. The resulting scheme can be seen as a (one-query) bit co-PIR as only D_{i^*,j^*} is erased from the perspective of the receiver. Importantly, we show that this scheme preserves security even against malicious receivers. This is because if the PIR message points to another block, then the malicious receiver obtains strictly lesser information and this does not violate the privacy of the honest sender.

Additionally, in terms of communication the scheme preserves i) short message from the receiver as the PIR receiver's message is small compared to the size of the database $|\mathbf{D}| = mk$, and ii) near optimal download rate as the sender's PIR message only grows with k.

In terms of computation, the scheme preserves the computational complexity for the receiver. However, the sender now as to run k PIR second message which makes its work to grow proportionally with $|\mathbf{D}| \cdot k$. Setting k to be sublinear in m yields subquadratic work in the size of the database for the sender.

Multiple-Query co-PIR via Recursion. We now discuss how to obtain a co-PIR where the receiver's input is a set S of indices instead of a single index.

Assume that the message of the sender can be decomposed into bit ciphertexts. That is, copir_2 can be decomposed into $(h, \alpha_1, \ldots, \alpha_m)$ where h is a header of size $\mathsf{poly}(\lambda)$ and each α_i decrypts to $D_i \in \{0,1\}$, where $\mathbf{D} = (D_1, \ldots, D_m)$ is the sender's input.

The crucial idea of this transformation is that, since the underlying one-query co-PIR has near optimal download rate, the sender can recurse the co-PIR without any blowup in the communication. Concretely the protocol works as follows:

- The receiver sends t first one-query co-PIR messages $\{\mathsf{copir}_{1,i}\}_{i\in[t]}$ to the sender, each one encoding an index a_i to be erased.
- The sender computes the first one-query co-PIR message $\mathsf{copir}_{2,1}$ using the input database $\mathbf{D} \in \{0,1\}^m$ and $\mathsf{copir}_{1,1}$. Recall that $\mathsf{copir}_{2,1}$ can be decomposed into $(h_1, \alpha_1^{(1)}, \ldots, \alpha_m^{(1)})$. The sender now creates a second $\mathsf{copir}_{2,2}$ using a new database $\mathbf{D}_1 = (\alpha_1^{(1)}, \ldots, \alpha_m^{(1)})s$ and $\mathsf{copir}_{1,2}$. The sender repeats this process until it obtains $\mathsf{copir}_{2,t}$ (together with all previous headers) and sends this to the receiver.
- The receiver can recursively decrypt each $\mathsf{copir}_{2,t+1-i}$ for $i \in [t]$. At each step, the a_{t+1-i} position of $(\alpha_1^{(t+1-i)}, \ldots, \alpha_m^{(t+1-i)})$ is erased and information about $D_{a_{t+1-i}}$ is statistically erased.

Since the underlying one-query co-PIR has near optimal download rate, each iteration of the recursion maintains this property as long as t is sublinear in the size of the initial database $\mathbf{D}$. Furthermore, if the starting co-PIR is statistically secure against malicious receivers, then so is the transformed co-PIR.

Achieving Statistical Sender Privacy Against Malicious Receivers. So far we have only discussed how to achieve semi-honest statistical security. It remains to show how to turn the protocol statistically secure for the sender against malicious receivers who might send malformed first round messages.

If we are able to guarantee that the receiver's message is well-formed, then we can use the semi-honest (statistical) security to argue malicious (statistical) security. As a first approach, we will discuss how to use a statistically sender secure *conditional disclosure of secrets* (CDS) to achieve the stronger notion of security.

Let $\mathcal{L}$ be an NP language. Recall that in a CDS scheme, the receiver holding a witness w for a statement x, sends a first message cds_1 to the sender that commits to w. The sender holding a message m computes a second CDS message cds_2 which allows the receiver to retrieve m iff $x \in \mathcal{L}$ and w is a valid witness. In terms of security, we want that if $x \notin \mathcal{L}$, then m is statistically hidden from the receiver.

It is well-known that statistically sender secure CDS schemes for NC1 can be constructed using (low-rate) SSP OT and information theoretic garbled circuits [3,4,32]. Moreover, any NP language can be verified by a NC1 circuit [24].

In order to achieve statistical sender security against malicious receivers, we will use a CDS that guarantees that the receiver's message is well-formed.

Consider the following language

$$\mathcal{L}_{\mathsf{CoPIR}'} = \{\mathsf{copir}_1 : \exists (S, r) \text{ s.t. } \mathsf{copir}_1 \leftarrow \mathsf{CoPIR}'.\mathsf{Query}(S; r)\}$$

that is the language of well formed receiver's messages, where CoPIR' is the semi-honest protocol[6] described in the previous sections. Additionally, recall that our co-PIR scheme has a decomposability feature that the sender's message copir_2 can be decomposed into $(\alpha_1, \ldots, \alpha_m)$ where each α_i encodes $\mathbf{D}_i$.

The statistically secure protocol can be roughly described as follows:

- The receiver sends a co-PIR message $\mathsf{copir}_1 \leftarrow \mathsf{CoPIR}'.\mathsf{Query}(S; r)$ for a set of indices S of size t using random coins r. It additionally sends a first message cds_1 for language $\mathcal{L}_{\mathsf{CoPIR}'}$ using (S, r) as the witness.
- The sender computes $\mathsf{copir}_2 \leftarrow \mathsf{CoPIR}'.\mathsf{Send}(\mathsf{copir}_1, \mathbf{D})$ and decomposes copir_2 into $(\alpha_1, \ldots, \alpha_m)$. It now samples random $\beta_1, \ldots, \beta_t$ and computes

  $$\mathbf{v} = (\alpha_1, \ldots, \alpha_m) + (\beta_1, \ldots, \beta_t, 0, \ldots, 0)$$

  that is the first t coordinates of copir_2 are hidden using $\beta_1, \ldots, \beta_t$. It now sends a CDS message $\mathsf{cds}_2 \leftarrow \mathsf{CDS}.\mathsf{Send}(\mathsf{cds}_1, (\beta_1, \ldots, \beta_t))$ encrypting the values $(\beta_1, \ldots, \beta_t)$.

If copir_1 is well-formed then the receiver can retrieve the values $\beta_1, \ldots, \beta_t$, recover copir_2 and retrieve $(\alpha_1, \ldots, \alpha_m)$. In this case, we can use the semi-honest (statistical) security of the underlying CoPIR' to argue that the scheme is statistically secure. On the other hand, if copir_1 is malformed, then the values $\beta_1, \ldots, \beta_t$ are statistically hidden from the receiver given that CDS is statistically secure. In this case, the values $\alpha_1, \ldots, \alpha_t$ are statistically hidden from the receiver's point of view and thus, the first t positions of $\mathbf{D}$ are statistically hidden.

In terms of communication, the scheme has near optimal download rate as the CDS communication only depends on t (i.e., the size of the receiver's message) and this is typically set to be sub-linear in the size of the database.

While this gives us a generic solution to achieve SSP co-PIR, it incurs in a huge overhead as we need to make non black-box use of the underlying semi-honest co-PIR.

A Black-Box Solution. To achieve a better concrete efficiency, we show how to build a black-box CDS scheme specifically for our purposes.

Recall that the receiver's message is composed by a ciphertext encrypting a square matrix of size k.[7] That is, a well formed receiver's message consists of $\mathsf{ct} \leftarrow \mathsf{LHE}.\mathsf{Enc}(\mathsf{pk}, b \cdot \mathbf{I})$ where $b \in \{0, 1\}$ and $\mathbf{I}$ is the identity matrix. However, if the receiver behaves maliciously, then it can encrypt any matrix $\mathbf{A}$ so that it learns partial (or total) information about the erased block.

---

[6] Technically speaking, we need the co-PIR scheme to be semi-malicious secure but for the sake of this overview, we will ignore this difference. Our co-PIR scheme constructed before satisfies semi-malicious security.

[7] The receiver's message is actually composed by several of these ciphertexts but for simplicity we assume that we only have one ciphertext.

Algebraic Restriction Codes. This is where algebraic restriction (AR) [1] codes come into play. Roughly speaking, an AR code restricts the class of functions that an adversary can apply over an encoded value.

More precisely, let $\hat{\mathbf{y}}_i \leftarrow \mathsf{AR.Encode}(\mathbf{y}_i)$ for $i = 1, 2$. The work of [1] provides a construction of AR codes that restrict the class of any linear function $g(\hat{\mathbf{y}}_1, \hat{\mathbf{y}}_2) = \hat{\mathbf{y}}_1 \cdot \mathbf{A} + \hat{\mathbf{y}}_2$ over the encoded values to the class of $f(\mathbf{y}_1, \mathbf{y}_2) = \mathbf{y}_1 \cdot (c \cdot \mathbf{I}) + \mathbf{y}_2$ where $\mathbf{I}$ is the identity matrix and $c \in \mathbb{Z}_p$. The security of AR codes allow to statistically simulate the evaluation of g over two encoded values $\hat{\mathbf{y}}_1, \hat{\mathbf{y}}_2$ given just the output of the decoding $f(\mathbf{y}_1, \mathbf{y}_2)$ where f is a function that depends on g.

A CDS from AR Codes. Our main idea is to recast the construction of [1] in terms of CDS. Specifically, the sender sets

$$\mathbf{y}_1 = \begin{pmatrix} \mathbf{r}_0 \\ \mathbf{r}_1 \end{pmatrix} \text{ and } \mathbf{y}_1 = \begin{pmatrix} \mathbf{m} \\ \mathbf{m} - \mathbf{r}_1 \end{pmatrix}$$

where $\mathbf{r}_0, \mathbf{r}_1 \leftarrow\!\!\$\, \mathbb{Z}_p^k$ and $\mathbf{m}$ is the message that the sender wants to send.

However, instead of evaluating $F(\mathbf{X}) = \mathbf{y}_1 \cdot \mathbf{X} + \mathbf{y}_2$ (that depends on $\mathbf{y}_1, \mathbf{y}_2$) over ct, it first AR encodes both $\mathbf{y}_1, \mathbf{y}_2$, applies $G(\mathbf{X}) = \hat{\mathbf{y}}_1 \cdot \mathbf{X} + \hat{\mathbf{y}}_2$ and finally homomorphically decodes the result.[8]

The AR codes security guarantees that the receiver will decrypt to something of the form

$$\mathbf{y}_1 \cdot (c\mathbf{I}) + \mathbf{y}_2 = \begin{pmatrix} c\mathbf{r}_0 + \mathbf{m} \\ c\mathbf{r}_1 + \mathbf{m} - \mathbf{r}_1 \end{pmatrix}.$$

If $c = 0, 1$ then the receiver can retrieve $\mathbf{m}$. However, if $c \neq 0, 1$ then the message $\mathbf{m}$ is statistically hidden from the receiver.

2.4 Consistency of Inputs

Recall that we need a mechanism to ensure that the same set is used by a malicious receiver to generate a PIR and a co-PIR message. First, note that the underlying PIR also needs to be statistically sender secure, and this can be instantiated using the scheme of [1]. Our second crucial observation is that the co-PIR receiver message comprises of a public key pk and encryptions of $a_i \cdot \mathbf{I}$ for $a_i \in \{0, 1\}$ which means that the co-PIR messages are identical to the PIR messages of the scheme of [1]![9] This means that the receiver does not have to send separate PIR messages: the sender can just interpret the co-PIR messages as PIR messages and this guarantees consistency of inputs.

[8] For this to work, we need the decoding function of the AR codes to be a linear function and this is indeed the case for AR codes from [1].

[9] Our actual co-PIR scheme is a bit more complex as it also contains PIR messages as a result of the block-to-bit transformation. However, our co-PIR scheme is still "PIR-compatible" for a variant of the PIR scheme of [1].

2.5 Well-Formedness of Ciphertexts

The last missing piece is how to ensure that the ciphertexts encrypting the LPN secrets are well-formed. These ciphertexts need to have a special structure i.e., they need to be encrypting bits, but in the current form, there is nothing that prevents the adversary from sending malformed ciphertexts and learn additional information.

Unfortunately, we cannot use a generic CDS protocol as we will lose optimal sender's message length or statistical security against the receivers. This is where we use rate-1 CDS. A rate-1 CDS is a standard statistical sender secure CDS with one additional efficiency property: we require the size of the sender's message to be $|m| + o(|m|)$ for sufficiently long m (which is larger than the size of the NP verification).

Assume for now that we have a download rate-1 CDS scheme which is statistically secure against malicious receivers. The sender encrypts its OT message using this CDS, and this message will be released to the receiver iff the ciphertexts are well-formed. Since the CDS scheme is rate-1, there is no blowup in the size of the sender's message. Moreover, the receiver's CDS message is small as its size only depends on the size of the LPN secrets and the size of the NP relation to be verified is independent of the size of the sender's input.

To construct such a rate-1 CDS scheme, we plug the (download rate-1) OT scheme of [1] together with the encryption scheme of [35] which yields a CDS scheme for branching programs (which contains NC1 circuits) and this is sufficient for our purposes.

2.6 Future Directions

Except for the use of the general purpose rate-1 CDS scheme used in the last step, our scheme uses only black-box techniques in the sense that it does not use explicit circuit-level description of cryptographic primitives. Coming up with a black-box technique that guarantees well-formedness of the ciphertexts of the receiver is a interesting open problem.

3 Preliminaries

Due to space constraints the preliminaries are presented in the full version of the paper. Here we just present non standard notation.

Let $\mathsf{Diag}(n, \mathbf{v})$ be the algorithm that takes a vector $\mathbf{v} = (v_1, \ldots, v_n) \in \{0,1\}^n$ and outputs a matrix

$$\mathbf{D} = \begin{pmatrix} v_1 & & 0 \\ & \ddots & \\ 0 & & v_n \end{pmatrix} \in \{0,1\}^{n \times n},$$

i.e. $\mathbf{D} \in \{0,1\}^{n \times n}$ is a diagonal matrix with the components of $\mathbf{v}$ on its diagonal.

Addtionally let $\mathsf{SingleRowMatrix}(\ell, n, i, \mathbf{v})$ be the algorithm that takes $i \in [\ell]$ and a row-vector $\mathbf{v} \in \{0,1\}^n$ and outputs a matrix

$$\mathbf{V} = \begin{pmatrix} 0 & \dots & 0 \\ \vdots & & \vdots \\ 0 & \dots & 0 \\ - & \mathbf{v} & - \\ 0 & \dots & 0 \\ \vdots & & \vdots \\ 0 & \dots & 0 \end{pmatrix} \in \{0,1\}^{\ell \times n},$$

i.e. the i-th row of $\mathbf{V}$ is $\mathbf{v}$, but $\mathbf{V}$ is 0 everywhere else.

4 Definition of Co-Private Information Retrieval

We start by defining co-PIR in an identical way as in [18]. A co-PIR is a primitive that allows a sender to transmit a database to a receiver, except for some positions which will be (statistically) erased.

Definition 4 (Co-PIR). *Let $\mathbb{H}$ be a group. A co-private information retrieval (co-PIR) scheme is parametrized by a integer $m = \mathsf{poly}(\lambda)$ and is given by a tuple of algorithms* $(\mathsf{Query}, \mathsf{Send}, \mathsf{Rec})$ *with the following sintax:*

- $\mathsf{Query}(1^\lambda, S)$ *takes as input the security parameter λ and a subset of indices $S = \{i_1, \dots, i_t\} \subseteq [m]$ of size t. It outputs a first co-PIR message* copir_1 *and a private state* st.
- $\mathsf{Send}(\mathsf{copir}_1, \mathbf{D})$ *takes as input a first co-PIR message* copir_1 *and a database* $\mathbf{D} \in \mathbb{H}^m$.[10] *It outputs a second co-PIR message* copir_2.
- $\mathsf{Rec}(\mathsf{copir}_2, \mathsf{st})$ *takes as input a second co-PIR message* copir_2 *and a private state* st. *It outputs a database $\tilde{\mathbf{D}} \in \mathbb{H}^m$.*

A co-PIR scheme should fulfill the following properties.

Definition 5 (Correctness). *A co-PIR scheme is said to be correct if for any $m = \mathsf{poly}(\lambda)$ and $S \subseteq [m]$*

$$\Pr\left[\mathbf{D}_{\bar{S}} = \tilde{\mathbf{D}}_{\bar{S}} : \begin{array}{c} (\mathsf{copir}_1, \mathsf{st}) \leftarrow \mathsf{Query}(1^\lambda, S) \\ \mathsf{copir}_2 \leftarrow \mathsf{Send}(\mathsf{copir}_1, \mathbf{D}) \\ \tilde{\mathbf{D}} \leftarrow \mathsf{Rec}(\mathsf{copir}_2, \mathsf{st}) \end{array}\right] = 1$$

where $\bar{S} = [m] \setminus S$. In other words, $\mathbf{D}_i = \tilde{\mathbf{D}}_i$ for all $i \notin S$.

We also define a slightly stronger notion of security that we call locally correct.

[10] We use the term bit co-PIR to denote the case when $\mathbb{H} = \{0, 1\}$. Otherwise, we use the term block co-PIR.

Definition 6 (Locally correctness). *A co-PIR scheme is locally correct if the following holds: i)* copir_2 *is of the form* $(\alpha_1, \ldots, \alpha_m)$*, and ii) The* Rec *algorithm can be divided into subalgorithms* Rec_i *such that* $\mathbf{D}_i \leftarrow \mathsf{Rec}_i(\alpha_i, \mathsf{st})$ *for all* $i \notin S$*.*

Definition 7 (Efficiency). *A co-PIR scheme is said to be efficient if the it fulfills the following requirements:*

- $|\mathsf{copir}_1| = \mathsf{polylog}(|\mathbf{D}|) \cdot \mathsf{poly}(\lambda, |S|)$.[11]
- ***Download rate 1:*** *If* t *is sublinear in* $|\mathbf{D}|$ *(that is* $t = o(|\mathbf{D}|)$*) then*

$$\lim_{\lambda \to \infty} \sup \frac{|\mathsf{copir}_2|}{|\mathbf{D}|} \to 1$$

for sufficiently large $|\mathbf{D}|$ *where* $\mathbf{D} \in \mathbb{H}^m$ *and* $\mathsf{copir}_2 \leftarrow \mathsf{Send}(\mathsf{copir}_1, \mathbf{D})$.[12]

Definition 8 (Receiver security). *A co-PIR scheme* CoPIR *is said to be receiver secure if for all* $m = \mathsf{poly}(\lambda)$*, any subsets* $S_1, S_2 \subseteq [m]$ *we have that for any adversary* $\mathcal{A}$

$$\left| \begin{array}{c} \Pr\left[1 \leftarrow \mathcal{A}(k, \mathsf{copir}_1) : (\mathsf{copir}_1, \mathsf{st}) \leftarrow \mathsf{Query}(1^\lambda, S_1)\right] - \\ \Pr\left[1 \leftarrow \mathcal{A}(k, \mathsf{copir}_1) : (\mathsf{copir}_1, \mathsf{st}) \leftarrow \mathsf{Query}(1^\lambda, S_2)\right] \end{array} \right| \leq \mathsf{negl}(\lambda).$$

Sender Security. We define two notions for statistical sender security. The first one, which is the strongest one, considers malicious and computationally unbounded receivers.

Definition 9 (Statistical sender security). *A co-PIR is said to be statistically sender secure if there is a (possibly computationally inefficient) extractor* $\mathsf{CoPIR.Ext}$ *such that for any message* copir_1 *and any pair of databases* $(\mathbf{D}, \mathbf{D}')$

$$\mathsf{Send}(\mathsf{copir}_1, \mathbf{D}) \approx_s \mathsf{Send}(\mathsf{copir}_1, \mathbf{D}')$$

where $S \leftarrow \mathsf{CoPIR.Ext}(\mathsf{copir}_1)$ *and* $\mathbf{D}'_i = \mathbf{D}_i$ *for* $i \notin S$*. Here,* S *is a set of size at most* t*.*

We also consider a relaxation of sender security that only considers semi-honest and computationally unbounded receivers.

---

[11] We usually consider co-PIR protocols where the first message depends polylogarithmically on the size of $\mathbf{D}$, similarly to PIR protocols. However, for our OT application in Sect. 10, it is enough to consider copir_1 to depend sublinearly on the size of $\mathbf{D}$.

[12] In a co-PIR, we allow the sender's message to be of the same size of the sender's input (or even slightly larger by an additive term depending on t) instead of the usual rate-1 definition which compares the sender's message with the receiver's input. This is the reason why we e define a co-PIR to be rate-1 only for $t = o(\mathbf{D})$ erased positions, which is enough for our applications.

Definition 10 (Semi-honest statistical sender security). *A one-query co-PIR scheme* CoPIR *is said to be semi-honest sender secure if for all* $S \subseteq [m]$ *of size* t *we have that*

$$\mathsf{Send}(\mathsf{copir}_1, \mathbf{D}) \approx_s \mathsf{Send}(\mathsf{copir}_1, \mathbf{D}')$$

for all $\mathbf{D}, \mathbf{D}' \in \mathbb{H}^m$ *such that* $\mathbf{D}'_i = \mathbf{D}_i$ *for* $i \notin S$*, and all* $\mathsf{copir}_1 \leftarrow \mathsf{Query}(1^\lambda, S)$.

A co-PIR fulfilling the latter security definition is called a semi-honest co-PIR.

One-Query co-PIR. We also define a one-query co-PIR scheme, that is, a co-PIR where the receiver's query is composed by a single index.

Definition 11 (One-query co-PIR). *A one-query co-PIR scheme is identical to a co-PIR except that the input of the receiver is composed by a single index. That is, the set* S *in Definition 4 is of the form* $S = \{i^*\}$*. Correctness, statistical sender security and receiver security are defined in an analogous way.*

Self-reducibility. Another property that we will need is self-reducibility.[13] This ensures that the output of a one-query co-PIR has the same form as the database and thus can be input into a new one-query co-PIR.

Definition 12 (Self-reducibility). *A one-query co-PIR scheme is said to be self-reducible if the sender's message is of the form* $\mathsf{copir}_2 = (\mathsf{head}, \alpha_1, \ldots, \alpha_m)$*. Moreover, for any* $i^* \in [m]$*, any two databases* $\mathbf{D}, \mathbf{D}'$ *such that* $\mathbf{D}_i = \mathbf{D}'_i$ *for all* $i \neq i^*$ *and any* copir_1 *message we have that*

$$(\mathsf{head}, \alpha_1, \ldots, \alpha_{i^*-1}, \alpha_{i^*+1}, \ldots, \alpha_m) \approx_s (\mathsf{head}', \alpha'_1, \ldots, \alpha'_{i^*-1}, \alpha'_{i^*+1}, \ldots, \alpha'_m)$$

where $\mathsf{copir}_2 = (\mathsf{head}, \alpha_1, \ldots, \alpha_m) \leftarrow \mathsf{Send}(\mathsf{copir}_1, \mathbf{D})$, $\mathsf{copir}'_2 = (\mathsf{head}', \alpha'_1, \ldots, \alpha'_m) \leftarrow \mathsf{Send}(\mathsf{copir}_1, \mathbf{D}')$.

In other words, self-reducibility states that all information about the block/bit D_i of the database is contained in a single block/bit of the copir_2 message. This property will be essential for recursion.[14]

[13] The work of [14] defines an identical property for OT.

[14] In this definition we assume that the i-th block/bit of copir erases D_i. However, this does not need to be the case in general: it might happen that the i-th block/bit of copir erases D_j, which is what happens with our construction in Sect. 6. However, both definitions are equivalent up to a reordering of the database.

PIR Compatibility. Let PIR be a PIR scheme and CoPIR be a co-PIR scheme. We say that CoPIR is PIR-compatible if the first message $\mathsf{copir}_1 \leftarrow \mathsf{CoPIR.Query}(1^\lambda, S)$ can be used as a first message of the PIR scheme. That is, we can parse copir_1 as q and compute $\mathsf{r} \leftarrow \mathsf{PIR.Send}(\mathbf{D}, \mathsf{q})$ while preserving correctness, receiver security and (statistical) sender security.

5 Semi-honest One-Query Co-PIR

We first present a construction of a one-query co-PIR that achieves semi-honest statistical sender security.

Before presenting our scheme we show how we can convert a LHE scheme over $\mathbb{Z}_2$ that supports ciphertext shrinking into an LHE scheme over $\mathbb{F}_q$ where $q = 2^\mu$ for some $\mu = \mathsf{poly}(\lambda)$. Here, we rely on the fact that multiplication over $\mathbb{F}_q$ can be expressed as a linear function over the field $\mathbb{Z}_2$. That is, suppose that an element $x \in \mathbb{F}_q$ is of the form $x = x_1 + x_2\alpha + \cdots + x_\mu \alpha^{\mu-1}$ where each $x_i \in \mathbb{Z}_2$ and α is a symbol. Then, for elements $a, x \in \mathbb{F}_q$ the product

$$xa = f_{1,a}(\mathbf{x}) + f_{2,a}(\mathbf{x})\alpha + \cdots + f_{\mu,a}(\mathbf{x})\alpha^{\mu-1}$$

where $\mathbf{x} = (x_1, \ldots, x_\mu)$ and each $f_{i,a} : \mathbb{Z}_2^\mu \to \mathbb{Z}_2$ is a $\mathbb{Z}_2$-linear function which depends solely on a. This means that there is a square matrix $\mathbf{A}$ (determined by a) such that the coefficients of the product $x \cdot a$ over $\mathbb{F}_q$ are the coefficients of $\mathbf{x} \cdot \mathbf{A}$ over $\mathbb{Z}_2$.

We now define the following functions.

- $\mathsf{FieldMult}(a \in \mathbb{F}_q, \mu)$ takes as input an element $a \in \mathbb{F}_q$ where $q = 2^\mu$. It outputs a matrix $\mathbf{A} \in \{0,1\}^{\mu \times \mu}$ such that the coefficients of $\mathbf{x}\mathbf{A} \in \{0,1\}^\mu$ correspond to the coefficients of $x \cdot a$ over $\mathbb{F}_q$ (here $\mathbf{x}$ is a binary vector whose coefficients are the ones of $x \in \mathbb{F}_q$).

Ingredients. We need the following ingredients: Let $k, m \in \mathsf{poly}(\lambda)$, $\mu > \lceil \log m \rceil$ and $q = 2^\mu$. Let

- $\mathsf{LHE} = (\mathsf{KeyGen}, \mathsf{Enc}, \mathsf{Eval}, \mathsf{Shrink}, \mathsf{DecShrink})$ be a rate-1 packed LHE scheme over $\mathbb{Z}_2$.
- $\mathsf{bin} : [m] \to \{0,1\}^\mu$ be the function that outputs the binary decomposition.

Construction 1. *We now present the full construction.*
$\mathsf{Query}(1^\lambda, i^* \in [m])$*:*

- *Compute* $\mathbf{i}^* = (i_1^*, \ldots, i_\mu^*) \leftarrow \mathsf{bin}(i^*)$.
- *For all* $\ell \in [\mu]$ *set*

$$\mathbf{T}_\ell^* = i_\ell^* \cdot \mathbf{I}_\ell = \begin{pmatrix} i_\ell^* & \mathbf{0} & \ldots & \mathbf{0} \\ \mathbf{0} & i_\ell^* & \ldots & \mathbf{0} \\ \vdots & & \ddots & \vdots \\ \mathbf{0} & \ldots & \mathbf{0} & i_\ell^* \end{pmatrix} \in \{0,1\}^{k \times k}$$

where $\mathbf{I}_k$ *is the identity matrix of size* k.

- *Create* $(\mathsf{pk}, \mathsf{sk}) \leftarrow \mathsf{LHE.KeyGen}(1^\lambda, k)$.
- *For all* $\ell \in [\mu]$ *compute* $\mathsf{ct}_\ell \leftarrow \mathsf{LHE.Enc}(\mathsf{pk}, \mathbf{T}^*_\ell)$.[15]
- *Output* $\mathsf{copir}_1 = (\mathsf{pk}, \{\mathsf{ct}_\ell\}_{\ell\in[\mu]})$ *and* $\mathsf{st} = (\mathsf{sk}, i^*)$.

$\mathsf{Send}\left(\mathsf{copir}_1, \mathbf{D} \in \left(\mathbb{F}_q^k\right)^m\right)$*:*

- *Parse* copir_1 *as* $(\mathsf{pk}, \mathsf{ct})$. *Additionally, parse* $\mathbf{D} = (\mathbf{D}_1, \ldots, \mathbf{D}_m)$ *where each* $\mathbf{D}_i = (d_{i,1}, \ldots, d_{i,k}) \in \mathbb{F}_q^k$ *and* $d_{i,j} \in \mathbb{F}_q$ *for all* $j \in [k]$.
- *For all* $i \in [m]$ *and* $j \in [k]$ *determine* $\mathbf{A}_{i,j} \leftarrow \mathsf{FieldMult}(d_{i,j}, \mu)$. *Parse* $\mathbf{A}_{i,j} = \begin{pmatrix} - \mathbf{a}_{i,j,1} - \\ \vdots \\ - \mathbf{a}_{i,j,\mu} - \end{pmatrix} \in \{0,1\}^{\mu\times\mu}$.
- *For all* $i \in [m]$, $j \in [k]$ *and* $\ell \in [\mu]$ *compute* $\mathbf{C}_{i,j,\ell} \leftarrow \mathsf{SingleRowMatrix}(k, \mu, j, \mathbf{a}_{i,j,\ell})$.
- *For all* $i \in [m]$, *compute* $\mathbf{e}_i = (e_{i,1}, \ldots, e_{i,\mu}) \leftarrow \mathsf{bin}(i)$. *Additionally for all* $\ell \in [\mu]$ *set* $\mathbf{U}_{i,\ell} = \mathsf{Diag}(k, e_{i,\ell})$.
- *For all* $i \in [m]$ *consider the following* $\mathbb{Z}_2$ *function* $f_i : (\{0,1\}^{k\times k})^\mu \to \{0,1\}^{k\times\mu}$ *defined by*

$$f_i(\mathbf{X}_1, \ldots, \mathbf{X}_\mu) = \sum_{j=1}^{k}\sum_{\ell=1}^{\mu} (\mathbf{U}_{i,\ell} - \mathbf{X}_\ell) \cdot \mathbf{C}_{i,j,\ell}.$$

- *For all* $i \in [m]$ *compute* $\tilde{\mathsf{ct}}_i \leftarrow \mathsf{LHE.Eval\&Shrink}(\mathsf{pk}, f_i, (\mathsf{ct}_1, \ldots, \mathsf{ct}_\mu))$.
- *Output* $\mathsf{copir}_2 = \{\tilde{\mathsf{ct}}_i\}_{i\in[m]}$.

$\mathsf{Rec}(\mathsf{copir}_2, \mathsf{st})$*:*

- *Parse* copir_2 *as* $\{\tilde{\mathsf{ct}}_i\}_{i\in[m]}$ *and* st *as* (sk, i^*).
- *For all* $i \in [m] \setminus \{i^*\}$ *compute* $\mathbf{W}_i \leftarrow \mathsf{LHE.Dec}(\mathsf{sk}, \tilde{\mathsf{ct}}_i)$. *For each* $j \in [k]$ *parse each row* $\mathbf{w}_{i,j} \in \{0,1\}^\mu$ *of* $\mathbf{W}_i$ *as an element* $w_{i,j} \in \mathbb{F}_q$.
- *For all* $i \in [m]\setminus\{i^*\}$, *set* $\mathbf{e}_i \leftarrow \mathsf{bin}(i)$. *Parse* $\mathbf{e}_i$ *and* $\mathbf{i}^*$ *as* $\mathbb{F}_q$ *elements (that is,* $\hat{e}_i, \hat{i}^* \in \mathbb{F}_q$ *are the elements whose coefficients correspond to the coefficients of* $\mathbf{e}_i, \mathbf{i}^* \in \{0,1\}^\mu$*). Compute* $\tilde{\mathbf{D}}_i = (\hat{e}_i - \hat{i}^*)^{-1} \cdot (w_{i,1}, \ldots, w_{i,k})$ *over* $\mathbb{F}_q$. *Note that* $\tilde{\mathbf{D}}_i \in \mathbb{F}_q$.
- *Output* $\tilde{\mathbf{D}} = (\tilde{\mathbf{D}}_1, \ldots, \tilde{\mathbf{D}}_{i^*-1}, \mathbf{0}, \tilde{\mathbf{D}}_{i^*+1}, \ldots, \tilde{\mathbf{D}}_m)$.

The analysis of the scheme is presented in the full version of the paper.

6 Bit One-Query Co-PIR from Block One-Query Co-PIR

This construction is presented in the full version of the paper. The main idea behind it is that part of the erased block can be transmitted to the receiver via a PIR without incuring in additional communication. Some amount of care needs to be taken in order to preserve the PIR-compatibility of the scheme. We prove that the transformation preserves semi-honest security but it also preserves statistical sender security if the underlying PIR is statistical sender secure.

[15] Recall that an ecryption of a matrix is defined as individual packed encryptions of each column.

7 Semi-Honest Co-PIR from Semi-Honest One-Query Co-PIR

We now show how to bootstrap a one-query co-PIR into a multiple-query co-PIR. This construction works by recursing the one-query co-PIR multiple times and, at each step, one position of the database is erased. Since the underlying one-query co-PIR has rate 1, then there is no blowup in communication when we recurse it.

Construction 2. *Let* $\{\mathbb{H}_i\}_{i\in[t]}$ *be groups. For* $i \in [t]$ *let* $\mathsf{1QCoPIR}^{(i)} = (\mathsf{Query}, \mathsf{Send}, \mathsf{Rec})$ *be a one-query co-PIR scheme such that the outputs of* $\mathsf{1QCoPIR}^{(i)}.\mathsf{Send}$ *are of the form* $(\mathsf{head}, \alpha_1, \ldots, \alpha_m)$ *where* $\alpha_j \in \mathbb{H}_i$.

$\mathsf{Query}(1^\lambda, S)$*:*

- *Parse* $S = \{a_1, \ldots, a_t\}$.
- *For* $i \in [t]$ *compute* $(\mathsf{copir}_{1,i}, \mathsf{st}_i) \leftarrow \mathsf{1QCoPIR}^{(i)}.\mathsf{Query}(1^\lambda, a_i)$.
- *Output* $\mathsf{copir}_1 = \{\mathsf{copir}_{1,i}\}_{i\in[t]}$ *and* $\mathsf{st} = \{\mathsf{st}_i\}_{i\in[t]}$.

$\mathsf{Send}(\mathsf{copir}_1, \mathbf{D} \in \mathbb{H}^m)$*:*

- *Parse* copir_1 *as* $\{\mathsf{copir}_{1,i}\}_{i\in[t]}$. *Set* $\mathsf{DB}_0 = \mathbf{D}$.
- *For* $i \in [t]$ *do the following:*
  - *Compute* $\mathsf{copir}_{2,i} \leftarrow \mathsf{1QCoPIR}^{(i)}.\mathsf{Send}(\mathsf{copir}_{1,i}, \mathsf{DB}_{i-1})$.
  - *Parse* $\mathsf{copir}_{2,i}$ *as* $(\mathsf{head}_i, \alpha_{i,1}, \ldots, \alpha_{i,m})$.
  - *Set* $\mathsf{DB}_i = (\alpha_{i,1}, \ldots, \alpha_{i,m})$.
- *Set* $\mathsf{DB}^* = \mathsf{DB}_t$.
- *Output* $\mathsf{copir}_2 = (\mathsf{DB}^*, \mathsf{head}_1, \ldots, \mathsf{head}_t)$.

$\mathsf{Rec}(\mathsf{copir}_2, \mathsf{st})$*:*

- *Parse* copir_2 *as* DB^* *and* st *as* $\{\mathsf{st}_i\}_{i\in[t]}$.
- *Set* $\mathsf{DB}'_t = \mathsf{DB}^*$.
- *For* $i = t$ *to* 1, *set* $\mathsf{copir}'_{2,i} = (\mathsf{head}_i, \mathsf{DB}'_i)$ *and compute* $\mathsf{DB}'_{i-1} \leftarrow \mathsf{1QCoPIR}^{(i)}.\mathsf{Rec}(\mathsf{copir}'_{2,i}, \mathsf{st}_i)$.
- *Output* $\tilde{\mathbf{D}} = \mathsf{DB}'_0$.

The analysis of the scheme is presented in the full version of the paper.

8 Conditional Disclosure of Secrets for DDH-Based Encryption

In this section we present a black-box construction of a CDS for a specific language. Namely, our scheme guarantees that an El-Gamal public key is wellformed and that a certain ciphertext encrypts a bit. The scheme fulfills statistical sender privacy.

The main idea of this construction is to use AR codes to guarantee that the receiver's message is wellformed. The full construction and analysis is presented in the full version of the paper.

9 Statistical Sender Secure Co-PIR

In this section we present a scheme for statistical sender secure co-PIR. Our scheme works by bootstrapping a semi-honest co-PIR into a statistical sender secure one. We also show in the full version of the paper an alternative construction for SSP co-PIR from SSP PIR, albeit at the cost of slightly worse overall computational complexity.

We now show how to boostrap a semi-honest co-PIR into a statistical sender secure co-PIR using a CDS. Essentially, the CDS will ensure that the first message of the receiver is well-formed.

Let CoPIR be a semi-honest co-PIR scheme parametrized by m. Consider the following languange $\mathcal{L}_{\mathsf{CoPIR}}$ parametrized by CoPIR

$$\mathcal{L}_{\mathsf{CoPIR}} = \left\{\mathsf{copir}_1 : \exists (S, r) \in [m]^t \times \{0,1\}^\lambda \text{ s.t. } \mathsf{copir}_1 \leftarrow \mathsf{CoPIR.Query}(1^\lambda, S; r)\right\}.$$

Clearly this is a NP languange thus there exists a statistical sender secure CDS scheme for this particular languange [33,44].

Ingredients. Let $\mathbb{H}$ be a group. Let

- $\mathsf{CoPIR} = (\mathsf{Query}, \mathsf{Send}, \mathsf{Rec})$ be a co-PIR scheme where the outputs of $\mathsf{CoPIR.Send}$ are of the form $(\alpha_1, \dots, \alpha_m)$ where $\alpha_i \in \mathbb{H}$.
- $\mathsf{CDS} = (\mathsf{Enc}, \mathsf{Send}, \mathsf{Release})$ be a statistical sender secure CDS scheme for the the language $\mathcal{L}_{\mathsf{CoPIR}}$. Looking ahead, we will use the CDS construction from Sect. 8 to obtain a black-box construction.

Construction 3. *We now describe the construction in full detail.*
$\mathsf{Query}(1^\lambda, S)$*:*

- *Parse* $S = \{a_1, \dots, a_t\}$.
- *Compute* $(\mathsf{copir}'_1, \mathsf{st}') \leftarrow \mathsf{CoPIR.Query}(1^\lambda, S; r)$ *using random coins* $r \in \{0,1\}^\lambda$.
- *Compute* $(\mathsf{cds}_1, \mathsf{st}'') \leftarrow \mathsf{CDS.Enc}(1^\lambda, (S, r))$.
- *Output* $\mathsf{copir}_1 = (\mathsf{copir}'_1, \mathsf{cds}_1)$ *and* $\mathsf{st} = (\mathsf{st}', \mathsf{st}'')$.

$\mathsf{Send}(\mathsf{copir}_1, \mathbf{D} \in \mathbb{G}^m)$*:*

- *Parse* copir_1 *as* $(\mathsf{copir}'_1, \mathsf{cds}_1)$.
- *Compute* $\mathsf{copir}'_2 \leftarrow \mathsf{CoPIR.Send}(\mathsf{copir}_1, \mathbf{D})$.
- *Parse* copir'_2 *as* $(\alpha_1, \dots, \alpha_m)$ *and set* $\mathsf{DB} = (\alpha_1, \dots, \alpha_m)$.
- *For all* $i \in [t]$ *sample* $\beta_i \leftarrow_{\$} \mathbb{H}$.
- *Set* $\mathsf{DB}^* = \mathsf{DB} + (\beta_1, \dots, \beta_t, 0 \dots, 0)$.
- *Compute* $\mathsf{cds}_2 \leftarrow \mathsf{CDS.Send}(\mathsf{cds}_1, \mathcal{L}_{\mathsf{CoPIR}}, (\beta_1, \dots, \beta_t))$.
- *Output* $\mathsf{copir}_2 = (\mathsf{DB}^*, \mathsf{cds}_2)$.

$\mathsf{Rec}(\mathsf{copir}_2, \mathsf{st})$*:*

- *Parse* copir_2 *as* $(\mathsf{DB}^*, \mathsf{cds}_2)$ *and* st *as* $(\mathsf{st}', \mathsf{st}'')$.
- *Compute* $(\beta'_1, \dots, \beta'_t) \leftarrow \mathsf{CDS.Release}(\mathsf{cds}_2, \mathsf{st}'')$.

- *Compute* $\mathsf{DB}' \leftarrow \mathsf{DB}^* - (\beta'_1, \ldots, \beta'_t, 0, \ldots, 0)$.
- *Set* $\mathsf{copir}'_2 = \mathsf{DB}'$ *and compute* $\tilde{\mathbf{D}} \leftarrow \mathsf{CoPIR.Rec}(\mathsf{copir}'_2, \mathsf{st}')$.
- *Output* $\tilde{\mathbf{D}}$.

Due to space constrains, the analysis of the scheme is deferred to the full version of the paper.

10 Statistical Sender Private Oblivious Transfer with Optimal Rate

As an application for our statistical sender secure co-PIR scheme, we build an OT scheme. This OT scheme has overall rate 1 and achieves statistical sender privacy.

Before presenting our construction, we present some notation that we will use throughout this section.

- $\mathsf{RowMatrix}(\ell, n, \mathbf{v}_1, \ldots, \mathbf{v}_\ell)$: Takes row-vectors $\mathbf{v}_1, \ldots, \mathbf{v}_\ell \in \{0,1\}^n$ and outputs a matrix
$$\mathbf{V} = \begin{pmatrix} - \mathbf{v}_1 - \\ \vdots \\ - \mathbf{v}_\ell - \end{pmatrix},$$
i.e. for every $i \in [\ell]$ the i-th row of $\mathbf{V}$ is the row-vector $\mathbf{v}_i$.

Ingredients. We will need the following ingredients for our protocol:

- A PIR scheme $\mathsf{PIR} = (\mathsf{Query}, \mathsf{Send}, \mathsf{Retrieve})$.
- A (bit) co-PIR scheme $\mathsf{CoPIR} = (\mathsf{Query}, \mathsf{Send}, \mathsf{Rec})$ that is PIR-compatible parametrized by m.
- A rate-1 circuit-private LHE scheme $\mathsf{LHE} = (\mathsf{KeyGen}, \mathsf{Enc}, \mathsf{Eval}, \mathsf{Shrink}, \mathsf{DecShrink})$ with plaintext space $\{0,1\}^\ell$ and for which shrinked ciphertexts have the form $\mathsf{ct} = (g, d_1, \ldots, d_\ell)$ where $g \in \mathbb{G}$ is a group element (for some large enough group $\mathbb{G}$, namely a DDH group) and $d_i \in \{0,1\}$.
- A download rate-1 CDS scheme $\mathsf{CDS} = (\mathsf{Enc}, \mathsf{Send}, \mathsf{Release})$ for the language
$$\mathcal{L} = \left\{ \mathsf{pk}, \{\mathsf{ct}_i\}_{i \in [\ell]} : \exists (r, \mathbf{s}_i, r_i) \text{ s.t. } \begin{array}{r} (\mathsf{pk}, \mathsf{sk}) \leftarrow \mathsf{LHE.KeyGen}(1^\lambda, \ell; r) \\ \mathbf{S}_i = \mathsf{SingleRowMatrix}(\ell, n, i, \mathbf{s}_i) \\ \mathsf{ct}_i \leftarrow \mathsf{LHE.Enc}(\mathsf{pk}, \mathbf{S}_i; r_i) \end{array} \right\}$$
for some $\mathbf{s}_i \in \{0,1\}^n$.
- The binary $\mathsf{LPN}(n, m, \rho)$ problem with dimension $n = \mathsf{poly}(\lambda)$, $m = n \cdot \ell \cdot \mathsf{poly}(\lambda)$ samples and slightly sub-constant noise-rate $\rho = m^{1-\epsilon}$.

Construction 4 (Optimal-rate SSP OT).
We now describe the scheme in full detail. $\mathsf{OTR}(1^\lambda, \mathbf{b} \in \{0,1\}^{m\ell})$:

- *Parse* $\mathbf{b} = (\mathbf{b}_1, \dots, \mathbf{b}_\ell)$, *where the* $\mathbf{b}_i \in \{0,1\}^m$ *are blocks of size* m.
- *Choose* $\mathbf{A} \leftarrow_\$ \{0,1\}^{n\times m}$ *uniformly at random and compute a pair of public and secret key* $(\mathsf{pk}, \mathsf{sk}) \leftarrow \mathsf{LHE.KeyGen}(1^\lambda, \ell; r)$ *using random coins* $r \in \{0,1\}^\lambda$.
- *For all* $i \in [\ell]$, *choose* $\mathbf{s}_i \leftarrow_\$ \{0,1\}^n$, *and* $\mathbf{e}_i \leftarrow_\$ \chi_{m,t}$, *compute* $\mathbf{c}_i \leftarrow \mathbf{s}_i\mathbf{A} + \mathbf{e}_i + \mathbf{b}_i$, *and set* $\mathbf{S}_i \leftarrow \mathsf{SingleRowMatrix}(\ell, n, i, \mathbf{s}_i)$. *Compute a matrix-ciphertext* $\mathsf{ct}_i \leftarrow \mathsf{LHE.Enc}(\mathsf{pk}, \mathbf{S}_i; r_i)$ *using random coins* $r_i \in \{0,1\}^\lambda$.
- *Compute* $(\mathsf{cds}_1, \tilde{\mathsf{st}}) \leftarrow \mathsf{CDS.Enc}(1^\lambda, w)$ *where* $w = (r, \{\mathbf{S}_i, r_i\}_{i\in[\ell]})$.
- *For all* $i \in [\ell]$ *set* $J_i = \mathsf{Supp}(\mathbf{e}_i)$ *to be the support of* $\mathbf{e}_i$. *Compute* $(\mathsf{copir}_{1,i}, \mathsf{st}_i) \leftarrow \mathsf{CoPIR.Query}(J_i)$.[16]
- *Output* $\mathsf{ot}_1 = \big(\mathsf{pk}, \mathbf{A}, \{\mathsf{ct}_i, \mathbf{c}_i, \mathsf{copir}_{1,i}\}_{i\in[\ell]}, \mathsf{cds}_1\big)$ *and* $\mathsf{st} = (\mathsf{sk}, \{\mathsf{st}_i, J_i\}_{i\in[\ell]}, \tilde{\mathsf{st}})$.

$\mathsf{OTS}(\mathsf{ot}_1, (\mathbf{m}_0, \mathbf{m}_1) \in (\{0,1\}^{m\ell})^2)$:

- *Parse* $\mathbf{m}_0 = (\mathbf{m}_{0,1}, \dots, \mathbf{m}_{0,\ell})$ *and* $\mathbf{m}_1 = (\mathbf{m}_{1,1}, \dots, \mathbf{m}_{1,\ell})$, *where each* $\mathbf{m}_{b,i} = (m_{b,i,1}, \dots, m_{b,i,m}) \in \{0,1\}^m$. *Parse* $\mathsf{ot}_1 = \big(\mathsf{pk}, \mathbf{A}, \{\mathsf{ct}_i, \mathbf{c}_i, \mathsf{copir}_{1,i}\}_{i\in[\ell]}, \mathsf{cds}_1\big)$.
- *For* $i \in [\ell]$ *set* $\mathbf{z}_i = \mathbf{m}_{0,i}$.
- *Set* $\mathbf{Z} = \mathsf{RowMatrix}(\ell, m, \mathbf{z}_1, \dots, \mathbf{z}_\ell)$.
- *For all* $i \in [\ell]$ *set* $\mathbf{C}_i = \mathsf{SingleRowMatrix}(\ell, m, i, \mathbf{c}_i)$ *and* $\mathbf{D}_i = \mathsf{Diag}(m, \mathbf{m}_{1,i} - \mathbf{m}_{0,i})$.
- *Define the* $\mathbb{Z}_2$*-linear function* $f : (\{0,1\}^{\ell\times n})^\ell \to \{0,1\}^{\ell\times m}$ *via*

$$f(\mathbf{X}_1, \dots, \mathbf{X}_\ell) = \left(\sum_{i=1}^{\ell}(-\mathbf{X}_i\mathbf{A} + \mathbf{C}_i)\cdot \mathbf{D}_i\right) + \mathbf{Z}.$$

Additionally, define the $\mathbb{Z}_2$*-linear function* $g : (\{0,1\}^{\ell\times n})^\ell \to \{0,1\}^{\ell\times m}$ *via*

$$g(\mathbf{X}_1, \dots, \mathbf{X}_\ell) = \left(\sum_{i=1}^{\ell}(-\mathbf{X}_i\mathbf{A} + \mathbf{C}_i + \mathbf{U}_i)\cdot \mathbf{D}_i\right) + \mathbf{Z}.$$

where $\mathbf{U}_i \leftarrow \mathsf{SingleRowMatrix}(\ell, m, i, \mathbf{1})$ *and* $\mathbf{1} = (1, \dots, 1)$ *is the vector of length* m *which is* 1 *everywhere.*
- *Compute* $\mathsf{CT}_1 \leftarrow \mathsf{LHE.Eval\&Shrink}(\mathsf{pk}, f, \mathsf{ct}_1, \dots, \mathsf{ct}_\ell)$ *and* $\mathsf{CT}_2 \leftarrow \mathsf{LHE.Eval\&Shrink}(\mathsf{pk}, g, \mathsf{ct}_1, \dots, \mathsf{ct}_\ell)$.
- *Parse* CT_1 *as* $\{g_i, d_{i,1}, \dots, d_{i,\ell}\}_{i\in[m]}$ *where each* $g_i \in \mathbb{G}$ *and* $d_{i,j} \in \{0,1\}$. *Similarly parse* CT_2 *as* $\{h_i, f_{i,1}, \dots, f_{i,\ell}\}_{i\in[m]}$ *each* $h_i \in \mathbb{G}$ *and* $f_{i,j} \in \{0,1\}$.
- *For all* $i \in [\ell]$ *set* $\mathbf{D}_i = (d_{1,i}, \dots, d_{m,i})$ *and* $\mathbf{F}_i = (f_{1,i}, \dots, f_{m,i})$. *Compute* $\mathsf{copir}_{2,i} \leftarrow \mathsf{CoPIR.Send}(\mathsf{copir}_{1,i}, \mathbf{D}_i)$ *and* $\mathsf{r}_i \leftarrow \mathsf{PIR.Send}(\mathsf{q}_i, \mathbf{F}_i)$ *where* $\mathsf{copir}_{1,i}$ *is parsed as the PIR message* q_i.
- *Set* $\mathsf{ot}_2' = \{g_i, \mathsf{copir}_{2,i}, h_i, \mathsf{r}_i\}_{i\in[\ell]}$.
- *Compute* $\mathsf{cds}_2 \leftarrow \mathsf{CDS.Send}(\mathsf{cds}_1, \mathcal{L}, \mathsf{ot}_2')$.
- *Output* $\mathsf{ot}_2 = \mathsf{cds}_2$.

[16] Recall that, since the CoPIR scheme is PIR-compatible then $\mathsf{copir}_{1,i}$ also corresponds to a first message PIR with input J_i.

$\mathsf{OTD}(\mathsf{ot}_2, \mathsf{st})$:

- *Parse* ot_2 *as* cds_2 *and* $\mathsf{st} = (\mathsf{sk}, \{\mathsf{st}_i, J_i\}_{i\in[\ell]}, \tilde{\mathsf{st}})$.
- *Compute* $\mathsf{ot}_2' \leftarrow \mathsf{CDS.Release}(\mathsf{cds}_2, \tilde{st})$. *Parse* ot_2' *as* $\{g_i, \mathsf{copir}_{2,i}, h_i, \mathsf{r}_i\}_{i\in[\ell]}$.
- *For all* $i \in [\ell]$ *compute* $\tilde{\mathbf{D}}_i = (\tilde{d}_{1,i}, \ldots, \tilde{d}_{m,i}) \leftarrow \mathsf{CoPIR.Retrieve}(\mathsf{copir}_{2,i}, \mathsf{st}_i)$.
- *Set* $\tilde{\mathsf{CT}}_1$ *to be* $\{g_i, \tilde{d}_{i,1}, \ldots, \tilde{d}_{i,\ell}\}_{i\in[m]}$. *Compute* $\mathbf{W} \leftarrow \mathsf{LHE.DecShrink}(\mathsf{sk}, \tilde{\mathsf{CT}}_1)$ *where* $\mathbf{W} \in \{0,1\}^{\ell\times m}$. *Parse* $\mathbf{W} = (w_{i,j})_{i\in[\ell],j\in[m]}$ *where* $w_{i,j} \in \{0,1\}$
- *For all* $i \in [\ell]$ *compute* $(v_{i,J_i[1]}, \ldots, v_{i,J_i[t]}) \leftarrow \mathsf{PIR.Retrieve}(\mathsf{r}_i, \mathsf{st}_i)$. *Additionally for all* $j \in [t]$, *compute* $y_{i,J_i[j]} \leftarrow \mathsf{LHE.Dec}(h_{J_i[j]}, v_{i,J_i[j]})$.
- *Set* $\mathbf{M} = (m_{i,j})_{i\in[\ell],j\in[m]} \in \{0,1\}^{\ell\times m}$ *where*

$$m_{i,j} = \begin{cases} y_{i,J_i[l]} & \textit{if } l = J_i[l] \\ w_{i,j} & \textit{otherwise} \end{cases} .$$

- *Output* $\mathbf{M}$.

The full analysis of the scheme is presented in the full version of the paper.

11 Two-Party Secure Computation with Overall Communication of $\mathcal{O}(|\mathcal{C}|) + \mathsf{poly}(\lambda)$

We now show an application of our optimal overall rate SSP OT. This application is in constructing a 2-Party secure computation (2PC) scheme with overall communication of $\mathcal{O}(|\mathcal{C}|) + \mathsf{poly}(\lambda)$, where $\mathcal{C}$ is the circuit to be computed and provides statistical semi-honest security against one of the parties and computational semi-honest security against the other party.

The protocol is just the classical GMW protocol [28] in the OT correlations model where the OT correlations are generated using our SSP OT.

Specifically, to compute a secret sharing of the AND of two wires whose values are themselves secret shared as (a_1, a_2) and (b_1, b_2) respectively, the parties first compute locally $a_1 \cdot b_1$ and $a_2 \cdot b_2$. One of the parties acts as the sender and the other acts as the receiver in two instances of 1-out-of-2 OT. Assume w.l.o.g. that P_1 acts as the sender and P_2 acts as the receiver. P_2 uses a_2 and b_2 as its choice bits and P_1 uses $(r_1, b_1 + r_1)$ and $(r_2, a_1 + r_2)$ respectively as the sender messages. P_2 obtains $a_2b_1 + r_1$ and $a_1b_2 + r_2$ as the outputs of the two OT executions. P_1 sets the share of the AND to be $a_1b_1 + r_1 + r_2$ and P_2 sets its share to be $a_2b_2 + a_1b_2 + r_1 + a_2b_1 + r_2$. Note that instantiating the GMW protocol with an OT scheme that does not have overall rate-1 incurs an communication complexity of $\mathsf{poly})|\mathcal{C}|, \lambda)$.

Lemma 13 ([28]). *Given a circuit* $\mathcal{C} : \{0,1\}^n \times \{0,1\}^m \to \{0,1\}$, *there exists a two-party* $O(|\mathcal{C}|)$*-round protocol in the OT-correlation model such that*

- *The protocol provides semi-honest statistical security.*
- *The communication complexity is upper-bounded by* $6|\mathcal{C}| + n + m + \mathsf{poly}(\lambda)$.
- *Both parties share* $2|\mathcal{C}|$ *OT correlations.*

For each gate, the parties need to perform 2 chosen input OTs. If they share 2 random OT correlations, these can be derandomized using the standard transformation from random OT to chosen input OT which takes 3 bits of communication per OT. Thus, the total communication is 6 bits per gate. If we setup the OT correlations using our SSP OT scheme, we obtain the following corollary.

Corollary 14. *Given a circuit $\mathcal{C} : \{0,1\}^n \times \{0,1\}^m \rightarrow \{0,1\}$, there exists a two-party α-round protocol in the standard model such that*

- *The protocol is semi-honest secure against one of the parties and statistically semi-honest secure against the other one.*
- *The communication complexity is upperbounded by $10|\mathcal{C}| + n + m + \mathsf{poly}(\lambda)$.*

The $2 \cdot |\mathcal{C}|$ OT correlations can be shared using the OT scheme from Sect. 10 incurring in total communication approaching $4|\mathcal{C}| + \mathsf{poly}(\lambda)$ for large enough $|\mathcal{C}|$. Plugging this with the lemma above, we obtain a scheme with total communication $10|\mathcal{C}| + n + m + \mathsf{poly}(\lambda)$. Moreover, statistical security for one of the parties follow from the SSP property of the underlying OT.

Acknowledgements. Pedro Branco was partially funded by the German Federal Ministry of Education and Research (BMBF) in the course of the 6GEM research hub under grant number 16KISK038. Nico Döttling: Funded by the European Union (ERC, LACONIC, 101041207). Views and opinions expressed are however those of the author(s) only and do not necessarily reflect those of the European Union or the European Research Council. Neither the European Union nor the granting authority can be held responsible for them. Akshayaram Srinivasan was supported in part by a SERB startup grant and Google India Research Award.

References

1. Aggarwal, D., Döttling, N., Dujmovic, J., Hajiabadi, M., Malavolta, G., Obremski, M.: Algebraic restriction codes and their applications. In: Braverman, M. (ed.) 13th Innovations in Theoretical Computer Science Conference (ITCS 2022). Leibniz International Proceedings in Informatics (LIPIcs), vol. 215, pp. 1–15. Schloss Dagstuhl - Leibniz-Zentrum für Informatik, Dagstuhl, Germany (2022). https://drops.dagstuhl.de/opus/volltexte/2022/15598
2. Aiello, B., Ishai, Y., Reingold, O.: Priced oblivious transfer: how to sell digital goods. In: Pfitzmann, B. (ed.) EUROCRYPT 2001. LNCS, vol. 2045, pp. 119–135. Springer, Heidelberg (2001). https://doi.org/10.1007/3-540-44987-6_8
3. Applebaum, B.: Garbled circuits as randomized encodings of functions: a primer. In: Tutorials on the Foundations of Cryptography. ISC, pp. 1–44. Springer, Cham (2017). https://doi.org/10.1007/978-3-319-57048-8_1
4. Applebaum, B., Ishai, Y., Kushilevitz, E.: Cryptography in NC^0. In: 45th FOCS, pp. 166–175. IEEE Computer Society Press, October 2004
5. Badrinarayanan, S., Fernando, R., Jain, A., Khurana, D., Sahai, A.: Statistical ZAP arguments. In: Canteaut, A., Ishai, Y. (eds.) EUROCRYPT 2020, Part III. LNCS, vol. 12107, pp. 642–667. Springer, Cham (2020). https://doi.org/10.1007/978-3-030-45727-3_22

6. Badrinarayanan, S., Garg, S., Ishai, Y., Sahai, A., Wadia, A.: Two-message witness indistinguishability and secure computation in the plain model from new assumptions. In: Takagi, T., Peyrin, T. (eds.) ASIACRYPT 2017, Part III. LNCS, vol. 10626, pp. 275–303. Springer, Cham (2017). https://doi.org/10.1007/978-3-319-70700-6_10
7. Badrinarayanan, S., Patranabis, S., Sarkar, P.: Statistical security in two-party computation revisited. In: Kiltz, E., Vaikuntanathan, V. (eds.) Theory of Cryptography. Lecture Notes in Computer Science, vol. 13748, pp. 181–210. Springer Nature Switzerland, Cham (2022). https://doi.org/10.1007/978-3-031-22365-5_7
8. Bitansky, N., Freizeit, S.: Statistically sender-private OT from LPN and derandomization. Cryptology ePrint Archive, Paper 2022/185 (2022). https://eprint.iacr.org/2022/185
9. Boyle, E., Couteau, G., Gilboa, N., Ishai, Y.: Compressing vector OLE. In: Lie, D., Mannan, M., Backes, M., Wang, X. (eds.) ACM CCS 2018, pp. 896–912. ACM Press, October 2018
10. Boyle, E., et al.: Efficient two-round OT extension and silent non-interactive secure computation. In: Cavallaro, L., Kinder, J., Wang, X., Katz, J. (eds.) ACM CCS 2019, pp. 291–308. ACM Press, November 2019
11. Boyle, E., Couteau, G., Gilboa, N., Ishai, Y., Kohl, L., Scholl, P.: Efficient pseudorandom correlation generators: silent OT extension and more. In: Boldyreva, A., Micciancio, D. (eds.) CRYPTO 2019, Part III. LNCS, vol. 11694, pp. 489–518. Springer, Cham (2019). https://doi.org/10.1007/978-3-030-26954-8_16
12. Boyle, E., Couteau, G., Gilboa, N., Ishai, Y., Kohl, L., Scholl, P.: Correlated pseudorandom functions from variable-density LPN. In: 61st FOCS, pp. 1069–1080. IEEE Computer Society Press, November 2020
13. Boyle, E., Couteau, G., Gilboa, N., Ishai, Y., Kohl, L., Scholl, P.: Efficient pseudorandom correlation generators from ring-LPN. In: Micciancio, D., Ristenpart, T. (eds.) CRYPTO 2020. LNCS, vol. 12171, pp. 387–416. Springer, Cham (2020). https://doi.org/10.1007/978-3-030-56880-1_14
14. Boyle, E., Couteau, G., Meyer, P.: Sublinear secure computation from new assumptions. In: Kiltz, E., Vaikuntanathan, V. (eds.) Theory of Cryptography. Lecture Notes in Computer Science, vol. 13748, pp. 121–150. Springer Nature Switzerland, Cham (2022). https://doi.org/10.1007/978-3-031-22365-5_5
15. Boyle, E., Gilboa, N., Ishai, Y.: Breaking the circuit size barrier for secure computation under DDH. In: Robshaw, M., Katz, J. (eds.) CRYPTO 2016, Part I. LNCS, vol. 9814, pp. 509–539. Springer, Heidelberg (2016). https://doi.org/10.1007/978-3-662-53018-4_19
16. Boyle, E., Gilboa, N., Ishai, Y.: Group-based secure computation: optimizing rounds, communication, and computation. In: Coron, J.-S., Nielsen, J.B. (eds.) EUROCRYPT 2017, Part II. LNCS, vol. 10211, pp. 163–193. Springer, Cham (2017). https://doi.org/10.1007/978-3-319-56614-6_6
17. Brakerski, Z., Branco, P., Döttling, N., Garg, S., Malavolta, G.: Constant ciphertext-rate non-committing encryption from standard assumptions. In: Pass, R., Pietrzak, K. (eds.) TCC 2020, Part I. LNCS, vol. 12550, pp. 58–87. Springer, Cham (2020). https://doi.org/10.1007/978-3-030-64375-1_3
18. Brakerski, Z., Branco, P., Döttling, N., Pu, S.: Batch-OT with optimal rate. In: Dunkelman, O., Dziembowski, S. (eds.) Advances in Cryptology - EUROCRYPT 2022. Lecture Notes in Computer Science, vol. 13276, pp. 157–186. Springer International Publishing, Cham (2022). https://doi.org/10.1007/978-3-031-07085-3_6

19. Brakerski, Z., Döttling, N.: Two-message statistically sender-private OT from LWE. In: Beimel, A., Dziembowski, S. (eds.) TCC 2018, Part II. LNCS, vol. 11240, pp. 370–390. Springer, Cham (2018). https://doi.org/10.1007/978-3-030-03810-6_14
20. Brakerski, Z., Döttling, N., Garg, S., Malavolta, G.: Leveraging linear decryption: rate-1 fully-homomorphic encryption and time-lock puzzles. In: Hofheinz, D., Rosen, A. (eds.) TCC 2019, Part II. LNCS, vol. 11892, pp. 407–437. Springer, Cham (2019). https://doi.org/10.1007/978-3-030-36033-7_16
21. Brakerski, Z., Koppula, V., Mour, T.: NIZK from LPN and trapdoor hash via correlation intractability for Approximable relations. In: Micciancio, D., Ristenpart, T. (eds.) CRYPTO 2020, Part III. LNCS, vol. 12172, pp. 738–767. Springer, Cham (2020). https://doi.org/10.1007/978-3-030-56877-1_26
22. Chase, M., Garg, S., Hajiabadi, M., Li, J., Miao, P.: Amortizing rate-1 OT and applications to PIR and PSI. In: Nissim, K., Waters, B. (eds.) TCC 2021, Part III. LNCS, vol. 13044, pp. 126–156. Springer, Cham (2021). https://doi.org/10.1007/978-3-030-90456-2_5
23. Döttling, N., Garg, S., Ishai, Y., Malavolta, G., Mour, T., Ostrovsky, R.: Trapdoor hash functions and their applications. In: Boldyreva, A., Micciancio, D. (eds.) CRYPTO 2019, Part III. LNCS, vol. 11694, pp. 3–32. Springer, Cham (2019). https://doi.org/10.1007/978-3-030-26954-8_1
24. Garg, S., Gentry, C., Halevi, S., Raykova, M., Sahai, A., Waters, B.: Candidate indistinguishability obfuscation and functional encryption for all circuits. In: 54th FOCS, pp. 40–49. IEEE Computer Society Press, October 2013
25. Garg, S., Hajiabadi, M., Ostrovsky, R.: Efficient range-trapdoor functions and applications: rate-1 OT and more. In: Pass, R., Pietrzak, K. (eds.) TCC 2020, Part I. LNCS, vol. 12550, pp. 88–116. Springer, Cham (2020). https://doi.org/10.1007/978-3-030-64375-1_4
26. Gentry, C., Halevi, S.: Compressible FHE with applications to PIR. In: Hofheinz, D., Rosen, A. (eds.) TCC 2019, Part II. LNCS, vol. 11892, pp. 438–464. Springer, Cham (2019). https://doi.org/10.1007/978-3-030-36033-7_17
27. Goldreich, O., Goldwasser, S., Micali, S.: How to construct random functions. J. ACM **33**(4), 792–807 (1986). https://doi.org/10.1145/6490.6503
28. Goldreich, O., Micali, S., Wigderson, A.: How to play any mental game or a completeness theorem for protocols with honest majority. In: Aho, A. (ed.) 19th ACM STOC, pp. 218–229. ACM Press, May 1987
29. Goyal, V., Jain, A., Jin, Z., Malavolta, G.: Statistical zaps and new oblivious transfer protocols. In: Canteaut, A., Ishai, Y. (eds.) EUROCRYPT 2020, Part III. LNCS, vol. 12107, pp. 668–699. Springer, Cham (2020). https://doi.org/10.1007/978-3-030-45727-3_23
30. Halevi, S., Kalai, Y.T.: Smooth projective hashing and two-message oblivious transfer. J. Cryptol. **25**(1), 158–193 (2012)
31. Ishai, Y., Kilian, J., Nissim, K., Petrank, E.: Extending oblivious transfers efficiently. In: Boneh, D. (ed.) CRYPTO 2003. LNCS, vol. 2729, pp. 145–161. Springer, Heidelberg (2003). https://doi.org/10.1007/978-3-540-45146-4_9
32. Ishai, Y., Kushilevitz, E.: Randomizing polynomials: a new representation with applications to round-efficient secure computation. In: 41st FOCS, pp. 294–304. IEEE Computer Society Press, November 2000
33. Ishai, Y., Kushilevitz, E.: Perfect Constant-round secure computation via perfect randomizing polynomials. In: Widmayer, P., Eidenbenz, S., Triguero, F., Morales, R., Conejo, R., Hennessy, M. (eds.) ICALP 2002. LNCS, vol. 2380, pp. 244–256. Springer, Heidelberg (2002). https://doi.org/10.1007/3-540-45465-9_22

34. Ishai, Y., Kushilevitz, E., Ostrovsky, R., Sahai, A.: Cryptography with constant computational overhead. In: Ladner, R.E., Dwork, C. (eds.) 40th ACM STOC, pp. 433–442. ACM Press, May 2008
35. Ishai, Y., Paskin, A.: Evaluating branching programs on encrypted data. In: Vadhan, S.P. (ed.) TCC 2007. LNCS, vol. 4392, pp. 575–594. Springer, Heidelberg (2007). https://doi.org/10.1007/978-3-540-70936-7_31
36. Jain, A., Jin, Z.: Non-interactive zero knowledge from sub-exponential DDH. In: Canteaut, A., Standaert, F.-X. (eds.) EUROCRYPT 2021, Part I. LNCS, vol. 12696, pp. 3–32. Springer, Cham (2021). https://doi.org/10.1007/978-3-030-77870-5_1
37. Jain, A., Kalai, Y.T., Khurana, D., Rothblum, R.: Distinguisher-dependent simulation in two rounds and its applications. In: Katz, J., Shacham, H. (eds.) CRYPTO 2017, Part II. LNCS, vol. 10402, pp. 158–189. Springer, Cham (2017). https://doi.org/10.1007/978-3-319-63715-0_6
38. Kalai, Y.T., Khurana, D., Sahai, A.: Statistical witness indistinguishability (and more) in two messages. In: Nielsen, J.B., Rijmen, V. (eds.) EUROCRYPT 2018, Part III. LNCS, vol. 10822, pp. 34–65. Springer, Cham (2018). https://doi.org/10.1007/978-3-319-78372-7_2
39. Kalai, Y.T., Lombardi, A., Vaikuntanathan, V., Wichs, D.: Boosting batch arguments and ram delegation. Cryptology ePrint Archive, Paper 2022/1320 (2022). https://eprint.iacr.org/2022/1320
40. Khurana, D., Mughees, M.H.: On statistical security in two-party computation. In: Pass, R., Pietrzak, K. (eds.) TCC 2020, Part II. LNCS, vol. 12551, pp. 532–561. Springer, Cham (2020). https://doi.org/10.1007/978-3-030-64378-2_19
41. Khurana, D., Sahai, A.: How to achieve non-malleability in one or two rounds. In: Umans, C. (ed.) 58th FOCS, pp. 564–575. IEEE Computer Society Press, October 2017
42. Micciancio, D., Sorrell, J.: Simpler statistically sender private oblivious transfer from ideals of cyclotomic integers. In: Moriai, S., Wang, H. (eds.) ASIACRYPT 2020, Part II. LNCS, vol. 12492, pp. 381–407. Springer, Cham (2020). https://doi.org/10.1007/978-3-030-64834-3_13
43. Naor, M., Pinkas, B.: Efficient oblivious transfer protocols. In: Kosaraju, S.R. (ed.) 12th SODA, pp. 448–457. ACM-SIAM, January 2001
44. Ostrovsky, R., Paskin-Cherniavsky, A., Paskin-Cherniavsky, B.: Maliciously circuit-private FHE. In: Garay, J.A., Gennaro, R. (eds.) CRYPTO 2014. LNCS, vol. 8616, pp. 536–553. Springer, Heidelberg (2014). https://doi.org/10.1007/978-3-662-44371-2_30
45. Peikert, C., Waters, B.: Lossy trapdoor functions and their applications. In: Ladner, R.E., Dwork, C. (eds.) 40th ACM STOC, pp. 187–196. ACM Press, May 2008
46. Rabin, M.O.: How to exchange secrets with oblivious transfer. Cryptology ePrint Archive (2005)

Malicious Secure, Structure-Aware Private Set Intersection

Gayathri Garimella, Mike Rosulek(✉), and Jaspal Singh

Oregon State University, Corvallis, USA
rosulekm@eecs.oregonstate.edu

Abstract. Structure-Aware private set intersection (sa-PSI) is a variant of PSI where Alice's input set A has some publicly known structure, Bob's input B is an unstructured set of points, and Alice learns the intersection $A \cap B$. sa-PSI was recently introduced by Garimella *et al.* (Crypto 2022), who described a semi-honest protocol with communication that scales with the description size of Alice's set, instead of its cardinality. In this paper, we present the first sa-PSI protocol secure against malicious adversaries.

sa-PSI protocols are built from function secret sharing (FSS) schemes, and the main challenge in our work is ensuring that multiple FSS sharings encode the *same* structured set. We do so using a cut-and-choose approach. In order to make FSS compatible with cut-and-choose, we introduce a new variant of function secret sharing, called *derandomizable* FSS (dFSS).

We show how to construct dFSS for union of geometric balls, leading to a malicious-secure sa-PSI protocol where Alice's input is a union of balls. We also improve prior FSS constructions, giving asymptotic improvements to semi-honest sa-PSI.

1 Introduction

Private Set Intersection (PSI) enables two parties Alice (with private input set A) and Bob (with private input set B) to learn the intersection $A \cap B$ of their sets, while ensuring that no party learns anything beyond the intersection. All standard PSI protocols have communication and computation complexity proportional to the cardinality of the input sets [11,22,23,28,37,40,44].

Structure Aware Private Set intersection, proposed by Garimella *et al.* in [24], is a variant of PSI where one party's input set has a publicly known structure. Formally, Alice has input $A \in \mathcal{S}$ from a known family $\mathcal{S}$ of sets, Bob has input B (an arbitrary set), and Alice learns $A \cap B$. The goal is for the communication cost to scale with the description size of A rather than its cardinality. The main result in [24] is a generic framework that reduces structure-aware PSI to the task of designing an efficient (in terms of share size and evaluation) function secret sharing (FSS) scheme for the same family $\mathcal{S}$ of sets.

G. Garimella, M. Rosulek and J. Singh—Authors partially supported by NSF award S2356A.

H. Handschuh and A. Lysyanskaya (Eds.): CRYPTO 2023, LNCS 14081, pp. 577–610, 2023.
https://doi.org/10.1007/978-3-031-38557-5_19

Structure-aware PSI is a powerful idea; suppose the publicly known structure is a union of n disjoint, fixed-radius balls in some distance metric. PSI of such sets solves the problem of fuzzy PSI, where Alice and Bob can identify which pairs of their points are within some small fixed distance of each other. Structure-aware PSI would have communication that scales with the description size n instead of the *total volume* of the balls.

1.1 Our Contributions

The protocol construction in [24] is secure in the semi-honest model. Our main contribution is to carefully extend their framework for structure-aware PSI to be secure in the presence of malicious adversaries. We incorporate a cut-and-choose style check to thwart any malicious behavior. For this, we require additional properties from the underlying boolean FSS and introduce a new variant called *derandomizable* function secret sharing (dFSS). We formally characterize dFSS and show new constructions.

Intuition Behind Derandomizable FSS. In our protocol (following the outline of [24]) the receiver Alice is supposed to generate many FSS sharings of her PSI input set. A malicious Alice may generate invalid FSS shares, and/or generate FSS sharings of inconsistent sets. We want to prevent and detect this kind of misbehavior, using a cut-and-choose technique.

In a cut-and-choose, we expect Alice to generate more FSS sharings than needed, then convince Bob that most of them were generated correctly, by "opening" them—i.e., by revealing both of its shares. However, the FSS shares are shares of Alice's private input, so revealing both shares has the unpleasant side-effect of revealing Alice's private input.

We avoid this issue with the following idea: Instead of generating FSS shares of her input, Alice can generate shares of some suitable "random objects R_i." Revealing both shares reveals only R_i, and not Alice's input.

But our protocol requires FSS shares that represent Alice's input. Hence, we require an FSS scheme with the following property: Given one FSS share of R_i, and given a public "offset" value $A - R_i$, the two shareholders compute secret shares of an output that corresponds to the object A, not the object R_i. We call such an FSS scheme **derandomizable**.

Derandomizable FSS allows Bob to check that FSS shares are well-formed (by opening some of them in a cut-and-choose). However, it does not immediately help Bob check that different FSS shares encode the same object—we address that in the details of our protocol. This property of derandomizing FSS keys was first observed by Boyle et al. [9] for the class of point functions, where they use this idea to reduce online complexity of secure 2 party computation of certain types of FSS gates. We formalize this derandomizable property of FSS and design it for a wider collection of sets.

Malicious-Secure, Structure-Aware PSI. We show a malicious-secure structure-aware PSI protocol in the UC model, given a dFSS for $\mathcal{S}$. Our protocol requires

construction	dFSS?	share size	eval cost
disjoint balls: basic FSS [8]	yes	$O(n\kappa u^d)$	$O(nu^d)$
disjoint balls: [24]	no	$O(n(4\log\delta)^d\kappa)$	$O((2\log\delta)^d)$
disjoint balls: ours	yes	$O(n\kappa(ud + (\log\delta)^d))$	$O((2\log\delta)^d)$
balls with centers $> 4\delta$ apart: [24]	no	$O(nd2^d\kappa\log\delta)$	$O(d\log\delta)$
balls with centers $> 8\delta$ **apart: ours**	yes	$O(nd\kappa\log\delta)$	$O(d\log\delta)$
axis-disjoint balls: [24]	no	$O(nd\kappa\log\delta)$	$O(d\log\delta)$

Fig. 1. FSS share size for n balls (ℓ_∞ norm) of radius δ in d dimensions, over u-bit integers. Evaluation time is for evaluating on one point.

additively homomorphic commitments and committed oblivious transfer. The communication complexity of the protocol is $\mathcal{O}(\kappa(\sigma + d + \kappa + |B|))$, where σ is the share size of dFSS, d is the description size of a structured set, κ is the security parameter.

New dFSS Definition and Techniques. We introduce the notion of derandomizable bFSS (dFSS) and present the following generic transformation results. Given dFSS for collections of sets $\mathcal{S}_1, \mathcal{S}_2$ we can construct:

- dFSS for **complement** set $\overline{\mathcal{S}_1} = \{S \mid \overline{S} \in \mathcal{S}_1\}$
- dFSS for **cross product** of the sets $\mathcal{S}_1 \times \mathcal{S}_2$
- dFSS for **point function tensor product** $\mathsf{PT} \otimes \mathcal{S}_1 = \{(\mathcal{U}\backslash\{x\}) \times S | x \in \mathcal{U}, S \in \mathcal{S}\}$, where PT represents a family of singleton sets/point functions over $\mathcal{U}$.

Next, we present a new spatial hashing technique for constructing dFSS for (two classes of) disjoint union of sets:

- Union of disjoint δ–radius balls in ℓ_∞ metric space. Our share size is $\mathcal{O}(n\kappa(ud + (\log\delta)^d))$, where κ is the security parameter, $[2^u]^d$ is the input domain (*i.e.*, d-dimensional points with u-bit coordinates) and n is the number of balls.
- Union of δ–radius balls with pairwise distance between the balls' centers $> 8\delta$ in ℓ_∞ metric space. Our share size is $\mathcal{O}(\kappa nud)$.

Finally, our new dFSS constructions can be used to improve the *semi-honest* sa-PSI protocol [24]. If Alice's input is the union of n disjoint balls of fixed radius δ in ℓ_∞ metric space, we achieve the following improvement in communication -

- $\mathcal{O}(\kappa(n(4\log\delta)^d + |B|)) \to \mathcal{O}(\kappa(nu + n(\log\delta)^d + |B|))$, where the universe set is $[2^u]^d$.
- $\mathcal{O}(\kappa(nd(\log\delta)^d + |B|)) \to \mathcal{O}(\kappa(nud + |B|))$, when input balls have pairwise distance $> 8\delta$,

A more detailed comparison of FSS evaluation cost and share size is presented in Fig. 1. Using these improved dFSS constructions for union of ℓ_∞ balls, our malicious secure structure-aware PSI protocol has only a 6–7$\times$ communication overhead compared to the semi-honest secure protocol of [24] (see Fig. 2).

structured input set	Communication cost (in GB)	
	[24] (semi-honest secure)	Ours (malicious secure)
disjoint union of ℓ_∞ balls	101.1	662.4
union of balls with centers $> 8\delta$ apart	13.2	85.6

Fig. 2. PSI concrete communication cost comparison with [24]. Here Alice's structured set (of size $\approx 10^7$) contains $n = 2700$ ℓ_∞ balls in 2 dimensions, each with radius $\delta = 30$ in universe of size 2^{32} along each dimension, and Bob inputs an unstructured set of size 10^6.

1.2 Related Work

Early solutions [29,35] for 2-party PSI are based on Diffie-Hellman (and secure against semi-honest adversaries). In the last few years, we have seen many protocol paradigms emerge, based on techniques like key agreement [17,28,31], bloom filters [18,42], oblivious polynomial evaluation via additively homomorphic encryption [14,33], circuit-based [22,27,39,40], vector oblivious linear function evaluation [44] to name a few.

However, truly practical and scalable solutions for PSI are mostly designed in the OT paradigm. Their efficiency comes from OT extension [30], which reduces the *marginal* cost of each OT instance to cheap symmetric-key operations (*e.g.*, calls to AES). These OT instances enable the comparisons necessary for PSI. Pinkas, Schneider, and Zohner [41] were the first to propose basing PSI directly on OT. The approach was later refined in a series of works [11,23,34,36–38,43,44].

Structure-Aware PSI. Recently, Garimella et al. [24] introduced structure-aware PSI, where Alice has structured input and Bob has an unstructured set of points and the communication cost of the protocol scales with the description size instead of cardinality of the structured set. Note that *silent OT* [4–6,12,45], which allows parties to generate essentially unlimited oblivious transfer instances with no communication, does **not** solve the problem of structure-aware PSI. Silent OT generates only *random* OT correlations, which must be converted to chosen-input OT instances using communication [1], which is proportional to the cardinality of sets.

Malicious Model. To the best of our knowledge, the first specialized protocol (*i.e.*, with less than quadratic complexity) for PSI in the malicious setting is due to [21]. Other approaches proposed for malicious 2-party PSI, use techniques like Diffie-Hellman key agreement, oblivious linear function evaluation and Homomorphic Encryption (*e.g.*, [13,16,25,26,31]). More recent works [23,37,42–44] use OT extension for malicious security.

FSS. Function secret sharing was first introduced by Boyle et al. [7], who proposed efficient FSS constructions for point functions, comparison functions and a few other interesting classes. These original FSS constructions were further optimized in a sequence of works for point functions, multi-point functions, comparison functions and d dimensional intervals [3,8,10]. [Weak] Boolean FSS bFSS was introduced by Garimella et al. [24], and they present efficient weak bFSS constructions for union of disjoint ℓ_∞-balls and union of δ-radius ℓ_∞-balls with pairwise distance $> 4\delta$. The new spatial hashing based dFSS constructions we introduce exponentially improve on these bFSS constructions.

A number of works from the literature study the problem of verifiable function secret sharing - which allows the two parties holding FSS keys to verify their keys were correctly generated by the Share function [2,8,15]. However, all these works are limited to studying verifiable FSS for only point and multi-point functions, and for a special form of comparison/interval functions. Furthermore, to verify that these keys are correct with respect to an input domain D requires computational complexity proportional to $|D|$ - making this verification cost high for a large domain size. In our malicious secure PSI framework, we verify if the keys are correctly generated with communication complexity proportional to just the FSS share sizes, instead of their domain.

Boyle et al. [9] study a notion of derandomizable FSS for the families of offset functions. This class includes point, comparison, interval, and d-dimensional interval functions. Our notion of dFSS requires a similar derandomizability property as well as an "extractability" property (defined in Sect. 3). Our definitions and constructions are not limited to families of offset functions. E.g., union of disjoint, fixed-radius d-dimensional balls is not an offset family.

2 Preliminaries

2.1 Secure Computation in the Presence of Malicious Adversaries

We define security in the ideal/real world paradigm. The ideal world assumes a trusted third party that computes our chosen functionality f given the parties' choice of inputs. In the real protocol execution, the parties interact with each other according to some prescribed protocol (Π) to correctly compute the functionality f. When a *malicious* adversary corrupts a specific party, it learns its entire state, set of all received messages during execution and can cause the party to deviate arbitrarily (from expected protocol behavior) in its interaction with the honest party. In our setting, we assume the malicious adversary *statically* corrupts either the *sender* or the *receiver* at the start of the protocol. Informally, a protocol is considered secure if every attack in the real world can be simulated in the ideal world implying that the adversary never learns more than what he sees in an ideal execution of the protocol.

Definition 1. *A protocol Π is said to securely compute f in the presence of malicious adversaries if for every probabilistic polynomial time (PPT) adversary $\mathcal{A}$, there is a probabilistic polynomial time simulator Sim such that*

$$\Pr_{real}[\Pi, \mathcal{Z}, \mathcal{A}]_{x,y} \approx \Pr_{ideal}[\mathcal{F}, \mathcal{Z}, \mathsf{Sim}]_{x,y}$$

i.e. no probabilistic polynomial time distinguisher $\mathcal{Z}$ has non-negligible advantage.

2.2 Committed Oblivious Transfer

The functionality is presented in Fig. 3. A sender inputs a pair of messages m_0, m_1, a receiver inputs a bit b, and the transfer function outputs m_b to the receiver. The open function can be invoked by the sender to reveal both messages m_0, m_1 to the receiver.

Parameter: message length l

Choose:

1. Receive (choose, id, b) from the receiver, where $b \in \{0,1\}$.
2. If no message of the form $(\mathsf{choose}, id, .)$ is present in memory, store (choose, id, b) and send (choose, id) to the sender.

Transfer:

1. Receive $(\mathsf{transfer}, id, m_0, m_1)$ from the sender, where $m_0, m_1 \in \{0,1\}^l$.
2. If no messages of the form $(\mathsf{transfer}, id, m_0, m_1)$ is present in memory and a message of the form (choose, id, b) is stored, send $(\mathsf{transfer}, id, m_b)$ to the receiver.

Open:

1. Receive (open, id) from the sender
2. Output stored message $(\mathsf{transfer}, id, m_0, m_1)$ to the receiver

Fig. 3. Ideal functionality $\mathcal{F}_{\mathsf{COT}}$

2.3 Homomorphic Commitment Scheme

The functionality is presented in Fig. 4. The functionality allows a sender and receiver to commit and open to messages. The functionality is additively homomorphic so it can reveal/open the difference of any two committed values within a session.

2.4 Cuckoo Hashing

A cuckoo hash table $\mathcal{C}$ is a randomized data structure of size m that is used to encode a set of elements (key-value pairs) X of size n parametrized by three hash functions $\mathcal{H} = (\mathsf{H}_1, \mathsf{H}_2, \mathsf{H}_3)$ with $\mathsf{H}_1, \mathsf{H}_2, \mathsf{H}_3 : \{0,1\}^* \rightarrow [m]$:

$$\mathcal{C} \leftarrow \mathsf{Cuckoo}^m_{\mathsf{H}_1,\mathsf{H}_2,\mathsf{H}_3}(X)$$

A cuckoo table $\mathcal{C} = (C_1, \ldots, C_m)$ holds every element of X where for each $(x, y) \in X$ there is some $i \in \{1,2,3\}$ such that $C_{h_i(x)} = y$. Some positions of $\mathcal{C}$ will not matter, corresponding to empty bins. We pick the parameter m such that every element from X finds a place in the cuckoo table except with negligible probability. Concretely, we set $m = 1.27n$.

Parameter: Message space represented by some field $\mathbb{F}$.
$\mathcal{F}_{\mathsf{hcom}}$ interacts with a sender P_s, a receiver P_r and an adversary $\mathcal{S}$ and it has the following three phases:

Commit:

1. Upon receiving a message $(\mathsf{com}, sid, idx, P_s, P_r, m)$ from P_s, where $m \in \mathbb{F}$, record the tuple (idx, P_s, P_r, m) and send the message $(\mathsf{receipt}, sid, idx, P_s, P_r)$ to P_r and S.
2. Ignore any future commit messages with the same idx from P_s to P_r.
3. If a message $(\mathsf{aborts}, sid, idx)$ is received from $\mathcal{S}$, the functionality halts.

Open:

1. On receiving a message $(\mathsf{reveal}, sid, idx)$ from P_s: If a tuple (idx, P_s, P_r, m) was previously recorded, then send message $(\mathsf{ok}, sid, idx, P_s, P_r, m)$ to P_r and $\mathcal{S}$. Otherwise, ignore.
2. On receiving a message $(\mathsf{reveal}, sid, idx_0, idx_1)$ from P_s: If tuples (idx_0, P_s, P_r, m_0), (idx_1, P_s, P_r, m_1) were previously recorded, then send message $(\mathsf{ok}, sid, idx_0, idx_1, P_s, P_r, (m_0 - m_1))$ to P_r and $\mathcal{S}$. Otherwise, ignore.

Fig. 4. Ideal functionality $\mathcal{F}_{\mathsf{HCom}}$

2.5 Function Secret Sharing

Boolean Function Secret Sharing [24]**.** Weak boolean function secret sharing (p, ρ)-bFSS is a relaxation of the standard FSS definition, it can allow for FSS evaluation with output length ρ and a bounded false positive rate p. In this work, we don't allow for false positives and only consider ρ-bFSS with output length relaxation. Our full definition is in Appendix A.

3 Derandomizable bFSS

In this work, we introduce *derandomizable FSS*, a new variant of weak boolean FSS with some additional properties. First, we always translate our input into a group $\mathbb{G}$ via an encoding function. A given input can have multiple encodings, however, all of them must decode back to the same input.

Definition 2 (Encoding Function/Scheme). *For a group $\mathbb{G}$, a family of sets $\mathcal{S}$, we can deterministically encode a set $\mathsf{Encode} : \mathcal{S} \to \mathbb{G}$, if there exists $\mathsf{Encode}^{-1} : \mathbb{G} \to \mathcal{S}$ such that:*

$$Pr\left(\mathsf{Encode}^{-1}(\mathsf{Encode}(S)) = S\right) = 1$$

In our ρ-dFSS definition, RShare generates key shares for a uniformly random element $R \in \mathbb{G}$ from the encoding space. The evaluation function DEval takes an additional parameter $\mathsf{offset} \in \mathbb{G}$ and evaluates the input on key shares corresponding to group element $(\mathsf{offset} + R)$ where $+$ is the group operation. Finally, we require that we can extract the group element (which encodes the structured input) from the key shares. These properties will jointly enable randomizing and de-randomizing our structured input required for our malicious-secure sa-PSI protocol.

Definition 3 (Derandomizable bFSS syntax). *Let $\mathcal{S} \subseteq 2^{\mathcal{U}}$ denote a family of sets over input domain $\mathcal{U} = \mathbb{G}$, an encode function $\mathsf{Encode} : \mathcal{S} \rightarrow \mathbb{G}$ and security parameter κ. A 2-party derandomizable ρ-dFSS scheme with algorithms (RShare, Extract, DEval) has the following syntax:*

- $(k_0, k_1, R) \leftarrow \mathsf{RShare}(1^\kappa)$: *is a randomized algorithm that outputs a uniformly random group element $R \in \mathbb{G}$ and its associated (k_0, k_1) key shares.*
- $R \leftarrow \mathsf{Extract}(k_0, k_1)$: *is a deterministic function that takes key shares as input. It outputs the group element R associated with the k_0, k_1 (output by RShare).*
- $y_{idx} \leftarrow \mathsf{DEval}(1^\kappa, idx, k_{idx}, x, \mathsf{offset})$: *is a deterministic algorithm with inputs security parameter, party index $idx \in \{0,1\}$, the key share k_{idx}, the input point of evaluation $x \in \mathcal{U}$ and a group element offset $\mathsf{offset} \in \mathbb{G}$. It outputs a string $y_{idx} \in \{0,1\}^\rho$.*

Definition 4 (Derandomizable bFSS security). *A derandomizable 2-party ρ-dFSS scheme (RShare, Extract, DEval) for $\mathcal{S} \subseteq 2^{\mathcal{U}}$ is* **secure** *if it satisfies the following conditions:*

- ***Correctness for yes-instances:*** *For any $S \in \mathcal{S}$, $x \in S$:*

$$\Pr\left(y_0 \oplus y_1 = 0^\rho \;\middle|\; \begin{array}{l} (k_0, k_1, R) \leftarrow \mathsf{RShare}(1^\kappa) \\ y_0 \leftarrow \mathsf{DEval}(1^\kappa, k_0, x, \mathsf{Encode}(S) - R) \\ y_1 \leftarrow \mathsf{DEval}(1^\kappa, k_1, x, \mathsf{Encode}(S) - R) \end{array} \right) = 1 - \mathsf{negl.}(\kappa)$$

- ***Correctness for no-instances:*** *For every set $S \in \mathcal{S}$, $\underline{x \in \mathcal{U} \backslash S}$:*

$$\Pr\left(y_0 \oplus y_1 \neq 0^\rho \;\middle|\; \begin{array}{l} (k_0, k_1, R) \leftarrow \mathsf{RShare}(1^\kappa) \\ y_0 \leftarrow \mathsf{DEval}(1^\kappa, 0, k_0, x, \mathsf{Encode}(S) - R) \\ y_1 \leftarrow \mathsf{DEval}(1^\kappa, 1, k_1, x, \mathsf{Encode}(S) - R) \end{array} \right) = 1$$

- ***Privacy:*** *For every set $S \in \mathcal{S}$ and index $idx \in \{0,1\}$ there exists a simulator Sim such that the following distributions are computationally indistinguishable in the security parameter:*

$$\boxed{\begin{array}{l} (k_0, k_1, R) \leftarrow \mathsf{RShare}(1^\kappa) \\ \text{return } (k_{\mathsf{idx}}, \mathsf{Encode}(S) - R) \end{array}} \cong_\kappa \mathsf{Sim}(1^\kappa, idx)$$

- ***Extractability:*** *there exists an efficient function Extract, such that for any pair of strings k_0, k_1 and $R \in \mathbb{G}$*

$$\bot \neq R \leftarrow \mathsf{Extract}(k_0, k_1) \iff \exists r \text{ such that } (k_0, k_1, R) \xleftarrow{r} \mathsf{RShare}(1^\kappa)$$

$(\Longleftarrow)$ For every output (k_0, k_1, R) of RShare, Extract outputs R given the k_0, k_1 key shares.

($\implies$) For every output R of Extract, there exists randomness r such that RShare will output (k_0, k_1, R).

Definition 5. *A derandomizable 2-party ρ-dFSS scheme is called* ***a strong*** **dFSS** *if $\rho = 1$, else its referred to as a* ***weak*** **dFSS**.

Definition 6. *A derandomizable 2-party ρ-dFSS scheme for a collection of sets is said to have pseudo-random keys if the output of the simulator in Definition 4 is pseudo-random.*

4 Malicious-Secure Structure-Aware PSI

In this section, we discuss the main ideas of our malicious-secure sa-PSI protocol. We provide a full protocol description, proof of security and an asymptotic analysis of our communication cost.

4.1 Overview and Intuition

Let's start by reviewing the semi-honest sa-PSI protocol [24]. The receiver (Alice) generates κ independent FSS sharings $(k_0^{(i)}, k_1^{(i)}) \leftarrow \mathsf{Share}(A)$ of her structured input A and the sender (Bob) samples a uniformly random string $s \leftarrow \{0,1\}^\kappa$. Now, both parties run κ instances of OT so that Bob learns one of the two FSS shares $k_*^{(i)} = k_{s_i}^{(i)}$ for each of his choice bits s_i. Bob can define an OPRF function as:

$$F(x) = \mathsf{H}\Big(\mathsf{Eval}(k_*^{(1)}, x), \mathsf{Eval}(k_*^{(2)}, x), \ldots, \mathsf{Eval}(k_*^{(\kappa)}, x)\Big),$$

where H is a random oracle. Bob can compute $F(x)$ for any value x of his choice. On the other hand, F is defined using Bob's choice bits s, in such a way that Alice can compute $F(x)$ only when $x \in A$. When $x \in A$, Bob's choice bits have no effect—i.e., $\mathsf{Eval}(k_0^{(i)}, x) = \mathsf{Eval}(k_1^{(i)}, x)$—by the property of the ρ-bFSS. In this case, Alice can compute $F(x)$ as $\mathsf{H}\big(\mathsf{Eval}(k_0^{(1)}, x), \ldots, \mathsf{Eval}(k_0^{(\kappa)}, x)\big)$. If $x \notin A$, then each of Bob's choice bits changes one of the argument terms to H, so Alice would need to correctly guess all κ of Bob's choice bits in order to call H on the correct input to compute $F(x)$. Now we have a PSI protocol in the usual way [20]: Bob sends $\{F(b) \mid b \in B\}$ to Alice, who can only recognize those OPRF outputs that correspond to her input set A.

What goes wrong with a malicious adversary? A corrupt Alice can send incorrect or inconsistent ρ-bFSS key shares to the OT instances. Bob would like to verify that Alice's OT inputs are well-formed FSS shares consistent with her chosen structured input. A potential approach is cut-and-choose, where Bob challenges Alice with a set of randomly chosen indices to "open" (learn both key shares) and "check" (if it correctly encodes Alice's input), and aborts if any of the opened key shares are inconsistent. However, observe that a direct application of cut-and-choose violates Alice's input privacy. Bob can re-construct the input from any pair of well-formed ρ-dFSS keys he learns during the "open" phase. To get around this issue, we introduce a new variant of weak boolean FSS called *derandomizable* FSS (Sect. 3) with some additional useful properties.

In a dFSS scheme, the key sharing phase is randomized to generate shares of a uniformly random element (say R) from the same family of sets as the input (A). The evaluation step is modified to include an "offset" or "correction" ($A - R$) to de-randomize the evaluation from an FSS share of R to an FSS share of the chosen input (A). Within our PSI context, Alice (with chosen input $A \in \mathcal{S}$) will now generate ℓ ($> \kappa$ for cut-and-choose) dFSS shares of uniformly random elements $R_i \in \mathcal{S}$ from the same family of sets as her input. Bob picks some subset of indices (OpenSet) and checks if the shares are well-formed and correspond to an element from $\mathcal{S}$, otherwise aborts. All the unopened OTs (termed EvalSet in the protocol) will be used to define the OPRF function, similar to the semi-honest protocol.

Alice sends "offset" ($A - R_i$) for all indices (in EvalSet), so that Bob can de-randomize his received FSS shares to Alice's input. However, Alice can still cheat by de-randomizing different R_i's to different A values. To fix this, Alice must initially commit to her input encoding and all the randomly sampled R_i sets, under an additively homomorphic commitment scheme. Later, during the evaluation stage, she homomorphically decommits to the required "offsets". Now, Bob can be convinced that *all* offsets de-randomize the FSS shares to the same underlying input.

4.2 Protocol

Now, we take a closer look at the protocol and highlight some useful aspects.

Objects and Encodings. We have written the "offset" value $A - R_i$, which implies that there is a group structure over the set of objects. For this reason, we make an important distinction between the primary objects (**sets** of points) and **encodings** of those objects. For example, if the set of points is a geometric ball, then a good encoding may be the coordinates of the ball's center. The group operation on encodings is vector addition of points in the ambient geometry.

The encoding of a single ball is naturally deterministic, but in other settings an object may have many valid encodings. Our dFSS construction for union of balls is such an example. Given n balls, we assign them to one of m bins using cuckoo hashing. Even with the hashing functions fixed, there are typically several legal ways to assign objects into bins using cuckoo hashing. The encoding of the set is (essentially) a vector of length m, where the ith component holds the center of the ball assigned to the ith bin (or a dummy center).

Most of the reasoning about our FSS constructions is in the "encoding domain." The PSI protocol can force a corrupt Alice to use some element of the encoding domain as her PSI input. However, not all such elements are actually encodings of a valid set. Consider the example where the valid sets are disjoint unions of n balls. Our FSS construction maps those n balls to m bins, and we must have $m = (1 + O(1)) \cdot n > n$ for cuckoo hashing to succeed with high probability for the honest parties. However, there are values in the encoding space that correspond to the union of up to m balls. Therefore, the choice of encoding determines if an adversary is able to have more balls in its input set than the honest parties.

Cut-and-Choose. In Fig. 6 we present our cut and choose parameters for ℓ OT instances. We allow Bob to check ℓ_1 OT instances ($\mathsf{OpenSet}$) and evaluate on the remaining ℓ_2 OT instances ($\mathsf{EvalSet}$) where $\ell = \ell_1 + \ell_2$. A corrupt Alice wins the cut-and-choose if *all* ℓ_1 OTs are correct and less than κ OT instances of $\mathsf{EvalSet}$ are correct (argument to H to compute the $\mathsf{OPRF}()$ has low entropy). In more detail, we maximize the number of indices c that are faulty so that less than κ OT instances of $\mathsf{EvalSet}$ are correct, and count the number of ways to pick $\mathsf{OpenSet}$ such that has no bad indices c out of the total number of ways to pick $\mathsf{OpenSet}$. Both these requirements must be met with negligible probability in the security parameter.

$$\max_{c:c>\ell_2-\kappa} \frac{\binom{\ell-c}{\ell 1}}{\binom{\ell}{\ell_1}} \leq 1/2^{\lambda}$$

OPRF Notation. For ease of presentation, we slightly modify our notation for OPRF outputs $F(x)$. Because of cut-and-choose, only a subset of FSS instances are used for evaluation. We write the argument to the hash function H as a set rather than a string:

$$F(x) = \mathsf{H}\Big(x;\ \big\{(i, \mathsf{DEval}(k_*^{(i)}, b, \mathsf{offset}_i)) \mid i \in \mathsf{EvalSet}\big\}\Big)$$

When we write an expression like this, we mean that the items of the set (pairs) are serialized into a string in a canonical way—*i.e.*, by sorting the pairs by their first component.

Now, we present the full details of our framework for malicious-secure Structure-Aware PSI in Fig. 7 and prove that our protocol securely realizes our ideal functionality in Fig. 5. The protocol is in the random oracle model and makes calls to the ideal functionality for Committed OT ($\mathcal{F}_{\mathsf{COT}}$) and an Additively Homomorphic Commitment scheme ($\mathcal{F}_{\mathsf{HCom}}$).

Parameters: Given a family of subsets $\mathcal{S} \subseteq 2^{\mathcal{U}}$ over the universe $\mathcal{U}$ and an encode function $\mathsf{Encode} : \mathcal{S} \to \mathbb{G}$.

Functionality:

1. If Alice is honest, then receive from her an input set $A \in \mathcal{S}$. Otherwise if Alice is corrupt, receive from her an encoding $E \in \mathbb{G}$ and define $A = \mathsf{Encode}^{-1}(E)$.
2. Receive input $B \subseteq \mathcal{U}$ from Bob.
3. Give output $A \cap B$ and $|B|$ to Alice.

Fig. 5. Ideal functionality $\mathcal{F}_{\mathsf{saPSI}}$ for Structure-Aware PSI in malicious model.

Parameters:

- Computational security parameter κ and statistical security parameter λ
- Family of sets $\mathcal{S}$ with corresponding ρ-dFSS scheme (RShare, Encode, DEval)
- Random oracle $\mathsf{H} : \{0,1\}^* \rightarrow \{0,1\}^{2\kappa}$
- Committed oblivious transfer functionality $\mathcal{F}_{\mathsf{COT}}$ (Figure 3)
- Additively homomorphic commitment functionality $\mathcal{F}_{\mathsf{HCom}}$ (Figure 4)
- $\ell = (\ell_1 + \ell_2)$ OT instances where $\max_{c:c>\ell_2-\kappa} \frac{\binom{\ell-c}{\ell_1}}{\binom{\ell}{\ell_1}} \leq 1/2^{\lambda}$. As a concrete example, $(\ell_1, \ell_2) = (60, 220)$ suffices for $(\kappa, \lambda) = (128, 40)$.

Fig. 6. Parameters for Malicious-Secure Structure Aware PSI

4.3 Security Against Malicious Behavior

Theorem 1. *Given a ρ-dFSS scheme for a family of subsets $\mathcal{S} \subseteq 2^{\mathcal{U}}$ over input domain $\mathcal{U}$. Protocol π_{sa-PSI} (in Fig. 7) UC-securely realizes $\mathcal{F}_{\mathsf{sa\text{-}PSI}}$ in the presence of a malicious adversary in the $\mathcal{F}_{\mathsf{COT,\ HCom}}$-hybrid random oracle model.*

Proof. **Bob is Corrupt.** In the ideal world execution, the simulator does the following steps to simulate a corrupt Bob's protocol view -

- Simulator observes Bob's queries to $\mathcal{F}_{\mathsf{Com}}$ in step 1 and extracts OpenSet.
- Send acknowledgements $(\mathsf{receipt}, sid_a, \ell, P_a, P_b)$ and $\{(\mathsf{receipt}, sid_a, i, P_a, P_b) \mid i \in [\ell]\}$ to simulate the ideal functionality $\mathcal{F}_{\mathsf{HCom}}$ responses in step 2.
- Observes Bob's choice bit string s to the $\mathcal{F}_{\mathsf{COT}}$ ideal functionality. For the ith OT instance -
  - If $i \in \mathsf{OpenSet}$: sample $(k_0^{(i)}, k_1^{(i)}, R_i) \leftarrow \mathsf{RShare}(1^\kappa)$.
  - If $i \notin \mathsf{OpenSet}$: call the simulator $(k_*^{(i)} = k_{s_i}^{(i)}, \mathsf{offset}_i) \leftarrow \mathsf{Sim}(1^\kappa, s_i)$ that guarantees privacy of the underlying ρ-dFSS scheme.
  - Send $(\mathsf{transfer}, i, k_*^{(i)} = k_{s_i}^{(i)})$ to Bob on behalf of $\mathcal{F}_{\mathsf{COT}}$.
  - Include $(\mathsf{ok}, sid_a, \ell, i, P_a, P_b, \mathsf{offset}_i)$ in the set of messages to Bob in step 7 of the protocol.
- For $i \in \mathsf{OpenSet}$: send $(\mathsf{transfer}, i, k_0^{(i)}, k_1^{(i)})$ and acknowledge $(\mathsf{ok}, sid_a, i, P_a, P_b, R_i)$ to Bob.
- Let $\mathsf{OPRF}(b) = \mathsf{H}\big(b;\ \{(i, \mathsf{DEval}(k_*^{(i)}, b, \mathsf{offset}_i)) \mid i \in \mathsf{EvalSet}\}\big)$. The simulator observes Bob's queries to the random oracle and defines set

  $$\mathcal{B} = \{b \mid \text{Bob made a random oracle query of the form } H(b,\cdot) \text{ and } \mathsf{OPRF}(b) \in \tilde{B}\}$$

  where $\tilde{B}$ is the message sent by Bob in step 8.
- Simulator sends Bob's effective input $\mathcal{B}$ to $\mathcal{F}_{\mathsf{sa\text{-}PSI}}$. The functionality returns $A \cap \mathcal{B}$ to Alice.

Now, we show a sequence of hybrids from the real-world to ideal world execution.

- *Hybrid 0:* We start with the real interaction where Alice interacts with her actual input A.

Inputs: Alice (P_a) has input $A \in \mathcal{S}$ and Bob (P_b) has input B.

Protocol:

1. Bob does the following -
   - Picks a string $s \leftarrow \{0,1\}^\ell$ uniformly at random.
   - Picks indices $\mathsf{OpenSet} \subset [\ell]$ and sends $(\mathsf{com}, sid_b, 0, P_b, P_a, \mathsf{OpenSet})$ to $\mathcal{F}_{\mathsf{Com}}$.
2. Alice makes ℓ calls to $\mathsf{RShare}(1^\kappa)$ from the ρ-dFSS scheme. Then commits to the generated sets and an encoding of her input.
   - For $i \in [\ell]$: do $(k_0^{(i)}, k_1^{(i)}, R_i) \leftarrow \mathsf{RShare}(1^\kappa)$.
   - For $i \in [\ell]$: send $(\mathsf{com}, sid_a, i, P_a, P_b, R_i)$ to $\mathcal{F}_{\mathsf{HCom}}$.
   - Alice sends $(\mathsf{com}, sid_a, \ell, P_a, P_b, \mathsf{Encode}(A))$ to $\mathcal{F}_{\mathsf{HCom}}$.
3. Alice as OT sender and Bob as OT receiver run ℓ (parallel) instances of committed oblivious transfer $\mathcal{F}_{\mathsf{COT}}$ (Figure 3). In the ith instance -
   - Alice inputs the keys shares. She sends $(\mathsf{transfer}, i, k_0^{(i)}, k_1^{(i)})$ to $\mathcal{F}_{\mathsf{COT}}$.
   - Bob sends $(\mathsf{choose}, i, s_i)$ to $\mathcal{F}_{\mathsf{COT}}$ which returns $(\mathsf{transfer}, i, k_*^{(i)} = k_{s_i}^{(i)})$.
4. Bob sends $(\mathsf{reveal}, sid_b, 0)$ to $\mathcal{F}_{\mathsf{HCom}}$ to reveal $\mathsf{OpenSet}$ to Alice.
5. If Alice receives $(\mathsf{ok}, sid_b, 0, P_b, P_a, \mathsf{OpenSet})$ from $\mathcal{F}_{\mathsf{HCom}}$, then -
   - For $i \in \mathsf{OpenSet}$: send (open, i) to $\mathcal{F}_{\mathsf{COT}}$; Bob learns $(k_0^{(i)}, k_1^{(i)})$.
   - For $i \in \mathsf{OpenSet}$: send $(\mathsf{reveal}, sid_a, i)$ to $\mathcal{F}_{\mathsf{Com}}$; Bob can now learn R_i.
6. Now, Bob does the following check -
   - For $i \in \mathsf{OpenSet}$: $R_i \stackrel{?}{=} \mathsf{Extract}(k_0^{(i)}, k_1^{(i)})$ and aborts if function call fails.
7. Alice reveals the offsets to Bob -
   - For all $j \in \mathsf{EvalSet}$: send $(\mathsf{reveal}, sid_a, \ell, j)$ to $\mathcal{F}_{\mathsf{HCom}}$.
   - Bob receives $(\mathsf{ok}, sid_a, \ell, j, P_a, P_b, \mathsf{offset}_j)$, $\mathsf{offset}_j = (\mathsf{Encode}(A) - R_j)$.
8. Bob computes $\widetilde{B}$, defined below, and sends it (permuted uniformly at random) to Alice. Set D is serialized to a string by sorting its elements by their first components.

$$\widetilde{B} = \left\{ \mathsf{H}(b;\ D) \ \middle|\ b \in B \right\};\ \text{where } D = \{(i, \mathsf{DEval}(k_*^{(i)}, b, \mathsf{offset}_i)) \mid i \in \mathsf{EvalSet}\}$$

9. Alice computes the **PSI output** as

$$\left\{ a \in A \ \middle|\ \mathsf{H}\big(a;\ \{(i, \mathsf{DEval}(k_0^{(i)}, a, \mathsf{offset}_i)) \mid i \in \mathsf{EvalSet}\}\big) \in \widetilde{B} \right\}$$

Fig. 7. Protocol description for Structure-Aware PSI in the Malicious model.

- *Hybrid 1:* Extract $\mathsf{OpenSet}$ from Bob's queries to $\mathcal{F}_{\mathsf{COT}}$. In this hybrid, look at indices $i \notin \mathsf{OpenSet}$: replace $(k_0^{(i)}, k_1^{(i)}, R_i) \leftarrow \mathsf{RShare}(1^\kappa)$ with $(k_{s_i}^{(i)}, \mathsf{offset}_i) \leftarrow \mathsf{Sim}(1^\kappa, s_i)$ a call to simulator of the underlying dFSS scheme. Here, Bob's input s_i to $\mathcal{F}_{\mathsf{COT}}$ is used to simulate $k_{s_i}^{(i)}$ ($\mathcal{F}_{\mathsf{COT}}$ output sent to Bob) and offset_i (sent to Bob in step 7). The simulator knows the cut-and-choose indices $\mathsf{OpenSet}$ in advance, and hence it will never need to show the "other FSS share" for these indices. By the privacy property of the dFSS scheme (Definition 3), this hybrid is indistinguishable from the real Hinteraction.

- *Hybrid 2:* In this hybrid, we replace the actual interaction with $\mathcal{F}_{\mathsf{HCom}}$ in step 2 by sending acknowledgements $(\mathsf{receipt}, sid_a, \ell, P_a, P_b)$ and $(\mathsf{receipt}, sid_a, i, P_a, P_b)$ for all $i \in [\ell]$ to Bob, so that the actual values being committed are not used in this step. This hybrid is identically distributed with the previous hybrid since Alice is honest.
- *Hybrid 3:* Now, we modify how honest Alice computes the output of the protocol. Let $\mathsf{OPRF}(b) = \mathsf{H}\big(b;\ \{(i, \mathsf{DEval}(k_*^{(i)}, b, \mathsf{offset}_i)) \mid i \in \mathsf{EvalSet}\}\big)$. We track the queries made by Bob to the random oracle $\mathsf{OPRF}(b)$ until Bob sends $\tilde{B}$ in step 8 of the protocol. Now we define set -

  $$\mathcal{B} = \{b \mid \text{Bob made a random oracle query of form } H(b, \cdot) \text{ and } \mathsf{OPRF}(b) \in \tilde{B}\}$$

  and change Alice's output to $A \cap \mathcal{B}$.
  It remains to show that for any $a \in A$ it belongs to modified output $A \cap \mathcal{B}$ if and only if it belongs to $A \cap B$, except with negligible probability. We have the following cases -
  1. $a \in \mathcal{B}$: $\mathsf{H}\big(a;\ \{(i, \mathsf{DEval}(k_*^{(i)}, a, \mathsf{offset}_i)) \mid i \in \mathsf{EvalSet}\}\big) =$ $\mathsf{H}\big(a;\ \{(i, \mathsf{DEval}(k_0^{(i)}, a, \mathsf{offset}_i)) \mid i \in \mathsf{EvalSet}\}\big)$ if and only if $a \in A \cap B$ by the correctness property of the dFSS scheme.
  2. $a \notin \mathcal{B}$ because $\mathsf{OPRF}(a) \notin \tilde{B}$: as a result $a \notin A \cap \mathcal{B}$ and $a \notin A \cap B$.
  3. $a \notin \mathcal{B}$ because Bob did not query the random oracle on $\mathsf{OPRF}(a)$: here $a \notin A \cap \mathcal{B}$; but the probability that $a \in A \cap B$ is $\frac{|\tilde{B}|}{2^\kappa}$ because Alice's query to random oracle $\mathsf{OPRF}(a)$ is "freshly" random.

  This hybrid differs from the previous hybrid only if case 3 is true which happens with negligible probability.

Alice is Corrupt. In order to simulate Alice's view in the ideal execution, the simulator does the following:

- Sample $\mathsf{OpenSet} \subset [\ell]$ uniformly at random and send $(\mathsf{receipt}, sid_b, 0, P_b, P_a)$ to Alice. All the remaining indices are in $\mathsf{EvalSet} = [\ell] \backslash \mathsf{OpenSet}$.
- Extract $\{R_0, R_1, \ldots, R_{\ell-1}\}$ from messages $\{(\mathsf{com}, sid_a, i, P_a, P_b, R_i) \mid i \in [\ell]\}$ to $\mathcal{F}_{\mathsf{HCom}}$.
- Extract Alice's encoding E of her input from her request $(\mathsf{com}, sid_a, \ell, P_a, P_b, E)$ to $\mathcal{F}_{\mathsf{HCom}}$.
- Extract ℓ key pairs from $(\mathsf{transfer}, i, k_0^{(i)}, k_1^{(i)})$ sent by Alice to $\mathcal{F}_{\mathsf{COT}}$. Send acknowledgements $\{(\mathsf{receipt}, sid_b, i, P_b, P_a) \mid i \in [\ell]\}$ on behalf of the $\mathcal{F}_{\mathsf{COT}}$ to Alice.
- Let $\mathsf{Good} = \{i \mid i \in [\ell] \text{ and } R_i \stackrel{?}{=} \mathsf{Extract}(k_0^{(i)}, k_1^{(i)})\}$.
- If $|\mathsf{Good} \cap \mathsf{OpenSet}| = |\mathsf{OpenSet}|$ and $|\mathsf{Good} \cap \mathsf{EvalSet}| < \kappa$, the simulator aborts. That is, if all opened indices are Good and not enough indices in EvalSet are Good, the simulator aborts.
- Send input encoding E to $\mathcal{F}_{\mathsf{sa\text{-}PSI}}$ and learn output $A \cap B$ where $A = \mathsf{Encode}^{-1}(E)$. Now, simulate Bob's final protocol message as:

  $$\Big\{\mathsf{H}(b;\ D_b)\ \Big|\ b \in A \cap B\Big\} \cup \Big\{r_i\ \Big|\ i \in \{1, \ldots, |B \backslash A|\}\Big\}$$

where $r_i \xleftarrow{\$} \{0,1\}^{2\kappa}$ and

$$D_b = \{(i, \mathsf{DEval}(k_0^{(i)}, b, \mathsf{offset}_i))\}_{i \in \{\mathsf{EvalSet} \cap \mathsf{Good}\}} \\ \cup \{(i, \mathsf{DEval}(k_*^{(i)}, b, \mathsf{offset}_i))\}_{i \in \{\mathsf{EvalSet} \setminus \mathsf{Good}\}}$$

Through a series of hybrids we transform the real protocol execution into a simulated execution in the ideal world.

- *Hybrid 0:* We start with the actual protocol interaction where Bob participates with his input set B.
- *Hybrid 1:* We define $\mathsf{Good} = \{i \mid i \in [\ell] \text{ and } R_i \stackrel{?}{=} \mathsf{Extract}(k_0^{(i)}, k_1^{(i)})\}$ to be the collection of indices where we can successfully extract the set from the FSS shares. In this hybrid, we abort if $|\mathsf{Good} \cap \mathsf{OpenSet}| = |\mathsf{OpenSet}|$ and $|\mathsf{Good} \cap \mathsf{EvalSet}| < \kappa$. In Fig. 6, we select parameters $|\mathsf{OpenSet}| = \ell_1$ and $|\mathsf{EvalSet}| = \ell_2$ so that abort occurs with negligible probability, making this hybrid indistinguishable from the previous hybrid.
- *Hybrid 2:* In this hybrid, we modify the message sent by Bob in step 8 of the protocol. In the previous hybrid, the message is defined as:

  $$\widetilde{B} = \left\{\mathsf{H}(b;\ D_b)\ \middle|\ b \in A \cap B\right\} \cup \left\{\mathsf{H}(b;\ D_b)\ \middle|\ b \in B \backslash A\right\}$$

  where $D_b = \{(i, \mathsf{DEval}(k_*^{(i)}, b, \mathsf{offset}_i)) \mid i \in \mathsf{EvalSet}\}$.
  For the case $b \notin A$: if index $i \in \mathsf{Good}$ then $\mathsf{DEval}(k_0^{(i)}, b, \mathsf{offset}_i) \neq \mathsf{DEval}(k_1^{(i)}, b, \mathsf{offset}_i)$ by the correctness of the underlying ρ-dFSS scheme. When $b \notin A$ we can write

  $$\mathsf{DEval}(k_*^{(i)}, a, \mathsf{offset}_i) = \mathsf{DEval}(k_0^{(i)}, b, \mathsf{offset}_i) \oplus s_i \cdot g_i$$

  where g_i is a characteristic vector that indicates whether i is Good or not and s_i is Bob's choice bit. For Alice to guess $\mathsf{OPRF}(b)$ she will have to simultaneously guess Bob's choice bits for *all* indices $i \in \{\mathsf{EvalSet} \cap \mathsf{Good}\}$. From the previous hybrid, we know that $|\mathsf{EvalSet} \cap \mathsf{Good}| > \kappa$, giving Alice negligible advantage. Therefore, we replace the H outputs for $b \in B \backslash A$ with uniform outputs $r_i \xleftarrow{\$} \{0,1\}^{2\kappa}$ as shown below -

  $$\widetilde{B} = \left\{\mathsf{H}(b;\ D_b)\ \middle|\ b \in A \cap B\right\} \cup \left\{r_i\ \middle|\ i \in \{1, \ldots, |B \backslash A|\}\right\}$$

  where $D_b = \{(i, \mathsf{DEval}(k_*^{(i)}, b, \mathsf{offset}_i)) \mid i \in \mathsf{EvalSet}\}$.
  For the case $b \in A$: if index $i \in \mathsf{Good}$ then $\mathsf{DEval}(k_0^{(i)}, b, \mathsf{offset}_i) = \mathsf{DEval}(k_1^{(i)}, b, \mathsf{offset}_i)$ by the correctness of the underlying ρ-dFSS scheme. For all indices $i \in \{\mathsf{EvalSet} \cap \mathsf{Good}\}$ Alice can express $\mathsf{DEval}(k_*^{(i)}, a, \mathsf{offset}_i) = \mathsf{DEval}(k_0^{(i)}, b, \mathsf{offset}_i)$. However, for the small set of indices $i \in \{\mathsf{EvalSet} \backslash \mathsf{Good}\}$ Alice must still guess Bob's choice bits. We reflect this change in the message sent by Bob as follows -

  $$\left\{\mathsf{H}(b;\ D_b)\ \middle|\ b \in A \cap B\right\} \cup \left\{r_i\ \middle|\ i \in \{1, \ldots, |B \backslash A|\}\right\}$$

where $r_i \xleftarrow{\$} \{0,1\}^{2\kappa}$ and

$$D_b = \{(i, \mathsf{DEval}(k_0^{(i)}, b, \mathsf{offset}_i))\}_{i \in \{\mathsf{EvalSet} \cap \mathsf{Good}\}} \\ \cup \{(i, \mathsf{DEval}(k_*^{(i)}, b, \mathsf{offset}_i))\}_{i \in \{\mathsf{EvalSet} \setminus \mathsf{Good}\}}$$

Communication Analysis: We suggest practical instantiations for the various components of our protocol. The $\mathcal{F}_{\mathsf{COT}}$ functionality can be realized by the committed OT construction in Jawurek et al. [32], in which the communication cost of choose, transfer and open is bounded by $\mathcal{O}(\kappa + l)$, where l is the length of the message. The $\mathcal{F}_{\mathsf{HCom}}$ functionality can be realized by the homomorphic commitment protocol of Frederiksen et al. [19], which supports additive homomorphisms over any field $\mathbb{F}$. The communication cost for each commit and open is bounded by $\mathcal{O}(t\lambda \log |\mathbb{F}|)$ and $\mathcal{O}(t \log |\mathbb{F}|)$ respectively, where t is the length of batch codes used in their construction and λ is the statistical security parameter. However, for batch invocations of commit and open their protocol achieves rate ≈ 1.

The step-by-step communication cost breakdown of our protocol is as follows:

- Step 1: Communication costs $\mathcal{O}(\kappa + t)$ for sending a commitment to the OpenSet
- Step 2: Committing to offsets and keys output by RShare: $\mathcal{O}(\ell(\sigma + \kappa))$, where σ is the FSS share size.
- Step 3: transfer and choose COT cost: $\mathcal{O}(\ell(\sigma + \kappa))$
- Step 4: decommitting OpenSet costs $\mathcal{O}(\kappa)$
- Step 5: For each element in OpenSet, Alice opens the key pair, and for elements not in OpenSet she opens the offsets: $\mathcal{O}(\ell(\kappa + \sigma + \log |\mathbb{G}|))$
- Step 7: Communication for this step is $\mathcal{O}(|\mathsf{EvalSet}|(\kappa + \log |\mathbb{G}|))$
- Step 8: Bob sends a set of hash values, each of length 2κ: total cost $\mathcal{O}(|B|\kappa)$, where B is Bob's unstructured set

With cut-and-choose parameter $\ell = \mathcal{O}(\kappa)$, the total communication complexity of the protocol is $\mathcal{O}(\kappa(\sigma + \log |\mathbb{G}| + \kappa + |B|))$.

5 dFSS Constructions

5.1 dFSS from Known bFSS Constructions

Many known bFSS constructions can be easily transformed into an equivalent dFSS. In this section we present derandomizable bFSS variants for singletons (point functions), intervals, and fixed-radius ℓ_∞-balls in d dimensions, with each set including the empty set. The idea for these constructions is to make RShare output bFSS shares of a random set from the collection. The correctness and privacy of the underlying bFSS also ensures correctness and privacy of the dFSS. Further if the Share function of bFSS is **invertible** - given FSS keys k_0 and k_1 we can output the corresponding set input to Share, making the dFSS construction extractable.

The universe set $\mathcal{U} = \{0, 1, \ldots, 2^u - 1\}^d = [2^u]^d$ is parameterized by u, d. We will use the shorthand notation $\mathcal{U}_{u,d}$ to represent the same set throughout this section.

Define $\mathsf{PT}_{u,d}$ to be the family of singleton sets for the universe set $\mathcal{U}_{u,d}$ including the empty set. Define $\mathsf{INT}_{u,\delta}$ to be the family of 1-dimensional modular intervals of length δ—i.e., sets of the form $[a, b] = \{(a + i) \mod 2^u | 0 \leq i \leq \delta\}$, where $a, b \in [2^u]$ and $b = (a + \delta) \mod 2^u$, including the empty set. Define $\mathsf{BALL}_{u,d,\delta}$ to be the family of radius-δ ℓ_∞-balls in the domain $\mathcal{U}_{u,d}$, including the empty set. $\mathcal{B}_\infty(\mathsf{ctr}, \delta)$ represents a single ℓ_∞ ball of radius δ centered at ctr—*i.e.*, all points within ℓ_∞-distance δ of ctr. Similar to the collection of interval functions, the collection $\mathsf{BALL}_{u,d,\delta}$ contains ℓ_∞ balls that wrap naturally around any edge of the d-dimensional universe set. Let $\mathsf{map} : \mathcal{U}_{u,d} \to [2^{ud}]$ be any bijective mapping.

Theorem 2. *Given a strong ρ-bFSS construction for singleton sets, 1-dimensional interval and d dimensional intervals with an invertible Share function, there exists a corresponding ρ-dFSS for $\{PT_{u,d}, INT_{\delta,u}, BALL_{\delta,u,d}\}$.*

Its proof can be found in Appendix B.1.

The best known constructions for collection of sets $\{\mathsf{PT}_{u,d}, \mathsf{INT}_{u,\delta}, \mathsf{BALL}_{u,d,\delta}\}$ [3,8] have invertible Share functions - i.e. given the FSS keys, we can efficiently compute the secret shared set. For the point function construction [8] for example, Eval involves computing a path in a GGM-PRF like tree, corresponding to the input x. By construction, the two parties can secret share 1 for each node in the path corresponding to some special point x^*, and other nodes secret share 0. Hence the Extract function can identify x^* (defining the singleton set), given both keys k_0, k_1, and by identifying the path corresponding to x^* in both trees one bit at a time.

From these previous known bFSS constructions [3,8] and Theorem 2 we have the following corollaries:

Corollary 3. *There exists a 1-dFSS with pseudo-random keys for $PT_{u,d}$, $INT_{u,\delta}$ and $BALL_{u,d,\delta}$ with share sizes $O(\kappa ud)$, $O(\kappa u)$ and $O(\kappa u^d)$ respectively.*

5.2 Generic Transformations

In this section we present some generic transformations for dFSS.

Theorem 4. *Given a 1-dFSS for a collection of sets $\mathcal{S}$ with share size σ, there exists a 1-dFSS for the collection $\overline{\mathcal{S}} = \{S | \overline{S} \in \mathcal{S}\}$ with share size σ.*

This new dFSS can be constructed, by making one of the parties output the complement of their DEval output for collection $\mathcal{S}$.

For collections $\mathcal{S}_1, \mathcal{S}_2$, we define the collection

$$\mathsf{sum}[\mathcal{S}_1, \mathcal{S}_2] = \{S_1 \triangle S_2 = (S_1 \backslash S_2) \cup (S_2 \backslash S_1) | S_1 \in \mathcal{S}_1 \text{ and } S_2 \in \mathcal{S}_2\}$$

Then we have the following theorem:

Theorem 5. *Given a* 1*-dFSS* F_1, F_2 *for a collection of sets* $\mathcal{S}_1, \mathcal{S}_2$ *with share size* σ_1, σ_2 *respectively, there exists a* 1*-dFSS* $\mathsf{sum}[F_1, F_2]$ *for the collection* $\mathsf{sum}[\mathcal{S}_1, \mathcal{S}_2]$ *with share size* $\sigma_1 + \sigma_2$*.*

Further note that, if F_1 and F_2 correspond to dFSS for disjoint sets S_1 and S_2 respectively, then $\mathsf{sum}[F_1, F_2]$ corresponds to a dFSS for the disjoint union $S_1 \cup S_2$. Further in this paper, we'll also use the following shorthand notation:

$$\mathsf{sum}[F_1, F_2, \ldots, F_t] = \mathsf{sum}[F_1, \mathsf{sum}[F_2, \ldots, \mathsf{sum}[F_{t-1}, F_t]]]$$

Both the above theorems follow easily from the derandomizability property of the underlying dFSS, and from the complement and sum bFSS constructions in [24]. From the same construction we also have that the Eval cost of the sum dFSS would be the sum of the Eval cost of its component dFSS.

bFSS from dFSS. There is a direct transformation of a dFSS scheme for a collection of sets to a bFSS scheme for the same. A formal description of the construction and the proof of the following theorem is provided in Appendix B.2.

Theorem 6. *Given a* ρ*-dFSS for* $\mathcal{S}$ *with share size* σ*, there exists a corresponding* ρ*-bFSS construction for* $\mathcal{S}$ *with share size* σ*.*

Concat Technique. Given dFSS for two collections $\mathcal{S}_1, \mathcal{S}_2$, this technique gives a dFSS for their cross product $\mathcal{S}_1 \times \mathcal{S}_2$. Here the simple trick is to just concat the outputs of DEval of the two dFSS constructions. This is the same technique as the concat technique introduced in [24]. See Appendix B.3 for a more detailed description of the construction and the proof of the following theorem:

Theorem 7. *Given* ρ_1*-dFSS* F_1 *for* $\mathcal{S}_1$ *with share size* σ_1 *and* ρ_2*-dFSS* F_2 *for* $\mathcal{S}_2$ *with share size* σ_2*, there exists a* $(\rho_1 + \rho_2)$*-dFSS* $\mathsf{concat}[F_1, F_2]$ *for* $\mathcal{S}_1 \times \mathcal{S}_2$ *with share size* $\sigma_1 + \sigma_2$*. Furthermore, if* F_1 *and* F_2 *dFSS have pseudo-random keys, then so does* $\mathsf{concat}[F_1, F_2]$*.*

Using this concat technique we can get a dFSS for an ℓ_∞ ball, which can be viewed as a cross products of d intervals.

Corollary 8. *There exists a* d*-dFSS for* $\mathsf{BALL}_{u,d,\delta}$ *with share size* $O(\kappa u d)$

Tensor Technique. The point function tensor technique was first introduced by Boyle et al. [8] - where given an FSS for some class of functions $\mathcal{F}$ with pseudo-random keys, FSS for point functions PT, there exists an FSS for the class of functions $\mathsf{PT} \otimes \mathcal{F}$ - which contains functions of the form:

$$\mathsf{PT} \otimes \mathcal{F} = \{g_{\alpha,f} \mid f_{\alpha,1} \in PT, f \in \mathcal{F}\}$$

$$g_{\alpha,f}(x,y) = \begin{cases} f(y) & \text{if } x = \alpha \\ 0 & \text{otherwise} \end{cases}$$

In the original construction, we can replace the FSS for $\mathcal{F}$ with a dFSS for some structure $\mathcal{S}$ to get a dFSS for the following tensor structure:

$$\mathsf{PT} \otimes \mathcal{S} = \{\mathcal{U} \backslash \{\alpha\} \times S \mid \alpha \in \mathcal{U}, S \in \mathcal{S}\}$$

Theorem 9. *Given a ρ-dFSS F with pseudo-random keys for $\mathcal{S}$ with share size σ, a strong dFSS P for PT_u with share size $O(u\kappa)$, and a pseudo-random generator, there exists a ρ-dFSS $(P \otimes F)$ for the collection $\mathsf{PT} \otimes \mathcal{S}$ with share size $O(\kappa(\log|\mathcal{U}| + \sigma))$*

In the above construction, if the encoding group of $\mathsf{PT}, \mathcal{S}$ are $\mathbb{G}_{\mathsf{PT}}, \mathbb{G}_{\mathcal{S}}$ respectively, then the encoding group of $\mathsf{PT}\otimes\mathcal{S}$ is $\mathbb{G}_{\mathsf{PT}} \times \mathbb{G}_{\mathcal{S}}$. In the following subsection, we'll also assume this tensor construction DEval has an auxiliary output, where this output bit corresponds to the output of just the singleton dFSS P in the tensor construction $P \otimes F$. We'll refer to this modified eval as DEval^{aux}. From our tensor construction, we also get the following result:

Corollary 1. *Given a ρ-dFSS with pseudo-random keys for $\mathcal{S}$ with share size σ, and a pseudo-random generator, there exists a ρ-dFSS for $\overline{\mathsf{PT}} \otimes \mathcal{S} = \{\{\alpha\} \times S \mid \alpha \in \mathcal{U}, S \in \mathcal{S}\}$ with share size $O(\kappa(\log|\mathcal{U}| + \sigma))$*

This essentially follows from the fact that the tensor construction from Theorem 9 gives an auxiliary output for the strong dFSS for collection PT- allowing us to take the compliment wrt the universe $\mathcal{U}$ in the first component of the input.

The above dFSS (secret sharing $\{x\} \times S$) for input (x, y) evaluated to 0 i.e. corresponds to the element being contained in the secret shared set $\iff x = \alpha$ and $y \in S$.

5.3 An Improved Spatial Hashing Technique

So far we've developed strong and weak dFSS schemes for a fixed radius ball in ℓ_∞ metric space. We'll use them as building blocks in this section to develop dFSS schemes for union of disjoint n balls.

Let F be a strong dFSS scheme for a single ball, then the generic transformation $\mathsf{sum}[F^n] = \mathsf{sum}[F, F, \ldots, F \text{ (n times)}]$ can be used to construct a strong dFSS for a set of n disjoint balls from the same domain. For this trivial construction, the computation cost of Eval would be n times the Eval cost of a single ball.

Improving on this construction, Garimella et al. [24] introduce a *spatial hashing* technique, which gives a bFSS construction for union of n disjoint fixed radius balls in a metric space, where the Eval cost is 2^d times the Eval cost for a single ball, with the FSS key size increasing by a factor of $O(4^d)$, where d is the number of dimensions in the input domain. Assume the entire input space is divided into contiguous fixed size grid cells of side length 2δ - where δ is the radius of the input balls. In this spatial hashing construction, we prepare bFSS keys for each cell that intersects with an input ball, and pack them into an oblivious-key value storage (OKVS) [23] - giving the bFSS keys for union of balls. Here the

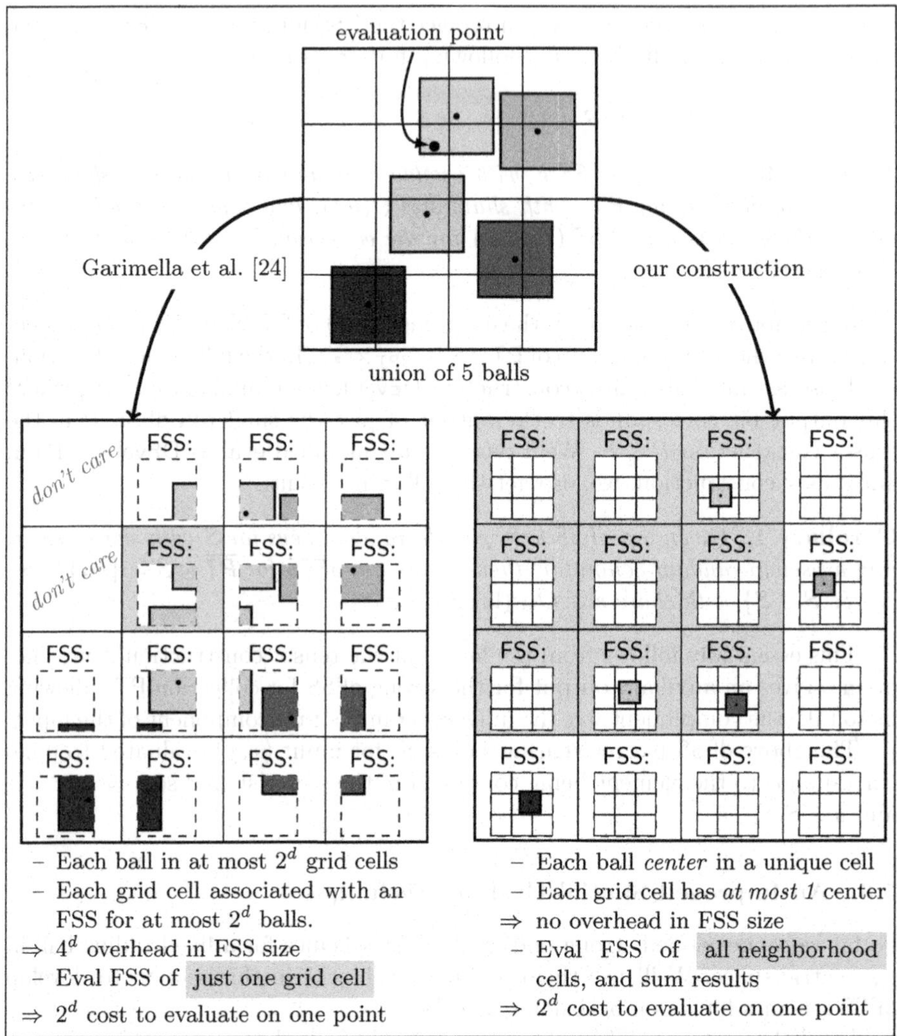

Fig. 8. Illustration of the construction of Garimella et al. [24] and our improved construction, for the union of n balls.

grid coordinate is treated as the OKVS key, and the corresponding bFSS key is treated as its value. In this construction, we "shatter" each input ball, across all the 2^d intersecting grid cells - hence a bFSS key for an input ball is prepared and used for each of its neighboring cells. This blows up the size of the bFSS keys for the union of balls by a factor of 2^d. The other factor of 2^d comes from the fact that we insert $2^d n$ key-value pairs into the OKVS (Fig. 8).

They key features of the [24] spatial hashing protocol are also presented in Fig. 9. It depicts the "shattering" technique we described pictorially on an example union of five l_∞ balls in 2 dimensions.

Next we'll introduce an *improved* spatial hashing construction for union of balls, which has two fold advantages over the [24] construction:

- We present a dFSS instead of a bFSS scheme scheme for a union of balls. Which makes the proposed construction applicable for both the malicious and semi-honest structure-aware PSI setting.
- We avoid the use of the "shattering" technique, where each input ball is secret-shared once for each neighboring cell. This improves the FSS key size - giving it just a constant overhead compared to the trivial sum construction

High Level Intuition for Our Spatial Hashing Construction. To construct dFSS for a union of radius-δ ℓ_∞-balls, we first impose a grid structure on the input domain $\mathcal{U} = [2^u]^d$ - partitioning the input space into contiguous d dimensional grid cells, where each cell is an ℓ_∞-ball of radius δ i.e. each cell is a d dimensional cube with side length $2d$.

The dFSS key for both parties in our construction would be a cuckoo table (with 3 hash functions), where each corresponding entry of the two cuckoo tables contain dFSS keys for a single ball. In particular, we'd want the dFSS for an input ball with center ctr to be located in either of the following three locations in the cuckoo table: $H_0(\mathsf{cell}(\mathsf{ctr})), H_1(\mathsf{cell}(\mathsf{ctr}))$ or $H_2(\mathsf{cell}(\mathsf{ctr}))$, where H_i is a cuckoo hash function for $i \in \{0, 1, 2\}$ and cell function outputs the grid cell containing the input point. We refer to these grid cells containing input ball centers as *active cells.* In this construction we essentially prepare FSS keys for just the active grid cells and pack them in a cuckoo table.

To check if a point x is contained in any of the n input balls, we need to just check if the neighboring cells of x have a center of an input ball which contain x - since no input ball with center outside this neighborhood can ever contain x. Let the set of grid cells defining the neighborhood of x be $\eta(x)$. Then given a dFSS F for a single ball, we can define the Eval for a union of balls on an input point x as follows:

1. First query the cuckoo table for each grid cell in $\eta(x)$, for each of the three hash functions. This outputs $3|\eta(x)|$ FSS keys of individual balls, which can be arranged into a vector $\boldsymbol{v}$.
2. Output $\mathsf{sum}[F^{3|\eta(x)|}].\mathsf{Eval}(\boldsymbol{v}, x)$

This proposed technique of constructing FSS keys for just active cells, and evaluating only in a neighborhood is also illustrated in Fig. 9 for an example input.

Compared to the trivial construction, where sum was used to take the disjoint union of n balls, in our construction above, we use the sum construction for taking the disjoint union of just the balls in the neighborhood of x. The derandomizablility of this scheme follows from the fact that the dFSS keys inserted into the cuckoo table are derandomizable. For this scheme the encoding group is $\mathbb{G}^m$, where $\mathbb{G}$ is the encoding group of a single ball (corresponding to a single entry of the cuckoo table), and m is the size of the cuckoo table.

Domain Reduction Optimization. For the above mentioned improved spatial hashing construction, the dFSS key size would be proportional to $(\log|\mathcal{U}|)^d$ - a factor that comes from the fact that we assume each input ball is from the domain $\mathcal{U}$ and from Corollary 3. The input balls however, are of fixed radius δ - implying each input ball would be entirely contained in the neighborhood of its center. For an ℓ_∞ ball, this neighborhood is precisely a d dimensional cube of side length 6δ. We'll next improve the FSS key size for our spatial hashing construction by reducing the domain size of each input ball from the universe to just its neighborhood. This would reduce the dFSS key size, making it proportional to just $(\log(6\delta))^d$ instead of $(\log|\mathcal{U}|)^d$.

Let F be the dFSS for a single ball, and P be a dFSS for point functions. While in the above proposed spatial hashing construction we entered dFSS keys of a single ball (F) in each cuckoo entry. In our optimized spatial hashing construction, we'll put keys of dFSS $(\overline{P} \otimes F)$, where F corresponds to the dFSS for the input ball (let say at center ctr), and P corresponds to the dFSS for the point function $\mathsf{cell}(\mathsf{ctr})$. We evaluate this dFSS on input (y, x) - where x is an element of $\mathcal{U}$, and y is any cell in the neighborhood $\eta(x)$. Then from Corollary 1 this 1-dFSS outputs 0 if and only if $y = \mathsf{cell}(\mathsf{ctr})$ and x is contained in the ball centered at ctr. Hence, the output of this modified construction always matches that of the above construction without the domain reduction optimization as well. Furthermore, now since the dFSS F is guarded by a point function P - we can restrict the input domain of F to just a d dimensional cube of side length 6δ (containing the cells that intersect with the input ball). This is due to the fact the dFSS F evaluation matter only when you guess the cell containing the ball at center ctr correct, and otherwise the evaluation outputs 0. Note that in this optimization, we cannot use the sum construction to take the disjoint union over the neighborhood of x since the input to dFSS $(\overline{P} \otimes F)$ is not the same for each cell in the neighborhood. We illustrate this more clearly in our protocol description.

Formal dFSS Description. While the approach above was described for disjoint union of ℓ_∞ balls, we can extend it to other collections of union of sets as well. We'll next present some formal definitions to help define these collections of sets and our proposed dFSS construction for them.

Definition 7. *A collection of sets $\mathcal{S}$ in universe $\mathcal{U} = [2^u]^d$ is said to be a **translatable** collection if for some set $S \subset \mathcal{U}$, $\mathcal{S} = \{t + S \mid t \in \mathcal{U}\}$, where $t + S = \{t + s \mid s \in S\}$.*

Specifically note PT, INT, BALL are all translatable collections. We can define any arbitrary point of a translatable set to be a *representative element* (analogous to the "center" of a ball), so that a translated set can be specified by only the position of the representative element.

Definition 8. *For any translatable collection $\mathcal{S}$, an efficient and invertible function $\mathsf{rep} : \mathcal{S} \to \mathcal{U}$ is said to be a representative function for $\mathcal{S}$ if $\mathsf{rep}(t + S) = t + \mathsf{rep}(S)$ for any $S \in \mathcal{S}, t \in \mathcal{U}$.*

As an example, for a point function/singleton set $\{x\}$ we make x the representative, and for an ℓ_∞ ball we can define its center to be a representative.

Given a collection of sets $\mathcal{S}$, we define the collection $\mathsf{disjoint\text{-}union}_n(\mathcal{S})$ to contain a collection of n disjoint sets from the collection $\mathcal{S}$. More formally we have:

Definition 9. *For any collection of sets* $\mathcal{S}$. $\mathsf{disjoint\text{-}union}_n(\mathcal{S}) = \{\{S_i\}_{i\in[n]} \mid S_i \in \mathcal{S}, S_i \cap S_j = \emptyset$ *for* $i \neq j\}$

We can partition the space $\mathcal{U} = [2^u]^d$ into contiguous *grid cells*, which are d-dimensional ℓ_∞-balls of radius δ. We uniquely *label* each grid cell by the point contained in it with least distance from the origin. Define a function cell_δ (parameterized by the grid size) that maps any point in the universe $\mathcal{U}$ to its unique grid cell label. Hence the function $\mathsf{cell}_\delta^{-1}$ maps a grid cell label to the set of points contained in it.

Definition 10. *For any vector* $\boldsymbol{x} = (x_1, x_2, \ldots, x_d) \in \mathcal{U}$, *define the function that maps a point to its grid cell label as:* $\mathsf{cell}_\delta(\boldsymbol{x}) = \lfloor \boldsymbol{x}/2\delta \rfloor = (\lfloor x_1/2\delta \rfloor, \ldots, \lfloor x_d/2\delta \rfloor)$. *We also define* $\mathsf{cell}_\delta^{-1}(\boldsymbol{x}) = [x_1, x_1+2\delta) \times [x_2, x_2+2\delta) \times \ldots \times [x_d, x_d+2\delta)$, *which maps any grid cell label to the set of points contained in that grid cell.*

Definition 11. *Define* $G(\delta, u, d)$ = *set of all grid cells* $= \{\mathsf{cell}_\delta^{-1}(\mathsf{cell}(\boldsymbol{x})) \mid \boldsymbol{x} \in \mathcal{U}\}$

We next define an active cell, as a grid cell that contains the representative element of some translatable set from the union of sets. As presented in the high level overview of the technique, we require each active cell to contain at max a single representative for a set.

Definition 12. *For some* $\{S_i\}_{i\in[n]} \in \mathsf{disjoint\text{-}union}_n(\mathcal{S})$, *a cell* $c \in G(\delta, u, d)$ *is termed* ***active****, if* $\mathsf{rep}(S_j) \in c$ *for some* $j \in [n]$. *Further we say the disjoint union set* $\{S_i\}_{i\in[n]}$ *has* ***unique active cells*** *if the number of active cells are* n.

Next we define the neighborhood $\eta(x)$ of any input x - which includes the set of all grid cells that could contain the representative of a translatable set that might contain x. We'll use this set to define the DEval function.

Definition 13. *For some translatable collection* $\mathcal{S}, x \in [2^u]^d$, *define* $\eta(x) = \{c \in G(\delta, u, d) \mid c = \mathsf{rep}(S)$ *and* $x \in S$ *for some* $S \in \mathcal{S}\}$

For example, for collection of sets $\mathsf{BALL}_{u,d,\delta}$, then $\eta(x)$ contains the cell $\mathsf{cell}(x)$ and each of its neighboring cells; and for collection of sets $PT_{u,d}$, $\eta(x)$ is just the singleton set containing $\mathsf{cell}(x)$.

Defining Encoding Group. Let $\mathcal{S}$ be a translatable collection of sets with encoding group $\mathbb{G}_\mathcal{S}$, G_{PT} be the encoding group for the collection of point functions, and let grid parameter δ be set such that every set in $\mathcal{S}' = \mathsf{disjoint\text{-}union}(\mathcal{S})$ has unique active cells. Then we'll define the encoding group for $\mathcal{S}'$ as $\mathbb{G} =$

$(\mathbb{G}_{\mathsf{PT}} \times \mathbb{G}_{\mathcal{S}})^m$, where m would correspond to the size of a 3 hash-function cuckoo table, used to store n items. Intuitively, each element of this vector encoding is a pair - where the first element encodes a grid cell, and the second element encodes the representative of the input set present at that grid cell.

The encode function Encode on input $\{S_i\}_{[n]} \in \mathsf{disjoint\text{-}union}(\mathcal{S})$ is defined as follows:

1. $X \leftarrow \{(\mathsf{cell}(\mathsf{rep}(S_i)), (\mathsf{Encode}_{\mathsf{PT}}(\mathsf{cell}(\mathsf{rep}(S_i)), \mathsf{Encode}_{\mathcal{S}}(S_i))) \,|1 \le i \le n\}$
2. **Output** cuckoo table $T = \mathsf{Cuckoo}^m_{\mathsf{H}_0,\mathsf{H}_1,\mathsf{H}_2}(X)$

By the correctness of cuckoo hashing, for any $S \in \{S_i\}_{[n]}$, its encoding is located in one of the following indexes in table T: $H_0(\mathsf{cell}(\mathsf{rep}(S)))$, $H_1(\mathsf{cell}(\mathsf{rep}(S)))$, $H_2(\mathsf{cell}(\mathsf{rep}(S)))$.

This Encode function is also efficiently invertible as follows:

$$\mathsf{Encode}^{-1}(T) = \{S \in \mathcal{S} | (c, S) \leftarrow \mathsf{Encode}^{-1}_{\mathcal{S}}(T[i]) \text{ and } c = \mathsf{cell}(\mathsf{rep}(S)), i \in [n]\} \tag{1}$$

For this encoding scheme we formally present a strong dFSS for disjoint union of a collection of translatable sets in Fig. 9.

Theorem 10. *For $\mathcal{U} = [2^u]^d$, Given a strong dFSS for a translatable collection $\mathcal{S}$ with share size σ, and for some grid parameter δ giving unique active cells, there exists a strong dFSS for $\mathsf{disjoint\text{-}union}_n(\mathcal{S})$ with share size $O(n(\sigma + \kappa ud))$.*

Proof.
- **Correctness:** For any input union of sets $S^* = \{S_i \in \mathcal{S} | i \in [n]\}$, and input $x \in \mathcal{U}$.
  For any $c \in \eta(x)$ and $i \in \{0, 1, 2\}$, define y_j^{idx} as the idx^{th} party's y' value computed in DEval for the $j = (c, i)^{th}$ iteration of the for-loops. And define $y_j = y_j^0 + y_j^1$.
  Then by the correctness of the dFSS $\overline{P} \otimes F$, $y_j = 0$ iff cell c contains the representative of a translatable set in S^* that contains x. The xor of y with $y_j \oplus 1$, essentially updates the shared y value between the two parties with the complement of the y_j bit. Hence, if c does not contain the center of an input ball, or if x is not contained in the translatable set with a representative in c - then the secret shared value of y is not updated. Since all the translatable sets are disjoint, the value of secret shared y is updated from 0 to 1 **only** if x is contained in a translatable set with a representative in its neighborhood. Finally, note we xor with 1^{idx} - ensuring a complement of the final output - i.e. the 1-dFSS outputs 0 only if x is contained in a translatable set in S^*.
- **Privacy:** Given the simulator Sim for the tensor compliment $\overline{P} \otimes F$, and a cuckoo table of size m, the simulator for $\mathsf{disjoint\text{-}union}_n(\mathcal{S})$ outputs an m sized vector, where each of its entries is an independent output of Sim.
- **Extractability:** This follows directly from the extractability of the tensor dFSS $\overline{PT} \otimes F$.

Corollary 11. *There exist a 1-dFSS for union of n disjoint ℓ_∞-balls of radius δ in $\mathcal{U} = \{0, 1, \ldots, 2^u - 1\}^d$ with share size $O(n\kappa(ud + (\log \delta)^d))$*

```
Let m be the size of a 3 hash (H_0, H_1, H_2) cuckoo table containing n elements
Given a 1-dFSS F for a translatable structure S and a 1-dFSS P for PT_{u,d}

RShare(1^κ):
  v_0, v_1, v_R - size m arrays
  for i ∈ [m]:
    (v_0[i], v_1[i], v_R[i]) ← (P̄ ⊗ F).RShare(1^κ)
  return (v_0, v_1, v_R)

Extract(1^κ, k_0, k_1):
  Parse k_0, k_1 as cuckoo encodings
  Initialize empty |k_0| sized vector v_R
  For i ∈ [|k_0|]:
    v_R[i] ← (P̄ ⊗ F).Extract(k_0[i], k_1[i])
  ¿if v_R[i] = ⊥, return ⊥
  return v_R

DEval(1^κ,idx,v, x, offset):
  y ← 0
  For c ∈ η(x) :
    For i ∈ {0, 1, 2}
    y' ← ((P̄ ⊗ F).DEval(v[H_i(c)], (c, x) − offset[H_i(c)]))
    // y' for both parties is a secret sharing of 0 iff x is
    // contained in a translatable set located in cell c
    y ← y ⊕ y' ⊕ 1^idx
  // the 1^idx xor component is used to take the FSS complement
  return y ⊕ 1^idx
```

Fig. 9. spatial-hashing$_\delta$ construction for the collection of sets disjoint-union($\mathcal{S}$) with grid size δ in domain $\mathcal{U} = \{0, 1, \ldots, 2^u - 1\}^d$

Proof. For union of radius-δ balls, we set the grid parameter to δ to ensure unique active cells. For a universe of size 6δ, from Corollary 3 we get a strong dFSS for $\mathsf{BALL}_{6\delta,d,\delta}$ with share size $O(\kappa(\log\delta)^d)$. The corollary follows from Theorem 10.

Weak Spatial Hashing. We can further optimize the spatial hashing construction for the case where the translatable sets in the disjoint union are sufficiently "far apart". Suppose we consider a disjoint union $S^* = \{S_i \mid i \in [n]\}$ of translatable sets, such that for each $x \in \mathcal{U}$, $\eta(x)$ contains at most a single active cell. We define this collection of sets as sparse-union($\mathcal{S}$), and its encoding group and Encode function is the same as the previous spatial hashing construction. For this collection, we'll show how to construct dFSS using just a weak dFSS for the translatable collection of sets. In particular, this construction would give us a weak dFSS for union of fixed radius ℓ_∞ balls with share size being linearly proportional to the dimension d, subject to the constraint that the distance between each pair of input balls is at least 8 times their radius.

This construction is similar to the previously proposed spatial hashing construction with some subtle differences which we list next: (as an example here we take the underlying translatable set to be a ball in some metric space)

- Let F be the dFSS for a single ball, and P be a dFSS for point functions. While in the above spatial hashing construction we entered keys of dFSS $(\overline{P} \otimes F)$ in the cuckoo table, where F corresponds to the dFSS for the input

ball (let say at center ctr), and P corresponds to the dFSS for the point function cell(ctr). In this construction, we'll instead enter keys for the tensor construction $(P \otimes F)$, which also has an auxiliary DEval output corresponding to the point function P.
We evaluate this dFSS on input of the form (y, x) - where x is an element of $\mathcal{U}$, and y is any cell in the neighborhood $\eta(x)$. Then from Theorem 9 this weak dFSS outputs an all zero string if and only if $y \neq$ cell(ctr) or x is contained in the ball centered at ctr.

- The final output of the proposed dFSS on any input x has two components (which are concatenated). The first component is 0 if and only if there exists an active cell in $\eta(x)$ - which can be computed using the auxiliary output of the $(P \otimes F)$ dFSS in each entry of the cuckoo table. The second component is an all zero string if either $\eta(x) = \emptyset$ or if x is not contained in the ball with center in its neighborhood. This second component is computed directly from the output of $(P \otimes F)$ dFSS. Hence, this weak dFSS would output an all zero string only if $\eta(x)$ is non-empty and it contains a center of a ball containing x.

The formal description of this weaker spatial hashing construction is given in Fig. 10

Theorem 12. *For $\mathcal{U} = \{0, 1, \ldots, 2^u - 1\}^d$, Given ρ-dFSS for a translatable collection $\mathcal{S}$ with share size σ, and for some grid parameter δ, there exists a $(\rho + 1)$-dFSS for sparse-union$_n(\mathcal{S})$ with share size $O(n(\sigma + \kappa u d))$.*

Using this theorem and the weak dFSS for $\mathsf{BALL}_{6\delta,d,\delta}$ we get a dFSS for a sparse union of ℓ infinity balls with share size that's linear in d. We define the ℓ_∞ distance between a pair of balls in $\mathsf{BALL}_{6\delta,d,\delta}$ to be the distance between their centers. Then we have the following corollary:

Corollary 13. *There exists a $(d + 1)$-dFSS for the union of n, ℓ_∞-balls of radius δ, with pairwise distance $> 8\delta$, in $\mathcal{U} = \{0, 1, \ldots, 2^u - 1\}^d$, with share size $O(\kappa n u d)$.*

5.4 Discussion on Co-domain of Encode^{-1}

Given a dFSS for collection of sets $\mathcal{S}$ with encode function Encode : $\mathcal{S} \rightarrow \mathbb{G}$. For each $S \in \mathcal{S}$, we have Encode^{-1}(Encode(S)) $= S$. In our PSI protocol however, a malicious Alice may commit offsets corresponding to some element in the encoding space $g \in \mathbb{G}$. Note that for $\mathcal{S} \in \{\mathsf{PT}_{u,d}, \mathsf{INT}_{d,\delta}, \mathsf{BALL}_{u,d,\delta}\}$, for any $g \in \mathbb{G}$, Encode$^{-1}(g) \in \mathcal{S}$—i.e., Encode is a bijection for these collections. Hence for $\mathcal{S} \in \{\mathsf{PT}_{u,d}, \mathsf{INT}_{d,\delta}, \mathsf{BALL}_{u,d,\delta}\}$ the corrupt party cannot input a set outside the expected collection.

For union of n disjoint ℓ_∞ balls with encoding function Encode : disjoint-union$_n(\mathsf{BALL}_{u,d,\delta}) \rightarrow \mathbb{G}$ and for any $g \in G$, from Eq. 1, we have that Encode$^{-1}(g)$ may contain at most one input ball for each entry in the cuckoo table. Hence a corrupt party may be able to input a set of at most m balls in our PSI protocol, where m is the size of the cuckoo table to store n items.

Let m be the size of a 3 hash (H_0, H_1, H_2) cuckoo table containing n elements
Given a ρ-dFSS F for a translatable structure $\mathcal{S}$ and a 1-dFSS P for $\mathsf{PT}_{u,d}$

```
RShare(1^κ):
  v_0, v_1, v_R - size m arrays
  for i ∈ [m]:
    (v_0[i], v_1[i], v_R[i]) ← (P ⊗ F).RShare(1^κ)
  return (v_0, v_1, v_R)

Extract(1^κ, k_0, k_1):
  Parse k_0, k_1 as cuckoo encodings
  Initialize empty |k_0| sized vector v_R
  For i ∈ [|k_0|]:
    v_R[i] ← (P ⊗ F).Extract(k_0[i], k_1[i])
    if v_R[i] = ⊥, return ⊥
  return v_R

DEval(1^κ,idx,v, x, offset):
  y ← (0,0)
  For c ∈ η(x) :
    For i ∈ {0,1,2}
    (y_0, y_1) ← ((P ⊗ F).DEval^aux(v[H_i(c)], (c,x) − offset[H_i(c)]))
   // here y_0 corresponds to the auxiliary output
    y ← y ⊕ (y_0, y_1)
  return (y[0] ⊕ 1^idx)||y[1]
```

Fig. 10. Weak spatial hashing construction for the collection of sets sparse-union$(\mathcal{S})$ with grid size δ in domain $\mathcal{U} = \{0, 1, \ldots, 2^u - 1\}^d$

Appendix

A Weak Boolean FSS Definition

Here we present the original weak boolean FSS formulation from [24] with no false positives.

Definition 14 (bFSS syntax). *Let $\mathcal{S} \subseteq 2^{\mathcal{U}}$ denote a family of sets over input domain $\mathcal{U}$, security parameter κ. A 2-party ρ-bFSS scheme with algorithms (Share, Eval) has the following syntax:*

- $(k_0, k_1) \leftarrow \mathit{Share}(1^\kappa, S)$*: is an algorithm with input the security parameter and (the description of) a set $S \in \mathcal{S}$ and it outputs key shares (k_0, k_1).*
- $y_{idx} \leftarrow \mathit{Eval}(1^\kappa, idx, k_{idx}, x)$*: is a deterministic algorithm with input security parameter κ, party index $idx \in \{0, 1\}$, key share k_{idx} and any $x \in \mathcal{U}$. It outputs a binary string y_{idx} of length ρ.*

Definition 15 (bFSS security). *A 2-party ρ-bFSS scheme (Share, Eval) for $\mathcal{S} \subseteq 2^{\mathcal{U}}$ is **secure** if is satisfies the following conditions:*

- ***Correctness for yes-instances:*** *For every $S \in \mathcal{S}$, $x \in S$:*

$$\Pr\left(y_0 \oplus y_1 = 0^\rho \;\middle|\; \begin{array}{l} (k_0, k_1) \leftarrow \mathit{Share}(1^\kappa, S) \\ y_0 \leftarrow \mathit{Eval}(1^\kappa, 0, k_0, x) \\ y_1 \leftarrow \mathit{Eval}(1^\kappa, 1, k_1, x) \end{array} \right) = 1$$

Given a bFSS F for singleton set with $\mathcal{U} = [2^{ud}+1]$

$\mathsf{RShare}(1^\kappa)$:	$\mathsf{DEval}(1^\kappa, \mathsf{idx}, k, \mathsf{offset}, x)$:
Pick random encoding $r \leftarrow_R \mathcal{U}$	$y_{\mathsf{idx}} \leftarrow F.\mathsf{Eval}(1^\kappa, \mathsf{idx}, k, \mathsf{map}(x) - \mathsf{offset})$
$(k_0, k_1) \leftarrow F.\mathsf{Share}(1^\kappa, a)$	return y_{idx}
return (k_0, k_1, r)	

Fig. 11. (RShare,DEval) functions of a dFSS for $\mathsf{PT}_{u,d}$

- ***Correctness for no-instances:*** *For every set $S \in \mathcal{S}$, $x \in \mathcal{U} \backslash S$:*

$$\Pr\left(y_0 \oplus y_1 \neq 0^\rho \;\middle|\; \begin{array}{l} (k_0, k_1) \leftarrow Share(1^\kappa, S) \\ y_0 \leftarrow Eval(1^\kappa, 0, k_0, x) \\ y_1 \leftarrow Eval(1^\kappa, 1, k_1, x) \end{array} \right) = 1$$

- ***Privacy:*** *For every set $S \in \mathcal{S}$ and index $idx \in \{0, 1\}$ there exists a simulator Sim such that the following distributions are computationally indistinguishable in the security parameter:*

$$\boxed{\begin{array}{l} (k_0, k_1) \leftarrow \mathsf{Share}(1^\kappa, S) \\ \text{return } k_{\mathsf{idx}} \end{array}} \cong_\kappa Sim(1^\kappa, idx)$$

B dFSS Proofs/Constructions

B.1 dFSS for Singleton Sets, Intervals and a d-Dimensional Ball

The construction for the following theorem can be found in Fig. 11.

Theorem 2. *Given a strong ρ-bFSS construction for singleton sets, 1-dimensional interval and d dimensional intervals with an invertible Share function, there exists a corresponding ρ-dFSS for $\{PT_{u,d}, INT_{\delta,u}, BALL_{\delta,u,d}\}$.*

Proof. We'll show how this theorem holds for the class of point functions, but a similar proof would follow for the other two collections as well.

To encode collection of point functions, we define its encoding group $\mathbb{G}_{\mathsf{PT}}$ as $[2^{ud}+1]$. The group element 2^{ud} would encode the null set. Which helps us define the Encode function as follows:

$$\mathsf{Encode}_{\mathsf{PT}}(\{x\}) = \mathsf{map}(x) \text{ for } x \in \mathcal{U}_{u,d} \text{ and } \mathsf{Encode}_{\mathsf{PT}}(\emptyset) = 2^{ud}$$

Furthermore, we can define $\mathsf{Encode}_{\mathsf{PT}}^{-1}$ using the inverse of map. The proposed construction is presented in Fig. 11. Here the RShare outputs keys for a random singleton set, which is later derandomized in DEval to a chosen element by using an appropriate offset. Note, here we can encode a null set as well, by making the offset derandomize the singleton set to $\{2^{ud}\}$ - which is outside the domain of the dFSS. Next we show how each of the dFSS properties are satisfied (Fig. 12).

Given a dFSS F for some $\mathcal{S}$ with encode function Encode

$\underline{\mathsf{Share}(1^\kappa, S \in \mathcal{S})}$:
$(k_0, k_1, R) \leftarrow F.\mathsf{RShare}(1^\kappa)$
$\mathsf{offset} = \mathsf{Encode}(S) - R$
return $((k_0, \mathsf{offset}), (k_1, \mathsf{offset}))$

$\underline{\mathsf{Eval}(1^\kappa, \mathsf{idx}, key = (k_{\mathsf{idx}}, \mathsf{offset}), x)}$:
return $F.\mathsf{DEval}(1^\kappa, \mathsf{idx}, k_{\mathsf{idx}}, \mathsf{offset}, x)$

Fig. 12. (Share,Eval) of a bFSS for a collection of sets given a dFSS F for the same structure

- **Correctness:** For any $x, x^* \in PT_{u,d}$, and offset $\mathsf{offset} = \mathsf{Encode}_{\mathsf{PT}}(x^*) - r$, define y_{idx} to be $F.\mathsf{Eval}(1^\kappa, \mathsf{idx}, k, \mathsf{map}(x) - \mathsf{offset})$. Then $y_0 \oplus y_1 = 1 \iff \mathsf{map}(x) = \mathsf{map}(x^*)$ by the correctness of the underlying bFSS scheme, and else $y_0 \oplus y_1 = 1$.
  If the underlying bFSS has a correctness error - in the sense that the keys k_0, k_1 evaluate to a null set with negligible probability, then the dFSS would give incorrect output for the element x^* if its not $\emptyset$. This leads to a negligible error for a *yes-instance* of this dFSS. This negligible error does arise in point function constructions in [3,8], which we'll assume in this work.
  For a *no-instance* of this dFSS, there is never any error in the output. Since the output $y_0 \oplus y_1$ is always zero when input $x \neq x^*$.
- **Security:** This follows directly from the privacy of the underlying bFSS, and by the fact that r acts as a one-time in the offset $\mathsf{Encode}(x^*) - r$.
- **Extractability:** The Extract functions outputs the secret shared singleton element r, given the two keys k_0, k_1. It can be constructed using the invertible Share function as follows:

$$\mathsf{Extract}(k_0, k_1) = \mathsf{Encode}(\mathsf{Share}^{-1}(1^\kappa, k_0, k_1))$$

Similarly a bFSS for 1 dimensional interval and d dimensional fixed radius ℓ_∞ can give us a corresponding dFSS by "reducing the domain size" to ensure a null set can be encoded by a set outside the specified domain of dFSS.

B.2 bFSS from dFSS

Theorem 6. *Given a ρ-dFSS for $\mathcal{S}$ with share size σ, there exists a corresponding ρ-bFSS construction for $\mathcal{S}$ with share size σ.*

Proof. Note that each of these Encode function are efficiently invertible. The RShare, DEval for all these collections have the same structure, depicted in Fig. 11.

- **Correctness:** The term $\sum_{\mathsf{idx} \in \{0,1\}} \mathsf{Eval}(\mathsf{idx}, (k_{\mathsf{idx}}, \mathsf{Encode}(S) - R), x) = \sum_{\mathsf{idx} \in \{0,1\}} \mathsf{Eval}(\mathsf{idx}, k_{\mathsf{idx}}, \mathsf{Encode}(S) - R, x)$. Hence this follows directly from the correctness definition of dFSS.
- **Security:** The simulator for the bFSS simply runs the simulator for the dFSS.

```
RShare(1^κ):
  Initialize k_0, k_1, R as empty associated arrays
  (k_0[0], k_1[0], R[0]) ← F_1.RShare(1^κ)
  (k_0[1], k_1[1], R[1]) ← F_2.RShare(1^κ)
  return (k_0, k_1, R)

Extract(1^κ, k_0, k_1):
  return (F_1.Extract(1^κ, k_0[0],k_1[0]),
  F_2.Extract(1^κ, k_0[1],k_1[1]))

DEval(1^κ,idx,k_idx, offset, x):
  y_1 ← F_1.DEval(1^κ,idx,k_idx[0], offset[0],x)
  y_2 ← F_2.DEval(1^κ,idx,k_idx[1], offset[1], x)
  return y_1||y_2
```

Fig. 13. dFSS for cross product $S_1 \times S_2$ given dFSS for S_1 and S_2

B.3 concat

Theorem 7. *Given ρ_1-dFSS F_1 for $\mathcal{S}_1$ with share size σ_1 and ρ_2-dFSS F_2 for $\mathcal{S}_2$ with share size σ_2, there exists a $\rho_1 + \rho_2$-dFSS concat$[F_1, F_2]$ for $\mathcal{S}_1 \times \mathcal{S}_2$ with share size $\sigma_1 + \sigma_2$. Furthermore, if F_1 and F_2 dFSS have pseduo-random keys, then so does concat$[F_1, F_2]$.*

Proof. Given encode functions $\mathsf{Encode}_1 : \mathcal{S}_1 \to \mathbb{G}_1$ and $\mathsf{Encode}_2 : \mathcal{S}_2 \to \mathbb{G}_2$ for dFSS F_1 and F_2 respectively, we define encode function for concat $[F_1, F_2]$ $\mathsf{Encode} : \mathcal{S}_1 \times \mathcal{S}_2 \to \mathbb{G}_1 \times \mathbb{G}_2$ as:

$$\mathsf{Encode}(S_1, S_2) = (\mathsf{Encode}_1(S_1), \mathsf{Encode}_2(S_2))$$

Note that this Encode function is efficiently invertible if the two component Encode functions are. Encodings with respect to the new Encode function form a group which is a direct product of the groups for the component FSS.

- **Correctness:** The correctness of $F = \mathsf{concat}[F_1, F_2]$ reduces to the correctness of F_1 and F_2. The first k_1 bits of the term $y = \sum_{\mathsf{idx}\in\{0,1\}} F.\mathsf{DEval}(\mathsf{idx}, (k_{\mathsf{idx}}\ , \mathsf{Encode}(S_1, S_2) - (R_1, R_2)), (x, y))$ equal $\sum_{\mathsf{idx}\in\{0,1\}} F_1.\mathsf{Eval}(\mathsf{idx}, (k_{\mathsf{idx}}, \mathsf{Encode}(S_1) - R_1), x)$ and the last k_2 bit of y equal $\sum_{\mathsf{idx}\in\{0,1\}} F_2.\mathsf{Eval}(\mathsf{idx}, (k_{\mathsf{idx}}, \mathsf{Encode}(S_2) - R_2), x)$. Hence, $y = 0^{k_1+k_2}$ for $(x, y) \in S_1 \times S_2$. And if $x \notin S_1$, the first k_1 bits are not all zero bits with probability at least p_1, and if $x \notin S_2$, the last k_2 bits are not all zero bits with probability at least p_2.
- **Security:** The simulator Sim for concat$[F_1, F_2]$ invokes the simulators for F_1 and F_2, which output (k_0, offset_0) and (k_1, offset_1). Then Sim outputs $((k_0, k_1), (\mathsf{offset}_0, \mathsf{offset}_1))$.
- **Extractability:** This is reduced to the extractability property of the two underlying dFSS F_1 and F_2 as shown in Fig. 13.

References

1. Beaver, D.: Precomputing oblivious transfer. In: Coppersmith, D. (ed.) CRYPTO 1995. LNCS, vol. 963, pp. 97–109. Springer, Heidelberg (1995). https://doi.org/10.1007/3-540-44750-4_8
2. Boneh, D., Boyle, E., Corrigan-Gibbs, H., Gilboa, N., Ishai, Y.: Lightweight techniques for private heavy hitters. In: 2021 IEEE Symposium on Security and Privacy (SP), pp. 762–776. IEEE (2021)
3. Boyle, E., et al.: Function secret sharing for mixed-mode and fixed-point secure computation. In: Canteaut, A., Standaert, F.-X. (eds.) EUROCRYPT 2021. LNCS, vol. 12697, pp. 871–900. Springer, Cham (2021). https://doi.org/10.1007/978-3-030-77886-6_30
4. Boyle, E., Couteau, G., Gilboa, N., Ishai, Y.: Compressing vector OLE. In: Lie, D., Mannan, M., Backes, M., Wang, X. (eds.) ACM CCS 2018, pp. 896–912. ACM Press, October 2018
5. Boyle, E., et al.: Efficient two-round OT extension and silent non-interactive secure computation. In: Cavallaro, L., Kinder, J., Wang, X., Katz, J. (eds.) ACM CCS 2019, pp. 291–308. ACM Press, November 2019
6. Boyle, E., Couteau, G., Gilboa, N., Ishai, Y., Kohl, L., Scholl, P.: Efficient pseudorandom correlation generators: silent OT extension and more. In: Boldyreva, A., Micciancio, D. (eds.) CRYPTO 2019, Part III. LNCS, vol. 11694, pp. 489–518. Springer, Cham (2019). https://doi.org/10.1007/978-3-030-26954-8_16
7. Boyle, E., Gilboa, N., Ishai, Y.: Function secret sharing. In: Oswald, E., Fischlin, M. (eds.) EUROCRYPT 2015. LNCS, vol. 9057, pp. 337–367. Springer, Heidelberg (2015). https://doi.org/10.1007/978-3-662-46803-6_12
8. Boyle, E., Gilboa, N., Ishai, Y.: Function secret sharing: improvements and extensions. In: Proceedings of the 2016 ACM SIGSAC Conference on Computer and Communications Security, pp. 1292–1303 (2016)
9. Boyle, E., Gilboa, N., Ishai, Y.: Secure computation with preprocessing via function secret sharing. In: Hofheinz, D., Rosen, A. (eds.) TCC 2019. LNCS, vol. 11891, pp. 341–371. Springer, Cham (2019). https://doi.org/10.1007/978-3-030-36030-6_14
10. Boyle, E., Gilboa, N., Ishai, Y., Kolobov, V.I.: Programmable distributed point functions. Cryptology ePrint Archive (2022)
11. Chase, M., Miao, P.: Private set intersection in the internet setting from lightweight oblivious PRF. In: Micciancio, D., Ristenpart, T. (eds.) CRYPTO 2020, Part III. LNCS, vol. 12172, pp. 34–63. Springer, Cham (2020). https://doi.org/10.1007/978-3-030-56877-1_2
12. Couteau, G., Rindal, P., Raghuraman, S.: Silver: silent VOLE and oblivious transfer from hardness of decoding structured LDPC codes. In: Malkin, T., Peikert, C. (eds.) CRYPTO 2021, Part III. LNCS, vol. 12827, pp. 502–534. Springer, Cham (2021). https://doi.org/10.1007/978-3-030-84252-9_17
13. Dachman-Soled, D., Malkin, T., Raykova, M., Yung, M.: Efficient robust private set intersection. In: Abdalla, M., Pointcheval, D., Fouque, P.-A., Vergnaud, D. (eds.) ACNS 2009. LNCS, vol. 5536, pp. 125–142. Springer, Heidelberg (2009). https://doi.org/10.1007/978-3-642-01957-9_8
14. Dachman-Soled, D., Malkin, T., Raykova, M., Yung, M.: Secure efficient multiparty computing of multivariate polynomials and applications. In: Lopez, J., Tsudik, G. (eds.) ACNS 2011. LNCS, vol. 6715, pp. 130–146. Springer, Heidelberg (2011). https://doi.org/10.1007/978-3-642-21554-4_8

15. de Castro, L., Polychroniadou, A.: Lightweight, maliciously secure verifiable function secret sharing. In: Dunkelman, O., Dziembowski, S. (eds.) EUROCRYPT 2022. LNCS, vol. 13275, pp. 150–179. Springer, Cham (2022). https://doi.org/10.1007/978-3-031-06944-4_6
16. De Cristofaro, E., Kim, J., Tsudik, G.: Linear-complexity private set intersection protocols secure in malicious model. In: Abe, M. (ed.) ASIACRYPT 2010. LNCS, vol. 6477, pp. 213–231. Springer, Heidelberg (2010). https://doi.org/10.1007/978-3-642-17373-8_13
17. De Cristofaro, E., Tsudik, G.: Practical private set intersection protocols with linear complexity. In: Sion, R. (ed.) FC 2010. LNCS, vol. 6052, pp. 143–159. Springer, Heidelberg (2010). https://doi.org/10.1007/978-3-642-14577-3_13
18. Dong, C., Chen, L., Wen, Z.: When private set intersection meets big data: an efficient and scalable protocol. In: Sadeghi, A.-R., Gligor, V.D., Yung, M. (eds.) ACM CCS 2013, pp. 789–800. ACM Press, November 2013
19. Frederiksen, T.K., Jakobsen, T.P., Nielsen, J.B., Trifiletti, R.: On the complexity of additively homomorphic UC commitments. In: Kushilevitz, E., Malkin, T. (eds.) TCC 2016. LNCS, vol. 9562, pp. 542–565. Springer, Heidelberg (2016). https://doi.org/10.1007/978-3-662-49096-9_23
20. Freedman, M.J., Ishai, Y., Pinkas, B., Reingold, O.: Keyword search and oblivious pseudorandom functions. In: Kilian, J. (ed.) TCC 2005. LNCS, vol. 3378, pp. 303–324. Springer, Heidelberg (2005). https://doi.org/10.1007/978-3-540-30576-7_17
21. Freedman, M.J., Nissim, K., Pinkas, B.: Efficient private matching and set intersection. In: Cachin, C., Camenisch, J.L. (eds.) EUROCRYPT 2004. LNCS, vol. 3027, pp. 1–19. Springer, Heidelberg (2004). https://doi.org/10.1007/978-3-540-24676-3_1
22. Garimella, G., Mohassel, P., Rosulek, M., Sadeghian, S., Singh, J.: Private set operations from oblivious switching. In: Garay, J.A. (ed.) PKC 2021, Part II. LNCS, vol. 12711, pp. 591–617. Springer, Cham (2021). https://doi.org/10.1007/978-3-030-75248-4_21
23. Garimella, G., Pinkas, B., Rosulek, M., Trieu, N., Yanai, A.: Oblivious key-value stores and amplification for private set intersection. In: Malkin, T., Peikert, C. (eds.) CRYPTO 2021, Part II. LNCS, vol. 12826, pp. 395–425. Springer, Cham (2021). https://doi.org/10.1007/978-3-030-84245-1_14
24. Garimella, G., Rosulek, M., Singh, J.: Structure-aware private set intersection, with applications to fuzzy matching. In: Dodis, Y., Shrimpton, T. (eds.) CRYPTO 2022. LNCS, vol. 13507, pp. 323–352. Springer, Cham (2022). https://doi.org/10.1007/978-3-031-15802-5_12
25. Ghosh, S., Nilges, T.: An algebraic approach to maliciously secure private set intersection. In: Ishai, Y., Rijmen, V. (eds.) EUROCRYPT 2019, Part III. LNCS, vol. 11478, pp. 154–185. Springer, Cham (2019). https://doi.org/10.1007/978-3-030-17659-4_6
26. Hazay, C., Lindell, Y.: Efficient protocols for set intersection and pattern matching with security against malicious and covert adversaries. In: Canetti, R. (ed.) TCC 2008. LNCS, vol. 4948, pp. 155–175. Springer, Heidelberg (2008). https://doi.org/10.1007/978-3-540-78524-8_10
27. Huang, Y., Evans, D., Katz, J.: Private set intersection: are garbled circuits better than custom protocols? In: NDSS 2012. The Internet Society, February 2012
28. Huberman, B.A., Franklin, M., Hogg, T.: Enhancing privacy and trust in electronic communities. In: ACM Conference On Electronic Commerce. ACM (1999)

29. Huberman, B.A., Franklin, M., Hogg, T.: Enhancing privacy and trust in electronic communities. In: Proceedings of the 1st ACM Conference on Electronic Commerce, pp. 78–86 (1999)
30. Ishai, Y., Kilian, J., Nissim, K., Petrank, E.: Extending oblivious transfers efficiently. In: Boneh, D. (ed.) CRYPTO 2003. LNCS, vol. 2729, pp. 145–161. Springer, Heidelberg (2003). https://doi.org/10.1007/978-3-540-45146-4_9
31. Jarecki, S., Liu, X.: Fast secure computation of set intersection. In: Garay, J.A., De Prisco, R. (eds.) SCN 2010. LNCS, vol. 6280, pp. 418–435. Springer, Heidelberg (2010). https://doi.org/10.1007/978-3-642-15317-4_26
32. Jawurek, M., Kerschbaum, F., Orlandi, C.: Zero-knowledge using garbled circuits: how to prove non-algebraic statements efficiently. In: Sadeghi, A.-R., Gligor, V.D., Yung, M. (eds.) 2013 ACM SIGSAC Conference on Computer and Communications Security, CCS'13, Berlin, Germany, November 4–8, 2013, pp. 955–966. ACM (2013). https://doi.org/10.1145/2508859.2516662
33. Kissner, L., Song, D.: Privacy-preserving set operations. In: Shoup, V. (ed.) CRYPTO 2005. LNCS, vol. 3621, pp. 241–257. Springer, Heidelberg (2005). https://doi.org/10.1007/11535218_15
34. Kolesnikov, V., Kumaresan, R., Rosulek, M., Trieu, N.: Efficient batched oblivious PRF with applications to private set intersection. In: Weippl, E.R., Katzenbeisser, S., Kruegel, C., Myers, A.C., Halevi, S. (eds.) ACM CCS 2016, pp. 818–829. ACM Press, October 2016
35. Meadows, C.: A more efficient cryptographic matchmaking protocol for use in the absence of a continuously available third party. In: 1986 IEEE Symposium on Security and Privacy, pp. 134–134. IEEE (1986)
36. Pinkas, B., Rosulek, M., Trieu, N., Yanai, A.: SpOT-light: lightweight private set intersection from sparse OT extension. In: Boldyreva, A., Micciancio, D. (eds.) CRYPTO 2019, Part III. LNCS, vol. 11694, pp. 401–431. Springer, Cham (2019). https://doi.org/10.1007/978-3-030-26954-8_13
37. Pinkas, B., Rosulek, M., Trieu, N., Yanai, A.: PSI from PaXoS: fast, malicious private set intersection. In: Canteaut, A., Ishai, Y. (eds.) EUROCRYPT 2020, Part II. LNCS, vol. 12106, pp. 739–767. Springer, Cham (2020). https://doi.org/10.1007/978-3-030-45724-2_25
38. Pinkas, B., Schneider, T., Segev, G., Zohner, M.: Phasing: private set intersection using permutation-based hashing. In: Jung, J., Holz, T. (eds.) USENIX Security 2015, pp. 515–530. USENIX Association, August 2015
39. Pinkas, B., Schneider, T., Tkachenko, O., Yanai, A.: Efficient circuit-based PSI with linear communication. In: Ishai, Y., Rijmen, V. (eds.) EUROCRYPT 2019, Part III. LNCS, vol. 11478, pp. 122–153. Springer, Cham (2019). https://doi.org/10.1007/978-3-030-17659-4_5
40. Pinkas, B., Schneider, T., Weinert, C., Wieder, U.: Efficient circuit-based PSI via cuckoo hashing. In: Nielsen, J.B., Rijmen, V. (eds.) EUROCRYPT 2018, Part III. LNCS, vol. 10822, pp. 125–157. Springer, Cham (2018). https://doi.org/10.1007/978-3-319-78372-7_5
41. Pinkas, B., Schneider, T., Zohner, M.: Faster private set intersection based on OT extension. In: 23rd USENIX Security Symposium (USENIX Security 2014), pp. 797–812 (2014)
42. Rindal, P., Rosulek, M.: Improved private set intersection against malicious adversaries. In: Coron, J.-S., Nielsen, J.B. (eds.) EUROCRYPT 2017, Part I. LNCS, vol. 10210, pp. 235–259. Springer, Cham (2017). https://doi.org/10.1007/978-3-319-56620-7_9

43. Rindal, P., Rosulek, M.: Malicious-secure private set intersection via dual execution. In: Thuraisingham, B.M., Evans, D., Malkin, T., Xu, D. (eds.) ACM CCS 2017, pp. 1229–1242. ACM Press, October 2017
44. Rindal, P., Schoppmann, P.: VOLE-PSI: fast OPRF and circuit-PSI from vector-OLE. In: Canteaut, A., Standaert, F.-X. (eds.) EUROCRYPT 2021, Part II. LNCS, vol. 12697, pp. 901–930. Springer, Cham (2021). https://doi.org/10.1007/978-3-030-77886-6_31
45. Schoppmann, P., Gascón, A., Reichert, L., Raykova, M.: Distributed vector-OLE: improved constructions and implementation. In: Cavallaro, L., Kinder, J., Wang, X., Katz, J. (eds.) ACM CCS 2019, pp. 1055–1072. ACM Press, November 2019

Threshold Cryptography

Secure Multiparty Computation from Threshold Encryption Based on Class Groups

Lennart Braun(✉), Ivan Damgård, and Claudio Orlandi

Aarhus University, Aarhus, Denmark
{braun,ivan,orlandi}@cs.au.dk

Abstract. We construct the first actively-secure threshold version of the cryptosystem based on class groups from the so-called CL framework (Castagnos and Laguillaumie, 2015).

We show how to use our threshold scheme to achieve general universally composable (UC) secure multiparty computation (MPC) with only transparent set-up, i.e., with no secret trapdoors involved.

On the way to our goal, we design new zero-knowledge (ZK) protocols with constant communication complexity for proving multiplicative relations between encrypted values. This allows us to use the ZK proofs to achieve MPC with active security with only a constant factor overhead.

Finally, we adapt our protocol for the so called "You-Only-Speak-Once" (YOSO) setting, which is a very promising recent approach for performing MPC over a blockchain. This is possible because our key generation protocol is simpler and requires significantly less interaction compared to previous approaches: in particular, our new key generation protocol allows the adversary to bias the public key, but we show that this has no impact on the security of the resulting cryptosystem.

1 Introduction

In secure multiparty computation (MPC), a set of N parties jointly compute an agreed function on inputs privately held by the parties. For security, we require that the result is correct and that the only new information revealed is the intended output. This should be true even if up to t parties are corrupted by an adversary, for some parameter $1 \leq t < N$.

The CDN Framework. In recent years, we have seen an explosion of results that improve the efficiency of general MPC protocols. One tool that is featured prominently in many recent works is Threshold Linearly Homomorphic Encryption (TLHE). In such a scheme there is a common public key pk, while the secret decryption key is shared among the parties using an appropriate secret-sharing scheme. It is assumed that we have a secure decryption protocol which on input a ciphertext $c = \mathsf{Enc}(\mathsf{pk}, m)$ returns the encrypted message m while revealing nothing else. Furthermore we assume that messages come from a ring, typically $\mathbb{Z}_n$ for some natural number n and that we have corresponding multiplication

H. Handschuh and A. Lysyanskaya (Eds.): CRYPTO 2023, LNCS 14081, pp. 613–645, 2023.
https://doi.org/10.1007/978-3-031-38557-5_20

and exponentiation operations on ciphertexts such that for any messages a, b and public constant α in the ring, we have

$$\mathsf{Enc}(\mathsf{pk}, a) \cdot \mathsf{Enc}(\mathsf{pk}, b)^{\alpha} = \mathsf{Enc}(\mathsf{pk}, a + \alpha b).$$

This set-up, together with a set of appropriate zero-knowledge protocols, allows to implement MPC for general functions. This idea was first introduced by Cramer et al. in [17]. The construction is known as the CDN framework because it works for any TLHE scheme, given the right set of zero-knowledge protocols. These include, for instance, proof of plaintext knowledge for a given ciphertext. While the required protocols can always be realized using generic techniques for zero-knowledge, some cryptosystems, such as Paillier encryption [34], allow very efficient Σ-protocols for this purpose, such that the overhead required for the proofs is only a constant factor, compared to simply sending the required ciphertexts.

The CDN framework was defined for honest majority, but it is well-known in the folklore that it can also easily be adapted to work for dishonest majority, although only security with abort can then be obtained. In the years following the introduction of CDN, interest in the framework declined somewhat, for several reasons. For honest majority, it was realized that more efficient protocols can be obtained from techniques based on secret-sharing. For dishonest majority the BeDOZa/SPDZ protocols [6,21] introduced the idea of pushing the use of the expensive public key operations into a preprocessing phase where the inputs and function to compute need not be known. The preprocessing produces correlated randomness (typically so-called Beaver's multiplication triples [5]) that is used once the function and inputs are known, and then, in the on-line phase, only very simple information-theoretic techniques are needed. The most practical instantiations of SPDZ perform preprocessing using somewhat-homomorphic Lattice-based encryption [4,30,31]. This works well for relatively small plaintext spaces, say $\mathbb{F}_q$ for a 128-bit prime q, but gets very cumbersome for large q. While the preprocessing could also be done using the CDN approach based on Paillier encryption, this forces the plaintext ring to be $\mathbb{Z}_n$ for an RSA modulus n and this is not a good fit for all applications. In particular, the modulus, and hence the plaintext domain is not even known before the key generation is done, whereas other approaches can work for a predefined plaintext ring. Finally, one needs the modulus to be generated in a trusted way, which either requires a trusted authority or a (notoriously cumbersome) secure protocol for generating n. In summary, for large plaintext rings, there is a lack of a satisfactory approach to perform general preprocessing.

YOSO MPC. Interest in the CDN framework was recently renewed by the introduction of the You Only Speak Once (YOSO) model for MPC, by Gentry et al. in [29]. This model assumes a large universe of M parties, here referred to as servers, that are all willing to help execute a secure computation. The main idea is to have the secure computation be done by a committee of N servers where $N \ll M$, and where the committee will change over time. The goal is to hide from the adversary who is in the committee. If this can be done, we can hope to do MPC with communication complexity that scales sublinearly with M, even if the adversary can corrupt, say, just under $M/2$ of the servers – since then a randomly chosen but small committee will have honest majority with large probability.

However, the adversary is most likely able to tell who is in the committee as soon as these servers start sending messages and could then attack them. Hence the YOSO paradigm: a committee should only send one round of messages, and then the committee changes. The new committee will of course need to receive private information, so to realize this, one needs receiver anonymous communication channels (RACC). One can think of this as a primitive that outputs N public encryption keys such that the adversary does not know who they belong to (as long as the owner is not corrupt), and such that the majority of the owners are honest. In [29] a construction of RACC was proposed.

The bottleneck in a YOSO protocol is clearly the private communication between committees. The secret state one needs to maintain should therefore be as small as possible. This means that secret-sharing-based protocols and protocols in the preprocessing model are not well suited for YOSO, as parties need to remember a large number of shares. In contrast, a protocol following the CDN paradigm works much better: the only secret state that must be maintained consists of each party's share of the secret key. The rest of the state consists of public ciphertexts. This was pointed out already in [29], where a concrete construction was done from the Paillier-based instantiation of CDN. However, the construction assumed as set-up an honestly generated public key and a sharing of the secret key for the first committee. Doing CDN-style MPC in the YOSO model without trusted set-up was left as an open problem.

Our Contribution. The contributions of our work are as follows:

1. We construct the first actively-secure threshold version of the class-group-based LHE from the so-called CL framework [12]. This allows e.g., to address the problem related to the plaintext space mentioned above, since the CL cryptosystem can be used for plaintext space $\mathbb{F}_q$ where q can be (almost) any prime.
2. We propose a novel threshold key-generation protocol for the CL cryptosystem that is simpler and requires significantly less interaction than the state-of-the-art from [28]. This is essential to enable usage of the cryptosystem in the YOSO setting. The simplification is of independent interest as it also applies to other cryptosystems, including standard ElGamal based on DDH.
3. We identify a problem with Feldman-style secret sharing over a group of unknown order as introduced by Rabin [36].[1] This is an essential tool used by our key-generation protocol. We fix the problem, patching the protocol (which becomes only slightly more complicated) and we can prove it secure under the assumption that the group order is hard to compute.
4. We design new zero-knowledge protocols for proving multiplicative relations between CL-encrypted values, with only constant factor overhead.

[1] We describe the issue in detail in the full version [9].

5. We introduce a new computational assumption, which we call the *rough order assumption*, stating that class groups with no small prime factors in their order are hard to distinguish from general class groups. Assuming this, we can considerably simplify our zero-knowledge protocols and their security proofs. We believe this is of independent interest as it will apply to other constructions based on class groups.
6. We build an UC-secure MPC protocol with transparent setup following the CDN paradigm. The protocol uses our novel TLHE scheme and ZK protocols described above. Transparent set-up in this context means that we do not need to assume a trusted party that generates the set-up and must keep some trapdoor information secret. Essentially, we just need to select some parameters from public randomness e.g., using a random oracle.
7. Finally, we adapt our MPC protocol to the YOSO setting, including the threshold key generation protocol. This solves the open problem mentioned above, from [29].

It would be easy to adapt our MPC protocol to the dishonest-majority setting, e.g., using the SPDZ paradigm (but we do not explicitly describe it in this paper). While this might not be so interesting in the YOSO context, it would have some benefit in the traditional MPC setting, since it would allow using any $\mathbb{F}_q$ (where q is a large prime) as plaintext ring, and as explained above, this can be an advantage over previous approaches for large q.

1.1 Technical Overview

As mentioned, we start from the CL cryptosystem as suggested in [12] and further investigated in [10,11,13]. The cryptosystem is based on (subgroup of) a class group $G \simeq F \times H$ where F has known order q and the order of H is hard to compute. Such a group is specified by choosing initially a public number called the discriminant. This number is sampled transparently e.g., no hidden factorization is required.

A public key is a pair $\mathsf{pk} = (g, h)$ of elements in H, where the secret key is the discrete log of h base g. An encryption of $m \in \mathbb{F}_q$ with randomness r is of the form $\mathsf{Enc}(\mathsf{pk}, m; r) = (g^r, f^m h^r)$, where $f \in F$ is a generator of F or order q, and where in addition discrete logs base f are easy to compute. Decryption and the homomorphic properties follow almost immediately. CPA security follows from an appropriate assumption on subgroup indistinguishability. For the application of this system to MPC, there are a number of technical challenges to overcome, as we explain below.

Distributed Key Generation. To avoid trusted set-up in the CDN paradigm, we need a distributed key generation protocol, where a public key is formed and parties obtain shares of the corresponding secret key. Now, encryption in the CL framework is essentially ElGamal encryption adapted to the class-group setting. So a natural first attempt is to have each player perform a Feldman-style verifiable secret sharing of their contribution to the key [25], and then essentially add up all valid contributions.

In a Feldman VSS, the dealer publishes g^x and $\{g^{\alpha_k}\}_{k=1}^t$ where the α_k's are coefficients of a degree-t polynomial to be used for secret sharing x among the parties. Evaluating the polynomials in the exponent, it is possible to publicly compute values $y_j = g^{s_j}$, where s_j is the share of party P_j and this allows verification of the share that P_j receives in private. However, it turns out that there is a problem with this type of secret sharing in our setting: it takes place over a group of unknown order (as first done in [36]) so parties cannot reduce modulo the order, meaning that we can only do integer arithmetic in the exponent. Therefore we must use the integer variant of Shamir secret sharing, i.e., polynomials with integer coefficients. Feldman's original suggestion was to use a group of known public order, such as a prime order subgroup of $\mathbb{Z}_p^*$ for a prime p. In such a setting, it is the case that from any $t+1$ shares $\{s_j\}$ that satisfy $y_i = g^{s_i}$, one can reconstruct the correct secret x, and this can be concluded without relying on any computational assumptions. But this is not true for the case where integer secret sharing is used over an unknown order group. Intuitively, the reason is that we use integer secret sharing, but the verification of shares only guarantees that they are correct modulo the group order, not that they are the correct integers. It turns out that this can be used to mount a subtle attack against the protocols in the literature (which seems to have gone unnoticed since [36]): As we describe in detail in the full version [9], a corrupt dealer who knows the group order can break reconstruction. This means that reconstruction cannot be shown secure unless we rely on the assumption that the group order is hard to compute. We fix this issue by having the dealer prove in zero-knowledge that they know the discrete log of g^x. Then, if any value is reconstructed that is different from what we extract from the dealer, we would get a multiple of the group order which we assume is infeasible to compute.[2]

Once we have a working version of Feldman VSS we can use the linearity properties and essentially add all valid contributions to the key to get the final key pair. However, this leads to a second challenge: as pointed out in [28], the approach based on Feldman VSS allows the adversary to bias the public key by selecting the contributions of the corrupt players after seeing what the honest players send. It is then not clear that the resulting encryption scheme is still secure. In [28] the problem was solved by designing a different protocol that guarantees a uniform public key, but this protocol is more complex, requires several rounds and is not suitable for the YOSO setting. Our approach is to instead take a closer look at the key generation using only Feldman VSS. We observe that the adversary's influence on this protocol can be shown to be equivalent to a modified CPA game where the adversary is first shown a public key pk, then selects a number δ, and the final public key is then $\mathsf{pk}' = \mathsf{pk} \cdot g^\delta$; the CPA game now continues as usual with pk' as the public key. Next, we show that

[2] In follow-up work, we have observed that for the particular application to key generation, a slightly weaker reconstruction property suffices, namely that the product of x and a public constant modulo the group order can be reconstructed. This can be achieved without the dealer proving knowledge of x and hence the key generation can be made more efficient.

for the cryptosystem in question, given an adversary who can win this modified CPA game, we can construct one that wins the standard CPA game. Hence, our encryption scheme is CPA secure, even if the public key is biased in the way our simpler protocol allows. This observation is of independent interest, as it applies also to standard ElGamal encryption based on DDH (described in the full version [9]). We note that in [28], it was shown that a biased public key is good enough for some signature schemes, but the problem for encryption schemes was left open.

Zero-Knowledge Protocols. An efficient zero-knowledge protocol for proof of plaintext knowledge was already suggested in [11]. In addition, we need a protocol for the following setting: given ciphertext $c = \mathsf{Enc}(\mathsf{pk}, a)$, a party P can choose b, compute $d = \mathsf{Enc}(\mathsf{pk}, b)$ and $e = c^b \cdot \mathsf{Enc}(\mathsf{pk}, 0) = \mathsf{Enc}(\mathsf{pk}, a \cdot b)$ and prove in zero-knowledge that d and e were correctly computed. Since $e = c^b \cdot \mathsf{Enc}(\mathsf{pk}, 0)$ and b also appears in the exponent in $\mathsf{Enc}(\mathsf{pk}, b)$, it turns out we can use a Schnorr-style Σ-protocol to prove this relation [18].

Usually, one would want these protocols to have standard knowledge soundness, and it is well known that achieving this, as well as constant factor overhead protocols, leads to technical difficulties in groups of unknown order. More specifically, the extractor needs to compute inverses modulo the group order which cannot be done efficiently. This issue can sometimes be avoided by relying on the assumption that the adversary cannot compute non-trivial roots of a given group element. But even this will not work in our setting: we need to work with ciphertexts - and hence group elements - that are chosen by the adversary, and for those we can of course not assume that the adversary cannot compute roots. While it is possible to work around this using more complicated protocols, we observe that there is a much cleaner way to solve the problem:

We take a close look at the soundness property we need for our MPC protocol. It turns out to be sufficient that an adversarially generated ciphertext is proved to be well formed, and that we can extract the plaintext from the proof. This is weaker than full knowledge soundness that would equire us to also extract the ciphertext's randomness from the proof. It then turns out that we can prove the soundness property we need under the sole assumption that the order of the group we work in is "rough", i.e., has only large prime factors in its order. This is not necessarily true for class groups in general, but we introduce a new computational assumption stating that discriminants for class groups with rough order are indistinguishable from discriminants in general. This is then the only assumption we need for soundness. While this is admittedly a new and not yet well studied assumption, we believe that it will have impact in future work since it allows a much cleaner design and analysis of zero-knowledge protocols which would otherwise be quite cumbersome to analyse. (However, at the cost of more complicated protocols and analysis, we could instead use the more well-known strong root assumption.)

YOSO MPC. All this leads to a general MPC protocol following the CDN paradigm, which we adapt to the YOSO setting in the final part of the paper. This solves the open problem from [29], in that we obtain a CDN-style MPC protocol without trusted set-up. We do this following the approach of [29] but replacing Pailler encryption by class-group-based encryption (which does not require any trusted set-up for key generation), however, the major difference is that the Feldman VSS used in the key generation must also be adapted to YOSO. In the original VSS, the dealer sends shares privately to the share holders. Instead, we let the dealer publish ciphertexts containing shares intended for the next committee, as well as zero-knowledge proof that the ciphertexts are correct. Now, the VSS consists of publishing one message which fits well the YOSO setting.

1.2 Other Related Work

Class groups have been used as tool to achieve transparent setups for other cryptographic primitives including: SNARKS [3], pseudorandom correlation functions [2], verifiable delay functions [8,35,39], and much more.

In concurrent work, Kolby et al. [32] show that it is possible to achieve guaranteed output delivery in a constant number of rounds without relying on trusted setup in the YOSO model. In particular, they propose two protocols based on garbled circuits and fully-homomorphic encryption which achieve constant round communication. They also propose a non constant-round protocol (which is used to bootstrap the constant-round protocols that require setup) which has some similarities with our work since it also uses linearly homomorphic encryption based on class groups in the YOSO context. However, the work in [32] does not construct a TLHE scheme nor a YOSO key generation protocol. Instead, they assign a key pair from the basic scheme to each committee member and instruct committee members to send to the next committee by secret sharing their data and encrypting the shares for the receivers. This does achieve general MPC in YOSO without set-up, but this comes at a price: the amount of data that must be privately passed between committees is proportional to the size of the circuit being computed. In contrast, in a solution using a TLHE scheme, one can pass information by posting public ciphertexts encrypted under the global public key, and the data will then be accessible to any committee that has shares of the private key. Hence, these shares are the only private data we need to maintain. In [24], Erwig et al. present a threshold cryptosystem for the YOSO setting based on the discrete logarithm problem in prime order groups.

Recently, in concurrent and independent work, Castagnos et al. [14] created a threshold linearly homomorphic encryption scheme with $\mathbb{Z}_{2^k}$ as plaintext space using a new variant of the CL framework. While this enables new applications where arithmetic modulo a 2-power is needed, the construction requires a class group where the discriminant is an RSA modulus whose factors must not be known to the adversary. So this scheme does not allow transparent set-up.

2 Preliminaries

Notation. The following shorthands are used to describe ranges of integers: $[n] := \{1, \dots, n\}$, $[a, b] := \{a, \dots, b\}$, and $[a, b) := \{a, \dots, b-1\}$. We use a computational security parameter λ and a statistical security parameter σ. Our protocols are defined for N parties $P_1, \ldots, P_N$ out of whom up to t parties can be corrupted. We use $\mathcal{C}$ and $\mathcal{H}$ to denote the subsets of corrupted and honest parties, respectively. We frequently use $\Delta := N! = 1 \cdot 2 \cdots N$.

The CL Framework for Unknown Order Groups. The framework was introduced by Castagnos et al. [12], and enhanced in [10,11,13]. The following description is based on [10, Def. 4] and [38].

Group Structure. The framework specifies two algorithms, CLGen and $\mathsf{CLSolve}$. CLGen takes a computational security parameter 1^λ and a prime $q > 2^\lambda$, and outputs a tuple $\mathsf{pp}_{\mathsf{cl}} := (q, \bar{s}, f, g_q, \widehat{G}, F; \rho) \leftarrow \mathsf{CLGen}(1^\lambda, q)$, where ρ denotes the randomness used by CLGen.[3] We define a UC functionality $\mathcal{F}_{\mathsf{CL}}$ that generates and distributes $\mathsf{pp}_{\mathsf{cl}}$. Here, $(\widehat{G}, \cdot)$ is a finite abelian group of order $\hat{n} := q \cdot \hat{s}$. The factor $\hat{s}$ remains unknown, but we are given an upper bound $\bar{s} \geq \hat{s}$. Moreover $\gcd(q, \hat{s}) = 1$, and the size of $\hat{s}$ depends on the security parameter λ. Taking the qth powers gives us the subgroup $\widehat{G}^q \subset \widehat{G}$, and $F = \langle f \rangle \subset \widehat{G}$ is the unique subgroup of order q. Hence, $\widehat{G}$ factors as $\widehat{G} \simeq \widehat{G}^q \times F$. While $\widehat{G}$ acts as base group, we are more interested in the cyclic subgroup $G \subset \widehat{G}$ of order $n := q \cdot s$. Whereas elements of $\widehat{G}$ are efficiently recognizable, this does not hold for elements of $G \subset \widehat{G}$. Again, $G^q = \langle g_q \rangle$ denotes the (cyclic) subgroup of qth powers, and G factors as $G \simeq G^q \times F$ with $g := g_q \cdot f$ being a generator of G. Given the output of CLGen, the second algorithm $\mathsf{CLSolve}$ deterministically and efficiently solves the discrete logarithm problem in the subgroup F.

Distributions. Protocols in the CL framework make use of distributions $\mathcal{D}$ and $\mathcal{D}_q$ over the integers, such that $\{g^x \mid x \leftarrow \mathcal{D}\}$ and $\{g_q^x \mid x \leftarrow \mathcal{D}_q\}$ induce almost uniform distributions over G and G^q, respectively. E.g., $\mathcal{D}$ can be instantiated by sampling a uniform integer from the interval $\{0, \ldots, q\bar{s}/(4\delta) - 1\}$. Then $\{g^x \mid x \leftarrow \mathcal{D}\}$ is δ-close, i.e., has statistical distance at most δ, to the uniform distribution over G [38, S. 3.1.3]. To get a statistical distance of at most $2^{-\sigma}$, we can set the upper bound of the interval to $q\bar{s} \cdot 2^{\sigma-2} - 1$.

Assumptions. We make use of the well-known unknown order assumption (ORD) for class groups stating that it is hard to find a multiple of $\mathrm{ord}(h)$ for any $h \in (\widehat{G} \setminus F)$. We also use the hard subgroup membership assumption (HSM) by [13] which says random elements of G and $\widehat{G}^q$ are indistinguishable. We refer to the full version [9] for the formal definitions of ORD and HSM. The next assumption says that class groups with no small prime factors in their order are indistinguishable from class groups in general.

Definition 1 (Rough Order Assumption). *Let λ be a security parameter, $|q| \geq \lambda$ prime, $C \in \mathbb{N}$, and $\mathcal{A}$ be a PPT algorithm. Define $\mathcal{D}_C^{\mathsf{rough}}$ to be the uniform distribution over the set* $\{\rho \in \{0,1\}^\lambda \mid (q, \bar{s}, f, g_q, \widehat{G}, F; \rho) \leftarrow \mathsf{CLGen}(1^\lambda, q; \rho) \wedge$

---

[3] [11, Sec. 3.2] remarks that the randomness used in their instantiation of CLGen is not crucial for security, but traditionally random discriminants are used for class-group-based crypto. Hence, we can use publicly known randomness $\rho \in \{0,1\}^\lambda$.

$\forall$ *prime* $p < C \; : \; p \nmid \mathrm{ord}(\widehat{G})\}$*, The experiment samples* $\rho_0 \in_R \{0,1\}^\lambda$*,* $\rho_1 \leftarrow \mathcal{D}_C^{\mathsf{rough}}$*, and* $b \in_R \{0,1\}$*, and runs* $b^* \leftarrow \mathcal{A}(1^\lambda, \rho_b, \mathsf{CLSolve}(\cdot))$*. We say* $\mathcal{A}$ *solves the* C-rough order *(*RO_C*)* problem *if it outputs* $b^* = b$*. We define its advantage* $\mathsf{Adv}_{\mathcal{A}}^{RO_C}$ *as its success probability. We say the* RO_C *assumption holds if* $\mathsf{Adv}_{\mathcal{A}}^{RO_C}$ *is negligible in* λ *for all PPT algorithms* $\mathcal{A}$*.*

This is a new assumption, and as such is not yet well studied. Our reasons for believing it is plausible are as follows: except for 2-powers, we do not know how to compute any non-trivial information on class group orders despite many years of research. Furthermore, Cohen and Lenstra [15] give heuristic arguments indicating that the fraction of discriminants less than some bound B for which a prime p divides the order of the corresponding class group is roughly the same as for random integers, as long as p is much smaller than B. This can be taken as evidence that random class group orders behave similarly to random integers w.r.t. the sizes of their prime factors. This would mean that a significant (and certainly non-negligible) fraction of class groups have C-rough order, as long as C is small compared to B, which is certainly the case for our parameters. Thus we are not comparing class groups in general to a vanishingly small (or even empty) subset. This also means that if our assumption would fail dramatically, so that a distinguisher with advantage essentially 1 was found, this would actually be great news, as this would allow us to sample class groups with rough order by trial and error.

Another thing to note is that the challenger in the security game corresponding to the assumption is not efficient, as we do not know how to sample class groups with C-rough order efficiently. This means the assumption has to be used with care, as indeed we do: the assumption is only used in the proof and nothing that would need to be implemented depends on the challenger. Incidentally, we are not the first to propose such an assumption: the gap-DDH assumption also has an inefficient challenger [33].

Proofs and Arguments in the CL Framework. [10] give a Σ-like protocol to prove knowledge of plaintext and randomness corresponding to ciphertexts of the HSM-CL encryption scheme of [13] (see Sect. 3), that can be simplified to proofs for discrete logarithms. To allow 2-special soundness in the unknown order setting, these protocols are restricted to binary challenges and, thus, need to be repeated to obtain a negligible soundness error.

In [11], the authors overcome this efficiency issue by basing the soundness on computational assumptions. Even with a large challenge spaces they show how to either extract a witness or to break either the strong root or the low order assumption. Since we only need limited or no extraction, we base the soundness of our arguments on the RO_C assumption instead.

3 The Linearly Homomorphic Encryption Scheme

In [13], Castagnos et al. presented the HSM-CL linearly homomorphic encryption scheme, which we denote as $\Pi_{\mathsf{hsm\text{-}cl}}$. It provides IND-CPA security under the HSM assumption. A public key has the form $g_q^{\mathsf{sk_{cl}}}$, where the secret key is sampled as $\mathsf{sk_{cl}} \leftarrow \mathcal{D}_q$. A message $m \in \mathbb{F}_q$ is encrypted with randomness $r \leftarrow \mathcal{D}_q$ as $\mathsf{Enc}(\mathsf{pk_{cl}}, m; r) = (g_q^r, f^m \cdot \mathsf{pk_{cl}}^r)$.

We use ct to denote a ciphertext and overload the $\cdot$ and $+$ operators to denote homomorphic operations: $a \cdot \mathsf{ct}_x + \mathsf{ct}_y + b$ denotes a sequence of scalar multiplication, and addition of ciphertexts and constants without randomization, and $a \cdot_R^{r_1} \mathsf{ct}_x +_R^{r_2} \mathsf{ct}_y +_R^{r_3} b$ is the same sequence randomized with r_1, r_2, r_3 (which we might omit if not explicitly needed).

We need to make some modification to the original HSM-CL encryption scheme $\Pi_{\mathsf{hsm\text{-}cl}}$ to make it work with our protocols and the proof strategy for our MPC protocol. The new procedures are specified in Fig. 1. Starting from the original scheme $\Pi_{\mathsf{hsm\text{-}cl}} = (\mathsf{Setup}, \mathsf{KeyGen}, \mathsf{Enc}, \mathsf{Dec})$, we construct the new encryption scheme $\Pi^*_{\mathsf{hsm\text{-}cl}}$ in two steps:

1. The original KeyGen procedure samples key pairs that are distributed almost-uniformly in G^q. Our distributed key generation protocol, however, allows the adversary to bias the distribution of the generated keys, as we will discuss in Sect. 6. We show that despite this bias the encryption scheme $\Pi^1_{\mathsf{hsm\text{-}cl}} := (\mathsf{Setup}, \mathsf{BiasedKeyGen}^{\mathcal{A}}, \mathsf{Enc}, \mathsf{Dec})$ is still secure.
2. The proof strategy for our MPC protocol (given in Sect. 7) follows [21] and requires an encryption scheme with a particular property: There needs to be a second key generation algorithm that produces lossy public keys. These need to be indistinguishable to normal public keys, but encryptions under these keys should be statistically indistinguishable to encryptions of zero. Hence, we define a special key generation algorithm $\mathsf{BiasedSpecialKeyGen}_b^{\mathcal{A}}$ that outputs a public key $\widetilde{\mathsf{pk}}_{\mathsf{cl}}$ which includes a ciphertext ct_P which is an encryption of b. In the real protocol $b = 1$ so encryption with SEnc uses the homomorphic property to multiply the message with ct_P. In the proof, when $b = 0$, a lossy public key is produced instead. Therefore, encrypting an arbitrary message always results in an encryption of 0. Moreover, during the generation of ct_P the adversary can once more bias the distribution, which also needs to be handled by the security proof. Our final encryption scheme is defined as $\Pi^*_{\mathsf{hsm\text{-}cl}} := (\mathsf{Setup}, \mathsf{BiasedSpecialKeyGen}_1^{\mathcal{A}}, \mathsf{SEnc}, \mathsf{Dec})$.

The main result of this section is the following Theorem 1. In the following, we prove a series of lemmas that, when combined, yield the theorem as a corollary.

Theorem 1 (Security of $\Pi^*_{\mathsf{hsm\text{-}cl}}$). *Under the HSM assumption, $\Pi^*_{\mathsf{hsm\text{-}cl}}$*

1. provides indistinguishability under chosen-plaintext attacks (IND-CPA), and
2. has lossy public keys which are indistinguishable from real public keys.

Handling Biased Keys. Our efficient distributed key generation protocol allows the adversary to bias the distribution of the keys. We prove that the bias does not affect the security, and exploit the homomorphic properties to reduce its security to that of $\Pi_{\mathsf{hsm\text{-}cl}}$.

$\underline{\mathsf{BiasedKeyGen}^{\mathcal{A}}(\mathsf{pp_{cl}})}$

1. Sample $\alpha \leftarrow \mathcal{D}_q$.
2. Set $\mathsf{pk}^*_{\mathsf{cl}} := g_q^{\alpha}$.
3. $\delta \leftarrow \mathcal{A}(\mathsf{pp_{cl}}, \mathsf{pk}^*_{\mathsf{cl}})$.
4. $\mathsf{sk_{cl}} := \alpha + \delta$ and $\mathsf{pk_{cl}} := g_q^{\mathsf{sk_{cl}}} = g_q^{\alpha+\delta}$.
5. Output $(\mathsf{pk_{cl}}, \mathsf{sk_{cl}})$.

$\underline{\mathsf{SEnc}(\widetilde{\mathsf{pk}}_{\mathsf{cl}}, m \in \mathbb{F}_q; r)}$

1. Parse $\widetilde{\mathsf{pk}}_{\mathsf{cl}} = (\mathsf{pk_{cl}}, \mathsf{ct}_P)$.
2. Output $\mathsf{ct} := m \cdot_R^r \mathsf{ct}_P$.

$\underline{\mathsf{BiasedSpecialKeyGen}_b^{\mathcal{A}}(\mathsf{pp_{cl}})}$ for $b \in \{0,1\}$

1. $(\mathsf{pk_{cl}}, \mathsf{sk_{cl}}) \leftarrow \mathsf{BiasedKeyGen}^{\mathcal{A}}(\mathsf{pp_{cl}})$.
2. Sample $\beta \leftarrow \mathcal{D}_q$.
3. Set $\mathsf{ct}^*_P := (g_q^{\beta}, f^b \cdot \mathsf{pk}_{\mathsf{cl}}^{\beta})$.
4. $\varepsilon \leftarrow \mathcal{A}(\mathsf{pp_{cl}}, \mathsf{pk_{cl}}, \mathsf{ct}^*_P)$.
5. $\widetilde{\mathsf{pk}}_{\mathsf{cl}} := (\mathsf{pk_{cl}}, (g_q^{\beta+\varepsilon}, f^b \cdot \mathsf{pk}_{\mathsf{cl}}^{\beta+\varepsilon}))$.
6. Output $(\widetilde{\mathsf{pk}}_{\mathsf{cl}}, \mathsf{sk_{cl}})$.

Fig. 1. Modified key generation, and encryption algorithms that allow an adversary $\mathcal{A}$ to influence the distribution of public keys in a limited way.

Lemma 2 (IND-CPA Security of $\Pi^1_{\mathsf{hsm\text{-}cl}}$). *If $\Pi_{\mathsf{hsm\text{-}cl}}$ is indistinguishabile under chosen-plaintext attacks (IND-CPA) then so is $\Pi^1_{\mathsf{hsm\text{-}cl}}$.*

Proof. We prove the claim by showing that any adversary $\mathcal{B}$ that wins the IND-CPA game for $\Pi^1_{\mathsf{hsm\text{-}cl}}$ with advantage $\mathsf{Adv}_{\mathcal{B}}^{\mathsf{hsm\text{-}cl},1}$ can be transformed into an adversary $\mathcal{A}$ for $\Pi_{\mathsf{hsm\text{-}cl}}$ with the same advantage $\mathsf{Adv}_{\mathcal{A}}^{\mathsf{hsm\text{-}cl}} = \mathsf{Adv}_{\mathcal{B}}^{\mathsf{hsm\text{-}cl},1}$. Given an adversary $\mathcal{B}$, we create $\mathcal{A}$ as follows: Initially $\mathcal{A}$ receives public parameters $\mathsf{pp_{cl}}$ and a public key $\mathsf{pk_{cl}}$ from the challenger. It gives $\mathsf{pk_{cl}}$ to $\mathcal{B}$, which responds with δ. Define the biased public key $\mathsf{pk}'_{\mathsf{cl}} := \mathsf{pk_{cl}} \cdot g_q^{\delta}$. This phase corresponds to the $\mathsf{BiasedKeyGen}^{\mathcal{B}}(\mathsf{pp_{cl}})$ procedure. Then $\mathcal{B}$ selects $m_0, m_1 \in \mathbb{F}_q$, which $\mathcal{A}$ forwards to the challenger. The challenger samples $b \in_R \{0,1\}$, encrypts m_b and sends the resulting $\mathsf{ct} = (\mathsf{ct}_1, \mathsf{ct}_2)$ to $\mathcal{A}$. $\mathcal{A}$ sends $\mathsf{ct}' = (\mathsf{ct}'_1, \mathsf{ct}'_2) = (\mathsf{ct}_1, \mathsf{ct}_2 \cdot \mathsf{ct}_1^{\delta})$ to $\mathcal{B}$. Finally, $\mathcal{B}$ outputs a bit $b' \in \{0,1\}$, and $\mathcal{A}$ forwards this output to the challenger.

The challenger creates the ciphertext $\mathsf{ct} = (g_q^r, \mathsf{pk}_{\mathsf{cl}}^r \cdot f^{m_b})$, where r denotes the randomness used during the encryption. We have $\mathsf{pk}'_{\mathsf{cl}} = \mathsf{pk_{cl}} \cdot g_q^{\delta}$ and

$$\mathsf{ct}' = \left(g_q^r, (\mathsf{pk}_{\mathsf{cl}}^r \cdot f^{m_b}) \cdot (g_q^r)^{\delta}\right) = \left(g_q^r, (\mathsf{pk_{cl}} \cdot g_q^{\delta})^r \cdot f^{m_b}\right) = \left(g_q^r, (\mathsf{pk}'_{\mathsf{cl}})^r \cdot f^{m_b}\right).$$

Therefore, ct' is a valid encryption of m_b under the biased public key $\mathsf{pk}'_{\mathsf{cl}}$ with the same distribution as it would normally have. Overall, $\mathcal{A}$ wins the game iff $\mathcal{B}$ answers correctly, which happens with probability $1/2 + \mathsf{Adv}_{\mathcal{B}}^{\mathsf{hsm\text{-}cl},1}$. Hence, the advantage in the case of biased keys is the same as in the standard scheme. □

Special Public Keys. In Fig. 1 we specify the key generation algorithm $\mathsf{BiasedSpecialKeyGen}_b^{\mathcal{A}}$ parametrized by a bit $b \in \{0,1\}$. $\mathsf{BiasedSpecialKeyGen}_1^{\mathcal{A}}$ produces working public keys, whereas $\mathsf{BiasedSpecialKeyGen}_0^{\mathcal{A}}$ produces lossy public keys. Each special public key $\widetilde{\mathsf{pk}}_{\mathsf{cl}}$ consists of a normal public key $\mathsf{pk_{cl}}$ and a ciphertext ct_P that is an encryption of $b \in \{0,1\}$. First we show that the distributions of working public keys ($b = 1$) and lossy public keys ($b = 0$) produced by $\mathsf{BiasedSpecialKeyGen}_b^{\mathcal{A}}$ are indistinguishable.

Lemma 3 ($\Pi^*_{hsm\text{-}cl}$ has Indistinguishable Lossy Keys). *If $\Pi^1_{hsm\text{-}cl}$ is IND-CPA secure, then $\Pi^*_{hsm\text{-}cl}$ has lossy public keys which are indistinguishable from real public keys.*

Since working and lossy public keys are encryptions of 1 and 0, an efficient distinguisher would break IND-CPA security of $\Pi^1_{\mathsf{hsm\text{-}cl}}$. The complete proof is given in the full version [9]. Now we show that the final encryption scheme $\Pi^*_{\mathsf{hsm\text{-}cl}}$ is actually IND-CPA secure.

Lemma 4 (IND-CPA Security of $\Pi^*_{hsm\text{-}cl}$). *If $\Pi^*_{hsm\text{-}cl}$ has indistinguishable lossy public keys as defined in Lemma 3, then $\Pi^*_{hsm\text{-}cl}$ provides indistinguishability under chosen-plaintext attacks (IND-CPA).*

IND-CPA security of $\Pi^*_{\mathsf{hsm\text{-}cl}}$ follows from the fact that real keys are indistinguishable from lossy keys, and the fact that when lossy keys are used then the encryptions are (statistically) independent of the encrypted message. The full proof is given in the full version [9]. Now Theorem 1 follows as a corollary of the lemmas in this section.

4 Secret Sharing over the Integers

For our threshold encryption scheme in Sect. 6, we need a threshold secret sharing scheme to share a secret key of the $\Pi^*_{\mathsf{hsm\text{-}cl}}$ encryption scheme. Any majority of at least $t+1 > N/2$ parties needs to be able to (implicitly) reconstruct the secret key to decrypt ciphertexts.

Since we work in an unknown order setting, the secret key of $\Pi^*_{\mathsf{hsm\text{-}cl}}$ is an integer and not a field element. Hence, the standard Shamir's secret sharing scheme [37] over a finite field does not work for us: We need a secret sharing scheme that is suitable for sharing integers (from a bounded interval). Moreover, Lagrange interpolation requires division, but we cannot simply divide modulo the unknown group order to reconstruct the secret key in the exponent.

Similar problems have appeared in the construction of threshold RSA systems, where the group order is also unknown unless the factorization of the modulus is revealed [23,27,36]. It is usually solved by multiplying the Lagrange coefficients with a suitable factor to eliminate the denominator. We also use a Shamir-style secret sharing scheme over $\mathbb{Z}$ with a polynomial of degree t.

The next challenge is to make sure that the dealer distributes consistent shares that allow reconstruction of the secret, and that during reconstruction every party publishes its correct share. We use a variant of Feldman's verifiable secret sharing scheme [25] adapted to the our class group setting in a similar way as [36] for threshold RSA.

Secret Sharing over $\mathbb{Z}$. To share a secret from a bounded range $\alpha \in [0, 2^\ell)$ with $(t+1)$-out-of-N reconstruction, we could use a random degree-t polynomial $f(X)$ such that $f(0) = \alpha$ and giving P_i the share $y_i := f(i)$ for $i \in [N]$. First, note that $f(i)$ reveals $\alpha \bmod i$. Hence, we share $\tilde{\alpha} := \alpha \cdot \Delta$ instead, where $\Delta := N!$. Then, we also need to make sure that the random coefficients of f are sampled from a large enough interval to hide α.

Protocol 1 (Shamir's Secret Sharing over $\mathbb{Z}$). Let N be the number of parties, t the corruption threshold, ℓ a bound on the secret size, and σ a statistical security parameter. Moreover, let $\ell_0 \in \mathbb{N}$ be a parameter. To share a secret $\alpha \in [0, 2^{\ell})$ the dealer proceeds as follows:

1. Let $\tilde{\alpha} := \alpha \cdot \Delta$ with $\Delta := N!$.
2. Sample $\mathbf{r} = (r_1, \ldots, r_t) \in_R [0, 2^{\ell_0+\sigma})^t$
3. Set $f(X) := \tilde{\alpha} + r_1 \cdot X + \cdots + r_t \cdot X^t$.
4. Send $y_i := f(i)$ over a private channel to party P_i for $i \in [N]$.

We denote this as $\mathsf{Share}(\alpha, \mathbf{r})$ when α is shared using the random coins $\mathbf{r}$, and use $\mathsf{Share}_i(\alpha, \mathbf{r})$ to denote the share of P_i.

Privacy. Statistically no information about the shared secret should be revealed by any set of up to t shares. We formally define and prove privacy for Protocol 1 in the full version [9], similarly to linear integer secret sharing schemes [19,22].[4]

Integer Reconstruction. By Lagrange interpolation, any subset S of at least $t+1$ parties can combine their shares to reconstruct the secret. We have

$$f(X) = \sum_{i \in S} y_i \cdot \ell_i^S(X) \quad \text{with} \quad \ell_i^S(X) = \prod_{j \in S \setminus \{i\}} \frac{x_j - X}{x_j - x_i}. \tag{1}$$

We also write the Lagrange coefficients at 0 (jointly often referred to as reconstruction vector) as $\ell_i^S := \ell_i^S(0)$. Clearly reconstruction also works for integer polynomials f, but the Lagrange coefficients are not necessarily integers. If we need to reconstruct without division, then we can multiply Lagrange coefficients by Δ, since $\Delta \cdot \ell_i^S(X) \in \mathbb{Z}[X]$ for all i and S, although we are reconstructing the value $\Delta \cdot f(X)$ instead of $f(X)$. Hence, we can use Shamir's secret sharing over the integers to reconstruct a secret $\alpha \cdot \Delta^2$ in the exponent of a group element with unknown order. Similarly, we can also recover the polynomial itself from a sufficient number of shares. In the full version [9] we show that we can reconstruct $\Delta \cdot f$ by using $\mathbb{Z}$ linear combinations of the shares.

Feldman VSS. We now adapt Feldman's verifiable secret sharing scheme [25] to the class group setting. In [36], Rabin has already provided a variant of this for threshold RSA, but our techniques are slightly different.[5] In the following, we assume that public parameters $\mathsf{pp_{cl}}$ are given together with a designated group element $g_{\mathsf{F}} \in (\widehat{G} \setminus F)$.

Protocol 2 (Feldman VSS). To share a secret $\alpha \in [0, 2^{\ell})$, the dealer shares it as $(y_1, \ldots, y_N) \leftarrow \mathsf{Share}(\alpha, \mathbf{r})$ (see Protocol 1). It sends y_i privately to P_i, and

[4] We can see Protocol 1 as a linear integer secret sharing (LISS) [19,22] variant, with the difference that we reconstruct $\alpha \cdot \Delta^2$ The distribution matrix is a Vandermonde matrix, and the distribution vector is the vector of coefficients of the polynomial.

[5] [36] uses generators $g_0, g := g_0^{\Delta^2}$ of maximal order in $\mathbb{Z}_n^*$ and then g as base in the Feldman scheme. Rabin does not prove the reconstruction property, but claims it follows directly from Feldman's work. We could not reproduce the proof and, therefore, use a slightly different construction.

additionally, broadcasts values $C_0 := g_{\mathsf{F}}^{\alpha}$ and $C_k := g_{\mathsf{F}}^{\Delta \cdot r_k}$ for $k \in [t]$, where $\Delta := N!$. Party P_i verifies its share y_i by checking that

$$g_{\mathsf{F}}^{\Delta \cdot y_i} \stackrel{?}{=} C_0^{\Delta^2} \cdot \prod_{k=1}^{t} (C_k)^{(i^k)} \tag{2}$$

holds, and broadcasts a complaint otherwise. Moreover, the dealer needs to prove in zero-knowledge that $C_0, \ldots, C_t \in \langle g_{\mathsf{F}} \rangle$, e.g., by proving knowledge of discrete logarithms of all C_i to base g_{F}. During reconstruction, Eq. (2) can be used to verify that the parties publish the correct shares. For the sharing procedure we write $(y_1, \ldots, y_N; C_0, \ldots, C_t) \leftarrow \mathsf{F\text{-}Share}(\alpha; \mathbf{r}; g_{\mathsf{F}})$, and $\{\bot, \top\} \leftarrow \mathsf{F\text{-}Check}(i, y_i; C_0, \ldots, C_t; g_{\mathsf{F}})$ denotes the verification.

We prove in the full version [9] that Protocol 2 has the desired reconstruction properties:

Lemma 5 (Feldman Reconstruction). *If* $\gcd(\Delta, \operatorname{ord}(g_{\mathsf{F}})) = 1$, *and under the (ORD) assumption, we have*

(i) Given $C_0, \ldots, C_t \in \langle g_{\mathsf{F}} \rangle$, a proof of knowledge of the discrete logarithm of C_0, and $t+1$ shares $y_{i_1}, \ldots, y_{i_{t+1}}$ such that Equation (2) *holds. Then there exists an efficient algorithm which the parties can use to find (except with negligible probability) a value $\alpha \in \mathbb{Z}$ such that $C_0 = g_{\mathsf{F}}^{\alpha}$.*

(ii) Moreover, any collection of $t+1$ shares which pass the check in Equation (2) *can be used to recover the same value α* $\pmod{\operatorname{ord}(g_{\mathsf{F}})}$.

Why is the assumption $\gcd(\Delta, \operatorname{ord}(g_{\mathsf{F}}))$ sensible? To obtain such a g_{F}, one can raise a given element $g'_{\mathsf{F}} \in \widehat{G} \setminus F$ to large enough powers of all primes up to N. This eliminates all small prime factors in the order of g_{F}. Otherwise, if a base $g_{\mathsf{F}} \in G^q$ is already given, one can rely on the RO_{N+1} assumption (Definition 1). This allows us to pretend that $\gcd(\Delta, \operatorname{ord}(g_{\mathsf{F}})) = 1$ holds, because the adversary cannot distinguish the two cases.

Simulating VSS with Fixed C_0. In the simulation of higher level protocols (see Sect. 6), we need to fake a Feldman VSS towards the adversary where the checking value C_0 cannot be chosen freely, but needs to be a prescribed value. First, we use Protocol 1 to share an arbitrary value $\tilde{\alpha}$ such that the corrupted parties obtains shares $(x_1, y_1), \ldots, (x_t, y_t) \in \mathbb{Z}^2$, We use the following lemma, which we prove in the full version [9], to find values $C_1, \ldots, C_t \in \langle g_{\mathsf{F}} \rangle$ that matches the adversary's view:

Lemma 6 (Feldman Simulation). *Given $C_0 \in \langle g_{\mathsf{F}} \rangle$ and $(x_1, y_1), \ldots, (x_t, y_t) \in \mathbb{Z}^2$, $1 \leq x_1 < \cdots < x_t \leq N$, we can efficiently find $C_1, \ldots, C_t \in \langle g_{\mathsf{F}} \rangle$ such that $\mathsf{F\text{-}Check}(x_j, y_j; C_0, \ldots, C_t, g_{\mathsf{F}})$ is satisfied for all (x_j, y_j), $j \in [t]$. Moreover, the values $C_1, \ldots, C_t \in \langle g_{\mathsf{F}} \rangle$ have, conditioned on C_0 and $(x_j, y_j)_{j \in [t]}$, the same distribution as produced by* F-Share.

5 Zero-Knowledge

For our protocols we need zero-knowledge arguments for several different relations. First, we need arguments for the discrete logarithm and equal discrete logarithm relations, $\mathsf{R}_{\mathsf{DLog}}$ and $\mathsf{R}_{\mathsf{EqDLog}}$. These relations are defined with respect to CL public parameters $\mathsf{pp}_{\mathsf{cl}}$ which we leave implicit in the notation.

$$\mathsf{R}_{\mathsf{DLog}} := \{(g,h);x \mid g,h \in \widehat{G} \wedge x \in \mathbb{Z} \wedge h = g^x\} \tag{3}$$

$$\mathsf{R}_{\mathsf{EqDLog}} := \{(g_1,g_2,h_1,h_2);x \mid ((g_i,h_i);x) \in \mathsf{R}_{\mathsf{DLog}} \text{ for } i = 1,2\} \tag{4}$$

We use $\Pi^{\mathsf{bin}}_{\mathsf{DLog}}$ and $\Pi^{\mathsf{bin}}_{\mathsf{EqDLog}}$ to denote the standard Σ protocols for these relations with binary challenges and parallel repetitions. Then, we also need proofs of plaintext knowledge (PoPK) for $\Pi^*_{\mathsf{hsm\text{-}cl}}$ ciphertexts, that allow the extraction of the plaintext, as well as proofs of correct multiplication (PoCM). We use Σ-like protocols [16], which can be specified by three PPT algorithms (Commit, Respond, Verify) and a challenge space. In this work we consider *zero-knowledge arguments* of the same shape that satisfy statistical special honest-verifier zero-knowledge (SHVZK) and completeness for witnesses of a bounded size, as well as computational soundness for language membership, since in most cases it is not necessary to extract the (full) witness. Formal definitions are given in the full version [9]. In Sect. 5 we obtain arguments for general relations of class group elements, and Sect. 5 covers the protocols for $\Pi^*_{\mathsf{hsm\text{-}cl}}$ ciphertexts.

ZK Arguments for General Relations. Here we consider proofs for general relations R, which are conjunctions of n statements containing m secrets:

$$\mathsf{R} = \Big\{(Y_i, \mathbf{X}_i)_{i\in[n]}; \mathbf{w} \;\Big|\; \bigwedge_{i=1}^{n} [Y_i = \prod_{j=1}^{m} X_{i,j}^{w_j}] \wedge \text{ all } X \in \widehat{G}^{n(m+1)} \wedge \mathbf{w} \in \mathbb{Z}^m\Big\}. \tag{5}$$

The statement $X := (Y_i, \mathbf{X}_i)_{i\in[n]}$ consists of elements of $\widehat{G}$ either defined by the context, or chosen by $\mathcal{P}$, and the witness $\mathbf{w}$ usually consists of integers from a bounded range $w_j \in [-S, +S]$. The protocols are sound with respect to R, but completeness and SHVZK are only guaranteed for witnesses from this interval.[6]

For such a relation, we can write the canonical Σ protocol $\mathsf{C\Sigma P(R)}$ where $A, C \in \mathbb{N}$ are parameters:

- $\mathsf{Commit}(X, \mathbf{w})$: Sample $\mathsf{stt} := (r_1, \ldots, r_m) \in_R [A]^m$, compute $t_i := \prod_{j=1}^m X_{i,j}^{r_j}$ for $i \in [n]$, and output $(\mathsf{stt}, \mathsf{com} := (t_i)_{i\in[n]})$.
- The challenge is sampled $\mathsf{chl} \in_R [C]$.
- $\mathsf{Respond}(X, \mathbf{w}, \mathsf{stt}, \mathsf{chl})$: Compute $u_j := r_j + \mathsf{chl} \cdot w_j$ for $j \in [m]$, and output $\mathsf{res} := (u_1, \ldots, u_m)$.
- $\mathsf{Verify}(X, \mathsf{com}, \mathsf{chl}, \mathsf{res})$: If $Y_i, X_{i,j} \in \widehat{G}$ for $i \in [n], j \in [m]$, $u_j \in [-SC, +SC + A]$ for $j \in [m]$, and $t_i \cdot Y_i^{\mathsf{chl}} = \prod_{j=1}^m X_{i,j}^{u_j}$ for $i \in [n]$ output $\top$, otherwise $\perp$.
- $\mathsf{Simulate}(X, \mathsf{chl})$: Sample $\mathsf{res} := (u_1, \ldots, u_m) \in_R [-SC, +SC + A]^m$, compute $t_i := Y_i^{-\mathsf{chl}} \cdot \prod_{j\in[m]} X_{i,j}^{u_j}$ for $i \in [n]$, and output $(\mathsf{com} := (t_i)_{i\in[n]}, \mathsf{res})$.

For this class of protocols, we can show the following properties:

[6] For simplicity, we use the same bounds $[-S, +S]$ for each secret, but we could also specify separate bounds for each secret $s_j \in [-S_j, +S_j]$ and sample the randomness $r_j \in_R [A_j]$ s.t. S_jC/A_j is negligible for every $j \in [m]$. This makes the protocol description more complicated, but it would be more efficient when we have secrets of different sizes.

Theorem 7. *If* R *be a relation as described in Eq. 5, then:*

(i) $\mathsf{C\Sigma P(R)}$ *is sound for* R *with soundness error* $1/C + \mathsf{negl}(\lambda)$ *under the* RO_C *assumption.* [7]
(ii) $\mathsf{C\Sigma P(R)}$ *is complete for* R *if* $\mathbf{w} \in [-S, +S]^m$.
(iii) $\mathsf{C\Sigma P(R)}$ *is statistical special honest-verifier zero-knowledge if* $\mathbf{w} \in [-S, +S]^m$ *and* SC/A *is negligible.*

Proof. While the proofs of completeness and SHVZK are standard (given in the full version [9]), the soundness proof (i) is more involved and relies on our RO_C assumption:

Consider a malicious PPT prover $\mathcal{P}^*$ that generates an instance X such that there is no witness $\mathbf{w}$ such that $(X, \mathbf{w}) \in \mathsf{R}$. Now $\mathcal{P}^*$ can guess $\mathcal{V}$'s random challenge $\mathsf{chl} \in_R [C]$ with probability $1/C$ and use the simulator (cf. (iii)) to obtain a transcript which makes $\mathcal{V}$ accept.

Assume towards contradiction that $\mathcal{P}^*$ had a success probability that is strictly larger than $1/C$, and suppose $\mathrm{ord}(\widehat{G})$ was C-rough. Then, by averaging, there exists a first message com such that there exist third messages $\mathsf{res}, \mathsf{res}'$ for two different challenges $\mathsf{chl} \neq \mathsf{chl}'$ such that $\mathcal{V}$ accepts both $(\mathsf{com}, \mathsf{chl}, \mathsf{res})$ and $(\mathsf{com}, \mathsf{chl}', \mathsf{res}')$.

Note that all relevant group elements live in the subgroup $\langle Y_i, X_{i,j}\rangle_{i,j} \subseteq \widehat{G}$. Let $\ell := \mathrm{ord}(\langle Y_i, X_{i,j}\rangle_{i,j}) \mid \prod_i \mathrm{ord}(Y_i) \cdot \prod_{i,j} \mathrm{ord}(X_{i,j})$. Since $\mathrm{ord}(\widehat{G})$ is C-rough, ℓ must also be C-rough. Hence, as $|\mathsf{chl} - \mathsf{chl}'| < C$, $(\mathsf{chl} - \mathsf{chl}')$ is invertible modulo ℓ, i.e., we can find an integer $(\mathsf{chl} - \mathsf{chl}')^{-1} \in \mathbb{Z}$ such that $(\mathsf{chl} - \mathsf{chl}') \cdot (\mathsf{chl} - \mathsf{chl}')^{-1} = 1 \pmod{\ell}$. Therefore we have

$$\left[t_i \cdot Y_i^{\mathsf{chl}} = \prod_{i \in [m]} X_{i,j}^{u_j}\right] \wedge \left[t_i \cdot Y_i^{\mathsf{chl}'} = \prod_{i \in [m]} X_{i,j}^{u'_j}\right] \implies$$

$$Y_i^{\mathsf{chl} - \mathsf{chl}'} = \prod_{i \in [m]} X_{i,j}^{u_j - u'_j} \iff Y_i = \prod_{i \in [m]} X_{i,j}^{(u_j - u'_j) \cdot (\mathsf{chl} - \mathsf{chl}')^{-1}},$$

where all the exponents are considered integers. By setting $w_j := (u_j - u'_j) \cdot (\mathsf{chl} - \mathsf{chl}')^{-1}$ for $j \in [m]$ and $\mathbf{w} := (w_1, \ldots, w_m)$ we have found a witness such that $(X, \mathbf{w}) \in \mathsf{R}$ and, therefore, reached a contradiction.

So such a $\mathcal{P}^*$ cannot exist or $\mathrm{ord}(\widehat{G})$ is not C-rough after all. Hence, if we had such a $\mathcal{P}^*$, we could distinguish groups $\widehat{G}$ that do not have a C-rough order. By the RO_C assumption, such a distinguisher has at most negligible advantage. We conclude that $\mathsf{C\Sigma P(R)}$ has a soundness error of $1/C + \mathsf{negl}(\lambda)$. □

Corollary 8. *The protocols* $\Pi_{\mathsf{DLog}} := \mathsf{C\Sigma P}(\mathsf{R}_{\mathsf{DLog}})$ *and* $\Pi_{\mathsf{EqDLog}} := \mathsf{C\Sigma P}(\mathsf{R}_{\mathsf{EqDLog}})$ *are zero-knowledge arguments with* $\mathsf{D} := [-S, +S]$ *for the relations* $\mathsf{R}_{\mathsf{DLog}}$ *and* $\mathsf{R}_{\mathsf{EqDLog}}$*, respectively.*

[7] Note that the soundness property does not require the existence of a witness $\mathbf{w}$ such that each w_j is within the range $[-S, +S]$.

Proofs of Plaintext Knowledge and Correct Multiplication. For our MPC protocol in Sect. 7, we need additional protocols that are not only sound, but also allow for partial extraction of the witnesses. First, we need the parties to prove that whenever they publish a ciphertext, it is a) well-formed and b) they know the corresponding plaintext.

$$\mathsf{R}_{\mathsf{Enc}} = \{\mathsf{ct}; (m, s) \mid \mathsf{ct}_1 = \mathsf{ct}_{P1}^m \cdot \tilde{g}_q^s \wedge \mathsf{ct}_2 = \mathsf{ct}_{P2}^m \cdot \mathsf{pk}_{\mathsf{cl}}^s\} \tag{6}$$

The relation $\mathsf{R}_{\mathsf{Enc}}$ is parametrized by public parameters $\mathsf{pp}_{\mathsf{cl}}$ and a special public key $\widetilde{\mathsf{pk}_{\mathsf{cl}}} = (\mathsf{pk}_{\mathsf{cl}}, \mathsf{ct}_P)$, where $\mathsf{ct}_P = (\mathsf{ct}_{P1}, \mathsf{ct}_{P2})$ is an encryption of 1 (or 0 in the case of a lossy public key, see Sect. 3), but we generally omit them from the notation. We do not require a full argument of knowledge, since we only need to extract the encrypted message $a \in \mathbb{F}_q$, but not the randomness s. Therefore, we give a specialized definition:

Definition 2 (Proof of Plaintext Knowledge). *Let Π be a zero-knowledge argument for the relation $\mathsf{R}_{\mathsf{Enc}}$ (Equation* (6)*) (defined for a valid public key $\widetilde{\mathsf{pk}_{\mathsf{cl}}}$) with witness domain $\mathsf{D} := \mathbb{F}_q \times \mathrm{dom}(\mathcal{D}_q)$. Let $\mathsf{sk}_{\mathsf{cl}}$ be a secret key matching the public key in $\mathsf{R}_{\mathsf{Enc}}$. We say Π is a* Proof of Plaintext Knowledge (PoPK) *if additionally there exists an efficient algorithm* Extract *and the following holds: Given two accepting transcripts* $(\mathsf{com}, \mathsf{chl}, \mathsf{res}), (\mathsf{com}, \mathsf{chl}', \mathsf{res}')$ *corresponding to a ciphertext* ct *such that* $\mathsf{chl} \neq \mathsf{chl}'$*, then*

(i) ct *can be correctly decrypted* $\mathsf{Dec}(\mathsf{sk}_{\mathsf{cl}}, \mathsf{ct}) = m \in \mathbb{F}_q$*,*
(ii) and the same value m can be extracted from the transcripts: $\mathsf{Extract}(\mathsf{ct}, (\mathsf{com}, \mathsf{chl}, \mathsf{res}), (\mathsf{com}, \mathsf{chl}', \mathsf{res}')) = m$.

We show in the full version [9] that the canonical protocol $\mathsf{C\Sigma P}(\mathsf{R}_{\mathsf{Enc}})$ satisfies the above condition and define the corresponding extractor Extract. Extraction of the message $m \in \mathbb{F}_q$ works, because it appears in the exponent of f of known order q. We cannot extract the randomness s, however, since we can neither invert $\mathsf{chl} - \mathsf{chl}'$ modulo the unknown order of g_q nor expect division over the integers to work. However, by using the RO_C assumption we are able to pretend that certain inverses exist modulo $\mathrm{ord}(g_q)$.

Theorem 9. *The protocol $\Pi_{PoPK} := \mathsf{C\Sigma P}(\mathsf{R}_{\mathsf{Enc}})$ is a Proof of Plaintext Knowledge under the RO_C assumption.*

In the multiplication part of our MPC protocol, a party needs to multiply a publicly known ciphertext ct_b (which we assume to be valid) with a private value $a \in \mathbb{F}_q$ that is additionally encrypted as ct_a to produce a new ciphertext ct_c. We formalize this in the following relation, where s is the randomness used to encrypt a, and s' is the randomness used to randomize the resulting ciphertext.

$$\begin{aligned}\mathsf{R}_{\mathsf{Mult}} = \{(\mathsf{ct}_a, \mathsf{ct}_b, \mathsf{ct}_c); (a, s, s') \mid (\mathsf{ct}_a; (a, s)) \in \mathsf{R}_{\mathsf{Enc}} \wedge \\ \mathsf{ct}_{c,1} = \mathsf{ct}_{b,1}^a \cdot \tilde{g}_q^{s'} \wedge \mathsf{ct}_{c,2} = \mathsf{ct}_{b,2}^a \cdot \mathsf{pk}_{\mathsf{cl}}^{s'}\}\end{aligned} \tag{7}$$

Definition 3 (Proof of Correct Multiplication). *Let Π be a zero-knowledge argument for the relation $\mathsf{R}_{\mathsf{Mult}}$ (Eq.* (7)*) (defined for a valid public* *key* $\widetilde{\mathsf{pk}_{\mathsf{cl}}}$*) with witness domain* $\mathsf{D} := \mathbb{F}_q \times \mathrm{dom}(\mathcal{D}_q)^2$. *We say* Π *is a* Proof of Correct Multiplication (PoCM) *if additionally it satisfies the PoPK extraction property (Definition 2) with respect to* ct_a.

Since $\mathsf{R}_{\mathsf{Mult}}$ is an extension of $\mathsf{R}_{\mathsf{Enc}}$, Theorem 9 immediately carries over:

Corollary 10. *The protocol* $\Pi_{\mathsf{Mult}} := \mathsf{C\Sigma P}(\mathsf{R}_{\mathsf{Mult}})$ *is a Proof of Correct Multiplication under the* RO_C *assumption.*

6 Threshold Linearly Homomorphic Encryption

Here, we present our novel threshold encryption scheme based on the linearly homomorphic encryption scheme $\Pi_{\mathsf{hsm\text{-}cl}}$ of [11,13]. To obtain a more efficient protocol we use the modified $\Pi^*_{\mathsf{hsm\text{-}cl}}$ encryption scheme (Sect. 3).

Ideal Functionality. We specify a UC functionality $\mathcal{F}_{\mathsf{TE}}$ in Fig. 2. Apart from the Init procedure, it allows the parties to generate a key pair $(\widetilde{\mathsf{pk}_{\mathsf{cl}}}, \mathsf{sk}_{\mathsf{cl}})$ such that the special public key $\widetilde{\mathsf{pk}_{\mathsf{cl}}}$ is made public, but nobody learns the corresponding secret key $\mathsf{sk}_{\mathsf{cl}}$. The KeyGen method allows the simulator $\mathcal{S}$ to influence the distribution of the generated key pair as specified by $\mathsf{BiasedSpecialKeyGen}_1^{\mathcal{S}}$ (Fig. 1). Moreover, the functionality allows parties to decrypt $\Pi_{\mathsf{hsm\text{-}cl}}$ ciphertexts using the stored secret key. Defining a single functionality that contains both the key generation and the decryption simplifies the simulation proof, since the environment never sees the honest parties' shares of the secret key. A similar approach is taken, e.g., in [1] for UC threshold Schnorr signatures.

Ideal Threshold Encryption Functionality $\mathcal{F}_{\mathsf{TE}}$

Init On input $(\mathsf{Init}, 1^\lambda, q)$ from all parties, $\mathcal{F}_{\mathsf{TE}}$ generates $\mathsf{pp}_{\mathsf{cl}} \leftarrow \mathsf{CLGen}(1^\lambda, q)$. It stores $\mathsf{pp}_{\mathsf{cl}}$ and outputs them to all parties. This method must be called exactly once, and before any other call.

KeyGen On input (KeyGen) from all parties, $\mathcal{F}_{\mathsf{TE}}$ runs $(\widetilde{\mathsf{pk}_{\mathsf{cl}}}, \mathsf{sk}_{\mathsf{cl}}) \leftarrow \mathsf{BiasedSpecialKeyGen}_1^{\mathcal{S}}(\mathsf{pp}_{\mathsf{cl}})$ with $\mathcal{S}$. When $\mathcal{S}$ responds with continue, $\mathcal{F}_{\mathsf{TE}}$ sends $\widetilde{\mathsf{pk}_{\mathsf{cl}}}$ to all parties. This method must be called exactly once, and before any call to Decrypt.

Decrypt On input (Decrypt, $\mathsf{ct} = (\mathsf{ct}_1, \mathsf{ct}_2) \in \widehat{G}^2$) from all parties, $\mathcal{F}_{\mathsf{TE}}$ computes $M := \mathsf{ct}_2 \cdot \mathsf{ct}_1^{-\mathsf{sk}_{\mathsf{cl}}}$ and sends M to $\mathcal{S}$.[a] If $\mathcal{S}$ responds with abort, $\mathcal{F}_{\mathsf{TE}}$ aborts. Otherwise, if it responds with continue, $\mathcal{F}_{\mathsf{TE}}$ sends $m \leftarrow \mathsf{CLSolve}(\mathsf{pp}_{\mathsf{cl}}, M)$ to all parties.

[a] We leak M instead of m to also be able to simulate the decryption in case ct is not a valid ciphertext since if $M \notin F \implies \mathsf{CLSolve}(\mathsf{pp}_{\mathsf{cl}}, M) = \bot$.

Fig. 2. Ideal Threshold Encryption Functionality

Protocol Π_{TE} (Part I)

The parties maintain a set $\mathcal{Q}$ of qualified parties initially containing all parties. After a party gets disqualified, it will be ignored by all honest parties.

Init Send $(\mathsf{Gen}, 1^\lambda, q)$ to $\mathcal{F}_{\mathsf{CL}}$ which returns $\mathsf{pp}_{\mathsf{cl}} = (q, \bar{s}, f, g_q, \widehat{G}, F; \rho)$.

KeyGen 1. Generation of a key pair $(\mathsf{pk}_{\mathsf{cl}}, \mathsf{sk}_{\mathsf{cl}})$. All P_i proceed in parallel:

(a) Sample the contribution to the secret key $\alpha_i \leftarrow \mathcal{D}_q$.

(b) Share α_i as $(y_{i,1}, \ldots, y_{i,N}; C_{i,0}, \ldots, C_{i,t}) \leftarrow \mathsf{F\text{-}Share}(\alpha_i; \mathbf{r}_i; g_q)$. such that $y_{i,j}$ is privately sent to P_j, and $C_{i,0}, \ldots, C_{i,t}$ are broadcasted.

(c) Compute $(\mathsf{com}^1_{i,k}, \mathsf{stt}^1_{i,k}) \leftarrow \Pi_{\mathsf{DLog}}.\mathsf{Commit}(C_{i,k}, r_{i,k})$ for $k \in [t]$ and $(\mathsf{com}^1_{i,0}, \mathsf{stt}^1_{i,0}) \leftarrow \Pi^{\mathsf{bin}}_{\mathsf{DLog}}.\mathsf{Commit}(C_{i,0}, \alpha_i)$. Broadcast $(\mathsf{com}^1_{i,k})_{k \in [0,t]}$.

(d) Send $(\mathsf{Rand}, [C])$ to $\mathcal{F}_{\mathsf{Rand}}$ so that all parties receive $\mathsf{chl}^1 \in_R [C]$.

(e) Broadcast $\mathsf{res}^1_{i,k} \leftarrow \Pi_{\mathsf{DLog}}.\mathsf{Respond}(C_{i,k}, r_{i,k}, \mathsf{stt}^1_{i,k}, \mathsf{chl}^1)$ for $k \in [t]$ and $\mathsf{res}^1_{i,0} \leftarrow \Pi^{\mathsf{bin}}_{\mathsf{DLog}}.\mathsf{Respond}(C_{i,0}, \alpha_i, \mathsf{stt}^1_{i,0}, \mathsf{chl}^1)$.

(f) Verify shares received from $P_j \neq P_i$: Check if

i. $\mathsf{F\text{-}Check}(i, y_{j,i}; C_{j,0}, \ldots, C_{j,t}; g_q) \stackrel{?}{=} \top$, and

ii. $\Pi_{\mathsf{DLog}}.\mathsf{Verify}(C_{j,k}, \mathsf{com}^1_{j,k}, \mathsf{chl}^1, \mathsf{res}^1_{j,k}) \stackrel{?}{=} \top$ for all $k \in [t]$, and $\Pi^{\mathsf{bin}}_{\mathsf{DLog}}.\mathsf{Verify}(C_{j,0}, \mathsf{com}^1_{j,0}, \mathsf{chl}^1, \mathsf{res}^1_{j,0}) \stackrel{?}{=} \top$.

If only Step 1(f)i failed, then broadcast a complaint against P_j.

(g) For every complaint received by $P_j \neq P_i$, broadcast the value $y_{i,j}$.

(h) If Step 1(f)ii failed for P_j, or if P_j broadcasted a value $y_{j,l}$ in response to P_l that does not satisfy Step 1(f)i, remove P_j from $\mathcal{Q}$.

2. Computing the public key and shares of the secret key

(a) All parties compute the public key $\mathsf{pk}_{\mathsf{cl}} := \prod_{P_j \in \mathcal{Q}} C_{j,0}$ where the secret key is defined as $\mathsf{sk}_{\mathsf{cl}} := \sum_{P_j \in \mathcal{Q}} \alpha_i$.

(b) Each P_i computes its share $\gamma_i := \sum_{P_j \in \mathcal{Q}} y_{j,i}$ of $\mathsf{sk}_{\mathsf{cl}}$.

(c) All parties compute $\Gamma_i := \prod_{P_j \in \mathcal{Q}} C_{j,0}^{\Delta^2} \cdot \prod_{k=1}^{t} C_{j,k}^{(i^k)}$ for each P_i.

3. Continued in Figure 4.

Fig. 3. Distributed Key Generation and Decryption protocols for $\Pi_{\mathsf{hsm\text{-}cl}}$

Distributed Key Generation (DKG). We present our protocol in Fig. 3. in the $(\mathcal{F}_{\mathsf{CL}}, \mathcal{F}_{\mathsf{Rand}})$-hybrid model, where $\mathcal{F}_{\mathsf{Rand}}$ is a standard coin tossing functionality. The DKG protocol consists of two parts: First the parties generate a key pair $(\mathsf{pk}_{\mathsf{cl}}, \mathsf{sk}_{\mathsf{cl}})$ such that the secret key $\mathsf{sk}_{\mathsf{cl}}$ is distributed among all parties. Then, they generate ct_P which is an encryption of 1 under the public key $\mathsf{pk}_{\mathsf{cl}}$.

Recall that a key pair is of the form $(\mathsf{sk}_{\mathsf{cl}}, \mathsf{pk}_{\mathsf{cl}} = g_q^{\mathsf{sk}_{\mathsf{cl}}})$, where $\mathsf{sk}_{\mathsf{cl}}$ is a sufficiently large random integer. Each party first samples their contribution α_i to the secret key, and then uses a variant of Feldman VSS (cf. Sect. 4) with base g_q to share it with all other parties. The properties of the VSS scheme and complaint resolution guarantee that for every P_i we have either a consistent secret sharing of α_i, or P_i is disqualified and ignored for the remainder of the key generation. The secret key is now well-defined as $\mathsf{sk}_{\mathsf{cl}} = \sum_{P_i \in \mathcal{Q}} \alpha_i$, and each of these α_i can

Protocol Π_{TE} (Part II)

KeyGen (continued) 3. Generation of ct_P. All P_i proceed in parallel:

(a) Sample the contribution to the randomness $\beta_i \leftarrow \mathcal{D}_q$.

(b) Share β_i as $(z_{i,1}, \ldots, z_{i,N}; D_{i,0}, \ldots, D_{i,t}) \leftarrow \mathsf{F\text{-}Share}(\beta_i; \mathsf{s}_i; g_q)$ such that $z_{i,j}$ is privately sent to P_j, and $D_{i,0}, \ldots, D_{i,t}, D'_{i,0} := \mathsf{pk}_{\mathsf{cl}}^{\beta_i}$ are broadcasted.

(c) Compute $(\mathsf{com}^2_{i,0}, \mathsf{stt}_{i,0}) \leftarrow \Pi^{\mathsf{bin}}_{\mathsf{EqDLog}}.\mathsf{Commit}((D_{i,0}, \mathsf{pk}_{\mathsf{cl}}, D'_{i,0}), s_{i,0})$, and $(\mathsf{com}^2_{i,k}, \mathsf{stt}_{i,k}) \leftarrow \Pi_{\mathsf{DLog}}.\mathsf{Commit}(D_{i,k}, s_{i,k})$ for $k \in [1,t]$, and broadcast $\mathsf{com}^2_{i,0}, \ldots, \mathsf{com}^2_{i,t}$.

(d) Send $(\mathsf{Rand}, [C])$ to $\mathcal{F}_{\mathsf{Rand}}$ so that all parties receive $\mathsf{chl}^2 \in_R [C]$.

(e) Broadcast $\mathsf{res}^2_{i,0} \leftarrow \Pi^{\mathsf{bin}}_{\mathsf{EqDLog}}.\mathsf{Respond}((D_{i,0}, \mathsf{pk}_{\mathsf{cl}}, D'_{i,0}), s_{i,0}, \mathsf{stt}^2_{i,0}, \mathsf{chl}^2)$, and $\mathsf{res}^2_{i,k} \leftarrow \Pi_{\mathsf{DLog}}.\mathsf{Respond}(D_{i,k}, s_{i,k}, \mathsf{stt}^2_{i,k}, \mathsf{chl}^2)$ for $k \in [1,t]$.

(f) Verify shares received from $P_j \neq P_i$: Check if

  i. $\mathsf{F\text{-}Check}(j, z_{j,i}; D_{j,0}, \ldots, D_{j,t}; g_q) \stackrel{?}{=} \top$, and

  ii. $\Pi^{\mathsf{bin}}_{\mathsf{EqDLog}}.\mathsf{Verify}((D_{j,0}, \mathsf{pk}_{\mathsf{cl}}, D'_{j,0}), \mathsf{com}^2_{i,0}, \mathsf{chl}^2, \mathsf{res}^2_{i,0}) \stackrel{?}{=} \top$, and
  $\Pi_{\mathsf{DLog}}.\mathsf{Verify}(D_{j,k}, \mathsf{com}^2_{j,k}, \mathsf{chl}^2, \mathsf{res}^2_{j,k}) \stackrel{?}{=} \top$ for all $k \in [1,t]$,

  If only Step 3(f)i failed, then broadcast a complaint against P_j.

(g) For every complaint received by $P_j \neq P_i$, broadcast the value $z_{i,j}$.

(h) If Step 3(f)ii failed for P_j, or if P_j broadcasted a value $z_{j,l}$ in response to P_l that does not satisfy Step 3(f)i, reset $D_{j,0} := D'_{j,0} := 1$.

Finally, everyone computes $\mathsf{ct}_P := \left(\prod_{P_i \in \mathcal{Q}} D_{i,0}, f \cdot \prod_{P_i \in \mathcal{Q}} D'_{i,0}\right)$.

Decrypt To jointly decrypt a $\Pi_{\mathsf{hsm\text{-}cl}}$ ciphertext $\mathsf{ct} = (\mathsf{ct}_1, \mathsf{ct}_2) \in \widehat{G}^2$, all P_i proceed in parallel as follows:

1. Compute $w_i := \mathsf{ct}_1^{\gamma_i \cdot \Delta}$ and $(\mathsf{com}_i, \mathsf{stt}_i) \leftarrow \Pi_{\mathsf{EqDLog}}.\mathsf{Commit}((\mathsf{ct}_1, \Gamma_i, w_i), \gamma_i \cdot \Delta)$. Broadcast w_i and com_i.
2. Send $(\mathsf{Rand}, [C])$ to $\mathcal{F}_{\mathsf{Rand}}$ so that all parties receive $\mathsf{chl} \in_R [C]$.
3. Broadcast $\mathsf{res}_i \leftarrow \Pi_{\mathsf{EqDLog}}.\mathsf{Respond}((\mathsf{ct}_1, \Gamma_i, w_i), \gamma_i \cdot \Delta, \mathsf{stt}_i, \mathsf{chl})$.
4. Define $S := \{P_i \mid \Pi_{\mathsf{EqDLog}}.\mathsf{Verify}((\mathsf{ct}_1, \mathsf{pk}_j, w_j), \mathsf{com}_j, \mathsf{chl}, \mathsf{res}_j) = \top\}$.
5. Compute $W := \prod_{P_j \in S} w_j^{(\ell_j^S \cdot \Delta)}$ and $\overline{M} := \mathsf{ct}_2^{\Delta^3} \cdot W^{-1}$.
6. Output $m := \mathsf{CLSolve}(\mathsf{pp}_{\mathsf{cl}}, \overline{M}) \cdot \Delta^{-3} \bmod q$.

Fig. 4. Distributed Key Generation and Decryption protocols for $\Pi_{\mathsf{hsm\text{-}cl}}$

be reconstructed by a majority of all parties. Each party additionally obtains a share γ_i of $\mathsf{sk}_{\mathsf{cl}}$ such that any set of at least $(t+1)$ parties can reconstruct $\mathsf{sk}_{\mathsf{cl}}$. Moreover, each party has learned $\mathsf{pk}_i := g_q^{\alpha_i}$ for $P_i \in \mathcal{Q}$ and can compute the public key as $\mathsf{pk} = \prod_{P_i \in \mathcal{Q}} \mathsf{pk}_i$. Note that the Feldman VSS already reveals the parties' contributions to the public key pk_i. Hence, a rushing adversary is able to bias the resulting key based on the honest parties contributions.[8]

[8] The protocol of [28] prevents this kind of bias in the setting of prime-order groups. We could instantiate their protocol also in the unknown order setting, but the setup would be significantly more complicated.

The aim of the second part is to generate a ciphertext $\mathsf{ct}_P = (\mathsf{ct}_1, \mathsf{ct}_2) = (g_q^\beta, f \cdot \mathsf{pk}_{\mathsf{cl}}^\beta)$, where β is again a large random value. Since ct_1 is basically an ephemeral public key, the protocol is very similar to the key generation part of Π_{TE}: Every party samples their contribution β_i to the randomness β, and proves that their contribution $g_q^{\beta_i}$ has the right form. The difference is that now we also need to compute ct_2. Hence, each party also computes $\mathsf{pk}_{\mathsf{cl}}^{\beta_i}$ and uses Π_{EqDLog} to prove that their contributions to ct_1 and ct_2 are consistent. Moreover, parties that misbehave are not disqualified, but their contributions to ct_1 and ct_2 are essentially removed by setting them to 1. While it is not necessary that β_i can be reconstucted by a majority of the parties, we nevertheless share it with a Feldman VSS. This is only necessary for the proof, since it allows the simulator to reconstruct the β_i of the corrupted $P_i \in \mathcal{C}$. Alternatively, an online-extractible proof for the $\mathsf{R}_{\mathsf{EqDLog}}$ relation would suffice as well. Finally, the parties can multiply f into the result to get an encryption of 1.

Distributed Decryption. To decrypt a ciphertext ct, each party P_i computes a partial decryption $w_i := \mathsf{ct}_1^{\gamma_i \cdot \Delta}$, and proves that they used their share of $\mathsf{sk}_{\mathsf{cl}}$ via Π_{EqDLog}. Since at least $t+1$ parties do this honestly, they can reconstruct $\mathsf{sk}_{\mathsf{cl}}$ in the exponent of ct_1 and perform the remainder of the $\Pi_{\mathsf{hsm\text{-}cl}}$ decryption.

Theorem 11. *The protocol Π_{TE} (Fig. 3) securely realizes the functionality $\mathcal{F}_{\mathsf{TE}}$ (Fig. 2) in the $(\mathcal{F}_{\mathsf{CL}}, \mathcal{F}_{\mathsf{Rand}})$-hybrid model with secure channels and broadcast with static and computational security tolerating up to $t < N/2$ corruptions under the ORD and RO_{N+1} assumptions when $1/C = \mathsf{negl}(\lambda)$.*

Proof. For an explanation of the correctness of the protocol, see the full version [9].

Simulation. We set up the simulation as follows: The environment $\mathcal{Z}$ selects a set $\mathcal{C}$ of at most $t < N/2$ parties to corrupt. $\mathcal{Z}$ sends $(\mathsf{corrupt}, P_i)$ for each $P_i \in \mathcal{C}$ to the simulator $\mathcal{S}$ who forwards it to $\mathcal{F}_{\mathsf{TE}}$. Now $\mathcal{S}$ controls the communication of the P_i to $\mathcal{F}_{\mathsf{TE}}$. $\mathcal{S}$ sets up simulated copies of the all parties, and forwards the instructions of $\mathcal{Z}$ for the corrupted parties to their simulated counterparts.

To prove adaptive security for their DKG protocol, Abe et al. [1] used the single-inconsistent-player (SIP) variant of UC. We only aim for static security, but use the same underlying idea in the standard UC model: $\mathcal{S}$ selects a distinguished honest party $P_h \in \mathcal{H}$, and lets all other honest parties $\mathcal{H} \setminus \{P_h\}$ act according to Π_{TE}. The messages sent by P_h, however, are chosen such that the resulting view of the environment is consistent with the values output by $\mathcal{F}_{\mathsf{TE}}$. Hence, $\mathcal{S}$ does not always know the witnesses needed to perform the zero-knowledge arguments. Instead it uses the corresponding simulators and programs the $\mathcal{F}_{\mathsf{Rand}}$ functionality with the used challenges. Since $\mathcal{S}$ controls the honest majority of (simulated) parties, it knows enough shares to extract the contributions α_i of the corrupted parties from the VSS. The full $\mathcal{S}$ is given in Figs. 5 and 6.

Set of Qualified Parties and Secret Key are Well-Defined. All honest parties have computed the same set $\mathcal{Q}$ after Step 1h of Π_{TE}, because disqualifi-

Simulator for Π_{TE} (Part I)

Init Simulate the generation of $\mathsf{pp_{cl}}$ by running $\mathsf{pp_{cl}} \leftarrow \mathsf{CLGen}(1^\lambda, q)$.

KeyGen 1. Simulate generation of $\mathsf{pk_{cl}}$. Run $\mathsf{BiasedKeyGen}^{\mathcal{S}}$ with $\mathcal{F}_{\mathsf{TE}}$.

(a) Send (KeyGen) to $\mathcal{F}_{\mathsf{TE}}$ and receive the intermediate public key $\mathsf{pk}^*_{\mathsf{cl}}$.

(b) For all $P_i \in \mathcal{H} \setminus \{P_h\}$, simulate Steps 1a to 1c according to Π_{TE}.

(c) For P_h, instead send $C_{h,0}, \ldots, C_{h,t}$ computed as follows:

i. Sample $\alpha_h \leftarrow \mathcal{D}_q$ and share it as $(y_{h,1}, \ldots, y_{h,N}) \leftarrow \mathsf{Share}(\alpha_h; \mathbf{r}_h)$.

ii. Set $C_{h,0} := \mathsf{pk}^*_{\mathsf{cl}} \cdot \prod_{P_i \in \mathcal{H} \setminus \{P_h\}} C_{i,0}^{-1}$.

iii. Use Lemma 6 to get $C_{h,1}, \ldots, C_{h,t}$ such that $\mathsf{F\text{-}Check}(j, y_{h,j}; C_{h,0}, \ldots, C_{h,t}; g_q)$ holds for all $P_j \in \mathcal{C}$.

iv. Sample $\mathsf{chl}^1 \in_R [C]$, run $(\mathsf{com}^1_{h,0}, \mathsf{res}^1_{h,0}) \leftarrow \Pi^{\mathsf{bin}}_{\mathsf{DLog}}.\mathsf{Simulate}(C_{h,0}, \mathsf{chl}^1)$, and $(\mathsf{com}^1_{h,k}, \mathsf{res}^1_{h,k}) \leftarrow \Pi_{\mathsf{DLog}}.\mathsf{Simulate}(C_{h,k}, \mathsf{chl}^1)$ for $k \in [t]$. Send $(\mathsf{com}^1_{h,k})_{k \in [0,t]}$

(d) Receive shares and checking values $(y_{i,j}; C_{i,0}, \ldots, C_{i,t})$ and $(\mathsf{com}^1_{i,0}, \ldots, \mathsf{com}^1_{i,t})$ from all $P_i \in \mathcal{C}$ for all $P_j \in \mathcal{H}$.

(e) Simulate the call to $\mathcal{F}_{\mathsf{Rand}}$ and send chl^1 to all parties.

(f) For all $P_i \in \mathcal{H} \setminus \{P_h\}$, compute $\mathsf{res}^1_{i,0} \leftarrow \Pi^{\mathsf{bin}}_{\mathsf{DLog}}.\mathsf{Respond}(C_{i,0}, \alpha_i, \mathsf{stt}^1_{i,0}, \mathsf{chl}^1)$ and $\mathsf{res}^1_{i,k} \leftarrow \Pi_{\mathsf{DLog}}.\mathsf{Respond}(C_{i,k}, r_{i,k}, \mathsf{stt}^1_{i,k}, \mathsf{chl}^1)$ for $k \in [t]$. Send $(\mathsf{res}^1_{i,k})_{k \in [0,t]}$ for all $P_i \in \mathcal{H}$ and receive $(\mathsf{res}^1_{i,k})_{k \in [0,t]}$ from all $P_i \in \mathcal{C}$.

(g) Simulate the complaint resolution:

i. Respond honestly to all complaints against honest parties.

ii. Broadcast a complaint on behalf of $P_j \in \mathcal{H}$ if they received an invalid share $y_{i,j}$ from $P_i \in \mathcal{C}$.

iii. If a $P_i \in \mathcal{C}$ responds to a complaint with a a corrected value $y'_{i,j}$: Remove P_i from $\mathcal{Q}$ if $y'_{i,j}$ is invalid. Otherwise, reset $y_{i,j} := y'_{i,j}$.

(h) Reconstruct α_i from the shares $\{(j, y_{i,j})\}_{P_j \in \mathcal{H}}$ for each $P_i \in \mathcal{C} \cap \mathcal{Q}$.

(i) Set $\delta := \sum_{P_i \in \mathcal{C} \cap \mathcal{Q}} \alpha_i$, and send δ to $\mathcal{F}_{\mathsf{TE}}$.

(j) Define $\mathsf{pk_{cl}} := \prod_{P_j \in \mathcal{Q}} C_{j,0} = \mathsf{pk}^*_{\mathsf{cl}} \cdot g_q^\delta$, and set $\gamma_i := \sum_{P_j \in \mathcal{Q}} y_{j,i}$ and $\Gamma_i := g_q^{\gamma_i \cdot \Delta}$ for all P_i.

2. Continued in Figure 6.

Fig. 5. Simulator for the key generation protocol in Π_{TE}

cation of parties depend only on information that was broadcasted, and is thus consistent among all honest parties. Moreover, no honest party gets disqualified. Since honest parties adhere to the protocol, no other honest parties would complain against them. If a corrupted party complains against an honest party, it will respond with that party's share which satisfies F-Check, so no other honest party will consider it disqualified. Let $P_i \in \mathcal{Q}$ be still qualified party. If $P_i \in \mathcal{H}$, then the honest parties have $\geq t+1$ valid shares of α_i. If $P_i \in \mathcal{C}$ is corrupted and not disqualified, then it has responded with valid shares to all complaints, and, by soundness of Π_{DLog} and $\Pi^{\mathsf{bin}}_{\mathsf{DLog}}$, we have $C_{i,0}, \ldots, C_{i,t} \in G^q$ except with negligible probability. Thus, each honest party $P_j \in \mathcal{H}$ has either directly received

Simulator for Π_{TE} (Part II)

KeyGen (continued) 2. Simulate generation of ct_P. Continue of $\mathsf{BiasedSpecialKeyGen}_1^S$ with $\mathcal{F}_{\mathsf{TE}}$.

(a) Receive the intermediate ciphertext $\mathsf{ct}_P^* = (\mathsf{ct}_1^*, \mathsf{ct}_2^*)$.
(b) For all $P_i \in \mathcal{H} \setminus \{P_h\}$, Simulate Steps 3a to 3c according to Π_{TE}:
(c) For P_h, instead send $D_{h,0}, \ldots, D_{h,t}, D'_{h,0}$ computed as follows:
   i. Sample $\beta_h \leftarrow \mathcal{D}_q$ and share it as $(z_{h,1}, \ldots, z_{h,N}) \leftarrow \mathsf{Share}(\beta_h; \mathbf{r}_h)$.
   ii. Set $D_{h,0} := \mathsf{ct}_1^* \cdot \prod_{P_i \in \mathcal{H}\setminus\{P_h\}} D_{i,0}^{-1}$.
   iii. Set $D'_{h,0} := \mathsf{ct}_2^* \cdot f^{-1} \cdot \prod_{P_i \in \mathcal{H}\setminus\{P_h\}} D'^{-1}_{i,0}$.
   iv. Use Lemma 6 to get $D_{h,1}, \ldots, D_{h,t}$ such that $\mathsf{F\text{-}Check}(j, z_{h,j}; D_{h,0}, \ldots, D_{h,t}; g_q)$ holds for all j such that $P_j \in \mathcal{C}$.
   v. Sample $\mathsf{chl}^2 \in_R [C]$, run
      A. $(\mathsf{com}_{h,0}^2, \mathsf{chl}^2, \mathsf{res}_{h,0}^2) \leftarrow \Pi_{\mathsf{EqDLog}}^{\mathsf{bin}}.\mathsf{Simulate}((D_{h,0}, \mathsf{pk}_{\mathsf{cl}}, D'_{h,0}), \mathsf{chl}^2)$, and
      B. $(\mathsf{com}_{h,k}^2, \mathsf{chl}^2, \mathsf{res}_{h,k}^2) \leftarrow \Pi_{\mathsf{DLog}}.\mathsf{Simulate}(D_{h,k}, \mathsf{chl}^2)$ for $k \in [1, t]$,
   and send $\mathsf{com}_{h,k}^2$ for $k \in [0, t]$.
(d) Receive shares and checking values $(z_{i,j}; D_{i,0}, \ldots, D_{i,t})$, $D'_{i,0}$, and $(\mathsf{com}_{i,0}^2, \ldots, \mathsf{com}_{i,t}^2)$ from all $P_i \in \mathcal{C}$ for all $P_j \in \mathcal{H}$.
(e) Simulate the call to $\mathcal{F}_{\mathsf{Rand}}$ and send chl^2 to all parties.
(f) For all $P_i \in \mathcal{H} \setminus \{P_h\}$, compute
   i. $\mathsf{res}_{i,0}^2 \leftarrow \Pi_{\mathsf{EqDLog}}^{\mathsf{bin}}.\mathsf{Respond}((D_{i,0}, \mathsf{pk}_{\mathsf{cl}}, D'_{i,0}), r_{i,0}, \mathsf{stt}_{i,0}^2, \mathsf{chl}^2)$, and
   ii. $\mathsf{res}_{i,k}^2 \leftarrow \Pi_{\mathsf{DLog}}.\mathsf{Respond}(D_{i,k}, r_{i,k}, \mathsf{stt}_{i,k}^2, \mathsf{chl}^2)$ for $k \in [1, t]$.
   Send $\mathsf{res}_{i,k}^2$ for all $P_i \in \mathcal{H}$ and receive $\mathsf{res}_{i,k}^2$ from all $P_i \in \mathcal{C}$ (for $k \in [0, t]$).
(g) Simulate the complaint resolution as in Step 1g above, but instead of disqualifying misbehaving $P_j \in \mathcal{C}$, reset $D_{j,0} := D'_{j,0} := 1$ and $\beta_j := 0$.
(h) Reconstruct β_i from the shares $\{(j, z_{i,j})\}_{P_j \in \mathcal{H}}$ for all other $P_i \in \mathcal{C} \cap \mathcal{Q}$.
(i) Set $\varepsilon := \sum_{P_i \in \mathcal{C} \cap \mathcal{Q}} \beta_i$, and send ε to $\mathcal{F}_{\mathsf{TE}}$.
(j) Define $\mathsf{ct}_P := \left(\prod_{P_j \in \mathcal{Q}} D_{j,0}, F \cdot \prod_{P_j \in \mathcal{Q}} D'_{j,0}\right) = \left(\mathsf{ct}_1^* \cdot g_q^{\varepsilon}, \mathsf{ct}_2^* \cdot \mathsf{pk}_{\mathsf{cl}}^{\varepsilon}\right)$. Send continue to $\mathcal{F}_{\mathsf{TE}}$.

Decrypt 1. Send (Decrypt, $\mathsf{ct} = (\mathsf{ct}_1, \mathsf{ct}_2) \in \widehat{G}^2$) on behalf of the corrupted parties to $\mathcal{F}_{\mathsf{TE}}$ and receive the partially decrypted message M.

2. Compute $\overline{M} := M^{\Delta^3}$ and $W := \mathsf{ct}_2^{\Delta^3} \cdot \overline{M}^{-1}$.
3. Set $A := \{0\} \cup \{i \mid P_i \in \mathcal{C}\}$ such that $|A| = t + 1$.
4. Compute $\overline{w}_i := \mathsf{ct}_1^{\gamma_i}$ and $w_i := \overline{w}_i^{\Delta}$ for $P_i \in \mathcal{C}$.
5. Set $\overline{w}_0 := \mathsf{ct}_2 \cdot M^{-1}$.
6. Compute $w_i := \overline{w}_0^{\ell_0^A(h)\cdot\Delta} \cdot \prod_{P_j \in \mathcal{C}} \overline{w}_j^{\ell_j^A(h)\cdot\Delta}$ for each $P_i \in \mathcal{H}$.
7. Sample $\mathsf{chl} \in_R [C]$.
8. For all $P_i \in \mathcal{H}$ run $(\mathsf{com}_i, \mathsf{chl}, \mathsf{res}_i) \leftarrow \Pi_{\mathsf{EqDLog}}.\mathsf{Simulate}((\mathsf{ct}_1, \Gamma_i, w_i), \mathsf{chl})$.
9. Send (w_i, com_i) for all $P_i \in \mathcal{H}$.
10. Simulate the call to $\mathcal{F}_{\mathsf{Rand}}$ and send chl to all parties.
11. Send res_i for all $P_i \in \mathcal{H}$.
12. Send continue to $\mathcal{F}_{\mathsf{TE}}$.

Fig. 6. Simulator for the decryption protocol in Π_{TE}

a valid share $y_{i,j}$ from P_i in Step 1b, or a valid share $y_{i,j}$ has been broadcasted by P_i in Step 1g after P_j had issued a complaint in Step 1f. Hence, the honest parties know $\geq t+1$ consistent shares. By Lemma 5, this determines α_i.

We can apply Lemma 5 here, because we use the Feldman VSS with base g_q and we use with $\Pi^{\mathsf{bin}}_{\mathsf{DLog}}$ a proof of knowledge for C_0. By the RO_{N+1} assumption (Def. 1), the parameters $\mathsf{pp}_{\mathsf{cl}}$ are indistinguishable to parameters where g_q has an order which is co-prime to Δ.

Indistinguishability of the Simulation of KeyGen. Following the KeyGen protocol, the simulation also consists of two phases: The first concerns simulating the generation of a key pair $(\mathsf{pk}_{\mathsf{cl}}, \mathsf{sk}_{\mathsf{cl}})$; the second handles the generation of ct_P. In the following, we cover both parts separately.

In the first part, the messages sent by the simulated parties $P_i \in \mathcal{H} \setminus \{P_h\}$ are distributed exactly as in the real execution since $\mathcal{S}$ lets them behave according to protocol. The only deviation happens in Step 1c of the simulation:

1. $\mathcal{S}$ lets P_h send a value $C_{h,0}$ that is distributed correctly given the intermediate public key $\mathsf{pk}^*_{\mathsf{cl}}$ generated by $\mathcal{F}_{\mathsf{TE}}$. The other values $C_{h,1}, \ldots, C_{h,k}$ are produced using Lemma 6. Hence, the $C_{h,1}, \ldots, C_{h,k}$ have the correct distribution given $C_{h,0}$ and the corrupted parties' shares $\{y_j \mid P_j \in \mathcal{C}\}$; they are actually fully determined if $|\mathcal{C}| = t$).
   In the real protocol, it holds $C_{h,0} = g_q^{\alpha_h}$, where α_h is the value shared by P_h, but in the simulation, $C_{h,0}$ and the shared α_h are unrelated. Since the Feldman VSS reveals no other information about α_h and the environment sees at most t shares of the corrupted parties $P_i \in \mathcal{C}$, it cannot detect the difference.
2. Additionally, the proofs by P_h are simulated which is possible, since $\mathcal{S}$ can sample the challenge chl^1 in advance and then program $\mathcal{F}_{\mathsf{Rand}}$ to output it in Step 1e. By SHVZK of Π_{DLog} and $\Pi^{\mathsf{bin}}_{\mathsf{DLog}}$, the simulated proofs are indistinguishable from normally computed proofs.

Since $\mathcal{S}$ controls the honest parties, it has $t+1$ shares of α_i for each qualified $P_i \in \mathcal{Q}$. Thus, $\mathcal{S}$ can extract the contributions of the corrupted, but still qualified parties' contributions in Step 1h, and submit their sum δ in Step 1i to $\mathcal{F}_{\mathsf{TE}}$ to complete the $\mathsf{BiasedKeyGen}^{\mathcal{S}}$ procedure.

Note that when $\mathcal{S}$ defines the values γ_i and Γ_i for each parties, then, by construction, $(\gamma_1, \ldots, \gamma_N)$ is a secret sharing of $\sum_{P_i \in \mathcal{Q}} \alpha_i \neq \mathsf{sk}_{\mathsf{cl}}$.

The second half of the simulation is very similar to the first. The only difference is that the parties now need to generate a ciphertext $\mathsf{ct}_P = (\mathsf{ct}_1, \mathsf{ct}_2)$ consisting of two components. Again the $\mathcal{S}$ lets all $P_i \in \mathcal{H} \setminus \{P_h\}$ follow the protocol and chooses P_h's values such that the honest parties' contributions match what $\mathcal{F}_{\mathsf{TE}}$ outputs as preliminary ciphertext ct^*_P. Then it uses the Feldman shares to extract the randomness contributions β_i from all corrupted parties that were not caught misbehaving. For all other parties β_i is reset to 0 according to the protocol, so that they become irrelevant.

Hence, we conclude that overall the environment's view in the KeyGen simulation is indistinguishable from its view of a real protocol execution.

Indistinguishability of the Simulation of Decrypt. First, recall that, in the simulation, $(\gamma_1, \ldots, \gamma_N)$ is a secret sharing of $\alpha := \sum_{P_i \in \mathcal{Q}} \alpha_i$, *not* of $\mathsf{sk_{cl}}$, which is unknown to $\mathcal{S}$.

If $\mathcal{S}$ would let the honest parties execute the protocol using their shares γ_h, then the decrypted value will most likely be invalid and not match the output of $\mathcal{F}_{\mathsf{TE}}$, since the ciphertext would essentially be decrypted with a random secret key α, which is unrelated to $\mathsf{sk_{cl}}$. Instead it uses the partially decrypted message M received from $\mathcal{F}_{\mathsf{TE}}$ to compute messages w_i for $P_i \in \mathcal{H}$ that are consistent with M and the adversary's view. Note that the t shares γ_i of the corrupted parties $P_i \in \mathcal{C}$ and the actual secret key $\mathsf{sk_{cl}}$ uniquely define what the honest parties need to send, since all points are supposed to lie on some degree-t polynomial $\bar{f}$.

Hence, we use Lagrange interpolation in the exponent of ct_1 to find values consistent with $\bar{f}$ such that $\bar{f}(0) = \mathsf{sk_{cl}}$ and $\bar{f}(i) = \gamma_i$ for $P_i \in \mathcal{C}$. By definition of M, we have $M = \mathsf{ct}_2 \cdot \mathsf{ct}_1^{-\mathsf{sk_{cl}}} \iff \mathsf{ct}_1^{\mathsf{sk_{cl}}} = \mathsf{ct}_2 \cdot M^{-1}$, and set $\overline{w}_0 := \mathsf{ct}_2 \cdot M^{-1}$. If the corrupted parties would behave correctly, they would send $w_i := \mathsf{ct}_1^{\gamma_i \cdot \Delta}$. Since Lagrange interpolation in the exponent already adds a factor Δ, we work with $\overline{w}_i := \mathsf{ct}_1^{\gamma_i}$. For each $P_i \in \mathcal{H}$, we set

$$w_i := \overline{w}_0^{\ell_0^A(i)\cdot\Delta} \cdot \prod_{P_j \in \mathcal{C}} \overline{w}_j^{\ell_j^A(i)\cdot\Delta} = \mathsf{ct}_1^{\mathsf{sk_{cl}}\cdot\ell_0^A(i)\cdot\Delta} \cdot \prod_{P_j \in \mathcal{C}} \mathsf{ct}_1^{\gamma_j\cdot\ell_j^A(i)\cdot\Delta}$$
$$= \mathsf{ct}_1^{\mathsf{sk_{cl}}\cdot\ell_0^A(i)\cdot\Delta + \sum_{P_j \in \mathcal{C}} \gamma_j\cdot\ell_j^A(i)\cdot\Delta} = \mathsf{ct}_1^{\bar{f}(j)\cdot\Delta}.$$

Hence, w_i is exactly, what the adversary expects the honest parties to send given the view of the corrupted parties and the result of the decryption.

Now $\mathcal{S}$ does not know the discrete logarithms of the w_i to base ct_1, it uses the SHVZK simulator for Π_{EqDLog} to simulate proof transcripts in Step 8 for a randomly chosen challenge $\mathsf{chl} \in [C]$, and then programs the simulated $\mathcal{F}_{\mathsf{Rand}}$ to output chl as challenge. By SHVZK, the simulated messages $(\mathsf{com}_i)_{P_i\in\mathcal{H}}, (\mathsf{res}_i)_{P_i\in\mathcal{H}}$ are statistically indistinguishable from the messages appearing in an honestly generated proof. □

Guaranteed Output Delivery. Assuming public parameters $\mathsf{pp_{cl}}$ available, our protocol achieves *guaranteed output delivery (GOD)*: The adversary cannot prevent the honest parties from successfully completing the protocol to generate a shared key or decrypt a ciphertext. This holds because the simulator $\mathcal{S}$ defined in the proof of Theorem 11 never lets $\mathcal{F}_{\mathsf{TE}}$ abort, but always instructs it to deliver the output to the honest parties after a constant number of rounds.

7 MPC

We follow the approach of Damgård et al. [20] and define an arithmetic black box functionality (ABB) $\mathcal{F}^q_{\mathsf{ABB}}$ for reactive secure computation over the field $\mathbb{F}_q$ (formally stated in the full version [9]). It allows parties to privately Input field elements to the ABB and to let it publicly Output stored values to all parties. Moreover, $\mathcal{F}_{\mathsf{ABB}}^q$ allows to compute Linear combinations on stored values with public coefficients, and to Multiply stored values. For all methods, $\mathcal{F}_{\mathsf{ABB}}^q$ conducts the operation if it receives corresponding messages from at least $t+1$ parties. This ensures that the (at most) t corrupted parties cannot prevent the honest parties from proceeding with the computation.

We realize this functionality with the protocol Π_{ABB}^q, and state its security in Theorem 12. We refer to the full version [9] for the formal protocol specification and the full security proof. The construction of Π_{ABB}^q essentially follows the CDN [20] paradigm: All values in the computation are encrypted with $\Pi_{\mathsf{hsm\text{-}cl}}^*$ and the parties use $\mathcal{F}_{\mathsf{TE}}$ to generate a public key and decrypt ciphertexts. Whenever a party publishes a ciphertext or performs a multiplication it uses Π_{PoPK} and Π_{Mult} to prove correctness. We use that $\Pi_{\mathsf{hsm\text{-}cl}}^*$ has lossy public keys to prove indistinguishability of the simulation in the SPDZ-style [21].

Theorem 12 (Security of Π_{ABB}^q). *The protocol Π_{ABB}^q securely realizes the functionality $\mathcal{F}_{\mathsf{ABB}}^q$ in the $(\mathcal{F}_{\mathsf{Rand}}, \mathcal{F}_{\mathsf{TE}})$-hybrid model with broadcast with static and computational security tolerating up to $t < N/2$ corruptions given that Π_{PoPK} and Π_{Mult} are proofs of plaintext knowledge and correct multiplication.*

8 YOSO MPC

The YOSO framework (as defined in [29]) is defined for a universe of M players (servers), and we use their model for computationally secure YOSO protocols. This concretely means that the parties in the protocol we specify are actually roles that in an actual execution will be assigned to physical servers by a *Role Assignment Mechanism.* It further means that a public encryption key is assigned to each party (role). In an actual execution, the physical server assigned to play a role will learn the corresponding secret key, but the adversary will not learn the identity of the server until it speaks. This mechanism is abstracted away in the model. We can therefore think of a large set of parties, they each own a key pair and can only speak once. Furthermore, if we divide the parties into disjoint committees with N members each, we can assume that each committee has honest majority if we choose N large enough.

A construction of a role assignment mechanism was presented in [7]. Their implementation allows us to choose the encryption scheme freely, so in this paper we will use the CL encryption scheme. However we will use separate class-group set-up, where the plaintext space is numbers mod q', where q' is chosen large enough compared to q. We will specify below what this means more precisely.

In the YOSO framework, we assume that public information can be reliably posted for everyone to see: the motivation for this is that the framework is intended for doing MPC on a blockchain. When we say in the following that something is "publicly known" or "on public display", this means it has been posted or can be efficiently computed from what is posted. Further, a committee is only allowed to speak once, that is, committee members decrypt whatever ciphertext is intended for them, read the public information, post a single message and do nothing further. The idea is that this allows us to assume that even an adaptive adversary who can corrupt a large fraction of the physical servers, will not be able to corrupt a majority of any committee. See [29] for details.

Committees will be denoted by COM_i, for $i = 0, 1, \ldots$, and their public keys will be denoted by $\mathsf{pk}_1^i, \ldots, \mathsf{pk}_N^i$. In the protocol, committees will do their work in numeric order, starting with COM_0. We assume that the role assignment mechanism is called such that when COM_i is about to start, the public keys of (at least) $\mathsf{COM}_{i+1}, \mathsf{COM}_{i+2}, \mathsf{COM}_{i+3}, \mathsf{COM}_{i+4}$ are publicly known.

In the following, we show how to adapt our honest majority MPC protocol to the YOSO setting. For this, we will need non-interactive zero-knowledge arguments of knowledge (NIAoK) for various statements. Any instantiation will do, as long as it is simulation extractable[9], meaning that you can extract a witness from a proof that verifies, even if the prover has access to simulated proofs. We also require that only transparent set-up is needed, as our overall goal is MPC with transparent set-up. In this paper, we describe Σ-protocols for all the statements needed, so one approach is to make these non-interactive using the random oracle model and the Fischlin-transform [26] which will have the required properties. By careful protocol redesign and analysis, we believe it would be possible to use the more efficient Fiat-Shamir transform, but leave this for future work. Another option is to use a recent construction of SNARKS with transparent set-up based on class groups [3]. We will denote a non-interactive argument on public instance x and witness w by $\mathsf{NIAoK}(x, w; eq(x, w))$, where $eq(x, w)$ is the equation that x and w are proven to satisfy.

Key Generation. We assume the specification of the class group and the generators is given (recall that this set-up is transparent). We first need a protocol that allows a committee to obtain shares of a random value η, while leaking only g_q^η to the adversary.

We will need this for key generation, but also for other purposes, and in fact it is a simple adaptation of Steps 1 and 2 of the distributed key generation protocol Π_{TE} (Fig. 3). It involves two committees COM_u and COM_v, where COM_u will generate the randomness required, and COM_v will receive the shares.

The idea is that members of the first committee COM_u will do a Feldman secret-sharing of their contribution to η, see Protocol 2. The shares will be intended for COM_v, so members of COM_u will encrypt the shares under $\mathsf{pk}_1^v, \ldots, \mathsf{pk}_N^v$, do a non-interactive ZK proof that these are correct, and post the ciphertexts and proofs. See the full version [9] for more details. The plaintext modulus q' for the pk_v^i's is chosen such that q' is larger than any honestly generated share. Then members of COM_v will add the valid contributions together to get g_q^η and shares of η. The protocol is shown in Fig. 7. Towards understanding the protocol, note that P_i in the first step does an integer secret sharing of η_i as a part of the Feldman procedure, resulting in shares $y_{i,j}$. Correctness of a share can be verified by the equation $g_q^{\Delta y_{i,j}} = C_{i,0}^{\Delta^2} \cdot \prod_{k=1}^t C_{i,k}^{j^k}$, as the right hand side

[9] Actually a weak form of extraction (see Sect. 5) will suffice, where we only extract a part of the witness. This is because the MPC protocol we describe here is a simple adaptation of Π_{ABB}^q for the non-YOSO model.

effectively evaluates the underlying polynomial in the exponent. After the protocol, every party who looks at the public information will be able to compute g_q^η and the Γ_j's, using the equations in the last step of the protocol.

Protocol CreateVSS

Create and send shares Each member P_i of COM_u samples the contribution to the secret $\eta_i \leftarrow \mathcal{D}_q$, and samples $s_{i,j} \leftarrow \mathcal{D}_q{}'$. Then it shares η_i as $(y_{i,1},\ldots,y_{i,N};C_{i,0},\ldots,C_{i,t}) \leftarrow \mathsf{F\text{-}Share}(\eta_i;\mathbf{r}_i;g_q)$, computes $\mathsf{ct}_{i,j} = \mathsf{Enc}(\mathsf{pk}_j^v, y_{i,j}; s_{i,j})$ for $j \in [N]$. Finally, P_i posts:

- $(C_{i,0},\ldots,C_{i,t})$
- $\mathsf{NIAoK}(C_{i,0},\eta_i;C_{i,0} = g_q^{\eta_i})$
- $\mathsf{NIAoK}(C_{i,k},r_{i,k};C_{i,k} = g_q^{\Delta r_{i,k}})$ for $k \in [t]$, where $\Delta = N!$
- $\mathsf{NIAoK}((\mathsf{pk}_j^v,\{C_{i,k}\},\mathsf{ct}_{i,j}),(y_{i,j},s_{i,j});\mathsf{ct}_{i,j} = \mathsf{Enc}(\mathsf{pk}_j^v,y_{i,j};s_{i,j}),\ g_q^{\Delta y_{i,j}} = C_{i,0}^{\Delta^2}\cdot\prod_{k=1}^t C_{i,k}^{j^k})$, for $j \in [M]$

Receive Shares Each member P_j of COM_v does the following:

1. Check all the proofs posted by COM_u and form a set $\mathcal{Q}$ of members (of COM_u) for which the proofs validate (NB: all honest P_j will agree on $\mathcal{Q}$).
2. Decrypt $\mathsf{ct}_{i,j}$ to get $y_{i,j}$.
3. Compute a share of η as $\gamma_j = \sum_{i\in\mathcal{Q}} y_{i,j}$, where $\eta := \sum_{i\in\mathcal{Q}} \eta_i$.
4. Compute $g_q^\eta = \prod_{i\in\mathcal{Q}} C_{i,0}$.
5. Compute a public verification value corresponding to γ_j, namely

$$\Gamma_j = g_q^{\Delta\gamma_j} = \prod_{i\in\mathcal{Q}} g_q^{\Delta y_{i,j}} = \prod_{i\in\mathcal{Q}} C_{i,0}^{\Delta^2}\cdot\prod_{k=1}^{t} C_{i,k}^{j^k}.$$

Fig. 7. Create verifiable secret-sharing for a committee

Definition 4. *We say that* a committee COM_ℓ holds $\mathsf{VSS}(\eta;\mathsf{f})$ *if it is the case that* f *is an integer polynomial of degree at most* t*, where* $\mathsf{f}(0) = \Delta\eta$*, each committee member* P_i *has a share* $\mathsf{f}(i)$*, and the value* $g_q^{\Delta\mathsf{f}(i)}$ *is on public display. Furthermore, also* g_q^η *is publicly known.*

With this notation, the CreateVSS protocol can be described as a protocol that is executed by two committees COM_u and COM_v, and which results in COM_v holding $\mathsf{VSS}(\eta;\mathsf{f})$ for some random value η, where only g_q^η is leaked to the adversary. Note that the underlying structure is linearly homomorphic: if a committee holds $\mathsf{VSS}(\eta;\mathsf{f})$ and $\mathsf{VSS}(\eta';\mathsf{f}')$, it effectively also holds $\mathsf{VSS}(\eta+\eta';\mathsf{f}+\mathsf{f}')$, by adding the underlying shares and multiplying the public values. We use CreateVSS for distributed key generation (Fig. 8). It needs to be executed by committees 0–3, as this step must happen before anything else.

Protocol DistKeyGen

Create and share the secret key Committees COM_0 and COM_1 run CreateVSS so that COM_1 holds $\mathsf{VSS}(\eta; \mathsf{f})$, and we set $\mathsf{pk}_{\mathsf{cl}} := g_q^{\eta}$ and $\mathsf{sk}_{\mathsf{cl}} := \eta$.
Create a special ciphertext The goal is to generate a ciphertext $\mathsf{ct}_P = (\mathsf{ct}_1, \mathsf{ct}_2) = (g_q^{\beta}, f \cdot \mathsf{pk}_{\mathsf{cl}}^{\beta})$, where β is a large random value. Our construction in Step 3 of Π_{TE} does this in the standard non-YOSO setting. We adapt it for YOSO in exactly the same way as we adapted Steps 1 and 2 to get CreateVSS. The resulting protocol is executed by next two committees $\mathsf{COM}_2, \mathsf{COM}_3$. They can clearly do this based only on the public key $\mathsf{pk}_{\mathsf{cl}}$. As a result, ct_P is now on public display, so now $\widetilde{\mathsf{pk}}_{\mathsf{cl}} = (\mathsf{pk}_{\mathsf{cl}}, \mathsf{ct}_P)$ is publicly known.

Fig. 8. Distributed key generation in the YOSO setting

Resharing the Secret Key. We need a protocol for passing the shares of the secret key from one committee COM_v to another committee $\mathsf{COM}_{v'}$. The idea is for an earlier committee COM_u to share the same random value for both COM_v and $\mathsf{COM}_{v'}$, and this will help to do the transfer. The Reshare protocol (Fig. 9) will be called several times, so the indices u, v, v' should be thought of as parameters, that will be determined by the global MPC protocol. Execution of Reshare adds a factor of Δ to the secret key held by the receiving committee, but this is not a problem, as we shall see.

Threshold Decryption. Note that our threshold decryption protocol for the standard setting (Fig. 4) is already a one round protocol, once we make the proofs of equality of discrete logs non-interactive. We need the protocol to work for a committee who holds $\mathsf{VSS}(\Delta^{\ell}\mathsf{sk}_{\mathsf{cl}}, \mathsf{f})$ for some ℓ, because each execution of Reshare adds a factor of Δ. This is not a problem, we will obtain the plaintext times a factor of $\Delta^{\ell} \bmod q$, and this factor can be divided out locally.

MPC. To realize the arithmetic black-box functionality in the YOSO setting, in particular secure multiplication, we follow the standard approach of generating so-called multiplication triples. That is, triples $(\mathsf{ct}_1, \mathsf{ct}_2, \mathsf{ct}_3)$ of ciphertexts containing plaintext values a, b, c where a, b are random and $c = ab$. We first construct a protocol for generating such triples while leaking nothing but the ciphertexts.

The basic steps of the final MPC protocol are found in the full version [9] and are a straightforward adaptation of Π^q_{ABB} which we described for the standard non-YOSO model. We assume here a global scheduling of which committees do the various types of work, where the first 4 committees do the key generation. After this, committees only need to work to do multiplications and output. Assume we are about to do a number of multiplications on encrypted values and that COM_i is the committee with the largest index who holds shares of the secret key but has not spoken yet. Now, $\mathsf{COM}_{i+1}, \mathsf{COM}_{i+2}$ will generate an appropriate number of multiplication triples, and COM_{i+3} will do the first part

Protocol Reshare

Create mask for the secret key We execute CreateVSS twice, one instance is done by $\mathsf{COM}_u, \mathsf{COM}_v$ and one by $\mathsf{COM}_u, \mathsf{COM}_{v'}$, with two adjustments: First, the two instances are correlated such that the shared secret value η is the same in both cases: as part of CreateVSS, each member P_i must make public $g_q^{\eta_i}$, where η_i is their additive contribution to the secret η. The receiving committees check that this value is the same in both instances and discard the contribution if not. Second, each η_i is chosen as a random number of bitlength σ larger than the maximal length of $\mathsf{sk}_{\mathsf{cl}}$. Also, the coefficient in the polynomials used are chosen to be σ bits longer than those used in the DistKeyGen protocol.
Open masked key We can now assume that COM_u holds $\mathsf{VSS}(\mathsf{sk}_{\mathsf{cl}}, \mathsf{f})$ as well as $\mathsf{VSS}(\eta, \mathsf{g})$. It therefore also holds $\mathsf{VSS}(\mathsf{sk}_{\mathsf{cl}} - \eta, \mathsf{f} - \mathsf{g})$. Each member P_j of COM_u posts its share $(\mathsf{f} - \mathsf{g})(j)$. Note that this share can be publicly verified, as $g_q^{\Delta \cdot (\mathsf{f}-\mathsf{g})(j)}$ is publicly known.
Adjust shares Members of $\mathsf{COM}_{u'}$ can now identify (at least) $t+1$ posted correct shares and reconstruct (by "integer interpolation") $\Delta(\mathsf{sk}_{\mathsf{cl}} - \eta)$. They then form $\mathsf{VSS}(\Delta(\mathsf{sk}_{\mathsf{cl}} - \eta), \mathsf{h}_0)$ where h_0 is a default polynomial, say the degree-0 polynomial that always takes the value $\Delta(\mathsf{sk}_{\mathsf{cl}} - \eta)$. This can then be added to $\Delta \cdot \mathsf{VSS}(\eta, \mathsf{h})$ received by the committee in the first step to form $\mathsf{VSS}(\Delta \mathsf{sk}_{\mathsf{cl}}, \mathsf{h} + \mathsf{h}_0)$.

Fig. 9. Transfer secret-sharing to a new committee

of the Reshare protocol, in the role of the auxiliary committee COM_u, and using COM_i and COM_{i+4} as the sending and receiving committees. Now, COM_i can do its part of the multiplication and post the resulting data, as well as data from the Reshare protocol, allowing COM_{i+4} to get shares of the secret key. The system is now ready to do the next layer of multiplications, with COM_{i+1} assuming the role COM_i played before.

In the full version [9], we sketch how the security of the YOSO version of the protocol can be argued by a relatively straightforward adaptation of the proof for the non-YOSO version.

Acknowledgements. This research was supported by the Concordium Blockhain Research Center, Aarhus University, Denmark, the Carlsberg Foundation under the Semper Ardens Research Project CF18-112 (BCM), and the European Research Council (ERC) under the European Unions's Horizon 2020 research and innovation programme under grant agreement No 803096 (SPEC). We thank Guilhem Castagnos, Fabien Laguillaumie, and Ida Tucker for clarifications regarding the CL framework.

References

1. Abe, M., Fehr, S.: Adaptively secure Feldman VSS and applications to universally-composable threshold cryptography. In: Franklin, M. (ed.) CRYPTO 2004. LNCS, vol. 3152, pp. 317–334. Springer, Heidelberg (August 2004). https://doi.org/10.1007/978-3-540-28628-8_20
2. Abram, D., Damgård, I., Orlandi, C., Scholl, P.: An algebraic framework for silent preprocessing with trustless setup and active security. In: Dodis, Y., Shrimpton, T. (eds.) CRYPTO 2022, Part IV. LNCS, vol. 13510, pp. 421–452. Springer, Heidelberg (August 2022). https://doi.org/10.1007/978-3-031-15985-5_15
3. Arun, A., Ganesh, C., Lokam, S.V., Mopuri, T., Sridhar, S.: Dew: a transparent constant-sized polynomial commitment scheme. In: Boldyreva, A., Kolesnikov, V. (eds.) PKC 2023, Part II. LNCS, vol. 13941, pp. 542–571. Springer, Heidelberg (May 2023). https://doi.org/10.1007/978-3-031-31371-4_19
4. Baum, C., Cozzo, D., Smart, N.P.: Using TopGear in overdrive: a more efficient ZKPoK for SPDZ. In: Paterson, K.G., Stebila, D. (eds.) SAC 2019. LNCS, vol. 11959, pp. 274–302. Springer, Heidelberg (August 2019). https://doi.org/10.1007/978-3-030-38471-5_12
5. Beaver, D.: Efficient multiparty protocols using circuit randomization. In: Feigenbaum, J. (ed.) CRYPTO'91. LNCS, vol. 576, pp. 420–432. Springer, Heidelberg (August 1992). https://doi.org/10.1007/3-540-46766-1_34
6. Bendlin, R., Damgård, I., Orlandi, C., Zakarias, S.: Semi-homomorphic encryption and multiparty computation. In: Paterson, K.G. (ed.) EUROCRYPT 2011. LNCS, vol. 6632, pp. 169–188. Springer, Heidelberg (May 2011). https://doi.org/10.1007/978-3-642-20465-4_11
7. Benhamouda, F., et al.: Can a public blockchain keep a secret? In: Pass, R., Pietrzak, K. (eds.) TCC 2020, Part I. LNCS, vol. 12550, pp. 260–290. Springer, Heidelberg (November 2020). https://doi.org/10.1007/978-3-030-64375-1_10
8. Boneh, D., Bünz, B., Fisch, B.: A survey of two verifiable delay functions. Cryptology ePrint Archive, Report 2018/712 (2018), https://eprint.iacr.org/2018/712
9. Braun, L., Damgård, I., Orlandi, C.: Secure multiparty computation from threshold encryption based on class groups. Cryptology ePrint Archive, Report 2022/1437 (2022). https://eprint.iacr.org/2022/1437
10. Castagnos, G., Catalano, D., Laguillaumie, F., Savasta, F., Tucker, I.: Two-party ECDSA from hash proof systems and efficient instantiations. In: Boldyreva, A., Micciancio, D. (eds.) CRYPTO 2019, Part III. LNCS, vol. 11694, pp. 191–221. Springer, Heidelberg (August 2019). https://doi.org/10.1007/978-3-030-26954-8_7
11. Castagnos, G., Catalano, D., Laguillaumie, F., Savasta, F., Tucker, I.: Bandwidth-efficient threshold EC-DSA. In: Kiayias, A., Kohlweiss, M., Wallden, P., Zikas, V. (eds.) PKC 2020, Part II. LNCS, vol. 12111, pp. 266–296. Springer, Heidelberg (May 2020). https://doi.org/10.1007/978-3-030-45388-6_10
12. Castagnos, G., Laguillaumie, F.: Linearly homomorphic encryption from DDH. In: Nyberg, K. (ed.) CT-RSA 2015. LNCS, vol. 9048, pp. 487–505. Springer, Heidelberg (April 2015). https://doi.org/10.1007/978-3-319-16715-2_26
13. Castagnos, G., Laguillaumie, F., Tucker, I.: Practical fully secure unrestricted inner product functional encryption modulo p. In: Peyrin, T., Galbraith, S. (eds.) ASIACRYPT 2018, Part II. LNCS, vol. 11273, pp. 733–764. Springer, Heidelberg (December 2018). https://doi.org/10.1007/978-3-030-03329-3_25

14. Castagnos, G., Laguillaumie, F., Tucker, I.: Threshold linearly homomorphic encryption on $\mathbf{Z}/2^k\mathbf{Z}$. In: Agrawal, S., Lin, D. (eds.) ASIACRYPT 2022, Part II. LNCS, vol. 13792, pp. 99–129. Springer, Heidelberg (December 2022). https://doi.org/10.1007/978-3-031-22966-4_4
15. Cohen, H., Lenstra, H.W.: Heuristics on class groups of number fields. In: Number Theory Noordwijkerhout 1983 (1984)
16. Cramer, R.: Modular design of secure yet practical cryptographic protocols. Ph.D. thesis, Universiteit van Amsterdam (1997)
17. Cramer, R., Damgård, I., Nielsen, J.B.: Multiparty computation from threshold homomorphic encryption. In: Pfitzmann, B. (ed.) EUROCRYPT 2001. LNCS, vol. 2045, pp. 280–299. Springer, Heidelberg (May 2001). https://doi.org/10.1007/3-540-44987-6_18
18. Cramer, R., Damgård, I., Schoenmakers, B.: Proofs of partial knowledge and simplified design of witness hiding protocols. In: Desmedt, Y. (ed.) CRYPTO 1994. LNCS, vol. 839, pp. 174–187. Springer, Heidelberg (August 1994). https://doi.org/10.1007/3-540-48658-5_19
19. Cramer, R., Fehr, S.: Optimal black-box secret sharing over arbitrary Abelian groups. In: Yung, M. (ed.) CRYPTO 2002. LNCS, vol. 2442, pp. 272–287. Springer, Heidelberg (August 2002). https://doi.org/10.1007/3-540-45708-9_18
20. Damgård, I., Nielsen, J.B.: Universally composable efficient multiparty computation from threshold homomorphic encryption. In: Boneh, D. (ed.) CRYPTO 2003. LNCS, vol. 2729, pp. 247–264. Springer, Heidelberg (August 2003). https://doi.org/10.1007/978-3-540-45146-4_15
21. Damgård, I., Pastro, V., Smart, N.P., Zakarias, S.: Multiparty computation from somewhat homomorphic encryption. In: Safavi-Naini, R., Canetti, R. (eds.) CRYPTO 2012. LNCS, vol. 7417, pp. 643–662. Springer, Heidelberg (August 2012). https://doi.org/10.1007/978-3-642-32009-5_38
22. Damgård, I., Thorbek, R.: Linear integer secret sharing and distributed exponentiation. In: Yung, M., Dodis, Y., Kiayias, A., Malkin, T. (eds.) PKC 2006. LNCS, vol. 3958, pp. 75–90. Springer, Heidelberg (April 2006). https://doi.org/10.1007/11745853_6
23. Desmedt, Y., Frankel, Y.: Shared generation of authenticators and signatures (extended abstract). In: Feigenbaum, J. (ed.) CRYPTO'91. LNCS, vol. 576, pp. 457–469. Springer, Heidelberg (August 1992). https://doi.org/10.1007/3-540-46766-1_37
24. Erwig, A., Faust, S., Riahi, S.: Large-scale non-interactive threshold cryptosystems through anonymity. Cryptology ePrint Archive, Report 2021/1290 (2021), https://eprint.iacr.org/2021/1290
25. Feldman, P.: A practical scheme for non-interactive verifiable secret sharing. In: 28th FOCS. pp. 427–437. IEEE Computer Society Press (October 1987). https://doi.org/10.1109/SFCS.1987.4
26. Fischlin, M.: Communication-efficient non-interactive proofs of knowledge with online extractors. In: Shoup, V. (ed.) CRYPTO 2005. LNCS, vol. 3621, pp. 152–168. Springer, Heidelberg (August 2005). https://doi.org/10.1007/11535218_10
27. Frankel, Y., Gemmell, P., MacKenzie, P.D., Yung, M.: Optimal resilience proactive public-key cryptosystems. In: 38th FOCS. pp. 384–393. IEEE Computer Society Press (October 1997). https://doi.org/10.1109/SFCS.1997.646127
28. Gennaro, R., Jarecki, S., Krawczyk, H., Rabin, T.: Secure distributed key generation for discrete-log based cryptosystems. J. Cryptol. **20**(1), 51–83 (2006). https://doi.org/10.1007/s00145-006-0347-3

29. Gentry, C., et al.: YOSO: You only speak once - secure MPC with stateless ephemeral roles. In: Malkin, T., Peikert, C. (eds.) CRYPTO 2021, Part II. LNCS, vol. 12826, pp. 64–93. Springer, Heidelberg, Virtual Event (August 2021). https://doi.org/10.1007/978-3-030-84245-1_3
30. Gordon, S.D., Le, P.H., McVicker, D.: Linear communication in malicious majority MPC. Cryptology ePrint Archive, Report 2022/781 (2022), https://eprint.iacr.org/2022/781
31. Keller, M., Pastro, V., Rotaru, D.: Overdrive: making SPDZ great again. In: Nielsen, J.B., Rijmen, V. (eds.) EUROCRYPT 2018, Part III. LNCS, vol. 10822, pp. 158–189. Springer, Heidelberg (April/May 2018). https://doi.org/10.1007/978-3-319-78372-7_6
32. Kolby, S., Ravi, D., Yakoubov, S.: Towards efficient YOSO MPC without setup. Cryptology ePrint Archive, Report 2022/187 (2022), https://eprint.iacr.org/2022/187
33. Okamoto, T., Pointcheval, D.: The gap-problems: A new class of problems for the security of cryptographic schemes. In: Kim, K. (ed.) PKC 2001. LNCS, vol. 1992, pp. 104–118. Springer, Heidelberg (February 2001). https://doi.org/10.1007/3-540-44586-2_8
34. Paillier, P.: Public-key cryptosystems based on composite degree residuosity classes. In: Stern, J. (ed.) EUROCRYPT'99. LNCS, vol. 1592, pp. 223–238. Springer, Heidelberg (May 1999). https://doi.org/10.1007/3-540-48910-X_16
35. Pietrzak, K.: Simple verifiable delay functions. In: Blum, A. (ed.) ITCS 2019. vol. 124, pp. 60:1–60:15. LIPIcs (Jan 2019). https://doi.org/10.4230/LIPIcs.ITCS.2019.60
36. Rabin, T.: A simplified approach to threshold and proactive RSA. In: Krawczyk, H. (ed.) CRYPTO 1998. LNCS, vol. 1462, pp. 89–104. Springer, Heidelberg (1998). https://doi.org/10.1007/BFb0055722
37. Shamir, A.: How to share a secret. Commun. Assoc. Comput. Mach. **22**(11), 612–613 (1979)
38. Tucker, I.: Chiffrement fonctionnel et signatures distribuées fondés sur des fonctions de hachage à projection, l'apport des groupes de classes. Ph.D. thesis, École normale supérieure de Lyon (2020)
39. Wesolowski, B.: Efficient verifiable delay functions. In: Ishai, Y., Rijmen, V. (eds.) EUROCRYPT 2019, Part III. LNCS, vol. 11478, pp. 379–407. Springer, Heidelberg (May 2019). https://doi.org/10.1007/978-3-030-17659-4_13

Two-Round Stateless Deterministic Two-Party Schnorr Signatures from Pseudorandom Correlation Functions

Yashvanth Kondi(✉), Claudio Orlandi, and Lawrence Roy

Aarhus University, Aarhus, Denmark
{ykondi,orlandi}@cs.au.dk, ldr709@gmail.com

Abstract. Schnorr signatures are a popular choice due to their simplicity, provable security, and linear structure that enables relatively easy threshold signing protocols. The deterministic variant of Schnorr (where the nonce is derived in a stateless manner using a PRF from the message and a long term secret) is widely used in practice since it mitigates the threats of a faulty or poor randomness generator (which in Schnorr leads to catastrophic breaches of security). Unfortunately, threshold protocols for the deterministic variant of Schnorr have so far been quite inefficient, as they make non black-box use of the PRF involved in the nonce generation.

In this paper, we present the first two-party threshold protocol for Schnorr signatures, where signing is stateless and deterministic, and only makes black-box use of the underlying cryptographic algorithms.

We present a protocol from general assumptions which achieves covert security, and a protocol that achieves full active security under standard factoring-like assumptions. Our protocols make crucial use of recent advances within the field of *pseudorandom correlation functions (PCFs).*

As an additional benefit, only two-rounds are needed to perform distributed signing in our protocol, connecting our work to a recent line of research on the trade-offs between round complexity and cryptographic assumptions for threshold Schnorr signatures.

1 Introduction

Schnorr [Sch91] provides a simple method to leverage the hardness of computing discrete logarithms in some group of known prime order, to construct a provably unforgable signature scheme [PS96]. Although the adoption of Schnorr signatures was initially hampered by a patent, following the patent's expiration in 2008 its footprint in real-world use has been rapidly growing. For instance EdDSA [BDL+11] (a carefully parameterized instantion of Schnorr) already enjoys wide support in several standard libraries, and even more recently Schnorr signatures have seen interest from the Bitcoin community [WNR]. Along with their increasing deployment, interest in mechanisms for *key protection* of Schnorr signatures has grown in the recent past. One common method of mitigating single points of failure in the storage and use of such keys is via *threshold* signatures [Des88]. Informally, a threshold signature allows its key to be secret

H. Handschuh and A. Lysyanskaya (Eds.): CRYPTO 2023, LNCS 14081, pp. 646–677, 2023.
https://doi.org/10.1007/978-3-031-38557-5_21

shared amongst multiple devices, so that a qualified quorum of these devices must collaborate in order to perform signing operations with the key.

The linear nature of Schnorr's signature scheme is known to be conducive to simple distributed signing protocols, with several classic [SS01, NKDM03, GJKR07], and recent [MPSW19, KG20, NRS21, AB21] constructions. At a high level, a Schnorr signature under public key $\mathsf{pk} = \mathsf{sk} \cdot G$ is of the form $(R = r \cdot G, s = \mathsf{sk} \cdot e + r)$, where $e = H(R, pk, m)$, and so a multiparty signing protocol consists of sampling the nonce R with standard distributed key generation techniques [Ped91] and computing s by taking a linear combination the shares of sk and r.

Deterministic Nonce Derivation. Schnorr's original proposal required the random sampling of r, and a line of works on secret key recovery from nonce bias [HS01, ANT+20, MH20] has shown that even a slight noticeable deviation from the uniform distribution can induce catastrophic failure. Taken in combination with empirical observations on the ubiquity of randomness failures in practice [Hen22], this sensitivity to nonce bias makes the nonce sampling step a significant potential attack surface for Schnorr signatures. In order to mitigate this threat, early proposals [Bar97, Wig97] called for *deterministic* nonce generation.

Statelessness. One may consider deriving nonces by maintaining a stateful pseudorandom number generator, for example. However such an approach then becomes vulnerable to state reuse, which implies nonce reuse in this context. Reliably maintaining state can be surprisingly non-trivial in a variety of scenarios, and is studied under the umbrella of *state continuity* [PLD+11, SP16, MAK+17] in the systems literature. One such scenario that is particularly relevant to modern cloud deployment conditions is that of incorrectly instantiating Virtual Machines [EZJ+14, KASN15]—stale state is not typically detectable within the context provided to cryptographic APIs.

This problem could in principle be addressed by general solutions for state continuity based on trusted hardware [PLD+11, SP16]. However, such solutions come with extra hardware costs and qualitative disadvantages due to heuristic hardware-based trust assumptions, in addition to suffering a high latency for simple operations (over 60ms to increment an SGX Trusted Monotonic Counter [BCLK17]). We refer the reader to Garillot et al. [GKMN21] for a more detailed discussion.

Modern instantiations of Schnorr's scheme such as EdDSA are therefore both *deterministic*, and *stateless*—nonces are derived by applying a hash function (or PRF) on the message being signed, along with a long-term secret. In particular, given a PRF $\mathsf{F} : \{0,1\}^* \mapsto \mathbb{Z}_q$ the signer samples a PRF seed $\mathsf{sd} \leftarrow \{0,1\}^\kappa$ during key generation, and computes $r \leftarrow \mathsf{F}_{\mathsf{sd}}(m)$ to use in signing the message. Our goal in this work is to translate this template for stateless derandomization to the distributed setting, which is known to be a challenging problem [MPSW19]. We focus on the two-party setting in this work, as it is the base case for the challenging dishonest majority setting, and is already sufficient for a number of useful applications including cryptocurrency wallets, two-factor authentication, etc. As one indicator of real-world interest in solutions to this problem, the recent draft NIST Internal Report on Threshold EdDSA/Schnorr signatures [BD22] and subsequent call for multiparty threshold schemes considers stateless deterministic signing as a potentially desirable mode of operation.

1.1 Distributed Schnorr Signing with Stateless Determinism

We first explain the obstacle to translating the benefits of the simple stateless deterministic nonce derivation technique described above to the distributed signing setting, and then we discuss existing approaches to the problem.

The Obstacle. Consider a setting in which parties P_0, P_1 have signing key shares $\mathsf{sk}_0, \mathsf{sk}_1$, and wish to sign a message m under their joint signing key $\mathsf{sk} = \mathsf{sk}_0 + \mathsf{sk}_1$. The protocol of Nicolosi et al. [NKDM03] roughly proceeds as follows: each P_i samples $r_i \leftarrow \mathbb{Z}_q$ and computes $R_i = r_i \cdot G$, and P_0 first sends a commitment $C = \mathsf{Com}(R_0)$ to P_1. Upon receiving C, party P_1 sends R_1 to P_0, who then establishes the signing nonce $R = R_0 + R_1$, which in turn determines $e = H(R, \mathsf{pk}, m)$. Finally, P_0 computes $s_0 = \mathsf{sk}_0 \cdot e + r_0$ locally and sends this value (along with the opening of C to R_0) to P_1, who is able to compute $s_1 = \mathsf{sk}_1 \cdot e + r_1$ and complete the signature $(R = R_0 + R_1, s = s_0 + s_1)$.

A naive method to statelessly derandomize such a protocol would be to instruct each P_i to sample a long-term secret seed sd_i, and begin the protocol by computing $r_i = \mathsf{F}_{\mathsf{sd}_i}(m)$ using a pseudorandom function F rather than sampling one afresh. This naive approach already solves the problem in the semi-honest setting. However, it runs into the following issue for malicious security: a corrupt P_1 could initiate two signature sessions to sign the same message, behaving honestly in the first instance, and in the second instance using $r_1^* \neq \mathsf{F}_{\mathsf{sd}_1}(m)$ in place of the correct r_1 (equivalently $R_1^* \neq R_1$). As P_0's choice of r_0 depends only on (sd_0, m), its nonce share R_0 stays the same in both instances. This leads to different nonces $R = R_0 + R_1$ and $R^* = R_0 + R_1^*$ with corresponding $e = H(R, \mathsf{pk}, m)$ and $e^* = H(R^*, \mathsf{pk}, m)$ in the two instances, which induces P_0 to reveal $s_0 = \mathsf{sk}_0 e + r_0$ and $s_0^* = \mathsf{sk}_0 e^* + r_0$ to P_1. As s_0, s_0^* constitute two independent linear combinations of the same two values (one of which is sk_0), P_1 can simply solve for sk_0 and recover the whole signing key. This flavour of issue was first documented by Maxwell et al. [MPSW19], and has been notoriously difficult to mitigate.

Existing Approaches. To our knowledge, there are only two papers in the literature that present techniques to mitigate the above issue: those of Nick et al. [NRSW20], and Garillot et al. [GKMN21]. Both works take a GMW-type approach [GMW87] of having each party prove in zero-knowledge that it executed the naive semi-honest stateless deterministic protocol correctly. Conceptually, the approach is simple: each P_i provides a one-time commitment to its long-term seed sd_i—perhaps during distributed key generation—and subsequently when signing a message, each P_i proves in zero-knowledge that its claimed nonce R_i is indeed of the form $R_i = \mathsf{F}_{\mathsf{sd}_i}(m) \cdot G$, where sd_i is contained in the commitment.

This simple approach is non-trivial to implement with concrete efficiency, as the statement being proven consists of an algebraic component (by virtue of the elliptic curve operations), and a complex non-algebraic one (due to the PRF). Nick et al. [NRSW20] reconcile this difference by designing a custom arithmetization-friendly PRF to use along with a succinct proof system, i.e. Bulletproofs [BBB+18]. On the other hand, Garillot et al. [GKMN21] take the opposite approach; they start with a standard block-cipher based PRF—such as AES or SHA—and optimize garbled circuit based ZK proofs [JKO13] for this setting.

Both approaches (and indeed any approach based on the GMW paradigm) are bottlenecked by having to prove cryptographic statements involving F in zero-knowledge; the efficiency of such approaches inherently depends on the circuit complexity of pseudorandom functions. It is therefore natural to ask,

Can we design a distributed, stateless, deterministic, Schnorr signing scheme that makes only blackbox use of cryptographic primitives?

Our Results. In this work, we develop a new methodology for distributing Schnorr signing while retaining stateless determinism, that makes blackbox use of an increasingly general cryptographic primitive—*pseudorandom correlation functions*, or PCFs [BCG+20]. Just as the single party algorithm is easily derandomized with PRFs, we invoke PCFs to natively translate the derandomization technique to the distributed setting. Roughly, PCFs are the multiparty analogue of PRFs—they compress exponentially large correlated random tapes into short keys. This way, the random tape for all signing nonces is effectively committed during distributed key generation; when signing a message the parties access the relevant portion to obtain their nonce shares, and use the correlation to validate each other's shares.

The complexity of the correlation determines the efficiency of the PCF, and so we show that the relatively simple Vector Oblivious Linear Evaluation (VOLE) correlation suffices for our task. We present two instantiations of our methodology:

- Our first construction is based on the SoftSpoken VOLE PCF by Roy [Roy22], and makes blackbox use of any PRF. While the original construction worked only for small fields, we generalize it to arbitrary ones to be able to use it in our context. The computation overhead of this approach is barely noticeable relative to the naive semi-honest protocol (only additions in $\mathbb{Z}_q$), and the bandwidth overhead is a single group element. However, it only achieves *covert* security [AL07].
- Our second construction achieves full malicious security, and correspondingly requires a VOLE PCF for a large field. Our starting point is the Paillier

encryption based PCF of Orlandi et al. [OSY21]. Since their PCF generates correlation modulo a biprime, we need to carefully devise a technique to obtain VOLE correlations modulo a prime while preserving active security which can be used in our context. We construct a secure translation and consistency checking mechanism for this purpose, whose security we reduce to the Decisional Composite Residuosity (DCR) and Strong RSA assumptions. Besides instantiating a fundamentally new approach, our construction achieves the lowest bandwidth consumption of any known stateless deterministic Schnorr signing scheme (only a few hundred bytes), at reasonable computation overhead (a few exponentiations). We report on a proof-of-concept implementation in Sect. 5.2.

As an interesting additional benefit, our constructions achieve two-round signing, which has been notoriously difficult to accomplish even in the randomized setting [DEF+19]. Existing two-round signing protocols either rely on interactive assumptions or the Algebraic Group Model [KG20,NRS21,AB21], or make use of non-black-box zero-knowledge proofs of cryptographic statements [NRSW20]. We give a comparison of our approaches to those from the literature in Table 1.

Table 1. Comparison of different techniques to distribute Schnorr signing. Computation complexity is not represented in this table, as it is best measured empirically, and most works are not implemented. Note that our protocols invoke an ideal oracle $\mathcal{F}_{\mathsf{Setup}}^{\mathsf{PCF}}$ during key generation, which is not the focus in this work. Bandwidth cost represents data transmitted per party when signing with a 256-bit elliptic curve, and is either derived analytically here (see the full version of this paper for [Lin22,NRS21] and Sects. 4.1 and 5.1 for our work) or taken from previous work. "Blackbox" refers to the use of cryptographic tools as a black box, in order to avoid dependence on their circuit complexity. For instance, Schnorr's proof of knowledge of discrete logarithm is blackbox as it uses the group as an oracle, whereas proving statements that involve the circuit representation of group operations is not.

	Stateless & Deterministic	Rounds	Bandwidth (KB)	Assumptions	Blackbox	Security
[Lin22]	✗	3	0.9	RO	✓	Malicious
[NRS21]	✗	2	0.1	RO+OMDL	✓	Malicious
[NRSW20]	✓	2	1.1	RO+DDH[a]	✗	Malicious
[GKMN21]	✓	3	307	RO+PRF	✗	Malicious
This work	✓	2	0.1	OT+PRF	✓	Covert
This work	✓	2	0.5	RO+DCR+Strong RSA	✓	Malicious

[a] DDH in a custom elliptic curve, not the same one as the signature.

Key Generation/Setup. Our protocols make use of an ideal setup oracle $\mathcal{F}_{\mathsf{Setup}}^{\mathsf{PCF}}$ to sample and distribute the PCF keys. In principle, this oracle can be realized by MPC to obtain a fully distributed protocol. The focus of this work is on the signing phase, and so we do not discuss the concrete efficiency or optimizations in realizing $\mathcal{F}_{\mathsf{Setup}}^{\mathsf{PCF}}$. Moreover, as discussed by Abram et al. [ANO+22], in many practical applications of threshold cryptography there is a natural "trusted dealer" that can execute $\mathcal{F}_{\mathsf{Setup}}^{\mathsf{PCF}}$, namely the owner of the cryptocurrency wallet distributing its secret key.

Future Work. As shown in Table 1, our results achieve *either* malicious security, or security under generic assumptions (OT and PRF). Achieving both at the same time remains an interesting open question.

1.2 Our Techniques

In this work, we retain the approach of having each P_i prove that their claimed nonce was derived correctly, but we do not look to the literature on zero-knowledge proofs to instantiate such an object. Instead, we view this problem through the lens of Pseudorandom Correlation Functions (PCFs) [BCG+20]. Informally, a two-party PCF produces two keys k_0, k_1 so that for any public $x \in \{0,1\}^\kappa$, it holds that $a_0 = \mathsf{PCF.Eval}(k_0, x)$ and $a_1 = \mathsf{PCF.Eval}(k_1, x)$ are correlated per some useful function. As an example, a PCF for the (Random) Oblivious Transfer correlation would enforce that $a_0 = (m_0, m_1) \in \{0,1\}^{2\times\kappa}$, and $a_1 = (b, m_b) \in \{0,1\} \times \{0,1\}^\kappa$. The 'pseudorandomness' property intuitively guarantees that (a_0, a_1) is distributed pseudorandomly in the appropriate domain.

Feasibility of the Ideal PCF. We begin by considering what the ideal PCF might look like for the task of nonce derivation. Consider a "nonce correlation", which enforces that (a_0, a_1) are of the form $a_0 \in \mathbb{Z}_q$ and $a_1 = a_0 \cdot G \in \mathbb{G}$. It is immediate how such a PCF would be useful in the design of two-party Schnorr signing—to sign a message m, each P_i derives its nonce as $r_i = \mathsf{PCF.Eval}(k_{i,0}, m)$ while P_{1-i} derives the corresponding $R_i = \mathsf{PCF.Eval}(k_{i,1}, m)$. As each party P_i can derive the other's nonce share R_{1-i} locally via the PCF, the common nonce $R = R_0 + R_1$ is established non-interactively just by fixing the message, and it only remains for the parties to locally compute and exchange their s_i values. This gives a conceptually simple non-interactive stateless deterministic two-party Schnorr signing protocol. While it is feasible to construct such a PCF via generic techniques [DHRW16,BCG+20], it is unclear how to instantiate it with reasonable concrete efficiency, or even blackbox in the group $\mathbb{G}$.

The VOLE PCF is Nearly Ideal. The Vector Oblivious Linear Evaluation (VOLE) correlation enforces that (a_0, a_1) be of the form $a_0 = (u, v)$ and $a_1 = (w, \Delta)$ such that $w - v = u\Delta$, where Δ is fixed across all evaluations with the same key pair. If the correlation holds mod q, the value u can be used as r_i directly, and v, w, Δ can serve to *authenticate* $R_i = u \cdot G$. In particular, if P_0 and P_1 derive (a_0, a_1) as above, and P_0 sends $R_0 = u \cdot G$ and $V = v \cdot G$ to P_1, party P_1 can then check the correlation *in the exponent*, i.e. validate $w \cdot G - V \stackrel{?}{=} \Delta \cdot R_i$. The probability that P_0 tricks P_1 into accepting a false $R_0^* \neq R_0$ is essentially equivalent to the probability that P_0 is able to guess Δ.

The VOLE PCF is therefore conducive to a two-round Schnorr signing protocol: each P_i derives $r_i, v_i, w_{1-i}, \Delta_{1-i}$ locally—correlated as $w_i - v_i = r_i \Delta$ for each $i \in \{0,1\}$—and sends the corresponding R_i, V_i to P_{1-i}. Upon receiving R_{1-i}, V_{1-i}, each P_i validates the correlation with w_{1-i}, Δ_i in the exponent, and sets $R = R_0 + R_1$. The parties then locally compute and exchange their respective $s_i = \mathsf{sk}_i \cdot e + r_i$ values, and complete the signature as $(R, s = s_0 + s_1)$.

First Instantiation: SoftSpoken VOLE. As a building block for OT extension, Roy [Roy22] introduced a PCF for the VOLE correlation called SoftSpoken VOLE, which makes blackbox use of any PRF. However, this PCF was designed to create VOLE correlations in $\mathbb{F}_{2^{O(\log \kappa)}}$ as a generalization of the IKNP OT extension technique [IKNP03]. In order to use it in our context, we generalize the SoftSpoken VOLE technique so that it can produce such correlations in any field, even exponentially large ones. However, an important caveat of this adjustment is that while u is uniform in say $\mathbb{Z}_q$, in order for the PCF evaluation to be efficient (i.e. polynomial in κ), the Δ component of the correlation is restricted to a polynomially large subset of $\mathbb{Z}_q$. This means that a corrupt P_i^* could fool P_{1-i} into accepting an incorrect R_i^* with small but noticeable probability, and thus our first instantiation only achieves covert security.

Second Instantiation: Paillier PCF. Orlandi et al. [OSY21] presented a PCF for the VOLE correlation based on Paillier's encryption scheme. For concreteness, assume that P_0 owns k_0, and P_1 owns k_1 which allow them to non-interactively generate shares $w - v$ of $u\Delta$ in $\mathbb{Z}_N$. Although the PCF can produce exponentially large Δ values, the correlations it produces hold over the ring $\mathbb{Z}_N$ where N is the product of two large primes—this factorization of N is known only to the party that holds key k_0. We therefore have to design an additional protocol to carefully 'translate' this correlation from $\mathbb{Z}_N$ to a correlation in $\mathbb{Z}_q$.

This translation problem turns out to be surprisingly non-trivial, as demonstrated by our initial failed approaches. We first explored techniques such as rounded division ($u' = \lfloor \frac{uq}{N} \rceil$) and remainder ($u' = (u \bmod N) \bmod q$) to convert from $\mathbb{Z}_N$ to $\mathbb{Z}_q$. Any such conversion introduces errors into the shares, which is quite difficult to securely correct to a valid correlation over $\mathbb{Z}_q$. Consider an IKNP OT extension [IKNP03] type approach, where P_0 sends a "correction word" to account for the error. The challenge then is to ensure that P_0 is unable to send a malformed correction word without being detected. One might try adding a VOLE consistency checking protocol to verify the correlation, but validity of the correlation alone does not suffice in our setting; P_0 must be unable to *change* its output $u' \in \mathbb{Z}_q$ in repeated invocations of the protocol. One approach that we explored at this point is having P_0 prove that the corrected u' is "small", i.e. fully reduced modulo q. However this led us to a general issue with (approximate) range proofs: any such proof system that we could develop achieved at most a soundness of $\frac{1}{2}$ per repetition. This stems from an issue where P_0 can add an error of $\frac{1}{2}$ mod N at some point in the protocol, which has a noticeable chance of escaping detection when multiplied by a (small) even number. We refer the reader to Couteau et al. [CKLR21, Section 2.1] for a detailed discussion of this flavour of issue.

In Sect. 5 we present our solution to this translation problem that finally worked. Roughly, our translation to $\mathbb{Z}_q$ mechanism works as follows: First, the parties translate their shares over $\mathbb{Z}_N$ into shares over $\mathbb{Z}$, removing the modulus by using a technique from the Paillier HSS constructions of [OSY21,RS21]. This requires sending a correction, to force u to be small compared to N. Then, the parties take their shares modulo q to get shares suitable for use in two-party Schnorr. To handle P_0's possible lies, we introduce some carefully crafted checks which only allow P_0 to lie by a multiple of some parameter M, which we require to be divisible by q (thus having no impact on the final result). The most important of these checks is an "integer consistency check" in the exponent, using a different group generated by $g \in (\mathbb{Z}_{N_\mathsf{V}})^\times$, where N_V is another semiprime, making g's order be unknown. Performing a check over $\mathbb{Z}$ instead of $\mathbb{Z}_N$ avoids the issue of wraparound, as multiplying two large numbers cannot output a small number. We defer a more detailed technical description to Sect. 5.

1.3 Related Work

As discussed earlier, to our knowledge the works of Nick et al. [NRSW20] and Garillot et al. [GKMN21] are the only ones to present distributed Schnorr signing protocols where signing is stateless and deterministic. Both use zero-knowledge proofs to prove the consistency of claimed nonces with respect to committed nonce derivation keys. Our full security PCF construction achieves better communication complexity than both, while staying within the realm of standard assumptions.

Smart and Alaoui [ST19], and Dalskov et al. [DOK+20] observed that SPDZ-style MACs can be checked in the exponent, and showed how to apply this principle in the context of distributing the computation of ECDSA signatures. Our techniques in this paper can be viewed as a PCF interpretation of a similar idea, i.e. that VOLE correlations can be useful for authentication in the exponent.

Abram et al. [ANO+22] used Pseudorandom Correlation *Generators* (PCGs) to generate useful correlations to distribute the computation of ECDSA. Like us, they follow a pseudorandom correlation paradigm in a threshold signature context, however the setting in their paper is entirely different; their work optimizes storage and 'online' bandwidth complexity of distributing ECDSA, and their techniques rely on maintaining state.

Bonte et al. [BST21] investigate the cost of using MPC to distribute the EdDSA signing algorithm, which derives nonces by hashing the message to be signed with a long-term secret. While the ideal functionality that they achieve is stateless and deterministic, the *protocol* itself is not—i.e. their protocol relies on keeping state and/or sampling fresh randomness online.

Several works on threshold ECDSA make use of Paillier encryption [GG18, LN18, CGG+20] for Oblivious Linear Evaluation (OLE). Their techniques are fundamentally different; they rely on a classic OLE protocol that leverages the additive homomorphism of Paillier encryption [Gil99], and make use of expensive range proofs to enforce the correctness of the OLE. In contrast, our full security construction does not directly make use of the homomorphism of Paillier encryption, and rather than use range proofs to enforce honesty, we design a custom mechanism to guarantee that the VOLE correlation is correctly 'translated' from $\mathbb{Z}_N$ to $\mathbb{Z}_q$.

2 Definitions

Notation. We define the modulus operation to be symmetric, meaning that $a \bmod b \in [-\frac{b}{2}, \frac{b}{2}) \cap \mathbb{Z}$. This works together with rounding $\lfloor \frac{a}{b} \rceil$ as quotient and remainder: $a = b\lfloor \frac{a}{b} \rceil + a \bmod b$.

2.1 Semiprime-Related Assumptions

There are many cryptographic schemes built on using a semiprime's factorization as the trapdoor. Here, we will present the assumptions we need. First, we need to choose a distribution for the semiprimes.

$N, \varphi \leftarrow$ **RSA.Gen**(1^κ): Sample primes $p, q \in (2^{\ell(\kappa)/2-1}, 2^{\ell(\kappa)/2})$ uniformly at random. Output $N = pq \in (2^{\ell(\kappa)-2}, 2^{\ell(\kappa)})$ and $\varphi = (p-1)(q-1)$.

$N, \varphi \leftarrow$ **RSA.GenSafe**(1^κ): Sample *safe* primes $p, q \in (2^{\ell(\kappa)/2-1}, 2^{\ell(\kappa)/2})$ uniformly at random. I.e. sample primes p, q such that $\frac{p-1}{2}$ and $\frac{q-1}{2}$ are also prime. Compute N, φ as in RSA.Gen.

The polynomial $\ell(\kappa)$ should be chosen to make the related hardness assumptions achieve κ-bit security.[1]

First, we the DCR assumption for the security of the Paillier cryptosystem.

Definition 2.1. The decisional composite residuosity (DCR) assumption states that the following distributions are indistinguishable. RSA.Gen

$(N, \phi) \leftarrow \mathsf{RSA.Gen}(1^\kappa)$ $r \leftarrow (\mathbb{Z}_{N^2})^\times$ return N, r	$(N, \phi) \leftarrow \mathsf{RSA.Gen}(1^\kappa)$ $r \leftarrow (\mathbb{Z}_{N^2})^\times$ return N, r^N

Second, we will use a consistency check based on a group of unknown order, for which we use multiplication modulo a semiprime (similarly to [DF02]). For security, we need two properties. First, it must be hard to find roots of unity other than ± 1, i.e., to find elements $x \in (\mathbb{Z}_N)^\times \setminus \{\pm 1\}$ of low multiplicative order. If N is sampled with GenSafe, the only small order possible is 2, and a square root of unity would allow N to be factored. Second, it must be hard to compute modular roots. We use a version of the RSA assumption.

[1] Assuming that the adversary uses the general number field sieve, $\ell(\kappa) = \widetilde{\Theta}(\kappa^3)$.

Definition 2.2. The Strong RSA assumption states that all PPT adversaries $\mathcal{A}$ must have negligible chance of winning the following game.

$$\boxed{\begin{array}{l}(N,\phi) \leftarrow \mathsf{RSA.GenSafe}(1^\kappa)\\ g \leftarrow (\mathbb{Z}_N)^\times\\ (z,e) \leftarrow \mathcal{A}(N)\\ \text{win if } |e| > 1 \text{ and } z^e = g\end{array}}$$

2.2 Pseudorandom Correlation Functions

We will use the Pailler-based pseudorandom correlation function (PCF) of [OSY21]. There are a couple of issues, however, with applying their definition to Pailler PCF for VOLE correlations. First, the output ring of the correlation, $\mathbb{Z}_N$ for a semiprime N, is sampled randomly. However, there is no feature in their definition that allows the group to be sampled. Second, the master secret key msk for VOLE is Δ, and it is supposed to be both output as part of y_1. But their reverse sampling definition requires that the output distribution be the same for two different choices of msk.

Below we have modified their definitions to fix these issues.

Definition 2.3. Let $1 \leq \ell_0(\kappa), \ell_1(\kappa) \leq \mathsf{poly}(\kappa)$ be output-length functions, and let $\mathcal{M}_i$ be a set of allowed master keys for party i. Let $(\mathsf{Setup}, \mathcal{Y})$ be a tuple of probabilistic algorithms, such that

- $\mathsf{Setup}(1^\kappa, \mathsf{msk}_0 \in \mathcal{M}_0, \mathcal{M}_1)$ samples a distribution key pk and an (optional) trapdoor sk.
- $\mathcal{Y}(\mathsf{pk}, \mathsf{msk}_0, \mathsf{msk}_1)$, returns a pair of outputs $(y_0, y_1) \in \{0,1\}^{\ell_0(\kappa)} \times \{0,1\}^{\ell_1(\kappa)}$.

We say that the tuple $(\mathsf{Setup}, \mathcal{Y})$ defines a reverse sampleable correlation with setup if there exists a probabilistic polynomial time algorithm $\mathsf{RSample}$ such that

- $\mathsf{RSample}(\mathsf{pk}, \mathsf{msk}_0, \mathsf{msk}_1, \sigma \in \{0,1\}, y_\sigma \in \{0,1\}^{\ell_\sigma(\kappa)})$ returns $y_{1-\sigma} \in \{0,1\}^{\ell_{1-\sigma}(\kappa)}$ such that for all $\mathsf{msk}_0 \in \mathcal{M}_0, \mathsf{msk}_1 \in \mathcal{M}_1$ and all $\sigma \in \{0,1\}$, the distributions of $(\mathsf{pk}, \mathsf{sk}, y_\sigma, y_{1-\sigma})$ and $(\mathsf{pk}, \mathsf{sk}, y_\sigma, y^*)$ are statistically close, where:

$$\left\{ (\mathsf{pk}, \mathsf{sk}, y_0, y_1, y^*) \;\middle|\; \begin{array}{lcl} (\mathsf{pk}, \mathsf{sk}) & \leftarrow & \mathsf{Setup}(1^\kappa, \mathsf{msk}_0, \mathsf{msk}_1) \\ (y_0, y_1) & \leftarrow & \mathcal{Y}(\mathsf{pk}, \mathsf{msk}_0, \mathsf{msk}_1) \\ y^* & \leftarrow & \mathsf{RSample}(\mathsf{pk}, \mathsf{msk}_0, \mathsf{msk}_1, \sigma, y_\sigma) \end{array} \right\}$$

To show how this reverse sampling definition works, we next give the distribution for VOLE correlations.

Definition 2.4. A reverse sampleable correlation $(\mathsf{Setup}, \mathcal{Y})$ is a *VOLE correlation* if $\mathcal{M}_0 = \{\perp\}$, $\mathcal{M}_1 \subseteq \mathbb{Z}$, pk outputs a public modulus N, and the distribution $\mathcal{Y}(N, \perp, \Delta)$ samples $u, v \leftarrow \mathbb{Z}_N$, computes $w := u\Delta + v$, and outputs $((u,v), w)$.

Definition 2.5. Let $(\mathsf{Setup}, \mathcal{Y})$ fix a reverse-sampleable correlation with setup which has output length functions $\ell_0(\kappa), \ell_1(\kappa)$ and sets $\mathcal{M}_0, \mathcal{M}_1$ of allowed master keys, and let $\kappa \leq n(\kappa) \leq \mathsf{poly}(\kappa)$ be an input length function. Let $(\mathsf{PCF.Gen}, \mathsf{PCF.Eval})$ be a pair of algorithms with the following syntax:

- $\mathsf{PCF.Gen}(\mathsf{pk}, \mathsf{sk}, \mathsf{msk}_0, \mathsf{msk}_1)$ is a probabilistic polynomial time algorithm that outputs a pair of keys (k_0, k_1);
- $\mathsf{PCF.Eval}(\sigma, k_\sigma, x)$ is a deterministic polynomial-time algorithm that on input $\sigma \in \{0,1\}$, key k_σ and input value $x \in \{0,1\}^{n(\kappa)}$, outputs a value $y_\sigma \in \{0,1\}^{\ell_\sigma(\kappa)}$.

We say ($\mathsf{PCF.Gen}$, $\mathsf{PCF.Eval}$) is a (weak) pseudorandom correlation function (PCF) for $\mathcal{Y}$, if the following conditions hold:

- Pseudorandom $\mathcal{Y}$-correlated outputs. For every $\mathsf{msk}_0 \in \mathcal{M}_0$, $\mathsf{msk}_1 \in \mathcal{M}_1$, and non-uniform adversary $\mathcal{A}$ of size $\mathsf{poly}(\kappa)$, and every $Q = \mathsf{poly}(\kappa)$, it holds that

$$|\Pr[\mathrm{Exp}_0^{pr}(\kappa) = 1] - \Pr[\mathrm{Exp}_1^{pr}(\kappa) = 1]| \leq negl(\kappa)$$

  for all sufficiently large κ, where $\mathrm{Exp}_b^{pr}(\kappa)$ for $b \in \{0,1\}$ is defined as follows. (In particular, where the adversary is given access to $Q(\kappa)$ samples.)

$\mathrm{Exp}_0^{pr}(\kappa)$:	$\mathrm{Exp}_1^{pr}(\kappa)$:
$(\mathsf{pk}, \mathsf{sk}) \leftarrow \mathsf{Setup}(1^\kappa, \mathsf{msk}_0, \mathsf{msk}_1)$	$(\mathsf{pk}, \mathsf{sk}) \leftarrow \mathsf{Setup}(1^\kappa, \mathsf{msk}_0, \mathsf{msk}_1)$
	$(k_0, k_1) \leftarrow \mathsf{PCF.Gen}(\mathsf{pk}, \mathsf{sk}, \mathsf{msk}_0, \mathsf{msk}_1)$
for $i = 1$ to $Q(\kappa)$:	for $i = 1$ to $Q(\kappa)$:
$x^{(i)} \leftarrow \{0,1\}^{n(\kappa)}$	$x^{(i)} \leftarrow \{0,1\}^{n(\kappa)}$
$(y_0^{(i)}, y_1^{(i)}) \leftarrow Y(1^\kappa, \mathsf{msk})$	for $\sigma \in \{0,1\}$: $y_\sigma^{(i)} \leftarrow \mathsf{PCF.Eval}(\sigma, k_\sigma, x^{(i)})$
$b \leftarrow \mathcal{A}(1^\kappa, \mathsf{pk}, (x^{(i)}, y_0^{(i)}, y_1^{(i)})_{i \in [Q(\kappa)]})$	$b \leftarrow \mathcal{A}(1^\kappa, \mathsf{pk}, (x^{(i)}, y_0^{(i)}, y_1^{(i)})_{i \in [Q(\kappa)]})$
return b	return b

- Security. For each $\sigma \in \{0,1\}$ there is a simulator $\mathcal{S}_\sigma$s such that for every $\mathsf{msk}_0 \in \mathcal{M}_0$, $\mathsf{msk}_1 \in \mathcal{M}_1$, any every non-uniform adversary $\mathcal{A}$ of size $B(\kappa)$, and every $Q = \mathsf{poly}(\kappa)$, it holds that

$$|\Pr[\mathrm{Exp}_0^{sec}(\kappa) = 1] - \Pr[\mathrm{Exp}_1^{sec}(\kappa) = 1]| \leq negl(\kappa)$$

  for all sufficiently large κ, where $\mathrm{Exp}_b^{sec}(\kappa)$ for $b \in \{0,1\}$ is defined as follows (again, with $Q(\kappa)$ samples).

$\mathrm{Exp}_0^{sec}(\kappa)$:	$\mathrm{Exp}_1^{sec}(\kappa)$:
$(\mathsf{pk}, \mathsf{sk}) \leftarrow \mathsf{Setup}(1^\kappa, \mathsf{msk}_0, \mathsf{msk}_1)$	$(\mathsf{pk}, \mathsf{sk}) \leftarrow \mathsf{Setup}(1^\kappa, \mathsf{msk}_0, \mathsf{msk}_1)$
$(k_0, k_1) \leftarrow \mathsf{PCF.Gen}(\mathsf{pk}, \mathsf{sk}, \mathsf{msk}_0, \mathsf{msk}_1)$	$k_\sigma \leftarrow \mathcal{S}_\sigma(\mathsf{pk}, \mathsf{sk}, \mathsf{msk}_\sigma)$
for $i = 1$ to $Q(\kappa)$:	for $i = 1$ to $Q(\kappa)$:
$x^{(i)} \leftarrow \{0,1\}^{n(\kappa)}$	$x^{(i)} \leftarrow \{0,1\}^{n(\kappa)}$
	$y_\sigma^{(i)} \leftarrow \mathsf{PCF.Eval}(\sigma, k_\sigma, x^{(i)})$
$y_{1-\sigma}^{(i)} \leftarrow \mathsf{PCF.Eval}(1-\sigma, k_{1-\sigma}, x^{(i)})$	$y_{1-\sigma}^{(i)} \leftarrow \mathsf{RSample}(1^\kappa, \mathsf{msk}_0, \mathsf{msk}_1, \sigma, y_\sigma^{(i)})$
$b \leftarrow \mathcal{A}(1^\kappa, \mathsf{pk}, k_\sigma, (x^{(i)}, y_{1-\sigma}^{(i)})_{i \in [Q(\kappa)]})$	$b \leftarrow \mathcal{A}(1^\kappa, \mathsf{pk}, k_\sigma, (x^{(i)}, y_{1-\sigma}^{(i)})_{i \in [Q(\kappa)]})$
return b	return b

2.3 Discrete Log Pseudorandom Correlation Functions

As we wish to enable a diversity of techniques and instantiations for our approach, rather than present a protocol that uses a specific type of PCF directly, we instead make use of an intermediate object that we define here, called an $(\varepsilon, \mathbb{G})$-$\mathsf{PCF}_{\mathsf{DL}}$. Roughly, an $(\varepsilon, \mathbb{G})$-$\mathsf{PCF}_{\mathsf{DL}}$ produces two keys $(k_\mathsf{P}, k_\mathsf{V})$ through a setup algorithm. Given public input m (which can be for e.g. a message to be signed), k_P can be used to derive a $r_m \in \mathbb{Z}_q$ and an accompanying π_R, which serves as a proof that the nonce $R_m = r_m \cdot G$ was correctly derived. These nonces must be pseudorandom, and the probability that a verifier is fooled into accepting an incorrect $R^*_m \neq R_m$ is bounded by ε.

We formalize these intuitive properties below, accounting for subtleties that will be important for the simulation of our UC-secure signing protocol.

Definition 2.6. An $(\varepsilon, \mathbb{G})$-$\mathsf{PCF}_{\mathsf{DL}}$ is characterized by five algorithms $(\mathsf{Setup}, \mathsf{P}, \mathsf{V}, \mathcal{S}, \mathcal{V})$. The algorithms P and V are not provided with random tapes. The security parameter is taken to be equal to the size of the group, i.e. $\kappa = |\mathbb{G}|$. These algorithms must satisfy the following properties:

- **Completeness**: For any efficient adversary $\mathcal{A}$ interacting with the oracle $\mathcal{O}_{\mathsf{compl}}$, the chance of an abort is negligible.

$$\boxed{\begin{array}{l} (k_{\mathsf{P}}, k_{\mathsf{V}}) \leftarrow \mathsf{Setup}(\kappa) \\ \underline{\mathcal{O}_{\mathsf{compl}}(m)}: \\ \quad (r_m, \pi_R) \leftarrow \mathsf{P}(k_{\mathsf{P}}, m) \\ \quad R_m = r_m \cdot G \\ \quad \text{abort if } \mathsf{V}(k_{\mathsf{V}}, m, R_m, \pi_R) \neq 1 \\ \quad \text{return } r_m, \pi_R \end{array}}$$

- **ε-Soundness**: For any efficient algorithm $\mathcal{A}$:

$$\Pr\left[R^* \neq R_m \ \wedge\ \mathsf{V}(k_{\mathsf{V}}, m, R^*, \pi^*_R) = 1 \ :\ \begin{array}{rcl} (k_{\mathsf{P}}, k_{\mathsf{V}}) & \leftarrow & \mathsf{Setup}(\kappa) \\ (m, R^*, \pi^*_R) & \leftarrow & \mathcal{A}(k_{\mathsf{P}}) \\ (r_m, \pi_R) & \leftarrow & \mathsf{P}(k_{\mathsf{P}}, m) \\ R_m & = & r_m \cdot G \end{array} \right] \leq \varepsilon(\kappa)$$

- **Pseudorandom Nonces With Simulatable Proofs**: Define two oracles, the first being $\mathcal{O}_{\mathsf{P}}(k_{\mathsf{P}})$, which on query $m \in \{0,1\}^\kappa$ computes $(r_m, \pi_R) \leftarrow \mathsf{P}(k_{\mathsf{P}}, m)$ and returns (R_m, π_R) where $R_m = r_m \cdot G$. The second oracle $\mathcal{O}_{\mathcal{S}}(k_{\mathsf{V}})$ is defined as follows:
  1. Upon initialization, sample a random tape $\rho \in \{0,1\}^\kappa$ for $\mathcal{S}$
  2. Upon receiving a query $m \in \{0,1\}^*$, if R_m is undefined, then sample $R_m \leftarrow \mathbb{G}$ and $\pi_R \leftarrow \mathcal{S}(k_{\mathsf{V}}, m, R_m, ; \rho)$
  3. Return (R_m, π_R)

  There is a negligible function negl such that for any efficient adversary $\mathcal{A}$,

$$\left| \begin{array}{l} \Pr[\mathcal{A}^{\mathcal{O}_{\mathcal{S}}(k_{\mathsf{V}})}(k_{\mathsf{V}}) = 1 \ :\ (k_{\mathsf{P}}, k_{\mathsf{V}}) \leftarrow \mathsf{Setup}(\kappa)] \\ - \Pr[\mathcal{A}^{\mathcal{O}_{\mathsf{P}}(k_{\mathsf{P}})}(k_{\mathsf{V}}) = 1 \ :\ (k_{\mathsf{P}}, k_{\mathsf{V}}) \leftarrow \mathsf{Setup}(\kappa)] \end{array} \right| \leq \mathsf{negl}(\kappa)$$

- **Simulatable Proof Validation**: Define the oracle $\mathcal{O}_{\mathcal{V}}(k_{\mathsf{P}}, \cdot)$ as follows: Upon receiving (m, R^*_m, π^*_R) as input:
  1. If `flag` is already defined, and `flag` $\neq 1$, then ignore the query.
  2. Otherwise if `flag` is undefined, sample a random integer `coin` $\leftarrow [1, 1/\varepsilon(\kappa)]$.
  3. Set `flag` $=$ `coin` $\cdot\, \mathcal{V}(k_{\mathsf{P}}, m, R^*_m, \pi^*_R)$, and return `flag` $\stackrel{?}{=} 1$.

The oracles $\mathcal{O}_{\mathcal{V}}(k_{\mathsf{P}}, \cdot)$ and $\mathsf{V}(k_{\mathsf{V}}, \cdot)$ are indistinguishable to any efficient $\mathcal{A}(k_{\mathsf{P}})$ that queries only *incorrect* nonces (i.e. $R^*_m \neq r_m \cdot G$ where $(r_m, \cdot) \leftarrow \mathsf{P}(k_{\mathsf{P}}, m)$) over choice of $(k_{\mathsf{P}}, k_{\mathsf{V}}) \leftarrow \mathsf{Setup}(\kappa)$.

Remark 2.7. Simulatable Proof Validation follows directly from ε-Soundness when ε is negligible in κ. This is due to a canonical $\mathcal{V}$ that simply rejects all incorrect R^*_m—by soundness, it follows that *any* incorrect R^*_m will be accepted by a verifier only with negligible probability.

Remark 2.8. The P and V algorithms are deterministic, and do not allow state by syntax, which will result in a stateless deterministic distributed Schnorr protocol later on.

3 Deterministic Signing from Pseudorandom Discrete Logarithm Nonce Derivation Functions

Given an $(\varepsilon, \mathbb{G})$-$\mathsf{PCF}_{\mathsf{DL}}$, we show how to distribute the computation of Schnorr signatures so that the signing protocol enjoys stateless determinism. We begin by describing the ideal UC functionality that we will realize.

Functionality 3.1. $\mathcal{F}^{\varepsilon}_{\mathsf{Schnorr}}$. **Threshold Schnorr Signing With Error**

This two-party functionality is parameterized by the group $(\mathbb{G}, G, q)$, error ε such that $\eta = 1/\varepsilon$ is an integer, and the hash function H. All messages are adversarially delayed.

Key Generation: Run once.

1. Upon receiving $(sid, \texttt{init})$ from both parties, sample $\mathsf{sk} \leftarrow \mathbb{Z}_q$, and compute $\mathsf{pk} = \mathsf{sk} \cdot G$
2. In case an entry prefixed by sid does not already exist, send $(sid, \texttt{public-key}, \mathsf{pk})$ to both parties, and store $(sid, \texttt{keys}, \mathsf{pk}, \mathsf{sk})$ in memory.

Signing a message: Run arbitrarily many times.

1. Ignore any queries prefixed by sid if $(sid, \texttt{keys}, \mathsf{pk}, \mathsf{sk})$ does not exist in memory.
2. Upon receiving $(sid, \texttt{sign}, m)$ from both parties, if m has not previously been signed, sample $r_m \leftarrow \mathbb{Z}_q$ and store $(sid, \texttt{nonce}, m, r_m)$ in memory. Otherwise retrieve $(sid, \texttt{nonce}, m, r_m)$ from memory.
3. Compute $R_m = r_m \cdot G$ and in case P_i is corrupt, send it $(sid, \texttt{nonce}, R_m)$ and wait for $(sid, \texttt{proceed}, m)$.
4. Compute
$$s = \mathsf{sk} \cdot H(R_m, \mathsf{pk}, m) + r_m$$
and send $(sid, \texttt{sig}, R_m, s)$ to both parties.

Cheat: If P_i is corrupt, it may send $(sid, \texttt{cheat}, m)$ instead of $(sid, \texttt{proceed}, m)$ upon receiving $(sid, \texttt{nonce}, R_m)$. If initialized and `cheat` has not previously been sent, then:

1. Uniformly sample a random integer $\texttt{coin} \leftarrow [1, \eta]$
2. If $\texttt{coin} = 1$ then P_i is given control of this functionality (i.e. henceforth P_i receives all messages and responds on behalf of $\mathcal{F}^{\varepsilon}_{\mathsf{Schnorr}}$) without notifying P_{1-i}.
3. Otherwise, send $(sid, \texttt{cheat-detected})$ to both P_0 and P_1, and stop accepting further instructions.

Observe that if $\varepsilon(\kappa)$ is negligible in κ, then $\mathcal{F}^{\varepsilon}_{\mathsf{Schnorr}}$ is effectively equivalent to the standard Schnorr signing functionality (up to syntax); sending $(sid, \texttt{cheat}, m)$ to $\mathcal{F}^{\varepsilon}_{\mathsf{Schnorr}}$ in this case is equivalent to instructing the standard Schnorr signing functionality to abort.

Our protocol makes use of an $\mathcal{F}^{\mathsf{PCF}}_{\mathsf{Setup}}$ hybrid functionality, which upon receipt of the initialization commands for an *sid* (i.e. `prover-init` and `verifier-init`) simply executes the Setup algorithm of the $(\varepsilon, \mathbb{G})$-$\mathsf{PCF}_{\mathsf{DL}}$ and returns the resulting k_{P} and k_{V} to the appropriate parties. We give the exact description in the full version. While such a functionality can always be instantiated generically by MPC, we discuss instantiations tailored to each $(\varepsilon, \mathbb{G})$-$\mathsf{PCF}_{\mathsf{DL}}$ construction in their respective sections. The focus of this work is on the round complexity and stateless determinism of the *signing* protocol, and so we do not prioritize the optimization of the instantiation of the one-time setup phase. We now give the our distributed Schnorr signing protocol.

Protocol 3.2. π_{Sch}**. Stateless Deterministic Threshold Schnorr Signing**

This two-party protocol is parameterized by the group $(\mathbb{G}, G, q)$, where $|\mathbb{G}| = \kappa$, an $(\varepsilon, \mathbb{G})$-$\mathsf{PCF}_{\mathsf{DL}}$ characterized by algorithms $(\mathsf{Setup}, \mathsf{P}, \mathsf{V}, \mathcal{S}, \mathcal{V})$, and optionally $\varepsilon_\kappa = \varepsilon(\kappa)$ such that $\eta = 1/\varepsilon_\kappa$ is an integer. This protocol additionally makes use of ideal functionalities $\mathcal{F}^{\mathsf{PCF}}_{\mathsf{Setup}}$ and $\mathcal{F}^{\mathsf{R}_{DL}}_{\mathsf{Com-ZK}}$, which are ommitted in this version in the interest of space.

All superscripts in the protocol descriptions are indices.

Key Generation: For $i \in \{0, 1\}$, each P_i does the following:
1. Send $(sid_i, \texttt{prover-init})$ and $(sid_{1-i}, \texttt{verifier-init})$ to $\mathcal{F}^{\mathsf{PCF}}_{\mathsf{Setup}}$ and wait for responses $(sid, \texttt{prover-key}, k^i_{\mathsf{P}})$ and $(sid, \texttt{verifier-key}, k^{1-i}_{\mathsf{V}})$ respectively.
2. Sample $\mathsf{sk}_i \leftarrow \mathbb{Z}_q$, compute $\mathsf{pk}_i = \mathsf{sk}_i \cdot G$ and send $(\texttt{commit}, sid_i, \mathsf{pk}_i, \mathsf{sk}_i)$ to $\mathcal{F}^{\mathsf{R}_{DL}}_{\mathsf{Com-ZK}}$
3. Wait for $(\texttt{committed}, sid_{1-i})$ from $\mathcal{F}^{\mathsf{R}_{DL}}_{\mathsf{Com-ZK}}$ and send $(\texttt{open}, sid_i)$
4. Wait for $(\texttt{opened}, sid_{1-i}, \mathsf{pk}_{1-i})$ and set $\mathsf{pk} = \mathsf{pk}_0 + \mathsf{pk}_1$

Signing a message m**:** For $i \in \{0, 1\}$, each P_i does the following:

1. Compute $(r^i_m, \pi^i_R) \leftarrow \mathsf{P}(k^i_{\mathsf{P}})$ and $R^i_m = r^i_m \cdot G$
2. Send (R^i_m, π^i_R) to P_{1-i} and wait for (R^{1-i}_m, π^{1-i}_R) in response

3. If $\mathsf{V}(k^i_{\mathsf{V}}, m, R^{1-i}_m, \pi^{1-i}_R) = 0$, then abort. Otherwise, set $R_m = R^0_m + R^1_m$
4. Send $s_i = \mathsf{sk}_i \cdot H(R_m, \mathsf{pk}, m) + r^i_m$ to P_{1-i}, and wait for s_{1-i} in response
5. Compute $s = s_0 + s_1$, and output (s, R_m) after verifying that it is a Schnorr signature on m.

Theorem 3.3. π_{Sch} UC-realizes $\mathcal{F}^{\varepsilon}_{\mathsf{Schnorr}}$ in the $\mathcal{F}^{\mathsf{PCF}}_{\mathsf{Setup}}, \mathcal{F}^{\mathsf{R}_{DL}}_{\mathsf{Com-ZK}}$-hybrid model in the presence of up to one static active corruption, assuming that $(\mathsf{Setup}, \mathsf{P}, \mathsf{V}, \mathcal{S}, \mathcal{V})$ is an $(\varepsilon, \mathbb{G})$-$\mathsf{PCF}_{\mathsf{DL}}$.

Proof. (Sketch) We briefly describe how to simulate the view of a corrupt P_i.
Key Generation. For each $i \in \{0, 1\}$, the simulator runs $(k^i_{\mathsf{P}}, k^i_{\mathsf{V}}) \leftarrow \mathsf{Setup}(1^\kappa)$. The keys $(k^i_{\mathsf{P}}, k^{1-i}_{\mathsf{V}})$ are given to P_i on behalf of $\mathcal{F}^{\mathsf{PCF}}_{\mathsf{Setup}}$. Additionally, $(\mathsf{pk}_i, \mathsf{sk}_i)$ is received from P_i on behalf of $\mathcal{F}^{\mathsf{R}_{DL}}_{\mathsf{Com-ZK}}$. Upon receiving pk from $\mathcal{F}^{\varepsilon}_{\mathsf{Schnorr}}$, compute $\mathsf{pk}_{1-i} = \mathsf{pk} - \mathsf{pk}_i$ and send pk_{1-i} to P_i on behalf of $\mathcal{F}^{\mathsf{R}_{DL}}_{\mathsf{Com-ZK}}$.
Signing a Message m**.**

1. Upon receiving the nonce R_m from $\mathcal{F}^{\varepsilon}_{\mathsf{Schnorr}}$, compute $(r^i_m, \pi^i_R) \leftarrow \mathsf{P}(k^i_{\mathsf{P}})$ and $R^i_m = r^i_m \cdot G$.
2. Compute $R^{1-i}_m = R_m - R^i_m$ and $\pi^{1-i}_R \leftarrow \mathcal{S}(k_{\mathsf{P}}, R^{1-i}_m)$, and send (R^{1-i}_m, π^{1-i}_R) to P_i on behalf of P_{1-i}.
3. Upon receiving (R^{i*}_m, π^{i*}_R) from P_i,
   (a) If $R^{i*}_m = R^i_m$ and $\mathsf{V}(k_{\mathsf{V}}, m, R^i_m, \pi^{i*}_R) = 1$ then send `proceed` to $\mathcal{F}^{\varepsilon}_{\mathsf{Schnorr}}$, and receive the signature (R, s) in response. Compute $s_{1-i} = s - (\mathsf{sk}_i \cdot H(R_m, \mathsf{pk}, m) + r^i_m)$ and send s_{1-i} to P_i.
   (b) Otherwise when $R^{i*}_m \neq R^i_m$, if no cheat has been attempted before, then send `cheat` to $\mathcal{F}^{\varepsilon}_{\mathsf{Schnorr}}$. If the cheat is successful (or has been successful in the past), and $\mathcal{V}(k_{\mathsf{P}}, m, R^{i*}_m, \pi^{i*}_R) = 1$, obtain sk and r_m from the $\mathcal{F}^{\varepsilon}_{\mathsf{Schnorr}}$, set $R'_m = R^{1-i}_m + R^{i*}_m$, and $\mathsf{sk}_{1-i} = \mathsf{sk} - \mathsf{sk}_i$ and $r^{1-i}_m = r_m - r^i_m$. Compute $s_{1-i} = \mathsf{sk}_{1-i} \cdot H(R'_m, \mathsf{pk}, m) + r^i_m$ and send s_{1-i} to P_i. Additionally, upon receiving s_i from P_i, instruct $\mathcal{F}^{\varepsilon}_{\mathsf{Schnorr}}$ to send $(R'_m, s_i + s_{1-i})$ to P_{1-i}.
   (c) Abort in any case not explicitly handled above.

Indistinguishability of Simulation. The simulation of the key generation phase is merely syntactically different from the real protocol. In the simulation of the signing phase, (R^{1-i}_m, π^{1-i}_R) is distributed indistinguishably from the real protocol by virtue of the Pseudorandom Nonces With Simulatable Proofs property. As for (R^{i*}_m, π^{i*}_R) being 'accepted', there are two main cases:

- $R^{i*}_m = R^i_m$, in which case the real protocol and simulation behave identically (i.e. they proceed or abort conditional on $\mathsf{V}(k_{\mathsf{V}}, m, R^i_m, \pi^{i*}_R)$).
- $R^{i*}_m \neq R^i_m$, in which case the real protocol proceeds conditional on $\mathsf{V}(k_{\mathsf{V}}, m, R^{i*}_m, \pi^{i*}_R)$, whereas the simulation proceeds conditional on $\texttt{coin} = 1$ where `coin` is a random integer sampled from $[1/\eta]$ by $\mathcal{F}^{\varepsilon}_{\mathsf{Schnorr}}$ *and* $\mathcal{V}(k_{\mathsf{P}}, m, R^{i*}_m, \pi^{i*}_R) = 1$. These two methods of validating (R^{i*}_m, π^{i*}_R) are indistinguishable, by the Simulatable Proof Validation property. Note that since

this property only accounts for *incorrect* nonces, in the reduction to this property, one must be able to simulate the output of $\mathsf{V}(k_{\mathsf{V}})$ when it is sent correct nonces. We claim that this oracle can be simulated in the reduction by simply always accepting correct nonces (even if the accompanying π_R^* is incorrect), at no loss of advantage. This is because a correct R_m accompanied by an π_R^* that was not computed honestly induces one of two outcomes: (1) the honest V accepts anyway, in which case the reduction made the correct choice, or (2) the honest V aborts, in which case the adversary (and hence the reduction) would have failed anyway.

Finally, conditional on (R_m^{i*}, π_R^{i*}) having been 'accepted', both the simulation and and the real protocol compute s_{1-i} in the exact same way (up to syntax). □

Corollary 3.4. π_{Sch} *UC-realizes* $\mathcal{F}_{\mathsf{Schnorr}}$ *in the presence of up to one static active corruption, assuming that* $(\mathsf{Setup}, \mathsf{P}, \mathsf{V}, \mathcal{S})$ *is an* $(\varepsilon, \mathbb{G})$-$\mathsf{PCF}_{\mathsf{DL}}$ *where* ε *is negligible in* κ.

4 Covert Security from SoftSpoken VOLE

With our $(\varepsilon, \mathbb{G})$-$\mathsf{PCF}_{\mathsf{DL}}$ abstraction and the protocol π_{Sch} to use it in place, we turn our focus to how to instantiate an $(\varepsilon, \mathbb{G})$-$\mathsf{PCF}_{\mathsf{DL}}$. As a first construction, we adapt the SoftSpoken VOLE PCF of Roy [Roy22] to our context. Roughly, k_{P} consists of $\eta = 1/\varepsilon(\kappa)$ independently sampled PRF keys, and k_{V} consists of all but one of them—the missing index is labelled Δ, and k_{P} contains no information about Δ. In order to evaluate $(\varepsilon, \mathbb{G})$-$\mathsf{PCF}_{\mathsf{DL}}$ at a public point m, P simply adds up the result of evaluating the PRF with each of the keys to derive r_m, and computes π_R by taking a linear combination of the PRF evaluations. Given Δ and all but the Δth PRF keys, V uses the structure of the SoftSpoken VOLE PCF to derive w correlated with π_R, R_m, Δ and verifies the correlation in the exponent. The omission of the Δth PRF key in k_{V} keeps R_m pseudorandom, and soundness follows from the fact that forging an π_R for an incorrect R_m is exactly equivalent to guessing Δ. We give our entire construction below.

Algorithm 4.1. $\mathsf{ssPCF}_{\varepsilon,\mathbb{G},\mathsf{F}}$. $(\varepsilon, \mathbb{G})$-$\mathsf{PCF}_{\mathsf{DL}}$ **from SoftSpoken VOLE**

This algorithm is parameterized by the group $(\mathbb{G}, G, q)$, where $|\mathbb{G}| = \kappa$, and $\varepsilon_\kappa = \varepsilon(\kappa)$ such that $\eta = 1/\varepsilon_\kappa$ is an integer. Additionally, this algorithm makes blackbox use of a pseudorandom function $\mathsf{F} : \{0,1\}^\kappa \to \mathbb{Z}_q$

$\mathsf{Setup}(\kappa)$:

1. Sample a random integer index $\Delta \leftarrow [\eta]$
2. Sample η keys, $\{k_i\}_{i\in[\eta]} \leftarrow \{0,1\}^{\kappa\times\eta}$
3. Assemble and output $k_{\mathsf{P}} = \{k_i\}_{i\in[\eta]}$, and $k_{\mathsf{V}} = \left(\Delta, \{k_i\}_{i\in[\eta]\setminus\Delta}\right)$

$\mathsf{P}(k_{\mathsf{P}}, m)$: Output $r_m = -\sum_{i\in[\eta]} \mathsf{F}_{k_i}(m)$, and $\pi_R = \left(\sum_{i\in[\eta]} i \cdot \mathsf{F}_{k_i}(m)\right) \cdot G$

$\mathsf{V}(k_{\mathsf{V}}, m, R, \pi_R)$:

1. Compute $w = \sum_{i \in [\eta] \setminus \Delta} (i - \Delta) \cdot \mathsf{F}_{k_i}(m)$
2. Output 1 iff $w \cdot G \stackrel{?}{=} \pi_R - \Delta \cdot R_m$, and 0 otherwise

Theorem 4.2. Algorithm $\mathsf{ssPCF}_{\varepsilon,\mathbb{G},\mathsf{F}}$ is a $(\varepsilon, \mathbb{G})$-$\mathsf{PCF}_{\mathsf{DL}}$ for any $\mathbb{G}$ and $\varepsilon(\kappa) \in \mathsf{poly}(\kappa)$, assuming that F is a pseudorandom function.

Proof. **Completeness.** Observe that since $(i - \Delta) = 0$ when $i = \Delta$, for any $(R_m, \pi_R) \leftarrow \mathsf{P}(k_\mathsf{P} = \{k_i\}_{i \in [\eta]})$ it holds that

$$\begin{aligned} w \cdot G &= \left(\sum_{i \in [\eta] \setminus \Delta} (i - \Delta) \cdot \mathsf{F}_{k_i}(m) \right) \cdot G = \left(\sum_{i \in [\eta]} (i - \Delta) \cdot \mathsf{F}_{k_i}(m) \right) \cdot G \\ &= \left(\sum_{i \in [\eta]} i \cdot \mathsf{F}_{k_i}(m) \right) \cdot G - \Delta \cdot \left(\sum_{i \in [\eta]} \mathsf{F}_{k_i}(m) \right) \cdot G \\ &= \pi_R - \Delta \cdot R_m \end{aligned}$$

which is exactly the condition that induces V to output 1, proving completeness.

Soundness. First, note that any given prover's key k_P allows for η different corresponding k_V values, each of which is equally likely. For a given k_P and message m, we will call a nonce $R \in \mathbb{G}$ 'honest' if $(r_m, \pi_R) = \mathsf{P}(k_\mathsf{P}, m)$ and $r_m \cdot G = R$, and 'malformed' otherwise. A given k_P, m induces a unique honest nonce and proof which we will denote (R_m, π_R^m). Now, consider the following claims:

Claim 4.3. *For a given prover's key $k_\mathsf{P} = \{k_i\}_{i \in [\eta]}$, message m, and honest nonce R_m, there is a unique value $\pi_R^m \in \mathbb{G}$ such that $\mathsf{V}(k_\mathsf{V}, m, R^*, \pi_R^m) = 1$.*

Claim 4.4. *For a given prover's key $k_\mathsf{P} = \{k_i\}_{i \in [\eta]}$, message m, and malformed nonce R^*, each possible choice of verification key $k_\mathsf{V} = (\Delta, \{k_i\}_{i \in [\eta] \setminus \Delta})$ implies a unique value $\pi_{R,\Delta}^* \in \mathbb{G}$ such that $\mathsf{V}(k_\mathsf{V}, m, R^*, \pi_{R,\Delta}^*) = 1$.*

Both of the above claims follow from the fact that for any $R^* = R_m + D$, the proof $\pi_{R,\Delta}^* \in \mathbb{G}$ that induces the verifier to accept is given by:

$$\begin{aligned} \pi_{R,\Delta}^* &= w \cdot G + \Delta \cdot R^* \\ &= \pi_R^m - \Delta \cdot R_m + \Delta \cdot R^* \\ &= \pi_R^m + \Delta \cdot D \end{aligned}$$

therefore if $D = 0$ the only accepting proof is π_R^m independent of Δ, otherwise $\pi_{R,\Delta}^*$ is unique for each choice of $\Delta \in [\eta]$.

Corollary 4.5. *Denote by* $\mathsf{fooled}_\mathcal{B}$ *the event that* $(m, R^*, \pi_R^*) \leftarrow \mathcal{B}(k_\mathsf{P})$ *induces* $\mathsf{V}(k_\mathsf{V}, m, R^*, \pi_R^*) = 1$, *where* $(k_\mathsf{P}, k_\mathsf{V}) \leftarrow \mathsf{Setup}(\kappa)$. *Then,* $\Pr[\mathsf{fooled}_\mathcal{B}] \leq 1/\eta$ *for any algorithm* $\mathcal{B}$.

The corollary follows immediately from Claim 4.4 and the fact that there are η different, equally likely choices of k_{V} for each k_{P}.

Corollary 4.5 therefore gives us that for any algorithm $\mathcal{A}$:

$$\Pr\left[R^* \neq R_m \ \wedge\ \mathsf{V}(k_{\mathsf{V}}, m, R^*, \pi_R^*) = 1 \ :\ \begin{array}{rcl} (k_{\mathsf{P}}, k_{\mathsf{V}}) & \leftarrow & \mathsf{Setup}(\kappa) \\ (m, R^*, \pi_R^*) & \leftarrow & \mathcal{A}(k_{\mathsf{P}}) \\ (r_m, \pi_R) & \leftarrow & \mathsf{P}(k_{\mathsf{P}}, m) \\ R_m & = & r_m \cdot G \end{array}\right]$$
$$= \Pr[\mathsf{fooled}_{\mathcal{A}^*}] \leq 1/\eta = \varepsilon(\kappa)$$

and this satisfies soundness.

Extending the above soundness proof to Simulatable Proof Validation is straightforward—given a dishonest (R_m^*, π_R^*) the algorithm $\mathcal{V}$ simply enumerates all possible $\pi_{R,\Delta}^*$ values (as per Claim 4.4), and outputs 1 if π_R^* is among them, and 0 otherwise.

Pseudorandom Nonces With Simulatable Proofs. We first define the simulator $\mathcal{S}$ as follows.

$\mathcal{S}(k_{\mathsf{V}}, m, R_m; \rho)$:

1. Parse $(\Delta, \{k_i\}_{i \in [\eta] \setminus \Delta})$ from k_{V}, and compute $w = \sum_{i \in [\eta] \setminus \Delta} (i - \Delta) \cdot \mathsf{F}_{k_i}(m)$
2. Output $\pi_R = w \cdot G + \Delta \cdot R_m$

We now show that with the above simulator, $\mathcal{O}_{\mathsf{P}}(k_{\mathsf{P}})$ and $\mathcal{O}_{\mathcal{S}}(k_{\mathsf{V}})$ are computationally indistinguishable assuming that F is a pseudorandom function. Consider a hybrid oracle $\mathcal{O}_{\mathcal{H}1}(k_{\mathsf{P}}, k_{\mathsf{V}})$ defined as follows:

1. Compute $r_{m,\Delta} = \mathsf{F}_{k_\Delta}(m)$
2. Compute $r_m = -r_{m,\Delta} - \sum_{i \in [\eta] \setminus \Delta} \mathsf{F}_{k_i}(m)$ (equivalent to $\mathsf{P}(k_{\mathsf{P}})$)
3. Set $R_m = r_m \cdot G$, and compute $\pi_R = \mathcal{O}_{\mathcal{S}}(k_{\mathsf{V}})$
4. Output (R_m, π_R)

Claim 4.6. *The oracles $\mathcal{O}_{\mathcal{H}1}$ and $\mathcal{O}_{\mathsf{P}}$ are distributed identically, i.e. for any adversary $\mathcal{A}$,*

$$\left|\begin{array}{l} \Pr[\mathcal{A}^{\mathcal{O}_{\mathcal{H}1}(k_{\mathsf{P}}, k_{\mathsf{V}})}(k_{\mathsf{V}}) = 1 \ :\ (k_{\mathsf{P}}, k_{\mathsf{V}}) \leftarrow \mathsf{Setup}(\kappa)] \\ \quad - \Pr[\mathcal{A}^{\mathcal{O}_{\mathsf{P}}(k_{\mathsf{P}})}(k_{\mathsf{V}}) = 1 \ :\ (k_{\mathsf{P}}, k_{\mathsf{V}}) \leftarrow \mathsf{Setup}(\kappa)] \end{array}\right| = 0$$

The above claim follows from the fact that r_m is computed in exactly the same way by both $\mathcal{O}_{\mathsf{P}}$ and $\mathcal{O}_{\mathcal{H}1}$, and that the computation of π_R by $\mathcal{S}$ (denote it $\pi_R^{\mathcal{S}}$)

is equivalent to the way that P computes it (denote it π_R^{P}), in particular:

$$\begin{aligned}\pi_R^S &= w \cdot G + \Delta \cdot R_m \\ &= \sum_{i \in [\eta] \setminus \Delta} (i - \Delta) \cdot \mathsf{F}_{k_i}(m) + \Delta \cdot \sum_{i \in [\eta]} \mathsf{F}_{k_i}(m) \\ &= \sum_{i \in [\eta]} ((i - \Delta) \cdot \mathsf{F}_{k_i}(m) + \Delta \cdot \mathsf{F}_{k_i}(m)) \\ &= \sum_{i \in [\eta]} i \cdot \mathsf{F}_{k_i}(m) \\ &= \pi_R^{\mathsf{P}}\end{aligned}$$

Now we define the next hybrid oracle $\mathcal{O}_{\mathcal{H}2}(k_{\mathsf{V}})$ as follows:

1. Sample $r_{m,\Delta} \leftarrow \mathbb{Z}_q$
2. Compute $r_m = -r_{m,\Delta} - \sum_{i \in [\eta] \setminus \Delta} \mathsf{F}_{k_i}(m)$
3. Set $R_m = r_m \cdot G$, and compute $\pi_R = \mathcal{O}_{\mathcal{S}}(k_{\mathsf{V}})$
4. Output (R_m, π_R)

Claim 4.7. *Assuming that* F *is a pseudorandom function, the oracles* $\mathcal{O}_{\mathcal{H}1}$ *and* $\mathcal{O}_{\mathcal{H}2}$ *are computationally indistinguishable. i.e. There is a negligible function* negl *such that for any efficient adversary* $\mathcal{A}$*:*

$$\left| \begin{array}{l} \Pr[\mathcal{A}^{\mathcal{O}_{\mathcal{H}2}(k_{\mathsf{V}})}(k_{\mathsf{V}}) = 1 \ : \ (k_{\mathsf{P}}, k_{\mathsf{V}}) \leftarrow \mathsf{Setup}(\kappa)] \\ - \Pr[\mathcal{A}^{\mathcal{O}_{\mathcal{H}1}(k_{\mathsf{P}}, k_{\mathsf{V}})}(k_{\mathsf{V}}) = 1 \ : \ (k_{\mathsf{P}}, k_{\mathsf{V}}) \leftarrow \mathsf{Setup}(\kappa)] \end{array} \right| \leq \mathsf{negl}(\kappa)$$

The above claim follows from a straightforward perfect reduction to the PRF game. Notice that the difference between $\mathcal{O}_{\mathcal{H}2}$ and $\mathcal{O}_{\mathcal{S}}$ is merely syntactic. From Claims 4.6 and 4.7, we have that

$$\left| \begin{array}{l} \Pr[\mathcal{A}^{\mathcal{O}_{\mathcal{S}}(k_{\mathsf{V}})}(k_{\mathsf{V}}) = 1 \ : \ (k_{\mathsf{P}}, k_{\mathsf{V}}) \leftarrow \mathsf{Setup}(\kappa)] \\ - \Pr[\mathcal{A}^{\mathcal{O}_{\mathsf{P}}(k_{\mathsf{P}})}(k_{\mathsf{V}}) = 1 \ : \ (k_{\mathsf{P}}, k_{\mathsf{V}}) \leftarrow \mathsf{Setup}(\kappa)] \end{array} \right| \leq \mathsf{negl}(\kappa)$$

for some negligible function negl. This completes the proof of the Pseudorandom Nonces With Simulatable Proofs property, and hence proves the theorem. □

4.1 Efficiency

A single P evaluation costs η F invocations, one (fixed base) exponentiation in $\mathbb{G}$, and 2η additions in $\mathbb{Z}_q$—the partial sums produced when computing r_m can be saved and reused to compute π_R. A verification by V costs $\eta - 1$ F invocations, η *small* $\mathbb{Z}_q$ multipications, as many $\mathbb{Z}_q$ additions, and two $\mathbb{G}$ exponentiations (one fixed base and one variable base). The dominant computation cost for say $\varepsilon = 10\%$ (i.e. a 90% chance of a cheater being caught) in most situations will likely be the three $\mathbb{G}$ exponentiations—i.e. roughly the same computation cost profile as generating and then verifying a Schnorr signature.

In terms of bandwidth, π_R consists of a single $\mathbb{G}$ element, i.e. half the size of a Schnorr signature in most common representations.

5 Full Security from Pseudorandom Correlation Functions

Algorithm 5.1 provides a formal description of our protocol. We provide some intuitions here: in a nutshell, the PCF setup provides P and V with keys k_0, k_1 which allow them to non-interactively generate shares $w - v$ of $u\Delta$ in $\mathbb{Z}_{N_\mathsf{P}}$. The main challenge we need to solve is to translate these shares into $\mathbb{Z}_q$, where q is the prime used in Schnorr signatures. Roughly, our translation mechanism works as follows: First, the parties translate their correlated shares into shares over $\mathbb{Z}$, removing the modulus by using a technique similar to what is used in the Paillier HSS constructions of [OSY21,RS21]. Essentially, note that shares $w - v$ of $u\Delta$ (modulo N_P) are very likely to be shares of $u\Delta$ without any modulus, as long as $|u\Delta| \ll N_\mathsf{P}$. However, u is uniformly random in $\mathbb{Z}_{N_\mathsf{P}}$, so party P must partially derandomize u to get a correlation for a smaller value u_{lo}. That is, P expresses u in terms of its quotient and residue w.r.t. a second modulus $M \ll \frac{N_\mathsf{P}}{\Delta}$, i.e. (u_{hi}, u_{lo}) such that $u_{hi} \cdot M + u_{lo} = u$. Then, P reveals u_{hi} so both parties can locally compute shares $w_{lo} - v$ of $u_{lo}\Delta$. Taking these shares modulo q then gives the desired VOLE correlation, with $r = u_{lo} \bmod q$.

But what if P is malicious and tries to cheat? Note that P could send an incorrect u_{hi} to get shares of $u_{lo}\Delta$ modulo N_P, where $u_{lo} = u_{lo}^* + M(u_{hi}^* - u_{hi})$, and (u_{hi}^*, u_{lo}^*) are what these would be if P were honest. We combine three protections to stop P from cheating. First, we have $q \mid M$, so that if the parties get shares of $u_{lo}\Delta$ over $\mathbb{Z}$ (i.e., if u_{lo} is small) then the cheating makes no difference, as $u_{lo} \equiv u_{lo}^* \mod q$ anyway. Second, we add an "integer consistency check" in the exponent, using a different group generated by $g \in (\mathbb{Z}_{N_\mathsf{V}})^\times$, where N_V is a semiprime so that g's order is unknown. We let P send $g^{u_{lo}}$ and g^v, and V checks that $g^{w_{lo}-v} = g^{u_{lo}\Delta}$. To pass this check, a corrupted P must guess a linear function of Δ that equals the number of times $u_{lo}\Delta \bmod N_\mathsf{P}$ wraps around, which is only possible when u_{lo} is very close to a multiple of N_P. Finally, V enforces an upper bound on $|u_{hi}|$ so that the only values of u_{lo} near a multiple of N_P are near 0 (i.e., the case we already solved by requiring $q \mid M$).

Dealing with a corrupted V is much easier, and only requires setting M to be large enough so that $g^{u_{lo}}$ and $u_{lo} \bmod q$ are statistically independent.

Algorithm 5.1. $\mathsf{modPCF}_{\mathbb{G},\mathsf{PCF}}$**.** $(\varepsilon, \mathbb{G})$-$\mathsf{PCF}_{\mathsf{DL}}$ **from Paillier PCF**

Parameters and constants:

1. A random oracle $H\colon \{0,1\}^* \to \{0,1\}^{n(\kappa)}$.
2. A group $\mathbb{G}$ of odd order q, written additively. We require that $q < 2^{\ell(\kappa)/2-2}$.
3. The number $\eta \geq 2\ln(2)\ell' 2^\kappa$ of possible verifier secrets Δ. We require that $\eta < 2^{\ell(\kappa)/2-2}$ and that q has no factors below η.
4. The Paillier key size, $\ell' \geq \log_2(q\eta) + \kappa + \ell(\kappa) + 2$.

$\mathsf{Setup}(\kappa)$: 1. Sample $(N_\mathsf{P}, \varphi_\mathsf{P}) \leftarrow \mathsf{RSA.Gen}(1^{\kappa'})$, where $\kappa' > \kappa$ is chosen so that $\ell(\kappa') = \ell'$.

2. Sample $(N_V, \varphi_V) \leftarrow \mathsf{RSA.GenSafe}(1^\kappa)$ and $g \leftarrow (\mathbb{Z}_{N_V})^\times$.
3. Setup the smaller modulus $M := qN_V$.
4. Sample the verifier secret index $\Delta \leftarrow [-\frac{\eta}{2}, \frac{\eta}{2}) \cap \mathbb{Z}$.
5. Set up the PCF: $(k_0, k_1) \leftarrow \mathsf{PCF.Gen}(1^\kappa, N_P, \varphi_P, \perp, \Delta)$.
6. Output $k_P = (k_0, N_P, N_V, M, g)$, and $k_V = (k_1, N_P, N_V, M, g, \Delta)$.

$\mathsf{P}((k_0, N_P, N_V, M, g), m)$: 1. Compute $(u, v) := \mathsf{PCF.Eval}(0, k_0, H(m))$.
2. Find $u_{hi} := \lfloor \frac{u}{M} \rceil$, $u_{lo} := u - Mu_{hi} = u \bmod M$.
3. Compute the proof $s := g^{u_{lo}}$ and $t := g^v$.
4. Output $r_m := u \bmod q$, and $\pi_R := (u_{hi}, s, t, v \cdot G)$.

$\mathsf{V}((k_1, N_P, N_V, M, g, \Delta), m, R_m, \pi_R)$: 1. Compute $w := \mathsf{PCF.Eval}(1, k_1, H(m))$.
2. Let $(u_{hi}, s, t, V) := \pi_R$.
3. Correct w as $w_{lo} := (w - Mu_{hi}\Delta) \bmod N_P$.
4. Output 1 if all of the following checks pass. Otherwise output 0.
   (a) $|u_{hi}| \leq \frac{N_P}{2M}$
   (b) $g^{w_{lo}} \stackrel{?}{=} \pm t\, s^\Delta$
   (c) $w_{lo} \cdot G \stackrel{?}{=} V + \Delta \cdot R_m$

5.1 Efficiency

Notice that t and V are only used to check an equality. This allows an optimization where P sends $h_{tV} = H'(|t|, V)$ instead of t and V, and V checks that $h_{tV} \stackrel{?}{=} H'(|g^{w_{lo}} s^{-\Delta}|, w_{lo} \cdot G - \Delta \cdot R_m)$. This is still sound, because in the soundness proof we can extract $|t| = \pm t$ and V from h_{tV}.

We now give a summary of the complexity of the protocol with the hash optimization, for both communication and computation. The proof π_R that P sends contains u_{hi} for $\log_2(N_P/M)$ bits, s for $\log_2(N_V)$ bits, and h_{tV} for 2κ bits. The total is $C = \ell' - \log_2(q) + 2\kappa$ bits, because $M = qN_V$. Set $\eta = 2\ln(2)\ell' 2^\kappa$.[2] We get that $\ell' - \log_2(\ell') \geq \log_2(q) + 2\kappa + \ell(\kappa) + 3 + \log_2(\ln(2))$. Since $A - \log_2(A) \geq B$ can be solved by $A = B + \log_2(2B)$ when $B \geq 2$, and since $\log_2(\ln(2)) < 0$, we can set

$$\ell' \geq \log_2(q) + 2\kappa + \ell(\kappa) + 4 + \log_2(\log_2(q) + 2\kappa + \ell(\kappa) + 3).$$

Since $q \ll \ell(\kappa)$ for our application, we have that $\ell(\kappa)$ is bigger than all the other terms put together, which let's us simplify by choosing a slightly bigger ℓ'. We can compute the total communication cost using ℓ'.

$$\ell' = \log_2(q) + 2\kappa + \ell(\kappa) + \log_2(\ell(\kappa)) + 5$$
$$C = \ell(\kappa) + \log_2(\ell(\kappa)) + 5 + 4\kappa$$

[2] η really should be rounded up to an integer, but this makes almost no difference.

For computation, P performs two exponentiations in $(\mathbb{Z}_{N_\mathsf{P}^2})^\times$ (for the PCF) and two in $(\mathbb{Z}_{N_\mathsf{V}})^\times$ (for the check), while V computes one exponentiation in $(\mathbb{Z}_{N_\mathsf{P}^2})^\times$ and two in $(\mathbb{Z}_{N_\mathsf{V}})^\times$. The CRT optimization can be applied to P's exponentiations in $(\mathbb{Z}_{N_\mathsf{P}^2})^\times$ and to V's exponentiations in $(\mathbb{Z}_{N_\mathsf{V}})^\times$, since they know the factorizations of their respective moduli.

We illustrate our scheme's efficiency with concrete parameters for the $\kappa =$ 128-bit security level. To evaluate $\ell(\kappa)$, we follow NIST's recommendations for RSA key sizes, which is 3072 bits for 128-bit security [Bar20, Table 2]. Let $q \approx 2^{252}$ be the prime order subgroup used for the Ed25519 signature scheme [BDL+11]. We then get $\ell' = 3597$ bits (rounding up), with a total communication cost of $C = 3601$ bits, or 451 bytes. When used with Protocol 3, each party must send an additional curve point and element of $\mathbb{Z}_q$, so the per-party communication cost is 514 bytes.

A Note on Setup Efficiency. As written, the setup functionality samples N_P and N_V itself, which appears to require distributed sampling of an RSA modulus. However, observe that the factorization of the moduli need not be hidden from both parties simultaneously—N_P's factorization is known by the prover, and it is fine to give N_V's to the verifier. This opens the door for protocols where the appropriate party simply samples the RSA modulus itself, and proves that it is well-formed (as is common in widely deployed Paillier-based Threshold ECDSA protocols [CGG+20]). As the focus is on the signing protocols in this work, rather than the instantiation of the setup functionality, we leave optimizing the setup phase for future work.

5.2 Implementation

We made a prototype implementation using the GMP library. When running on a single thread of a laptop (with a Ryzen 7 5800H processor), the prover takes 56ms while the verifier takes 130ms, leading to a per-party computation time of 188ms per ed25519 signature. These estimates indicate that our construction is considerably more computationally efficient than prior work based on Bulletproofs: from [NRSW20, Table 1], their prover runs in 943ms and the verifier between 10–50 ms depending on the batch size, making our protocol approximately 5 times faster in total. Of course the benchmarks are not directly comparable as they are measured in different environments, but they provide an overall picture of the efficiency comparison. We do not estimate our construction to be computationally lighter than prior work based on garbled circuits [GKMN21], which is however much heavier on bandwidth consumption than this work.

Theorem 5.2. Algorithm $\mathsf{modPCF}_{\mathbb{G},\mathsf{PCF}}$ is a $(\varepsilon, \mathbb{G})$-$\mathsf{PCF}_\mathsf{DL}$, assuming that PCF is a pseudorandom correlation function for a VOLE reverse sampleable correlation.

The proof is given in the following sections, split between the three properties.

5.3 Completeness

Theorem 5.3. $\mathsf{modPCF}_{\mathbb{G},\mathsf{PCF}}$ satisfies completeness, as defined in $(\varepsilon, \mathbb{G})$-$\mathsf{PCF}_{\mathsf{DL}}$. More specifically, assume that at most Q unique queries to H are made (either by the adversary or P). Then the chance of failure is at most $Q(\frac{1}{2}+\eta^{-1})2^{-\kappa} + \mathsf{Adv}_{\mathsf{PCF.Pseudorandom}}$.

Proof. We will ignore the output (r_m, π_R) from $\mathcal{O}_{\mathsf{compl}}$, instead proving that $\mathsf{modPCF}_{\mathbb{G},\mathsf{PCF}}$ will remain complete even when $\mathcal{A}$ is given k_{P}. In the worst case, every message m input to H will be given to $\mathcal{O}_{\mathsf{compl}}$, and because the time of abort does not matter, we can assume m is given to $\mathcal{O}_{\mathsf{compl}}$ at the same time as $H(m)$ is sampled. Therefore, we compute an upper bound A on the probability of abort for $\mathcal{O}_{\mathsf{compl}}(m)$, assuming that that $H(m)$ is freshly random. The overall game then aborts with probability at most QA, by the union bound.

First, let's check the bounds on u_{lo} and u_{hi}. We have $|u_{lo}| = |u_i \bmod M| \leq \frac{M}{2}$, because we are using a symmetric modulus operation. Also,

$$|u_{hi}| = \left|\left\lfloor \frac{u}{M} \right\rceil\right| \leq \left\lceil \frac{N_{\mathsf{P}}}{2M} \right\rceil \leq \left\lfloor \frac{N_{\mathsf{P}}}{2M} \right\rfloor + 1,$$

so check (a) will pass except for when $|u_{hi}|$ takes the maximal value $\lfloor \frac{N_{\mathsf{P}}}{2M} \rfloor + 1$. If it fails,

$$|u| \geq \left\lfloor \frac{N_{\mathsf{P}}}{2M} \right\rfloor M + \frac{M}{2} > \frac{N_{\mathsf{P}}}{2M} M - M + \frac{M}{2} = \frac{N_{\mathsf{P}} - M}{2}.$$

Therefore, u would be in a set of size at most $2(\frac{N_{\mathsf{P}}}{2} - \frac{N_{\mathsf{P}}-M}{2}) = M$, which has probability at most

$$\frac{M}{N_{\mathsf{P}}} < q 2^{\ell(\kappa)-\ell'+2} < q 2^{-\log_2(q\eta)-\kappa} = \eta^{-1} 2^{-\kappa}, \tag{1}$$

by the pseudorandomness of PCF.

Next, for checks (b) and (c) we need the following lemma.

Lemma 5.4 ([RS21, Lemma 19]). *For any $N_{\mathsf{P}} \in \mathbb{Z}^+$, $x \in \mathbb{Z}$, and uniformly random $r \in \mathbb{Z}_{N_{\mathsf{P}}}$, we have*

$$\Pr\left[x = (r + x) \bmod N_{\mathsf{P}} - r \bmod N_{\mathsf{P}}\right] = \max\left(1 - \frac{|x|}{N_{\mathsf{P}}}, 0\right).$$

We will use this lemma on the correlation between w_{lo} and v. Notice that

$$w_{lo} - v \equiv w - v - u_{hi} M \Delta \equiv u\Delta - u_{hi} M \Delta \equiv u_{lo}\Delta \mod N_{\mathsf{P}},$$

and $|u_{lo}\Delta| \leq M\frac{\eta}{2}$ is small compared to N_{P}. By the pseudorandomness of PCF, v will be uniform. As both v and w_{lo} are reduced modulo N_{P}, by Lemma 5.4 we can remove the modulus to get $w_{lo} - v = u_{lo}\Delta$, except with probability $\frac{M\eta}{2N_{\mathsf{P}}} \leq 2^{-\kappa-1}$. Checks (b) and (c) then must be satisfied, as they are $g^{w_{lo}} \stackrel{?}{=} g^{v+\bar{u}\Delta}$ and $w_{lo} \cdot G \stackrel{?}{=} (v + \Delta u) \cdot G$ respectively. For check (c), notice that $u = u_{lo} + M u_{hi} \equiv u \bmod q$ because $q \mid M$.

Therefore, we have the bound $A = (\frac{1}{2}+\eta^{-1})2^{-\kappa}$, which after multiplying by Q matches the theorem statement. □

5.4 Soundness

Theorem 5.5. $\mathsf{modPCF}_{\mathbb{G},\mathsf{PCF}}$ satisfies ε-**Soundness**, for

$$\varepsilon = Q(2^{-\kappa} + 5\eta^{-1}) + 2\eta^{-1} + 2^{-\ell(\kappa)/2+3} < Q(2^{-\kappa} + 6\eta^{-1}),$$

plus the advantages against the underlying hardness assumptions: $\Theta(\mathsf{Adv}_{\mathsf{StrongRSA}}) + \mathsf{Adv}_{\mathsf{PCF.Security}} + \mathsf{Adv}_{\mathsf{PCF.Pseudorandom}}$. Here, we assume that at most Q unique queries to H are made.

Proof. Our proof overall is structured as a hybrid argument. The first hybrid, $\mathcal{H}_1$, is a straightforward change from PCF evaluation to reverse sampling, based on the security of PCF. First, change k_0 to be sampled with $\mathsf{PCF}.\mathcal{S}_0(N_\mathsf{P}, \phi, \bot)$, and remove the call to PCF.Gen. Let $(u, v) = \mathsf{PCF.Eval}(0, k_0, H(m))$ be the correlation that would be computed by an honest prover. Then change V to equivalently compute w as $v + u\Delta$, instead of evaluating the PCF with k_1 (which is no longer defined). Define $u_{lo} = u - Mu_{hi}$, where u_{hi} is the value sent by the adversary. Then

$$w_{lo} = (w - Mu_{hi}\Delta) \bmod N_\mathsf{P} = (v + u_{lo}\Delta) \bmod N_\mathsf{P}.$$

Let

$$\mathcal{D} = \{\Delta \in [-\frac{\eta}{2}, \frac{\eta}{2}) \mid g^{(v+u_{lo}\Delta) \bmod N_\mathsf{P}} = \pm t\, s^{\Delta}\},$$

and replace check (b) with the equivalent check $\Delta \in \mathcal{D}$.

Claims. With the notation defined in $\mathcal{H}_1$, we can now analyze the consistency check in $\mathsf{modPCF}_{\mathbb{G},\mathsf{PCF}}$. The bulk of our proof will be about finding the size and structure of $\mathcal{D}$, as this is what determines whether the attacker can succeed in lying about R_m. We first give a series of claims that should hold when the consistency check passes, except with negligible probability. More precisely, a claim stating X means that Pr[consistency check passes $\wedge \neg X$] is negligible. The final claim will be that the scheme is sound, i.e., R_m must take its honest value. We will justify these claims with hybrids, changing the protocol until all of the claims are true unconditionally.

Claim 5.6. *In addition to the actually checked value Δ, $\mathcal{D}$ contains a second element $\Delta' \neq \Delta$.*

Claim 5.7. *From Δ, Δ', we can efficiently find nonzero integers a, b such that $g^a = \pm s^b$, where $|a| \leq N_\mathsf{P}$ and $|b| \leq \eta$.*

Claim 5.8. *From Δ, Δ', we can efficiently extract integers $\bar{u}_{lo} = a/b$ and $\bar{v}$ such that $s = \pm g^{\bar{u}_{lo}}$ and $t = \pm g^{\bar{v}}$.*

Claim 5.9. *g^2 generates the subgroup of perfect squares in $(\mathbb{Z}_{N_\mathsf{V}})^\times$.*

Claim 5.10. *$\bar{u}_{lo} \equiv u_{lo} \mod N_\mathsf{P}$ and $\bar{v} \equiv v \mod N_\mathsf{P}$.*

Claim 5.11. $\mathcal{D} = \left\{\Delta \in [-\frac{\eta}{2}, \frac{\eta}{2}) \mid |\bar{v} + \bar{u}_{lo}\Delta| \leq \frac{N_\mathsf{P}}{2}\right\}$,

Claim 5.12. *We can assume without loss of generality that $\Delta' = \Delta \pm 1$.*

Claim 5.13. $\bar{u}_{lo} = u_{lo}$.

Claim 5.14. $R_m = r_m \cdot G$.

Now we present the remaining hybrids to show that these claims hold.

$\mathcal{H}_2$. Change the verifier to abort if $|\mathcal{D}| < 2$, and otherwise sample $\mathcal{D}'$ as a uniformly random element of $\mathcal{D}\backslash\{\Delta\}$. This makes Claim 5.6 hold trivially. This change is only distinguishable when $|\mathcal{D}| \leq 1$, in which case the adversary has to guess that Δ is the unique value in $\mathcal{D}$, when Δ is uniformly random over η possibilities. Therefore, passing check (b) has probability at most η^{-1} in $\mathcal{H}_1$, and zero probability in $\mathcal{H}_2$. This bounds the advantage at η^{-1}. Claim 5.7 also holds in this hybrid. Because $\Delta, \Delta' \in \mathcal{D}$, we have $g^{(v+u_{lo}\Delta) \bmod N_{\mathsf{P}}} = \pm t\, s^{\Delta}$, and the same for Δ'. Taking the ratio between the two equations gives $g^a = \pm s^b$, where

$$a = (v + u_{lo}\Delta') \bmod N_{\mathsf{P}} - (v + u_{lo}\Delta) \bmod N_{\mathsf{P}}, \qquad b = \Delta' - \Delta.$$

The bounds are $|a| \leq N_{\mathsf{P}}$ and $|b| \leq \eta$, because a is the difference of two values below N_{P} and b is the difference of two values below η.
Note that this hybrid is not efficiently computable. We will fix this in a later hybrid, but until then we will use only statistical security (like here), or give a reduction that avoids this issue.

$\mathcal{H}_3$. Add checks requiring that $b \mid a$ and $s = \pm g^{\bar{u}_{lo}}$. Here, we let

$$\bar{u}_{lo} = \frac{a}{b} \quad \text{and} \quad \bar{v} = (v + u_{lo}\Delta) \bmod N_{\mathsf{P}} - \bar{u}_{lo}\Delta. \tag{2}$$

That is, $\bar{u}_{lo}$ and $\bar{v}$ are defined to be the slope and intercept of the line through $(\Delta, (v + u_{lo}\Delta) \bmod N_{\mathsf{P}})$ and $(\Delta', (v + u_{lo}\Delta') \bmod N_{\mathsf{P}})$. Then $s = \pm g^{\bar{u}_{lo}}$ implies that $t = \pm g^{\bar{v}}$. Therefore, Claim 5.8 holds as of this hybrid. The indistinguishability of this hybrid follows from a reduction to Strong RSA. This reduction is deferred to the full version of this paper.

$\mathcal{H}_4$. Require that g^2 generates the subgroup of perfect squares in $(\mathbb{Z}_{N_{\mathsf{V}}})^{\times}$, which can be checked efficiently using that we know a prime factorization $p' \cdot q'$ of N_{V}, and that p' and q' are safe primes. This makes Claim 5.9 hold trivially. The order of the group of perfect squares is $(\frac{p'-1}{2}) \cdot (\frac{q'-1}{2})$, which is a semiprime. Therefore, g^2 generates it with probability $\left(1 - \frac{2}{p'-1}\right)\left(1 - \frac{2}{q'-1}\right) \geq 1 - 2^{-\ell(\kappa)/2+3}$, so this change is indistinguishable.
Proof of Claim 5.10. Using Claim 5.8, we now have $\Delta^* \in \mathcal{D}$ if and only if

$$g^{(v+u_{lo}\Delta^*) \bmod N_{\mathsf{P}}} = \pm g^{\bar{v}+\bar{u}_{lo}\Delta^*}$$

Since g^2 generates the perfect squares of $(\mathbb{Z}_{N_{\mathsf{V}}})^{\times}$, which has odd order $\varphi_{\mathsf{V}}/4$, squaring both sides gives

$$(v + u_{lo}\Delta^*) \bmod N_{\mathsf{P}} \equiv \bar{v} + \bar{u}_{lo}\Delta^* \mod \varphi_{\mathsf{V}}/4. \tag{3}$$

Additionally, this last equation holds without the modulus for $\Delta^* = \Delta$ and $\Delta^* = \Delta'$, because $\bar{u}_{lo}$ and $\bar{v}$ come from interpolating a line through these two points over $\mathbb{Z}$ (see Eq. (2)). Taking both sides modulo N_P gives

$$\begin{aligned} v + u_{lo}\Delta &\equiv \bar{v} + \bar{u}_{lo}\Delta && \mod N_\mathsf{P} \\ v + u_{lo}\Delta' &\equiv \bar{v} + \bar{u}_{lo}\Delta' && \mod N_\mathsf{P} \\ (u_{lo} - \bar{u}_{lo})(\Delta' - \Delta) &\equiv 0 && \mod N_\mathsf{P}. \end{aligned}$$

Since $\Delta' - \Delta \neq 0$ is smaller than $\eta < 2^{\ell(\kappa)/2-2} < 2^{\ell'/2-1} < \min(p, q)$, $\Delta' - \Delta$ is coprime to N_P. Therefore, $u_{lo} \equiv \bar{u}_{lo} \mod N_\mathsf{P}$, and so $v \equiv \bar{v} \mod N_\mathsf{P}$ as well.

Proof of Claim 5.11. We can now substitute $\bar{u}_{lo}, \bar{v}$ for u_{lo}, v in Eq. (3), simplifying it to get

$$\begin{aligned} (\bar{v} + \bar{u}_{lo}\Delta^*) \bmod N_\mathsf{P} - \bar{v} - \bar{u}_{lo}\Delta^* &\equiv 0 \mod \varphi_\mathsf{V}/4 \\ -N_\mathsf{P}\left\lfloor \frac{\bar{v} + \bar{u}_{lo}\Delta^*}{N_\mathsf{P}} \right\rceil &\equiv 0 \mod \varphi_\mathsf{V}/4 \\ \left\lfloor \frac{\bar{v} + \bar{u}_{lo}\Delta^*}{N_\mathsf{P}} \right\rceil &\equiv 0 \mod \varphi_\mathsf{V}/4. \end{aligned}$$

We used that N_P is coprime to $\varphi_\mathsf{V}/4$ because they are both semiprimes and N_P's prime factors are much larger than $\varphi_\mathsf{V}/4$. Recall that $(v + u_{lo}\Delta) \bmod N_\mathsf{P} - \bar{v} - \bar{u}_{lo}\Delta$, so we can upper bound the value being rounded:

$$\left| \frac{\bar{v} + \bar{u}_{lo}\Delta^*}{N_\mathsf{P}} \right| = \left| \frac{(v + u_{lo}\Delta^*) \bmod N_\mathsf{P} + \bar{u}_{lo}(\Delta^* - \Delta)}{N_\mathsf{P}} \right| \leq \frac{1}{2} + \eta < \varphi_\mathsf{V}/4,$$

since $\bar{u}_{lo} \leq |a| \leq N_\mathsf{P}$. Therefore, we can remove the modulus, showing that $\Delta^* \in \mathcal{D}$ implies $\left\lfloor \frac{\bar{v} + \bar{u}_{lo}\Delta}{N_\mathsf{P}} \right\rceil = 0$, or equivalently $|\bar{v} + \bar{u}_{lo}\Delta| \leq \frac{N_\mathsf{P}}{2}$. Conversely, if $|\bar{v} + \bar{u}_{lo}\Delta| \leq \frac{N_\mathsf{P}}{2}$ then $g^{(v+u_{lo}\Delta^*) \bmod N_\mathsf{P}} = g^{(\bar{v}+\bar{u}_{lo}\Delta^*) \bmod N_\mathsf{P}} = g^{\bar{v}+\bar{u}_{lo}\Delta^*}$, so $\Delta^* \in \mathcal{D}$.

$\mathcal{H}_5$. Instead of sampling $\mathcal{D}'$ as a uniformly random element of $\mathcal{D} \setminus \{\Delta\}$, just check the two neighboring elements $\Delta \pm 1$. By Claim 5.11, $\mathcal{D}$ is an interval, and by Claim 5.6 it contains at least two elements. Therefore, any element $\Delta \in \mathcal{D}$ has a neighboring element $\Delta' \in \mathcal{D}$, so this change is indistinguishable. All the preceding claims merely require that Δ and Δ' be distinct elements of $\mathcal{D}$, so they will still hold with this choice of Δ'. Therefore, Claim 5.12 holds. Note that this hybrid is now efficiently computable, by removing the sampling introduced in $\mathcal{H}_2$.

$\mathcal{H}_6$. In this hybrid, add a new check requiring that $\bar{u}_{lo} = u_{lo}$ so that Claim 5.13 is trivially true. To notice this change, the adversary must find $\bar{u}_{lo} \neq u_{lo}$ while passing the check $\Delta \in \mathcal{D}$. They have probability at most $\frac{|\mathcal{D}|}{\eta}$ of passing, so we want to upper bound $|\mathcal{D}|$. By Claim 5.11, Δ must be in a width $\frac{N_\mathsf{P}}{\bar{u}_{lo}}$ interval, which can contain at most $\frac{N_\mathsf{P}}{\bar{u}_{lo}} + 1$ integers.
The adversary is limited in how it can pick $\bar{u}_{lo}$. By Claim 5.10, $\bar{u}_{lo} \equiv u_{lo}$

mod N_{P}, and we defined $u_{lo} = u - Mu_{hi}$. We also have $|u_{hi}| \le \frac{N_{\mathsf{P}}}{2M}$ from check (a). Therefore, $|u_{lo}| \le |u| + M|u_{hi}| \le |u| + \frac{N_{\mathsf{P}}}{2}$. The adversary must shift u_{lo} by at least N_{P} in either direction to get $\bar{u}_{lo} \neq u_{lo}$, so $|\bar{u}_{lo}| \ge N_{\mathsf{P}} - |u_{lo}| \ge \frac{N_{\mathsf{P}}}{2} - |u|$.

The only control that the adversary exercises over u is through the message m, as u is the honest output from the PCF. For the ith random oracle query $H(m_i)$, let P_{m_i} be the probability that the adversary selects m_i and passes the check. Then $\eta P_{m_i} \le \mathbb{E}\left[\frac{N_{\mathsf{P}}}{\frac{N_{\mathsf{P}}}{2} - |u_{m_i}|} + 1\right]$, where $(u_{m_i}, v_{m_i}) = \mathsf{PCF.Eval}(0, k_0, H(m_i))$. By the pseudorandomness of PCF, $|u_{m_i}|$ is indistinguishable from a uniformly random integer in $[0, \frac{N_{\mathsf{P}}-1}{2}]$. Therefore,

$$\begin{aligned}
\eta P_{m_i} &\le 1 + \frac{2}{N_{\mathsf{P}}+1} \sum_{j=0}^{\frac{N_{\mathsf{P}}-1}{2}} \frac{N_{\mathsf{P}}}{\frac{N_{\mathsf{P}}}{2} - j} \\
&= 1 + \frac{4N_{\mathsf{P}}}{N_{\mathsf{P}}+1} + \frac{2}{N_{\mathsf{P}}+1} \sum_{x=0}^{\frac{N_{\mathsf{P}}-3}{2}} \frac{N_{\mathsf{P}}}{\frac{N_{\mathsf{P}}}{2} - x} \\
&\le 5 + \int_0^{\frac{N_{\mathsf{P}}-1}{2}} \frac{2}{\frac{N_{\mathsf{P}}}{2} - x} dx \\
&= 5 + 2\ln(N_{\mathsf{P}}/2) - 2\ln(1/2) = 5 + 2\ln(N_{\mathsf{P}}).
\end{aligned}$$

The second inequality uses the summation as a left Riemann sum; this gives a lower bound on the integral because $\frac{N_{\mathsf{P}}}{\frac{N_{\mathsf{P}}}{2} - x}$ is an increasing function. Finally, apply the union bound over all queries i to upper bound the distinguisher's advantage at $Q\frac{5+2\ln(N_{\mathsf{P}})}{\eta} \le Q(5\eta^{-1} + 2^{-\kappa})$, where Q is the total number of queries to H.

$\mathcal{H}_7$. In this final hybrid, we require that Claim 5.14 be true. That is, we make V fail whenever R_m is not its honest value $r_m \cdot G = u \cdot G$. This makes the soundness game trivially impossible for the adversary to attack. We will bound the chance that the adversary passes all the previous checks, but fails this final check.

Let $A = R_m - u \cdot G$ and $B = V - \bar{v} \cdot G$. Then check (c) becomes

$$\begin{aligned}
B + \bar{v} \cdot G + \Delta \cdot A + \Delta u \cdot G &= w_{lo} \cdot G \\
B + \Delta \cdot A &= ((\bar{v} + \bar{u}_{lo}\Delta) \bmod N_{\mathsf{P}} - \bar{v} - \Delta\bar{u}_{lo}) \cdot G \\
B + \Delta \cdot A &= -N_{\mathsf{P}}\left\lfloor \frac{\bar{v} + \bar{u}_{lo}\Delta}{N_{\mathsf{P}}} \right\rfloor \cdot G = 0,
\end{aligned}$$

because $\bar{u}_{lo} = u_{lo} = u - Mu_{hi} \equiv u \mod q$ since $q \mid M$. Next, since q has no prime factors below η, $\Delta \cdot A$ will uniquely identify Δ when $A \neq 0$. When $A = 0$, $R_m = r_m \cdot G$ and so the newly added check will pass. Therefore, any adversary distinguishing $\mathcal{H}_7$ from $\mathcal{H}_6$ has advantage at most η^{-1}. □

5.5 Pseudorandom Nonces

Theorem 5.15. $\mathsf{modPCF}_{\mathbb{G},\mathsf{PCF}}$ satisfies the pseudorandomness property defined in $(\varepsilon, \mathbb{G})$-$\mathsf{PCF}_{\mathsf{DL}}$. Assuming that at most Q unique queries to H are made, by either the adversary or the oracles, the distinguisher advantage is bounded by

$$Q((1+\eta^{-1})2^{-\kappa-1} + 2^{-\ell(\kappa)/2+2}) < Q2^{-\kappa}$$

plus the advantage against PCF, which is $\mathsf{Adv}_{\mathsf{PCF.Security}} + \mathsf{Adv}_{\mathsf{PCF.Pseudorandom}}$.

Proof. Let the simulator $\mathcal{S}(k_{\mathsf{V}}, m, R_m)$ work as follows.

1. Compute the verifier's share $w := \mathsf{PCF.Eval}(1, k_1, H(m))$.
2. Sample $u \leftarrow [-\frac{N_{\mathrm{round}}}{2}, \frac{N_{\mathrm{round}}}{2}) \cap \mathbb{Z}$, where $N_{\mathrm{round}} = M\lfloor \frac{N_{\mathsf{P}}}{M} \rceil$ is the multiple of M nearest to N_{P}.
3. Compute u_{hi}, u_{lo}, and s as in the prover.
4. Compute $w_{lo} := (w - M u_{hi} \Delta) \bmod N_{\mathsf{P}}$ as in the verifier, then set $t := g^{w_{lo}} s^{-\Delta}$ and $V := w_{lo} \cdot G - \Delta \cdot R_m$.
5. Output $\pi_R := (u_{hi}, s, t, V)$.

We need to show that the simulation $\mathcal{O}_{\mathcal{S}}(k_{\mathsf{V}})$ is indistinguishable from the real prover $\mathcal{O}_{\mathsf{P}}(k_{\mathsf{P}})$. To do so, we give a hybrid proof, going from the real prover to the simulation. We assume that the queries to H are exactly the queries to $\mathcal{O}_{\mathsf{P}}(k_{\mathsf{P}})$, as the adversary can always be made to query $\mathcal{O}_{\mathsf{P}}(k_{\mathsf{P}})$ at the extra locations. During the proof, we focus on only a single execution of $\mathcal{O}_{\mathsf{P}}(k_{\mathsf{P}})$ and a single oracle query $H(m)$, so all statistical bounds must be multiplied by Q in the overall advantage.

$\mathcal{H}_1$. By the security of the PCF, we can replace the prover's PCF evaluations $(u, v) \leftarrow \mathsf{PCF.Eval}(0, k_0, H(m))$ with computing the verifier's share w and sampling $(u, v) \leftarrow \mathsf{RSample}(1^\kappa, \Delta, 1, w)$. More concretely, $\mathsf{RSample}$ chooses u uniformly in $[-\frac{N_{\mathsf{P}}}{2}, \frac{N_{\mathsf{P}}}{2}) \cap \mathbb{Z}$ and finds the corresponding $v := (w - u\Delta) \bmod N_{\mathsf{P}}$. We also have to change k_1 to be sampled with $\mathsf{PCF}.\mathcal{S}_1(N_{\mathsf{P}}, \phi, \Delta)$, and remove k_0 and the call to $\mathsf{PCF.Gen}$.

$\mathcal{H}_2$. Sample $u \leftarrow [-\frac{N_{\mathrm{round}}}{2}, \frac{N_{\mathrm{round}}}{2}) \cap \mathbb{Z}$ instead. This has advantage at most

$$\frac{|N_{\mathsf{P}} - N_{\mathrm{round}}|}{N_{\mathsf{P}}} = \frac{|N_{\mathsf{P}} \bmod M|}{N_{\mathsf{P}}} \leq \frac{M}{2N} < \eta^{-1} 2^{-\kappa-1},$$

by Eq. (1).

$\mathcal{H}_3$. Instead of computing $t := g^v$ and $V := v \cdot G$, calculate them based on the consistency checks as $t := g^{w_{lo}} s^{-\Delta}$ and $V := w_{lo} \cdot G - \Delta \cdot R_m$. These formulas are equivalent as long as $w_{lo} = v + u_{lo}\Delta$ (without any modulus). As argued in Theorem 5.3, this holds except with probability $2^{-\kappa-1} + \mathsf{Adv}_{\mathsf{PCF.Pseudorandom}}$.

$\mathcal{H}_4$. Currently $u_{lo} = u \bmod M$ is uniformly random in $\mathbb{Z}_M$. Add a bad event asserting that $u_{lo} \in [-\frac{M_{\varphi_{\mathsf{V}}}}{2}, \frac{M_{\varphi_{\mathsf{V}}}}{2})$, where $M_{\varphi_{\mathsf{V}}} = q\varphi_{\mathsf{V}}$. The bad event occurs with probability

$$\frac{M - M_{\varphi_{\mathsf{V}}}}{M} = \frac{N_{\mathsf{V}} - \varphi_{\mathsf{V}}}{N_{\mathsf{V}}} = \frac{1}{p'} + \frac{1}{q'} - \frac{1}{N_{\mathsf{V}}} < 2^{-\ell(\kappa)/2+2},$$

where $p' \cdot q'$ is the prime factorization of N_V.
Assuming that this bad event does not occur, we can divide u_{lo} into two components using the Chinese remainder theorem, which applies because q and φ_V) are coprime. That is, φ_V has prime factoriztaion $4 \cdot (\frac{p'-1}{2}) \cdot (\frac{q'-1}{2})$ because p' and q' are safe primes, and q is an odd number below $2^{\ell(\kappa)/2-1} < \min(\frac{p'-1}{2}, \frac{q'-1}{2})$. Therefore, the possible values of u_{lo} are in bijection with pairs (u_q, u_{φ_V}), where $u_q = u_{lo} \bmod q$ and $u_{\varphi_V} = u_{lo} \bmod \varphi_V$. The only places u_{lo} is used are in $s := g^{u_{lo}}$ and $r_m := u \mod q$. Instead, compute these with u_{φ_V} and u_q, respectively.

$\mathcal{H}_5$. Instead of computing $u_q = u_{lo} \bmod q$, sample $u_q \leftarrow \mathbb{Z}_q$ (while leaving u_{lo} unchanged). This is indistinguishable because u_q is uniformly random in both hybrids, and because u and u_{lo} are not used directly.

$\mathcal{H}_6$. Factor out the computation of R_m into $\mathcal{O}_\mathcal{S}$. The simulator $\mathcal{S}$ is now exactly the modified prover, so we are now at the simulated distribution.

□ +

Acknowledgments. The research described in this paper received funding from: the Concordium Blockhain Research Center, Aarhus University, Denmark; the Carlsberg Foundation under the Semper Ardens Research Project CF18-112 (BCM); the European Research Council (ERC) under the European Unions's Horizon 2020 research and innovation programme under grant agreement No 803096 (SPEC); the Danish Independent Research Council under Grant-ID DFF-0165-00107B (C3PO).

References

[AB21] Kılınç Alper, H., Burdges, J.: Two-round trip schnorr multi-signatures via delinearized witnesses. In: Malkin, T., Peikert, C. (eds.) CRYPTO 2021. LNCS, vol. 12825, pp. 157–188. Springer, Cham (2021). https://doi.org/10.1007/978-3-030-84242-0_7

[AL07] Aumann, Y., Lindell, Y.: Security against covert adversaries: efficient protocols for realistic adversaries. In: Vadhan, S.P. (ed.) TCC 2007. LNCS, vol. 4392, pp. 137–156. Springer, Heidelberg (2007). https://doi.org/10.1007/978-3-540-70936-7_8

[ANO+22] Abram, D., Nof, A., Orlandi, C., Scholl, P., Shlomovits, O.: Low-bandwidth threshold ECDSA via pseudorandom correlation generators. In: 43rd IEEE Symposium on Security and Privacy, SP 2022, San Francisco, CA, USA, 22–26 May 2022, pp. 2554–2572. IEEE (2022)

[ANT+20] Aranha, D.F., Novaes, F.R., Takahashi, A., Tibouchi, M., Yarom, Y.: LadderLeak: breaking ECDSA with less than one bit of nonce leakage. In: ACM CCS 2020, November 2020

[Bar97] Barwood, G.: Digital signatures using elliptic curves, message 32f519ad.19609226@news.dial.pipex.com posted to sci.crypt., (1997)

[Bar20] Barker, E.: Recommendation for key management: Part 1 - general. Technical Report NIST Special Publication (SP) 800–57, Part 1, Rev. 5, National Institute of Standards and Technology, Gaithersburg, MD (2020)

[BBB+18] Bünz, B., Bootle, J., Boneh, D., Poelstra, A., Wuille, P., Maxwell, G.: bulletproofs: short proofs for confidential transactions and more. In: 2018 IEEE Symposium on Security and Privacy, May 2018

[BCG+20] Boyle, E., Couteau, G., Gilboa, N., Ishai, Y., Kohl, L., Scholl, P.: Correlated pseudorandom functions from variable-density LPN. In: 61st FOCS, November (2020)

[BCLK17] Brandenburger, M., Cachin, C., Lorenz, M., Kapitza, R.: Rollback and forking detection for trusted execution environments using lightweight collective memory. In: DSN 2017 (2017)

[BD22] Brandão, L.T.A.N., Davidson, M.: NISTIR 8214B, Notes on Threshold EdDSA/Schnorr Signatures (2022). https://csrc.nist.gov/publications/detail/nistir/8214b/draft

[BDL+11] Bernstein, D.J., Duif, N., Lange, T., Schwabe, P., Yang, B-Y :. High-speed high-security signatures. In CHES 2011, September/October (2011)

[BST21] Bonte, C., Smart, N.P., Tanguy, T.: Thresholdizing hasheddsa: MPC to the rescue. Int. J. Inf. Sec. **20**(6), 879–894 (2021)

[CGG+20] Canetti, R., Gennaro, R., Goldfeder, S., Makriyannis, N., Peled, U.: UC non-interactive, proactive, threshold ECDSA with identifiable aborts. In: ACM CCS 2020, November 2020

[CKLR21] Couteau, G., Klooß, M., Lin, H., Reichle, M.: Efficient Range Proofs with Transparent Setup from Bounded Integer Commitments. In: Canteaut, A., Standaert, F.-X. (eds.) EUROCRYPT 2021, Part III. LNCS, vol. 12698, pp. 247–277. Springer, Cham (2021). https://doi.org/10.1007/978-3-030-77883-5_9

[DEF+19] Drijvers, M., et al.: On the security of two-round multi-signatures. In: 2019 IEEE Symposium on Security and Privacy, May 2019

[Des88] Desmedt, Y.: Society and group oriented cryptography: a new concept. In: Pomerance, C. (ed.) CRYPTO 1987. LNCS, vol. 293, pp. 120–127. Springer, Heidelberg (1988). https://doi.org/10.1007/3-540-48184-2_8

[DF02] Damgård, I., Fujisaki, E.: A statistically-hiding integer commitment scheme based on groups with hidden order. In: Zheng, Y. (ed.) ASIACRYPT 2002. LNCS, vol. 2501, pp. 125–142. Springer, Heidelberg (2002). https://doi.org/10.1007/3-540-36178-2_8

[DHRW16] Dodis, Y., Halevi, S., Rothblum, R.D., Wichs, D.: Spooky Encryption and Its Applications. In: Robshaw, M., Katz, J. (eds.) CRYPTO 2016, Part III. LNCS, vol. 9816, pp. 93–122. Springer, Heidelberg (2016). https://doi.org/10.1007/978-3-662-53015-3_4

[DOK+20] Dalskov, A., Orlandi, C., Keller, M., Shrishak, K., Shulman, H.: Securing DNSSEC keys via threshold ECDSA from generic MPC. In: Chen, L., Li, N., Liang, K., Schneider, S. (eds.) ESORICS 2020, Part II. LNCS, vol. 12309, pp. 654–673. Springer, Cham (2020). https://doi.org/10.1007/978-3-030-59013-0_32

[EZJ+14] Everspaugh, A., Zhai, Y., Jellinek, R., Ristenpart, T., Swift, M.: Not-so-random numbers in virtualized Linux and the whirlwind RNG. In: 2014 IEEE Symposium on Security and Privacy, May 2014

[GG18] Gennaro, R., Goldfeder, S.: Fast multiparty threshold ECDSA with fast trustless setup. In: ACM CCS 2018, October 2018

[Gil99] Gilboa, N.: Two party RSA key generation. In: Wiener, M. (ed.) CRYPTO 1999. LNCS, vol. 1666, pp. 116–129. Springer, Heidelberg (1999). https://doi.org/10.1007/3-540-48405-1_8

[GJKR07] Gennaro, R., Jarecki, S., Krawczyk, H., Rabin, T.: Secure distributed key generation for discrete-log based cryptosystems. J. Cryptology **20**(1), 51–83 (2006). https://doi.org/10.1007/s00145-006-0347-3

[GKMN21] Garillot, F., Kondi, Y., Mohassel, P., Nikolaenko, V.: Threshold Schnorr with stateless deterministic signing from standard assumptions. In: Malkin, T., Peikert, C. (eds.) CRYPTO 2021. LNCS, vol. 12825, pp. 127–156. Springer, Cham (2021). https://doi.org/10.1007/978-3-030-84242-0_6

[GMW87] Goldreich, O., Micali, S., Wigderson, A.: How to prove all NP statements in zero-knowledge and a methodology of cryptographic protocol design (Extended Abstract). In: Odlyzko, A.M. (ed.) CRYPTO 1986. LNCS, vol. 263, pp. 171–185. Springer, Heidelberg (1987). https://doi.org/10.1007/3-540-47721-7_11

[Hen22] Heninger, N.: RSA, DH and DSA in the Wild. In: Bos, J., Stam, M. (eds.), Computational Cryptography, chapter 6, pp. 140–181. Cambridge University Press (2022)

[HS01] Howgrave-Graham, N., Smart, N.P.: Lattice attacks on digital signature schemes. Des. Codes Cryptogr. **23**(3), 283–290 (2001)

[IKNP03] Ishai, Y., Kilian, J., Nissim, K., Petrank, E.: Extending oblivious transfers efficiently. In: Boneh, D. (ed.) CRYPTO 2003. LNCS, vol. 2729, pp. 145–161. Springer, Heidelberg (2003). https://doi.org/10.1007/978-3-540-45146-4_9

[JKO13] Jawurek, M., Kerschbaum, F., Orlandi, C.: Zero-knowledge using garbled circuits: how to prove non-algebraic statements efficiently. In: ACM CCS 2013, November 2013

[KASN15] Kumari, R., Alimomeni, M., Safavi-Naini, R.: Performance analysis of Linux RNG in virtualized environments. In: ACM Workshop on Cloud Computing Security Workshop - CCSW 2015, New York, USA (2015)

[KG20] Komlo, C., Goldberg, I.: FROST: flexible round-optimized Schnorr threshold signatures. SAC **2020**(October), 21–23 (2020)

[Lin22] Lindell, Y.: Simple three-round multiparty schnorr signing with full simulatability. Cryptology ePrint Archive, Report 2022/374 (2022). http://eprint.iacr.org/2022/374

[LN18] Lindell, Y., Nof, A.: Fast secure multiparty ECDSA with practical distributed key generation and applications to cryptocurrency custody. In: ACM CCS 2018, October 2018

[MAK+17] Matetic, S., et al.: ROTE: rollback protection for trusted execution. In: USENIX Security 2017, August 2017

[MH20] De Micheli, G., Heninger, N.: Recovering cryptographic keys from partial information, by example. Cryptology ePrint Archive, Report 2020/1506 (2020). https://eprint.iacr.org/2020/1506

[MPSW19] Maxwell, G., Poelstra, A., Seurin, Y., Wuille, P.: Simple schnorr multi-signatures with applications to bitcoin. Des. Codes Cryptography **87**(9), 2139–2164 (2019)

[NKDM03] Nicolosi, A., Krohn, M.N., Dodis, Y., Mazieres, D.: Proactive two-party signatures for user authentication. In: NDSS 2003, February 2003

[NRS21] Nick, J., Ruffing, T., Seurin, Y.: MuSig2: simple two-round Schnorr multi-signatures. In: Malkin, T., Peikert, C. (eds.) CRYPTO 2021. LNCS, vol. 12825, pp. 189–221. Springer, Cham (2021). https://doi.org/10.1007/978-3-030-84242-0_8

[NRSW20] Nick, J., Ruffing, T., Seurin, Y., Wuille, P.: MuSig-DN: schnorr multi-signatures with verifiably deterministic nonces. In: ACM CCS 2020, November 2020

[OSY21] Orlandi, C., Scholl, P., Yakoubov, S.: The rise of Paillier: homomorphic secret sharing and public-key silent OT. In: Canteaut, A., Standaert, F.-X. (eds.) EUROCRYPT 2021, Part I. LNCS, vol. 12696, pp. 678–708. Springer, Cham (2021). https://doi.org/10.1007/978-3-030-77870-5_24

[Ped91] Pedersen, T.P.: A threshold cryptosystem without a trusted party. In: Davies, D.W. (ed.) EUROCRYPT 1991. LNCS, vol. 547, pp. 522–526. Springer, Heidelberg (1991). https://doi.org/10.1007/3-540-46416-6_47

[PLD+11] Parno, B., Lorch, J.R., Douceur, J.R., Mickens, J.W., McCune, J.M.: Memoir: practical state continuity for protected modules. In: 2011 IEEE Symposium on Security and Privacy, May 2011

[PS96] Pointcheval, D., Stern, J.: Security proofs for signature schemes. In: Maurer, U. (ed.) EUROCRYPT 1996. LNCS, vol. 1070, pp. 387–398. Springer, Heidelberg (1996). https://doi.org/10.1007/3-540-68339-9_33

[Roy22] Roy, L.: SoftSpokenOT: communication-computation tradeoffs in OT extension. In: CRYPTO 2022 (2022)

[RS21] Roy, L., Singh, J.: Large message homomorphic secret sharing from DCR and applications. In: Malkin, T., Peikert, C. (eds.) CRYPTO 2021, Part III. LNCS, vol. 12827, pp. 687–717. Springer, Cham (2021). https://doi.org/10.1007/978-3-030-84252-9_23

[Sch91] Schnorr, C.P.: Efficient signature generation by smart cards. J. Cryptology **4**(3), 161–174 (1991). https://doi.org/10.1007/BF00196725

[SP16] Strackx, R., Piessens, F.: Ariadne: a minimal approach to state continuity. In: USENIX Security 2016, August 2016

[SS01] Stinson, D.R., Strobl, R.: Provably secure distributed Schnorr signatures and a (t, n) threshold scheme for implicit certificates. In: ACISP 01, July 2001

[ST19] Smart, N.P., Alaoui, Y.T.: Distributing any elliptic curve based protocol. In: 17th IMA International Conference on Cryptography and Coding, December 2019

[Wig97] Wigley, J.: Removing need for RNG in signatures, message 5gov5d$pad@wapping.ecs.soton.ac.uk posted to sci.crypt (1997). https://groups.google.com/group/sci.crypt/msg/a6da45bcc8939a89

[WNR] Wuille, P., Nick, J., Ruffing, T.: BIP 340: Schnorr signatures for secp256k1. https://github.com/bitcoin/bips/blob/master/bip-0340.mediawiki

Fully Adaptive Schnorr Threshold Signatures

Elizabeth Crites[1(✉)], Chelsea Komlo[2], and Mary Maller[3]

[1] University of Edinburgh, Edinburgh, UK
ecrites@ed.ac.uk

[2] University of Waterloo & Zcash Foundation, Waterloo, Canada
ckomlo@uwaterloo.ca

[3] Ethereum Foundation & PQShield, London, UK
mary.maller@ethereum.org

Abstract. We prove adaptive security of a simple three-round threshold Schnorr signature scheme, which we call Sparkle. The standard notion of security for threshold signatures considers a *static* adversary – one who must declare which parties are corrupt at the beginning of the protocol. The stronger *adaptive* adversary can at any time corrupt parties and learn their state. This notion is natural and practical, yet not proven to be met by most schemes in the literature.

In this paper, we demonstrate that Sparkle achieves several levels of security based on different corruption models and assumptions. To begin with, Sparkle is statically secure under minimal assumptions: the discrete logarithm assumption (DL) and the random oracle model (ROM). If an adaptive adversary corrupts fewer than $t/2$ out of a threshold of $t+1$ signers, then Sparkle is adaptively secure under a weaker variant of the one-more discrete logarithm assumption (AOMDL) in the ROM. Finally, we prove that Sparkle achieves *full* adaptive security, with a corruption threshold of t, under AOMDL in the algebraic group model (AGM) with random oracles. Importantly, we show adaptive security without requiring secure erasures. Ours is the first proof achieving full adaptive security without exponential tightness loss for *any* threshold Schnorr signature scheme; moreover, the reduction is tight.

1 Introduction

A threshold signature scheme allows a set of n possible signers to jointly produce a signature over a message and with respect to a single public key, so long as at least a threshold $t+1$ of signers participate. Importantly, threshold signature schemes are secure even if t signers are under adversarial control. A recent line of work has explored multi-party signature schemes whose output is a standard (single-party) Schnorr signature [33,35,39]. Schnorr signatures admit an efficient and compact representation even in the multi-party setting, which makes them of particular interest for practical use [17].

Static vs. Adaptive Security. Most threshold signature schemes in the literature are proven *statically* secure. In the static setting, an adversary must declare

H. Handschuh and A. Lysyanskaya (Eds.): CRYPTO 2023, LNCS 14081, pp. 678–709, 2023.
https://doi.org/10.1007/978-3-031-38557-5_22

which parties it wishes to corrupt in advance of any messages being sent. This model places an artificial restriction on the adversary's capabilities: in reality, malicious actors may observe a system before targeting specific parties. Thus, adaptive security is a strictly stronger notion, and indeed there are schemes that are statically but not adaptively secure [14]. While there are generic methods for transforming a statically secure scheme into an adaptively secure one [16], such as guessing the corrupted parties and aborting if incorrect, these methods incur undesirable performance overhead and a tightness loss of $\binom{n}{t}$. This grows exponentially in the number of parties, and no adaptive guarantees can be made for larger n. Adaptive security without exponential tightness loss is challenging to achieve. A number of other techniques for proving adaptive security have been proposed, but similarly require undesirable tradeoffs. Prior methods include erasure of secret state [16], which is not easily enforced in practice, or heavyweight tools, such as non-committing encryption [31].

In this work, we investigate the adaptive security of a simple three-round threshold Schnorr signature scheme, which we call Sparkle, under different corruption models and security assumptions. Achieving adaptive security is not just of theoretical interest: NIST recently published a call for threshold EdDSA/Schnorr schemes and included adaptive security as a main goal [11,12], ideally supporting up to $n = 1024$ or more parties. Our techniques are likely of independent interest, as this paper introduces the first proof achieving full adaptive security without exponential tightness loss for *any* threshold Schnorr signature scheme; moreover, the reduction is tight.

Concurrent Security. A *concurrent* adversary may open an arbitrary number of signing sessions simultaneously and unforgeability should still hold. Concurrent security is also a difficult property to achieve, and indeed a host of threshold, blind, and multi-signature schemes were demonstrated to be broken by concurrent (ROS) attacks first observed by DEFKLNS19 [19] and exhibited in polynomial time by BLLOR21 [8]. Our security reductions for Sparkle hold against a concurrent and adaptive adversary. Combining concurrency and adaptivity in a multi-party, multi-round signature protocol is the main technical achievement of this work.

Schnorr Threshold Signature Sparkle. In this paper, we prove the adaptive security of a simple three-round threshold Schnorr signature scheme Sparkle that follows a commit-reveal paradigm. To begin with, we prove the static security of Sparkle from minimal assumptions: that the discrete logarithm assumption (DL) holds in the random oracle model (ROM). This is the same assumption and model for which Schnorr signatures themselves are proven secure. Our security reduction incurs no additional tightness loss compared to the security reduction for plain Schnorr signatures [41]. We compare the efficiency of Sparkle with existing two- and three-round threshold Schnorr signatures in Table 1.

Adaptive Security of Sparkle. We next consider an adaptive adversary who may corrupt up to $t/2$ out of a threshold of $t+1$ parties over the course of the protocol. We prove that Sparkle is adaptively secure in the random oracle model under AOMDL, a weaker variant of the one-more discrete logarithm assumption

Scheme	Static Assumptions	Sign					Combine	
		Performance			Bandwidth		Performance	
		rounds	exp	H	$\mathbb{G}$	$\mathbb{F}$	exp	H
FROST [33]	OMDL+ROM	2	$t+2$	$t+1$	2	1	t	t
FROST2 [5]	OMDL+ROM	2	3	2	2	1	1	1
Lindell22 [35]	DL+ROM	3	$11t+1$	$18t+10^7$	11	25	0	0
Sparkle	DL+ROM	3	1	$t+2$	1	2	0	0

Fig. 1. Efficiency of Two- and Three-Round Schnorr Threshold Signature Schemes. All output a standard Schnorr signature. We only compare schemes that are secure against ROS attacks [8]. The number of network rounds between participants is given in the rounds column. exp stands for the number of group exponentiations. The total number of group and field elements sent by each signer is denoted by $\mathbb{G}$ and $\mathbb{F}$, respectively. H denotes the total number of hashing operations performed. The cost of signature verification is identical for each scheme, and is simply the cost of verifying a single Schnorr signature. Estimates for Lindell22 are made with respect to a 128-bit security level for Fischlin [22], where $r = 8$ is the number of commitments for a Fischlin proof and the length of the zero vector is $b = 16$, such that $b \cdot r = 128$.

formalized in [39]. Importantly, we do so without requiring secure erasure of secret state. In the $t+1$-aomdl game, the adversary is given as input an AOMDL challenge that is a vector of group elements of length $t+1$. The adversary is given access to a discrete logarithm oracle, which returns the discrete logarithm of a group element chosen by the adversary. To win the $t+1$-aomdl game, the adversary must output all $t+1$ discrete logarithms of its challenge, having queried its DL oracle a maximum of t times. The AOMDL assumption is stronger than the discrete logarithm assumption because of the adversary's ability to request for up to t discrete logarithm solutions before returning the $t+1$ discrete logarithms of its challenge. On the other hand, the AOMDL assumption is strictly weaker than standard OMDL [7] because the adversary only receives the discrete logarithm of linear combinations of its challenge elements, which allows the oracle to run in polynomial time and makes it a falsifiable assumption [4,29,32].

In the case where the adversary can corrupt up to a full t parties, it is not clear how to prove the adaptive security of Sparkle under AOMDL+ROM alone. The reason is that in order to extract an AOMDL solution, the adversary is rewound once, and there is no guarantee that the adversary will corrupt the same set of parties after the fork as it did during the first iteration of the protocol. When the adversary can corrupt only $t/2$ parties, this causes no issues, as the total number of corruptions over both iterations does not exceed t. If the adversary could corrupt more parties, the reduction would query its DL oracle more than t times and would lose the $t+1$-aomdl game.

We thus look towards the algebraic group model (AGM) [23] for proving our strongest adaptivity result. The AGM assumes that whenever an adversary outputs a group element, it also outputs an algebraic representation specifying how

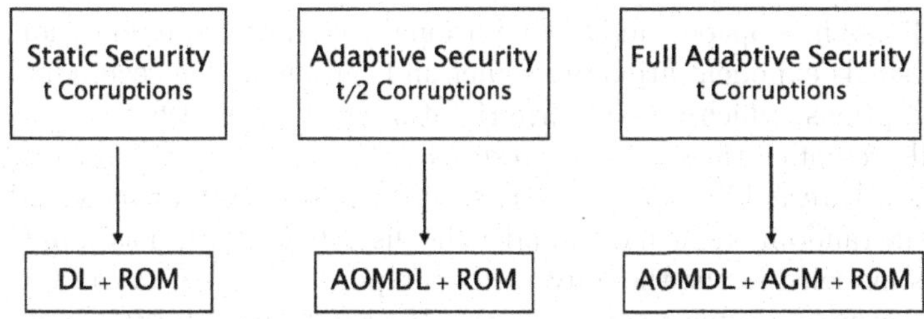

Fig. 2. Comparison of security models and assumptions for our threshold Schnorr signature scheme Sparkle. The signing threshold is $t+1$. DL is the Discrete Logarithm Assumption, and AOMDL is the Algebraic One-More Discrete Logarithm Assumption. ROM is the Random Oracle Model, and AGM is the Algebraic Group Model.

the group element depends on previously seen values. In the AGM, we are able to prove full adaptive security of Sparkle, with corruption threshold t, under the AOMDL assumption and random oracles. Our security reduction is *straight-line*, i.e., does not rewind the adversary, and so avoids counting the number of corruptions over different forks of the adversary's execution.

2 Related Work

Threshold Schnorr Signatures. Closest to the design of Sparkle is the MSDL scheme presented by Boneh, Drijvers, and Neven [10], the three-round MuSig scheme by Maxwell, Poelstra, Seurin, and Wuille [38], and the 2Schnorr scheme by Nicolosi, Krohn, Dodis, and Mazières [40]. However, MSDL and MuSig consider only the multi-signature setting (n-out-of-n), and 2Schnorr considers only the 2-out-of-2 setting. Concurrent to this work, Makriyannis [37] defines a commit-reveal threshold Schnorr signature scheme similar to Sparkle and proves security with respect to an idealized notion of threshold signatures by CGGMP21 [15]. They consider adaptive security but employ the guessing argument that incurs exponential tightness loss relative to the number of parties.

Stinson and Strobl [44] present a threshold Schnorr scheme secure in the random oracle model under the discrete logarithm assumption. However, their scheme requires performing a three-round distributed key generation protocol (DKG) [27] to generate the nonce for each signature, which adds considerable network overhead: at a minimum, it requires participants to perform four rounds in total. Further, the proof of security assumes only a static adversary.

Komlo and Goldberg [33] present a two-round threshold Schnorr signature FROST. Unlike prior threshold Schnorr schemes in the literature [26], FROST is secure against a concurrent adversary and is not susceptible to ROS attacks [8]. FROST2, introduced in [5], is an optimized version of FROST that reduces the number of exponentiations required for signing from $t+1$ to one. (See Table 1 for a comparison of efficiency.) However, both FROST and FROST2 are proven secure assuming a static adversary and the one-more discrete logarithm assumption

(OMDL) [5]. While Sparkle adds an additional round of communication, it only requires a single exponentiation per signer and can be proven secure under standard assumptions, which are also criteria of interest in [11,12].

Lindell presents a three-round threshold Schnorr signature [35] with the goal of defining a threshold scheme that is secure against ROS attacks and proven secure in the random oracle model under the discrete logarithm assumption only. Security is modeled in the the universally composable framework (UC) [13] and therefore captures a concurrent adversary. However, the security proof assumes the adversary is static, and no claims are made regarding adaptive security. Sparkle similarly relies on only ROM and DL assumptions, but does not require the use of online-extractable zero-knowledge proofs [22], and hence is both significantly more efficient and a simpler design.

Adaptive Security of Threshold Signatures. While adaptive security for threshold schemes is a well-known topic in the literature, to the best of our knowledge, no proof of adaptive security without exponential tightness loss exists for a threshold Schnorr signature scheme that is secure against ROS attacks.

Generalized techniques for transforming statically secure threshold schemes into adaptively secure schemes have been defined in the literature [16,31,36]. However, these techniques introduce prohibitive performance overhead, such as requiring a robust distributed key generation mechanism (DKG) for nonce generation.

Almansa, Damgård, and Nielsen [2] present a threshold RSA scheme with proactive and adaptive security, but these results do not translate to the discrete logarithm setting. Libert, Joye, and Yung [34] present a variant of the threshold BLS [9] scheme that is adaptively secure. However, their variant is incompatible with single-party BLS verification, an often-critical goal for threshold schemes in practice. Bacho and Loss [3] demonstrate the adaptive security of threshold BLS directly in the AGM from the $t+1$-omdl assumption. Their reduction is tight. Interestingly, they demonstrate that the $t+1$-omdl assumption is the minimum assumption under which threshold BLS can be proven adaptively secure.

Definitions. In this work, we employ a game-based approach to defining the static and adaptive security of a threshold signature, formalizing prior notions presented in the literature [34]. Alternative definitions of adaptive security in the UC setting have been proposed by CGGMP21 [15]. They prove their threshold ECDSA scheme adaptively secure assuming that ECDSA is secure, in addition to other non-interactive and falsifiable assumptions. However, their construction focuses on n-out-of-n multi-party signing, and their techniques critically do not translate to the t-out-of-n setting unless $\binom{n}{t}$ is small. Our fully adaptive t-out-of-n construction requires the algebraic group model, and incorporating algebraic adversaries into the UC setting is known to be a hard problem [1].

On the other hand, Lindell [35] shows that their protocol UC-realizes the Schnorr functionality with aborts, in the presence of an adversary that non-adaptively corrupts t parties. Secure evaluation of the Schnorr functionality is stronger than unforgeability. As noted in [15], it is arguably overly strong in the sense that it necessitates certain design decisions, such as incorporating online-extractable zero-knowledge proofs. Indeed, [35] elected for Fischlin proofs (see Table 1). The only method to bias the nonces in both Sparkle and [35] is to abort; this is not the case in FROST [33]. However, all three works allow aborts, and therefore the distribution of the secret randomness cannot be considered uniform [20].

3 Preliminaries

3.1 General Notation

Let $\kappa \in \mathbb{N}$ denote the security parameter and 1^κ its unary representation. A function $f : \mathbb{N} \to \mathbb{R}$ is called *negligible* if for all $c \in \mathbb{R}, c > 0$, there exists $k_0 \in \mathbb{N}$ such that $|f(k)| < \frac{1}{k^c}$ for all $k \in \mathbb{N}, k \geq k_0$. For a non-empty set S, let $x \leftarrow\$ S$ denote sampling an element of S uniformly at random and assigning it to x. We use $[n]$ to represent the set $\{1, \ldots, n\}$ and $[0..n]$ to represent the set $\{0, \ldots, n\}$. We represent vectors as $\boldsymbol{a} = (a_1, \ldots, a_n)$.

Let PPT denote probabilistic polynomial time. Algorithms are randomized unless explicitly noted otherwise. Let $y \leftarrow A(x; \omega)$ denote running algorithm A on input x and randomness ω and assigning its output to y. Let $y \leftarrow\$ A(x)$ denote $y \leftarrow A(x; \omega)$ for a uniformly random ω. The set of values that have non-zero probability of being output by A on input x is denoted by $[A(x)]$.

Group Generation. Let GrGen be a polynomial-time algorithm that takes as input a security parameter 1^κ and outputs a group description $(\mathbb{G}, p, g)$ consisting of a group $\mathbb{G}$ of order p, where p is a κ-bit prime, and a generator g of $\mathbb{G}$.

Polynomial Interpolation. A polynomial $f(x) = a_0 + a_1 x + a_2 x^2 + \ldots + a_t x^t$ of degree t over a field $\mathbb{F}$ can be interpolated by $t + 1$ points. Let $\eta \subseteq [n]$ be the list of $t + 1$ distinct indices corresponding to the x-coordinates $x_i \in \mathbb{F}, i \in \eta$ of these points. Then the Lagrange polynomial $L_i(x)$ has the form:

$$L_i(x) = \prod_{j \in \eta; j \neq i} \frac{x - x_j}{x_i - x_j} \tag{1}$$

Given a set of $t+1$ points $(x_i, f(x_i))_{i \in [t+1]}$, any point $f(x_\ell)$ on the polynomial f can be determined by Lagrange interpolation as follows:

$$f(x_\ell) = \sum_{k \in \eta} f(x_k) \cdot L_k(x_\ell)$$

3.2 Definitions and Assumptions

Assumption 1 (Discrete Logarithm Assumption (DL)) *Let the advantage of an adversary $\mathcal{A}$ playing the discrete logarithm game* $\mathsf{Game}^{\mathsf{dl}}$*, as defined in Fig. 3, be as follows:*

$$\mathsf{Adv}^{\mathsf{dl}}_{\mathcal{A}}(\kappa) = \left|\Pr[\mathsf{Game}^{\mathsf{dl}}_{\mathcal{A}}(\kappa) = 1]\right|$$

MAIN $\mathsf{Game}^{\mathsf{dl}}_{\mathcal{A}}(\kappa)$	MAIN $\mathsf{Game}^{t+1\text{-}\mathsf{a\ omdl}}_{\mathcal{A}}(\kappa)$	$\mathcal{O}^{\mathsf{dl}}(X,\ \alpha, \{\beta_i\}_{i=0}^{t})$
$(\mathbb{G}, p, g) \leftarrow\$ \mathsf{GrGen}(1^\kappa)$	$(\mathbb{G}, p, g) \leftarrow\$ \mathsf{GrGen}(1^\kappa)$	// $X = g^\alpha \prod_{i=0}^{t} X_i^{\beta_i}$
$x \leftarrow\$ \mathbb{Z}_p$; $X \leftarrow g^x$	$Q \leftarrow \emptyset$	$q \leftarrow q + 1$
$x' \leftarrow\$ \mathcal{A}((\mathbb{G}, p, g), X)$	$q \leftarrow 0$	$x \leftarrow \alpha + \sum_{i=0}^{t} x_i \beta_i$
if $x' = x$	**for** $i \in [0..t]$ **do**	**return** x
return 1	$x_i \leftarrow\$ \mathbb{Z}_p$; $X_i \leftarrow g^{x_i}$	$x \leftarrow \mathsf{dlog}(X)$
return 0	$Q[X_i] = x_i$	**return** x
	$\boldsymbol{x} \leftarrow (x_0, \ldots, x_t)$	
	$\boldsymbol{X} \leftarrow (X_0, X_1, \ldots, X_t)$	
	$\boldsymbol{x}' \leftarrow \mathcal{A}^{\mathcal{O}^{\mathsf{dl}}}((\mathbb{G}, p, g), \boldsymbol{X})$	
	if $\boldsymbol{x}' = \boldsymbol{x} \wedge q < t + 1$	
	return 1	
	return 0	

Fig. 3. The Discrete Logarithm (DL), One-More Discrete Logarithm (OMDL), and Algebraic One-More Discrete Logarithm (AOMDL) games. $\mathbb{G}$ is a cyclic group with prime order p and generator g. dlog is an algorithm that finds the discrete logarithm relation of the input X and g. The differences between the OMDL and AOMDL games are highlighted in gray; the key distinction is that in the AOMDL game, the adversary can only query for linear combinations of its challenge group elements; in the OMDL game, the environment must return the discrete logarithm of an arbitrary group element.

The discrete logarithm assumption holds if for all PPT adversaries $\mathcal{A}$, $\mathsf{Adv}^{dl}_{\mathcal{A}}(\kappa)$ is negligible.

Assumption 2 (One-More Discrete Logarithm Assumption (OMDL)) [7] *Let the advantage of an adversary $\mathcal{A}$ playing the $t+1$-one-more discrete logarithm game $\mathsf{Game}^{t+1\text{-omdl}}$, as defined in Fig. 3, be as follows:*

$$\mathsf{Adv}^{t+1\text{-}omdl}_{\mathcal{A}}(\kappa) = \left|\Pr[\mathsf{Game}^{t+1\text{-omdl}}_{\mathcal{A}}(\kappa) = 1]\right|$$

The one-more discrete logarithm assumption holds if for all PPT adversaries $\mathcal{A}$, $\mathsf{Adv}^{t+1\text{-}omdl}_{\mathcal{A}}(\kappa)$ is negligible.

Algebraic One-More Discrete Logarithm Assumption (AOMDL). The algebraic one-more discrete logarithm assumption (AOMDL) was formalized by Jonas, Ruffing, and Seurin [39]. We highlight differences with the OMDL assumption in Fig. 3. Note that while the OMDL assumption is not falsifiable (because the adversary is allowed to query for the discrete logarithm of any arbitrary group element), the AOMDL assumption is falsifiable. This is because the input to the discrete logarithm oracle is a linear combination of all challenges issued to the adversary, so it is guaranteed that the environment runs in PPT when its respective adversary runs in PPT. Hence, the AOMDL assumption is a strictly weaker assumption than standard OMDL.

An adversary in the AOMDL game is initialized in exactly the same manner as an OMDL adversary, with the same winning condition. The only distinction between the games is the inputs to and outputs from the discrete logarithm oracle. In the AOMDL setting, the adversary provides a vector $(\alpha, \beta_0 \ldots, \beta_t)$ of coefficients to the discrete logarithm oracle. The oracle then responds with the integer linear combination of these coefficients with respect to the discrete logarithm of the set of challenges $(X_0, \ldots, X_t)$. It is easy to see that the AOMDL game can be used to win the OMDL game, by the adversary simply querying $\mathcal{O}^{\mathsf{dl}}$ with a bit vector, to return the discrete logarithm of the term whose coefficient is set to one.

Assumption 3 (Algebraic One-More Discrete Logarithm Assumption) [39] *Let the advantage of an adversary $\mathcal{A}$ playing the $t+1$-algebraic one-more discrete logarithm game* $\mathsf{Game}^{t+1\text{-}\mathsf{aomdl}}$*, as defined in Fig. 3, be as follows:*

$$Adv_{\mathcal{A}}^{t+1\text{-}aomdl}(\kappa) = \left|\Pr[\mathsf{Game}_{\mathcal{A}}^{t+1\text{-}\mathsf{aomdl}}(\kappa) = 1]\right|$$

The algebraic one-more discrete logarithm assumption holds if for all PPT adversaries $\mathcal{A}$, $Adv_{\mathcal{A}}^{t+1\text{-}aomdl}(\kappa)$ is negligible.

Assumption 4 (Algebraic Group Model (AGM) [23]**)** *An adversary is algebraic if for every group element $Z \in \mathbb{G} = \langle g \rangle$ that it outputs, it is required to output a representation $\boldsymbol{a} = (a_0, a_1, a_2, \ldots)$ such that $Z = g^{a_0} \prod Y_i^{a_i}$, where $Y_1, Y_2, \cdots \in \mathbb{G}$ are group elements that the adversary has seen thus far.*

Definition 1 (Schnorr Signatures [42]**).** *The Schnorr signature scheme consists of algorithms* $(\mathsf{Setup}, \mathsf{KeyGen}, \mathsf{Sign}, \mathsf{Verify})$*, defined as follows:*

- $\mathsf{Setup}(1^\kappa) \to \mathsf{par}$*: On input a security parameter, run* $(\mathbb{G}, p, g) \leftarrow\!\!\$\ \mathsf{GrGen}(1^\kappa)$ *and select a hash function* $\mathsf{H} : \{0,1\}^* \to \mathbb{Z}_p$*. Output public parameters* $\mathsf{par} \leftarrow ((\mathbb{G}, p, g), \mathsf{H})$ *(which are given implicitly as input to all other algorithms).*
- $\mathsf{KeyGen}(1^\kappa) \to (\mathsf{pk}, \mathsf{sk})$*: On input a security parameter, sample a secret key* $x \leftarrow\!\!\$\ \mathbb{Z}_p$ *and compute a public key* $X \leftarrow g^x$*. Output key pair* $(\mathsf{pk}, \mathsf{sk}) \leftarrow (X, x)$*.*
- $\mathsf{Sign}(\mathsf{sk}, m) \to \sigma$*: On input the secret key* $\mathsf{sk} = x$ *and a message m, sample a nonce* $r \leftarrow\!\!\$\ \mathbb{Z}_p$ *and compute a nonce commitment* $R \leftarrow g^r$*, the challenge* $c \leftarrow \mathsf{H}(X, m, R)$*, and the response* $z \leftarrow r + cx$*. Output signature* $\sigma \leftarrow (R, z)$*.*
- $\mathsf{Verify}(\mathsf{pk}, m, \sigma) \to 0/1$*: On input the public key* $\mathsf{pk} = X$*, a message m, and a purported signature* $\sigma = (R, z)$*, compute* $c \leftarrow \mathsf{H}(X, m, R)$ *and output* 1 *(accept) if* $RX^c = g^z$*; else, output* 0 *(reject).*

A Schnorr signature is a Sigma protocol zero-knowledge proof of knowledge of the discrete logarithm of the public key X, made non-interactive and bound to the message m by the Fiat-Shamir transform [21]. Schnorr signatures are secure under the discrete logarithm assumption in the random oracle model [41].

Definition 2 (Shamir Secret Sharing [43]). *Shamir secret sharing is an $(n, t+1)$-threshold secret sharing scheme consisting of algorithms* (IssueShares, Recover), *defined as follows:*

- IssueShares$(x, n, t+1) \to \{(1, x_1), \ldots, (n, x_n)\}$: *On input a secret x, number of participants n, and threshold $t+1$, perform the following. First, define a polynomial $f(Z) = x + a_1 + a_2 Z^2 + \cdots + a_t Z^t$ by sampling t coefficients at random: $a_1, \ldots, a_t \leftarrow\$ \mathbb{Z}_p$. Then, set each participant's share $x_i, i \in [n]$, to be the evaluation of $f(i)$:*
$$x_i \leftarrow x + \sum_{j \in [t]} a_j i^j$$
Output $\{(i, x_i)\}_{i \in [n]}$.
- Recover$(t+1, \{(i, x_i)\}_{i \in \mathcal{S}}) \to \perp / x$: *On input threshold $t+1$ and a set of shares $\{(i, x_i)\}_{i \in \mathcal{S}}$, output $\perp$ if $\mathcal{S} \not\subseteq [n]$ or if $|\mathcal{S}| < t+1$. Otherwise, recover x as follows:*
$$x \leftarrow \sum_{i \in \mathcal{S}} \lambda_i x_i$$
where the Lagrange coefficient for the set $\mathcal{S}$ is defined by
$$\lambda_i = \prod_{j \in \mathcal{S}, j \neq i} \frac{j}{i-j}$$

4 Threshold Signature Schemes

We begin with the definition of a threshold signature scheme. We build upon prior definitions in the literature [24,25,28], but define an additional algorithm for combining signatures that is separate from the signing rounds. It may be performed by one of the signers or some external party. We then provide game-based definitions of static and adaptive security for threshold signatures. Our definitions model a three-round signing protocol but can be adapted to schemes with fewer or more rounds.

Definition 3 (Threshold Signatures). *A threshold signature scheme* TS *is a tuple of polynomial-time algorithms* TS = (Setup, KeyGen, (Sign, Sign$'$, Sign$''$), Combine, Verify), *defined as follows:*

- Setup$(1^\kappa) \to$ par: *Takes as input a security parameter and outputs public parameters* par *(which are given implicitly as input to all other algorithms).*
- KeyGen$(n, t+1) \to (\tilde{X}, \{\tilde{X}_i\}_{i \in [n]}, \{x_i\}_{i \in [n]})$: *A probabilistic algorithm that takes as input the number of signers n and the threshold $t+1$ and outputs the public key $\tilde{X}$ representing the set of n signers, the set $\{\tilde{X}_i\}_{i \in [n]}$ of public keys for each signer, and the set $\{x_i\}_{i \in [n]}$ of secret shares for each signer. It is assumed that participant i is sent its respective share x_i privately.*

- $(\mathsf{Sign}, \mathsf{Sign}', \mathsf{Sign}'') \rightarrow \{\rho_i, \rho_i', \rho_i''\}_{i \in \mathcal{S}}$: *A set of probabilistic algorithms where each subsequent algorithm represents a single stage in an interactive signing protocol, performed by each signing party in a signing set* $\mathcal{S} \subseteq [n], |\mathcal{S}| \geq t+1$ *with respect to a message* m*, defined as follows:*

$$\begin{aligned}(\rho_i, \mathsf{st}_i) &\leftarrow \mathsf{Sign}(m, \mathcal{S})\\ (\rho_i', \mathsf{st}_i) &\leftarrow \mathsf{Sign}'(\mathsf{st}_i, x_i, \{\rho_j\}_{j \in \mathcal{S}})\\ \rho_i'' &\leftarrow \mathsf{Sign}''(\mathsf{st}_i, x_i, \{\rho_j'\}_{j \in \mathcal{S}})\end{aligned}$$

  $\rho_i, \rho_i', \rho_i''$ *are protocol messages, and* st_i *is the state of signing party* i *in* $\mathcal{S}$*.*
- $\mathsf{Combine}(\{(\rho_i', \rho_i'')\}_{i \in \mathcal{S}}) \rightarrow (m, \sigma)$: *A deterministic algorithm that takes as input the set of protocol messages* (ρ_i', ρ_i'') *sent by each party during the* Sign' *and* Sign'' *stages and outputs a signature* σ*.*
- $\mathsf{Verify}(\tilde{X}, m, \sigma) \rightarrow 0/1$: *A deterministic algorithm that takes as input the public key* $\tilde{X}$*, a message* m*, and purported signature* σ *and outputs* 1 *(accept) if the signature verifies; else, it outputs* 0 *(reject).*

Remark 1 (Distributed key generation). Our definition assumes a centralized key generation algorithm KeyGen to generate the public key $\tilde{X}$ and set of shares $\{\tilde{X}_i, x_i\}_{i \in [n]}$. However, our scheme and proofs can be adapted to use a fully decentralized distributed key generation protocol (DKG). We refer to [3] for a discussion on how to achieve adaptively secure DKGs.

Correctness. A threshold signature scheme is *correct* if for all security parameters κ, all allowable $1 \leq t+1 \leq n$, all $\mathcal{S}$ such that $t+1 \leq |\mathcal{S}| \leq n$, all messages $m \in \{0,1\}^*$, and for $(\tilde{X}, \{\tilde{X}_i, x_i\}_{i \in [n]}) \leftarrow\$ \mathsf{KeyGen}(n, t+1)$, if all signers in $\mathcal{S}$ input (x_i, m) to the signing protocol $(\mathsf{Sign}, \mathsf{Sign}', \mathsf{Sign}'')$, then every signer will output a signature share that, when combined with all other shares, results in a signature σ satisfying $\mathsf{Verify}(\tilde{X}, m, \sigma) = 1$.

4.1 Static Security

We present a game-based definition of static security for threshold signatures analogous to existential unforgeability against chosen message attack (EUF-CMA) for standard signature schemes [30]. The static security game is defined formally in Fig. 4, where it contains all but the dashed boxes. In addition to the security parameter κ, the game additionally accepts a parameter τ, which specifies the fraction of t signers that the adversary may corrupt. A static adversary can corrupt a full t signers out of at least $t+1$ signers in a session, so the fraction is $\tau = 1$.

In the static unforgeability game, the challenger generates public parameters par and returns them to the adversary. The adversary must now choose the set of corrupt participants cor, which are fixed for the duration of the protocol. The challenger then runs KeyGen to derive the joint public key $\tilde{X}$ representing the set of n signers, the individual public key shares $\{\tilde{X}_i\}_{i \in [n]}$, and the secret key

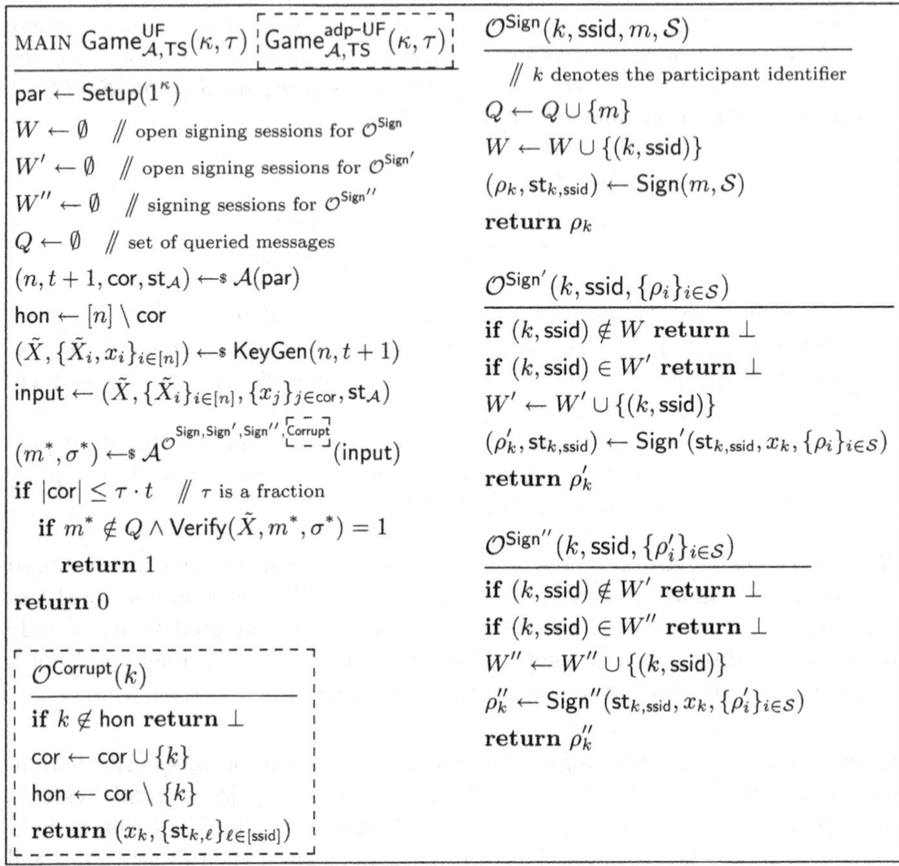

Fig. 4. Static and adaptive unforgeability games for a threshold signature scheme with three signing rounds. The public parameters par are implicitly given as input to all algorithms, and ρ, ρ', ρ'' represent protocol messages defined within the construction. The static game contains all but the dashed boxes, and the adaptive game adds the dashed boxes. τ specifies the fraction of t signers that the adversary may corrupt. For example, $\tau = 1$ means the adversary can corrupt a full t signers, and $\tau = 1/2$ means it can corrupt $t/2$ signers.

shares $\{x_i\}_{i\in[n]}$. It returns $\tilde{X}$, $\{\tilde{X}_i\}_{i\in[n]}$, and the set of corrupt shares $\{x_j\}_{j\in\mathsf{cor}}$ to the adversary.

After key generation has concluded, the adversary can query honest signers $k \in \mathsf{hon}$ at each step in the signing protocol by querying oracles $\mathcal{O}^{\mathsf{Sign}}, \mathcal{O}^{\mathsf{Sign}'}, \mathcal{O}^{\mathsf{Sign}''}$, and has full power over choosing the set of signers $\mathcal{S}$ and the message m to be signed. The signing session identifier is denoted by ssid.

The adversary wins if it can produce a valid forgery $\sigma^* = (R^*, z^*)$ with respect to the joint public key $\tilde{X}$ on a message m^* that has not been previously queried.

The adversary may be *rushing*, meaning it can wait to produce its outputs after having seen the honest outputs first (represented by protocol messages ρ, ρ', ρ'' in Fig. 4). The adversary may also be *concurrent*, meaning it can open simultaneous signing sessions at once, or choose not to complete a signing session (e.g., the adversary might query $\mathcal{O}^{\mathsf{Sign}}, \mathcal{O}^{\mathsf{Sign}'}$, but not $\mathcal{O}^{\mathsf{Sign}''}$, before it starts a new session). By modeling a concurrent adversary, we ensure that our notion of security protects against practical attacks that can occur in such a setting [8].

Definition 4 (Static Security). *Let the advantage of an adversary $\mathcal{A}$ playing the static security game $\mathsf{Game}^{\mathsf{UF}}_{\mathcal{A}}(\kappa, \tau)$, as defined in Fig. 4, be as follows:*

$$\mathsf{Adv}^{st\text{-}sec}_{\mathcal{A},\mathsf{TS}}(\kappa, \tau) = \left|\Pr[\mathsf{Game}^{\mathsf{UF}}_{\mathcal{A},\mathsf{TS}}(\kappa, \tau) = 1]\right|$$

A threshold signature scheme TS *is* statically secure *if for all PPT adversaries $\mathcal{A}$, $\mathsf{Adv}^{st\text{-}sec}_{\mathcal{A}}(\kappa, \tau)$ is negligible.*

4.2 Adaptive Security

We build upon the notion of adaptive security for threshold signature schemes by Libert, Joye, and Yung [34]. We provide a formal game-based definition, which is specified in Fig. 4. The adaptive unforgeability game contains the same inputs and algorithms as the static game, but additionally includes a corruption oracle $\mathcal{O}^{\mathsf{Corrupt}}$.

In the adaptive setting, the adversary is not restricted to choosing its set of corrupt participants cor only at the beginning of the game. Instead, the adversary can at any time choose to corrupt an honest party by querying $\mathcal{O}^{\mathsf{Corrupt}}$, receiving in return the honest party's secret key and state across all signing sessions.

In addition to producing a valid forgery, the adversary must meet the winning condition that the set of corrupted participants at the end of the experiment is within the expected bound, i.e., less than $\tau \cdot t$, with respect to the corruption ratio τ. An adaptive adversary may, for example, corrupt $t/2$ (i.e., $\tau = 1/2$) or a full t (i.e., $\tau = 1$) signers out of at least $t + 1$ signers in a session.

Definition 5 (Adaptive Security). *Let the advantage of an adversary $\mathcal{A}$ playing the static security game $\mathsf{Game}^{\mathsf{adp\text{-}UF}}_{\mathcal{A},\mathsf{TS}}(\kappa, \tau)$, as defined in Fig. 4, be as follows:*

$$\mathsf{Adv}^{adp\text{-}sec}_{\mathcal{A},\mathsf{TS}}(\kappa, \tau) = \left|\Pr[\mathsf{Game}^{\mathsf{adp\text{-}UF}}_{\mathcal{A},\mathsf{TS}}(\kappa, \tau) = 1]\right|$$

A threshold signature scheme TS *is* adaptively secure *if for all PPT adversaries $\mathcal{A}$, $\mathsf{Adv}^{adp\text{-}sec}_{\mathcal{A}}(\kappa, \tau)$ is negligible.*

5 Schnorr Threshold Signature Scheme Sparkle

Sparkle is a simple three-round Schnorr threshold signature scheme (Fig. 5). We employ a centralized key generation algorithm KeyGen to generate the public key $\tilde{X}$ and set of shares $\{\tilde{X}_i, x_i\}_{i \in [n]}$. The public parameters par generated during setup are provided as input to all other algorithms and protocols. We assume an external mechanism to choose the set of signers $\mathcal{S} \subseteq \{1, \ldots, n\}$, where $t + 1 \leq |\mathcal{S}| \leq n$ and $\mathcal{S}$ is ordered to ensure consistency.

Intuitively, Sparkle follows a commit-reveal paradigm for its three-round signing protocol. In the first round, each participant in the signing set $\mathcal{S}$ commits to their nonce $R_i = g^{r_i}$ by publishing $\mathsf{cm}_i \leftarrow \mathsf{H}_{\mathsf{cm}}(m, \mathcal{S}, R_i)$, where m is the message. In the second round, each participant reveals R_i in the clear. In the third round, each participant computes the aggregate nonce $\tilde{R} = \prod_{i \in \mathcal{S}} R_i$, the Schnorr challenge $c \leftarrow \mathsf{H}_{\mathsf{sig}}(\tilde{X}, m, \tilde{R})$ using $\tilde{R}$, and their signature share z_i. The signature shares are additively combined via the Combine algorithm to produce the Schnorr signature $\sigma = (\tilde{R}, z = \sum_{i \in \mathcal{S}} z_i)$.

This commit-reveal strategy ensures two security properties. First, requiring each participant to publish a commitment in the first round, before revealing their R_i, prevents a rushing adversary from adaptively choosing R_j as a function of other participants' R_i values. Second, as we will see later in the proofs of adaptive security, it allows the reduction to effectively handle corruptions at any point in the signing process, without requiring the erasure of secret state.

Parameter Generation. On input a security parameter 1^κ, the setup algorithm runs $(\mathbb{G}, p, g) \leftarrow\!\!\$\ \mathsf{GrGen}(1^\kappa)$, and selects two hash functions $\mathsf{H}_{\mathsf{cm}}, \mathsf{H}_{\mathsf{sig}} : \{0,1\}^* \to \mathbb{Z}_p$. It outputs public parameters $\mathsf{par} \leftarrow ((\mathbb{G}, p, g), \mathsf{H}_{\mathsf{cm}}, \mathsf{H}_{\mathsf{sig}})$.

Key Generation. On input the number of signers n and the threshold $t + 1$, the key generation algorithm first generates the secret key $x \leftarrow\!\!\$\ \mathbb{Z}_p$ and corresponding public key as $\tilde{X} \leftarrow g^x$. It then performs a Shamir secret sharing of x (Def. 2): $\{(i, x_i)\}_{i \in [n]} \leftarrow\!\!\$\ \mathsf{IssueShares}(x, n, t+1)$. Each participant's public key is computed as $\tilde{X}_i \leftarrow g^{x_i}$ and it outputs $(\tilde{X}, \{\tilde{X}_i, x_i\}_{i \in [n]})$.

Signing Round 1 (Sign)**.** On input a message m and a signing set $\mathcal{S}$, each participant $i \in \mathcal{S}$ samples $r_i \leftarrow\!\!\$\ \mathbb{Z}_p$, computes $R_i \leftarrow g^{r_i}$ and $\mathsf{cm}_i \leftarrow \mathsf{H}_{\mathsf{cm}}(m, \mathcal{S}, R_i)$, and outputs their commitment cm_i.

Signing Round 2 (Sign$'$)**.** On input commitments $\{\mathsf{cm}_j\}_{j \in \mathcal{S}}$, each participant $i \in \mathcal{S}$ outputs their nonce R_i.

Signing Round 3 (Sign$''$)**.** On input nonces $\{R_j\}_{j \in \mathcal{S}}$, each participant $i \in \mathcal{S}$ first checks that the commitments received in the first round are valid, i.e., $\mathsf{cm}_j = \mathsf{H}_{\mathsf{cm}}(m, \mathcal{S}, R_j)$ for all $j \in \mathcal{S}$. If not, return $\perp$. Else, each participant computes the aggregate nonce $\tilde{R} = \prod_{j \in \mathcal{S}} R_j$, $c \leftarrow \mathsf{H}_{\mathsf{sig}}(\tilde{X}, m, \tilde{R})$, and partial signature $z_i \leftarrow r_i + c\lambda_i x_i$, where λ_i is the Lagrange coefficient for participant i with respect to signing set $\mathcal{S}$. Each participant outputs z_i.

Combining Signatures. On input nonces $\{R_j\}_{j \in \mathcal{S}}$ and partial signatures $\{z_j\}_{j \in \mathcal{S}}$, the combiner computes $\tilde{R} \leftarrow \prod_{j \in \mathcal{S}} R_j$ and $z \leftarrow \sum_{j \in \mathcal{S}} z_j$, and outputs $\sigma \leftarrow (\tilde{R}, z)$.

```
Setup(1^κ)
  (G, p, g) ←$ GrGen(1^κ)
  // select two hash functions
  H_cm, H_sig : {0,1}* → Z_p
  par ← ((G, p, g), H_cm, H_sig)
  return par

KeyGen(n, t+1)
  x ←$ Z_p;  X̃ ← g^x
  {(i, x_i)}_{i∈[n]} ←$ IssueShares(x, n, t+1)
  // Shamir secret sharing of x
  for i ∈ [n]  X̃_i ← g^{x_i}
  return (X̃, {X̃_i, x_i}_{i∈[n]})

Sign(m, S)
  // local signer has index k
  r_k ←$ Z_p;  R_k ← g^{r_k}
  cm_k ← H_cm(m, S, R_k)
  ρ_k ← cm_k
  st_k ← (cm_k, R_k, r_k, m, S)
  return (ρ_k, st_k)

Sign'(st_k, x_k, {ρ_i}_{i∈S})
  parse cm_i ← ρ_i for all i ∈ S
  parse (cm_k, R_k, r_k, m, S) ← st_k
  return ⊥ if cm_k ∉ {cm_i}_{i∈S}
  ρ'_k ← R_k
  st_k ← (cm_k, R_k, r_k, m, S, {ρ_i}_{i∈S})
  return (ρ'_k, st_k)

Sign''(st_k, x_k, {ρ'_i}_{i∈S})
  // Sign'' must be called once per st_k
  parse (cm_k, R_k, r_k, m, S, {ρ_i}_{i∈S}) ← st_k
  parse R_i ← ρ'_i for all i ∈ S
  return ⊥ if R_k ∉ {R_i}_{i∈S}
  for i ∈ S do
    return ⊥ if cm_i ≠ H_cm(m, S, R_i)
  R̃ ← ∏_{i∈S} R_i
  c ← H_sig(X̃, m, R̃)
  z_k ← r_k + c λ_k x_k
  // λ_k is the Lagrange coefficient for k w.r.t. S
  ρ''_k ← z_k
  return ρ''_k

Combine({(ρ'_i, ρ''_i)}_{i∈S})
  parse R_i ← ρ'_i, z_i ← ρ''_i for all i ∈ S
  R̃ ← ∏_{i∈S} R_i;  z ← Σ_{i∈S} z_i
  σ ← (R̃, z)
  return σ

Verify(X̃, m, σ)
  parse (R̃, z) ← σ
  c ← H_sig(X̃, m, R̃)
  if R̃ X̃^c = g^z
    return 1
  return 0
```

Fig. 5. The Sparkle threshold signature scheme. The public parameters par are implicitly given as input to all algorithms and protocols. We assume an external mechanism to choose the set of signers $\mathcal{S} \subseteq \{1, \ldots, n\}$, where $t+1 \leq |\mathcal{S}| \leq n$ and $\mathcal{S}$ is ordered to ensure consistency. Note that verification is identical to a standard (single-party) Schnorr signature as in Definition 1.

Verification. On input the joint public key $\tilde{X}$, a message m, and a purported signature $\sigma = (\tilde{R}, z)$, the verifier computes $c \leftarrow \mathsf{H}_{\mathsf{sig}}(\tilde{X}, m, \tilde{R})$ and accepts if $\tilde{R}\tilde{X}^c = g^z$.

Correctness of Sparkle is straightforward to verify. Note that verification of the signature σ is identical to verification of a standard (single-party) Schnorr signature (Def. 1) with respect to the joint public key $\tilde{X}$ and aggregate nonce $\tilde{R}$.

6 Static Security Under Standard Assumptions

In this section, we show that Sparkle is statically secure under the discrete logarithm assumption (DL) in the random oracle model (ROM). Static security allows an adversary to control up to t parties, but they must be declared at the beginning of the protocol (Fig. 4).

Theorem 1. Sparkle *is statically secure under DL in the ROM.*

We formally prove Theorem 1 in Sect. 9.

Proof Outline. Let $\mathcal{A}$ be a PPT adversary against the static unforgeability of Sparkle (Fig. 4). We construct a PPT reduction $\mathcal{B}$ against the DL assumption (Fig. 3) that uses $\mathcal{A}$ as a subroutine as follows. $\mathcal{B}$ takes as input a DL challenge $\dot{X}$ and aims to output $\dot{x}$ such that $\dot{X} = g^{\dot{x}}$. $\mathcal{B}$ sets the joint public key $\tilde{X} \leftarrow \dot{X}$ and performs a standard simulation of Shamir secret sharing. $\mathcal{B}$ then returns $\tilde{X}$, public key shares $\{\tilde{X}_i\}_{i \in [n]}$, and secret key shares $\{x_j\}_{j \in \mathsf{cor}}$ to $\mathcal{A}$.

$\mathcal{B}$ simulates signing without knowing the secret keys $\{x_k\}_{k \in \mathsf{hon}}$ of the honest parties as follows. $\mathcal{B}$ can simulate R_k for all $k \in \mathsf{hon}$ as $R_k \leftarrow g^{z_k}\tilde{X}_k^{-c\lambda_k}$ for random $z_k \leftarrow\!\!\$\, \mathbb{Z}_p$ so that the partial signature z_k output in Round 3 verifies. However, c must equal $\mathsf{H}_{\mathsf{sig}}(\tilde{X}, m, \tilde{R})$ for aggregate $\tilde{R}$. Luckily, $\mathcal{B}$ can compute $\tilde{R} = \prod_{i \in \mathcal{S}} R_i$, where $\mathcal{S}$ is the signing set, by extracting R_j for all $j \in \mathsf{cor}$ from $\mathcal{A}$'s $\mathsf{H}_{\mathsf{cm}}(m, \mathcal{S}, R_j)$ queries in Round 1. So, $\mathcal{B}$ samples a random value for $c \leftarrow\!\!\$\, \mathbb{Z}_p$, computes R_k for all $k \in \mathsf{hon}$ as above, and programs $c \leftarrow \mathsf{H}_{\mathsf{sig}}(\tilde{X}, m, \tilde{R})$ – all before $\mathcal{A}$ sees the honest R_k's output at the end of Round 2. This leaves just one problem: $\mathcal{B}$ needs to output $\mathsf{cm}_k = \mathsf{H}_{\mathsf{cm}}(m, \mathcal{S}, R_k)$ in Round 1 *before* being able to carry out the above steps. But $\mathcal{B}$ can simply output a random value $\mathsf{cm}_k \leftarrow\!\!\$\, \mathbb{Z}_p$ in Round 1 and program $\mathsf{cm}_k \leftarrow \mathsf{H}_{\mathsf{cm}}(m, \mathcal{S}, R_k)$ in Round 2.

$\mathcal{B}$ then *rewinds* $\mathcal{A}$, programming the single point $c' \leftarrow\!\!\$\, \mathbb{Z}_p; c' \leftarrow \mathsf{H}_{\mathsf{sig}}(\tilde{X}, m^*, \tilde{R}^*)$ on the second iteration of $\mathcal{A}$. By the local forking lemma [6], $\mathcal{A}$'s two forgeries $(m^*, (\tilde{R}^*, z^*)), (m', (\tilde{R}', z'))$ satisfy $(\tilde{R}^*, m^*) = (\tilde{R}', m')$ with non-negligible probability. Thus, $\mathcal{B}$ can compute $\dot{x} = \frac{z^* - z'}{c^* - c'}$ and win the DL game.

7 Adaptive Security Against up to $t/2$ Corruptions

In this section, we prove the adaptive security of Sparkle against up to $t/2$ corruptions under the algebraic one-more discrete logarithm assumption (AOMDL)

(Fig. 3) in the random oracle model (ROM). The reason the allowed corruption is $t/2$ is that, in order to extract an AOMDL solution, the reduction needs to rewind the adversary once, and there is no guarantee that the adversary will corrupt the same set of parties after the fork as it did during the first iteration of the adversary. When the adversary can corrupt only $t/2$ parties, this causes no issues, as the total number of corruptions over both iterations does not exceed t. If the adversary could corrupt more parties, then the reduction would query its discrete logarithm oracle more than t times and would lose the $t+1$-aomdl game.

Theorem 2. Sparkle *is adaptively secure against* $t/2$ *corruptions under AOMDL in the ROM.*

We formally prove Theorem 2 in Sect. 9.

Proof Outline. Let $\mathcal{A}$ be a PPT adversary against the adaptive unforgeability of Sparkle (Fig. 4). We construct a PPT reduction $\mathcal{B}$ against the $t+1$-aomdl assumption (Fig. 3) that uses $\mathcal{A}$ as a subroutine as follows. $\mathcal{B}$ takes as input a $t+1$-aomdl challenge $(Y_0, Y_1, \ldots, Y_t)$ and aims to output y_i such that $Y_i = g^{y_i}$ for all $i \in [0..t]$ without querying its DL oracle more than t times. For all $i \in [n]$, $\mathcal{B}$ sets each public key share as $\tilde{X}_i \leftarrow Y_0 Y_1^i \cdots Y_t^{i^t}$. The joint public key is $\tilde{X} \leftarrow Y_0$. $\mathcal{B}$ queries its DL oracle on $\tilde{X}_j$ (with representation $(1, j, \ldots, j^t)$) to get x_j for the initial corrupted set cor. $\mathcal{B}$ then returns $(\tilde{X}, \{\tilde{X}_i\}_{i\in[n]}, \{x_j\}_{j\in \mathsf{cor}})$ to $\mathcal{A}$.

$\mathcal{B}$'s simulation of signing is similar to the proof of static security. In particular, $\mathcal{B}$ again simulates R_k for honest $k \in \mathsf{hon}$ as $R_k \leftarrow g^{z_k}\tilde{X}_k^{-c\lambda_k}$ in Round 2. If $\mathcal{A}$ corrupts an honest party k after Round 2 has begun, then $\mathcal{B}$ queries its DL oracle on $\tilde{X}_k$ (with rep. $(1, k, \ldots, k^t)$) to get x_k, computes $r_k \leftarrow z_k - c\lambda_k x_k$, and returns x_k along with the honest party's state $\mathsf{st}_{k,\mathsf{ssid}} = \{\mathsf{cm}_k, R_k, r_k, \ldots\}$ across all signing sessions to $\mathcal{A}$. However, $\mathcal{A}$ may choose to corrupt some honest k *before* Round 2, or even before it outputs its own cm_j's in Round 1. In this case, $\mathcal{B}$ samples a random $r_k \leftarrow\!\!\$\ \mathbb{Z}_p$, sets $R_k \leftarrow g^{r_k}$, and programs $\mathsf{cm}_k \leftarrow \mathsf{H}_{\mathsf{cm}}(m, \mathcal{S}, R_k)$ for the random cm_k it output in Round 1. It then queries its DL oracle on $\tilde{X}_k$ (with rep. $(1, k, \ldots, k^t)$) to get x_k and returns it and $\mathsf{st}_{k,\mathsf{ssid}} = \{\mathsf{cm}_k, R_k, r_k, \ldots\}$ across all signing sessions to $\mathcal{A}$. As in the proof of static security, $\mathcal{B}$ rewinds $\mathcal{A}$ in order to extract $x = y_0$ from $\mathcal{A}$'s two forgeries. Assume w.l.o.g. that $\mathcal{A}$ corrupts t parties over the two iterations. ($\mathcal{A}$ can corrupt up to $t/2$ parties in each iteration, and $\mathcal{B}$ can corrupt the remaining itself.) For simplicity, say the corrupt indices are $\mathsf{cor} = \{1, \ldots, t\}$. Then $\mathcal{B}$ has made t DL queries on $g^{x_k} = Y_0 Y_1^k \cdots Y_t^{k^t}$. This forms a system of linear equations:

$$\begin{pmatrix} x \\ x_1 \\ \vdots \\ x_t \end{pmatrix} = \begin{pmatrix} 1 & 0 & \cdots & 0 \\ 1 & 1 & \cdots & 1^t \\ \vdots & \vdots & \ddots & \vdots \\ 1 & t & \cdots & t^t \end{pmatrix} \begin{pmatrix} y_0 \\ y_1 \\ \vdots \\ y_t \end{pmatrix}$$

This is a Vandermonde matrix and is therefore invertible. $\mathcal{B}$ knows $(x, x_1, \ldots, x_t)$, and so can solve for $(y_0, y_1, \ldots, y_t)$ to win the $t+1$-aomdl game.

8 Adaptive Security Against t Corruptions

We now prove our strongest result: that Sparkle is secure against t adaptive corruptions. In particular, if exactly $t+1$ parties engage in signing, all but one of them could be malicious and the unforgeability of Sparkle would still hold. We prove this result under the AOMDL assumption (Fig. 3) in the AGM with random oracles. We also provide a proof of static security under the DL assumption in the AGM and ROM, intended as a warm-up for our adaptive proof, in the full version of the paper [18].

Theorem 3. Sparkle *is adaptively secure against t corruptions under the AOMDL assumption in the AGM and ROM.*

We formally prove Theorem 3 in Sect. 9.

Proof Outline. Let $\mathcal{A}$ be an algebraic adversary against the adaptive unforgeability of Sparkle (Fig. 4). We construct a PPT reduction $\mathcal{B}$ against the $t+1$-aomdl assumption (Fig. 3) that uses $\mathcal{A}$ as a subroutine as follows. $\mathcal{B}$ takes as input a $t+1$-aomdl challenge $(Y_0, Y_1, \ldots, Y_t)$ and aims to output y_i such that $Y_i = g^{y_i}$ for all $i \in [0..t]$ without querying its DL oracle more than t times. $\mathcal{B}$ simulates key generation, signing, and corruption as in the $t/2$-adaptive proof, but does not rewind $\mathcal{A}$, so $\mathcal{A}$ may corrupt a full t parties.

$\mathcal{A}$'s forgery $(m^*, (\tilde{R}^*, z^*))$ verifies as $\tilde{R}^* = g^{z^*}\tilde{X}^{-c^*}$, where $\mathcal{A}$ provided a representation of $\tilde{R}^*$ when querying $c^* = \mathsf{H}_{\mathsf{sig}}(\tilde{X}, m^*, \tilde{R}^*)$:

$$\tilde{R}^* = g^{\gamma^*}\tilde{X}^{\xi^*}\tilde{X}_1^{\xi_1^*}\cdots\tilde{X}_n^{\xi_n^*}\prod_{i=1}^{q_S} R_{i,1}^{\rho_{i,1}^*}\cdots R_{i,n}^{\rho_{i,n}^*}$$

where $\{R_{i,k}\}_{i\in[q_S]}$ are the honest nonces returned by the Sign' oracle over q_S signing queries. Each $R_{i,k}$ verifies as $R_{i,k} = g^{z_{i,k}}\tilde{X}_k^{-c_i\lambda_{i,k}}$, where $c_i = \mathsf{H}_{\mathsf{sig}}(\tilde{X}, m_i, \tilde{R}_i)$. Equating the two expressions for $\tilde{R}^*$ and rearranging, we have:

$$g^{z^*}g^{-\gamma^*}\prod_{i=1}^{q_S} g^{-z_{i,1}\rho_{i,1}^*}\cdots g^{-z_{i,n}\rho_{i,n}^*}$$
$$= \tilde{X}^{c^*}\tilde{X}^{\xi^*}\tilde{X}_1^{\xi_1^*}\cdots\tilde{X}_n^{\xi_n^*}\prod_{i=1}^{q_S}(\tilde{X}_1^{-c_i\lambda_{i,1}})^{\rho_{i,1}^*}\cdots(\tilde{X}_n^{-c_i\lambda_{i,n}})^{\rho_{i,n}^*}$$

$\mathcal{B}$ queries its DL oracle on $\tilde{X}_j$ (with representation $(1, j, \ldots, j^t)$) to obtain $\{x_j\}_{j\in\mathsf{cor}}$ for the t corrupt parties. For all $k \in [n]$, $\tilde{X}_k = \tilde{X}Y_1^kY_2^{k^2}\cdots Y_t^{k^t}$, and for all $i \in [t]$, $Y_i = \tilde{X}^{L'_{0,i}}\prod_{j\in\mathsf{cor}} g^{x_j L'_{j,i}}$, where $L'_{j,i}$ is the ith coefficient of the Lagrange polynomial $L'_j(Z)$ for the set $0\cup\mathsf{cor}$. Plugging these in and rearranging, we have:

$$g^{\eta^*} = \tilde{X}^{c^*+\xi^*}\prod_{k=1}^{n}\tilde{X}^{\mu_k^*}g^{\nu_k^*}$$

where $\eta^* = z^* - \gamma^* - \sum_{i=1}^{q_S}(z_{i,1}\rho^*_{i,1} + \cdots + z_{i,n}\rho^*_{i,n})$, $\mu^*_k = 1 + \sum_{i=1}^{t} L'_{0,i}k^i$, and $\nu^*_k = \sum_{i=1}^{t}\left(\sum_{j\in\mathsf{cor}} x_j L'_{j,i}\right)k^i$. Then:

$$x = \frac{\eta^* - \sum_{k=1}^{n}\nu^*_k}{c^* + \xi^* + \sum_{k=1}^{n}\mu^*_k}$$

$\mathcal{A}$ fixed $\tilde{R}^*$ and thus $\eta^*, \{\nu^*_i\}_{i\in[n]}, \xi^*, \{\mu^*_i\}_{i\in[n]}$ as it queried $\mathsf{H}_{\mathsf{sig}}(\tilde{X}, m^*, \tilde{R}^*)$ to receive random c^*. Thus, the denominator is nonzero with overwhelming probability and $\mathcal{B}$ can solve for x. $\mathcal{B}$ can then compute $(y_0, y_1, \ldots, y_t)$ as in the $t/2$-adaptive proof to win the $t+1$-aomdl game.

9 Static and Adaptive Security Proofs

In this section, we provide formal proofs of static and adaptive security for Sparkle. In particular, we prove the following: (1) static security (against up to t corruptions) (Theorem 1) under DL+ROM, (2) adaptive security against up to $t/2$ corruptions (Theorem 2) under AOMDL+ROM, and (3) adaptive security against up to t corruptions (Theorem 3) under AOMDL+AGM+ROM.

9.1 Proof of Static Security

Proof. (of Theorem 1.) Let $\mathcal{A}$ be a PPT adversary attempting to break the static unforgeability of Sparkle (Fig. 4) that makes up to q_H queries to H_{cm} and $\mathsf{H}_{\mathsf{sig}}$, and q_S queries to its signing oracles. Without loss of generality, we assume $\mathcal{A}$ queries $\mathsf{H}_{\mathsf{sig}}$ on its forgery $(\tilde{X}, m^*, \tilde{R}^*)$. Then, let $q = q_H + q_S + 1$. We construct a PPT reduction $\mathcal{B}$ against the DL assumption (Fig. 3) that uses $\mathcal{A}$ as a subroutine such that

$$\mathsf{Adv}^{st\text{-}sec}_{\mathcal{A}}(\kappa, 1) \le \sqrt{q\mathsf{Adv}^{\mathsf{dl}}_{\mathcal{B}}(\kappa) + \mathsf{negl}(\kappa)}$$

Here, $\tau = 1$ to allow $\mathcal{A}$ to corrupt a full $\tau \cdot t = t$ parties. The reduction $\mathcal{B}$ runs $\mathcal{A}$ two times. On the second iteration, $\mathcal{B}$ programs $\mathsf{H}_{\mathsf{sig}}$ to output a different random value on a single point so that it can extract a discrete logarithm solution from $\mathcal{A}$'s two forgeries. $\mathcal{B}$ perfectly simulates $\mathsf{Game}^{\mathsf{UF}}_{\mathcal{A}}(\kappa, 1)$. However, $\mathcal{B}$ can only extract a discrete logarithm if $\mathcal{A}$'s forgery $(m^*, (\tilde{R}^*, z^*))$ at the end of each iteration verifies and includes the same nonce $\tilde{R}^*$. By the local forking lemma [6], this occurs with probability less than $\frac{1}{q}(\mathsf{Adv}^{st\text{-}sec}_{\mathcal{A}}(\kappa, 1))^2$.

The Reduction $\mathcal{B}$: We define the reduction $\mathcal{B}$ playing game $\mathsf{Game}^{\mathsf{dl}}_{\mathcal{B}}(\kappa)$ as follows. $\mathcal{B}$ is responsible for simulating key generation and oracle responses for queries to $\mathcal{O}^{\mathsf{Sign}}, \mathcal{O}^{\mathsf{Sign}'}, \mathcal{O}^{\mathsf{Sign}''}$, H_{cm}, and $\mathsf{H}_{\mathsf{sig}}$. Let $\mathsf{Q}_{\mathsf{cm}}, \mathsf{Q}_{\mathsf{sig}}$ be the set of $\mathsf{H}_{\mathsf{cm}}, \mathsf{H}_{\mathsf{sig}}$ queries and their responses, respectively. $\mathcal{B}$ initializes them to the empty set and maintains them across both iterations of the adversary. $\mathcal{B}$ may program the random oracles $\mathsf{H}_{\mathsf{cm}}, \mathsf{H}_{\mathsf{sig}}$. Let Q be the set of messages that have been queried in $\mathcal{O}^{\mathsf{Sign}}$ as in $\mathsf{Game}_{\mathcal{A}}^{\mathsf{UF}}(\kappa, 1)$. $\mathcal{B}$ initializes Q to the empty set. At the beginning of the second iteration of $\mathcal{A}$, $\mathcal{B}$ resets Q to the empty set.

DL Input. $\mathcal{B}$ takes as input the group description $\mathcal{G} = (\mathbb{G}, p, g)$ and a DL challenge $\dot{X}$. $\mathcal{B}$ aims to output $\dot{x}$ such that $\dot{X} = g^{\dot{x}}$.

Static Corruption. $\mathcal{B}$ runs $\mathcal{A}()$. $\mathcal{A}$ chooses the total number of potential signers n, the threshold $t + 1 \le n$, and the set of corrupt parties $\mathsf{cor} \leftarrow \{j\}, |\mathsf{cor}| \le t$, which are fixed for the rest of the protocol. $\mathcal{B}$ sets $\mathsf{hon} \leftarrow [n] \setminus \mathsf{cor}$ and must reveal the secret keys of the corrupt parties to $\mathcal{A}$, which $\mathcal{B}$ does in the next step.

Simulating KeyGen. $\mathcal{B}$ simulates the key generation algorithm (Fig. 5) using its DL challenge $\dot{X}$ as follows.

1. $\mathcal{B}$ sets the joint public key $\tilde{X} \leftarrow \dot{X}$.
2. $\mathcal{B}$ simulates a Shamir secret sharing of the discrete logarithm of $\tilde{X}$ by performing the following steps. (See Sect. 3 for notation.) Assume without loss of generality that $|\mathsf{cor}| = t$.
   (a) $\mathcal{B}$ samples t random values $x_j \leftarrow\!\!\$\; \mathbb{Z}_p$ for $j \in \mathsf{cor}$.
   (b) Let f be the polynomial whose constant term is the challenge $f(0) = \dot{x}$ and for which $f(j) = x_j$ for all $j \in \mathsf{cor}$. $\mathcal{B}$ computes the $t + 1$ Lagrange polynomials $\{L'_0(Z), \{L'_j(Z)\}_{j \in \mathsf{cor}}\}$ relating to the set (of x-coordinates) $0 \cup \mathsf{cor}$.
   (c) For all $1 \le i \le t$, $\mathcal{B}$ computes
$$Y_i = \tilde{X}^{L'_{0,i}} \prod_{j \in \mathsf{cor}} g^{x_j L'_{j,i}}$$
   where $L'_{j,i}$ is the ith coefficient of $L'_j(Z) = L'_{j,0} + L'_{j,1}Z + \cdots + L'_{j,t}Z^t$.
   (d) For all $1 \le i \le n$, $\mathcal{B}$ computes
$$\tilde{X}_i = \tilde{X} Y_1^i Y_1^{i^2} \cdots Y_t^{i^t}$$
   which is implicitly equal to $g^{f(i)}$.

The joint public key is $\tilde{X} = g^{f(0)} = \dot{X}$ with corresponding secret key $x = \dot{x}$. $\mathcal{B}$ runs $\mathcal{A}^{\mathcal{O}^{\mathsf{Sign}, \mathsf{Sign}', \mathsf{Sign}''}}(\tilde{X}, \{\tilde{X}_i\}_{i \in [n]}, \{x_j\}_{j \in \mathsf{cor}})$.

Simulating Random Oracle Queries. $\mathcal{B}$ handles $\mathcal{A}$'s random oracle queries throughout the protocol by lazy sampling, as follows.

$\underline{\mathsf{H}_{\mathsf{cm}}}$: When $\mathcal{A}$ queries H_{cm} on $(m, \mathcal{S}, R)$, $\mathcal{B}$ checks whether $(m, \mathcal{S}, R, \mathsf{cm}) \in \mathsf{Q}_{\mathsf{cm}}$ and, if so, returns cm. Else, $\mathcal{B}$ samples $\mathsf{cm} \leftarrow\!\!\$\; \mathbb{Z}_p$, appends $(m, \mathcal{S}, R, \mathsf{cm})$ to Q_{cm}, and returns cm.

$\underline{\mathsf{H}_{\mathsf{sig}}}$: When $\mathcal{A}$ queries $\mathsf{H}_{\mathsf{sig}}$ on (X, m, R), $\mathcal{B}$ checks whether $(X, m, R, c) \in \mathsf{Q}_{\mathsf{sig}}$ and, if so, returns c. Else, $\mathcal{B}$ samples $c \leftarrow\!\!\$\; \mathbb{Z}_p$, appends (X, m, R, c) to $\mathsf{Q}_{\mathsf{sig}}$, and returns c.

Simulating Sparkle Signing. $\mathcal{B}$ handles $\mathcal{A}$'s signing queries as follows.

Round 1 ($\mathcal{O}^{\mathsf{Sign}}$): In the first round of signing for session ssid, each party i in the signing set $\mathcal{S}$ sends a commitment cm_i. When $\mathcal{A}$ queries $\mathcal{O}^{\mathsf{Sign}}$ on $(k, \mathsf{ssid}, m, \mathcal{S})$ for honest $k \in \mathsf{hon}$, $\mathcal{B}$ samples $\mathsf{cm}_k \leftarrow\!\!\$\, \mathbb{Z}_p$, appends $(m, \mathcal{S}, \cdot, \mathsf{cm}_k)$ to Q_{cm}, sets $\mathsf{st}_{k,\mathsf{ssid}} \leftarrow (\mathsf{cm}_k, \cdot, \cdot, m, \mathcal{S})$, and returns cm_k to $\mathcal{A}$.

Round 2 ($\mathcal{O}^{\mathsf{Sign}'}$): In the second round of signing for session ssid, each party i in the signing set $\mathcal{S}$ takes as input the set of commitments $\{\mathsf{cm}_i\}_{i \in \mathcal{S}}$ and reveals its nonce R_i such that $\mathsf{cm}_i = \mathsf{H}_{\mathsf{cm}}(m, \mathcal{S}, R_i)$. When $\mathcal{A}$ queries $\mathcal{O}^{\mathsf{Sign}'}$ on $(k, \mathsf{ssid}, \{\mathsf{cm}_i\}_{i \in \mathcal{S}})$ for $k \in \mathsf{hon}$, then for all $j \in \mathcal{S} \cap \mathsf{cor}$, $\mathcal{B}$ looks up cm_j for a record $(m, \mathcal{S}, R_j, \mathsf{cm}_j) \in \mathsf{Q}_{\mathsf{cm}}$.

If there exists $j' \in \mathcal{S}$ such that $(m', \mathcal{S}', \cdot, \mathsf{cm}_{j'}) \in \mathsf{Q}_{\mathsf{cm}}$ and $(m', \mathcal{S}') \neq (m, \mathcal{S})$, or if there exists some $j' \in \mathcal{S}$ for which no record $(m, \mathcal{S}, \cdot, \mathsf{cm}_{j'}) \in \mathsf{Q}_{\mathsf{cm}}$ exists, then $\mathcal{B}$ chooses $R_k \leftarrow\!\!\$\, g^{r_k}$ randomly, updates $\mathsf{st}_{k,\mathsf{ssid}} \leftarrow (\mathsf{cm}_k, R_k, r_k, m, \mathcal{S})$, programs $\mathsf{cm}_k \leftarrow \mathsf{H}_{\mathsf{cm}}(m, \mathcal{S}, R_k)$ and returns R_k.

Else if this is the first query in the signing session, $\mathcal{B}$ samples $c \leftarrow\!\!\$\, \mathbb{Z}_p$. For all $k \in \mathsf{hon}$, $\mathcal{B}$ samples $z_k \leftarrow\!\!\$\, \mathbb{Z}_p$, computes $R_k \leftarrow g^{z_k} \tilde{X}_k^{-c\lambda_k}$ (λ_k is the Lagrange coefficient for party k in the set $\mathcal{S}$), and programs $\mathsf{cm}_k \leftarrow \mathsf{H}_{\mathsf{cm}}(m, \mathcal{S}, R_k)$ (updating $(m, \mathcal{S}, R_k, \mathsf{cm}_k) \in \mathsf{Q}_{\mathsf{cm}}$). Then $\mathcal{B}$ computes $\tilde{R} = \prod_{i \in \mathcal{S}} R_i$ and programs $c \leftarrow \mathsf{H}_{\mathsf{sig}}(\tilde{X}, m, \tilde{R})$. (However, if $\mathcal{A}$ has already queried $\mathsf{H}_{\mathsf{sig}}$ on $(\tilde{X}, m, \tilde{R})$, then $\mathcal{B}$ aborts.)

Finally, $\mathcal{B}$ sets $\mathsf{st}_{k,\mathsf{ssid}} \leftarrow (\mathsf{cm}_k, R_k, z_k, c\lambda_k, m, \mathcal{S}, \{\mathsf{cm}_i\}_{i \in \mathcal{S}})$, and returns R_k to $\mathcal{A}$. If this is not the first query, $\mathcal{B}$ looks up $\mathsf{st}_{k,\mathsf{ssid}} \leftarrow (\mathsf{cm}_k, R_k, z_k, c\lambda_k, m, \mathcal{S}, \{\mathsf{cm}_i\}_{i \in \mathcal{S}})$ and returns R_k.

Round 3 ($\mathcal{O}^{\mathsf{Sign}''}$): In the third round of signing for session ssid, each party i in the signing set $\mathcal{S}$ produces a partial signature on the message m. When $\mathcal{A}$ queries $\mathcal{O}^{\mathsf{Sign}''}$ on $(k, \mathsf{ssid}, \{R_i\}_{i \in \mathcal{S}})$ for $k \in \mathsf{hon}$, $\mathcal{B}$ looks up $\mathsf{st}_{k,\mathsf{ssid}} \leftarrow (\mathsf{cm}_k, R_k, z_k, c\lambda_k, m, \mathcal{S}, \{\mathsf{cm}_i\}_{i \in \mathcal{S}})$, checks whether $\mathsf{cm}_i = \mathsf{H}_{\mathsf{cm}}(m, \mathcal{S}, R_i)$ for all $i \in \mathcal{S}$ and returns $\perp$ if not. If $\mathsf{cm}_i = \mathsf{H}_{\mathsf{cm}}(m, \mathcal{S}, R_i)$ but $\mathcal{A}$ never queried H_{cm} on input $(m, \mathcal{S}, R_i)$, $\mathcal{B}$ aborts. Else, $\mathcal{B}$ sets $\mathsf{st}_{k,\mathsf{ssid}} \leftarrow ()$ and returns z_k.

Output. At the end of the game, $\mathcal{A}$ produces a forgery $(m^*, \sigma^*) = (m^*, (\tilde{R}^*, z^*))$ and wins if $\mathsf{Verify}(\tilde{X}, m^*, \sigma^*) = 1$ and $m^* \notin Q$.

Extracting the Discrete Logarithm of $\dot{X}$. $\mathcal{B}$'s simulation of key generation and signing is perfect, and $\mathcal{B}$ aborts with negligible probability. Indeed, $\mathcal{B}$ aborts in Round 3 if $\mathcal{A}$ reveals R_j such that $\mathsf{cm}_j = \mathsf{H}_{\mathsf{cm}}(m, \mathcal{S}, R_j)$ but $\mathcal{A}$ never queried H_{cm} on $(m, \mathcal{S}, R_j)$. This requires $\mathcal{A}$ to have guessed cm_j ahead of time, which occurs with negligible probability $1/p$.

$\mathcal{B}_2$ also aborts in Round 2 if $\mathcal{A}$ had previously queried $\mathsf{H}_{\mathsf{sig}}$ on $(\tilde{X}, m, \tilde{R})$. In that case, $\mathcal{B}$ had returned a random $c \leftarrow \mathsf{H}_{\mathsf{sig}}(\tilde{X}, m, \tilde{R})$, so the reduction fails. However, this implies that $\mathcal{A}$ guessed R_k before $\mathcal{B}$ revealed it, which occurs with negligible probability $1/p$.

It remains to show that $\mathcal{B}$ can extract the discrete logarithm of $\dot{X}$ from $\mathcal{A}$'s two valid forgeries. $\mathcal{A}$'s first forgery $(m^*, (\tilde{R}^*, z^*))$ satisfies $\tilde{R}^* \tilde{X}^{c^*} = g^{z^*}$, where $c^* = \mathsf{H}_{\mathsf{sig}}(\tilde{X}, m^*, \tilde{R}^*)$. Here, z^* does not suffice for $\mathcal{B}$ to extract the discrete logarithm of $\tilde{X}$ because it does not necessarily know the discrete logarithm of $\tilde{R}^*$.

Thus, $\mathcal{B}$ chooses $c' \leftarrow_{\$} \mathbb{Z}_p$ and programs $\mathsf{H_{sig}}$ to output c' on input $(\tilde{X}, m^*, \tilde{R}^*)$. $\mathcal{B}$ resets Q to the empty set, but the sets $\mathsf{Q_{cm}}$, $\mathsf{Q_{sig}}$ are kept for the second iteration of the adversary. $\mathcal{B}$ then runs $\mathcal{A}$ again on the same random coins.

After the second iteration, suppose $\mathcal{A}$ terminates with $(m', (\tilde{R}', z'))$. If $(m', \tilde{R}') = (m^*, \tilde{R}^*)$ and $\mathcal{A}$'s forgeries both verify, then $\mathcal{B}$ returns $\dot{x} = \frac{z^* - z'}{c^* - c'}$ such that $\tilde{X} = g^{\dot{x}}$ and wins $\mathsf{Game}^{\mathsf{dl}}_{\mathcal{B}}(\kappa)$. If $(m', \tilde{R}') \neq (m^*, \tilde{R}^*)$ or $\mathcal{A}$'s forgery does not verify, then $\mathcal{B}$ must abort. By the local forking lemma [6], this happens with probability less than $\frac{1}{q}(\mathsf{Adv}^{st\text{-}sec}_{\mathcal{A}}(\kappa, 1))^2$. If $\mathcal{A}$ succeeds having not queried $\mathsf{H_{cm}}$ on $(m, \mathcal{S}, R_j)$, then $\mathcal{B}$ aborts. This occurs with probability less than $\frac{q_H}{p}$. Thus,

$$\frac{1}{q}(\mathsf{Adv}^{st\text{-}sec}_{\mathcal{A}}(\kappa, 1))^2 \leq \mathsf{Adv}^{\mathsf{dl}}_{\mathcal{B}}(\kappa) + \mathsf{negl}(\kappa)$$

9.2 Proof of Adaptive Security for up to $t/2$ Corruptions

Proof. (of Theorem 2.) Let $\mathcal{A}$ be a PPT adversary attempting to break the adaptive unforgeability of Sparkle (Fig. 4) that makes up to q_H queries to $\mathsf{H_{cm}}$ and $\mathsf{H_{sig}}$, and q_S queries to its signing oracles. Without loss of generality, we assume $\mathcal{A}$ queries $\mathsf{H_{sig}}$ on its forgery $(\tilde{X}, m^*, \tilde{R}^*)$. Then, let $q = q_H + q_S + 1$. We construct a PPT reduction $\mathcal{B}$ against the $t+1$-aomdl assumption (Fig. 3) that uses $\mathcal{A}$ as a subroutine such that

$$\mathsf{Adv}^{adp\text{-}sec}_{\mathcal{A}}(\kappa, 1/2) \leq \sqrt{q\mathsf{Adv}^{t+1\text{-}\mathsf{aomdl}}_{\mathcal{B}}(\kappa) + \mathsf{negl}(\kappa)}$$

Here, $\tau = 1/2$ to restrict $\mathcal{A}$ to corrupt $\tau \cdot t = t/2$ parties. The reduction $\mathcal{B}$ runs $\mathcal{A}$ two times. Over the two iterations, $\mathcal{B}$ makes no more than t queries to its discrete logarithm oracle $\mathcal{O}^{\mathsf{dl}}$ and aims to output $t+1$ discrete logarithms that constitute a valid solution to the AOMDL challenge. If $\mathcal{B}$ makes fewer than t queries while responding to $\mathcal{A}$'s oracle queries, then it makes the additional queries necessary to extract an AOMDL solution. On the second iteration of $\mathcal{A}$, $\mathcal{B}$ programs $\mathsf{H_{sig}}$ to output a different random value on a single point so that it can extract one of the $t+1$ discrete logarithm solutions from $\mathcal{A}$'s two forgeries. $\mathcal{B}$ perfectly simulates $\mathsf{Game}^{\mathsf{adp\text{-}UF}}_{\mathcal{A}}(\kappa, 1/2)$. However, $\mathcal{B}$ can only extract a solution if $\mathcal{A}$'s forgery $(m^*, (\tilde{R}^*, z^*))$ at the end of each iteration verifies and includes the same nonce $\tilde{R}^*$. By the local forking lemma [6], this occurs with probability less than $\frac{1}{q}(\mathsf{Adv}^{adp\text{-}sec}_{\mathcal{A}}(\kappa, 1/2))^2$.

The Reduction $\mathcal{B}$: We define the reduction $\mathcal{B}$ playing game $\mathsf{Game}^{t+1\text{-}\mathsf{aomdl}}_{\mathcal{B}}(\kappa)$ as follows. $\mathcal{B}$ is responsible for simulating key generation and oracle responses for queries to $\mathcal{O}^{\mathsf{Sign}}, \mathcal{O}^{\mathsf{Sign}'}, \mathcal{O}^{\mathsf{Sign}''}, \mathcal{O}^{\mathsf{Corrupt}}, \mathsf{H_{cm}}$, and $\mathsf{H_{sig}}$. Let $\mathsf{Q_{cm}}, \mathsf{Q_{sig}}$ be the set of $\mathsf{H_{cm}}, \mathsf{H_{sig}}$ queries and their responses, respectively. $\mathcal{B}$ initializes them to the empty set and maintains them across both iterations of the adversary. $\mathcal{B}$ may program the random oracles $\mathsf{H_{cm}}, \mathsf{H_{sig}}$. Let Q be the set of messages that have been queried in $\mathcal{O}^{\mathsf{Sign}}$ as in $\mathsf{Game}_{\mathcal{A}}^{\mathsf{adp\text{-}UF}}(\kappa, 1/2)$. $\mathcal{B}$ initializes Q to the empty set. At the beginning of the second iteration of $\mathcal{A}$, $\mathcal{B}$ resets Q to the empty set.

AOMDL Input. $\mathcal{B}$ takes as input the group description $\mathcal{G} = (\mathbb{G}, p, g)$ and an AOMDL challenge of $t+1$ values $(Y_0, \ldots, Y_t)$. As in $\mathsf{Game}_{\mathcal{B}}^{t+1\text{-}\mathsf{aomdl}}(\kappa)$, $\mathcal{B}$ has access to a discrete logarithm oracle $\mathcal{O}^{\mathsf{dl}}$, which it may query up to t times. $\mathcal{B}$ aims to output $(y_0, \ldots, y_t)$ such that $Y_i = g^{y_i}$ for all $0 \leq i \leq t$.

Initial Corruption. $\mathcal{B}$ runs $\mathcal{A}()$. $\mathcal{A}$ chooses the total number of potential signers n, the threshold $t+1 \leq n$, and the initial set of corrupt parties $\mathsf{cor} \leftarrow \{j\}, |\mathsf{cor}| \leq t/2$. $\mathcal{B}$ sets $\mathsf{hon} \leftarrow [n] \setminus \mathsf{cor}$ and must reveal the secret keys of the corrupt parties to $\mathcal{A}$, which $\mathcal{B}$ does in the next step.

Simulating KeyGen. $\mathcal{B}$ simulates the key generation algorithm (Fig. 5) using its AOMDL challenge $(Y_0, \ldots, Y_t)$ as follows. For all $1 \leq i \leq n$, $\mathcal{B}$ sets the public key share as

$$\tilde{X}_i = Y_0 Y_1^i \cdots Y_t^{i^t}$$

which is implicitly equal to $g^{f(i)}$. The joint public key is $\tilde{X} = g^{f(0)} = Y_0$ with corresponding secret key $x = y_0$. $\mathcal{B}$ obtains the initial corrupt secret key shares by querying $x_j = f(j) \leftarrow \mathcal{O}^{\mathsf{dl}}(\tilde{X}_j)$ (with representation $(1, j, \ldots, j^t)$) for all $j \in \mathsf{cor}$. $\mathcal{B}$ runs $\mathcal{A}^{\mathcal{O}^{\mathsf{Sign}, \mathsf{Sign}', \mathsf{Sign}'', \mathsf{Corrupt}}}(\tilde{X}, \{\tilde{X}_i\}_{i \in [n]}, \{x_j\}_{j \in \mathsf{cor}})$.

Simulating Random Oracle Queries. $\mathcal{B}$ handles $\mathcal{A}$'s random oracle queries throughout the protocol by lazy sampling, as follows.

$\underline{\mathsf{H}_{\mathsf{cm}}}$: When $\mathcal{A}$ queries H_{cm} on $(m, \mathcal{S}, R)$, $\mathcal{B}$ checks whether $(m, \mathcal{S}, R, \mathsf{cm}) \in \mathsf{Q}_{\mathsf{cm}}$ and, if so, returns cm. Else, $\mathcal{B}$ samples $\mathsf{cm} \leftarrow\!\!\$\, \mathbb{Z}_p$, appends $(m, \mathcal{S}, R, \mathsf{cm})$ to Q_{cm}, and returns cm.

$\underline{\mathsf{H}_{\mathsf{sig}}}$: When $\mathcal{A}$ queries $\mathsf{H}_{\mathsf{sig}}$ on (X, m, R), $\mathcal{B}$ checks whether $(X, m, R, c) \in \mathsf{Q}_{\mathsf{sig}}$ and, if so, returns c. Else, $\mathcal{B}$ samples $c \leftarrow\!\!\$\, \mathbb{Z}_p$, appends (X, m, R, c) to $\mathsf{Q}_{\mathsf{sig}}$, and returns c.

Simulating Sparkle Signing. $\mathcal{B}$ handles $\mathcal{A}$'s signing queries as follows.

Round 1 ($\mathcal{O}^{\mathsf{Sign}}$): In the first round of signing for session ssid, each party i in the signing set $\mathcal{S}$ sends a commitment cm_i. When $\mathcal{A}$ queries $\mathcal{O}^{\mathsf{Sign}}$ on $(k, \mathsf{ssid}, m, \mathcal{S})$ for honest $k \in \mathsf{hon}$, $\mathcal{B}$ samples $\mathsf{cm}_k \leftarrow\!\!\$\, \mathbb{Z}_p$, appends $(m, \mathcal{S}, \cdot, \mathsf{cm}_k)$ to Q_{cm}, sets $\mathsf{st}_{k,\mathsf{ssid}} \leftarrow (\mathsf{cm}_k, \cdot, \cdot, m, \mathcal{S})$, and returns cm_k to $\mathcal{A}$.

Round 2 ($\mathcal{O}^{\mathsf{Sign}'}$): In the second round of signing for session ssid, each party i in the signing set $\mathcal{S}$ takes as input the set of commitments $\{\mathsf{cm}_i\}_{i \in \mathcal{S}}$ and reveals its nonce R_i such that $\mathsf{cm}_i = \mathsf{H}_{\mathsf{cm}}(m, \mathcal{S}, R_i)$. When $\mathcal{A}$ queries $\mathcal{O}^{\mathsf{Sign}'}$ on $(k, \mathsf{ssid}, \{\mathsf{cm}_i\}_{i \in \mathcal{S}})$ for $k \in \mathsf{hon}$, then for all $j \in \mathcal{S} \cap \mathsf{cor}$, $\mathcal{B}$ looks up cm_j for a record $(m, \mathcal{S}, R_j, \mathsf{cm}_j) \in \mathsf{Q}_{\mathsf{cm}}$.

If there exists $j' \in \mathcal{S}$ such that $(m', \mathcal{S}', \cdot, \mathsf{cm}_{j'}) \in \mathsf{Q}_{\mathsf{cm}}$ and $(m', \mathcal{S}') \neq (m, \mathcal{S})$, or if there exists some $j' \in \mathcal{S}$ for which no record $(m, \mathcal{S}, \cdot, \mathsf{cm}_{j'}) \in \mathsf{Q}_{\mathsf{cm}}$ exists, then $\mathcal{B}$ chooses $R_k \leftarrow g^{r_k}$ randomly, updates $\mathsf{st}_{k,\mathsf{ssid}} \leftarrow (\mathsf{cm}_k, R_k, r_k, m, \mathcal{S})$, programs $\mathsf{cm}_k \leftarrow \mathsf{H}_{\mathsf{cm}}(m, \mathcal{S}, R_k)$ and returns R_k.

Else if this is the first query in the signing session, $\mathcal{B}$ samples $c \leftarrow_{\$} \mathbb{Z}_p$. For all $k \in \mathsf{hon}$, $\mathcal{B}$ samples $z_k \leftarrow_{\$} \mathbb{Z}_p$, computes $R_k \leftarrow g^{z_k}\tilde{X}_k^{-c\lambda_k}$ (λ_k is the Lagrange coefficient for party k in the set $\mathcal{S}$), and programs $\mathsf{cm}_k \leftarrow \mathsf{H}_{\mathsf{cm}}(m, \mathcal{S}, R_k)$ (updating $(m, \mathcal{S}, R_k, \mathsf{cm}_k) \in \mathsf{Q}_{\mathsf{cm}}$). Then $\mathcal{B}$ computes $\tilde{R} = \prod_{i \in \mathcal{S}} R_i$ and programs $c \leftarrow \mathsf{H}_{\mathsf{sig}}(\tilde{X}, m, \tilde{R})$. (However, if $\mathcal{A}$ has already queried $\mathsf{H}_{\mathsf{sig}}$ on $(\tilde{X}, m, \tilde{R})$, then $\mathcal{B}$ aborts.)

Finally, $\mathcal{B}$ sets $\mathsf{st}_{k,\mathsf{ssid}} \leftarrow (\mathsf{cm}_k, R_k, z_k, c\lambda_k, m, \mathcal{S}, \{\mathsf{cm}_k\}_{k \in \mathcal{S}})$, and returns R_k to $\mathcal{A}$. If this is not the first query, $\mathcal{B}$ looks up $\mathsf{st}_{k,\mathsf{ssid}} \leftarrow (\mathsf{cm}_k, R_k, z_k, c\lambda_k, m, \mathcal{S}, \{\mathsf{cm}_k\}_{k \in \mathcal{S}})$ and returns R_k.

Round 3 ($\mathcal{O}^{\mathsf{Sign}''}$): In the third round of signing for session ssid, each party i in the signing set $\mathcal{S}$ produces a partial signature on the message m. When $\mathcal{A}$ queries $\mathcal{O}^{\mathsf{Sign}''}$ on $(k, \mathsf{ssid}, \{R_i\}_{i \in \mathcal{S}})$ for $k \in \mathsf{hon}$, $\mathcal{B}$ looks up $\mathsf{st}_{k,\mathsf{ssid}} \leftarrow (\mathsf{cm}_k, R_k, z_k, c\lambda_k, m, \mathcal{S}, \{\mathsf{cm}_i\}_{i \in \mathcal{S}})$, checks whether $\mathsf{cm}_i = \mathsf{H}_{\mathsf{cm}}(m, \mathcal{S}, R_i)$ for all $i \in \mathcal{S}$ and returns $\perp$ if not. If $\mathsf{cm}_i = \mathsf{H}_{\mathsf{cm}}(m, \mathcal{S}, R_i)$ but $\mathcal{A}$ never queried H_{cm} on input $(m, \mathcal{S}, R_i)$, $\mathcal{B}$ aborts. Else, $\mathcal{B}$ sets $\mathsf{st}_{k,\mathsf{ssid}} \leftarrow ()$ and returns z_k.

Simulating Corruption Queries ($\mathcal{O}^{\mathsf{Corrupt}}$): $\mathcal{A}$ may at any time corrupt an honest party k by querying $\mathcal{O}^{\mathsf{Corrupt}}(k)$. Upon receiving a corruption query, $\mathcal{B}$ first checks that $k \in \mathsf{hon}$, returning $\perp$ if not. Otherwise, $\mathcal{B}$ queries its DL oracle $\mathcal{O}^{\mathsf{dl}}$ on $\tilde{X}_k = g^{f(k)}$ (with representation $(1, k, \ldots, k^t)$) to obtain the secret key $x_k = f(k)$. Then, for each $\mathsf{st}_{k,\mathsf{ssid}}$, $\mathcal{B}$ does the following:

- If $\mathsf{st}_{k,\mathsf{ssid}} = (\mathsf{cm}_k, \cdot, \cdot, m, \mathcal{S})$, then $\mathcal{B}$ chooses $r_k \leftarrow_{\$} \mathbb{Z}_p$, sets $R_k \leftarrow g^{r_k}$, and programs $\mathsf{cm}_k \leftarrow \mathsf{H}_{\mathsf{cm}}(m, \mathcal{S}, R_k)$. It then updates $\mathsf{st}_{k,\mathsf{ssid}} \leftarrow (\mathsf{cm}_k, R_k, r_k, m, \mathcal{S})$.
- If $\mathsf{st}_{k,\mathsf{ssid}} = (\mathsf{cm}_k, R_k, z_k, c\lambda_k, m, \mathcal{S}, \{\mathsf{cm}_i\}_{i \in \mathcal{S}})$, then $\mathcal{B}$ computes $r_k = z_k - c\lambda_k x_k$ (now that it knows x_k) and updates $\mathsf{st}_{k,\mathsf{ssid}} \leftarrow (\mathsf{cm}_k, R_k, r_k, m, \mathcal{S}, \{\mathsf{cm}_i\}_{i \in \mathcal{S}})$.
- If $\mathsf{st}_{k,\mathsf{ssid}} = ()$, then return $()$. This case occurs if signing session ssid has already been completed (i.e., a valid signature was issued).

Finally, $\mathcal{B}$ sets $\mathsf{hon} \leftarrow \mathsf{hon} \setminus \{k\}$ and $\mathsf{cor} \leftarrow \mathsf{cor} \cup \{k\}$ and returns $x_k, \{\mathsf{st}_{k,\ell}\}_{\ell \in [\mathsf{ssid}]}$ to $\mathcal{A}$.

Output. At the end of the game, $\mathcal{A}$ produces a forgery $(m^*, \sigma^*) = (m^*, (\tilde{R}^*, z^*))$ and wins if $\mathsf{Verify}(\tilde{X}, m^*, \sigma^*) = 1, m^* \notin Q$, and $|\mathsf{cor}| \leq t/2$.

Extracting the Discrete Logarithm of Y_0. $\mathcal{B}$'s simulation of key generation and signing is perfect, and $\mathcal{B}$ aborts with negligible probability. Indeed, $\mathcal{B}$ aborts in Round 3 if $\mathcal{A}$ reveals R_j such that $\mathsf{cm}_j = \mathsf{H}_{\mathsf{cm}}(m, \mathcal{S}, R_j)$ but $\mathcal{A}$ never queried H_{cm} on $(m, \mathcal{S}, R_j)$. This requires $\mathcal{A}$ to have guessed cm_j ahead of time, which occurs with negligible probability $1/p$.

$\mathcal{B}_2$ also aborts in Round 2 if $\mathcal{A}$ had previously queried $\mathsf{H}_{\mathsf{sig}}$ on $(\tilde{X}, m, \tilde{R})$. In that case, $\mathcal{B}$ had returned a random $c \leftarrow \mathsf{H}_{\mathsf{sig}}(\tilde{X}, m, \tilde{R})$, so the reduction fails. However, this implies that $\mathcal{A}$ guessed R_k before $\mathcal{B}$ revealed it, which occurs with negligible probability $1/p$.

Next, we show that $\mathcal{B}$ can extract the discrete logarithm of Y_0 from $\mathcal{A}$'s two valid forgeries. $\mathcal{A}$'s first forgery $(m^*, (\tilde{R}^*, z^*))$ satisfies $\tilde{R}^*\tilde{X}^{c^*} = g^{z^*}$, where $c^* =$

$\mathsf{H}_{\mathsf{sig}}(\tilde{X}, m^*, \tilde{R}^*)$. Here, z^* does not suffice for $\mathcal{B}$ to extract the discrete logarithm of $\tilde{X} = Y_0$ because it does not necessarily know the discrete logarithm of $\tilde{R}^*$. Thus, $\mathcal{B}$ chooses $c' \leftarrow_{\$} \mathbb{Z}_p$ and programs $\mathsf{H}_{\mathsf{sig}}$ to output c' on input $(\tilde{X}, m^*, \tilde{R}^*)$. $\mathcal{B}$ resets Q to the empty set, but the sets Q_{cm}, $\mathsf{Q}_{\mathsf{sig}}$ are kept for the second iteration of the adversary. $\mathcal{B}$ then runs $\mathcal{A}$ again on the same random coins.

After the second iteration, suppose $\mathcal{A}$ terminates with $(m', (\tilde{R}', z'))$. If $(m', \tilde{R}') = (m^*, \tilde{R}^*)$ and $\mathcal{A}$'s forgeries both verify, then $\mathcal{B}$ returns $y_0 = x = \frac{z^* - z'}{c^* - c'}$ such that $Y_0 = \tilde{X} = g^x$. If $(m', \tilde{R}') \neq (m^*, \tilde{R}^*)$ or $\mathcal{A}$'s forgery does not verify, then $\mathcal{B}$ must abort. By the local forking lemma [6], this happens with probability less than $\frac{1}{q}(\mathsf{Adv}_{\mathcal{A}}^{adp\text{-}sec}(\kappa, 2))^2$. If $\mathcal{A}$ succeeds having not queried H_{cm} on $(m, \mathcal{S}, R_j)$, then $\mathcal{B}$ aborts. This occurs with probability less than $\frac{q_H}{p}$. Thus,

$$\frac{1}{q}(\mathsf{Adv}_{\mathcal{A}}^{adp\text{-}sec}(\kappa, 2))^2 \leq \Pr[\mathcal{B} \text{ extracts } y_0] + \mathsf{negl}(\kappa)$$

If $\mathcal{B}$ extracts y_0, then we use this to extract a full AOMDL solution as follows.

Extracting an AOMDL Solution. The reduction $\mathcal{B}$ must now extract the remaining $y_1, \ldots, y_t$ such that $Y_i = g^{y_i}$.

Assume without loss of generality that $\mathcal{A}$ makes t corruptions over the two iterations. (If not, $\mathcal{B}$ can corrupt the remaining number at the end, by querying its DL oracle until it reaches t secret keys.) Recall that $\mathcal{B}$ set $\tilde{X}_i = Y_0 Y_1^i \cdots Y_t^{i^t}$ and made t DL queries $g^{x_{i_1}}, \ldots, g^{x_{i_t}}$:

$$g^{x_{i_1}} = Y_0 Y_1^{i_1} \cdots Y_t^{{i_1}^t}$$
$$\vdots$$
$$g^{x_{i_t}} = Y_0 Y_1^{i_t} \cdots Y_t^{{i_t}^t}$$

Recall also that $\tilde{X} = Y_0$. This forms the following system of linear equations:

$$x = y_0$$
$$x_{i_1} = y_0 + i_1 y_1 \cdots + {i_1}^t y_t$$
$$\vdots$$
$$x_{i_t} = y_0 + i_t y_1 \cdots + {i_t}^t y_t$$

Equivalently,

$$\begin{pmatrix} x \\ x_{i_1} \\ \vdots \\ x_{i_t} \end{pmatrix} = \begin{pmatrix} 1 & 0 & \cdots & 0 \\ 1 & i_1 & \cdots & {i_1}^t \\ \vdots & \vdots & \ddots & \vdots \\ 1 & i_t & \cdots & {i_t}^t \end{pmatrix} \begin{pmatrix} y_0 \\ y_1 \\ \vdots \\ y_t \end{pmatrix}$$

$\mathcal{B}$ knows all of the values on the left-hand side. The matrix

$$V = \begin{pmatrix} 1 & 0 & \cdots & 0 \\ 1 & i_1 & \cdots & {i_1}^t \\ \vdots & \vdots & \ddots & \vdots \\ 1 & i_t & \cdots & {i_t}^t \end{pmatrix}$$

is a Vandermonde matrix and is therefore invertible. Thus, $\mathcal{B}$ can solve for $(y_0, y_1, \ldots, y_t)$ and win the $t+1$-aomdl game.

9.3 Proof of Adaptive Security for up to t Corruptions

Proof. (of Theorem 3.) Let $\mathcal{A}$ be an algebraic adversary attempting to break the adaptive unforgeability of Sparkle (Fig. 4). We construct a PPT reduction $\mathcal{B}$ against the $t+1$-aomdl assumption (Fig. 3) that uses $\mathcal{A}$ as a subroutine such that

$$\mathsf{Adv}_{\mathcal{A}}^{adp\text{-}sec}(\kappa, 1) \leq \mathsf{Adv}_{\mathcal{B}}^{t+1\text{-aomdl}}(\kappa) + \mathsf{negl}(\kappa)$$

Here, $\tau = 1$ to allow $\mathcal{A}$ to corrupt a full $\tau \cdot t = t$ parties.

The Reduction $\mathcal{B}$: We define the reduction $\mathcal{B}$ playing game $\mathsf{Game}_{\mathcal{B}}^{t+1\text{-aomdl}}(\kappa)$ as follows. $\mathcal{B}$ is responsible for simulating key generation and oracle responses for queries to $\mathcal{O}^{\mathsf{Sign}}, \mathcal{O}^{\mathsf{Sign}'}, \mathcal{O}^{\mathsf{Sign}''}, \mathcal{O}^{\mathsf{Corrupt}}, \mathsf{H}_{\mathsf{cm}}$, and $\mathsf{H}_{\mathsf{sig}}$. Let $\mathsf{Q}_{\mathsf{cm}}, \mathsf{Q}_{\mathsf{sig}}$ be the set of $\mathsf{H}_{\mathsf{cm}}, \mathsf{H}_{\mathsf{sig}}$ queries and their responses, respectively. $\mathcal{B}$ may program the random oracles $\mathsf{H}_{\mathsf{cm}}, \mathsf{H}_{\mathsf{sig}}$. Let Q be the set of messages that have been queried to $\mathcal{O}^{\mathsf{Sign}}$ as in game $\mathsf{Game}_{\mathcal{A}}^{\mathsf{adp\text{-}UF}}(\kappa, 1)$. $\mathcal{B}$ initializes $\mathsf{Q}_{\mathsf{cm}}, \mathsf{Q}_{\mathsf{sig}}, Q$ to the empty set.

AOMDL Input. $\mathcal{B}$ takes as input the group description $\mathcal{G} = (\mathbb{G}, p, g)$ and an AOMDL challenge of $t+1$ values $(Y_0, \ldots, Y_t)$. As in $\mathsf{Game}_{\mathcal{B}}^{t+1\text{-aomdl}}(\kappa)$, $\mathcal{B}$ has access to a discrete logarithm oracle $\mathcal{O}^{\mathsf{dl}}$, which it may query up to t times. $\mathcal{B}$ aims to output $(y_0, \ldots, y_t)$ such that $Y_i = g^{y_i}$ for all $i \in [0..t]$.

Initial Corruption. $\mathcal{B}$ runs $\mathcal{A}()$. $\mathcal{A}$ chooses the total number of potential signers n, the threshold $t+1 \leq n$, and the initial set of corrupt parties $\mathsf{cor} \leftarrow \{j\}, |\mathsf{cor}| \leq t$. $\mathcal{B}$ sets $\mathsf{hon} \leftarrow [n] \setminus \mathsf{cor}$ and must reveal the secret keys of the corrupt parties to $\mathcal{A}$, which $\mathcal{B}$ does in the next step.

Simulating KeyGen. $\mathcal{B}$ simulates the key generation algorithm (Fig. 5) using its AOMDL challenge $(Y_0, \ldots, Y_t)$ as follows. For all $i \in [n]$, $\mathcal{B}$ sets the public key share as

$$\tilde{X}_i = Y_0 Y_1^i \cdots Y_t^{i^t}$$

which is implicitly equal to $g^{f(i)}$. The joint public key is $\tilde{X} = g^{f(0)} = Y_0$ with corresponding secret key $x = y_0$. $\mathcal{B}$ obtains the initial corrupt secret key shares by querying $x_j = f(j) \leftarrow \mathcal{O}^{\mathsf{dl}}(\tilde{X}_j)$ (with representation $(1, j, \ldots, j^t)$) for all $j \in \mathsf{cor}$. $\mathcal{B}$ runs $\mathcal{A}^{\mathcal{O}^{\mathsf{Sign}, \mathsf{Sign}', \mathsf{Sign}'', \mathsf{Corrupt}}}(\tilde{X}, \{\tilde{X}_i\}_{i \in [n]}, \{x_j\}_{j \in \mathsf{cor}})$.

Simulating Random Oracle Queries. $\mathcal{B}$ handles $\mathcal{A}$'s random oracle queries throughout the protocol by lazy sampling, as follows.

$\underline{\mathsf{H}_{\mathsf{cm}}}$: When $\mathcal{A}$ queries H_{cm} on $(m, \mathcal{S}, R)$, $\mathcal{B}$ checks whether $(m, \mathcal{S}, R, \mathsf{cm}) \in \mathsf{Q}_{\mathsf{cm}}$ and, if so, returns cm. Else, $\mathcal{B}$ samples $\mathsf{cm} \leftarrow\!\!\$\, \mathbb{Z}_p$, appends $(m, \mathcal{S}, R, \mathsf{cm})$ to Q_{cm}, and returns cm.

$\underline{\mathsf{H}_{\mathsf{sig}}}$: When $\mathcal{A}$ queries $\mathsf{H}_{\mathsf{sig}}$ on (X, m, R), $\mathcal{B}$ checks whether $(X, m, R, c) \in \mathsf{Q}_{\mathsf{sig}}$ and, if so, returns c. Else, $\mathcal{B}$ samples $c \leftarrow\!\!\$\, \mathbb{Z}_p$, appends (X, m, R, c) to $\mathsf{Q}_{\mathsf{sig}}$, and returns c.

Simulating Sparkle Signing. $\mathcal{B}$ handles $\mathcal{A}$'s signing queries as follows.

Round 1 ($\mathcal{O}^{\mathsf{Sign}}$): In the first round of signing for session ssid, each party i in the signing set $\mathcal{S}$ sends a commitment cm_i. When $\mathcal{A}$ queries $\mathcal{O}^{\mathsf{Sign}}$ on $(k, \mathsf{ssid}, m, \mathcal{S})$ for honest $k \in \mathsf{hon}$, $\mathcal{B}$ samples $\mathsf{cm}_k \leftarrow\!\!\$\, \mathbb{Z}_p$, appends $(m, \mathcal{S}, \cdot, \mathsf{cm}_k)$ to Q_{cm}, sets $\mathsf{st}_{k,\mathsf{ssid}} \leftarrow (\mathsf{cm}_k, \cdot, \cdot, m, \mathcal{S})$, and returns cm_k.

Round 2 ($\mathcal{O}^{\mathsf{Sign}'}$): In the second round of signing for session ssid, each party i in the signing set $\mathcal{S}$ takes as input the set of commitments $\{\mathsf{cm}_i\}_{i \in \mathcal{S}}$ and reveals its nonce R_i such that $\mathsf{cm}_i = \mathsf{H}_{\mathsf{cm}}(m, \mathcal{S}, R_i)$. When $\mathcal{A}$ queries $\mathcal{O}^{\mathsf{Sign}'}$ on $(k, \mathsf{ssid}, m, \mathcal{S}, \{\mathsf{cm}_i\}_{i \in \mathcal{S}})$ for $k \in \mathsf{hon}$, then for all $j \in \mathcal{S} \cap \mathsf{cor}$, $\mathcal{B}$ looks up cm_j for a record $(m, \mathcal{S}, R_j, \mathsf{cm}_j) \in \mathsf{Q}_{\mathsf{cm}}$.

If there exists $j' \in \mathcal{S}$ such that $(m', \mathcal{S}', \cdot, \mathsf{cm}_{j'}) \in \mathsf{Q}_{\mathsf{cm}}$ and $(m', \mathcal{S}') \neq (m, \mathcal{S})$, or if there exists some $j' \in \mathcal{S}$ for which no record $(m, \mathcal{S}, \cdot, \mathsf{cm}_{j'}) \in \mathsf{Q}_{\mathsf{cm}}$ exists, then $\mathcal{B}$ chooses $R_k \leftarrow\!\!\$\, g^{r_k}$ randomly, updates $\mathsf{st}_{k,\mathsf{ssid}} \leftarrow (\mathsf{cm}_k, R_k, r_k, m, \mathcal{S})$, programs $\mathsf{cm}_k \leftarrow \mathsf{H}_{\mathsf{cm}}(m, \mathcal{S}, R_k)$, and returns R_k.

Else if this is the first query in the signing session, $\mathcal{B}$ samples $c \leftarrow\!\!\$\, \mathbb{Z}_p$. For all $k \in \mathsf{hon}$, $\mathcal{B}$ samples $z_k \leftarrow\!\!\$\, \mathbb{Z}_p$, computes $R_k \leftarrow g^{z_k} \tilde{X}_k^{-c\lambda_k}$ (λ_k is the Lagrange coefficient for party k in the set $\mathcal{S}$), and programs $\mathsf{cm}_k \leftarrow \mathsf{H}_{\mathsf{cm}}(m, \mathcal{S}, R_k)$ (updating $(m, \mathcal{S}, R_k, \mathsf{cm}_k) \in \mathsf{Q}_{\mathsf{cm}}$). Then $\mathcal{B}$ computes $\tilde{R} = \prod_{i \in \mathcal{S}} R_i$ and programs $c \leftarrow \mathsf{H}_{\mathsf{sig}}(\tilde{X}, m, \tilde{R})$. (However, if $\mathcal{A}$ has already queried $\mathsf{H}_{\mathsf{sig}}$ on $(\tilde{X}, m, \tilde{R})$, then $\mathcal{B}$ aborts.)

Finally, $\mathcal{B}$ sets $\mathsf{st}_{k,\mathsf{ssid}} \leftarrow (\mathsf{cm}_k, R_k, z_k, c\lambda_k, m, \mathcal{S}, \{\mathsf{cm}_i\}_{i \in \mathcal{S}})$, and returns R_k to $\mathcal{A}$. If this is not the first query, $\mathcal{B}$ looks up $\mathsf{st}_{k,\mathsf{ssid}} \leftarrow (\mathsf{cm}_k, R_k, z_k, c\lambda_k, m, \mathcal{S}, \{\mathsf{cm}_i\}_{i \in \mathcal{S}})$ and returns R_k.

Round 3 ($\mathcal{O}^{\mathsf{Sign}''}$): In the third round of signing for session ssid, each party i in the signing set $\mathcal{S}$ produces a partial signature on the message m. When $\mathcal{A}$ queries $\mathcal{O}^{\mathsf{Sign}''}$ on $(k, \mathsf{ssid}, \{R_i\}_{i \in \mathcal{S}})$ for $k \in \mathsf{hon}$, $\mathcal{B}$ looks up $\mathsf{st}_{k,\mathsf{ssid}} \leftarrow (\mathsf{cm}_k, R_k, z_k, c\lambda_k, m, \mathcal{S}, \{\mathsf{cm}_i\}_{i \in \mathcal{S}})$, checks whether $\mathsf{cm}_i = \mathsf{H}_{\mathsf{cm}}(m, \mathcal{S}, R_i)$ for all $i \in \mathcal{S}$ and returns $\perp$ if not. If $\mathsf{cm}_i = \mathsf{H}_{\mathsf{cm}}(m, \mathcal{S}, R_i)$ but $\mathcal{A}$ never queried H_{cm} on input $(m, \mathcal{S}, R_i)$, $\mathcal{B}$ aborts. Else, $\mathcal{B}$ sets $\mathsf{st}_{k,\mathsf{ssid}} \leftarrow ()$, and returns z_k.

Simulating Corruption Queries ($\mathcal{O}^{\mathsf{Corrupt}}$): $\mathcal{A}$ may at any time corrupt an honest party k by querying $\mathcal{O}^{\mathsf{Corrupt}}(k)$. Upon receiving a corruption query, $\mathcal{B}$ first checks that $k \in \mathsf{hon}$, returning $\perp$ if not. Otherwise, $\mathcal{B}$ queries its DL oracle $\mathcal{O}^{\mathsf{dl}}$ on $\tilde{X}_k = g^{f(k)}$ (with representation $(1, k, \ldots, k^t)$) to obtain the secret key $x_k = f(k)$. Then, for each $\mathsf{st}_{k,\mathsf{ssid}}$, $\mathcal{B}$ does the following:

- If $\mathsf{st}_{k,\mathsf{ssid}} = (\mathsf{cm}_k, \cdot, \cdot, m, \mathcal{S})$, then $\mathcal{B}$ chooses $r_k \leftarrow_{\$} \mathbb{Z}_p$, sets $R_k \leftarrow g^{r_k}$, and programs $\mathsf{cm}_k \leftarrow \mathsf{H}_{\mathsf{cm}}(m, \mathcal{S}, R_k)$. It then updates $\mathsf{st}_{k,\mathsf{ssid}} \leftarrow (\mathsf{cm}_k, R_k, r_k, m, \mathcal{S})$.
- If $\mathsf{st}_{k,\mathsf{ssid}} = (\mathsf{cm}_k, R_k, z_k, c\lambda_k, m, \mathcal{S}, \{\mathsf{cm}_i\}_{i\in\mathcal{S}})$, then $\mathcal{B}$ computes $r_k = z_k - c\lambda_k x_k$ (now that it knows x_k) and updates $\mathsf{st}_{k,\mathsf{ssid}} \leftarrow (\mathsf{cm}_k, R_k, r_k, m, \mathcal{S}, \{\mathsf{cm}_i\}_{i\in\mathcal{S}})$.
- If $\mathsf{st}_{k,\mathsf{ssid}} = ()$, then return $()$. This case occurs if signing session ssid has already been completed (i.e., a valid signature was issued).

Finally, $\mathcal{B}$ sets $\mathsf{hon} \leftarrow \mathsf{hon} \setminus \{k\}$ and $\mathsf{cor} \leftarrow \mathsf{cor} \cup \{k\}$ and returns $x_k, \{\mathsf{st}_{k,\ell}\}_{\ell\in[\mathsf{ssid}]}$ to $\mathcal{A}$.

Output. At the end of the game, $\mathcal{A}$ produces a forgery $(m^*, \sigma^*) = (m^*, (\tilde{R}^*, z^*))$ and wins if $\mathsf{Verify}(\tilde{X}, m^*, \sigma^*) = 1$, $m^* \notin Q$, and $|\mathsf{cor}| \leq t$.

Extracting an AOMDL Solution. $\mathcal{B}$'s simulation of key generation and signing is perfect, and $\mathcal{B}$ aborts with negligible probability. Indeed, $\mathcal{B}$ aborts in Round 3 if $\mathcal{A}$ reveals R_j such that $\mathsf{cm}_j = \mathsf{H}_{\mathsf{cm}}(m, \mathcal{S}, R_j)$ but $\mathcal{A}$ never queried H_{cm} on $(m, \mathcal{S}, R_j)$. This requires $\mathcal{A}$ to have guessed cm_j ahead of time, which occurs with negligible probability $1/p$.

$\mathcal{B}_2$ also aborts in Round 2 if $\mathcal{A}$ had previously queried $\mathsf{H}_{\mathsf{sig}}$ on $(\tilde{X}, m, \tilde{R})$. In that case, $\mathcal{B}$ had returned a random $c \leftarrow \mathsf{H}_{\mathsf{sig}}(\tilde{X}, m, \tilde{R})$, so the reduction fails. However, this implies that $\mathcal{A}$ guessed R_k before $\mathcal{B}$ revealed it, which occurs with negligible probability $1/p$.

It remains to show that $\mathcal{B}$ can extract an AOMDL solution from $\mathcal{A}$'s output. Assume without loss of generality that $\mathcal{A}$ makes t corruptions over the course of the protocol. (If not, $\mathcal{B}$ can corrupt the remaining number at the end, by querying its DL oracle until it reaches t secret keys.) Recall that $\mathcal{B}$ set $\tilde{X}_i = Y_0 Y_1^i \cdots Y_t^{i^t}$ and made t DL queries $g^{x_{i_1}}, \ldots, g^{x_{i_t}}$:

$$g^{x_{i_1}} = Y_0 Y_1^{i_1} \cdots Y_t^{{i_1}^t}$$

$$\vdots$$

$$g^{x_{i_t}} = Y_0 Y_1^{i_t} \cdots Y_t^{{i_t}^t}$$

Recall also that $\tilde{X} = Y_0$. This forms the following system of linear equations:

$$x = y_0$$

$$x_{i_1} = y_0 + i_1 y_1 \cdots + {i_1}^t y_t$$

$$\vdots$$

$$x_{i_t} = y_0 + i_t y_1 \cdots + {i_t}^t y_t$$

Equivalently,

$$\begin{pmatrix} x \\ x_{i_1} \\ \vdots \\ x_{i_t} \end{pmatrix} = \begin{pmatrix} 1 & 0 & \cdots & 0 \\ 1 & i_1 & \cdots & {i_1}^t \\ \vdots & \vdots & \ddots & \vdots \\ 1 & i_t & \cdots & {i_t}^t \end{pmatrix} \begin{pmatrix} y_0 \\ y_1 \\ \vdots \\ y_t \end{pmatrix} \tag{2}$$

$\mathcal{B}$ knows all of the values $\{x_j\}_{j\in\mathsf{cor}} = \{x_{i_1},\ldots,x_{i_t}\}$ on the left-hand side, but not x. However, $\mathcal{B}$ can compute x as follows.

Extracting the Discrete Logarithm of $\tilde{X} = Y_0$. $\mathcal{A}$'s forgery verifies as:

$$\tilde{R}^* = g^{z^*}\tilde{X}^{-c^*} \tag{3}$$

where $c^* = \mathsf{H}_{\mathsf{sig}}(\tilde{X}, m^*, \tilde{R}^*)$. On the other hand, when $\mathcal{A}$ made its query $\mathsf{H}_{\mathsf{sig}}(\tilde{X}, m^*, \tilde{R}^*)$, it provided a representation of $\tilde{R}^*$ in terms of all of the group elements it had seen so far, namely $(g, \tilde{X}, \tilde{X}_1, \ldots, \tilde{X}_n, \{R_{i,1},\ldots,R_{i,n}\}_{i\in[q_S]})$, where $\{R_{i,k}\}_{i\in[q_S]}$ are the honest nonces returned by the Sign' oracle over the q_S signing queries that $\mathcal{A}$ makes. We assume without loss of generality that $\mathcal{A}$ completes every signing session. (Otherwise, $\mathcal{B}$ can perform any unmet Sign' and Sign'' queries itself.) Thus, $\mathcal{A}$ provided $(\gamma^*, \xi^*, \xi_1^*, \ldots, \xi_n^*, \{\rho_{i,1}^*, \ldots, \rho_{i,n}^*\}_{i\in[q_S]})$ such that:

$$\tilde{R}^* = g^{\gamma^*}\tilde{X}^{\xi^*}\tilde{X}_1^{\xi_1^*}\cdots\tilde{X}_n^{\xi_n^*}\prod_{i=1}^{q_S} R_{i,1}^{\rho_{i,1}^*}\cdots R_{i,n}^{\rho_{i,n}^*}$$

Each $R_{i,k}$ verifies as $R_{i,k} = g^{z_{i,k}}\tilde{X}_k^{-c_i\lambda_{i,k}}$, where $c_i = \mathsf{H}_{\mathsf{sig}}(\tilde{X}, m_i, \tilde{R}_i)$. Thus,

$$\tilde{R}^* = g^{\gamma^*}\tilde{X}^{\xi^*}\tilde{X}_1^{\xi_1^*}\cdots\tilde{X}_n^{\xi_n^*}\prod_{i=1}^{q_S}(g^{z_{i,1}}\tilde{X}_1^{-c_i\lambda_{i,1}})^{\rho_{i,1}^*}\cdots(g^{z_{i,n}}\tilde{X}_n^{-c_i\lambda_{i,n}})^{\rho_{i,n}^*}$$

Equating this with Eq. (3), we have:

$$g^{z^*}\tilde{X}^{-c^*} = g^{\gamma^*}\tilde{X}^{\xi^*}\tilde{X}_1^{\xi_1^*}\cdots\tilde{X}_n^{\xi_n^*}\prod_{i=1}^{q_S}(g^{z_{i,1}}\tilde{X}_1^{-c_i\lambda_{i,1}})^{\rho_{i,1}^*}\cdots(g^{z_{i,n}}\tilde{X}_n^{-c_i\lambda_{i,n}})^{\rho_{i,n}^*}$$

Rearranging, we have:

$$g^{z^*}g^{-\gamma^*}\prod_{i=1}^{q_S} g^{-z_{i,1}\rho_{i,1}^*}\cdots g^{-z_{i,n}\rho_{i,n}^*}$$
$$= \tilde{X}^{c^*}\tilde{X}^{\xi^*}\tilde{X}_1^{\xi_1^*}\cdots\tilde{X}_n^{\xi_n^*}\prod_{i=1}^{q_S}(\tilde{X}_1^{-c_i\lambda_{i,1}})^{\rho_{i,1}^*}\cdots(\tilde{X}_n^{-c_i\lambda_{i,n}})^{\rho_{i,n}^*} \tag{4}$$

Let $\eta^* = z^* - \gamma^* - \sum_{i=1}^{q_S}(z_{i,1}\rho_{i,1}^* + \cdots + z_{i,n}\rho_{i,n}^*)$ and $\zeta_k^* = \xi_k^* - \sum_{i=1}^{q_S} c_i\lambda_{i,k}\rho_{i,k}^*$ for all $k \in [n]$. Then Eq. (4) can be rewritten as:

$$g^{\eta^*} = \tilde{X}^{c^*+\xi^*}\tilde{X}_1^{\zeta_1^*}\cdots\tilde{X}_n^{\zeta_n^*} \tag{5}$$

Recall that $\tilde{X}_i = \tilde{X}Y_1^iY_2^{i^2}\cdots Y_t^{i^t}$ for all $i \in [n]$ and that $Y_i = \tilde{X}^{L'_{0,i}}\prod_{j\in\mathsf{cor}} g^{x_jL'_{j,i}}$ for all $i \in [t]$. Thus,

$$\tilde{X}_k = \tilde{X}\prod_{i=1}^{t}\left(\tilde{X}^{L'_{0,i}}\prod_{j\in\mathsf{cor}} g^{x_jL'_{j,i}}\right)^{k^i}$$

Let $\mu_k^* = 1 + \sum_{i=1}^t L'_{0,i} k^i$ and $\nu_k^* = \sum_{i=1}^t \left(\sum_{j \in \mathsf{cor}} x_j L'_{j,i} \right) k^i$. Then $\tilde{X}_k$ can be rewritten as:

$$\tilde{X}_k = \tilde{X}^{\mu_k^*} g^{\nu_k^*}$$

and Eq. (5) can be rewritten as:

$$g^{\eta^*} = \tilde{X}^{c^* + \xi^*} \prod_{k=1}^{n} \tilde{X}^{\mu_k^*} g^{\nu_k^*}$$

Rearranging, we have:

$$g^{\eta^* - \sum_{k=1}^n \nu_k^*} = \tilde{X}^{c^* + \xi^* + \sum_{k=1}^n \mu_k^*}$$

and

$$\dot{x} = \frac{\eta^* - \sum_{k=1}^n \nu_k^*}{c^* + \xi^* + \sum_{k=1}^n \mu_k^*}$$

$\mathcal{A}$ fixed $\tilde{R}^*$ and thus $\eta^*, \{\nu_i^*\}_{i \in [n]}, \xi^*, \{\mu_i^*\}_{i \in [n]}$ as it queried $\mathsf{H}_{\mathsf{sig}}(\tilde{X}, m^*, \tilde{R}^*)$ to receive random c^*. Thus, the denominator is nonzero with overwhelming probability and $\mathcal{B}$ can solve for x.

The matrix

$$V = \begin{pmatrix} 1 & 0 & \cdots & 0 \\ 1 & i_1 & \cdots & i_1{}^t \\ \vdots & \vdots & \ddots & \vdots \\ 1 & i_t & \cdots & i_t{}^t \end{pmatrix}$$

in Eq. 2 is a Vandermonde matrix and is therefore invertible. Thus, $\mathcal{B}$ can solve for $(y_0, y_1, \ldots, y_t)$ and win the $t+1$-aomdl game.

Acknowledgements. Elizabeth Crites was supported by Input Output through their funding of the Blockchain Technology Lab at the University of Edinburgh.

References

1. Abdalla, M., Barbosa, M., Katz, J., Loss, J., Xu, J.: Algebraic adversaries in the universal composability framework. In: Tibouchi, M., Wang, H. (eds.) ASIACRYPT 2021. LNCS, vol. 13092, pp. 311–341. Springer, Cham (2021). https://doi.org/10.1007/978-3-030-92078-4_11
2. Almansa, J.F., Damgård, I., Nielsen, J.B.: Simplified Threshold RSA with Adaptive and Proactive Security. In: Vaudenay, S. (ed.) EUROCRYPT 2006. LNCS, vol. 4004, pp. 593–611. Springer, Heidelberg (2006). https://doi.org/10.1007/11761679_35
3. Bacho, R., Loss, J.: On the adaptive security of the threshold BLS signature scheme. In: IACR Cryptol. ePrint Arch. CCS 2022 (2022), 534 (2022). https://doi.org/10.1145/3548606.3560656

4. Bauer, B., Fuchsbauer, G., Plouviez, A.: The one-more discrete logarithm assumption in the generic group model. In: Tibouchi, M., Wang, H. (eds.) ASIACRYPT 2021. LNCS, vol. 13093, pp. 587–617. Springer, Cham (2021). https://doi.org/10.1007/978-3-030-92068-5_20
5. Bellare, M., Crites, E.C., Komlo, C., Maller, M., Tessaro, S., Zhu, C.: Better than advertised security for non-interactive threshold signatures. In: Dodis, Y., Shrimpton, T. (eds.) CRYPTO 2022, Santa Barbara, CA, USA, August 15–18, 2022. 13510. LNCS. pp. 517–550. Springer, Cham (2022). https://doi.org/10.1007/978-3-031-15985-5_18
6. Bellare, M., Dai, W., Li, L.: The local forking lemma and its application to deterministic encryption. In: Galbraith, S.D., Moriai, S. (eds.) ASIACRYPT 2019. LNCS, vol. 11923, pp. 607–636. Springer, Cham (2019). https://doi.org/10.1007/978-3-030-34618-8_21
7. Bellare, M., Namprempre, C., Pointcheval, D., Semanko, M.: The one-more-RSA-inversion problems and the security of chaum's blind signature scheme. J. Cryptology **16**(3), 185–215 (2003). https://doi.org/10.1007/s00145-002-0120-1
8. Benhamouda, F., Lepoint, T., Loss, J., Orrù, M., Raykova, M.: On the (in)security of ROS. In: Canteaut, A., Standaert, F.-X. (eds.) EUROCRYPT 2021. LNCS, vol. 12696, pp. 33–53. Springer, Cham (2021). https://doi.org/10.1007/978-3-030-77870-5_2
9. Boldyreva, A.: Threshold signatures, multisignatures and blind signatures based on the Gap-Diffie-Hellman-group signature scheme. In: Desmedt, Y.G. (ed.) PKC 2003. LNCS, vol. 2567, pp. 31–46. Springer, Heidelberg (2003). https://doi.org/10.1007/3-540-36288-6_3
10. Boneh, D., Drijvers, M., Neven, G.: Compact Multi-signatures for Smaller Blockchains. In: Peyrin, T., Galbraith, S. (eds.) ASIACRYPT 2018. LNCS, vol. 11273, pp. 435–464. Springer, Cham (2018). https://doi.org/10.1007/978-3-030-03329-3_15
11. Brandão, L., Davidson, M.: Notes on threshold EdDSA/Schnorr signatures (2022). https://nvlpubs.nist.gov/nistpubs/ir/2022/NIST.IR.8214B.ipd.pdf
12. Brandão, L., Peralta, R.: NIST first call for multi-party threshold schemes (2023). https://nvlpubs.nist.gov/nistpubs/ir/2023/NIST.IR.8214C.ipd.pdf
13. Canetti, R.: Universally composable security: a new paradigm for cryptographic protocols. In: FOCS, pp. 136–345, 14–17 October 2001, Las Vegas, Nevada, USA. IEEE Computer Society (2001). https://doi.org/10.1109/SFCS.2001.959888
14. Canetti, R., Feige, U., Goldreich, O., Naor. M.: Adaptively secure multi-party computation. In: Miller, G.L. (ed.) STOC 1996, Philadelphia, Pennsylvania, USA, 22–24 May 1996, pp. 639–648. ACM (1996). https://doi.org/10.1145/237814.238015
15. Canetti, R., Gennaro, R., Goldfeder, S., Makriyannis, N., Peled. U.: UC Non-interactive, proactive, threshold ECDSA with identifiable aborts. In: IACR Cryptol. ePrint Arch, CCS 2020 (2021). https://doi.org/10.1145/3372297.3423367
16. Canetti, R., Gennaro, R., Jarecki, S., Krawczyk, H., Rabin, T.: Adaptive security for threshold cryptosystems. In: Wiener, M. (ed.) CRYPTO 1999. LNCS, vol. 1666, pp. 98–116. Springer, Heidelberg (1999). https://doi.org/10.1007/3-540-48405-1_7
17. Connolly, D., Komlo, C., Goldberg, I., Wood, C.: Two-round threshold Schnorr signatures with FROST. (2022). https://datatracker.ietf.org/doc/draft-irtf-cfrg-frost/
18. Crites, E., Komlo, C., Maller, M.: Fully adaptive Schnorr threshold signatures. cryptology ePrint Archive, Paper 2023/445. (2023). https://eprint.iacr.org/2023/445

19. Drijvers, M., et al.: On the security of two-round multi-signatures. In: SP 2019, San Francisco, CA, USA, 19–23 May 2019. pp. 1084–1101. IEEE (2019). https://doi.org/10.1109/SP.2019.00050
20. Edgington, B.: Upgrading Ethereum (2023). https://eth2book.info/bellatrix/part2/building_blocks/randomness/
21. Fiat, A., Shamir, A.: How To prove yourself: practical solutions to identification and signature problems. In: Odlyzko, A.M. (ed.) CRYPTO 1986. LNCS, vol. 263, pp. 186–194. Springer, Heidelberg (1987). https://doi.org/10.1007/3-540-47721-7_12
22. Fischlin, M.: Communication-efficient non-interactive proofs of knowledge with online extractors. In: Shoup, V. (ed.) CRYPTO 2005. LNCS, vol. 3621, pp. 152–168. Springer, Heidelberg (2005). https://doi.org/10.1007/11535218_10
23. Fuchsbauer, G., Kiltz, E., Loss, J.: The algebraic group model and its applications. In: Shacham, H., Boldyreva, A. (eds.) CRYPTO 2018. LNCS, vol. 10992, pp. 33–62. Springer, Cham (2018). https://doi.org/10.1007/978-3-319-96881-0_2
24. Gennaro, R., Goldfeder, S.: Fast multiparty threshold ECDSA with fast trustless setup. In: Lie, D., Mannan, M., Backes, M., Wang, X. (eds.) CCS 2018, Toronto, ON, Canada, 15–19 October 2018, pp. 1179–1194. ACM (2018). https://doi.org/10.1145/3243734.3243859
25. Gennaro, R., Jarecki, S., Krawczyk, H., Rabin, T.: Robust threshold DSS signatures. In: Inf. Comput. 164(1), 54–84 (2001). https://doi.org/10.1006/inco.2000.2881
26. Gennaro, R., Jarecki, S., Krawczyk, H., Rabin, T.: Secure applications of pedersen's distributed key generation protocol. In: Joye, M. (ed.) CT-RSA 2003. LNCS, vol. 2612, pp. 373–390. Springer, Heidelberg (2003). https://doi.org/10.1007/3-540-36563-X_26
27. Gennaro, R., Jarecki, S., Krawczyk, H., Rabin, T.: Secure distributed key generation for discrete-log based cryptosystems. J. Cryptol. **20**(1), 51–83 (2007). https://doi.org/10.1007/s00145-006-0347-3
28. Gennaro, R., Rabin, T., Jarecki, S., Krawczyk, H.: Robust and efficient sharing of RSA Functions. J. Cryptol. **20**(3), 393 (2007). https://doi.org/10.1007/s00145-007-0201-2
29. Gentry, C., Wichs, D.: Separating succinct non-interactive arguments from all falsifiable assumptions. In: Fortnow, L., Vadhan. S.P. (eds.) STOC 2011, San Jose, CA, USA, 6–8 June 2011, pp. 99–108. ACM (2011). https://doi.org/10.1145/1993636.1993651
30. Goldwasser, S., Micali, S., Rivest, R.L.: A digital signature scheme secure against adaptive chosen-message attacks. SIAM J. Comput. **17**(2), 281–308 (1988). https://doi.org/10.1137/0217017
31. Jarecki, S., Lysyanskaya, A.: Adaptively secure threshold cryptography: introducing concurrency, removing erasures. In: Preneel, B. (ed.) EUROCRYPT 2000. LNCS, vol. 1807, pp. 221–242. Springer, Heidelberg (2000). https://doi.org/10.1007/3-540-45539-6_16
32. Koblitz, N., Menezes, A.: Another look at non-standard discrete log and Diffie-Hellman problems. In: J. Math. Cryptol. **2**(4), 311–326 (2008). https://doi.org/10.1515/JMC.2008.014
33. Komlo, C., Goldberg, I.: FROST: flexible round-optimized schnorr threshold signatures. In: Dunkelman, O., Jacobson, Jr., M.J., O'Flynn, C. (eds.) SAC 2020. LNCS, vol. 12804, pp. 34–65. Springer, Cham (2021). https://doi.org/10.1007/978-3-030-81652-0_2

34. Libert, B., Joye, M., Yung, M.: Born and raised distributively: fully distributed non-interactive adaptively-secure threshold signatures with short shares. Theoret. Comput. Sci. **645**, 1–24 (2016). https://doi.org/10.1016/j.tcs.2016.02.031
35. Lindell. Y.: Simple three-round multiparty Schnorr signing with full simulatability. In: IACR Cryptol. ePrint Arch, p. 374 (2022). https://eprint.iacr.org/2022/374
36. Lysyanskaya, A., Peikert, C.: Adaptive security in the threshold setting: from cryptosystems to signature schemes. In: Boyd, C. (ed.) ASIACRYPT 2001. LNCS, vol. 2248, pp. 331–350. Springer, Heidelberg (2001). https://doi.org/10.1007/3-540-45682-1_20
37. Makriyannis, N.: On the Classic Protocol for MPC Schnorr Signatures. Cryptology ePrint Archive, Paper 2022/1332. (2022). https://eprint.iacr.org/2022/1332
38. Maxwell, G., Poelstra, A., Seurin, Y., Wuille, P.: Simple Schnorr multi-signatures with applications to Bitcoin. Des. Codes Cryptogr. **87**(9), 2139–2164 (2019). https://doi.org/10.1007/s10623-019-00608-x. DESI 2019
39. Nick, J., Ruffing, T., Seurin, Y.: MuSig2: Simple Two-Round Schnorr Multi-signatures. In: Malkin, T., Peikert, C. (eds.) CRYPTO 2021. LNCS, vol. 12825, pp. 189–221. Springer, Cham (2021). https://doi.org/10.1007/978-3-030-84242-0_8
40. Nicolosi, A., Krohn, M.N., Dodis, Y., Mazèeres, D.: Proactive two-party signatures for user authentication. In: Proceedings of the Network and Distributed System Security Symposium, NDSS 2003, San Diego, California, USA. The Internet Society, (2003). https://www.ndss-symposium.org/ndss2003/proactive-two-party-signatures-user-authentication/
41. Pointcheval, D., Stern, J.: Security arguments for digital signatures and blind signatures. J. Cryptology **13**(3), 361–396 (2000). https://doi.org/10.1007/s001450010003
42. Schnorr, C.P.: Efficient signature generation by smart cards. J. Cryptology **4**(3), 161–174 (1991). https://doi.org/10.1007/BF00196725
43. Shamir, A.: How to share a secret. Commun. ACM **22**(11), 612–613 (1979). https://doi.org/10.1145/359168.359176
44. Stinson, D.R., Strobl, R.: Provably secure distributed schnorr signatures and a (t, n) threshold scheme for implicit certificates. In: Varadharajan, V., Mu, Y.(eds.) ACISP 2001. LNCS, vol. 2119, pp. 417–434. Springer, Heidelberg (2001). https://doi.org/10.1007/3-540-47719-5

Snowblind: A Threshold Blind Signature in Pairing-Free Groups

Elizabeth Crites[1(✉)], Chelsea Komlo[2,3], Mary Maller[4,5], Stefano Tessaro[6], and Chenzhi Zhu[6]

[1] University of Edinburgh, Edinburgh, UK
ecrites@ed.ac.uk
[2] University of Waterloo, Waterloo, Canada
ckomlo@uwaterloo.ca
[3] Zcash Foundation, McLean, USA
[4] Ethereum Foundation, Zug, Switzerland
mary.maller@ethereum.org
[5] PQShield, Oxford, UK
[6] Paul G. Allen School of Computer Science and Engineering, University of Washington, Seattle, USA
{tessaro,zhucz20}@cs.washington.edu

Abstract. Both threshold and blind signatures have, individually, received a considerable amount of attention. However little is known about their combination, i.e., a threshold signature which is also blind, in that no coalition of signers learns anything about the message being signed or the signature being produced. Several applications of blind signatures (e.g., anonymous tokens) would benefit from distributed signing as a means to increase trust in the service and hence reduce the risks of key compromise. This paper builds the first blind threshold signatures in pairing-free groups. Our main contribution is a construction that transforms an underlying blind non-threshold signature scheme with a suitable structure into a threshold scheme, preserving its blindness. The resulting signing protocol proceeds in three rounds, and produces signatures consisting of one group element and two scalars. The underlying non-threshold blind signature schemes are of independent interest, and improve upon the current state of the art (Tessaro and Zhu, EUROCRYPT '22) with shorter signatures (three elements, instead of four) and simpler proofs of security. All of our schemes are proved secure in the Random Oracle and Algebraic Group Models, assuming the hardness of the discrete logarithm problem.

1 Introduction

Blind signatures [11] allow a *user* to interact with a *signer* to obtain a valid signature on a chosen message. The signer learns nothing about the message being signed, and cannot link any signature back to the interaction that produced it. Blind signatures are a key ingredient in e-cash systems [11,12], and play a major role in a number of recent applications and products in industry, such as privacy-preserving ad-click measurement [29], Apple's iCloud Private Relay [21],

H. Handschuh and A. Lysyanskaya (Eds.): CRYPTO 2023, LNCS 14081, pp. 710–742, 2023.
https://doi.org/10.1007/978-3-031-38557-5_23

Google One's VPN Service [44], and various forms of anonymous tokens [20, 42]. Variants of RSA blind signatures [26] are also covered by an RFC draft [13].

The main aim of this paper is to mitigate the risk of signer's compromise in blind signatures by following the popular approach of distributing the signer's operation across a number of issuers, each holding a share of the secret key, as in threshold signatures [14, 15]. This raises the natural question of how easy it is to implement threshold *blind* signatures, a blind analogue of the classical notion of threshold signatures, which has received significantly less attention. Crucially, unlike standard threshold signatures, the signers learn nothing about the message being signed. Moreover, resulting signatures need to remain unlinkable.

It is possible to combine ideas from [9] to obtain a threshold-blind version of BLS [10], as done explicitly in [43]. BLS signing is non-interactive and therefore, by default, concurrently secure. Other works also give pairing-based schemes [24]. Here, in contrast, we focus on designs based on standard, *pairing-free*, elliptic curves. These are appealing, as highly-verified standard cryptographic libraries (such as NSS and BoringSSL) do not provide support for pairing-friendly curves. RSA signatures [34] are pairing free and non-interactive; however, signature sizes are much larger than those defined over elliptic curves. For example, RSA signatures are 6 times larger than Schnorr signatures at the same security level. Our schemes add only one field element to Schnorr signatures, making them an attractive alternative. Designing pairing-free schemes comes with a number of technical challenges to achieve concurrent security and prevent so-called ROS attacks [8], which have affected both threshold and blind signatures alike.

OUR CONTRIBUTIONS. We develop Snowblind, a construction of threshold blind signatures which compiles a suitable underlying (non-threshold) blind signature scheme into a (blind) threshold signing protocol. The resulting signing protocol proceeds in three rounds between the coordinator and the servers. Our instantiations of Snowblind produce signatures that consist of three group elements, and the underlying signature scheme is marginally more complex than standard Schnorr signatures. The unforgeability of these instantiations is proved in the Algebraic Group Model (AGM) [16], assuming the hardness of the discrete logarithm problem. We also assume random oracles.

These schemes satisfy a strong notion of (statistical) blindness that holds even if *all* servers collude. We also present formal security definitions, generalizing the notions of one-more unforgeability and blindness to the threshold setting.

An important remark here is that while the AGM is undoubtedly undesirable, it has been necessary in all recent constructions of pairing-free blind signatures based on the hardness of DL-related problems [17, 22, 41]. Avoiding its use in the concurrent setting is a well-known and very challenging theoretical question.

IMPROVING BLIND SIGNATURES. Snowblind relies on new, non-threshold, three-move blind signature schemes of independent interest. The technical challenges to build such schemes are captured already by a non-blind *interactive* signing protocol for Schnorr signatures. Here, the signer initially sends $A \leftarrow g^a$ to the user, where $a \leftarrow\!\!\$\ \mathbb{Z}_p$. Subsequently, the user responds with a challenge $c \leftarrow \mathsf{H}_{\mathsf{sig}}(m, A)$, and the signer sends $z = a + c \cdot \mathsf{sk}$, where $\mathsf{sk} \in \mathbb{Z}_p$ is the secret key. In particular, $\mathsf{pk} = g^{\mathsf{sk}}$ is the public key, and (A, z) is a valid Schnorr signature for m.

Benhamouda et al. [8] show that this protocol is completely insecure against a malicious user that interacts *concurrently* with the signer: After obtaining $\ell \geq \log p$ initial values $A_1, \ldots, A_\ell$, one can efficiently compute suitable challenges $c_1, \ldots, c_\ell$ such that their responses yield $\ell + 1$ valid signatures, hence violating *one-more unforgeability*. The attacker achieves this by solving the related ROS problem, for which [8] gives a polynomial-time algorithm.

Tessaro and Zhu [41] recently proposed an approach to mitigate the above attack by having the signer initially send a *pair*

$$A = g^a \ , \ \ B \leftarrow g^b h^y \ ,$$

where $a, b, y \leftarrow\$ \mathbb{Z}_p$. Then, upon receiving the challenge $c \leftarrow \mathsf{H}_{\mathsf{sig}}(m, A, B)$, the signer responds with

$$z \leftarrow a + c \cdot y \cdot \mathsf{sk} \ , \ \ y \ , \ \ b \ .$$

The final signature is (A, z, b, y).

This protocol can easily be made blind. In [41], the user masks the values (A, B, c, b, y, z) using randomness r_1, r_2, α, β as follows:

$$\bar{A} = g^{r_1} A^{\alpha/\beta} \ , \qquad \bar{B} = g^{r_2} B^{\alpha} \ , \qquad \bar{b} = r_2 + \alpha b \ ,$$
$$\bar{c} = c/\beta \ , \qquad \bar{y} = \alpha y \ , \qquad \bar{z} = r_1 + (\alpha/\beta) z \ .$$

The final blinded signature is $(\bar{A}, \bar{z}, \bar{b}, \bar{y})$, which is perfectly blinded by the randomness r_1, r_2, α, β.

The crucial point here is that B is a *perfectly hiding* Pedersen commitment to y, and therefore y can be thought as randomly sampled *after* the challenge c is returned to the signer. The format of the final response z, thanks to this "fresh-looking" random y, compromises the linear structure of interactive Schnorr signing which enables ROS attacks. In [41], this scheme is proved one-more unforgeable in the AGM+ROM assuming the hardness of the discrete logarithm problem, along with the hardness of a variant of the ROS problem, called WFROS. However, in contrast to ROS, the WFROS problem is shown *unconditionally* to be exponentially hard.

In this paper, we improve upon [41] along two orthogonal axes:

- We show that the above signing protocol can produce signatures for a different base scheme which consists of *three* elements (one group element, and two scalars), instead of four. Note that [41] also proposes a variant of their scheme with shorter signatures, relying however on the stronger generic group model [27,38].
- We also propose an alternative approach to incorporating the value y in the signing process, where the signer final response uses $z = a + (c + y^k) \cdot \mathsf{sk}$, where $k \geq 2$ such that the map $y \mapsto y^k$ is a permutation in $\mathbb{Z}_p$. (This happens exactly when $\mathsf{gcd}(p-1, k) = 1$.) An important feature of this approach is that it also offers a significantly simpler proof than that of [41], which in particular merely relies on the hardness of the ROS problem for dimension *one*, which is known to be exponentially hard.

Table 1. Pairing-free blind signatures with concurrent security. All schemes are proved OMUF secure in the AGM+ROM, under the given assumption(s). $\mathbb{G}$ denotes a group element, $\mathbb{Z}_p$ denotes a scalar. κ indicates a κ-bit string, where κ is the security parameter. The ROS assumption is subject to a polynomial-time attack for more than $\log p$ concurrent sessions. The mROS assumption is subject to (lightly) sub-exponential attacks [17]. All schemes, except Abe's, have perfect blindness.

	PK Size	Sig size	Communication	Assumption
Blind Schnorr [17]	$1\ \mathbb{G}$	$1\ \mathbb{G} + 1\ \mathbb{Z}_p$	$1\ \mathbb{G} + 2\ \mathbb{Z}_p$	OMDL+ROS
Clause Blind Schnorr [17]	$1\ \mathbb{G}$	$1\ \mathbb{G} + 1\ \mathbb{Z}_p$	$2\ \mathbb{G} + 4\ \mathbb{Z}_p$	OMDL+mROS
Abe [1,22]	$3\ \mathbb{G}$	$2\ \mathbb{G} + 6\ \mathbb{Z}_p$	$3\ \mathbb{G} + 6\ \mathbb{Z}_p + \kappa$	DL
Tessaro-Zhu [41]	$1\ \mathbb{G}$	$1\ \mathbb{G} + 3\ \mathbb{Z}_p$	$2\ \mathbb{G} + 4\ \mathbb{Z}_p$	DL
This work	$1\ \mathbb{G}$	$1\ \mathbb{G} + 2\ \mathbb{Z}_p$	$2\ \mathbb{G} + 4\ \mathbb{Z}_p$	DL

The resulting schemes are the state-of-the-art with respect to schemes with security based solely on discrete-log related assumptions in pairing-free groups. We discuss related work more in depth in Sect. 1.1 below, and give an efficiency comparison in Table 1.

A THRESHOLD VERSION. Our main technical contribution is a threshold signing protocol for the above blind signature schemes. We assume that there are multiple issuers who each possess secret shares and a single user. Our threshold protocol requires three rounds of interaction. The signing is asynchronous and all interactions are initiated by the user. In particular issuers do not speak directly to each other. If the user goes offline then no signature is produced but there are no other negative consequences. In particular we require that signatures are unforgeable unless the user has queried at least one honest party in the third and final round of interaction.

The Snowblind signature scheme is relatively simple. The final signature is identical to the base signature (1 group element and 2 field elements). The basic idea (which will require some adjustments) is rather simple. First a *threshold* of issuers sends a pair

$$A_i = g^{a_i}\ ,\ \ B_i \leftarrow g^{b_i} h^{y_i}\ ,$$

where $a_i, b_i, y_i \leftarrow\!\!\$\ \mathbb{Z}_p$. Then these first-round messages are aggregated by the user into the product $A = \prod_i A_i$ and $B = \prod_i B_i$. Then, upon receiving the challenge $c \leftarrow \mathsf{H}_{\mathsf{sig}}(m, A, B)$, the issuers would like to directly send

$$z_i \leftarrow a_i + f(c, y) \cdot \mathsf{sk}_i\ ,\ \ y_i\ ,\ \ b_i\ ,$$

where $f(c, y) = c \cdot y$ or $f(c, y) = c + y^k$, depending on which base scheme we pick. However, they do not yet know $b = \sum_i b_i$ or $y = \sum_i y_i$. Thus instead they first reveal all b_i, y_i to the user, who sends b, y back. In the final third round the issuers return the z_i's. This protocol can also be easily made blind by masking the values (A, B, c, z, y, b) in the same way as the base blind scheme.

A few more (minor) adjustments need to be made for the scheme to be proved secure. A first one is concerned with the Pedersen commitments not being online extractable – we will resolve this by including an additional extractable commitment cm_i to y_i, along with B_i. The second is that we will need the involved issuers to agree on the set of involved issuers, their commitments cm_i, and the challenge c, before their reveal their own z_i. This will require using an additional (non-threshold, non-blind) signature scheme.

PROVING SECURITY OF SNOWBLIND. Our key technical challenge is now in proving the one-more unforgeability (OMUF) of the above scheme. In particular, the base blind signature schemes discussed above do not have simple security reductions, and we were reluctant to add additional complexity to these arguments. A better approach is to attempt to reduce the OMUF of the threshold blind signature to the OMUF of the blind signature. Unfortunately this modular approach does not quite work. In particular, the reduction has to query its final-round OMUF oracle in the second round of signing in order to simulate responses. Thus when an adversary responds with $\ell+1$ signatures having made fewer than ℓ queries (over unique sessions) to the final round, the reduction could have made $\ell+1$ queries to its final-round oracle and thus would not output a valid forgery. Preventing the adversary from forging signatures when it only queries the preliminary rounds (i.e. the rounds before the final round) is important in our asynchronous and concurrent model, where we can make no termination guarantees.

Instead, we consider a less round-efficient base blind signature scheme that mimics the structure of our threshold scheme. In this alternative scheme, rather than sending (z, b, y) in the second round, the issuer sends (b, y) but withholds z for now. Then in a third round it reveals z. We prove the OMUF of this scheme in the algebraic group model under the discrete logarithm assumption. Security of the base two-round scheme is implied by the security of this three-round scheme because the user sends no additional information between the second and third rounds. More importantly, we can prove the security of our threshold scheme based on the security of this three-round scheme. In particular the reduction only queries its final-round OMUF oracle when the adversary queries its OMUF oracle in the final round on at least one honest party.

1.1 Related Work

We give a brief overview of the most relevant related works in greater detail.

BLIND SIGNATURES IN PAIRING-FREE GROUPS. There are very efficient blind signature schemes based on pairings (starting from the work of [9], which in turn is based on [10]) and RSA [6,11] which fall outside the scope of this paper.

The space of blind signatures in pairing-free groups is more complex, especially when focusing on schemes that achieve OMUF concurrent security in the context of one-more unforgeability. As explained above, at first glance, Schnorr signatures [35] appear simple to translate into a blind setting. However, a recent algorithm [8] for solving the ROS problem [36] results in a complete break of security for a sufficient number of concurrent sessions (at least $\log p$, where p is the group order), whereas one can expect only sub-exponential security for a smaller number of concurrent sessions. (This has been proved in the AGM [17], where the security of blind Schnorr signatures is reduced to the hardness of ROS, which is sub-exponential for the case necessary to support fewer than $\log p$ sessions.)

Blind Schnorr signatures are also proved [22] to be sequentially OMUF secure in the AGM, although sequential security is too weak to support most applications of blind signatures without introducing significant performance bottlenecks. The situation is similar for a larger class of signatures based on identification schemes, which includes in particular Okamoto-Schnorr blind signatures [28]. For these, however, OMUF security for a bounded number of concurrent sessions (fewer than $\log p$) can be proved without the AGM, although with very poor concrete guarantees, via a complex rewinding argument [19]. Their sequential security follows instead from a simpler use of the Forking Lemma [32]. We note that the AGM is necessary for Schnorr signatures, as opposed to Okamoto-Schnorr, due to the lower bound of Baldimtsi and Lysyanskaya [3].

Table 1 discusses the more limited set of works achieving *concurrent* OMUF security in the pairing-free setting. All of these works rely on security proofs in the AGM+ROM. The first concurrently OMUF secure scheme is due to Abe [1]– its original proof (which did not rely on the AGM) was found to be incorrect, and a proof in the AGM+ROM was only recently given in [22]. This scheme is rather inefficient, and only achieves computational blindness (under the Decisional Diffie-Hellman assumption).[1] Fuchsbauer, Plouviez, and Seurin [17] introduced a new signing protocol for plain Schnorr signatures, called "Clause Blind Schnorr," where the output of the signing protocol is a signature that is valid under plain Schnorr verification. However, their security proof relies on the hardness of a variant of ROS (called mROS) for which sub-exponential attacks exist – instantiating their scheme on a 256-bit curve would only achieve (roughly) 80 bits of security. Finally, Tessaro and Zhu [41] recently proposed the only scheme which achieves concurrent security and perfect blindness, while producing signatures smaller than those of Abe's scheme. They do so by relying on a variant of the ROS problem, called WFROS, for which they prove an unconditional lower bound.

Kastner et al. recently corrected the OMUF security reduction [22] for the Abe-Okamoto partially blind signature scheme [2]. However their techniques do not extend to the concurrent setting.

Concurrently to this work, Fuchsbauer and Wolf [18] present a blind signature scheme that outputs a signature which can be verified with the single-party Schnorr verification algorithm. However, their constructions require zero-knowledge proofs that the challenge – that is itself the output from a hash function – is derived correctly, which requires significant performance overhead and

[1] One motivation for statistical and/or perfect blindness is the looming threat of quantum attacks, which would affect the blindness of current schemes more than they would affect one-more unforgeability, for which the use of quantum-safe assumptions, while important, still remains less critical.

additional complexity. Also concurrently to this work, Barretto and Zanon [4] present blind signatures that are concurrently secure in the random oracle model; however, they rely on a non-black-box adversary. They do not consider the threshold setting.

THRESHOLD SIGNATURES. Most relevant to us, there has been significant work on obtaining efficient threshold signature schemes for Schnorr signatures. For example, FROST [5,23] presents a two-round threshold signature scheme that is concurrently secure. Other concurrently-secure Schnorr threshold signatures exist that trade off efficiency for robustness [40] or a direct reduction to standard assumptions in the random oracle model [25]. However, a naive approach to blinding these schemes can open the door to ROS attacks [8].

Threshold blind signatures have been considered in prior literature, notably in a setting that requires pairings [24]. Our schemes, however, are pairing-free.

THRESHOLD CREDENTIAL ISSUANCE. Coconut [39] is a Threshold Issuance Anonymous Credential (TIAC) system that enables a set of certification authorities to jointly and blindly issue credentials. While the construction is practical, it was presented without a formal security analysis. Rial and Piotrowska [33] proved a modified scheme secure in the UC setting. Both schemes are built upon a threshold variant of Pointcheval-Sanders (PS) signatures [31], which rely on pairings.

2 Preliminaries

NOTATION. Let $\kappa \in \mathbb{N}$ denote the security parameter and 1^κ its unary representation. A function $\nu : \mathbb{N} \to \mathbb{R}$ is called *negligible* if for all $c \in \mathbb{R}, c > 0$, there exists $k_0 \in \mathbb{N}$ such that $|\nu(k)| < \frac{1}{k^c}$ for all $k \in \mathbb{N}, k \geq k_0$. For a non-empty set S, let $x \leftarrow\!\!\$\, S$ denote sampling an element of S uniformly at random and assigning it to x. We use $[n]$ to represent the set $\{1, \ldots, n\}$ and represent vectors as $\vec{a} = (a_1, \ldots, a_n)$. We denote $\mathbb{Z}_p^* = \mathbb{Z}_p \setminus \{0\}$.

Let PPT denote probabilistic polynomial time. Algorithms are randomized unless explicitly noted otherwise. Let $y \leftarrow A(x; \omega)$ denote running algorithm A on input x and randomness ω and assigning its output to y. Let $y \leftarrow\!\!\$\, A(x)$ denote $y \leftarrow A(x; \omega)$ for a uniformly random ω.

Code-based games are used in security definitions [7]. A game $\mathsf{Game}^{\mathsf{sec}}_{\mathcal{A}}(\kappa)$, played with respect to a security notion sec and adversary $\mathcal{A}$, has a MAIN procedure whose output is the output of the game.

GROUP GENERATORS AND DISCRETE LOGS. Throughout this paper, a *group (parameter) generator* GrGen is a polynomial-time algorithm that takes as input a security parameter 1^κ and outputs a group description $\mathcal{G} = (\mathbb{G}, p, g)$ consisting of a group $\mathbb{G}$ of order p, where p is a κ-bit prime, and a generator g of $\mathbb{G}$.

Definition 1 (Discrete Logarithm Assumption (DL)). *The discrete logarithm assumption holds with respect to* GrGen *if for all PPT adversaries* $\mathcal{A}$, *the advantage* $\mathsf{Adv}^{\mathsf{dlog}}_{\mathcal{A},\mathsf{GrGen}}(\kappa) = \Pr[\mathcal{G} \leftarrow\!\!\$\, \mathsf{GrGen}(1^\kappa);\ x \leftarrow\!\!\$\, \mathbb{Z}_p;\ x \leftarrow\!\!\$\, \mathcal{A}(\mathcal{G}, g^x)]$ *is negligible.*

THE ALGEBRAIC GROUP MODEL. We will make use of the algebraic group model (AGM) [16] throughout this paper, which in particular only proves security for *algebraic* adversaries. Somewhat informally, we say that an adversary is *algebraic* if for every group element $Z \in \mathbb{G} = \langle g \rangle$ that it outputs, it is required to output a representation $\vec{a} = (a_0, a_1, a_2, \dots)$ such that $Z = g^{a_0} \prod Y_i^{a_i}$, where $Y_1, Y_2, \dots \in \mathbb{G}$ are group elements that the adversary has seen thus far.

POLYNOMIAL INTERPOLATION. Let $\mathbb{F}$ be a field of size at least t, and let $\mathcal{S} \subseteq \mathbb{F}$ be such that $|\mathcal{S}| = t$. Then, any set of at least t evaluations $(i, P(i))_{i\in\mathcal{S}}$ for a polynomial $P(z) = a_0 + a_1 z + a_2 z^2 + \ldots + a_{t-1}z^{t-1}$ of degree $t-1$ over $\mathbb{F}$ can be interpolated to evaluate the polynomial on any other point $z_0 \in \mathbb{F}$ as $P(z_0) = \sum_{i\in\mathcal{S}} P(k) \cdot L_i(z_0)$, where $L_i(z)$ is the Lagrange coefficient of form

$$L_i(z) = \prod_{j\in\mathcal{S}; j\neq i} \frac{z-j}{i-j}\,. \tag{1}$$

(Here, the set $\mathcal{S}$ is usually implicit in L_i.)

SHAMIR SECRET SHARING. We will employe Shamir's secret sharing scheme [37] in our threshold blind signature construction.

- $\mathsf{Share}(x, n, t) \to \{(1, x_1), \dots, (n, x_n)\}$: Define a polynomial $P(z) = x + a_1 z + a_2 z^2 + \dots + a_{t-1} z^{t-1}$ by sampling $t-1$ random coefficients $a_1, \dots, a_{t-1} \leftarrow_\$ \mathbb{Z}_p$. Output the set of participant shares $\{(i, x_i)\}_{i\in[n]}$, where each $x_i, i \in [n]$, is the evaluation of $P(i)$: $x_i \leftarrow x + \sum_{j\in[t-1]} a_j i^j$.
- $\mathsf{Recover}(t, \{(i, x_i)\}_{i\in\mathcal{S}}) \to x$: The recover algorithm takes as input t shares and returns the original secret. Recover x as follows: $x \leftarrow \sum_{i\in\mathcal{S}} \lambda_i^{\mathcal{S}} x_i$, where the Lagrange coefficient for the set $\mathcal{S}$ is defined by $\lambda_i^{\mathcal{S}} = L_i(0) = \prod_{j\in\mathcal{S}, j\neq i} \frac{j}{j-i}$.

3 Definitions

3.1 Blind Signatures

A **blind signature scheme** BS allows a user to interact with an issuer to obtain a valid signature over a message m unknown to the issuer. Importantly, when later presented with this signature, the issuer cannot link it to any particular signing execution. BS is parameterized by the number of rounds r required to perform the signing protocol. The public parameters par are generated by a trusted party and given as input to all other algorithms. A public/private key pair is generated by running $(\mathsf{pk}, \mathsf{sk}) \leftarrow_\$ \mathsf{BS.KeyGen}()$. To collectively produce a signature, the issuer and user engage in an interactive signing protocol as shown in Eq. 2, wherein the issuer takes as input the secret key sk, but not the message, and the user takes as input the public key pk and the message m. At the end of the signing protocol, the user outputs the blind signature σ, that is valid if $\mathsf{BS.Verify}(\mathsf{pk}, \sigma, m) = 1$.

Definition 2. *A* **blind signature scheme** BS *parameterized by the number of signing rounds r is a tuple of polynomial-time algorithms* $\mathsf{BS} = (\mathsf{BS.Setup}, \mathsf{BS.KeyGen}, \{\mathsf{BS.ISign}_j\}_{j=1}^r, \{\mathsf{BS.USign}_j\}_{j=1}^r, \mathsf{BS.Verify})$, *as follows.*

$\mathsf{BS.Setup}(1^\kappa) \rightarrow \mathsf{par}$: *Accepts as input a security parameter κ and outputs public parameters* par, *which are then implicitly provided as input to all other algorithms.*

$\mathsf{BS.KeyGen}() \rightarrow (\mathsf{pk}, \mathsf{sk})$: *A probabilistic algorithm that generates and outputs a keypair, where* pk *is the public key and* sk *is the secret key.*

The interaction between the user and the issuer to sign a message $m \in \{0,1\}^*$ with respect to pk *is defined by the following experiment:*

$$
\begin{aligned}
&(\mathsf{st}^I, \mathsf{pm}_1^I) \leftarrow \mathsf{BS.ISign}_1(\mathsf{sk})\ ,\ (\mathsf{st}^U, \mathsf{pm}_1^U) \leftarrow \mathsf{BS.USign}_1(\mathsf{pk}, m, \mathsf{pm}_1^I)\\
&(\mathsf{st}^I, \mathsf{pm}_j^I) \leftarrow \mathsf{BS.ISign}_j(\mathsf{st}^I, \mathsf{pm}_{j-1}^U)\ ,\ (\mathsf{st}^U, \mathsf{pm}_j^U) \leftarrow \mathsf{BS.USign}_j(\mathsf{st}^U, \mathsf{pm}_{j-1}^I)\\
&\mathsf{pm}_r^I \leftarrow \mathsf{BS.ISign}_r(\mathsf{st}^I, \mathsf{pm}_{r-1}^U)\ ,\ \bot/\sigma \leftarrow \mathsf{BS.USign}_r(\mathsf{st}^U, \mathsf{pm}_r^I)
\end{aligned} \tag{2}
$$

In the above experiment, st^I *is the internal state of the issuer,* st^U *is the internal state of the user.* pm^I *is a protocol message sent by the issuer, and* pm^U *is a protocol message sent by the user.*

$\mathsf{BS.Verify}(\mathsf{pk}, \sigma, m) \rightarrow \{0,1\}$: *A deterministic algorithm that outputs a bit indicating if the signature is valid with respect to the message and public key.*

A blind signature scheme is *correct* if for every $m \in \{0,1\}^*$ and for $(\mathsf{pk}, \mathsf{sk}) \leftarrow_\$ \mathsf{BS.KeyGen}()$, the experiment in (2) returns σ such that $\mathsf{BS.Verify}(\mathsf{pk}, \sigma, m) = 1$. For security, a blind signature scheme must be *one-more unforgeable* and *blind*, which we describe next.

ONE-MORE UNFORGEABILITY. The standard notion of security for non-blind signature schemes, EUF-CMA security, cannot be applied to the blind setting, as the reduction cannot detect if the signature output by the adversary is a forgery or a valid signature. Instead, one must employ the notion of *one-more unforgeability*. Intuitively, one-more unforgeability requires an adversary that is allowed to query the signing oracle ℓ times to produce $\ell + 1$ valid signatures, guaranteeing that at least one is forged. We consider the setting where ℓ is unbounded and determined dynamically, as opposed to requiring a fixed ℓ.

We show the one-more unforgeability experiment $\mathsf{Game}_{\mathcal{A},\mathsf{BS}}^{\mathrm{omuf}}(\kappa)$ in the full version.

Definition 3 (One More Unforgeability). *Let the advantage of an adversary $\mathcal{A}$ against the one-more unforgeability game* $\mathsf{Game}_{\mathcal{A},\mathsf{BS}}^{\mathrm{omuf}}(\kappa)$ *be as follows:*

$$\mathsf{Adv}_{\mathcal{A},\mathsf{BS}}^{\mathrm{omuf}}(\kappa) = \Pr[\mathsf{Game}_{\mathcal{A},\mathsf{BS}}^{\mathrm{omuf}}(\kappa) = 1]$$

A blind signature scheme BS *is* one-more unforgeable *if for all PPT adversaries $\mathcal{A}$, there exists a negligible function ν such that* $\mathsf{Adv}_{\mathcal{A},\mathsf{BS}}^{\mathrm{omuf}}(\kappa) < \nu(k)$.

Blindness. We employ a similar notion of blindness as in prior literature [17, 41], and rely on a right-or-left indistinguishability-based definition. Intuitively, a signature scheme achieves blindness if the adversary has negligible chance of distinguishing two signatures with respect to two messages of its choosing. Our schemes satisfy the stronger notion of *perfect blindness*, where the adversary's advantage is zero.

We show the blindness experiment $\mathsf{Game}^{\mathrm{blind}}_{\mathcal{A},\mathsf{BS}}(\kappa)$ in the full version.

Definition 4 (Perfect Blindness). *Let the advantage of an adversary* $\mathcal{A}$ *against the blindness game* $\mathsf{Game}^{\mathrm{blind}}_{\mathcal{A},\mathsf{BS}}(\kappa)$ *be as follows:*

$$\mathsf{Adv}^{\mathrm{blind}}_{\mathcal{A},\mathsf{BS}}(\kappa) = |\Pr[\mathsf{Game}^{\mathrm{blind}}_{\mathcal{A},\mathsf{BS}}(\kappa) = 1] - 1/2|$$

A blind signature scheme BS *satisfies* perfect blindness *if for all PPT adversaries* $\mathcal{A}$, $\mathsf{Adv}^{\mathrm{blind}}_{\mathcal{A},\mathsf{BS}}(\kappa) = 0$.

3.2 Threshold Blind Signatures

A threshold blind signature is an interactive signing protocol between a single user and multiple issuers, each with a share of the secret signing key. Similar to blind signatures, a threshold blind signature scheme should satisfy *correctness*, *blindness*, and *one-more unforgeability*. We present formal security definitions, generalizing the notions of one-more unforgeability and blindness from the single-party setting to the threshold setting. Game-based notions of security for threshold blind signatures have been given in prior literature [24], however, our notions explicitly model important details such as concurrency and session management.

A threshold blind signature scheme TB is similarly parameterized by the number of signing rounds r. The public parameters par are generated by a trusted party and given as input to all other algorithms. Key generation is described in a centralized manner with respect to the number of issuers n and threshold t, where public/private key pairs are generated for all n issuers, as well as the joint public key representing all n issuers. To collectively produce a signature, a quorum $\mathcal{S}$ of issuers interact with the user in an interactive signing protocol as defined in Eq. 3, wherein each issuer takes as input its secret key $\mathsf{sk_i}$, but not the message, and the user takes as input the public key pk, the message m, and the signing set $\mathcal{S}$. For a valid signature to be issued, it must be the case that $t \leq \mathcal{S} \leq n$. At the end of the signing protocol, the user outputs the threshold blind signature σ and each issuer learns the set $\mathcal{S}$ of issuers that are involved in the signing protocol. The signature σ on m is valid if $\mathsf{TB.Verify}(\mathsf{pk}, m, \sigma) = 1$.

Definition 5. *A* **threshold blind signature scheme** TB *parameterized by the number of signing rounds* r *is a tuple of polynomial-time algorithms* $\mathsf{TB} = (\mathsf{TB.Setup}, \mathsf{TB.KeyGen}, \{\mathsf{TB.ISign}_j\}_{j=1}^r, \{\mathsf{TB.USign}_j\}_{j=1}^r, \mathsf{TB.Verify})$, *as follows.*

$\mathsf{TB.Setup}(1^\kappa) \to \mathsf{par}$: *Accepts as input a security parameter* κ *and outputs public parameters* par, *which are then implicitly provided as input to all other algorithms.*

$\mathsf{TB.KeyGen}(n,t) \rightarrow (\mathsf{pk}, \{\mathsf{pk}_1,\ldots,\mathsf{pk}_n\}, \{\mathsf{sk}_1,\ldots,\mathsf{sk}_n\}, \mathsf{aux})$: *A probabilistic algorithm that accepts as input the number of signers* n *and the threshold* t*. Outputs the public key* pk *representing the set of all signers, the set* $\{\mathsf{pk}_1,\ldots,\mathsf{pk}_n\}$ *of public keys representing each issuer, the set* $\{\mathsf{sk}_1,\ldots,\mathsf{sk}_n\}$ *of secret keys for each issuer, and additional auxiliary information* aux.

The interaction between the user and a set of issuers $\mathcal{S}, t \leq |\mathcal{S}| \leq n$*, to sign a message* $m \in \{0,1\}^*$ *with respect to* pk *is defined by the following experiment:*

$$
\begin{aligned}
&(\mathsf{st}_\mathsf{i}^I, \mathsf{pm}_{1,\mathsf{i}}^I) \leftarrow \mathsf{TB.ISign}_1(\mathsf{i}, \mathsf{sk}_\mathsf{i}, \mathsf{aux})\ ,\ (\mathsf{st}^U, \mathsf{pm}_1^U) \leftarrow \mathsf{TB.USign}_1(\mathsf{pk}, \mathsf{aux}, m, \mathcal{S}, \{\mathsf{pm}_{1,\mathsf{i}}^I\}_{\mathsf{i}\in\mathcal{S}})\\
&(\mathsf{st}_\mathsf{i}^I, \mathsf{pm}_{j,\mathsf{i}}^I) \leftarrow \mathsf{TB.ISign}_j(\mathsf{i}, \mathsf{st}_\mathsf{i}^I, \mathsf{pm}_{j-1}^U)\ ,\ (\mathsf{st}^U, \mathsf{pm}_j^U) \leftarrow \mathsf{TB.USign}_j(\mathsf{st}^U, \{\mathsf{pm}_{j-1,\mathsf{i}}^I\}_{\mathsf{i}\in\mathcal{S}})\\
&(\mathsf{pm}_{r,\mathsf{i}}^I, \mathcal{S}) \leftarrow \mathsf{TB.ISign}_r(\mathsf{i}, \mathsf{st}_\mathsf{i}^I, \mathsf{pm}_{r-1}^U)\ ,\ \bot/\sigma \leftarrow \mathsf{TB.USign}_r(\mathsf{st}^U, \{\mathsf{pm}_{r,\mathsf{i}}^I\}_{\mathsf{i}\in\mathcal{S}})
\end{aligned} \tag{3}
$$

Note that in the last round, $\mathsf{TB.ISign}_r$ *also outputs* $\mathcal{S}$ *indicating that issuer* i *learns the set of issuers involved in the signing protocol.*

$\mathsf{TB.Verify}(\mathsf{pk}, \sigma, m) \rightarrow \{0,1\}$: *A deterministic algorithm that outputs a bit indicating if the signature is valid with respect to the message and public key.*

A threshold blind signature scheme is *correct* if for all allowable $1 \leq t \leq n$, for all $t \leq \mathcal{S} \leq n$, all messages $m \in \{0,1\}^*$, and for $(\mathsf{pk}, \{\mathsf{pk}_1,\ldots,\mathsf{pk}_n\}, \{\mathsf{sk}_1,\ldots,\mathsf{sk}_n\}, \mathsf{aux}) \leftarrow\!\!\$\ \mathsf{TB.KeyGen}(n,t)$, the experiment in (3) returns σ such that $\mathsf{TB.Verify}(\mathsf{pk}, \sigma, m) = 1$.

Distributed key generation. Our definition considers a centralized key generation algorithm $\mathsf{TB.KeyGen}$ to generate the public key pk and set of shares $\{\mathsf{pk}_i, \mathsf{sk}_i\}_{i\in[n]}$. However, our scheme and proofs can be adapted to use a fully decentralized distributed key generation protocol, such as the Pedersen DKG [30].

One-More Unforgeability. We show the one-more unforgeability game for a threshold blind signature in Fig. 1. Compared to the single-signer notion of unforgeability, the adversary is allowed to participate in the signing protocol in the role of both user and issuer. The adversary is allowed to choose the parameters n and t, as well as the set of honest signers honest and the set of corrupt signers $\mathsf{corrupt}$, not to exceed $t-1$. The environment then performs key generation in a centralized manner with respect to these parameters. The adversary is given as input the public parameters, the joint public key pk, the set of public key shares for each participant $\{\mathsf{pk}_\mathsf{i}\}_{\mathsf{i}\in[n]}$, and the set of secret key shares for the corrupted parties $\{\mathsf{sk}_\mathsf{i}\}_{\mathsf{i}\in\mathsf{corrupt}}$. Additionally, the adversary is given an auxiliary string aux. When playing the role of the user, the adversary can query the signing oracle $\mathcal{O}^{\mathsf{ISign}_k}$ for each round k in the protocol, for any issuer $\mathsf{i} \in \mathsf{honest}$, session identifier sid, and protocol message pm^U of its choosing.

The adversary wins the one-more unforgeability game if it outputs a set of $\ell+1$ valid signatures with respect to the joint public key pk, for messages of its choosing, where ℓ denotes the number of signatures that are legitimately obtained by the adversary. For a particular signing set $\mathcal{S}$ and a session identifier

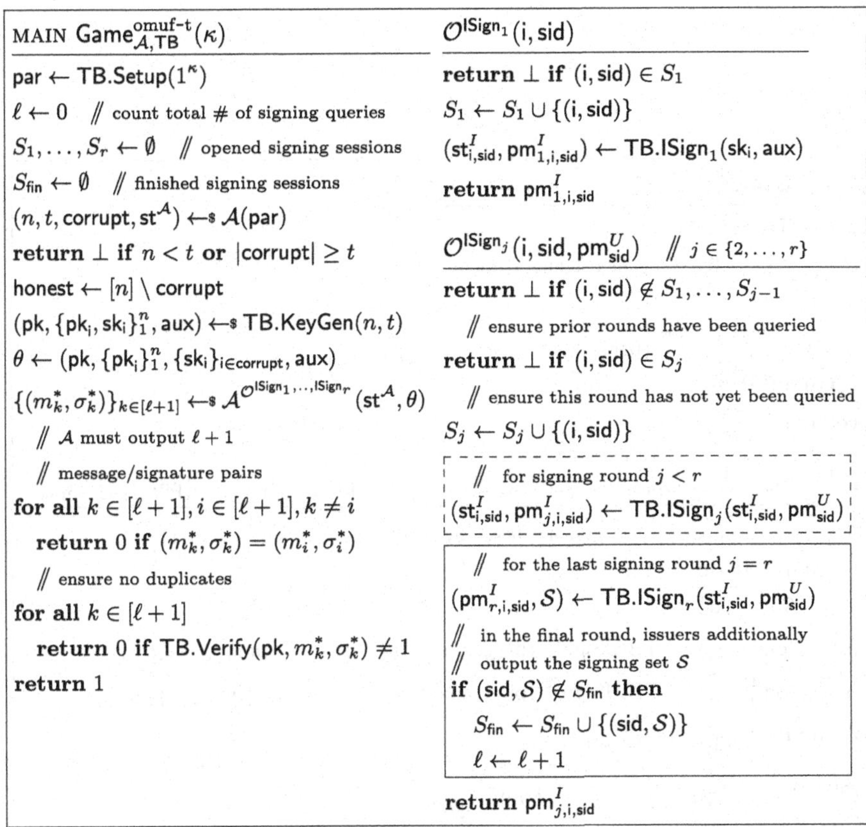

Fig. 1. The one-more unforgeability game for a threshold blind signature scheme. The dashed box appears only for Round $2 \leq j < r$, and the solid box appears only for Round r. The public parameters par are implicitly given as input to all algorithms.

sid, there is at most one signature issued, contingent on the adversary completing the signing session with at least one of the honest issuers.

Definition 6 (One-More Unforgeability). *Let the advantage of an adversary $\mathcal{A}$ against the one-more unforgeability game* $\mathsf{Game}^{\mathrm{omuf\text{-}t}}_{\mathcal{A},\mathsf{TB}}(\kappa)$*, as defined in Fig. 1, be as follows:*

$$\mathsf{Adv}^{\mathrm{omuf\text{-}t}}_{\mathcal{A},\mathsf{TB}}(\kappa) = |\Pr[\mathsf{Game}^{\mathrm{omuf\text{-}t}}_{\mathcal{A},\mathsf{TB}}(\kappa) = 1]|$$

A threshold blind signature scheme TB *satisfies* one-more unforgeability *if for all PPT adversaries $\mathcal{A}$,* $\mathsf{Adv}^{\mathrm{omuf\text{-}t}}_{\mathcal{A},\mathsf{TB}}(\kappa)$ *is negligible.*

Blindness. We now extend the definition of blindness to the threshold setting. The key difference in the threshold blindness experiment is that the user interacts with *multiple* issuers, as opposed to a single issuer. Hence, the adversary

MAIN $\mathsf{Game}^{\text{blind-t}}_{\mathcal{A},\mathsf{TB}}(\kappa)$

$\mathsf{par} \leftarrow \mathsf{TB.Setup}(1^\kappa)$
$S_1, \ldots, S_r \leftarrow \emptyset$ // opened signing sessions
$b \leftarrow_\$ \{0,1\}$
$b' \leftarrow_\$ \mathcal{A}^{\mathcal{O}^{\mathsf{USign}_1,\ldots,\mathsf{USign}_r}}(\mathsf{par})$
return 0 **if** $b' \neq b$
return 1

$\mathcal{O}^{\mathsf{USign}_1}(\mathsf{sid}, \mathsf{pk}_{\mathsf{sid}}, \mathsf{aux}_{\mathsf{sid}}, m_{0,\mathsf{sid}}, m_{1,\mathsf{sid}}, \mathcal{S}_{0,\mathsf{sid}}, \mathcal{S}_{1,\mathsf{sid}}, \{\mathsf{pm}^I_{0,\mathsf{i},\mathsf{sid}}\}_{\mathsf{i}\in\mathcal{S}_{0,\mathsf{sid}}}, \{\mathsf{pm}^I_{1,\mathsf{i},\mathsf{sid}}\}_{\mathsf{i}\in\mathcal{S}_{1,\mathsf{sid}}})$

// $\mathcal{S}_{i,\mathsf{sid}} \subseteq [n]$ is the set of signers chosen by $\mathcal{A}$ for signing session $i \in \{0,1\}$.
return $\bot$ **if** $\mathsf{sid} \in S_1$
$S_1 \leftarrow S_1 \cup \{\mathsf{sid}\}$
$(\mathsf{st}^U_{0,\mathsf{sid}}, \mathsf{pm}^U_{0,1,\mathsf{sid}}) \leftarrow \mathsf{TB.USign}^{(1)}_1(\mathsf{pk}_{\mathsf{sid}}, \mathsf{aux}_{\mathsf{sid}}, m_{b,\mathsf{sid}}, \mathcal{S}_{0,\mathsf{sid}}, \{\mathsf{pm}^I_{0,\mathsf{i},\mathsf{sid}}\}_{\mathsf{i}\in\mathcal{S}_{0,\mathsf{sid}}})$
$(\mathsf{st}^U_{1,\mathsf{sid}}, \mathsf{pm}^U_{1,1,\mathsf{sid}}) \leftarrow \mathsf{TB.USign}^{(2)}_1(\mathsf{pk}_{\mathsf{sid}}, \mathsf{aux}_{\mathsf{sid}}, m_{1-b,\mathsf{sid}}, \mathcal{S}_{1,\mathsf{sid}}, \{\mathsf{pm}^I_{1,\mathsf{i},\mathsf{sid}}\}_{\mathsf{i}\in\mathcal{S}_{1,\mathsf{sid}}})$
return $(\mathsf{pm}^U_{0,1,\mathsf{sid}}, \mathsf{pm}^U_{1,1,\mathsf{sid}})$

$\mathcal{O}^{\mathsf{USign}_j}(\mathsf{sid}, \{\mathsf{pm}^I_{0,\mathsf{i},\mathsf{sid}}\}_{\mathsf{i}\in\mathcal{S}_{0,\mathsf{sid}}}, \{\mathsf{pm}^I_{1,\mathsf{i},\mathsf{sid}}\}_{\mathsf{i}\in\mathcal{S}_{1,\mathsf{sid}}})$ // $j \in \{2,\ldots,r\}$

return $\bot$ **if** $\mathsf{sid} \notin S_1, \ldots, S_{j-1}$ // ensure prior rounds have been queried
return $\bot$ **if** $\mathsf{sid} \in S_j$ // ensure this round has not yet been queried
$S_j \leftarrow S_j \cup \{\mathsf{sid}\}$
$\boxed{\sigma_{b,\mathsf{sid}}}$ $(\mathsf{st}^U_{0,\mathsf{sid}}, \mathsf{pm}^U_{0,j,\mathsf{sid}})$ $\leftarrow \mathsf{TB.USign}^{(1)}_j(\mathsf{st}^U_{0,\mathsf{sid}}, \{\mathsf{pm}^I_{0,\mathsf{i},\mathsf{sid}}\}_{\mathsf{i}\in\mathcal{S}_{0,\mathsf{sid}}})$
$\boxed{\sigma_{1-b,\mathsf{sid}}}$ $(\mathsf{st}^U_{1,\mathsf{sid}}, \mathsf{pm}^U_{1,j,\mathsf{sid}})$ $\leftarrow \mathsf{TB.USign}^{(2)}_j(\mathsf{st}^U_{1,\mathsf{sid}}, \{\mathsf{pm}^I_{1,\mathsf{i},\mathsf{sid}}\}_{\mathsf{i}\in\mathcal{S}_{1,\mathsf{sid}}})$
$\boxed{\textbf{return } (\bot,\bot) \textbf{ if } \sigma_{0,\mathsf{sid}} = \bot \textbf{ or } \sigma_{1,\mathsf{sid}} = \bot}$
return $\boxed{(\sigma_{0,\mathsf{sid}}, \sigma_{1,\mathsf{sid}})}$ $(\mathsf{pm}^U_{0,j,\mathsf{sid}}, \mathsf{pm}^U_{1,j,\mathsf{sid}})$

Fig. 2. The blindness game for a threshold blind signature scheme. The public parameters par are implicitly given as input to all algorithms. Dashed boxes denote Rounds 2 to $r-1$, and solid boxes denote Round r only.

$\mathsf{Setup}(1^\kappa)$	$\mathsf{Sign}(\mathsf{sk}, m)$
$(\mathbb{G}, p, g) \leftarrow\$ \mathsf{GrGen}(1^\lambda)$	$r, y \leftarrow\$ \mathbb{Z}_p^*;\ R \leftarrow g^r h^y$
$h \leftarrow\$ \mathbb{G}$	$c \leftarrow \mathsf{H}_{\mathsf{sig}}(\mathsf{pk}, m, R)$
Select $\mathsf{H}_{\mathsf{sig}} : \{0,1\}^* \rightarrow \mathbb{Z}_p$	$z \leftarrow r + f(c, y) \cdot \mathsf{sk}$
$\mathsf{par} \leftarrow ((\mathbb{G}, p, g, h), \mathsf{H}_{\mathsf{sig}})$	$\sigma \leftarrow (R, z, y)$
return par	**return** σ
$\mathsf{KeyGen}()$	$\mathsf{Verify}(\mathsf{pk}, m, \sigma)$
$\mathsf{sk} \leftarrow\$ \mathbb{Z}_p;\ \mathsf{pk} \leftarrow g^{\mathsf{sk}}$	**parse** $(R, z, y) \leftarrow \sigma$
return (pk, sk)	**return** 0 **if** $y = 0$
	$c \leftarrow \mathsf{H}_{\mathsf{sig}}(\mathsf{pk}, m, R)$
	return 0 **if** $R \cdot \mathsf{pk}^{f(c,y)} \neq g^z h^y$
	return 1

Fig. 3. Our base (non-blind) signature scheme. We can instantiate it with any bivariate function f such that $f(X, y)$ is invertible for all $y \in \mathbb{Z}_p^*$. The public parameters par are implicitly given as input to all algorithms.

queries the oracle $\mathcal{O}^{\mathsf{USign}_1}$ with a public key and two messages of its choosing. Additionally, the adversary is allowed to choose disjoint signing sets $\mathcal{S}_0, \mathcal{S}_1 \subseteq [n]$ and two sets of protocol messages. Hence, the adversary could corrupt *all* issuers, not just a threshold number of them, and the scheme should still preserve blindness. The blindness game for threshold blind signatures is specified in Fig. 2. Our scheme satisfies the stronger notion of *perfect blindness*, where the adversary's advantage in winning the blindness game is zero.

Definition 7 (Perfect Blindness). *Let the advantage of an adversary $\mathcal{A}$ against the threshold blindness game $\mathsf{Game}^{\mathrm{blind\text{-}t}}_{\mathcal{A},\mathsf{TB}}(\kappa)$, as defined in Fig. 2, be as follows:*

$$\mathsf{Adv}^{\mathrm{blind\text{-}t}}_{\mathcal{A},\mathsf{TB}}(\kappa) = |\Pr[\mathsf{Game}^{\mathrm{blind\text{-}t}}_{\mathcal{A},\mathsf{TB}}(\kappa) = 1] - 1/2|$$

A threshold blind signature scheme TB *satisfies* perfect blindness *if for all PPT adversaries $\mathcal{A}$, $\mathsf{Adv}^{\mathrm{blind\text{-}t}}_{\mathcal{A},\mathsf{TB}}(\kappa) = 0$.*

4 Blind Signature Scheme BS

In this section, we present our construction of a blind signature scheme BS. We begin by constructing a base (non-blind) scheme (Fig. 3), from which our blind signature scheme is derived. The base scheme can be instantiated in two different ways, which are parameterized by a non-linear function $f : \mathbb{Z}_p \times \mathbb{Z}_p \rightarrow \mathbb{Z}_p$.

Explicitly, we consider two possibilities: $f_1(c, y) = c + y^5$ and $f_2(c, y) = cy$. A signature is then given by $\sigma = (R, z, y)$, where

$$R = g^r h^y \qquad \text{and} \qquad z = r + f(c, y) \cdot \mathsf{sk}$$

for $c = \mathsf{H}_{\mathsf{sig}}(\mathsf{pk}, m, R)$. We prove the EUF-CMA security in the full version. We then blind the base scheme by replacing the Sign algorithm with an interactive protocol between an issuer running ISign and a user running USign, wherein the issuer does not learn the message m. The signature size with either function f is one group element plus two scalars, which is only one more scalar than a Schnorr signature [35].

Our blind signature scheme BS is specified in Fig. 4. Of technical interest is the fact the security reductions for the two parametrization options f_1 and f_2 use very different techniques, and yet achieve identical efficiency and security assumptions.

The issuer in the blind protocol behaves identically for either function f. Initially, the issuer sends some g^a and $g^b h^y$ for random a, b, y. The user returns a blinded challenge c. In the second round, the issuer returns the opening (b, y) in the clear, and the response $z = a + f(c, y) \cdot \mathsf{sk}$. This is described formally in Fig. 4.

The user in the blind protocol behaves slightly differently for f_1 and f_2. In Fig. 4, we show the corresponding algorithms USign_1 and USign_2 for each function f. Let us informally describe the user for f_1. In USign_1, the user computes a nonce and challenge as

$$\bar{R} = g^{r + \alpha^5 a + \alpha^5 \beta \mathsf{sk} + \alpha b} h^{\alpha y} \qquad \text{and} \qquad \bar{c} = \mathsf{H}_{\mathsf{sig}}(\mathsf{pk}, m, \bar{R})$$

blinded by the random values r, α, β. Note that, up to this point, the random value y is completely hidden from the user. Thus, a malicious user is unable to include factors of g^{y^5} in the nonce $\bar{R}$, preventing potential ROS attacks. Now, the user returns $c = \bar{c}\alpha^{-5} + \beta$ to the issuer, which is randomized by α and β. Then, in USign_2, upon receiving (z, b, y) the user sets

$$\bar{z} \leftarrow r + \alpha^5 z + \alpha b \qquad \text{and} \qquad \bar{y} = \alpha y$$

where $\bar{y}$ is randomized by α. Now $\bar{z}$ is the unique value that satisfies the verifier's equation given $\bar{R}, \bar{z}$. Thus, the final signature $\sigma = (\bar{R}, \bar{z}, \bar{y})$ reveals no information about the session.

If instead f_2 is used, in USign_1 the user computes a nonce and challenge as

$$\bar{R} = g^{r + \alpha\beta^{-1} a + \alpha b} h^{\alpha y} \qquad \text{and} \qquad \bar{c} = \mathsf{H}_{\mathsf{sig}}(\mathsf{pk}, m, \bar{R})$$

blinded by the random values r, α, β. The user returns $c = \beta\bar{c}$ to the issuer, which is randomized by β. Then, in USign_2, upon receiving (z, b, y) the user sets

$$\bar{z} \leftarrow r + \alpha\beta^{-1} z + \alpha b \qquad \text{and} \qquad \bar{y} = \alpha y$$

where $\bar{y}$ is randomized by α. Now $\bar{z}$ is the unique value that satisfies the verifier's equation given $\bar{R}, \bar{z}$. Thus, the final signature $(\bar{R}, \bar{z}, \bar{y})$ reveals no information

BS.Setup(1^κ)

$(\mathbb{G}, p, g) \leftarrow_\$ \mathsf{GrGen}(1^\kappa)$; $h \leftarrow_\$ \mathbb{G}$

Select $\mathsf{H}_{\mathsf{sig}} : \{0,1\}^* \to \mathbb{Z}_p^*$

$\mathsf{par} \leftarrow ((\mathbb{G}, p, g, h), \mathsf{H}_{\mathsf{sig}}$

return par

BS.KeyGen()

$\mathsf{sk} \leftarrow_\$ \mathbb{Z}_p$; $\mathsf{pk} \leftarrow g^{\mathsf{sk}}$

return (sk, pk)

BS.Verify(pk, m, σ)

parse $(\bar{R}, \bar{z}, \bar{y}) \leftarrow \sigma$

$\bar{c} \leftarrow \mathsf{H}_{\mathsf{sig}}(\mathsf{pk}, m, \bar{R})$

if $\bar{y} = 0$ **or** $\bar{R} \cdot \mathsf{pk}^{f(\bar{c},\bar{y})} \neq g^{\bar{z}} h^{\bar{y}}$

  return 0

return 1

BS.ISign(sk)		BS.USign(pk, m)
$a, b, \leftarrow_\$ \mathbb{Z}_p$; $y \leftarrow_\$ \mathbb{Z}_p^*$		
$A \leftarrow g^a$; $B \leftarrow g^b h^y$	$\xrightarrow{A,B}$	$(\mathsf{st}^U, c) \leftarrow_\$ \mathsf{USign}_1(\mathsf{pk}, m, A, B)$
$z \leftarrow a + f(c, y) \cdot \mathsf{sk}$	$\xleftarrow{c}$	
	$\xrightarrow{z,b,y}$	**return** $\mathsf{USign}_2(\mathsf{st}^U, z, b, y)$

$f_1(c, y)$

return $c + y^5$

$\mathsf{BS}[f_1].\mathsf{USign}_1(\mathsf{pk}, m, A, B)$

$\alpha \leftarrow_\$ \mathbb{Z}_p^*$; $r, \beta \leftarrow_\$ \mathbb{Z}_p$

$\bar{R} \leftarrow g^r A^{\alpha^5} \mathsf{pk}^{\alpha^5 \beta} B^\alpha$

$\bar{c} \leftarrow \mathsf{H}_{\mathsf{sig}}(\mathsf{pk}, m, \bar{R})$

$c \leftarrow \bar{c}\alpha^{-5} + \beta$

$\mathsf{st}^U \leftarrow (\bar{R}, r, \alpha, \beta)$

return (st^U, c)

$\mathsf{BS}[f_1].\mathsf{USign}_2(\mathsf{st}^U, z, b, y)$

return $\perp$ **if** $B \neq g^b h^y$

return $\perp$ **if** $g^z \neq A\mathsf{pk}^{c+y^5}$

$\mathsf{st}^U \leftarrow (\bar{R}, r, \alpha, \beta)$

$\bar{z} \leftarrow r + \alpha^5 z + \alpha b$; $\bar{y} \leftarrow \alpha y$

$\sigma \leftarrow (\bar{R}, \bar{z}, \bar{y})$

return $\perp$ **if** $\mathsf{BS.Verify}(\mathsf{pk}, m, \sigma) = 0$

return σ

$f_2(c, y)$

return $c \cdot y$

$\mathsf{BS}[f_2].\mathsf{USign}_1(\mathsf{pk}, m, A, B)$

$\alpha, \beta \leftarrow_\$ \mathbb{Z}_p^*$; $r \leftarrow_\$ \mathbb{Z}_p$

$\bar{R} \leftarrow g^r A^{\alpha\beta^{-1}} B^\alpha$

$\bar{c} \leftarrow \mathsf{H}_{\mathsf{sig}}(\mathsf{pk}, m, \bar{R})$

$c \leftarrow \beta\bar{c}$

$\mathsf{st}^U \leftarrow (\bar{R}, r, \alpha, \beta)$

return (st^U, c)

$\mathsf{BS}[f_2].\mathsf{USign}_2(\mathsf{st}^U, z, b, y)$

return $\perp$ **if** $B \neq g^b h^y$

return $\perp$ **if** $g^z \neq A\mathsf{pk}^{c \cdot y}$

$\mathsf{st}^U \leftarrow (\bar{R}, r, \alpha, \beta)$

$\bar{z} \leftarrow r + \alpha\beta^{-1} z + \alpha b$; $\bar{y} \leftarrow \alpha y$

$\sigma \leftarrow (\bar{R}, \bar{z}, \bar{y})$

return $\perp$ **if** $\mathsf{BS}_2.\mathsf{Verify}(\mathsf{pk}, m, \sigma) = 0$

return σ

Fig. 4. Top: The two-round blind signature scheme BS[GrGen, f]. Bottom: Two ways of instantiating f and the corresponding $\mathsf{USign}_1, \mathsf{USign}_2$. The power 5 may be replaced with any power $q < \mathsf{poly}(\kappa)$ for which $\gcd(q, p-1) = 1$.

$\mathsf{BSr3.ISign}(\mathsf{sk})$		$\mathsf{BSr3.USign}(\mathsf{pk}, m)$
$a, b, y \leftarrow\!\!\$\ \mathbb{Z}_p$		
$A \leftarrow g^a;\ B \leftarrow g^b h^y$	$\xrightarrow[A,B]{}$	pick $s \in \mathbb{Z}_p$ arbitrarily
	$\xleftarrow[c,s]{}$	$(\mathsf{st}^U, c) \leftarrow\!\!\$\ \mathsf{BS}[f].\mathsf{USign}_1(\mathsf{pk}, m, A, h^s B)$
	$\xrightarrow[b,y]{}$	
	$\xleftarrow[\perp]{}$	
$z \leftarrow a + f(c, y+s) \cdot \mathsf{sk}$	$\xrightarrow[z]{}$	**return** $\mathsf{BS}[f].\mathsf{USign}_2(\mathsf{st}^U, z, b, y+s)$

Fig. 5. The signing protocol of blind signature scheme $\mathsf{BSr3}[f]$, which is a three-round version of $\mathsf{BS}[f]$. Two instantiations of f, $\mathsf{BS}[f].\mathsf{USign}_1$ and $\mathsf{BS}[f].\mathsf{USign}_2$ are shown in Fig. 4.

about the session. When we instantiate our blind signature with f_2, the scheme draws many parallels with [41]; however, the resulting signature is more efficient.

We prove that BS is perfectly blind and one-more unforgeable under the discrete logarithm assumption in the AGM and the ROM. When $f(c, y) = c+y^5$, correct simulation computes 5th roots, so these roots must exist and be unique. We chose the power 5 in our construction for ease of exposition and because they often exist in practice; however, our proofs hold for any prime p and power $q < \mathsf{poly}(\kappa)$ for which unique roots exist (i.e., when $\mathsf{gcd}(q, p-1) = 1$).

Single use and secure state keeping. Our schemes require choosing values uniformly at random, and require that these values be used *strictly* once; otherwise, all security is lost. Like many multi-round protocols, this assumption requires secure state keeping. Our definitions model this state keeping via session identifiers, and implementations of our schemes will similarly need to ensure secure state keeping, to prevent nonce misuse.

4.1 One-More Unforgeability

To demonstrate the one-more unforgeability of BS, we introduce a three-round variant BSr3 (Fig. 5). BS.Setup, BS.KeyGen and BS.Verify are identical in both schemes, but the signing protocols differ in two ways. First, the user can additionally pick a scalar s that varies y generated by the signer. Second, z is sent to the user in an additional round. We show that the unforgeability of BSr3 implies the unforgeability of BS in Lemma 1. Indeed, the signing oracles in the one-more unforgeability game of BS can be simulated by the signing oracles in the one-more unforgeability game of BSr3. We introduce BSr3 as an intermediate step towards proving security for our threshold blind signature scheme Snowblind, presented in the next section. The relationships between our blind and threshold blind constructions and the assumptions on which they rely are outlined in Fig. 6.

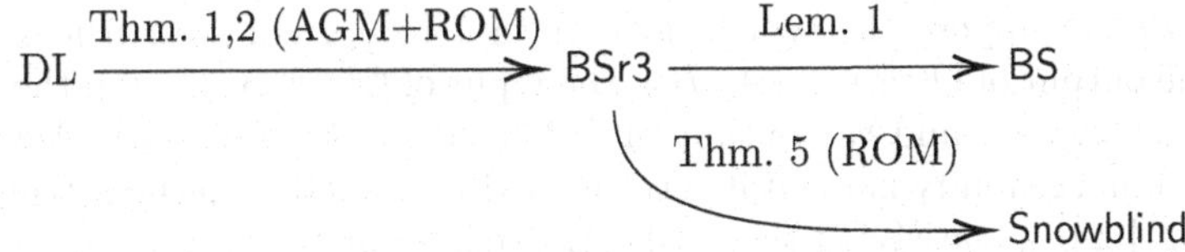

Fig. 6. Underlying assumptions for our blind and threshold blind signature constructions. DL denotes the Discrete Logarithm problem, AGM denotes the Algebraic Group Model, and ROM denotes the Random Oracle Model.

Lemma 1. *Let* GrGen *be a group generator. For any* $f \in \{f_1, f_2\}$, *and nay adversary* $\mathcal{A}$ *for the game* $\mathsf{Game}^{\mathrm{omuf}}_{\mathcal{A},\mathsf{BS}[\mathsf{GrGen},f]}$ *there exists an adversary* $\mathcal{B}$ *for the game* $\mathsf{Game}^{\mathrm{omuf}}_{\mathcal{B},\mathsf{BSr3}[\mathsf{GrGen},f]}$ *making the same number of oracle queries as* $\mathcal{A}$ *running in a similar running time as* $\mathcal{A}$ *such that*

$$\mathsf{Adv}^{\mathrm{omuf}}_{\mathcal{A},\mathsf{BS}[\mathsf{GrGen},f]}(\kappa) = \mathsf{Adv}^{\mathrm{omuf}}_{\mathcal{B},\mathsf{BSr3}[\mathsf{GrGen},f]}(\kappa)$$

Proof. Let $\mathcal{A}$ be an adversary against the one-more unforgeability of the two-round protocol in Fig. 4. We construct an adversary $\mathcal{B}$ against the one-more unforgeability of the three-round protocol in Fig. 5 as follows.

$\mathcal{B}$ has access to its own signing oracles, denoted by $\hat{\mathcal{O}}^{\mathsf{ISign}_1,\mathsf{ISign}_2,\mathsf{ISign}_3}$. Upon receiving a challenge public key pk, $\mathcal{B}$ runs $\mathcal{A}^{\mathcal{O}^{\mathsf{ISign}_1,\mathsf{ISign}_2}}(\mathsf{pk})$. When $\mathcal{A}$ queries $\mathcal{O}^{\mathsf{ISign}_1}$, $\mathcal{B}$ queries $\hat{\mathcal{O}}^{\mathsf{ISign}_1}$ and receives (A, B), which it returns to $\mathcal{A}$. When $\mathcal{A}$ queries $\mathcal{O}^{\mathsf{Sign}_2}$ on c, $\mathcal{B}$ queries its $\hat{\mathcal{O}}^{\mathsf{ISign}_2}$ oracle on $(c, 0)$ to get (b, y). Next, $\mathcal{B}$ queries $\hat{\mathcal{O}}^{\mathsf{Sign}_3}$ and receives z. $\mathcal{B}$ returns (b, y, z) to $\mathcal{A}$. When $\mathcal{A}$ returns a forgery $\{(m_k, \sigma_k)\}_{k=1}^{\ell+1}$, $\mathcal{B}$ outputs the same forgery.

If $\mathcal{A}$ succeeds, then both $\mathcal{A}$ and $\mathcal{B}$ have made fewer than ℓ final-round queries, and $\mathcal{B}$'s forgery also verifies. Thus, $\mathsf{Adv}^{\mathrm{omuf}}_{\mathcal{A},\mathsf{BS}[\mathsf{GrGen},f]}(\kappa) = \mathsf{Adv}^{\mathrm{omuf}}_{\mathcal{B},\mathsf{BSr3}[\mathsf{GrGen},f]}(\kappa)$. □

We prove that BSr3 is one-more unforgeable under the discrete logarithm assumption in the algebraic group model (AGM) and random oracle model (ROM) for both instantiations of f and provide proof outlines here. The game models the hash function $\mathsf{H}_{\mathsf{sig}}$ as a random oracle, which on each different input outputs an uniformly random value over $\mathbb{Z}_p^*$, and to which the adversary is given oracle access. The full proofs can be found in the full version.

Theorem 1. *Let* GrGen *be a group generator. For any algebraic adversary* $\mathcal{A}$ *for the game* $\mathsf{Game}^{\mathrm{omuf}}_{\mathcal{A},\mathsf{BSr3}[\mathsf{GrGen},f_1]}$ *making at most* q_S *signing queries and* q_H *queries to the random oracle, there exists adversaries* $\mathcal{B}_0, \mathcal{B}_1, \mathcal{B}_2$ *for the discrete logarithm problem running in a similar running time as* $\mathcal{A}$ *such that*

$$\mathsf{Adv}^{\mathrm{omuf}}_{\mathcal{A},\mathsf{BSr3}[\mathsf{GrGen},f_1]}(\kappa) \leq q_S \mathsf{Adv}^{\mathrm{dlog}}_{\mathcal{B}_0,\mathsf{GrGen}}(\kappa) + \mathsf{Adv}^{\mathrm{dlog}}_{\mathcal{B}_1,\mathsf{GrGen}}(\kappa) + \mathsf{Adv}^{\mathrm{dlog}}_{\mathcal{B}_2,\mathsf{GrGen}}(\kappa) + \frac{q_S + 2 + 4q_H + q_S q_H^2}{p}$$

where p *denotes the group size.*

Proof Outline. Suppose the session id is from 1 to q_S. For session id $i \in [q_S]$, denote the output of $\mathcal{O}^{\mathsf{ISign}_1}$ as (A_i, B_i), the input of $\mathcal{O}^{\mathsf{ISign}_2}$ as (c_i, s_i), the output of $\mathcal{O}^{\mathsf{ISign}_2}$ as (b_i, y_i), and the output of $\mathcal{O}^{\mathsf{ISign}_3}$ as z_i. An adversary $\mathcal{A}$ wins the one-more unforgeability game if it returns distinct forged signatures $\{(m_k^*, \sigma_k^* = (\bar{R}_k^*, \bar{z}_k^*, \bar{y}_k^*)\}_{k\in[\ell+1]}$ satisfying the verification equation:

$$\bar{R}_k^* = g^{\bar{z}_k^*} h^{\bar{y}_k^*} \mathsf{pk}^{-(\bar{c}_k^* + (\bar{y}_k^*)^5)}$$

where $\bar{c}_k^* = \mathsf{H}_{\mathsf{sig}}(\mathsf{pk}, m_k^*, \bar{R}_k^*)$. An algebraic adversary must also output a representation of each $\bar{R}_k^*$:

$$\bar{R}_k^* = g^{\varsigma_k^*} h^{\eta_k^*} \mathsf{pk}^{\chi_k^*} \prod_{i\in[q_S]} A_i^{\rho_{k,i}^*} B_i^{\tau_{k,i}^*} .$$

To prove the theorem, we define a series of games, beginning with the one-more unforgeability game $\mathsf{Game}^{\mathsf{omuf}}_{\mathcal{A},\mathsf{BSr3}}$ and concluding with a game Game_2 in which $\mathcal{A}$ wins if the following conditions hold: (1) $\rho_{k,i}^* = 0$ for each (A_i, B_i) queried in the first round with no corresponding (i, c_i) query in the second round, and (2) $\bar{y}_k^*$ satisfies the following equation:

$$\bar{y}_k^* = \eta_k^* + \sum_{i\in[q_S]} y_i \tau_{k,i}^* .$$

Intuitively, these conditions say that each $\bar{R}_k^*$ must have a representation over completed signing sessions only and that $\bar{R}_k^*$ must commit to $\bar{y}_k^*$. We show that if $\mathcal{A}$ wins Game_2, its responses must satisfy a polynomial expression in the secret key sk, and a reduction $\mathcal{B}_2$ can use this expression to compute sk with overwhelming probability.

We first jump to a hybrid game Game_1 in which condition (1) holds but not (2). To do this we design a reduction $\mathcal{B}_0$ that randomly selects a signing query $i' \in [q_S]$ for which the condition fails, and can compute the discrete logarithm of $A_{i'}$ with overwhelming probability. To jump from Game_1 to Game_2, we show that if $\mathcal{A}$ wins Game_1, its responses must satisfy a polynomial expression in the discrete logarithm ω of h, which a reduction $\mathcal{B}_1$ can use to compute ω with overwhelming probability.

The most technical aspect of our proof is constructing the reduction $\mathcal{B}_2$. Indeed, we demonstrate that whenever $\mathcal{A}$ wins Game_2, then either $\mathcal{B}_2$ returns the secret key as

$$\mathsf{sk} = \frac{-\varsigma_k^* - \sum_{i\in S_3}(z_i \rho_{k,i}^* + b_i \tau_{k,i}^*) + \bar{z}_k^*}{\chi_k^* + \bar{c}_k^* + (\eta_k^* + \sum_{i\in[q_S]} y_i \tau_{k,i}^*)^5 - \sum_{i\in S_3}(c_i + (y_i + s_i)^5)\rho_{k,i}^*} ,$$

where S_3 is defined in the game denoting the set of completed signing sessions, or the denominator is zero:

$$\chi_k^* + \bar{c}_k^* + (\eta_k^* + \sum_{i\in[q_S]} y_i \tau_{k,i}^*)^5 - \sum_{i\in S_3}(c_i + (y_i + s_i)^5)\rho_{k,i}^* = 0 . \qquad (4)$$

We then proceed with a timing argument that shows Eq. (4) holds with probability less than the probability that the *one-dimensional* ROS problem has a solution. The one-dimensional ROS problem is proven to be statistically hard in [17, Lemma 2]. □

Theorem 2. *Let* GrGen *be a group generator. For any algebraic adversary $\mathcal{A}$ for the game* $\mathsf{Game}^{\mathrm{omuf}}_{\mathcal{A},\mathsf{BSr3}[\mathsf{GrGen},f_2]}$ *making at most q_S signing queries and q_H queries to the random oracle, there exists adversaries $\mathcal{B}_0, \mathcal{B}_1, \mathcal{B}_2$ for the discrete logarithm problem running in a similar running time as $\mathcal{A}$ such that*

$$\mathsf{Adv}^{\mathrm{omuf}}_{\mathcal{A},\mathsf{BSr3}[\mathsf{GrGen},f_2]}(\kappa) \le q_S \cdot \mathsf{Adv}^{\mathrm{dlog}}_{\mathcal{B}_0,\mathsf{GrGen}}(\kappa) + \mathsf{Adv}^{\mathrm{dlog}}_{\mathcal{B}_1,\mathsf{GrGen}}(\kappa) + \mathsf{Adv}^{\mathrm{dlog}}_{\mathcal{B}_2,\mathsf{GrGen}}(\kappa) + \frac{(q_S+1)(q_H+q_S+1)^2}{p-1}$$

where p denotes the group size.

Proof Outline. We follow the same technique as f_1 to construct $\mathcal{B}_0, \mathcal{B}_1, \mathcal{B}_2$ and switch to Game_2 in which: (1) $\rho^*_{k,i} = 0$ for each (A_i, B_i) queried in the first round with no corresponding query for i in the third round, and (2) $\bar{y}^*_k$ satisfies $\bar{y}^*_k = \eta^*_k + \sum_{i\in[q_S]} y_i \tau^*_{k,i}$. In Game_2 we can similarly show that either the reduction $\mathcal{B}_2$ returns the secret key sk, or

$$\chi^*_k + \bar{c}^*_k(\eta^*_k + \sum_{i\in[q_S]} y_i \tau^*_{k,i}) - \sum_{i\in S_3} c_i(y_i + s_i)\rho^*_{k,i} = 0\,. \tag{5}$$

Our proof that Eq. (5) holds with negligible probability differs substantially from our proof for f_1. Here, we reduce it to a modified version of the WFROS problem [41] which has been shown to be information-theoretically hard. The reduction and the hardness proof of the modified WFROS problem follow from similar ideas from [41]. More details are given in the full version. □

Remark 1. The main difference between the modified WFROS problem and the original WFROS game is that the adversary is allowed to send an additional offset s_i in each query to one of the oracles, which leads to an additional loss factor of q_S in the advantage bound. However, this is because we are proving the OMUF of the more complex three-round scheme BSr3 which is stronger than the OMUF of BS. In fact, we can remove the q_S factor and get the same bound as [41] for the OMUF advantage of BS[GrGen, f_2].

4.2 Blindness

The following two theorems establish the perfect blindness of BS[GrGen, f_1] and BS[GrGen, f_2]. (The proofs are very similar.)

Theorem 3. *Let* GrGen *be a group generator. Then, the blind signature scheme* BS[GrGen, f_1] *is perfectly blind.*

Proof. Let $\mathcal{A}$ be an adversary playing $\mathsf{Game}^{\text{blind}}_{\mathcal{A},\mathsf{BS}[f_1]}(\kappa)$ against the blind signature scheme as described in Fig. 4. Without loss of generality, we assume the randomness of $\mathcal{A}$ is fixed. As we prove perfect blindness, we can focus on adversaries that only run one signing session, i.e., they use a single sid, as security for a more general adversary follows by a standard hybrid argument. Further, we also assume that $\mathcal{A}$ always finishes both signing sessions and receives valid signatures (σ_0, σ_1) from $\mathcal{O}^{\mathsf{USign}_2}$. (Otherwise, the output of $\mathcal{O}^{\mathsf{USign}_1}$ are two blinded challenges which are both uniformly random over $\mathbb{Z}_p$, and blindness trivially holds.)

Let V_A denote the set of all possible views of $\mathcal{A}$ that can occur after one single interaction with $\mathcal{O}^{\mathsf{USign}_1}, \mathcal{O}^{\mathsf{USign}_2}$. In particular, any such view $\Delta \in V_A$ takes form $\Delta = (\mathsf{pk}, m_0, m_1, T_0, T_1, \sigma_0, \sigma_1)$. Here, $\sigma_i = (\bar{R}_i, \bar{c}_i, \bar{z}_i, \bar{y}_i)$, where $\bar{c}_i = \mathsf{H}_{\mathsf{sig}}(\mathsf{pk}, m_i, \bar{R}_i)$. (Note that $\bar{c}_i$ is redundant here, and does not need to be included, but it will make the argument easier.) Moreover, T_0 and T_1 are the signing protocol transcripts for the left and right interactions, respectively, and take form $T_i = (A_i, B_i, c_i, z_i, b_i, y_i)$. We need to show that the distribution of the actual adversarial view, which we denote as v_A, is the same when $b = 0$ and $b = 1$. Because we assume the randomness of $\mathcal{A}$ is fixed, the distribution of v_A only depends on the randomness $\eta = (r_0, \alpha_0, \beta_0, r_1, \alpha_1, \beta_1)$ required to respond to $\mathcal{O}^{\mathsf{USign}_1}$ and $\mathcal{O}^{\mathsf{USign}_2}$ queries, and we write $v_A(\eta)$ to make this fact explicit.

Concretely, fix some $\Delta \in V_A$. We now show that there exists a unique η that makes it occur, i.e., $v_A(\eta) = \Delta$, regardless of whether we are in the $b = 0$ or in the $b = 1$ case. In particular, we claim that, in both cases $b = 0, b = 1$, $v_A(\eta) = \Delta$ if and only if for $i \in \{0, 1\}$, η satisfies

$$\begin{aligned} r_i &= \bar{z}_{\omega_i} - z_i \alpha_i^5 - \alpha_i b_i \\ \alpha_i &= \bar{y}_{\omega_i} / y_i \\ \beta_i &= c_i - \bar{c}_{\omega_i} \alpha_i^{-5} , \end{aligned} \tag{6}$$

where $\omega_0 = b$ and $\omega_1 = 1 - b$.

In the "only if" direction, from Fig. 4, it is clear that when $v_A(\eta) = \Delta$, then η satisfies all constraints in Eq. 6.

To prove the "if" direction, assume that η satisfies all constraints in Eq. 6. We need to show that $v_A(\eta) = \Delta$. This means in particular verifying that the challenges output by $\mathcal{O}^{\mathsf{USign}_1}$ are indeed (c_0, c_1) and the signatures output by $\mathcal{O}^{\mathsf{USign}_2}$ are indeed (σ_0, σ_1).

Note that because we only consider Δ's that result in $\mathcal{O}^{\mathsf{USign}_2}$ not producing output $(\bot, \bot)$, for $i \in \{0, 1\}$, we have $\bar{y}_i \neq 0$, as well as,

$$g^{z_i} = A_i \mathsf{pk}^{c_i + y_i^5} , \quad B_i = g^{b_i} h^{y_i} , \quad \bar{R}_{\omega_i} = g^{\bar{z}_{\omega_i}} h^{\bar{y}_{\omega_i}} \mathsf{pk}^{-\bar{c}_{\omega_i} - \bar{y}_{\omega_i}^5} .$$

Therefore, using Eq. 6,

$$\begin{aligned} \bar{R}_{\omega_i} &= g^{r_i + z_i \alpha_i^5 + \alpha_i b_i} h^{\alpha_i y_i} \mathsf{pk}^{\alpha_i^5 (\beta_i - c_i - y_i^5)} \\ &= B_i^{\alpha_i} g^{r_i + z_i \alpha_i^5} \mathsf{pk}^{\alpha_i^5 (\beta_i - c_i - y_i^5)} \\ &= g^{r_i} A_i^{\alpha_i^5} B_i^{\alpha_i} \mathsf{pk}^{\alpha_i^5 \beta_i} . \end{aligned}$$

Consequently, for $i \in \{0,1\}$, $\mathcal{O}^{\mathsf{USign}_1}$ outputs the challenge

$$\alpha_i^{-5}\mathsf{H}_{\mathsf{sig}}(\mathsf{pk}, m_{\omega_i}, g^{r_i}A^{\alpha_i^5}\mathsf{pk}^{\alpha^5\beta_i}B^{\alpha_i}) + \beta_i = \alpha_i^{-5}\mathsf{H}_{\mathsf{sig}}(\mathsf{pk}, m_{\omega_i}, \bar{R}_{\omega_i}) + \beta_i = c_i ,$$

i.e., the two challenges are consistent with the view Δ. Furthermore, for $i \in \{0,1\}$, the signatures $(\tilde{\sigma}_1, \tilde{\sigma}_2)$ output by $\mathcal{O}^{\mathsf{USign}_2}$ are such that

$$\tilde{\sigma}_{\omega_i} = (g^{r_i}A_i^{\alpha_i^5}B_i^{\alpha_i}\mathsf{pk}^{\alpha_i^5\beta_i}, r_i + \alpha_i^5 z_i + \alpha_i b_i, \alpha_i y_i) = (\bar{R}_{\omega_i}, \bar{z}_{\omega_i}, \bar{y}_{\omega_i}) = \sigma_{\omega_i} ,$$

i,.e., these are exactly the signatures from Δ. □

Theorem 4. *Let* GrGen *be a group generator. Then, the blind signature scheme* BS[GrGen, f_2] *is perfectly blind.*

The proof is very similar to that of Theorem 3, and we defer it to the full version.

5 Threshold Blind Signature Scheme Snowblind

Here we present Snowblind, an efficient threshold blind signature scheme (Fig. 7). Snowblind extends single-party blind signing to the multi-issuer setting. In this setting, the user determines the signing set $\mathcal{S}$, such that $t \leq |\mathcal{S}| \leq n$. The user plays the role of the coordinator of the protocol; each issuer interacts directly with the user, and the user relays protocol messages between issuers for each round, for a total of three signing rounds. At the end of the protocol, the user aggregates the signature shares received from each issuer and publishes the resulting signature.

We provide a modular approach to proving the one-more unforgeability (OMUF) of Snowblind (Fig. 1). Indeed, we are able to reduce the OMUF of Snowblind to the OMUF of our three-round blind signature scheme BSr3 in Sect. 4, which more closely resembles the structure of Snowblind. We cannot directly reduce to the OMUF of our more efficient two-round scheme BS because in the simulation, the BS adversary might make more queries to its final-round signing oracle than the Snowblind adversary does, resulting in an invalid forgery. Preventing the adversary from forging signatures when it only queries the preliminary rounds is important in our asynchronous and concurrent model, where we can make no termination guarantees.

Concretely, we employ a centralized key generation mechanism, but, alternatively, a distributed key generation protocol (DKG) could be used. The public parameters par generated during setup are provided as input to all other algorithms and protocols. We assume some external mechanism to choose the set of signers $\mathcal{S} \subseteq \{1, \ldots, n\}$, where $t \leq |\mathcal{S}| \leq n$ and $\mathcal{S}$ is ordered to ensure consistency. Snowblind additionally makes use of a standard EUF-CMA-secure single-party signature scheme DS, used to authenticate messages sent in the signing rounds.

Parameter Generation. On input the security parameter 1^κ, the setup algorithm runs $(\mathbb{G}, p, g) \leftarrow\$ \mathsf{GrGen}(1^\kappa)$ and selects a random group element $h \leftarrow\$ \mathbb{G}$

$\mathsf{Snowblind.Setup}(1^\kappa)$

$(\mathbb{G}, p, g) \leftarrow\!\!\$\ \mathsf{GrGen}(1^\kappa);\ h \leftarrow\!\!\$\ \mathbb{G}$

select two hash functions $\mathsf{H_{cm}}, \mathsf{H_{sig}} : \{0,1\}^* \to \mathbb{Z}_p^*$

$\mathsf{par_{sig}} \leftarrow \mathsf{DS.Setup}(1^\kappa)$

return $\mathsf{par} \leftarrow ((\mathbb{G}, p, g, h), \mathsf{H_{cm}}, \mathsf{H_{sig}}, \mathsf{par_{sig}})$

$\mathsf{Snowblind.KeyGen}(n, t)$

$\mathsf{sk} \leftarrow\!\!\$\ \mathbb{Z}_p;\ \mathsf{pk} \leftarrow g^{\mathsf{sk}}$

$\{(\mathsf{i}, \mathsf{sk_i})\}_{\mathsf{i} \in [n]} \leftarrow\!\!\$\ \mathsf{Share}(\mathsf{sk}, n, t)$

  // *Shamir secret sharing of* sk

for $\mathsf{i} \in [n]$ **do**

  $\mathsf{pk_i} \leftarrow g^{\mathsf{sk_i}};\ (\hat{\mathsf{pk}}_\mathsf{i}, \hat{\mathsf{sk}}_\mathsf{i}) \leftarrow \mathsf{DS.KeyGen}()$

$\mathsf{aux} \leftarrow \{\hat{\mathsf{pk}}_\mathsf{i}\}_{\mathsf{i} \in [n]}$

return $(\mathsf{pk}, \{\mathsf{pk_i}\}_{\mathsf{i} \in [n]} \{\mathsf{sk_i}, \hat{\mathsf{sk}}_\mathsf{i}\}_{\mathsf{i} \in [n]}, \mathsf{aux})$

$\mathsf{Snowblind.Verify}(\mathsf{pk}, m, \sigma)$

parse $(\bar{R}, \bar{z}, \bar{y}) \leftarrow \sigma$

$\bar{c} \leftarrow \mathsf{H_{sig}}(\mathsf{pk}, m, \bar{R})$

if $\bar{y} = 0$ **or** $\bar{R} \cdot \mathsf{pk}^{f(\bar{c}, \bar{y})} \neq g^{\bar{z}} h^{\bar{y}}$

  return 0

return 1

$\mathsf{Snowblind.ISign}(\mathsf{i}, \mathsf{sk_i}, \mathsf{aux})$		$\mathsf{Snowblind.USign}(\mathsf{pk}, \mathsf{aux}, m, \mathcal{S})$
parse $\{\hat{\mathsf{pk}}_\mathsf{i}\}_{\mathsf{i} \in [n]} \leftarrow \mathsf{aux}$		parse $\{\hat{\mathsf{pk}}_\mathsf{i}\}_{\mathsf{i} \in [n]} \leftarrow \mathsf{aux}$
abort if $\mathsf{i} \notin \mathcal{S}$	$\xleftarrow{\mathcal{S}}$	
$a_\mathsf{i}, b_\mathsf{i} \leftarrow\!\!\$\ \mathbb{Z}_p;\ y_\mathsf{i} \leftarrow\!\!\$\ \mathbb{Z}_p^*$		
$\mathsf{cm_i} \leftarrow \mathsf{H_{cm}}(\mathsf{sid}, \mathsf{i}, y_\mathsf{i})$		
$A_\mathsf{i} \leftarrow g^{a_\mathsf{i}};\ B_\mathsf{i} \leftarrow g^{b_\mathsf{i}} h^{y_\mathsf{i}}$	$\xrightarrow{A_\mathsf{i}, B_\mathsf{i}, \mathsf{cm_i}}$	$A \leftarrow \prod_{j \in \mathcal{S}} A_j,\ B \leftarrow \prod_{j \in \mathcal{S}} B_j$
$\mathsf{msg} \leftarrow (\mathsf{sid}, \mathcal{S}, c, \{\mathsf{cm}_j\}_{j \in \mathcal{S}})$	$\xleftarrow{c, \{\mathsf{cm}_j\}_{j \in \mathcal{S}}}$	$(\mathsf{st}^U, c) \leftarrow\!\!\$\ \mathsf{BS}[f].\mathsf{USign}_1(\mathsf{pk}, m, A, B)$
$\sigma_i \leftarrow \mathsf{DS.Sign}(\hat{\mathsf{sk}}_\mathsf{i}, \mathsf{msg})$	$\xrightarrow{b_\mathsf{i}, y_\mathsf{i}, \sigma_\mathsf{i}}$	
abort if $\exists\, j$ such that $\mathsf{cm}_j \neq \mathsf{H_{cm}}(\mathsf{sid}, j, y_j)$ **or** $\mathsf{DS.Verify}(\hat{\mathsf{pk}}_j, \mathsf{msg}, \sigma_j) \neq 1$	$\xleftarrow{\{\sigma_j, y_j\}_{j \in \mathcal{S}}}$	
$y \leftarrow \sum_{j \in \mathcal{S}} y_j$		$y \leftarrow \sum_{j \in \mathcal{S}} y_j$
$z_i \leftarrow a_i + f(c, y) \cdot (\lambda_\mathsf{i}^{\mathcal{S}} \mathsf{sk_i})$	$\xrightarrow{z_i}$	$z = \sum_{j \in \mathcal{S}} z_j;\ b \leftarrow \sum_{j \in \mathcal{S}} b_j$
		$(\bar{R}, \bar{z}, \bar{y}) \leftarrow \mathsf{BS}[f].\mathsf{USign}_2(\mathsf{st}^U, z, b, y)$
		return $\sigma \leftarrow (\bar{R}, \bar{z}, \bar{y})$

Fig. 7. The signing protocol of the threshold blind signature scheme Snowblind[GrGen, DS, f] derived from our blind signature scheme BSr3[f] (Fig. 5), where DS is an arbitrary EUF-CMA-secure digital signature scheme. sid denotes the id of the signing session. Snowblind assumes an external mechanism to choose the set $\mathcal{S} \subseteq \{1, \ldots, n\}$ of signers, where $t \leq |\mathcal{S}| \leq n$. $\mathcal{S}$ is required to be ordered to ensure consistency. Each issuer must respond to each round in a session no more than once or else all security is lost. Implementations of our scheme should ensure secure state keeping as described in our definitions.

as well as two hash functions $\mathsf{H}_{\mathsf{cm}}, \mathsf{H}_{\mathsf{sig}} : \{0,1\}^* \rightarrow \mathbb{Z}_p$. It also runs the setup algorithm for a signature scheme $\mathsf{par}_{\mathsf{sig}} \leftarrow \mathsf{DS.Setup}(1^\kappa)$ used for authentication in Signing Rounds 1 and 2. It outputs public parameters $\mathsf{par} \leftarrow ((\mathbb{G}, p, g, h), \mathsf{H}_{\mathsf{cm}}, \mathsf{H}_{\mathsf{sig}}, \mathsf{par}_{\mathsf{sig}})$.

Key Generation. On input the number of signers n and the threshold t, this algorithm first generates the secret key $\mathsf{sk} \leftarrow\!\!\$\, \mathbb{Z}_p$ and joint public key $\mathsf{pk} \leftarrow g^{\mathsf{sk}}$. It then performs Shamir secret sharing of sk: $\{(\mathsf{i}, \mathsf{sk_i})\}_{\mathsf{i}\in[n]} \leftarrow\!\!\$\, \mathsf{Share}(\mathsf{sk}, n, t)$. It computes the corresponding public key for each participant as $\mathsf{pk_i} \leftarrow g^{\mathsf{sk_i}}$. It then runs the key generation algorithm $(\hat{\mathsf{pk}}_\mathsf{i}, \hat{\mathsf{sk}}_\mathsf{i}) \leftarrow \mathsf{DS.KeyGen}()$. It sets $\mathsf{aux} \leftarrow \{\hat{\mathsf{pk}}_\mathsf{i}\}_{\mathsf{i}\in[n]}$. To guarantee identification of misbehaving issuers by verifying each issuer's signature share (i.e., identifiable abort), aux may additionally include the set of public key shares $\{\mathsf{pk}_1, \ldots, \mathsf{pk}_n\}$. Finally, it outputs $(\mathsf{pk}, \{\mathsf{pk_i}\}_{\mathsf{i}\in[n]}\{\mathsf{sk_i}, \hat{\mathsf{sk}}_\mathsf{i}\}_{\mathsf{i}\in[n]}, \mathsf{aux})$.

Signing Round 1. In the first round, the issuers compute a shared nonce $A = g^a$ and $B = g^b h^y$. On input a signing set $\mathcal{S}$ determined by the user, each issuer $\mathsf{i} \in \mathcal{S}$, chooses random values $a_\mathsf{i}, b_\mathsf{i} \leftarrow\!\!\$\, \mathbb{Z}_p, y_\mathsf{i} \leftarrow\!\!\$\, \mathbb{Z}_p^*$, computes a commitment $\mathsf{cm_i} \leftarrow \mathsf{H}_{\mathsf{cm}}(\mathsf{sid}, \mathsf{i}, y_\mathsf{i})$ and two nonces $A_\mathsf{i} \leftarrow g^{a_\mathsf{i}}, B_\mathsf{i} \leftarrow g^{b_\mathsf{i}} h^{y_\mathsf{i}}$, and outputs $(A_\mathsf{i}, B_\mathsf{i}, \mathsf{cm_i})$.
The user receives the set of all $\{(A_j, B_j, \mathsf{cm}_j)\}_{j\in\mathcal{S}}$, from which it computes the aggregate nonces $A \leftarrow \prod_{j\in\mathcal{S}} A_j, B \leftarrow \prod_{j\in\mathcal{S}} B_j$. The user then computes the blinded challenge $c \leftarrow\!\!\$\, \mathsf{BS}[f].\mathsf{USign}_1(\mathsf{pk}, m, A, B)$ on the message m and outputs it together with the set of commitments $\{\mathsf{cm}_j\}_{j\in\mathcal{S}}$. Here $\mathsf{BS}[f].\mathsf{USign}_1$ is the same algorithm as described for the non-threshold blind signature in Fig. 4.

Signing Round 2. In the second round, the issuers jointly reveal b and y such that $B = g^b h^y$. On input the set of commitments $\{\mathsf{cm}_j\}_{j\in\mathcal{S}}$ and challenge c, each issuer $\mathsf{i} \in \mathcal{S}$ forms the message $\mathsf{msg} = (\mathsf{sid}, \mathcal{S}, c, \{\mathsf{cm}_j\}_{j\in\mathcal{S}})$ and runs the signing algorithm $\sigma_i \leftarrow \mathsf{DS.Sign}(\hat{\mathsf{sk}}_\mathsf{i}, \mathsf{msg})$, used to authenticate the messages sent in Signing Rounds 1 and 2. Each issuer then outputs their committed values $b_\mathsf{i}, y_\mathsf{i}$ and signature σ_i.
The user receives the set of all $\{b_j, y_j, \sigma_j\}_{j\in\mathcal{S}}$ and echoes $\{y_j, \sigma_j\}_{j\in\mathcal{S}}$ back to all parties in the signing set.

Signing Round 3. In the third and final round, the issuers jointly compute $z \leftarrow a + f(c, y) \cdot \mathsf{sk}$. On input $\{(\sigma_j, y_j)\}_{j\in\mathcal{S}}$, each issuer i first checks that the commitments received in the first round are valid, i.e., $\mathsf{cm}_j = \mathsf{H}_{\mathsf{cm}}(\mathsf{sid}, j, y_j)$ for all $j \in \mathcal{S}$ and aborts if for some j, $\mathsf{cm}_j \neq \mathsf{H}_{\mathsf{cm}}(\mathsf{sid}, j, y_j)$.
This ensures that no malicious issuer can cancel out the honest contributions to y.
It then checks that all signatures σ_j verify: $\mathsf{DS.Verify}(\hat{\mathsf{pk}}_j, \mathsf{msg}, \sigma_j) = 1$ and aborts if not. The signature ensures that the honest signing parties all agree on the shared y.
Otherwise, issuer i computes the aggregate y-value $y \leftarrow \sum_{j\in\mathcal{S}} y_j$. It then computes the value $f(c, y)$ according to the chosen base blind signature scheme (Fig. 4) and $z_\mathsf{i} \leftarrow a_\mathsf{i} + f(c, y) \cdot (\lambda_\mathsf{i}^{\mathcal{S}} \mathsf{sk_i})$, where $\lambda_\mathsf{i}^{\mathcal{S}}$ is the ith Lagrange coefficient corresponding to $\mathcal{S}$. The Lagrange coefficients are computed as

shown in Eq. (1). Finally, the issuer outputs z_i.
The user receives the set of all $\{z_j\}_{j\in\mathcal{S}}$, from which it computes the aggregate z-value $z \leftarrow \sum_{j\in\mathcal{S}} z_j$ and $y \leftarrow \sum_{j\in\mathcal{S}} y_j$. The user then computes and outputs the blind signature $\sigma \leftarrow \mathsf{BS}[f].\mathsf{USign}_2(z, b, y)$.

Verification. On input the joint public key pk, a message m, and a signature $\sigma = (\bar{R}, \bar{z}, \bar{y})$, the verifier computes $c \leftarrow \mathsf{H}_{\mathsf{sig}}(\mathsf{pk}, m, \bar{R})$ and accepts if $\bar{R} \cdot \mathsf{pk}^{f(\bar{c},\bar{y})} = g^{\bar{z}} h^{\bar{y}}$ and $\bar{y} \neq 0$.

Note that verification of the threshold signature σ is identical to verification of the single-party signatures with respect to the aggregate nonce $\bar{R}$ and joint public key pk.

Complexity Analysis. For a signing session between the user and a set of issuers $\mathcal{S}$, each issuer sends two group elements and one scalar in the first round, two scalars and one signature in the second round, and one scalar in the third round. Therefore, the total communication complexity of each issuer is $2\mathbb{G}+4\mathbb{Z}_p+\mathsf{sig}$, where $\mathbb{G}$ denotes a group element, $\mathbb{Z}_p$ denotes a scalar, and sig denotes a signature of DS. The user sends the set $\mathcal{S}$ in the first round, $(1+|\mathcal{S}|)$ scalars in the second round, and $|\mathcal{S}|$ signatures and $|\mathcal{S}|$ scalars in the third round. Therefore, the total communication complexity of the user is $(2|\mathcal{S}| + 1)\mathbb{Z}_p + |\mathcal{S}|\mathsf{sig}$ plus $|\mathcal{S}| \log(n)$ bits.

For computation, the total computation complexity of each issuer is $3\mathsf{GExp}+\mathsf{GMul}+3\mathsf{SMul}$ plus one signing operation and $|\mathcal{S}|$ verifications of DS, where GExp denotes one group exponentiation, GMul denotes one group multiplication, and SMul denotes one scalar multiplication. The total computation complexity of the user is $6\mathsf{GExp} + (2n+4)\mathsf{GMul} + 6\mathsf{SMul}$.

One-More Unforgeability. We reduce the OMUF of $\mathsf{Snowblind}$ to the OMUF of our three-round blind signature defined in Fig. 5 and EUF-CMA security of the underlying signature scheme DS, which is formally stated in the following theorem. The OMUF game models the hash functions H_{cm} and $\mathsf{H}_{\mathsf{sig}}$ as random oracles, to which the adversary is given oracle access.

Theorem 5. *Let* GrGen *be a group generator and* DS *be a digital signature scheme. For any adversary* $\mathcal{A}$ *for the game* $\mathsf{Game}^{\text{omuf-t}}_{\mathsf{Snowblind}[\mathsf{GrGen},f,\mathsf{DS}]}$ *making at most* q_S *queries to* $\mathcal{O}^{\mathsf{ISign}_1}$ *and* q_H *queries to the random oracles, there exists an adversary* $\mathcal{B}$ *for the game* $\mathsf{Game}^{\text{omuf}}_{\mathsf{BSr3}[\mathsf{GrGen},f]}$ *making at most* q_S *queries to* $\mathcal{O}^{\mathsf{ISign}_1}$ *and* q_H *queries to the random oracle running in a similar running time as* $\mathcal{A}$ *and an adversary* $\mathcal{C}$ *for the game* $\mathsf{Game}^{\text{euf-cma}}_{\mathsf{DS}}$ *making at most* q_S *queries to* $\mathcal{O}^{\mathsf{Sign}}$ *running in a similar running time as* $\mathcal{A}$ *such that*

$$\mathsf{Adv}^{\text{omuf-t}}_{\mathcal{A},\mathsf{Snowblind}[\mathsf{GrGen},f,\mathsf{DS}]}(\kappa) \leq \mathsf{Adv}^{\text{omuf}}_{\mathcal{B},\mathsf{BSr3}[\mathsf{GrGen},f]}(\kappa) + \mathsf{Adv}^{\text{euf-cma}}_{\mathcal{C},\mathsf{DS}}(\kappa) + \frac{(2q_S + q_H + 1)(nq_S + q_H)}{p-1}$$

where n *denotes the number of signers and* p *denotes the group size.*

Let us give some intuition behind the security reduction of Theorem 5. We design a reduction $\mathcal{B}$ that takes as input a public key pk for the 3-round blind signature. $\mathcal{B}$ simulates the key generation process such that the threshold public key is equal to pk. The secret shares of the corrupt parties are chosen by $\mathcal{B}$. The secret keys of the honest parties are unknown by $\mathcal{B}$, but $\mathcal{B}$ internally computes γ_k and δ_k so that $\mathsf{pk}_\mathsf{k} = \mathsf{pk}^{\gamma_\mathsf{k}} g^{\delta_\mathsf{k}}$ for all $\mathsf{k} \in \mathsf{honest}$, where honest denotes the set of honest signers.

We then specify how $\mathcal{B}$ simulates the signature oracles in a manner which is statistically indistinguishable from the real oracles. For simplicity of the explanation here, let us consider a signing session for $\mathcal{S}$ that consists of only honest signers. In the first signing round, $\mathcal{B}$ embeds exactly one $\hat{\mathcal{O}}^{\mathsf{ISign}_1}$ response $(\hat{A}, \hat{B})$ into the messages from honest signers. For each $\mathsf{i} \in \mathcal{S}$, $\mathcal{B}$ sets $A_\mathsf{i} = \hat{A}^{\gamma_\mathsf{i} \lambda_\mathsf{i}^{\mathcal{S}}} g^{\tilde{a}_\mathsf{i}}$ and $B_\mathsf{i} = \hat{B}^{\frac{1}{|\mathcal{S}|}} g^{\tilde{b}_\mathsf{i}} h^{\tilde{y}_\mathsf{i}}$, where $\tilde{a}_\mathsf{i}, \tilde{b}_\mathsf{i}, \tilde{y}_\mathsf{i}$ are sampled randomly.

In the second signing round, $\mathcal{B}$ sets $\hat{s} = \sum_{\mathsf{i} \in \mathcal{S}} \tilde{y}_\mathsf{i}$, queries $\hat{\mathcal{O}}^{\mathsf{ISign}_2}$ on $(c, \hat{s})$, and receives $\hat{b}, \hat{y}$. Then $\mathcal{B}$ sets $b_\mathsf{i} = \frac{\hat{b}}{|\mathcal{S}|} + \tilde{b}_\mathsf{i}$, $y_\mathsf{i} = \frac{\hat{y}}{|\mathcal{S}|} + \tilde{y}_\mathsf{i}$. It is easy to see that $B_\mathsf{i} = g^{b_\mathsf{i}} h^{y_\mathsf{i}}$.

In the third signing round $\mathcal{B}$ gets $\hat{z}$ by querying $\hat{\mathcal{O}}^{\mathsf{ISign}_3}$. Then $\mathcal{B}$ sets $z_\mathsf{i} = \lambda_\mathsf{i}^{\mathcal{S}} \gamma_\mathsf{i} \hat{z} + \tilde{a}_\mathsf{i} + f(c, y) \lambda_\mathsf{i}^{\mathcal{S}} \delta_\mathsf{i}$, where $y = \sum_{\mathsf{i} \in \mathcal{S}} y_\mathsf{i} = \hat{y} + \hat{s}$. It is not hard to see that z_i is correct since $\hat{z} = \hat{a} + f(c, \hat{y} + \hat{s})\mathsf{sk}$ and thus

$$g^{z_\mathsf{i}} = g^{[\lambda_\mathsf{i}^{\mathcal{S}} \gamma_\mathsf{i} \hat{a} + \tilde{a}_\mathsf{i}] + [\lambda_\mathsf{i}^{\mathcal{S}} f(c,y)(\gamma_\mathsf{i} \mathsf{sk} + \delta_\mathsf{i})]} = A_\mathsf{i} \cdot (\mathsf{pk}_\mathsf{i})^{\lambda_\mathsf{i}^{\mathcal{S}} f(c,y)} .$$

Proof (of Theorem 5). For $\mathcal{A}$ described in the theorem, we construct an adversary $\mathcal{B}$ for $\mathsf{Game}_{\mathsf{BSr3}}^{\mathrm{omuf}}$ as follows. $\mathcal{B}$ is responsible for simulating oracle responses for the three rounds of signing, and queries to H_cm and H_sig. $\mathcal{B}$ may program H_cm and H_sig. $\mathcal{B}$ has access to its own random oracle, denoted by $\hat{\mathsf{H}}_\mathsf{sig}$, and signing oracles, denoted by $\hat{\mathcal{O}}^{\mathsf{ISign}_1}$, $\hat{\mathcal{O}}^{\mathsf{ISign}_2}$, and $\hat{\mathcal{O}}^{\mathsf{ISign}_3}$, from $\mathsf{Game}_{\mathsf{BSr3}}^{\mathrm{omuf}}$. $\mathcal{B}$ cannot program $\hat{\mathsf{H}}_\mathsf{sig}$ because it is part of $\mathcal{B}$'s challenge. Let Q_cm be the set of H_cm queries and their responses.

To start with, $\mathcal{B}$ receives as input group parameters $\mathcal{G} = (\mathbb{G}, p, g)$ and a challenge public key $\overline{\mathsf{pk}}$ issued by the BSr3 OMUF game. $\mathcal{B}$ randomly samples $h \leftarrow\!\!\$\ \mathbb{G}$. Then, $\mathcal{B}$ initializes Q_cm and $\mathsf{SignQuery}$ to empty sets and also initializes S_1, S_2, S_3 and ℓ as in $\mathsf{Game}_{\mathsf{Snowblind}}^{\mathrm{omuf\text{-}t}}$.

Key Generation. After receiving $(n, t, \mathsf{corrupt}, \mathsf{st}^\mathcal{A})$ from $\mathcal{A}$, assuming without loss of generality that $|\mathsf{corrupt}| = t - 1$, $\mathcal{B}$ simulates the key generation algorithm as follows. First, $\mathcal{B}$ sets the joint public key $\mathsf{pk} \leftarrow \overline{\mathsf{pk}}$. $\mathcal{B}$ then simulates a Shamir secret sharing of the discrete logarithm of pk by performing the following steps.

1. For all $\mathsf{j} \in \mathsf{corrupt}$, $\mathcal{B}$ samples a random value $x_\mathsf{j} \leftarrow\!\!\$\ \mathbb{Z}_p$ and defines the secret key as $\mathsf{sk}_\mathsf{j} \leftarrow x_\mathsf{j}$ and corresponding public key as $\mathsf{pk}_\mathsf{j} \leftarrow g^{x_\mathsf{j}}$.
2. To generate the public keys of the honest parties $\mathsf{k} \in \mathsf{honest} = [n] \setminus \mathsf{corrupt}$, $\mathcal{B}$ proceeds as follows:
   (a) For all $i \in \tilde{\mathcal{S}} := \mathsf{corrupt} \cup \{0\}$, it computes the Lagrange polynomials evaluated at point k: $\tilde{\lambda}_{\mathsf{k}i} = L_i^{\tilde{\mathcal{S}}}(\mathsf{k}) = \prod_{j \in \tilde{\mathcal{S}}, j \neq i} \frac{(j - \mathsf{k})}{(j - i)}$.

(b) It takes the public keys of the corrupted parties $\{\mathsf{pk_j}\}_{\mathsf{j}\in\mathsf{corrupt}}$ and the joint public key pk and computes: $\mathsf{pk_k} = \mathsf{pk}^{\tilde{\lambda}_{\mathsf{k}0}} \prod_{\mathsf{j}\in\mathsf{corrupt}} \mathsf{pk_j}^{\tilde{\lambda}_{\mathsf{kj}}}$. $\mathcal{B}$ internally sets $\gamma_\mathsf{k} \leftarrow \tilde{\lambda}_{\mathsf{k}0}$ and $\delta_\mathsf{k} \leftarrow \sum_{\mathsf{j}\in\mathsf{corrupt}} x_\mathsf{j}\tilde{\lambda}_{\mathsf{kj}}$ so that $\mathsf{pk_k} = \mathsf{pk}^{\gamma_\mathsf{k}} g^{\delta_\mathsf{k}}$ for all $\mathsf{k} \in \mathsf{honest}$.

3. For all $\mathsf{i} \in [n]$, $\mathcal{B}$ runs $(\hat{\mathsf{pk}}_\mathsf{i}, \hat{\mathsf{sk}}_\mathsf{i}) \leftarrow_\$ \mathsf{DS.KeyGen}()$.

$\mathcal{B}$ runs $\mathcal{A}^{\mathcal{O}^{\mathsf{ISign}_1,\mathsf{ISign}_2,\mathsf{ISign}_3},\mathsf{H_{cm}},\mathsf{H_{sig}}}(\mathsf{st}^\mathcal{A}, \mathsf{pk}, \{\mathsf{pk_i}\}_{i\in[n]}, \{\mathsf{sk_j}, \hat{\mathsf{sk}}_\mathsf{j}\}_{\mathsf{j}\in\mathsf{corrupt}}, \mathsf{aux})$ where $\mathsf{aux} \leftarrow \{\hat{\mathsf{pk}}_\mathsf{i}\}_{\mathsf{i}\in[n]}$. $\mathcal{B}$ simulates the oracles as follows. In the following, we use the same notations as the Snowblind protocol to denote variables from the game $\mathsf{Game}^{\mathsf{omuf\text{-}t}}_{\mathsf{Snowblind}}$. We use $\hat{A}, \hat{B}, \hat{b}, \hat{y}, \hat{z}, \hat{s}$ to denote variables from the game $\mathsf{Game}^{\mathsf{omuf}}_{\mathsf{BSr3}}$ and $\tilde{(\cdot)}$ to denote variables generated by $\mathcal{B}$ itself during the simulation.

Hash Queries. When $\mathcal{A}$ queries $\mathsf{H_{cm}}$ on $(\mathsf{sid}, \mathsf{i}, y)$, $\mathcal{B}$ checks whether $((\mathsf{sid}, \mathsf{i}, y), \mathsf{cm}) \in \mathsf{Q_{cm}}$ for some cm and, if so, returns cm. Else, $\mathcal{B}$ samples $\mathsf{cm} \leftarrow_\$ \mathbb{Z}_p$, appends $((\mathsf{sid}, \mathsf{i}, y), \mathsf{cm})$ to $\mathsf{Q_{cm}}$, and returns cm.

When $\mathcal{A}$ queries $\mathsf{H_{sig}}$ on (pk, m, R), $\mathcal{B}$ returns $c \leftarrow \hat{\mathsf{H}}_{\mathsf{sig}}(\mathsf{pk}, m, R)$.

Signing Round 1 ($\mathcal{O}^{\mathsf{ISign}_1}$ Queries). When $\mathcal{A}$ queries $\mathcal{O}^{\mathsf{ISign}_1}$ on $(\mathsf{i}, \mathsf{sid}, \mathcal{S})$, $\mathcal{B}$ returns $\perp$ if $(\mathsf{i}, \mathsf{sid}) \in S_1$ or $\mathsf{i} \notin \mathcal{S}$. If $(\mathsf{sid}, \mathcal{S}) \in \mathsf{SignQuery}$, which means $\mathcal{A}$ has made a query $(\mathsf{k}, \mathsf{sid}, \mathcal{S})$ for an honest party $\mathsf{k} \in \mathsf{honest} \cap \mathcal{S}$ for the same sid and $\mathcal{S}$ before, then $\mathcal{B}$ looks up the previously computed values $(\tilde{A}_\mathsf{i}^{(\mathsf{sid},\mathcal{S})}, \tilde{B}_\mathsf{i}^{(\mathsf{sid},\mathcal{S})}, \tilde{\mathsf{cm}}_\mathsf{i}^{(\mathsf{sid},\mathcal{S})})$.

Otherwise, $\mathcal{B}$ sets $\mathsf{SignQuery} \leftarrow \mathsf{SignQuery} \cup \{(\mathsf{sid}, \mathcal{S})\}$, creates a session id for the game $\mathsf{Game}^{\mathsf{omuf}}_{\mathsf{BSr3}}$ as $\mathsf{sid}^{(\mathsf{sid},\mathcal{S})}_{\mathsf{BSr3}} \leftarrow (\mathsf{i}, \mathsf{sid})$, and queries $\hat{\mathcal{O}}^{\mathsf{ISign}_1}$ on $\mathsf{sid}^{(\mathsf{sid},\mathcal{S})}_{\mathsf{BSr3}}$ and receives a nonce pair $(\hat{A}, \hat{B})$. Then, for each $\mathsf{k} \in \mathsf{hon}_\mathcal{S}$, $\mathcal{B}$ samples $\tilde{a}_\mathsf{k}^{(\mathsf{sid},\mathcal{S})}$, $\tilde{b}_\mathsf{k}^{(\mathsf{sid},\mathcal{S})} \leftarrow_\$ \mathbb{Z}_p, \tilde{y}_\mathsf{k}^{(\mathsf{sid},\mathcal{S})}, \tilde{\mathsf{cm}}_\mathsf{k}^{(\mathsf{sid},\mathcal{S})} \leftarrow_\$ \mathbb{Z}_p^*$ and computes

$$\tilde{A}_\mathsf{k}^{(\mathsf{sid},\mathcal{S})} \leftarrow \hat{A}^{\gamma_\mathsf{k}\lambda_\mathsf{k}^\mathcal{S}} g^{\tilde{a}_\mathsf{k}^{(\mathsf{sid},\mathcal{S})}}, \quad \tilde{B}_\mathsf{k}^{(\mathsf{sid},\mathcal{S})} \leftarrow \hat{B}^{\frac{1}{|\mathsf{hon}_\mathcal{S}|}} g^{\tilde{b}_\mathsf{k}^{(\mathsf{sid},\mathcal{S})}} h^{\tilde{y}_\mathsf{k}^{(\mathsf{sid},\mathcal{S})}}, \quad \tilde{s}^{(\mathsf{sid},\mathcal{S})} \leftarrow \sum_{\mathsf{k}\in\mathsf{hon}_\mathcal{S}} \tilde{y}_\mathsf{k}^{(\mathsf{sid},\mathcal{S})}$$

Finally, $\mathcal{B}$ sets $\mathcal{S}_{\mathsf{i},\mathsf{sid}} \leftarrow \mathcal{S}$, $S_1 \leftarrow S_1 \cup \{(\mathsf{i}, \mathsf{sid})\}$, and returns $(A_\mathsf{i} \leftarrow \tilde{A}_\mathsf{i}^{(\mathsf{sid},\mathcal{S})}, B_\mathsf{i} \leftarrow \tilde{B}_\mathsf{i}^{(\mathsf{sid},\mathcal{S})}, \mathsf{cm_i} \leftarrow \tilde{\mathsf{cm}}_\mathsf{i}^{(\mathsf{sid},\mathcal{S})})$ to $\mathcal{A}$.

Signing Round 2 ($\mathcal{O}^{\mathsf{ISign}_2}$ queries). When $\mathcal{A}$ queries $\mathcal{O}^{\mathsf{ISign}_2}$ on $(\mathsf{i}, \mathsf{sid}, c, \{\mathsf{cm}_j\}_{j\in\mathcal{S}})$ where $\mathcal{S} = \mathcal{S}_{\mathsf{i},\mathsf{sid}}$, $\mathcal{B}$ checks if $(\mathsf{i}, \mathsf{sid}) \in S_1$, $(\mathsf{i}, \mathsf{sid}) \notin S_2$, and $\mathsf{cm_i} = \tilde{\mathsf{cm}}_\mathsf{i}^{(\mathsf{sid},\mathcal{S})}$ and returns $\perp$ if not. If $\mathcal{B}$ has not queried $\hat{\mathcal{O}}^{\mathsf{ISign}_2}$ for session id $\mathsf{sid}^{(\mathsf{sid},\mathcal{S})}_{\mathsf{BSr3}}$, then, for each $j \in \mathcal{S} \cap \mathsf{corrupt}$, $\mathcal{B}$ finds y_j such that $((\mathsf{sid}, j, y_j), \mathsf{cm}_j) \in \mathsf{Q_{cm}}$ and sets $\hat{s} = \tilde{s}^{(\mathsf{sid},\mathcal{S})} + \sum_{j\in\mathcal{S}\cap\mathsf{corrupt}} y_j$. If there exists more than one such y_j for some j, $\mathcal{B}$ aborts and we denote this abort event as $\mathsf{HashColl}$. If such y_j does not exists for some j, $\mathcal{B}$ sets $\hat{s} = 0$ and we denote this event as $\mathsf{BadCm}^{(\mathsf{sid},\mathcal{S})}$. Then, $\mathcal{B}$ queries $\hat{\mathcal{O}}^{\mathsf{ISign}_2}$ on $(\mathsf{sid}^{(\mathsf{sid},\mathcal{S})}_{\mathsf{BSr3}}, (c, \hat{s}))$ and receives $\hat{b}, \hat{y}$. If $\mathcal{B}$ has queried $\hat{\mathcal{O}}^{\mathsf{ISign}_2}$ for session id $\mathsf{sid}^{(\mathsf{sid},\mathcal{S})}_{\mathsf{BSr3}}$, $\mathcal{B}$ retrieves $\hat{b}, \hat{y}$ from the previous query.

Then, $\mathcal{B}$ sets $b_\mathsf{i} = \frac{\hat{b}}{|\mathsf{hon}_\mathcal{S}|} + \tilde{b}_\mathsf{i}^{(\mathsf{sid},\mathcal{S})}$, $y_\mathsf{i} = \frac{\hat{y}}{|\mathsf{hon}_\mathcal{S}|} + \tilde{y}_\mathsf{i}^{(\mathsf{sid},\mathcal{S})}$ and appends $((\mathsf{sid}, \mathsf{i}, y_\mathsf{i}), \tilde{\mathsf{cm}}_\mathsf{i}^{(\mathsf{sid},\mathcal{S})})$ to $\mathsf{Q_{cm}}$. If there exists $((\mathsf{sid}, \mathsf{i}, y_\mathsf{i}), \mathsf{cm}) \in \mathsf{Q_{cm}}$ such that $\mathsf{cm} \neq \tilde{\mathsf{cm}}_\mathsf{i}^{(\mathsf{sid},\mathcal{S})}$, $\mathcal{B}$ aborts and we denote the abort event as YColl. If $y_\mathsf{i} = 0$, $\mathcal{B}$ aborts and we denote the abort event as YZero. Then, $\mathcal{B}$ sets $\mathsf{msg}_{\mathsf{i},\mathsf{sid}} \leftarrow (\mathsf{sid}, \mathcal{S}, c, \{\mathsf{cm}_j\}_{j\in\mathcal{S}})$, computes $\sigma_\mathsf{i} \leftarrow \mathsf{DS.Sign}(\hat{\mathsf{pk}}_\mathsf{i}, \mathsf{msg}_{\mathsf{i},\mathsf{sid}})$, $S_2 \leftarrow S_2 \cup \{(\mathsf{i}, \mathsf{sid})\}$, and returns $(b_\mathsf{i}, y_\mathsf{i}, \sigma_\mathsf{i})$.

Signing Round 3 ($\mathcal{O}^{\mathsf{ISign}_3}$ queries). When $\mathcal{A}$ queries $\mathcal{O}^{\mathsf{ISign}_3}$ on $(\mathsf{i}, \mathsf{sid}, \{\sigma_j, y_j\}_{j\in\mathcal{S}})$ where $\mathcal{S} = \mathcal{S}_{\mathsf{i},\mathsf{sid}}$, $\mathcal{B}$ retrieves $(\mathsf{sid}, \mathcal{S}, c, \{\mathsf{cm}_j\}_{j\in\mathcal{S}}) \leftarrow \mathsf{msg}_{\mathsf{i},\mathsf{sid}}$, checks

1. if $(\mathsf{i}, \mathsf{sid}) \in S_2$ and $(\mathsf{i}, \mathsf{sid}) \notin S_3$ # Round 2 has completed but Round 3 has not completed yet.
2. if $\mathsf{cm}_j = \mathsf{H}_{\mathsf{cm}}(\mathsf{sid}, j, y_j)$ for all $j \in \mathcal{S}$ # In Round 2, for all corrupt j the record $((\mathsf{sid}, j, y_j), \mathsf{cm}_j)$ does exists.
3. if $\mathsf{DS.Verify}(\mathsf{pk}_j, \mathsf{msg}_{\mathsf{i},\mathsf{sid}}, \sigma_j)$ for all $j \in \mathcal{S}$ # All honest parties in $\mathcal{S}$ received the same $(\mathcal{S}, c, \{\mathsf{cm}_j\}_{j\in\mathcal{S}})$ for sid.

and returns $\perp$ if not. If all the checks pass but $\mathsf{BadCm}^{(\mathsf{sid},\mathcal{S})}$ occurs, $\mathcal{B}$ aborts and we denote this abort event as $\mathsf{ForgeCm}$. If all the checks pass but there exists $\mathsf{k} \in \mathsf{hon}_\mathcal{S}$ such that $\mathsf{msg}_{\mathsf{k},\mathsf{sid}} = \perp$ or $\mathsf{msg}_{\mathsf{k},\mathsf{sid}} \neq \mathsf{msg}_{\mathsf{i},\mathsf{sid}}$, $\mathcal{B}$ aborts and we denote this abort event as $\mathsf{ForgeSig}$.

Otherwise, $\mathcal{B}$ gets $\hat{z}$ by querying $\hat{\mathcal{O}}^{\mathsf{ISign}_3}$ on $\mathsf{sid}_{\mathsf{BSr3}}^{(\mathsf{sid},\mathcal{S})}$ if it has not done the query before. Else $\mathcal{B}$ recalls $\hat{z}$ from the previous query. Finally $\mathcal{B}$ returns $z_\mathsf{i} \leftarrow \lambda_\mathsf{i}^{\mathcal{S}}\gamma_\mathsf{i}\hat{z} + \tilde{a}_\mathsf{i}^{(\mathsf{sid},\mathcal{S})} + f(c, y)\lambda_\mathsf{i}^{\mathcal{S}}\delta_\mathsf{i}$, where $y = \sum_{i\in\mathcal{S}} y_i$.

Output. When $\mathcal{A}$ returns $\{(m_k^*, \sigma_k^*)\}_{k\in[\ell+1]}$, $\mathcal{B}$ then outputs $\{(m_k^*, \sigma_k^*)\}_{k\in[\ell+1]}$.

Analysis of $\mathcal{B}$. To complete the proof, we show that (1) whenever $\mathcal{A}$ wins the game simulated by $\mathcal{B}$, $\mathcal{B}$ also wins; (2) if none of the abort events occurs, $\mathcal{B}$ simulates the game $\mathsf{Game}^{\mathsf{omuf\text{-}t}}_{\mathsf{Snowblind[GrGen},f,\mathsf{DS]}}$ perfectly; (3) $\mathcal{B}$ only aborts with negligible probability.

(1) From the simulation, $\mathcal{B}$ makes at most one query to $\hat{\mathcal{O}}^{\mathsf{ISign}_I}$ when $\mathcal{A}$ makes one query to $\mathcal{O}^{\mathsf{ISign}_I}$ for $I = 1, 2$. Also, for each $(\mathsf{sid}, \mathcal{S})$, $\mathcal{B}$ makes at most one query to $\hat{\mathcal{O}}^{\mathsf{ISign}_3}$ if $\mathcal{A}$ make queries to $\mathcal{O}^{\mathsf{ISign}_3}$ corresponding to $(\mathsf{sid}, \mathcal{S})$. Therefore, $\mathcal{B}$ at most makes q_S queries to $\hat{\mathcal{O}}^{\mathsf{ISign}_1}$ and at most ℓ queries to $\hat{\mathcal{O}}^{\mathsf{ISign}_3}$. Also, it is clear $\mathcal{B}$ at most makes q_H queries to $\hat{\mathsf{H}}_{\mathsf{sig}}$.

Since $\mathcal{B}$ sets $\mathsf{pk} = \overline{\mathsf{pk}}$ and all random oracle queries to $\mathsf{H}_{\mathsf{sig}}$ are forwarded to $\hat{\mathsf{H}}_{\mathsf{sig}}$, each valid message-signature pair for pk is also valid for $\overline{\mathsf{pk}}$ in the game $\mathsf{Game}^{\mathsf{omuf}}_{\mathsf{BSr3[GrGen},f]}$. Therefore, if $\mathcal{A}$ wins, $\mathcal{B}$ wins the game $\mathsf{Game}^{\mathsf{omuf}}_{\mathsf{BSr3[GrGen},f]}$. Denote Win as the event $\mathcal{A}$ wins $\mathsf{Game}^{\mathsf{omuf\text{-}t}}_{\mathcal{A},\mathsf{Snowblind}}(\kappa)$ simulated by $\mathcal{B}$ and $\mathsf{Abort} := \mathsf{YZero} \vee \mathsf{YColl} \vee \mathsf{HashColl} \vee \mathsf{ForgeCm} \vee \mathsf{ForgeSig}$, and we have $\Pr[\mathsf{Win} \wedge (\neg\mathsf{Abort})] \leq \mathsf{Adv}^{\mathsf{omuf}}_{\mathcal{B},\mathsf{BSr3[GrGen},f]}$.

(2) It is clear that the key generation and signing round 1 are simulated perfectly. For signing round 2, on a query for $(\mathsf{i}, \mathsf{sid}, \mathcal{S})$, if $\mathcal{B}$ does not abort, we know y_i and b_i are computed correctly since $B_\mathsf{i} = \tilde{B}_\mathsf{i}^{(\mathsf{sid},\mathcal{S})} = \hat{B}^{\frac{1}{|\mathsf{hon}_\mathcal{S}|}} g^{\tilde{b}_\mathsf{i}} h^{\tilde{y}_\mathsf{i}^{(\mathsf{sid},\mathcal{S})}} = g^{\frac{\hat{b}}{|\mathsf{hon}_\mathcal{S}|}+\tilde{b}_\mathsf{i}} h^{\frac{\hat{y}}{|\mathsf{hon}_\mathcal{S}|}+\tilde{y}_\mathsf{i}^{(\mathsf{sid},\mathcal{S})}} = g^{b_\mathsf{i}} h^{y_\mathsf{i}}$. Also, since $\tilde{y}_\mathsf{i}$ is randomly sampled from $\mathbb{Z}_p$ and YZero does not occur, we know y_i is uniformly distributed in $\mathbb{Z}_p^*$, which implies the simulation of signing round 2 is perfect. Also, given $\mathsf{HashColl}$ does not occur, the simulation of H_{cm} is perfect.

For signing round 3, on a query for $(\mathsf{i}, \mathsf{sid}, \mathcal{S})$, we only need to show that if none of the abort events occurs, then $g^{z_\mathsf{i}} = A_\mathsf{i}\mathsf{pk}_\mathsf{i}^{f(c,y)\lambda_\mathsf{i}^{\mathcal{S}}}$. Since ForgeCm does not occur, we know for each $j \in \mathcal{S} \cap \mathsf{corrupt}$, y_j received in round 3 is exactly the same as the one $\mathcal{B}$ finds in round 2. Since ForgeSig does not occur, we know for each $\mathsf{k} \in \mathsf{hon}_\mathcal{S}$, y_k received in round 3 is exactly the one $\mathcal{B}$ computes in round 2. Therefore, we have

$$y = \sum_{j\in\mathcal{S}\cap\mathsf{corrupt}} y_j + \sum_{\mathsf{k}\in\mathsf{hon}_\mathcal{S}} y_\mathsf{k} = \sum_{j\in\mathcal{S}\cap\mathsf{corrupt}} y_j + \sum_{\mathsf{k}\in\mathsf{hon}_\mathcal{S}} (\frac{\hat{y}}{|\mathsf{hon}_\mathcal{S}|} + \tilde{y}_\mathsf{k}^{(\mathsf{sid},\mathcal{S})})$$
$$= \hat{y} + \left(\tilde{s}^{(\mathsf{sid},\mathcal{S})} + \sum_{j\in\mathcal{S}\cap\mathsf{corrupt}} y_j\right) = \hat{y} + \hat{s} \; .$$

Since $g^{\hat{z}} = \hat{A}\mathsf{pk}^{f(c,\hat{y}+\hat{s})}$ and $A_\mathsf{i} = \tilde{A}_\mathsf{i}^{(\mathsf{i},\mathsf{sid})} = \hat{A}^{\lambda_\mathsf{i}^{\mathcal{S}}\gamma_\mathsf{i}} g^{\tilde{a}_\mathsf{i}}$, we have

$$g^{z_\mathsf{i}} = g^{\lambda_\mathsf{i}^{\mathcal{S}}\gamma_\mathsf{i}\hat{z}+\tilde{a}_\mathsf{i}+f(c,y)\lambda_\mathsf{i}^{\mathcal{S}}\delta_\mathsf{i}} = \hat{A}^{\lambda_\mathsf{i}^{\mathcal{S}}\gamma_\mathsf{i}} g^{\tilde{a}_\mathsf{i}+f(c,y)\lambda_\mathsf{i}^{\mathcal{S}}\delta_\mathsf{i}} \mathsf{pk}^{f(c,\hat{y}+\hat{s})\lambda_\mathsf{i}^{\mathcal{S}}\gamma_\mathsf{i}}$$
$$= \hat{A}^{\lambda_\mathsf{i}^{\mathcal{S}}\gamma_\mathsf{i}} g^{\tilde{a}_\mathsf{i}} (\mathsf{pk}^{\gamma_\mathsf{i}} g^{\delta_\mathsf{i}})^{f(c,y)\lambda_\mathsf{i}^{\mathcal{S}}} = A_\mathsf{i}\mathsf{pk}_\mathsf{i}^{f(c,y)\lambda_\mathsf{i}^{\mathcal{S}}} \; .$$

Therefore, $\mathcal{B}$ simulates the game $\mathsf{Game}^{\mathrm{omuf}}_{\mathsf{BSr3}[\mathsf{GrGen},f]}$ perfectly if $\mathcal{B}$ does not abort, which implies

$$\mathsf{Adv}^{\mathrm{omuf\text{-}t}}_{\mathcal{A},\mathsf{Snowblind}[\mathsf{GrGen},f,\mathsf{DS}]}(\kappa) \leq \Pr[\mathsf{Win} \wedge (\neg\mathsf{Abort})] + \Pr[\mathsf{Abort}]$$

(3) For YZero, since $\tilde{y}_\mathsf{i}$ is randomly sampled from $\mathbb{Z}_p$ indepedent of $\hat{y}$ and the number of $\mathcal{O}^{\mathsf{ISign}_2}$ valid queries is bounded by q_S, we have $\Pr[\mathsf{YZero}] \leq \frac{q_S}{p}$. For YColl, since when y_i is computed, given the view of $\mathcal{A}$, $\tilde{y}_\mathsf{i}$ is uniformly distributed over $\mathbb{Z}_p$, which implies y_i is uniformly distributed over $\mathbb{Z}_p$. Since $|\mathsf{Q}_{\mathsf{cm}}| \leq nq_S + q_H$,[2] the probability that YColl occurs in one query is bounded by $\frac{nq_S+q_H}{p}$. Therefore, we have $\Pr[\mathsf{YColl}] \leq \frac{q_S(nq_S+q_H)}{p}$.

HashColl corresponds to the event that there exists $\mathsf{sid}, j, y, y', \mathsf{cm}$ such that $j \in \mathsf{corrupt}$, $((\mathsf{sid}, j, y), \mathsf{cm}) \in \mathsf{Q}_{\mathsf{cm}}$, $((\mathsf{sid}, j, y'), \mathsf{cm}) \in \mathsf{Q}_{\mathsf{cm}}$, and $y \neq y'$. For each query (sid, j, y) to H_{cm} where $j \in \mathsf{corrupt}$, since the number of entries Q_{cm} that corresponds to (sid, j) is bounded by q_H, the probability that $\mathsf{H}_{\mathsf{cm}}(\mathsf{sid}, j, y)$ collides with an existing entry in Q_{cm} corresponds to (sid, j) is bounded by $\frac{q_H}{p-1}$. Since the number of such query is bounded by q_H, we have $\Pr[\mathsf{HashColl}] \leq \frac{q_H^2}{p-1}$.

If ForgeCm occurs, we know $\mathsf{BadCm}^{(\mathsf{sid},\mathcal{S})}$ occurs for some $(\mathsf{sid}, \mathcal{S})$. Given the event $\mathsf{BadCm}^{(\mathsf{sid},\mathcal{S})}$ occurs, ForgeCm occurs during the $\mathcal{O}^{\mathsf{ISign}_3}$ query corresponding to $(\mathsf{sid}, \mathcal{S})$ only if $\mathcal{A}$ makes a new query (sid, j, y) to H_{cm} and gets back with cm where j and cm are fixed after $\mathsf{BadCm}^{(\mathsf{sid},\mathcal{S})}$ occurs, the probability of which, thus, is bounded by $\frac{q_H}{p-1}$. Therefore, $\Pr[\mathsf{ForgeCm}] \leq \frac{q_S q_H}{p-1}$.

Finally, the event that ForgeSig occurs implies $\mathcal{A}$ breaks EUF-CMA security of DS for some public key $\hat{\mathsf{pk}}_\mathsf{k}$. Therefore, we can construct an adversary $\mathcal{C}$ for

[2] For each $\mathcal{O}^{\mathsf{ISign}_2}$ query at most n entries are added, and for each H_{cm} query at most one entry is added.

the game $\mathsf{Game}_{\mathsf{DS}}^{\text{euf-cma}}$ as follows. To start with, $\mathcal{C}$ receives a public key $\hat{\mathsf{pk}}^*$ from $\mathsf{Game}_{\mathsf{DS}}^{\text{euf-cma}}$ and runs $\mathcal{A}$ by simulating the game $\mathsf{Game}_{\mathsf{DS}}^{\text{euf-cma}}$ faithfully except $\mathcal{C}$ randomly samples $\mathsf{k}^* \leftarrow\!\!\$\; [n] \setminus \mathsf{corrupt}$ and sets $\hat{\mathsf{pk}}_{\mathsf{k}^*} = \hat{\mathsf{pk}}^*$. Whenever $\mathcal{C}$ need to generate a signature for public key $\hat{\mathsf{pk}}_{\mathsf{k}^*}$, $\mathcal{C}$ makes a query to $\mathcal{O}^{\mathsf{Sign}}$. $\mathcal{C}$ also maintains $\mathsf{msg}_{\mathsf{i},\mathsf{sid}}$, which is defined in the construction of $\mathcal{B}$. Then, if $\mathsf{ForgeSig}$ occurs, there exists $\mathsf{k} \in [n] \setminus \mathsf{corrupt}$ and sid such that $\mathcal{A}$ sends a signature for $m_{\mathsf{k},\mathsf{sid}}$ and public key $\hat{\mathsf{pk}}_{\mathsf{k}}$ but never receives a signature for $m_{\mathsf{k},\mathsf{sid}}$ before. Therefore, if $\mathsf{k} = \mathsf{k}^*$, $\mathcal{C}$ can win the game $\mathsf{Game}_{\mathsf{DS}}^{\text{euf-cma}}$. It is easy to see that $\mathcal{C}$ makes at most q_S query to $\mathcal{O}^{\mathsf{Sign}}$. Since the probability that $\mathsf{k} = \mathsf{k}^*$ is at least $1/n$, we have $\Pr[\mathsf{ForgeSig}] \leq n\mathsf{Adv}_{\mathcal{C},\mathsf{DS}}^{\text{euf-cma}}$, which concludes the theorem. □

Blindness. The following theorem implies that our threshold scheme satisfies perfect blindness as long as the underlying base scheme is perfectly blind. The proof proceeds by a straighforward simulation argument.

Theorem 6. *For any* GrGen*,* f*, and* DS*, the scheme* $\mathsf{Snowblind}[\mathsf{GrGen}, f, \mathsf{DS}]$ *is perfectly blind if* $\mathsf{BS}[\mathsf{GrGen}, f]$ *is perfectly blind.*

Proof. The main idea is to show that for any adversary $\mathcal{A}$, there exists an adversary $\mathcal{B}$ such that $\mathsf{Adv}_{\mathcal{A},\mathsf{Snowblind}[\mathsf{GrGen},f,\mathsf{DS}]}^{\text{blind-t}}(\kappa) = \mathsf{Adv}_{\mathcal{B},\mathsf{BS}[\mathsf{GrGen},f]}^{\text{blind}}(\kappa)$.

It is not hard to see, by a standard hybrid argument, that it suffices to look at adversaries $\mathcal{A}$ that only query a single sid in $\mathsf{Game}_{\mathcal{A},\mathsf{Snowblind}}^{\text{blind-t}}(\kappa)$, i.e., they only attack a single session.

We construct $\mathcal{B}$ which has access to oracles $\hat{\mathcal{O}}^{\mathsf{USign}_1,\mathsf{USign}_2}$ and internally runs $\mathcal{A}$ by simulating the oracles $\mathcal{O}^{\mathsf{USign}_1,\ldots,\mathsf{USign}_4}$ as follows. Suppose $\mathcal{A}$ starts a signing session by querying $\mathcal{O}^{\mathsf{USign}_1}$ on input $(\mathsf{sid}, \mathsf{pk}, \mathsf{aux}, m_0, m_1, \mathcal{S}_0, \mathcal{S}_1)$. Since USign_1 takes no issuer's message as input and returns the signer set $\mathcal{S}$, $\mathcal{B}$ simulates $\mathcal{O}^{\mathsf{USign}_1}$ the same as $\mathsf{Game}_{\mathsf{Snowblind}}^{\text{blind-t}}$. For a query to $\mathcal{O}^{\mathsf{USign}_2}$ on input $(\mathsf{sid}, \{(A_{0,\mathsf{i}}, B_{0,\mathsf{i}}, \mathsf{cm}_{0,\mathsf{i}})\}_{\mathsf{i}\in\mathcal{S}_0}, \{(A_{1,\mathsf{i}}, B_{1,\mathsf{i}}, \mathsf{cm}_{1,\mathsf{i}})\}_{\mathsf{i}\in\mathcal{S}_1})$, $\mathcal{B}$ computes $A_I = \prod_{\mathsf{i}\in\mathcal{S}_I} A_{I,\mathsf{i}}$ and $B_I = \prod_{\mathsf{i}\in\mathcal{S}_I} B_{I,\mathsf{i}}$ for $I \in \{0,1\}$, queries $(c_0, c_1) \leftarrow \hat{\mathcal{O}}^{\mathsf{USign}_1}(\mathsf{sid}, \mathsf{pk}, m_0, m_1(A_0, B_0), (A_1, B_1))$, and finally returns $((c_0, \{\mathsf{cm}_{0,\mathsf{i}}\}_{\mathsf{i}\in\mathcal{S}_0}), (c_1, \{\mathsf{cm}_{1,\mathsf{i}}\}_{\mathsf{i}\in\mathcal{S}_1}))$. For a query to $\mathcal{O}^{\mathsf{USign}_3}$ on input $(\mathsf{sid}, \{(y_{0,\mathsf{i}}, b_{0,\mathsf{i}}, \sigma_{0,\mathsf{i}})\}_{\mathsf{i}\in\mathcal{S}_0}, \{(y_{1,\mathsf{i}}, b_{1,\mathsf{i}}, \sigma_{1,\mathsf{i}})\}_{\mathsf{i}\in\mathcal{S}_1})$, $\mathcal{B}$ returns $(\{(y_{0,\mathsf{i}}, \sigma_{0,\mathsf{i}})\}_{\mathsf{i}\in\mathcal{S}_0}, \{(y_{1,\mathsf{i}}, \sigma_{1,\mathsf{i}})\}_{\mathsf{i}\in\mathcal{S}_1})$. For a query to $\mathcal{O}^{\mathsf{USign}_3}$ on input $(\mathsf{sid}, \{z_{0,\mathsf{i}}\}_{\mathsf{i}\in\mathcal{S}_0}, \{z_{1,\mathsf{i}}\}_{\mathsf{i}\in\mathcal{S}_1})$, $\mathcal{B}$ computes $b_I = \sum_{\mathsf{i}\in\mathcal{S}_I} b_{I,\mathsf{i}}$, $y_I = \sum_{\mathsf{i}\in\mathcal{S}_I} y_{I,\mathsf{i}}$, $z_I = \sum_{\mathsf{i}\in\mathcal{S}_I} z_{I,\mathsf{i}}$ for $I \in \{0,1\}$ and returns $\hat{\mathcal{O}}^{\mathsf{USign}_2}(\mathsf{sid}, (z_0, b_0, y_0), (z_1, b_1, y_1))$.

Finally, after $\mathcal{A}$ returns b', $\mathcal{B}$ returns b'. It is clear that if $b = I$ for $I \in \{0,1\}$ in the game $\mathsf{Game}_{\mathsf{BS}}^{\text{blind}}$, $\mathcal{B}$ simulates the game $\mathsf{Game}_{\mathsf{Snowblind}}^{\text{blind-t}}$ for $b = I$ perfectly. Therefore, $\mathcal{B}$ has the same advantage as $\mathcal{A}$. □

Acknowledgements. Elizabeth Crites is supported by Input Output through their funding of the Blockchain Technology Lab at the University of Edinburgh. Tessaro and Zhu are supported in part by NSF grants CNS-2026774, CNS-2154174, a JP Morgan Faculty Award, a CISCO Faculty Award, and a gift from Microsoft.

References

1. Abe, M.: A secure three-move blind signature scheme for polynomially many signatures. In: Pfitzmann, B. (ed.) EUROCRYPT 2001. LNCS, vol. 2045, pp. 136–151. Springer, Heidelberg (2001). https://doi.org/10.1007/3-540-44987-6_9
2. Abe, M., Okamoto, T.: Provably secure partially blind signatures. In: Bellare, M. (ed.) CRYPTO 2000. LNCS, vol. 1880, pp. 271–286. Springer, Heidelberg (2000). https://doi.org/10.1007/3-540-44598-6_17
3. Baldimtsi, F., Lysyanskaya, A.: On the security of one-witness blind signature schemes. In: Sako, K., Sarkar, P. (eds.) ASIACRYPT 2013, Part II. LNCS, vol. 8270, pp. 82–99. Springer, Heidelberg (2013). https://doi.org/10.1007/978-3-642-42045-0_5
4. Barreto, P.L., Zanon, G.H.M.: Blind signatures from zero-knowledge arguments. Cryptology ePrint Archive, Paper 2023/067 (2023). https://eprint.iacr.org/2023/067
5. Bellare, M., Crites, E.C., Komlo, C., Maller, M., Tessaro, S., Zhu, C.: Better than advertised security for non-interactive threshold signatures. In: Dodis, Y., Shrimpton, T. (eds.) CRYPTO 2022. LNCS, vol. 13510, pp. 517–550. Springer, Cham (2022). https://doi.org/10.1007/978-3-031-15985-5_18
6. Bellare, M., Namprempre, C., Pointcheval, D., Semanko, M.: The one-more-RSA-inversion problems and the security of Chaum's blind signature scheme. J. Cryptol. **16**(3), 185–215 (2003). https://doi.org/10.1007/s00145-002-0120-1
7. Bellare, M., Rogaway, P.: The security of triple encryption and a framework for code-based game-playing proofs. In: Vaudenay, S. (ed.) EUROCRYPT 2006. LNCS, vol. 4004, pp. 409–426. Springer, Heidelberg (2006). https://doi.org/10.1007/11761679_25
8. Benhamouda, F., Lepoint, T., Loss, J., Orrù, M., Raykova, M.: On the (in)security of ROS. In: Canteaut, A., Standaert, F.-X. (eds.) EUROCRYPT 2021. LNCS, vol. 12696, pp. 33–53. Springer, Cham (2021). https://doi.org/10.1007/978-3-030-77870-5_2
9. Boldyreva, A.: Threshold signatures, multisignatures and blind signatures based on the gap-Diffie-Hellman-group signature scheme. In: Desmedt, Y.G. (ed.) PKC 2003. LNCS, vol. 2567, pp. 31–46. Springer, Heidelberg (2003). https://doi.org/10.1007/3-540-36288-6_3
10. Boneh, D., Lynn, B., Shacham, H.: Short signatures from the weil pairing. In: Boyd, C. (ed.) ASIACRYPT 2001. LNCS, vol. 2248, pp. 514–532. Springer, Heidelberg (2001). https://doi.org/10.1007/3-540-45682-1_30
11. Chaum, D.: Blind signatures for untraceable payments. In: Chaum, D., Rivest, R.L., Sherman, A.T. (eds.) CRYPTO 1982, Santa Barbara, California, USA, 23–25 August 1982, pp. 199–203. Plenum Press, New York (1982). https://doi.org/10.1007/978-1-4757-0602-4_18
12. Chaum, D., Fiat, A., Naor, M.: Untraceable electronic cash. In: Goldwasser, S. (ed.) CRYPTO 1988. LNCS, vol. 403, pp. 319–327. Springer, New York (1990). https://doi.org/10.1007/0-387-34799-2_25
13. Denis, F., Jacobs, F., Wood, C.A.: RSA Blind Signatures. Internet-Draft draft-IRTF-CFRG-RSA-blind-signatures-02. Work in Progress. Internet Engineering Task Force (2021). https://datatracker.ietf.org/doc/html/draft-irtf-cfrg-rsa-blind-signatures-02
14. Desmedt, Y.: Society and group oriented cryptography: a new concept. In: Pomerance, C. (ed.) CRYPTO 1987. LNCS, vol. 293, pp. 120–127. Springer, Heidelberg (1988). https://doi.org/10.1007/3-540-48184-2_8

15. Desmedt, Y., Frankel, Y.: Threshold cryptosystems. In: Brassard, G. (ed.) CRYPTO 1989. LNCS, vol. 435, pp. 307–315. Springer, New York (1990). https://doi.org/10.1007/0-387-34805-0_28
16. Fuchsbauer, G., Kiltz, E., Loss, J.: The algebraic group model and its applications. In: Shacham, H., Boldyreva, A. (eds.) CRYPTO 2018. LNCS, vol. 10992, pp. 33–62. Springer, Cham (2018). https://doi.org/10.1007/978-3-319-96881-0_2
17. Fuchsbauer, G., Plouviez, A., Seurin, Y.: Blind Schnorr signatures and signed ELGamal encryption in the algebraic group model. In: Canteaut, A., Ishai, Y. (eds.) EUROCRYPT 2020. LNCS, vol. 12106, pp. 63–95. Springer, Cham (2020). https://doi.org/10.1007/978-3-030-45724-2_3
18. Fuchsbauer, G., Wolf, M.: (concurrently secure) blind schnorr from schnorr. Cryptology ePrint Archive, Paper 2022/1676 (2022). https://eprint.iacr.org/2022/1676
19. Hauck, E., Kiltz, E., Loss, J.: A modular treatment of blind signatures from identification schemes. In: Ishai, Y., Rijmen, V. (eds.) EUROCRYPT 2019. LNCS, vol. 11478, pp. 345–375. Springer, Cham (2019). https://doi.org/10.1007/978-3-030-17659-4_12
20. Hendrickson, S., Iyengar, J., Pauly, T., Valdez, S., Wood, C.A.: Private Access Tokens. Internet-Draft draft-private-access-tokens-01. Work in Progress. Internet Engineering Task Force (2021). https://datatracker.ietf.org/doc/html/draft-private-access-tokens-01
21. icloud private relay overview. https://www.apple.com/privacy/docs/iCloud_Private_Relay_Overview_Dec2021.PDF. Accessed 03 Feb 2023
22. Kastner, J., Loss, J., Xu, J.: The Abe-Okamoto partially blind signature scheme revisited. In: Agrawal, S., Lin, D. (eds.) ASIACRYPT 2022, Part IV. LNCS, vol. 13794, pp. 279–309. Springer, Cham (2022). https://doi.org/10.1007/978-3-031-22972-5_10
23. Komlo, C., Goldberg, I.: FROST: flexible round-optimized schnorr threshold signatures. In: Dunkelman, O., Jacobson, Jr., M.J., O'Flynn, C. (eds.) SAC 2020. LNCS, vol. 12804, pp. 34–65. Springer, Cham (2021). https://doi.org/10.1007/978-3-030-81652-0_2
24. Kuchta, V., Manulis, M.: Rerandomizable threshold blind signatures. In: Yung, M., Zhu, L., Yang, Y. (eds.) INTRUST 2014. LNCS, vol. 9473, pp. 70–89. Springer, Cham (2015). https://doi.org/10.1007/978-3-319-27998-5_5
25. Lindell, Y.: Simple three-round multiparty schnorr signing with full simulatability. IACR Cryptology ePrint Archive, p. 374 (2022). https://eprint.iacr.org/2022/374
26. Lysyanskaya, A.: Security analysis of RSA-BSSA. Cryptology ePrint Archive, Paper 2022/895, PKC 2023 (2022). https://doi.org/10.1007/978-3-031-31368-4_10
27. Maurer, U.: Abstract models of computation in cryptography. In: Smart, N.P. (ed.) Cryptography and Coding 2005. LNCS, vol. 3796, pp. 1–12. Springer, Heidelberg (2005). https://doi.org/10.1007/11586821_1
28. Okamoto, T.: Provably secure and practical identification schemes and corresponding signature schemes. In: Brickell, E.F. (ed.) CRYPTO 1992. LNCS, vol. 740, pp. 31–53. Springer, Heidelberg (1993). https://doi.org/10.1007/3-540-48071-4_3
29. PCM: Click fraud prevention and attribution sent to advertiser. https://webkit.org/blog/11940/pcm-click-fraud-prevention-and-attribution-sent-to-advertiser/. Accessed 03 Feb 2023
30. Pedersen, T.P.: Non-interactive and information-theoretic secure verifiable secret sharing. In: Feigenbaum, J. (ed.) CRYPTO 1991. LNCS, vol. 576, pp. 129–140. Springer, Heidelberg (1992). https://doi.org/10.1007/3-540-46766-1_9

31. Pointcheval, D., Sanders, O.: Short randomizable signatures. In: Sako, K. (ed.) CT-RSA 2016. LNCS, vol. 9610, pp. 111–126. Springer, Cham (2016). https://doi.org/10.1007/978-3-319-29485-8_7
32. Pointcheval, D., Stern, J.: Security arguments for digital signatures and blind signatures. J. Cryptol. **13**(3), 361–396 (2000). https://doi.org/10.1007/s001450010003
33. Rial, A., Piotrowska, A.M.: Security analysis of coconut, an attribute-based credential scheme with threshold issuance. IACR Cryptology ePrint Archive, p. 11 (2022). https://eprint.iacr.org/2022/011
34. Rivest, R.L., Shamir, A., Adleman, L.M.: A method for obtaining digital signatures and public-key cryptosystems. Commun. ACM **21**(2), 120–126 (1978). https://doi.org/10.1145/359340.359342
35. Schnorr, C.P.: Efficient identification and signatures for smart cards. In: Brassard, G. (ed.) CRYPTO 1989. LNCS, vol. 435, pp. 239–252. Springer, New York (1990). https://doi.org/10.1007/0-387-34805-0_22
36. Schnorr, C.P.: Security of blind discrete log signatures against interactive attacks. In: Qing, S., Okamoto, T., Zhou, J. (eds.) ICICS 2001. LNCS, vol. 2229, pp. 1–12. Springer, Heidelberg (2001). https://doi.org/10.1007/3-540-45600-7_1
37. Shamir, A.: How to share a secret. Commun. ACM **22**(11), 612–613 (1979). https://doi.org/10.1145/359168.359176
38. Shoup, V.: Lower bounds for discrete logarithms and related problems. In: Fumy, W. (ed.) EUROCRYPT 1997. LNCS, vol. 1233, pp. 256–266. Springer, Heidelberg (1997). https://doi.org/10.1007/3-540-69053-0_18
39. Sonnino, A., Al-Bassam, M., Bano, S., Meiklejohn, S., Danezis, G.: Coconut: threshold issuance selective disclosure credentials with applications to distributed ledgers. In: 26th Annual Network and Distributed System Security Symposium, NDSS 2019, San Diego, California, USA, 24–27 February 2019. The Internet Society (2019). https://www.ndss-symposium.org/ndss-paper/coconut-threshold-issuance-selective-disclosure-credentials-with-applications-to-distributed-ledgers/
40. Stinson, D.R., Strobl, R.: Provably secure distributed schnorr signatures and a (t, n) threshold scheme for implicit certificates. In: Varadharajan, V., Mu, Y. (eds.) ACISP 2001. LNCS, vol. 2119, pp. 417–434. Springer, Heidelberg (2001). https://doi.org/10.1007/3-540-47719-5_33
41. Tessaro, S., Zhu, C.: Short pairing-free blind signatures with exponential security. In: Dunkelman, O., Dziembowski, S. (eds.) EUROCRYPT 2022. LNCS, vol. 13276, pp. 782–811. Springer, Cham (2022). https://doi.org/10.1007/978-3-031-07085-3_27
42. Trust tokens. https://developer.chrome.com/docs/privacy-sandbox/trust-tokens/. Accessed 03 Feb 2023
43. Vo, D.-L., Zhang, F., Kim, K.: A new threshold blind signature scheme from pairings. In: Proceedings of the 2003 Symposium on Cryptography and Information Security (SCIS 2003) (2003)
44. VPN by google one, explained. https://one.google.com/about/vpn/howitworks. Accessed 02 Feb 2023

Practical Schnorr Threshold Signatures Without the Algebraic Group Model

Hien Chu[1(✉)], Paul Gerhart[1], Tim Ruffing[2], and Dominique Schröder[1]

[1] Friedrich-Alexander-Universität Erlangen-Nürnberg, Erlangen, Germany
hien.chu@fau.de

[2] Blockstream Research, Victoria, Canada

Abstract. Threshold signatures are digital signature schemes in which a set of n signers specify a threshold t such that any subset of size t is authorized to produce signatures on behalf of the group. There has recently been a renewed interest in this primitive, largely driven by the need to secure highly valuable signing keys, e.g., DNSSEC keys or keys protecting digital wallets in the cryptocurrency ecosystem. Of special interest is FROST, a practical Schnorr threshold signature scheme, which is currently undergoing standardization in the IETF and whose security was recently analyzed at CRYPTO'22.

We continue this line of research by focusing on FROST's unforgeability combined with a practical distributed key generation (DKG) algorithm. Existing proofs of this setup either use non-standard heuristics, idealized group models like the AGM, or idealized key generation. Moreover, existing proofs do not consider all practical relevant optimizations that have been proposed. We close this gap between theory and practice by presenting the Schnorr threshold signature scheme Olaf, which combines the most efficient known FROST variant FROST3 with a variant of Pedersen's DKG protocol (as commonly used for FROST), and prove its unforgeability. Our proof relies on the AOMDL assumption (a weaker and falsifiable variant of the OMDL assumption) and, like proofs of regular Schnorr signatures, on the random oracle model.

Keywords: Threshold Signatures · Schnorr Signatures · FROST

1 Introduction

Threshold signatures [22,23] are digital signature schemes in which a set of n signers can specify a threshold t such that any subset of size t is authorized to produce signatures on behalf of the group. The security of threshold schemes states that the scheme remains secure even in a compromise of up to a certain threshold number of parties.

While threshold signatures have a long history dating back to the late 1980s s s and early 1990s [22,23,44,45], there has recently been a renewed interest in this primitive. This renewed attention is largely driven by the need to secure highly valuable signing keys, e.g., DNSSEC keys [19] or keys protecting digital wallets

H. Handschuh and A. Lysyanskaya (Eds.): CRYPTO 2023, LNCS 14081, pp. 743–773, 2023.
https://doi.org/10.1007/978-3-031-38557-5_24

in the cryptocurrency ecosystem [40], as well as the standardization efforts by IETF [17] and the NIST call for threshold multi-party schemes [13], indicating how quickly this field is moving into practical implementation.

Several threshold versions of various digital signatures have been proposed over the years, including threshold RSA signatures [21,34,51], DSA/ECDSA signatures [5,15,16,19,20,24,27–29,35,40,46,54], BLS signatures [12], and Schnorr signatures [30,32,33,37,39,52]. Among these, Schnorr threshold signatures have gained significant attention in recent years after the expiration of the patent on (regular single-signer) Schnorr signatures [49], in particularly due to their simple and linear algebraic structure. This structure makes it possible to construct threshold signatures that look and verify like a regular Schnorr signature, making them useful in scenarios where verification algorithms are fixed, and where privacy of signers and compactness of signatures is a concern. For instance, the Bitcoin network added support for Schnorr signature verification with the activation of the Taproot softfork in November 2021 with the explicit goal of enabling the use of Schnorr threshold signatures [53]. Since only the verification algorithm is fixed in the consensus rules and threshold signatures are simply normal Schnorr signatures, blockchain verifiers do need to be concerned with the specific details of threshold signing, and in fact cannot even tell from a valid signature whether it has been produced by a single signer or by some group of signers using a threshold signature scheme. Moreover, users can easily profit from any advances in Schnorr threshold signatures by simply switching to new signing protocols, without the need to change the Bitcoin network, which can be a tedious and protracted process that requires broad consensus in the ecosystem.

Most of the current attention to Schnorr threshold signature scheme focuses on the state-of-the-art scheme FROST by Komlo and Goldberg [37], which is in the process of being standardized by IETF [17] and for which multiple independent implementation efforts exist [1–4]. FROST's signature protocol is semi-interactive and highly efficient. It requires only one preprocessing round and one actual signing round, with the preprocessing round being possible before knowing the message to be signed. In addition, FROST is the first Schnorr threshold signature scheme that can accommodate arbitrary selections of t and n, provided that $t \leq n$. This includes choices where $t - 1 \geq n/2$, which ensures that even if f signers are malicious and form a dishonest majority ($n/2 \leq f \leq t-1$), the scheme is supposed to remain unforgeable.

PROVING THE SECURITY OF FROST: A CHALLENGING TASK. However, while FROST is highly efficient, proving it unforgeable turned out to be a challenging task. To make things worse, an entire jungle of different FROST variants appears in the literature. Komlo and Goldberg [37] proposed the initial variant, now called FROST1, and gave a non-standard heuristic argument[1] for its unforgeability when used with PedPoP, a variant of Pedersen DKG [31,45] with proofs

[1] That is, the heuristic argument did not consist of using commonly used idealized model such as the random oracle model, the generic group model or the algebraic group model but was constructed particularly for their proof.

of possession (PoPs), i.e., proofs of knowledge of the individual contributions to the joint public key.

Crites, Komlo, and Maller [18] and Bellare, Tessaro, and Zhu [11][2] analyze an optimized variant, which saves some exponentiations in the signing protocol. However, the optimized variant as formulated by Crites, Komlo, and Maller [18] (called FROST2-CKM in the following) has an additional check in signing protocol algorithm, which makes honest signers abort if two signers submit the same protocol message in the first round. Crites, Komlo, and Maller [18] prove that FROST2-CKM with PedPoP is unforgeable in the random oracle model (ROM) under the OMDL assumption and under the Schnorr knowledge of exponent assumption (Schnorr-KoE), which they introduce and justify in the algebraic group model (AGM) [25]. They further conjecture that the duplicate check is an artifact of their proof technique and can be avoided using techniques by Bellare, Tessaro, and Zhu [11], who analyze a variant (called FROST2-BTZ in the following), which does not have the duplicate check but is otherwise identical to FROST2-CKM. Bellare, Tessaro, and Zhu [11] introduce a hierarchy of unforgeability notions and prove that FROST1 and FROST2-BTZ with an idealized key generation (i.e., trusted setup) are unforgeable (fulfilling different notions in their hierarchy) under the one-more discrete logarithm (OMDL) assumption in the random oracle model (ROM).[3]

Most recently, Ruffing et al. [48] propose yet another variant FROST3, which promises significant bandwidth savings in the preprocessing phase by the ability to aggregate protocol messages before broadcasting them to the signers, but they do not give a proper formal proof and merely sketch a reduction to the unforgeability of FROST2-BTZ (whose proof relies on idealized key generation).

In a nutshell, this means that practitioners are left with the unsatisfactory situation that all existing proofs either rely on an idealized group model such as the AGM, on an idealized model of trusted key generation, or other non-standard heuristics. Moreover, none of the existing proofs properly cover the security of FROST3, which is the most efficient known variant of FROST.

THE AGM AND ITS LIMITATIONS. The algebraic group model (AGM) [25] is an idealized model similar to the generic group model (GGM) [41,50] in that the attacker does not get direct access to the group and its representation but can perform group operations with an external oracle. In contrast to the GGM, the attacker can exploit the encoding of group elements and derive (new) group elements via group operations for elements they have received earlier [36]. The recent work of Zhang, Zhou, and Katz [36] challenged the current formalization of the AGM as "hardness in the AGM may not imply hardness in the GGM". Thus, having a proof with fewer assumptions and idealized models would be important to enhance our understanding of security in the real world.

---

[2] A merged version of these two works appeared at CRYPTO 2022 [7].

[3] While the idealized key generation can in principle by instantiated using a fully simulatable DKG [31,33,38], we are not aware of any suitable DKG that has been proven secure in a dishonest majority setting ($n/2 \leq t-1$).

Our Solution: From FROST to Olaf. The main focus of our work is to provide a proof of FROST which does not rely on the AGM or idealized key generation. Our starting point is FROST3. While FROST3 is highly efficient, there has been no satisfying security analysis of it yet. To avoid idealized key generation, we combine FROST3 with a simplified variant SimplPedPoP of PedPoP. We call that combination Olaf, and we prove it unforgeable without relying on the AGM. We stress that our proof still relies on the ROM, but this is expected given that all known proofs of regular Schnorr signatures rely on the ROM, even if they use the AGM additionally [26].[4]

Mixed Forking – Our Proof Technique. The security proof of previous works [7] used the AGM within the DKG to extract the secret keys for the forged signature. A natural approach to avoid the AGM and extract the keys is to make use of the forking lemma in the random oracle model and provide a reduction to the underlying one-more discrete logarithm (OMDL) assumption [8,10]. However, this is non-trival because we need to consider the PedPoP DKG and the signing protocol together. The rationale behind this is that PedPoP (like Pedersen DKG) lacks the ability to be simulated. Hence, it becomes crucial to examine the combination of the DKG and the signing protocol as a unified execution in order to thoroughly analyze its properties. Unfortunately, the known variants of the forking lemmas [8,10] cannot be applied directly to this joint execution: The forking lemma of Bellare and Neven (BN) [9], building on the lemma of Pointcheval and Stern [47], allows extracting after one fork has happened, which means that an attacker can only split into two paths, each corresponding to a possible outcome of the protocol. This approach starts only two executions of the adversary, which is what existing forking proofs of FROST rely on. However, multiple extractions are impossible, meaning we would learn only one secret. Applying this technique t times as needed the simulation of the DKG in sequence to extract t times (from $t-1$ PoPs sent by the $t-1$ signers controlled by the adversary plus one forgery) leads to a total of 2^t simultaneous protocol executions. Therefore, any reduction that tried to extract t different values by applying the BN forking lemma t times would incur an exponential loss.

A second natural approach is the usage of the multi-forking lemma due to Bagherzandi, Cheon, and Jarecki (BCJ) [6] that allows efficient post-execution extraction of multiple values via forking. This means that a reduction can extract t different values simultaneously. In contrast to the previous lemma, this technique allows the extraction of t different values at one time, without the need for 2^t executions of an adversary. Although the multi-forking lemma successfully resolves the simulation issue concerning PedPoP, it cannot be employed for simulating the signature scheme. This limitation arises from the fact that the lemma entails the generation of a polynomial number of adversary executions ($\gg 2$), all potentially making signing queries. Consequently, it poses compatibility challenges with existing forking proofs of FROST. Therefore, none of the

[4] There is a claimed proof of Schnorr signatures in the GGM which does not rely on the ROM [42], but it has been found to be flawed [14].

above forking lemmas satisfies our needs completely. To overcome these technical difficulties, we use both forking lemmas, and we refer to this proof technique as *mixed forking.*

2 Technical Overview

The goal of our work is to prove the unforgeability of Olaf under the algebraic one-more discrete logarithm (AOMDL) assumption without relying on the AGM. The AOMDL assumption [43] is a weaker and falsifiable version of the OMDL assumption, which we will explain in Sect. 3.

Overview over OMDL Proofs for Schnorr-Style Signatures. Generally speaking, unforgeability proofs for Schnorr-style signatures based on the (A)OMDL assumption in the random oracle model follow a similar approach. The public key pk is the first output of the (A)OMDL challenge oracle, and the goal of the security reduction is to compute the discrete logarithm sk of pk. A signature for a message m, a secret key sk and the corresponding public key pk has the form $\sigma = (R, s) = (g^r, r + sk \cdot c)$, where $c = \mathsf{H}_{\text{sig}}(pk, g^r, m)$. The reduction has to provide a signing oracle for the adversary. To answer queries to the j-th signing oracle queries for an adversarially chosen message m_j without knowing the secret key sk, the reduction first requests a fresh challenge $R_j = g^{r_j}$ from the (A)OMDL challenge oracle as a commitment. Afterward, the reduction requests $R_j \cdot pk^c = g^{r_j + sk \cdot c}$ to the ODLog oracle provided by the (A)OMDL game. Upon this request, the ODLog oracle then returns the value $s_j = r_j + sk \cdot c$, such that (R_j, s_j) is a valid signature for the message m_j. Eventually, the adversary outputs its signature forgery $\sigma = (R, s)$. Then, the reduction forks the adversary, e.g., using the forking lemma by Bellare and Neven [9] (a generalization of the forking lemma by Pointcheval and Stern [47]), to obtain a second forgery $\sigma' = (R, s')$ on the same commitment R but a different hash value $c' \neq c'$. Using both forgeries, the reduction can extract the secret key sk by computing $sk = (s - s')/(c - c')$.

Transferring this Technique to Threshold Signatures. This forking technique proves effective in the context of Schnorr signatures within a single-signer scenario, and it can be modified to work with Schnorr threshold signature schemes: Instead of using a single group element R, it is necessary that the scheme uses two group elements D, E that will be combined into a single element R. (This is what FROST does.) On a very high level, two group elements are necessary because the adversary can force the reduction to answer a signing query corresponding to the same values D, E in both forks.

However, when considering the DKG additionally, a further distinction arises: Solving the equation of both forgery signatures releases the full signing key sk corresponding to the joint public key representing the entire group of signers. Yet, the reduction needs to learn the additive secret key share sk_i for some $i \in \{1, \ldots, n\}$, for which holds $sk = \sum_{i=1}^{n} sk_i$ to win the (A)OMDL game. Learning this share sk_i from the combined one sk is solely feasible if the reduction possesses the secret keys belonging to all remaining signers, including those controlled by the adversary.

Learning the Signing Key Shares of the Adversary. The recent work of Crites, Komlo, and Maller [18] addresses the issue of acquiring the adversary's secret shares using the Pedersen DKG protocol with proofs of possession (PedPoP) in place of the conventional Pedersen DKG protocol. PedPoP uses the same key sharing technique as the Pedersen DKG, but each participating signer $\mathcal{S}_i$ has to provide a proof of possession (PoP), i.e., a Schnorr proof of knowledge of the secret key share sk_i corresponding to the public key share g^{sk_i}. Intuitively, Crites, Komlo, and Maller utilize the algebraic representation of the Schnorr PoPs provided by the AGM to compute the secret key shares. Since our goal is to prove the protocol secure whilst avoiding the AGM, we can not follow this approach. Instead, we use a forking technique to extract the secret key shares utilizing the Schnorr PoPs.

Extracting $t-1$ PoPs Avoiding the AGM. As already mentioned, we want to extract $t-1$ PoPs by forking the adversary (which controls $t-1$ malicious signers). This is the point we encounter technical problems: Using the forking lemma by Bellare and Neven (BN) [9] to extract $t-1$ different PoPs sequentially would yield a security loss exponential in t. Therefore, we use the multi-forking lemma of Bagherzandi, Cheon, and Jarecki (BCJ) [6] to extract all $t-1$ PoPs simultaneously after the DKG phase is done. Doing so, we extract all $t-1$ adversarially chosen signing key shares sk_i.

The Drawback of Multi-forking. Even if this lemma provides us efficiently with all needed shares, it also creates a new problem: The underlying technique of BCJ executes many multiple executions of the adversary simultaneously until enough executions are successfully. Following this approach, the multiple executions of the adversary can all query a signing oracle after DKG is done. The number of these queries may exceed the maximum number of allowed queries to the ODLog oracle. Indeed, as we explained above, previous approaches crucially rely on the fact that only two executions of the adversary, corresponding to two group elements D and E, are run (as with the BN forking lemma).

Mixed Forking. To overcome this issue, we use a two-step approach that mixes both forking lemmas: As a first step, we apply the BN forking lemma to a wrapped version $\mathcal{B}$ of the adversary $\mathcal{A}$, obtaining an algorithm $\mathcal{C}$ that extracts the combined signing key sk. Here, $\mathcal{B}$ simulates the unforgeability game to $\mathcal{A}$ and answers signing queries using the discrete logarithm oracle provided by the (A)ODML game. As a second step, we apply the BCJ multi-forking lemma to $\mathcal{C}$, obtaining an algorithm $\mathcal{D}$ that simultaneously extract all $n-1$ signing key shares sk_i from the DKG phase. Having available all adversarial signing key shares and the combined signing key, our algorithm $\mathcal{D}$ can now extract the remaining signing key shares and solve all discrete logarithm challenges. However, $\mathcal{D}$ is not yet a working reduction to the (A)OMDL assumption: While it has a non-negligible probability ϵ of solving all discrete logarithm challenges, it does not solve the (A)OMDL problem because it still makes too many requests to the ODLog oracle: While each execution of $\mathcal{C}$ know runs only two executions of the adversary $\mathcal{A}$, algorithm $\mathcal{D}$ uses the BCJ multi-forking technique and thus runs many executions of $\mathcal{C}$ (and thus $\mathcal{D}^*$ runs many executions of $\mathcal{A}$ in total).

Reducing the Number of Discrete Logarithm Queries. To solve this last problem, we run $\mathcal{D}$ with a subtle modification, resulting in a full reduction $\mathcal{D}^*$: Only in one execution of $\mathcal{C}$ started by $\mathcal{D}^*$ will signing queries be answered using the ODLog oracle. The signing oracle queries that occur in all other executions of $\mathcal{C}$ started by the BCJ multi-forking lemma are not answered at all. Instead, these other executions are simply aborted after all executions of $\mathcal{A}$ therein have completed the DKG, i.e., before signing queries are allowed. Intuitively, this is not a problem because $\mathcal{D}^*$ only starts many executions of $\mathcal{C}$ to extract from the PoPs, which the adversary $\mathcal{A}$ is forced to send already during DKG. As our analysis shows, this is indeed sufficient, and reduction $\mathcal{D}^*$ has the same success probability ϵ as $\mathcal{D}^*$. However, this second reduction solves the (A)OMDL problem, as only two executions of the adversary $\mathcal{A}$ will ever make signing queries.

3 Preliminaries

Notation and Group Description. We denote by $x \leftarrow y$ the assignment of value y to variable x, and we denote by $x \leftarrow\!\!\$\, X$ the uniform sampling of x from the set X. We utilize the symbol $\mathcal{G} := (\mathbb{G}, p, g)$ to denote a set of group parameters, where $\mathbb{G}$ is a cyclic group of order p, where p is a λ-bit prime, and g is a generator of $\mathbb{G}$. Given an element $X \in \mathbb{G}$, we let $\log_g(X)$ denote the discrete logarithm of X with base g, i.e., $\log_g(X)$ is the value $x \in \mathbb{Z}_p$, such that $X = g^x$.

Algebraic One-More Discrete Logarithm (AOMDL). Our threshold signature scheme's security is established through the utilization of the algebraic one-more discrete logarithm (AOMDL) assumption [43], which serves as a falsifiable counterpart to the non-falsifiable OMDL assumption. Similar to the OMDL assumption, the AOMDL assumption allows an adversary $\mathcal{A}$ on input the group description $\mathcal{G}$ to query a challenge oracle OCH, which outputs group elements, and a discrete logarithm oracle $\mathsf{ODLog}(X, \ldots)$ oracle, which returns $\log_g(X)$. The adversary may obtain c challenges from the OCH oracle and wins, if it outputs the discrete logarithms of all c instances, but asked the ODLog oracle at most $q < c$ times. Yet, in contrast to the OMDL assumption, the adversary $\mathcal{A}$ has to provide an algebraic representation of the group element X on which it queries the ODLog oracle. This algebraic representation makes the AOMDL assumption falsifiable, as it allows the ODLog oracle and thus the defining game to be computable in PPT. Therefore, a security reduction to the AOMDL assumption is preferable over a security reduction to the OMDL assumption, because it gives us a stronger result than a reduction to the OMDL assumption.

Game $\mathsf{AOMDL}_{\mathbb{G}}^{\mathcal{A}}$	Oracle $\mathsf{ODLog}(X, (\alpha, (\beta_i)_{1\le i\le c}))$	Oracle OCH
$c \leftarrow 0;\ q \leftarrow 0$	// $X = g^{\alpha} \prod_{i=1}^{c} X_i^{\beta_i}$ for $X_i = g^{x_i}$	$c \leftarrow c+1$
$(y_1, \ldots, y_c) \leftarrow \mathcal{A}^{\mathsf{OCH},\mathsf{ODLog}}$	$q \leftarrow q+1$	$x_c \leftarrow\$\ \mathbb{Z}_p$
return $q < c \wedge (\bigwedge_{i=1}^{c} x_i = y_i)$	**return** $\alpha + \sum_{i=1}^{c} \beta_i x_i$	$X \leftarrow g^{x_c}$
	return $\log_g(X)$	**return** X

Fig. 1. Game $\mathsf{AOMDL}_{\mathbb{G}}^{\mathcal{A}}$ for the AOMDL assumption. The changes from the ordinary OMDL game to the AOMDL game are in gray.

We emphasize that our approach does not employ the algebraic group model (AGM). Furthermore, our reduction to the algebraic one-more discrete logarithm (AOMDL) assumption differs conceptually from utilizing the AGM. The AGM offers the advantage of assuming an algebraic adversary against a cryptographic scheme, simplifying the reduction process. However, for a security proof based on the AOMDL assumption, we are required to construct an algebraic *reduction.* This is an additional requirement for our reduction compared to the case of the OMDL assumption. Thus, our task of providing a reduction becomes more challenging when considering the AOMDL assumption, and we do not rely on the AGM in our approach.

Definition 1 (AOMDL Problem). *Given a group description* $\mathbb{G}$*, let* $\mathsf{AOMDL}_{\mathbb{G}}^{\mathcal{A}}$ *be as defined in Fig. 1. The algebraic one-more discrete logarithm (AOMDL) problem is* (τ, ϵ)*-hard for* $\mathbb{G}$ *if, for any algorithm* $\mathcal{A}$ *running in time* τ*, the advantage of* $\mathcal{A}$ *is*

$$\mathsf{Adv}_{\mathcal{A},\mathbb{G}}^{\mathsf{AOMDL}} := \Pr\left[\mathsf{AOMDL}_{\mathbb{G}}^{\mathcal{A}} = \mathsf{true}\right] \le \epsilon.$$

THRESHOLD SIGNATURE SCHEMES. Threshold signature schemes allow a group of n possible signers $\mathcal{S}_1, \ldots, \mathcal{S}_n$ to collectively sign a message m without the need for all signers to be present or active simultaneously.

In such a scheme, a signature is created by combining signature shares from a subset of the group, where the subset size t is typically smaller than the total number of users. Our definition of threshold signatures takes care of the key generation process, for which we require an interactive distributed key generation protocol (DKG) [31]. A DKG allows multiple parties to generate a shared key without any single party having access to the full key. Furthermore, we call a threshold signature scheme *semi-interactive* if the signing process involves a preprocessing round and a signing round. In the following, we assume that the bitstring encoding of an indexed set such as $\{\rho_i\}_{i\in S}$ or $\{\sigma_i\}_{i\in S}$ includes an encoding of the index set S.

Definition 2 (Threshold Signatures). *A* semi-interactive threshold signature scheme $\mathsf{TS} = (\mathsf{Setup}, \mathsf{KeyGen}, \mathsf{PreRound}, \mathsf{PreAgg}, \mathsf{SignRound}, \mathsf{SignAgg}, \mathsf{Verify})$ *consists of algorithms as follows:*

$par \leftarrow \mathsf{Setup}(n, t)$: *The* setup algorithm Setup *takes as input the number n of signers and the signing threshold t, and outputs public parameters par. From now on, par is an implicit input to all subsequent algorithms.*

$(pk, sk_i) \leftarrow \mathsf{KeyGen}(i)$: *The* key generation protocol KeyGen *is an interactive algorithm of which an instance is run by each signer $\mathcal{S}_1, \ldots, \mathcal{S}_n$ concurrently. Concretely, signer $\mathcal{S}_i$ runs* KeyGen(i), *which takes as input a signer index i and outputs a public key pk and the secret key sk_i of $\mathcal{S}_i$.*

$(state_i, \rho_i) \leftarrow \mathsf{PreRound}(pk)$: *The* preprocessing *algorithm is run by signer $\mathcal{S}_i$. It takes as input a public key pk and outputs a secret state $state_i$ and a presignature share ρ_i.*

$\rho \leftarrow \mathsf{PreAgg}(pk, \{\rho_i\}_{i \in S})$: *The deterministic* presignature aggregation *algorithm* PreAgg *takes as input a public key pk, a set $\{\rho_i\}_{i \in S}$ of presignature shares and outputs a (full) presignature ρ.*

$\sigma_i \leftarrow \mathsf{SignRound}(sk_i, pk, S, state_i, \rho, m)$: *The* Signature share algorithm *is run by signer $\mathcal{S}_i$. It takes as input a secret key sk_i, a public key pk, an index set $S \subseteq \{1, \ldots, n\}$ of signer indices with $|S| = t$, a secret state $state_i$, a presignature ρ, and a message m. It outputs a signature share σ_i.*

$\sigma \leftarrow \mathsf{SignAgg}(pk, \rho, \{\sigma_i\}_{i \in S}, m)$: *The deterministic* signature aggregation *algorithm takes a public key pk, a (full) presignature ρ, a set $\{\sigma_i\}_{i \in S}$ of signature shares and outputs a (full) signature σ.*

$b \leftarrow \mathsf{Verify}(pk, m, \sigma)$: *The verification algorithm takes as input a public key pk, a message m, and a signature σ. It outputs a boolean b, where $b =$* true *means that the signature is valid and* false *that it is invalid.*

Unforgeability Definition. We now provide an unforgeability definition for semi-interactive threshold signatures. Intuitively, we call a semi-interactive threshold signature scheme TS unforgeable if there exists no adversary that wins the game TS-UF with better than non-negligible probability.

Playing TS-UF, an adversary $\mathcal{A}$ controls up to t signers and has access to a preprocessing oracle PreRound and a signing oracle OSignRound. Our model assumes that presignature aggregation and signature aggregation are performed by an untrusted coordinator, so leave these tasks entirely to $\mathcal{A}$. Moreover, since the corresponding algorithms take only public inputs, we do not need to need provide oracles for them.

To setup keys, the adversary can run an instance of the key generation protocol KeyGen with every honest signer. We do not assume any implicit synchronization mechanism between honest signers. Instead, it is the responsibility of KeyGen to ensure synchronization explicitly. That means for example that it is in general possible in our game that at some point in time, some honest signer $\mathcal{S}_i$ has finished key generation already and is available for signing queries, while some other honest $\mathcal{S}_j$ has not finished key generation yet. Moreover, two honest signers $\mathcal{S}_i$ and $\mathcal{S}_j$ may in general output two different joint public keys $pk_i \neq pk_j$ (in which case the adversary may forge under either public key). We believe that the latter should never happen in any meaningful and secure key generation protocol. Yet, our way of modeling ensures that it is the responsibility of the

Game $\mathsf{TS\text{-}UF}^{\mathcal{A}}_{\mathsf{TS},n,t,CS}$

// CS is a set of indices of corrupted signers.
// It holds $CS \subseteq \{1,\ldots,n\} \wedge |CS| < t$.
$HS \leftarrow \{1,\ldots,n\} \setminus CS$ // Honest signers
$\mathit{Started}, \mathit{SK}, \mathit{PK}, \mathit{PreStates}, \mathit{Sigs} \leftarrow \emptyset$
$\mathit{par} \leftarrow \mathsf{Setup}(n,t)$
$(m^*, \sigma^*, i) \leftarrow \mathcal{A}^{\mathsf{OKeyGen},\mathsf{OPreRound},\mathsf{OSignRound}}(\mathit{par})$
return $\mathsf{Verify}(\mathit{PK}[i], m^*, \sigma^*) \wedge |\mathit{Sigs}[m^*]| = 0$

Oracle $\mathsf{OKeyGen}(i)$

if $i \notin HS \vee i \in \mathit{Started}$ **then return** $\bot$
$\mathit{Started} \leftarrow \mathit{Started} \cup \{i\}$
// Run $\mathsf{KeyGen}(i)$ with $\mathcal{A}$ controlling network connections
// between signer S_i and all signers S_j, $j \in \{1,\ldots,n\} \setminus \{i\}$,
// and in a separate thread concurrently to other oracle calls.
$(pk_i, sk_i) \leftarrow \langle \mathsf{KeyGen}(i), \mathcal{A} \rangle$
$\mathit{PK}[i] \leftarrow pk_i$; $\mathit{SK}[i] \leftarrow sk_i$
return pk_i

Oracle $\mathsf{OPreRound}(i, j)$

if $i \notin HS \vee \mathit{PK}[i] = \bot$ **then return** $\bot$
if $\mathit{PreStates}[i][j] \neq \bot$ **then return** $\bot$
$pk_i \leftarrow \mathit{PK}[i]$
$(\mathit{state}_i, \rho_i) \leftarrow \mathsf{PreRound}(pk_i)$
$\mathit{PreStates}[i][j] \leftarrow \mathit{state}_i$
return ρ_i

Oracle $\mathsf{OSignRound}(i, j, S, \rho, m)$

if $i \notin HS \vee \mathit{PK}[i] = \bot$ **then return** $\bot$
if $\mathit{PreStates}[i][j] = \bot$ **then return** $\bot$
$\mathit{state}_i \leftarrow \mathit{PreStates}[i][j]$
$sk_i \leftarrow \mathit{SK}[i]$; $pk_i \leftarrow \mathit{PK}[i]$
$\sigma_i \leftarrow \mathsf{SignRound}(sk_i, pk_i, \mathit{state}_i, \rho, m)$
$\mathit{Sigs}[m] \leftarrow \mathit{Sigs}[m] \cup \{i\}$
return σ_i

Fig. 2. Unforgeability game TS-UF for semi-interactive threshold signature schemes.

scheme to exclude (or otherwise handle) these cases of inconsistency between honest signers.

To win, $\mathcal{A}$ has to come up with a message, forgery pair (m^*, σ^*) that verifies and which is non-trivial, i.e., for which it has not learned any partial signature. This specific definition of a non-trivial forgery corresponds to the weakest notion TS-UF-0 in the hierarchy by Bellare, Tessaro, and Zhu [11]. Yet, our definition differs from theirs because key generation is idealized in their work.

Definition 3 (Unforgeability). *Let* $\mathsf{TS} = (\mathsf{Setup}, \mathsf{KeyGen}, \mathsf{PreRound}, \mathsf{PreAgg}, \mathsf{SignRound}, \mathsf{SignAgg}, \mathsf{Verify})$ *be a semi-interactive threshold signature scheme. Fix integers* $n \geq t \geq 1$, *and let the game* TS-UF *be defined as in Fig. 2. The scheme* TS *is* $(n, t, \tau, q_s, q, \epsilon)$-unforgeable under chosen-message attack (TS-UF) *if for any adversary* $\mathcal{A}$ *running in time* τ, *making at most* q_s *queries to each of* OPreRound *and* OSignRound, *and making at most* q_h *queries to each random oracle, and any set of corrupted parties* CS *with* $|CS| < t$, *the advantage of* $\mathcal{A}$ *is*

$$\mathsf{Adv}^{\mathsf{TS\text{-}UF}}_{\mathcal{A},\mathsf{TS},n,t,CS} := \Pr\left[\mathsf{TS\text{-}UF}^{\mathcal{A}}_{\mathsf{TS},n,t,CS} = \mathsf{true}\right] \leq \epsilon.$$

4 SimplPedPoP: A Simplified Pedersen PKG with PoPs

We introduce and employ a simplified version of the PedPoP distributed key generation (DKG) protocol [18,37]. We refer to this protocol as SimplPedPoP and provide a comprehensive description in Fig. 3. Unlike in PedPoP, but like in the original Pedersen DKG [31,45], we transmit the secret shares during the initial round of the protocol.

The Pedersen DKG [31,45] enables a group of n signers to collaboratively compute a public key pk, where any subset of t or more signers can collectively reconstruct the corresponding secret key $x = \log_g X$. At a high level, this is achieved through a combination of additive sharing and Shamir secret sharing, following these steps: Each signer $\mathcal{S}_i$ generates a random local polynomial $f_i(Z)$ of degree $t-1$ over the field $\mathbb{Z}_p$. Here, $f_i(Z) = a_{i,0} + a_{i,1}Z + \cdots + a_{i,t-1}Z^{t-1}$ represents the local polynomial for signer $\mathcal{S}_i$. By summing up all the local polynomials, we obtain the global polynomial $f(Z) = \sum_{i=0}^{n} f_i(Z) = a_0 + a_1 Z + \cdots + a_{t-1}Z^{t-1}$. Consequently, the joint secret key x is derived as the value $a_0 = f(0)$. During a successful execution of the protocol, each signer $\mathcal{S}_i$ receives Shamir secret shares from other signers $\mathcal{S}_j$, allowing them to compute the value $f(i)$. This would in principle allow t signers to reconstruct of $x = a_0 = f(0)$ via Lagrange interpolation, but in a threshold signing protocol, signers will want to avoid reconstruction of x and instead use Lagrange interpolation to compute only functions of x.

The PedPoP variant [18,37] of Pedersen DKG makes each signer additionally send a proof of possession (PoP), i.e., a Schnorr proof of knowledge of their share $f_i(0)$, which ensures that the protocol is secure even in a dishonest majority case $t - 1 \geq n/2$.

Our SimplPedPoP protocol reuses these ideas, but differs when it comes to ensuring agreement, i.e., ensuring that all honest signers agree *i)* on all common

Interactive Algorithm SimplPedPoP(i)

Signer $\mathcal{S}_i$ is connected to each other signer $\mathcal{S}_j$ via secure point-to-point channels, which guarantee authentication and confidentiality. This can, e.g., be realized with a public-key infrastructure (PKI).

1. Signer $\mathcal{S}_i$ chooses a random polynomial $f_i(Z)$ over $\mathbb{Z}_p$ of degree $t-1$
$$f_i(Z) = a_{i,0} + a_{i,1}Z + \cdots + a_{i,t-1}Z^{t-1}$$
and computes $A_{i,k} = g^{a_{i,k}}$ for $k = 0, \ldots, t-1$. Denote $x_i = a_{i,0}$ and $X_i = A_{i,0}$. Signer $\mathcal{S}_i$ computes a proof of possession of X_i as a Schnorr signature (on an empty message) as follows. Signer $\mathcal{S}_i$ samples $\tilde{r}_i \leftarrow \mathbb{Z}_p$ and sets $\tilde{R}_i \leftarrow g^{\tilde{r}_i}$. Signer $\mathcal{S}_i$ computes $\tilde{c}_i \leftarrow \mathsf{H}_{\text{reg}}(X_i, \tilde{R}_i, i)$ and sets $\tilde{s} \leftarrow \tilde{r} + \tilde{c}_i x_i$. Signer $\mathcal{S}_i$ then derives a commitment $(A_{i,0}, \ldots, A_{i,t-1})$ and sends $((\tilde{R}_i, \tilde{s}_i), (A_{i,0}, \ldots, A_{i,t-1}))$ to all signers $\mathcal{S}_j$ for $j \in \{1, \ldots, n\} \setminus \{i\}$.
Moreover, signer $\mathcal{S}_i$, for every $j \in \{1, \ldots, n\}$ (including $j = i$ itself), computes secret shares $\tilde{x}_{i,j} = f_i(j)$, and sends $\tilde{x}_{i,j}$ to signer $\mathcal{S}_j$.
2. Upon receiving proofs of possession, commitments and secret shares from all other signers, signer $\mathcal{S}_i$ verifies the Schnorr signatures by computing $\tilde{c}_j \leftarrow \mathsf{H}_{\text{reg}}(X_i, \tilde{R}_i, i)$ and checking that
$$\tilde{R}_j A_{j,0}^{\tilde{c}_j} = g^{\tilde{s}_j} \text{ for } j \in \{1, \ldots, n\} \setminus \{i\}.$$
Moreover, signer $\mathcal{S}_i$ verifies the shares received from the other signers by checking
$$g^{\tilde{x}_{j,i}} = \prod_{k=0}^{t-1} A_{j,k}^{i^k}.$$
If any check fails, signer $\mathcal{S}_i$ aborts.
Otherwise, $\mathcal{S}_i$ runs interactive algorithm $\mathsf{Eq}(i, t_i)$ with all other signers $\mathcal{S}_j$ for $j \in \{1, \ldots, n\} \setminus \{i\}$ on local input
$$\eta_i \leftarrow \{(\tilde{R}_j, \tilde{s}_j), (A_{j,0}, \ldots, A_{j,t-1})\}_{j=1}^{n}.$$
3. When $\mathsf{Eq}(i, \eta_i)$ outputs true for $\mathcal{S}_i$, then $\mathcal{S}_i$ terminates the SimplPedPoP protocol successfully by outputting the joint public key $X \leftarrow \prod_{j=1}^{n} X_j$ and the local secret key $\tilde{x}_i \leftarrow \sum_{j=1}^{n} \tilde{x}_{j,i}$. When $\mathsf{Eq}(i, t_i)$ outputs false, then $\mathcal{S}_i$ aborts.

Fig. 3. Interactive Algorithm SimplPedPoP.

parameters such as the joint public key pk, and *ii)* on the fact that all honest signers received proper secret shares. To this end, signers in SimplPedPoP simply abort when they do not receive proper secret shares, and each signer $\mathcal{S}_i$ runs an interactive equality check protocol $b \leftarrow \mathsf{Eq}(i, \eta_i)$ with all other signers on the common parameters η_i as seen by respective $\mathcal{S}_i$ in as a second step in the protocol. We require the following two abstract properties from the equality check protocol Eq.

Agreement: If an honest party outputs true, then every honest party will output true.

Integrity: If an honest party outputs true, then for every pair of honest parties $\mathcal{S}_i$ and $\mathcal{S}_j$, we have $\eta_i = \eta_j$ for their inputs.

We formulate agreement, which will not be required for unforgeability but is nevertheless highly desirable, deliberately such that it is orthogonal to message timing and synchrony assumptions (e.g., synchronous vs. asynchronous networks), because these assumptions may be very different for different applications.

Agreement and integrity ensure that if an honest signer $\mathcal{S}_i$ terminates the DKG protocol successfully, then all honest signers terminate successfully, and their public and secret outputs are as expected, and in particular, they agree on the joint public key pk. By abstracting the implementation details of the equality check, our protocol becomes adaptable to various scenarios. Let us consider two examples:

- In a scenario where a single user employs multiple signing devices (e.g., hardware wallets for cryptocurrencies) to set up a threshold signing, the devices can simply display the common parameters (or a hash of them) to the user. The user can manually verify the equality of these parameters and confirm their consistency to all devices by pressing a button or otherwise providing explicit confirmation.
- In a network-based DKG scenario, the equality check can be instantiated by having each signer transmit their local value of the common parameters (or a hash thereof) using a reliable broadcast protocol. Subsequently, the recipients can compare their local value with the received values to check for equality among all participants.

These approaches allow flexibility in implementing the equality check, catering to scenarios where manual verification or network-based broadcasts are suitable.

Simply aborting the protocol (or just never terminating it) in case of failure differs from the original Pedersen DKG and PedPoP. These existing protocols are constructed such that a protocol run can continue even if some malicious signer sends invalid secret shares or equivocates to make honest signers fail to achieve agreement. This accommodates the need for DKG protocols to offer some kind of termination or liveness property in practice.

However, we believe that for many applications, setting up keys is a one-time procedure for which aborting and asking for manual intervention in case of failure not only acceptable, but in fact even desirable: Coming back to the first aforementioned example scenario, if different signing devices display different hashes, the user knows for sure that one device is faulty, and it may not be desirable to continue the process with the existing set of devices. In contrast, a DKG protocol that guarantees termination would simply mask the error.

We would like to stress that none of our proof techniques crucially rely on the fact that we have chosen to work with a modified variant of PedPoP, and though a formal treatment is not in the scope of our work, we believe that it is straight-forward to adapt our unforgeability proof to work with PedPoP.

5 Olaf: A Practical Schnorr Threshold Signature Scheme

The Olaf threshold signature scheme is a semi-interactive Schnorr threshold signature scheme. It is in essence the FROST3 [48] scheme, which improves over previous variants of FROST by the ability to aggregate presignature shares before broadcasting them to signers, with key generation implemented via SimplPedPoP. Since our unforgeability proof covers this specific combination of SimplPedPoP and FROST3, we choose a separate name Olaf for the combination, to stress that the schemes should be regarded as a unit in terms of provable security.

$\mathsf{Olaf} := \mathsf{Olaf}_{\mathbb{G}}$ is parameterized by a group $\mathbb{G}$. We provide pseudocode descriptions of all algorithms in Fig. 4. Most importantly, Olaf outputs a Schnorr signature $\sigma = (R, s)$ which can be verified by the joint public key X like an ordinary single-signer Schnorr signature.

Since the scope of our work is unforgeability rather than robustness, we omit the algorithm ShareVal present in the original description of FROST3 [48], whose purpose is to verify signatures shares sent by individual signers and thereby to ensure that the signing protocol provides identifiable aborts. Nonetheless, the results by Ruffing et al. [48] on the robustness of FROST3 carry over to Olaf directly.

6 Security Analysis of Olaf

FORKING LEMMAS. In this section, we formally prove the security of Olaf using both the forking lemma by Bellare and Neven (BN) [9] (Lemma 1 below) and the multi-forking lemma by Bagherzandi, Cheon, and Jarecki (BCJ) [6] (Lemma 2 below). These represent different trade-offs between tightness and time complexity. Whereas the BCJ multi-forking lemma allows forking on multiple points without an exponential loss, it starts a polynomial number of executions of the forked algorithm instead of just two as in the BN forking lemma.

Lemma 1 (BN Forking Lemma [9]**).** *Let $q \geq 1$ be an integer. Let $\mathcal{A}$ be a probabilistic algorithm that takes as input a main input inp generated by some probabilistic algorithm* InpGen()*, elements $h_1, \ldots, h_q$ from some sampleable set H, and random coins from some sample able set $R_{\mathcal{A}}$, and returns either a distinguished failure symbol $\perp$, or a tuple (f, ϕ), where $f \in \{1, \ldots, q\}$ and ϕ is some*

$\mathsf{Setup}(n, t)$

$(\mathbb{G}, p, g) \leftarrow \mathbb{G}$
if $n > p$ **then return** $\perp$
// Select hash functions
$\mathsf{H}_{\text{non}}, \mathsf{H}_{\text{sig}} : \{0,1\}^* \to \mathbb{Z}_p$
$par \leftarrow (n, t, (\mathbb{G}, p, g), \mathsf{H}_{\text{non}}, \mathsf{H}_{\text{sig}})$
return par

$\mathsf{KeyGen}(i)$

// interactive algorithm
$(X, \overline{x}_i) \leftarrow \mathsf{SimplPedPoP}(i)$
$(pk, sk_i) \leftarrow (X, \overline{x}_i)$
return (pk, sk_i)

$\mathsf{PreRound}(pk)$

$X \leftarrow pk$
$d_i, \leftarrow\!\$\, \mathbb{Z}_p\, ;\ e_i, \leftarrow\!\$\, \mathbb{Z}_p$
$D_i \leftarrow g^{d_i}\, ;\ E_i \leftarrow g^{e_i}$
$state_i \leftarrow (d_i, e_i)$
$\rho_i \leftarrow (D_i, E_i)$
return $(state_i, \rho_i)$

$\mathsf{PreAgg}(pk, \{\rho_i\}_{i \in S})$

$X \leftarrow pk$
$\{(D_i, E_i)\}_{i \in S} \leftarrow \{\rho_i\}_{i \in S}$
$D \leftarrow \prod_{i \in S} D_i$
$E \leftarrow \prod_{i \in S} E_i$
$\rho \leftarrow (D, E)$
return ρ

$\mathsf{Lagrange}(S, i)$

$\Lambda_i \leftarrow \prod_{j \in S \setminus \{I\}} j/(j-i)$
return Λ_i

$\mathsf{SignRound}(sk_i, pk, S, state_i, \rho, m)$

// called at most once
// per secret state $state_i$
$\overline{x}_i \leftarrow sk_i\, ;\ X \leftarrow pk$
$(D, E) \leftarrow \rho$
$(d_i, e_i) \leftarrow state_i$
$b \leftarrow \mathsf{H}_{\text{non}}(X, S, \rho, m)$
$R \leftarrow DE^b$
$c \leftarrow \mathsf{H}_{\text{sig}}(X, R, m)$
$\Lambda_i \leftarrow \mathsf{Lagrange}(S, i)$
$\sigma_i \leftarrow d_i + be_i + c\Lambda_i\overline{x}_i$
return σ_i

$\mathsf{SignAgg}(pk, \rho, \{\sigma_i\}_{i \in S}, m)$

$X \leftarrow pk$
$(D, E) \leftarrow \rho$
$b \leftarrow \mathsf{H}_{\text{non}}(X, S, \rho, m)$
$R \leftarrow DE^b$
$s' \leftarrow \sum_{i \in S} \sigma_i$
$\sigma \leftarrow (R, s)$
return σ

$\mathsf{Verify}(pk, m, \sigma)$

$X \leftarrow pk$
$(R, s) \leftarrow \sigma$
$c \leftarrow \mathsf{H}_{\text{sig}}(X, R, m)$
return $(g^s = RX^c)$

Fig. 4. Threshold Signature Scheme $\mathsf{Olaf}_{\mathbb{G}}$.

Algorithm $\mathsf{Fork}_H^{\mathcal{A}}(inp)$

$\rho \leftarrow\$ R_{\mathcal{A}}\,;\ h_1,\ldots,h_q \leftarrow\$ H$
$\omega \leftarrow \mathcal{A}(inp,(h_1,\ldots,h_q);\rho)$
if $\omega = \bot$ **then return** $\bot$
$(f,\phi) \leftarrow \omega$
$h'_1,\ldots,h'_q \leftarrow\$ H$
$\omega' \leftarrow \mathcal{A}(inp,(h_1,\ldots,h_{f-1},h'_f,\ldots,h'_q);\rho)$
if $\omega' = \bot$ **then return** $\bot$
$(f',\phi') \leftarrow \omega'$
if $f \neq f' \vee h_f = h'_f$ **then return** $\bot$
$out \leftarrow (h_f,\phi)\,;\ out' \leftarrow (h'_f,\phi')$
return (f, out, out')

Fig. 5. Forking algorithm $\mathsf{Fork}_{H,R}^{\mathcal{A}}$ from Lemma 1.

Algorithm $\mathsf{MFork}_H^{\mathcal{A}}(inp)$

$\rho \leftarrow\$ R_{\mathcal{A}}\,;\ h_1,\ldots,h_q \leftarrow\$ H$
$\omega \leftarrow \mathcal{A}(inp,(h_1,\ldots,h_q);\rho)$
if $\omega = \bot$ **then return** $\bot$
$(F,\{\phi_f\}_{f\in F},\theta) \leftarrow \omega$
$mout \leftarrow \{(h_f,\phi_f)\}_{f\in F}\,;\ mout' \leftarrow \emptyset$
for $f \in F$ **do**
  $succ \leftarrow \mathsf{false}\,;\ k \leftarrow 0\,;\ k_{\max} \leftarrow |F|\cdot 8q/acc\cdot \ln(|F|\cdot 8/acc)$
  repeat
    $k \leftarrow k+1\,;\ h'_f,\ldots,h'_q \leftarrow\$ H$
    $\omega' \leftarrow \mathcal{A}(inp,(h_1,\ldots,h_{f-1},h'_f,\ldots h'_q);\rho)$
    if $\omega' = \bot$ **then continue**
    $(F',\{\phi'_f\}_{f\in F'},\theta') \leftarrow \omega'$
    if $f \in F' \wedge h'_f \neq h_f$ **then**
      $mout' \leftarrow mout' \cup \{(h'_f,\phi'_f)\}\,;\ succ \leftarrow \mathsf{true}$
  until $succ = \mathsf{true} \vee k > k_{\max}$
  if $succ = \mathsf{false}$ **then return** $\bot$
return $(F, mout, mout')$

Fig. 6. Forking algorithm $\mathsf{MFork}^{\mathcal{A}}$ from Lemma 2.

side output. The accepting probability of $\mathcal{A}$, denoted acc, is defined as the probability (over inp $\leftarrow$ $\mathsf{InpGen}()$, $h_1, \ldots, h_q \leftarrow\$ H$, and the random coins of $\mathcal{A}$) that $\mathcal{A}$ returns a non-$\perp$ output. Consider algorithm $\mathsf{Fork}_H^{\mathcal{A}}$ as defined in Fig. 5, and let frk be the probability (over inp $\leftarrow$ $\mathsf{InpGen}()$ and the random coins of $\mathsf{Fork}_H^{\mathcal{A}}$) that $\mathsf{Fork}_H^{\mathcal{A}}$ returns a non-$\perp$ output. Then

$$frk \geq acc\left(\frac{acc}{q} - \frac{1}{|H|}\right).$$

Lemma 2 (BCJ Multi-Forking Lemma [6]**).** *Let $q \geq 1$ be an integer. Let $\mathcal{A}$ be a probabilistic algorithm which takes as input a main input inp generated by some probabilistic algorithm $\mathsf{InpGen}()$, elements $h_1, \ldots, h_q$ from some sampleable set H, and random coins from some sampleable set $R_{\mathcal{A}}$, and returns either a distinguished failure symbol $\perp$, or a tuple $(F, \{\phi_j\}_{j \in F}, \theta)$, where $F \subseteq \{1, \ldots, q\}$ and $F \neq \emptyset$, and $\{\phi_j\}_{j \in F}$ and θ are some side outputs. The accepting probability of $\mathcal{A}$, denoted acc, is defined as the probability (over inp $\leftarrow$ $\mathsf{InpGen}()$, $h_1, \ldots, h_q \leftarrow\$ H$, and the random coins of $\mathcal{A}$) that $\mathcal{A}$ returns a non-$\perp$ output. Consider algorithm $\mathsf{MFork}^{\mathcal{A}}$ as defined in Fig. 6, and let mfrk be the probability (over inp $\leftarrow$ $\mathsf{InpGen}()$ and the random coins of $\mathsf{MFork}^{\mathcal{A}}$) that $\mathsf{MFork}^{\mathcal{A}}$ returns a non-$\perp$ output. Assume $|H| > |F| \cdot 8q/acc$. Then*

$$mfrk \geq \frac{acc}{8}.$$

Note that our formulation of Lemma 2 has an additional side output θ, which is independent of $j \in F$ and not present in the original formulation of the lemma. It is easy to see that this modification does not invalidate the lemma. Indeed, θ can be thought of as included in ϕ_j for every $j \in F$ (but we would like to avoid this approach to keep the notation simple).

SECURITY ANALYSIS. We prove the following result about the unforgeability of Olaf under the AOMDL assumption.

Theorem 1. *Fix $n \geq t \geq 1$ and a group description $\mathcal{G} = (\mathbb{G}, p, g)$ such that p is a λ-bit prime. For any adversary $\mathcal{A}$ running in expected time τ, making at most q_s queries to each of $\mathsf{OPreRound}$ and $\mathsf{OSignRound}$, making at most q_h queries to each random oracle, and having an advantage of $\epsilon = \mathsf{Adv}^{\mathsf{TS\text{-}UF}}_{\mathcal{A},\mathsf{Olaf},n,t,CS}$ such that $\lambda > \log_2((8q^3t + 6q)/\epsilon^2)$, there exists an algorithm $\mathcal{D}^*$ running in expected time not more than*

$$\tau' \approx \frac{8q^2t^2}{\epsilon^2 - 3q \cdot 2^{1-\lambda}} \cdot \ln \frac{8q^2t}{\epsilon^2 - 3q \cdot 2^{1-\lambda}} \cdot (\tau_{\mathsf{TS\text{-}UF}} + \tau)$$

and having an advantage of $\epsilon' = \mathsf{Adv}^{\mathsf{AOMDL}}_{\mathcal{D}^*,\mathcal{G}}$ such that

$$\epsilon' \geq \frac{\epsilon^2}{8q} - \frac{6 + q^2}{2^{\lambda-3}},$$

where $q = 3q_h + 2q_s + t$ and $\tau_{\mathsf{TS\text{-}UF}}$ is the running time of game $\mathsf{TS\text{-}UF}_{\mathsf{Olaf},n,t,CS}$ ignoring the time to run $\mathcal{A}$ within the game.

Proof Overview. We construct a sequence of algorithms. First, we construct a wrapper $\mathcal{B}$ around $\mathcal{A}$, which simulates game $\mathsf{TS\text{-}UF}^{\mathcal{A}}_{\mathsf{TS},n,t,CS}$ towards $\mathcal{A}$ and embeds a discrete logarithm challenge X^* as the additive share of a single honest signer in the key generation. That means that $\mathcal{B}$ cannot handle signing queries honestly, and will need to query the challenge oracle provided by the AOMDL game when simulating presigning queries to be able to use the discrete logarithm oracle provided by the AOMDL game to simulate signing queries. Algorithm $\mathcal{B}$ returns the PoPs sent by $\mathcal{A}$ during key generation, the forgery output by $\mathcal{A}$, and some auxiliary information.

In a first forking step, we use $\mathcal{B}$ to construct an algorithm $\mathcal{C}$, which runs forking algorithm $\mathsf{Fork}^{\mathcal{B}}_{H}$, forking $\mathcal{B}$ on the $\mathsf{H}_{\mathsf{sig}}$ query corresponding to the forgery. This enables $\mathcal{C}$ to compute and return a discrete logarithm x of the public key X as common in proofs of Schnorr signatures.

In a second forking step, we use $\mathcal{C}$ to construct an algorithm $\mathcal{D}$, which runs the multiple-forking algorithm $\mathsf{MFork}^{\mathcal{C}}_{H}$, forking $\mathcal{C}$ on all $\mathsf{H}_{\mathsf{reg}}$ queries corresponding to PoPs sent by $\mathcal{A}$. This enables $\mathcal{D}$ to compute the additive shares that the adversary contributed to x. By subtracting these from x, algorithm $\mathcal{D}$ obtains the discrete logarithm x^* of X^*. With this knowledge, $\mathcal{D}$ can solve for all additional discrete logarithm challenges it obtained during the simulation of signing queries. However, due to the fact $\mathcal{D}$ runs many instances of $\mathcal{C}$, which all run two instances of $\mathcal{B}$, which all make use of the discrete logarithm oracle to answer signing queries, $\mathcal{D}$ in total makes too many queries to this oracle.

As a final step, we construct an algorithm $\mathcal{D}^*$, which is like $\mathcal{D}$ but aborts all but one execution of $\mathcal{C}$ after key generation, i.e., after all PoPs from $\mathcal{A}$ have been received. Since one full execution of $\mathcal{C}$ is enough to extract x, and all other aborted executions run far enough such that $\mathcal{D}^*$ can still extract from the PoPs, the outputs of $\mathcal{D}^*$ and $\mathcal{D}$ are the same. However, the full execution of $\mathcal{C}$ in $\mathcal{D}^*$ makes only two queries to the discrete logarithm oracle per signing query, i.e., as many as challenge oracle queries made. Since $\mathcal{D}^*$ has additionally solved the challenge X^*, it wins AOMDL.

Proof. We construct a series of algorithms. In the entire proof, we call the probability that some algorithm $\mathcal{A}$ returns a non-$\perp$ output the *accepting probability* $acc_{\mathcal{A}}$ of $\mathcal{A}$. Whenever some algorithm calls an oracle $\mathsf{ODLog}(X, (\alpha, (\beta_i)_{1 \le i \le c}))$, it will be clear from the way X is constructed how to represent X as a linear combination of the generator g and obtained discrete logarithm challenges. Thus, for the sake of readability, we allow ourselves to omit the representation argument $(\alpha, (\beta_i)_{1 \le i \le c})$.

Construction of Algorithm $\mathcal{B}$. We describe how to construct algorithm $\mathcal{B}$. Let $HS = \{1, \dots, n\} \setminus CS$. Algorithm $\mathcal{B}$ takes as input

$$inp_{\mathcal{B}} = (X^*, \{U_{i,j}\}_{i \in HS, j \in \{1, \dots 2q_s\}}, (h_{\mathrm{reg},1}, \dots, h_{\mathrm{reg},q})),$$

where $X^* \leftarrow\$ \mathbb{G}$ and $U_{i,j} \leftarrow\$ \mathbb{G}$ for all $i \in HS, j \in \{1, \dots 2q_s\}$ and $h_{\mathrm{reg},i} \leftarrow\$ \mathbb{Z}_p$. It also takes as input a stream $(h_1, \dots, h_q) \leftarrow\$ \mathbb{Z}_p^q$.

The inputs X^* and $U_{i,j}$ represent $|HS| \cdot q_s + 1$ discrete logarithm challenges that will be obtained via $|HS| \cdot q_s + 1$ oracle calls OCH by the caller of $\mathcal{B}$. Accordingly, $\mathcal{B}$ has access to a discrete logarithm oracle ODLog provided by the caller. (When we apply a forking lemma to $\mathcal{B}$, we can think of this deterministic oracle as part of $\mathcal{B}$ because the lemma does not require $\mathcal{B}$ to be PPT.)

Algorithm $\mathcal{B}$ initializes associative arrays $T_{\text{reg}}, T_{\text{non}}$ and T_{sig}. For these arrays, which store programmed values for respectively $\mathsf{H}_{\text{reg}}, \mathsf{H}_{\text{non}}$ and H_{sig}, we write assignments in form "$T(x) \leftarrow y$" for an array T, and we write "$T(x) = \bot$" if there is no value stored under key x. It also initializes two counters $\mathit{ctrh} \leftarrow 0$ and $\mathit{ctrh}_{\text{reg}} \leftarrow 0$, and a flag $\mathit{Ev}_1 \leftarrow \mathsf{false}$ that will help keep track of a bad event. Algorithm $\mathcal{B}$ initializes sets $\mathit{Started} \leftarrow \emptyset$ for keeping track of signers who started key generation, $S \leftarrow \emptyset$ for keeping track of open signing sessions, $\mathit{Sigs} \leftarrow \emptyset$ for keeping track of completed signing sessions, $Q \leftarrow \emptyset$ for keeping track of queries to ODLog, and a counter $\mathit{sidctr} \leftarrow 0$ for signing queries $\mathsf{OPreRound}$. It also picks $\kappa \leftarrow\$ HS$. Then, it picks random coins $\rho_{\mathcal{A}}$ and runs $\mathcal{A}((\mathbb{G}, p, g), t, n; \rho_{\mathcal{A}})$, answering oracle queries as follows.

- Key generation queries $\mathsf{OKeyGen}(i)$: If $i \in \mathit{Started}$, then $\mathcal{B}$ returns $\bot$. Otherwise, $\mathcal{B}$ lets $\mathit{Started} \leftarrow \mathit{Started} \cup \{i\}$.
  If $i = \kappa$, then $\mathcal{B}$ lets $\{\gamma_j, \delta_j\}_{j \in HS} \leftarrow \mathsf{Sim}(X^*)$ as defined in Fig. 7 to embed the challenge X^* as $\mathcal{S}_\kappa$'s additive share of the public key.
  If $i \neq \kappa$, $\mathcal{B}$ follows $\mathsf{SimplPedPoP}_i$ honestly except that it never receives any secret shares from $\mathcal{S}_\kappa$ during step 2 (Fig. 3) and moves on to the equality check unconditionally. It consequently outputs no secret key sk_i at step 3.
  In any case ($i = \kappa$ or $i \neq \kappa$), $\mathcal{B}$ lets $X_i \leftarrow \prod_j^n A_{j,0}$, where $A_{j,0}$ are either as in Sim or as in $\mathsf{SimplPedPoP}_i$. If $i = \min(HS)$, $\mathcal{B}$ collects all PoPs $\{(\tilde{R}_j, \tilde{s}_j)\}_{j \in CS}$ that $\mathcal{A}$ sends while $\mathsf{OKeyGen}(i)$ is running.
- Hash queries $\mathsf{H}_{\text{reg}}(X_i, \tilde{R}_i, i)$: If $T_{\text{reg}}(X_i, \tilde{R}_i, i) = \bot$, then $\mathcal{B}$ increments $\mathit{ctrh}_{\text{reg}}$, assigns $T_{\text{reg}}(X_i, \tilde{R}_i, i) \leftarrow h_{\mathit{ctrh}_{\text{reg}}}$. It returns $T_{\text{reg}}(X_i, \tilde{R}_i, i)$ as query answer.
- Hash queries $\mathsf{H}_{\text{non}}(X, S, \rho, m)$: If $T_{\text{non}}(X, S, \rho, m) = \bot$, then $\mathcal{B}$ increments ctrh, assigns $T_{\text{non}}(X, S, \rho, m) \leftarrow h_{\mathit{ctrh}}$. If $T_{\text{sig}}(X, R, m) = \bot$, then $\mathcal{B}$ makes an internal query to $\mathsf{H}_{\text{sig}}(X, R, m)$. Finally, it returns $T_{\text{non}}(X, S, \rho, m)$.
- Hash queries $\mathsf{H}_{\text{sig}}(X, R, m)$: If the value $T_{\text{sig}}(X, R, m) = \bot$, then $\mathcal{B}$ increments ctrh, assigns $T_{\text{sig}}(X, R, m) \leftarrow h_{\mathit{ctrh}}$. It returns $T_{\text{sig}}(X, R, m)$.
- Preprocessing queries $\mathsf{OPreRound}(i, j)$: $\mathcal{B}$ increments sidctr, adds sidctr to S, and returns $D_i \leftarrow U_{2\mathit{sidctr}-1}, E_i \leftarrow U_{2\mathit{sidctr}}$.
- Signing queries $\mathsf{OSignRound}(i, j, S, \rho, m)$: If $X_i = \bot$ or $j \notin S$, then $\mathcal{B}$ returns $\bot$. Otherwise, $\mathcal{B}$ removes j from S, lets $\mathit{Sigs}[m] \leftarrow \mathit{Sigs}[m] \cup \{i\}$ and proceeds as follows. Let $D_i \leftarrow U_{i,2j-1}, E_i \leftarrow U_{i,2j}$ and $(D, E) \leftarrow \rho$. $\mathcal{B}$ lets $b \leftarrow T_{\text{non}}(X, S, (D, E), m)$ and $T_{\text{sig}}(X, R, m)$ (if any of these values is $\bot$, it first queries H_{non} or H_{sig} internally for the corresponding input). It then makes a query to the DL oracle to obtain $\sigma_I \leftarrow \mathsf{ODLog}\left(D_i E_i^b \left((X^*)^{\gamma_i} g^{\delta_i}\right)^{c\Lambda_i}\right)$. It lets $Q \leftarrow Q \cup \{((i, j, \sigma_i, b, c, \Lambda_i)\}$ and returns σ_i.

It can be verified that, unless Ev_1 is set to true, algorithm $\mathcal{B}$ provides a perfect simulation of game $\mathsf{TS\text{-}UF}^{\mathcal{A}}_{\mathsf{TS},n,t,CS}$. Note that $\mathcal{B}$ programs random oracles H_{non}

and $\mathsf{H}_{\mathsf{sig}}$ with a single stream of hash values $h_1, \ldots, h_q$. This is to ensure that, when $\mathcal{B}$ will be forked on a $\mathsf{H}_{\mathsf{sig}}$ value, not only all $\mathsf{H}_{\mathsf{sig}}$ values, but also all $\mathsf{H}_{\mathsf{non}}$ values will be refreshed after the forking point in the second execution of $\mathcal{B}$.

Since SimplPedPoP runs an equality check protocol Eq (ensuring integrity) on inputs the common parameters $\{(\tilde{R}_j, \tilde{s}_j), (A_{j,0}, \ldots, A_{j,t-1})\}_{j=1}^n$, we know that before any query $\mathsf{OSignRound}(i, \ldots)$ which is not rejected due to $X_i \neq \perp$, all PoPs $\{(\tilde{R}_j, \tilde{s}_j)\}_{j \in CS}$ sent by $\mathcal{A}$ have been received by all honest signers, i.e., in particular by $\mathcal{S}_{\min(HS)}$. (Also, all honest signers have received identical PoPs, but we do not need this fact.) Moreover, the equality check protocol ensures that whenever two honest parties $i, j \in HS$ simulated by $\mathcal{B}$ output public keys X_i and X_j in the key generation, we know that $X_i = X_j$. Thus, we can just write X from now on.

If $\mathcal{A}$ returns $\perp$, then $\mathcal{B}$ outputs $\perp$. Otherwise, $\mathcal{B}$ checks the validity of the PoPs as follows. If $T_{\mathsf{reg}}(X_i, \tilde{R}_i, i) = \perp$, it makes an internal query to $\mathsf{H}_{\mathsf{reg}}(X_i, \tilde{R}_i)$ which ensures that $T_{\mathsf{reg}}(X_i, \tilde{R}_i, i)$ is defined for each $i \in CS$, lets $\tilde{c}_i \leftarrow T_{\mathsf{reg}}(X_i, \tilde{R}_i, i)$. If for some $i \in CS$, $g^{\tilde{s}_i} \neq \tilde{R}_i X_i^{\tilde{c}_i}$, $\mathcal{B}$ outputs $\perp$.

Otherwise, denote by $(i, m, (R, s))$ the output of $\mathcal{A}$, (i.e., (R, s) is a purported forgery for the message m). Then, $\mathcal{B}$ checks the validity of the forgery as follows. If $T_{\mathsf{sig}}(X, R, m) = \perp$, it makes an internal query to $\mathsf{H}_{\mathsf{sig}}(X, R, m)$, and lets $c \leftarrow T_{\mathsf{sig}}(X, R, m)$. If $g^s \neq RX^c$, i.e., the forgery is not a valid signature, or if $|Sigs[m]| > 0$, i.e., the forgery is invalid because the adversary made OSignRound queries for m, $\mathcal{B}$ outputs $\perp$.

Otherwise, it takes the following additional steps. Algorithm $\mathcal{B}$ lets F be the set such that for each index $f \in F$, array entry $T_{\mathsf{reg}}(X_{\iota^{-1}(f),0}, \tilde{R}_{\iota^{-1}(f)}, \iota(f))$ was assigned input h_f for some bijective re-indexing $\iota : F \rightarrow CS$. (In more detail, since the signer index i is the last argument to $\mathsf{H}_{\mathsf{reg}}$, we know that every two distinct signers $\mathcal{S}_i$ and $\mathcal{S}_{i'}$ for $i, i' \in CS$ with $i \neq i'$ have T_{reg} values h_f and $h_{f'}$ with $f \neq f'$, i.e., there is an injective function $\iota^{-1} : CS \rightarrow \{1, \ldots, q\}$, and $\mathcal{B}$ lets $F \leftarrow \iota^{-1}(CS)$, so that $\iota : F \rightarrow CS$ is bijective.) Denote by f_{sig} the index such that $T_{\mathsf{sig}}(X, R, m) = h_{f_{\mathsf{sig}}}$. Algorithm $\mathcal{B}$ outputs $(f_{\mathsf{sig}}, (s, (F, \{\phi_f\}_{f \in F}, \{x_i\}_{i \in HS}, Q)))$.

It remains to upper bound $\Pr[Ev_1]$. The group element $\tilde{R}_\kappa$ related to Ev_1 event is assigned to $g^{\tilde{s}_\kappa}(X^*)^c$, which is uniformly random in $\mathbb{G}$ as $\tilde{s}_\kappa$ is uniformly random over $\mathbb{Z}_p$ and independent of $(X^*)^c$. In addition, there are always at most q queries to $\mathsf{H}_{\mathsf{reg}}$, and hence, $\Pr[Ev_1]$ occurs with probability at most $q/2^{\lambda-1}$.

We show that $\mathcal{B}$ receives enough values for programming random oracles by bounding $ctrh_{\mathsf{reg}}$ and $ctrh$. $\mathsf{H}_{\mathsf{reg}}$ is called at most q_h times by $\mathcal{A}$ and at most $|CS| < t$ times when verifying the proofs of possession, hence $ctrh_{\mathsf{reg}} \leq q_h + t \leq q$ at the end of the execution. $\mathsf{H}_{\mathsf{non}}$ is called at most q_h times by the adversary and at most once per OSignRound query, hence at most $q_h + q_s$ times in total. Finally, $\mathsf{H}_{\mathsf{sig}}$ is called at most q_h times by the adversary, at most once per $\mathsf{H}_{\mathsf{non}}$ query, at most once per OSignRound query, and at most once when verifying the forgery, hence at most $2q_h + q_s + 1$ times in total. Hence, $ctrh \leq 3q_h + 2q_s + 1 \leq q$ at the end of execution, where we used $t \geq 1$.

Algorithm $\mathsf{Sim}(X^*)$

$X_\kappa \leftarrow X^*$
// There is an implicit polynomial f_κ with coefficients $a_{i,k}$ such that...
for $j \in CS$ **do**
  // $\ldots f_\kappa(j) = \tilde{x}_{\kappa,j}$, and ...
  $\tilde{x}_{\kappa,j} \leftarrow\!\$\; \mathbb{Z}_p$
for $k \in \{1, \ldots, t-1\}$ **do**
  // $\ldots f_\kappa(0) = \log_g X^*$.
  $A_{\kappa,k} \leftarrow (X^*)^{\bar{\Lambda}_{k,0}} \prod_{j \in CS} g^{\tilde{x}_{\kappa,j} \bar{\Lambda}_{k,j}}$ // $a_{\kappa,k} = \log_g A_{\kappa,k}$.
  // Here, $\bar{\Lambda}_{k,j}$ are coefficients s.t. $a_{\kappa,k} = \sum_{j=0}^{t} \bar{\Lambda}_{k,j} \tilde{x}_{\kappa,j}$ and are computed as entries
  // of a matrix $\bar{\Lambda} = L^{-1}$, where L is the $(t-1) \times (t-1)$ matrix with $L_{i,k} = i^k$.
$\tilde{s}_\kappa, \tilde{c}_\kappa \leftarrow\!\$\; \mathbb{Z}_p, \tilde{R}_\kappa \leftarrow g^{\tilde{s}_\kappa} (X^*)^{\tilde{c}_\kappa}$
if $T_{\mathrm{reg}}(X^*, \tilde{R}_\kappa, \kappa) \neq \bot$ **then**
  $Ev_1 = \mathsf{true}$
$T_{\mathrm{reg}}(X^*, \tilde{R}_\kappa, \kappa) \leftarrow \tilde{c}_\kappa$
for $j \in CS$ **do**
  send $\left((\tilde{R}_\kappa, \tilde{s}_\kappa), (A_{\kappa,0}, \ldots, A_{\kappa,t-1})\right)$ **to** $\mathcal{S}_j$ // common parameters
  send $\tilde{x}_{\kappa,j}$ **to** $\mathcal{S}_j$ // secret shares
receive $(\tilde{R}_j, \tilde{s}_j)$ **from** $\mathcal{S}_j, j \in CS$
for $j \in HS$ **do**
  // $f_\kappa(j) = \tilde{x}_{\kappa,j}$ is the discrete logarithm of $(X^*)^{\gamma_j} g^{\delta_j}$.
  $\gamma_j \leftarrow \mathsf{Lagrange}(CS \cup \{j\}, j)$;
  $\delta_j \leftarrow -\gamma_j \sum_{k \in CS} \tilde{x}_{\kappa,k} \mathsf{Lagrange}(CS \cup \{j\}, k)$
$\eta_\kappa \leftarrow \{(\tilde{R}_j, \tilde{s}_j), (A_{j,0}, \ldots, A_{j,t-1})\}_{j=1}^{n}$
$b \leftarrow \mathsf{Eq}(\kappa, \eta_\kappa)$ // interactively with all other signers $\mathcal{S}_j$, $j \in \{1, \ldots, n\} \setminus \{\kappa\}$
if $b = \mathsf{false}$ **then return** $\bot$
return $\{\gamma_j, \delta_j\}_{j \in HS}$

Fig. 7. Algorithm Sim used for simulating $\mathsf{SimplPedPoP}(\kappa)$ in $\mathcal{B}$.

The accepting probability of $\mathcal{B}$ for randomly chosen inputs is

$$acc_{\mathcal{B}} = \mathsf{Adv}^{\mathsf{TS\text{-}UF}}_{\mathcal{A},\mathsf{Olaf},n,t,CS} - \Pr[Ev_1] \geq \epsilon - \frac{q}{2^{\lambda-1}}.$$

Construction of Algorithm $\mathcal{C}$. Algorithm $\mathcal{C}$ takes as input

$$inp_{\mathcal{C}} = (X^*, \{U_{i,j}\}_{i\in HS, j\in\{1,\ldots 2q_s\}}),$$

where $X^* \leftarrow\$\, \mathbb{G}$ and $U_{i,j} \leftarrow\$\, \mathbb{G}$ for all $i \in HS, j \in \{1, \ldots 2q_s\}$. It also takes as input a stream $(h_{\text{reg},1}, \ldots, h_{\text{reg},q}) \leftarrow\$\, \mathbb{Z}_p^q$.

Analogously to $\mathcal{B}$, the inputs X^* and $U_{i,j}$ represent $|HS| \cdot q_s + 1$ discrete logarithm challenges that will be obtained via $|HS| \cdot q_s + 1$ oracle calls OCH by the caller of $\mathcal{C}$, and $\mathcal{C}$ has access to a discrete logarithm oracle ODLog provided by the caller. (When we apply a forking lemma to $\mathcal{C}$, we can think of this deterministic oracle as part of $\mathcal{C}$ because the lemma does not require $\mathcal{C}$ to be PPT.)

Algorithm $\mathcal{C}$ is defined in Fig. 8, with $H = \mathbb{Z}_p$ and Fork as defined in Lemma 1. All ODLog oracle queries made by $\mathsf{Fork}^{\mathcal{B}}_H$ are relayed by $\mathcal{C}$ to its own ODLog oracle. In the following, we call the first execution of $\mathcal{B}$ started by $\mathsf{Fork}^{\mathcal{B}}_H$

Algorithm $\mathcal{C}(inp_{\mathcal{C}}, (h_{\text{reg},1}, \ldots, h_{\text{reg},q}))$

$(X^*, \{U_{i,j}\}_{i\in HS, j\in\{1,\ldots 2q_s\}}) \leftarrow inp_{\mathcal{C}}$

$inp_{\mathcal{B}} \leftarrow ((\mathbb{G}, p, g), X^*, \{U_{i,j}\}_{i\in HS, j\in\{1,\ldots 2q_s\}}, (h_{\text{reg},1}, \ldots, h_{\text{reg},q}))$

$\omega \leftarrow \mathsf{Fork}^{\mathcal{B}}_H(inp_{\mathcal{B}})$

if $\omega = \perp$ **then return** $\perp$

$(f_{\text{sig}}, out, out') \leftarrow \omega$

$(h_{f_{\text{sig}}}, (s, (F, \{\phi_f\}_{f\in F}), \{x_i\}_{i\in HS\setminus\{\kappa\}}, Q)) \leftarrow out$

$(h'_{f_{\text{sig}}}, (s', (F', \{\phi'_f\}_{f\in F'}), \{x'_i\}_{i\in HS\setminus\{\kappa'\}}, Q')) \leftarrow out'$

$x \leftarrow (s - s')/(h_{f_{\text{sig}}} - h'_{f_{\text{sig}}})$

// Relay only $(F, \{\phi_f\}_{f\in F}, \{x_i\}_{i\in HS\setminus\{\kappa\}})$, ignore $(F', \{\phi'_f\}_{f\in F'}, \{x'_i\}_{i\in HS\setminus\{\kappa\}})$

$\theta \leftarrow (\{x_i\}_{i\in HS\setminus\{\kappa\}}, Q, Q', x,)$

return $(F, \{\phi_f\}_{f\in F}, \theta)$

Fig. 8. Algorithm $\mathcal{C}$.

a primary execution of $\mathcal{B}$ (i.e., the one started in line 2 of algorithm $\mathsf{Fork}^{\mathcal{B}}_H$ leading to assignment of variable *out* in line 10), and we call the (one) other execution of $\mathcal{B}$ (leading to the assignment of variable *out′* in line 10) a secondary execution of $\mathcal{B}$. By construction of $\mathcal{B}$, the two outputs returned by $\mathsf{Fork}^{\mathcal{B}}$ are such that $g^s = RX^{h_{f_{\text{sig}}}}$ and $g^{s'} = R'X'^{h'_{f_{\text{sig}}}}$, where the non-primed values are from the primary execution of $\mathcal{B}$ and the primed values are those from the second execution of $\mathcal{B}$. Since the two executions of $\mathcal{B}$ run by $\mathsf{Fork}^{\mathcal{B}}_H$ are identical before the two assignments $T_{\text{sig}}(X, R, m) \leftarrow h_{f_{\text{sig}}}$ and $T'_{\text{sig}}(X', R', m') \leftarrow h'_{f_{\text{sig}}}$, the keys of the two assignments must be the same. Hence, $X = X'$ and $R = R'$. By construction of Fork, we know that $h_{f_{\text{sig}}} \neq h'_{f_{\text{sig}}}$. Therefore, $\mathcal{C}$ can compute $x = (s - s')/(h_{f_{\text{sig}}} - h'_{f_{\text{sig}}})$ as the discrete logarithm of $X = \prod_{i=1}^{n} X_i$.

By Lemma 1, $\mathcal{C}$'s accepting probability $acc_{\mathcal{C}}$ is the probability $frk_{\mathcal{B}}$ that $\mathsf{Fork}^{\mathcal{B}}$ does not output $\perp$, i.e.,

$$\begin{aligned} acc_{\mathcal{C}} = frk_{\mathcal{B}} &\geq acc_{\mathcal{B}} \cdot \left(\frac{acc_{\mathcal{B}}}{q} - \frac{1}{|H|} \right) \\ &\geq \left(\epsilon - \frac{q}{2^{\lambda-1}} \right) \cdot \left(\frac{\epsilon}{q} - \frac{2}{2^{\lambda-1}} \right) \\ &\geq \frac{\epsilon^2}{q} - \frac{3}{2^{\lambda-1}}. \end{aligned}$$

Construction of Algorithm $\mathcal{D}$. We first construct a helper algorithm $\mathcal{D}$. Algorithm $\mathcal{D}$ is a syntactically valid adversary against game $\mathsf{AOMDL}_{\mathbb{G}}^{\mathcal{D}}$ (but is not yet our final reduction to AOMDL). It is defined in Fig. 9, where $H = \mathbb{Z}_p$ and MFork is as defined in Lemma 2. All ODLog oracle queries made by $\mathsf{MFork}_H^{\mathcal{C}}$ are relayed by $\mathcal{D}$ to its own ODLog oracle, caching pairs of group elements and responses to avoid making multiple queries for the same group element.

In the following, we call the first execution of $\mathcal{C}$ started by $\mathsf{MFork}_H^{\mathcal{C}}$ (i.e., the one started in line 2 of algorithm $\mathsf{MFork}_H^{\mathcal{C}}$ leading to the assignment of variable *mout* in line 5) the primary execution of $\mathcal{C}$, and we call the other executions of $\mathcal{C}$ (leading to an addition to variable *mout'* in line 5 in case of success) secondary executions of $\mathcal{C}$.

Consider the outputs *mout* and *mout'* returned from $\mathsf{MFork}_H^{\mathcal{C}}$ to $\mathcal{D}$. Output *mout* is from the primary execution of $\mathcal{B}$ within the primary execution of $\mathcal{C}$; let us call this execution the non-primed execution of $\mathcal{B}$. Similarly, *mout'* is from the primary execution of $\mathcal{B}$ within the respective successful secondary execution of $\mathcal{C}$; let us call this execution the primed execution of $\mathcal{B}$. With this convention, we have by construction that *mout* and *mout'* returned from $\mathsf{MFork}^{\mathcal{C}}$ are such that

$$g^{\tilde{s}_f} = \tilde{R}_f X_k^{h_{\text{reg},f}} \text{ and } g^{\tilde{s}'_f} = \tilde{R}'_f X_k^{h'_{\text{reg},f}},$$

where the non-primed variables are from the non-primed execution, and the primed values are from the primed execution. (Note that algorithm $\mathcal{C}$ returns only $(F, \{\phi_f\}_{f \in F}, \{x_i\}_{i \in HS \setminus \{\kappa\}})$ from the primary execution of $\mathcal{B}$ to its caller $\mathsf{MFork}_H^{\mathcal{C}}$.)

By construction of $\mathcal{B}$ and $\mathcal{C}$, the non-primed execution and the respective successful non-primed execution of $\mathcal{B}$ leading to the addition of $(h_{\text{reg},f}, \tilde{s}'_f)$ to *mout'* are identical before the corresponding array assignments $T_{\text{reg}}(X_{\iota(f)}, \tilde{R}_{\iota(f)}, i) \leftarrow h_{\text{reg},f}$ and $T'_{\text{reg}}(X'_{\iota(f)}, \tilde{R}'_{\iota(f)}, i) \leftarrow h'_{\text{reg},f}$ for $f \in F$ and some bijective re-indexing $\iota : F \rightarrow CS$, and thus the array keys of the two assignments must be the same. Hence, $X_i = X'_i$ and $\tilde{R}_i = \tilde{R}'_i$ for every $i \in CS$. By construction of $\mathsf{MFork}_H^{\mathcal{C}}$,

Algorithm $\mathcal{D}$

$X^* \leftarrow \mathsf{OCH}$
for $i \in HS$ **do**
  for $j \in \{1, \ldots, 2q_s\}$ **do**
    $U_{i,2j-1} \leftarrow \mathsf{OCH}$
$inp_{\mathcal{C}} \leftarrow ((\mathbb{G}, p, g), X^*, \{U_{i,j}\}_{i \in HS, j \in \{1,\ldots 2q_s\}})$
$\omega \leftarrow \mathsf{MFork}_H^{\mathcal{C}}(inp_{\mathcal{C}})$
if $\omega = \bot$ **then return** $\bot$
$(F, mout, mout', \theta) \leftarrow \omega$
$(\{x_i\}_{i \in HS \setminus \{\kappa\}}, x, Q, Q') \leftarrow \theta$
$\{(h_{\text{reg},f}, s_f)\}_{f \in F} \leftarrow mout$
$\{(h'_{\text{reg},f}, s'_f)\}_{f \in F} \leftarrow mout'$
for $f \in F$ **do**
  $x_f \leftarrow (s_f - s'_f)/(h_{\text{reg},f} - h'_{\text{reg},f})$
$x_\kappa \leftarrow x - \left(\sum_{f \in F} x_f\right) - \left(\sum_{i \in HS \setminus \{\kappa\}} x_i\right)$
$x^* \leftarrow x_\kappa$
Compute $\{u_{i,j}\}_{i \in HS, j \in \{1,\ldots 2q_s\}}$ from Q and Q' // see text
return $(x^*, u_{1,1}, \ldots, u_{|HS|,2q_s})$ // AOMDL solution

Fig. 9. Algorithm $\mathcal{D}$.

we know that $h_{\text{reg},f} \neq h'_{\text{reg},f}$ for every $f \in F$. Therefore, $\mathcal{D}^*$ can compute $x_f \leftarrow (s_f - s'_f)/(h_f - h'_f)$ for each $f \in F$, and values x_f are (up to re-indexing) the discrete logarithms of X_i for $i \in CS$.

Let X be the public key, i.e., $X = \prod_{k=1}^{n} X_k$, and let $x = \log_g X$ be its discrete logarithm. Then, $\sum_{f \in F} x_f$ is the sum of all contributions of all parties $i \in CS$ to x. By construction, $\sum_{i \in HS \setminus \{\kappa\}} x_i$ is the sum of all contributions of all parties $i \in HS \setminus \{\kappa\}$ to x. Thus, x_κ as computed by $\mathcal{D}$ is the contribution of party κ, which is by construction the discrete logarithm of challenge X^*.

We now explain how algorithm $\mathcal{D}$ computes values $\{u_{i,j}\}_{i \in HS, j \in \{1,\ldots 2q_s\}}$. Algorithm $\mathcal{D}$ initializes $Ev_2 \leftarrow$ false to track a bad event. From the two of executions of $\mathcal{B}$ run by $\mathsf{Fork}_H^{\mathcal{B}}$ within the primary execution of $\mathcal{C}$, algorithm $\mathcal{D}$ has sets Q and Q', which kept track of queries to ODLog in the respective execution. Algorithm $\mathcal{D}$ iterates over $i \in HS$ and over $j \in \{1, \ldots, q_s\}$, and looks for tuples of the form $(i, j, \sigma_i, b, c, \Lambda_i) \in Q$ for some values $\sigma_i, b, c, \Lambda_i$, and $(i, j, \sigma'_i, b', c', \Lambda'_i) \in Q'$ for some values $\sigma'_i, b', c', \Lambda'_i$. These correspond to $\mathsf{OSignRound}(i, j, \ldots)$ queries handled in the two executions, such that the pair of group elements $(U_{i,2j-1}, U_{i,2j})$ was assigned to variables (D_i, E_i) and $(D_{i'}, E_{i'})$, respectively, by the corresponding $\mathsf{OPreRound}(i, \ldots)$ query. In other words, $\mathcal{D}$ will find at most one tuple $(i, j, \sigma_i, b, c, \Lambda_i) \in Q$ and at most one tuple

$(i, j, \sigma'_i, b', c', \Lambda'_i) \in Q'$ such that the two executions of $\mathcal{B}$ in the primary execution of $\mathcal{C}$ made ODLog queries

$$\sigma_i \leftarrow \mathsf{ODLog}\left(U_{i,2j-1} U_{i,2j}^{b} \left((X^*)^{\gamma_i} g^{\delta_i}\right)^{c\Lambda_i}\right)$$
$$\text{and} \quad \sigma'_i \leftarrow \mathsf{ODLog}\left(U_{i,2j-1} U_{i,2j}^{b'} \left((X^*)^{\gamma_i} g^{\delta_i}\right)^{c'\Lambda'_i}\right).$$

Assume now that both tuples are defined. Consider the forking index f_{sig}, and let f and f' be the indices such that $b \leftarrow T_{\text{non}}(X, S, (D, E), m)$ and $b' \leftarrow T'_{\text{non}}(X', S', (D', E'), m')$ were assigned values h_f and $h'_{F'}$, respectively. If $f > f_{\text{sig}} \wedge b = b'$, then $\mathcal{D}$ sets $Ev_2 \leftarrow \mathsf{true}$ and returns $\perp$.

- *Case $f = f_{\text{sig}}$:* By construction, $h_{f_{\text{sig}}}$ was stored in T_{sig} (and not in T_{non}). Thus, $f \neq f_{\text{sig}}$, which contradicts the case assumption.
- *Case $f = f_{\text{sig}} - 1$ and $T_{\text{sig}}(X, R, m) = \perp$ when $T_{\text{non}}(X, S, (D, E), m)$ was assigned:* Then in both executions, it was precisely the internal query from H_{non} to H_{sig} that caused the assignments $T_{\text{sig}}(X, R, m) \leftarrow h_{f_{\text{sig}}}$ and $T'_{\text{sig}}(X, R, m) \leftarrow h'_{f_{\text{sig}}}$, respectively. This implies that $\mathcal{A}$ has output a forgery on message m for which $i \in Sigs[m]$, and hence that $\mathcal{B}$ has returned $\perp$, a contradiction.
- *Case $f = f_{\text{sig}} - 1$ and $T_{\text{sig}}(X, R, m) \neq \perp$ when $\mathsf{H}_{\text{non}}(X, S, (D, E), m)$ was assigned:* Then the assignment $T_{\text{sig}}(X, R, m) \leftarrow h_k$ happened before the fork, i.e., $k < f_{\text{sig}}$. Since the executions are identical at this point, we have $c = T_{\text{sig}}(X, R, m) = h_k = T'_{\text{sig}}(X, R, m) = c'$.
  Moreover, the assignment $T_{\text{non}}(X, S, (D, E), m) = h_f$ happened before the fork, i.e., $f < f_{\text{sig}}$. Since the executions are identical at this point, we have for the corresponding assignment $T'_{\text{non}}(X', S', (D', E'), m')$ that the array keys are identical, which in particular implies $S = S'$. Thus, $\Lambda_i = \mathsf{Lagrange}(S, i) = \mathsf{Lagrange}(S', i) = \Lambda'_i$.
- *Case $f < f_{\text{sig}} - 1$:* Then the assignment $T_{\text{sig}}(X, R, m) \leftarrow h_k$ happened at the latest during the internal query from H_{non} to H_{sig}, i.e., for some $k \leq f + 1 < f_{\text{sig}}$. Since $k < f_{\text{sig}}$, we have $c = T_{\text{sig}}(X, R, m) = h_k = T'_{\text{sig}}(X, R, m) = c'$ as in the previous case.
  Moreover, $\Lambda_i = \mathsf{Lagrange}(S, i) = \mathsf{Lagrange}(S', i) = \Lambda'_i$ as in the previous case.
- *Case $f > f_{\text{sig}}$:* Then also $f' > f_{\text{sig}}$. This implies $b = h_f$ and $b' = h'_{f'}$. Unless Ev_2, this implies $b \neq b$. ($f' = f_{\text{sig}}$ is not possible because $h_{f_{\text{sig}}}$ was stored in T_{sig} and not in T_{non}. $f' < f_{\text{sig}}$ would imply $f = f'$ because the executions are identical when $T'_{\text{non}}(X', S', (D', E'), m') \leftarrow h_{F'}$ is assigned, and thus $f < f_{\text{sig}}$, which contradicts the case assumption.)

In any case, we have

$$b = b' \implies (c = c' \wedge \Lambda_i = \Lambda'_i). \qquad (*)$$

If both tuples $(i, j, \sigma_i, b, c, \Lambda_i)$ and $(i, j, \sigma'_i, b', c', \Lambda'_i)$ are defined and identical, then also the corresponding ODLog queries made by the two executions of $\mathcal{B}$ are identical, and due to the caching of result, $\mathcal{D}$ has, in fact, made only one query to its ODLog oracle. In this case, $\mathcal{D}$ emulates the second query by choosing new values (b', c', Λ_i') and querying its ODLog oracle with

$$\sigma_i' \leftarrow \mathsf{ODLog}\left(U_{i',2j-1}U_{i',2j}^{b'}\left((X^*)^{\gamma_i}g^{\delta_i}\right)^{c'\Lambda_i'}\right).$$

Similarly, if at most one of the tuples $(i, j, \sigma_i, b, c, \Lambda_i)$ and $(i, j, \sigma_i', b', c', \Lambda_i')$ is defined, then $\mathcal{D}$ emulates the missing ODLog queries by choosing any values b, c, Λ_i, or b', c', Λ_i', such that $b \neq b'$, and making the missing ODLog queries.

If both tuples $(i, j, \sigma_i, b, c, \Lambda_i)$ and $(i, j, \sigma_i', b', c', \Lambda_i')$ are defined and not identical, then we know $b \neq b'$ (because otherwise (*) would imply that they are identical).

In any case, algorithm $\mathcal{D}$ has now made two ODLog queries, which correspond to two tuples $(i, j, \sigma_i, b, c, \Lambda_i)$ and $(i, j, \sigma_i', b', c', \Lambda_i')$ such that $b \neq b'$. Algorithm $\mathcal{D}$ constructs a system of two linear equations of the following form with unknowns $u_{i,2j-1}$ and $u_{i,2j}$, the discrete logarithms of $U_{i,2j-1}$ and $U_{i,2j}$.

$$u_{i,2j-1} + b \cdot u_{i,2j} = \sigma_i - (\gamma_i x^* - \delta_i)c\Lambda_i$$
$$u_{i,2j-1} + b' \cdot u_{i,2j} = \sigma_i' - (\gamma_i x^* - \delta_i)c'\Lambda_i'$$

Since $b \neq b'$, the system has a unique solution $(u_{i,2j-1}, u_{i,2j})$, which $\mathcal{D}$ computes.

Clearly, if $\mathcal{D}$ does not output $\perp$, the total number of ODLog queries made *during the primary execution of* $\mathcal{C}$ plus those that $\mathcal{D}$ made additionally when computing $\{u_{i,j}\}_{i\in HS, j\in\{1,\dots 2q_s\}}$ is exactly $|HS| \cdot 2q_s$. (Note that $\mathcal{D}$ makes also ODLog queries in other executions of $\mathcal{C}$ and thus exceeds the number of $|HS| \cdot 2q_s$ queries that would be allowed to solve AOMDL. We will construct $\mathcal{D}^*$ below to fix this.)

To bound the accepting probability of $\mathcal{D}$, observe that $\mathcal{D}$ does so if $\mathsf{MFork}_H^{\mathcal{C}}$ succeeds and Ev_2 is not set to true. Ev_2 is set to true if, in the linear system corresponding to some $i \in HS$ and $j \in \{1, \dots, q_s\}$, there are two identical scalars $b = b'$ in the two executions of $\mathcal{B}$ belonging to the primary execution of $\mathcal{C}$. In these two executions of $\mathcal{B}$, at most $2q_s$ of the $|HS| \cdot 2q_s$ scalars are actually used when handling signing sessions (namely 2 per OSignRound queries); for all other scalars $\mathcal{B}$ takes care of ensuring $b = b'$ when emulating missing ODLog. Since the $2q_s$ scalars are drawn from $\mathbb{Z}_p$ with $p \leq 2^{\lambda-1}$ and $q_s \leq q$, we have

$$\Pr[Ev_2] \leq \frac{4q^2}{2^{\lambda-1}} = \frac{q^2}{2^{\lambda-3}}.$$

By assumption, $\lambda > \log_2((8q^3t + 6q)/\epsilon^2)$, which, as can be verified, implies $|H| > |F| \cdot 8q/acc_{\mathcal{C}}$. Then by Lemma 2, $\mathsf{MFork}_H^{\mathcal{C}}$ returns a non-$\perp$ output with probability $frk_{\mathcal{C}}$

$$frk_{\mathcal{C}} \geq \frac{acc_{\mathcal{C}}}{8} \geq \frac{\epsilon^2}{8q} - \frac{3}{2^{\lambda-4}}.$$

The acceptance probability of $\mathcal{D}$ is

$$acc_{\mathcal{D}} \geq frk_{\mathcal{C}} - \Pr[Ev_2] = \frac{\epsilon^2}{8q} - \frac{3}{2^{\lambda-4}} - \frac{q^2}{2^{\lambda-3}} = \frac{\epsilon^2}{8q} - \frac{6+q^2}{2^{\lambda-3}}.$$

Construction of Algorithm $\mathcal{D}^*$. We now construct an algorithm $\mathcal{D}^*$, which is an adversary against game $\mathsf{AOMDL}_{\mathbb{G}}^{\mathcal{D}^*}$. Algorithm $\mathcal{D}^*$ is defined like algorithm $\mathcal{D}$ with the following modification: Algorithm $\mathcal{D}^*$ aborts any executions of $\mathcal{B}$ in secondary executions of $\mathcal{C}$ whenever it has collected all PoPs $\{(\tilde{R}_j, \tilde{s}_j)\}_{j \in CS}$ that $\mathcal{A}$ sends during a $\mathsf{OKeyGen}$ query. Since $\mathsf{SimplPedPoP}$ ensures that every honest signer $\mathcal{S}_i$ responds to $\mathsf{SignRound}(i, \ldots)$ queries with a non-$\perp$ return value only after it has successfully run the equality check protocol with every other signer, any abort occurs before the respective execution of $\mathcal{B}$ performs its first ODLog query, which happens only while handling $\mathsf{OSignRound}(i, \ldots)$ queries with non-$\perp$ return values.

We show that this can be done without changing the acceptance probability of $\mathcal{D}$ as compared to $\mathcal{D}^*$. Consider the values used by $\mathcal{D}$: Algorithm $\mathcal{D}$ uses values F, $mout = \{(h_{\text{reg},f}, s_f)\}_{f \in F}$ and $mout' = \{(h'_{\text{reg},f}, s'_f)\}_{f \in F}$, but these values are already determined when $\mathcal{B}$ is aborted, so algorithm $\mathcal{D}$ can reconstruct them from the internal state of $\mathcal{B}$ at abortion time. Algorithm $\mathcal{D}$ also uses value θ, but this is from the primary execution of $\mathcal{C}$ which is unchanged in $\mathcal{D}^*$ as compared to $\mathcal{D}$. In particular, to compute values $\{u_{i,j}\}_{i \in HS, j \in \{1,\ldots 2q_s\}}$, algorithm $\mathcal{D}$ uses sets Q and Q', which are part of θ. In conclusion, aborting $\mathcal{B}$ in the secondary executions of $\mathcal{C}$ does not affect any values used by $\mathcal{D}$, and thus the outputs of $\mathcal{D}^*$ and $\mathcal{D}$ are the same and

$$acc_{\mathcal{D}^*} = acc_{\mathcal{D}}.$$

Let us estimate the running time $\tau_{\mathcal{D}^*}$ of $\mathcal{D}^*$. To start with, $\mathcal{D}^*$ runs no slower than its non-aborting version $\mathcal{D}$. With $k_{\max}$ from algorithm MFork, the running time of $\mathcal{D}$ is roughly $|F|^2 \cdot k_{\max}$ times the running time of algorithm $\mathcal{C}$, which in turn is roughly twice the running time of algorithm $\mathcal{B}$. The running time of $\mathcal{B}$ is roughly the running time $\tau_{\mathsf{TS\text{-}UF}}$ of game $\mathsf{TS\text{-}UF}_{\mathsf{Olaf},n,t,CS}$ (ignoring $\mathcal{A}$ within the game) plus the running time τ of $\mathcal{A}$ within the game. In summary, the running time $\tau_{\mathcal{D}^*}$ of $\mathcal{D}^*$ is not more than roughly

$$\begin{aligned}
\tau_{\mathcal{D}^*} &\leq \tau_{\mathcal{D}} \\
&\approx |F|^2 \cdot k_{\max} \cdot \tau_{\mathcal{C}} \\
&\approx 2|F|^2 \cdot k_{\max} \cdot \tau_{\mathcal{B}} \\
&\approx 2|F|^2 \cdot k_{\max} \cdot (\tau_{\mathsf{TS\text{-}UF}} + \tau_{\mathcal{A}}) \\
&= \frac{|F|^2 \cdot 8q}{acc_{\mathcal{C}}} \cdot \ln \frac{|F| \cdot 8}{acc_{\mathcal{C}}} \cdot (\tau_{\mathsf{TS\text{-}UF}} + \tau_{\mathcal{A}}) \\
&\leq \frac{8qt^2}{acc_{\mathcal{C}}} \cdot \ln \frac{8t}{acc_{\mathcal{C}}} \cdot (\tau_{\mathsf{TS\text{-}UF}} + \tau_{\mathcal{A}}) \\
&= \frac{8q^2t^2}{\epsilon^2 - 3q \cdot 2^{1-\lambda}} \cdot \ln \frac{8q^2t}{\epsilon^2 - 3q \cdot 2^{1-\lambda}} \cdot (\tau_{\mathsf{TS\text{-}UF}} + \tau_{\mathcal{A}}).
\end{aligned}$$

Let us count the number of OCH and ODLog queries made by algorithm $\mathcal{D}^*$: Algorithm $\mathcal{D}^*$ (like $\mathcal{D}$) makes $|HS| \cdot 2q_s + 1$ OCH queries in total. Due to the way $\mathcal{D}^*$ aborts executions of $\mathcal{B}$ early, only the primary execution of $\mathcal{C}$ reaches a stage where $\mathcal{B}$ makes ODLog queries. Since this one execution of $\mathcal{C}$ runs two executions of $\mathcal{B}$ (via $\mathsf{Fork}_H^{\mathcal{B}}$), and each $\mathcal{B}$ execution makes exactly $|HS| \cdot q_s$ ODLog queries (including the queries emulated later by $\mathcal{D}^*$), algorithm $\mathcal{D}^*$ makes exactly $|HS| \cdot 2q_s$ ODLog queries. Thus, when $\mathcal{D}^*$ returns a non-$\perp$ output, it solves the AOMDL problem with advantage

$$\mathsf{Adv}^{\mathsf{AOMDL}}_{\mathcal{D}^*,\mathbb{G}} = acc_{\mathcal{D}^*} = acc_{\mathcal{D}} \geq \frac{\epsilon^2}{8q} - \frac{6+q^2}{2^{\lambda-3}}.$$

□

Acknowledgments. We thank the anonymous reviewers for their very helpful comments and suggestions. This work was partially supported by Deutsche Forschungsgemeinschaft as part of the Research and Training Group 2475 "Cybercrime and Forensic Computing" (grant number 393541319/GRK2475/1-2019), and through grant 442893093, and by the state of Bavaria at the Nuremberg Campus of Technology (NCT). NCT is a research cooperation between the Friedrich-Alexander-Universität Erlangen-Nürnberg (FAU) and the Technische Hochschule Nürnberg Georg Simon Ohm (THN).

References

1. Implementation of FROST by Bank of Italy. https://github.com/bancaditalia/secp256k1-frost
2. Implementation of FROST by CoinBase. https://github.com/coinbase/kryptology/tree/v1.8.0/pkg/ted25519/frost
3. Implementation of FROST by Taurus SA. https://github.com/taurusgroup/frost-ed25519
4. Implementation of FROST in libsecp256k1-zkp. https://github.com/BlockstreamResearch/secp256k1-zkp/pull/138
5. Abram, D., Nof, A., Orlandi, C., Scholl, P., Shlomovits, O.: Low-bandwidth threshold ECDSA via pseudorandom correlation generators. In: 2022 IEEE Symposium on Security and Privacy, pp. 2554–2572. IEEE Computer Society Press (2022). https://doi.org/10.1109/SP46214.2022.9833559
6. Bagherzandi, A., Cheon, J.H., Jarecki, S.: Multisignatures secure under the discrete logarithm assumption and a generalized forking lemma. In: Ning, P., Syverson, P.F., Jha, S. (eds.) ACM CCS 2008, pp. 449–458. ACM Press (2008). https://doi.org/10.1145/1455770.1455827
7. Bellare, M., Crites, E.C., Komlo, C., Maller, M., Tessaro, S., Zhu, C.: Better than advertised security for non-interactive threshold signatures. In: Dodis, Y., Shrimpton, T. (eds.) CRYPTO 2022, Part IV. LNCS, vol. 13510, pp. 517–550. Springer, Heidelberg (2022). https://doi.org/10.1007/978-3-031-15985-5_18
8. Bellare, M., Namprempre, C., Pointcheval, D., Semanko, M.: The one-more-RSA-inversion problems and the security of Chaum's blind signature scheme. J. Cryptol. **16**(3), 185–215 (2003). https://doi.org/10.1007/s00145-002-0120-1

9. Bellare, M., Neven, G.: Multi-signatures in the plain public-key model and a general forking lemma. In: Juels, A., Wright, R.N., De Capitani di Vimercati, S. (eds.) ACM CCS 2006, pp. 390–399. ACM Press (2006). https://doi.org/10.1145/1180405.1180453
10. Bellare, M., Palacio, A.: GQ and Schnorr identification schemes: proofs of security against impersonation under active and concurrent attacks. In: Yung, M. (ed.) CRYPTO 2002. LNCS, vol. 2442, pp. 162–177. Springer, Heidelberg (2002). https://doi.org/10.1007/3-540-45708-9_11
11. Bellare, M., Tessaro, S., Zhu, C.: Stronger security for non-interactive threshold signatures: BLS and FROST. Cryptology ePrint Archive, Report 2022/833 (2022). https://eprint.iacr.org/2022/833
12. Boldyreva, A.: Threshold signatures, multisignatures and blind signatures based on the gap-Diffie-Hellman-group signature scheme. In: Desmedt, Y.G. (ed.) PKC 2003. LNCS, vol. 2567, pp. 31–46. Springer, Heidelberg (2003). https://doi.org/10.1007/3-540-36288-6_3
13. Brandao, L., Peralta, R.: NIST First Call for Multi-Party Threshold Schemes. https://csrc.nist.gov/publications/detail/nistir/8214c/draft
14. Brown, D.R.L.: A flaw in a theorem about Schnorr signatures. Cryptology ePrint Archive, Report 2015/509 (2015). https://eprint.iacr.org/2015/509
15. Canetti, R., Gennaro, R., Goldfeder, S., Makriyannis, N., Peled, U.: UC non-interactive, proactive, threshold ECDSA with identifiable aborts. In: Ligatti, J., Ou, X., Katz, J., Vigna, G. (eds.) ACM CCS 2020, pp. 1769–1787. ACM Press (2020). https://doi.org/10.1145/3372297.3423367
16. Castagnos, G., Catalano, D., Laguillaumie, F., Savasta, F., Tucker, I.: Bandwidth-efficient threshold EC-DSA. In: Kiayias, A., Kohlweiss, M., Wallden, P., Zikas, V. (eds.) PKC 2020, Part II. LNCS, vol. 12111, pp. 266–296. Springer, Cham (2020). https://doi.org/10.1007/978-3-030-45388-6_10
17. Connolly, D., Komlo, C., Goldberg, I., Wood, C.A.: Two-Round Threshold Schnorr Signatures with FROST. Internet-Draft draft-IRTF-CFRG-frost, Internet Engineering Task Force (2023). https://datatracker.ietf.org/doc/draft-irtf-cfrg-frost/. Work in Progress
18. Crites, E., Komlo, C., Maller, M.: How to prove schnorr assuming schnorr: Security of multi- and threshold signatures. Cryptology ePrint Archive, Paper 2021/1375 (2021). https://eprint.iacr.org/2021/1375
19. Dalskov, A., Orlandi, C., Keller, M., Shrishak, K., Shulman, H.: Securing DNSSEC keys via threshold ECDSA from generic MPC. In: Chen, L., Li, N., Liang, K., Schneider, S. (eds.) ESORICS 2020, Part II. LNCS, vol. 12309, pp. 654–673. Springer, Cham (2020). https://doi.org/10.1007/978-3-030-59013-0_32
20. Damgård, I., Jakobsen, T.P., Nielsen, J.B., Pagter, J.I., Østergaard, M.B.: Fast threshold ECDSA with honest majority. In: Galdi, C., Kolesnikov, V. (eds.) SCN 2020. LNCS, vol. 12238, pp. 382–400. Springer, Cham (2020). https://doi.org/10.1007/978-3-030-57990-6_19
21. De Santis, A., Desmedt, Y., Frankel, Y., Yung, M.: How to share a function securely. In: 26th ACM STOC, pp. 522–533. ACM Press (1994). https://doi.org/10.1145/195058.195405
22. Desmedt, Y.: Society and group oriented cryptography: a new concept. In: Pomerance, C. (ed.) CRYPTO 1987. LNCS, vol. 293, pp. 120–127. Springer, Heidelberg (1988). https://doi.org/10.1007/3-540-48184-2_8
23. Desmedt, Y., Frankel, Y.: Threshold cryptosystems. In: Brassard, G. (ed.) CRYPTO 1989. LNCS, vol. 435, pp. 307–315. Springer, New York (1990). https://doi.org/10.1007/0-387-34805-0_28

24. Doerner, J., Kondi, Y., Lee, E., shelat, a.: Threshold ECDSA from ECDSA assumptions: the multiparty case. In: 2019 IEEE Symposium on Security and Privacy, pp. 1051–1066. IEEE Computer Society Press (2019). https://doi.org/10.1109/SP.2019.00024
25. Fuchsbauer, G., Kiltz, E., Loss, J.: The algebraic group model and its applications. In: Shacham, H., Boldyreva, A. (eds.) CRYPTO 2018, Part II. LNCS, vol. 10992, pp. 33–62. Springer, Cham (2018). https://doi.org/10.1007/978-3-319-96881-0_2
26. Fuchsbauer, G., Plouviez, A., Seurin, Y.: Blind Schnorr signatures and signed ElGamal encryption in the algebraic group model. In: Canteaut, A., Ishai, Y. (eds.) EUROCRYPT 2020, Part II. LNCS, vol. 12106, pp. 63–95. Springer, Cham (2020). https://doi.org/10.1007/978-3-030-45724-2_3
27. Gągol, A., Kula, J., Straszak, D., Świętek, M.: Threshold ECDSA for decentralized asset custody. Cryptology ePrint Archive, Report 2020/498 (2020). https://eprint.iacr.org/2020/498
28. Gennaro, R., Goldfeder, S.: Fast multiparty threshold ECDSA with fast trustless setup. In: Lie, D., Mannan, M., Backes, M., Wang, X. (eds.) ACM CCS 2018, pp. 1179–1194. ACM Press (2018). https://doi.org/10.1145/3243734.3243859
29. Gennaro, R., Goldfeder, S., Narayanan, A.: Threshold-optimal DSA/ECDSA signatures and an application to bitcoin wallet security. In: Manulis, M., Sadeghi, A.-R., Schneider, S. (eds.) ACNS 2016. LNCS, vol. 9696, pp. 156–174. Springer, Cham (2016). https://doi.org/10.1007/978-3-319-39555-5_9
30. Gennaro, R., Jarecki, S., Krawczyk, H., Rabin, T.: Robust threshold DSS signatures. In: Maurer, U. (ed.) EUROCRYPT 1996. LNCS, vol. 1070, pp. 354–371. Springer, Heidelberg (1996). https://doi.org/10.1007/3-540-68339-9_31
31. Gennaro, R., Jarecki, S., Krawczyk, H., Rabin, T.: Secure distributed key generation for discrete-log based cryptosystems. In: Stern, J. (ed.) EUROCRYPT 1999. LNCS, vol. 1592, pp. 295–310. Springer, Heidelberg (1999). https://doi.org/10.1007/3-540-48910-X_21
32. Gennaro, R., Jarecki, S., Krawczyk, H., Rabin, T.: Secure applications of Pedersen's distributed key generation protocol. In: Joye, M. (ed.) CT-RSA 2003. LNCS, vol. 2612, pp. 373–390. Springer, Heidelberg (2003). https://doi.org/10.1007/3-540-36563-X_26
33. Gennaro, R., Jarecki, S., Krawczyk, H., Rabin, T.: Secure distributed key generation for discrete-log based cryptosystems. J. Cryptol. **20**(1), 51–83 (2006). https://doi.org/10.1007/s00145-006-0347-3
34. Gennaro, R., Rabin, T., Jarecki, S., Krawczyk, H.: Robust and efficient sharing of RSA functions. J. Cryptol. **13**(2), 273–300 (2000). https://doi.org/10.1007/s001459910011
35. Groth, J., Shoup, V.: Design and analysis of a distributed ECDSA signing service. Cryptology ePrint Archive, Report 2022/506 (2022). https://eprint.iacr.org/2022/506
36. Katz, J., Zhang, C., Zhou, H.S.: An analysis of the algebraic group model. In: Agrawal, S., Lin, D. (eds.) ASIACRYPT 2022. LNCS, vol. 13794, pp. 310–322. Springer, Cham (2022). https://doi.org/10.1007/978-3-031-22972-5_11
37. Komlo, C., Goldberg, I.: FROST: flexible round-optimized schnorr threshold signatures. In: Dunkelman, O., Jacobson, Jr., M.J., O'Flynn, C. (eds.) SAC 2020. LNCS, vol. 12804, pp. 34–65. Springer, Cham (2021). https://doi.org/10.1007/978-3-030-81652-0_2
38. Komlo, C., Goldberg, I., Stebila, D.: A formal treatment of distributed key generation, and new constructions. Cryptology ePrint Archive, Report 2023/292 (2023). https://eprint.iacr.org/2023/292

39. Lindell, Y.: Simple three-round multiparty schnorr signing with full simulatability. Cryptology ePrint Archive, Report 2022/374 (2022). https://eprint.iacr.org/2022/374
40. Lindell, Y., Nof, A.: Fast secure multiparty ECDSA with practical distributed key generation and applications to cryptocurrency custody. In: Lie, D., Mannan, M., Backes, M., Wang, X. (eds.) ACM CCS 2018, pp. 1837–1854. ACM Press (2018). https://doi.org/10.1145/3243734.3243788
41. Maurer, U.: Abstract models of computation in cryptography. In: Smart, N.P. (ed.) Cryptography and Coding 2005. LNCS, vol. 3796, pp. 1–12. Springer, Heidelberg (2005). https://doi.org/10.1007/11586821_1
42. Neven, G., Smart, N.P., Warinschi, B.: Hash function requirements for schnorr signatures. J. Math. Cryptol. **3**(1), 69–87 (2009). https://doi.org/10.1515/JMC.2009.004
43. Nick, J., Ruffing, T., Seurin, Y.: MuSig2: simple two-round schnorr multi-signatures. In: Malkin, T., Peikert, C. (eds.) CRYPTO 2021, Part I. LNCS, vol. 12825, pp. 189–221. Springer, Cham (2021). https://doi.org/10.1007/978-3-030-84242-0_8
44. Pedersen, T.P.: A threshold cryptosystem without a trusted party. In: Davies, D.W. (ed.) EUROCRYPT 1991. LNCS, vol. 547, pp. 522–526. Springer, Heidelberg (1991). https://doi.org/10.1007/3-540-46416-6_47
45. Pedersen, T.P.: Non-interactive and information-theoretic secure verifiable secret sharing. In: Feigenbaum, J. (ed.) CRYPTO 1991. LNCS, vol. 576, pp. 129–140. Springer, Heidelberg (1992). https://doi.org/10.1007/3-540-46766-1_9
46. Pettit, M.: Efficient threshold-optimal ECDSA. In: Conti, M., Stevens, M., Krenn, S. (eds.) CANS 2021. LNCS, vol. 13099, pp. 116–135. Springer, Cham (2021). https://doi.org/10.1007/978-3-030-92548-2_7
47. Pointcheval, D., Stern, J.: Security arguments for digital signatures and blind signatures. J. Cryptol. **13**(3), 361–396 (2000). https://doi.org/10.1007/s001450010003
48. Ruffing, T., Ronge, V., Jin, E., Schneider-Bensch, J., Schröder, D.: ROAST: robust asynchronous schnorr threshold signatures. In: Yin, H., Stavrou, A., Cremers, C., Shi, E. (eds.) ACM CCS 2022, pp. 2551–2564. ACM Press (2022). https://doi.org/10.1145/3548606.3560583
49. Schnorr, C.P.: Method for identifying subscribers and for generating and verifying electronic signatures in a data exchange system. European Patent 0383985A1
50. Shoup, V.: Lower bounds for discrete logarithms and related problems. In: Fumy, W. (ed.) EUROCRYPT 1997. LNCS, vol. 1233, pp. 256–266. Springer, Heidelberg (1997). https://doi.org/10.1007/3-540-69053-0_18
51. Shoup, V.: Practical threshold signatures. In: Preneel, B. (ed.) EUROCRYPT 2000. LNCS, vol. 1807, pp. 207–220. Springer, Heidelberg (2000). https://doi.org/10.1007/3-540-45539-6_15
52. Stinson, D.R., Strobl, R.: Provably secure distributed schnorr signatures and a (t, n) threshold scheme for implicit certificates. In: Varadharajan, V., Mu, Y. (eds.) ACISP 2001. LNCS, vol. 2119, pp. 417–434. Springer, Heidelberg (2001). https://doi.org/10.1007/3-540-47719-5_33
53. Wuille, P., Nick, J., Ruffing, T.: Schnorr signatures for secp256k1. Bitcoin Improvement Proposal 340 (2020). https://github.com/bitcoin/bips/blob/master/bip-0340.mediawiki
54. Yuen, T.H., Cui, H., Xie, X.: Compact zero-knowledge proofs for threshold ECDSA with trustless setup. In: Garay, J.A. (ed.) PKC 2021, Part I. LNCS, vol. 12710, pp. 481–511. Springer, Cham (2021). https://doi.org/10.1007/978-3-030-75245-3_18

Author Index

A
Abraham, Ittai 39
Abram, Damiano 489
Acharya, Anasuya 328
Applebaum, Benny 236

B
Bacho, Renas 71
Bienstock, Alexander 263
Boneh, Dan 171
Boyle, Elette 171
Branco, Pedro 548
Braun, Lennart 613

C
Chu, Hien 743
Ciampi, Michele 459
Cohen, Ran 3
Collins, Daniel 71
Corrigan-Gibbs, Henry 171
Crites, Elizabeth 678, 710

D
Damgård, Ivan 613
David, Bernardo 360
Deligios, Giovanni 360
Döttling, Nico 548

E
Escudero, Daniel 263

G
Garay, Juan 3
Garg, Sanjam 295
Garimella, Gayathri 577
Gaži, Peter 107
Gerhart, Paul 743
Gilboa, Niv 171
Goel, Aarushi 360
Goyal, Vipul 427

H
Halevi, Shai 203
Hazay, Carmit 328

I
Ishai, Yuval 171, 203, 360, 393, 515

J
Jain, Abhishek 295
Jovanovic, Philipp 39

K
Kelkar, Mahimna 515
Khurana, Dakshita 393
Klein, Ohad 139
Komargodski, Ilan 139
Komlo, Chelsea 678, 710
Kondi, Yashvanth 646
Konring, Anders 360
Kushilevitz, Eyal 203, 360

L
Liu-Zhang, Chen-Da 71, 360
Loss, Julian 71

M
Maller, Mary 39, 678, 710
Meiklejohn, Sarah 39
Mukherjee, Pratyay 295

N
Narayanan, Varun 360, 515
Nir, Oded 236

H. Handschuh and A. Lysyanskaya (Eds.): CRYPTO 2023, LNCS 14081, pp. 775–776, 2023.
https://doi.org/10.1007/978-3-031-38557-5

O
Orlandi, Claudio 613, 646
Ostrovsky, Rafail 459

P
Pinkas, Benny 236
Poburinnaya, Oxana 328
Polychroniadou, Antigoni 263

R
Rabin, Tal 203
Ren, Ling 107
Rosulek, Mike 577
Roy, Lawrence 646
Ruffing, Tim 743
Russell, Alexander 107

S
Sahai, Amit 393
Schröder, Dominique 743
Singh, Jaspal 577
Sinha, Rohit 295
Siniscalchi, Luisa 459
Srinivasan, Akshayaram 393, 427, 548
Stern, Gilad 39

T
Tessaro, Stefano 710

V
Venkitasubramaniam, Muthuramakrishnan 328

W
Waldner, Hendrik 459
Wang, Mingyuan 295, 427
Waters, Brent 489

Z
Zafar, Liav 515
Zhandry, Mark 489
Zhang, Yinuo 295
Zhu, Chenzhi 710
Zikas, Vassilis 3

Printed in the United States
by Baker & Taylor Publisher Services